FINANCIAL ACCOUNTING

PRINCIPLES AND PRACTICES

For the students of BCom, BBA, MBA, MFC, MIB, MHROD, CFA and other courses of different Indian Universities and Management Institutes

Prof. Jawahar Lal
Ex-Head, Department of Commerce
Ex-Dean, Faculty of Commerce and Business
Delhi School of Economics
University of Delhi
Delhi

Dr. Seema Srivastava
Assistant Professor
Department of Commerce
Moti Lal Nehru College (Day)
University of Delhi
Delhi

S Chand And Company Limited
(ISO 9001 Certified Company)

S Chand And Company Limited

(ISO 9001 Certified Company)

Head Office: D-92, Sector–2, Noida – 201301, U.P. (India), Ph. 91-120-4682700

Registered Office: A-27, 2nd Floor, Mohan Co-operative Industrial Estate, New Delhi – 110 044, Phone: 011-49731800

www.**schandpublishing.com**; e-mail: **info@schandpublishing.com**

Marketing Offices:

Chennai	:	Ph: 23632120; chennai@schandpublishing.com
Guwahati	:	Ph: 2738811, 2735640; guwahati@schandpublishing.com
Hyderabad	:	Ph: 40186018; hyderabad@schandpublishing.com
Jalandhar	:	Ph: 4645630; jalandhar@schandpublishing.com
Kolkata	:	Ph: 23357458, 23353914; kolkata@schandpublishing.com
Lucknow	:	Ph: 4003633; lucknow@schandpublishing.com
Mumbai	:	Ph: 25000297; mumbai@schandpublishing.com
Patna	:	Ph: 2260011; patna@schandpublishing.com

First Edition 2003
Subsequent Editions and Reprints 2006, 2008, 2009, 2010, 2012
Third Revised Edition 2014
Reprints 2014, 2016, 2018, 2021, 2022
Reprint 2024

ISBN : 978-81-219-2306-4

Product Code: H8FAC48ACCN10ENAC14O

PRINTED IN INDIA

By Vikas Publishing House Private Limited, Plot 20/4, Site-IV, Industrial Area Sahibabad, Ghaziabad – 201 010 and Published by S Chand And Company Limited, A-27, 2nd Floor, Mohan Co-operative Industrial Estate, New Delhi – 110 044.

PREFACE TO THE THIRD REVISED EDITION

It is our esteemed pleasure to place the third revised edition of the book **Financial Accounting, Principles and Practices** among the students and other readers. The previous edition of the book has been highly appreciated by the students and the academic community. This fact has inspired us to make the revised edition a more useful and student-friendly text.

ORGANIZATION AND COVERAGE

The third edition of the book has attempted to present discussions in a more logical, clear and comprehensive manner. The book has been restructured and rearranged into Five Parts comprising of 21 chapters.

- **Part-One: Fundamentals** has two chapters and makes an overview of financial accounting and discusses different Accounting Concepts and Accounting Standards.
- **Part-Two: Accounting Records and Systems** consists of nine chapters and explains Accounting Equation and Transaction Analysis, Journals, Cash Book and Subsidiary Books, Ledger Posting and Trial Balance, Bank Reconciliation Statement, Errors and their Rectifications, Preparation of Financial Statements: Profit and Loss Account and Balance Sheet, Depreciation Accounting and Inventory Valuation.
- **Part-Three: Company Accounts** contains five chapters, namely Accounting for Shares, Accounting for Debentures, Company Final Accounts, Accounting for Amalgamation and Valuation of Goodwill.
- **Part-Four: Financial Analysis** discusses the Statement of Changes in Financial Position, Cash Flow Statement and Financial Statement Analysis.
- **Part-Five: Specialised Topics** is devoted to the discussion of two specialised topics–Corporate Financial Reporting and Computerised Accounting (How to Use Tally).

Many portions in the book have been revised with a view to provide updated material to the students and readers. The following chapters have been thoroughly improved:

1. Financial Accounting: An Overview
2. Basic Accounting Concepts and Accounting Standards
3. Accounting for Shares
4. Corporate Financial Reporting

PEDAGOGY

The revised text continues to possess all pedagogical features associated with the previous edition such as:

- Chapter objectives (Learning Objectives) have been given at the beginning of each chapter. The chapter objectives have been integrated with the text presentation and the listing of objectives provides an outline of the chapters.

- The book gives a clear, concise and building block discussion in a logical and lively style to make the material real and interesting, and certainly more helpful to the students in learning and understanding it.
- The text contains several well-illustrated charts, diagrams and figures to help the students easily and quickly understand the concepts and relationships, and enable them to develop the ideas underlying the material as it is explained.
- Theory questions involving thought provoking and real-life theory questions are given at the end of each chapter.
- Self-evaluation exercises containing abundance of multiple choice questions, true or false, fill in the blanks have been added at the end of the chapters to help students review the key ideas contained in the chapters. Answers to self-evaluation exercises are also provided at the end of each chapter.
- Adequate exercises and problems have been given at the end of each chapter.
- The book provides glossary of useful technical terms in the area of financial accounting at the end of the book. The text is primarily designed for professional programmes of the Indian Universities, Management Institutes and Business Schools. This book will be very useful to the following programmes and courses :
  - MBA
  - BBA, BBS
  - MIB, MFC, MHROD, CFA
  - Other professional courses aiming to provide exposure in Financial Accounting to the participants to enable them to pursue a business and finance career.
  - B.Com. of Indian Universities having syllabus contents identical to topics covered in the book.

We would welcome and appreciate constructive suggestions from the readers to improve and enhance the quality of the book and make it an essential text for the students.

ACKNOWLEDGEMENTS

We wish to express our thanks to our colleagues and friends who have provided constructive comments and useful suggestions in the development of the manuscript.

We are also thankful to our family members Pratibha, Sanjay, Ashish, Rajnish, Anupriya, Akshita–for their support and encouragement in completing this project.

Prof. JAWAHAR LAL

Dr. SEEMA SRIVASTAVA

PREFACE TO THE FIRST EDITION

Financial Accounting is a growing, dynamic and stimulating field of study. To be effective, individuals and professionals in all areas of business, especially those in finance and accounting, must have sufficient understanding of financial accounting and principles underlying financial statements and other accounting information produced in this subject. The subject matter of financial accounting can be made more useful and understandable by a book that provides comprehensive and up-to-date coverage of the subject with clear and readable discussion that helps the learning process of students and readers.

The present book is a student-oriented text. It presents an all-encompassing and up-to-date discussion of the fundamental accounting concepts and principles in a business setting in a logical, concise, clear and lucid manner. It aims to help the students and readers develop a sound understanding of basic accounting principles and mechanics of the accounting process.

ORGANIZATION AND COVERAGE

The book comprises 17 chapters divided into five parts.

Part One: 'Fundamentals' has two chapters and makes an overview of financial accounting and discusses different accounting postulates, concepts, principles and standards.

Part Two: 'Accounting Records and Systems' consists of seven chapters and explains Accounting Equation and Transaction Analysis, Journals, Subsidiary Books, Ledger Posting, Errors and their Rectifications, Bank Reconciliation Statement, Trial Balance, Profit and Loss Account, Balance Sheet.

Part Three: 'Elements of Financial Statements' has three chapters and presents discussion on different elements of financial statements namely, Revenue, Expenses, Gains, Losses. It also examines Depreciation Accounting, Inventory Valuation.

Part Four: 'Company Accounts' consists of three chapters and explains the accounting treatment in different situations such as Issue of Shares, Issue of Debentures, Preparing Company Final Accounts.

Part Five: 'Specialised Topics' is devoted to the discussion of specialised topics and discusses Financial Statement Analysis and Computerised Accounting in a business environment.

PEDAGOGY

This book contains numerous pedagogical devices and techniques to provide a balanced blend of conceptual and procedural materials for the students. Some pedagogical features of the book are:

- Chapter objectives (Learning Objectives) have been given at the beginning of each chapter. The chapter objectives have been integrated with the text presentation and the listing of objectives provides an outline of the chapters.
- Clear, concise, building block discussion in a logical and lively style are presented in all the chapters which make the materials real and interesting and certainly more helpfui to the students in learning and understanding it.
- The text contains many well-illustrated charts, diagrams and figures designed to help the students easily and quickly understand concepts and relationships and enable them to develop the ideas underlying the material as it is explained.

- ➢ Summary is presented at the end of each chapter
- ➢ Theory Questions involving thought provoking and real-life theory questions are given at the end of all chapters.
- ➢ Self-Evaluation Exercises containing abundance of multiple choice, true or false, fill in the blanks have been added at the end of chapters to help students review the key ideas contained in the chapters. Answers to Self-Evaluation Exercises are also provided with the end-of chapter materials.
- ➢ Adequate exercises and problems have been given at the end of the chapters.
- ➢ The book provides glossary of useful technical terms in the area of financial accounting at the end of the book.

The text is primarily designed for many professional programmes of the Indian universities, management institutes and business schools. The book will be very useful to the following programmes and courses :

- ➢ BBA and MBA courses of GGS Indraprastha University, New Delhi.
- ➢ BBA programme of other Indian universities and management Institutes.
- ➢ CFA, DFA, MBA programmes of the Institute of Chartered Financial Analysis of India (ICFAI), Hyderabad.
- ➢ MBA, MFC, and other similar programmes of Indian universities/management institutes.
- ➢ Other professional courses aiming to provide exposure in Financial Accounting to the participants to enable them to pursue a business and finance career.

ACKNOWLEDGEMENTS

We wish to express our thanks to our colleagues and friends who have provided constructive comments and useful suggestions in the development of the manuscript.

AUTHORS

CONTENTS

PART–ONE : FUNDAMENTALS

1. Financial Accounting : An Overview **1.3—1.21**

2. Basic Accounting Concepts and Accounting Standards **2.1—2.25**

PART–TWO : ACCOUNTING RECORDS AND SYSTEMS

3. Accounting Equation and Transaction Analysis **3.3—3.17**

4. Accounting Mechanics I : Journals **4.1—4.22**

5. Cash Book and Subsidiary Books **5.1—5.19**

6. Accounting Mechanics II : Ledger Posting and Trial Balance **6.1—6.38**

7. Bank Reconciliation Statement **7.1—7.15**

8. Errors and their Rectifications **8.1—8.16**

9. Preparation of Financial Statements : Profit and Loss Account and Balance Sheet **9.1—9.90**

10. Depreciation Accounting **10.1—10.47**

11. Inventory Valuation **11.1—11.28**

PART–THREE : COMPANY ACCOUNTS

12. Accounting for Shares **12.3—12.51**

13. Accounting for Debentures **13.1—13.48**

14. Company Final Accounts **14.1—14.72**

15. Accounting for Amalgamation **15.1—15.42**

16. Valuation of Goodwill **16.1—16.12**

PART–FOUR : FINANCIAL ANALYSIS

17. Statement of Changes in Financial Position **17.3—17.25**

18. Cash Flow Statement **18.1—18.37**

19. Financial Statement Analysis **19.1—19.39**

PART–FIVE : SPECIALISED TOPICS

20. Corporate Financial Reporting **20.3—20.27**

21. Computerised Accounting (How to Use Tally) **21.1—21.49**

GLOSSARY **G-1—G-10**

PART – ONE

FUNDAMENTALS

- **Chapter 1** Financial Accounting: An Overview
- **Chapter 2** Basic Accounting Concepts and Accounting Standards

1

FINANCIAL ACCOUNTING: AN OVERVIEW

LEARNING OBJECTIVES

After reading this chapter, you should be able to:

- *Describe* the evolution of accounting
- *Define* accounting
- *Distinguish* between accounting and book-keeping
- *Explain* the role of accounting as an information system
- *Understand* accounting as the language of business
- *Identify* the different users of accounting information
- *Explain* the nature of financial accounting and management accounting
- *Elaborate* the three principal financial statements
- *Pinpoint* the three basic forms of organisation

EVOLUTION OF ACCOUNTING

Accounting has evolved in a manner similar to law, medicine and most other fields of human activity, in response to the social and economic needs of society. Book-keeping and accounting did not emerge as chance phenomena, but as a pragmatic response to a specific world need.[1] This is true not only of the days of Paciolo[2] but also important for present-day accounting survival. Sieveking, one of the few historians who have paid attention to the subject, says that book-keeping developed as a direct response to the establishment of partnership on a large scale.

For centuries after the system of double-entry book-keeping appeared, accounting was practised without a uniform methodology or any form of theory. It was only during the 19th century that a distinct move from book-keeping to accounting—a move from relatively simple recording and

1. Maurice Moonitz and A.C. Littleton, *Significant Accounting Essays,* Prentice-Hall, 1965. p. 12.
2. Francisan Monk, Paciolo, is looked upon as the father of modern accounting, His Summa, published in 1494, comprised the first text reference on book-keeping, Later book-keeping spread throughout the world through a series of Paciolo imitations.

analysis of transactions towards a comprehensive accounting information system—was effected. The close of 19th century was marked by the most extraordinary expansion of business.

Company form of organisation, a phenomenon which was becoming increasingly common in business world, grew at a great speed. Books about business transactions were written, conventions were followed and accounting was recognised as a system of analysing and maintaining records of business transactions.

In part, the new significance of accounting gained recognition because of separation between ownership and control and also due to diversification in ownership. The increased reliance on capital as a factor of production necessitated extensive record-keeping, and finally, in the 19th century, a theoretical framework began to evolve. This framework or methodology provided a technical means to measure, evaluate, and communicate information of economic and financial nature.

Modern business is marked by continuity, a never-ending flow of economic activities. Therefore, accounting has grown to meet a social requirement and to guide the business and industry accordingly. Accounting is moving away from its traditional procedural base, encompassing record-keeping and such related work as the preparation of budgets and final accounts, towards the adoption of a role which emphasises its social importance. Welsch and Anthony[3] comment:

> "The growth of business organisations in size, particularly publicly-held corporations, has brought pressure from stock-holders, potential investors, creditors, governmental agencies, and the public at large, for increased financial disclosure. The public's right to know more about organisations that directly and indirectly affect them (whether or not they are shareholders) is being increasingly recognised as essential. An open society is one that has a high degree of freedom at the individual level and typically evidences an effective commitment to measuring the quality of life attained. These characteristics make it essential that the members of that society be provided adequate, understandable, and dependable financial information from the major institutions that comprise it."

Profit calculation is no longer a simple comparison of financial values at the beginning and end of a transaction or series of transactions. It is now related to a complex set of allocations and valuations pertaining to the operational activities of a business enterprise. The concept of accountancy or accounting has broadened to include description of the recording, processing, classifying, evaluating, interpreting and supplying of economic–financial information for presentation of financial statements and decision-making purposes.

Further refinements in cost and management accounting followed later on in the 20th century along with large-scale production and high-capital investment. These developments created a need to allocate costs correctly over the units of production, and also to provide a measure of productivity and efficiency. Thereafter, cost accounting evolved naturally to meet recognized managerial requirements of pricing and costing for competitive purposes, and towards determining and setting forth of operational information for decision-making purposes.

Traditionally, governmental accounting was linked to taxation and revenue control, and to the recording of, and accountability for, receipts and expenditures. Development in budgeting in the 20th century created a much larger scope for government accounting. The national budget became a managerial and policy-making instrument and developed into a mechanism for the forward planning of receipts and expenditures. Budgeting has now developed to form one of the bases of—and is closely associated with—economic planning and programming.

The use of enterprise accounting for the purpose of macro (economic or national) accounting is largely a present-century development. For purposes of economic policy and economic planning, the national data—to a large extent derived from commercial data—have assumed greater significance.

---

3. Glenn A. Welsch and Robert N. Anthony, *Fundamentals of Financial Accounting,* Richard D. Irwin, 1971, p. 19.

This, in turn, has given rise to the concept of macro accounting which has presented the professional with a new sphere of operation and perspective. Macro accounting has particular importance in helping build the bridge between economics and accounting, and thus offers accounting a significant scope to make a contribution towards macro economic policy.[4]

Accounting, thus, has gone through many phases—simple double-entry book-keeping, enterprise, government, and cost and management accounting, and recently, social accounting. These phases have largely been a product of changing economic and social environments. As business and society have become more complex over the years, accounting has developed new concepts and techniques to meet the ever increasing needs for financial information.

DEFINITION OF ACCOUNTING

What is accounting? This basic question has never been answered precisely and many definitions of the term are available.

Back in 1941, the Committee on Terminology of the American Institute of Certified Public Accountants (AICPA) formulated the following definition,[5] which was widely quoted for many years:

> "Accounting is the art of recording, classifying and summarising in a significant manner, and in terms of money, transactions and events which are, in part at least, of a financial character, and interpreting the results thereof."

In 1966, The American Accounting Association (AAA), in order to emphasise the broader perspective of accounting, provided the following definition of accounting:[6]

> "Accounting is the process of identifying, measuring and communicating economic information to permit informed judgements and decisions by users of the information".

In 1970, the AICPA of the US defined accounting with reference to the concept of information:[7]

> "Accounting is a service activity. Its function is to provide quantitative information, primarily financial in nature, and about economic activities, that is intended to be useful in making economic decisions."

The term 'quantitative information' used in the above definition is wider in scope than financial or economic information. Both the definitions, AAA (1966) and AICPA (1970), emphasise on using the information for the purposes of decision-making.

Modern accounting, therefore, is not merely concerned with record-keeping but also with a whole range of activities involving planning, control, decision making, problem solving, performance measurement and evaluation, coordinating and directing, auditing, tax determination and planning, cost and management accounting.

The managers within an organisation and interested outside parties use accounting information in making decisions that affect the organisation. Today's accounting focusses on the ultimate needs of those who use accounting information, whether these users are inside or outside the business itself.

Others have also given their definitions of accounting, but none has succeeded in clearly establishing the nature and scope of accounting. Each definition has merit in that it describes

4. Dr. Adolf J. H. Enthoven, *Accounting Education in Economic Development,* North-Holland Publishing Co., 1981, p. 11.
5. Accounting Terminology Bulletin No. 1; *Review and Resume,* AICPA, 1953, para 9.
6. American Accounting Association, *A Statement of Basic Accounting Theory,* 1966, p. 1.
7. Accounting Principles Board, Statement No. 4, *Basic Concepts and Accounting Principles Underlying Financial Statement of Business Enterprises*, 1970, para 40.

essentially what accountants do, but the boundaries are fuzzy.[8] Of the several available definitions of accounting, the one developed by American Accounting Association is perhaps the best because of its focus on accounting as an aid to decision making.[9]

ACCOUNTING AND BOOK-KEEPING

Book-keeping should be distinguished from accounting which has been defined earlier. Book-keeping is a process of accounting concerned merely with recording transactions and keeping records. Book-keeping is a small and simple part of accounting. It is mechanical and repetitive while dealing with business transactions.

Accounting, on the other hand, aims at designing a satisfactory information system which may fulfil informational needs of different users and decision makers. Accounting primarily focusses on measurement, analysis, interpretation and use of information. It highlights the relevance and relationship of the information produced by the accounting process and effects of different accounting alternatives. Accounting includes budgeting, strategic planning, cost analysis, auditing, income-tax preparation, performance measurement, evaluation, control, preparing managerial reports for decision making, etc.

ACCOUNTING AS AN INFORMATION SYSTEM

The term 'system' may be defined as a set of elements which operate together in order to attain a goal. A system does not consist of random sets of elements but elements which may be identified as belonging together because of a common goal. A system contains three activities: (*i*) input, (*ii*) processing of input, and (*iii*) output.

Accounting comprises a series of linked activities. These accounting activities form a progression of steps, beginning with observing, then collecting, recording, analysing, and finally communicating information to users. In other words, the accounting process involves the accumulation, analysis, measurement, interpretation, classification, and summarisation of the results of each of the many business transactions that affected the entity during the year. After this processing, accounting then transmits or projects messages to potential decision makers. The messages are in the form of financial statements, and the decision makers are the users. Accounting generally does not generate the basic information (raw financial data), rather, the raw financial data results from the day-to-day transactions of the enterprise.

As an information system, accounting links an information source or transmitter (generally the accountant), a channel of communication (generally the financial statements) and a set of receivers (external users). When accounting is looked upon as a process of communication, it is defined as "the process of encoding observations in the language of the accounting system, of manipulating the signs and statements of the systems and decoding and transmitting the result.[10]

Figure 1.1 displays how accounting as an information system aids business and economic decisions made by user-decision-makers. In this service activity, as shown in Fig. 1.1, accounting assumes a link between business activities and transactions and the decision-makers. First, accounting measures business activities and transactions through recording data. Second, the recorded data is processed and stored until needed. Processing can be done in such a manner or format as to become

8. "A good definition, besides providing a description so that people have an understanding of what the object is, should establish clear-cut boundaries. Any object that falls within the boundaries of the set is identified as a member of the set and any object that falls outside is then not a member of the set". Vernon Kam, *Accounting Theory,* John-Wiley and Sons, 1990, p. 33.
9. Robert N. Anthony and James S. Reece, *Accounting Principles*, Richard D. Irwin 1991, p. 8.
10. R. J. Chambers, *Accounting, Evaluation and Economic Behaviour*, Scholars Book Company, 1974, p. 184.

useful information. Alternatively, sometimes, the processed data are further processed or prepared to provide the required information to the user. Thirdly, processed and prepared information is communicated to users and decision-makers in the forms of financial statements, other statements, reports, etc. In this accounting system, business transactions and activities are the input and statements and reports generated for the decision-makers comprise the output.

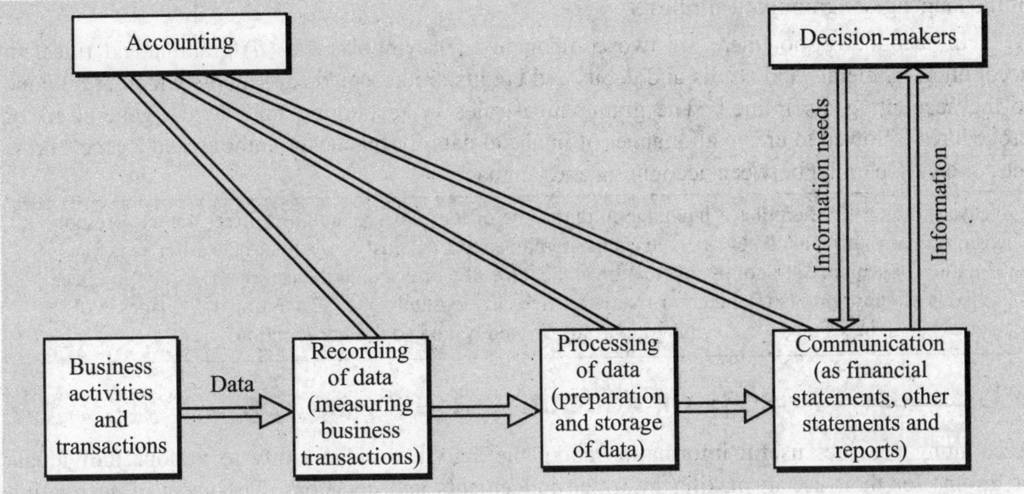

Fig. 1.1 Accounting as an information system in business and economic decision-making.

Thus, as an information system accounting has a basic goal, *i.e.*, to provide information. In order to accomplish this goal, the accounting system should be designed to classify financial information on a basis suitable for decision-making purposes and to process the tremendous quantities of data efficiently and accurately.

Also, the information system must be designed to report the results periodically, in a realistic and concise format that is comprehensible to users who generally have only a limited accounting knowledge. Furthermore, the information system must be designed to accommodate the special and complex needs of internal management of the enterprise on a continuing basis.

ACCOUNTING AS A LANGUAGE

Accounting is often called the 'language of business'. It is one means of communicating information about a business. As a new language is to be learnt to converse and communicate, so also accounting is to be learnt and practised to communicate vis-a-vis business events. Many accounting writers and researchers, as well as the accounting profession have referred to accounting as the language of business. For instance. Yuji Ijiri[11] observes:

> "As the language of business, accounting has many things in common with other languages. The various business activities of a firm are reported in accounting statements using accounting language, just as news events are reported in newspapers, in English or another language. To express an event in accounting or in English we must follow certain rules. Without following certain rules diligently, not only does one run the risk of being misunderstood but also risks a penalty for misrepresentation, lying or perjury. Comparability of statements is essential to the effective functioning of a language whether it is in English or in accounting. At the same time, language has to be flexible to adapt to a changing environment."

11. Yuji Ijiri, *Theory of Accounting Measurement,* Accounting Research Study No. 10. AAA, 1975, p. 14.

There are important similarities between a language and accounting. A language broadly has two components: (*i*) symbols, and (*ii*) rules to make it purposeful. Symbols are the meaningful units or words identifiable in any language, known as linguistic objects and which are used to convey particular meanings or concepts. The arrangement of symbols in a systematic manner becomes a language. The rules which influence the usage and pattern of the symbols are known as the grammar of the language or grammatical rules.

In accounting too, there are two components: (*i*) symbols, and (*ii*) grammatical rules. In accounting, numerals and words and debits and credits are accepted as symbols which are unique to the accounting discipline.[12] The grammatical rules in accounting refer to the general set of procedures followed to create all manner of financial data for business. Anthony and Reece[13] draw the following parallel between accounting and language:

> "Accounting .... resembles a language in that some of its rules are definite whereas others are not. Accountants differ as to how a given event should be reported, just as grammarians differ as to many matters of sentence structure, punctuation and choice of words. Nevertheless, just as many practices are clearly poor English (language), many practices are definitely poor accounting. Languages evolve and change in response to the changing needs of society, and so does accounting."

USERS OF ACCOUNTING INFORMATION

Accounting provides useful information about the activities of an entity to various individuals or groups for their use in making informed judgements and decisions. The users of accounting information can be broadly divided into three categories:

1. Management or managers
2. Users with direct financial interest
3. Users with indirect financial interest

Figure 1.2 shows different users of accounting information and different decisions made by them.

1. Management: Management is a group of people who are responsible for using the resources and managing the affairs of an entity to achieve certain predetermined goals and objectives. Managers perform many managerial functions such as planning, controlling, directing, measuring, evaluating and taking corrective action. Business managers need to decide continuously what to do, how to do it and whether the actual results tally the original plans and targets. Accounting provides timely and useful information to the management for planning, control, performance measurement, decision making and for performing many activities and functions in the company, Thus, management is one of the most important users of accounting information and a major function of accounting is to provide useful information to the managers and management.

2. Users with Direct Financial Interest: Users who have direct financial interest in a company include existing and potential investors and creditors. These users do not participate in the actual management of the company but have interest in how a business has performed because they have invested, or are thinking of investing in a company. Existing and potential investors are obviously interested in the past performance of a company and its earning potential and growth prospects in the future. For this, the company's financial statements and other information should be analysed to decide and select a profitable investment opportunity.

Similarly, the existing and potential creditors require accounting information to make sound credit decisions, *i.e.*, whether to lend money to a company. The creditors are interested in knowing

12. Daniel L. McDonald, *Comparative Accounting Theory,* Addison Wesley, 1972.
13. Robert N. Anthony and James S. Reece, *Accounting Principles,* Richard D. Irwin, 1991, p. 14.

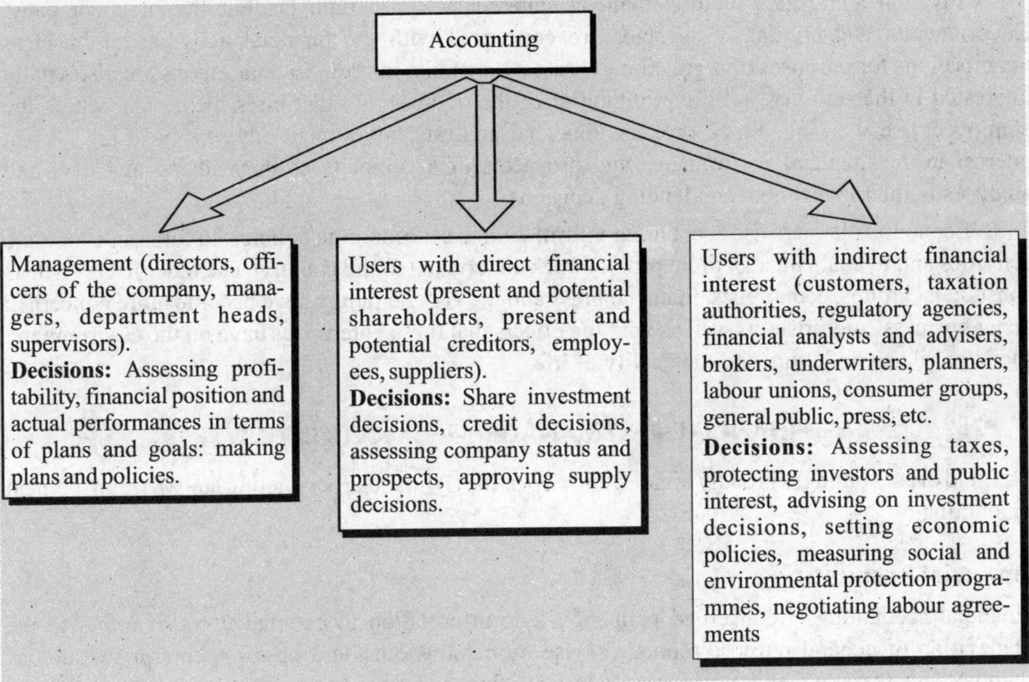

Fig. 1.2 Different users of accounting information

whether the company will have enough cash to pay interest charges and repay the debt on the due date. For this, the company's liquidity and cash flow position should be analysed. Banks, finance companies, mortgage companies, investment and insurance concerns, individual creditors and other similar individuals and groups who lend money need accounting information to analyse a company's profitability, liquidity and financial position before making a loan to the company.

Besides the investors and creditors, there are other users such as employees and suppliers who have direct financial interest in a company and accounting information as well, Employees' decisions may be based on perceptions of company's economic status acquired through financial statements. In particular, prospective and present employees may use the financial reports to assess risk and growth potential of a company, therefore job security and future promotional possibilities.

To suppliers, a business enterprise is a source of cash in the form of payment for goods or services supplied. Suppliers are also interested in a company's ability to generate adequate cash flows towards the payment of goods and services supplied which, in turn, can be decided on the basis of the company's financial statement.

3. Users with an Indirect Financial Interest: There are some other users who have indirect interest in a company's business or who use accounting information to help others having direct interest in a company's profitability and financial position. Such users are customers, taxation authorities, governmental and regulatory agencies, labour unions, financial analysts and advisers: stock exchanges and brokers, underwriters; economists: planners; consumer groups; general public and the financial press.

Customers may use financial statement data to forecast the likelihood and/or timing of a firm going bankrupt or being unable to meet its commitments. This information may be important in estimating the value of a warranty or in predicting the availability of supporting services or continuing supply of goods over an extended period of time.

Taxation authorities require financial statements to ascertain tax liability of a company. Governmental and regulatory agencies are concerned with the financial activities of business organisations for purposes of regulation to protect the public interest. Labour unions are also vitally interested in the stability and the profitability of the organisation that hires them or in which the employees are working. Stock brokers, financial analysts, investment advisers have an indirect interest in the financial performance and prospects of a company as they advise investors and creditors in their investment and lending decisions.

Economic planners use accounting information to set economic policies, to forecast economic activities and to evaluate economic programmes undertaken in the country. The other users such as consumers' groups, economists, financial press and the general public have become more concerned about business enterprises as well as with the effects that these enterprises have on the environment, social problems, inflation, and the quality of life.

FINANCIAL AND MANAGEMENT ACCOUNTING

The field of accounting is broadly divided into two parts: (*i*) financial accounting, and (*ii*) management accounting.

Financial Accounting

Financial accounting is concerned with providing information to external users. It refers to the preparation of general purpose reports for use by persons outside a business enterprise, such as shareholders (existing and potential), creditors, financial analysts, labour unions, government authorities, and the like. Financial accounting is oriented towards the preparation of financial statements which summarise the results of operations for selected periods of time and show the financial position of the business at particular dates. It involves recording, classifying and summarising of the effects of internal events and external transactions. The following are important to understand the scope and nature of financial accounting:

1. Contents: The end product of the financial accounting process comprises financial statements that communicate useful information to decision-makers. The financial statements reflect a combination of recorded facts, accounting conventions and personal judgements of the preparers. There are three primary financial statements for a profit-making entity in India, *viz.* the income statement (statement of revenues, expenses and profit), and the balance sheet (statement of assets, liabilities and owners equity), Cash Flow Statement as per AS 3 issued by the Institute of Chartered Accountants of India.

2. Accounting System: The accounting system includes various techniques and procedures used by the accountant (preparer) in measuring, describing and communicating financial data to users. Journals, ledgers, trial balance, financial statements are prepared using double entry accounting system.

3. Accounting Principles: Financial accounting follows a set of ground rules or accounting principles which are generally known as Generally Accepted Accounting Principles (GAAP). GAAP helps in the preparation of financial statements and in the choice of accounting methods, procedures and techniques.

4. Measurement Unit: Financial accounting measures all business transactions in terms of monetary unit of a society in which it operates. The common denominator or yardstick used for accounting measurement is, say, rupee in India and dollar in the US.

5. Users of Financial Accounting Information: As stated earlier, financial accounting information is intended to primarily serve external users. The Financial Accounting Standards Board of the US observes that financial accounting should provide information that is useful to present and potential investors and creditors and other users for making rational investments, credit and similar decisions.[14] Financial accounting information is used by a variety of groups, and for diverse purposes. Some users have direct interest in reported information. Examples of such users are owners, creditors and suppliers, potential owners, management, employees, customers. Some users need financial accounting information to help those who have direct interest in a business enterprise. Examples of such users are financial analysts and advisers, stock exchanges, financial press and reporting agencies, trade associations, labour unions, These user groups having direct/indirect interest have different objectives and diverse information needs. The emphasis in financial accounting has been on general-purpose information which, obviously, is not intended to satisfy any specialised needs of individual users or specific user groups.

Limitations of Financial Accounting

Financial accounting suffers from the following limitations which have been responsible for the emergence of cost and management accounting:

1. Financial accounting does not provide detailed cost information for different departments, processes, products, jobs in the production divisions. Similarly, separate cost data are not available for different services and functions in the administration division. Management may need information about different products, sales territories and sales activities which are also not available in financial accounting.

2. Financial accounting does not set up a proper system of controlling materials and supplies. Undoubtedly, if material and supplies are not controlled in a manufacturing concern, they will lead to losses on account of misappropriation, misutilisation, scrap, defectives, etc. They may, in turn, influence the reported net income of a business enterprise.

3. Recording and accounting for wages and labour is not carried out for different jobs, processes, products, departments. This creates problems in analysing the cost associated with different activities. This also does not provide a basis for rewarding workers and employees for the above-average performance.

4. It is difficult to know the behaviour of costs in financial accounting as expenses are not assigned to the product at each stage of production. Expenses are not classified into direct and indirect, and therefore, cannot be classified as controllable and uncontrollable. Control of cost which is the most important objective of all business enterprise cannot be achieved with the aid of financial accounting alone.

5. Financial accounting does not possess an adequate system of standards to evaluate the performance of departments and employees working in the departments. Standardisation is now applied to all elements of business. Standards need to be developed for materials, labour and overheads so that a firm can compare the work of labourers, workers, supervisors and executives with what should have been done in an allotted period of time.

6. Financial accounting contains historical cost information which is accumulated at the end of the accounting period. This accounting does not provide day-to-day information about costs and expenses. This is the reason why much dissatisfaction has been shown with external financial reporting. Historical cost is not a reliable basis for predicting future earnings, solvency, or overall managerial effectiveness. Historical cost information is relevant but not adequate for all purposes. It is now rightly contended that current cost information should be reported along with historical cost information.

7. Financial accounting does not provide information to analyse the losses due to various factors, such as idle plant and equipment, seasonal fluctuations in volume of business, etc. It does

14. Financial Accounting Standard Board, *Objectives of Financial Reporting by Business Enterprises.* Statements of Financial Accounting Concepts no. 1. FASB, 1978, Para 34.

not help management in taking important decisions about expansion of business, dropping a product line, starting with a new product, alternative methods of production, improvement in product, etc. Managerial decisions about these business matters have now become vital for the survival and growth of business enterprises.

MANAGEMENT ACCOUNTING

Management accounting refers to all types of accounting information and reports for the internal use of managements. Management accounting is concerned with providing information to managers to carry out their managerial responsibilities and functions such as planning, execution, control and decision-making. The Institute of Management Accountants (US) defines management accounting as:

> "... the process of identification, measurement, accumulation, analysis, preparation and communication of financial information used by management to plan, evaluate and control within the organisation and to assure appropriate use and accountability for its resources."

Management accounting provides both historical and estimated data which the management uses in evaluating and controlling performances, and in planning future operations. For instance, accounting information may be used by top management in determining the selling price of a new product. A finance manager may use a statement of projected cash receipts and disbursements in deciding if short-term borrowing is necessary. Production managers, by comparing past performances with planned objectives, can take steps to reduce wastages, unfavourable trends, and to increase productivity and induce favourable trends.

A sales manager may use a report and compare cost of producing and selling different products and then recommend to the top management the prices to be charged and the products to be pushed through by the sales force. The different users (managers) within an enterprise can specify the types of information they need for their decisions and management accounting accordingly may prepare or supply information to satisfy their needs.

Management accounting uses the information and statements prepared in financial accounting plus it prepares and provides additional information and reports to the management. In providing this additional information, management accounting is not governed by any definite set of accounting principles. Since the additional data are used only by management, the management accounting provides the data in the format that is most useful for management.

SIMILARITIES BETWEEN FINANCIAL ACCOUNTING AND MANAGEMENT ACCOUNTING

Both financial accounting and management accounting are part of the total accounting information system. Both deal with economic events. Both try to quantify the results of economic activity and transactions. Both are concerned with financial statements, revenues, expenses, assets, liabilities and cash flows.

The accounting information system that accumulates and classifies information, generates financial statements is the same system that is used for most of the reports and analyses which are prepared under management accounting. Further, the reports prepared in management accounting and financial accounting are based on the same database. This is the reason why the accounting system in an organisation, when it collects and classifies information, does so in a manner and format which can be appropriate for both the accounting systems. To achieve this dual purpose in developing the database, many business enterprises expand this database so as to fulfil adequately the informational needs of their managers and decision-makers.

For example, investors and other users are primarily interested in the overall profitability of a company. However, the managers within the company are more interested in the profitability of individual products. In this situation, the accounting system can be developed and designed so as to provide both total company profits as well as profits from individual products. The vital point about an accounting system is its flexibility.

More specifically, financial accounting and management accounting are also similar with respect to determination and measurement of costs, their assignment to different accounting periods and allocation of costs to different departments and segments. The concepts and principles which are used in the area of financial accounting for the purposes of cost accumulation and cost allocation may also be suitable for management accounting. It means any method, principle or concept which is developed for financial accounting can also be used for preparing reports and analyses falling under management accounting.

DIFFERENCES BETWEEN FINANCIAL ACCOUNTING AND MANAGEMENT ACCOUNTING

The following are the differences between financial accounting and management accounting.

1. Primary Users of Information: The users of financial accounting statements are mainly external to the business enterprise. External users include shareholders, creditors, financial analysts, government authorities, stock exchanges, labour unions, etc. The financial statements prepared in financial accounting are relevant to managements but are not adequate for the purpose of planning, control and decision-making.

Management accounting prepares reports and supplies information to the management for planning, controlling and decision-making. The information generated under the management accounting system is used by members of management at different levels in conformity with their information requirements for analysing business operations and for planning and control purposes. Thus, different sets of information could be developed under management accounting and supplied to different persons responsible for various activities in the organisation.

2. Accounting Method: Financial accounting follows the double-entry system for recording, classifying and summarising business transactions. Management accounting is not based on the double-entry system. The data under management accounting may be gathered for small or large segments or activities of an organisation and monetary as well as other measures and, information can be used for different activities in the firm.

3. Accounting Principles: Financial accounting data is primarily meant for external users. The Generally Accepted Accounting Principles (GAAP)* are important in financial accounting, and are used extensively while recording, classifying, summarising, and reporting business transactions. The use of GAAP adds credibility and reliability to financial statements and creates confidence among the financial statement users.

On the contrary, management accounting is not bound to use GAAP. It can use any accounting technique or practice which generates useful information. Besides, data developed in management accounting may comprise facts, estimates, projections, analyses, etc.

4. Unit of Measurement: All information under financial accounting is in terms of money. That is, transactions measured in terms of money have already occurred. In comparison, management accounting applies any measurement unit that is useful in a particular situation. Besides the monetary units, the management accountant may find it necessary to use measures such as number of

* Generally Accepted Accounting Principles (GAAP) includes conventions, rules and procedures used in financial accounting to process financial information and to define accepted accounting practice at a particular time.

employees, labour hours, machine hours and product units for the purpose of analysis and decision-making. The common objective in all measurement, reporting and data analysis in management accounting is usefulness for a particular, and mostly 'in house', purpose. Historical costs and past transactions are essential to financial accounting but may be secondary to management accounting as they are not of much use to management.

5. Time Span: Financial accounting data and statements are developed for a definite period, usually a year. It requires that financial statements be developed and presented at regular time intervals. Company annual reports may be prepared semi-annually or quarterly but the important point is that they are prepared on a regular basis.

Management Accounting reports and statements are prepared as and when they are needed. Reports may be prepared on a monthly, weekly or even a daily basis. Frequency of reports is determined by the planning, controlling and decision-making needs.

6. General Purpose Report vs. Specific Purpose Report: Financial accounting produces information and reports which are general purpose in nature in order to serve the informational needs of many external users such as shareholders, creditors, potential investors, customers, suppliers regulatory authorities, employees and the general public. Financial accounting is concerned with overall firm performance rather than individual segments or departments.

On the contrary, the reports and data developed under management accounting are known as specific-purpose reports designed for a particular user (manager) or particular decision. Management accounting uses internal reports to evaluate the performance of entities, product lines, departments and managers.

7. Historical vs. Futuristic Data: Financial accounting has a historical orientation and records and reports what has happened. Financial accounting concentrates on the results of past decisions. Management accounting has a futuristic orientation and concentrates on what is likely to happen in the future. This is due to the fact that management accounting emphasises on developing information for planning, control and decision-making purposes. Therefore, management accounting focusses on the future more than the financial accounting.

PRINCIPAL FINANCIAL STATEMENTS

The end product of the financial accounting process is a set of reports that are called financial statements. The following constitute the financial statements:

1. Profit and loss account
2. Balance sheet
3. Statement of Changes in Financial Position (SCFP)

Profit and loss account, also known as income statement, presents the results of operations of a business enterprise for a period of time. This statement shows net profit or net income of an entity for a period of time. Net profit or income is the difference between revenues and expenses. The profit and loss account indicates how successful a business enterprise has been in achieving its profit goal for a given time span. It also gives the sources and amounts of revenues earned and the different types and amounts of expenses. When expenses exceed revenues for a period, a business enterprise incurs a net loss.

Balance sheet shows the financial position of a business on a certain date. For this reason, it is often called the statement of financial position. Balance sheet indicates the investing and financing activities of a business enterprise at a point of time and shows a firm's assets, liabilities and equity capital usually at the close of the last day of a month or a year. Assets are economic resources and provide future benefits to a firm such as cash, inventories, building, plant, patent, goodwill, etc. Liabilities are outsiders' claims on the assets of a business enterprise such as creditors, accounts payables, salaries payable, income-tax payable, debentures. Liabilities include shareholders' equity as well which is in the forms of ordinary shares, preference shares, retained earnings. Shareholders' equity is the shareholders' or owners' claim on the assets of a firm. The shareholders' claims are only residual, *i.e.*, shareholders have claims against the assets of a company only after all creditors' claims have been met.

A Statement of Changes in Financial Position (SCFP) shows where the financial resources (funds) have come from (sources) and where they have gone (uses). SCFP is generally prepared on working capital basis and cash basis. Working capital-based SCFP explains increase or decrease in working capital for a specified period of time. It reports:

(*a*) amount of changes in working capital associated with the operating activities of a firm.

(*b*) long-term financing or other sources that cause an increase in the working capital.

(*c*) long-term investment activities or other uses that cause a reduction in the working capital.

Cash basis SCFP, popularly known as cash flow statement, summarise the flow of cash in and out of the firm over a period of time. It focusses on various items which bring out changes in the cash balance between two balance sheet dates. Cash flow statement covers all items which increase or decrease the cash of a business enterprise. In USA, UK and other countries, statement of cash flows is legally required to be prepared by companies along with income statement and balance sheet. In India also, cash flow statement is required to be given in published company annual reports by the Indian companies whose securities are listed on the Stock Exchanges.

Among the above statements, balance sheet is considered a status or stock report and the other two statements—income statement and statement of changes in financial position—are known as flow reports. Balance sheets, as stocks reports, show the information about the resources of an organisation at a specified moment of time. The income statement and statement of changes in financial position (working capital and cash basis), as the flow reports, show the activities of the enterprises over a period of time, say for a year, half-year, or a quarter. Figure 1.3 summarises the information provided by the financial statements.

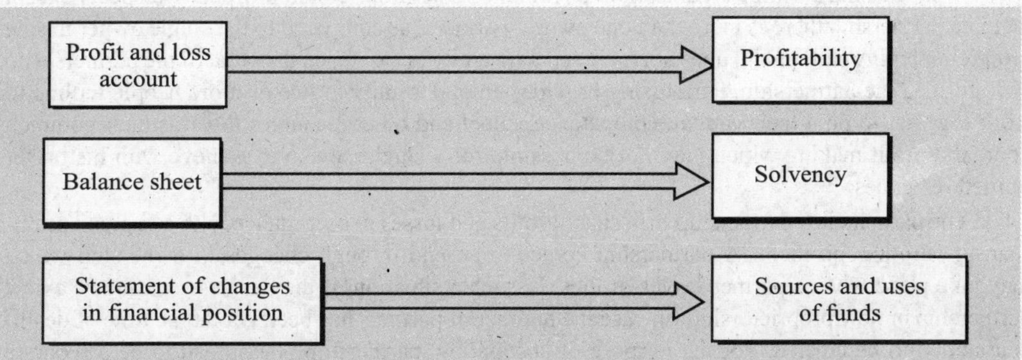

Fig. 1.3 Information provided by the financial statements

FORMS OF BUSINESS ORGANISATION

There are three basic forms of organisation—sole proprietorship, partnership and company form of organisation. In accounting, these forms of organisation are considered as having a separate entity from the owners for the purpose of recording business transactions and preparing financial statements. However, legally, only a company enjoys a separate entity from the shareholders–owners.

Table 1.1 gives the distinguishable characteristics of sole proprietorship, partnership and company.

Table 1.1 Comparative features of the forms of business organisation

Features	Sole proprietorship	Partnership	Company
1. Legal status	Not a separate legal entity	Not a separate legal entity	Separate legal entity
2. Transfer of ownership	Sale by owner to a new person/entity	Change in any partner's share creates new partnership	Transfer of ownership through sale of shares
3. Duration or life	Limited by desire or death of sole proprietor	Limited by desire or death of any partner	Indefinite, possibly unlimited
4. Ownership risk or liability	Unlimited, owner's personal property can be used to pay off business liabilities	Unlimited, except as provided in Limited Liability Partnership Act 2008	Limited to investment made by shareholders in the company
5. Accounting treatment basis	Separate economic unit	Separate economic unit	Separate economic unit

A sole proprietorship is a business established by a single person. The single individual manages the affairs of business and performs all planning, controlling and decision-making activities. All profits earned in the business accrue to the individual and similarly is personally liable for all the obligations and liabilities relating to the business. Legally, a sole proprietor does not have a separate entity from that of his proprietorship. The sole proprietorship comes to an end at the mere desire of sole proprietor or at his or her death or incapacity. For the purposes of recording transactions and accounting, the sole proprietorship is assumed to have separate entity from that of the sole proprietor.

A partnership form of organisation is similar to sole proprietorship in many respects except that in a partnership there is more than one owner (partners) as compared to the single owner in sole proprietorship. A partnership does not have separate entity or existence than that of the partners who have formed the partnership. Partnership provides an opportunity to two or more people willing to work together to pool their capital, competence, talent and other resources towards their common good and profit making which may not be possible for a single person to achieve with his or her limited resources.

The partners in a partnership firm share profits and losses in accordance with an agreed profit-sharing ratio among them. A partnership comes to an end through changes in ownership which may take place when a partner leaves or dies. In such a situation, if the business continues, a new partnership or new proprietorship (in case the number of partners has been two at the time of death) is assumed to be created. For the purpose of accounting, partnership is assumed to be a separate entity vis-a-vis the partners. Limited Liability Partnership (LLP) Act 2008 applies to partnership firm in India. As per its provisions, every partner of an LLP is, for the purpose of the business of the LLP, the agent of LLP, but not of other partners. The provisions do not affect the personal liability of a partner for his own wrongful act or omission, but a partner is not personally liable for the wrongful act or omission of any other partner of the LLP. The liabilities of the LLP and partners who are found to have acted with intent to defraud creditors or for any fraudulent purpose is unlimited for all or any of the debts or other liabilities of the LLP. A partner is not personally liable directly or indirectly for an obligation solely by reason of being a partner of the LLP.

A company form of organisation is formed through the shares issued by the company to the public. Thus, the capital of a company is raised by issuing shares and the persons who purchase the shares are known as shareholder-owners. Legally, a company has an entity separate from its shareholders. Shareholders do not participate directly in the management and control of the company. Instead, they elect a board of directors which is given the responsibility of managing the company for the benefit of shareholders. Shareholders' liability is limited; limited to the extent of the total face value of shares purchased by them. That is, shareholders' personal property cannot be used for the company's liabilities. Shareholders can transfer/sell their shares to other persons without affecting the company's operations. Thus, the life of a company is unlimited and is not affected by the death, retirement, or incapacity of company directors/shareholders or any other persons. Because of the limited liability, shareholders are often willing to invest in riskier, but potentially profitable, companies. Compared with sole proprietorship and partnership, companies have many advantages which enable them to collect capital for the formation, expansion and growth of the company.

THEORY QUESTIONS

1. What are the objectives of accounting, financial accounting and management accounting?
2. Distinguish between management accounting and financial accounting.
3. Which decision-makers use accounting information?
4. What objectives does management seek to achieve by using accounting information?
5. Why are investors and creditors interested in the financial statements of a business enterprise?
6. What groups besides managers, investors and creditors use accounting information?
7. What are the main financial statements obtained through the financial accounting process?
8. Why is balance sheet sometimes called the statement of financial position?
9. Contrast the purposes of the balance sheet from those of the income statement.
10. Suggest reasons why the format and content of financial accounting statements and reports tend to be more standardised than is the case for management accounting reports.
11. "Accounting is an information system." Explain this statement.
12. Discuss the different forms of organisation.
13. List and briefly describe the main audiences for financial accounting information.
14. Accounting is said to be the language of business. What does it try to communicate and how?
15. Rajan is the accountant of a small company making two or three different types of household tools. He systematically and accurately collects and records all the transactions of the company, and prepares statements, so that the management knows the annual profit and the financial position.

    "What more can a good accountant do?" ponders Rajan. From your understanding of the scope of accounting, advise him in what other ways he might be of service to the management.
16. Why is accounting regarded as an aid to management? Explain briefly.
    (BBA, GGSIP University, December 2000)
17. Write notes on Limitations of Accounting. **(BBA, GGSIP University, December 2002)**
18. (*a*) Define Accounting. Discuss the functions of Accounting, (*b*) Bring out the difference between Management Accounting and Financial Accounting.
    (BBA, GGSIP University, December 2004)
19. (*a*) What do you mean by Accounting? Who are the parties interested in accounting information? (*b*) What are the limitations of accounting?
    (BBA, GGSIP University, December 2006)
20. "Accounting is the language of the business." Comment.
    (BBA, GGSIP University, December 2007)

21. Distinguish between financial accounting and management accounting.
(BBA, GGSIP University, December 2007, December 2008)

22. "Accounting begins where book-keeping ends." Comment.
(BBA, GGSIP University, December 2008)

23. Answer the following:
(*a*) Is accounting science or art?
(*b*) What is the relation of accounting with management?
(BBA, GGSIP University, December 2009)

24. Write notes on: End users of accounting information.
(BBA, GGSIP University, December 2009)

25. "Book-keeping and accounting are not synonymous terms."
(BBA, GGSIP University, December 2010)

SELF-EVALUATION EXERCISES

I. Select the correct answer for the following multiple-choice questions.

1. A profit-making business that is a separate legal entity and in which ownership is in the form of shares is known as
(*a*) Sole proprietorship (*b*) Trust
(*c*) Partnership (*d*) Company

2. The properties owned by a business enterprise are called
(*a*) Assets (*b*) Liabilities
(*c*) Capital (*d*) Owner's equity

3. A list of assets, liabilities and owner's equity of a business enterprise as of a specific date is
(*a*) Balance sheet (*b*) Income statement
(*c*) Cash flow statement (*d*) None of the above

4. Which of the following is an important reason for studying accounting?
(*a*) The information provided by accounting is useful in making many economic decisions.
(*b*) Accounting plays an important role in society.
(*c*) The study of accounting could lead to a challenging career.
(*d*) All of the above are important reasons.

5. Which of the following groups uses accounting information for planning a company's profitability?
(*a*) Investors (*b*) Creditors
(*c*) Management (*d*) Regulatory agencies

6. Economic events that affect the financial position of a business are called
(*a*) Separate entities (*b*) Business transactions
(*c*) Money measures (*d*) Financial actions

7. Which of the following forms of organisation is not treated as a separate economic unit in accounting?
(*a*) Sole proprietorship (*b*) Committee
(*c*) Partnership (*d*) Company

8. If a company has liabilities of ₹ 19,000 and owner's equity of ₹ 57,000, the assets of the company are

(*a*) ₹ 38,000 (*b*) ₹ 76,000
(*c*) ₹ 57,000 (*d*) ₹ 19,000

9. The payment of a liability will
(*a*) increase both assets and liabilities (*b*) increase assets and decrease liabilities
(*c*) decrease assets and increase liabilities (*d*) decrease assets and decrease liabilities

10. The purchase of an asset for cash will
(*a*) increase and decrease assets at the same time
(*b*) increase both assets and liabilities
(*c*) increase assets and owner's equity
(*d*) increase assets and decrease liabilities

11. The balance sheet is related to the income statement in the same way that
(*a*) a point in time is related to a period of time
(*b*) a period of time is related to a point in time
(*c*) a point in time is related to another point in time
(*d*) a period of time is related to another period of time

12. Expenses and withdrawals appear, respectively, on which of the following financial statements?
(*a*) Balance sheet and income statement
(*b*) Income statement and balance sheet
(*c*) Statement of owner's equity and balance sheet
(*d*) Income statement and statement of owner's equity

13. Which of the following types of accountants should be completely independent of the firm or organisation whose financial data is being examined?
(*a*) Controller (*b*) Chartered accountant
(*c*) Internal auditor (*d*) Firm's budget director

II. Answer True or False:

1. Those needing financial information in their decision-making include business managers, investors, bankers, government administrators, and many others.

2. The primary function of accountants is to provide financial information about the activities and current position of an organisation.

3. There is little public discussion and concern about accounting today: accounting is left largely to accountants.

4. One main reason for studying accounting is to learn which measurement methods are used in presenting financial reports: most users of financial reports should be familiar with the measurement methods used to determine the values presented in financial reports.

5. All accounting entities are profit motivated.

6. Business entities usually borrow money first; after they have secured this capital, they try to get owners to invest additional money in the business.

7. The three basic types of business entities are: (*a*) sole proprietorships, (*b*) mutual cooperative associations, and (*c*) company,

8. The most practical way for a large number of investors to pool their capital to operate a business is to form a partnership.

9. Financial reports consist of two basic parts: (*a*) formal financial statements, and (*b*) a report from the employees of the business concerning working conditions and the labour policies of the business.
10. The three principal financial statements that are included in the financial reports of a business are: (*a*) balance sheet, (*b*) income statement, and (*c*) statement of changes in financial position.
11. The basic information components of the income statement are: (*a*) sales revenue, (*b*) liabilities, and (*c*) profit.
12. Expenses are deducted from sales revenue to determine profit; for a business entity, this profit is called net income.
13. When owners put money in a business, the money is called capital, to emphasise that the money is being committed to investment uses by the business.
14. The statement of changes in financial position reports the sources and uses of capital during the year.
15. The main purpose of reporting financial statements to the owners and those who lend money to the business is to keep them informed about the current financial performance and financial condition of the entity.

III. Indicate which type of business entity best fits each of the characteristics listed below:

SP = Sole (or Single) Proprietorship
P = Partnership
C = Company

(*a*) Only one owner has invested money (capital) in the business
(*b*) Issues shares to its owners when they invest capital
(*c*) Recognised by law as a distinct legal entity
(*d*) Each unit of ownership has one vote
(*e*) One owner may have a great voice in management and a larger share of profit, which is determined by the arrangement among the owners.
(*f*) Limited by the amount of capital that one person can invest in the business.

IV. Indicate the financial statement in which each type of financial information listed below is reported:

BS = Balance sheet (also called the statement of financial condition)
IS = Income statement
SCFP = Statement of changes in financial position

(*a*) Revenue from sales to customers
(*b*) The cumulative profit earned, which was not distributed to owners but kept in the business over all the years the business has been operating
(*c*) Obligations of the business for borrowing money
(*d*) Economic resources owned by the business entity
(*e*) Expenses during the period
(*f*) Net income earned during one period
(*g*) Sources of capital to the entity during the period
(*h*) Net loss suffered during the period, if no profit is earned
(*i*) Purchase of assets during the period by the entity to increase its productive capacity
(*j*) Amounts owned by the entity resulting from the purchases on credit

V. Indicate whether each of the following is in the field of financial accounting (FA) or management accounting (MA):

(*a*) Preparing external financial statements that are reported to investors.
(*b*) Preparing internal reports based on the organisational structure of the business entity
(*c*) Preparing condensed financial statements for the business entity as a whole
(*d*) Budgeting
(*e*) Developing detailed cost methods
(*f*) Standard costs
(*g*) Controlled by generally accepted accounting principles
(*h*) Auditing of financial reports by independent CAs
(*i*) Writing of additional commentary to accompany the external financial statements

VI. Match each description with its related term or abbreviation

Related Term	***Description***
1. Sole proprietorship	(A) Collection, analysis, measurement, recording and reporting information about an entity to decision-makers
2. Company	(B) A business owned by two or more persons
3. Accounting	(C) An incorporated entity that issues shares as evidence of ownership
4. Partnership	(D) Chartered accountant
5. ICAI	(E) An unincorporated business owned by one person.
6. CA	(F) Accounting Standards Board
7. ASB	(G) Institute of Chartered Accountants of India.

ANSWERS TO SELF-EVALUATION EXERCISES

I.

1. (*d*)	**2.** (*a*)	**3.** (*a*)	**4.** (*d*)	**5.** (*c*)	**6.** (*b*)
7. (*b*)	**8.** (*b*)	**9.** (*d*)	**10.** (*a*)	**11.** (*a*)	**12.** (*d*)

II.

1. True	**2.** True	**3.** False	**4.** True	**5.** False	**6.** False
7. False	**8.** False	**9.** False	**10.** True	**11.** False	**12.** True
13. True	**14.** True	**15.** True			

III.	(*a*) SP	(*b*) C	(*c*) C	(*d*) C	(*e*) P	(*f*) C
IV.	(*a*) IS	(*b*) BS	(*c*) BS	(*d*) BS	(*e*) IS	(*f*) IS
	(*g*) SCFP	(*h*) IS	(*i*) SCFP	(*j*) BS		
V.	(*a*) FA	(*b*) MA	(*c*) FA	(*d*) MA	(*e*) MA	(*f*) MA
	(*g*) FA	(*h*) FA	(*i*) FA			

VI.

1. (E)	**2.** (C)	**3.** (A)	**4.** (B)	**5.** (G)	**6.** (D)
7. (F)					

[illegible]

[illegible]

[illegible]

2

BASIC ACCOUNTING CONCEPTS AND ACCOUNTING STANDARDS

LEARNING OBJECTIVES

After reading this chapter, you should be able to:

- Define Postulates, Assumptions, Concepts, Principles and Convention.
- Explain basic accounting concepts such as entity, going concern, money measurement, accounting period, cost, dual-aspect, conservatism, matching, realization, consistency, materiality, full disclosure.
- Understand Generally Accepted Accounting Principles (GAAP).
- Discuss the provisions and guidelines given in AS 1 Disclosure of Accounting Policies.
- Define accounting standard.
- Explain benefits of accounting standards.
- Understand status of Accounting Standards in India.
- Discuss compliance with Accounting Standards in India.
- Understand the objectives of International Accounting Standards Board (IASB).
- Know how international accounting standards are developed.
- Prepare a list of IASs and IFRSs issued by IASB.

POSTULATES, ASSUMPTIONS, CONCEPTS, PRINCIPLES AND CONVENTIONS

Terms such as postulates, assumptions, concepts, principles and conventions (and others such as procedures, rules) are widely used, but with no general agreement as to their precise meaning. Often, what is referred to as 'Postulates' or 'Assumptions' by some writers, are termed as 'Concepts' or 'Principles' by others and *vice versa*. Similarly, what are understood by same as 'Accounting Conventions' are forcefully recognized as 'Accounting Principles' or 'Accounting Concepts' and *vice versa*. Thus, it can be observed that finding a precise terminology has always been one of the most difficult tasks in accounting. Further, the lack of agreement about precise meaning has affected, to some extent, the attempts made towards developing a theory for financial accounting.

The purpose of this chapter is not to engage the readers in a debate of suitable terminology but to explain something which are widely accepted as of greatest importance and widest applicability, whether as postulates, assumptions, concepts, principles or conventions. But before this, an attempt has been made to define the terms postulates, assumptions, concepts, principles and conventions.

Postulates

Accounting postulates are basic assumptions which are generally accepted as self-evident truths in accounting. Postulates are established or general truths which do not require any evidence to prove them. They are the propositions taken for granted.

American Institute of Certified Public Accountants (US) Observes

"Postulates are few in number and are the basic assumptions on which principles rest. They necessarily are derived from the economic and political environment and from the modes of thought and customs of all segments of the business community. The profession, however, should make clear their understanding and interpretation of what they are, to provide a meaningful foundation for the formulation of principles and the development of rules or other guides for the application of principles in specific situations."[1]

According to Kohler[2]

"The truth of a postulate, like that of other assumptions, is taken for granted as something generally admitted as self-evident... Postulates are chosen for their convenience and fruitfulness in organising and promoting inquiry or useful action. Postulates may be expected to change as activities within the field are modified, and as the public interest in the field alters its views concerning the value of the field to society."

Assumptions

Assumptions in accounting are considered and accepted as postulates. There is a wider consensus that both postulates and assumptions carry the same meaning and importance in the accounting context. Assumptions are premises, self-evident truths, statements accepted without proof as a basis for a line of reasoning or course of action. Applicability and utility of assumptions are deemed to be self-evident and consequences associated with applying assumptions justify their exploration and use.

Concepts

Accounting concepts are also self-evident statements or truths. Accounting concepts are so basic that one should accept them as valid without any questioning. Accounting concepts provide the conceptual guidelines for application in the financial accounting process, *i.e.*, for recording, measurement, analysis and communication of information about an organisation. These concepts provide help in resolving future accounting issues on a permanent or a longer basis, rather than trying to deal with each issue on an *adhoc* basis. The concepts are important because they (*a*) help explain the 'why' of accounting, (*b*) provide guidance when new accounting situations are encountered, and (*c*) significantly reduce the need to memorise accounting procedures when learning about accounting.[3]

Principles

Accounting principles are general decision rules derived from the accounting concepts. According to AICPA (US), a principle means, "a general law or rule adopted or professed as a guide to action:

1. American Institute of Certified Public Accountants, The Basic Postulates of Accounting, AICPA, 1961, p. 7.
2. Eric L. Kohler, A Dictionary for Accountants, Prentice Hall, 1983, p. 361.
3. Glewn A. Welsch and Daniel G. Short, Fundamentals of Financial Accounting, Irwin, 1987, p. 144.

a settled ground or basis of conduct or practice." Accounting principles are characterised as 'how to apply' concepts. Anthony and Reece[4] comment:

"Accounting principles are man-made. Unlike the principles of physics, chemistry and other natural science, accounting principles were not deducted from basic axioms, nor can they be verified by observation and experiment. Instead, they have evolved. This evolutionary process is going on constantly; accounting principles are not eternal truths."

A principle is an explanation concisely framed in words to compress an important relationship among accounting ideas into a few words. Principles are concise explanations. Accounting principles do not suggest exactly as to how each transaction will be recorded. This is the reason that accounting practices differ from one enterprise to another. The differences in accounting practices are also due to the fact that GAAP provides flexibility in the recording and reporting of business transactions.

Accounting principles influence the development of accounting techniques which are specific rules to record specific transactions and events in an organisation.

Conventions

Convention is referred to as a statement or a rule of practice adopted by common consent, express or implied. It can be distinguished from an Assumption, Axiom or Postulate in that it need not represent what is thought to be self-evident truth[5]. For example, it is a convention (established by long usage) that debits are placed on the left hand side of a 'T' account and credits on the right hand side. The opposite would be an equally useful convention.

A convention may be said to exist when it is known that an alternative equally logical rule or procedure is available but is not used because of considerations of habit, cost, time or convenience. Convention dictates many of the activities in accounting such as measures of materiality, the style and content of financial statements. Modified conventions emerge in the world of accounting from time to time. They are generally attributed to the growth of the public interest in the improvement of financial reporting.

BASIC ACCOUNTING CONCEPTS

Accounting principles are built on a foundation of a few basic concepts. These concepts are so basic that most preparers of financial statements do not consciously think of them. As stated earlier, they are regarded as self-evident. Some accounting researchers and theorists argue that certain of the present accounting concepts are wrong and should be changed. Nevertheless, in order to understand accounting as it now exists, one must understand the underlying concepts currently used.

Basic accounting concepts discussed herein may not be identical to those listed by other authors or groups. However, these are the concepts that are widely accepted and used in practice by preparers of financial statements and by auditors while verifying such statements. The basic accounting concepts are as follows:

1. Entity Concept: The entity concept assumes that the financial statements and other accounting information are for the specific business enterprise which is distinct from its owners. Consequently, the analysis of business transactions involving costs and revenue is expressed in terms of the changes in the firm's financial conditions. Similarly, the assets and liabilities devoted to business activities are entity assets and liabilities. The transactions of the enterprise are to be reported rather than the transaction of the enterprise's owners. This concept, therefore, enables the accountant to distinguish between personal and business transactions. The concept applies to sole

4. Robert N. Anthony and James S. Reece, Accounting Principles, Irwin, 1991, p. 15.
5. R.H. Parker, MacMillan Dictionary of Accounting, MacMillan, 1984, p. 46.

proprietorship, partnership, companies, and small and large enterprise. It may also apply to a segment of a firm, such as division, or several firms, such as when inter-related firms are consolidated.

2. Going-Concern Concept: A business entity is viewed as continuing in operation in the absence of evidence to the contrary.[6] Because of the relative permanence of enterprises, financial accounting is formulated assuming that the business will continue to operate for an indefinitely long period in the future.

The going-concern concept justifies the valuation of assets on a non-liquidation basis and it calls for the use of historical cost for many valuations. Also, the fixed assets and intangibles are amortised over their useful life rather than over a shorter period in expectation of early liquidation.

The going-concern concept leads to the proposition that individual financial statements are part of a continuous, inter-related series of statements. This further implies that data communicated are tentative and that current statements should disclose adjustments to past year statements revealed by more recent developments.

3. Money Measurement Concept: A unit of exchange and measurement is necessary to account for the transactions of business enterprises in a uniform manner. The common denominator chosen in accounting is the monetary unit. Money is the common denominator in terms of which the exchangeability of goods and services, including labour, natural resources and capital, are measured. Money measurement concept holds that accounting is a measurement and communication process of the activities of the firm that are measurable in monetary terms. Obviously, financial statements should indicate the money used.

Money measurement concept implies two limitations of accounting. First, accounting is limited to the production of information expressed in terms of a monetary unit: it does not record and communicate other relevant but non-monetary information. Secondly, the monetary measurement concept concerns the limitations of the monetary unit itself as a unit of measure. The primary characteristics of the monetary unit—purchasing power, or the quantity of goods or services that money can acquire—is of concern. Traditionally, financial accounting has dealt with this problem by stating that this concept assumes either that the purchasing power of the monetary unit is stable over time or that the changes in prices are not significant. While still accepted for current financial reporting, the stable monetary unit concept is the object of continuous and persistent criticism.

4. Accounting Period Concept: Financial accounting provides information about the economic activities of an enterprise for specified time periods that are shorter than the life of the enterprise. Normally, the time periods are of equal length to facilitate comparison.

The time period is identified in the financial statements. The time periods are usually of twelve months. Sometimes quarterly or half-yearly statements are also issued. These are considered interim and different from annual statements. For managerial use, statements covering shorter periods such as a month or a week may also be prepared.

5. Cost Concept: The cost concept requires that assets be recorded at the exchange price, *i.e.*, acquisition cost or historical cost. Historical cost is recognised as the appropriate valuation basis for recognition of the acquisition of all goods and services, expenses, costs and equities. For accounting purposes, business transactions are normally measured in terms of the actual prices or costs at the time the transaction occurs, *i.e.*, financial accounting measurements are primarily based on exchange prices at which economic resources and obligations are exchanged. Thus, the amounts at which assets are listed in the accounts of a firm do not indicate what the assets could be sold for.

6. A related proposition is that if liquidation appears imminent, financial information may be prepared on the assumption that liquidation will take place.

The historical cost concept implies that since the business is not going to sell its asset as such there is little point in revaluing assets to reflect current values. In addition, for practical reasons, the accountant prefers the reporting of actual costs to market values which are difficult to verify.

6. Dual-Aspect Concept: This concept lies at the heart of the whole accounting process. The accountant records events affecting the wealth of a particular entity. The question is—which aspect of this wealth are important? Since an accounting entity is an artificial creation, it is essential to know to whom its resources belong to or what purpose they serve. It is also important to know what kind of resources it controls, *e.g.*, cash, buildings or land. Accounts recording systems have therefore developed so as to show two main things: (*a*) the source of wealth, and (*b*) the form it takes.

Suppose Mr. X decides to establish a business and transfers ₹ 1,00,000 from his private bank account to a separate business account. He might record this event as follows:

Business Entity Records

Liabilities	*Assets*
Source of wealth	Form of wealth
X's capital ₹ 1,00,000	Cash at bank ₹ 1,00,000

Clearly, the source of wealth must be numerically equal to the form of wealth. Since they are simply different aspects of the same thing, *i.e.*, in the form of an equation: *S* (sources) must equal *F* (forms).

Moreover, any transaction or event affecting the wealth of entity must have two aspects recorded in order to maintain the equality of both sides of the accounting equation. If business has acquired an asset, it must have resulted in one of the following:

(*a*) Some other asset has been given up.

(*b*) The obligation to pay for it has arisen.

(*c*) There has been a profit, leading to an increase in the amount that the business owes to the proprietor.

(*d*) The proprietor has contributed money for the acquisition of asset.

This does not mean that a transaction will affect both the source and form of wealth. There are four categories of events affecting the accounting equation:

(*a*) Both, sources and forms of wealth, increase by the same amount.

(*b*) Both, sources and forms of wealth, decrease by the same amount.

(*c*) Some forms of wealth increase while others decrease without any change in the source of wealth.

(*d*) Some sources of wealth increase while others decrease without any change in the form in which wealth is held.

The example given above illustrates category (*a*) since the commencing transaction for the entity results in the source of wealth, and form of wealth, cash, both increasing from zero to ₹ 1,00,000. By contrast, *X* might decide to withdraw ₹ 20,000 cash from the business. Then financial position of business entity would result in:

Liabilities	*Assets*
Source of wealth	Form of wealth
X's capital ₹ 80,000	Cash ₹ 80,000

It is essential to appreciate why both sides of the equation decrease. By taking out cash, *X* automatically reduces his supply of private finance to the business by the same amount.

Suppose now that Mr. *X* buys stocks of goods for ₹ 30,000 with the available cash. His supply of capital does not change, but the composition of the business assets does.

Source of wealth	₹	Form of wealth	₹
X's capital	80,000	Stock	30,000
		Cash	50,000
	80,000		80,000

The two aspects of this transaction are not in the same direction but compensatory, an increase in stocks of setting a decrease in cash. Similarly, sources of wealth also may be affected by a transaction. Thus, if *X* gives his son *Y*, a ₹ 20,000 share in the business by transferring part of his own interest, the effect is as follows:

Source of wealth	₹	Form of wealth	₹
X's capital	60,000	Stocks	30,000
Y's capital	20,000	Cash	50,000
	80,000		80,000

If, however, *X* gives *Y* ₹ 20,000 in cash privately and *Y* then puts it into the business, both sides of equation would be affected. *Y*'s capital of ₹ 20,000 being balanced by an extra ₹ 20,000 in cash, *X*'s capital remaining at ₹ 80,000.

7. Accrual Concept: According to Financial Accounting Standards Board (US): "Accrual accounting attempts to record the financial effects on an enterprise of transactions and other events and circumstances that have cash consequences for the enterprise in the periods in which those transactions, events and circumstances occur rather than only in the periods in which cash is received or paid by the enterprise. Accrual accounting is concerned with the process by which cash expended on resources and activities is returned as more (or perhaps less) cash to the enterprise, not just with the beginning and end of that process. It recognises that the buying, producing, selling and other operations of an enterprise during a period, as well as other events that affect enterprise performance often do not coincide with the cash receipts and payments of the periods."

Realization concept and matching concept are central to accrual accounting. Accrual accounting measures income for a period as the difference between the revenues recognized in that period and the expenses that are matched with those revenues. Under accrual accounting the period's revenues generally are not the same as the period's cash receipts from customers, and the period's expenses generally are not the same as the period's cash disbursements.

Cash-Basis Accounting: Under cash-basis accounting, sales are not recorded until the period in which they are received in cash. Similarly, costs are deducted from sales in the period in which they are paid for cash disbursements. Thus, neither the realization nor matching concept applies in cash-basis accounting.

In practice, "pure" cash-basis accounting is rare. This is because a pure cash-basis approach would require treating the acquisition of inventories as a reduction in profit when the acquisition costs are paid rather than when the inventories are sold. Similarly, costs of acquiring items of plant and equipment would be treated as profit reductions when paid in cash rather than in the later periods when these long-lived items are used. Clearly, such a pure cash-basis approach would result in balance sheets and income statements that would be of limited usefulness. Thus, what is commonly called *cash-basis accounting* is actually a mixture of cash basis for some items (especially sales and period costs) and accrual basis for other items (especially product costs and long-lived assets). This mixture is also sometimes called **modified cash-basis accounting** to distinguish it from a pure cash-basis method.[7]

7. Robert N. Anthony, David F. Hawking and Kenneth A. Merchant, Accounting, Text and Cases, McGraw Hill, 2008, p. 68.

Cash-basis accounting is seen most often in small firms that provide services and therefore do not have significant amounts of inventories. Examples include restaurants, beauty parlours and barber shops, and income tax preparation firms. Since most of these establishments do not extend credit to their customers, cash-basis profit may not differ dramatically from accrual-basis income. Nevertheless, cash-basis accounting is *not* permitted by GAAP for any type of business entity.

8. Conservatism[8] Concept: This principle is often described as "anticipate no profit, and provide for all possible losses." This characterisation might be viewed as the reactive version of the minimax managerial philosophy, *i.e.*, minimise the chance of maximum losses. The concept of accounting conservatism suggests that when and where uncertainty and risk exposure so warrant, accounting takes a wary and watchful stance until the appearance of evidence to the contrary. Accounting conservatism does not mean intentionally understating income and assets, it applies only to situations in which there are reasonable doubts. For example, inventories are valued at the lower ends of cost or market value.

In its application to the income statement, conservatism encourages the recognition of all losses that have occurred or are likely to occur but does not acknowledge gains until actually realised. The early amortisation of intangible assets and the restrictions against recording appreciation of assets have also, at least to some extent, been motivated by conservatism. Failure to recognise revenue until a sale has taken place is still another manifestation of conservatism.

9. Matching Concept: The matching concept in financial accounting is the process of matching (relating) accomplishments or revenues (as measured by the selling prices of goods and services delivered) with efforts or expenses (as measured by the cost of goods and services used) to a particular period for which the income is being determined. This concept emphasises which items of cost are expenses in a given accounting period. That is, costs are reported as expenses in the accounting period in which the revenue associated with those costs is reported. For example, when the sales value of some goods is reported as revenue in a year, the cost of those goods would be reported as expenses in the same year.

Matching concepts need to be fulfilled only after realisation concept has been completed by the accountant: first revenues are measured in accordance with the realisation concept and then costs are associated with these revenues. *Costs are matched with revenues, not the other way around.* The matching process, therefore, requires cost allocation which is significant in historical cost accounting. Past (historical) costs are examined and are subjected to a procedure whereby elements of cost regarded as having expired service potential are allocated or matched against relevant revenues. The remaining elements of costs which are regarded as continuing to have future service potential are carried forward in the historical balance sheet and are termed as assets. *Thus, the balance sheet is nothing more than a report of unallocated past costs waiting expiry of their estimated future service potential before being matched with suitable revenues.*

10. Realization or Recognition Concept: The realization or recognition concept indicates the amount of revenue that should be recognised from a given sale. Realization rules help the accountant in determining that a revenue or expense has occurred, so that it can be measured, recorded, and reported in financial reports.

Realization refers to inflows of cash or claims to cash (*e.g.*, accounts receivable) arising from the sale of goods or services. Thus, if a customer buys ₹ 500 worth of items at a grocery store, paying cash, the store realizes ₹ 500 from the sale. If a clothing store sells a suit for ₹ 3,000, the purchaser agreeing to pay within 30 days, the store realizes ₹ 3,000 (in receivables) from the sale, *provided*

8. According to some writers 'prudence' is a better word than conservatism, Uncertainties inevitably surround many transactions and this should be recognised by exercising prudence in preparing financial statements. Prudence does not, however, justify the creation of secret or hidden reserves.

that the purchaser has a good credit record so that payment is reasonably certain (conservatism concept).

The realization concept states that the amount recognised as revenue is the amount that is reasonably certain to be realized—that is, that customers are reasonably certain to pay. Of course, there is room for differences in judgment as to how certain "reasonably certain" is. However, the concept does clearly allow for the amount of revenue recognized to be less than the selling price of the goods and services sold.[9] The obvious situation is the sale of merchandise at a discount—at an amount less than its normal selling price. In such cases, revenue is recorded at the lower amount, not the normal price.

11. Consistency Concept: This concept requires that once an organisation has decided on one method, it should use the same method for all subsequent transactions and events of the same nature unless it has sound reasons to change methods. If accounting methods are frequently changed, comparison of financial statements for one period with those of another period would be difficult. The consistent use of accounting methods and procedures over time will check the distortion of profit and loss account and the balance sheet and the possible manipulation of these statements. Consistency is necessary to help external users in comparing financial statements of a given firm over time and in making sound economic decisions.

12. Materiality Concept: In law there is a doctrine called *de minimis non curat lex*, which means that the court will not consider trivial matters. Similarly, the accountant does not attempt to record events so insignificant that the work of recording them is not justified by the usefulness of the results.

Materiality concept implies that the transactions and events that have immaterial or insignificant effects should not be recorded and reported in the financial statements. It is argued that the recording of insignificant events cannot be justified in terms of its subsequent poor utility to users. For example, conceptually, a brand-new pad of paper is an asset of the entity. Every time someone writes on a page of the pad, part of this asset is used up, and retained earnings decrease correspondingly. Theoretically, it would be possible to ascertain the number of partly used pads that are owned by the entity at the end of the accounting period and to show this amount as an asset. But the cost of such an effort would obviously be unwarranted, and no accountant would attempt to do this. Accountants take the simpler, even though less exact, course of action and treat the asset as being used up (expensed) either at the time the pads were purchased or at the time they were issued from supplies inventory to the user.

Unfortunately, there is no agreement on the meaning of materiality and the exact line separating material events from immaterial events. The decision depends on judgment and commonsense. It is for the preparer of accounts to interpret what is and what is not material. Probably the materiality of an event or transaction can be decided in terms of its impact on the financial position, results of operations, changes in the financial position of an organisation and on evaluation or decisions made by users.

13. Full Disclosure Concept: The full disclosure concept requires that a business enterprise should provide all relevant information to external users for the purpose of sound economic decisions. This concept implies that no information of substance or of interest to the average investors will be omitted or concealed from an entity's financial statements.

GENERALLY ACCEPTED ACCOUNTING PRINCIPLES (GAAP)

Financial accounting follows a set of ground rules or accounting principles in presenting financial information which are known as Generally Accepted Accounting Principles (GAAP). In fact, to be

9. Robert N. Anthony, David F. Hawking and Kenneth A. Merchant, *Ibid*, p. 56.

useful, financial accounting information should be collected, classified, summarised and reported objectively. Those who use such information and rely on such data have a right to be assured that the data are reliable, free from bias and in consistencies, whether deliberate or otherwise. For this reason, financial accounting depends on certain guidelines or standards that have proved useful over the years in accounting and reporting information. In this task, GAAP plays a vital role and financial accounting information can be meaningful only when prepared according to some agreed upon standards and procedures, *i.e.*, Generally Accepted Accounting Principles.

Accounting Principles Board[10] of the USA Observes

"Generally Accepted Accounting Principles incorporate the consensus at a particular time as to which economic resources and obligations should be recorded as assets and liabilities by financial accounting, which changes in assets and liabilities should be recorded, when these changes are to be recorded, how the assets and liabilities and changes in them should be measured, what information should be disclosed and which financial statements should be prepared."

GAAP are simply guides to action and may change over time. They are not immutable laws like those in the physical science. Sometimes specific principles must be altered or new principles must be formulated to fit changed economic circumstances or changes in business practices. Accounting principles originate from problem situations such as changes in the law, tax regulations, new business organisational arrangements, or new financing or ownership techniques.

Certain accounting techniques or procedures are tried in response to the effect such problems have on financial reports. Through comparative use and analysis, one or more of these techniques are judged most suitable, obtain substantial authoritative support and are then considered a generally accepted accounting principle.

Walgenbach[11], *et al.* comment

> "Because no basic natural accounting law exists, accounting principles have developed on the basis of their usefulness. Consequently, the growth of accounting is more closely related to experience and practice than to the foundation provided by ultimate law. As such, accounting principles tend to envolve rather than be discovered, to be flexible rather than precise and to be subject to regular evaluation rather than be ultimate or final."

In India, organisations such as the Accounting Standards Board (ASB), Institute of Chartered Accountants of India, Department of Corporate Affairs (Government of India), Securities and Exchange Board of India (SEBI), Institute of Costs and Works Accountants of India, Institute of Company Secretaries, Stock Exchanges, and the literature each of these publishes, are instrumental in the development of most accounting principles. In the US, Financial Accounting Standards Board (FASB), American Institute of Certified Public Accountants (AICPA). Securities and Exchange Commission (SEC), Internal Revenue Service and the American Accounting Association are instrumental in the formulation of accounting principles. At the international level, International Accounting Standards Board (IASB) has taken upon the responsibility of formulating accounting standards for use by all the countries of the world.

AS-1: DISCLOSURE OF ACCOUNTING POLICIES

The Institute of Chartered Accountants of India (ICAI) issued AS-1 titled 'Disclosure of Accounting Policies' in November 1979. This standard is now mandatory and deals with the disclosure of significant accounting policies followed in preparing and presenting Financial Statements.

10. Accounting Principles Board, Statement No. 4, AICPA, 1970.
11. Paul H. Walgenbach, Ernst I. Hanson and Norman E. Dittrich, Financial Accounting, An Introduction, Harcourt Brace Jovanovich, 1988, p. 443.

In general, accounting policies are not at present regularly and fully disclosed in all financial statements. Many enterprises include in the Notes on the Accounts, description of some of the significant accounting policies.

Even among the few enterprises that presently include in their annual reports a separate statement of accounting policies, considerable variation exists. The statement of accounting policies forms part of the accounts in some cases while in others it is given as supplementary information.

The purpose of AS-1 is to promote better understanding of financial statements by establishing through an accounting standard the disclosure of significant accounting policies and the manner in which accounting policies are disclosed in the financial statements. Such disclosure would also facilitate a more meaningful comparison between financial statements of different enterprises.

AS-1 contains explanations on following points:

Fundamental Accounting Assumptions

1. Certain fundamental accounting assumptions underlie the preparation and presentation of financial statements. They are usually not specifically stated because their acceptance and use are assumed. Disclosure is necessary if they are not followed.

The following have been generally accepted as fundamental accounting assumptions:

(*a*) *Going Concern*: The enterprise is normally viewed as a going concern, that is, as continuing in operation for the foreseeable future. It is assumed that the enterprise has neither the intention nor the necessity of liquidation or of curtailing materially the scale of the operations.

(*b*) *Consistency*: It is assumed that accounting policies are consistent from one period to another.

(*c*) *Accrual*: Revenues and costs are accrued, that is, recognised as they are earned or incurred (and not as money is received or paid) and recorded in the financial statements of the periods to which they relate. (The considerations affecting the process of matching costs with revenues under the accrual assumption are not dealt with in this statement).

2. Nature of Accounting Policies

(*i*) The accounting policies refer to the specific accounting principles and the methods of applying those principles adopted by the enterprise in the preparation and presentation of financial statements.

(*ii*) There is no single list of accounting policies which are applicable to all circumstances. The differing circumstances in which enterprises operate in a situation of diverse and complex economic activity make alternative accounting principles and methods of applying those principles acceptable. The choice of the appropriate accounting principles and the methods of applying those principles in the specified circumstances of each enterprise calls for considerable judgement by the management of the enterprise.

(*iii*) The various statements of the Institute of Chartered Accountants of India combined with the efforts of government and other regularity agencies and progressive managements have reduced in recent years the number of acceptable alternatives particularly in the case of corporate enterprises. While continuing efforts in this regard in future are likely to reduce the number still further, the availability of alternative accounting principles and methods of applying these principles is not likely to be eliminated altogether in view of the differing circumstances faced by the enterprises.

3. Areas in which differing accounting policies are encounted: The following are examples of the areas in which different accounting policies may be adopted by different enterprises.

- Method of depreciation, depletion and amortisation
- Treatment of expenditure during construction

- Conversion of translation of foreign currency items
- Valuation of inventories
- Treatment of goodwill
- Valuation of investments
- Treatment of retirement benefits
- Recognition of profit on long-term contracts
- Valuation of fixed assets
- Treatment of contingent liabilities

The above list of examples is not intended to be exhaustive.

4. Considerations in the Selection of Accounting Policies: The primary consideration in the selection of accounting policies by an enterprise is that the financial statements prepared and presented on the basis of such accounting policies should represent a true and fair view of the state of affairs of the enterprise as at the balance sheet date and of the profit or loss for the period ended on that date.

For this purpose, the major considerations governing the selection and application of accounting policies are:

(*a*) *Prudence*: In view of the uncertainty attached to future events, profits are not anticipated but recognized only when realised though not necessarily in cash. Provision is made for all known liabilities and losses even though the amount cannot be determined with certainty and represents only a best estimate in the light of available information.

(*b*) *Substance over Form*: The accounting treatment and presentation in financial statements of transactions and events should be governed by their substance and not merely by the legal form.

(*c*) *Materiality*: Financial statements should disclose all "material" items, *i.e.*, items the knowledge of which might influence the decisions of the user of the financial statements.

5. Disclosure of Accounting Policies

(*i*) To ensure proper understanding of financial statements, it is necessary that all significant accounting policies adopted in the preparation and presentation of financial statements should be disclosed.

(*ii*) Such disclosure should form part of the financial statements.

(*iii*) It would be helpful to the reader of financial statements if they are all disclosed as such in one place instead of being scattered over several statements, schedules and notes.

(*iv*) Examples of matters in respect of which disclosure of accounting policies adopted will be required are contained in point no. 3. This list of examples is not, however, intended to be exhaustive.

(*v*) Any change in an accounting policy which has a material effect should be disclosed. The amount by which any item in the financial statements is affected by such change should also be disclosed to the extent ascertainable. Where such amount is not ascertainable, wholly or in part, the fact should be indicated. If a change is made in the accounting policies which has no material effect on the financial statements for the current period but which is reasonably expected to have a material effect in later periods, the fact of such change should be appropriately disclosed in the period in which the change is adopted.

(*vi*) Disclosure of accounting policies or of changes therein cannot remedy a wrong or inappropriate treatment of the item in the accounts.

6. Accounting Standard in AS-1

(*i*) All significant accounting policies adopted in the preparation and presentation of financial statements should be disclosed.

(*ii*) The disclosure of the significant accounting policies as such should form part of the financial statements and the significant accounting policies should normally be disclosed in one place.

(*iii*) Any change in the accounting policies which has material effect in the current period or which is reasonably expected to have a material effect in later periods should be disclosed. In the case of a change in accounting policies which has a material effect in the current period, the amount by which any item in the financial statements is affected by such change should also be disclosed to the extent ascertainable. Where such amount is not ascertainable, wholly or in part, the fact should be indicated.

(*iv*) If the fundamental accounting assumptions, *viz*., Going Concern, Consistency and Accrual are followed in financial statements, specific disclosure is not required. If a fundamental accounting assumption is not followed, the fact should be disclosed.

ACCOUNTING STANDARDS

Definition of Accounting Standard

The use of word 'Standard' in accounting literature is of a recent origin. What is described as 'standard' today, used to be generally known as 'principles' a few years ago. The British introduced the term 'standards' in place of 'principles' when they set up their Accounting Standards Steering Committee at the end of 1969, and the Americans adopted the same term ('standard') in 1973, when the Accounting Principles Board was wound up and the Financial Accounting Standards Board was created. In India, this term has mainly become popular since the formation of Accounting Standards Board (ASB) in April 1977 by the Institute of Chartered Accountants of India.

The term 'Accounting Standard' may be defined as written statements issued from time to time by institutions of the accounting profession or institutions in which it has sufficient involvement and which are established expressly for this purpose. They are written documents, policy documents issued by expert accounting body or by Government or other regulatory body covering the aspects of recognition, measurement, treatment, presentation and disclosure of accounting transaction in the financial statement.

The objective of accounting standards is to standardize the diverse accounting policies and practices with a view to eliminate to the extent possible the non-comparability of financial statements and increase relevance and reliability of financial statements.

Accounting standards mainly deal with financial measurements and disclosures used in producing a set of fairly presented financial statements. In this respect, accounting standards can be thought of as a system of measurements and disclosure. They also draw the boundaries within which acceptable conduct lies and in that and many other respects, they are similar in nature to laws.

BENEFITS OF ACCOUNTING STANDARDS

The benefits of accounting standards may be listed as follows.

1. To Improve the Credibility and Reliability of Financial Statements: Financial statements of business enterprises are used by a diverse group of users for making sound economic decision. The users are shareholders (existing and potential), trade creditors, customers, suppliers, employees, taxation authorities and other interested parties. It is necessary, therefore, that the financial statements the users use and upon which they rely, present a fair picture of the position and progress of the enterprises. It is the function of accounting (and auditing) standards to create this general sense of confidence by providing a framework within which credible financial statements can be produced. Accounting standards are required to meet a basic need of managers, investors and creditors to compare results and financial conditions of different segments of firms, different periods of a firm, different firms and different industries. In the absence of standards, there would be no incentives to encourage an enterprise to conform to any particular model for the sake of comparison. Thus, the main aim of accounting standards is to protect users' interest by providing them with information in which they can have confidence.

2. Benefits to Preparers and Auditors: Preparers and auditors, with the passage of time and changing climate of opinion, have to work in an environment where they face the threat of stern sanctions and a bad name to their professions. These result partly from changed penalties and remedies available under the company law and partly from the greater willingness of aggrieved parties to take their causes before the courts. The risk of these developments is considerable to auditors whether in terms of uncovered financial exposure to liability or adverse effects on professional reputation resulting from unfavourable publicity.

Particularly dangerous are causes of undetected fraud, and audited accounts, which are held to be misleading due to insufficient disclosure or use of inappropriate accounting principles. Given the increasing risks, the accounting profession realised that it needed to have the accounting standards for their own benefits.

3. Determining Managerial Accountability: Accounting standards facilitate in determining specific corporate accountability and regulation of the company. They help in assessing managerial skill in maintaining and improving the profitability of the company, depicting the progress of the company, its solvency and liquidity.

Generally they are important factors in assessing the effectiveness of management's performance of its duties and leadership. Standards aim to ensure consistency and comparability in place of (imposed) uniformity in financial reporting to permit better comparisons in profitability, financial position, future prospects and other performance indicators associated with different business firms.

ACCOUNTING STANDARDS IN INDIA

The Institute of Chartered Accountants of India constituted the Accounting Standards Board (ASB) in April 1977, recognising the need to harmonise the diverse accounting policies and practices in India and keeping in view the international development in the field of accounting. The ASB is entrusted with the following functions:

1. To formulate accounting standards which may be established by the council of ICAI in India. While formulating standards, the ASB is required to take into consideration the applicable laws, customs and usages and business environment; it is also required to give due consideration to International Accounting Standards issued by IASC (now IASB) and to integrate them, to the extent possible, in the light of the conditions and practices prevailing in India.
2. To propagate the Accounting Standards and persuade the concerned parties to adopt them in the preparation and presentation of financial statements.
3. To issue guidance notes on the Accounting Standards and give clarifications on issues arising therefrom.
4. To review the accounting standards at periodic intervals.

The date from which a particular standard will come to effect, as well as the class of enterprises to which it will apply, will also be specified by the Institute. Unless otherwise stated, no standard will have retrospective application. Normally, before formulating the standards, ASB will hold discussions with the representatives of the government, public sector undertakings, industry and other organisations, for ascertaining their views. An exposure draft of the proposed standards will be prepared and issued for comments by members of the institute and the public at large. After considering the comments received, the draft of the proposed standard will be finalised by ASB and submitted to the council which will study it, modify it if necessary and issue it under its own authority.

ACCOUNTING STANDARDS ISSUED BY ASB (INDIA)

The Institute of Chartered Accountants of India has issued so far 32 Accounting Standards. They are displayed in Exhibit 2.1.

Exhibit 2.1 Status of the Accounting Standards issued by the Institute of Chartered Accounts of India

Number of the Accounting Standards (AS) (1)	Title of the Accounting Standard (2)	Date from which Mandatory (Accounting periods commencing on or after) (3)
AS-1	Disclosure of Accounting Policies	01.04.1993
AS-2 (Revised)	Valuation of Inventories	01.04.1999
AS-3 (Revised)	Cash Flow Statement	01.04.2001
AS-4 (Revised)	Contingencies and Events occurring after the Balance Sheet Date	01.04.1998
AS-5 (Revised)	Net Profit or Loss for the period. Prior Period items and Changes in Accounting Policies	01.04.1996
AS-6 (Revised)	Depreciation Accounting	01.04.1995
AS-7 (Revised)	Accounting for Construction Contracts	01.04.2003
AS-8	Withdrawn and included in AS-26.	
AS-9	Revenue Recognition	01.04.1993
AS-10	Accounting for Fixed Assets	01.04.1993
AS-11 (Revised)	The Effects of Changes in Foreign Exchange Rates (Revised 2003)	01.04.2004
AS-12	Accounting for Government Grants	01.04.1994
AS-13	Accounting for Investments	01.04.1995
AS-14	Accounting for Amalgamations	01.04.1995
AS-15	Accounting for Retirement Benefits in the Financial Statements of Employers	01.04.1995
AS-16	Borrowing Costs	01.04.2000
AS-17	Segment Reporting	01.04.2001
AS-18	Related Party Disclosures	01.04.2001
AS-19	Leases	01.04.2001
AS-20	Earning per Share	01.04.2001
AS-21	Consolidated Financial Statement	01.04.2001
AS-22	Accounting for Taxes on Income	01.04.2001
AS-23	Accounting for Investment in Associates in Consolidated Financial Statements	01.04.2002
AS-24	Discontinuing Operations	01.04.2004
AS-25	Interim Financial Reporting	01.04.2002

Number of the Accounting Standards (AS) (1)	Title of the Accounting Standard (2)	Date from which Mandatory (Accounting periods commencing on or after) (3)
AS-26	Intangible Assets	01.04.2003
AS-27	Financial Reporting of Interests in Joint Venture	01.04.2002
AS-28	Impairment of Assets	01.04.2004
AS-29	Provisions, Contingent Liabilities and Contingent Assets	01.04.2004
AS-30	Financial Instruments: Recognition and Measurement and Limited Revision to AS-2, AS-11 (Revised 2003), AS-21, AS-23, AS-26, AS-27, AS-28	01.04.2011
AS-31	Financial Instruments—Presentation	01.04.2011
AS-32	Financial Instruments—Disclosures	01.04.2011

In addition to these standards, the Institute of Chartered Accountants of India has issued statements, guidance notes and opinions which seek to bring about uniformity in corporate accounting and reporting practices.

COMPLIANCE WITH ACCOUNTING STANDARDS

Compliance with accounting standards has been made mandatory. Sub-section (3A) to Section 211 (inserted by the Companies Amendment Act, 1999) requires that every profit and loss account and balance sheet shall comply with the accounting standards. Accounting standards means the standards of accounting recommended by the Institute of Chartered Accountants of India (ICAI) and prescribed by the Central Government in consultation with the National Advisory Committee on Accounting Standards (NACAS) constituted under sub-section 210A(1).

Until the Central Government proscribes accounting standards under this section, accounting standards issued by the ICAI shall be deemed to be the accounting standards.

As per newly inserted clause 50 of the Listing Agreement it is mandatory for the companies listed in a recognized stock exchange to comply with all applicable accounting standards in the preparation and presentation of financial statements.

(i) Establishment of NACAS: Section 210A (inserted *vide* the Companies Amendment Act, 1999) discusses about the establishment of the NACAS. The Central Government is empowered by virtue of the provision of section 210A(1) to establish NACAS which would advise the Central Government on the formulation and laying down of accounting policies and accounting standards for adoption by companies or class of companies under the Act. The NACAS shall give its recommendation to the Central Government on such matters of accounting policies and standards and auditing as may be referred to it for advice from time to time.

The ICAI is free to set Accounting Standards as it has been doing since 1977. For the purpose of the Companies Act, the Central Government enjoys the authority to prescribe such accounting standards which are recommended by the ICAI. While prescribing any accounting standard, the Central Government may consult the NACAS.

(ii) Deviation from accounting standards: Sub-section (3B) to section 211 requires that in case the profit and loss account and balance sheet of a company do not comply with the requirements of the accounting standards, disclosure should be made stating:

- Deviations from the accounting standards;
- The reasons for such deviation; and
- The financial effect, if any, arising due to such deviation.

The disclosure requirement as stated in section 211 (3A) will bring transparency but such deviations may be material enough to affect the truth and fairness of the financial statements. Accordingly, it is necessary for the statutory auditors to give negative report in case truth and fairness of the financial statements are violated by virtue of such deviations. This needs a change in the auditors reporting norm.

(*iii*) *Duties of the statutory auditors with regard to mandatory accounting standards*: The statutory auditors are required to make qualification in their report in case any item is treated differently from the prescribed treatment in the relevant accounting standard. However, while qualifying they should consider the materiality of the relevant item.

In case of non-disclosure of significant accounting policies the auditors are required to specify the fact in their report. The ICAI suggests that it should be on the following lines:

"The company has disclosed those accounting policies the disclosure of which is required by the Companies Act, 1956. Other significant accounting policies, *viz*., those relating to method of accounting followed for recognising revenue of the long term construction contracts and recognition of warranty expenses have not been disclosed nor have all the policies been disclosed at one place, which is contrary to Accounting Standard-1, 'Disclosure of Accounting Policies' issued by the ICAI."

Similarly, an auditor is required to specify the fact in case a non-corporate body prepares financial statements on cash basis. The ICAI suggests that specifying the fact is sufficient and the auditors may state that accounts give true and fair view on the cash basis if it is so.

The newly inserted sub-section (3) of section 227 requires the auditors to report whether, in his opinion, the profit and loss account and balance sheet comply with the accounting standards referred to in section 211 (3C).

(*iv*) *Income-tax Act, 1961*: Pursuant to an amendment to the Income-tax Act, 1961 in 1995, it has been provided that the Central Government may notify in the official Gazette from time to time accounting standards to be followed by any class of assessees or in respect of any class of income. Two accounting standards, *viz*. (1) Disclosure of Accounting Policies and (2) Disclosure of Prior Period and Extraordinary items and changes in accounting policies have been issued. These standards are more or less in conformity with the parallel standards issued by the ICAI. The main reason advanced for the necessity for the amendment of the Income-tax Act was the belief that the standards issued by the ICAI permitted alternative treatment in various situations. ICAI has already initiated action to reduce the alternatives.

The RBI as a regulatory authority also issues directions to banks and financial institutions as also to Non-Banking Finance Companies (NBFCs) on the manner in which certain accounting matters should be dealt with.

An equally significant development is the establishment by the Securities and Exchange Board of India (SEBI) of a Standing Committee on Accounting Standards. This committee monitors the existence of relevant accounting standards and their harmonization with the corresponding International Accounting Standards. It mandates the adherence to the standards and enforces the same through the listing agreements between the companies and stock exchanges. Therefore, at least in so far as listed companies are concerned, a better enforcement mechanism has been put in place.

INTERNATIONAL ACCOUNTING STANDARDS COMMITTEE (IASC) AND IASB

The IASC Foundation is an independent body, not controlled by any particular Government or professional organisation. Its main purpose is to oversee the IASB in setting the accounting principles which are used by business and other organisations around the world concerned with financial reporting.

The IASC was formed in 1973 through an agreement made by professional accountancy bodies from Australia, Canada, France, Germany, Ireland, Japan, Mexico, the Netherlands, the UK and the USA.

In November 1999, the IASC board itself approved the constitutional changes necessary for its own restructuring. In May 2000, the IFAC unanimously approved the restructuring. The constitution of the old IASC was revised to reflect the new structure. A new IASC Foundation was incorporated (under the laws of the US state of Delaware), and its trustees were appointed. By early 2001, the members of the IASB and the SAC were appointed, and the new structure became operational. Later that year, the IASB moved into new quarters in London. The technical staff of the IASB comprises of over 20 accounting professionals—roughly quadruple the former IASC's professional staff.

The objectives of the IASB stated in its Constitution (2000) are:

(*a*) to develop in the public interest, a single set of high-quality, understandable and enforceable global accounting standards that require high quality, transparent and comparable information in financial statements and other financial reporting to help participants in the world's capital markets and other users make economic decisions;

(*b*) to promote the use and rigorous application of those standards; and

(*c*) to bring about convergence of national accounting standards and International Accounting Standards to high-quality solutions.

PROCESS OF DEVELOPING INTERNATIONAL ACCOUNTING STANDARDS

In developing international accounting standards, the IASC, now IASB, follows the following procedures:

1. The IASC board selects a topic and assigns it to a steering committee which is made of four representatives, at least one of which is a board member and at least one of which is from a developing country.
2. The steering committee studies the issues involved and presents to the board a point outline on the topic.
3. The board gives its comments to the steering committee which then prepares a preliminary draft of the proposed standard.
4. The board reviews preliminary draft of the new standard and then circulates it among all the member bodies for their comments.
5. Based on these comments, the steering committee prepares a revised draft and a final exposure draft is submitted to the board for approval.
6. If approved by a two-thirds vote of the board, the exposure draft will be sent to IASC members. The exposure draft is published in all member countries and world-wide public comments are invited from all interested parties, both professional and non-professional.
7. At the conclusion of the exposure period, usually six months, the comments submitted are considered by the steering committee, and then a final standard is drafted.
8. The steering committee submits the revised draft of the final standard to the board for its approval; and if approved by at least 8 of the 14 members of the board, it will be issued as a new IFRS.

The old IASC called its standards International Accounting Standards. The new name for standards issued by the IASB is International Financial Reporting Standards (IFRS). In one of its earliest actions, the IASB voted to make clear that the IASs issued by the former IASC continue with full force and effect unless and until the IASB amends or replaces them. The IASB announced that the term 'IFRS' should be understood to include IAS.

IASs and IFRSs

From its inception in 1973 until it was reorganised into the International Accounting Standards Board (IASB) in early 2001, the IASC developed 41 standards, known as International Accounting Standards. Many of those were revised one or more times over the years. Several were superseded or merged in with other standards. Since 2001, the IASB has revised a number of IASs and has begun a second series of standards known as International Financial Reporting Standards (IFRSs), starting again with number 1. Table 2.1 sets out a complete list of the IASs and IFRSs. Those not identified as superseded or withdrawn continue in force.

Table 2.1 IAS and IFRS

IAS 1	*Presentation of Financial Statements*
IAS 2	*Inventories*
IAS 3	*Consolidated Financial Statements.* Originally issued in 1976, effective 1977. No longer effective. Superseded in 1989 by IAS 27 and IAS 28.
IAS 4	*Depreciation Accounting.* Withdrawn in 1999, replaced by IAS 16 , IAS 22 and IAS 38, all of which were issued or revised in 1998.
IAS 5	*Information to be Disclosed in Financial Statements.* Originally issued in 1976, effective 1997. No longer effective. Superseded by IAS 1 in 1997.
IAS 6	*Accounting Responses to Changing Prices.* Superseded by IAS 15, which has been withdrawn.
IAS 7	*Cash Flow Statements.*
IAS 8	*Accounting Policies, Changes in Accounting Estimates, and Errors.*
IAS 9	*Accounting for Research and Development Activities.* Superseded by IAS 38, effective 1999.
IAS 10	*Events after the Balance Sheet Date.*
IAS 11	*Construction Contracts.*
IAS 12	*Income Taxes.*
IAS 13	*Presentation of Current Assets and Current Liabilities.* Superseded by IAS 1.
IAS 14	*Segment Reporting.*
IAS 15	*Information Reflecting the Effecting of Changing Prices.* Withdrawn by the IASB in 2003.
IAS 16	*Property, Plant and Equipment.*
IAS 17	*Leases.*
IAS 18	*Revenue.*
IAS 19	*Employee Benefits.*
IAS 20	*Accounting for Government Grants and Disclosure of Government Assistance.*
IAS 21	*The Effects of Change in Foreign Exchange Rates.*
IAS 22	*Business Combinations.* Superseded by IFRS 3, effective in 2005.
IAS 23	*Borrowing Costs.*
IAS 24	*Related Party Disclosures.*
IAS 25	*Accounting for Investments.* Superseded by IAS 39 and IAS 40, effective in 2001.
IAS 26	*Accounting and Reporting by Retirement Benefit Plans.*
IAS 27	*Consolidated and Separate Financial Statements.*
IAS 28	*Investments in Associates.*
IAS 29	*Financial Reporting in Hyper Inflationary Economies.*
IAS 30	*Disclosures in the Financial Statements of Banks and Similar Financial Institutions.*
IAS 31	*Interests in Joint Ventures.*
IAS 32	*Financial Instruments: Disclosure and Presentation.*
IAS 33	*Earnings per Share.*
IAS 34	*Interim Financial Reporting.*
IAS 35	*Discounting Operations.* Superseded by IFRS 5, effective in 2005.
IAS 36	*Impairment of Assets.*
IAS 37	*Provisions, Contingent Liabilities and Contingent Assets.*
IAS 38	*Intangible Assets.*
IAS 39	*Financial Instruments: Recognition and Measurement.*

IAS 40	*Investment Property.*
IAS 41	*Agriculture.*
IFRS 1	*First-time Adoption of International Financial Reporting Standards.*
IFRS 2	*Share-based Payment.*
IFRS 3	*Business Combinations.*
IFRS 4	*Insurance Contracts.*
IFRS 5	*Non-current Assets Held for Sale and Discontinued Operations.*
IFRS 6	*Exploration for and Evaluation of Mineral Resources.*
IFRS 7	*Financial Instruments: Disclosures.*
IFRS 8	*Operating Segments.*
IFRS 9	*Financial Instruments.*

IAS 3, 4, 5, 6, 9, 13, 14, 15, 22, 25, 30 and 35 have been superseded.

THEORY QUESTIONS

1. Define Postulates, Concepts, Principles and Conventions.

2. Explain any four of the following concepts/conventions with suitable examples:
(*a*) Money Measurement (*b*) Consistency
(*c*) Going Concern (*d*) Disclosure
(*e*) Conservatism.

3. Briefly explain the following:
(*a*) Consistency (*b*) Realisation concept
(*c*) Materiality (*d*) Going Concern.

4. Explain matching concept and realisation concept.

5. Distinguish between Accrual Basis of Accounting and Cash Basis of Accounting.

6. Explain Going Concern concept and Realisation concept.

7. Write notes on:
(*i*) Money Measurement Concept (*ii*) Business Entity Concept.

8. Explain the following:
Dual-Aspect Concept and Conservatism.

9. Distinguish between Accrual Basis of Accounting and Cash Basis of Accounting.

10. Write short notes on:
(*i*) Money Measurement Concept (*ii*) Convention of Full Disclosure.

11. Write notes on:
(*i*) Business Entity Concept (*ii*) Consistency.

12. Recognising that the values of land have been increasing in the recent years, Anil, owner of Anil Construction Ltd., increased the balance sheet amount of land from ₹ 50 lacs to ₹ 6 Crore. Explain the Accounting concept which has been violated.

13. Briefly explain:
(*i*) Going Concern Concept (*ii*) Conservatism.

14. Define the following terms:
(*a*) Postulates (*b*) Assumptions (*c*) Concepts (*d*) Principles
(*e*) Convention.

15. Distinguish between Accounting Concepts and Accounting Principles.

16. What is a Realization or Recognition Concept?

17. What are the constraints in Materiality Concept?

18. Explain the concept of Generally Accepted Accounting Principles (GAAP).

19. What are fundamental Accounting Assumptions as per AS1 (India)?

20. What are different areas in Accounting where different Accounting policies are encountered?

21. Define Accounting Standard.

22. List the benefits of Accounting Standards.

23. How many accounting standards have been issued by ICAI?

24. What are the provisions with regard to compliance of accounting standards in India?

25. What are the duties of auditor with regard to compliance of accounting standards in India?

26. A company charges to expense all items (appearing like assets) that costs ₹ 1,000 or less. Which concept supports this policy?

27. Certain generally accepted accounting principles or concepts have been violated in each of the situations described below:

Indicate for each situation which concept or principle has been violated.

(*a*) When the Alpha company acquired its branch office building for ₹ 50,000, the total amount of cash outlay was recorded as rent expense.

(*b*) The personal automobile of Rajiv Dhawan, major shareholder of a company, is listed among the company assets.

(*c*) Land acquired at a cost of ₹ 25 lakhs in 2005 is up to ₹ 45 lakhs.

(*d*) Equipment acquired on January 15, for ₹ 7,00,0000 is recorded on December 31 balance sheet at ₹ 84,00,000. Mr. Ashok Johnson, the managing director of the company explains that since at the date of acquisition, the consumer price index was 100 and had increased to 120 by year-end, the appropriate value for financial statement presentation would accordingly be ₹ 84,00,000.

(*e*) A calculator purchased in early March for ₹ 1,150 can be purchased at year-end for ₹ 925. The company has used the later value on the balance sheet date.

(*f*) Land bought on July 1 for ₹ 5,15,000 is valued on the December 31 balance sheet at ₹ 7,05,000, a value obtained by considering recent land sales in the vicinity.

(*g*) A lawn mower used by Mr. Rakesh, the managing director of the company, for his residence is included among the December 31 assets of the company.

28. What is meant by Accounting Standards? Explain briefly the merits of issuing accounting standards.

29. Define the term 'Accounting Standard'. How does a standard differ from a concept?

30. Explain in detail the convention of materiality. Why is it considered so significant in accounting?

31. Write a note on the significance of Accounting Standards. Are all Indian Accounting standards mandatory?

32. Briefly describe the purpose of accounting standards. How many accounting standards have been formulated by Accounting Standards Board of the Institute of Chartered Accountants of India till date?

33. Write a note on the convention of conservatism. Does it lead to understatement of income?

34. What is the legal status of accounting standards in India?

35. Distinguish between Postulates, Concepts, Principles and Conventions.

36. Explain the following accounting terms:

(*a*) Entity Concept (*b*) Going-Concern Concept

(*c*) Dual-Aspect Concept (*d*) Matching Concept

(*e*) Accrual Concept (*f*) Cost Concept.

37. Explain the significance of separate entity postulate in recording transactions and events of an entity.

38. Why is the Going-Concern postulate central to accounting practice?

39. What limitations does the money measurement concept impose on accounting?

40. "Many important events that influence the prospects for the entity are not recorded in the financial records." Comment and give examples.

41. Would an account record the personal assets and liabilities of the owners in the account of the business? Explain.

42. "It is not important to know when cash is received and when payment is made." Comment.

43. What are accounting standards? Explain their significance.

44. In what way accounting standards are helpful to accountants, auditors and managers?

45. Write an explanatory note on accounting standards setting in India.

46. Explain the progress made by ASB in standards setting.

47. Financial statements are prepared using generally accepted accounting principles. What does this term mean? Why are these principles necessary?

48. Explain the guidelines contained in AS-I Disclosure of Accounting Policies issued by ICAI.

49. State the principles of accounting. **(MBA, JNTU, Hyderabad, Feb. 2007)**

50. Explain generally accepted accounting principles. **(MBA, JNTU, Hyderabad, Feb. 2007)**

51. "According to business entity concept of accounting, the owner's capital in the business is treated as a liability of the business." Comment. **(BBA, GGSIP University, March 2000)**

52. Distinguish between Cash and Accrual Basis of Accounting. **(BBA, GGSIP University, March 2000, December 2002)**

53. Write short notes on:

(*a*) Dual-aspect Concept of Accounting (*b*) Accounting Standards.

(BBA, GGSIP University, March 2008)

54. Write short notes on:

(*a*) Accounting Standards (*b*) Going-Concern Concept.

(BBA, GGSIP University, December 2002)

55. What are Accounting Concepts and Conventions? List them. **(BBA, GGSIP University, December 2004)**

56. "Accounting records the qualitative aspect of business enterprises." Do you agree? Why or why not? **(BBA, GGSIP University, December 2006)**

57. (*a*) Explain the matching cost and revenue concept of accounting, (*b*) Give a brief description of the procedure for issuing accounting standards in India. **(BBA, GGSIP University, December 2006)**

58. "Since the life of the business is assumed to be indefinite, the financial statements of the business should be prepared only when it goes into liquidation." Comment. **(BBA, GGSIP University, December 2007)**

59. Explain the role played by the Institute of Chartered Accountants of India in formulation of accounting standards. **(BBA, GGSIP University, December 2007)**

60. What are the objectives of IASB? How many accounting standards have been issued by the IASB so far? **(BBA, GGSIP University, December 2008)**

61. Write notes on 'Matching Principle.' **(BBA, GGSIP University, December 2009)**

62. Comment on the following:

"Measurement of business income requires matching revenues with related cost or expense." **(BBA, GGSIP University, December 2010)**

63. Explain the following accounting concepts:

(*a*) Money measurement concept (*b*) Business entity concept

(*c*) Going-concern concept (*d*) Realization concept

(*e*) Cost concept. **(BBA, GGSIP University, December 2010)**

64. What is IASB? What are its objectives?

65. What is the process of developing international accounting standards?

66. How many IFRSs have been issued so far?

SELF-EVALUATION EXERCISES

I. Select the correct answer for the following multiple-choice questions:

1. The accounting principle of matching is best demonstrated by

(*a*) Not recognising any expense unless some revenue is realised

(*b*) Associating effort (cost) with accomplishment (revenue)

(*c*) Recognising prepaid rent received as revenue

(*d*) Establishing a reserve for possible future market decline in inventory account.

2. Which of the following cost items would be matched with current revenues on a basis other than association of cause and effect?

(*a*) Goodwill (*b*) Sales commission

(*c*) Cost of goods sold (*d*) Purchases on credit.

3. The immediate recognition of loss is supported by the underlying principle of

(*a*) Matching (*b*) Consistency (*c*) Judgement (*d*) Conservatism.

4. The entity postulate

(*a*) Refers to the name of the company required in the heading of the balance sheet

(*b*) Refers to the owners of the entity, who must account for their interest in the entity in their personal holdings

(*c*) Indicates that the accounting unit on which the financial reports are based is the business itself, separate from its owners

(*d*) Holds that the business is made up of many separate components that are accounted for separately but reported collectively in the financial statements.

5. The time period postulate

(*a*) Refers to the limited life of a joint venture

(*b*) Suggests that companies need to prepare financial reports on a periodic basis, when all operating cycles are complete

(*c*) Suggests that companies prepare financial reports on the basis of a systematic time internal, even though the operating cycle(s) of the entity may be incomplete

(*d*) Refers to the fact that adjusting entries must be made before financial statements are prepared periodically.

6. The valuation of a promise to receive cash in the future at present value on the financial statements of a business entity is valid by virtue of which accounting postulate or principle?

(*a*) Entity (*b*) Materiality (*c*) Matching (*d*) Going-concern.

7. The determination of the expenses for an accounting period is based largely on the application of which principle?

(*a*) Cost (*b*) Consistency (*c*) Matching (*d*) Time period.

8. A sole proprietor decided to use the same bank account for his personal affairs as for his business. Which of the following accounting principles is violated?

(*a*) Going concern (*b*) Entity (*c*) Measuring unit (*d*) Objectivity.

9. Generally Accepted Accounting Principles

(*a*) Define accounting practice at a point in time

(*b*) Are similar in nature to the principles of chemistry or physics

(*c*) Are rarely changed

(*d*) Are not affected by changes in the way business operates.

10. Assigning revenues to the accounting period in which the goods were delivered or the services performed and expenses to the accounting period in which they were used to produce revenues is known as the

(*a*) Accounting period problem (*b*) Continuity assumption

(*c*) Matching rule (*d*) Recognition.

II. Certain accounting postulates and principles have had an important impact on the development on Generally Accepted Accounting Principles. Below is a list of these assumptions and concepts as well as a list of statements describing certain accounting practices.

(*a*) Entity (*b*) Continuity (*c*) Period of time (*d*) Historic cost

(*e*) Monetary unit (*f*) Conservatism

1. The business rather than its owners is the reporting unit.

2. Accounting measurements are reported in rupees.

3. The year is the normal reporting unit.

4. In the absence of evidence to the contrary, the business will operate long enough to carry out its existing commitments.

5. Exchange price is retained in the accounting recording.

6. An accounting alternative is selected that is least likely to overstate assets and income.

***Required*:** Select the accounting postulate or principle that justifies each accounting practice mentioned.

III. Answer True or False:

1. Generally Accepted Accounting Principles are the basic rules governing the preparation of external financial statements.

2. Every conceivable accounting problem for all types of business can be solved by referring to a comprehensive book of accounting principles to find the exact GAAP that determines the proper method of accounting.

3. Because business entities are profit motivated, their financial statements are oriented mainly to the measurement of profit.

4. The going-concern assumption is especially important in accounting for long-term assets used for many years by a business.

5. Matching sales revenue with expenses to measure the profit earned becomes more and more reliable and accurate the longer the period over which profit is measured; measuring profit for one year is more reliable and accurate than for one month or one quarter in most cases.
6. In the UK, the accounting unit of measure is the pound; in the US is the dollar, in Germany it is the Mark, in France the Franc and in India the Rupee. These are examples of the monetary unit measurement concept in accounting.
7. If inflation occurs, thereby reducing the purchasing power value of the Rupee, the accountant adjusts the primary financial statements of the business to account for the loss in the value of the monetary unit.
8. Consistency of accounting methods from period to period is strongly favoured, because it keeps the business entity's financial statements on a comparable basis over time.
9. Financial reports should provide adequate disclosure and be released on a timely basis.
10. All three of the principle financial statements reported by a business entity are financial summaries of the activities and operations of the entity during a period of time.
11. Financial statements are prepared in conformity with Generally Accepted Accounting Principles. These principles are the basic 'ground rules' for financial reporting.
12. Even though two businesses both follow Generally Accepted Accounting Principles, their financial statements may not both use exactly the same accounting methods.
13. External financial statements are sent to the shareholders in the business entity, who are treated as outsiders and not as the managers of the business.
14. Financial reports sent to owners are different from those sent to entities or individuals who lend money to the business.
15. The chief accountant and the chief executive of the business entity have a shared responsibility to see that its financial reports are presented fairly *vis-a-vis* the investors in the business.
16. Generally speaking, the financial statements reported externally to investors are very similar to those reported internally to managers of the business entity.

IV. Certain underlying considerations have had an important impact on the development of Generally Accepted Accounting Principles. Below is a list of these underlying considerations, as well as a list of statements describing them.

(*a*) Going concern or continuity
(*b*) Monetary unit
(*c*) Conservatism
(*d*) Matching
(*e*) Full disclosure
(*f*) Materiality
(*g*) Transaction approach
(*h*) Accrual basis
(*i*) Industry practices
(*j*) Verifiability
(*k*) Consistency
(*l*) Realisation
(*m*) Historic cost
(*n*) Time period
(*o*) Business entity.

1. The business for which the financial statements are prepared is separate and distinct from the owners of the entity.
2. The assumption is made that the entity in question will remain in business for an indefinite period of time.
3. Accountants need some standard of measure to bring financial transactions together in a meaningful way.
4. Revenue should be recognised when the earning process is virtually complete and the exchange value can be objectively determined.

5. This concept deals with when to recognise the costs that are associated with the recognised revenue.
6. Accounting reports must disclose all facts that may influence the judgment of an informed reader.
7. This principle involves the relative size and importance of an item to a firm.
8. The accountant is required to adhere as closely as possible to verifiable data.
9. Lead to accounting reports that do not conform to the general theory that underlies accounting.
10. The accountant records only events that affect the financial position of the entity and, at the same time, can be reasonably determined in monetary terms.
11. Revenue must be recognised when it is realised and expenses are recognised when incurred.
12. The entity must give the same treatment to comparable transactions from period to period.
13. The measurement with the least favourable effect on net income and financial position in the current period must be selected.
14. Of the various values that could be used, this value has been selected because it is objective and determinable.
15. With this assumption, inaccuracies of accounting for the entity short of its complete lifespan are accepted.

Required: Place the appropriate letter identifying each statement made above.

ANSWERS TO SELF-EVALUATION EXERCISES

I.

1. (*b*)	**2.** (*a*)	**3.** (*d*)	**4.** (*c*)	**5.** (*c*)	**6.** (*d*)
7. (*c*)	**8.** (*b*)	**9.** (*a*)	**10.** (*c*)		

II.

1. Entity	**2.** Monetary unit	**3.** Period of time
4. Continuity	**5.** Historic cost	**6.** Conservatism

III.

1. True	**2.** False	**3.** True	**4.** True	**5.** True	**6.** True
7. False	**8.** True	**9.** True	**10.** False	**11.** True	**12.** True
13. True	**14.** False	**15.** True	**16.** False		

IV.

1. (*o*)	**2.** (*a*)	**3.** (*g*)	**4.** (*l*)	**5.** (*d*)	**6.** (*e*)
7. (*f*)	**8.** (*j*)	**9.** (*i*)	**10.** (*b*)	**11.** (*h*)	**12.** (*k*)
13. (*c*)	**14.** (*m*)	**15.** (*n*)			

PART – TWO

ACCOUNTING RECORDS AND SYSTEMS

- **Chapter 3** Accounting Equation and Transaction Analysis
- **Chapter 4** Accounting Mechanics I: Journals
- **Chapter 5** Cash Book and Subsidiary Book
- **Chapter 6** Accounting Mechanics II: Ledger Posting and Trial Balance
- **Chapter 7** Bank Reconciliation Statement
- **Chapter 8** Errors and their Rectification
- **Chapter 9** Preparation of Financial Statements: Profit and Loss Account and Balance Sheet
- **Chapter 10** Depreciation Accounting
- **Chapter 11** Inventory Valuation

3

ACCOUNTING EQUATION AND TRANSACTION ANALYSIS

LEARNING OBJECTIVES

After reading this chapter, you should be able to:

- Explain the concept of accounting equation.
- List some items of assets and liabilities.
- Discuss effects of financial transactions on accounting equation *i.e.*, transaction analysis.

The end result of the accounting process for a business entity is the financial statements such as balance sheet, profit and loss account, statement of changes in financial position. These statements are presented in condensed (highly summarised) form and cannot be prepared until the financial transactions of the business entity have been recorded, classified and summarised. The framework of the financial statements and the elements shown in these statements rests on important and basic relationship, referred to as basic or fundamental accounting equation, basic accounting model. This basic equation is expressed by the balance sheet equation, and therefore, is known as the balance sheet equation also. The balance sheet equation indicates that

Sources of Funds = Uses of Funds

Or

Equities = Assets

Or

Proprietor's Equity (Capital) + Outside Liability = Assets

The above accounting equation signifies that assets of a business are always equal to the total of outside liabilities and proprietor's equity. It means that the accounting equation should always be in balance. This fundamental equality is always true because the left side of the equation is simply another view of the right side. This is because whatever funds are raised by the business, either through capital or business operations or from outsider will be tied up in one or other form of uses (assets). Assets represent resources owned by the business entity; equity represents the claims of those who supplied the assets. Thus, the fundamental accounting equation emphasises accounting equivalence or duality concept *i.e.*, each financial transaction has a dual nature and affects both the assets and liabilities side of the balance sheet.

Algebraically the equations can be expressed as:

$$A = L + P$$

where A = assets

L = outside liabilities

P = Proprietor's equity

The above equation can also be expressed as

$$P = A - L \quad ...(1)$$

$$L = A - P \quad ...(2)$$

$$A - L - P = \text{Zero} \quad ...(3)$$

Assets and Liabilities

The aforesaid Accounting Equation is concerned with assets and equities (outside liabilities and proprietor's equity). Following is the list of some assets and equities:

Assets:

1. Cash
2. Cash at Bank
3. Bills Receivable
4. Prepaid expenses
5. Debtors or accounts receivable
6. Stock (stock of raw materials, work-in-progress, finished goods etc.)
7. Loose tools
8. Office equipments and furniture
9. Patents, copyrights
10. Machinery
11. Buildings
12. Land
13. Goodwill

Equities (Outside liabilities and Proprietor's equity).

(*a*) Outside liabilities

1. Bank overdraft
2. Outstanding expenses
3. Bills payable
4. Creditors on accounts
5. Loan—short-term as well as long-term
6. Debentures

(*b*) Proprietorship equity

(*i*) Capital (Plus additions less withdrawals)

(*ii*) Reserves and surplus of profits/accumulated profits.

Effects of Financial Transactions on Accounting Equation

Every business transaction can be analysed by or expressed in terms of its effect on the balance sheet equation. A business transaction results into a change in all or any of the components of the equation. Whatever may be the change, the Accounting Equation remains in balance. Different types of business transactions may result into a maximum of nine possible effect combinations on the components of accounting equation.

These nine possible combinations of changes or effects are:

(*i*) Increase in one asset; decrease in another asset.
(*ii*) Increase in one liability; decrease in another liability.
(*iii*) Increase in one item of proprietor's equity; decrease in another item of proprietor's equity.
(*iv*) Increase in one item of proprietor's equity; decrease in liability.
(*v*) Increase in a liability; decrease in proprietor's equity.
(*vi*) Increase in asset; increase in liability.
(*vii*) Increase in asset; increase in proprietor's equity.
(*viii*) Decrease in asset; decrease in liability.
(*ix*) Decrease in asset; decrease in proprietor's equity.

Transaction Analysis

Determining the effect of a business transaction on assets, liabilities and equities of the accounting equation is called transaction analysis. A transaction analysis shows increases and decreases in the assets, liabilities or proprietor's equity of a business entity. Where these effects are presented in an account form, they are shown by a simultaneous debit and credit in the relevant accounts of assets, liabilities and/or equities.

Some illustrations are given here to explain the transaction analysis and the effects of business transactions on the accounting equation.

Transaction 1: Transaction 1 – *X* starts business and invests ₹ 1,00,000 as his capital.

(Amount in ₹)

Assets		= Liabilities + Proprietor's equity
	Cash = –	*X*'s capital
Effect of transaction	1,00,000 = –	1,00,000
New Balance	1,00,000 = –	1,00,000

Transaction 2: On April 2, the firm purchases furniture for ₹ 40,000 for cash.

Assets		= Liabilities + Proprietor's equity	
Cash + furniture		= –	*X*'s capital
Old Balance	1,00,000	= –	1,00,000
Effect of Transaction	– 40,000 + 40,000	= –	1,00,000
New Balance	60,000 + 40,000	= –	1,00,000

Transaction 3: On April 3, the firm purchases merchandise (goods) costing ₹ 30,000 for cash.

Assets		= Liabilities + Proprietor's equity	
Cash + furniture + Merchandise		= –	*X*'s capital A/c
Old Balance	60,000 + 40,000	= –	1,00,000
Effect of transaction	–30,000 + 30,000	= –	1,00,000
New Balance	30,000 + 40,000 + 30,000	= –	1,00,000

Transaction 4: On April 4, the firm purchases merchandise costing ₹ 40,000 on credit.

Assets		= Liabilities + Proprietor's equity
Cash + furniture + Merchandise		= Creditors + *X*'s capital
Old Balance	30,000 + 40,000 + 30,000	= – + 1,00,000
Effect of transaction	+ 40000	= + 40,000
New balance 30000 + 40000 + 70000		= 40,000 + 1,00,000

Transaction 5: On April 6, the firm sells merchandise for ₹ 30000 on credit to Mr. *A*, costing ₹ 20,000

Assets	=	Liabilities + Proprietor's equity
Cash + Debtors + Merchandise + Furniture	=	Creditors + *X*'s capital + Surplus Profit
Old Balance 30,000 + – + 70,000 + 40000	=	40,000 + 1,00,000
Effect of transactions + 30,000 – 20,000	= –	10,000
New Balance 30,000 + 30,000 + 50,000 + 40,000 = 40,000 + 1,00,000 + 10,000		

Transaction 6: On April 15, the firm receives ₹ 20,000 cash from Debtor.

Assets	=	Liabilities + Proprietor's equity
Cash + Debtor + Merchandise + Furniture	=	Creditor + *X*'s Cap + Surplus Profit
Old Balance 30,000 + 30,000 + 50,000 + 40,000	=	40,000 + 1,00,000 + 10,000
Effect of transaction + 20000 – 20000	=	– –
New Balance 50,000 + 10,000 + 50,000 + 40,000 = 40,000 + 1,00,000 + 10,000		

Transaction 7: On April 16, the firm pays ₹ 40,000 to its creditors.

Assets	=	Liabilities + Proprietor's equity
Cash + Debtors + Merchandise + Furniture	=	Creditors + *X*'s capital + Surplus/Profit
Old Balance 50,000 + 10,000 + 50,000 + 40,000	=	40,000 + 1,00,000 + 10,000
Effect of transaction – 40000	=	40000 – –
New Balance 10,000 + 10,000 + 50,000 + 40,000	=	1,00,000 + 10,000

Transaction 8: On April 17, the firm pays ₹ 2,000 as rent.

Assets	=	Liabilities + Proprietor's equity
Cash + Debtors + Merchandise + Furniture	=	Creditor + *X*'s Cap + Surplus/Profit
Old Balance 10000 + 10000 + 50,000 + 40,000	=	+ 1,00,000 + 10,000
Effect of transaction – 2000	=	–2000
New Balance 8000 + 10,000 + 50,000 + 40,000	=	1,00,000 + 8000

Profit and Loss A/c for the year ending ...

	₹		₹
To purchases A/c	30,000	By Sales A/c	30,000
To purchases A/c	40,000	By closing stock	50,000
To G/P c/d	10,000		
	80,000		80,000

	₹		₹
To Rent A/c To Net profit	2,000 8,000	By Gross profit b/d	10,000
	10,000		10,000

Balance Sheet as on ...

Liabilities	₹	Assets	₹
Capital	1,00,000	Cash	8,000
		Furniture	40,000
Profit	8,000	Debtors	10,000
		Closing Stock (*merchandise*)	50,000
	1,08,000		1,08,000

Illustration 1: Show the Accounting equation on the basis of the following transactions:

(*i*) I started business with cash ₹ 1,00,000

(*ii*) Purchased goods on credit from Mohan – ₹ 40,000

(*iii*) Sold goods for cash ₹ 26000 (Cost ₹ 22000).

Solution: **(Amount in ₹)**

	Transaction	Assets			= Liabilities + Proprietor's equity
1.	*X* started business with cash	Bank + Goods	=		Creditors + Capital
		₹ 1,00,000 + 0			0 + ₹ 1,00,000
	Beginning Equation	1,00,000 + 0	=		0 + ₹ 1,00,000
2.	Purchased goods on credit from Mohan	(+) 40,000	= (+) 40,000		
	New Equation	1,00,000 + 40,000	= 40,000		+ 1,00,000
3.	Sold goods for cash ₹ 26,000 (cost ₹ 22,000)	(+) 26000	(–) 22000	=	+ 4,000
	Ending Equation	1,26,000	+ 18,000	= 40,000	+ 1,04,000

Illustration 2: On January 1, 2012, a company Super Consultants India Ltd. was incorporated. The following transactions occurred during January 2012.

January:

1. Business was started with capital of ₹ 1,00,000 cash.
4. Equipment was rented (and paid) for the month at a cost of ₹ 12,000.
8. Paper & stationery purchased on credit ₹ 8,000.
15. The company charged ₹ 30,000 as consulting fees from the customers during January. This amount is due to be received next month.
20. Miscellaneous expenses of ₹ 6,000 were paid.
29. Land was purchased by borrowing ₹ 4,00,000 from a bank. The loan is due to be repaid in five years. Interest payments are due at the end of each month beginning July 31.
30. Salaries of ₹ 7,000 for the month were paid.
31. **Lesson** fees were billed to customers in the amount of ₹ 28,000. (They are due to be received next month).

Prepare a summary of the preceding transactions. Determine balances after each transaction to show that the basic equation is in balance.

Prepare an income statement, a statement of retained earnings, balance sheet for January 2002.

Solution:

Super Consultants India Ltd.
Summary of Transactions
January 2012

(Amount in ₹)

Date	Cash +	Assets Accounts receivables	+ Land	= Liabilities + Equity = A/cs payables	+ Loan	Capital	+ Profit or Retained Earning
1	1,00,000			=			1,00,000
4	– 12,000						–12,000
8	88,000			+ 8000		1,00,000	–12,000
							– 8,000
	88,000			800		1,00,000	–20,000
15		+ 30,000					+30,000
	88,000	30,000		= 8,000		1,00,000	+10,000
20							
	– 6,000						–6,000
	82,000	30,000		= 8,000		1,00,000	+4,000
29			+ 4,00,000		+ 4,00,000		
	82,000	30,000	4,00,000	= 8,000	4,00,000	1,00,000	4,000
30							
	– 7,000					– 7,000	
31	75,000	30,000	4,00,000	= 8,000	4,00,000	1,00,000	–3,000
		+ 28,000					+28,000
	75,000	58,000	4,00,000	= 8,000	4,00,000	1,00,000	25,000

Income Statement for the Month Ended January 31, 2012

Revenues	₹
Consulting fees	30,000
Lesson Fees	28,000
Total Revenues	58,000
Less: Expenses:	
Rent expense	12,000
Paper & Stationery	8,000
Salaries	7,000
Misc. expenses	6,000
	33,000
Net Income	25,000

Statement of Retained Earnings

	Retained earnings as on January 1.....	NIL
Add:	Net Income for January 2002	₹ 25,000
	Total	25,000
Less =	dividends	NIL
	Retained earnings, January 31	25,000

Balance Sheet as on January 31, 2012

Liabilities	₹	Assets	₹
Capital	1,00,000	Cash	75,000
Retained earnings	25,000	Accounts Receivable	58,000
Accounts payables	8,000	Land	4,00,000
Loan	4,00,000		
	5,33,000		5,33,000

Illustration 3: Prove that accounting equation is satisfied in all the following transactions of Mr. *X*:

(*i*) Commenced business with cash—₹ 80,000
(*ii*) Purchased goods for cash—₹ 40,000 and on credit ₹ 30,000
(*iii*) Sold goods for cash—₹ 40,000 costing ₹ 25,000
(*iv*) Paid salary—₹ 2,000, and salary outstanding ₹ 1,000
(*v*) Bought scooter for personal use for cash at ₹ 20,000.

Solution: **(Amount in ₹)**

	Transaction	Cash	Assets = Liabilities + Owners' Equity			
			Goods	Creditors	+ Salary outstanding	+ Capital
(*i*)	*X* commenced business with cash, beginning equation	80,000	—	—	—	80,000
(*ii*)	Purchased goods for cash and on credit	–40,000	+70,000	= 30,000		—
(*iii*)	Sold goods for cash (₹ 40,000) costing ₹ 25,000	40,000	–25,000	= – –	+15,000	
	New equation	80,000	+45,000	30,000	–	+95,000
(*iv*)	Paid salary of ₹ 2,000 and salary outstanding is ₹ 1,000	–2,000	–	–	+1,000	–3,000
	New equation	78,000	+45,000	= 30,000	1,000	+92,000
(*v*)	Bought scooter for personal use for cash	–20,000				–20,000
	Ending equation	58,000	+45,000	= 30,000	= 1,000	+72,000

Illustration 4: Show the accounting equation on the basis of the following transactions:

	₹
(*i*) *Y* started business with cash	90,000
(*ii*) Purchased goods on credit	50,000
(*iii*) Purchased furniture for cash	10,000
(*iv*) Sold goods costing ₹ 20,000 for	40,000

(*v*) Sold goods costing ₹ 20,000 on credit for	42,000
(*vi*) Bought goods worth ₹ 20,000 (₹ 15,000 paid in cash and balance on credit)	
(*vii*) Drawn for personal use	5,000
(*viii*) Paid as rent	1,000
(*ix*) Paid for salaries	3,000
(*x*) Paid for creditors	40,000
(*xi*) Received from debtors	12,000

Solution: **(Amount in ₹)**

	Transaction	Assets = Liabilities + Owner's Equity						
		Cash +	**Goods +**	**Debtors**	**+ Furniture**	**=**	**Creditors +**	***Y*'s capital**
1.	*Y* started business with cash							
	Beginning equation	90,000				=		90,000
2.	Purchased goods on credit	–	+ 50,000	+ –	+ –	=	50,000	+ –
	New equation	90,000	+ 50,000	+ –	+ –	=	50,000	+ 90,000
3.	Purchased furniture for cash	–10,000	+ –	+ – +	10,000	=	–	+ –
	New equation	80,000	+ 50,000	+ – +	10,000	=	50,000	+ 90,000
4.	Sold goods costing ₹ 20,000 for ₹ 40,000	+ 40,000	– 20,000	+ – +	–	=	– +	20,000
	New equation	1,20,000	+ 30,000	+ – +	10,000	=	50,000	+1,10,000
5.	Sold goods costing ₹ 20,000 for ₹ 42,000 on credit	–	– 20,000	+ 42,000	+ –	=	– +	22,000
	New equation	1,20,000	+ 10,000	+ 42,000	+ 10,000	=	50,000	+ 1,32,000
6.	Bought goods worth ₹ 20,000 (₹ 15,000 paid in cash, balance on credit)	–15,000	+ 20,000	+ –	+ –	=	+ 5,000	+ –
	New equation	1,05,000	+ 30,000	+ 42,000	+ 10,000	=	55,000	+ 1,32,000
7.	Drew for personal use	–5000	+ –	+ –	+	=	–	–5,000
	New equation	1,00,000	+ 30,000	+ 42,000	+ 10,000	=	55,000	+ 1,27,000
8.	Paid as rent	–1,000	+ –	+ –	+ –	=	–	– 1,000
	New equation	99,000	+ 30,000	+ 42,000	+ 10,000	=	55,000	+ 1,26,000
9.	Paid for salaries	–3,000	+ –	+ –	+ –	=	–	– 3,000
	New equation	96,000	+ 30,000	+ 42,000	+ 10,000	=	55,000	+ 1,23,000
10.	Paid to creditors	– 40,000	+ –	+ –	+ –	=	– 40,000	+ –
	New equation	56,000	+ 30,000	+ 42,000	+ 10,000	=	15,000	+ 1,23,000
11.	Received from Debtors	+ 12000	+ –	– 12,000	+ –	=	–	+ –
	Ending equation	68,000	+ 30,000	+ 30,000	+ 10,000	=	15,000	+ 1,23,000

Illustration 5: Show the accounting equation on the basis of the following transactions and present a balance sheet on the basis of the ending equation:

	(₹)
(*i*) Mohan commenced business with cash	70,000
(*ii*) Purchased goods on credit	14,000
(*iii*) Withdrew for private use	3,000
(*iv*) Goods purchased for cash	10,000
(*v*) Paid wages	2,000
(*vi*) Paid to creditors	10,000
(*vii*) Sold goods on credit (Cost price—₹ 10,000)	15,000
(*viii*) Sold goods for cash (Cost price—₹ 3,000)	6,000
(*ix*) Purchased furniture for cash	2,000

Solution: **(Amount in ₹)**

Transaction	Assets				= Liabilities + Owner's Equity		
	Cash +	Goods +	Debtors	+ Furniture		Creditors +	Mohan's Capital
1. Mohan commenced Business with cash	70,000	+ –	+ –	+ –	=	– +	70,000
Beginning equation	70,000	+ –	+ –	+ –	=	– +	70,000
2. Purchased goods on credit	–	+ 14,000	+ –	+ –	=	14,000	+ –
New equation	70,000	+ 14,000	+ –	+ –	=	14,000	+ 70,000
3. Withdrawn for private use	– 3,000	+ –	+ –	+ –	=	– +	– 3,000
New equation	67,000	+14,000	+ –	+ –	=	14,000	+ 67,000
4. Goods purchased for cash	– 10,000	+ 10,000	+ –	+ –	=	– +	–
New equation	57,000	+ 24,000	+ –	+ –	=	14,000	+ 67,000
5. Paid wages	–2,000	+ –	+ –	+ –	=	14,000	+ –2,000
New equation	55,000	+ 24,000	–	–	=	14,000	+ 65,000
6. Paid to creditors	–10,000	+ –	+ –	+	=	–10,000	+ –
New equation	45,000	+ 24,000	+ –	+ –	=	4,000	+ 65,000
7. Sold goods on credit for ₹ 15,000 (Cost ₹ 10,000)	–	– 10,000	+ 15,000	+ –	=	–	+ 5,000
New equation	45,000	+ 14,000	+ 15,000	+ –	=	4,000	+ 70,000
8. Sold goods for cash ₹ 6,000 costing ₹ 3,000	+ 6,000	–3,000	+ –	+ –	=	–	+ 3,000
New equation	51,000	+ –11,000	+ 15,000	+	=	4,000	+ 73,000
9. Purchased furniture for cash	–2,000	+ –	+ –	+ 2,000	=	–	+ –
Ending equation	49,000	+ 11,000	+ 15,000	+ 2,000	=	4,000	+ 73,000

Balance Sheet

Liabilities	₹	Assets	₹
Creditor	4,000	Cash	49,000
Mohan's capital	73,000	Goods	11,000
		Debtors	15,000
		Furniture	2,000
	77,000		77,000

THEORY QUESTIONS

1. What is the fundamental accounting equation? Express it in two different forms.
2. What are the two classifications of equities in a balance sheet?
3. What do you understand by transaction analysis? Illustrate.
4. Each business transaction has two elements. Explain.
5. Indicate whether each of the following would increase, decrease or have no effect on owner's equity:
   (*a*) Purchased supplies for cash
   (*b*) Withdrew supplies for personal use
   (*c*) Paid salaries
   (*d*) Purchased equipment for cash
   (*e*) Invested cash in business
   (*f*) Rendered service to customers, on account
   (*g*) Rendered service to customers, for cash
6. Give one suitable transaction that would result into each of the following:
   (*i*) Increase in an asset and decrease in another asset
   (*ii*) Increase in one liability and decrease in another liability
   (*iii*) Increase in liability and decrease in proprietor's equity
   (*iv*) Increase in one asset and increase in liability
7. Certain generally accepted accounting principles or concepts have been violated in each of the situations described below.

   Indicate for each situation which concept or principle has been violated.
   (*a*) When the Alpha company acquired its branch office building for ₹ 50,000, the total amount of cash outlay was recorded as rent expense.
   (*b*) The personal automobile of Rajiv Dhawan, major shareholder of a company, is listed among the company assets.
   (*c*) Land acquired at a cost of ₹ 2,50,000 in 1995 is up to ₹ 4,25,000.
   (*d*) Equipment acquired on January 15 for ₹ 70,000 is recorded on December 31 balance sheet at ₹ 84,000. Mr. Ashok Johnson, the managing director of the company, explains that since at the date of acquisition, the consumer price index was 100 and had increased to 120 by year-end, the appropriate value for financial statement presentation would accordingly be ₹ 84,000.
   (*e*) A calculator purchased in early March for ₹ 1,150 can be purchased at year-end for ₹ 925. The company has used the latter value on the balance sheet date.

(*f*) Land bought on July 1 for ₹ 5,15,000 is valued on the December 31 balance sheet at ₹ 7,05,000, a value obtained by considering recent land sales in the vicinity.

(*g*) A lawnmower used by Mr. Rakesh, the managing director of the company, for his residence is included among the December 31 assets of the company.

8. What is an accounting equation? Explain with suitable examples.

9. "All transactions are subject to accounting equatiion." Comment on this statement.

10. Give the example of different transactions which may influence assets, liabilities and owner's funds.

11. "Assets and liabilities both are claims, one in favour of business, the other against business." Explain this statement.

12. What is transaction analysis? Explain with suitable examples.

13. Explain with examples as to how accounting equation is not influenced by occurrence of some transactions.

14. What is Accounting Equation? **(BBA, GGSIP University, December 2004)**

SELF-EVALUATION EXERCISES

I. Select the correct answer for the following multiple choice questions:

1. Dual aspect concept results in the accounting equation:

(*a*) Capital + liabilities = Assets (*b*) Revenue = Expenses

(*c*) Capital + Profit = Assets + Expenses (*d*) None of the above.

2. On sale of old furniture, owner's equity would:

(*a*) increase (*b*) decrease

(*c*) remain unchanged (*d*) may or may not change.

3. The outside liabilities of a business are ₹ 20,000. The proprietor's capital is ₹ 50,000. The total assets of the firm are:

(*a*) ₹ 50,000 (*b*) ₹ 30,000 (*c*) ₹ 70,000 (*d*) ₹ 20,000.

4. On 31st December, 2012, assets of the business are ₹ 3,00,000 and its capital is ₹ 1,00,000. Its liabilities on that date will be

(*a*) ₹ 4,00,000 (*b*) 2,00,000 (*c*) 1,00,000 (*d*) None of the above

5. Withdrawals by the proprietor would

(*a*) reduce both assets and owner's equity

(*b*) reduce assets and increase liabilities

(*c*) reduce owner's equity and increase liability

(*d*) no change.

6. Which of the following changes would constitute valid accounting transactions?

(*a*) Increase in a liability, increase in an asset

(*b*) Increase in an asset, decrease in proprietorship

(*c*) Increase in a liability, decrease in an asset

(*d*) Decrease in an asset, decrease in proprietorship.

7. Which of the following transactions does not affect the balance sheet totals?

(*a*) Purchasing ₹ 5,000 supplies on credit.

(*b*) Paying a ₹ 30,000 note payable

(*c*) Collection ₹ 40,000 from debtors.

(*d*) Withdrawal of ₹ 8000 by the firm's owner.

8. The ending balance of owner's equity is ₹ 21,000. During the year, the owner contributed ₹ 6,000 and withdrew ₹ 4,000. If the firm had ₹ 8,000 net income for the year, what was the owner's beginning equity?

(*a*) ₹ 19,000 (*b*) ₹ 11,000 (*c*) ₹ 21,000 (*d*) ₹ 23,000.

9. Beginning and ending total assets were ₹ 25,000 and ₹ 32,000, respectively, for the current year. At year-end, owner's equity was ₹ 20,000 and liabilities were ₹ 4,000 larger than at the beginning of the year. If owner's withdrawals exceeded contributions by ₹ 2,000, what was the net income or net loss for the year?

(*a*) ₹ 5,000 net loss (*b*) ₹ 9,000 net income

(*c*) ₹ 13,000 net income (*d*) ₹ 5,000 net income.

II. Answer True or False:

1. Transactions cause the financial condition of the business to change.

2. Some transactions are not of any concern to the accountant and they are not recorded in accounts books.

3. Partnership and sole proprietorship do not issue shares.

4. The accounting equation can be thought of as a very condensed version of the balance sheet.

5. The total value of a business entity's assets could be more than the total claims on the assets by liabilities and owner's equity.

6. Double-entry accounting means that both the assets of the entity and the claims on the assets are accounted for.

7. It is better to state the accounting equation as ASSETS = LIABILITIES + OWNER'S EQUITY rather than ASSETS – LIABILITIES = OWNER'S EQUITY.

8. Paying cash for the purchase of fixed assets does not change the total assets of the business; furthermore, there are no changes on the other side of the balance sheet (in liabilities and owner's equity).

9. If transactions are recorded correctly, the accounting equation and the statement of financial condition should always be in balance, that is, the total of both sides should be equal.

EXERCISES AND PROBLEMS

I. Show the Accounting Equation on the basis of the following transactions:

	(₹)
1. Ravi started business with cash	40,000
2. Purchased goods on credit	10,000
3. Received commission	250
4. Paid rent	1,000
5. Purchased goods for cash	14,000
6. Withdrew cash for private use	1,500
7. Sold goods on credit (Cost price ₹ 15,000)	20,000
8. Purchased furniture for cash	3,000
9. Paid to creditors	7,500

Ans: (Assets ₹ 45,250; Liabilities ₹ 2,500; Capital ₹ 42,750).

II. Show the Accounting Equation on the basis of the following transactions:

	(₹)
1. Mohan commenced business with cash	15,000
2. He purchased goods on credit	5,000
3. He sold goods for cash (costing ₹ 2,500) for	3,000
4. Purchased furniture for cash	1,500
5. Sold goods to Rakesh on credit (costing ₹ 400) for	500
6. Paid salaries	250
7. Received cash from Rakesh	500
8. Withdrew cash for private use	1,200
9. Received rent from tenants	1,500
10. Purchased goods from Mukesh for cash	500

Ans: (Assets = ₹ 20,650; Liabilities ₹ 5,000; Capital ₹ 15,650).

III. Prove that Accounting Equation is satisfied in all the following transactions of Manu:

1. Commenced business with cash ₹ 3,00,000
2. Paid rent in advance ₹ 2,500
3. Purchased goods for cash ₹ 1,50,000 and credit ₹ 1,00,000
4. Sold goods for cash ₹ 1,50,000 costing ₹ 1,00,000
5. Paid salary ₹ 2500 and salary outstanding ₹ 500
6. Bought motorcycle for personal use ₹ 25,000

Ans: (Assets ₹ 4,22,500; Liabilities ₹ 1,00,000; capital ₹ 3,22,500).

IV. Prepare Accounting Equation from the following:

1. Started business with cash ₹ 1,00,000 and goods ₹ 40,000
2. Bought goods for cash ₹ 30,000 and on credit for ₹ 20,000
3. Goods costing ₹ 48,000 sold at a profit of 33 1/3%. Half the payment received in cash
4. Purchased furniture for office use ₹ 12,000 and for household use of Sudhir ₹ 8,000

Ans: (Assets ₹ 1,68,000; Liabilities ₹ 20,000, Capital ₹ 1,48,000).

V. Show the effect of the following transactions on assets, liabilities and capital using the Accounting Equation:

1. Started business with cash ₹ 60,000
2. Rent received ₹ 2,000
3. Accrued interest ₹ 500
4. Commission received in advance ₹ 1,000
5. Amount withdrawn ₹ 5,000

Ans: (Assets ₹ 58,500; Liabilities ₹ 1,000; Capital ₹ 57,500).

VI. Anu has following transactions in an accounting year:

1. Commenced business with cash ₹ 25,000.
2. Paid wages ₹ 1,000
3. Salaries outstanding ₹ 100
4. Prepaid Insurance ₹ 350

5. Interest due but not paid ₹ 50
6. Rent paid in advance ₹ 75

Ans: (Assets ₹ 24,000; Liabilities ₹ 150; Capital ₹ 23,850).

VII. Prove that the accounting equation is satisfied in all the following transactions:

1. Started business with cash ₹ 1,20,000
2. Purchased a typewriter for cash for ₹ 8,000 for office use
3. Purchased goods for ₹ 50,000 for cash
4. Purchased goods for ₹ 40,000 on credit
5. Goods costing ₹ 60,000 sold for ₹ 80,000 on credit
6. Paid for rent ₹ 1,500 and for salaries ₹ 2,000
7. Received ₹ 800 for commission
8. Withdrew for private use ₹ 5,000 in cash

Ans: (Assets ₹ 1,72,300; Liabilities ₹ 40,000; Capital ₹ 1,32,300).

VIII. Develop Accounting equation for the following transactions:

	(₹)
1. Rohit started business with cash	1,50,000
2. He purchased goods from Ram on credit	50,000
3. Paid carriage	500
4. Sold goods for (profit ₹ 3,000)	9,000
5. Received security deposits from tenants	1,500
6. Invested in shares (personal)	50,000
7. Introduced fresh capital	25,000
8. Goods destroyed by fire	2,500

Ans: (Assets ₹ 1,76,500; Liabilities ₹ 51,500; Capital ₹ 1,25,000).

IX. Prepare Accounting Equation from the following:

1. Invested ₹ 3,00,000 in cash
2. Purchased an old car for ₹ 56,000 cash
3. Received cash as salary ₹ 72,000
4. Purchased a home for ₹ 3,00,000, giving ₹ 1,00,000 in cash and balance through a loan
5. Purchased securities for cash ₹ 1,50,000
6. Received cash for dividend on securities ₹ 4,000
7. Paid cash for household expenses ₹ 6,000
8. Paid cash ₹ 10,000 for loan and ₹ 6,000 for interest
9. Sold securities costing ₹ 20,000 for ₹ 30,000

Ans: (Assets ₹ 5,64,000; Liabilities ₹ 1,90,000; Capital ₹ 3,74,000).

X. Prakash started a business with a cash investment of ₹ 70,000. Following transactions took place:

1. Paid three months advance rent for office accommodation ₹ 4,200
2. Bought office car ₹ 42,000
3. Puchased office furniture ₹ 14,000
4. Bought office typewriter from Alpine Supply Company ₹ 6,000

5. Sold extra office furniture at cost to Ajay for ₹ 2,000. Ajay paid ₹ 1,200 in cash and accepted a bill at three months for the balance
6. Ajay paid the amount of the bill at maturity and Prakash paid half the amount he owed to Alpine Supply Company
7. Collected ₹ 1,20,000 as commission
8. Paid telephone bill amounting to ₹ 300.

Develop Accounting Equation.

ANSWERS TO SELF-EVALUATION EXERCISES

I.

1. (*a*) **2.** (*d*) **3.** (*c*) **4.** (*b*) **5.** (*a*) **6.** (*a*), (*d*)
7. (*c*) **8.** (*b*) **9.** (*d*)

II.

1. True **2.** False **3.** True **4.** True **5.** False **6.** True
7. False **8.** True **9.** True.

4

ACCOUNTING MECHANICS I : JOURNALS

LEARNING OBJECTIVES

After reading this chapter, you should be able to:

- Understand the meaning of account.
- Explain the meaning of debit and credit.
- Discuss rules of debit and credit.
- List type of accounts.
- Present discussion on journalising the transaction.

In the previous chapter, it was explained that, within the framework of basic accounting equation and duality concept, sources of funds must always equal uses of funds. That is,

Total Liabilities = Total Assets

Or

Owners' Equity + Outside Liability = Assets

It is also evident from the earlier discussions that any of the following is a source of funds in business:

- Incurring Liability (including owner's equity)
- Earning Revenue
- Making Profits

It stands to reason that a decrease in liability, revenue or profit must be a use of funds being the opposite of a source. Similarly, any of the following is a use of funds:

- Acquiring Assets
- Incurring Expenses
- Incurring Losses

Also a decrease in assets, expenses or losses must be a source of funds, being the opposite of a use.

Thus, no matter what event transpires in the business, it must be possible to capture that event in the balance sheet in such a way that the liabilities (sources) and assets (uses) remain equal.

THE ACCOUNT

The account is the basic building block of any accounting system. An account is a standardised format used to maintain separate record and to accumulate data for each of the individual items in order to facilitate the preparation of periodic financial statements and to provide a continuous check on the accuracy of the recording of transactions. An account exists, therefore, for each asset, liability, owner capital, revenue and expense item. The account is used to record increases and decreases in these items (asset, liability, owner capital, revenue and expense) resulting from business transactions. The account (of an item) shows the following things:

1. The account title, which is the name of a particular accounting element, such as Cash Account.
2. A place to record increases in the monetary amounts in the account.
3. A place to record decreases in the monetary amounts in the account.
4. Dates and descriptive notations.
5. Cross-references to other accounting records.

To illustrate the nature of the account, an example of Cash Account is given below:

Cash Account

Debit **Credit**

Date	Particulars	Ledger Folio	Amount (₹)	Date	Particulars	Ledger Folio	Amount (₹)
2003				2003			
Jan. 1	To balance b/d		50,000	Jan. 12	By salaries		11,000
Jan. 15	To debtors		21,000	Jan. 27	By rent		17,000
Jan. 25	To sales		35,000	Jan. 31	By balance c/d		78,000
	Total:		1,06,000		**Total:**		1,06,000
Feb. 1	To balance b/d		78,000				

On the left side of the Cash Account, there are three accounting entries, one representing the beginning balance and the other two entries representing increases to this account. On the right side there are three accounting entries, two entries representing decreases to this account and the third entry representing the closing balance. The left-side entries begin with the prefix "to" and right-side entries begin with the prefix "by". One may notice that the total of the left side of the cash account is ₹ 1,06,000 and the total of the right side is ₹ 28,000. The net difference between increases and decreases in the cash account is an increase and that is why the balance of ₹ 78,000 is located on the increases in cash side. In the account plus (+) and minus (–) signs are not needed. Of course, total decreases in cash could not have exceeded total increases; as we cannot spend more cash than we have. The balance in an account is the difference between increases and decreases. The cash account (or any other account) thus shows the four money elements:

1. Beginning balance
2. Increases or additions
3. Decreases or deductions
4. Closing balance

The form of the account looks like the letter T. For this reason it is referred to as a T-Account. The T-Account form is used by accountants for preparing accounts, actual record keeping, analysing accounting problems and by accounting teachers for teaching accounting.

DEBIT AND CREDIT

As stated earlier, accounts are prepared to provide help in the preparation of financial statements and to check the correctness of transactions recorded by a business enterprise. It is obvious that the financial statements can be prepared only after accounts for different elements (transactions) have been prepared which have to be reported on the financial statements.

Checking the accuracy of recorded transactions and the accounting system is done in terms of basic accounting equation (discussed in the previous chapter) and rules of debit and credit.

The terms debit and credit are used to describe the left-hand and the right-hand sides of an account, as shown below. The verb "to debit" means to make entry in the left-hand side of an account and the verb "to credit" means to make an entry in the right-hand side of an account. The terms debit and credit have no other meaning in accounting.

(Any Type of Account)

Debit	**Credit**
Always the left side	Always the right side

The abbreviations Dr. and Cr. are used in place of Debit and Credit. An entry made on the left-hand side is a debit to the account and entry recorded on the right-hand side is a credit to the account. About the debit and credit, a writer has commented in the following manner:

"When the book lies open in front of you and you look at the book (not the book at you) then the side where you have your heart is the left or Debit side. The side away from your heart is the right side and is called Credit."[1]

All accounts show entries recording increases and decreases. In some accounts (such as Cash Account illustrated earlier), increases are recorded on the left-hand side (Debit side) of the account and decreases are recorded on the right-hand side (Credit side) of the account. In other accounts, the reverse is true. It means debits and credits by themselves do not indicate increases or decreases. Reference must be made to a specific account to determine if the debits or credits represent increases or decreases.

The five major categories of accounts are illustrated below showing debits and credits related to increases or decreases.

1. Asset Accounts

Debit Side	**Credit Side**
Shows increases Normal Balance-Debit	Shows Decreases

2. Liabilities Account

Debit Side	**Credit Side**
Shows decreases	Shows increases Normal balance-Credit

3. Owners' Equity Account

Debit Side	**Credit Side**
Shows decreases	Shows increases Normal balance-Credit

1. Paul H. Walgenbach, Ernest I Hanson and Norman E. Dittrich, Financial Accounting, Harcourt Brace Jovanovich, 1988, p. 42.

4. Revenue Account

Debit Side	Credit Side
Shows decreases	Shows increases Normal balance-Credit

5. Expenses Account

Debit Side	Credit Side
Shows increases Normal balance-Debit	Shows decreases

Normal balance refers to positive balance of an account. For any account, generally speaking, the total of the increases to the account exceeds the total of the decreases to the account. The resulting balance is a positive balance rather than a negative balance. For example, a typical asset account (such as plant Account) have total debits in excess of total credits and consequently have a normal debit balance. After observing the above five types of account, the following inferences are drawn:

1. Debit is always the left side of all account, and credit is always the right side of the account.
2. Increases in assets and expenses accounts are always debit entries.
3. Increases in liabilities, owners' equity and revenue accounts are always credit entries.
4. Decreases are always recorded on the side opposite increases.
5. The normal balance of any account is on the side on which increases are recorded.
6. Assets and expense accounts normally have debit balances. The liabilities, owners' equity and revenue accounts generally have credit balances.

It should be understood that all the above types of accounts are part of the basic balance sheet equation, Assets = Liabilities + Owners' Equity. That is, each financial transaction has two parts, as observed in Chapter 3. For example, if an asset is increased, then if the balance sheet equation is to remain in balance, something else must happen, namely, one of the following:

1. Another asset must decrease, or
2. A liability must increase, or
3. Owners' equity must increase.

In all the above situations, debit will always equal the credit and the basic balance sheet equation will remain in balance.

Illustration of Debit and Credit Rules and Recording of Transactions in the Accounts

The following illustration is taken to explain the application of debit and credit rules (entries) in the various accounts, using T accounts for simplicity and understanding. Prior to making debit and credit entries, a transaction should be analysed to determine which accounts must be increased or decreased. After this has been determined, the rules of debit and credit are applied to record the appropriate increases and decreases to the accounts.

Transaction 1: Ashok invested ₹ 80,000 of his funds in a new business entitled Alpha Co. Ltd.

Asset (Increase)
Cash A/c

(Amount in ₹)

	Debit	Credit
(1)	80,000	

Equity (Increase)
Capital A/c

Debit			Credit
		(1)	80,000

This transaction increases both the assets and equities of the firm. According to rules of debit and credit, debits will increase assets and credits will increase equity accounts of the firm.

Transaction 2: Alpha Co. Ltd. purchased the following assets for cash: Supplies ₹ 9,000, office equipment ₹ 7,000, Tools ₹ 6,000.

Assets (Increases)
Supplies A/c

	Debit		Credit
(2)	9,000		

Office Equipment A/c

	Debit		Credit
(2)	7,000		

Tools A/c

	Debit		Credit
(2)	6,000		

Assets (Decreases)
Cash A/c

	Debit		Credit
(2)	80,000	(2)	22,000

Three assets—supplies, office equipment and tools—are purchased by the firm in cash, reducing the asset cash by ₹ 22,000. Assets are increased by debits and reduced by credits. Therefore, the three asset accounts—supplies, office equipment and tools—are debited, each for its respective amount and cash is credited for the total of ₹ 22,000.

Transaction 3: Alpha Co. acquired land for ₹ 75,000 for storing purposes, paying ₹ 15,000 in cash and issuing bills payable for the difference.

Asset (Increase, Decrease)
Cash A/c

	Debit		Credit
(1)	80,000	(2) (3)	22,000 15,000

Land A/c

	Debit		Credit
(3)	75,000		

Liability (Increases)
Account Payable A/c

	Debit		Credit
		(3)	60,000

The asset land account is debited by ₹ 75,000 (increases) and the asset cash account is credited by ₹ 15,000 (decreases). Bills payable account is credited by ₹ 60,000 (increase in liabilities). This transaction shows that increases in assets are recorded by debits, decreases in assets by credits and increases in liabilities by credits.

Transaction 4: Alpha Co. paid ₹ 12,000 for three months' rent in advance.

Asset (Increase)
Prepaid Rent A/c

	Debit		Credit
(4)	12,000		

Assets (Decrease)
Cash A/c

	Debit		Credit
(1)	80,000	(2)	22,000
		(3)	15,000
		(4)	12,000

Rent paid in advance (or any expense paid in advance) is an asset or resource having future economic benefit as it gives right to the firm to occupy the rented property. As increases in assets are recorded by debits and decreases in assets are recorded by credits, prepaid rent is debited for ₹ 12,000 and cash is credited for ₹ 12,000.

Transaction 5: Alpha Co. received ₹ 9,500 as payment for consultancy services rendered by the firm to the customers.

Assets (Increase)
Cash A/c

	Debit		Credit
(1)	80,000	(2)	22,000
		(3)	15,000
(5)	9,500	(4)	12,000

Equity (Increases)
Consultancy Services A/c

	Debit		Credit
		(5)	9,500

This transaction increases the asset cash and equity of the firm by the revenue received for services rendered. Assets are increased by debits and revenues are increased by credits. Therefore, a debit of ₹ 9,500 to cash and a credit of ₹ 9,500 to Receipts for consultancy services are made to record the transaction.

Transaction 6: Alpha Co. rendered consultancy services to its customers for ₹ 13,500 on credit and the customers will pay later.

Assets (Increase)
Account Receivable

	Debit		Credit
(6)	13,500		

Equity (Increases)
Consultancy Services

	Debit		Credit
		(5)	9,500
		(6)	13,500

The firm has given consultancy services to the customers who will pay in future. Since the services has been completed, revenue is earned. A future economic benefit has been received and therefore an asset account—Accounts Receivable—is created in exchange for the services rendered. Assets are increased by debits. Revenues are increased by credits.

Transaction 7: Alpha Co. paid ₹ 12,000 for the land earlier purchased on credit for ₹ 60,000.

Assets (Decrease)
Cash A/c

	Debit		Credit
(1)	80,000	(2)	22,000
(5)	9,500	(3)	15,000
		(4)	12,000
		(7)	12,000

Liabilities (Decrease)
Accounts Payable A/c

	Debit		Credit
(7)	12,000	(3)	60,000

The asset cash and liability bills payable are reduced by ₹ 12,000 each by this transaction. Assets are decreased by credits; liabilities are decreased by debits.

Transaction 8: Additional tools are purchased on credit, for ₹ 1,500.

Assets (Increase)
Tools A/c

	Debit		Credit
(2)	6,000		
(8)	1,500		

Accounts Payable A/c

	Debit		Credit
		(8)	15,000

This transaction increases the asset Tools and the liability Accounts Payable each by ₹ 1,500. Assets are increased by debits. Liabilities are increased by credits.

Transaction 9: Alpha Co. paid utilities expense of ₹ 1,000.

Assets (Decrease)
Cash A/c

	Debit		Credit
(1)	80,000	(2)	22,000
(5)	9,500	(3)	15,000
		(4)	12,000
		(7)	12,000
		(9)	1,000

A separate expense account is created for each expense item. This transaction increases the utility Expense and reduces the asset cash by ₹ 1,000. Expenses are increased by debits and assets are decreased by credits.

Transaction 10: Alpha Co. received ₹ 7,500 in cash from customers for whom consultancy services were earlier rendered (Transaction 6).

Assets (Increase)
Cash

	Debit		Credit
(1)	80,000	(2)	22,000
(5)	9,500	(3)	15,000
(10)	7,500	(4)	12,000
		(7)	12,000
		(9)	1,000

Assets (Decrease)
Accounts Receivable

	Debit		Credit
(6)	13,500	(10)	7,500

Payments by customers reduce the asset accounts receivable and increase the asset cash. Assets are increased by debits and decreased by credits.

Transaction 11: Depreciation of ₹ 7,500 is recorded on the office equipment.

Assets (Decrease)
Depreciation

	Debit		Credit
		(12)	7,500

Equity (Decreases)

	Debit		Credit
(12)	7,500		

Depreciation expense is recorded by increasing an expense and reducing an asset. The reduction of the asset is accomplished by the use of a contra-asset account. Expenses are increased by debits. Assets are reduced by credits.

Transaction 12: Ashok withdrew ₹ 2,000 from the firm for personal use.

Assets (Decrease)
Cash A/c

	Debit		Credit
(1)	80,000	(2)	22,000
(5)	9,500	(3)	15,000
(10)	7,500	(4)	12,000
		(7)	12,000
		(9)	1,000
		(12)	2,000

Equity (Decreases)
Drawing A/c

	Debit		Credit
(12)	2,000		

This transaction reduces cash and decreases equity of the firm by ₹ 2,000. Assets are reduced by credits and liabilities are reduced by debits. For withdrawals made by the proprietor, a separate account—Drawing Account—is opened. Drawing is a contra account because its balance represents a reduction of equity (capital) account. Debiting the drawing account to reflect the reduction in owner's equity has the same effect as debiting the owner's capital account directly because, at the end of the period, after net profit is added to the owner's capital account, the debit balance in the drawing account is deducted to arrive at the ending amount of owner's capital.

Transaction 13: ₹ 4,000 of the prepaid rent (₹ 12,000) had expired; as mentioned in Transaction 4.

Assets (Decrease)
Prepaid Rent A/c

	Debit		Credit
(4)	12,000	(13)	4,000

Equity (Decreases)
Rent Expense A/c

	Debit		Credit
(13)	4,000		

In transaction 4 the firm paid ₹ 12,000 for three months' rent in advance. At the end of one month. ₹ 4,000 rent has expired and no longer represents an asset. Assets are decreased by credits and liability is decreased by debits. Expenses reduce the equity of the firm.

TYPES OF ACCOUNTS

The accounts maintained by a business organisation are classified into three types as shown in the figure.

Personal Account: It deals with accounts of individuals like creditors, debtors, bank etc. It shows the balance due to these individuals or due from them on a particular date.

Real Account: It represents assets like plant and machinery, land and buildings, goodwill etc. As on a particular date, this account shows the worth of the asset.

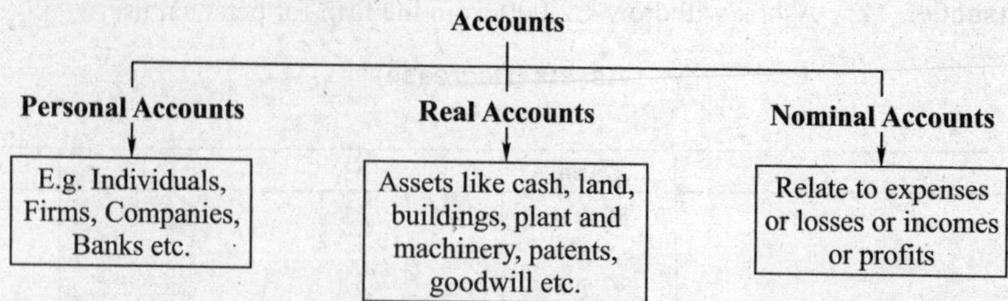

Nominal Account: It consists of different types of expenses or incomes or loss or profit. These accounts show the amount of income earned or expenses incurred for a particular period, say a month, a year, etc.

LEDGER

Ledger contains a classified summary of all transactions recorded in the cash book and journal. A ledger is not an independent record. The transactions recorded in a ledger are derived from either the cash book or the journal.

JOURNALISING THE TRANSACTIONS

Recording the dual aspects of a transaction is known as journalising. Normally, in a business it is impossible to record every transaction as a journal entry. Hence, special journals such as purchases book, sales book etc. are used. Only certain special transactions are recorded in the journal book. However, for a clear understanding of the readers, the journal entries for various transactions are explained below. Let us apply the rules of debit and credit for a few sample transactions after ascertaining dual aspects.

Transaction (1)	Aspects (2)	Account Debited (3)	Reason for the debit (4)	Account Credited (5)	Reason for the credit (6)
ABC Ltd. received ₹ 5,000 from Gupta & Company	Aspect 1—Cash of ₹ 5,000 is received. Aspect 2—The amount is given by Gupta & Co.	Cash A/c	Cash A/c is a real A/c. The rule of 'Debit what comes in' applies	Gupta & Co.	Gupta & Co. A/c is a personal A/c. The rule of 'credit the giver' applies.
PQR Ltd. purchased ₹ 6,000 worth of goods from *X* Co.	Aspect 1—Goods worth ₹ 6,000 is received Aspect 2—The goods are supplied by *X* Co.	Purchases A/c	Purchase A/c is a real A/c. The rule of 'Debit what comes in' applies	*X* Co. A/c	*X* Co. A/c a personal A/c. The rule of 'credit the giver' applies
XYZ Ltd. paid the salaries of ₹ 15,500 to its staff for the month through bank transfer.	Aspect 1—Payment of an expense of ₹ 15,500. Aspect 2—Bank balance is reduced by ₹ 15,500.	Salaries A/c	Salaries A/c is a nominal A/c. The rule of 'Debit all expenses' applies.		Bank A/c is a Real A/c. The rule of 'credit what goes out' applies

Illustration 1: Journalise the following transactions in the books of Basu:

(*a*) Basu sold goods to Chowdhary for ₹ 75,000 against a cheque.

(*b*) Received as commission ₹ 40,000.

(*c*) Bank paid ₹ 30,000 directly for insurance premium of Basu.

(*d*) Cash deposited into Bank ₹ 5,00,000.

(*e*) Withdrawn cash from Bank for personal expenses ₹ 85,000.

Solution: **Journal Entries**

S. No.	Particulars	L.F.	Amount Dr. (₹)	Amount Cr. (₹)
(*a*)	Bank A/c	Dr.	75,000	
	To Sales A/c			75,000
	(Being the goods sold to Chowdhary against a cheque)			
(*b*)	Cash A/c	Dr.	40,000	
	To Commission A/c			40,000
	(Being the commission received)			
(*c*)	Insurance Premium A/c	Dr.	30,000	
	To Bank A/c			30,000
	(Being the Insurance Premium paid directly through Bank)			
(*d*)	Bank A/c	Dr.	5,00,000	
	To Cash A/c			5,00,000
	(Being the cash deposited in the bank)			
(*e*)	Drawings A/c	Dr.	85,000	
	To Bank A/c			85,000
	(Being the cash withdrawn from bank for personal use)			
	Total		2,80,000	2,80,000

Illustration 2: Journalise the following transactions in the books of Shri Shiv Kumar Gupta:

2012	Particulars	(₹)
Jan. 1	Commenced business with	50,000
Jan. 2	Goods purchased for cash	30,000
Jan. 3	Paid freight	2,000
Jan. 7	Goods sold to Rajani Kant on credit	13,000
Jan. 8	Paid for stationery	1,000
Jan. 9	Paid for Rent	5,000
Jan. 10	Cash received from Mohan Das	15,400
	Allowed him discount	600
Jan. 17	Paid Premium	4,000
Jan. 19	Paid postage	100
Jan. 20	Rakesh was declared Insolvent, fifty paise in the rupee was received from his estate, total debt being ₹ 10,000	
Jan. 29	Paid for Salaries	8,000

Solution: **Journal**

Date 2012	Particulars	L.F.	Dr. Amount (₹)	Cr. Amount (₹)
Jan. 1	Cash A/c			
	To Capital A/c	Dr.	50,000	
	(Started business with ₹ 50,000)			50,000
Jan. 2	Purchases A/c	Dr.	30,000	
	To Cash			30,000
	(Being the amount of Cash purchases)			

Date 2012	Particulars	L.F.	Dr. Amount (₹)	Cr. Amount (₹)
Jan. 3	Freight A/c Dr. To Cash (Being the payment for freight)		2,000	2,000
Jan. 7	Rajani Kant Dr. To Sales A/c (Being the sales of Goods on credit)		13,000	13,000
Jan. 8	Stationery A/c Dr. To Cash A/c (Being the amount of stationery paid)		1,000	1,000
Jan. 9	Rent A/c Dr. To Cash A/c (Being the amount of rent paid)		5,000	5,000
Jan. 10	Cash A/c Dr. Discount A/c Dr. To Mohan Das (Being cash received from Mohan Das)		15,400 600	16,000
Jan. 17	Premium A/c Dr. To Cash (Being the payment for premium)		4,000	4,000
Jan. 19	Postage A/c Dr. To Cash (Being the payment for postage)		100	100
Jan. 20	Cash A/c Dr. Bad debts A/c Dr. To Rakesh (Being the recovery of 50 paise in the rupee from Rakesh, total debt being ₹ 10,000)		5,000 5,000	10,000
Jan. 29	Salaries A/c Dr. To Cash (Being the payment for salaries)		8,000	8,000
	Total		1,39,100	1,39,100

Illustration 3: Journalise the following transactions:

2012		(₹)
July 1	*X* started business with cash	80,000
July 3	Goods purchased for cash	30,000
July 5	Goods purchased from *A*	5,000
July 7	Goods sold for cash	10,000
July 10	Goods sold to *P*	30,000
July 12	Cash paid to *A*	3,000
July 15	Cash received from *P*	10,000
July 21	Paid for wages	1,500
July 25	Purchased furniture from Sunil Kumar for cash	5,000
July 28	Paid rent	5,000
July 31	Paid for salaries	2,000

Solution: **Journal**

Date 2012	Particulars	L.F.	Dr. Amount (₹)	Cr. Amount (₹)
July 1	Cash A/c Dr. To Capital A/c (Started business with cash)		80,000	80,000
July 3	Purchases A/c Dr. To Cash (Being the purchase of goods for cash)		30,000	30,000
July 5	Purchases A/c Dr. To *A* (Being goods purchased from *A*)		5,000	5,000
July 7	Cash A/c Dr. To Sales A/c (Being goods sold on cash)		10,000	10,000
July 10	*P* Dr. To Sales A/c (Being goods sold to *P*)		30,000	30,000
July 12	*A* Dr. To Cash A/c (Being cash paid to *A*)		3,000	3,000
July 15	Cash A/c Dr. To *P* (Being cash received from *P*)		10,000	10,000
July 21	Wages A/c Dr. To Cash A/c (Being wages paid)		1,500	1,500
July 25	Furniture A/c Dr. To Cash A/c (Being furniture purchased from Sunil Kumar)		5,000	5,000
July 28	Rent A/c Dr. To Cash (Being rent paid)		5,000	5,000
July 31	Salaries A/c Dr. To Cash (Being salaries paid)		2,000	2,000

Illustration 4: Journalise the following transactions in the books of Khanu and Co.:

2012		(₹)
Jan. 2	Started the business with	8,00,000
Jan. 3	Bought furniture for	1,20,000
Jan. 6	Bought stationery for	5,000
Jan. 7	Purchased goods for cash at	2,00,000
Jan. 9	Sold goods for cash worth	50,000
Jan. 11	Sold to R. Desai goods worth	1,00,000
Jan. 14	Bought goods from Mundra Bros. at	80,000
Jan. 18	Paid office cleaning charges of	1,500
Jan. 20	Bought goods from Hari worth	1,00,000
Jan. 22	Sold to Sharma and Co. goods worth	60,000
Jan. 24	Received from R. Desai	50,000

2012		(₹)
Jan. 25	Paid to Hari	90,000
Jan. 28	Bought typewriter for	80,000
Jan. 31	Paid house rent of	7,500
Jan. 31	Paid light charges of	5,000
Jan. 31	Paid salary amounting to	50,000
Jan. 31	Received commission of	15,000

Solution: **Journal**

Date 2012	Particulars		L.F.	Dr.	Cr.
Jan. 2	Cash A/c To Capital A/c (Started business with ₹ 8,000)	Dr.		8,00,000	8,00,000
Jan. 3	Furniture A/c To Cash (Purchased Furniture)	Dr.		1,20,000	1,20,000
Jan. 6	Stationery A/c To Cash (Purchased stationery)	Dr.		5,000	5,000
Jan. 7	Purchases A/c To Cash A/c (Being the purchase of goods)	Dr.		2,00,000	2,00,000
Jan. 9	Cash A/c To Sales A/c (Being the sale of goods)	Dr.		50,000	50,000
Jan. 11	R. Desai To Sales A/c (Being the sale of goods to R. Desai)	Dr.		1,00,000	1,00,000
Jan. 14	Purchases A/c To Mundra Brothers (Being the purchases of goods from Mundra Brothers)	Dr.		80,000	80,000
Jan. 18	Office cleaning charges A/c To Cash (Being the office cleaning charges paid)	Dr.		1,500	1,500
Jan. 20	Purchases A/c To Hari (Being the purchase of goods)	Dr.		1,00,000	1,00,000
Jan. 22	Sharma & Co. To Sales A/c (Being the sale of goods)	Dr.		60,000	60,000
Jan. 24	Cash A/c To R. Desai (Being amount received from R. Desai)	Dr.		50,000	50,000
Jan. 25	Hari To Cash A/c (Being the amount paid to Hari)	Dr.		90,000	90,000
Jan. 28	Typewriter A/c To Cash A/c (Being the purchase of typewriter)	Dr.		80,000	80,000

Date 2012	Particulars	L.F.	Dr.	Cr.
Jan. 31	Rent A/c Dr. Lighting A/c Dr. Salary A/c Dr. To Cash (Being the payment made for rent, lighting and salary)		7,500 5,000 50,000	 62,500
Jan. 31	Cash A/c Dr. To Commission A/c (Being the amount of commission received)		15,000	 15,000

THEORY QUESTIONS

1. Explain the nature of an account. What information is recorded in an account? Illustrate with an example.
2. Explain the meaning of the terms debit and credit.
3. What are the rules of debit and credit for different accounts?
4. Debits and credits are used to increase and decrease accounts. How is it possible for one of these items, say, debits, to be able to both increase and decrease accounts?
5. What are normal balances? How are they determined?
6. Identify the following as asset, liability, owner's equity, revenue or expense accounts and indicate whether a debit entry or credit entry increases the balance of the account.

   Accounts receivable

   Accounts payable

   Cash

   Professional fees

   Owner's capital

   Advertising expense

   Supplies on hand

   Plant

   Owners' drawings
7. What is the justification for using a separate owner's drawing account?
8. "During the year the total owner's equity of Alpha Co increased from ₹ 1,00,000 to ₹ 1,50,000. Therefore, the annual earnings must have been ₹ 50,000." Is this statement necessarily true? Explain.
9. "Every journal entry made to the journal in a financial accounting system must have at least one debit and one credit." Do you agree or not? Explain.
10. For accounting purposes, what is an account? Explain why accounts are used in an accounting system.
11. Complete the following matrix by entering either debit or credit in each cell:

Item	Increases	Decreases
Assets		
Liabilities		
Owner's Equity		
Revenue		
Expenses		

12. Complete the following matrix by entering either increases or decreases in each cell:

Item	Debit	Credit
Assets		
Liabilities		
Owner's Equity		
Revenue		
Expenses		

13. What is a journal entry?
14. Explain the rules of debit and credit.
15. What do debits and credits mean in different types of accounts?
16. What is an account? How would you classify different accounts maintained by a business enterprise?
17. Give the rules of debit and credit and explain them with suitable examples.
18. "All transactions have double aspects." Comment giving examples.
19. What is double entry system? What are its benefits? Give examples.
20. "All transactions have debit as well as credit." Explain with illustrations.
21. Indicate the nature (debit or credit) of normal balance in the following accounts: (*i*) Personal accounts of a debtor (*ii*) Furniture A/c (*iii*) Merchandise A/c (*iv*) Salaries A/c (*v*) Rent payable A/c (*vi*) Bills payable A/c.
22. What are the usual entries that are passed through Journal proper?
23. "Real Accounts always show debit balances." Comment. **(BBA, GGSIP University, March 2000)**
24. "Bank account is a real account". Comment. **(BBA, GGSIP University, December 2002)**
25. What is a Prime Book of Entry? Classify the various business transactions and give rules for debit and credit. **(BBA, GGSIP University, December 2004)**
26. What are the rules of double entry system in relation to debit and credit? **(BBA, GGSIP University, December 2009)**
27. Distinguish between real accounts and nominal accounts. **(BBA, GGSIP University, December 2010)**

SELF-EVALUATION EXERCISES

I. Select the correct answer for the following multiple choice questions:

1. In recording transactions
   (*a*) The word "debit" means to increase and the word "credit" means to decrease.
   (*b*) Assets, expenses, and owners' drawing accounts are debited for increases.
   (*c*) Liabilities, revenue, and owners' drawing accounts are debited for increases.
   (*d*) Assets, expenses and owners' capital accounts are debited for increases.
2. The first step in the accounting cycle is to
   (*a*) Record transactions in journals
   (*b*) Analyse transactions from source documents
   (*c*) Post journal entries to general ledger accounts
   (*d*) Adjust the general ledger accounts

3. A journal entry that contains more than just two accounts is called
   (*a*) A posted journal entry (*b*) An adjusting journal entry
   (*c*) An erroneous journal entry (*d*) A compound journal entry
4. Which of the following is a contra asset account?
   (*a*) Recovery of Unrealized Loss on Short-term Investments.
   (*b*) Unrealized Loss on Short-term Investments.
   (*c*) Loss on Sale of Investments.
   (*d*) Allowance to Reduce Short-term Investments to Market.
5. The separate record maintained for each item that appears on the financial statements is the:
   (*a*) ledger (*b*) account
   (*c*) chart of accounts (*d*) none of the above
6. A debit may signify:
   (*a*) an increase in an asset account (*b*) a decrease in an asset account
   (*c*) an increase in a liability account (*d*) an increase in the capital account
7. The type of account with a normal credit balance is:
   (*a*) an asset (*b*) a dividend (*c*) a revenue (*d*) an expense
8. The receipt of cash from customers in payment of their accounts would be recorded by a:
   (*a*) debit to cash: credit to Accounts Receivable
   (*b*) debit to Accounts Receivable; credit to Cash
   (*c*) debit to Cash; credit to Accounts Payable
   (*d*) debit to Accounts Payable; credit to Cash
9. The left side of an account is referred to as
   (*a*) the balance (*b*) a debit (*c*) a credit (*d*) a footing
10. Which of the following is a liability account?
    (*a*) Accounts Receivable (*b*) Withdrawals
    (*c*) Rent Expense (*d*) Accounts Payable
11. A purchase of office equipment on credit requires a credit to
    (*a*) Office Equipment (*b*) Cash
    (*c*) Accounts Payable (*d*) Equipment Expense
12. Payment for a two-year insurance policy requires a debit to
    (*a*) Prepaid Insurance (*b*) Insurance Expense
    (*c*) Cash (*d*) Accounts Payable
13. An agreement to spend ₹ 10,000 a month on advertising beginning next month requires:
    (*a*) a debit to Advertising Expense (*b*) a credit to Cash
    (*c*) no entry (*d*) a debit to Prepaid Advertising
14. Transactions are initially recorded in the
    (*a*) trial balance (*b*) T account (*c*) general journal (*d*) ledger
15. The normal account balances for Equipment and Accumulated Depreciation, Equipment are
    (*a*) debit and credit, respectively (*b*) credit and debit, respectively
    (*c*) debits (*d*) credits

II. Answer True or False:

1. Immediately after purchasing fixed assets, the financial condition of a business is worse than it was just before the purchase.

2. An account is the basic record-keeping unit in which the increases and decreases caused by transactions are recorded; on the basis of these recorded decreases and increases, an account's balance at a particular date can be determined.
3. Accounts reported in the external Balance sheet are the summarized totals of all the detailed accounts of the same type that are kept by the business entity.
4. The accounts used by a particular business for recording increases and decreases, as distinguished from the accounts reported in its balance sheet and income statements, have a uniform and standardized format. A blank account sheet for an asset is the same as a blank account sheet for a liability, owners equity, revenue, or expense.
5. All debits are increases to accounts, and all credits are decreases to accounts: these are the basic rules of debits and credits.
6. Debits equal credits in recording transactions, because the rules for debits and credits are designed in such a way that this always holds true.
7. All debits are shown on the left side of *T* accounts, and all credits are shown on the right side.
8. Recording revenue and expenses directly in the Retained Earnings account is not very practical, so separate revenue and expense accounts are used.
9. An increases to an expense account is recorded as a debit to that expense account, because expenses decrease Retained Earnings and decreases to this account are debits.
10. At the end of each year, in a separate step, the difference between all the revenue and expense accounts is entered in the Retained Earnings account.
11. Keeping separate revenue and expense accounts, instead of direct entry in the Retained Earnings account, causes the accounting equation to be out of balance.
12. Journal entries are the first step in the accounting cycle.
13. Journal entries include specific accounts and definite monetary amounts of increase or decrease to the accounts.
14. Journal entries do not have to follow debit and credit rules; debit and credit rules only apply to posting the journal entries in the accounts.
15. A debit is essentially a value increase or value decrease to an account. Whether it is an increase or a decrease depends on which account is being credited.

III. Match each item listed under Terminology with its appropriate description given herein:

Terminology	Description
1. Journal entry	A. Fundamental accounting model
2. Note payable	B. The three required periodic financial statements.
3. Assets = Liabilities	C. The two equalities in accounting the results of transaction analysis.
4. Expenses	D. An accounting method of expressing the results of transaction analysis
5. Accounts payable	E. The account that is credited when money is borrowed from a bank.
6. $A = L + OE$ and Debits = Credits	F. The account that is credited when a sale is made.
7. Balance sheet, income statement, statement of changes in financial position.	G. The account that is debited when an expense is incurred.

8.	Revenues	H.	The account that is debited when a credit sale is made.
9.	Accounts receivable	I.	The account that is credited when an expense is incurred on credit.
10.	Double-entry system.	J.	Application of the fundamental accounting model – Assets = Liabilities + Owners Equity.

IV. Fill in the blanks with appropriate words:

1. Cash receipts and payments are recorded in .... book.
2. Non-Cash transactions are normally recorded through ....
3. Motor vehicles account is .... account (personal/real/nominal account).
4. Credit purchases of goods are recorded in .... book.
5. The receipt of a benefit is termed as ....
6. A debit in a nominal account denotes an ....
7. Accounts of .... always show a debit balance.

EXERCISES AND PROBLEMS

1. Journalise the following transactions in the books of Hari:

2012		₹
April 1.	Hari started business with cash	60,00,000
2.	Purchased furniture for cash	10,00,000
4.	Purchased goods for cash	25,00,000
5.	Bought goods from Kamlesh	1,50,000
6.	Sold goods for cash	36,00,000
8.	Sold good to Ram	30,00,000
10.	Paid cash to Kamal	15,00,000
14.	Received cash from Ram	18,00,000
16.	Purchased goods from Sohan	6,00,000
18.	Purchased goods from Sohan for cash	8,00,000
20.	Paid rent for the office	1,00,000
26.	Received commission	75,000
27.	Paid salary to Gopal	1,20,000
28.	Received cash from Ram	12,00,000
29.	Withdrew cash from office for personal use	4,00,000
30.	Wages paid	7,20,000

2. Journalise the following transactions in the books of Sumit:

2012		₹
Jan. 1	Sumit started business with cash	10,00,000
2	Paid into bank	6,00,000
3	Bought goods from Mohan on credit	2,00,000
4	Purchased furniture	20,000
	purchased adding machine	80,000
	purchased typewriter	60,000
6	Paid for postage	1,500
8	Sold goods for cash	40,000

2012		₹
9	Sold goods on credit to Mahesh & Co.	1,00,000
15	Paid to Mohan	1,95,000
	Discount allowed by them	5,000
25	Sold goods to Ray & Co.	56,000
26	Received cheque from Mahesh & Co. in full settlement of amount due to them	97,500
31	Paid for electric charge	1,000
	Paid rent by cheque	20,000

3. Pass Journal Entries in the books of Onkar Nath from the following transactions:

2012	
Jan. 1	Onkar Nath started business with cash ₹ 40,000; Goods ₹ 40,000 and furniture ₹ 10,000
2	Sold goods to Ramal for cash ₹ 10,000
4	Ramlal returned goods worth ₹ 2,000
8	Received from Ramlal ₹ 7,990 in full settlement of his account
10	Purchased goods from Brij of the list price of ₹ 10,000 at 15% trade discount
13	Returned goods to Brij of the list price of ₹ 1,000
16	Settled the account of Brij by paying cash, under a discount of 10%
18	Bought a 'table fan' for ₹ 1,200 for the domestic use of Onkar Nath
25	Paid Trade Expenses ₹ 700 and Travelling Expenses ₹ 380

4. Record the following transactions:

1. Gee commences business with a capital of ₹ 25,00,000 trading under the name of Jain General Store.
2. Paid into State Bank of India ₹ 5,00,000.
3. Bought goods from Chandara for ₹ 10,00,000.
4. Bought furniture from Sharda and Co. for ₹ 3,00,000.
5. Sold goods to Paras for ₹ 50,000.
6. Received a sum of ₹ 1,00,000 being rent for the portion of a building let out.
7. Gee contracted with Deep Construction Co. for the renovation of the building at an estimated cost of ₹ 5,00,000.
8. Bought Shares in Siyaram Ltd. for ₹ 5,00,000.
9. Paid Gee's life insurance premium ₹ 15,000.
10. Bank collected dividends on our investments ₹ 50,000.

5. Pass Journal Entries for the following transactions:

1. Provide depreciation on Furniture ₹ 500 and on Machinery ₹ 2,000.
2. Received cash ₹ 1,000 for bad debts written off last year.
3. Ajay Singh was declared bankrupt. He owed ₹ 2,500 to us. This amount was written off as bad.
4. ₹ 20,000 for wages and ₹ 4,000 for salaries are outstanding.
5. Purchased furniture for ₹ 6,000 for the proprietor and paid the amount by cheque.

6. Journalise the following:

1. Bought goods from Kapil for ₹ 40,000 at a trade discount of 10% and cash discount of 2%, paid 60% of the amount immediately.

2. Received a cheque from *Y* for ₹ 8,000, this cheque was deposited into bank the next day.
3. Cheque received from *Y* was dishonoured.
4. Old newspapers sold ₹ 50.
5. Purchased goods from *X* and paid by cheque ₹ 7,000.
6. Sold half of the above goods to *P* at a profit of 30% on cost.

7. Journalise the following transactions:

2012	
Jan. 1	Mohan Bros. commenced business with capital of ₹ 50,000 and goods worth ₹ 30,000.
Jan. 11	Sold old machinery to Nathu for ₹ 2,500.
Jan. 15	Goods worth ₹ 5,000 given as charity.
Jan. 20	Proprietor withdrew for private use ₹ 2,000 from office and ₹ 3,000 from bank.
Jan. 25	Cash purchases were of ₹ 10,000, cash Sales of ₹ 8,000.
Jan. 30	Rent due has been decided to pay in the next accounting year amounting to ₹ 1,000.
	Interest on capital ₹ 500.

8. Journalise the following transactions:
   1. Amit is declared insolvent. Received from his official Receiver a first and final composition of 60 paise in the rupee on a debt of ₹ 4,000.
   2. Paid ₹ 250 in cash as wages on installation of a machine.
   3. Provide 10% depreciation on furniture costing ₹ 5,000.
   4. Sold goods to Manu list price ₹ 4,000, trade discount 10% and cash discount 5%. He paid the amount on the same day and availed the cash discount.
   5. Out of rent paid this year, ₹ 1,000 is related to next year.

9. Pass Journal Entries:
   1. Received ₹ 980 from Viru in full settlement of debt to his account for ₹ 1,000.
   2. Received interest on loan from the debtor ₹ 150.
   3. ₹ 550 due from Ram is a bad debt.
   4. Provide interest on capital (₹ 50,000) at 6% for six months.
   5. Supplied goods costing ₹ 600 to Kunti, issued invoice at 10% above cost less 5% trade discount.
   6. Bought goods from Om and Co. goods worth ₹ 30,000 at 15% trade discount and 2% cash discount terms and paid them half the amount in cash.

10. Journalise the transactions:
    1. Goods for ₹ 2,500 were given away as charity.
    2. Goods worth ₹ 2,500 were distributed as free samples.
    3. Goods worth ₹ 5,000 and cash ₹ 4,000 were stolen by an employee.
    4. Goods worth ₹ 1,000 were destroyed by fire. Half of money received from Insurance Co.
    5. Interest charged on drawings @ 5% when total drawings were ₹ 10,000.

ANSWERS TO SELF-EVALUATION EXERCISES

I.	II.	III.	IV.
1. (*b*)	1. False	1. D	1. Cash
2. (*b*)	2. True	2. E	2. Journal
3. (*d*)	3. True	3. A	3. Real
4. (*d*)	4. True	4. G	4. Purchases
5. (*b*)	5. False	5. I	5. Debtor
6. (*a*)	6. True	6. J	6. Expense/Loss
7. (*c*)	7. True	7. B	7. Assets.
8. (*a*)	8. True	8. F	
9. (*b*)	9. True	9. H	
10. (*d*)	10. True	10. C	
11. (*c*)	11. False		
12. (*a*)	12. True		
13. (*c*)	13. True		
14. (*c*)	14. False		
15. (*a*)	15. True		

5

CASH BOOK AND SUBSIDIARY BOOK

LEARNING OBJECTIVES

After reading this chapter, you should be able to:

- *Explain* the nature of Cash Book, Petty Cash Book
- *Discuss* different types of journal books such as Purchase Book, Purchase Return Book, Sales Book, Sales Return Book, Bills Receivable Book, Bills Payable Book, Journal Proper.

CASH BOOK

Cash Book records all receipts of and payments in cash. Usually the deposits into bank accounts maintained by a business firm, withdrawals from such accounts and cheque payments are also recorded in the Cash Book. Sometimes a separate book for recording receipts and payments by cheques/DDs etc., is kept, known as the Bank Book. A Cash Book which is used to record both cash and bank transactions is referred to as a Two-Column Cash Book. The format of this cash book is given below:

Cash Book of Ramesh & Co.

Dr. Cr.

Date 2012	Receipts	Cash (₹)	Bank (₹)	Date 2012	Payments	Cash (₹)	Bank (₹)
April 1	To balance b/d	1,500	13,000	April 2	By Wages	50	
6	To Sales	800		5	By electricity		400
7	To Arvind Co.		2000	8	By Plumbing repairs	400	
11	To Bela Corporation		2,350	15	By *Y* Ltd.		10,800
20	To Sales	500		30	By balance c/d	2,350	6,150
		2,800	17,350			2,800	17,350

Cash Discounts

Sometimes, in order to encourage early payments due from customers, a company may offer a certain percentage of the amount as a discount. For example, if a customer owes the company ₹ 1,000, the company may allow 2% discount if the payment is made before a certain date. In such a case, the customer would pay an actual cash of ₹ 980 only (₹ 1,000–2% of ₹ 1,000) and ₹ 20 would be treated as discount expense by the company. In the same way, a company might be given some discounts by its creditors for early payment of the amounts payable by it. A cash discount may be distinguished from a trade discount which is given on the invoice price, especially when orders for large quantities are placed. The trade discount is therefore reflected as a reduction in the sale price itself.

A Cash Book can also be used to record the cash discounts that are allowed to customers for prompt payments and the cash discounts that are received on payments made to suppliers within a stipulated time period. Since discounts will be allowed to customers at the time of receipt of money and received from suppliers at the time of payment of dues, it is convenient to maintain the column for discounts allowed on the receipts side of the Cash Book and the column for discount received on the payments side. A Cash Book in which the cash and bank transactions and the details of cash discounts are recorded is referred to as a Three-Column Cash Book. An illustrative format of this type of Cash Book is given below:

Cash Book of Ramesh & Co.

Dr. **Cr.**

Date	Receipts	Dis.	Cash	Bank	Date	Payment	Dis.	Cash	Bank
2012					**2012**				
April 1	To balance b/d		1,500	13,000	April 2	By Wages		50	
6	To Sales		800		5	By electricity			400
7	To Arvind Co.	50		2,000	8	By Plumbing repairs		400	
11	To Bela Corp.	60		2,350	15	By *Y* Ltd.	150		10,800
20	To Sales		500		30	By balance c/d		2,350	6,150
		110	2,800	17,350			150	2,800	17,350

The Cash Book normally also carries Columns for Cash Memo No., Ledger Folio, Vouchers No. etc.

The unique feature of the Cash Book is that it performs the functions of a Journal and the General Ledger with regard to the Cash and Bank transactions. In other words, Cash Book is the book of first entry for all such transactions and the ledger accounts for cash in hand and cash at bank will not be maintained in the General Ledger.

Petty Cash Book

When the petty cash fund is operated as an imprest fund, the recording of the petty expenses paid will be made in the petty cash book. This would also avoid recording too many small value transactions in the main cash book. The petty cash book would contain a number of analytical columns for grouping the various expenses under a few classifications which would facilitate subsequent posting into the General Ledger; A specimen petty cash book is given below:

Analytical Petty Cash Book of Ramesh & Co.

Amt. Recd. ₹	Date	Particulars	Total amount ₹	Postage & Stationery ₹	Carriage ₹	Travelling ₹	Sundry Exp. ₹
	2012						
3,000	April 01	To Bank A/c (cheque encashed)					
	April 17	By postal stamps	800	800			
	April 10	By stationery	320	320			

Amt. Recd. ₹	Date	Particulars	Total amount ₹	Postage & Stationery ₹	Carriage ₹	Travelling ₹	Sundry Exp. ₹
	April 15	By carriage	160		160		
	April 20	By Auto fare of salesman	200			200	
	April 22	By telegram	50	50			
	April 27	By tea to customers	150				150
	April 30	By stationery	360	360			
		Total	2,040	1,530	160	200	150
	April 30	By balance c/d	960				
3,000			3,000				
	2012						
960	May 1	To Balance b/d					
2,040	May 1	To Bank A/c (Cheque encashed)					

The Imprest System

When an analytical petty cash book is maintained for recording the petty expenses, it will be practically more convenient to consider the petty cash as a separate account and take cheques issued for the petty cash imprest as a debit to petty cash account and all petty expenses paid as credits in petty cash account. The journal entries in the months of April and May 2012 in the books of Ramesh Co. will be as follows:

Date	Particulars		Dr.	Cr.
April 1	Petty Cash Account	Dr.	3,000	
	To Bank Account			3,000
	(being the imprest amount released for petty expenses)			
April 30	Postage and Stationery A/c	Dr.	1,530	
	Carriage Account	Dr.	160	
	Travelling Expenses Account	Dr.	200	
	Sundry Expenses Account	Dr.	150	
	To petty Cash Account			204
	(being the petty expenses incurred during April)			
May 1	Petty Cash Account	Dr.	2040	
	To Bank Account			2040
	(being the reimbursement of petty expenses)			

If credit for all the expenses is also given in the Cash Account (or Bank A/c) then the Cash A/c will be understated (due to two credits–one in respect of release of imprest and the other in respect of actual expenses), and to counterbalance the understatement, the balance in Petty Cash Account must be added to that of the Cash Account.

JOURNAL

The Books of Accounts maintained by an organisation other than the cash book may be classified into Journals and Ledgers. The Journal is used as the book of first entry for all transactions which cannot be recorded in the Cash Book. In other words, all non-cash transactions should be recorded in the journal. For practical convenience the journal is maintained by using a number of books called the subsidiary books. For example, the following subsidiary books may constitute the journal for an enterprise.

(*i*) Purchase Book

(*ii*) Purchase Returns Book

(*iii*) Sales Book
(*iv*) Sales Returns Book
(*v*) Bills Receivable Book
(*vi*) Bills Payable Book
(*vii*) Journal Proper.

Specimen formats of these books and brief explanations regarding their use are given in the following sections:

Purchases Book

Also known as the Purchases Journal, this book is used to record credit purchases of goods only. The term 'goods' covers only those items procured by the business for resale.

Purchase Book of Johnson Co.

Date 2012	Name of Supplier	Ledger Folio	Inward Invoice No.	Amount ₹
April 12	*Y* Limited		3,354	10,95,000
12	Sharp Enterprises		401	2,70,000
20	Best and Company		5,542	3,90,000
	Total			17,55,000

Purchase Returns Book

This subsidiary book is used to record the goods purchased on credit and sent back to suppliers as they are found not conforming to specifications or for any other reason.

Purchase Returns Book of Johnson Co.

Date 2012	Name of Supplier	Ledger Folio	Debit Note No.	Amount ₹
April 15	Sharp Enterprises		80	1,00,000
25	Best and Company		81	90,000
	Total			1,90,000

Sales Book

Also known as the Sales Journal, this subsidiary book is used to record all sale of goods on credit.

Sales Book of Johnson Co.

Date 2012	Name of Customer	Ledger Folio	Outward Invoice No.	Amount (₹)
April 3	Beta Corporation		1001	2,41,000
5	Zeta Company		1002	3,94,000
6	Quality Dealers		1003	4,90,000
15	Sooraj Traders		1004	1,80,000
25	Star Enterprises		1005	19,50,000
	Total			32,55,000

Sales Returns Book

This book is used to record the transactions relating to goods sold on credit and received back from the customers as not conforming to the specifications or for any other reason.

Sales Returns Book of Johnson Co.

Date	Name of Customer	Ledger Folio	Credit Note No.	Amount (₹)
2012				
April 10	Zeta Company		10	54,000
27	Star Enterprises		11	2,00,000
	Total			2,54,000

Bills Receivable Book

The Bills Receivable of an enterprise consist of all Promissory Notes given or Bills of Exchange accepted by customers in respect of amounts due from them. The Bills Receivable Book is used to record all such Promissory Notes given or such Bills of Exchange accepted by customers.

Bills Receivable Book of Johnson Co.

Date	From whom received	Acceptor	Date of Bills	Term	Date of Maturity	Where payable	Amount ₹	How disposed
April 12	Quality Dealers	Quality Dealers	8.4.12	90 days	10.7.12	Bank of India, Bombay	4,90,000	Discounted on 20.4.12
18	Sooraj Traders	Sooraj Traders	16.4.12	60 days	10.6.12	Union Bank of Bombay	1,80,000	
							6,70,000	

Bills Payable Book

The Bills Payables consist of all Promissory Notes given or Bills of Exchange accepted by the business in respect of amounts owing to its suppliers. The Bills Payable Book is used to record all such Promissory Notes given or Bills of Exchange accepted by the business.

Bills Payable Book of Johnson Co.

Date	Name of the drawer	Payee	Date of Bills	Term	Date of Maturity	Where payable	Amount ₹	Remark
2012								
April 25	Best & Co.	Best & Co.	25.4.12	90 days	27.7.12	Canara Bank, Bombay	3,00,000	

Journal Proper

This Book is used to record all transactions which cannot be included in the cash book or any of the other six subsidiary books discussed above. The transactions that will be recorded in Journal Proper are: purchase or sale of fixed assets and investments on credit, adjusting entries, rectification entries etc.

Journal Proper of Johnson Co.

Date	Particulars	Ref.	L.F.	Debit ₹	Credit ₹
April 10	Furniture and Fittings A/c To Furniture Mart A/c (being the purchase of furniture on credit)	Dr.		4,00,000	4,00,000
30	Repairs to Machinery A/c To Machinery A/c (being the rectification of a wrong posting of a repair expense to asset A/c)	Dr.		5,00,000	5,00,000

Illustration 1: From the following transactions of M/s J Choudhary, write up his cash book (three-column form) bringing down the balance as on May 31, 2012.

May 1 Balance at bank	1,50,000
May 2 Drew from bank for office use	50,000
May 3 Bought office furniture for cash	32,000
May 8 Paid wages in cash	15,000
May 14 Drew from bank from office use	25,000
May 16 Sold goods for cash	22,000
May 19 Received a cheque from B Batiwala & Co in settlement of their account of ₹ 75,000 less 5 per cent	
May 23 Bought goods for cash	45,000
May 25 Drew cheque for self	40,000
May 31 Paid Agrawal's account ₹ 40,000 by cheque less 2½ per cent	

Solution:

Cash Book

Date	Particulars	L.F.	Dis. ₹	Cash ₹	Bank ₹	Date	Particulars	L.F.	Dis. ₹	Cash ₹	Bank ₹
May 1	To Balance b/d				1,50,000	May 2	By Cash A/c	C			50,000
May 2	To Bank A/c	C		50,000		May 3	By Furniture A/c			32,000	
May 14	To Bank A/c	C		25,000		May 8	By Wages A/c			15,000	
May 16	To Sales A/c			22,000		May 14	By Cash A/c				25,000
May 19	To Batiwala & Co.		3,750		71,250	May 23	By Purchases A/c			45,000	
						May 25	By Drawing A/c				40,000
						May 31	By Agrawal		1,000		39,000
						May 31	By Balance c/d			5,000	67,250
			3,750	97,000	2,21,250				1,000	97,000	2,21,250
June 1	To Balance b/d			5,000	67,250						

Illustration 2: Enter the following transactions in the purchase day book:

2012

Jan. 2 Bought of G Saha and Co. 60 yards of long cloth @ ₹ 140 per yard.

Jan. 8 Purchased from B Chandra & Co. piece goods for ₹ 20,000.

Jan. 16 Purchased from A. Basu & Co. 100 yards of shirting @ ₹ 300 per yard less trade discount @ 2%

Jan. 28 Bought of SK Sarkar & Sons, 200 yards of terycot @ ₹ 1,200 per yard less 2½ per cent trade discount.

Solution:

Purchase Book

Date	Particulars	L.F.	Details	Amount ₹
2012 Jan. 2	G. Saha 60 yds of long cloth @ ₹ 140 per yard			8,400
Jan. 8	B. Chandra & Co. piece goods			20,000
Jan. 16	A. Basu & Co. 100 yards of shirting @ ₹ 300 per yard *Less*: Trade discount @ 2%		30,000 600	29,400
Jan. 28	SK Sarkar & Sons 200 yards of terycot @ ₹ 1,200 per yard *Less*: Trade discount @ 2½%		2,40,000 6,000	2,34,000
	Total			2,91,800

Illustration 3: Prepare a sales day book from the following transactions:

Jan. 2, 2012 Sold to Nilima, spices worth ₹ 80,000 less 10% trade discount.

July 4, 2012 Sold to Sadhana, sugar worth ₹ 40,000, extra charges ₹ 1,000.

July 5, 2012 Sold to Mohan, wheat worth ₹ 20,000 forwarding expenses ₹ 1,500.

Solution:

Sales Book

Date	Particulars	L.F.	Details ₹	Amount ₹
2012 July 12	Nilima Spices *Less*: Trade discount 10% (Sales of spices to Nilima worth ₹ 80,000, less 10% trade discount)		80,000 8,000	72,000
July 4	Sadhana Sugar *Add*: Extra charge (Sale of sugar worth ₹ 40,000 to Sadhana, extra charges being ₹ 1,000)		40,000 1,000	41,000
July 5	Mohan Wheat *Add*: Forwarding charges (Sale of wheat to Mohan for ₹ 20,000 forwarding charges being ₹ 1,500)		30,000 1,500	21,500
	Total			1,34,500

Illustration 4. Prepare the sales day book from the following transactions:

2012

Feb. 1 Sold goods to Ram, 200 metres cloth @ ₹100 per metre less trade discount 7%.

Feb. 3 Sold to Rahim, 500 metres cloth @ ₹ 200 per metre less trade discount 5% packing charges ₹ 3,000.

Feb. 4 Sold to Shyam, 2,000 metres cloth @ ₹ 200 per metre less trade discount 5% other charges made of ₹ 2,500.

Feb. 7 Sold to Jadu, 300 metres cloth @ ₹ 250 per metre less trade discount of 10%.

Solution: **Sales Book**

Date	Particulars	Details ₹	Amount ₹
2012			
Feb. 1	Ram, 200 metres cloth @ ₹ 100 per metre	20,000	
	Less: Trade discount 7%	1,400	18,600
Feb. 3	Rahim, 500 metres cloth @ ₹ 200 per metre	1,00,000	
	Less: Trade discount 5%	5,000	
		95,000	
	Add: Packing charges	3,000	98,000
Feb. 4	Shyam, 2000 metres cloth @ ₹ 200 per metre	4,00,000	
	Less: Trade discount 5%	20,000	
		3,80,000	
	Add: Other charges	2,500	3,82,500
Feb. 7	Jadu, 300 metres cloth @ ₹ 250 per metre	75,000	
	Less: Trade discount 10%	7,500	67,500
	Total		5,66,600

Illustration 5: Prepare purchase returns book (returns outward) from the following particulars:

July 1 Returned to Sumit Prakash 50 m of cloth @ ₹ 20 per metre
July 15 Bharat Kumar & Sons 10 sarees @ ₹ 300 per saree
July 20 Prem Chandra 200 m of cloth @ ₹ 70 per metre
July 31 Bihari Brothers 100 m of cloth @ ₹ 100 per metre

Solution: **Purchase Returns Book**

Date	Particulars	Details ₹	Amount ₹
July 1	Sumit Prakash 50 m of cloth @ ₹ 20 per metre		1,000.00
July 15	Bharat Kumar & Sons 10 sarees @ ₹ 300 per saree		3,000.00
July 20	Prem Chandra 200 m of cloth @ ₹ 70 per metre		14,000.00
July 31	Bihari Brothers 100 m of cloth @ ₹ 100 per metre		10,000.00
			28,000.00

Illustration 6: Enter the following transactions in the appropriate book:

2012

Aug. 01 Returned to us by Harish Gupta & Co. 200 bags coffee @ ₹ 100 per bag.
Aug. 17 Returned by Bipin Pal & Brothers, 300 chests of tea @ ₹ 70 per chest.
Aug. 31 Returned by Bhagwan Das 50 tins of ghee @ ₹ 1,000 per tin.

Solution: **Returns Inwards Book**

Date	Particulars	Details ₹	Amount ₹
2012			
Aug. 01	Harish Gupta & Co., 200 bags coffee @ ₹ 100 per bag		20,000
Aug. 17	Bipin Pal & Brothers, 300 chests of tea @ ₹ 70 per chest		21,000
Aug. 31	Bhagwan Das, 50 tins of ghee @ ₹ 1,000 per tin		50,000
	Total		91,000

Illustration 7: Enter the following transactions in the sales book of M/s Prem Kumar of New Delhi:

2012

May 7 Sold to Manish Gupta, Delhi
100 bags of rice @ ₹ 450 per bag
10 bags of wheat @ ₹ 500 per bag

May 9 Sold to Rajinder Singh, Patiala
80 bags of rice @ ₹ 500 per bag
30 bags of rice @ ₹ 550 per bag
Trade discount allowed @ 10%

May 11 Sold to Ranvir Singh, Agra
100 bags of wheat @ ₹ 550 per bag
Trade discount allowed 10%

Solution: **Sales Book**

Date	Particulars	Details ₹	Amount ₹
2012			
May 7	**Manish Gupta, Delhi:**		
	100 bags of rice @ 450 per bag	45,000	
	10 bags of wheat @ 500 per bag	5,0000	50,000
May 9	**Rajinder Singh, Patiala:**		
	80 bags of rice @ 500 per bag	40,000	
	30 bags of rice @ 550 per bag	16,500	
		56,500	
	Less: Trade discount 10%	5,650	50,850
May 11	**Ranvir Singh, Agra:**		
	100 bags of wheat @ ₹ 550 per bag	55,000	
	Less: Trade discount @ 10%	5,500	49,500
	Total (Credited to sales A/c)		1,50,350

Illustration 8: Enter the following transactions in the purchases book of M/s Vijay Chandra:

2012

May 7 Bought of Prem Das, Delhi; on credit:
100 copies of Principles of Accounting Part I by C.L. Khanna @ ₹ 50 per copy
Trade discount allowed 10%

May 11 Bought of P. Chand and Co. Delhi on credit:
200 copies of Mercantile Law by P.S. Guglani @ ₹ 60 per copy
Less: 10% trade discount

May 13 Bought of Ravinder Kumar, Agra, on credit:
100 copies of History of India Part I
by Mohan Das @ ₹ 70 less 10% discount

Solution: **Purchase Book**

Date	Particulars	Details ₹	Amount ₹
2012	**Prem Das, Delhi**		
May 7	100 copies of principle of accounting by C.L. Khanna @ ₹ 50 per copy	5,000	4,500
	Less: 10% discount	500	

Date	Particulars	Details ₹	Amount ₹
	P. Chand & Co., Delhi		
May 11	200 copies of Mercantile Law by P.S. Guglani @ ₹ 60 per copy	12,000	
	Less: 10% trade discount	1,200	10,800
	Ravinder Kumar, Agra		
May 13	100 copies of history of India Pt. I by Mohan Das @ ₹ 70 per copy	7,000	
	Less: 10% trade discount	700	6,300
	Total (Debited to purchase A/c)		21,600

Illustration 9: Prepare a Cash Book from the following transactions:

2012		(₹)
Jan. 1	Cash in hand	1,000
Jan. 1	Cash at bank	15,000
Jan. 3	Received from Mohan	12,850
	and allowed him Discount	150
Jan. 4	Cash Sales	20,000
Jan. 5	Paid for Rent	4,000
Jan. 6	Cash purchasing	26,000
Jan. 7	Paid to Harish by Cheque	10,000
Jan. 8	Stationery purchased	2,000
Jan. 9	Goods sold for cash	25,000
Jan. 10	Paid salary	6,000
Jan. 12	Paid to Ram Prakash	20,500
	Discount allowed by him	500
Jan. 15	Cash Sales	10,000
Jan. 16	Received a cheque from Prem Das and allowed discount	15,600
Jan. 22	Paid charity	1,000
Jan. 25	Paid to travelling expenses	3,000
Jan. 29	Paid into Bank	5,000

Solution: **Cash Book**

Date 2012	Particulars	L.F.	Dis. (₹)	Cash (₹)	Bank (₹)	Date 2012	Particulars	L.F.	Dis. (₹)	Cash (₹)	Bank (₹)
Jan. 1	To Balance b/d	—	—	1,000	15,000	Jan. 5	By Rent	—	—	4,000	
Jan. 3	To Mohan	—	150	12,850	—	Jan. 6	By Purchase	—	—	26,000	
Jan. 4	To Sales	—	—	20,000	—	Jan. 7	By Harish	—	—	—	10,000
Jan. 9	To Sales	—	—	25,000	—	Jan. 8	By Stationery	—	—	2,000	—
Jan. 15	To Sales	—	—	10,000	—	Jan. 10	By Salary	—	—	6,000	—
Jan. 16	To Prem Das	—	400	—	15,600	Jan. 12	By Ram Prakash	—	500	20,500	
Jan. 29	To Cash	—	—	C	5,000	Jan. 22	By Charity	—	—	1,000	
						Jan. 25	By Travelling	—	—	3,000	
						Jan. 29	By Bank	—	—	5,000	
						Jan. 31	By Balance c/d	—		1,350	25,600
	Total		550	68,850	35,600		**Total**		500	68,850	35,600
Feb. 1	To Balance b/d			1,350	25,600						

Illustration 10: Enter the following in the purchases journal of M/s Modern Furniture Suppliers, Poona:

April Bought on credit from M/s Prakash and Company at a Trade Discount of 10%:
12 dozen Easy chairs at the rate of ₹ 1,150 per dozen.
6 dozen Folding chairs at the rate of ₹ 1,250 per dozen
10 dining Tables at the rate of ₹ 1,450 each.

April 15 Purchases from Shetten and Company, Hubli:
20 Steel cupboards at the rate of ₹ 1,450 each at a Trade Discount of 10% plus Transport charges ₹ 900.

Solution: In the Books of M/s Modern Furniture Suppliers.

Purchases Book

Date	Particulars	L.F.	Details (₹)	Amount (₹)
April 1	**M/s Prakash and Company:**			
	12 dozen Easy Chairs @ ₹ 1,150 per dozen		13,800	
	6 dozen Folding Chairs @ ₹ 1,250 per dozen		7,500	
	10 Dining tables @ ₹ 1,450 each		14,500	
			35,800	
	Less: 10% Discount		3,580	32,220
April 15	**Shetten and Company, Hubli:**			
	20 Steel Cupboards @ ₹ 1,450 each		29,000	
	Less: 10% Trade Discount		2,900	
			26,100	
	Transport Charges		900	27,000
	Total			59,220

Illustration 11: Compile a cash book with cash and Bank columns from the following transactions:

		₹
June 1	Cash Balance	50,000
	Bank Balance	1,75,000
June 5	Cash received from sale of Shares	5,50,000
June 6	Paid into Bank	5,00,000
June 7	Paid S. Bose by cheque	1,25,000
June 20	Received from A. Mukerji by a cheque for ₹ and deposited the same in bank.	60,000

Solution:

Dr. Receipts **Cash Book** Payments Cr.

Date	Particulars	L.F.	Dis. (₹)	Cash (₹)	Bank (₹)	Date	Particulars	L.F.	Dis. (₹)	Cash (₹)	Bank (₹)
June 1	To Balance b/d			50,000	1,75,000	June 6	By Bank A/c			5,00,000	
June 5	To Sale of Shares A/c			5,50,000		June 7	By S. Bose				1,25,000
June 6	To Cash A/c	C			5,00,000						
June 20	To A. Mukerji				60,000	June 30	By Balance c/d			1,00,000	6,10,000
				6,00,000	7,35,000	June 30				6,00,000	7,35,000
July 1	To Balance b/d			1,00,000	6,10,000						

Illustration 12: Write out an analytical petty cash book from the following transactions:

2012

August 1 Issued a cheque for ₹ 10,000 to the petty cashier.
2 Paid electricity charges ₹ 325
4 Paid telephone charges ₹ 250
8 Paid for printing ₹ 375
15 Paid for stationery ₹ 600
20 Purchased post cards ₹ 300

Solution: **Petty Cash Book**

Receipts	Date	Voucher Particulars	Total	Elect.	Tele.	Printing	Stat.	Post cards
10,000	Aug. 1	To Cash						
	Aug. 2	By Electricity charges	325	325				
	Aug. 4	By Telephone charges	250		250			
	Aug. 8	By Printing	375			375		
	Aug. 15	By Stationery	600				600	
	Aug. 20	By Post Cards	300					300
			1,850	325	250	375	600	300
		By Balance c/d	8,150					
10,000			10,000					
8,150		By Balance b/d						
1,850		To Cash						

THEORY QUESTIONS

1. What are the books of original entry?
2. List the various subsidiary books.
   What is the purpose of each subsidiary book? Give specimen of purchase book and sales book and enter four imaginary transactions therein.
3. What is a cash book? What are different types of cash book. How is it balanced?
4. What is contra entry? How are contra entries recognised?
5. What is imprest system of petty cash? What are its advantages?
6. "The cash book generally shows a debit balance". Comment.
7. What do you understand by 'Subsidiary books'? What are the objects of preparing such books?
8. Explain the following subsidiary books. Give their specimen also:
   (*i*) Sales Book (*ii*) Purchase Book (*iii*) Purchase Returns Book
9. What do you understand by special purpose subsidiary books?
10. What is a petty cash book? How will you maintain the petty Cash Book on imprest system?
11. What do you mean by 'balancing of account'? What are the two types of balances?
12. What is Journal Proper?
13. Comment on the following:
    (*a*) "Trade discount is not recorded in Journal proper".
    (*b*) "Cash book is both a book of prime entry and a ledger account".
    (*c*) "A contra entry is made in the cash book when the owner introduces additional capital". **(BBA, GGSIP University, December 2006)**
14. Write notes on Petty Cash Book. **(BBA, GGSIP University, December 2008)**
15. Write notes on three-column cash book. **(BBA, GGSIP University, December 2009)**

SELF-EVALUATION EXERCISES

I. Select the correct answer for the following multiple choice questions:

1. An entry to debit petty cash is made when
   (*a*) a petty cash fund is established
   (*b*) a petty cash fund is replenished
   (*c*) a petty cash fund is established and when it is replenished
   (*d*) a shortage in the petty cash fund is recorded.

2. A petty cash fund is
   (*a*) used to pay relatively small amounts
   (*b*) established by estimating the amount of cash needed for disbursements of relatively small amounts during a specified period
   (*c*) reimbursed when the amount of money in the fund is reduced to a predetermined minimum amount
   (*d*) all of the above.

3. The purchase book records
   (*a*) all purchases (*b*) all purchases of merchandise
   (c) credit purchases of merchandise (*d*) cash purchases of merchandise.

4. The sales book records
   (*a*) all sales (*b*) all sales of merchandise
   (*c*) cash sales of merchandise (*d*) credit sales of merchandise

5. A cash book is
   (*a*) subsidiary only
   (*b*) ledger account
   (*c*) book of first entry and also a ledger account.
   (*d*) none of the above

II. Fill in the blanks with appropriate words:

1. Cash purchases are entered in ....

2. Acceptances received from customers are recorded in ....

3. Return of goods purchased from suppliers are recorded in ....

4. Payments for petty expenses are recorded in........................books on........................

EXERCISES AND PROBLEMS

1. From the following transactions prepare a single-column Cash Book:

2012		₹
March 1	Commenced business with cash	20,00,000
2	Bought goods for cash	5,00,000
5	Sold goods for cash	4,00,000
10	Goods purchased from Ravi on credit	10,00,000
13	Paid to Ravi	7,00,000
15	Cash Sales	8,00,000
18	Purchased furniture for office	6,00,000

20 Paid Wages	38,000
24 Paid Rent	40,000
26 Received Commission	60,000
28 Withdrew for personal expenses	1,00,000
31 Paid Salary	90,000

(**Ans:** Cash Balance ₹ 1,92,000).

2. Gopi commenced business on 1st April, 2002 with ₹ 4,00,000 as capital. He had the following cash transactions:

Prepare double-column cash book:

2012		₹
April 1	Purchased furniture and paid cash	50,000
1	Purchased goods	60,000
4	Sold goods for cash	30,000
5	Purchased goods	40,000
5	Paid cash to Ram Mohan	1,12,000
5	He allowed discount	2,000
6	Received cash from Krishna and Co.	1,20,000
	Allowed discount	4,000
7	Paid for petty expenses	3,000
8	Cash Purchase	30,000
9	Cash Sales	40,000
11	Received from Mohan Bros.	1,20,000
13	Paid for typewriter	1,60,000
15	Paid for telephone	40,000
15	Paid Ali and Sons	80,000
	They allowed discount	1,600

(**Ans:** Cash Balance ₹ 1,35,000)

3. Enter the following transactions in the Cash Book with discount columns:

2012		(₹)
April 1	Balance from the last month	3,758.34
2	Received cash from S.K. Agarwal	6,800.00
4	Purchased a radio set for private use	2,000.00
5	Purchased goods for cash	3,000.00
6	Cash Sales	3,720.00
	Paid Salaries	300.00
8	Received from Mukesh	2,000.00
9	Paid Naresh Chand in full settlement of his account of ₹ 500	450.00
12	Paid for V.V.P. for goods from Chandigarh	487.16
13	Sent money order to Satish	300.00
	Money order commission	5.00
14	Krishan paid cash to us	2,472.50
	Discount allowed	27.50
18	Cash Purchases	580.00

21	Paid for General Expenses	29.00
24	Received from Anand Prakash	561.20
28	Paid for stationery	50.00
30	Paid water bill	21.50
31	Paid for charity	10.00
	Purchased a transistor for his son	400.00

(**Ans:** Cash Balance ₹ 12,579.38).

4. Record the following transactions in three-column Cash Book:

2012			₹
June	1	Cash in hand	3,151.20
		Cash at bank	91,401.10
	2	Received a cheque from Ramesh and deposited into bank	990.00
	5	Bought goods for ₹ 2,000 and paid by cheque, discount allowed 1%	
	15	Paid trade expenses	120.00
	16	Paid taxes	400.00
	17	Paid insurance charges	100.00
	25	Sold goods for ₹ 12,500, received cheque and allowed discount 1%	
	27	Cheque received on 25th deposited into bank	
	28	Received cheque from John and Co.	6,000.00
	30	Purchased 100 National Plan Certificates for ₹ 100 each @ ₹ 95 each and paid for them by cheque.	

(**Ans:** Cash Balance ₹ 2531.20; Bank Balance ₹ 93,286.10).

5. Prepare a three-column Cash Book:

2012			₹
June	1	Cash Balance	1,00,000
		Bank Balance	3,50,000
	5	Cash received from sale of shares	11,00,000
	6	Paid into Bank	10,00,000
	7	Paid Jyoti by cheque	2,50,000
	9	Paid wages in cash	60,000
	20	Received from Tareen by a cheque and sent to bank	1,20,000
	21	Drawn from bank	1,00,000
	29	Paid office salaries in cash	80,000
	30	Sold goods for cash and banked the same	1,60,000
		Paid rent by cheque	20,000
		Paid into Bank	1,50,000

(**Ans:** Cash Balance ₹ 10,000; Bank Balance ₹ 14,10,000).

6. Enter the following transactions in Cash Book:

2012

June 1 Balance of Cash in Hand ₹ 24,000, overdraft at Bank ₹ 3,000

2 Deposited into Bank ₹ 20,000.

Sold goods for Cash ₹ 56,000 and paid half the proceeds into Bank.

5 Received a money order from Sanjay ₹ 1,000

8 Received ₹ 5,600 from Anuj. Paid ₹ 2,000 into Bank.

10 Received a cheque for ₹ 14,000 from Dhruv and Cash ₹ 1,800 in full settlement of ₹ 16,000 due from him.

12 Paid ₹ 13,200 to Manoj and Co., half cash and half by cheque.

13 Cheque received from Dhruv deposited into Bank.

15 Paid for purchase of Machinery ₹ 40,000.

16 Paid wages for erection of above Machinery ₹ 2,000.

17 Cheque issued for ₹ 12,000 in favour of Saini and Co. for purchase of furniture.

20 Purchased goods from Kamal Garments for ₹ 20,000 on credit.

Received a Bank Draft for ₹ 9,600 from Danu and Co. in full settlement of ₹ 10,000 due from them. Sent the draft to bank.

24 Bank issued a draft for ₹ 20,000 in favour of Kamal Garments on our request. Bank charged ₹ 50 for issuing the draft.

26 Drew from bank for petty Cash ₹ 200

28 Paid salary by cheque ₹ 12,000

30 Bank charges ₹ 100 and Interest ₹ 3,240 charged by bank.

Deposited into bank the entire balance after retaining ₹ 8,000 at office.

(**Ans:** Cash Balance ₹ 8,000; Bank Balance ₹ 18,210).

7. From the following transactions prepare three-column Cash Book:

2012		**(₹)**
May 1	Cash in hand	4,80,000
2	Bank Overdraft	30,40,000
2	Fresh Capital introduced	20,00,000
3	Deposited into Bank	15,00,000
5	An amount of ₹ 4,20,000 due from Asha written off as bad debts in the previous year, now recovered.	
6	Withdrew from bank for the payment of Life Insurance premium	3,00,000
8	Received a cheque from Manu for ₹ 6,00,000 and deposited the same into bank.	
10	Sold goods to Vijay on credit	30,00,000
12	Received a cheque for ₹ 28,00,000 from Vijay in full settlement.	
15	Cheque received from Vijay sent to Bank.	
18	Vijay's cheque returned by Bank dishonoured. Bank charged ₹ 2,500 on this cheque.	
19	Received a cheque for ₹ 6,80,000 from Vipin which was endorsed to Amarpal on the same day.	
25	Withdrew cash from Bank ₹ 5,00,000 for paying gift to his daughter on her birthday.	
26	Bought goods from Garg General Store for ₹ 10,00,000 on credit and they allowed us trade discount of 25%.	
28	Paid to Garg General Stores in cash in full settlement.	7,00,000
28	Sale of old machinery, payment received in cash ₹ 7,70,000	
30	Paid Salary by cheque ₹ 1,50,000. Paid Rent in cash ₹ 2,20,000.	
31	Paid into Current Account the entire balance after retaining ₹ 5,00,000 at office.	

(**Ans:** Cash Balance (Dr.) ₹ 5,00,000; Bank Overdraft ₹ 11,42,500).

Petty Cash Book

8. Prepare the columnar Petty Cash Book of Sanjay Ltd. for the month of January 2002 under the imprest system. The petty cash limit fixed was ₹ 2,500 and the cashier draws money under imprest petty cash system as and when the balance available with him is below ₹ 500. Petty cash transactions for the month of January 2012 are given below:

		(₹)
Jan. 1	Opening balance	2,500
2	Paid towards conveyance charges	420
3	Purchase of stationery	830
5	Wages to Sweeper	210
7	Paid towards conveyance charges	620
8	Postage stamps purchased	1,100
11	Wages to Sweeper	420
14	Telegram charges paid	95
16	Conveyance charges paid	225
20	Wages to Sweeper	490
20	Postage stamps purchased	810
23	Telegram charges	140
26	Entertainment expenses	313
26	Wages to Sweeper	630
27	Taxi charges paid	276
28	Postage stamps purchased	360
31	Entertainment expenses	270
31	Wages to Sweeper	420

9. Prepare Petty Cash Book from the following:

		(₹)
June 1	Received from Cashiers ₹ 1,500 as petty Cash	
2	Postage	90
3	Travelling	60
4	Cleaning	75
7	Petrol for Van	110
8	Travelling	125
9	Stationery	85
11	Cleaning	90
14	Postage	25
15	Travelling	40
18	Stationery	45
18	Cleaning	115
20	Postage	65
24	Delivery van service	220
26	Petrol	90
27	Cleaning	105
29	Postage	25
30	Petrol	140

10. Prepare a Purchase Book from the following transactions:

2012

June 5 Bought of Kishan and Co. Agra:
20 quintal Sugar @ ₹ 1,200 per quintal.
40 bags Rice each containing one quintal @ ₹ 1,500 per quintal Trade Discount 15%

June 10 Purchased from Chadha and Sons, Mathura:
Desi Ghee 20 tins, each containing 16 kg., @ ₹ 120 per kg.
Kerosene Oil, 1,000 litres @ ₹ 6 per litre.
Trade Discount 10%

June 14 Purchased from Sunil Kumar, Delhi:
Wheat 30 quintals @ ₹ 500 per quintal; Gram 20 quintals @ ₹ 1,200 per quintal, Rice 10 quintals @ ₹ 1,400 per quintal;
Cartage and other expenses paid in cash ₹ 700.

June 20 Purchased for cash from Roop Chand, Delhi:
50 Bales of Cotton @ ₹ 1,500 per bale

June 25 Bought Furniture for office use from Furniture House, Meerut on credit:
20 Godrej Chairs @ ₹ 300 per chair.
2 Godrej Tables @ ₹ 1,600 per table.

(**Ans.** Total of purchases Book ₹ 1,64,360).

11. Enter the following transactions in Sales Book of M/s Mira Lal and Sons, Calcutta:

2012

May 5 Sold to Sudesh Stationery House, Calcutta:
100 Dozen Pencils @ ₹ 20 per dozen.
40 dozen Pens @ ₹ 5 per pen.
Trade Discount 10%

May 8 Sold to Kapur Stationery Shop, Indore:
20 Dozen Note Books @ ₹ 60 per dozen.
30 Gross Rubbers @ ₹ 10 per dozen.

May 20 Sold old newspapers for ₹ 300

May 24 Sold to Jain Stationery House, Lucknow for Cash:
50 dozen Pencils @ ₹ 22 per dozen.

May 28 Sold to Ghulam Ali and Sons, Agra:
20 Reams of Paper @ ₹ 80 per ream, discount 15%

May 31 Sold old furniture to Kamal Nath and Co., Alipur on credit ₹ 2,200

(**Ans:** Total of Sales Book ₹ 10,120).

12. Prepare Purchases and Sales Book in the books of Deep Book Depot from the following transactions:

Jan. 1 Bought of Sunil, Bombay on credit:
200 copies Physics by Resnick Holidey @ ₹ 75 each
200 copies Mathematics Without Fears by N. Arora @ ₹ 50 each

Jan. 2 Sold to Shri Ram:
48 copies Physics @ ₹ 75 each
50 copies Mathematics without Fears @ ₹ 50 each

Jan. 8 Bought of Sultan Chand, Delhi:
80 copies Economics by K.K. Dewet @ ₹ 100 each
Less: 15% Trade Discount

Jan. 12 Sold to Saxen Bros.
40 copies Economics @ ₹ 100 each

Jan. 18 Sold to Kalicharan
40 copies Physics @ ₹ 75 each

Jan. 22 Bought of Rahul
200 copies M.S.L.C. Arithmetic @ ₹ 40 each
Less: Trade Discount 20%

Jan. 25 Bought of Hari Ram, Delhi on credit:
100 copies History of England @ ₹ 50 each
Less: 15% Trade Discount

Jan. 31 Sold to Arun:
50 copies M.S.L.C. Arithmetic @ ₹ 40 each

13. Prepare Returns Inward and Returns Outward Books from the following:

2012

Jan. 3 Returned to Lakhani:
50 pairs of chappals being not up to the approved sample @ ₹ 42 per pair.
Less: Trade Discount 20%

Jan. 10 Murari and Co., Fatehpuri, returned to us:
10 pairs of shoes for being defective @ ₹ 120 per pair
Less: Trade Discount 10%

Jan. 15 Returned to Baluja Shoe Co.:
20 pairs of ladies chappals @ ₹ 36 per pair
Less: 15%

Jan. 22 Pratik and Sons, Roop Nagar, returned to us:
50 pairs of shoes @ ₹ 150 per pair

Jan. 27 Manas Shoe Co., Model Town, returned to us:
20 pairs of sandals @ ₹ 85 per pair

Jan. 31 Returned to Bata Shoe Co. defective shoes worth ₹ 1,200.

(**Ans.** Returns Outward Book ₹ 3,492; Returned Inward Book ₹ 10,280).

ANSWERS TO SELF-EVALUATION EXERCISES

I	II
1. (*a*)	**1.** Cash Book
2. (*d*)	**2.** Bills Receivable Book
3. (*c*)	**3.** Purchase Returns Book
4. (*d*)	**4.** Petty Cash Book
5. (*c*)	Imprest System

6

ACCOUNTING MECHANICS II: LEDGER POSTING AND TRIAL BALANCE

LEARNING OBJECTIVES

After reading this chapter, you should be able to:

- Know what is a Ledger?
- Discuss the rules of posting of different account books.

LEDGER

An accounting system typically contains a large number of accounts. Collectively these individual accounts are contained in a record known as the ledger. A ledger is simply the grouping of the accounts that are used to prepare financial statements for a business. A ledger account is a summary device and it is shaped like the letter T and called a T account. Ledger is a principal book of an enterprise though it is not an independent record. It contains all the accounts in which all the business transactions pertaining to a business enterprise are recorded. The main function of the ledger is to classify and summarise all the items appearing in journal and other books of original entry under appropriate accounts so that at the end of the accounting period, each account contains the entire information of all transactions relating to it.

Relationship between Journal and Ledger

Journal and ledger are the most important books maintained in an enterprise. They are closely interrelated. Business transactions are recorded first in Journal and other books of original entry and then from these books they are transferred to Ledger. Journal records transactions in a chronological order while the ledger records the transactions in a classified form. Journal, being the book of original entry, is more reliable as compared to ledger.

A journal is not useful in answering a question such as, what is the balance of cash at a certain date? This question is answered by referring to the ledger, which summarises the cumulative effect of recorded transactions in separate accounts. This is accomplished by transferring or posting information from the journal into appropriate accounts in the ledger.

POSTING

Posting is a process of transferring debits and credits from the Journal and other books of original entry to other respective accounts in the Ledger. The aim of posting is to make a classified and summarised record of business transactions in appropriate accounts.

Rules Regarding Posting

The following rules are observed while posting/transferring the transactions in the ledger:

1. Separate accounts should be opened in the ledger for posting the different transactions recorded in the book of original entry.
2. All the transactions pertaining to one account should be posted in the same account.
3. Two aspects of the business transaction—debit aspect and credit aspect—should be posted on the debit side and credit side of the account respectively.

POSTING OF DIFFERENT ACCOUNT BOOKS

Cash Book

Rules regarding posting of cash book are given below:

(*i*) Transactions recorded on the debit side of cash book are posted on the credit side of accounts opened in the ledger.

(*ii*) Transactions recorded on the credit side of the cash book are posted on the debit side of different accounts in the ledger.

(*iii*) Contra entries appearing in the cash book are not posted.

(*iv*) Totals of discount columns of the cash book are posted in the discount account opened in the ledger. Debit side total is posted on the debit side and credit side total is posted on the credit side of the discount account.

(*v*) Balance in the cash column and bank column of the cash book is not posted anywhere. It is shown on the asset side of the Balance Sheet.

PETTY CASH BOOK

Transaction recorded in the Petty Cash Book are posted on the debit side of the accounts opened for the purpose. Balance of Petty Cash Book is not posted anywhere. It is shown on the asset side of the Balance Sheet.

PURCHASES BOOK

In Purchases Books, credit purchases of goods in which the enterprise deals are recorded. Accounts of all those persons who have supplied goods are to be opened and credited with the amount of purchases made from them. Total of purchases book is to be posted on the debit side of purchases account. This is illustrated below:

Dr. (₹) Harish Jain, Delhi (₹) Cr.

			20.5.2012	By Purchases A/c	10,000

Dr. Summant Prasad Cr.

			31.5.2012	By Purchases A/c	20,000

Dr. Purchase A/c Cr.

1.6.2012	To Sundries A/c	30,000			

PURCHASES RETURN BOOK

Purchases Return Book, also called Returns Outward Book, records returns of purchase made to suppliers. Personal accounts of all those persons to whom goods have been returned are debited and total of purchase returns book is credited to purchases returns account as illustrated below.

Dr. **Harish Jain, Delhi** **Cr.**

15.7.2012	To Purchases Returns A/c	1,000	1.7.2012	By Purchases A/c	10,000

Dr. **Summant Prasad** **Cr.**

20.6.2012	To Purchase Return A/c	3,000	31.5.2012	By Purchases	20,000

Dr. **Purchases Returns A/c** **Cr.**

			31.7.2012	By Sundries	4,000

SALES BOOK

Sales Book records all credit sales. While posting Sales Book to ledger, personal accounts of the customers are opened and debited by the amount of sales made to them. Total of Sales Book is credited to Sales Account. This is illustrated below:

Dr. **Ram Pershad** **Cr.**

2.7.2012	To Sales A/c	15,000			

Dr. **Devi Prasad** **Cr.**

25.6.2012	To Sales A/c	20,000			

Dr. **Sales A/c** **Cr.**

			15.7.2012	By Sundries	35,000

SALES RETURNS BOOK/RETURNS INWARD BOOK

When goods are returned by customers, they are recorded in sales returns book/returns inward book. While posting Sales Returns Book to Ledger, personal accounts of the customers are credited and total of Sales Returns Book is debited to Sales Returns A/c. This is illustrated below:

Dr. **Ram Pershad** **Cr.**

2.7.2012	To Sales A/c	15,000	14.7.2012	By Sales Returns A/c	4,000

Dr. **Devi Pershad** **Cr.**

25.6.2012	To Sales A/c	20,000	10.7.2012	By Sales Return A/c	4,000

Dr. **Sales Return A/c** **Cr.**

15.7.2012	To Sundries A/c	8,000			

BILLS RECEIVABLE BOOK

In bills receivable book, bills received by the enterprise are recorded. While posting bills receivable book, personal accounts of the persons giving the bills are credited. Total of bills receivable book is debited to Bills Receivable A/c. This is illustrated below.

Dr. **Sunder Kumar** **Cr.**

			2012 July 10	By B/R A/c	10,000

Dr. **Suresh Chander** **Cr.**

			2012 July 7	By B/R	15,000

Dr. **Bills Receivable A/c** **Cr.**

15.7.2012	To Sundries	25,000			

BILLS PAYABLE BOOK

The enterprise may accept so many bills in the business. Acceptances given are recorded in Bills Payable Book. While posting Bills Payable Book acceptances given are debited to the personal accounts of the persons to whom they have been given and total of Bills Payable Book is posted to the credit side of Bills Payable A/c. This is illustrated below:

Dr. **Ram Pershad** **Cr.**

2.7.2012	To B/P A/c	8,000			

Dr. **Chandra Mohan** **Cr.**

10.7.2012	To B/P A/c	7,000			

Dr. **Bills Payable A/c** **Cr.**

			15.7.2012	By Sundries	15,000

POSTING OF JOURNAL

When we journalise a transaction we write out in the journal as to which account is to be debited and which account is to be credited. The same information is transferred to Ledger in the two concerned accounts. This is illustrated below:

Furniture A/c To Jain & Co. (Being furniture bought from Jain & Co. on credit)	Dr.	70,000	70,000
Depreciation A/c To Furniture A/c (Being depreciation on furniture)	Dr.	7,000	7,000

Dr. **Furniture A/c** **Cr.**

To Jain & Co.	70,000	By Depreciation A/c	7,000

Dr. **Depreciation A/c** **Cr.**

To Furniture A/c	7,000		

Dr. **Jain & Co.** **Cr.**

		By Furniture A/c	70,000

BALANCING OF AN ACCOUNT

Balancing of an account implies a process of ascertaining the net balance of an account after considering and comparing the total of both sides, *viz*, debit side and credit side. The Balance is put on the side which is smaller and the two totals—debit side and credit side—are made equal. Against the balance a reference is put that it has been carried forward (c/f) or carried down (c/d). The balance of an account will be termed as debit balance if the total of debit side is greater than the total of credit side. On the other hand, if total of credit side is greater than total of debit side, balance will be a credit balance. This is illustrated below:

Mohan

		(₹)			(₹)
5.5.2012	To B/R A/c	7,000	1.5.2012	By Purchase A/c	15,000
6.5.2012	To Purchases	2,000	16.5.2012	By Purchases A/c	25,000
17.5.2012	To Bank A/c	15,000			
31.5.2012	To Balance c/d	16,000			
		40,000			40,000
			1.6.2012	By Balance b/d	16,000

Furniture A/c

		(₹)			(₹)
1.5.2012	To Bank A/c	16,000	31.5.2012	By Balance c/d	16,000
		16,000			16,000
1.6.2012	To Balance b/d	16,000			

TRIAL BALANCE

When all accounts of the ledger are in balance, a Trial Balance is prepared. A Trial Balance is a listing of all the accounts and their respective balances. Trial Balance is a statement of debit balance and credit balance extracted from ledger accounts on a particular date. A Trial Balance is, thus, a summary of all the Ledger Balances outstanding as on a particular date.

Proforma of a Trial Balance is as follows:

Trial Balance as at ......

Ledger Accounts	Debit Balance	Credit Balance

It must be stated here that total of debit balance column must be equal to total of credit balance column. This is so because under double entry system, for each item of debit there is a corresponding credit and secondly all the transactions recorded in the books of original entry are transferred to ledger.

Objectives of Preparing a Trial Balance

The following are the objectives of preparing a Trial Balance:

1. To check the arithmetical accuracy of accounting entries posted in the ledger—When the trial balance tallies, it is an indication of the fact that ledger accounts are arithmetically accurate. It also indicates that: (*i*) For each transaction, the debits and credits were recorded in equal amounts. (*ii*) The balance (debit balances and credit balances) for each account was calculated correctly. (*iii*) The balances of the various debit and credit accounts have been correctly added together to arrive at the total equality of the debits and credits. Of course there may be certain errors in the books of accounts inspite of the agreement of Trial Balance. These have been discussed later in a subsequent chapter.

2. To Provide a Basis for Financial Statements—Trial Balance is a first step towards preparation of financial statements of an organisation. If trial balance is not prepared, it will be impossible to prepare the financial statement.
3. Trial Balance serves as a summary of all the ledger accounts and provides a complete picture of each account in the ledger.

Illustration 1: During January 2012, Anil Kumar transacted the following business. You are required to make journal entries for the transactions and prepare cash book and other necessary ledger accounts based on the journal entries.

		(₹)
January 2012		
1.	Commenced business with cash	20,000
2.	Purchased goods on credit from Shyam	15,000
3.	Purchased goods for cash	500
4.	Paid Gopal an advance for goods ordered	1,000
5.	Received cash from Murthy as advance for goods ordered by him	1,500
6.	Purchased furniture for office use for cash	1,000
7.	Paid wages	250
8.	Received commission (in cash)	300
9.	Goods returned to Shyam	100
10.	Goods sold to Kamal	5,000
11.	Paid for postage and telegrams	100
12.	Goods returned by Kamal	250
15.	Paid for stationery	100
18.	Paid into bank	250
20.	Goods sold for cash	375
22.	Bought goods for cash	500
25.	Paid salaries	350
28.	Paid rent	250
31.	Drew cash for personal use	500

Solution:

Journal Entries

Date 2012	Particulars		Debit (₹)	Credit (₹)
Jan. 1	Cash Account To Capital Account (Being the cash brought into business as capital)	Dr.	20,000	20,000
Jan. 2	Purchases Account To Shyam's Account (Being the goods purchased on credit)	Dr.	15,000	15,000
Jan. 3	Purchases Account To Cash Account (Being the goods purchased for cash)	Dr.	500	500
Jan. 4	Gopal Account To Cash Account (Being the amount paid to Gopal)	Dr.	1,000	1,000
Jan. 5	Cash Account To Murthy Account (Being the cash received from Murthy)	Dr.	1,500	1,500

Date 2012	Particulars		Debit (₹)	Credit (₹)
Jan. 6	Furniture Account To Cash Account (Being the furniture purchased for office use for cash)	Dr.	1,000	1,000
Jan. 7	Wages Account To Cash Account (Being the wages paid)	Dr.	250	250
Jan. 8	Cash Account To Commission Received A/c (Being the commission received)	Dr.	300	300
Jan. 9	Shyam Account To Purchase Returns Account (Being goods returned to Shyam)	Dr.	100	100
Jan. 10	Kamal Account To Sales Account (Being goods sold to Kamal on credit)	Dr.	5,000	5,000
Jan. 11	Postage and Telegrams Account To Cash Account (Being the amount paid for postage and telegram)	Dr.	100	100
Jan. 12	Sales Returns Account To Kamal Account (Being the goods returned by Kamal)	Dr.	250	250
Jan. 15	Stationery Account To Cash Account (Being the amount paid for stationery)	Dr.	100	100
Jan. 18	Bank Account To Cash Account (Being the amount deposited into the bank)	Dr.	250	250
Jan. 20	Cash Account To Sales Account (Being the goods sold for cash)	Dr.	375	375
Jan. 22	Purchases Account To Cash Account (Being the goods purchased for cash)	Dr.	500	500
Jan. 25	Salaries Account To Cash Account (Being the amount paid as salaries)	Dr.	350	350
Jan. 28	Rent Account To Cash Account (Being the rent paid)	Dr.	250	250
Jan. 31	Drawings Account To Cash Account (Being the cash drawn for personal use)	Dr.	500	500

Ledger Accounts

Dr. **Cash Book** **Cr.**

Date	Receipts	L/F	Cash (₹)	Bank (₹)	Date	Payments	L/F	Cash (₹)	Bank (₹)
2012					**2012**				
Jan. 1	To Capital A/c		20,000		Jan. 3	By Purchase A/c		500	
Jan. 5	To Murthy A/c		1,500		Jan. 4	By Gopal A/c		1,000	

Date	Receipts	L/F	Cash (₹)	Bank (₹)	Date	Payments	L/F	Cash (₹)	Bank (₹)
Jan. 8	To Commission A/c		300		Jan. 6	By Furniture A/c		1,000	
Jan. 18	To Cash A/c C			250	Jan. 7	By Wages A/c		250	
Jan. 20	To Sales A/c		375		Jan. 12	By Postage & Telegrams		100	
					Jan. 15	By Stationery A/c		100	
					Jan. 18	By Bank A/c C		250	
					Jan. 22	By Purchase A/c		500	
					Jan. 25	By Salaries A/c		350	
					Jan. 28	By Rent A/c		250	
					Jan. 31	By Drawings A/c		500	
					Jan. 31	By Balance c/d		17,375	250
			22,175	250				22,175	250

Note: The letter 'C' in the Ledger Folio column denotes a contra entry. This is an entry for which the debit and credit aspects are found in the cash book itself.

Purchase Book

Dr.

Date 2012	Name of Supplier	Ledger Folio	Inward Invoice No.	Amount (₹)
Jan. 2	Shyam			15,000
	Total			15,000

Dr. **Purchase Returns Book** Cr.

Date 2012	Name of Supplier	Ledger Folio	Debit Note No.	Amount (₹)
Jan. 9	Shyam			100
	Total			100

Sales Book

Date 2012	Customer	Invoice No.	Amount (₹)
Jan. 10	Kamal		5,000
	Total		5,000

Dr. **Sales Return Book** Cr.

Date 2012	Name of Customer	Ledger Folio	Outward Invoice No.	Amount (₹)
Jan. 12	Kamal			250
	Total			250

General Ledger

Capital Account

2012		(₹)	2012		(₹)
Jan. 31	To Balance c/d	20,000	Jan. 1	By Cash A/c	20,000
		20,000			20,000
			Feb. 1	By Balance b/d	20,000

Shyam's Account

2012		(₹)	2012		(₹)
Jan. 9	To Purchase returns	100	Jan. 2	By Purchase A/c	15,000
Jan. 31	To Balance c/d	14,900			
		15,000			15,000
			Feb. 1	By Balance b/d	14,900

Dr. **Purchases Account** Cr.

2012		(₹)	2012		(₹)
Jan. 2	To Shyam A/c	15,000	Jan. 31	By Balance c/d	16,000
Jan. 3	To Cash	500			
Jan. 22	To Cash	500			
		16,000			16,000
Feb. 1	By Balance b/d	16,000			16,000

Dr. **Sales Account** Cr.

2012		(₹)	2012		(₹)
Jan. 31	To Balance c/d	5,375	Jan. 10	By Kamal A/c	5,000
			Jan. 20	By Cash	375
		5,375			5,375
			Feb. 1	By Balance b/d	5,375

Dr. **Purchase Returns Account** Cr.

2012		(₹)	2012		(₹)
Jan. 31	To Balance c/d	100	Jan. 9	By Shyam A/c	100
		100			100
			Feb. 1	By Balance b/d	100

Dr. **Sales Returns Account** Cr.

2012		(₹)	2012		(₹)
Jan. 12	To Kamal A/c	250	Jan. 31	By Balance c/d	250
		250			250
Feb. 1	To Balance b/d	250			250

Dr. **Gopal's Account** Cr.

2012		(₹)	2012		(₹)
Jan. 4	To Cash A/c	1,000	Jan. 31	By Balance c/d	1,000
		1,000			1,000
Feb. 1	To Balance b/d	1,000			1,000

Dr. **Wages Account** Cr.

2012		(₹)	2012		(₹)
Jan. 7	To Cash A/c	250	Jan. 31	By Balance c/d	250
		250			250
Feb. 1	To Balance b/d	250			250

Commission Received Account

2012		(₹)	2012		(₹)
Jan. 31	To Balance c/d	300	Jan. 8	By Cash A/c	300
		300			300
			Feb. 1	By Balance b/d	300

Dr. **Kamal's Account** Cr.

2012		(₹)	2012		(₹)
Jan. 10	To Sales A/c	5,000	Jan. 12	By Sales Returns A/c	250
			Jan. 31	By Balance c/d	4,750
		5,000			5,000
Feb. 1	To Balance b/d	4,750			

Postage and Telegrams Account

2012		(₹)	2012		(₹)
Jan. 11	To Cash A/c	100	Jan. 31	By Balance c/d	100
		100			100
Feb. 1	To Balance b/d	100			

Stationery Account

2012		(₹)	2012		(₹)
Jan. 15	To Cash A/c	100	Jan. 31	By Balance c/d	100
		100			100
Feb. 1	To Balance b/d	100			

Salaries Account

2012		(₹)	2012		(₹)
Jan. 25	To Cash A/c	350	Jan. 31	By Balance c/d	350
		350			350
Feb. 1	To Balance b/d	350			

Dr. **Rent Account** Cr.

2012		(₹)	2012		(₹)
Jan. 28	To Cash A/c	250	Jan. 31	By Balance c/d	250
		250			250
Feb. 1	To Balance b/d	250			

Dr. **Drawing Account** Cr.

2012		(₹)	2012		(₹)
Jan. 31	To Cash A/c	500	Jan. 31	By Balance c/d	500
		500			500
Feb. 1	To Balance b/d	500			

Dr. **Murthy's Account** **Cr.**

2012		(₹)	2012		(₹)
Jan. 31	To Balance c/d	1,500	Jan. 5	By Cash A/c	1,500
		1,500			1,500
			Feb. 1	To Balance b/d	1,500

Dr. **Furniture Account** **Cr.**

2012		(₹)	2012		(₹)
Jan. 6	To Cash A/c	1,000	Jan. 3	By Balance c/d	1,000
		1,000			1,000
Feb. 1	To Balance b/d	1,000			

Illustration 2: Enter the following into sales book and show the ledger postings:

25.6.2012 Sold to Ladies Corner, 5 bales of Laxmi Sari @ ₹ 200 per sari less trade discount of 20%. Each bale contained 100 pieces of sari measuring 6 metres each. Excise duty of 10%, sales tax 5%, octroi 15 paise per metre.

30.6.2012 Sold to Mahila Mahal, 3,000 piece of blouse @ 36 per dozen. Blouses were sent in packets, each containing 10 units. Extra charge was levied for packing ₹ 5 per packet.

2.7.2012 Sold to Lahana Dress Co., 50 ladies coats @ ₹ 150 each, less trade discount of 15%. Other charges levied-₹ 200.

Solution:

Sales Book

Date 2012	Particulars	L.F.	Details (₹)	Amount (₹)
June 25	**Ladies Corner:**			
	5 Bales of Laxmi Sari @ 200 per sari; each bale contains 100 saries measuring 6 m each		1,00,000	
	Less: Discount 20%		20,000	
	Add: Excise duty 10% (10% of ₹ 1,00,000)		10,000	
	Sales tax 5% (5% of ₹ 80,000)		4,000	
	Octroi 15 paise per m		450	94,450
June 30	**Mahila Mahal:**			
	3,000 pieces of blouse @ ₹ 360 per dozen		90,000	
	Add: Packing charges		1,500	91,500
July 2	**Lahana Dress:**			
	50 Ladies coats @ ₹ 150 each		7,500	
	Less: Trade discount 15%		1,125	
			6,375	
	Add: Other charges		200	6,575
	Total			1,92,525

Ledger

Dr. **Ladies Corner** **Cr.**

Date 2012	Particulars	Amount (₹)	Date	Particulars	Amount (₹)
June 25	To Sales A/c	94,450			

Mahila Mahal

Date 2012	Particulars	Amount (₹)	Date	Particulars	Amount (₹)
June 30	To Sales A/c	91,500			

Lahana Dress

Date 2012	Particulars	Amount (₹)	Date	Particulars	Amount (₹)
July 2	To Sales A/c	6,575			

Sales A/c

Date 2012	Particulars	Amount (₹)	Date	Particulars	Amount (₹)
			July 2	By Sundries	1,92,525

Illustration 3: Record the following transactions in the purchase day book and show the ledger postings.

(*a*) 16.10.2012: Purchased 480 kg butter from M/s. Dairy Products Co. @ ₹ 78 per kg less 15%.

(*b*) 20.12.2012: Purchased 56 kg ghee from Bharat Vegetable Products @ ₹ 120 per kg less 17.5%

(*c*) 22.10.2012: Purchased 46 kg butter from Bowbazaar Milk Cooperative Ltd. @ ₹ 72.5 a kg less 12.5%

Solution: **Purchase Book**

Date 2012	Particulars	L.F.	Dr. Amount (₹)	Cr. Amount (₹)
Oct. 16	**M/s Dairy Products Co.:** 480 kg Butter @ 78 per kg *Less*: Discount 15%		37,440 5,616	31,824
Oct. 20	**Bharat Vegetable Products:** 56 kg ghee @ ₹ 120 per kg *Less*: Discount 17.5%		6,720 1,176	5,544
Oct. 22	Bowbazar Milk Coop. Ltd.: 46 kg butter @ ₹ 72.5 per kg *Less*: Discount 12.5%		3,335 416.9	2,918.1
	Total			40,286.1

Ledger

M/s Dairy Products Co.

Date 2012	Particulars	Amount (₹)	Date 2012	Particulars	Amount (₹)
			Oct. 16	By Purchases A/c	31,824
		M/s Bharat Vegetable Products			
			Oct. 20	By Purchases A/c	5,544
		Bowbazar Milk Coop. Ltd.			
			Oct. 22	By Purchases A/c	2,918.1

Purchase A/c

Date 2012	Particulars	Amount (₹)	Date 2012	Particulars	Amount (₹)
Oct. 31	To Sundries	40,286.1			

Illustration 4: From the following, prepare return books, and show the ledger:

March 2012

5 Returned 10 shirts to Kundu Bros. @ ₹ 50 each, less 10% trade discount

8 Kamal & Co. returned goods worth ₹ 1,500

9 Returned goods to A. Roy, ₹ 750

12 Returned 60 packing boxes, ₹ 50 each, to J. Roy

14 S. Das returned 20 baba suits @ ₹ 120 each

15 Received return of blouse 30 pieces @ ₹ 70 each from Silk House.

Solution:

Returns Inward Book

Date 2012	Particulars	L.F.	Details	Total (₹)
Mar. 8	**Kamal & Co.:** Goods returned			1,500.00
Mar. 14	**S. Das:** 20 baba suits @ 120 each			2,400.00
Mar. 15	**Silk House:** 30 Blouse pieces @ ₹ 70 each			2,100.00
	Total			6,000.00

Returns Outward Book

Date 2012	Particulars	L.F.	Details	Total (₹)
Mar. 5	**Kundu Brothers:** 10 shirts @ ₹ 50 each *Less*: 10% trade discount			500.00 50.00
				450.00
Mar. 9	**A. Roy:** Goods returned			750.00
Mar. 12	**J. Roy:** 60 packing boxes @ ₹ 50 each			3,000.00

Ledger

Date 2012	Particulars	F	Amount (₹)	Date 2012	Particulars	F	Amount (₹)
				March 8	Kamal & Co. By Returns Inward A/c		1,500
				March 14	S. Das & Co. By Returns Inward A/c		2,400
				March 15	Silk House By Returns Inwards A/c		2,100

Returns Inward A/c

Date 2012							
Mar. 31	To Sundries		6,000				

Kundu Bros.

Date 2012	Particulars	F	Amount (₹)	Date 2012	Particulars	F	Amount (₹)
Mar. 5	To Returns Outwards		450.00	A. Roy			
Mar. 9	To Returns Outwards A/c		750.00				
Mar. 12	To Returns Outward A/c		3,000.00	J. Roy			

Returns Outward A/c

				Mar. 31	By Sundries		4,200

Illustration 5: From the following information, prepare a suitable Cash Book:

April 2012		(₹)
1.	Cash at hand	2,200
2.	Cash at bank	8,700
3.	Bought goods from Rahim	7,300
4.	Cash sales banked	5,500
8.	Sold goods to Das	8,200
9.	Received cheque in full settlement of Das's A/c	8,000
10.	Paid to settle Rahim's A/c	7,000
12.	Purchased office furniture by cheque	3,500
13.	Bought goods from PK Ghosh	10,400
15.	Paid carriages	200
18.	Bank collected dividend	500
20.	Withdrawn from bank	2,000
25.	Paid wages	1,500
27.	Paid to PK Ghosh by cheque	1,000

Show also the Ledger accounts that will be prepared from the cash book.

Solution:

Cash Book

Date 2012	Particulars	L.F.	Dis. ₹	Cash ₹	Bank ₹	Date 2012	Particulars	L.F.	Dis. ₹	Cash ₹	Bank ₹
April 1	To Balance b/d			2,200	8,700	April 10	By Rahim A/c		300	—	7,000
April 4	To Sales A/c				5,500	April 12	By Furniture A/c				3,500
April 9	To Das		200		8,000	April 15	By Carriage A/c			200	
April 8	To Dividend A/c				500	April 20	By Cash A/c	C			2,000
April 20	To Bank A/c	C		2,000							
						April 25	By Wages A/c			1,500	
						April 27	By PK Ghosh				1,000
						April 30	By Balance c/d			2,500	9,200
			200	4,200	22,700				300	4,200	22,700
May 1	To Balance b/d			2,500	9,200						

Ledger

Sales A/c

Date 2012	Particulars	L.F.	Amount (₹)	Date 2012	Particulars	L.F.	Amount (₹)
				April 4	By Bank A/c		5,500
			Das A/c				
April 8	To Sales A/c		8,200	April 9	By Bank A/c		8,000
				April 9	By Discount A/c		200
			8,200				8,200
			Rahim's A/c				
April 10	To Bank A/c		7,000	April 2	By Purchase A/c		7,300
	To Discount A/c		300				
			7,300				7,300
			Furniture A/c				
April 12	To Bank A/c		3,500				
			Carriage A/c				
April 15	To Cash A/c		200				
			Wages A/c				
April 25	To Cash A/c		1,500				
			PK Ghosh				
April 27	To Bank A/c		1,000				

Dividend A/c

	April 18	By Bank A/c	₹ 500

Discount Allowed A/c

To Das	₹ 200	

Discount Received A/c

	By Rahim	₹ 1,300

Notes: 1. Contra entries are not posted to ledger.

2. Purchases from Rahim and Sales to Das will be posted from purchases book and sales book, respectively.

PREPARATION OF TRIAL BALANCE

Illustration 6: The following were the transactions of a firm dealing in furniture:

March 2012		(₹)
1	Started business with cash	2,00,000
	Bank	8,00,000
	Furniture (goods)	5,00,000
3	Bought furniture from Ratan Bros.	2,00,000
4	Bought furniture for the office	1,00,000
6	Sold furniture to J. Mitra	2,00,000
8	Bought furniture	1,80,000

March 2012		(₹)
10	Returned furniture to Ratan Bros.	5,000
12	J. Mitra returned furniture	20,000
14	Paid taxi fare	1,000
15	Sold to J. Kabiraj furniture for ₹ 50,000, less trade discount @ 10%	
17	Received commission from J. Das	1,500
18	Paid to Ratan Bros. by cheque	1,00,000
19	Sent to bank	20,000
20	Received a cheque for ₹ 42,500 from L. Kabiraj in full settlement of his account	
22	Received a cheque for ₹ 50,000 from J. Mitra and deposited the same into bank	
23	Loan to Naren	15,000
24	J. Mitra's cheque dishonoured	
25	Furniture taken away for personal use	40,000
26	Received interest	1,000
27	Received dividend	2,500
29	Paid for postage stamps	500
30	Paid house rent by cheque	10,000
31	Cash withdrawn from bank	2,00,000
31	Paid salary	30,000
31	Paid for taxes	15,000

Journalise the above transactions in the books of the firm and show the ledger postings. Also prepare a trial balance as on March 31, 2012.

Solution: **Journal**

Date 2012	Particulars	L.F.	Dr. (₹)	Cr. (₹)
Mar. 1	Cash A/c Bank A/c Stock A/c To Capital A/c (Brought into the business as capital)	Dr. Dr. Dr.	2,00,000 8,00,000 5,00,000	15,00,000
Mar. 3	Purchases A/c To Ratan Bros. (Being the purchase of goods (furniture)	Dr.	2,00,000	2,00,000
Mar. 4	Furniture A/c To Bank A/c (Being the purchase of furniture for office)	Dr.	1,00,000	1,00,000
Mar. 6	J. Mitra To Sales A/c (Being the sale of goods (furniture) to J. Mitra)	Dr.	2,00,000	2,00,000
Mar. 8	Purchase A/c To Bank A/c (Being the purchase of goods)	Dr.	1,80,000	1,80,000
Mar. 10	Ratan Bros. To Returns Outward A/c (Being goods (furniture) returned to Ratan Bros.)	Dr.	5,000	5,000
Mar. 12	Returns Inward A/c To J. Mitra (Goods returned by Mitra)	Dr.	20,000	20,000

Date 2012	Particulars	L.F.	Dr. (₹)	Cr. (₹)
Mar. 14	Conveyance A/c Dr. To Cash A/c (Being the payment of taxi fare)		1,000	 1,000
Mar. 15	J. Kabiraj Dr. To Sales A/c (Being the sale of goods worth ₹ 50,000 to J. Kabiraj, trade discount being 10%)		45,000	 45,000
Mar. 17	Bank A/c Dr. To Commission (Received commission from J. Das)		1,500	 1,500
Mar. 18	Ratan Bros. Dr. To Bank A/c (Being payment made to Ratan Bros.)		1,00,000	 1,00,000
Mar. 19	Bank A/c Dr. To Cash A/c (Being money sent to bank)		20,000	 20,000
Mar. 20	Bank A/c Dr. Discount A/c Dr. To Kabiraj (Being a cheque for ₹ 42,500 received from J. Kabiraj in full settlement of his account)		42,500 2,500	 45,000
Mar. 22	Bank A/c Dr. To J. Mitra (Being cheque received from J. Mitra)		50,000	 50,000
Mar. 23	Loan to Naren A/c Dr. To Bank A/c (Money given to Naren)		15,000	 15,000
Mar. 24	J. Mitra Dr. To Bank A/c (Being the cheque of J. Mitra dishonoured)		50,000	 50,000
Mar. 25	Drawing A/c Dr. To Purchases A/c (Being goods (furniture) taken for personal use)		40,000	 40,000
Mar. 26	Bank A/c Dr. To Interest A/c (Being interest received)		1,000	 1,000
Mar. 27	Bank A/c Dr. To Dividend A/c (Being the amount of dividend received)		2,500	 2,500
Mar. 29	Postage A/c Dr. To Cash A/c (Payment for postage stamps)		500	 500
Mar. 30	Rent A/c Dr. To Bank A/c (Being the payment of house rent)		10,000	 10,000
Mar. 31	Cash A/c Dr. To Bank A/c (Cash withdrawn from bank)		2,00,000	 2,00,000
Mar. 31	Salary A/c Dr. Tax A/c Dr. To Cash A/c (Being the payment for salary and taxes)		30,000 15,000	 45,000

Ledger

Cash A/c

Date 2012	Particulars	L.F.	Amount (₹)	Date 2012	Particulars	L.F.	Amount (₹)
Mar. 1	To Capital A/c		2,00,000	Mar. 14	By Conveyance A/c		1,000
Mar. 31	To Bank A/c		2,00,000	Mar. 19	By Bank		20,000
				Mar. 29	By Postage		500
				Mar. 31	By Salary A/c		30,000
				Mar. 31	By Taxes A/c		15,000
				Mar. 31	By Balance c/d		3,33,500
			4,00,000				4,00,000
April 1	To Balance b/d		3,33,500				

Bank A/c

Date 2012	Particulars	L.F.	Amount (₹)	Date 2012	Particulars	L.F.	Amount (₹)
Mar. 1	To Capital A/c		8,00,000	Mar. 5	By Furniture		1,00,000
Mar. 17	To Commission A/c		1,500	Mar. 8	By Purchase		1,80,000
Mar. 19	To Cash A/c		20,000	Mar. 18	By Ratan Bros.		1,00,000
Mar. 20	To J. Kabiraj		42,500	Mar. 23	By Loan to Naren		15,000
Mar. 22	To J. Mitra		50,000	Mar. 24	By J. Mitra		50,000
Mar. 26	To Interest A/c		1,000	Mar. 30	By Rent A/c		10,000
Mar. 27	To Dividend A/c		2,500	Mar. 31	By Cash A/c		2,00,000
				Mar. 31	By Balance c/d		2,62,500
			9,17,500				9,17,500
April 1	To Balance b/d		2,62,500				

Capital A/c

Date 2012	Particulars	L.F.	Amount (₹)	Date 2012	Particulars	L.F.	Amount (₹)
Mar. 31	To Balance c/d		15,00,000	Mar. 1	By Cash		2,00,000
					By Bank		8,00,000
					By Stock		5,00,000
			15,00,000	April 1	By Balance b/d		15,00,000

Stock A/c

Date 2012	Particulars	L.F.	Amount (₹)	Date 2012	Particulars	L.F.	Amount (₹)
Mar. 1	To Capital A/c		5,00,000	Mar. 25	By Drawings A/c		40,000
				Mar. 31	By Balance c/d		4,60,000
			5,00,000				5,00,000
April 1	To Balance b/d		4,60,000				

Purchase A/c

Date 2012	Particulars	L.F.	Amount (₹)	Date 2012	Particulars	L.F.	Amount (₹)
Mar. 3	To Ratan Bros.		2,00,000	Mar. 31	By Balance c/d		3,80,000
Mar. 8	To Bank A/c		1,80,000				
			3,80,000				3,80,000
April 1	To Balance c/d		3,80,000				

Ratan A/c

Date 2012	Particulars	L.F.	Amount (₹)	Date 2012	Particulars	L.F.	Amount (₹)
Mar. 10	To Returns Outward A/c		5,000	Mar. 3	By Purchase A/c		2,00,000
Mar. 18	To Bank A/c		1,00,000				
Mar. 31	To Balance c/d		95,000				
			2,00,000				2,00,000
				April 1	By Balance b/d		95,000

Furniture A/c

Date 2012	Particulars	L.F.	Amount (₹)	Date 2012	Particulars	L.F.	Amount (₹)
Mar. 5	To Bank		1,00,000	Mar. 31	By Balance c/d		1,00,000
April 1	To Balance b/d		1,00,000				1,00,000

J. Mitra

Date 2012	Particulars	L.F.	Amount (₹)	Date 2012	Particulars	L.F.	Amount (₹)
Mar. 6	To Sales A/c		2,00,000	Mar. 12	By Returns Inward A/c		20,000
Mar. 24	To Bank A/c		50,000	Mar. 22	By Bank A/c		50,000
				Mar. 31	By Balance c/d		1,80,000
			2,50,000				2,50,000
April 1	To Balance b/d		1,80,000				

Sales A/c

Date 2012	Particulars	L.F.	Amount (₹)	Date 2012	Particulars	L.F.	Amount (₹)
Mar. 31	To Balance c/d		2,45,000	Mar. 6	By Mitra		2,00,000
				Mar. 15	By J. Kabiraj		45,000
			2,45,000				2,45,000
				April 1	By Balance b/d		2,45,000

Returns Outward A/c

Date 2012	Particulars	L.F.	Amount (₹)	Date 2012	Particulars	L.F.	Amount (₹)
Mar. 31	To Balance c/d		5,000	Mar. 10	By Ratan Bros.		5,000
				April 1	By Balance b/d		5,000

Returns Inward A/c

Date 2012	Particulars	L.F.	Amount (₹)	Date 2012	Particulars	L.F.	Amount (₹)
Mar. 12	To J. Mitra		20,000	Mar. 31	By Balance c/d		20,000
April 1	To Balance b/d		20,000				

Conveyance A/c

Date 2012	Particulars	L.F.	Amount (₹)	Date 2012	Particulars	L.F.	Amount (₹)
Mar. 10	To Cash A/c		1,000	Mar. 31	By Balance c/d		1,000
April 1	To Balance b/d		1,000				

J. Kabiraj

Date 2012	Particulars	L.F.	Amount (₹)	Date 2012	Particulars	L.F.	Amount (₹)
Mar. 15	To Sales A/c		45,000	Mar. 20	By Bank A/c		42,500
				Mar. 20	By Discount A/c		2,500
			45,000				45,000

Commission A/c

Date 2012	Particulars	L.F.	Amount (₹)	Date 2012	Particulars	L.F.	Amount (₹)
Mar. 31	To Balance c/d		1,500	Mar. 17	By Bank A/c		1,500
				April 1	By Balance b/d		1,500

Discount Allowed A/c

Date 2012	Particulars	L.F.	Amount (₹)	Date 2012	Particulars	L.F.	Amount (₹)
Mar. 20	To J. Kabiraj		2,500	Mar. 31	By Balance c/d		2,500
April 1	To Balance b/d		2,500				

Loan to Naren A/c

Date 2012	Particulars	L.F.	Amount (₹)	Date 2012	Particulars	L.F.	Amount (₹)
Mar. 23	To Bank A/c		15,000	Mar. 31	By Balance c/d		15,000
April 1	To Balance b/d		15,000				

Drawings A/c

Date 2012	Particulars	L.F.	Amount (₹)	Date 2012	Particulars	L.F.	Amount (₹)
Mar. 25	To Purchases A/c		40,000	Mar. 31	By Balance c/d		40,000
April 1	To Balance b/d		40,000				

Interest A/c

Date 2012	Particulars	L.F.	Amount (₹)	Date 2012	Particulars	L.F.	Amount (₹)
Mar. 31	To Balance c/d		1,000	Mar. 26	By Bank		1,000
				April 1	By Balance b/d		1,000

Dividend A/c

Date 2012	Particulars	L.F.	Amount (₹)	Date 2012	Particulars	L.F.	Amount (₹)
Mar. 31	To Balance c/d		2,500	Mar. 27	By Bank		2,500
				April 1	By Balance b/d		2,500

Postage A/c

Date 2012	Particulars	L.F.	Amount (₹)	Date 2012	Particulars	L.F.	Amount (₹)
Mar. 29	To Cash A/c		500	Mar. 31	By Balance c/d		500
Mar. 31	To Balance b/d		500				

Rent A/c

Date 2012	Particulars	L.F.	Amount (₹)	Date 2012	Particulars	L.F.	Amount (₹)
Mar. 30	To Bank A/c		10,000	Mar. 31	By Balance c/d		10,000
April 1	To Balance b/d		10,000				

Salary A/c

Date 2012	Particulars	L.F.	Amount (₹)	Date 2012	Particulars	L.F.	Amount (₹)
Mar. 31	To Cash A/c		30,000	Mar. 31	By Balance c/d		30,000
April 1	To Balance b/d		30,000				

Taxes A/c

Date 2012	Particulars	L.F.	Amount (₹)	Date 2012	Particulars	L.F.	Amount (₹)
Mar. 31	To Cash A/c		15,000	Mar. 31	By Balance c/d		15,000
April 1	To Balance b/d		15,000				

Trial Balance as on March 31, 2012

Particulars	Dr. Balance (₹)	Cr. Balance (₹)
Cash A/c	3,33,500	
Bank A/c	2,62,500	
Capital A/c		15,00,000
Stock A/c	4,60,000	
Purchase A/c	3,80,000	
Ratan Bros		95,000
Furniture A/c	1,00,000	
J. Mitra	1,80,000	
Salary A/c	30,000	
Sales A/c		2,45,000
Returns Outward A/c		5,000
Returns Inward A/c	20,000	
Conveyance A/c	1,000	
Commission A/c		1,500
Discount A/c	2,500	
Loan to Naren A/c	15,000	
Drawings A/c	40,000	
Interest A/c		1,000
Dividend A/c		2,500
Postage A/c	500	
Rent A/c	10,000	
Taxes A/c	15,000	
Total	18,50,000	18,50,000

Illustration 7: Journalise the following transactions, post them into the ledger and prepare a trial balance:

1.09.2012 Started business by bringing in cash worth ₹ 2,00,000 out of which paid into bank—₹ 80,000

02.09.2012 Bought furniture for ₹ 20,000 and machinery ₹ 40,000.

03.09.2012 Purchased goods for ₹ 56,000.

06.09.2012 Sold goods for ₹ 32,000

08.09.2012 Purchased goods from Jain & Co. on credit for ₹ 44,000

10.09.2012 Paid telephone rent for the year by cheque ₹ 2,000

11.09.2012 Bought one typewriter for ₹ 8,400 from Standard Typewriter Co. on credit.

15.09.2012 Sold goods to Shiva worth ₹ 48,000

17.09.2012 Sold goods to Kumar for cash at ₹ 8,000

19.09.2012 Amount withdrawn from bank for personal use ₹ 6,000

20.09.2012 Withdrew from bank for business use ₹ 14,000

21.09.2012 Received cash from Shiva ₹ 47,600 and discount allowed ₹ 400

22.09.2012 Paid into bank ₹ 23,200

23.09.2012 Bought 100 shares in PQ & Co. Ltd. at ₹ 120 per share and brokerage paid ₹ 80

25.09.2012 Goods worth ₹ 4,000 which were defective were returned to Jain & Co. and the balance amount due to them was settled by issuing a cheque in their favour.

28.09.2012 Sold 40 shares of PQ & Co. Ltd. at ₹ 130 per share and brokerage paid ₹ 80

28.09.2012 Bought goods worth ₹ 8,400 from Peter and supplied them to Paul for ₹ 12,000

30.09.2012 Paul returned goods worth ₹ 400

Goods worth ₹ 280 returned to Peter.

Issued a cheque for ₹ 4,000 in favour of the landlord towards rent.

30.09.2012 Paid salaries to staff ₹ 6,000.

Received from travelling salesman ₹ 8,000 for goods sold by him after deducting his travelling expenses ₹ 400

30.09.2012 Paid for donations ₹ 402

Stationery ₹ 1,800

Postage ₹ 996

Solution:

Journal Entries

Date	Particulars	L.F.	Dr. Amount (₹)	Cr. Amount (₹)
1.09.2012	Cash A/c Dr. To Capital A/c (Being cash brought in as capital))		2,00,000	2,00,000
1.09.2012	Bank Account Dr. To Cash A/c (Being cash deposited in bank)		80,000	80,000
2.09.2012	Furniture A/c Dr. Machinery A/c Dr. To Cash A/c (Being Furniture & Machinery purchased)		20,000 40,000	60,000
3.9.2012	Purchases Account Dr. To Cash Account (Goods purchased for cash)		56,000	56,000

Date	Particulars	L.F.	Dr. Amount (₹)	Cr. Amount (₹)
6.9.2012	Cash Account Dr. To Sales Account (Goods sold for cash)		32,000	32,000
8.9.2012	Purchases Account Dr. To Jain & Co. A/c (Goods purchased on credit)		44,000	44,000
10.9.2012	Telephone Rent Account Dr. To Bank Account (Telephone rent paid by cheque)		2,000	2,000
11.9.2012	Office Equipment Account Dr. To Standard Typewriter Co. A/c (Typewriter purchased on credit)		8,400	8,400
15.9.2012	Shiva's Account Dr. To Sales Account (Goods sold on credit)		48,000	48,000
17.9.2012	Cash Account Dr. To Sales Account (Goods sold for cash)		8,000	8,000
19.9.2012	Drawing Account Dr. To Bank Account (Amount withdrawn from bank for personal use)		6,000	6,000
20.9.2012	Cash Account Dr. To Bank Account (Cash withdrawn for business use)		14,000	14,000
21.9.2012	Cash Account Dr. Discount Allowed A/c Dr. To Shiva's Account (Amount received from Shiva and discount allowed)		47,600 400	48,000
22.9.2012	Bank Account Dr. To Cash Account (Cash paid into bank)		23,200	23,200
23.9.2012	Investment Account Dr. To Cash A/c (Purchase of 100 shares in PQ & Co. Ltd. at ₹ 120 and brokerage paid for ₹ 80 *i.e.*, cost of investment ₹ 120.80 per share)		12,080	12,080
25.9.2012	Jain & Co. Account Dr. To Purchase Returns Account To Bank Account (Defective goods worth ₹ 4,000 returned to Jain & Co. and balance due settled by cheque)		44,000	4,000 40,000
28.9.2012	Cash Account Dr. To Investments Account To Profit on Sale of Investments account (Sale of 40 shares at ₹ 130 per share and brokerage paid ₹ 80)		5,120	4,832 288
28.9.2012	Purchase Account Dr. To Peter's Account (Goods purchased from Peter on credit)		8,400	8,400
28.9.2012	Paul's Account Dr. To Sales Account (Goods sold on credit to Paul)		12,000	12,000

Date	Particulars	L.F.	Dr. Amount (₹)	Cr. Amount (₹)
30.9.2012	Sales Returns Account To Paul's Account (Defective goods returned by Paul)	Dr.	400	400
30.9.2012	Peter's Account To Purchase Returns Account (Defective goods returned to Peter)	Dr.	280	280
30.9.2012	Rent Account To Bank A/c (Issued a cheque to the landlord towards rent)	Dr.	4,000	4,000
30.9.2012	Salaries A/c To Cash A/c (Being salaries paid to staff)	Dr.	6,000	6,000
30.9.2012	Cash A/c Travelling Expenses A/c To Cash A/c (Cash received from salesman for goods sold by him less travelling expenses)	Dr. Dr.	8,000 400	8,400
30.9.2012	Donation A/c Stationery A/c Postage A/c To Cash A/c (Amount paid towards donation, stationery and postage)	Dr. Dr. Dr.	402 800 996	2,198

Note: Sold 40 shares of PQ & Co. Ltd. at ₹ 130 per share and brokerage paid ₹ 80.

(*i*) Cash A/c Dr. = (₹ 130 × 40 shares) – ₹ 80 = ₹ 5,120

(*ii*) Profit on sale of investment:

Total profit on sale of investment = ₹ 400

Less: Brokerage paid at the time of sale = –80

320

Less: Brokerage paid at the time of purchase added to cost of investments (40 shares × 80 P.) –32

288

(*iii*) Investment A/c:

(40 shares × ₹ 120.80) = ₹ 4,832

Cost of investment = ₹ 120 + Brokerage paid per share

= ₹ 120 + .80 = ₹ 120. 80 per share

Ledger Accounts

Cash A/c

Date	Particulars	Amount (₹)	Date	Particulars	Amount (₹)
1.9.2012	To Capital A/c	2,00,000	1.9.2012	By Bank A/c	80,000
6.9.2012	To Sales A/c	32,000	2.9.2012	By Furniture A/c	20,000
17.9.2012	To Sales A/c	8,000	2.9.2012	By Machinery A/c	40,000
20.9.2012	To Bank A/c	14,000	3.9.2012	By Purchase A/c	56,000
21.9.2012	To Shiva's A/c	47,600	22.9.2012	By Bank A/c	23,200

Date	Particulars	Amount (₹)	Date	Particulars	Amount (₹)
28.9.2012	To Investment A/c	4,832	23.9.2012	By Investment A/c	12,080
28.9.2012	To Profit on Sales of Investment A/c	288	30.9.2012	By Salaries A/c	6,000
30.9.2012	To Sales A/c	8,000	30.9.2012	By Donation A/c	402
			30.9.2012	By Stationery A/c	1,800
			30.9.2012	By Postage A/c	996
			30.9.2012	By Balance c/d	74,242
	Total	3,14,720			3,14,720

Purchase Returns A/c

Date	Particulars	Amount (₹)	Date	Particulars	Amount (₹)
30.9.2012	To Balance c/d	4,280	25.9.2012	By Jain & Co. A/c	4,000
			30.9.2012	By Peter's A/c	280
	Total	4,280			4,280

Sundry Debtors A/c

Shiva's A/c

Date	Particulars	Amount (₹)	Date	Particulars	Amount (₹)
15.9.2012	To Sales A/c	48,000	21.9.2012	By Sales Returns A/c	47,600
			21.9.2012	By Discount A/c	400
	Total	48,000			48,000

Paul's A/c

Date	Particulars	Amount (₹)	Date	Particulars	Amount (₹)
28.9.2012	To Sales A/c	12,000	30.9.2012	By Sales Returns A/c	400
	By Balance c/d	11,600			
	Total	12,000			12,000

Jain & Co. A/c

Date	Particulars	Amount (₹)	Date	Particulars	Amount (₹)
25.9.2012	To Purchase Return A/c	4,000	8.9.2012	By Purchase A/c	44,000
25.9.2012	To Bank A/c	40,000			
	Total	44,000			44,000

Peter's A/c

Date	Particulars	Amount (₹)	Date	Particulars	Amount (₹)
30.9.2012	To Purchase Return A/c	280	28.9.2012	By Purchase A/c	8,400
	To Balance b/d	8,120			
	Total	8,400			8,400

Purchases A/c

Date	Particulars	Amount (₹)	Date	Particulars	Amount (₹)
3.9.2012	To Cash Book	56,000	30.9.2012	By Balance c/d	1,08,400
8.9.2012	To Jain & Co.	44,000			
28.9.2012	To Peter's A/c	8,400			
		1,08,400			1,08,400
1.10.2012	To Balance b/d	1,08,400			

Standard Typewriter

Date	Particulars	Amount (₹)	Date	Particulars	Amount (₹)
	To Balance c/d	8,400	11.9.2012	By Office Equipment	8,400
		8,400			8,400
				By Balance b/d	8,400

Drawings A/c

Date	Particulars	Amount (₹)	Date	Particulars	Amount (₹)
19.9.2012	To Bank A/c	6,000	30.9.2012	By Balance c/d	6,000
	Total	6,000			6,000

Discount Allowed A/c

Date	Particulars	Amount (₹)	Date	Particulars	Amount (₹)
19.9.2012	To Shiva's A/c	400	30.9.2012	By Balance c/d	400
	Total	400			400

Investment A/c

Date	Particulars	Amount (₹)	Date	Particulars	Amount (₹)
23.9.2012	To Cash A/c	12,080	28.9.2012	By Cash A/c	4,832
			30.9.2012	By Balance c/d	7,248
	Total	12,080			12,080

Profit on Investment A/c

Date	Particulars	Amount (₹)	Date	Particulars	Amount (₹)
3.9.2012	To Balance c/d	288	28.9.2012	By Cash A/c	288
	Total	288			288

Rent A/c

Date	Particulars	Amount (₹)	Date	Particulars	Amount (₹)
30.9.2012	To Bank A/c	4,000	30.9.2012	By Balance c/d	4,000
	Total	4,000			4,000

Travelling Expenses A/c

Date	Particulars	Amount (₹)	Date	Particulars	Amount (₹)
30.9.2012	To Sales A/c	400	30.9.2012	By Balance c/d	400
	Total	400			400

Donation A/c

Date	Particulars	Amount (₹)	Date	Particulars	Amount (₹)
30.9.2012	To Cash A/c	402	30.9.2012	By Balance c/d	402
	Total	402			402

Stationery A/c

Date	Particulars	Amount (₹)	Date	Particulars	Amount (₹)
30.9.2012	To Cash A/c	1,800	30.9.2012	By Balance c/d	800
	Total	1,800			800

Postage A/c

Date	Particulars	Amount (₹)	Date	Particulars	Amount (₹)
30.9.2012	To Cash A/c	996	30.9.2012	By Balance c/d	996
	Total	996			996

Salaries A/c

Date	Particulars	Amount (₹)	Date	Particulars	Amount (₹)
30.9.2012	To Cash A/c	6,000	30.9.2012	By Balance c/d	6,000
	Total	6,000			6,000

Sales A/c

Date	Particulars	Amount (₹)	Date	Particulars	Amount (₹)
30.9.2012	To Balance c/d	1,08,400	6.9.2012	By Cash A/c	32,000
			15.9.2012	By Shiva's A/c	48,000
			17.9.2012	By Cash A/c	8,000
			28.9.2012	By Paul's A/c	12,000
			30.9.2012	By Cash A/c	8,000
			30.9.2012	By Travelling Expenses A/c	400
	Total	1,08,400			1,08,400

Sales Returns A/c

Date	Particulars	Amount (₹)	Date	Particulars	Amount (₹)
30.9.2012	To Paul's A/c	400	30.9.2012	By Balance c/d	400
	Total	400			400

Furniture A/c

Date	Particulars	Amount (₹)	Date	Particulars	Amount (₹)
2.9.2012	To Cash A/c	20,000	30.9.2012	By Balance c/d	20,000
	Total	20,000			20,000

Machinery A/c

Date	Particulars	Amount (₹)	Date	Particulars	Amount (₹)
2.9.2012	To Cash A/c	40,000	30.9.2012	By Balance c/d	40,000
	Total	40,000			40,000

Capital A/c

Date	Particulars	Amount (₹)	Date	Particulars	Amount (₹)
30.9.2012	To Balance c/d	2,00,000	1.9.2012	By Cash A/c	2,00,000
	Total	2,00,000			2,00,000

Telephone Rent A/c

Date	Particulars	Amount (₹)	Date	Particulars	Amount (₹)
10.9.2012	To Bank A/c	2,000	30.9.2012	By Balance c/d	2,000
	Total	2,000			2,000

Office Equipment A/c

Date	Particulars	Amount (₹)	Date	Particulars	Amount (₹)
11.9.2012	To Standard Typewriter Co. A/c	8,400	29.9.2012	By Balance c/d	8,400
	Total	8,400			8,400

Bank A/c

Date	Particulars	Amount (₹)	Date	Particulars	Amount (₹)
1.9.2012	To Cash A/c	80,000	10.9.2012	By Telephone Rent A/c	2,000
22.9.2012	To Cash A/c	23,200	19.9.2012	By Drawings	6,000
			20.9.2012	By Cash A/c	14,000
			25.9.2012	By Jain & Co.	40,000
			30.9.2012	By Rent	4,000
			30.9.2012	By Balance c/d	37,200
	Total	1,03,200			1,03,200

Trial Balance as on 30.9.2012

Particulars	Debit Amount (₹)	Credit Amount (₹)
Cash	74,242	
Capital		2,00,000
Bank	37,200	

Particulars	Debit Amount (₹)	Credit Amount (₹)
Furniture	20,000	
Machinery	40,000	
Telephone rent	2,000	
Office equipment	8,400	
Standard Typewriter		8,400
Discount	400	
Drawings	6,000	
Investments	7,248	
Profit on investments		288
Peter		8,120
Paul	11,600	
Rent	4,000	
Salaries	6,000	
Travelling expenses	400	
Donations	402	
Stationery	1800	
Postage	996	
Purchase	1,08,400	
Purchase return		4,280
Sales		1,08,400
Sales returns	400	
Total	3,29,488	3,29,488

Illustration 8: The balance sheet of a company as on March 31, 2012 is given below:

	(₹)	(₹)
Cash	21,000	
Accounts receivable	45,000	
Inventory	5,000	
Prepaid rent	1,000	
Accounts payable		12,500
Share capital		50,000
Profit and loss account		9,500
Total	72,000	72,000

Following is the summary of transactions that occurred during April:

(*a*) Collections of accounts receivable ₹ 44,000

(*b*) Payments of accounts payable ₹ 12,000

(*c*) Acquisition of inventory on credit ₹ 40,000

(*d*) Inventory costing ₹ 35,000 was sold on credit for ₹ 42,500

(*e*) Recognition of rent expense for April ₹ 500

(*f*) Wages paid in cash for April ₹ 4,000

(*g*) Dividends declared and disbursed to shareholders in April ₹ 9,000

Prepare all ledger accounts after including the opening balances as on March 31, 2012.

Ledger Accounts

Cash A/c

Dr. Cr.

Date	Particulars	Amount (₹)	Date	Particulars	Amount (₹)
1.4.2012	To Balance b/d	21,000	April	By A/c's payable	12,000
	To A/c's Receivable	44,000		By Wages	4,000
				By Dividends	9,000
				By Balance c/d	40,000
	Total	65,000			65,000

Inventory A/c

Date	Particulars	Amount (₹)	Date	Particulars	Amount (₹)
1.4.2012	To Balance b/d	5,000	April	By Customer's A/c	35,000
	To Supplier	40,000		By Balance c/d	10,000
	Total	45,000			45,000

Account Payable A/c

Date	Particulars	Amount (₹)	Date	Particulars	Amount (₹)
April	To Cash	12,000	1.4.2012	Balance b/d	12,500
	Balance c/d	40,500	April	By Inventory	40,000
	Total	52,500			52,500

Profit and Loss A/c

Date	Particulars	Amount (₹)	Date	Particulars	Amount (₹)
	To Rent Expenses	500	1.4.2012	By Balance b/d	9,500
	To Wages Expense	4,000		By Customer's A/c	7,500
	To Dividends	9,000			
	To Balance c/d	3,500			
	Total	17,000			17,000

Accounts Receivable Accounts

Date	Particulars	Amount (₹)	Date	Particulars	Amount (₹)
1.4.2012	To Balance b/d	45,000	April	By Cash	44,000
	To Inventory A/c	35,000		By Balance c/d	43,500
	To P&L A/c	7,500			
	Total	87,500			87,500

Wages Accounts

Date	Particulars	Amount (₹)	Date	Particulars	Amount (₹)
April	To Cash	4,000	1.4.2012	By P&L A/c	4,000
	Total	4,000			4,000

Prepaid Rent A/c

Date	Particulars	Amount (₹)	Date	Particulars	Amount (₹)
1.4.2012	To Balance b/d	1,000	30.4.2012	By Rent A/c	500
				By Balance c/d	500
	Total	1,000			1,000

Share Capital A/c

Date	Particulars	Amount (₹)	Date	Particulars	Amount (₹)
	To Balance c/d	50,000	1.4.2012	By Balance b/d	50,000
	Total	50,000			50,000

Rent Expenses A/c

Date	Particulars	Amount (₹)	Date	Particulars	Amount (₹)
	To Prepaid A/c	500		By P&L A/c	500
	Total	500			500

Dividend A/c

Date	Particulars	Amount (₹)	Date	Particulars	Amount (₹)
April 1	To Cash A/c	9,000		By P&L A/c	9,000
	Total	9,000			9,000

Trial Balance as on April 30, 2012

Particulars	(₹)	(₹)
Cash	40,000	
Accounts receivable	43,500	
Inventory	10,000	
Prepaid rent	500	
Accounts payable		40,500
Share capital		50,000
Profit and loss account		3,500
Total	94,000	94,000

Illustration 9: From the following list of balances, prepare a trial balance as on 30.6.2012:

	Particulars	(₹)
1.	Opening stock	3,600
2.	Wages	2,000
3.	Sales	24,000
4.	Bank loan	880
5.	Coal and Coke	600
6.	Purchase	15,000
7.	Repairs	400

	Particulars	(₹)
8.	Carriage	300
9.	Income tax	300
10.	Debtors	4,000
11.	Leasehold premises	1,200
12.	Cash in hand	40
13.	Plant & Machinery	1,500
14.	Loose tools	360
15.	Lighting	460
16.	Creditors	1,600
17.	Capital	8,000
18.	Miscellaneous receipts	120
19.	Office salaries	500
20.	Office furniture	120
21.	Patents	200
22.	Goodwill	3,000
23.	Cash at bank	1,020

Solution: **Trial Balance as on 30.6.2012**

S. No.	Head of accounts	LF	Debit Balance (₹)	Credit Balance (₹)
1.	Opening stock		3,600	
2.	Wages		2,000	
3.	Sales			24,000
4.	Bank loan			880
5.	Coal and coke		600	
6.	Purchases		15,000	
7.	Repairs		400	
8.	Carriage		300	
9.	Income tax		300	
10.	Debtors		4,000	
11.	Leasehold premises		1,200	
12.	Cash in hand		40	
13.	Plant & Machinery		1,500	
14.	Loose tools		360	
15.	Lighting		460	
16.	Creditors			1,600
17.	Capital			8,000
18.	Miscellaneous receipts			120
19.	Office salaries		500	
20.	Office furniture		120	
21.	Patents		200	
22.	Goodwill		3,000	
23.	Cash at bank		1,020	
	Total		34,600	34,600

Illustration 10: The accountant of a business firm wrongly prepared the following trial balance. You are required to draw up a trial balance correctly stating reasons in brief.

S. No.	Head of Accounts	Debit Balance (₹)	Credit Balance (₹)
1.	Capital		60,000
2.	Stock at commencement	5,000	
3.	Discount allowed		500
4.	Commission received		700
5.	Fixed assets		60,000
6.	Sales	85,000	
7.	Purchase		45,000
8.	Return outwards		1,000
9.	Returns inwards	2,000	
10.	Carriage inwards		600
11.	Carriage outwards		700
12.	Wages and salary	25,000	
13.	Bills receivable	7,000	
14.	Debtors	9,000	
15.	Bills payable		7,000
16.	Rent	3,000	
17.	Interest paid		2,000
18.	Cash	800	
19.	Creditors	6,900	
20.	Stock at the end	33,800	
	Total	1,77,500	1,77,500

Solution: **Trial Balance as on......**

S. No.	Head of Accounts	Debit Balance (₹)	Credit Balance (₹)
1.	Capital		60,000
2.	Stock at commencement	5,000	
3.	Discount allowed	500	
4.	Commission received		700
5.	Fixed assets	60,000	
6.	Sales		85,000
7.	Purchase	45,000	
8.	Return outwards		1,000
9.	Returns inwards	2,000	
10.	Carriage inwards	600	
11.	Carriage outwards	700	
12.	Wages and salary	25,000	
13.	Bills receivable	7,000	
14.	Debtors	9,000	
15.	Bills payable		7,000
16.	Rent	3,000	
17.	Interest paid	2,000	
18.	Cash	800	
19.	Creditors		6,900
	Total	1,60,600	1,60,600

Reasons:

1. Discount allowed is an expense and therefore it has a debit balance.
2. Fixed assets always reflect debit balance, because assets coming in are debited.
3. Sales has credit balance.
4. Purchases has a debit balance.
5. Carriage inwards is an expense and has a debit balance.
6. Carriage outwards is an expense and has a debit balance.
7. Interest paid is an expense and has a debit balance.
8. Creditor is a liability and has a credit balance.
9. Closing stock is not an account, so it cannot have any balance, and consequently, it does not find a place in the trial balance. Only when closing stock is adjusted against purchases, it appears in the trial balance.

THEORY QUESTIONS

1. What is the objective of posting?
2. Distinguish between a journal and a ledger. Explain their functions.
3. Explain the terms ledger and trial balance. What are the reasons for preparing a trial balance?
4. What is trial balance? What are the objectives of preparing a trial balance?
5. "A trial balance is a list showing all account titles in the ledger and the total of debits and credits in each account." Do you agree with this statement? Why or why not?
6. What type of errors could cause a trial balance not to balance?
7. A trial balance may be in balance but the accounts may be incorrect. How is this possible?
8. "If a trial balance tallies it can be concluded that there are no errors in the books of accounts."
9. Explain the errors which affect the agreement of trial balance.
10. Explain the errors which are not disclosed in spite of the agreement of a trial balance.
11. What do you understand by posting of a transaction?
12. How would you post cash book and petty cash book?
13. How would you post the transactions recorded in the following books:

    1. Purchases books 2. Sales book 3. Journal
    4. Bills receivable books 5. Bills payable book
14. Listed below are the total debits and credits from three trial balances that do not balance. For each case, indicate the type of error you would initially attempt to locate.

	Debit total	***Credit total***
(*a*)	₹ 25,500	₹ 25,400
(*b*)	₹ 43,470	₹ 43,230
(*c*)	₹ 80,614	₹ 80,974

15. A number of events common to the accounting function of a business entity are presented below. Prepare a list of these events as they would occur in their logical order.

    (*a*) Determining ledger account balances (*b*) Analysing the transaction
    (*c*) Preparing a balance sheet (*d*) Preparing a trial balance
    (*e*) Occurrence of a business transaction (*f*) Posting from the journal to the ledger
    (*g*) Preparing profit and loss account (*h*) Journalising transactions
    (*i*) Preparing balance sheet.

16. Explain the stages involved in the preparation of Trial Balance.
(MBA, JNTU, Hyderabad Jan. 2006)

17. "Trial balance simply helps in testing the arithmetical accuracy of accounting entries." Comment. **(BBA, GGSIP University, December 2000)**

18. Distinguish between Trial Balance and Balance Sheet.
(BBA, GGSIP University, December 2007, December 2009)

19. "Agreement of Trial Balance is not conclusive proof of accuracy in record keeping and posting of transactions in the ledger." Comment. **(BBA, GGSIP University, December 2008)**

SELF-EVALUATION EXERCISES

I. Select the correct answer for the following multiple-choice questions:

1. Ledger is a book of
(*a*) Original entry (*b*) Secondary entry
(*c*) All cash transactions (*d*) Subsidiary entry

2. Which of the following is not true of a trial balance?
(*a*) It proves that the total debits equal total credits, if it balances.
(*b*) It facilitates preparation of financial statements.
(*c*) It proves that no errors have been made in recording transactions, if it balances.
(*d*) It will not detect an error where the accounts debited and credited are reversed in recording a particular transaction.

3. The ending balance of the accounts receivable account was ₹ 12,000. Services billed to customers for the period were ₹ 21,500 and collections on account from customers were ₹ 23,600. The beginning balance of account receivable was
(*a*) ₹ 33,500 (*b*) 14,100 (*c*) ₹ 9,900 (*d*) ₹ 33,100

4. Posting refers to the process of transferring information from
(*a*) Journal to general ledger accounts (*b*) General ledger accounts to journals
(*c*) Source documents to journals (*d*) Journals to source documents

5. The form listing the balances and the titles of the accounts in the ledger on a given date is
(*a*) Income statement (*b*) Balance sheet
(*c*) Retained earnings statement (*d*) Trial balance

6. If the merchandise inventory at the end of the year is overstated by ₹ 7,500, the error will cause an
(*a*) Overstatement of cost of merchandise sold for the year by ₹ 7,500
(*b*) Understatement of gross profit for the year by ₹ 7,500
(*c*) Overstatement of net income for the year by ₹ 7,500
(*d*) Understatement of net income for the year by ₹ 7, 500

7. Deciding whether an expenditure for a desk is properly recorded as store equipment or office equipment is an example of a
(*a*) Recognition problem (*b*) Valuation problem
(*c*) Classification problem (*d*) Communication problem

8. The equality of debits and credits can be tested periodically by preparing a
(*a*) Trial balance (*b*) T account
(*c*) General journal (*d*) Ledger

9. Which of the following describes the proper sequence of actions in the accounting cycle?
   (*a*) Post, enter, analyse, prepare, close, adjust
   (*b*) Analyse, enter, post, adjust, prepare, close
   (*c*) Prepare, enter, post, adjust, analyse, close
   (*d*) Enter, post, close, prepare, adjust, analyse
10. On a bank reconciliation which of the following would be added to the balance by bank?
    (*a*) Outstanding cheques (*b*) Deposits in transit
    (*c*) Service charges (*d*) Interest on balance
11. Which of the following items appearing on a bank reconciliation would require an adjusting entry?
    (*a*) Outstanding cheques (*b*) Deposits in transit
    (*c*) Interest on balance (*d*) Adjusted cash balance
12. A transaction recorded on the debit side of cash book is transferred to the ledger
    (*a*) On the debit side of the account (*b*) On the credit side of the account
    (*c*) Is not posted anywhere
13. A transaction recorded on the credit side of cash book is transferred to the ledger
    (*a*) On debit side of the account (*b*) On credit side of the account
    (*c*) Is not posted anywhere
14. Balance of cash book is posted to the ledger
    (*a*) In the cash account (*b*) In bank account
    (*c*) Nowhere
15. Balance of petty cash book is posted to ledger
    (*a*) In the cash account (*b*) In the bank a/c
    (*c*) Nowhere
16. Total of purchases book is posted to the ledger
    (*a*) On the debits side of purchases a/c (*b*) On the credit side of purchases a/c
    (*c*) Nowhere
17. Total of purchases returns book is posted to the ledger
    (*a*) On the credit side of the purchases
    (*b*) On the credit side of purchases returns a/c
    (*c*) On the debit side of purchases returns a/c
18. Transactions recorded in the sales book are posted to the ledger:
    (*a*) On the debit side of customers' accounts
    (*b*) On the credit side of customers' accounts
    (*c*) Nowhere
19. Sales book total is posted to the ledger
    (*a*) On the debit side of sales returns a/c (*b*) On credit side of sales a/c
    (*c*) Nowhere
20. Total of sales returns book is posted to the ledger
    (*a*) On the debit side of sales returns a/c (*b*) On the credit side of sales returns a/c
    (*c*) Nowhere
21. Acceptances received and recorded in bills receivable are transferred to ledger
    (*a*) On the debit side of relevant personal accounts

(*b*) On the credit side of relevant personal accounts
(*c*) Nowhere

22. Total of bills receivable book is posted to the ledger
(*a*) On the debit side of bills receivable a/c (*b*) On the credit side of bills receivable a/c
(*c*) Nowhere

23. Total of bills payable book is posted to the ledger
(*a*) On the debit side of bills payable a/c (*b*) On the credit side of bills payable a/c
(*c*) Nowhere

24. Which of the following errors will not affect the trial balance?
(*a*) Wrong balancing of an account
(*b*) Writing an amount in the wrong account but on the correct side.
(*c*) Wrong totalling of an account.

25. Agreement of trial balance ensures:
(*a*) Arithmetical accuracy of recording transactions in the book of original entry
(*b*) Arithmetical accuracy of all accounting records
(*c*) Arithmetical accuracy of posting the entry to the ledger

II. Answer True or False:

1. Posting transactions in accounts may be done before or after making journal entries for the transactions, whichever is more convenient.
2. The use of posting reference column is important to make sure every entry is recorded in the accounts and to prevent an entry being posted twice.
3. The balance in the accounts receivable account can be correctly defined as uncollected sales revenue, *i.e.*, that part of sales revenue that has not been received yet in the form of cash.
4. If a company makes all its sales on credit, the total cash receipts from its customers during the year may actually be less than the total sales revenue for the year.
5. Accounts receivable is a 'near cash' account which is reported second after cash in the balance sheet because it will be converted into cash in the short run.
6. The journal entries for sales are based on certain information in the sales invoice for each sale; the sales invoice is the main source document used to record the journal entry for each sales transaction.
7. Retailers sell products to their customers in more or less the same condition that they buy the products from their suppliers; the products are not changed during the time a retailer holds the goods.
8. The purchases account is debited (+) with the cost of goods bought during the year, instead of debiting (–) the inventories account.
9. The balance in the accounts payable account can be correctly defined as unpaid purchases, *i.e.*, that part of the total purchases on credit that has not been paid yet.
10. A company's total cash receipts from all sources during the year may be more than its total sales revenue for the year.
11. Ledger means the complete collection of accounts from which the entity's financial statements are prepared.
12. Assume that a trial balance shows that the total of all debit balance accounts is within a few rupees of the total of all credit balance accounts; this is a tolerable amount of difference and the accountant would proceed to the next step in the accounting cycle.

13. A trial balance is very important because it reveals all accounting errors that have been made during the period.

III. Match the following phrases with the descriptions of the accounting processing cycle:

Phrases of the accounting information processing cycle (sequential order)		Description of phases	
1.	Data collection	(A)	Income statement, balance sheet, SCFP
2.	Transaction analysis	(B)	Transfer of amount for each account affected by the transaction results in a reclassification of the data.
3.	Journalising	(C)	A listing of each account and its debit or credit ending balance: checks debits=credits.
4.	Posting	(D)	Source documents that underlie each transaction
5.	Trial balance	(E)	A chronological record is prepared that reflects the economic effects of each transaction.
6.	Financial statements	(F)	A careful study of each transaction and determination of its economic effects on the entity.

ANSWERS TO SELF-EVALUATION EXERCISES

I.

1. (*b*)	**2.** (*c*)	**3.** (*b*)	**4.** (*a*)	**5.** (*d*)	**6.** (*c*)
7. (*c*)	**8.** (*a*)	**9.** (*b*)	**10.** (*b*)	**11.** (*c*)	**12.** (*b*)
13. (*a*)	**14.** (*c*)	**15.** (*c*)	**16.** (*a*)	**17.** (*b*)	**18.** (*a*)
19. (*b*)	**20.** (*a*)	**21.** (*b*)	**22.** (*a*)	**23.** (*b*)	**24.** (*b*)
25. (*c*)					

II.

1. False	**2.** True	**3.** True	**4.** True	**5.** True	**6.** True
7. True	**8.** False	**9.** True	**10.** True	**11.** True	**12.** False
13. False					

III.

1. (D)	**2.** (E)	**3.** (F)	**4.** (B)	**5.** (C)	**6.** (A)

7

BANK RECONCILIATION STATEMENT

LEARNING OBJECTIVES

After reading this chapter, you should be able to:

- *Understand* a Bank Reconciliation statement.
- *List* the reasons for difference between bank balances of Cash book and Pass book.
- *Indicate* procedure of preparing reconciliation statement?

The Bank Reconciliation Statement is an aid used to ensure the accuracy of transactions appearing in the bank column of the Cash Book. Such transactions can be verified through an external record, namely, the bank statement received periodically from the banker. While the business keeps a record of its transactions through the bank columns in the cash book, the banker in turn maintains the bank's transactions with the business in his ledger. An extract from this ledger showing details of the transactions during a specified period is sent at frequent intervals by the bank to the business and this extract is referred to as a bank statement.

Reasons for Difference Between Bank Balances as per Cash Book and Pass Book

The relationship between the customer and the banker is that of a creditor and a debtor. So, if the bank columns of the cash book show a debit balance as on a specified date, the bank statement should show an equal amount of credit balance as on that date and vice-versa. However, the balances shown by the two independent records may not always agree due to the following:

(*i*) Cheques issued by the business to its suppliers or other parties may not have been presented for payment.

(*ii*) Cheques received from customers and deposited may not have been collected by the banker.

(*iii*) Deposits may have been directly made by the customers into the bank account of the enterprise.

(*iv*) Collection charges, service charges and interest on overdraft charged by the banker. The business can ascertain the exact amount of charges and record them in the cash book only after the receipt of the bank statement.

(*v*) Interest credited by bank for the balance maintained with it and any other income such as interest on securities, dividend etc. collected by the bank on behalf of the business can be ascertained only from the bank statement.

(*vi*) Wrong entries made by the business in the Cash Book or errors committed by the bank in its ledger.

(*vii*) Omission of entries in the two sets of books.

(*viii*) Dishonour of customers cheques deposited in the bank account.

RECONCILIATION STATEMENT

On receipt of the bank statement, a comparison of the entries in the Cash Book with those appearing in the bank statement will help in identifying the items causing the difference in the two balances. While the difference due to (*i*) and (*ii*) above will be eliminated in the near future (that is, creditors will soon present their cheques for payment and customer cheques will be collected by the bank in due course), the difference due to items (*iii*) to (*v*) can be eliminated only if such items are recorded in the Cash Book. In addition, business must rectify any errors in the Cash Book, include any transactions omitted and record the dishonour, if any, of customers cheques. After these adjustments have been recorded, a statement will be prepared to reconcile the balance as shown by the Cash Book with that shown by the Pass Book. This statement is referred to as Bank Reconciliation Statement. It must be understood that this reconciliation statement will contain only details of

(*a*) Cheques issued and not presented

(*b*) Cheques deposited and remaining uncollected

(*c*) Errors in the bank statement and

(*d*) Omission of entries in the bank statement

The Bank Reconciliation statement is thus an additional tool available to check the accuracy of the bank columns of the cash book.

Illustration 1: On 31st March, 2012 the Cash Book of Rohit Kumar showed a total bank balance of ₹ 48,000 (debit). However his Pass Book showed a credit balance of ₹ 45,000 as on the same date. A detailed comparison of entries revealed the following:

(*a*) Customers cheques amounting to ₹ 9,500 had not been collected and credited by the bank as on 31.3.2012.

(*b*) Certain cheques amounting to ₹ 6,000 had not been presented for payment as on 31.3.2012.

(*c*) Bank charges of ₹ 500 and interest on investments of ₹ 3,000 collected by the Bank appear in Pass Book only.

(*d*) A customer had paid into bank directly a sum of ₹ 6,000 on March 30, 2012. This was not recorded in the Cash Book.

(*e*) A cheque for ₹ 8,000 received from a customer and deposited with bank had been dishonoured. Entry for dishonour had not been recorded in the Cash Book.

Solution: Bank Reconciliation Statement as at 31st March, 2012

Particulars	(+) Items	(–) Items
Balance as per cash book	48,000	
Less: Cheques deposited but not yet credited		9,500
Add: Cheques issued but not presented for payment	6,000	
Less: Bank charges debited in pass book		500
Add: Interest on Investment Credited in Pass Book	3,000	
Add: Direct payment made in bank a/c and not recorded in cash book	6,000	
Less: Cheque dishonoured and debited in Pass Book		8,000
Total	63,000	18,000
Balance as per pass book	45,000	

Illustration 2: Find out the balance as per pass book from the following particulars:

(*i*) Bank Overdraft as per cash book on 30th April, 2012 ₹ 2,000.

(*ii*) Cheques issued but not presented for payment ₹ 1,350.

(*iii*) Cheques deposited but not yet collected by the banker ₹ 560.

(*iv*) Bank charges ₹ 80 made by the bank not yet entered in the cash book.

(*v*) Interest on Investments collected by the bankers and credited in the pass book amounted to ₹ 905.

Solution: Bank Reconciliation Statement as on 30th April, 2012

Particulars	Plus amount (₹)	Minus amount (₹)
Overdraft as per cash book		2,000
Cheques issued but not yet presented for payment	1,350	
Cheques deposited but not yet collected		560
Bank charges		80
Interest on Investment collected by the bank	905	
Overdraft as per pass book	1,385	
	2,640	2,640

Illustration 3: On 31st March, 2012 the pass book showed a credit balance of ₹ 10,500. The following information is also available.

1. Cheques amounting to ₹ 2,750 were deposited in the bank but cheques of ₹ 750 had not been cleared up to 31st March.
2. Cheques amounting to ₹ 3,500 were issued, but cheque for ₹ 1,200 had not been presented for payment in the bank up to 31st March.
3. Bank had given a debit of ₹ 35 for Sundry charges.
4. Bank had received directly from customers ₹ 800 and dividend of ₹ 130 up to 31st March. Find out the balance as per the cash book.

Solution: Bank Reconciliation Statement as on 31st March, 2012

Particulars	Plus amount (₹)	Minus amount (₹)
Balance as per pass book	10,500	
Cheques paid into bank but not yet cleared	750	
Cheques issued but not presented for payment		1,200
Bank charges	35	
Bank received directly from customers		800
Dividend received directly by bank		130
Balance as per cash book		9,155
	11,285	11,285

Illustration 4: On 31st December 2012, there was credit balance of ₹ 12,000 in the pass book of Mr. Ram Prakash. He issued cheques of ₹ 3,000/- on 26.12.2012 out of which a cheque of ₹ 1,800/- was presented for payment on 31st Dec. 2012. Bank debited ₹ 20/- for expenses and credited ₹ 170 for interest for which no record has been made in the cash book. Ram Prakash received a cheque of ₹ 320/- from a customer but he forget to send it to bank though it was entered in the bank column of cash book.

Prepare bank reconciliation statement.

Solution: Bank Reconciliation Statement as on 31st December, 2012

Particulars	Plus amount (₹)	Minus amount (₹)
Balance as per pass book	12,000	
Cheques issued but not yet presented for payment (3,000 – 1,800)		1,200
Bank charges	20	
Interest directly credited by bank		170
Cheque received but not yet sent for collection	320	
Balance as per cash book		10,970
	12,340	12,340

Illustration 5: On 31.3.2012 the balance at the bank as shown by the pass book was ₹ 10,500. The balance did not agree with the Cash Book. The following points were discovered:

(*a*) On 28th March 2012, three cheques of ₹ 500, ₹ 600 and ₹ 1,200 were deposited but these cheques were not credited by the bank during the period.

(*b*) On 27th March 2012, cheques issued ₹ 750 and ₹ 350 to the creditors were not presented to the bank for payment.

(*c*) Interest amounting to ₹ 150 was credited in the Pass Book but was not entered in the cash book.

Ascertain the balance as per cash book.

Solution: Bank Reconciliation Statement as on 31st March, 2012

Particulars	Plus amount (₹)	Minus amount (₹)
Balance as per pass book	10,500	
Cheques paid into bank but not yet cleared (500 + 600 + 1,200)	2,300	
Cheques issued but not yet presented for payment (750 + 350)		1,100
Interest credited by bank		150
Balance as per cash book		11,550
	12,800	12,800

Illustration 6: On January 31, 2012 Martin's cash book showed a bank overdraft of ₹ 98,700. On comparison he finds the following:

(*a*) Out of total cheques of ₹ 8,900 issued on January 27, one cheque of ₹ 7,400 was presented for payment on February 4, and another cheque of ₹ 1,500 handed over to the customer, was returned by him, and in lieu of that, a new cheque of the same amount was issued to him on February 1. No entry for the return was made.

(*b*) Of the total cash and cheques worth ₹ 6800 deposited in the bank on January 24, one cheque of ₹ 2,600 was cleared on February 1, and another of ₹ 500 was returned by the bankers on February 2.

(*c*) Bank charges ₹ 35 and bank interest ₹ 2,860 appearing in the pass book are not yet recorded in the cash book.

(*d*) Cheque deposited in his account no. 2 ₹ 1,550 wrongly credited to this account by the bank.

(*e*) A cheque of ₹ 800 drawn on this account was wrongly debited in account no. 2 by the bank

(*f*) A cheque of ₹ 160 issued for this account was recorded by mistake in each book in bank column for no. 2 account, was presented for payment on February 2.

Solution: Bank Reconciliation Statement as on January 31, 2012

	(₹)	(₹)
Overdraft as per cash book		98,700
Less: Cheques issued but not presented for payment (₹ 7,400 + ₹ 1,500)	8,900	
Cheque deposited in account no. 2 wrongly credited to this account	1,550	
Cheque drawn on this account wrongly debited to account no. 2	800	
Add: Cheque deposited but not credited to date (₹ 2,600 + ₹ 500)		3,100
Bank charges and Interest appearing in the pass book (₹ 35 + 2, 860)		2,895
	11,250	1,04,695
Debit balance as per pass book (Overdraft)	93,445	
	1,04,695	1,04,695

Illustration 7: Mr. Jones is having two accounts (A and B) with the Central Bank of India. On 31.12.2012 his ledger shows a balance of ₹ 5000 in account A and an overdraft of ₹ 2,250 in account B. On verifying the ledger entries with the respective bank statements, the following mistakes were noticed.

1. A deposit of ₹ 1,500 made into A on 20.12.2012 has been entered in the ledger in account B.
2. A withdrawal of ₹ 500 from account A on 2.1.2012 has been entered in the ledger in account B.
3. Two cheques of ₹ 500 and ₹ 750 deposited in A account on 1.12.2012 (and entered in the books in B account) have been dishonoured by the bankers. The entries for the dishonour of these cheques have been entered in the books in B account.
4. In the account A and B, Mr. Jones has issued on 29.12.2012 cheques for ₹ 10,000 and 1,000, respectively, and these have not been cashed till 31.12.2012.
5. Incidental charges of ₹ 10 and 25 charged in the account A and B , respectively, have not been entered in the book.
6. The deposits of ₹ 5,000 and ₹ 3,500 made into the account A and B both on 30.12.2012 have not been credited by the bank till 31.12. 2012.
7. The bank has credited an interest of ₹ 50 for account A and has charged interest of ₹ 275 for account 'B' which have not been recorded in the books.

Draw the bank reconciliation statements for the above two accounts.

Solution:

Bank Reconciliation Statement of Mr. Jones as on December 31, 2012

		A		B	
		Dr.	**Cr.**	**Dr.**	**Cr.**
	Balance as per ledger	5,000	—	—	2,250
(1)	*Add*: Amount wrongly entered to the debit of account B in the ledger	1,500	—	—	1,500
(2)	*Less*: Withdrawal wrongly entered in account B in the ledger	—	500	500	—
(3)	No effect				
(4)	*Add*: Cheques issued but not encashed	10,000		1,000	
(5)	*Less*: Incidental charges		10		25
(6)	*Less*: Deposits not given effect to overdraft as per passbook (in B)		5,000		3,500
(7)	*Add*: Interest on accounts	50			275
	Balance (good) as per pass book (in A)		11,040	6,050	—
		16,550	16,500	7,550	7,550

Note: An item entered wrongly in the cash book does not affect the balance in bank passbook. Hence, no adjustment is needed.

Illustration 8: The following is a summary of a cash book as presented to you for December 2012:

	(₹)		(₹)
Receipts	1,469	Balance brought forward	761
Balance, carried forward	554	Payments	1,262
	2,023		2,023

All receipts are banked and payments made by cheque. On investigation you discover:

1. Bank charges of ₹ 136 entered on the bank statement had not been entered in cash book.
2. Cheques drawn amounting to ₹ 267 had been presented to the bank for payment.
3. Cheques received totalling ₹ 762 had been entered in the cash book and paid in to the bank, but had not been credited by the bank until January 2012.
4. A cheque for ₹ 22 had been entered as a receipt in the cash book instead of as a payment.
5. A cheque for ₹ 25 had been debited by the bank in error.
6. A cheque received for ₹ 80 had been returned by the bank and marked 'No funds available', No adjustment had been made in the cash book.
7. All dividends receivable are credited directly to the bank amount. During December, amounts totalling ₹ 62, were credited by the bank and no entries made in the cash book.
8. A cheque drawn for ₹ 6 had been incorrectly entered in the cash book as ₹ 66.
9. The balance brought forward should have been ₹ 71.
10. The bank statement as on December 31, 2012 showed an overdraft of ₹ 1,162.

You are required to:

(*a*) Show the adjustments required in the cash book.

(*b*) Prepare a bank reconciliation statement as on December 31, 2012.

Solution: (*a*) **Cash Book**

	(₹)		(₹)
Dividends received during December (7)	62	Balance brought forward	554
Adjustment cheque drawn for ₹ 6 entered as ₹ 66 (8)	60	Bank charges (1)	136
Adjustment of balance brought toward on December 1, 2002 (9)	50	Adjustment repaid cheque entered as receipt (4)	44
Balance carried forward	142	Adjustment regarding cheque returned (6)	80
	814		814

(*b*) Bank Reconciliation Statement (On December 31, 2012)

	(₹)	(₹)
Balance as per bank statement on December 31, 2002		1,162 (overdrawn)
Add: Cheque issued but not yet presented (2)		267
		1,429
Less: Deposits not yet credited (3)	762	
Cheque debited in error (5)	25	787
Balance as per cash book on December 31, 2002		642 (overdrawn)

Illustration 9: When Transit Co. Ltd, received its bank statement showing favourable balance of ₹ 7,392 for the period ended June 30, 2012, this did not agree with the balance shown in the cash book.

An examination of the cash book and bank statement disclosed the following:

1. A deposit of ₹ 492 paid in on June 29, 2012 had not been credited by the bank until July 1, 2012.
2. Bank charges amounting to ₹ 17 had not been entered in the cash book.
3. A debit of ₹ 42 appeared on the bank statement for an unpaid cheque, which had been returned marked 'out of date'. The cheque had been re-dated by the customer of Transit Co. Ltd. and paid into the bank again on July 3, 2012.
4. A standing order for payment of an annual subscription amounting to ₹ 10 had not been entered in the cash book.
5. On June 25, the managing director had given the cashier a cheque for ₹ 100 to pay into his personal account at the bank. The cashier had paid it into the company's account by mistake.
6. On June 27, two customers of Transit Co. Ltd had paid direct to the company's bank account ₹ 499 and ₹ 157, respectively, for goods supplied. The advices were not received by the company until July 1, and were entered in the cash book under that date.
7. On March 30, 2012, the company had entered into a hire purchase agreement to pay by banker's order a sum of ₹ 26, on the tenth day of each month commencing April. No entries had been made in the cash book.
8. ₹ 364 paid into the bank had been entered twice in the cash book.
9. Cheques issued amount to ₹ 4,672 had not been presented to the bank for payment until after June 30, 2012.
10. A customer of the company, who received a cash discount of 2.5% on his account of ₹ 200, paid the company a cheque on June 10. The cashier, in error, entered the gross amount in the bank column of the cash book.

After making the adjustments you are required:

(*a*) to show the necessary adjustments in the cash book of Transit Co. Ltd. bringing down the correct balance on June 30, 2012.

(*b*) to prepare a bank reconciliation statement.

Solution: **Transit Co. Ltd. Cash Book**

	(₹)		(₹)
Balance brought forward	2,972	Bank charges	17
Sunday debtors (₹ 499 + 157)	656	Annual subscription	10
Managing director's cheque	100	Refund of amount incorrectly banked	100
		Hire-purchase vendor	78
		Adjustment regarding cheques entered twice	364
		Discount allowed	5
		Balance carried forward	3,154
	3,728		3,728

Bank Reconciliation Statement as on June 30, 2012

	(₹)	(₹)
Balance as per cash book on June 30, 2012	4,672	3,154
Add: Cheques issued but not yet presented	100	4,772
		7,926
Less: Deposit not yet credited	492	
Cheque re-presented	42	534
Balance as per pass book		7,392

Illustration 10: On March 31, 2012 Krishna Kumar's cash book showed a bank balance (debit) of ₹ 24,250. However the bank statement showed a credit balance of ₹ 26,950 as on the same date. A detailed comparison of entries revealed the following:

(*a*) Customers' cheque amounting to ₹ 4,225 had not been collected by the bank as on 31.3. 2012.

(*b*) Certain cheques amounting ₹ 4,425 had not been presented for payment as on 31.3.2012.

(*c*) Bank charges of ₹ 500 and interest of ₹ 6,250 collected by the banker appear only in the bank statement.

(*d*) A wrong credit of ₹ 1,250 in the bank statement.

(*e*) Ramji Ltd, a customer had paid into bank directly a sum of ₹ 1,500 on March 29, 2012. This had not been recorded in the cash book.

(*f*) A cheque for ₹ 1,000 received from Bharat Ltd. a customer and deposited, had been returned unpaid. The dishonour of this cheque has not been entered in the cash book.

Prepare a bank reconciliation statement and also show cash book (with bank columns only).

Solution: **Cash Book of Krishna Kumar Bank Columns only**

2012	Receipts	Bank (₹)	2012	Payment	Bank (₹)
March 31	To Balance b/d	24,250	March 31	By Bank charges	500
March 31	To Interest received	1,250	March 31	By Bharat Ltd.	1,000
March 31	To Ramji Ltd.	1,500	March 31	By Balance c/d	25,500
		27,000			27,000

Bank Reconciliation Statement as on March 31, 2012

	(₹)	(₹)
Bank balance as per cash book		25,500
Add: Cheques issued and not presented	4,425	
Wrong credit in the bank statement	1,250	5,675
		31,175
Less: Cheques deposited and remaining uncollected		4,225
Bank balance as per bank statement		26,950

Illustration 11: Raj Mohan maintains two accounts, known as account no. 1 and account no. 2 with the bank of Baroda.

On December 31, 2012 the overdraft as per passbook for account no. 1 is ₹ 43,276. But the overdraft as per cash book is not the same and on comparing the pass book and cash book, he finds the following:

(*i*) Out of the total cheques of ₹ 3,700 deposited on December 27, 2012, one cheque amounting ₹ 1,325 was collected on January 4, 2013.

(*ii*) Out of the total cheques of ₹ 6,284, issued on December 22, 2012, two cheques of ₹ 750 each were not presented until December 31, 2012.

(*iii*) A cheque amounting ₹ 1,130 was sent to the supplier, through post on December 29, 2012 and it is expected to reach him only after January 3, 2013.

(*iv*) Bank charges amounting to ₹ 31.50 and interest charges amounting to ₹ 131 not yet recorded in the cash book.

(*v*) Mr. Raj Mohan has deposited a cheque in his account no. 2, for ₹ 500 on December 2, 2012, it was wrongly credited to account no. 1 by the bank.

(*vi*) A cheque deposited on December 15, 2012, for ₹ 250 was returned dishonoured by bankers on January 2, 2013.

(*vii*) A cheque of ₹ 100 issued for account no. 1 by mistake was recorded in bank column of the cash book for account no. 2, and this cheque was presented for payment on January 4, 2013.

From the above particulars prepare a bank reconciliation to find out the bank overdraft as per cash book.

Bank Reconciliation Statement as on December 31, 2012

	(₹)	(₹)
Bank overdraft as per pass book		43,276
Add: Cheques issued out not presented for Payment	1,500	
Add: Cheque sent to the supplier through post, but which did not reach him, hence not presented for payment	1,130	
Add: Cheque wrongly credited to account no. 1 by bank instead of account no. 2	500	3,130
		46,406
Less: Cheques deposited but not yet collected by the bank	1,325	
Less: Bank charges and interest not recorded in cash book (31.50 + 131)	162.50	
Less: Cheque deposited on December 15, 2012 but not cleared by the bank until December 31, 2012	250	1,737.50
		44,668.50

Note: Item no. (*vii*) will not make impact as on December 31, 2012 as it was presented for payment only on January 4, 2012.

Illustration 12: Prepare a bank reconciliation statement as on September 30, 2012 from the following entries in the bank column of the cash book and the corresponding pass book.

Cash Book Bank Column Only

		(₹)			(₹)
Sep. 1	To Balance	4,000	Sep. 4	By Drawings	350
Sep. 3	To Kamlesh	1,100	Sep. 8	By Suresh	1,650
Sep. 9	To Prabhu	750	Sep. 12	By Salary	1,400
Sep. 16	To Pawan	1,700	Sep. 16	By Manish	350
Sep. 23	To Satish	1,300	Sep. 23	By Shyam	2,100
Sep. 27	To Mohan	50	Sep. 27	By Kapil	1,000
Sep. 30	To Kapoor	175	Sep. 30	By Seeta	550
			Sep. 26	By Commission	50
			Sep. 30	By Balance carried over	1,125
		9,075			9,075

Bank Pass Book

Date 2012	Particulars	Debit (₹)	Credit (₹)	Balance (₹)
Sep. 1	By balance b/d			Cr. 4,000
Sep. 4	To cheque-drawing	350		Cr. 3,650
Sep. 5	By cheque-Kamlesh		1,100	Cr. 4,750
Sep. 9	To cheque-Suresh	1,650		Cr. 3,100
Sep. 11	By cheque-Prabhu		750	Cr. 3,850
Sep. 12	To cheque-Salary	1,400		Cr. 2,450

Date 2012	Particulars	Debit (₹)	Credit (₹)	Balance (₹)
Sep. 17	To cheque-Manish	850		Cr. 1,600
Sep. 20	By cheque-Satish		1,300	Cr. 2,900
Sep. 30	By dividend received		450	Cr. 3,350
	To bank charges	7.50		Cr. 3,342.50
	To electricity bill	30		Cr. 3,312.50
	To cheque-commission	50		Cr. 3,262.50

Solution: **Bank Reconciliation Statement as on 30.09.2012**

		(₹)
Add:	Balance as per bank column of cash book	1,125.00
	Cheque issued but not presented	
	Shyam–2,100	
	Kapil– 1,000	
	Seeta– 550	3,650
		4,775
Less:	Cheques deposited but not cleared	
	Pawan–1,700	
	Mohan– 50	
	Kapoor– 175	1,925
		2,850
Add:	Amount credited in pass book only: dividend received	450
		3,300
Less:	Amounts debited in pass book only	
	Bank charges 7.50	
	Electricity bill 30	37.50
	Balance as per pass book	3,262.50

Illustration 13: Prepare bank reconciliation statement as on November 30, 2012 from the following information:

(*a*) Balance as per passbook on 30.11.2012 overdrawn ₹ 40,000.

(*b*) On 5.10.2012 Mr. Ram deposited a cheque for collection of ₹ 2,000 and made entry in cash book which appears in the passbook on 6.12.2012 at ₹ 1,980.

(*c*) Cheques issued to parties but not presented for payment till 30.11.2012 are of ₹ 1,050, ₹ 1,670 and ₹ 1,800.

(*d*) Cheques deposited for collection but not collected by bankers till 30.11.2012 ₹ 17,520 and ₹ 820.

(*e*) Interest on investment collected by bankers on 30.11.2012 ₹ 1,910 entered in cash book on 4.12.2012 on receipt of bank intimation.

(*f*) Bank charges ₹ 180 (dated 27.11.2012) not entered in cash book.

(*g*) Cheque deposited for collection on 30.11.2012 but returned dishonoured on 6.12.2012 ₹ 1,890.

(*h*) Bankers have made a mistake in balancing by showing overdrawn balance in excess by ₹ 2,000 on 30.11.2012 which was rectified in bank passbook on 7.12.2012 when notified.

Bank Reconciliation Statement as on 30.11.2012

			(₹)	
	(a) Overdraft bank balance as per pass book			40,000
Add:	(c) Cheques issued but not presented for Payment till 30.11.2012	1,050		
		1,670		
		1,800	4,520	
	(e) Interest on investment collected by bankers entered in cash book after 30.11.2012		1,910	6,430
				46,430
Less:	(b) Cheque deposited but collected by bankers after 30.11.2012 and appears in the passbook at ₹ 1,980		2, 000	
	(d) Cheques deposited but not collected by bankers till 30.11.2012	17,520		
		820	18,340	
	(f) Bank charges not recorded in the cash book		180	
	(g) Cheque deposited but dishonoured		1,890	
	(h) Bank's mistake in balancing by showing overdrawn balance in excess		2,000	24,410
	Overdraft bank balance as per cash book			22,020

Illustration 14: A cash book shows an overdrawn position of ₹ 1,815 on March 31, 2012 although the bank statement shows only ₹ 1,689 overdrawn. Detailed examination of the two records revealed the following:

(*a*) A cheque for ₹ 780 in favour of Narayanan had been omitted by the bank from its statement, the cheque having been debited to another customer's A/c.

(*b*) The debit side of own book had been under cast by ₹ 150.

(*c*) A cheque for ₹ 91 drawn in payment of stationery account had been entered in the cash book as ₹ 64 and was shown correctly in bank statement.

(*d*) A cheque for ₹ 105 from Dinesh, having been paid into the bank was dishonoured and shown as such on bank statement, although no entry relating to dishonour had been made in the cash book

(*e*) The bank had debited a cheque for ₹ 63 in error. It should have been debited to Suresh's A/c.

(*f*) A dividend of ₹ 45 on equity shares had been directly collected by bank, but no entry has been made in cash book.

(*g*) A deposit of ₹ 540 on 31.3.2012 had not been credited by the bank.

(*h*) Interest of ₹ 114 had been directly debited by bank but not recorded in cash book.

You are required to prepare a bank reconciliation statement after necessary amendment in cash book as on March 31, 2012.

Solution:

Cash Book
(Bank column only)

Date	Receipts	Amount (₹)	Date	Payment	Amount (₹)
31.3.2012	To dividends	45	31.3.2012	By balance b/f (incorrect balance)	1,815
31.3.2012	To error in casting	150	31.3.2012	Stationery charges–cheque drawn for ₹ 91 wrongly recorded as ₹ 64 (91– 64)	27
31.3.2012	Balance c/d	1,866	31.3.2012	By Satish (cheque dishonoured)	105

Date	Receipts	Amount (₹)	Date	Payment	Amount (₹)
			31.3.2012	By bank interest-interest on over-draft	114
		2,061			2,061
			1.4.2012	By balance b/d (correct balance)	1,866

Bank Reconciliation Statement as on 31.3.2012

	Particulars	Amount (₹)	Amount (₹)
	Overdraft banks balance as per cash book (as amended) (Cr.)		1,866
Add:	A cheque for ₹ 63 wrongly debited by bank	63	
	A deposit not credited by bank	540	603
			2,469
Less:	A cheque in favour of Narayanan Associates not debited by bank		780
	Overdraft bank balance as per pass book (Dr.)		1,689

THEORY QUESTIONS

1. What is Bank Reconciliation Statement? What is the purpose of preparing it?
2. What are the reasons of difference between bank balances as per pass book and cash book?
3. What is Bank Reconciliation Statement?
4. Explain the reasons for difference in Cash Book and pass book balances.

MULTIPLE CHOICE QUESTIONS

Select the most appropriate answer for the following multiple choice questions:

1. A bank reconciliation is
   (*a*) A formal financial statement that lists all of a firm's bank account balances.
   (*b*) A merger of two banks that previously were competitors.
   (*c*) A statement sent monthly by a bank to a depositor that lists all deposits, cheques paid and other credits and charges to the depositor's account for the month.
   (*d*) A schedule that accounts for differences between a firm's cash balance as shown on its bank statement and the balance shown in its general ledger cash account.
2. In preparing a bank reconciliation statement the amount of cheques outstanding would be:
   (*a*) added to the bank balance according to the bank statement.
   (*b*) deducted from the bank balance according to the bank statement.
   (*c*) added to the bank balance according to the depositor's statement.
   (*d*) deducted from the bank balance according to the depositor's records.

EXERCISES AND PROBLEMS

1. From the following particulars, prepare a Bank Reconciliation Statement showing the balance as per Bank Pass Book on 31st March, 2012. The following cheques were paid into the firm's current account in March, 2012 but were credited by the bank in April 2012:
   Ashok ₹ 2,500, Mukesh ₹ 3,000, Sudesh ₹ 2,400.

The following cheques were issued by the firm in March 2012 and were cashed in April 2012: Kumud ₹ 3,000, Kamana ₹ 5,000, Ayesha ₹ 3,000.

A cheque for ₹ 1,000 which was received from a customer was entered in the bank column of the Cash Book in March, 2012, but the same was paid into bank in April, 2012.

The Pass Book shows a credit of ₹ 2,500 for interest and a debit of ₹ 500 for bank charges. The balance as per Cash Book was ₹ 1,80,000 on 31st March, 2012.

(**Ans:** Balance as per Pass Book ₹ 1,84,100).

2. On 31st December, 2012 the Pass Book of a merchant shows the credit balance of ₹ 6,714. The cheques and drafts sent to the bank but not collected and credited amounted ₹ 1,580 and three cheques drawn for ₹ 600, ₹ 300 and ₹ 400 respectively were not presented for payment till 31st January next year.

Bank has paid a bill payable amounting to ₹ 2,000 but it has not been entered in the Cash Book and a bill receivable of ₹ 1,000 which was discounted with the bank was dishonoured by the drawer on due date.

The bank has charged ₹ 26 as its commission for collecting outstation cheques and has allowed interest ₹ 20 on the trader's balance.

Prepare a Bank Reconciliation Statement and show the balance as shown in the Cash Book.

(**Ans:** Balance as per Cash Book ₹ 5,000).

3. On 30th June, 2012, the bank column of Sunil's Cash Book showed a debit balance of ₹ 16,500. On examination of the Cash Book and bank statement you find that:

(*a*) Out of total cheques amounting to ₹ 16,000 issued, cheques amounting to ₹ 11,600 have been presented for payment upto 30th June, 2012, cheques for ₹ 1,600 were presented in July, 2012 and the rest have not been presented at all.

(*b*) Out of total cheques amounting to ₹ 12,000 sent to bank for collection, cheques of ₹ 8,200 were credited in Pass Book upto 30th June, 2012, cheques amounting to ₹ 2,400 were credited in July 2012 and the rest have not been collected so far.

(*c*) On 28th June a customer deposited ₹ 7,000 direct in the bank account but it was entered only in the Pass Book.

(*d*) Debit side of Sunil's Cash Book (Bank Column) has been overcast by ₹ 200.

(*e*) No entry has been made in the Cash Book for the Rent of ₹ 1600 paid by bankers according to Sunil's standing instructions.

(*f*) The Pass Book showed a credit of ₹ 640 for interest and a debit of ₹ 80 for bank charges, but these have not been entered in the Cash Book.

Prepare a Bank Reconciliation Statement as on 30th June, 2012.

(**Ans:** Balance as per Pass Book ₹ 22,860).

4. From the following particulars prepare a Bank Reconciliation statement showing the balance as per Cash Book on 31.12.2012.

The following cheques were paid into bank in Dec., 2012 but were credited by bank in January 2012.

Sarika	₹ 3,500
Bhawana	₹ 2,500
Pooja	₹ 2,000

The following cheques were issued by the firm in December, 2012 but were presented in January, 2013:

Asha	₹ 4,000
Usha	₹ 4,500

A cheque for ₹ 1,000 which was received from a customer was entered in the bank column of the cash book in December 2012 but was omitted to be banked in Dec. 2012. The pass book shows a debit balance of ₹ 100 for bank charges and a credit balance of ₹ 2,000 for interest. Interest on investment ₹ 2,000 collected by bank appeared in the Pass Book. The bank balance as per Pass Book was ₹ 62,000 on 31st Dec. 2012.

(**Ans:** Balance as per Cash Book ₹ 59,000).

5. On 30th June 2012, the Cash Book of M/s Radhey and Sons showed a balance of ₹ 2,000 at Bank. They had sent cheques amounting to ₹ 10,000 to the bank before 30th June, but it appears from the Pass Book that cheques worth only ₹ 4,000 had been credited before that data. Similarly out of cheques of ₹ 5,000 issued during the month of June, cheques for ₹ 250 were presented and paid in July.

The Pass Book also showed the following payments:

(1) ₹ 320 as premium on the life policy according to standing instructions; and

(2) ₹ 2,000 against a pro-note, as per instructions.

The Pass Book showed that the bank had collected ₹ 600 as interest on Government Securities. The bank had charged interest ₹ 50 and bank charges ₹ 20. There was no entry in cash book for the payments, interest etc.

Prepare the Bank Reconciliation Statement as on 30th June 2012.

(**Ans:** Balance as Pass Book (Dr.) ₹ 11,080).

6. On checking Rajan's Cash Book with the Bank Statement of his overdraft current account for the month of November, 2012 you find the following:

(*a*) Cash Book showed an overdraft of ₹ 4,500

(*b*) The payment side of the Cash Book had been undercast by ₹ 150.

(*c*) A cheque of ₹ 750 drawn on his saving account has been shown as drawn on current account.

(*d*) Cheques amounting to ₹ 7,000 drawn and entered in the Cash Book had not yet been presented.

(*e*) Cheques amounting to ₹ 6,000 sent to the bank for collection, though entered in the Cash Book, had not been credited by the bank.

(*f*) Bank charges of ₹ 75 as per Bank Statement had not been taken into Cash Book.

(*g*) Dividends of the amount of ₹ 2,500 had been paid direct into the bank and not entered in the Cash Book.

You are required to prepare a Bank Reconciliation Statement on 30th Nov., 2012.

(**Ans:** Overdraft as per Pass Book ₹ 475).

7. A Bank Pass Book for Account No. 1 shows an overdraft of ₹ 6,500 on 31st March, 2012. This does not agree with the Cash Book balance. From the following particulars ascertain the Cash Book balance:

Cheques amounting to ₹ 15,000 were paid into bank in March out of which, it appears, only cheques amounting to ₹ 4,500 were credited by bank. Cheques issued during March amounted in all to ₹ 11,000. Out of these, cheques for ₹ 3,000 were unpaid on 31st March, 2012. The bank has wrongly debited Account No. 1 with ₹ 500 in respect of a cheque drawn on Account No. 2. The account stands debited with ₹ 150 for interest and with ₹ 30 for Bank charges. The bank has paid the annual subscription of ₹ 100 to a club according to the instructions. The entries for interest charges and subscription have not been made in the Cash Book.

(**Ans:** Dr. Balance as per Cash Book ₹ 1,780).

8. The bank pass book of Ravi showed an overdraft of ₹ 17,000 in his account, on 31st March 2012. On going through the pass book, the accountant found the following:

(*a*) A cheque of ₹ 550 credited in the pass book on 28th March, being dishonoured, is debited again in the pass book on 1 April 2012. There was no entry in cash book about the dishonour of the cheque until 15 April.

(*b*) Out of ₹ 10,500 paid in by Ravi in cash and by cheques on 31 March, cheques amounting to ₹ 4,000 were collected on 7 April.

(*c*) Bankers had credited his account with ₹ 1500 for interest by them on his behalf but the same had not been entered in his cash book.

(*d*) Out of cheques amounting to ₹ 3,900 drawn by him on 27 March a cheque for ₹ 1,250 was encashed on 3 April.

(*e*) Bankers seem to have given him wrong credit for ₹ 300 paid in by him in Account no. 2 and wrong debit.

Prepare Bank Reconciliation Statement on 31st March, 2012.

(**Ans:** Overdraft Balance as per Cash Book ₹ 15,580).

9. On 31st December 2012 the Cash Book showed an overdraft of ₹ 5,670.

From the following particulars make out a Bank Reconciliation Statement and ascertain the balance as per Bank Pass Book:

(*a*) Cheques drawn but not cashed before 31st Dec 2012 amounted to ₹ 3,946.

(*b*) Cheques paid into the Bank but not collected and credited before 31st Dec. 2012 amounted to ₹ 4,891.

(*c*) A bill receivable for ₹ 520 previously discounted with the Bank had been dishonoured and debited in the Pass Book.

(*d*) Debit is also made in the Pass Book for ₹ 120 on account of interest on overdraft and ₹ 55 on account of charges for collecting bills and cheques.

(*e*) The bank has collected interest on investment and credited ₹ 760 in the Pass Book.

(**Ans.** Overdraft as per Pass Book ₹ 6,550).

10. On 31st January, 2012 Cash Book showed a Bank overdraft of ₹ 12,500. On comparing it with the Pass Book, the following differences were noted:

(*a*) Cash and cheques amounting to ₹ 1,340 were sent to Bank on 27th January but cheques worth ₹ 230 were credited on 2nd February and one cheque for ₹ 45 was returned by them as dishonoured on 4th February.

(*b*) During the month of January, cheques issued to creditors amounted ₹ 1,670. Out of these, cheques worth ₹ 1,370 were presented for payment on 5th February.

(*c*) According to the standing orders, the Bankers have paid during the month of January the following:

(*a*) Life Insurance Premium ₹ 170

(*b*) Television Licence Fee ₹ 120

(*c*) Driving Licence Fee ₹ 22

(*d*) Bankers have collected ₹ 150 as dividend on the shares.

(*e*) Bankers have given a wrong credit for ₹ 150.

(*f*) Interest charged by the bank ₹ 125.

Prepare a Bank Reconciliation Statement as on 31st January, 2012.

(**Ans:** Overdraft Balance as per Pass Book ₹ 11,542).

ANSWERS TO MULTIPLE CHOICE QUESTIONS

1. (*d*) **2.** (*b*)

8

ERRORS AND THEIR RECTIFICATION

LEARNING OBJECTIVES

After reading this chapter, you should be able to:

- *List* the errors disclosed by and not disclosed by trial balance.
- *Understand* a suspense account?
- *Illustrate* the procedures of rectifying the errors.

The trial balance is prepared to ensure the arithmetical accuracy of the ledger of a business and also to ensure that for every debit entry a credit of an equal amount has been recorded. Thus, a trial balance in which the total of the debits does not equal the total of credits can be taken as an evidence for the existence of some errors in the records. On the other hand, a trial balance in which the total of the debits equal the total of credits is not a conclusive proof of the accuracy of the records. Certain errors may not effect the agreement of a trial balance as the erroneous entries may not violate the dual aspect concept. It means that even if the Trial Balance agrees, steps should be taken to ensure that the records are free from errors.

To understand the nature of errors and their rectification we may classify them into (*i*) errors disclosed by a Trial Balance and (*ii*) errors not disclosed by a Trial Balance.

Errors Disclosed by a Trial Balance

The errors which cause a mismatch in the trial balance totals are frequently referred to as errors disclosed in a Trial Balance. However, the mismatch does not automatically point to the actual errors. It is only the diligence and ingenuity of the person preparing the accounts which would help in the location of the errors.

The various errors which would cause a mismatch in the trial balance totals are as follows:

(*i*) **Wrong totalling in a subsidiary book:** For example, if the total of the purchase for a month is stuck as ₹ 26,150 instead of ₹ 26,250 then the debit in the purchases account would be ₹ 26,150 (as the total from the subsidiary book will be posted to the debit of the purchase account). The total of the credits posted in the individual suppliers a/c would be ₹ 26,250 and in the Trial Balance the total credits will exceed total debits by ₹ 100.

(*ii*) **Wrong calculation of balances in a ledger account:** For example, if the debit balance in the furniture a/c has been taken as ₹ 5,650 instead of ₹ 5,850 then the Trial Balance will show the total credits exceeding the total debits by ₹ 200.

(iii) **Partial omission of an entry:** If the debit or credit aspect of a transaction has been omitted to be recorded, the Trial Balance will disagree. For example, if a cash sales of ₹ 800 is omitted to be recorded in the Sales a/c then the total debits will exceed the total credits by ₹ 800.

(iv) **Posting an aspect of a transaction more than once:** For example, if an amount of ₹ 2,000 paid to XY Limited has been posted to the debit of XY Limited a/c twice, then the debits will exceed the credits by ₹ 2,000.

(v) **Debit entries wrongly recorded as credit entries of vice-versa:** For example, if an amount of ₹ 3,500 received from Z is posted to the credits of Z's a/c then the debits will exceed the credits by ₹ 7,000.

(vi) **Errors in totalling the debit column or the credit column of the Trial Balance:** Obviously, if a total mistake occurs while casting either the debit side or credit side of the Trial Balance, it will not tally.

(vii) **Balance of ledger accounts are wrongly transferred to the trial balance:** For example, the balance of ₹ 46,945 in the Plant and Machinery a/c is transferred to the trial balance as ₹ 46,495. This will cause the credits to exceed the debit by ₹ 450.

(viii) **Omitting to include an account's balance in the trial balance:** When an account which is outstanding in the ledger account is omitted to be include in the trial balance, it will not tally.

SUSPENSE ACCOUNT

When a combination of the various errors mentioned above have been committed, the mismatch in the totals of the Trial Balance will be totally different for the amounts of the individual transactions and only through scrutiny and checking of the books of accounts will help in detecting the errors. Sometimes, when the Trial Balance disagrees and sufficient time is not available to scrutinize the books, the accountant will include 'Suspense A/c' in the Trial Balance to make it agree and proceed with the preparation of Profit and 'Loss A/c' and Balance Sheet. For instance, if the totals of the credits in a Trial Balance exceeds the debits by ₹ 2,550 then a suspense a/c with a debit balance of 2,550 will be included in the Trial Balance. At a later date, the books may be scrutinised to detect the errors and the rectification entries passed to clear the balance in the Suspense A/c.

Errors not Disclosed by Trial Balance

Even though a trial balance may be in agreement, certain errors might have been committed while recording the transactions. Such errors are referred to as errors not disclosed by Trial Balance. The errors which will not cause a mismatch in the totals of a Trial Balance are as follows:

(a) **Omission of the recording of a transaction from the books of accounts:** If the withdrawal of goods worth ₹ 1,200 by the proprietor is omitted to be recorded in the books, the Trial Balance will still agree as both the debit and credit aspects have been omitted to be recorded.

(b) **Recording a transaction at an amount which is totally different from the actual amount:** If the purchases of goods worth ₹ 7,500 is recorded in the Purchase book as ₹ 5,700 the error will not cause the trial balance to disagree.

(c) **Compensating errors:** These are quite difficult to detect. If a cash discount of ₹ 215 allowed to a customer has been posted to the credit of his account as ₹ 251 and a cash sale of ₹ 2,851 has been posted to sales account as ₹ 2,815, then the excess credit caused by the first error would be exactly compensated by the lower credit recorded by the second error and the trial balance will be in agreement.

(d) **Posting of an aspect of a transaction on the correct side of wrong account:** If the amount of ₹ 800 received from MN Ltd. a debtor, is posted to the credit of NM Ltd. a/c, also a debtor,

the Trial Balance totals will still agree, because both are debit accounts and the total effect is the same.

(*e*) **Recording both aspects of a transaction more than once in the books of accounts:** If a sales of ₹ 3,500 made to PQR Ltd. is entered in the Sales Book twice, the error will not cause a mismatch in the totals of Trial Balance.

(*f*) **Errors of principle:** If the machinery a/c is debited for an amount of repair charges incurred for the machinery, the error will not be disclosed by the Trial Balance. This is because that both machinery a/c and repairs a/c are debit a/cs and it is a question of principle that repairs charges should not be debited to the machinery a/c. Hence, the total effect will be the same and therefore the Trial Balance will tally.

Illustration 1: Rectify the following errors and prepare suspense account:

(*i*) Goods purchased from Mani of ₹ 300 passed through Sales Book.

(*ii*) Received one bill from Arun ₹ 500 passed through bills payable book.

(*iii*) An item of ₹ 150 relating to prepaid rent account has omitted to be brought forward.

(*iv*) An item of ₹ 40 in respect of purchase returns instead of being debited to the personal account from returns outward book had been wrongly entered in the purchase book and posted therefrom wrongly to the debit of personal account.

(*v*) ₹ 500 paid to Mehta Bros. against our acceptance were debited to Malhotra Bros A/c.

(*vi*) Received final dividend of ₹ 20 from Ajit whose account had already been written off as bad debts, now credited to a newly opened account and was included in the list of creditors.

(*vii*) Bills received from Das for repairs done to radio ₹ 150 and radio supplied ₹ 950 was entered in the invoice book as ₹ 1,000.

Solution:

Sl. No.	Particulars	LF	Dr. Amount (₹)	Cr. Amount (₹)
(*i*)	Sales a/c Purchase a/c To Mani (Being the goods purchased wrongly passed through sales book)	Dr.	300	600
(*ii*)	Bills Receivable A/c Bills payable A/c To Arun (Being the rectification of Bills Receivable from Arun passed through Bills payable book)	Dr. Dr.	500 500	 1,000
(*iii*)	Prepaid rent A/c To Suspense (Being the omission of prepaid account in the books, now rectified by passing an entry)	Dr.	150	 150
(*iv*)	Suspense A/c To Purchase returns A/c To Purchase A/c (Being the error in respect of purchase returns wrongly entered in purchases book, now rectified)	Dr.	80	 40 40
(*v*)	Bills payable A/c To Malhotra Bros. (Being the acceptance from Mehta Bros. Wrongly debited to Malhotra Bros.)	Dr.	500	 500

Sl. No.	Particulars	LF	Dr. Amount (₹)	Cr. Amount (₹)
(*vi*)	Ajit To Bad debts recovered A/c (Being the bad debts recovered from Ajit wrongly included in the list of creditors)	Dr.	20	20
(*vii*)	Repairs A/c Furniture and Fitting A/c To Purchase A/c To Das (Being the bill received from Das for repairs done, has been wrongly entered in the purchases book with wrong amount)	Dr. Dr.	150 950	1,000 100

Suspense A/c

	(₹)		(₹)
To Balance (difference in trial balance)	70	By Prepaid Rent	150
To Purchase returns	40		
To Purchase	40		
Total	150		150

Illustration 2: An accountant who finds his Trial balance not agreeing opens a Suspense Account and rectifies the following errors:

(*i*) A cheque of ₹ 750 received for loss of stock by fire had been deposited in the proprietor's private Bank Account.

(*ii*) An item of purchase of ₹ 151 was entered in the purchase book as ₹ 15 and posted to the supplier's account ₹ 51.

(*iii*) A sales return of ₹ 500 was not entered in the financial accounts though it was duly taken in the stock book.

(*iv*) An amount of ₹ 300 was received in full settlement from a customer after he was allowed a discount of ₹ 50 but while writing the books, the amount received was entered in the discount column and discount allowed in the amount column.

(*v*) Bills receivable from Mr. A of ₹ 1,000 was posted to the credit of bills payable account and also credited to the account of Mr. A.

Show the suspense account and find out the opening balance.

Solution:

Sl. No.	Particulars	LF	Dr. Amount (₹)	Cr. Amount (₹)
(*i*)	Drawing A/c To Loss of Stock A/c (Being the rectification of a cheque wrongly passed to proprietor's private bank A/c)	Dr.	750	750
(*ii*)	Purchase A/c To Supplier's personal A/c To Suspense A/c (Being the rectification of undercasting of purchases amount in purchases book and supplier's A/c)	Dr.	136	100 36
(*iii*)	Sales Return A/c To Customer's A/c (Being the sales return transaction omitted to be recorded in books)	Dr.	500	500

Sl. No.	Particulars	LF	Dr. Amount (₹)	Cr. Amount (₹)
(iv)	Bank A/c To Discount allowed A/c (Being the amount received from a Customer wrongly entered in discount allowed column)	Dr.	250	250
(v)	Bills Payable A/c Bills Receivable A/c To Suspense A/c (Being bill received from Mr. A wrongly posted to Bills payable A/c and on credit ride of Mr. A's A/c)	Dr. Dr.	1,000 1,000	2,000

Suspense A/c

	(₹)		(₹)
To Balance (Difference transferred to trial balance)	2,036	By Purchases	36
		By Bills Payable	1,000
		By Bills Receivable	1,000
Total	2,036		2,036

Illustration 3: The credit column of a Trial balance as on 31st March, 2012 is short by ₹ 3,800.

On 1.4.2012 the following errors were discovered:

(*i*) A credit item of ₹ 9,300 has been debited to the personal account of Raman as ₹ 3,900.

(*ii*) ₹ 7,500 written off as depreciation on plant and machinery account has not been debited to depreciation account.

(*iii*) A discount of ₹ 4,500 allowed to Nataraj and Sons has been credited to them as ₹ 5,400.

(*iv*) The total of Sales Returns Book has been undercast by ₹ 1,000.

Pass the rectification entries. Assuming that the difference in Trial Balance is taken to a suspense account. You need not show the suspense account.

Solution:

Sl. No.	Particulars	LF	Dr. Amount (₹)	Cr. Amount (₹)
(i)	Suspense A/c To Raman's A/c (Being the rectification of a credit item of ₹ 93 wrongly debited as ₹ 39)	Dr.	13,200	13,200
(ii)	Depreciation A/c To Suspense A/c (Being the rectification of omission of posting to depreciation a/c)	Dr.	7,500	7,500
(iii)	Natraj & Sons A/c To Suspense A/c (Being the rectification of discount allowed of ₹ 45 credited as ₹ 54)	Dr.	900	900
(iv)	Sales Returns A/c To Suspense A/c (Being the rectification of undercasting of the sales returns book)	Dr.	1,000	1,000

Illustration 4: Write out the journal entries to rectify the following errors using suspense account:

(*a*) Goods of the value of ₹ 100 returned by Mr. Sharma were entered in the Sales Day Book and posted therefrom to the credit of his account.

(*b*) An amount of ₹ 150 entered in the Sales Returns Book has been posted to the Debit of Mr. Phillip, who returned the goods.

(*c*) A sale of ₹ 200 made to Mr. Gupta was correctly entered in the Sales Day Book but wrongly posted to the debit of Mr. Gupta's account for ₹ 20.

Solution:

Sl. No.	Particulars	LF	Dr. Amount (₹)	Cr. Amount (₹)
(*a*)	Sales A/c Sales Returns A/c To Suspense A/c (Being the goods returned by Mr. Sharma wrongly entered in Sales Day Book)	Dr. Dr.	100 100	 200
(*b*)	Suspense A/c To Mr. Philip (Being the goods returned by Mr. Philip wrongly posted to the debit of his account)	Dr.	300	 300
(*c*)	Mr. Gupta To Suspense A/c (Being the goods sold to Mr. Gupta posted to his account with wrong amount)	Dr.	180	 180

Illustration 5: Give the journal entries necessary to rectify the following errors detected in the books:

(*i*) A payment of ₹ 2,500 for purchase of a typewriter for office use has been debited to purchase account from the cash book.

(*ii*) A credit sale of ₹ 1,270 to Sri Chandra Bose has been posted to the debit of Sri Chandra Guha's account from the sales day book.

(*iii*) A payment of ₹ 960 for whitewashing the office room has been charged to building account.

Solution:

Sl. No.	Particulars	LF	Dr. Amount (₹)	Cr. Amount (₹)
1.	Typewriter A/c To Purchase A/c (Being the payment of ₹ 250 for purchase of typewriter debited to purchase A/c now rectified)	Dr.	2,500	 2,500
2	Sri Chandra Bose To Sri Chandra Guha (Being the wrong posting of credit sale to the debit of Sri Chandra Guha now rectified)	Dr.	1,270	 1,270
3.	Whitewashing charges A/c To Building A/c (Being the whitewashing charges wrongly debited to building A/c, now rectified)	Dr.	940	 940

Illustration 6: Give the correct journal entries for the following:

(*a*) Cost of repairing one machine, *i.e.*, ₹ 100 has been charged to machinery account.

(*b*) ₹ 50 paid to S. Roy in settlement of his account has been posted to the debit of purchase account.

(*c*) Goods sold on credit of ₹ 200 to B. Bose have been posted to the debit of general charges account.

(*d*) ₹ 250 received from B.K. Ghosh has been credited to account of K.B. Ghosh.

(*e*) Wages account includes ₹ 1,500 being wages paid to workmen engaged in construction work of the firm's new buildings.

Solution:

Sl. No.	Particulars	LF	Dr. Amount (₹)	Cr. Amount (₹)
(*a*)	Repairs A/c Dr. To Machinery A/c (Being the amount for repairs wrongly charged to machinery A/c now rectified)		100	100
(*b*)	S. Roy Dr. To Purchase A/c (Being the payment to S. Roy wrongly debited to purchases A/c, rectified)		50	50
(*c*)	B. Bose Dr. To General Charges A/c (Being the credit sale to B. Bose wrongly debited to general charges, now rectified)		200	200
(*d*)	K.B. Ghosh Dr. To B.K. Ghosh (Being ₹ 250 received from B.K. Ghosh wrongly credited to K.B. Ghosh, now rectified)		250	250
(*e*)	Building A/c Dr. To Wages A/c (Being the payment of wages for construction building debited to wages A/c, now rectified)		1,500	1,500

Illustration 7: Give the correct journal entries with respect to the under mentioned transactions in the books of a trader:

(*i*) The discount a/c was credited by ₹ 175, the amount representing the total of the discount column on debit side of the cash book.

(*ii*) The sales day book was undercast by ₹ 1,100.

(*iii*) The sales proceeds of old furniture amounting to ₹ 1,500 were credited to the sales account.

(*iv*) Bills receivable of ₹ 350 was posted as ₹ 503 on credit of the acceptor's account.

(*v*) Repairs worth ₹ 750 to motor car account were debited to the motor car A/c.

State how the above errors will effect the agreement of the trial balance.

Solution: **Journal**

Sl. No.	Particulars	LF	Dr. Amount (₹)	Cr. Amount (₹)
1.	Discount A/c Dr. To Suspense A/c (Being the total of discount on the debit side of cash book wrongly credited to discount A/c, now rectified)		350	350

Sl. No.	Particulars	LF	Dr. Amount (₹)	Cr. Amount (₹)
2.	Suspense A/c To Sales A/c (Being the undercasting of sales book, now rectified)	Dr.	1,100	1,100
3.	Sales A/c To Furniture A/c (Being the sale proceeds of old furniture wrongly credited to sales A/c, now rectified)	Dr.	1,500	1,500
4.	Acceptors A/c To Suspenses A/c (Being a bill receivable of ₹ 350 wrongly posted as 503 to the credit of acceptor's A/c now rectified)	Dr.	153	153
5.	Repairs A/c To Motor Car A/c (Being the repair of car debited to motor car A/c, now rectified)	Dr.	750	750

Suspense A/c

	(₹)		(₹)
To Sales A/c	1,100	By Balance b/d	597
		By Discount	350
		By Acceptors	153
	1,100		1,100

Note: The total of debit side of trial balance exceeds total of credit side by ₹ 597.

Illustration 8: Rectify the following errors:

1. Wages paid to the workers (₹ 250) for repairing the building have been debited to wages a/c.
2. A sum of ₹ 65 spent for repairing office furniture has been debited to furniture a/c.
3. Purchase of typewriter for ₹ 800 has been passed through the day book.
4. Rupees 75 paid as the examination fees of the proprietor's son has been posted to general expenses a/c.
5. Stock of goods valued at ₹ 950 donated to ND fund has been posted to general expenses a/c.
6. Rupees 5,400 received from M. Mehta were posted to the debit side of his account.
7. Rupees 1,000 being purchases return were posted to the purchase a/c.
8. Discount of ₹ 2,000 received was posted to the debit of discount a/c.
9. Rupees 3,740 paid for repairs to motor car were debited to motor car a/c as ₹ 1,740.

Solution: **Journal**

Sl. No.	Particulars	LF	Dr. Amount (₹)	Cr. Amount (₹)
1.	Repairs A/c To Wages A/c (Being the amount of wages paid for repairs wrongly debited to wages A/c, now rectified)	Dr.	250	250
2.	Repairs A/c To Furniture A/c (Being the sum spent for repairs of office furniture wrongly debited to furniture A/c, now rectified)	Dr.	65	65

Sl. No.	Particulars	LF	Dr. Amount (₹)	Cr. Amount (₹)
3.	Typewriter A/c Dr. To Purchase A/c (Being the purchase of typewriter wrongly passed through day book, now rectified)		800	 800
4.	Drawing A/c Dr. To General Expense A/c (Being the payment of examination fees of the proprietor's son wrongly debited to general expenses, now rectified)		75	 75
5.	Donations A/c Dr. To General Expenses A/c (Being the stock of goods donated to ND Funds wrongly debited to general expenses, now rectified)		950	 950
6.	Suspense A/c Dr. To M. Mehta A/c (Being the receipt of ₹ 5,400 from M. Mehta wrongly debited to his account, now rectified)		10,800	 10,800
7.	Suspense A/c Dr. To Purchase Return A/c To Purchase A/c (Being the amount of purchase returns wrongly debited to purchase now rectified)		2,000	 1,000 1,000
8.	Suspense A/c Dr. To Discount A/c (Being the discount of ₹ 2,000 was debited to discount A/c, now rectified)		4,000	 4,000
9.	Repairs A/c Dr. To Motor Car A/c To Suspense A/c (Being the payment of ₹ 3,740 for repairs to motor car wrongly debited to motor car as ₹ 1,740, now rectified)		3,740	 1,740 2,000

Illustration 9: The trial balance of M/s Ltd., as on March 31, 2012 did not balance. The difference amount of ₹ 76 was transferred to the credit of suspense account, and the accountant proceeded with the preparation of final accounts. After completion of final accounts, the following errors were discovered:

(*a*) Total of sales figure was taken as ₹ 58,726 instead of ₹ 58,762.

(*b*) A discount of ₹ 52 allowed to Mr. X was not recorded in the discount allowed account.

(*c*) The total of purchase returns book was undercast by ₹ 43.

(*d*) Sale of old furniture for ₹ 130 was wrongly entered in machinery a/c.

(*e*) A credit purchase for ₹ 49 made from Mr. Y was recorded in purchase book, but was omitted in Y's account.

(*f*) Rupees 320 received from P was posted to the credit of Mr. R.

(*g*) A credit sale made to Mr. S for ₹ 250 was recorded twice in his account.

(*h*) Depreciation on plant and machinery was wrongly recorded as ₹ 750 instead of ₹ 950.

(*i*) Rupees 50 of wages paid on March 30, 2012, are not debited to wages account.

Give Journal entries to rectify the above errors, and prepare suspense account.

Solution: **Rectification of Errors**

Sl. No.	Particulars	LF	Dr. Amount (₹)	Cr. Amount (₹)
(a)	Suspense A/c To Sales A/c (Being the sales figure undercast by ₹ 36)	Dr.	36	36
(b)	Discount A/c To Suspense A/c (Being the discount allowed not recorded earlier)	Dr.	52	52
(c)	Suspense A/c To Purchase Return A/c (Being the total purchase returns undercast by ₹ 43)	Dr.	43	43
(d)	Machinery A/c To Furniture A/c (Being the sale of furniture wrongly credited to machinery a/c earlier)	Dr.	130	130
(e)	Suspense A/c To Y's A/c (or Creditor A/c) (Being the credit purchase made from Y not recorded in his account)	Dr.	49	49
(f)	R A/c To P A/c (Being the entry to rectify the wrong credit given to R instead of P)	Dr.	320	320
(g)	Suspense A/c To S A/c (Being the entry to rectify the error of debiting S twice)	Dr.	250	250
(h)	Depreciation To Suspense A/c Being the entry to record depreciation figure correctly)	Dr.	200	200
(i)	Wages A/c To Suspense A/c (Being the entry to record the wages, which was not recorded earlier)	Dr.	50	50

Suspense A/c

	(₹)		(₹)
To Sales A/c	36	By Balance b/d	76
To Purchase return	43	By Discount allowed A/c	52
To Y's A/c	49	By Depreciation A/c	200
To S's A/c	250	By Wages A/c	50
Total	378		378

Illustration 10: You are presented with a trial balance showing a difference which has been carried to suspense account, and the following errors are revealed:

(*a*) Rupees 850 paid in cash for a typewriter was charged to office expenses account.

(*b*) A cash sale of ₹ 2,500 to Ram correctly entered in the cash book, was posted to the credit of Ram's account in the sale ledger.

(*c*) Goods amounting to ₹ 400 returned by Mohan were entered in the sales book and posted there from to the credit of Mohan's account.

(*d*) Bills receivable from Ravi for ₹ 1,500 posted to the credit of bills payable account and credited to Ravi's account.

(*e*) Goods amounting to ₹ 5,000 sold to Arun were correctly entered in the Sales book but posted to Arun's account for ₹ 9,000.

(*f*) Sales returns book was overcast by ₹ 50.

Journalise the necessary corrections and prepare the suspense account.

Solution: **Journal Entries**

Sl. No.	Particulars	LF	Dr. Amount (₹)	Cr. Amount (₹)
(*a*)	Office Equipment A/c To Office Expenses A/c (Purchase of a typewriter wrongly charged to office expenses, now rectified)	Dr.	850	850
(*b*)	Ram A/c To Sales A/c (Cash sale wrongly credited to customer's A/c, now rectified)	Dr.	2,500	2,500
(*c*)	Sales A/c Sales Return A/c To Suspense A/c (Goods returned by Mohan wrongly entered in the sales day book)	Dr. Dr.	400 400	800
(*d*)	Bill Payable A/c Bills Receivable A/c To Suspense A/c (Bills receivable from Ravi credited to bills payable A/c through correctly credited to Ravi, now rectified)	Dr. Dr.	1,500 1,500	3,000
(*e*)	Suspense A/c To Arun's A/c (Goods sold to Arun ₹ 5,000 wrongly posted to his account as ₹ 9,000, now rectified)	Dr.	4,000	4,000
(*f*)	Suspense A/c To Sales Return A/c (Error caused by overcasting the sales return book, now rectified)	Dr.	50	50

Suspense Account

Particulars	(₹)	Particulars	(₹)
To Sales return A/c	50	By difference in Trial Balance (*Balancing figure*)	250
To Arun A/c	4,000	Sales A/c	400
		Sales return A/c	400
		Bills payable A/c	1,500
		Bills Receivable A/c	1,500
Total	4,050		4,050

Illustration 11: Mr. Rajan closes his books on March 31 every year. In August 2012, he found that his books for the year 2011–12 contained some errors inspite of an agreed trial balance. The errors were:

(*a*) ₹ 1,600 paid for purchase of office furniture was posted to the purchase account.

(*b*) The sales book was overcast by ₹ 500.

(*c*) ₹ 550 paid for freight on machinery was debited to freight account for ₹ 1,050.

(*d*) Opening stock was overstated by ₹ 6,000 by a wrong casting in the inventory.

(*e*) An amount of ₹ 1,400 was received in full settlement from a customer after he was allowed a discount of ₹ 140 but while writing the books the amount received was entered in the discount column and the discount allowed was entered in the amount column.

(*f*) A Cheque of ₹ 14,660 received from Mr. Sunil, after allowing him discount of ₹ 140 was endorsed to Mr. Anil in full settlement for ₹ 15,000. The cheque was finally dishonoured but no entries for dishonour were passed in the books.

Give journal entries to rectify the above errors using the P&L adjustment account, where necessary.

Solution: **Journal Entries**

Sl. No.	Particulars	LF	Dr. Amount (₹)	Cr. Amount (₹)
(*a*)	Office furniture A/c	Dr.	1,600	
	To P&L Adjustment A/c			1,600
(*b*)	P&L Adjustment A/c	Dr.	500	
	To Suspense A/c			500
(*c*)	Machinery A/c	Dr.	550	
	Suspense A/c	Dr.	500	
	To P&L Adjustment A/c			1,050
(*d*)	P&L Adjustment A/c	Dr.	6,000	
	To Opening Stock			6,000
(*e*)	Cash A/c	Dr.	1,260	
	To P&L Adjustment			1,260
(*f*)	Sunil's A/c	Dr.	14,800	
	P&L Adjustment A/c		200	
	To Anil's A/c			15,000

The P&L adjustment a/c is used because the profits for 2011–12 are already arrived at in the balance sheet. Adjustment a/c can be adjusted against the balance in the P&L A/c.

Illustration 12: The account of a business firm prepared the trial balance and the total of debits equalled the total of credits. However, some of the errors subsequently discovered were as follows:

(*i*) The sales day book was overcast by ₹ 2,500.

(*ii*) Machinery maintenance expenditure of ₹ 17,500 had been debited to machinery a/c.

(*iii*) A Purchase return of ₹ 2,000 had been posted to the credit of the supplier account.

(*iv*) An amount of ₹ 10,000 received from a customer had been omitted to be posted to the customer's account.

(*v*) The purchases day book was undercast by ₹ 500.

After correcting the above errors the suspense account would have a balance of:

(*a*) ₹ 2,050 (Debit).

(*b*) ₹ 3,000 (Credit).

(*c*) Nil.

(*d*) ₹ 3,000 (Debit).

(*e*) None of the above.

Solution:

Suspense A/c

	(₹)		(₹)
To Customer A/c	10,000	By Sales A/c	2,500
		By Supplier A/c	4,000
		By Purchase A/c	500
		By Balance c/d	3,000
Total	10,000		10,000

Illustration 13: This trial balance of M/s P.M. Kashyap as on 31st March, 2012 did not tally. The difference of ₹ 15,100 was transferred to the credit of suspense a/c. After the completion of final accounts, the following errors were discovered.

(*a*) Total of Sales figure was taken as ₹ 56,000 instead of ₹ 65,000.

(*b*) The total of purchases Returns book was under cast by ₹ 100.

(*c*) Sale of old furniture for ₹ 900 was wrongly entered in machinery a/c.

(*d*) A credit purchase of ₹ 5,000 made from Mr. Y was recorded in purchases book but was not posted in Y's account.

(*e*) ₹ 1,000 received from A was posted to the credit of B.

(*f*) A credit sale of ₹ 2,000/- made to Mr. S was recorded twice in his account.

(*g*) Wages amounting to ₹ 1,000 were paid on 20th March, 2012. They were recorded in Cash Book but were not recorded in the wages a/c.

Give journal entries to record the above transactions and prepare the suspense a/c.

Solution:

Sl. No.	Particulars	LF	Dr. Amount (₹)	Cr. Amount (₹)
(*a*)	Suspense A/c To Sales A/c (Being the sales figure undercast by ₹ 9,000)	Dr.	9,000	9,000
(*b*)	Suspense A/c To Purchase Returns A/c (Being the total of purchases returns under cast by ₹ 100)	Dr.	100	100
(*c*)	Machinery A/c To Furniture (Being the sale of old furniture wrongly entered in Machinery A/c)	Dr.	900	900
(*d*)	Suspense A/c To Y (Being the credit purchase of ₹ 5,000 made from Y not recorded in his account earlier)	Dr.	5,000	5,000
(*e*)	B To A (Being the wrong credit given to B now rectified)	Dr.	1,000	1,000
(*f*)	Suspense A/c To S (Being the entry for rectifying the error of debiting S twice)	Dr.	2,000	2,000
(*g*)	Wages A/c To Suspense A/c (Being the amount of wages not recorded earlier)	Dr.	1,000	1,000

Suspense A/c

	(₹)		(₹)
To Sales A/c	9,000	By Balance b/d	15,100
To Purchase returns A/c	100	By Wages A/c	1,000
To Y	5,000		
To S	2,000		
Total	16,100		16,100

THEORY QUESTIONS

1. Explain the errors which affect the agreement of trial balance.
2. Explain the errors which are not disclosed despite the agreement of a trial balance.

EXERCISES AND PROBLEMS

1. Rectify the following errors:
   (*a*) A purchase of ₹ 200 from Ram was omitted to be entered in the Purchase book
   (*b*) A credit sale of ₹ 527 to John was recorded as ₹ 725.
   (*c*) A purchase of office furniture for ₹ 1,000 from Salwan Furniture was entered through Purchase Book.
   (*a*) Rent paid to landlord ₹ 600 was debited to his personal account.
   (*b*) Purchases Book was undercast by ₹ 200.
2. Give Journal Entries to rectify the following errors:
   (*i*) An account of ₹ 4,000 spent for the extension of machinery has been debited to wages A/c.
   (*ii*) ₹ 150 paid as cartage for the newly purchased furniture posted to cartage A/c.
   (*iii*) A builder's bill for ₹ 6,000 for erection of a small cycle shed was debited to repairs A/c.
   (*iv*) A cheque of ₹ 2,000 received from Ashok was dishonoured and had been posted to the debit side of 'Allowance A/c'.
   (*v*) ₹ 1,000 paid for the newly purchased 'cooler' posted to 'purchase account'.
3. Make the necessary correcting entries and show the Suspense Account.
   (*i*) The Purchases Book was undercast by ₹ 1,000.
   (*ii*) The Sales Book was overcast by ₹ 50.
   (*iii*) ₹ 20 received from Kiran were posted to the debit of his A/c.
   (*iv*) The total of the credit of Ajay's A/c has been over added by ₹ 500.
   (*v*) A discount of ₹ 18 allowed to a customer has been credited to his account as ₹ 81.
   (*vi*) Goods for ₹ 1,000 returned to Sharma, though entered in the Return Book has been posted to his account.
4. There was a difference of ₹ 725 in a Trial Balance. It has been transferred to credit side of suspense A/c. Later on following errors were discovered. Pass the rectifying entries and prepare suspense A/c.:
   (*a*) An amount of ₹ 375 has been posted in the debit side of commission account instead of ₹ 275.
   (*b*) Goods of ₹ 200 purchased from Deepak have been posted to his account as ₹ 250.

(*c*) Total of Sales Returns Book was overcast by ₹ 475.

(*d*) A credit amount of ₹ 50 was posted as ₹ 150 to the debit side of a personal account.

(*e*) Goods of ₹ 300 were sold to Nitin, but it was recorded in Purchase Book.

5. Pass rectification entries for the following transaction:

(*i*) A bill of exchange (received from Preeti) for ₹ 3,000 had been returned by the bank with whom, it had been discounted, as dishonoured and had been credited to Bank A/c and debited to Bill Receivable A/c.

(*ii*) A purchase of goods from Anku amounting to ₹ 300 has been wrongly passed through the Sales Book.

(*iii*) On 31st Dec. 2012 goods of the value of ₹ 200 were returned by Gopi Chand and were taken into stock on the same date, but no entry was passed in the books.

(*iv*) An amount of ₹ 2,000 due from Deepak, which has been written off as a Bad debt in a previous year, was unexpectedly recovered and has been posted to the personal account of Deepak.

(*v*) A cheque for ₹ 500 received from Manish was dishonoured and had been posted to the debit side of Sales Returns Account.

(*vi*) A Bill Receivable of ₹ 400 received from Ram was passed through the Bills Payable Book.

(*vii*) ₹ 480 paid for wages to workmen for making showcases had been charged to wages A/c.

(*viii*) ₹ 5,000 paid for the purchase of a Motor cycle for the proprietor had been charged to miscellaneous expenses A/c.

(*ix*) X was paid cash ₹ 5,600 but Y was debited by ₹ 5,000.

(*x*) Purchases Returns Book was carried forward as ₹ 132 instead of 123.

6. The books of a private firm have been posted upto 31st December, 2012, how would you correct the following errors which were subsequently found therein:

(*i*) An amount of ₹ 1,000 received from Motilal on 1st January, 2013 had been entered in the Cash Book as having been received on 31st December, 2012.

(*ii*) ₹ 750 paid for the purchase of a consumable durable for one of the partners has been charged to General Expenses A/c.

(*iii*) An addition in the returns inward book has been cast ₹ 100 short.

(*iv*) A cheque of ₹ 200 drawn for petty cash Account in the Ledger.

(*v*) ₹ 150 appearing in the discount column on the credit side of the cash book, had not been posted to a personal account.

Journalise the necessary corrections.

7. The book-keeper of a firm, having been unable to agree the Trial balance, raised a Suspense Account in which he entered the amount by which it was out of balance. The following errors were discovered:

(*a*) Goods bought from a supplier amounting to ₹ 77 had been noted to the credit of his account as ₹ 770.

(*b*) A dishonoured Bill of Exchange receivable for ₹ 800 returned to the firm's bank had been credited to the Bank A/c and debited to Bills Receivable Account. A cheque was received later from the customer for ₹ 800 and duly paid.

(*c*) An item of ₹ 80 entered in the Sales Return Book had been posted to the debit of the customer who returned the goods.

(*d*) An amount of ₹ 800 owing by a customer had been duly entered in his account, but not posted to the Discount Account.

(*e*) Bills Receivable from W ₹ 1,600 posted to the credit of Bills Payable Account and credited to W.

8. The accountant of a firm finds that the trial balance as on 31st December, 2012 is out by an excess debit of ₹ 566. He placed the amount in the Suspense Account. In the first week of January, 2013, he discovered the following errors. Pass journal entries necessary to rectify these errors and show the Suspense Account as it would appear at the end of the week. Do you have any comment to make?

(*a*) Cash paid to Amar Nath, ₹ 150, was posted on the credit of Amar Singh's Account as ₹ 114.

(*b*) Discount allowed by Jones ₹ 10, was not entered in the Cash book, but Jones stands debited correctly.

(*c*) No entry was made for goods worth ₹ 80 taken away by proprietor for personal use.

(*d*) ₹ 1,000 received from Jhaveri Bros for interest on loan advanced to them were recorded in the cash book. But the entry was not posted in the ledger.

(*e*) The total of Returns Outward Book was short by ₹ 200.

(**Hint:** At the end of the week, the Suspense Account will indicate a debit balance of ₹ 380. It means that there are still some errors left undetected, due to which trial balance will not tally).

9

PREPARATION OF FINANCIAL STATEMENTS: PROFIT AND LOSS ACCOUNT AND BALANCE SHEET

LEARNING OBJECTIVES

After reading this chapter, you should be able to:

- *Explain* the nature of adjustment entries.
- *Discuss* the accounting treatment of different adjustment entries.
- *Discuss* the preparation of Trading A/c, Profit and Loss A/c.
- *Understand concept of* a balance sheet.
- *Identify* different items of balance sheet.
- *List* the limitations of balance sheet.
- *Illustrate* the preparation of financial statements.

Preparation of Financial Statements: Profit and Loss Account and Balance Sheet

Trial Balance is first step towards preparation of financial statements—namely Trading and Profit and Loss Account and Balance Sheet. Trading and Profit and Loss Account are prepared in order to determine the income earned or loss incurred during the accounting period. Balance Sheet indicates the financial position of the enterprise. However, before preparing trading account, profit and loss account and balance sheet, certain adjustment entries are required.

Adjustment Entries

As stated earlier, financial accounting uses accrual basis of accounting which is supported by Generally Accepted Accounting Principles (GAAP). Under accrual basis of accounting:

1. Revenue are recognised when earned, without regard to the timing of cash receipts.
2. Expenses are recognised either (*a*) in the period in which related revenues are recognised or (*b*) when incurred, without regard to the timing of cash disbursements.

Another basis of accounting, which is not supported by GAAP is the cash basis. Unlike the accrual basis, the cash basis of accounting links revenues and expenses of an accounting period to the timing of cash flows. In cash basis accounting, revenue is recognised in the period in which cash is received and expenses is recognised at the time cash is paid. The cash basis of accounting is objective and relatively easy to use and is employed by individuals, individual professionals such as lawyers, accountants, teachers, small businesses. However, it is opposed to accrual basis of accounting as a basis of preparing financial statements of a business enterprise.

When the accrual basis of accounting is used, adjusting entries are required at the end of the period to record any previously unrecognised changes in assets, liabilities, revenues, or expenses. Adjusting entries are made to modify certain account balances at the end of the accounting period so that they will reflect fairly the situation as of the end of the period. Adjusting entries can be referred to as internal transactions, distinct from external transactions which are between a business entity and the parties external to the entity. It should be noted that the external (exchange) transactions are already found recorded in the accounting records and different ledger accounts.

The following are a few examples of situations where adjusting entries are needed and the accountant has to process these additional information before preparing the financial statements on the basis of trial balance:

(*a*) The accountant may know (or be instructed by the Accounts Manager) that the depreciation on building is to be charged at the rate of 10%.

(*b*) The accountant would ascertain that the salary of some workers for January in a particular year is unpaid at the end of the month.

(*c*) The accountant is informed by the store-keeper that the goods lying unsold in the store (representing closing stock) is worth ₹ 17 lakhs at cost.

(*d*) The accountant knows or is informed that the loan of ₹ 20,00,000 was taken at an interest of 12% per annum. He also knows that the interest accrued for January is unpaid as on January 31, since there is no ledger account for any interest paid.

(*e*) The accountant knows that the insurance premium was paid for the whole year whereas the accounts are being prepared for one month.

(*f*) The accountant is informed that ₹ 50,000 may not be collected from PQR Company owing to some technical dispute.

Thus, if profit and loss account is to report a realistic net profit (or net loss) based on accrual accounting, all revenues earned during the period and all expenses incurred must be shown. Therefore, revenues and expenses must be properly matched or aligned for the reporting period in question, popularly known as matching concept in the accounting literature.

Generally, four general types of adjustment (adjusting entries) are needed at the end of the accounting period prior to the preparation of financial statements:

1. Reflecting unrecorded revenue earned during the accounting period.
2. Reflecting unrecorded expenses incurred during the accounting period.
3. Reflecting or aligning recorded expenses with the appropriate accounting periods *i.e.*, considering expenditures benefiting more than one accounting period.
4. Reflecting or aligning recorded revenue with the appropriate accounting periods *i.e.*, considering revenues received in advance.

Adjustment in the first two categories—unrecorded revenues and unrecorded expenses—are referred to as accruals such as salaries and wages incurred but not paid, interest earned but not received. Adjustments in the last two categories—reflecting recorded costs and revenues with the appropriate periods—are referred to as deferrals such as prepaid expenses, unearned revenue and depreciation.

Adjusting Entries

Adjusting entries have following features:

1. Every adjusting entry affects both the trading and profit and loss account and the balance sheet.
2. Adjusting entries do not directly affect the cash account.
3. They are generally recorded at the end of the accounting period.
4. A profit and loss account balance (revenue or expense) is changed.
5. A balance sheet account balance (asset or liability) is changed.

TYPES OF ADJUSTMENT ENTRIES

The different items or situations which are subject to adjusting entries before preparing financial statements are explained below:

Closing Inventory

Under the periodic verification method, the closing inventory of every item is arrived at by physically counting the inventory available and assigning a value to the same. In concerns adopting the periodic verification method, the value of closing inventory will be brought into the books of accounts through the following journal entry:

Closing inventory A/c Dr.

To Trading A/c

While the closing inventory appears on the credit side of the trading account to reduce the cost of goods sold, it also appears as an asset in the Balance Sheet.

Outstanding or Accrued Expense

The nominal accounts record the actual expense paid during the accounting period. However, prior to the preparation of the financial statements, it must be ensured that all expenses which have fallen due to be paid but which have not been paid during the accounting period are also brought into the books to help in the proper matching of revenues and expenses. For example, ABC Trading Company had the practice of paying the salaries of the employees on 4th of the subsequent month. During the financial year ending 31st March, 2012 the salaries account shows a debit balance of ₹ 55,000. The salaries of ₹ 6,000 pertaining to March 2012 were paid on 4th April, 2012. While preparing the financial statements for the year ending 31st March, 2012, the salaries of ₹ 6,000 of March must also be included. This is done with the following adjusting journal entry:

Salaries A/c Dr. 6,000

To Outstanding Salaries A/c 6,000

The above journal entry increase the salaries to the correct amount of ₹ 61,000 and the outstanding salaries of ₹ 6,000 will be shown as a liability in the Balance Sheet.

The adjusting journal entry to record any outstanding accrued expense is

Expense A/c Dr.

To Outstanding Expense A/c

While the amount of expense taken from the Trial Balance will be increased by the amount outstanding and shown in the trading and Profit and Loss Account, the actual amount outstanding will be shown as a liability in the Balance Sheet.

In the subsequent accounting period, the outstanding expense liability will be transferred to the expense or nominal account and will be setoff by the entry of actual payments when it is made.

Prepaid Expense

Certain expenses paid may relate to more than one accounting period. In such cases, it is necessary to identify that portion of the expenditure for which the benefit is yet to be received by the concern and treat that part of the expenditure as prepaid.

ABC Trading Company took an insurance cover for all assets against fire on 1st October, 2013 and paid the annual premium of ₹ 2,400 on the same day. Since the benefit of the entire expenditure will expire only on 30th September, 2014 it is necessary to recognise this aspect while preparing the financial statements as on 31st March, 2014.

The amount of expense prepaid on 1st October, 2013 = (1/2 × 2,400 = ₹ 1,200)

The adjusting entry to record the prepaid insurance is

Prepaid Insurance A/c Dr. 1,200

To Insurance A/c 1,200

This ensures that the insurance expense is reported at the correct figure of ₹ 1,200 in the profit and loss account and the prepaid amount is shown as an asset in the balance sheet.

The journal entry to record any prepaid expense is,

Prepaid Expense A/c Dr.

To Expense A/c

In the subsequent accounting period, the balance in the prepaid expense account will be transferred back to the expense account.

Outstanding or Accrued Income

An income appearing in the ledger account may not represent the income that must have been received during the year. If a portion of an income has not yet been received or outstanding as at the end of the accounting period then the outstanding amount must be brought into books.

ABC Trading Company would have received the interest of ₹ 3,500 [50,000 × (14/100) × 1/2] during the accounting period ending 31st March 2013, the interest of ₹ 3,500 for the next six months will be received only in the subsequent accounting period. However, while preparing the financial statements, the total interest revenue to be recognise is the amount of ₹ 3,500 actually received plus the interest of ₹ 1,750 pertaining to the period 1st January, 2013 to 31st March, 2013.

The following adjusting entry will bring into books the amount of outstanding interest:

Outstanding Interest A/c Dr. 1,750

To Interest Received A/c 1,750

While the interest received will be increased to ₹ 5,250 and shown in the profit and loss account, the outstanding interest account will be listed as an asset in the Balance Sheet.

In the subsequent accounting period, the amount in the outstanding interest A/c will be transferred to interest received A/c and the actual receipt of the interest will offset the former transfer entry.

To record any outstanding income in the books of accounts, the journal entry is:

Outstanding Income A/c Dr.

To Income A/c

Income Received in Advance

While preparing the financial statements, adjustments may be necessary in respect of any income received in advance.

Law Publications has received subscriptions amounting to ₹ 50,000 during the financial year ending 31st December, 2012, out of this ₹ 2,500 represent subscriptions relating to the next financial year.

The entry to adjust for the income received in advance will be,

Subscriptions A/c Dr. 2,500

To Subscriptions received in Advance 2,500

With the posting of the above journal entry, the subscriptions account will be shown in the profit and loss account at the credit figure of ₹ 47,500 and in the balance sheet, the subscriptions received in advance as liability. Any income received in advance as a liability as benefits are yet to be conferred to the person from whom the amount has been received. The journal entry to record the adjustment of any income received in advance is

Income A/c Dr.

To Income Received in Advance A/c

Depreciation

Depreciation is the acquisition cost of an asset (less the expected salvage value) spread over the economic life of that asset. The purpose of charging depreciation over the economic life of the asset is to match the cost of the asset over the period for which revenue is earned by using the asset.

There are two methods of recording depreciation. Under the first method, the asset account is directly credited for the depreciation and the written down value is readily ascertained. The journal entry to record depreciation under the method is

Depreciation A/c Dr.

To Asset A/c

Under the second method, the depreciation charged is credited to a depreciation provision a/c and the written down value of the asset is shown in the balance sheet by deducting the provision from the original cost of the asset. The journal entry recorded under this method is

Depreciation A/c Dr

To Depreciation Provision A/c

Balance in Depreciation is transferred to Profit and Loss A/c. The accounting entry is as under:

Profit and Loss A/c Dr.

To Depreciation A/c

Depreciation provision account, if opened, will be shown by way of deduction from the relevant asset a/c in the balance sheet.

PROVISION FOR BAD DEBTS, CASH DISCOUNTS PAYABLE AND CASH DISCOUNTS RECEIVABLE

Bad Debts

The sales revenue recorded in the books of accounts of an organisation represent the amount realised or to be realised from the sale of goods. When goods are sold on credit it may sometimes happen that even though customers bought them with every intention of paying for them, due to certain subsequent change in circumstances, they may not be able to fulfil their obligations. For instance, if a customer, subsequent to the date of credit sales, is adjusted an insolvent and his estate cannot pay anything towards satisfaction of the amount due from him, then logically, the entry passed at the time of sale should be removed by reversing it, as the situation is similar to the sale not having taken place. In practice, however, instead of reversing the previous entry, the amount which cannot be recovered is considered as a loss called 'Bad debts'.

Example: ABC Ltd., had debtors outstanding to the extent of ₹ 7,50,000/- as on 31st March, 2013 Mr. X, who owed ₹ 15,000/- to the company has been adjudged insolvent and his estate is unable to pay anything.

The journal entry to record the above loss would be:

Bad debts A/c Dr. 15,000/-

To X A/c Cr. 15,000/-

Note that the sales account remains unchanged. However, in the income statement, while sales revenue will appear at the full figure, the bad debts will appear as a loss and thus the reduction in the amount realised will be accounted for. The Accounts Receivable account will also appear in the Balance Sheet at the realisable value of ₹ 7,35,000.

The journal entry for recording bad debts is:

Bad Debts A/c Dr.

To Accounts Receivable A/c

Provision for Bad and Doubtful Debts

We have already seen that according to the realisation concept, the amount to be recognised as revenue is the amount that is reasonably certain to be realised. When there is a possibility that all the sales revenue may not be realised in the future due to occurrence of bad debts, the sales revenue, then, in the income statement should reflect this position. However, in practice, the sales revenue is shown as the gross figure and any possible loss due to bad debts is shown as an expense.

When bad debts are expected to occur in the future, (*a*) the exact amount of loss may not be known and (*b*) a particular debtor's account cannot be identified to write off the expected loss or even if the debtor's account can be identified, a reduction in claim can be given effect to only when it becomes certain. To circumvent these problems, usually, a provision is made for the expected bad debts loss out of profits of the current year. This reduces the profit and hence the income statement conforms to the realisation principle and also prevents an estimated portion of profits from being distributed to the proprietors. For creating the provision for bad and doubtful debts, the journal entry is,

Profit and Loss A/c Dr.

To Provision for Bad Debts A/c.

Example: The Accounts Receivable of PQR Ltd. was ₹ 1,50,000/- as on 31st March, 2012. It was estimated that ₹ 5,000/- of the amount due may turn out to be uncollectable during the forthcoming year.

For creation of the provision the journal entry will be,

Profit and Loss A/c Dr. 5,000/-

To Provision for Bad Debts A/c 5,000/-

While the amount of the possible loss will appear on the debit side of the profit and loss account, the provision created, though a liability will be shown as a deduction from Accounts Receivable on the asset side of balance sheet. This would ensure that the current asset is shown at the realizable value.

Balance Sheet of PQR Ltd., as on 31.03.2012

Liabilities	Assets	(₹)	(₹)
	Accounts Receivable	1,50,000	
	Less provision for bad debts	5,000	1,45,000

Estimating Bad and Doubtful Debts:

Any one of the following methods may be used to estimate the amount of possible bad debts:

1. Bad debts may be estimated as a percentage of total sales during the year. This method can be used only when there are no cash sales or such sales are negligible.

2. Bad debts may be estimated as a percentage of credit sales.
3. Estimate bad debts as a percentage of receivable outstanding at the end of the accounting period.

The percentage used will be based on the judgement of the management and the past experience with regard to bad debts. Another logical way to estimate bad debts would be to draw up an aging schedule for the outstanding debtors and apply different percentages for amounts outstanding for various lengths of time.

Treatment of Bad Debts when a Provision for Bad Debts Exists

Let us extend the example of PQR Ltd., to the financial year ending 31st March, 2012.

The following details are available:

Bad Debts during the year ₹ 3,500

Accounts Receivable as on 31.3.2012 ₹ 1,70,000/-

PQR Ltd., would like to maintain the provision at 5% of Sundry Debtors.

The Accounts Receivable of ₹ 1,70,000/- as on 31/3/2012 is after account for the bad debts of ₹ 3,500/-. When bad debts occurred, the following entry would have been passed:

Bad Debts A/c Dr. 3,500/-

To Sundry Debtors A/c 3,500/-

Since provision for bad debts to the extent of ₹ 5,000/- already exists, the actual bad debts of ₹ 3,500/- will be transferred at the end of the year to this provision account and not to the profit and loss account.

The entry for the transfer will be:

Provision for the Bad Debts A/c Dr. ₹ 3,500

To Bad Debts A/c ₹ 3,500

At this point the provision A/c will appear as under:

Provision for Bad Debts A/c

31.03.2012	(₹)	1.4.2011	(₹)
To Bad Debts A/c	3,500.00	By Balance b/d	5,000/-

Since the provision has been utilised to the extent of ₹ 3,500/-, only ₹ 1,500/- is left for setting off any bad debts in the forthcoming year. However, PQR Ltd., wishes to maintain the provision at 5% on debtors. So, the balance required in the provision account as on 31.03.2012 is,

$$1,70,000 \times \frac{5}{100} = ₹\,8,500$$

To bring up the provision to the required balance a further appropriation of ₹ 7,000/- (₹ 8,500/- – ₹ 1,500/-) will have to be made from the profits and loss account. Entry will be,

Profit and Loss A/c Dr. 7,000.00

To Provision for Bad Debts A/c 7,000.00

The provision account after positing this entry will appear as follows:

Dr. **Provision for Bad Debts A/c** Cr.

	(₹)		(₹)
31.03.2012		1.4.2011	
To Bad Debts	3,500.00	By Balance b/d	5,000.00
31.3.2012		31.3.2012	
To Balance c/d	8,500.00	By Profit and Loss A/c	7,000.00
	12,000.00		12,000.00

The balance sheet will again show the Accounts Receivable at their realisable value.

Balance Sheet of PQR Ltd., as on 31.3.2012

Liabilities	Assets	(₹)	(₹)
	Accounts Receivable	1,70,000.00	
	Less: Provision for Bad Debts	8,500.00	1,61,500.00

We will extend the above example to yet another financial year.

The following details are available for the year ending 31.3.2013

Bad Debts during the year 1,000.00

Sundry Debtors as on 31.3.2013 1,10,000

PQR Ltd., would like to maintain the provision for bad debts as 5% of debtors.

As in the previous year, the total bad debts will be transferred to the provision for bad debts.

Provision for Bad Debts A/c Dr. 1,000.00

To Bed Debts A/c. 1,000.00

The provision account after the above transfer will appear as follows:

Dr. Provision for Bads Debts A/c Cr.

	(₹)		(₹)
31.03.2013 To Bad Debts A/c	1,000.00	1.4.2012 By Balance b/d	8,500.00

The provision required on the closing debtors will be,

$(5 \times 100) \times 1,10,000 = ₹\ 5,500/-$

The opening provision of ₹ 8,500/- has been utilised only to the extent of ₹ 1,000/- and therefore, ₹ 7,500/- is the amount available for further appropriation. Since the balance to be carried forward to the next accounting year is only ₹ 5,500/- a sum of ₹ 2,000/- (7,500/- less 5,500/-) can be transferred back to Profit and Loss A/c as excess provision which is not required to be carried forward. So, to retain a balance of ₹ 5,500/- in the provision account, the journal entry will be,

Provision for Bad Debts A/c Dr. 2,000.00

To Profit & Loss A/c 2,000.00

Dr. Provision for Bad Debts A/c Cr.

Date		(₹)	Date		(₹)
31.3.2013	To Bad Debts A/c	1,000/-	1.4.2012	By Balance b/d	8,500/-
31.3.2013	To Profit & Loss A/c	2,000/-			
31.3.2013	To Balance c/d	5,500/-			
		8,500/-			8,500/-

The balance sheet will show the realisable value of sundry debtors.

Balance Sheet of PQR Ltd., as on 31.3.2013

Liabilities	Assets	(₹)	(₹)
	Accounts Receivable	1,10,000	
	Less: Provision for Bad Debts	5,500	1,04,500/-

Recovery for Bad Debts Written Off

Sometimes, an amount written off as bad debts may be subsequently recovered. Any such recovery must be treated as a windfall and transferred to the profit and Loss A/c as a gain.

The journal entries will be,

At the time of receipt of the amount

Bank A/c or Cash A/c Dr.

To Bad Debts Recovered A/c

At the end of the financial year,

Bed Debts Recovered A/c Dr.

To Profit and Loss A/c

Provision for Discounts on Accounts Receivable

The organisations which allow the facility of making payments before the due date and enable their debtors to avail of cash discounts, must take into account the possible amount of discounts that may be allowed on closing debtors in the forthcoming year. This is necessary to show the closing debtors at their realisable value.

The principles for creation and maintenance of the provisions for discounts on debtors are the same as those discussed in the section on provision for bad debts. The only additional point to be noted is that discounts will be estimated on debts considered goods *i.e.*, closing sundry debtors minus provision for bad debts.

The illustration given clearly explains the methods of maintaining a provision for discounts on debtors. The following details are available for M Limited:

Year Ending

	31.3.2011 (₹)	31.3.2012 (₹)	31.3.2013 (₹)
Accounts Receivable	5,00,000	4,50,000	6,00,000
Discounts Allowed		1,000	8,000

While the company maintains 5% provision for bad debts, it would like to maintain 3% provision for discounts beginning from 31.3.2011.

The entries in the provision for discounts on receivable and the relevant extracts from the balance sheets are shown below:

Dr. Provision for Discounts on Accounts Receivable A/c Cr.

	(₹)		(₹)
31.3.2011		31.3.2011	
To Balance c/d	14,250	By Profit & Loss A/c	14,250
	14,250		14,250
31.3.2012		1.4.2011	
To Discount Allowed	1,000	By Balance b/d	14,250
To Profit and Loss A/c	425		
To Balance c/d	12,825		
	14,250		14,250
31.3.2013		1.4.2012	
To Discounts Allowed	8,000	By Balance c/d	12,825
To Balance c/d	17,100	By Profit and Loss A/c	12,275
Total	25,100		25,100

Working Notes:

31.3.2011	(₹)
Accounts Receivable	5,00,000
Less: Provision for bad debts at 5%	25,000
Debts considered goods	4,75,000
Provision for discounts on Accounts Receivable (3/100) × 4,75,000 =	14,250
31.3.2012	
Accounts Receivable	4,50,000
Less: Provision for bad debts at 5%	22,500
Debts considered good	4,27,500
Provision for discount on Accounts Receivable =	
(3/100) × 4,27,500 =	12,825
Opening Balance of Provision	14,250
Less: Discounts allowed during the year	1,000
	13,250

Since provision to be carried forward is only ₹ 12,825 an amount of ₹ 425 would be transferred to Profit and Loss A/c as excess provision.

31.3.2013	(₹)
Accounts Receivable	6,00,000
Less: Provision for Debts at 5%	30,000
Debts considered good	5,70,000
Provision for discounts on Receivable (3/100) × 5,70,000 =	17,100
Opening Balance of Provision	12,825
Less: Discounts allowed	8,000
	4,825

Additional amount to be transferred from
Profit and Loss A/c (17,100 – 4,825) = 12,275

Balance Sheet of M. Ltd. as on 31.3.2011

Assets	(₹)	(₹)
Accounts Receivable	5,00,000.00	
Less: Provision for Bad Debts	25,000.00	
	4,75,000.00	
Less: Provision for Discounts	14,250.00	4,60,750

Balance Sheet of M. Ltd. as on 31.3.2012

Assets	(₹)	(₹)
Accounts Receivable	4,50,000.00	
Less: Provision for Bad Debts	22,500.00	
	4,27,500.00	
Less: Provision for Discounts	12,825.00	4,14,675

Balance Sheet of M. Ltd. as on 31.3.2013

Assets	(₹)	(₹)
Accounts Receivable	6,00,000.00	
Less: Provision for Bad Debts	30,000.00	
	5,70,000.00	
Less: Provision for Discounts	17,100.00	5,52,900

Reserve for discounts on Accounts Payable

Organisations may like to show the sundry creditors in the balance sheet at the net payable value by estimating in advance the amount of cash discounts that may be received at the time of settlement amounts due. This is usually done by creating a reserve for discounts on creditors and then transferring the discounts received to such reserve. Since, income in respect of discounts receivable is recognised in advance, the journal entry for creating of the reserve will be:

Reserve for Discount on Accounts Payable A/c Dr.

To Profit and Loss A/c

The following illustration explains the mechanics of maintaining the reserve for discount on creditors.

The following details are available from the books of R. Limited.

Year Ending

	31.3.2011 (₹)	31.3.2012 (₹)	31.3.2013 (₹)
Accounts Payable	2,20,000.00	3,25,000.00	2,75,000.00
Discounts Received		3,200.00	900.00

R. Limited would like to maintain a reserve for discount on Accounts Payable at 2% beginning from 31.3.2011.

The reserve account and the relevant extracts from the balance sheet are shown below:

Dr. Reserve for Discounts on Accounts Payable A/c Cr.

	(₹)		(₹)
31.3.2011		31.3.2011	
To Profit and Loss A/c	4,400	By Balance c/d	4,400
	4,400		4,400
1.4.2011		31.3.2012	
To Balance b/d	4,400	By Discounts Received A/c	3,200
31.3.2012		31.3.2012	
To Profit and Loss A/c	5,300	By Balance c/d	6,500
	9,700		9,700
1.4.2013		31.3.2013	
To Balance b/d	6,500	By Discounts Received A/c	900
		31.3.2013	
		By Profit and Loss A/c	100
		31.3.2013	
		By Balance c/d	5,500
	6,500		6,500

Working Notes:

	(₹)
31.03.2011	
Accounts Payable	2,20,000
Reserve for discounts on Accounts Payable at 2%	4,400
31.3.2012	
Accounts Payable	3,25,000
Reserve for Discounts at 2%	6,500
Opening Balance of Reserve	4,400
Less: Discounts received	3,200
	1,200
Additional reserve required = 6,500 – 1,200 =	5,300
31.3.2013	
Accounts Payable	2,75,000
Reserve for Discounts at 2%	5,500
Opening Balance of Reserve	6,500
Less: Discounts received	900
	5,600

Since the available reserve exceeds the amount to be carried forward, the amount of excess ₹ 100 will be transferred to the profit and loss account to off-set the income taken in excess in the previous year.

Balance Sheet of R. Limited as on 31.3.2011

Liabilities	(₹)	(₹)	Assets	(₹)
Accounts payable	2,20,000			
Less: Reserve for Discounts	4,400	2,15,600		

Balance Sheet of R. Limited as on 31.3.2012

Liabilities	(₹)	(₹)	Assets	(₹)
Accounts payable	3,25,000			
Less: Reserve for Discounts	6,500	3,18,500		

Balance Sheet of R. Limited as on 31.3.2013

Liabilities	(₹)	(₹)	Assets	(₹)
Accounts payable	2,75,000			
Less: Reserve for Discounts	5,500	2,69,500		

CLOSING ENTRIES

The accounting treatment of the adjustments to be given effect to the various accounts for the preparation of financial statements have been discussed above. The next stage in the preparation of financial statements is the recording of the closing journal entries for the drawing up of the trading and profit and loss accounts. While the balance sheet is a mere listing of the assets and liabilities, the trading and profit and loss accounts are prepared in the form of ledger accounts and postings can be made into such accounts only if they have been entered in the book of prime entry of Journal. The trading and profit and loss accounts are nominal accounts and all expenses and incomes are transferred to this account. While expenses are shown on the debit side, the incomes are posted on the credit side.

Entries for the Preparation of Trading Account

(*i*) The purchases and sales returns must be transferred to the purchases and sales accounts respectively so that the net purchases and net sales can be determined. The entries for the transfer of returns are,

Purchases Returns A/c Dr.
 To Purchases A/c
Sales A/c Dr.
 To Sales Returns A/c.

(*ii*) For the transfer of opening stock, purchases and other direct expenses such as carriage inwards, wages etc., the entry is

Trading A/c Dr.
 To Opening Stock A/c
 To Purchase A/c
 To Direct Expenses A/c

(*iii*) For the transfer of net sales to trading account, the entry is,

Sales A/c Dr.
 To Trading A/c

(*iv*) The balance in the trading account is known and the gross profit/loss is determined. For transferring the gross profit/gross loss to profit and loss account, the entry is:

(*a*) In case of gross profit
 Trading A/c Dr.
 To Profit and Loss A/c
(*b*) In case of gross loss
 Profit and Loss A/c Dr.
 To Trading A/c

Entries for Preparation of Profit and Loss Account

(*i*) For transfer of all expenses, other than direct expenses, to profit and loss account the entry is,

Profit and Loss A/c Dr.
 To Expenses A/c

(*ii*) For transfer of all income, other than sales and related income, to profit and loss account the entry is,

Income A/c Dr.
 To Profit and Loss A/c

(*iii*) The credit balance in the profit and loss account represents the net profit earned and belongs to the proprietors. The entry for the transfer of net profit is,

Profit and Loss A/c Dr.
 To Capital A/c

The debit balance in profit and loss account represent the net loss. The entry for the transfer of net loss is

Capital A/c Dr.
 To Profit & Loss A/c

Adjustments in the Capital Account

The capital account of the proprietor as shown in the balance sheet should reveal the net amount owning to him by the business as on the closing date. The opening balance of the capital account must be adjusted for:

(*i*) Drawings
(*ii*) Net Profit earned during the year/Net loss occurred during the year
(*iii*) Salary, if any, due to the proprietor
(*iv*) Interest on capital, if any, due to the proprietor
(*v*) Interest on drawings, if any, due from the proprietor

We have already seen the entry needed to transfer the net profit/net loss to the capital account. The entries for the other adjustments will be as under:

For Transfer of drawings,

Capital A/c Dr.
To Drawings A/c

For providing for salary payable to proprietor

Proprietor's Salary A/c Dr.
To Capital A/c

The Proprietor's salary will be shown as an expenses in the profit and loss account.

For interest on capital

Interest on Capital A/c Dr.
To Capital A/c

The interest on capital will be shown as an expenses in the profit and loss account.

For interest on drawings,

Capital A/c Dr.
To Interest on Drawings A/c

The interest on drawings will be shown as an income in the profit and loss account.

While the entries for the adjustment of drawings and net profit/net loss in the capital account are in the nature of closing entries, all other items will be entered in the capital account only with the help of adjusting entries.

With the completion of the positing of adjusting and closing entries in the general ledger, balances will exist only for the assets, liabilities and capital account. These balances will be carried forward to the next accounting period. At the beginning of the subsequent accounting period, when a new general ledger is brought into use, the opening assets and liabilities will be brought into the ledger through an opening journal entry.

The opening journal entry is,

Assets A/c Dr.
To Liabilities A/c
To Capital A/c

CAPITAL AND REVENUE RECEIPTS AND EXPENDITURES

After explaining the adjusting and closing entries, it would be appropriate to discuss separately the different types of receipts and expenditures whose understanding are useful while preparing the financial statement of a business enterprises.

Expenditure

Expenditure can be classified into three categories:

1. **Capital Expenditure:** It means an expenditure which has been incurred for the purpose of acquiring an asset to be held in business on long term basis which results in increasing the earning capacity of the business. Some examples of capital expenditure are:
   (*a*) Expenditure incurred on the purchase of furniture, plant, copyright, patents, goodwill etc.
   (*b*) Expenditure incurred in increasing the capacity or efficiency of a fixed asset.
   (*c*) Expenditure incurred on purchase of shares and debentures of other companies for a long duration.
2. **Revenue Expenditure:** Expenditure incurred in running the business is termed as revenue expenditure. Examples of revenue expenditure are: rent, salaries, office expenses, cost of manufacturing and selling the product, repairs, depreciation etc.
3. **Deferred Revenue Expenditure:** It is that revenue expenditure which is incurred in one accounting period but the benefit of which is available in future periods. *e.g.*, Development costs in mines and plantations, discount on debentures in limited companies, market research, cost of experiments. Deferred revenue expenditure is written off over a number of years.

Receipts

Receipts are of two types: (1) Capital Receipts, and (2) Revenue Receipts.

1. **Capital Receipts:** Capital receipts consist of payments made to the enterprises either by share holders, or by proprietors of business, receipts from sale of fixed assets of a business or loan raised.

   It may be noted here that capital receipt is different from capital profit. For example if the price of machinery costing ₹ 20,000/- is sold for ₹ 21,000/-, there is a capital receipt of ₹ 21,000/- but capital profit is only ₹ 1,000/-. Suppose the same machinery is sold for ₹ 15,000/- then there is a capital receipt of ₹ 15,000/- but there is a capital loss of ₹ 5,000/-
2. **Revenue Receipts:** Any receipt which is not a capital receipt is termed as revenue receipt. Examples of revenue receipts are, Amount from sale of goods, Amount received from rendering services to other parties, Interest received, commission received.

   Capital receipts and Capital expenditure is not shown in Trading and Profit and Loss a/c. It is only revenue receipts and revenue expenditure of the current year which are shown in trading and profit and loss a/c. It may also be noted that capital profit is transferred to Capital Reserve whereas capital loss is charged to profit and loss a/c of the same year or over a few years in case it occurs in the course of purchase and sale of goods and services.

PREPARING TRADING ACCOUNT

Trading Account is prepared to know the gross profit/gross loss of a business enterprise arising out of trading operations. Then all administrative and selling expenses are deducted from gross profit to determine the net profit. Whether or not a separate Trading Account is prepared to determine gross profit or loss, the Net Profit/Net Loss remains the same.

It is necessary to emphasise here that Trading account is prepared on 'Accrual Basis'. The following is a simple example of a Trading Account.

Trading Account for the period ending March 2012

	(₹)	(₹)		(₹)	(₹)
To Opening Inventory:			By Sales	7,90,000	
Raw Materials	90,000		*Less*: Returns	10,000	7,80,000
Work-in-progress	70,000				
Finished goods	2,40,000	4,00,000	By Closing inventory:		
Purchases	500,000		Raw materials	40,000	
Less: Returns	15,000	4,85,000	Work-in-progress	80,000	
			Finished goods	3,00,000	4,20,000
Carriage inwards		10,000			
Wages		40,000			
Factory Expenses		20,000			
Fuel and Power		5,000			
Trading Expenses		15,000			
Gross Profit Transferred to P&L A/c		2,25,000			
		12,00,000			12,00,000

Important Points

Opening inventory is debited to Trading Account. Closing inventory is credited to Trading Account. (The information relating to opening inventory is usually provided in trial balance. The Closing stock figures is indicated in the 'Adjustments' outside the Trial Balance).

Purchases (Less Returns) are debited to Trading Account. Sales (less returns) are credited to Trading Account.

All expenses relating to trading and manufacturing activities are debited to Trading Account.

The Gross Profit (or Loss) is then transferred to Profit and Loss account.

Note that there is no hard and fast rule about segregation of expenses between Trading Account and Profit and Loss account. What is indicated above is based on generally accepted accounting principles. However, in specific circumstances it may become necessary to adopt a flexible approach. The question of segregation of expenses does not arise where only the Profit and Loss account is prepared without a separate Trading Account.

Preparing Profit and Loss Account

Given below is a simple example of a Profit and Loss Account. You may notice that it starts with gross profit (on credit side). If there is no separate Trading Account prepared, all the debits and credits of trading account appear individually in the Profit and Loss account. Where a separate Trading Account is prepared, only the figure of gross profit (or loss as the case may be) appears in the Profit and Loss account as a starting point.

The Profit and Loss account shown below is not a exhaustive list of expenses and incomes. It is a simplified version of a typical Profit and Loss account without taking any "adjustments" to be made into account.

Dr. Profit and Loss Account for the period ending March 2012 Cr.

	(₹)		(₹)
To Salaries	30,000	By Gross Profit	2,25,000
To Printing & Stationery	15,000	By Rent Received	2,000
To Postage and Telephone	2,500	By Other Income	10,000

	(₹)		(₹)
To Audit Fee	4,000		
To Office Rent	5,000		
To Insurance	10,000		
To Repair & Maintenance	5,000		
To General Expenses	4,000		
To Interest on Loans	8,000		
To Net Profit Transferred to Reserves or Capital	1,53,500		
	2,37,000		2,37,000

Profit and loss account may be prepared in the 'T' form (as shown above) or in the vertical form. If the profit and loss is prepared in the vertical form, the revenue are shown first and all expenses are shown as a deduction from the total revenues. A sample of vertical format is shown below:

Profit and Loss Account of .... for the year ended

Revenue

Sales

Other (Dividends, Interest etc.)

Expenses

Raw Materials Cost

Employee's remuneration and benefits

Other Expenses

Depreciation

Profit before Interest

Interest

Previous year's adjustment

Profit before Taxation

Income Tax

Net Profit available for appropriation

Appropriation

Interim dividend

Proposed final dividend

Transfer to General Reserve

WHAT IS A BALANCE SHEET?

A balance sheet, also commonly referred to as a statement of financial position, is a statement of assets and liabilities of business enterprises at a particular date. The balance sheet summarises and reveals the financial position of an enterprises on a particular date, by showing what is owns and what it owes. Because the balance sheet is a snap shot as of an instant in time, it is a status report rather than flow report.

The balance sheet is a fundamental or first accounting statement in the sense that every accounting transaction can be analysed in terms of its dual impact on the balance sheet. Moreover, most often, revenues and expenses are defined in terms of changes in assets and liabilities. Thus, a thorough understanding of the nature and measurement of assets and liabilities is needed to understand net income and its components. A Balance Sheet has no debit and credit side. It is a prepared on a particular date and as such, it shows the assets and liabilities of a business enterprises on that date. Even a single transaction will cause a change in the assets and liabilities of the enterprises as shown in the Balance Sheet. Therefore, it is true only for the date on which it has been prepared. It is called Balance Sheet because it is actually a sheet containing balances of ledger accounts which have not been closed by transfer to trading and profit and loss a/c.

The balance sheet is also called a statement of sources of funds (*i.e.*, liabilities or obligations) and utilisation of funds (*i.e.*, assets or resources). The financial position of an enterprises includes its economic resources (assets), economic obligations (liabilities), owner's equity and their relationship to each other on a particular date. The balance sheet reveals an enterprise's resource structure (major classes and amounts of assets) and its financial structure (major classes and amounts of liabilities and equity). As stated in Chapter 3, the balance sheet is a detailed summary of the basic accounting equation (which must always remain in balance):

Assets = Liabilities + Owner's Equity

The balance sheet is prepared in terms of certain accounting concepts such as: (*i*) Money measurement *i.e.*, amounts are expressed in money and reflect only those matters that can be measured in monetary terms, (*ii*) entity—*i.e.*, the balance sheet is prepared from the point of view of the business as a separate entity, distinguished from its owners and individuals associated with it, (*iii*) going concern *i.e.*, the balance sheet assumes that the enterprise is a going concern (*iv*) cost concept—*i.e.*, amounts stated in a balance sheet are regulated by the historical cost concept (*v*) dual-aspect—*i.e.*, assets listed on a balance sheet are equal in total to the liabilities and shareholders equity.

The proper heading of a balance sheet consists of (*a*) the name of organisation (*b*) the title of the statement, and (*c*) the date for which the statement is prepared.

To sum up, while preparing Profit and Loss Account and Balance Sheet, the following important points should be noted:

(*i*) Start with a tallied trial balance. It provides the arithmetical accuracy of entries made in the books namely cash book, journal and ledger. However, there are certain errors which are not disclosed by a trial balance.

(*ii*) On account of certain errors if the trial balance is not tallied, the Suspense Account is opened with the difference of two sides and the same is inserted on the side having difference. If suspense account shows:

(*a*) Debit balance, record it on the asset side of Balance Sheet.

(*b*) Credit balance, record it on the liabilities side of Balance Sheet.

The Suspense Account is closed after rectifying the errors. Real and Personal Accounts items alone are taken to Balance Sheet.

(*iii*) Adjustments given at the end of a trial balance should be given double-entry effect, otherwise accounts will not be complete. The balance sheet will not tally.

(*iv*) The treatment of adjustments for expenses and incomes in balance sheet is:

(*a*) Outstanding liabilities for expenses shown on liabilities side;

(*b*) Prepaid expenses shown on assets side;

(*c*) Income received in advance shown on liabilities side;

(*d*) Income earned but not received, and income accrued but not due, shown on assets side;

(*e*) Fixed assets are recorded at cost minus depreciation;

(*f*) Closing stock recorded at cost price or Net realisable value price whichever is less.

Balance sheet is just a statement of assets and liabilities. It is not an account like profit and loss account. Hence Debit (Dr.) or Credit (Cr.) do not figure in a balance sheet.

Profit and loss account is prepared for an accounting period. On the other hand a balance sheet is prepared as on a particular day (usually the last day of the accounting period).

ARRANGEMENT OF ASSETS AND LIABILITY ITEMS ON THE BALANCE SHEET

In the case of a company, The Companies Act 1956 provides that balance sheet should be prepared as per schedule VI (which has been revised in 2011) given therein and assets and liabilities should be written in the sequence (or order) shown in the Schedule. However, in the case of sole proprietorship, and partnership, no rule is provided for recording assets and liabilities on the balance sheet.

Generally assets and liabilities on a balance sheet may be written on

(*a*) liquidity basis and

(*b*) fixity basis.

Liquidity basis is that basis where assets and liabilities are arranged according to their realisability and payment preference. Fixity basis is the basis when assets and liabilities are arranged in the order of permanence. Proforma of balance sheet on liquidity basis and fixity basis are given below.

Proforma of a Balance Sheet (in order of Liquidity/Liquidity Basis)

Balance Sheet as at ....

Liabilities		Assets	
Current Liabilities:		**Current Assets:**	
Bank Overdraft	—	Cash in Hand	—
Outstanding Expenses	—	Cash at Bank	—
Bills Payable	—	Prepaid Expenses	—
Sundry Creditors	—	Sundry Debtors	—
Income Received in Advance	—	Accrued Income	—
	—	Bills Receivable	—
		Stock (closing)	—
Fixed or Non-Current Liabilities:		**Non-Current Assets (Fixed Assets):**	
Loan	—	Investment	—
Capital	—	Furniture and Fixture	—
Opening Balance	—	Plant and Machinery	—
Add: Net Profit (less loss)	—	Loose Tools	—
Less: Drawing	—	Building	—
		Land	—
		Goodwill	—

Proforma of Balance Sheet
(In order of Permanence/Fixity Basis)
Balance Sheet as at ....

Liabilities		Assets	
Capital		**Non-Current Assets/Fixed Deposit**	
Opening Balance	—	Goodwill	—
Add: Net Profit (Less Loss)		Land	—

Liabilities		Assets	
Less: Drawings	—	Building	—
		Plant and Machinery	—
Non-Current/Fixed Liabilities		Loose Tools	—
		Furniture & Fixture	—
Loan	—	Investments	—
Current Liabilities:		**Current Assets:**	
Income Received in Advance	—	Stock (Closing)	—
		Accrued Income	—
Sundry Creditors	—	Sundry Debtors	—
Bills Payable	—	Prepaid Expenses	—
Outstanding Expenses	—	Bills Receivable	
Bank Overdraft	—	Cash at Bank	—
		Cash in Hand	—

Note: The balance sheet can be prepared in a vertical format also. In a vertical form, a balance sheet generally appears as follows:

Balance Sheet of .... As on ....

1.	Fixed Assets		....
2.	Investments		....
3.	Current Assets	....	
	Less: Current Liabilities & Provisions	....	
	Net Current Assets		....
4.	Miscellaneous Expenditure		....
		Total Assets	....
5.	Shareholders' Fund:		
	Share Capital	....	
	Reserves and Surplus	....	....
6.	Secured Loan		....
7.	Unsecured Loans		....
		Total Liabilities	....

Note: The amount shown are normally rounded off the nearest rupee, or nearest lakh or nearest crore of rupees.

Meaning of Some Balance Sheet Items

The data shown in Balance Sheet and Profit and Loss account are not only the balances of individual accounts but some times they are grouped balance of many accounts and they lack uniformity and homogeneity. For the purpose of making comparisons and interpretation these items of data are to be split or broken up into many components, this processes is known as analysis. Financial analysis involves the division of facts on the basis of some definite plans, classifying them into classes on the basis of certain objectives and presenting them in most convenient, simple and understandable form *i.e.*, its classification and arrangement of data.

A clear and current understanding of the basic divisions of the balance sheet items and the meanings which they signify and the amount which they represent is very essential for the proper analysis and interpretation of financial statements. The various items of the balance sheet may be grouped as under:

Current Assets

All assets, which are acquired for reselling during the course of business are to be treated as current assets. These are acquired through cash and are easily convertible into cash. Examples are Cash and Bank balances, Inventory, Accounts Receivable etc.

Deferred Expenditure

It is shown at a point of time as assets in Balance Sheet. For example, research and development expenses of ₹ 1,00,000 resulting in a new product may be written off over 5 years. At the end of the first year, an amount of ₹ 80,000 being ₹ 1,00,000–₹ 20,000 will be shown in the Balance Sheet as deferred expenditure.

Current Liabilities

All short term obligations generally due and payable within one year are current liabilities. *e.g.* Bills payable, Accounts payable etc.

Non-Current Liabilities

All such liabilities payable over a longer period of time generally, after one year, are non-current liabilities. *e.g.*, Debentures, Long term loans etc.

Net Worth

Net worth is the amount of funds invested at the risk of the owners of the business concern. It is arrived after deducting all outside liabilities, both current and non-current, from total assets of the concern. Hence net worth equals the capital and Reserve of the concern.

Financial Analysts analyse the balance sheets and profit and loss accounts in great detail to assess the financial position of the companies by comparing the performance over a period of time and also by comparing performance of one company with others in similar business. Such comparisons with similar other companies are called inter-firm comparisons.

Financial Analysts use several financial ratios calculated from the data available in balance sheet and profit and loss account to assess the solvency, liquidity and profitability of an organisation.

The American terms of various assets and liabilities and some other items and their equivalent Indian terms are given below:

American Terminology	Indian Terminology
Accounts Receivable	Sundry Debtors/Debtors
Accounts Payable	Sundry Creditors/Creditors
Notes Receivable	Bills Receivable
Notes Payable	Bills Payable
Marketable Securities	Investments
Inventory	Inventory/Stock
Stock	Share
Stockholder	Shareholders
Common Stock	Equity Share or Equity Share Capital (As per the context)
Paid in Capital	Paid up Capital

American Terminology	Indian Terminology
Property, Plant and Machinery	Fixed Assets
Deferred Revenues	Incomes Received in Advance/Pre-received Income
Deferred Charges	Deferred Expenses/Deferred Revenue Expenditure
Gross Margin	Gross Profit
Sales Discount	Cash Discount Allowed
Retained Earnings	Credit Balance of P&L Account

Notes:

(*i*) The term 'deferred revenues' should not be confused with the term, 'deferred revenue expenditure'. In Indian terminology, deferred revenue expenditure means expenditure in respect of which benefits may be received over a period of time longer than a year.

(*ii*) In India, cash discounts allowed are usually shown as an expenditure in the Profit and Loss account and not netted out from sales.

ADJUSTMENT ITEMS

Treatment of various types of items that require adjustments for the preparation of a balance sheet are given as under:

Adjustment	Adjusting entry		Treatment in Balance Sheet
1. Outstanding expenses	Expenses a/c To Outstanding Exp. a/c	Dr.	Shown on the Liabilities side
2. Prepaid Expenses	Prepaid Expenses a/c To Expenses a/c	Dr.	Shown on the Asset side
3. Closing Stock	Closing Stock To Trading a/c	Dr.	Shown on the Asset side
4. Accrued Income	Accrued Income To Income a/c	Dr.	Shown on the Asset side
5. Depreciation	(*a*) Depreciation a/c To Assets a/c (*b*) Depreciation a/c To provision for depreciation	Dr. Dr.	Shown by way of deduction from the value of the Asset on the Asset side
6. Income Received in Advance	Income a/c To Income Received in Advance a/c	Dr.	Shown on the Liabilities side
7. Provision for Bad Debts	Profit & Loss a/c To Provision for Bad Debts	Dr.	Deducted from Sundry Debtors on the Asset side
8. Provision for Discount	Profit & Loss a/c To Provision for discount on Debtors	Dr.	Deducted from Sundry Debtors on the Asset side
9. Reserve for Discount on Creditors	Reserve for Discount on Creditors To Profit and Loss a/c	Dr.	Shown by way of Deduction from Sundry Creditors

Limitations of Balance Sheet

A balance sheet contains useful information about liquidity, operating capability and financial position of an enterprise and thus, is very useful to external users and others in making sound investment decisions. However, inspite of being a useful financial statement, it has some limitations, listed as below.

1. Balance Sheet is considered to be a static document and it reflects the position of the concern at a given date. The real position of the concern may be changing day-to-day, and the same is not depicted in Balance Sheet.
2. Balance Sheet is not a valuation statement. The values shown in it are not real values of assets. Thus exact position of the business cannot be gauged from balance sheet.
3. A balance sheet is prepared based on certain accounting policies. Such policies relate to inventory valuation (*i.e.*, closing stock), depreciation etc. Inventory may be valued using several methods like First-in-First Out (FIFO), Last-in-First-Out (LIFO), weighted average cost etc. Similarly, depreciation may be provided using straight line method or written down value method. The management may select accounting policies which may not reflect real financial position.

   Similarly, accounting policies may differ from company to company in respect of accounting for prepaid expenses, prior period adjustments, classification between revenue and capital expenditure, writing-off preliminary expenses etc.
4. Management may follow accounting procedures and treatments which may result into window dressing of balance sheets with a view to forecast a better picture to shareholders, bankers and financial institutions. It is a rosier picture that what it actually is. Window-dressing is accomplished in general ways, say, by not making adequate provisions (though prudence would require them) for expenses and potential losses, by taking into account income even before its actual accrual, by suppressing vital information, by playing around with inter-corporate adjustments etc.

Illustration 1: From the following figures, you are required to show:

(*a*) Provision for doubtful debts account

(*b*) Bad Debts account

(*c*) Profit and Loss account

Provision for Doubtful Debts 1.4.2012	₹ 1,000
Provision for Doubtful Debts 31.3.2013	₹ 2,000
Debts Written off in 2012–2013	₹ 1,200

Solution: **Provision for Doubtful Debts A/c**

Date 2013	Particulars	Amount ₹	Date 2012	Particulars	Amount ₹
Mar. 31	To Bad Debts written off	1,200		By Balance (given)	1,000
Mar. 31	To Balance (Closing)	2,000	Mar. 31	By Profit & Loss A/c (*Balancing Figure*)	2,200
		3,200			3,200

Bed Debts A/c

Date 2013	Particulars	Amount ₹	Date 2013	Particulars	Amount ₹
Mar. 31	To Balance (Given)	1,200	Mar. 31	By Provision for Bad Debts (transfer)	1,200
		1,200			1,200

Profit and Loss A/c

Date 2014	Particulars	Amount ₹	Date	Particulars	Amount ₹
Mar. 31	To Provision for Doubtful Debts	2,200			
		2,200			

Illustration 2: On 1st January, 2011 the reserve for Doubtful Debts account showed a balance of ₹ 10,000. During the year the bad debts written off amounted to ₹ 10,000/- and the Sundry Debtors at the end stood at ₹ 2,40,000/- on which the provision for doubtful debts was to be 5%.

During 2012 the bad debts written off amounted to ₹ 4,000/- and the closing balance of debtors was ₹ 1,40,000/-. The concern continued to provide for doubtful debts at 5% on closing balance of debtors.

Show the provisions for doubtful debts account for 2011 and 2012. All bad debts written off are adjusted through the Provision Account.

Solution: **Provision for Doubtful Debts A/c**

Date 2011	Particulars	Amount ₹	Date 2011	Particulars	Amount ₹
Dec. 31	To Bad Debts written off	10,000	Jan. 1	By Balance (given)	10,000
Dec. 31	To Balance (Closing) (5/100 × 2,40,000)	12,000	Dec. 31	By Profit & Loss A/c (*Balancing figure*)	12,000
		22,000			22,000
2012			**2012**		
Dec. 31	To Bad Debts	4,000	Jan. 1	By Balance b/d	12,000
Dec. 31	To Balance (Closing) (5/100 × 1,40,000)	7,000			
Dec. 31	To P&L A/c (*Bal. figure*)	1,000			
		12,000			12,000

Illustration 3: There were ₹ 2,500 bad debts during the year ended 31st March, 2012. An amount of ₹ 3,000/- for provision of bad debts is brought forward from last year. During the year ended at 31st March, 2012 provision of ₹ 1,750/- was made for bad and doubtful debts. Prepare bad debts account and provision for bad & doubtful debts account.

Solution: **Bad Debt A/c**

Date 2012	Particulars	Amount ₹	Date 2012	Particulars	Amount ₹
Mar. 31	To Balance (Given)	2,500	Mar. 31	By Provision for Bad Debts	2,500
		2,500			2,500

Provision for Bad & Doubtful Debts A/c

Date 2012	Particulars	Amount ₹	Date	Particulars	Amount ₹
March 31	To Bad Debts	2,500	Apr. 2011	By Balance b/d	3,000
	To Balance (Closing)	1,750	31.3.2012	By Profit & Loss A/c (*Balancing figure*)	1,250
		4,250			4,250

Illustration 4: The following figures appear in the books of a firm:

Provision for doubtful debts on 1.1.2012 ₹ 6,500

Bad debts written off during the year ₹ 4,000

Sundry debtors on 31.12.2012 ₹ 75,000. Of the sundry debtors ₹ 2,000 was bad and the provision for doubtful debts was to be maintained at 5% on sundry debtors. Pass Journal entries.

Solution: **Journal Entries**

Sl. No.	Particulars		Amount Dr. (₹)	Amount Cr. (₹)
1.	Bad Debts A/c To Sundry Debtors A/c (Being bad debts provided on debtors)	Dr.	4,000	4,000
2.	Provision for Bad & Doubtful Debts A/c To Bad Debt A/c (Being bad debts transferred)	Dr.	4,000	4,000
3.	Profit & Loss A/c To Provision for doubtful Debts A/c (Being provision on debtors transferred to P&L A/c)	Dr.	3,650	3,650
4.	Provision for Bad & Doubtful Debts A/c To Profit & Loss A/c (Being amount transferred to P&L A/c and Provision for doubtful debts)	Dr.	1,150	1,150

Illustration 5: The following balances appear in the trial balance of Joshi & Co. relating to the accounts for the year ending December 31, 2012:

Wages a/c ₹ 30,000

Salaries a/c ₹ 40,000

Rent a/c ₹ 5,000

Advertising a/c ₹ 17,000

It is found that following adjustments have not been made in the books:

1. Wages due but not paid ₹ 3,000
2. Salaries paid in advance ₹ 2,000
3. Unpaid Rent ₹ 1,000
4. Advertising expenses not recorded in the books ₹ 2,000

You are required to pass necessary journal entries to adjust these items. Also show how these items would appear in trading and profit and loss accounts and balance sheet.

Solution: **Journal Entries**

Sl. No.	Particulars		Amount Dr. (₹)	Amount Cr. (₹)
1.	Wages A/c To Outstanding wage A/c (Being the amount of outstanding wages)	Dr.	3,000	3,000
2.	Prepaid Salaries A/c To Salaries A/c (Being the salaries paid in advance)	Dr.	2,000	2,000
3.	Rent A/c To Outstanding Rent A/c (Being the amount of rent outstanding)	Dr.	1,000	1,000
4.	Advertising A/c To Outstanding Advertising A/c (Being the amount of advertising outstanding)	Dr.	2,000	2,000

Profit and Loss A/c for the year ended 31 December, 2012

		Amount (₹)			Amount (₹)
Wages	30,000				
Add: Outstanding	3,000	33,000			
Salaries	40,000				
Less: Paid in advance	2,000	38,000			
Rent	5,000				
Add: Unpaid	1,000	6,000			
Advertising	17,000				
Add: Unpaid	2,000	19,000			

Balance Sheet as on 31 December, 2012

Liabilities	(₹)	Assets	(₹)
Outstanding Expenses:		**Prepaid Expenses:**	
Wages	3,000	Salaries	2,000
Rent	1,000		
Advertising	2,000		

Illustration 6: The following balances appeared in the trial balance of X on December 31, 2012.

Debtors	₹ 1,00,000
Bad Debts	₹ 5,000
Provision for bad debts (1.1.2012)	₹ 6,000

It was found that bad debts worth ₹ 3,000 were not recorded in the books till Dec. 31, 2012. It was decided that a provision for bad debts equal to 8 per cent on the closing debtors will be adequate. You are required to prepare bad debts accounts and provision for bad debts account. Also show how these items would appear in profit and loss account and balance sheet.

Solution:

Bed Debts A/c (Amount in ₹)

31.12.2012	To Balance b/d	5,000	31.12.2012	By Provision for Bad Debts	8,000
31.12.2012	To Debtors A/c	3,000			
		8,000			8,000

Provision for Bad Debts A/c

	To Bad Debts	8,000		By Balance b/d	6,000
	To Balance c/d (New Provision)	7,760		By Profit and Loss A/c	9,760
		15,760			15,760

Profit & Loss A/c

	To Bad Debts	5,000			
	Add: Bad Debts	3,000			
		8,000			
	Add: New Provision	7,760			
		15,760			
	Less: Old Provision	6,000			9,760

Balance Sheet

Debtors	1,00,000	
Less: Bad Debts (not recorded)	3,000	
	97,000	
Less: Provision	7,760	89,240
Note: Debtors on 31.12.2007	1,00,000	
Less: Bad Debts not recorded	3,000	
	97,000	
New Provision for Bad Debts = 97,000 × 8/100 =	7,760	

Illustration 7: A firm had the following balances on April 1, 2006:

Provision for doubtful debts ₹ 6,500
Provision for discount on debtors ₹ 3,200
Reserve for discount on creditors ₹ 4,800

During the year ended March 31, 2007, bad debts amounted to ₹ 4,500, discounts allowed were ₹ 15,800 and discount received were ₹ 9,700. During the year 2007–08, bad debts amounting to ₹ 2,300 were written off while discount allowed and received were ₹ 12,500 and ₹ 8,900 respectively. Sundry debtors were ₹ 1,50,000 on 31.3.2007 and ₹ 90,000 on 31.3.2008. Sundry creditors were ₹ 1,05,000 and ₹ 1,26,000 on 31.3.2007 and 31.3.2008 respectively. It is the firm's policy to maintain a provision of 5 percent against bad and doubtful debts and 3 percent for discount on debtors and reserve of 2 percent on creditors. Show the necessary accounts for the year 2006–2007 and 2007–2008.

Solution:

Bad Debts A/c **(Amount in ₹)**

31.3.2007	To Sundry Debtors	4,500	2007	By Provision for Bad and Doubtful Debts	4,500
31.3.2008	To Sundry Debtors	2,300	31.3.2008	By Provision for Bad and Doubtful Debts	2,300

Provision for Bad and Doubtful Debts

31.3.2006	To Bad Debts transfer A/c		4,500	2006	By Balance b/d	6,500
31.3.2006	To Balance c/d		7,500	31.3.2007	By P&L A/c	5,500
			12,000			12,000
31.3.2008	To Bad Debts	2,300		April 1	By Balance b/d	7,500
	To P&L	700				
	To Balance c/d	4,500	7,500			7,500

Discount on Debtors A/c

31.3.2007	To Sundry Debtors	15,800	2007	By Provision for Discount on Debts	15,800
31.3.2008	To Sundry Debtors	12,500	31.3.2008	By Provision for Discount on Debtors	12,500

Provision for Discount on Debtors

31.3.2007	To Discount A/c	15,800	1.4.2007	By Balance c/d	3,200
31.3.2007	To Balance c/d	4,275	31.3.2001	By P&L A/c	16,875
		20,075			20,075
31.3.2008	To Discount A/c	12,500	1.4.2007	By Balance c/d	4,275
31.3.2008	To Balance c/d	2,565	31.3.2008	By P&L A/c	10,790
		15,065			15,065
			April 1	By Balance b/d	2,565

Discount on Sundry Creditors

31.3.2007	To Reserve for Discount on Sundry Creditors	9,700	1.4.2007	By Sundry Creditors	9,700
31.3.2008	To Reserve for Discount on Sundry Creditors	8,900	31.3.2008	By Sundry Creditors	8,900

Reserve for Discount on Sundry Creditors

1.4.2006	To Balance b/d	4,800	31.3.2007	By Discount on Sundry Creditors	9,700
31.3.2007	To P&L A/c	7,000	31.3.2007	By Balance c/d	2,100
		11,800			11,800
1.4.2007	To Balance b/d	2,100	31.3.2008	By Discount on Sundry Creditors	8,900
31.3.2008	To P&L A/c	9,320	31.3.2008	By Balance c/d	2,520
		11,420			11,420
1.4.2008	To Balance b/d	2,520			

Illustration 8: A machinery item was bought on 16.2.2002 and was sold on 15.10.2007. The following relevant information is available:

1. Cost of purchase of the machinery – ₹ 4,00,000
2. Transportation and installation costs – ₹ 20,000
3. Estimated useful life at the time of acquisition in 20 years.
4. Estimated scrap value at the time of disposal ₹ 1,000
5. The firm closes its books of account on March 31, every year
6. Depreciation was provided on the straight-line method; in the year of acquisition/disposal it is the policy of the firm to provide one-half of a year's depreciation.
7. Amount realised from sale of machine – ₹ 1,50,000

The accounting treatment for purchase and sale would be:

(*a*) Record ₹ 4,00,000 in machinery account as cost on acquisition and charge ₹ 1,44,300 as loss on sale.

(*b*) Record ₹ 4,20,000 in machinery account as cost on acquisition and charge ₹ 1,44,300 as loss on sale.

(*c*) Record ₹ 4,19,000 in machinery account as cost on acquisition and charge ₹ 1,44,300 as loss on sale.

(*d*) Debit ₹ 4,00,000 to machinery account on acquisition and credit ₹ 1,50,000 to the same account on sale.

(*e*) None of the above.

Required: Among the above choices, which one is correct?

Solution: Capitalisation of Machinery = ₹ (4,00,000 + 20,000)
= ₹ 4,20,000

Depreciation per year on straight line basis = ₹ (4,20,000 – 1,000)/20
= ₹ 20,950

Total Depreciation provided:

		(₹)
Year ended	31.03.2002 (1/2 × 20,950)	10,475/-
Year ended	31.03.2003	20,950/-
Year ended	31.03.2004	20,950/-

Year ended	31.03.2005	20,950/-
Year ended	31.03.2006	20,950/-
Year ended	31.03.2007	20,950/-
Year ended	31.03.2008 (1/2 × 20,000)	10,475/-
		1,25,700/-
Book value as on date of sale	= ₹ (4,20,000 – 1,25,700) =	₹ 2,94,300
Loss on Sale	= ₹ 2,94,3000 – 1,50,000 =	₹ 1,44,300

Choice B is correct

Illustration 9: A company had sales of ₹ 1,50,000 during 2007, receivable account has opening balance of ₹ 17,500 and provision for doubtful debts ₹ 2,500. Data for 2007: Collections on account receivable ₹ 1,35,000. Bad Debts expenses was estimated at 2% on credit sales. Write-offs of bad debts during 2007 were ₹ 3,500. The balance on 31.12.2007 in the accounts receivable account and provision for doubtful debts account respectively were:

(*a*) ₹ 3,25,000 (debit) and ₹ 89,000 (credit)
(*b*) ₹ 3,54,000 (debit) and ₹ 94,000 (credit)
(*c*) ₹ 29,000 (debit) and ₹ 2,000 (credit)
(*d*) ₹ 29,000 (debit) and ₹ 3,000 (credit)
(*e*) None of the above

Solution: The closing balances of the receivable accounts and provision for doubtful debts accounts can be ascertained by preparing these ledger accounts.

Receivable Accounts **(Amount in ₹)**

Dr. **Cr.**

1.1.2007	To Balance b/d	17,500	31.12.2007	By Bank A/c (Collection)	1,35,000
	To Sale c/d	1,50,000		By Bad Debts A/c	3,500
				By Balance c/d	29,000
		1,67,500			1,67,500

Dr. **Provision for Bad Debts Account** **Cr.**

31.12.2007	To Bad Debts A/c	3,500	01.01.2008	By Balance b/d	2,500
	To Balance c/d	2,000	31.12.2008	By Profit and Loss A/c	3,000
		5,500			5,500

Choice (*c*) is correct.

Illustration 10: In a firm a shortage of stock has arisen during the year ended September 30, 2011. The firm gathers the following information:

Opening Stock	–	₹ 87,500
Purchases	–	₹ 2,87,500
Closing Stock (on physical verification)	–	₹ 50,000

The goods are sold at a uniform mark-up of 20 per cent on selling price. The following details regarding Sundry Debtors are available:

Balance as on 01. 10. 2011	30,000
Balance as on 30.09.2012	27,500
Cash and cheques received from customers in the year	3,90,000
Sales returns	12,500

The shortage of stock is:
(*a*) ₹ 80,000
(*b*) ₹ 55,000
(*c*) ₹ 5,000
(*d*) ₹ 25,500
(*e*) None of the above.

Solution: **Sundry Debtors Account** **(Amount in ₹)**

Dr. **Cr.**

Particulars	(₹)	Particulars	(₹)
To Balance b/d	30,000	By Sales Returns	12,500
To Sales (*Balancing figure*)	4,00,000	By Cash & Bank	3,90,000
		By Balanced c/d	27,500
	4,30,000		4,30,000

Memorandum Trading Account

Particular	(₹)	Particulars	(₹)
To Opening Stock	87,500	By Sales	4,00,000
To Purchase	2,87,500	By Closing Stocks	55,000
To Gross Profit @ 20% of ₹ 4,00,000	80,000		
	4,55,000		4,55,000
Closing stock	55,000		
Less: Physical Stock	50,000		
Shortage of Stock	5,000		

Shortage of stock is ₹ 5,000. Hence, choice (*c*) is correct.

Illustration 11: The stocks held by a firm at their godown were completely damaged by fire on February 1, 2012.

The books of accounts, show the following information:

	(₹)
Sales—year ended December 31, 2007	2,00,000
Sales—January 2008	50,000
Purchases—year ended December, 2007	1,25,000
Purchases—January 2008	20,000
Stocks—1.1.2007	37,500
Stocks—31.12.2007	25,000

Taking the gross profit ratio to be constant from 2007 to January, 2008, insurance claim for inventory should be lodged for:

(*a*) ₹ 20,000 (*b*) ₹ 10,625
(*c*) ₹ 27,500 (*d*) ₹ 37,500
(*e*) None of the above.

Solution: **Workings:** Gross Profit for the year ended December 31, 2007 = ₹ 2,00,000 + 25,000 – (1,25,000 + 37,500) = ₹ 62,500

$$\text{Gross Profit margin (ratio)} = \frac{62,500 \times 100}{2,00,000} = 31.25\%$$

Gross Profit earned during January 2008

= ₹ 50,000 × 31.25% = ₹ 15,625

Value of Closing Stock as on January 31, 2008

= ₹ (25,000 + 20,000 + 15,625 – 50,000)

= ₹ 10,625

Choice (*b*) is correct.

Illustration 12: The sundry debtors account and sundry creditors account of a company are given below which are incomplete:

Sundry Debtors Account

	(₹)		(₹)
To Balance c/d	17,500	By Sales Returns	7,500
To Cash & Cheque Received	2,40,000	By Discount Allowed	1,000
To Bad Debts	2,500		
To Balance c/d	20,000		

Sundry Creditors Account

To Purchase Returns	1,500	By Balance c/d	7,500
To Discount Received	400	By Cash & Cheque paid	1,15,000
To Reserve for Discount	250		
To Balance c/d	12,500		

The following further information is made available:

(*i*) While the opening stock was ₹ 9,000, the closing stock has been ascertained at ₹ 12,500.

(*ii*) Expenses during the year:

Carriage inwards, ₹ 1,000

Salaries, ₹ 6,000

Depreciation, ₹ 1,77,500

(*iii*) You may take the opinion that closing balances of the sundry debtors and sundry creditors accounts given above as correct.

The Gross Profit for the year ended March 31, 2012 would be:

(*a*) ₹ 1,04,600

(*b*) ₹ 1,28,100

(*c*) ₹ 1,34,100

(*d*) ₹ 1,29,000

(*e*) None of the above

Solution:

Sundry Debtors Account

	(₹)		(₹)
To Balance b/d	17,500	By Cash & Cheque Received	2,40,000
To Sales (*Balancing figure*)	2,53,500	By Sales Returns	7,500
		By Discount Allowed	1,000
		By Bad Debts	2,500
		By Balance c/d	20,000
	2,71,000		2,71,000

Sundry Creditors Account

	(₹)		(₹)
To Cash & Cheque paid	1,15,000	By Balance b/d	7,500
To Purchase Returns	1,500	By Purchases (*Balancing figure*)	1,21,900
To discounts received	400		
To Balance c/d	12,500		
	1,29,400		1,29,400

Trading Account for the year ended March 31, 2012

		(₹)			(₹)
To Opening Stock	9,000		By Sales	2,53,500	
To Purchases	1,21,900		*Less*: Returns	7,500	2,46,000
Less: Returns	1,500	1,20,400	By Closing Stock		12,500
To Carriage Inward		1,000			
To Gross Profit		1,28,100			
		2,58,500			2,58,500

Illustration 13: From the following Trial Balance prepare Trading and Profit and Loss Account for the year ended 31st December, 2012 and Balance Sheet as on that date:

	Dr. (₹)	Cr. (₹)
Drawings	10,000	—
Stock on 1.1.2012	46,000	—
Purchases and Purchases Returns	1,50,200	600
Cash in Hand	3,400	—
Bank Balance	22,660	—
Freehold Premises	38,600	—
Trade Expenses	840	—
Printing, Stationery and Advertising	1,640	—
Professional Charges	280	—
Commission Received	—	3,300
Investments as on 1st January @ 10%	4,000	—
Interest on above	—	200
Sundry Debtors and Creditors	36,000	29,000
Wages	25,000	—
Salaries	14,000	—
Capital	—	1,14,000
Income Tax	1,600	—
Discount Allowed and Received	6,300	4,600
Sales Returns and Sales	550	2,08,950
Bills Receivable/Bills Payable	3,200	10,000
Office Furniture	3,050	—
Rent, Rates and Insurance	4,000	—
Bad Debts Provision	—	670
Total:	3,71,320	3,71, 320

Adjustments:

(*a*) Provide for wages ₹ 5,000.

(*b*) Write Off 5% depreciation on freehold premises and 10% on office furniture.
(*c*) Insurance to the extent of ₹ 200 relates to 2013.
(*d*) Stock on 31.12.2012 is ₹ 5,20,000.
(*e*) Charge interest on capital 5% and on drawings ₹ 300.
(*f*) Further bad debts are ₹ 1,000.
(*g*) Provide for doubtful debts @ 5% on sundry debtors.
(*h*) Make provision for discount on debtors and reserve for discount on creditors @ 2%.

Solution: Trading A/c for the year ending 31st December, 2012

		(₹)			(₹)
To Opening Stock		46,000	By Sales	2,08,950	
To Purchases	1,50,200		*Less*: Returns	550	2,08,400
Less: Return	600	1,49,600	By Closing Stock		52,000
To Wages	25,000				
Add: O/S	5,000	30,000			
To Gross Profit transferred to Profit and Loss A/c		34,800			
		2,60,400			2,60,400

Profit and Loss Account for the year ending 31st December, 2012

		(₹)			(₹)
To Trade Expenses		840	By Gross Profit		34,800
To Printing, Stationery and Advt.		1,640	By Commission		3,300
To Professional Fee		280	By Interest on Investments	200	
To Discount		6,300	*Add*: Accrued	200	
To Salaries		14,000			400
To Income Tax		1,600	By Discount		4,600
To Rent, Rates and Insurance	4,000		By Interest on Drawings		300
Less: Prepaid	200	3,800	By Reserve for Discount on Creditor		580
To Depreciation on freehold premises		1,930			
To Depreciation on Office furniture		305			
To Interest on Capital		5,700			
To Bad Debts	1,000				
Add: New Provision	1,750				
	2,750				
Less: Old Provision	670	2,080			
To Provision for discount on Debtors		665			
To Net Profit		4,840			
		43,980			43,980

Balance Sheet as at 31st December, 2012

Liabilities	(₹)	Assets		(₹)
Capital	1,14,000	Freehold premises	38,600	
Add: Interest on Capital	5,700	*Less*: Depreciation	1,930	36,670
	1,19,700	Office Furniture	3,050	

Liabilities		(₹)	Assets		(₹)
Less: Drawings	10,000		*Less*: Depreciation	305	2,745
	1,09,700		Investments	4,000	
Less: Interest on drawings	300		*Add:* Accrued interest	200	4,200
	1,09,400		Sundry Debtors	36,000	
Add: Net Profit	4,840	1,14,240	*Less*: Bad Debts	1,000	
Sundry Creditors	29,000			35,000	
Less: Provision for Discount	(580)	28,420	*Less*: New Provision	(1,750)	
Bills Payable		10,000		33,250	
O/S Wages		5,000	*Less*: Provision for Discount	(665)	32,582
			Bills Receivable		3,200
			Prepaid Insurance		200
			Closing Stock		52,000
			Cash in Hand		3,400
			Cash at Bank		22,660
		1,57,660			1,57,660

Illustration 14: The following Trial Balance was extracted from the books of Mr. X as on 31st December, 2012.

Debit Balance	Dr. (₹)		(₹)
Plant and Machinery	20,000	Opening Stock	34,200
Manufacturing Wages	34,500	Motor Car	12,000
Salaries	15,850	Sales Return	3,100
Furniture	10,000	Purchases	1,02,000
Freight on Purchases	1,860	Bad Debts	1,400
Freight on Sales	2,140	Interest and Bank Charges	400
Building	24,000	Cash at Bank	4,200
Manufacturing Expenses	9,500	Cash in Hand	1,120
Insurance and Tax	4,250	**Credit Balances**	
Goodwill	25,000	Capital Account	80,000
General Expenses	8,200	Sundry Creditors	44,560
Factory Fuel and Power	1,280	Bank Loan	15,000
Sundry Debtors	78,200	Purchases returns	1,740
Factory Lighting	950	Sales	2,50,850
		Reserve for Bad Debts	2,000

Prepare the Trading and Profit and Loss Account for the year ended 31st December, 2012 and the balance Sheet as on that date taking into consideration the following information:

(*a*) Stock in hand on 31st December, 2012 was valued at ₹ 30,500.

(*b*) Depreciate Plant and Machinery by 10%, Furniture by 5% and Motor car by ₹ 1,000

(*c*) Bring provision for Bad debts to 5% on Sundry Debtors.

(*d*) A commission of 1% on the gross profit is to be provided for Works Manager.

(*e*) A commission of 2% (two percent) on net profit (after charging the Works Manager commission but before charging General Managers Commission) is to be paid to the General Manager.

Solution: **Trading A/c for the year ending 31st December, 2012**

		(₹)			(₹)
To Opening Stock		34,200	By Sales	2,50,850	
To Purchases	1,02,000		*Less*: Returns	3,100	2,47,750
Less: Return	1,740	1,00,260	By Closing Stock		30,500
To Freight on Purchases		1,860			
To Manufacturing Wages		34,500			
To Manufacturing Expenses		9,500			
To Factory, Fuel & Power		1,280			
To Factory Lighting		950			
To Gross Profit transferred to Profit and Loss A/c		95,700			
		2,78,250			2,78,500

Profit and Loss Account for the year ending 31st December, 2012

		(₹)		(₹)
To Salaries		15,850	By Gross Profit	95,700
To Freight on Sales		2,140		
To Insurance & Tax		4,250		
To General Expenses		8,200		
To Bad Debts	1,400			
Add: New Provision	3,910			
	5,310			
Less: Old Provision	2,000	3,310		
To Intt./Bank Charge		400		
To Dep. On P & M		2,000		
To Dep. On Furniture		500		
To Dep. On Motor Car		1,000		
To Work Manager Commission		957		
To GM Commission		1,142		
To Net Profit		55,951		
		95,700		95,700

Balance Sheet as at 31st December, 2012

Liabilities		(₹)	Assets		(₹)
Capital	80,000		Plant & machinery	20,000	
Add: Net Profit	55,951	1,35,951	*Less*: Depreciation	(2,000)	18,000
Sundry Creditors		44,560	Furniture	10,000	
Bank Loan		15,000	*Less*: Depreciation	(500)	9,500
Work Manager Commission		957	Building		24,000
G.M. Commission		1,142	Motor Car	12,000	
			Less: Depreciation	1,000	11,000
			Goodwill		25,000
			Closing Stock		30,500
			Debtors	78,200	
			Less: New Provision	3,910	74,290
			Cash in Hand		4,200
			Cash at Bank		1,120
		1,97,610			1,97,610

Illustration 15: The following is the Trial Balance of Kamal Enterprises for the year ended 31st December, 2012. You are required to prepare a Profit and Loss Account and Balance Sheet after taking into account the adjustments given below:

Dr.	(₹)	Cr.	(₹)
Cash in Hand	500	Sales	1,50,300
Cash at Bank	1,200	Purchase Returns	5,000
Office Furniture	6,000	Accounts Payable	12,000
Accounts Receivable	15,000	Bills Payable	8,000
Commissions	1,200	Discount Received	1,000
Bills Receivable	3,500	Dividend Received	2,000
Power and Fuel	6,000	Rent Received	3,500
Plant & Machinery	24,000	Capital	27,000
Office Expenses	2,000		
Carriage Inwards	1,200		
Carriage Outwards	3,500		
Rent, Rates & Taxes	1,700		
Leasehold Premises	25,000		
Wages	30,000		
Salaries	7,000		
Opening Inventory	12,000		
Sales Returns	2,000		
Purchases	60,000		
Drawings	7,000		
	2,08,800		2,08,800

Adjustments:

1. Closing inventory as on 31.12.2013 ₹ 18,000.
2. Depreciate Plant and machinery at 10%.
3. Salaries outstanding ₹ 1,000, Power and Fuel outstanding ₹ 2,000.
4. ₹ 5,000 was spent on Plant and machinery but wrongly included in wages.
5. Provide for bad and doubtful debts for ₹ 1,500.
6. Discount earned but not received ₹ 100.
7. Commission due but not recorded ₹ 200.
8. Rent received includes ₹ 500 received in advance.

Solution: **Kamal Enterprises**

Trading and Profit and Loss Account for the year ending 31.12.2012

Dr. **Cr.**

	(₹)	(₹)		(₹)	(₹)
To Opening Inventory		12,000	By Sales	1,50,300	
To Purchases	60,000		*Less*: Returns	2,000	1,48,300
Less: Return	5,000	55,000	By Closing Inventory		18,000
To Wages	30,000				
Add: Spent on Plant & Machinery	5,000	25,000			
To Fuel and Power	6,000				
Add: Outstanding	2,000	8,000			
To Carriage Inwards		1,200			

	(₹)	(₹)		(₹)	(₹)
To Gross Profit c/d		65,100			
		1,66,300			1,66,300
To Office Expenses		2,000	By Gross Profit b/d		65,100
To Commission	1,200		By Discounts Recd.	1,000	
Add: Outstanding	200	1,400	*Add*: Discounts earned but not Received	100	1,100
To Carriage Outwards		3,500	By Dividend Recd.		2,000
To Rent, Rates & Taxes		1,700	By Rent Received	3,500	
To Salaries	7,000		*Less*: Received in Advance	500	3,000
Add: Outstanding	1,000	8,000			
To Provision for Bad & Doubtful Debt		1,500			
To Depreciation on Plant and Machinery (Calculated on ₹ 29,000)		29,000			
To Net Profit c/d		50,200			
		71,200			71,200

Dr. **Balance Sheet as on 31.12.2012** **Cr.**

Liabilities	(₹)	(₹)	Assets	(₹)	(₹)
To Capital	27,000		Plant & Machinery	29,000	
Add: Net Profit	50,200		*Less*: Depreciation	(2,900)	26,100
	77,200		Office Furniture		6,000
Less: Drawings	7,000	70,200	Leasehold Premises		25,000
Accounts Payable		12,000	Account Receivable	15,000	
Bills Payable		8,000	*Less*: Provision for Bad and Doubtful Debts	1,500	13,500
Salaries Outstanding		1,000	Discount Earned but not Received		100
Fuel and Power O/S		2,000	Bills Receivable		3,500
Commission due		200	Closing Inventory		18,000
Rent Received in Advance		500	Cash in Hand		500
			Cash at Bank		1,200
		93,900			93,900

Illustration 16: The following is the Trial Balance of Rajan Jewellers as on December 31, 2012:

Dr.	(₹)	Cr.	(₹)
Opening Inventory	72,000	Capital	5,00,000
Purchases	2,25,000	Sales	3,50,000
Furniture	15,000	Purchase Returns	1,800
Motor Car	30,000	Murthy	32000
Buildings	4,25,800	Vardan	24,000
Gangappa	12,000	Commission	7,500
Gorishankar	20,000		
Mathews	18,000		
Advertisement	22,000		

Dr.	(₹)	Cr.	(₹)
Repairs and Maintenance	13,000		
General Expenses	16,000		
Insurance	7,000		
Cash in hand	3,500		
Cash at Bank	6,000		
Salaries	30,000		
	9,15,300		9,15,300

Notes: To arrive at Accounts Receivable and Accounts Payable you have to add necessary ledger accounts.

You are required to draft Profit and Loss account and Balance Sheet as on 31st December, 2012.

1. Closing inventory as at 31.12.2012 ₹ 80,000.
2. Interest on Capital at 6%.
3. Prepaid advertisement ₹ 2,000.
4. Goods used for domestic purposes ₹ 1,800.
5. Outstanding Salaries ₹ 3,000.
6. Depreciation on Buildings at 5%, Furniture 5% and Motor Car at 10%.

Solution:

Rajan Jewellers

Trading and Profit and Loss Account for the year ending 31.12.2012

Dr. Cr.

	(₹)	(₹)		(₹)	(₹)
To Opening Inventory		72,000	By Sales		3,50,000
To Purchases	2,25,000		By Closing Inventory		80,000
Less: Return	1,800				
	2,23,200				
Less: Drawings	1,800	2,21,400			
To Gross Profit		1,36,600			
		4,30,000			4,30,000
To Advertisement	22,000		By Gross Profit		1,36,600
Less: Prepaid	(2,000)	20,000	By Commission		7,500
To General Expenses		16,000			
To Insurance		7,000			
To Repairs and Maintenance		13,000			
To Salaries	30,000				
Add: Outstanding	3,000	33,000			
To Interest on Capital		30,000			
To Depreciation On:					
Building	21,290				
Furniture	750				
Motor Car	3,000	25,040			
To Net Profit		60			
		1,44,100			1,44,100

Dr. **Balance Sheet as on 31.12.2012** **Cr.**

Liabilities	(₹)	(₹)	Assets	(₹)	(₹)
To Capital	5,00,000		Building	4,25,800	
Add: Net Profit	60		*Less*: Depreciation	21,290	4,04,510
Add: Interest on Capital	30,000		Furniture	15,000	
	5,30,060		*Less*: Depreciation	(750)	14,250
Less: Drawings	1,800	5,28,060	Motor car	30,000	
Accounts Payable:			*Less*: Depreciation	3,000	27,000
Murthy	32,000		**Accounts Receivable:**		
Varadan	24,000	56,000	Gangappa	12,000	
Outstanding Salaries		3,000	Gorishankar	20,000	
			Mathews	18,000	50,000
			Cash in Hand		3,500
			Cash at Bank		6,000
			Closing Inventory		80,000
			Prepaid Advertisement		2,000
		5,87,260			5,87,260

Illustration 17: On March 31, 2012 the following Trial Balance was extracted from the books of W Brothers:

	(₹)	(₹)
Capital A/c		1,00,000
Plant and Machinery	1,00,000	
Sales		4,07,000
Purchases	2,60,000	
Returns	6,000	5,750
Opening Stocks	40,000	
Discounts	350	
Bank Charges	75	
S. Debtors	45,000	
S. Creditors		35,000
Salaries	26,800	
Wages	30,000	
Carriage	1,950	
Bad Debts Provision		1,325
Rent, Rates & Taxes	10,000	
Advertising	2,000	
Cash in Hand	900	
Cash at Bank	6,000	
Furniture & Fitting	20,000	
	5,49,075	5,49,075

You are required to prepare final accounts for the year ended 31st March, 2012 and the balance sheet as on the date. The following adjustments are required:

1. Closing stock ₹ 35,000.
2. Depreciation on Plant and Machinery @ 15% p.a. and on furniture and fittings @ 10% p.a. to be provided.
3. Bad debts provision to be adjusted to ₹ 500.

4. Interest on capital to be allowed at 10% p.a.
5. 15% of the profit remaining after charging interest on capital to be carried to General reserve.

Solution:

Trading and Profit and Loss A/c of W. Brother for the year ending 31st March, 2012

		(₹)			(₹)
To Opening Stock		40,000	By Sales	4,07,000	
To Purchases	2,60,000		*Less*: Sales Returns	6,000	4,01,000
Less: Returns	5,750	2,54,250	By Closing Stock		35,000
To Carriage Inward		1,950			
To Wages		30,000			
To Gross Profit c/d		1,09,800			
		4,36,000			4,36,000
To Salaries		26,800	By Gross Profit b/d		1,09,800
To Rent, Rates & Taxes		10,000	By Provision for Bad Debt	1,325	
To Advertising		2,000	*Less*: New Provision	500	825
To Discount		350			
To Bank Charges		75			
To Depreciation on Plant and Machinery	15,000				
Furniture & Fittings	2,000	17,000			
To Interest on Capital		10,000			
To General Reserve (15% of ₹ 44,400)		6,660			
To Net Profit		37,740			
		1,10,625			1,10,625

Balance Sheet as on 31st March, 2012

		(₹)			(₹)
Sundry Creditors		35,000	Plant and Machinery	1,00,000	
General Reserve		6,660	*Less*: Depreciation	(15,000)	85,000
Capital	1,00,000		Furniture & Fixture	20,000	
Add: Net Profit	37,740		*Less*: Depreciation	(2,000)	18,000
Add: Interest on Capital	10,000	1,47,740	Stocks		35,000
			Sundry debtors	45,000	
			Less: Provision	500	44,500
			Cash at Bank		6,000
			Cash in Hand		900
		1,89,400			1,89,400

Illustration 18: From the following Trial Balance of Mr. Gopal for the year ending 31.3.2012 and additional information given, prepare Trading and Profit & Loss Account and Balance Sheet as at 31.3.2012:

Trial Balance

Particulars	Dr. (₹)	Cr. (₹)
Opening Stock	25,000	—
Capital	—	2,25,000
Debtors and Creditor	30,000	17,500
Purchases and Sales	2,00,000	3,50,000

Particulars	Dr. (₹)	Cr. (₹)
Returns	7,500	5,000
Carriage	4,000	—
Wages and Salaries	12,500	—
Commission	—	6,500
Machinery	40,000	—
Furniture	10,000	—
Bad debts	4,000	—
Provision for doubtful debts	—	5,000
B/R and B/P	15,000	3,500
Land and Buildings	2,00,000	—
Taxes and Insurance	8,500	—
Discount allowed	6,000	—
Bank	25,000	—
Drawings	25,000	—
	6,12,500	6,12,500

Additional Information:

(*a*) Value of the Closing Stock, as on 31st March, 2012 is ₹ 20,000.

(*b*) Wages and Salaries outstanding is ₹ 500 and Insurance prepaid is ₹ 2,000.

(*c*) Provide for doubtful debts on the debtors at the rate of 10%.

(*d*) Depreciate machinery and furniture at the rate of 10% and 15% respectively.

(*e*) Goods costing ₹ 12,000 were sold on the approval basis for ₹ 15,000 but these were not approved by the customers as yet.

Solution:

Trading and Profit & Loss Account for the year ending 31st March, 2012

Dr. Cr.

Particulars		(₹)	Particulars		(₹)
To Opening Stock		25,000	By Sales	3,50,000	
To Purchases	2,00,000		*Less*: Goods sent on approval	15,000	
Less: Returns	5,000	1,95,000	(on Selling Price)	3,35,000	
To Carriage		4,000	*Less*: Return	7,500	3,27,000
To Wages and Salaries:	12,500		By Closing Stock	20,000	
Add: Wages and Salaries O/S	500	13,000	*Add*: Stock on approval (at cost)	12,000	32,000
To Profit & Loss A/c		1,22,500	By Trading A/c		3,59,500
(Gross Profit transferred)		3,59,500	Gross Profit transferred		1,22,500
To Bad Debts	4,000		By Commission		6,500
Add: Provision for doubtful debts	1,500				
	5,500				
Less: Provision for doubtful debts	5,000	500			
To Taxes and Insurance	8,500				
Less: Prepaid Insurance	2,000	6,500			
To Discount allowed		6,000			
To Depreciation on:					
Machinery	4,000				
Furniture	1,500	5,500			
To Capital A/c					
Net Profit transferred		1,10,500			
		1,29,000			1,29,000

Balance Sheet as at 31.3.2012

Liabilities		₹	Assets		₹
Creditors		17,500	Bank		25,000
Bills Payable		3,500	Debtors	30,000	
Wages and Salaries O/S		500	*Less*: Goods sent on approval	15,000	
Capital	2,25,000			15,000	
Add: Net Profit	1,10,500		*Less*: Provision for doubtful debts	1,500	13,500
	3,35,000		Prepaid Insurance		2,000
Less: Drawings	25,000	3,10,500	Closing Stock	20,000	
			Add: Stock on Approval	12,000	32,000
			Bills Receivable		15,000
			Machinery	40,000	
			Less: Depreciation	4,000	36,000
			Furniture	10,000	
			Less: Depreciation	1,500	8,500
			Land and Buildings		2,00,000
		3,32,000			3,32,000

Illustration 19: From the following Trial Balance of Mr. Gaurav Singh for the year ending 31.3.2012 and additional information given, prepare Trading and Profit and Loss A/c and Balance Sheet as at 31.3.2012.

Trial Balance

Particulars	Dr. (₹)	Cr. (₹)
Opening Stock	62,500	—
Capital	—	4,64,000
Debtors and Creditors	75,000	43,750
Purchases and Sales	5,00,000	8,75,000
Carriage	10,000	—
Wages and Salaries	31,250	—
Commission	—	16,750
Machinery	1,38,750	—
Furniture	25,000	—
Bad Debts recovered	—	8,000
B/R and B/P	37,500	33,750
Land and Buildings	5,00,000	—
Taxes and Insurance	21,250	—
10% Bank Loan	—	50,000
Interest on Bank Loan	3,000	—
Bank	24,500	—
Drawings	62,500	—
	14,91,250	14,91,250

Additional Information:

(*i*) Value of the Closing Stock, as on 31st March, 2012 is ₹ 50,000.

(*ii*) Wages and Salaries outstanding is ₹ 12,500 and Insurance prepaid is ₹ 5,000.

(*iii*) Depreciate Machinery and Furniture @ 10% and 15% per annum respectively. Machinery included a machine which was purchased for ₹ 38,500 on 30th September, 2011.

(*iv*) Goods costing ₹ 10,000 were taken by the proprietor for his personal use, but no entry has been made in the books of accounts.

Solution:

Mr. Gaurav Singh Trading and Profit & Loss Account for the year ending 31st March, 2012

Dr. Particulars		Amount (₹)	Particulars	Cr. Amount (₹)
To Opening Stock		62,500	By Sales	8,75,000
To Purchases	5,00,000		By Closing Stock	50,000
Less: Transfer to Drawings A/c	1,000	4,90,000		
To Carriage		10,000		
To Wages and Salaries	31,250			
Add: Outstanding	12,500	43,750		
To Gross Profit c/d		3,18,750		
		9,25,000		9,25,000
To Taxes and Insurance	21,250		By Gross Profit b/d	3,18,750
Less: Insurance Prepaid	5,000	16,250	By Commission	16,750
To Interest on Bank Loan	3,000		By Bad Debts Recovered	8,000
Add: Outstanding	2,000	5,000		
To Depreciation on:				
Machinery				
₹ 1,00,000 × 10/100	10,000			
₹ 38,500 × 10/100 × 3/12	962			
Furniture	3,750	14,712		
To Net Profit transferred to Capital A/c		3,07,538		
		3,43,500		3,43,500

Balance Sheet as on 31.3.2012

Liabilities		Amount (₹)	Assets		Amount (₹)
10% Bank Loan		50,000	Bank		24,500
Interest on Loan due		2,000	B/R		37,500
B/P		33,750	Furniture	25,000	
Creditors		43,750	*Less*: Depreciation	3,750	21,250
Outstanding Wages and Salaries		12,500	Machinery	1,38,750	
Capital	4,64,000		*Less*: Depreciation	10,962	1,27,788
+ Net Profit	3,07,538		Debtors		75,000
	7,71,538		Land and Buildings		5,00,000
Drawings			Prepaid Insurance		5,000
₹ (62,500 + 10,000)	72,500	6,99,038	Closing Stock		50,000
		8,41,038			8,41,038

Illustration 20: The following is the schedule of balances on 31.3.2012 extracted from the books of Shri Gavaskar.

Particulars	Dr. (₹)	Cr. (₹)
Cash in Hand	1,400	
Cash at Bank	2,600	—
Sundry Debtors	86,000	—
Stock as on 1.4.2011	62,000	—

Particulars	Dr. (₹)	Cr. (₹)
Furniture and Fixture	21,400	—
Office Equipment	16,000	—
Buildings	60,000	—
Motor Car	20,000	—
Sundry Creditors	—	43,000
Loan	—	30,000
Reserve for Bad Debts	—	3,000
Purchases	1,40,000	—
Purchase returns	—	2,600
Sales	—	2,30,000
Sales returns	4,200	—
Salaries	11,000	—
Rent for godown	5,500	—
Interest on Loan	2,700	—
Rates and Taxes	2,100	—
Discount allowed to Debtors	2,400	—
Discount received from Creditors	—	1,600
Freight on Purchases	1,200	—
Carriage outwards	2,000	—
Drawings	12,000	—
Printing and Stationery	1,800	—
Electric charges	2,200	—
Insurance Premium	5,500	—
General Office Expenses	3,000	—
Bad Debts	2,000	—
Bank charges	1,600	—
Motor Car Expenses	3,600	—
Capital Account	—	1,62,000
	4,72,200	4,72,200

Prepare Trading and Profit & Loss Account for the year ended 31.3.2012 and the Balance Sheet as on that date after making provision for the following:

1. Depreciate:

(*a*) Building by 5%;

(*b*) Furniture and Fixture by 10%;

(*c*) Office equipment by 15%; and

(*d*) Motor Car by 20%.

2. Value of stock at the close of the year was ₹ 44,000.

3. Reserve for bad debts is to be maintained at 5% of Sundry Debtors.

4. Insurance premium includes ₹ 4,000 paid towards proprietor's life insurance policy and the balance of the insurance charges cover the period from 1.4.2011 to 30.6.2012.

Solution:

Dr. **Trading and Profit & Loss A/c of Shri Gavaskar for the year ended 31.3.2012** **Cr.**

Particulars		Amount (₹)	Particulars		Amount (₹)
To Opening Stock		62,000	By Sales	2,30,000	
To Purchases	1,40,000		*Less*: Returns	4,200	2,25,800
Less: Returns	2,600.	1,37,400	By Closing Stock		44,000
To Freight on Purchases		1,200			
To Profit & Loss A/c (Gross Profit)		69,200			
		2,69,800			2,69,800
To Salaries		11,000	By Trading A/c (Gross Profit)		69,200
To Rent for godown		5,500	By Discount Received		1,600
To Interest on Loan		2,700			
To Rates and Taxes		2,100			
To Discount allowed		2,400			
To Carriage outwards		2,000			
To Printing and Stationery		1,800			
To Electric charges		2,200			
To Insurance Premium	5,500				
Less: Drawings	4,000				
	1,500				
Less: Prepaid	300	1,200			
To Office Expenses		3,000			
To Bank Charges		1,600			
To Motor Car Expenses		3,600			
To Bad Debts	2,000				
Add: New Provision	4,300				
	6,300				
Less: Old Provision	3,000	3,300			
To Depreciation on:					
Buildings	3,000				
Furniture & Fixtures	2,140				
Office Equipment	2,400				
Motor Car	4,000	11,540			
To Net Profit transferred to Capital Account		16,860			
		70,800			70,800

Balance Sheet as on 31st March, 2012

Liabilities		Amount (₹)	Assets		Amount (₹)
Sundry Creditors		43,000	Cash in Hand		1,400
Loan		30,000	Cash at Bank		2,600
Capital	1,62,000		Sundry Debtors	86,000	
Add: Net Profit	16,860		*Less*: Provision	4,300	81,700
	1,78,860		Stock at the end		44,000
Less: Drawings:	12,000		Prepaid Insurance		300

Liabilities	Amount (₹)	Assets		Amount (₹)
L.I.C. Premium	4,000	Furniture and Fixtures	21,400	
	1,62,860		2,140	19,260
		Office Equipment	16,000	
		Less: Depreciation	2,400	13,600
		Buildings	60,000	
		Less: Depreciation	3,000	57,000
		Motor Car	20,000	
		Less: Depreciation	4,000	16,000
	2,35,860			2,35,860

Illustration 21: From the Trial Balance of 31.3.2012 and additional information given, prepare Trading and Profit and Loss Account and Balance Sheet as on 31.3.2012:

Trial Balance

Particulars	Debit (₹)	Credit (₹)
Capital	—	4,00,000
Drawings	50,000	—
Opening Stock	75,000	—
Purchases	4,20,000	—
Sundry Creditors	—	75,000
Sundry Debtors	1,20,000	—
Sales	—	8,10,000
Discounts	16,000	18,000
Commissions	12,000	14,000
Returns	16,000	20,000
Salaries	1,20,000	—
Rent, Rates and Taxes	40,000	—
Postage, Telegrams and Telephones	25,000	—
Loan	—	3,10,000
Interest	20,000	—
Furniture	3,50,000	—
Brand Names and Designs (Patents)	60,000	—
Advertisement	1,00,000	—
Cash in Hand	1,50,000	—
Cash at Bank	63,000	—
Freight Inward	20,000	—
Duty Drawbacks (Income)	—	10,000
	16,57,000	16,57,000

Other Information:

(*i*) Closing Stock ₹ 1,70,000.

(*ii*) Sales included Sales Tax ₹ 50,000.

(*iii*) Depreciate Furniture @ 10%.

(*iv*) Write-off Brand Names and Designs @ 20%.

(*v*) Advertisement to be written-off in 5 years.

(*vi*) Salaries outstanding ₹ 12,000 and Salaries paid in Advance ₹ 10,000.

Solution:

Trading and Profit & Loss Account for the year ended 31.3.2012

Dr. Cr.

Particulars		Amount (₹)	Particulars		Amount (₹)
To Opening Stock		75,000	**By Sales**	8,10,000	
To Purchases	4,20,000		*Less*: Returns	16,000	
Add: Freight Inward	20,000			7,94,000	
	4,40,000		*Less*: Sales tax	50,000	7,44,000
Less: Returns	20,000		By Closing Stock		1,70,000
	4,20,000				
Less: Duty Drawback*	10,000	4,10,000			
To Gross Profit transferred to Profit and Loss A/c		4,29,000			
		9,14,000			9,14,000
To Salaries	1,20,000		By Gross Profit		4,29,000
Add: Outstanding	12,000		By Discount Received		18,000
	1,32,000		By Commission Received		14,000
Less: Paid in Advance	10,000	1,22,000			
To Rent, Rates and Taxes		40,000			
To Postage, Telegrams and Telephone		25,000			
To Discount allowed		16,000			
To Commission allowed		12,000			
To Interest		20,000			
To Depreciation on Furniture		35,000			
To Amortization of Brand Names and Designs		12,000			
To Amortization of Advertisement (1/5 of ₹ 1,00,000)		20,000			
To Net Profit Transferred to Capital A/c		1,59,000			
		4,61,000			4,61,000

Balance Sheet as on 31st March, 2012

Liabilities		Amount (₹)	Assets		Amount (₹)
Capital	4,00,000		Furniture	3,50,000	
Add: Net Profit	1,59,000		*Less*: Depreciation	35,000	3,15,000
	5,59,000		Brand Names & Design	60,000	
Less: Drawings	50,000	5,09,000	*Less*: Amortization	12,000	48,000
Loan		3,10,000	Advertisement	1,00,000	
Sundry Creditors		75,000	*Less*: Amortization	20,000	80,000
Outstanding Salaries		12,000	Closing Stock		1,70,000
Provision for Sales-tax Liability		50,000	Sundry Debtors		1,20,000
			Prepaid Salaries		10,000
			Cash at Bank		63,000
			Cash in Hand		1,50,000
		9,56,000			9,56,000

Duty Drawback: This is paid to exporter as an incentive. It is duty levied on purchases and is returned subsequently. This can be treated as income or alternatively can be deducted from purchases.

Illustration 22: From the undermentioned trial balance of Banerjee, prepare the final accounts for the year ended 31st March, 2012 and the Balance Sheet as at that date:

Particulars	Debit (₹)	Credit (₹)
Land and Buildings	50,000	—
Purchases (Adjusted)	2,10,000	—
Stock (March 31st, 2012)	45,000	—
Returns	1,500	2,500
Wages	45,300	—
Salaries	39,000	—
Office Expenses	15,400	—
Carriage Inwards	1,200	—
Carriage Outwards	2,000	—
Discounts	750	1,200
Bad Debts	1,200	—
Sales	—	3,85,000
Capital Account	—	1,15,000
Chatterji's Loan A/c (taken on 1.10.2011 @ 18% p.a.)	—	25,000
Insurance	1,500	—
Commission	—	1,500
Plant and Machinery	50,000	—
Furniture and Fixtures	20,000	—
Bills Receivable	20,000	—
Sundry Debtors	40,000	—
Sundry Creditors	—	25,000
Cash at Bank	16,000	—
Office Equipment	12,000	—
Bills Payable	—	12,350
Expenses Payable	—	3,300
	5,70,850	5,70,850

The following adjustments be taken care of:

(*i*) Depreciate Land and Buildings @ 6%, Plant and Machinery @ 10%, Office Equipment @ 20% and Furniture and Fixtures @ 15%.

(*ii*) Create a provision for bad and doubtful debts at 2% on debtors.

(*iii*) Insurance premium includes ₹ 250 paid in advance.

(*iv*) Provide interest on capital @ 10% p.a. and salary to Banerjee ₹ 15,000.

Solution: **Trading and Profit & Loss Account of Mr. Banerjee for the year ending on 31.3.2012**

Dr. **Cr.**

Particulars		Amount (₹)	Particulars		Amount (₹)
To Purchases (Adju.)	2,10,000		By Sales	3,85,000	
Less: Returns	2,500	2,07,500	*Less*: Sales Return	1,500	3,83,500
To Wages		45,300			
To Carriage inwards		1,200			
To Gross Profit c/d		1,29,500			
		3,83,500			3,83,500

Particulars		Amount (₹)	Particulars	Amount (₹)
To Salaries		39,000	By Gross Profit b/d	1,29,500
To Office Expenses		15,400	By Discount	1,200
To Carriage Outwards		2,000	By Commission	1,500
To Discount		750		
To Insurance	1,500			
Less: Insurance prepaid	250	1,250		
To Bad Debts	1,200			
Add: Provision Required [₹ 40,000 × 2%]	800	2,000		
To Interest on: Chatterji's Loan O/S [₹ 25,000 @ 18% for 6 months]		2,250		
To Depreciation on:				
Land & Buildings	3,000			
Plant & Machinery	5,000			
Office Equipment	2,400			
Furniture & Fixtures	3,000	13,400		
To Interest on Capital		11,500		
To Salary to Banerjee		15,000		
To Transfer to General Reserve*[1]		2,965		
To Capital A/c Net Profit*[2]		26,685		
		1,32,200		1,32,200

Working Notes:

*[1] Profit before transfer to General Reserve = ₹ 29,650

[₹ (1,29,500 + 1,200 + 1,500 – 39,000 – 15,400 – 2,000 – 750 – 1,250 – 2,000 – 2,250 – 13,400 – 11,500 – 15,000) = ₹ 29,650]

Transferred to General Reserve $= ₹\ 29{,}650 \times \frac{10}{100} = ₹\ 2{,}965$

*[2] Net Profit = ₹ 29,650 – ₹ 2,965 = ₹ 26,685.

Balance Sheet of Mr. Banerji as on March 31st, 2012

Liabilities		Amount (₹)	Assets		Amount (₹)
Bills Payable		12,350	**Fixed Assets:**		
Sundry Creditors		25,000	Land and Buildings	50,000	
Expenses Payable		3,300	*Less*: Depreciation	3,000	47,000
Chatterji's Loan	25,000		Plant and Machinery	50,000	
Add: Int. Outstanding	2,250	27,250	*Less*: Depreciation	5,000	45,000
General Reserve		2,965	Furniture & Fixtures	20,000	
Capital Account	1,15,000		*Less*: Depreciation	3,000	17,000
Add: Interest on Capital	11,500		Office Equipment	12,000	
Salary	15,000		*Less*: Depreciation	2,400	9,600

Liabilities		Amount (₹)	Assets		Amount (₹)
Net Profit	26,685	1,68,185	**Current Assets:**		
			Stock		45,000
			Sundry Debtors	40,000	
			Less: Provision	800	39,200
			Bills Receivable		20,000
			Prepaid Insurance		250
			Cash at Bank		16,000
		2,39,050			2,39,050

Illustration 23: From the following Trial Balance of Shishir, you are required to prepare Final Accounts for the year ended 31 March, 2012 after making the necessary adjustments.

Particulars	Debit (₹)	Credit (₹)
Capital & Drawings Accounts	10,000	2,00,000
Freehold Property	60,000	—
Plant and Machinery	1,00,000	—
Salaries	14,000	—
Printing and Stationery	2,000	—
Furniture and Fixtures	4,000	—
Discount	1,500	—
Bills Payable	—	5,700
Debtors and Creditors	25,000	40,000
Insurance	3,000	—
Bad Debts	600	—
Office Rent	2,600	—
Loose Tools	2,000	—
Provision for Doubtful Debts	—	4,800
Loan to Sudhir @ 10% on 1st October, 2011	40,000	—
Interest on loan to Sudhir	—	1,000
Cash at Bank	25,000	—
Cash in Hand	10,500	—
Stock—31st March, 2012	74,000	—
Trading Profits	—	1,17,200
Outstanding Wages on 31st March, 2012	—	500
Insurance Claim received for Loss of Goods	—	5,000
Total:	3,74,200	3,74,200

Adjustments:

(*i*) Outstanding Salaries ₹ 700.

(*ii*) Prepaid Insurance ₹ 400.

(*iii*) Value of Loose Tools on 31st March, 2012—₹ 1,500.

(*iv*) A new machinery was purchased on credit and installed on 31st December, 2011 costing ₹ 15,000. No entry for the same has yet been made in the books.

(*v*) Depreciate (on Closing Balance)—Plant and Machinery at 10 per cent, Furniture and Fixtures at 5 per cent.

(*vi*) The provision for doubtful debts is to be maintained at 5 per cent on debtors.

Solution:

Profit and Loss Account of Mr. Shishir for the year ending on 31.3.2012

Dr. **Cr.**

Particulars		Amount (₹)	Particulars		Amount (₹)
To Salaries	14,000		By Trading A/c (Trading Profit)		1,17,200
Add: Outstanding	700	14,700	By Interest on loan	1,000	
To Printing and Stationery		2,000	*Add*: Accrued	1,000	2,000
To Discount		1,500	By Insurance Claim Received		5,000
To Insurance	3,000		By Provision for Doubtful Debts (31.3.2011)	4,800	
Less: Prepaid	400	2,600			
To Bad Debts		600	*Less*: Provision required (5% of ₹ 25,000)	1,250	3,550
To Office Rent		2,600			
To Depreciation on:					
Loose Tools	500				
Plants Machinery [1,15,000 × 10/100]	11,500				
Furniture and Fixtures [400 × 5/100]	200	12,200			
To Net Profit transferred to Capital Account		91,550			
		1,27,750			1,27,750

Balance Sheet as at 31st March, 2012

Liabilities		Amount (₹)	Assets		Amount (₹)
Capital	2,00,000		Freehold Property		60,000
Add: Net Profit	91,550		Plant and Machinery	1,00,000	
	2,91,550		Additions	15,000	
				1,15,000	
Less: Drawings	10,000	2,81,550	*Less*: Depreciation	11,500	1,03,500
Bills Payable		5,700	Furniture and Fixtures	4,000	
Creditors		40,000	*Less*: Depreciation	200	3,800
Creditors for Machinery		15,000	Loose Tools	2,000	
			Less: Depreciation	500	1,500
Outstanding Wages		500	Debtors	25,000	
Outstanding Salaries		700	*Less*: Provision	1,250	23,750
			Loan to Sudhir	40,000	
			Add: Interest Accrued	1,000	41,000
			Cash at Bank		25,000
			Cash in Hand		10,500
			Stock		74,000
			Prepaid Insurance		400
		3,43,450			3,43,450

Illustration 24: From the following Trial Balance of a trader on March 31st, 2012, prepare Trading and Profit & Loss Account for the year ending 31st March, 2012 and Balance Sheet as at that date after giving effect to the undermentioned adjustments:

Debit Balances	Amount (₹)	Credit Balances	Amount (₹)
Drawings	6,000	Bank Overdraft	25,000
Wages	15,500	Interest on Investment	5,800
Stock	12,800	Bills Payable	4,600
Loan to X	4,000	Interest on Loan to X	320
Rent	5,000	Capital	1,00,000
General Expenses	1,480	Reserve for Bad and doubtful debts	250
Investments	60,000	Sales	2,30,000
Purchases	1,60,000	Sundry Creditors	12,590
Freight and Carriage	2,100		
Goodwill	40,000		
Bills Receivable	6,200		
Rates and Taxes	1,800		
Sales Returns	2,100		
Insurance	900		
Cash & Bank Balance	3,700		
Postage & Telegram	3,800		
Land & Buildings	25,000		
Plant & Machinery	10,000		
Sundry debtors	16,500		
Packing Charges	400		
Bad debts	1,280		
	3,78,560		3,78,560

Adjustments:

(*i*) Closing Stock as on 31.3.2012—₹ 16,000.

(*ii*) Goods worth ₹ 700 were sent on 25.3.2012 as "Sale on Approval Basis" for ₹ 800 and the approval was not received before the end of the month.

(*iii*) 20% of the goodwill is to be written off.

(*iv*) Further bad debts were estimated at ₹ 350. Increase reserve for bad debts to the extent of ₹ 1,500.

(*v*) Depreciate Land and Building by 3% and Plant & Machinery by 10%.

(*vi*) Goods worth ₹ 800 were distributed as free samples.

Solution:

Trading and Profit & Loss Account
for the year ending on 31.3.2012

Dr. **Cr.**

Particulars		Amount (₹)	Particulars		Amount (₹)
To Opening Stock		12,800	By Sales	2,30,000	
To Purchases	1,60,000		*Less:* On Approval	800	
Less: Samples	800	1,59,200		2,29,200	
To Freight and Carriage		2,100	*Less:* Returns	2,100	2,27,700
To Wages		15,500	By Stock at the end	16,000	
To Gross Profit c/d		54,200	*Add:* On approval	700	16,700
		2,43,800			2,43,800
To Free Samples		800	By Gross Profit b/d		54,200
To Rent		5,000	By Interest on Investment		5,800

Particulars		Amount (₹)	Particulars	Amount (₹)
To General Expenses		1,480	By Interest on Loan	320
To Rates and Taxes		1,800		
To Insurance		900		
To Postage and Telegram		3,800		
To Packing charges		400		
To Bad Debts	1,280			
Add: Further bad debts	350			
Reserve (New)	1,500			
	3,130			
Less: Reserve for Bad & Doubtful debts (old)	250	2,880		
To Goodwill written off		8000		
To Depreciation on:				
Land and Buildings	750			
Plant and Machinery	1,000	1,750		
To Net Profit transferred to Capital Account		33,510		
		60,320		60,320

Balance Sheet as at 31st March, 2012

Liabilities		Amount (₹)	Assets		Amount (₹)
Capital	1,00,000		Goodwill	40,000	
Add: Net Profit	33,510		*Less*: w/o	8,000	32,000
	1,33,510		Land and Buildings	25,000	
Less: Drawings	6,000	1,27,510	*Less*: Depreciation	750	24,250
Bank Overdraft		25,000	Plant and Machinery	10,000	
Bills Payable		4,600	*Less*: Depreciation	1,000	9,000
Sundry Creditors		12,590	Investments		60,000
			Stock at the end		16,700
			Bills Receivable		6,200
			Sundry Debtors	16,500	
			Less: Sent on Approval	800	
				15,700	
			Less: Further bad debts	350	
				15,350	
			Less: Reserve for doubtful debts	1,500	13,850
			Cash and Bank		3,700
			Loan to X		4,000
		1,69,700			1,69,700

Illustration 25: Given below is the Trial Balance of Mr. Alok, a trader, as on 31.3.2012:

Particulars	Debit (₹)	Credit (₹)
Cash in Hand	5,000	–
Land and Building	80,000	
Plant and Machinery	50,000	

Particulars	Debit (₹)	Credit (₹)
Debtors and Creditors	25,000	40,000
Stock on 1.4.2011	10,000	
15% Investment on 1.4.2011	20,000	
Purchases and Sales	95,000	1,90,000
Bank Overdraft		20,000
Wages	28,000	
Salaries	16,000	
Rent, Rates and Taxes	15,000	
Bad Debts	6,000	
Drawings	5,000	
Bills Receivable and Bills Payable	15,000	21,000
Carriage Inwards	6,000	
Custom Duty on Purchases	16,000	
Life Insurance Premium	4,000	
Advertisement	30,000	
Provision for Doubtful Debts		2,000
Interest on investments		2,000
Trade expenses	11,000	
Furniture	20,000	
Sales Tax Payable		25,000
Capital		1,57,000
	4,57,000	4,57,000

Additional Information:

(*i*) Stock on 31.3.2012 was valued at ₹ 40,000.

(*ii*) Included in Debtors are ₹ 8,000 due from Ram and included in Creditors are ₹ 6,000 due to Ram.

(*iii*) Bills Receivable include a bill of ₹ 5,000 received from Varun, which has been dishonored.

(*iv*) Sales include ₹ 5,000 for the goods sold on approval basis. Gods are sold at a profit of 25% on cost. Approval was not received upto 31.3.2012.

(*v*) Wages include ₹ 5,000 spent on the erection of machinery.

(*vi*) Advertisement includes ₹ 20,000 spent at the time of launching a new product. It is the policy of the business to write off such expenses in 5 years.

(*vii*) Create a provision for doubtful debts at 5% on debtors.

(*viii*) Prepaid taxes amounted to ₹ 2,000.

(*ix*) Depreciate machinery by 10%.

Prepare Trading and Profit & Loss Account for the year ended 31st March, 2012 and a Balance Sheet on that date.

Solution:

Dr. Trading and Profit & Loss Account for the year ending on 31.3.2012 Cr.

Particulars		Amount (₹)	Particulars		Amount (₹)
To Opening Stock		10,000	By Sales	1,90,000	
To Purchases		95,000	*Less*: Sales on approval	5,000	1,85,000
To Wages	28,000		By Closing Stock	40,000	

Particulars		Amount (₹)	Particulars		Amount (₹)
Less: For Erection of machinery (capitalised)	5,000	23,000	*Add*: Cost of goods sold on approval*	4,000	44,000
To Carriage Inwards		6,000			
To Custom Duty on Purchases		16,000			
To Gross Profit c/d		79,000			
		2,29,000			2,29,000
To Salaries		16,000	By Gross Profit b/d		79,000
To Rent, Rates & Taxes	15,000		By Interest on investments	2,000	
Less: Prepaid	2,000	13,000	*Add*: Accrued interest	1,000	3,000
To Bad Debts	6,000				
Add: Provision for Doubtful Debts (New)*	950				
	6,950				
Less: Provision for Doubtful Debts (Old)	2,000	4,950			
To Advertisement	30,000				
Less: Carried forward	16,000	14,000			
To Trade expenses		11,000			
To Depreciation on machines		5,500			
To Net Profit transferred		17,550			
		82,000			82,000

Balance Sheet of Mr. Alok as on 31st March, 2012

Liabilities		Amount (₹)	Assets		Amount (₹)
Capital	1,57,000		Land and Building		80,000
Add: Net Profit	17,550		Plant and Machinery	50,000	
	1,74,550		*Add*: Wages	5,000	
Less: Life Insurance Premium	4,000			55,000	
	1,70,550		*Less*: Depreciation	5,500	49,500
Less: Drawings	5,000	1,65,550	Furniture		20,000
Creditors	40,000		Stock at the end ₹ [40,000 + 4,000]		44,000
Less: Due to Ram	6,000	34,000	15% Investment	20,000	
Bank Overdraft		20,000	*Add*: Accrued interest	1,000	21,000
Bills Payable		21,000	Bills Receivable	15,000	
Sales Tax Payable		25,000	*Less*: Dishonoured	5,000	10,000
			Debtors	25,000	
			Less: Sale on approval	5,000	
				20,000	
			Less: Due from Ram	6,000	
				14,000	
			Add: Varun (for Bill Dishonoured)	5,000	
				19,000	

Liabilities	Amount (₹)	Assets		Amount (₹)
		Less: Provision for Doubtful Debts	950	18,050
		Cash in hand		5,000
		Prepaid taxes		2,000
		Advertisement Suspense Account (Deferred)		16,000
	2,65,550			2,65,550

Working Notes:

$*_1$ Let the cost = ₹ 100; Profit = ₹ 25; Selling Price = ₹ 125

Cost of goods sold on approval = ₹ 5,000 × 100/125 = ₹ 4,000

$*_2$

	(₹)
Debtors	25,000
Less: Due from Ram	(6,000)
Less: Sale on Approval	(5,000)
Add: Varun for Bill Dishonoured	5,000
5% of ₹ 19,000 = ₹ 950	19,000

Illustration 26: Mr. Ajay Kumar, a shopkeeper, had prepared the following trial balance from his ledger as on 31st March, 2012:

Particulars	Debit (₹)	Credit (₹)
Purchase and Sales	6,20,000	8,30,000
Cash in hand	4,200	
Cash at Bank	24,000	
Stock of goods on 1.4.2011	1,00,000	
Capital Account		5,77,200
Drawings	8,000	
Salaries	64,000	
Postage and telephones	23,000	
Salesmen's commission	70,000	
Insurance	18,000	
Advertising	34,000	
Furniture	44,000	
Printing and Stationery	6,000	
Motor Car	96,000	
Bad Debts	4,000	
Cash Discount	8,000	
General Expenses	60,000	
Carriage Inwards	20,000	
Carriage Outwards	44,000	
Wages	40,000	
Debtors and Creditors	2,00,000	80,000
	14,87,200	14,87,200

You are required to prepare Trading and Profit & Loss Account for the year ended 31st March, 2012 and Balance Sheet as on that date. You are also given the following information:

(*i*) Stock on 31.3.2012 was ₹ 1,45,000.

(*ii*) Mr. Ajay Kumar had withdrawn goods worth ₹ 5,000 during the year.

(*iii*) Purchases include purchase of furniture worth ₹ 10,000.

(*iv*) Debtors are bad to the extent of ₹ 5,000.

(*v*) Creditors include a balance of ₹ 4,000 to the credit of Mr. Vijay in respect of which it has been decided and settled with the party to pay only ₹ 1,000.

(*vi*) Sales include goods worth ₹ 15,000 sent to Ram & Co. on approval and remaining unsold as on 31.3.2012. The cost of the goods was ₹ 10,000.

(*vii*) Provision for Bad Debts is to be created at 5% on Sundry Debtors.

(*viii*) Depreciate Furniture by 15% and Motor Car by 20%.

(*ix*) The salesmen are entitled to a commission of 10% on total sales.

Solution:

Trading and Profit & Loss Account
for the year ending 31.3.2012

Dr. **Cr.**

Particulars		Amount (₹)	Particulars		Amount (₹)
To Opening Stock		1,00,000	By Sales	8,30,000	
To Purchases	6,20,000		*Less*: Goods sent on approval	1,000	8,15,000
Less: Drawings	5,000		By Closing Stock	1,45,000	
	6,15,000		*Add*: Cost of Goods sent on approval	10,000	1,55,000
Less: Furniture	10,000	6,05,000			
To Carriage Inwards		20,000			
To Wages		40,000			
To Gross Profit b/d		2,05,000			
		9,70,000			9,70,000
To Salaries		64,000	By Gross Profit b/d		2,05,000
To Postage & telephones		23,000	By Creditors		3,000
To Salesmen's Commission	70,000		By Net Loss transferred to Capital A/c		1,75,800
Add: Outstanding Com.*	11,500	81,500			
To Insurance		18,000			
To Advertising		34,000			
To Printing & Stationery		6,000			
To Bad Debts	4,000				
Add: Further Bad Debts	5,000				
Add: Provision for Bad Debts*	9,000	18,000			
To Cash Discount		8,000			
To General Expenses		60,000			
To Carriage Outwards		44,000			
To Depreciation on:					
Furniture	8,100				
Motor car	19,200	27,300			
		3,83,800			3,83,800

Balance Sheet as at 31.3.2012

Liabilities		Amount (₹)	Assets		Amount (₹)
Creditors [₹ 80,000 – ₹ 3,000]		77,000	Cash in Hand		4,200
Outstanding Commission		11,500	Cash at Bank		24,000
Capital	5,77,200		Stock ₹ [1,45,000 + 10,000]		1,55,000
Less: Drawings ₹ [8,000 + 5,000]	13,000		Debtors	2,00,000	
			Less: Sale on approval	15,000	
	5,64,200			1,85,000	
Less: Net Loss	1,75,800	3,88,400	*Less:* Further Bad debts	5,000	
				1,80,000	
			Less: Provision for Bad debts	9,000	1,71,000
			Furniture	44,000	
			(+) Purchases	10,000	
				54,000	
			(–) Depreciation	8,100	45,900
			Motor Car	96,000	
			(–) Depreciation	19,200	76,800
		4,76,900			4,76,900

Working Notes:

* Outstanding Commission = [10% of (₹ 8,30,000 – ₹ 15,000)] – ₹ 70,000
= ₹ 81,500 – ₹ 70,000 = ₹ 11,500

* Provision for Bad Debts = 5% of [Debtors – (Further Bad Debts + Sale on approval)]
= 5% of ₹ [2,00,000 – (5,000 + 15,000)]
= 5% of ₹ [1,80,000]
= ₹ 9,000.

Illustration 27: The following Trial Balance was extracted from the books of Mr. Shyam Lal as on 31st December, 2012:

Particulars	Debit (₹)	Credit (₹)
Capital Account		1,00,000
Plant and Machinery	78,000	
Furniture	2,000	
Sales		1,27,000
Purchases	60,000	
Returns	1,000	750
Opening Stock	30,000	
Discount	425	800
Sundry Debtors and Creditors	45,000	25,000
Salaries	7,550	
Manufacturing Wages	10,000	
Carriage outwards	1,200	
Provision for Bad Debts		525
Rent, Rates and Taxes	10,000	
Advertisement	2,000	
Cash	6,900	
	2,54,075	2,54,075

Prepare Trading and Profit and Loss Account for the year ended 31st December, 2012 and Balance Sheet as on that date after taking into account the following adjustments:

(*i*) Closing stock was valued at ₹ 34,220.

(*ii*) Provision for Bad Debts is to be kept at ₹ 500.

(*iii*) Allow interest on capital at 10% p.a.

(*iv*) Furniture was old and the same was disposed off for ₹ 760 in exchange of new furniture costing ₹ 1,680. The net invoice of ₹ 920 was passed through Purchase Register (No depreciation need be charged on old and new furniture).

(*v*) Depreciate plant and machinery by 10% p.a.

(*vi*) The proprietor Mr. Shyam Lal has taken goods worth ₹ 5,000 for personal use and distributed goods worth ₹ 1,000 as samples.

Solution:

Trading and Profit & Loss Account for the year ending 31st December, 2012

Dr. **Cr.**

Particulars		Amount (₹)	Particulars		Amount (₹)
To Opening Stock		30,000	By Sales	1,27,000	
To Purchases	60,000		*Less:* Returns	1,000	1,26,000
Less: Returns	(750)		By Closing Stock		34,220
Furniture	(920)				
Samples	(1,000)				
Drawings	(5,000)	52,330			
To Wages		10,000			
To Gross Profit c/d		67,890			
		1,60,220			1,60,220
To Discount		425	By Gross Profit b/d		67,890
To Salaries		7,550	By Discount		800
To Carriage Outward		1,200	By Prov. for B/D		525
To Rent, Rates & Taxes		10,000			
To Advertisement		2,000			
To Interest on Cap.		10,000			
To Provision for B/D		500			
To Samples		1,000			
To Dep. on Plant		7,800			
To Net Profit		28,740			
		69,215			69,215

Balance Sheet as on 31st December, 2012

Liabilities		Amount (₹)	Assets		Amount (₹)
Capital	1,00,000		Plant	78,000	
Add: Interest	10,000		*Less:* Dep.	7,800	70,200
Net Profit	28,740		Furniture		2,920
Less: Drawings	(5,000)	1,33,740	Debtors	45,000	
Creditors		25,000	*Less:* Prob.	(500)	44,500
			Stock		34,220
			Cash		6,900
		1,58,740			1,58,740

Illustration 28: The following is the Trial Balance of Mr. Ram Lal as at 31st December, 2012:

Particulars	Debit (₹)	Credit (₹)
Ram Lal's Capital	—	86,690
Stock on 1.1.2012	46,800	—
Purchases and Sales	3,21,700	3,89,600
Returns	8,600	5,800
Freight and Carriage	18,600	—
Rent and Taxes	5,700	—
Salaries and Wages	9,300	—
Sundry Debtors and Creditors	24,000	14,800
Bank loan @ 6% p.a.	—	20,000
Bank Interest on loan	900	—
Printing and Advertising	14,600	—
Miscellaneous Income	—	250
Cash at Bank	8,000	—
Discount	1,800	4,190
Furniture and Fittings	5,000	—
General Expenses	11,450	—
Insurance	1,300	—
Postage and Telegrams	2,330	—
Cash in Hand	380	—
Travelling Expenses	870	—
Drawings	40,000	
	5,21,330	5,21,330

The following adjustments should be made:

(*i*) Included amongst the Debtors is ₹ 3,000 due from Suresh Kumar and included among the creditors ₹ 1,000 due to him.

(*ii*) Provision for Bad and Doubtful Debts be created at 5% and Reserve for Discount @ 2% on Sundry Debtors.

(*iii*) Depreciate Furniture and Fittings by 10%.

(*iv*) Personal Purchases amounting to ₹ 600 had been included in the Purchases Day Book.

(*v*) Interest on Bank Loan shall be provided for the whole year.

(*vi*) One quarter of the amount of Printing and Advertising is to be carried forward to next year.

(*vii*) Credit purchase invoice amounting to ₹ 400 had been omitted from the books.

(*viii*) Stock on 31st December, 2012 was ₹ 78,600.

Prepare Trading and Profit & Loss Account for the year ended 31st December, 2012 and Balance Sheet as on that date.

Solution:

Trading and Profit & Loss Account for the year ending 31st December, 2012

Dr. **Cr.**

Particulars		Amount (₹)	Particulars	Amount (₹)
To Opening Stock		46,800	By Sales	3,89,600
To Purchases	3,21,700		*Less*: Returns	8,600
Less: Returns	(5,800)			3,81,000

Particulars		Amount (₹)	Particulars	Amount (₹)
Drawings	(600)		By Closing Stock	78,600
Add: Omitted	400	3,15,700		
To Freight & Carriage		18,600		
To Gross Profit		78,500		
		4,59,600		4,59,600
To Rent & Taxes		5,700	By Gross Profit	78,500
To Salaries & Wages		9,300	By Discount	4,190
To Intt. on loan (900 + 300)		1,200	By Mis. Income	250
To Printing and stationary (14,600 – 3650)		10,950		
To Discount		1,800		
To Gen. Expenses		11,450		
To Insurance		1,300		
To Postage & Telegrams		2,330		
To Travelling Exp.		870		
To Provision for B/D		1,150		
To Provision for Discount		437		
To Depreciation on furniture		500		
To Net Profit		35,953		
		82,940		89,940

Balance Sheet as on 31st December, 2012

Liabilities	Amount (₹)	Assets		Amount (₹)
Capital	86,690	Furniture	5,000	
Add: N.P.	35,953	*Less*: Depreciation	500	4,500
	1,22,643	Debtors (24,000 – 1,000 – 1150 – 437)		21,413
Less: Drawings	40,600	Prepaid expense		3,650
	82,043	Stock		78,600
Creditors (14,800 – 1,000 + 400)	14,200	Bank		8,000
Loan (20,000 + 300)	20,300	Cash		380
	1,16,543			1,16,543

THEORY QUESTIONS

1. What basis of accounting is required by Generally Accepted Accounting Principles on the profit and loss account and balance sheet?
2. Explain the basic difference between accrual basis accounting and cash basis accounting. Which of the two is required by Generally Accepted Accounting Principles?
3. What are adjusting entries? Why are they needed for preparing financial statements?
4. List different types of adjusting entries.
5. What are prepaid expenses and unearned revenues?
6. What are accrued expenses and accrued revenues? Give an example of an adjustment to record each of these items.
7. At the end of an accounting period, certain accounts are adjusted. Why?
8. Explain the difference between deferrals and accruals as classification of adjusting entries.
9. "The net income of a business entity is determined by measuring the amount of revenue generated and subtracting expenses incurred, appropriately measured. As a consequence the

resulting difference, net profit, is a precise measure of operating performance for the period under consideration." Comment.

10. If a company fails to accrue salaries at the end of a month, what will be the effect of this omission on the financial statements?
11. Distinguish between: (*a*) capital and revenue expenditures. (*b*) capital and revenue receipts.
12. What is a trading account? What are its purposes?
13. What are the objectives of preparing profit and loss account?
14. Give a specimen of trading, profit and loss account, using imaginary figures.
15. What is a balance sheet? What are its characteristics?
16. Explain the rationale behind preparing a balance sheet. What are its limitation?
17. Explain the linkage between trial balance, profit and loss account and balance sheet.
18. A company balance sheet is a major financial statement. What information does it contain?
19. What are the purposes behind a balance sheet?
20. List the major sections (and the components of each section) of a balance sheet.
21. Following is a list of major classifications and subclassifications on the balance sheet. Number them in the order in which they normally appear on a balance sheet.
    Current liabilities
    Liabilities
    Owners' equity
    Long-term liabilities
    Long-term investments and funds
    Intangible assets
    Operational assets (property, plant, and equipment)
    Current assets
    Retained earnings
    Contributed capital
    Assets
    Other assets
    Deferred charges
22. Write notes on: Importance of difference between capital and revenue.
    [BBA, GGSIP University, March 2000, December 2000]
23. Explain the meaning of deferred revenue expenditure.
    [BBA, GGSIP University, December 2002, December 2008]
24. Give distinction between capital expenditure vs. Revenue Expenditure as well as Capital Receipts vs. Revenue Receipts with examples.
    [BBA, GGSIP University, December 2004, December 2006, December 2007, December 2009, December 2010]
25. Differentiate between Provision and Reserve. **[BBA, GGSIP University, December 2007]**

SELF-EVALUATION EXERCISES

SECTION A

I. Select the correct answer for the following multiple-choice questions:

1. If the supplies account, before adjustment on March 31, indicated a balance of ₹ 2,250 and an inventory of supplies on hand at March 31 totalled ₹ 950, the adjusting entry would be
   (*a*) Debit supplies ₹ 950; credit supplies expense ₹ 950

(*b*) Debit supplies ₹ 1,300; credit supplies expense ₹ 1,300
(*c*) Debit supplies expense ₹ 950; credit supplies ₹ 950
(*d*) Debit supplies expense ₹ 1,300; credit supplies ₹ 1,300

2. If the estimated amount of depreciation on equipment for a period is ₹ 2,000, the adjusting entry to record depreciation would be:
(*a*) Debit depreciation expense ₹ 2,000; credit equipment ₹ 2,000
(*b*) Debit equipment ₹ 2,000; credit depreciation expense ₹ 2,000
(*c*) Debit depreciation expense ₹ 2,000; credit accumulated depreciation ₹ 2,000
(*d*) Debit accumulated depreciation ₹ 2,000; credit depreciation expense ₹ 2,000

3. Which of the following accounts would be closed to the income summary account at the end of a period?
(*a*) Sales (*b*) Salary expense
(*c*) Both sales and salary expense (*d*) Neither sales nor salary expense

4. On a trading and profit and loss account the excess of net sales over the cost of merchandise sold is called:
(*a*) Operating income (*b*) Income from operations
(*c*) Gross profit (*d*) Net income

5. In general, the accounts in the income statement are known as
(*a*) Permanent accounts (*b*) Temporary accounts
(*c*) Unearned revenue accounts (*d*) Contra-asset accounts

6. Adjusting entries are essential to
(*a*) Matching rule (*b*) Accrual accounting
(*c*) A proper determination of net income (*d*) All of the above

7. The recording of wages earned but not yet paid is an example of an adjustment that
(*a*) Apportions revenues between two or more periods
(*b*) Recognises an accrued expense
(*c*) Recognises an unrecorded revenue
(*d*) None of the above

8. Prepaid insurance has an ending balance of ₹ 2,300. During the period, insurance of ₹ 1,200 expired. The adjusting entry would contain a debit
(*a*) To prepaid insurance for ₹ 1,200 (*b*) To insurance expense for ₹ 1,200
(*c*) To unexpired insurance for ₹ 1,100 (*d*) To insurance expense for ₹ 1,100

9. An important purpose of closing entries is
(*a*) To adjust the accounts in the ledger
(*b*) To set balance sheet accounts to zero in order to begin the next period
(*c*) To set income statement accounts to zero in order to begin the next period
(*d*) None of the above

10. After all closing entries have been posted, the balance of the income account will be
(*a*) A debit if a net income has been earned (*b*) A debit if a net loss has been incurred
(*c*) A credit if a net loss has been incurred (*d*) Zero

11. After closing entries have been posted which of the following accounts would have a non-zero balance?

(*a*) Service revenue earned (*b*) Depreciation expense
(*c*) Unearned service revenue (*d*) Service wages expense

12. The post-closing trial balance will
(*a*) Contain only income statement accounts
(*b*) Contain only balance sheet accounts
(*c*) Contain both income statement and balance sheet accounts
(*d*) Be prepared before closing entries are posted to the ledger

13. For which of the following adjustments would a reversing entry facilitate book-keeping procedures?
(*a*) Adjustment for depreciation expense
(*b*) Adjustment to allocate prepaid insurance to the current period
(*c*) Adjustment made as a result of inventory of supplies
(*d*) Adjustment for wages earned by employees but not yet paid

14. If beginning and ending merchandise inventories are ₹ 400 and ₹ 700, respectively, and cost of goods sold is ₹ 3,400 net purchase are
(*a*) ₹ 3,700 (*b*) ₹ 3,400
(*c*) ₹ 3,100 (*d*) Cannot be determined

15. The closing entries for a merchandising concern would contain a debit to
(*a*) Sales discounts (*b*) Purchases
(*c*) Freight in (*d*) Purchases discounts

16. Which of the following would appear as an operating expense on the income statement of a merchandising concern?
(*a*) Freight in (*b*) Freight out
(*c*) Sales returns and allowances (*d*) Purchases returns and allowances

17. Todd had a beginning credit balance of ₹ 21,000 in his capital account. At the close of the period Todd's drawing account had a debit balance of ₹ 2,200. On the end-of-period balance sheet, Todd's capital balance is ₹ 32,000. If Todd contributed an additional ₹ 2,000 to the firm during the period, the period's net income is
(*a*) ₹ 12,400 (*b*) ₹ 11,200 (*c*) ₹ 9,000 (*d*) ₹ 10,800

18. Which of the following is an example of an adjusting entry?
(*a*) Recording the purchase of supplies on account
(*b*) Recording depreciation expense on a truck
(*c*) Recording the billing of customers for services rendered
(*d*) Recording the payment of wages to employees

19. An adjusting entry to accrue wages earned but not yet paid is an example of
(*a*) Aligning recorded costs with the appropriate accounting periods
(*b*) Aligning recorded revenue with the appropriate accounting periods
(*c*) Reflecting unrecorded expenses incurred during the accounting period
(*d*) Reflecting unrecorded revenue earned during the accounting period

20. Which one of the following is correct?
(*a*) Gross profit + Sales + Direct expenses + Purchases + Closing stock = Opening stock
(*b*) Gross profit + Direct expenses + Purchases + Closing stock – Opening stock = Sales
(*c*) Gross profit + Direct expenses + Purchases + Opening stock – Closing stock = Sales

21. Which one of the following is correct?
(*a*) Gross profit + Purchases + Sales = Net profit
(*b*) Gross profit + Purchases + Administrative and other expenses = Net profit
(*c*) Gross profit + Sales + Administrative and other expenses = Net profit
(*d*) Gross profit – Administrative and selling expenses = Net profit

22. The adjustment to be made for interest on capital is
(*a*) Debit profit and loss account and deduct interest from capital
(*b*) Credit profit and loss account and deduct interest from capital
(*c*) Debit profit and loss account and add interest to capital
(*d*) Credit profit and loss account and deduct interest from capital

23. The adjustment to be made for provision for doubtful debt is
(*a*) Credit profit and loss account and deduct the provision from debtors
(*b*) Debit profit and loss account and deduct the provision from debtors
(*c*) Credit profit and loss account and add the provision to debtors
(*d*) Debit profit and loss account and add the provision to debtors

24. The adjustment to be made for interest on drawings is
(*a*) Debit profit and loss account and add interest to drawings
(*b*) Credit profit and loss account and add interest to drawings
(*c*) Debit profit and loss account and deduct interest from drawings
(*d*) Credit profit and loss account and deduct interest from drawings

25. The adjustment to be made for outstanding expenses is
(*a*) Add outstanding expenses to respective expenses and show it as asset
(*b*) Deduct outstanding expenses from respective expenses and show it as liability
(*c*) Add outstanding expenses to respective expenses and show it as liability
(*d*) Deduct outstanding expenses from respective expenses and show it as liability

26. Gross profit is equal to
(*a*) Net profit minus expenses
(*b*) Purchases plus stock minus net sales
(*c*) Net sales plus selling price of stock minus purchases
(*d*) Net sales minus cost price of sales

27. Net profit is equal to
(*a*) Gross profit minus expenses
(*b*) Net sales plus purchases minus gross profit
(*c*) Expenses minus gross profit
(*d*) Gross profit minus net sales plus purchases

Questions 28 to 29 relate to the following:

A trader buys ₹ 2,000 worth of goods paying ₹ 65 carriage on them. He sells the goods for ₹ 3,500 incurring expenses totalling ₹ 725.

28. The trader's gross profit is
(*a*) ₹ 1,500 (*b*) ₹ 1,435 (*c*) ₹ 1,345 (*d*) ₹ 710

29. The trader's net profit is
(*a*) ₹ 1,500 (*b*) ₹ 1,435 (*c*) ₹ 1,345 (*d*) ₹ 710

30. Which one of the following statements is correct?

(*a*) Gross profit on trading is entered on the right side of the trading account and carried down to the left side of the profit and loss account

(*b*) Gross profit on trading is entered on the left side of the trading account and carried down to the right side of the profit and loss account

(*c*) Net profit on trading is entered on the right side of the trading account and carried down to the left side of the profit and loss account

(*d*) Net profit on trading is entered on the left side of the trading account and carried down to the right side of the profit and loss account

31. The cost of sales is equal to

(*a*) Opening stock minus purchases

(*b*) Opening stock plus purchases

(*c*) Opening stock minus purchases plus closing stock

(*d*) Opening stock plus purchases minus closing stock

32. If the gross profit of a trader is ₹ 10,000 and the net profit is 75 per cent of the gross profit, his expenses total

(*a*) ₹ 7,500 (*b*) ₹ 2,500 (*c*) ₹ 750 (*d*) ₹ 250

33. If a trader's net sales amount to ₹ 18,000 and his gross profit is 60 per cent of sales and his net profit is 40 per cent of sales, his expenses are:

(*a*) ₹ 10,800 (*b*) ₹ 7,200 (*c*) ₹ 3,600 (*d*) ₹ 1,800

Questions 34 to 45 are based on the following:

Trading and profit and loss account for the year ended December 31, 2012 is as follows:

Dr. **Cr.**

	(₹)	(₹)		(₹)	(₹)
Opening Stock		900	Sales	19,860	
Purchases	12,150		*Less*: Returns Inwards	360	19,500
Less: Returns outwards	240	11,910			
Carriage Inwards		270			
		13,080			
Less: Closing Stock		1,650			
		11,430			
G/P c/d		8,070			
		19,500			19,500
Salaries		1,560	Gross Profit b/d		8,070
Depreciation		570			
Rent Paid	600				
Add: Accrued	120	720			
General Expenses		210			
Carriage Outwards		330			
Net Profit					
		8,070			8,070

34. The missing net profit figure should read

(*a*) ₹ 8,070 (*b*) ₹ 4,680 (*c*) ₹ 3,390 (*d*) ₹ 720

35. Total expenses other than cost of goods sold were
(*a*) ₹ 4,680 (*b*) ₹ 3,960 (*c*) ₹ 3,390 (*d*) ₹ 720

36. The cost of the goods sold totalled
(*a*) ₹ 19,860 (*b*) ₹ 19,500 (*c*) ₹ 13,080 (*d*) ₹ 11,430

37. Expense item of rent totalled
(*a*) ₹ 720 (*b*) ₹ 600 (*c*) ₹ 480 (*d*) ₹ 120

38. The turnover is
(*a*) ₹ 19,860 (*b*) ₹ 19,500 (*c*) ₹ 13,080 (*d*) ₹ 11,910

39. The net cost of purchases is
(*a*) ₹ 13,080 (*b*) ₹ 12,180 (*c*) ₹ 12,150 (*d*) ₹ 11,910

40. Purchases returned totalled
(*a*) ₹ 12, 270 (*b*) ₹ 11,910 (*c*) ₹ 600 (*d*) ₹ 240

41. Carriage outwards refers to the cost of
(*a*) Sending the goods sold (*b*) Collecting the purchases made
(*c*) Returning unwanted purchases (*d*) The return of unsold goods

42. Gross profit as a percentage of net sales is approximately
(*a*) 50% (*b*) 40% (*c*) 30% (*d*) 20%

43. Net profit as a percentage of net sales is approximately
(*a*) 45% (*b*) 35% (*c*) 25% (*d*) 15%

44. The value of unsold goods on December 31 was
(*a*) ₹ 12,150 (*b*) ₹ 11,910 (*c*) ₹ 1,650 (*d*) ₹ 900

45. The total of the trading account is
(*a*) ₹ 19,500 (*b*) ₹ 11,430 (*c*) ₹ 8,070 (*d*) ₹ 900

46. Depreciation results from
1. Wear and tear 2. Obsolescence 3. The passage of time
(*a*) 1, 2, 3 (*b*) 1 and 2 only (*c*) 1 only (*d*) 3 only

47. The double entry in the books for the annual amount of depreciation of an asset is
(*a*) Debit the profit and loss account, credit the asset account
(*b*) Credit the profit and loss account, debit the asset account
(*c*) Debit the bank account, credit the asset account
(*d*) Credit the bank account, debit the asset account

48. The book of prime entry necessary to introduce the annual depreciation is
(*a*) The cash book (*b*) The purchases book
(*c*) The ledger (*d*) The journal

49. Outstanding salaries appear in trial balance—₹ 2,000—it will be shown in
(*a*) Trading a/c (*b*) Profit and loss a/c (*c*) Balance sheet

50. Returns inwards will be shown as a deduction from
(*a*) Sales (*b*) Purchases (*c*) Returns outwards

51. Opening stock will be shown
(*a*) On the debit side of trading a/c (*b*) On the debit side of P&L A/c
(*c*) On the assets side of balance sheet

52. Closing stock appears in the trial balance—₹ 80,000. It will be shown

(*a*) On the credit side of trading a/c (*b*) On the credit side of profit and loss a/c

(*c*) On the assets side of balance sheet

53. P's trial balance contains the following information:

Bad debts, ₹ 3,000

Provision for bad debts ₹ 3,500

It is desired to make a provision of ₹ 4,000 at the end of the year. The amount to be debited to profit and loss a/c is

(*a*) ₹ 4,000 (*b*) ₹ 5,000 (*c*) ₹ 6,500 (*d*) ₹ 3,500

54. A's trial balance provides you the following information. Bad debts, ₹ 1,000. It is desired to maintain a provision for bad debts at ₹ 2,000. Amount debited to profit and loss a/c will be

(*a*) ₹ 1,000 (*b*) ₹ 3,000 (*c*) ₹ 4,000

55. D's trial balance contains the following information:

Bad debts, ₹ 500

Provision for bad debts ₹ 4,000

It is desired to maintain a provision of ₹ 3,000 at the end of the year

Accounting treatment of this adjustment is

(*a*) ₹ 1,500 to be debited to profit and loss a/c

(*b*) ₹ 500 to be debited to profit and loss a/c

(*c*) ₹ 500 to be credited to profit and loss a/c

(*d*) ₹ 3,500 to be debited to profit and loss a/c

56. A's trial balance contains the following information:

Discount allowed, ₹ 1,000

Provision for discount, ₹ 3,000

On accounts receivables

It is desired to make a provision for discount on accounts receivables, ₹ 3,500. The amount to be debited to profit and loss a/c is

(*a*) ₹ 4,500 (*b*) ₹ 4,000 (*c*) ₹ 1,500 (*d*) ₹ 500

57. F's trial balance contains the following information:

Discount received ₹ 1,200

Provision for discount on creditors ₹ 1,800

It is desired to maintain a provision for discount on creditors at ₹ 1,600

The amount to be credited to profit and loss a/c

(*a*) ₹ 1,000 (*b*) ₹ 1,400 (*c*) ₹ 200 (*d*) ₹ 2,200

II. Answer True or False:

1. Provision for doubtful debts represents the amount uncollectable.

2. Adjustment entries are made at the time of closing the business every day.

3. Drawings by proprietor is to be debited to profit and loss account.

4. Carriage inwards is an expense and carriage outwards is income.

5. Return outwards are nothing but sales returns.

6. Profit and loss account summarises the company's operations and profit or loss it has made during a period of time.

7. Cash balance at hand shows whether the business has earned profit or loss.

8. Free samples received are business gains.
9. If a trading asset is exchanged for a non-trading asset then the entry will be recorded in the journal proper.
10. When a bad debt is written off, the loss from it is equal to the profit expected from the particular business transaction with the debtor.
11. Goods lost by fire need not be accounted for since they are not sales.
12. Adjusting entries are necessary only when the mercantile system of accounting is being followed.
13. In the cash system of accounting, all pre-received incomes are current gains.
14. All accounts are closed by transfer either to the trading account or to the profit and loss account.
15. The opening entry is posted on the respective accounts as 'To/By balance b/f'.
16. All rectification entries are passed through the journal proper.
17. Reserve for doubtful debts account always has a credit balance.
18. Provisions for future bad debts and discounts reduce the correctness of profit or loss, as they are only estimates.
19. Provision for discount to debtors can be estimated only after computing the provision for doubtful debts.
20. Each partner's liability is limited to the extent of his capital contribution.
21. Partner's salaries are debited to the profit and loss account and credited to their respective personal accounts.
22. Interest on drawings charged to the partners increases the profit available for distribution to the partners.
23. The current account is maintained only on the fixed system of capital accounts.
24. The distinction between capital and revenue items is important because it is of fundamental importance to the determination of profits.
25. Interest paid on borrowings is a capital expenditure.
26. Capital expenditure should be shown in the books by debiting asset account and crediting supplier or cash account.
27. Furniture and fittings are classified as capital expenditure.
28. A fork lift truck purchased by a business is a capital expenditure.
29. Although there are differences between the two, both the prepaid expenses account and the buildings, machinery and equipment account involve the deferral or the delay of charging costs paid by the company to expense accounts, the costs are allocated to expenses in future periods, instead of being charged to expense when paid.
30. A company's total cash receipts from all sources during the year may be more than its total sales revenue for the year.
31. Assuming that all transactions during the year have been properly recorded in journal entries and that all these journal entries have been properly posted, the financial statements can be prepared from the company's accounts.
32. Making all the necessary adjusting entries at the end of the period is a very important step in the accounting cycle; if these entries were not made, the company's net income for the period probably would be wrong.
33. All expenses adjusting entries involve a credit (–) to an asset account.
34. Adjusting entries are made for net income purposes; there are no balance sheet reasons for making adjusting entries.

35. Determining which adjusting entries are required and the amounts for each entry is more the responsibility of the accountant than of the book keeper.
36. If the prepaid expense account were not used and if all pre-payments of expenses were immediately and entirely charged to expense, the total assets of the company at the end of the year would be understated (too low).
37. Debit (+) to the prepaid expenses account are later offset by credits (–) to the account, when expense entries are recorded.
38. The total cost of office supplies on hand at the start of the year plus those supplies purchased during the year is ₹ 3,500 and the cost of the office supplies still on hand at the end of the year is ₹ 400. Therefore, the proper amount of expense for the year is ₹ 3,900.
39. An adjusting entry at year-end is made for accrued expenses to record those expenses that the company has not paid or been billed for yet, but for which it has a liability to pay.
40. Adjusting entries would not be needed if the company's accounting system were better and if all transactions were recorded during the year.
41. Certain basic adjusting entries are made every year-end, and other adjusting entries may be required some years but not every year.
42. Assume that the accountant made a wrong computation and as a result the ending balance of the prepaid expenses account is overstated (too high) by ₹ 500; this means that the expenses for the year would be understated (too low) by ₹ 500.
43. If the adjusting entry for accrued expenses was overlooked by the accountant and not recorded, the company's total liabilities at year-end would be understated (too low) and its total expenses for the year would be understated (too low).
44. If the accountant made a wrong computation and, as a result, the ending balance of the accrued expenses account is overstated (too high) by ₹ 750, the expenses for the year would be understated (too low) by ₹ 750.
45. Computerised accounting system have no need for adjusting entries.
46. Bad debts is the term used to describe uncollectible accounts receivable.
47. The direct write-off method of recording bad debts expense is an acceptable accounting method.
48. When recording the bad debts expense entry by the allowance method, an estimate of the bad debts for the period must be made; the amount of the expense recorded may later turn out to be too high or too low.
49. The book value of accounts receivable is reduced when recording the bad debts expense by the allowance method, even though the accounts receivable account is not reduced.
50. After recording the bad debts expense adjusting entry for the period, allowance for doubtful accounts should have a credit balance.

III. Fill in the following blanks with appropriate word(s):

1. Goods spoiled and lost by fire are credited to________.
2. Withdrawal of goods from stock by the proprietor for personal use will reduce ________ and ________.
3. Administrative expenses are to be shown in________.
4. Return inwards is to be deducted from________.
5. Carriage outwards is to be________ to profit and loss account.
6. Gross profit can be ascertained by preparing ________ account.
7. The journal entries pertaining to cash, and credit transactions of goods in trade is called________.

8. Transactions that cannot be entered in the ______ as well as in the ______ are recorded in the journal proper.
9. Entries made in the journal proper to correct errors in the books are known as ______.
10. A ______ entry is one which is passed in the journal proper to shift the effects from one account to another, when the former becomes redundant.
11. All nominal accounts are ______ at the end of the year by transfer to the ______ account or ______ account, by virtue of a ______ entry.
12. The yearly balance of the commission account is transferred to the ______ at the end of the year.
13. The crediting of the drawings account and debiting of the capital account at the end of the year is an example of a ______ entry.
14. If the mercantile system of accounting is followed, then ______ entries are to be passed to account for any accruals and deferrals.
15. Unpaid rent of the earlier accounting year can be described as ______.
16. Closing, stock is accounted in the books by crediting the ______ account.
17. The balances of all the prepaid expenses in the ledger will be ______.
18. The rent receivable account can have only ______ or balance.
19. An opening entry is made when the entrepreneur ______ business or at the beginning of any financial year to bring forward the ______ and ______ of the previous year.
20. Amounts irrecoverable are ______ by transferring them from the respective debtor's account to the ______ account.
21. An estimate of future bad debts is known as a ______.
22. Future bad debts are usually projected as a ______ of debtors.
23. Bad debts written off during the year are transferred at the end of the year to the ______ account, or in the absence of it to the ______ account.
24. The provision for bad debts as well as the provision for discount on debtors are ______ from sundry debtors in the balance sheet.
25. At the end of the year the discount allowed account is transferred to the ______ account whereas the discount earned account is transferred to the ______ account, when provisions are maintained.
26. In the absence of provisions regarding future discounts allowed and earned, the discount allowed account and discount earned account at the end of the current year are to be transferred to the ______ and ______ sides, respectively, of the ______ account.
27. If the total of discounts allowed during the year plus the new provision for discounts on debtors exceeds the old provision for discounts on debtors, then the difference between the two will appear on the ______ side of the profit and loss account.
28. An expenditure which will benefit the future period is ______
29. Provision for doubtful debts shows ______ balance.

SECTION B

I. Select the correct answer for the following multiple-choice questions:

1. The balance sheet gives information regarding
   (*a*) Results of operations for a particular period
   (*b*) The financial position as on a particular date

(*c*) The operating efficiency of the firm
(*d*) Financial position during a particular period.

2. The item, closing inventory, is shown in balance sheet under
(*a*) Fixed assets (*b*) Current assets
(*c*) Current liabilities (*d*) Miscellaneous expenditure

3. Accounting policies may differ from one firm to another firm with respect of one of the following:
(*a*) Deciding credit and debit aspects of transactions
(*b*) Classification of assets and liabilities
(*c*) Classification of revenue and expenses
(*d*) Classification of revenue and expenditure

4. A balance sheet is
(*a*) A trial balance
(*b*) A trading account
(*c*) A statement showing the distributing of profits
(*d*) A list of assets and liabilities

5. On a balance sheet, the fixed assets are included at
(*a*) Cost price less depreciation (*b*) Book value
(*c*) Selling price (*d*) Replacement value

Questions 6 and 7 relate to the following:

1. stock 2. debtors 3. creditors
(*a*) 1, 2 and 3 (*b*) 1 and 2 only (*c*) 1 only (*d*) 3 only

6. Which is/are current liabilities?

7. Which is/are current assets?

Questions 8–14 relate to the following assets and liabilities:

	(₹)		(₹)
Capital	3,200		
Reserve	1300		
Stock	1,500	Machinery	2,000
Cash at bank	250	Debtors	750
Cash in hand	25	Fixtures and fittings	400
Trade creditors	1,225	Motor vehicle	800

8. The balance sheet totals are
(*a*) ₹ 5,725 (*b*) ₹ 4,425 (*c*) ₹ 3,950 (*d*) ₹ 3,000

9. Capital totals
(*a*) ₹ 4,700 (*b*) ₹ 4,500 (*c*) ₹ 3,500 (*d*) ₹ 3,200

10. Current liabilities are
(*a*) ₹ 3,000 (*b*) ₹ 12,925 (*c*) ₹ 1,925 (*d*) ₹ 750

11. Fixed assets total
(*a*) ₹ 3,950 (*b*) ₹ 3,200 (*c*) ₹ 1,150 (*d*) ₹ 400

12. Current assets are
(*a*) ₹ 3,000 (*b*) ₹ 2,525 (*c*) ₹ 1,775 (*d*) ₹ 1,225

13. Net working capital equals

(*a*) ₹ 3,200 (*b*) ₹ 1,775 (*c*) ₹ 1,300 (*d*) ₹ 275

14. The net assets figure is

(*a*) ₹ 5,725 (*b*) ₹ 4,500 (*c*) ₹ 3,000 (*d*) ₹ 1,300

15. If the capital of a business is ₹ 15,000 at the beginning of the year and ₹ 18,000 at the end, and the owner has withdrawn ₹ 4,500 the profit made is

(*a*) ₹ 13,500 (*b*) ₹ 10,500 (*c*) ₹ 7,500 (*d*) ₹ 3,000

Questions 16–19 are based on the following:

Balance Sheet as on December 31st, 2012

	(₹)	(₹)		(₹)
Capital a/c	10,000		Shop fittings	500
Balance Profit	400		Stock	2,500
	10,400		Trading debtors	650
Less: Drawings	200	10,200	Cash in bank	7,550
Trade creditors		1,000		
		11,200		11,200

16. Current liabilities total

(*a*) ₹ 11,200 (*b*) ₹ 10,400 (*c*) ₹ 10,200 (*d*) ₹ 1,000

17. Current assets total

(*a*) ₹ 11,200 (*b*) ₹ 10,700 (*c*) ₹ 10,550 (*d*) ₹ 3,000

18. The percentage return on total assets employed is approximately

(*a*) 10% (*b*) 85% (*c*) 5% (*d*) 4%

19. The book value of the fixed assets is

(*a*) ₹ 11,200 (*b*) ₹ 3,000 (*c*) ₹ 2,500 (*d*) ₹ 500

20. A bad debt is

(*a*) A large sum of money owed (*b*) A debt incurred by the employees

(*c*) A debt owed by one trader to another (*d*) Amount unrealised from debtors

21. Bad debts are written off by

(*a*) Debiting the debtors account and crediting bad debts account

(*b*) Crediting the debtor's account and debiting bad debts account

(*c*) Debiting the provision for bad debts account and crediting the debtor's account

(*d*) Crediting the provision for bad debts account and debiting the debtor's account

22. At the end of a financial year the entries made regarding bad debts are:

(*a*) Debit the debtor's account, credit provision for bad debts account

(*b*) Credit the debtor's account, debit provision for bad debts account

(*c*) Debit the profit and loss account, credit bad debts account

(*d*) Credit the profit and loss account, debits bad debts account

23. Provision for bad debts is made to

(*a*) Prevent bad debts arising

(*b*) Obtain a true debtor's figure for the balance sheet

(*c*) Even out actual bad debts incurring

(*d*) Encourage prompt payment of debts by debtors

24. The provision for bad debts account represents

(*a*) Some of the profit
(*b*) Some of the credit withheld
(*c*) The total of actual bad debts
(*d*) The total amount owing to the business.

25. On the balance sheet provision for bad debts is shown as

(*a*) Deduction from debtors
(*b*) A deduction from capital
(*c*) An addition to current liabilities
(*d*) A deduction from fixed assets

26. Provision for bad debts is made by

(*a*) Debiting the provision for debts account, crediting debtor's account
(*b*) Crediting the provision for bad debts account, debiting profit and loss account
(*c*) Debiting the provision for bad debts account, crediting profit and loss account
(*d*) Crediting the provision for bad debts account, debiting profit and loss account

27. If actual bad debts are less than the sum set aside then

(*a*) There will be a credit balance on the provision for bad debts account
(*b*) There will be a debit balance on the provision for bad debts account
(*c*) There will be a credit balance on the bad debts account
(*d*) There will be a debit balance on the bad debts account

28. If the provision for bad debts account has a credit balance of ₹ 55 and provision for the year is ₹ 310, the amount to be charged against the profit and loss account is

(*a*) ₹ 365
(*b*) ₹ 462
(*c*) ₹ 255
(*d*) ₹ 55

29. If the provision for bad debts account has a debit balance of ₹ 84 and provision is ₹ 462 the charge against the profit and loss account is

(*a*) ₹ 546
(*b*) ₹ 462
(*c*) ₹ 378
(*d*) ₹ 84

Questions 30 to 37 refer to the following:

In the first year of trading, W. Blake's receivables amount to the net figure of ₹ 4,500 after he has written off ₹ 85 actual bad debts. He decides to make a 5 per cent provision against any additional bad debts.

In the second year, his net receivables are now ₹ 6,000 after deducting and writing off ₹ 155 as actual bad debts. Again he provides 5 per cent against further bad debts.

In the third year, his net receivables are ₹ 4,000; provision is made again at 5 per cent and actual bad debts amount to ₹ 72.

30. At the end of the second year the balance of the bad debts account is

(*a*) ₹ 200
(*b*) ₹ 180
(*c*) ₹ 155
(*d*) ₹ 85

31. At the end of the second year the provision for bad debts account shows a balance of

(*a*) ₹ 525
(*b*) ₹ 300
(*c*) ₹ 200
(*d*) ₹ 75

32. At the end of the third year, the balance on the provision for bad debts account is

(*a*) ₹ 725
(*b*) ₹ 272
(*c*) ₹ 228
(*d*) ₹ 200

33. On the balance sheet at the end of the first year receivable will total

(*a*) ₹ 4,500
(*b*) ₹ 4,415
(*c*) ₹ 4,275
(*d*) ₹ 190

34. On the balance sheet at the end of the second year receivables will total

(*a*) ₹ 10,500
(*b*) ₹ 5,700
(*c*) ₹ 5,085
(*d*) ₹ 5,000

35. The value of receivables on the balance sheet at the end of the third year reads

(*a*) ₹ 1,450
(*b*) ₹ 3,800
(*c*) ₹ 3,728
(*d*) ₹ 272

36. The provision made for bad debts to be charged against the profit and loss account in the first year is

(*a*) ₹ 450 (*b*) ₹ 310 (*c*) ₹ 225 (*d*) ₹ 85

37. The provision made for bad debts to be charged against the profit and loss account in the second year is

(*a*) ₹ 600 (*b*) ₹ 300 (*c*) ₹ 180 (*d*) ₹ 230

38. Which one of the following statements is not correct?

(*a*) The provision for bad debts account is owed to the proprietor

(*b*) Bad debts could exceed the provision for bad debts

(*c*) Bad debts could be less than the provision for bad debts

(*d*) Provision for bad debts appears as a liabilities on the balance sheet

39. Y's trial balance contains the following information:

Bad debts	₹ 5,000
Provision bad debts	₹ 6,000
Sundry debtors	₹ 50,000

It is desired to create a provision for Bad debts at 10 per cent on Sundry debtors at the end of the year.

Sundry Debtors will appear in the balance sheet at a figure of

(*a*) 45,000 (*b*) 44,000 (*c*) 39,000 (*d*) 34,000

(*e*) 46,000

40. A's trial balance contains the following information:

Bad debits	₹ 5,000
Discount allowed	₹ 3,000
Provision for discount on debtors	₹ 3,300
Provision for bad debts	₹ 5,500
Sundry debtors	₹ 60,000

At the end of the year it is desired to maintain a provision for bad debts of ₹ 5,000 and provision for discount on debtor at ₹ 3,000.

Sundry debtors will appear in the balance sheet at a figure of

(*a*) ₹ 52,000 (*b*) ₹ 44,000 (*c*) ₹ 52,800 (*d*) ₹ 43,200

41. A's trial balance contains the following information

Sundry creditors	₹ 80,000
Discount received	₹ 5,000

Reserve for discount on creditors ₹ 5,500

It is desired to maintain a reserve for discount on creditors at ₹ 6,000

Sundry creditors will appear in the balance sheet at a figure of

(*a*) ₹ 69,000 (*b*) ₹ 74,500 (*c*) ₹ 63,500 (*d*) ₹ 74,000

II. Fill in the blanks:

1. All expenses incurred by the proprietor which are not related to business are treated as ______.
2. Properties and possessions of a business are termed as ______ of business.
3. Prepaid expenses appearing in trial balance will appear in ______.
4. Bills payable is classified as ______.
5. Changing the accounting policy to show rosy picture is called ______.

6. A balance sheet is a statement of what an enterprise ______ and what it ______ at a particular date.
7. ______ include cash and assets which can be normally converted into cash during the operating cycle of the business.
8. Fixed assets represent the employment of money on a ______ basis.
9. Assets are usually listed on a balance sheet under two main groups namely ______ and ______.
10. ______ account shows money or money's worth contributed by the proprietor to the business.
11. Excess debit over credit in the trading account represents a ______.
12. Carriage inwards account is transferred to the ______ account whereas carriage outwards account is transferred to the ______ account.
13. A gross profit is transferred to the ______ side of the profit and loss account.
14. If the opening and closing stock is ₹ 20,000 each, purchases are ₹ 50,000, manufacturing expenses are ₹ 10,000 and sales is ₹ 90,000 the gross profit will be ______.
15. If the gross profit is ₹ 11,000, administrative expenses are ₹ 3,000 and miscellaneous income is ₹ 700, the net profit will be ______.
16. An income received in advance will be ______ the respective income's account whereas an income receivable is ______.
17. Excess credit over debit in the profit and loss account indicates ______
18. Net profit/loss is transferred to the ______ account.
19. The balance sheet is ______ and not ______.
20. The balance sheet is a ______ of the assets, liabilities and capital of a concern, as on a particular date.
21. An expense payable account will show a ______ balance and will be shown on the ______ side of the balance sheet.
22. A debit balance in the suspense account will appear on the ___ side of the balance sheet.
23. Capital is the excess of ______ over ______.
24. The capital of a firm whose assets are ₹ 53,000 and liabilities are ₹ 19,000 is ______.
25. Amount of ______ is deducted from the value of respective assets in the balance sheet.
26. If the assets are ₹ 49,000 and the liabilities are ₹ 18,000 the total of the liabilities side of the balance sheet will be ______.
27. The capital of a proprietor ______ when the business makes a profit.
28. What is owed by a business to others is known as its ______.
29. The liability of a business ______ when it makes a profit.
30. Amounts irrecoverable are ______ by transferring them from the respective receivables account to the ______ account.
31. An estimate of future bad debts is known as a ______.
32. Bad debts written off during the year are transferred at the end of the year of the ______ account, or in the absence of it to the ______ account.
33. The provision for bad debts as well as the provision for discount on debtors are ______ from accounts receivables in the balance sheet.
34. At the end of the year the discount allowed account is transferred to the ______ account, whereas the discount earned account is transferred to the ______ account, when provisions are maintained.

35. In the absence of provision regarding future discount allowed and earned, the discount allowed account and discount earned account at the end of the current year are to be transferred to the ______ and ______ sides respectively of the ______ account.
36. If the total of discounts allowed during the year plus the new provision for discounts on debtors exceeds the old provision for discounts on debtors, then the difference between the two will appear on the ______ side of the profit and loss account.

III. Answer True or False:

1. Petty cash is an expense.
2. Provision for doubtful debts is added to sundry debtor's account in balance sheet.
3. Closing stock given in trial balance is to be credited to trading account.
4. Balance sheet is a position statement.
5. Assets that are meant to be converted into cash as soon as possible are termed as current assets.
6. Withdrawal of money or money's worth by the proprietor is reflected in drawings account.
7. Capital expenditure means expenditure incurred for the owners of the business.
8. The profit made by the assets and liabilities, and the debtors and creditors of the business can be fairly determined.
9. The giver of a benefit must be debited.
10. Nominal accounts fall within the category of impersonal accounts.
11. The double-entry rule for nominal accounts is "debit all expenses and gains and credit all incomes and losses".
12. A narration may not be written for entries that occur frequently.
13. Any number of entries can be combined, provided only that they occur on the same day.
14. The purchase of goods-in-trade and the subsequent resale of it (for profit) on the same day, can be conveniently combined.
15. The capital account is a record of the proprietor's investment in his business including amounts borrowed as a business loan for supplementing his investment.
16. Preparation of trading account precedes the drawing up of profit and loss account.
17. Carriage outward account does not appear in the trading account.
18. The expenses incurred in carriage for fetching the raw materials, etc., to the factory for production and finally delivering the finished goods to the buyers are all transferred to the trading account.
19. Depreciation appears in the profit and loss account.
20. Gross profit is transferred to the profit and loss account.
21. Bad receivable appearing in the trial balance must be deducted from accounts receivables in the balance sheet.
22. Some adjustments to final accounts may have only single effects.
23. If capital account is debited with ₹ 300 being the drawings over the year and reflects a net credit increase of ₹ 500 the net profit of the concern for the year transferred to the capital account is ₹ 1,800.
24. Final accounts can be prepared only after the suspense account becomes nil.
25. A capital expenditure, though it involves an outgo of cash does not appear in the profit and loss account.
26. Amounts due from customers are shown collectively in the balance sheet.

27. A net profit is a liability to the concern.
28. Some values reported in the balance sheet may be based on activities that took place several years ago.
29. The main reasons for the changes in a business entity's financial condition during the year are reported in its income statement of changes in Financial Position.
30. The balance sheet is sometime called a snapshot picture of the business entity's financial condition, because this financial statement is presented at a particular point in time.
31. The income statement may be for the year ending, say, December 31, 2012, and in the same set of financial statements the company's balance sheet may be at November 30, 2012.
32. The balance sheet has two sides, one showing its assets and the other showing sources of its total assets.
33. A classified balance sheet is one in which the items reported are grouped according to similar characteristics.
34. Only the book value or accounts receivable should be reported in the balance sheet, the balance of the account and the balance of the allowance for Doubtful Accounts should not be reported.
35. If no bad debts expense entries were recorded during the first year of business of a new company, its total assets and its owners equity at year-end would be overstated.
36. To be conservative, a company should deliberately over estimate its uncollectible accounts and bad debts expense.
37. The bad debts expense estimate may be based on an ageing analysis of the ending balance of Accounts Receivable, instead of the total credit sales for the period.
38. The bad debts expense estimate based on an ageing analysis of accounts receivable is quite different from the bad debts expense when it is based on total credit sales during the period.
39. Accrued expense, not having been billed to the business, are not really liabilities, and the company should not worry about these at year-end.
40. Recording many accrued expenses at year-end requires estimates; exact amounts are not available.
41. Over the entire life span of fixed assets, the total depreciation deducted for income tax is equal to that dedueted as expense in the yearly income statements.
42. The use of an accelerated depreciation method for income tax generally defers of delays paying the taxes until later years.
43. In the early years, the balance in the deferred income tax payable account decreases, but this is offset in the later years by increases in the account.
44. Deferred revenue is the liability account used to record revenue already received in cash but not yet earned by the business.
45. Accounts payable, accrued expenses, income-tax payable, and deferred income-tax payable all have one thing in common—they are non-interest bearing liabilities.

EXERCISES AND PROBLEMS

1. From the following Trial Balance of Shri Ram, prepare Trading and Profit and Loss Account for the year ended 31st December, 2012 and a Balance sheet as on that date:

Dr. Balances	(₹)	Cr. Balances	(₹)
Opening Stock	20,000	Sales	2,70,000
Purchases	80,000	Purchase Returns	4,000
Sales Return	6,000	Discount	5,200

Dr. Balances	(₹)	Cr. Balances	(₹)
Carriage Inwards	3,600	Sundry Creditors	25,000
Carriage outwards	800	Bills Payable	1,800
Wages	42,000	Capital	75,000
Salaries	27,500		
Plant & Machinery	90,000		
Furniture	8,000		
Sundry Debtors	52,000		
Bills Receivable	2,500		
Cash in Hand	6,300		
Travelling Expenses	3,700		
Lighting (factory)	1,400		
Rent & Taxes	7,200		
General Expenses	10,500		
Insurance	1,500		
Drawings	18,000		
Total	3,81,000	**Total**	3,81,000

Adjustments:

(*a*) Stock on 31st December, 2012 was valued at ₹ 24,000 (Market value ₹ 30,000)

(*b*) Wages outstanding for December, 2012 amounting to ₹ 3,000

(*c*) Salaries outstanding for December, 2012 amounted to ₹ 2,500

(*d*) Prepaid insurance amounted to ₹ 300.

(*e*) Provide depreciation on plant and machinery at 5% and on furniture at 20%.

(Gross Profit ₹ 1,42,000, Net Profit ₹ 87,700 Balance Sheet ₹ 1,77,000)

2. Following is the trial balance of Mr. A as at 31st December, 2012:

Dr. Balances	(₹)	Cr. Balances	(₹)
Mr. A's Building a/c	1,500	Capital Account	12,500
Purchase	4,000	Sales	28,020
Furniture	1,320	Returns outwards	800
Scooter	2,000		
Returns inward	1,150		
Stock on 1st January, 2001	16,900		
Bad Debts	150		
Carriage Inward	350		
General Expenses	600		
Bad Debts Provision			350
Bank Loan			2,500
Interest on Bank Loan	150		
Commission			450
Insurance & Taxes	1,000		
Scooter expenses	1,300		
Salaries	2,200		
Cash in Hand	1,000		
Debtors and Creditors	1,500		4,000
	48,620		48,620

Prepare the final accounts for the year ending 31st December, 2012 taking into accounts the following adjustments:

(*a*) Closing stock 31.12.2012 was valued at ₹ 2,170.

(*b*) Commission include ₹ 150 being commission received in advance.

(*c*) Salaries have been paid for 11 months

(*d*) Bank Loan has been taken at 10% p.a. interest.

(*e*) Depreciate building by 5% and Scooter by 15%

(*f*) Write off ₹ 100 as further bad debts and maintain bad debts provision at 5% on debtors.

(*g*) Scooter is used for business as well as for private purposes equally.

(Gross Profit ₹ 8,590/-, Net Profit ₹ 3,120/-, Balance Sheet ₹ 21,700/-).

3. From the following prepare Trading and Profit and Loss account for the year 2007 and Balance sheet as on 31st December, 2012:

	Dr. (₹)	Cr. (₹)
Building	25,000	—
Machinery	11,000	—
Furniture	5,000	—
Bank	4,500	—
Cash	5,500	—
Loan (Since 1.1.2012)	—	15,000
Capital	—	26,000
Debtors/Creditors	25,000	20,000
Opening Stock	6,000	—
Purchases/Returns	1,25,000	5,000
Sales/Returns	6,000	1,61,000
Rent	3,000	—
Establishment	3,000	—
P. F. deducted from Salaries	—	500
Interest (10%)	1,000	—
Electricity	500	—
Phone	500	—
Commission	3,000	—
Insurance Premium	500	—
Bad Debts	1,000	—
Bills Receivable	2,000	—
	2,27,500	2,27,500

Provide depreciation on building at 5% Machinery at 15% and furniture at 10%. Stock was not taken on 31.12.2012 but only 7.1.2013. The transactions from 1.1.2013 to 7.1.2013 are sale ₹ 12,500/- Purchase ₹ 7,500, stock on 7.1.2012 ₹ 9,000 and Gross Profit 20%. During the year machinery to the value of ₹ 5,000 was destroyed by fire and insurance claim was settled ₹ 4,000 and credited to machinery account. Also provide for Employer's share of P. F. ₹ 500; provision for bad debts at 5%, commission to the Manager at 10% on net profit after providing the commission.

(Gross Profit ₹ 40,500/-, Net Profit ₹ 15,000/-,
Balance Sheet ₹ 79,000/-, Closing Stock ₹ 23,000/-)

4. From the following trial balance prepare trading and profit and loss account and a balance sheet as on 31st December, 2012.

Dr. Balances	₹	Cr. Balances	₹
Purchases	90,000	Sales	1,77,000
Returns Inwards	2,250	Returns Outwards	3,100
Carriage on Purchases	1,300	Creditors	14,000
Carriage on Sales	750	Interest on Investments	1,800
Stock 1.1.2007	16,100	Provision for Bad Debts	1,450
Cash	1,500	Commission received	3,750
Building	75,000	Sales Tax Collected	3,000
Machinery	36,000	Accumulated depreciation	10,000
Fuel and Power	4,250	A's Capital	60,000
Debtors	40,750	B's Capital	45,000
Investment	18,000		
Rent	2,000		
General Expenses (including insurance premium of ₹ 1,000/- paid for one year ending 30th June 2007)	7,500		
Wages and Salaries	10,500		
Sales Tax Paid	2,200		
A's Drawings	5,000		
B's Drawings	6,000		
	3,19,100		3,19,100

Adjustments:

(*a*) Write off ₹ 750 as bad debts and create a provision for doubtful debts @ 5% on debtors.

(*b*) Provide 2% for discount on debtors and creditors.

(*c*) Depreciate building by 5% and machinery by 10%.

(*d*) Rent is payable at the rate of ₹ 200 per month.

(*e*) One third of the commission received is in respect of work to be done next year.

(*f*) Interest on Drawings is to be provided as follows:
Interest on A's Drawings: ₹ 250/- and Interest on B's Drawings ₹ 300/-

(*g*) Closing stock was valued at ₹ 28,350/-
(Gross Profit ₹ 84,050/-, Net Profit ₹ 69,620/-, Balance Sheet ₹ 1,96,590/-).

5. A book keeper has submitted to you the following trial balance wherein the totals of debit and credit balance are not equal:

	Dr. (₹)	Cr. (₹)
Capital	—	15,340
Cash in hand	—	60
Purchases	17,980	—
Sales	—	22,120
Cash at Bank	1,770	—
Fixtures & Fittings	450	—
Freehold Premises	3,000	—
Lighting and Heating	130	—
Bills Receivable	—	1,650
Returns Inwards	—	60

	Dr. (₹)	Cr. (₹)
Salaries	2,150	—
Creditors	—	3,780
Debtors	11,400	—
Stocks (1.1.2001)	6,000	—
Printing	450	—
Bills Payable	3,750	—
Rates, Taxes and Insurance	380	—
Discount Received/Allowed	890	400
	48,350	43,410

You are required to:

1. Draft the Trial Balance correctly.
2. Prepare a Trading and Profit and Loss Account and a Balance Sheet after taking into account the following adjustments:
   (*a*) Stock in hand 31.12.2007 was valued at ₹ 3,600.
   (*b*) Depreciate fixtures and fittings by ₹ 50.
   (*c*) ₹ 700 was due and unpaid in respect of salaries.
   (*d*) Rates and insurance had been paid in advance to extent of ₹ 80.
   (Gross Profit ₹ 1,680/-, Net Profit ₹ 980/-, Balance Sheet ₹ 21,960/-).

6. From the following Trial Balance, prepare Trading and Profit and Loss Account for the year ended 31st December, 2012 and Balance Sheet as on that date:

	Dr. (₹)	Cr. (₹)
Purchases and Sales	2,75,000	5,20,000
Returns Inwards	15,000	—
Returns Outwards	—	9,000
Carriage	12,400	—
Wages and Salaries	58,600	—
Trade Expenses	2,200	—
Rent	—	13,000
Insurance	2,000	—
Audit Fees	1,200	—
Debtors/Creditors	1,10,000	62,100
B/R and B/P	3,300	2,200
Printing and Advertising	5,500	—
Commission	—	1,000
Opening Stock	36,000	—
Cash in Hand	12,800	—
Cash at Bank	26,800	—
Bank Loan	—	20,000
Interest on Loan	1,500	—
Capital	—	2,50,000
Drawings	15,000	—
Fixed Assets	3,00,000	—
	8,77,300	8,77,300

Adjustments:

(*i*) Stock at the end ₹ 60,000/-.
(*ii*) depreciate fixed assets by 10%.
(*iii*) Commission earned but not received amounts to ₹ 400/-.
(*iv*) Rent received in advance ₹ 1,000/-.
(*v*) Interest on Bank Loan @ 15% p.a. is unpaid for the last six months.
(*vi*) Allow 8% interest on capital and charge ₹ 900/- as interest on Drawings.

(Gross Profit ₹ 1,92,000/-, Net Profit ₹ 1,42,400/-, Balance Sheet ₹ 4,83,300/-)

7. From the following Trial Balance prepare Trading and Profit and Loss Account and Balance Sheet as on 31.12.2012:

	Dr. (₹)	Cr. (₹)
Capital	—	5,000
Cash in Hand	750	—
Bank Overdraft 2%		1,000
Purchases and Sales	6,000	7,500
Returns	500	1,000
Establishment Charges	1,250	—
Taxes and Insurance	250	—
Bad Debts Reserve	—	500
Bad Debts	250	—
Sundry Debtors and Creditors	2,500	925
Commission	—	250
Investments	2,000	—
Stock on 1.1.2012	1,500	
Drawings	700	—
Furniture	300	—
Bills Receivable & Bills Payable	1,500	1,250
Collected Sales Tax	—	75
	17,500	17,500

Adjustments:

(*a*) Salary ₹ 50 and taxes ₹ 200 are outstanding but insurance ₹ 25 prepaid.
(*b*) Commission amounting to ₹ 50 has been received in advance for work to be done next year.
(*c*) Interest accrued on investments ₹ 105.
(*d*) Bad Debts Reserve is to be maintained at ₹ 500.
(*e*) Depreciation on furniture is to be charged at 10%.
(*f*) Stock on 31st December, 2012 was valued at ₹ 2,250.
(*g*) A fire occurred on 25th December, 2012 in the godown and stock of the value of ₹ 500 was destroyed. It was fully insured and insurance company admitted the claim in full.

(G.P. ₹ 3,250/-, N.P. ₹ 1,500/-, B/S ₹ 9,400/-).

8. Prepare Trading and Profit and Loss Account and Balance Sheet as on 31st December, 2012 from the following:

	(₹)		(₹)
Capital	41,000	Trade Expenses	7,700
Life Insurance Premium	1,400	Sundry Creditors	4,500
Plant and Machinery	2,500	Sales	62,000

	(₹)		(₹)
Stock in the beginning	7,500	Returns Outwards	500
Purchases	43,600	Special Rebates (Dr.)	400
Returns Inwards	3,000	Special Rebates (Cr.)	600
Sundry Debtors	10,500	Rent for Premises Sublet	500
Furniture	4,550	Lighting	200
Motor Car	20,000	Motor Car Expenses	3,150
Freight and duty	1,000	Bank Balance	7,600
Carriage in	400	Loan from Suresh @ 12% p.a.	5,000
Carriage out	150	Interest on Loan from Suresh (Dr.)	450

Adjustments:

1. Stock on 31st December, 2012 was valued at ₹ 12,500/-
2. Stock of ₹ 3,000 was burnt by fire on 25th December. It was fully insured and the Insurance company admitted the claim in full.
3. Goods worth ₹ 900 were distributed as free samples. Goods worth ₹ 750 were used for personal purposes by the Proprietor and Goods worth ₹ 250 were given away as charity.
4. Depreciate Motor Car by 15%
5. The Motor Car is used; partly for business and partly for domestic purposes; therefore, one third of the car expenses including car depreciation is to be proprietor's A/c.
6. Rent for 2 months is receivable on Premises sublet.
7. Balance at Bank on 31st December, 2012 as ascertained from the pass Book is ₹ 7,540/- the difference representing Bank Charges.
8. Included in Trade Expenses is Insurance Premium of ₹ 1,200/- paid for the year ending 31st March, 2012.

   (G.P. ₹ 24,400/-, N.P. ₹ 11,540/-, B/S ₹ 57,990).

9. Prepare Trading and profit and Loss Account for the year ended 31st December, 2012 and Balance sheet on that date:

	(₹)		(₹)
Capital	20,500	Purchases Returns	2,000
Creditors	15,000	Sales	1,44,800
Outstanding Expenses	3,400	Provision for Bad Debts	300
Rent Received	300	Advertisement Development	4,000
Plant and Machinery	10,000	Power	4,000
Goodwill	2,500	Depreciation of Machinery	500
Agents Samples	1,350	Salary	17,200
Opening Stock	16,000	Discount Received	900
Debtor	7,300	General Expenses	4,100
Cash at Bank	1,000	Prepaid Expenses	200
Cash in Hand	55	Salary to Agent	4,500
Drawings	2,500	Rent and Insurance	9,950
Purchases	85,500	Discount Allowed	2,500
Carriage Inward	750	Sales Return	300
Wages	11,500	Commission to Agents	1,445

Adjustments:

1. Closing Stock was valued at ₹ 15,700. Goods costing ₹ 1,000 was destroyed by fire. The insurance company admitted the claim of ₹ 790 only.

2. Write off ₹ 500 as Bad Debts and create a provision for doubtful debts on debtors at 5%.
3. Depreciate Agents samples by $33\frac{1}{3}\%$
4. Write off Advertisement Development by 25%.
5. Charge 5% Manager's Commission on Net Profits after charging his commission.
6. Proprietor withdraw ₹ 100 for his private use. This amount was included in General Expenses.
7. There is a contingent liability of ₹ 6,000 in respect of a court case.

(G.P. ₹ 45,450/-, N.P. ₹ 4,100/-, B/S ₹ 40,605).

10. On 31st December, 2012 the following trial balance has been extracted:

Dr. Balance	(₹)	Cr. Balance	(₹)
Drawings	3,000	Establishment	8,097
Sundry Debtors	19,100	Rates, Taxes and Insurance	3,891
Interest on Loan	200	Advertisement	2,264
Cash in Loan	3,050	**Cr. Balances**	
Stock (1.1.2012)	5,839	Capital A/c	30,000
Motor Vehicles	9,000	Sundry Creditors	8,401
Cash at Bank	4,555	Loan on Mortgage	8,500
Land and Building	12,000	Bad Debts Provision	710
Purchases	67,458	Sales	1,11,243
Sales Returns	7,821	Purchases Returns	1,346
Carriage in	3,929	Discounts	440
Carriage out	1,404	Bills Payable	2,714
General Expenses	4,489	Rent Received	250
Bills Receivable	6,882		

Adjustments:

1. Depreciate Land and Buildings at 5% and Motor Vehicle at 15%
2. Interest on Loan is @ 5% taken on 1st January, 2012.
3. Goods costing ₹ 600 were sent to customer on sale or return for ₹ 700 on 30th December, 2012 and has been recorded in the books as actual sale.
4. Salaries amounting to ₹ 700 and Rates amounting to ₹ 400 are due.
5. There has been a fire on 1st January, 2012 destroying goods worth ₹ 200/-
6. The Bad Debts provision is to be brought up to 5% on Sundry Debtors.
7. The stock in hand on 31st December, 2012 was valued at 6,850/-.
8. Goods costing ₹ 500 were taken away by the proprietor for his personal use, but no entry has been made in the books of accounts.
9. Prepaid Insurance amounted to ₹ 175.
10. Provide for Manager's commission at 5% on net profit after charging such commission.

(G.P. ₹ 34, 192/-, N.P. ₹ 10, 097/-, B/S ₹ 58,042).

11. From the following Trial Balance of Mr. Axe, prepare a Trading and Profit & Loss for the year ended on 31st December, 2012 and a Balance Sheet as on that date:

Dr. Balance	(₹)		(₹)
Materials Consumed	15,000	Bank Charges	30
Carriage	820	Coal, Gas and Water	220
Wages	3,610	B/R	400

Dr. Balance	(₹)		(₹)
Power and Fuel	540	**Cr. Balances**	
Trade	1,450	Axe's Capital A/c	18,000
Bad Debts	180	Sales	24,000
Returns	500	Loan from Kapil @ 12% (taken on 1.4.2001)	1,000
Fire Insurance	300	Bank	820
Rates & Taxes	520	Outstanding wages	340
Cash in Hand	160	Trade Expenses accrued but not paid	200
Stock on 31.12.2001	4,650	Discount	60
Plant & Machinery	8,000	Creditors	1,240
Interest on Kapil's Loan	60	Apprentice Premium	450
Debtors	5,400	B/P	370
Salaries	2,000	Provision for Doubtful Debts	760

Adjustments:

1. Carry forward the following unexpired amounts:
   (*a*) Fire Insurance ₹ 50
   (*b*) Rates & Taxes ₹ 120
   (*c*) Apprentice Premium ₹ 150
2. Wages include ₹ 500 spent on installation of a new machine on 1st January, 2012.
3. Depreciation is to be charged on Plant and machinery at 10% and Furniture at 20%. Loose Tools are re-valued at ₹ 1,200.
4. Make a Provision of ₹ 400 for doubtful debts on Debtors.
5. Accrued Income ₹ 230.

(G.P. ₹ 3,810/-, N.L. ₹ 1,250/-, B/S ₹ 20,900).

12. From the following ledger balances prepare Trading Account, Profit & Loss Account and a Balance Sheet as at 31st December, 2012:

Capital Account on 1.1.2012	50,000	Fire Insurance Premium A/c	900
Stock Account on 1.1.2012	8,000	Bad Debts A/c	2,100
Purchases Account	20,000	Discount Account (Dr.)	500
Sales Account	80,000	Apprenticeship Prem. (Cr.)	1,500
Returns Inwards A/c	1,500	Printing and Stationery A/c	250
Returns Outwards A/c	400	Rates and Taxes A/c	350
Carriage Outward A/c	2,500	Travelling Expenses A/c	150
Carriage Inward A/c	1,200	Sundry Trade Expenses A/c	200
Wages A/c	3,300	Business Premises A/c	55,000
Salaries A/c	5,500	Furniture & Fixture A/c	2,500
Rent A/c	1,100	Bills Receivable A/c	3,500
Freight and Dock Charges A/c	2,400	Bills Payable A/c	2,500
Sundry Debtors A/c	20,000	Investments A/c	3,000
Sundry Creditors A/c	15,800	Cash in Hand	250
Packing Machinery A/c	4,500	Cash at bank	3,500
Smith's Loan A/c	5,000	Proprietor's Withdrawals	3,000

Adjustments to be made are:

1. Stock in hand at 31st December, 2012 ₹ 7,000.
2. Wages to labourers for the last month are outstanding ₹ 300/-.
3. Salaries to Clerks for the month of December, 2012 are outstanding ₹ 500.
4. Rent of godowns for the last month is outstanding ₹ 100.
5. Fire Insurance Premium are ₹ 600 paid in July, 2012, to run for one year from 1st July, 2012 to 30th June, 2013.
6. Apprenticeship Premiums are for three years paid in advance on 1st January, 2012.
7. A stationery bill for ₹ 30 remains unpaid and unrecorded.
8. Depreciate: Business Premises by 5%; furniture and fixture by 10% packing machinery by 10%.
9. Interest on Investments at 5% for the half year to 31st December, 2012 has accrued.
10. Interest on Smith's Loan for one year has accrued at 7%.
11. Interest on capital to be allowed at 5% for the year.
12. Interest on Drawings to be charged to him, as ascertained for the year ₹ 80.

(G.P. ₹ 50,700/-, N.P. ₹ 31,875/-, B/S ₹ 1,01,525/-).

13. Prepare Trading and profit and Loss Account and Balance Sheet as on 31st December, 2012 from the following Balances of Mr. Roshan Seth:

	(₹)		(₹)
Capital	20,500	Stock on 1.1.2012	16,000
Creditors—Trade	15,000	Debtors	7,300
Creditors—Expenses	3,400	Cash at bank	1,000
Drawings	2,500	Cash in Hand	55
Purchases	85,500	Wages	11,500
Carriage Inwards	750	Power	4,500
Rent Received	300	Rent and Insurance	9,950
Purchases Returns	2,000	Salaries	17,200
Sales	1,44,800	Discount Received	900
Bad Debts Reserve on 1.1.2012	300	Sales Returns	300
Advertising Development	4,000	Traveller's Commission	1,445
Goodwill	2,500	Traveller's Salaries	4,450
Plant and Machinery	10,000	Discount Allowed	2,500
Traveller's Samples	1,350		

Adjustments:

1. The closing stock was ₹ 11,500 but there has been a loss by fire on December 20, 2012 to the extent of ₹ 10,000 not covered by insurance. Depreciate Plant and machinery by 10% and Traveller's Samples by $33\frac{1}{3}$%. Increase the bad Debts Provision to ₹ 1,000. Write off 20% of Advertising Development A/c. Annual Premium on insurance expiring 1st March, 2013 was ₹ 600/-. Provide for Manager's commission @ 5% on net profit.

(G.P. ₹ 49,750/-, N.P. ₹ 1,845/-, B/S ₹ 34,555).

14. From the following Trial Balance extracted from the books of Ram Singh, prepare a Trading and Profit and Loss Account for the year ended 30th September, 2012 and a Balance Sheet as on that date.

	(₹)	(₹)
Capital Account	—	45,000
Drawings Account	3,240	—
Land and Buildings	12,500	—
Plant & Machinery	7,135	—
Furniture and Fixtures	625	—
Carriage (Inwards)	2,185	—
Wages	10,735	—
Salaries	2,335	—
Bad Debts Provision as on 1.10.2011	—	1,235
Sales	—	45,615
Sales Returns	880	—
Bank Charges	70	—
Coal, Gas and Water	360	—
Rates & Taxes	420	—
Discounts Accounts Balance	—	60
Purchases	21,080	
Purchases Returns	—	4,230
Bills Receivable	635	—
Trade Expenses	995	—
Sundry Debtors	18,900	—
Sundry Creditors	—	6,085
Stock (1st October, 2011)	13,210	—
Apprentice Premium (paid by apprentice in factory)	—	250
Fire Insurance	245	—
Cash at Bank	6,500	—
Cash in Hand	425	—
	1,02,475	1,02,475

Adjustments:

1. Carry forward the following unexpired amounts:
   (*i*) Fire Insurance ₹ 62.50
   (*ii*) Rates and Taxes ₹ 120
   (*iii*) Apprentice premium ₹ 200
2. Transfer to Building Account ₹ 1,500 from purchases and ₹ 1,000 from wages, representing cost of material and labour spent on additions to Building made during the year.
3. Charge depreciation on Land and Building at 2.5% and on Plant and Machinery 10%.
4. Make a Provision of 5% on Sundry Debtors for bad debts.
5. Charge 5% Interest on capital but not on Drawings.
6. The value of stock as on 30th September, 2012 was ₹ 14,695.

(G.P. ₹ 18,590/-, N.P. ₹ 11, 769/-, B/S ₹ 62,064)

ANSWERS TO SELF-EVALUATION EXERCISES

Section A

I.

1. (*d*) 2. (*c*) 3. (*c*) 4. (*c*) 5. (*b*) 6. (*d*)

7. (*b*) **8.** (*b*) **9.** (*c*) **10.** (*d*) **11.** (*c*) **12.** (*b*)
13. (*d*) **14.** (*a*) **15.** (*d*) **16.** (*b*) **17.** (*b*) **18.** (*b*)
19. (*c*) **20.** (*c*) **21.** (*d*) **22.** (*c*) **23.** (*b*) **24.** (*b*)
25. (*c*) **26.** (*d*) **27.** (*a*) **28.** (*b*) **29.** (*d*) **30.** (*b*)
31. (*d*) **32.** (*b*) **33.** (*c*) **34.** (*b*) **35.** (*c*) **36.** (*d*)
37. (*a*) **38.** (*b*) **39.** (*b*) **40.** (*d*) **41.** (*a*) **42.** (*b*)
43. (*c*) **44.** (*c*) **45.** (*a*) **46.** (*a*) **47.** (*a*) **48.** (*d*)
49. (*c*) **50.** (*a*) **51.** (*a*) **52.** (*c*) **53.** (*d*) **54.** (*b*)
55. (*c*) **56.** (*c*) **57.** (*a*)

II.

1. False **2.** False **3.** False **4.** False **5.** False **6.** True
7. False **8.** False **9.** True **10.** False **11.** False **12.** True
13. True **14.** False **15.** True **16.** True **17.** True **18.** True
19. True **20.** False **21.** True **22.** True **23.** True **24.** True
25. False **26.** True **27.** True **28.** True **29.** True **30.** True
31. False **32.** True **33.** False **34.** False **35.** True **36.** True
37. True **38.** False **39.** True **40.** False **41.** True **42.** True
43. True **44.** False **45.** False **46.** True **47.** False **48.** True
49. True **50.** True

III.

1. Trading account **2.** Stock, capital **3.** Profit and loss account
4. Sales **5.** Debited **6.** Trading **7.** Journal proper
8. Subsidiary journals, cash book **9.** Rectification entries **10.** Transfer
11. Closed, trading, profit and loss, closing **12.** Profit and loss account
13. Transfer **14.** Adjusting **15.** A payable/current liability **16.** Trading
17. Debit/carried forward to next year/reflected on the asset side of balance sheet
18. Debit, nil **19.** Commences, assets, liabilities
20. Written off, bad debts **21.** Reserve/provision for doubtful/bad debts
22. Percentage **23.** Reserve for bad debts, profit and loss
24. Deducted **25.** Reserve for discount on debtors; reserve for discount on creditors
26. Debit, credit, profit and loss **27.** Debit
28. Capital expenditure **29.** Credit

Section B

I.

1. (*b*) **2.** (*b*) **3.** (*d*) **4.** (*d*) **5.** (*b*) **6.** (*d*)
7. (*b*) **8.** (*a*) **9.** (*b*) **10.** (*c*) **11.** (*b*) **12.** (*b*)
13. (*c*) **14.** (*b*) **15.** (*c*) **16.** (*d*) **17.** (*b*) **18.** (*d*)
19. (*d*) **20.** (*d*) **21.** (*b*) **22.** (*c*) **23.** (*b*) **24.** (*a*)
25. (*a*) **26.** (*d*) **27.** (*a*) **28.** (*c*) **29.** (*a*) **30.** (*c*)
31. (*c*) **32.** (*d*) **33.** (*c*) **34.** (*b*) **35.** (*b*) **36.** (*c*)
37. (*d*) **38.** (*d*) **39.** (*a*) **40.** (*a*) **41.** (*d*)

II.

1. Drawings **2.** Assets **3.** Balance Sheet
4. Current liability **5.** Window dressing **6.** Owns, owes
7. Current assets **8.** Long-term
9. Fixed assets, current assets **10.** Capital **11.** Loss **12.** Trading, profit and loss
13. Credit **14.** ₹ 30,000 **15.** ₹ 8,700 **16.** Deducted, added
17. Net profit **18.** Capital **19.** Statement of account, an account
20. Statement/list **21.** Credit, liability **22.** Asset
23. Assets, liabilities to outsiders **24.** ₹ 34,000
25. Depreciation **26.** ₹ 49,000 **27.** Increases **28.** Liability
29. Increases **30.** Written off, bad receivables
31. Reserve/provision for doubtful/bad receivables
32. Reserve for bad receivables: profit and loss **33.** Deducted
34. Reserve for discount on receivables, reserve for discount on payables
35. Debit, credit, profit and loss **36.** Debit

III.

1. False **2.** False **3.** False **4.** True **5.** True **6.** True
7. False **8.** True **9.** False **10.** True **11.** False **12.** True
13. False **14.** False **15.** False **16.** True **17.** True **18.** False
19. True **20.** True **21.** False **22.** True **23.** False **24.** False
25. True **26.** True **27.** True **28.** True **29.** True **30.** True
31. False **32.** True **33.** True **34.** False **35.** True **36.** False
37. True **38.** False **39.** False **40.** True **41.** True **42.** True
43. False **44.** True **45.** True

10

DEPRECIATION ACCOUNTING

LEARNING OBJECTIVES

After reading this chapter, you should be able to:

- *Identify* the type of long-term assets and related terms for their write-offs.
- *Explain* the accounting problem with regard to long-term assets.
- *Discuss* the meaning and causes of depreciation.
- *List* the factors that effect the computation of depreciation.
- *Examine* the statement, 'depreciation is a process of allocation, not of valuation'.
- *Discuss* straight-line method and accelerated methods of depreciation.
- *Identify* the advantages of accelerated methods of depreciation.
- *Explain* the factors influencing the selection of a depreciation method.

LONG-TERM ASSETS

This chapter discusses the accounting problems related to the use of long-term assets whose benefits to a firm extend over many accounting periods, specially the problem of depreciation accounting.

Before taking up depreciation, it should be understood that the costs relating to the use of long-term assets should be properly calculated and matched against the revenue earned so that periodic net income can be determined. These use costs or expenses or periodic write-offs are known by different names for different category of assets as shown here:

Types of Long-term Assets	Term of expense for write-off or use costs
1. Tangible assets:	
(*i*) Land	None
(*ii*) Plant, building, equipment tools, furniture, vehicles	Depreciation
(*iii*) Natural resources such as oil, timber, coal, ore, mineral deposits	Depletion
2. Intangible assets such as patent, copyrights, trade marks, goodwill	Amortisation

Among the above assets, land is a tangible asset that has an indefinite or unlimited useful life. Therefore, it is not subject to depreciation or periodic write-off to expenses.

Depletion is the name of expenses or write-off in the case of natural resources. Depletion refers to the systematic and rational allocation of the acquisition cost of natural resources to future periods in which the use of those natural resources contributes to revenue. Natural resources are exhausted or used up through mining, cutting, pumping, etc.

The term amortisation is used in case of intangible assets. Amortisation refers to the systematic and rational allocation of the acquisition cost of intangible assets to future periods in which the benefits contribute to revenue. It is the periodic write-off to expenses of the intangible asset's cost over its expected useful life.

The term depreciation refers to periodic allocation of the acquisition cost of a tangible long-term asset over its useful life. Depreciation has been discussed in detail later.

ACCOUNTING PROBLEM IN LONG-TERM ASSETS

Basically, there are two problems relating to accounting of long-term assets. First, what is the original acquisition cost of a particular long-term asset. Second, how should the amount of expense or periodic write-off be determined to allocate it against yearly revenue to reflect the asset's consumption. The other related issues are how should subsequent expenditures such as repairs, maintenance and additions be treated, how should disposal of long-term assets be recorded. These accounting problems are graphically presented in Fig. 10.1.

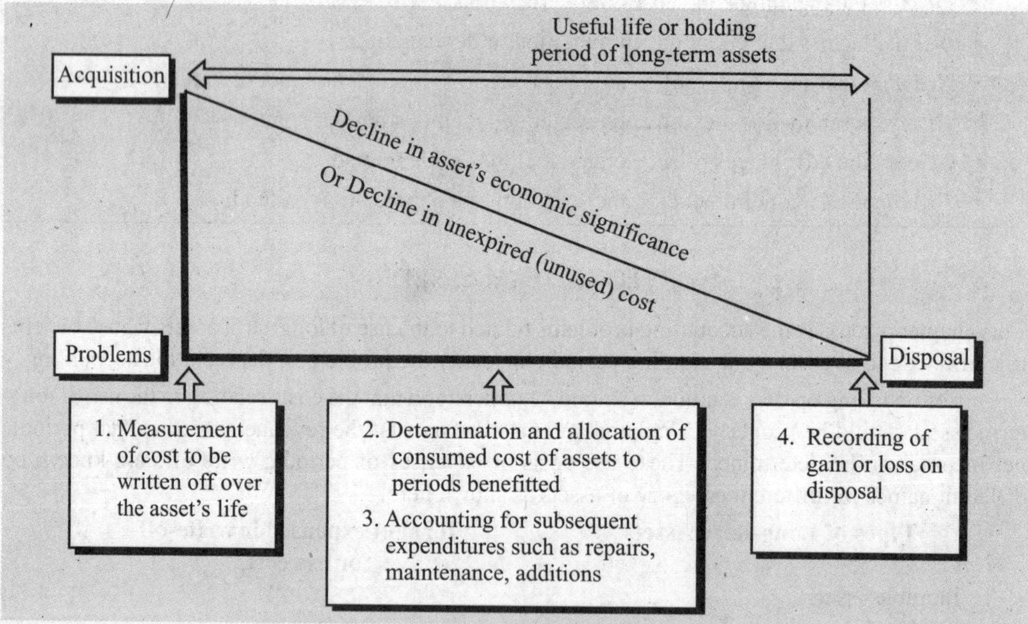

Fig. 10.1. Accounting problems of long-term assets

For accounting purposes, the acquisition cost of a long-term asset having a limited useful life indicates the prepaid cost of a bundle of future services or benefits that will help earn future revenues. Acquisition cost of long-term assets are like inventories and prepaid expenses. Acquisition cost includes all expenditures necessary to get the long-term assets in place and ready for use.

Cost of a long term asset is easy to determine when the asset is purchased for cash. In this case, cost of asset is equal to cash paid for the asset plus expenditures for freight, insurance while in transit, sales tax, special foundations, installation and other necessary costs. When a second-hand asset is purchased, the initial costs of getting it ready for use, such as expenditures for new parts, repairs and painting are added to the cost of the asset.

Some costs associated with the acquisition of an asset are not added to the cost if they are not found necessary to get the asset ready for use, and therefore, do not increase asset's usefulness. Expenditures resulting from carelessness or errors in installing the asset, from vandalism or from other unusual occurrences do not increase the usefulness of the assets and should be treated as an expense.

If a debt is incurred for the purchase of the asset, the interest charges are not the cost of the asset but the cost of borrowing money to purchase the asset. They are, therefore, an expense for the period. But interest incurred during the construction period of an asset is treated as part of the cost of an asset.

The cost of land includes not only the negotiated price but also other expenditures such as broker's commissions, title fees, surveying fees, lawyer's fees, accrued taxes paid by the purchaser, assessment for local improvements such as streets and sewage systems, cost of draining, clearing, levelling and grading. Any salvage recovered from the old building will be deducted from the cost of the land.

Improvement to land such as parking lots, private sidewalks, driveways, fences are not added to the cost of land but to a separate land improvement account. These expenditures are depreciated over the estimated lives of the improvements.

When an existing or old building or used machinery is purchased, its cost includes the purchase price plus all repair, renovation and other expenses incurred by the purchaser prior to use of the asset. Ordinary repair costs incurred after the asset is placed in use are normal operating expenses when incurred.

When a business constructs its own buildings, the cost includes all reasonable and necessary expenditures such as those for materials, labour, some related overhead and indirect costs, architects' fees, insurance during construction, interest on construction loans during the period of construction, lawyer's fees. If outside contractors are used in the construction, the net contract price plus other expenditures necessary to put the building in usable condition are included.

Sometimes, basket purchases (also known as group purchases, package purchases) of assets are made by the purchaser wherein two or more types of long-term asset are acquired in a single transaction, and for a lumpsum. In basket or package purchases, cost of each assets acquired must be measured and recorded separately. For example, assume that a purchaser has bought land and the building situated on the land for a lumpsum payments of ₹ 8,50,000. The total purchase price can be divided between these two assets on the basis of relative market or appraisal values, as shown here.

Assets	Estimated market value (₹)	Per cent of total (%)	Allocation of purchase price (₹)	Estimated useful life (₹)
Land	1,00,000	10	85,000	Indefinite
Building	9,00,000	90	7,65,000	30 yrs
	10,00,000	100	8,50,000	

When a long-term asset is purchased and a non-cash consideration is included in part or in full payment for it, the cash equivalent cost is measured as any cash paid plus current market value of the non-cash consideration given. Alternatively, if the market value of the non-cash consideration given cannot be determined, the current market value of the asset purchased is used for measurement purposes.

As a general rule, long-term assets are recorded at cost due to the basis criterion of objectivity. However, there could be some exceptions to this rule of cost basis. For example, if an asset is acquired by donation or by paying substantially less than the market value of the asset, then it is recorded at its fair market value. Similarly, if the value of land increases sharply after its acquisition due to some abnormal factors, such as discovery of mineral deposits or oil, the amount originally recorded as the cost of land may be increased to reflect current value of the land.

NATURE OF DEPRECIATION

As stated earlier, depreciation is a term applicable in case of plant, building, equipment, furniture, fixtures, vehicles, tools. These long-term or fixed assets have a limited useful life, *i.e.*, they will provide service to the entity (in the form of helping in the generation of revenue) over a limited number of future accounting periods. Depreciation implies allocating the cost of a tangible fixed or long-term asset over its useful life. Depreciation makes a part of the cost of asset chargeable as an expense in profit and loss account of the accounting periods in which the asset has helped in earning revenue.

Thus, allocating the capitalised cost of an asset into expense for different accounting periods is known as depreciation.

The Institute of Chartered Accountants of India defines depreciation as follows:

"Depreciation is a measure of the wearing out, consumption or other loss of value of depreciable asset arising from use, effluxion of time or obsolescence through technology and market changes. Depreciation is allocated so as to charge a fair proportion of the depreciable amount in each accounting period during the expected useful life of the asset. Depreciation includes amortisation of assets whose useful life is pre-determined".

SSAP 12 of the UK also defines the depreciation in the same manner.

"Depreciation is the measure of the wearing out, consumption or other loss of value of a fixed asset whether arising from use, effluxion of time or obsolescence through technology and market changes."

International Accounting Standards Committee (now IASB) defines this terms as follows:

"Depreciation is the allocation of the depreciable amount of an asset over its estimated useful life. Depreciation for the accounting period is charged to income either directly or indirectly".

Depreciation accounting is based on the matching concept wherein an attempt is made to match a part of acquisition cost of an asset (shown as depreciation expense) with the revenue generated by the use of such asset.

Causes for Depreciation

Depreciation implies a decline in the service potential of an asset and the decline in the service potential makes the asset have only a limited useful life. Unless the asset should eventually be retired from its planned use, there is no cause for depreciation. For example, services provided by land do not decrease over time, therefore, land is not depreciated and all costs are recovered when the land is sold.

There are many factors that cause decline in the service potential or economic utility of asset, and hence, become the causes of depreciation. However, the major causes are physical deterioration and obsolescence.

Physical deterioration of the asset results from use and physical factors such as normal wear and tear, chemical action such as rust, effects of wind and rain. To some extent, maintenance and repairs may partially check or offset deterioration. Therefore, while estimating the useful life and salvage value of the asset, a given level of maintenance is assumed. However, this does not eliminate the need for depreciation.

Obsolescence is another important cause for depreciation. Obsolescence is non-physical factor and means becoming out-of-date. With fast-changing technology as well as fast-changing demands, machinery and even buildings often become obsolete before they wear out. Inventions may result in new processes that reduce the unit cost of production to the point where continued operation of old equipment is not economical. Firms replace computers that work as well as when they were purchased because new, smaller computers occupy less space and compute faster.

It should also be noted that replacing the asset is not essential to the existence of depreciation. Depreciation is the expiration or disappearance of service potential from the time the plant asset is put into use until the time it is retired from service. Whether or not the asset is replaced does not effect the amount or treatment of its depreciation.

Accountants rightly do not differentiate between physical deterioration and obsolescence and are not interested in identifying the specific causes of depreciation for determining the amount of depreciation. These and other causes are only helpful in estimating an asset's useful life in which the accountants are interested because the useful life of an asset is used to measure the amount of depreciation.

FACTORS THAT AFFECT THE COMPUTATION OF DEPRECIATION

The computation of depreciation for an accounting period depends on the following factors:

1. **Depreciable Assets:** Depreciable assets are assets which:
   (*i*) are expected to be used during more than one accounting period;
   (*ii*) have a limited useful life; and
   (*iii*) are held by an enterprise for use in the production or supply of goods and services, for rental to others, or for administrative purposes and not for the purpose of sale in the ordinary course of business.
2. **Useful Life:** Useful life is either:
   (*i*) the period over which a depreciable asset is expected to be used by the enterprises; or
   (*ii*) the number of production or similar units expected to be obtained from the use of the asset by the enterprise.

   The useful life of a depreciable asset is shorter than its physical life and is:
   (*i*) pre-determined by legal or contractual limits, such as the expiry dates;
   (*ii*) directly governed by extraction or consumption;
   (*iii*) depend on the extent of use and physical deterioration on account of wear and tear which again depends on operational factors, such as, the number of shifts for which the asset is to be used, repair and maintenance policy of the enterprise, etc;
   (*iv*) reduced by obsolescence arising from such factors as:
   (*a*) technological changes
   (*b*) improvement in production methods
   (*c*) change in market demand for the product or service output of the asset
   (*d*) legal or other restrictions

   Estimation of the useful life of a depreciable asset or a group of similar depreciable assets is a matter of judgement ordinarily based on experience with similar types of assets. For an asset using new technology or used in the production of a new product or in the provision of a new service with which there is little experience, estimation of the useful life is more difficult but is nevertheless required.

Since the estimated useful life of the asset is determined at the time of acquisition it may become necessary to revise the estimate after a period of usage. According to AS 6, when the original estimated useful life is revised, the unamortised depreciable amount of the asset is charged to revenue over the revised remaining useful life. Another method to be adopted for taking into account the revised life of the asset is to recompute the aggregate depreciation charged to date on the basis of the revised useful life of the asset and to adjust the excess or short depreciation so determined in the accounting period of revision.

3. **Depreciable Amount:** Depreciable amount of a depreciable asset is its historic cost, or other amount substituted for historic cost in the financial statements, less the estimated residual value.

   Historic cost of a depreciable asset represents its money outlay or its equivalent in connection with its acquisition, installation and commissioning as well as for additions to or improvement thereof. The historic cost of a depreciable asset may undergo subsequent changes arising as a result of increase in long-term liability on account of exchange fluctuations, price adjustments, change in duties or similar factors.

4. **Residual Value:** The residual value of an asset is often insignificant and can be ignored in the calculation of the depreciable amount. If the residual value is likely to be significant, it is estimated at the date of acquisition, or the date of any subsequent revaluation of the asset, on the basis of the realisable value prevailing at the date for similar assets which have reached the end of their useful lives and have operated under conditions similar to those in which the asset will be used. The gross residual value in all cases is reduced by the expected costs of disposal at the end of the useful life of the asset.

   According to ICAI's AS 6 "Any addition or extension to an existing asset which is of a capital nature and which becomes an integral part of the existing asset is depreciated over the remaining useful life of that asset. As a practical measure, however, depreciation is sometimes provided on such addition or extension at the rate which is applied to an existing asset. Any addition or extension which retains a separate identity and is capable of being used after the existing asset is disposed off, is depreciated independently on the basis of an estimate of its own useful life".

'DEPRECIATION IS A PROCESS OF ALLOCATION NOT OF VALUATION'

The Statement that 'depreciation is a process of allocation not of valuation' is found in the following definition of AICPA (US):

"Depreciation accounting is a system of accounting which aims to distribute the cost... of tangible capital assets, less salvage (if any) over the estimated useful life of the unit in a systematic and rational manner. It is a process of allocation, not of valuation".

This definition represents depreciation as an allocation of cost and is based on the following assumptions:

(*i*) Depreciation is that part of the cost of a fixed asset which is not recoverable when the asset is finally put of use.

(*ii*) Depreciation is related to the expected benefits derived from the asset and it is possible to measure the benefits.

(*iii*) Depreciation accounting is not an attempt to measure the value of an asset at any point of time. But there is only an attempt to measure the value of the benefit the asset has provided during a given accounting period and that benefit is valued as portion of the cost of asset. In other words, the balance sheet value of depreciable asset is that portion of the original cost which has not been allocated as a periodic expense in the process of income measurement.

(*iv*) Depreciation accounting does not itself provide funds for the replacement of a depreciable asset, but the charging of depreciation ensures the maintenance, in fact, of the original money capital of the entity. Indeed, a provision for depreciation is not identified with cash or any other specific asset, or assets.

Allocation Process

Allocation in accounting refers to the process of partitioning a set or an amount and the assignment of resulting subsets or amounts to separate periods of time or classifications. Depreciation accounting attempts to allocate in a rational and systematic manner the difference between acquisition cost and estimated salvage value over the estimated useful life of the asset.

The main emphasis in depreciation accounting is on the computation of the periodic charge to be allocated as an expense and to be matched with revenues reported in each period. Depreciation considers the original cost as a deferred expense and the original cost is charged against the profits of the various periods by allocating it over a given period in a systematic manner.

Depreciation does not refer to physical deterioration of an asset or decrease in market value of an asset over time. If this is so, then it can be claimed that periodic repairs and sound maintenance policy may keep buildings and equipment is good running order or as good as new, and thus, physical deterioration can be stopped or checked. However, every building or machine, at sometimes or the other, has to be discarded and replaced. The need for depreciation is not eliminated by repairs and depreciation does not depend on physical deterioration alone or on no physical deterioration. Similarly, depreciation process is not affected by what happens to the price level, in general, or to the price of asset in particular. It is related to the income statement which shows the net income after accounting for depreciation. Depreciation is simply the allocation of the cost of a plant asset to the periods that benefit from the services of the asset.

The net income under allocation concept of depreciation would be overstated in times of rising prices. That is, the allocation concept does not consider the problem of asset replacement at a higher price in future. It is rightly argued that an additional reserve out of net profits can be provided for replacement of assets alongwith historic cost basis of providing depreciation. Alternatively, replacement cost can be made the basis of allocating the cost of an asset which would reflect current business situations and the net income would also be realistic. Whatever methods or adjustments are done, the allocation basis of determining depreciation is followed. However, when replacement cost is used in place of historic cost of asset, the objective of current revenue matching with current cost is also achieved.

Depreciation Not a Valuation Process

Depreciation is not a process of valuation. The valuation concept considers depreciation as the decline in the value of the asset over a period of time. It requires the valuation of assets at two points of time, and assuming decline in value, the amount of depreciation is determined as the difference between the value of asset at the beginning and the end of an accounting period. However, depreciation does not arise due to decline in value during that period, but rather from the process of ensuring a return of capital invested. If, in a given period an asset increases in value, there will still be depreciation during that period.

A depreciation problem will exist whenever (*i*) funds are invested in services to be rendered by a plant asset, and (*ii*) at some date in the future, the asset must be retired from service with a residual value less than it's original cost.

The valuation concept is related to the balance sheet which aims to reflect the values of different assets at a particular date or point in time.

The valuation concept implies that depreciation should reflect the decrease in value of the asset over a period of time. The term value means: (*i*) market value (*ii*) value to the owner. The valuation concept would provide a very unsatisfactory basis for distributing the depreciation charges. Decline in the value of asset with time is likely to be unequal and would make net income comparison difficult and unreliable. When the value of the new asset increases, it is not brought into accounting records because the increase in value may not be permanent and also no profits (due to increase in value of asset) should be taken into account unless they are realised.

Further, even if the market value of a plant or building increases, depreciation should be recorded as a result of allocation.

Eventually, the building will wear out, the plant will lose its utility or become obsolete regardless of interim fluctuations in market value.

Under ideal conditions, *i.e.*, when prices are stable, all facts are clear, estimates are correct, the amount of depreciation under the allocation process and valuation process are likely to be identical. In other words, after deducting the amount of depreciation under the allocation procedure from the cost of an asset at the beginning of the year, the resulting remaining cost of an asset will reflect the value of the asset at the balance sheet dates that one could obtain while following valuation process of determining depreciation.

For example, assume the cost of an asset to be ₹ 10,000 with zero scrap value. If the useful life of the asset is 10 years, the amount of depreciation under allocation process will be ₹ 1,000. Further, assume that price of this asset and prices, in general, are stable and the asset is available for purchase in the market. In this ideal situation, value of asset will decline because prices are stable and the asset will have wear and tear and will not maintain the same potential or utility when it was purchased. Since the useful life of the asset is 10 years, the value of asset should be zero at the end of 10 years. It means for each year, the amount of decline in value comes to ₹ 1,000 which is also the amount of depreciation under the allocation process.

However, the trouble is that practical conditions are far from ideal. It is difficult to determine depreciation on the changes in market value because a reliable, objective and practical source for such data is rarely found. Any attempt to accomplish the objectives of allocation and valuation, simultaneously, would be impossible and create confusion. The better approach, is, therefore, to ignore the valuation aspect and to concentrate on a satisfactory distribution of the cost of the asset.[1]

Cost allocation is a matching principle and the objective is to find a particular method that, more or less, coincides with the pattern of services or benefits provided by the asset to future periods of time. The Accounting Principles Board (US)[2] has said "the allocation method used should appear reasonable to an unbiased observer and should be followed systematically".

Need for Depreciation

The need for charging a reasonable amount of depreciation over the estimated useful life of the asset arises for the following purposes:

1. **To ascertain the true income:** The basic need of depreciation is to ascertain the true income. If depreciation is ignored, the loss that is occurring in respect of fixed assets will be ignored. The loss will suddenly loom large when the asset become useless or valueless. From another angle, when goods are produced it involves use of fixed assets–the reduction in their value should be treated as element of cost of production of goods. Therefore, depreciation should be debited to P&L A/c before profit is ascertained.

---

1. David R. Anderson, Practical Controllership.
2. APB Statement No. 4, *Basic Concept and Accounting Principles Underlying Financial Statement of Business Enterprises,* 1970, para 159.

2. **To show the asset at its proper value:** In the absence of depreciation charge, the asset will be shown at its acquisition cost every year in the balance sheet. If depreciation is not allowed, the Balance sheet would fail to show the true financial position. Therefore, depreciation must be accounted for in order to present the assets at their proper value.
3. **To maintain the capital invested:** Depreciation helps to maintain the capital invested in the asset intact in the business so that it can be reinvested in the profit earning process.
4. **To retain out of profit fund for replacement:** The other need for depreciation is to retain out of profit funds for replacement of assets. The amount debited in P&L A/c are retained in the business. These are available for replacement of the assets when its life is over.
5. **To allocate the cost of fixed asset to product:** The business firms, to find out the accurate cost of production, requires to allocate the cost of fixed asset to product.
6. **To compute tax liability:** In such a case the rate of depreciation is influenced by tax laws.

METHODS OF DEPRECIATION

There are different methods for allocating costs of fixed depreciable assets. Such allocation has a direct effect on the determination of net income because depreciation expense is a necessary charge and as such a deduction from the revenues in a given period.

Various methods of depreciation are generally classified as follows:

1. On the Basis of Time
   (*i*) Straight Line Method
   (*ii*) Decreasing Charge Depreciation
      (*a*) Written down value method
      (*b*) Double method
      (*c*) Sum of year digit method
2. On the Basis of Investment
   (*i*) Annuity Method
   (*ii*) Sinking Fund Method
3. On the Basis of Output

1. Straight line Method: This method assumes that depreciation is a function of time rather than use. This method is based on the assumption that each accounting period receives same a benefits from using the assets. It allocates an equal amount of depreciation in each accounting periods of the service life of the assets. Therefore, it is called Straight Line Method.

The formula for calculating depreciation charge for each accounting period is

$$\text{Annual Depreciation} = \frac{\text{Acquisition cost} - \text{Estimated scrap value}}{\text{Estimated Life in Years}}$$

Advantages:

(*i*) It is simple in use.
(*ii*) It realistically matches cost and revenue and determine income of each period easily.
(*iii*) There is no change either in the rate or the amount of depreciation over the useful life of the assets. Such a procedure provides for improved comparability.

Disadvantages:

(*i*) It ignores the cost of capital.
(*ii*) It is based on the wrong assumption of equal utility of the assets during the useful life.

(*iii*) It is also wrong to consider depreciation as a function of time rather than use.

(*iv*) The maintenance of asset is generally costly in the later years with the result that deductions from the revenue would be greater in later years than in the earlier years.

The journal entry for recording depreciation is

Depreciation A/c Dr.

To Asset A/c

Illustration 1: ABC Ltd. acquires a machine on 1st July, 2007 at a cost of ₹ 2,80,000 and spent ₹ 20,000 on its installation. The firm writes off depreciation at 10% of the original cost every year. The books are closed on 31st December every year. Prepare machinery A/c for 3 years.

Solution: **Machinery A/c**

Date	Particulars	(₹)	Date	Particulars	(₹)
2006	To Bank	2,80,000	2006	By Depreciation A/c	15,000
July 1	To Bank (installation Exps.)	20,000	Dec. 31	By Balance c/d	2,85,000
		3,00,000			3,00,000
2007			2007		
Jan. 1	To balance b/d	2,85,000	Dec. 31	By Depreciation A/c	30,000
			Dec. 31	By balance c/d	2,55,000
		2,85,000			2,85,000
2008			2008		
Jan. 1	To balance b/d	2,55,000	Dec. 31	By Depreciation A/c	30,000
			Dec. 31	By balance c/d	2,25,000
		2,55,000			2,55,000

Sale of Asset: If the asset is disposed of in the middle of the year, the amount realised should be credited to the asset a/c for the time it has been in use. Any balance left in the account of asset will be profit or loss and should be transferred to P&L A/c.

Illustration 2: On 1st Jan. 2009, a company purchased a machine costing ₹ 5,00,000. Its estimated working life is 20 years at the end of which it will fetch ₹ 20,000. Additions are made on 1 January, 2010 and 1 July, 2011 to the value of ₹ 80,000 (scrap value ₹ 4000) and ₹ 40,000 (scrap value ₹ 2,000) respectively.

The life of both the new machines is 20 years. Show machine a/c for first four years.

Solution: **Machine A/c**

2009	Particulars	(₹)	2009	Particulars	(₹)
Jan. 1	To Bank	5,00,000	Dec. 31	By Depreciation	24,000
			Dec. 31	By Balance c/d	4,76,000
		5,00,000			5,00,000
2010			2010		
Jan. 1	To balance b/d	4,76,000	Dec. 31	By Depreciation	27,800
Jan. 1	To Bank	80,000	Dec. 31	By balance c/d	5,28,200
		5,56,000			5,56,000
2011			2011		
Jan. 1	To balance b/d	5,28,200	Dec. 1	By Depreciation	
July 1	To Bank	40,000		(24,000 + 3800 + 950)	28,750
			Dec. 1	By Balance c/d	5,39,450
		5,68,200			5,68,200

2009	Particulars	(₹)	2009	Particulars	(₹)
2012			2012		
Jan. 1	To Bal b/d	5,39,450	Dec. 31	By Depreciation (24,000 + 3800 + 1900)	29,700
			Dec. 31	By Balance c/d	5,09,750
		5,39,450			5,39,450

Note: In case, no method of depreciation has been stated in an examination problem, it is appropriate to use straight line method.

Illustration 3: Rubal Ltd. purchased a machine costing ₹ 3,00,000 on 1st April, 2000 and an additional machine on 1st Oct., 2000 costing ₹ 2,00,000 and on 1 July, 2001 costing ₹ 1,00,000.

On 1st Jan. 2002, one third of Machine purchased on 1st April, 2000 was sold at ₹ 30,000.

Prepare machine A/c for 3 years, it is given that depreciation is charged @ 10% p.a. on straight line method.

Solution: **Machine A/c**

2000	Particulars	(₹)	1998	Particulars	(₹)
April 1	To Bank	3,00,000	Dec. 31	By Depreciation (22,500 + 5,000)	27,500
Oct. 1	To Bank	2,00,000	Dec. 31	By Balance c/d	4,72,500
		5,00,000			5,00,000
2001			2001		
Jan. 1	To balance b/d	4,72,500	Dec. 31	By Depreciation (30000 + 20000 + 5000)	55,000
July 1	To Bank A/c	1,00,000	Dec. 31	By balance c/d	5,17,500
		5,72,500			5,72,500
2002			2002		
Jan. 1	To balance b/d	5,17,500	Jan. 1	By Bank	30,000
				By P&L A/c (loss)	52,500
			Dec. 31	By Depreciation	50,000
				By Balance c/d	3,85,000
		5,17,500			5,17,500

2. Diminishing Balance Method: Under this method, a fixed percentage is applied to book value of the assets (cost of assets). In other words, the depreciation is calculated on the reducing balance (assets cost–depreciation) and not on the original cost. The procedure is that depreciation calculated is deducted from the cost of assets and balance known as the written down value. The written down value at the end of the estimated useful life of the assets should equal the estimated salvage or scrap value.

The formula for determining the rate of depreciation in diminishing balance method is as follows:

$$\text{Rate of depreciation} = 1 - \sqrt[n]{\frac{s}{c}}$$

Advantages:

1. It is easy to use.
2. There is same weightage, in totality, on profit and loss A/c, of depreciation.
3. It facilitates replacement of fixed assets as it makes more funds available at an early stage.

4. This method is permissible under the Income Tax Act.
5. The higher depreciation is charged in the earlier years when the machine is most efficient compared to later years.

Disadvantages:

1. Under this method, value of asset can never be zero.
2. It is difficult to calculate proper rate of depreciation.
3. There is no provision of interest on capital invested in use of assets.

Illustration 4: Y Ltd. Co. purchased a machine costing ₹ 3,00,000 on 1st January, 2007. The depreciation is to be charged at 20% p.a. on Diminishing Balance method.

Write up Machinery A/c for first four years.

Solution: **Machinery A/c**

2007	Particulars	(₹)	2007	Particulars	(₹)
Jan. 1	To Bank	3,00,000	Dec. 31	By Depreciation	60,000
			Dec. 31	By Balance c/d	2,40,000
		3,00,000			3,00,000
2008			2008		
Jan. 1	To balance	2,40,000	Dec. 31	By Depreciation	48,000
			Dec. 31	By balance c/d	1,92,000
		2,40,000			2,40,000
2009			2009		
Jan. 1	To balance b/d	1,92,000	Dec. 31	By Depreciation	38,400
			Dec. 31	By balance c/d	1,53,600
		1,92,000			1,92,000
2010			2010		
Jan. 1	To balance b/d	1,53,600	Dec. 31	By Depreciation	30,720
			Dec. 31	By Bal. c/d	1,22,880
		1,53,600			1,53,600

Illustration 5: X Ltd. bought a machinery for ₹ 30,000 on 1st April, 2007. One more machine was purchased on Oct. 1st, 2007 costing ₹ 20,000. On July 1st, 2008, a new machinery for ₹ 10,000 was added to the existing machinery.

On 1st January, 2009, one third of the machinery which was installed on April 1st, 2007 was sold for ₹ 3,000. Show the machinery A/c in the books of X Ltd. The rate of depreciation is 10% on reducing balance method.

Solution: **Machinery A/c**

Date	Particulars	(₹)	Date	Particulars	(₹)
2007			2007		
April 1	To Bank	30,000	Dec. 31	By Depreciation	2,750
Oct. 1	To Bank	20,000		By Balance c/d	47,250
		50,000			50,000
2008			2009		
Jan. 1	To Balance b/d	47,250	Dec. 31	By Depreciation	5,225
July 1	To Bank	10,000	Dec. 31	By Balance c/d	52,025
		57,250			57,250

Date	Particulars	(₹)	Date	Particulars	(₹)
2009			2009		
Jan. 1	To balance b/d	52,025	Jan. 1	By Depreciation	3,000
			Jan. 1	By P&L A/c (loss)	5,325
			Dec. 31	By Depreciation	4,370
			Dec. 31	By balance c/d	39,330
		52,025			52,025

Illustration 6: A machine is purchased for ₹ 3,00,000 and its estimated useful life is 3 years with scrap value ₹ 30,000. It is decided to depreciate the machine by diminishing balance method. Find out the rate of depreciation p.a.

Solution:

$S =$ ₹ 30,000 $\quad C =$ ₹ 3,00,000 $\quad n = 3$

$$r = 1 - n\sqrt{\frac{s}{c}} = 1 - 3\sqrt{\frac{30,000}{3,00,000}}$$

$$= 1 - 3\sqrt{\frac{1}{10}}$$

$$= \frac{1 - (\underline{1})\ 1/3}{10}$$

$$= 1.0 - .464$$

$$= .536$$

$$= 53.6\%.$$

Illustration 7: A Company had bought machinery for ₹ 2,00,000 including a boiler worth ₹ 20,000. The Machinery Account had been credited for depreciation on the reducing instalment system for the past four years at the rate of 10 per cent. During the fifth year, the boiler became useless on account of damage to some of its vital parts. The damaged boiler is sold in the very beginning of the fifth year for ₹ 4,000. Write up the Machinery Account for all these five year.

Solution:

Dr. **Machinery Account** **Cr.**

Date	Particulars	Amount (₹)	Date	Particulars	Amount (₹)
1st year	To Bank A/c	2,00,000	1st year	By Depreciation A/c	20,000
				By Balance c/d	1,80,000
		2,00,000			2,00,000
2nd year	To Balance b/d	1,80,000	2nd year	By Depreciation A/c	18,000
				By Balance c/d	1,62,000
		1,80,000			1,80,000
3rd year	To Balance b/d	1,62,000	3rd year	By Depreciation A/c	16,200
				By Balance c/d	1,45,800
		1,62,000			1,62,000
4th year	To Balance b/d	1,45,800	4th year	By Depreciation A/c	14,580
				By Balance c/d	1,31, 220
		1,45,800			1,45,800

Date	Particulars	Amount (₹)	Date	Particulars	Amount (₹)
5th year	To Balance b/d	1,31,220	5th year	By Bank –Sale	4,000
				By P&L A/c* (Loss on Sale of boiler)	9,122
				By Dep. A/c*	11,810
				By Balance c/d	1,06, 288
	Total	1,31,220			1,31,220

Working Notes:

	₹
* Loss on Sale:	20,000
Cost of boiler	
Less: Depreciation for four years (₹ 2,000 + ₹ 1,800 + ₹ 1,620 + ₹ 1,458)	6,878
Book Value at the beginning of 5th year	13,122
Less: Sale Proceeds	4,000
Loss on Sale of boiler	9,122

* **Depreciation for 5th year:**

Balance of remaining machinery at the beginning of 5th year

= ₹ 1,31, 220 – ₹ 13,122

= ₹ 1,18,098

Hence, Depreciation for the 5th year @ 10%

= ₹ 11,810 (to the nearest rupee)

Illustration 8: On 1st April, 2000, a firm purchased a machinery for ₹ 2,00,000. On 1st October, 2000, additional machinery costing ₹ 1,00,000 was purchased. On 1st October, 2001, the machinery purchased on 1st April, 2000 was sold for ₹ 90,000. On 1st October, 2002, new machinery was purchased for ₹ 2,50,000, while the machinery purchased on 1st October, 2000 was sold for ₹ 85,000 on the same day.

The firm provides depreciation on its machinery @10% per annum on original cost. It closes its books of accounts on 31st March every year. Show machinery account for three accounting years ending 31st March, 2003.

Solution:

Dr. **Machinery Account** **Cr.**

Date	Particulars	Amount (₹)	Date	Particulars		Amount (₹)
2000			2001			
April 1	To Bank A/c	2,00,000	March 31	By Dep. A/c ₹ 2,00,000 @10%	20,000	
Oct. 1	To Bank A/c	1,00,000		₹ 1,00,000 @ 10% for 6 months	5,000	25,000
				By Balance c/d		2,75,000
		3,00,000				3,00,000
2001			2001			
April 1	To Balance b/d	2,75,000	Oct. 1	By Bank A/c (Sale)		90,000
				By Dep. A/c ₹ 2,00,000 @ 10% for 6 months		10,000

Date	Particulars	Amount (₹)	Date	Particulars		Amount (₹)
				By Profit and Loss A/c (Loss on Sale *)		80,000
			2002 March 31	By Dep. A/c ₹ 1,00,000 @10%	10,000	
				By Balance c/d		85,000
		2,75,000				2,75,000
2002 April 1st	To Balance b/d	85,000	2002 Oct. 1	By Bank A/c		85,000
Oct. 1st	To Bank A/c	2,50,000	2003 March 31	By Dep. A/c ₹ 1,00,000 @ 10% for 6 months		5,000
	To P&L A/c Gain on Sale*$_2$	5,000		By Dep. A/c ₹ 2,50,000 @ 10% for 6 months		12,500
				By Balance c/d		2, 37,500
		3,40,000				3,40,000

Working Notes:

* Calculation of Loss on Sale of Machinery purchased on 1st April, 2000

		₹
Cost		2,00,000
Less: Depreciation [1.4.2000–31.3.2001]		20,000
		1,80,000
Less: Depreciation [1.4.2001–30.9.2001]		10,000
		1,70,000
Less: Sale Proceeds		90,000
Loss		– 80,000

* **Calculation of Profit on Sale of Machinery purchased on 1st October, 2000**

	₹	₹
Cost		1,00,000
Less: Depreciation		
[1.10.2000–31.3.2001]	5,000	
[1.4.2001–31.3.2002]	10,000	
[1.4.2002–30.9.2002]	5,000	20,000
Book Value on 1.10.2002		80,000
Sale Proceeds		85,000
∴ Profit on Sale of Machinery (₹ 85,000 – ₹ 80,000)		+ 5,000

Illustration 9: Mr. X purchased a second hand machinery on 1.2.2003 for ₹ 50,000; paid ₹ 11,000 for its over-hauling and ₹ 5,000 for its installation which was completed by 31.3.2003. The company provides depreciation on its machinery at 15% on diminishing balance method from the date it was put to use and closes its books on 31st December every year. On 1.10.2004, a repair work was carried out on the machine and ₹ 5,000 were paid for the same. The machine was sold on 31.10.2005, for a sum of ₹ 11,000 and an amount of ₹ 1,000 was paid as dismantling charges.

Prepare machinery account from 2003 to 2005.

Solution:

Dr. **Machinery Account** **Cr.**

Date	Particulars	Amount (₹)	Date	Particulars	Amount (₹)
2003			2003	By Depreciation A/c (15% on	
Feb. 1	To Bank A/c	50,000	Dec. 31	₹ 66,000) for 9 months)	7,425
Mar. 31	To Bank A/c [₹ 11,000 + ₹ 5,000]	16,000		By Balance c/d	58,575
2004		66,000	2004		66,000
Jan. 1	To Balance b/d	58,575	Dec. 31	By Depreciation A/c (15% on ₹ 55,875)	8,786
				By Balance c/d	49,789
2005		58,575	2005		58,575
Jan. 1	To Balance b/d	49,789	Oct. 31	By Depreciation A/c (15% on ₹ 49,789 for 10 months)	6,223
				By Bank A/c	10,000
				By Profit & Loss A/c (Loss) (*Balancing fig.*)	33,566
		49,789			49,789

Working Notes:

* Repair cost is not capitalised since it is a routine expense and it does not increase the capacity of the machine.

* Cost of dismantling has been deducted from the sale price for calculating loss on sale of machine.

Illustration 10: ABC Ltd. purchased second hand machinery on 1st April, 2006 for ₹ 3,70,000 and installed it at a cost of ₹ 30,000. On 1st October, 2007 it purchased another machinery for ₹ 1,00,000 and on 1st October, 1998, it sold off the first machine purchased in 2006, for ₹ 2,80,000.

On the same date it purchased a machinery for ₹ 2,50,000. On 1st October, 2009, the second machinery purchased for ₹ 1,00,000 was sold off for ₹ 20,000.

In the beginning depreciation was provided on Machinery at rate of 10% p.a. on the original cost each year on 31st March. From the year 2007–2008, however, the company changed the method of providing depreciation and adopted the written down value method, the rate of Depreciation being 15%.

Give machinery A/c for the period 2006–2010.

Solution: Working:

(*i*) *Machine sold on 1st October, 2008*

w.d.v. on April 1, 2008	3,06,000
Less: Dep. @ 15% p.a. for 6 months	22,950
	2,83,050
Less: Sale	2,80,000
Loss	3,080

(*ii*) *Machinery Sold in 1st October, 2009*

W.D.V. on April 1, 2009	78,625
Less: Dep. @ 15% p.a. for 6 months	5,897
	72,728

Less: Sale	20,000
Loss	52,728

Machinery A/c

Date	Particulars	Amount (₹)	Date	Particulars	Amount (₹)
2006			2007		
April 1	To Bank	3,70,000	March 31	By Depreciation A/c	40,000
April 1	To bank	30,000	March 31	By Balance c/d	3,60,000
		4,00,000			4,00,000
2007			2008		
April 1	To balance b/d	3,60,000	Mar. 1	By Depreciation A/c (54000 + 7500)	61,500
Oct. 1	To Bank	1,00,000			
			Mar. 1	By Balance c/d (3,06,00 + 92,500)	3,98,500
		4,60,000			4,60,000
2008			2009		
April 1	To balance b/d	3,98,500	Oct. 1	By Bank	2,80,000
Oct. 1	To Bank	2,50,000	Oct. 1	By Dep.	22,950
			Oct. 1	By P&L A/c (Loss)	3,050
			2009		
			Mar. 31	By Depreciation A/c (13875 + 18750)	32,625
			Mar. 31	By Balance c/d (78,625 + 231,250)	3,09,875
		6,48,500			6,48,500
2009			2009		
April 1	To Balance b/d	3,09,875	Oct. 1	By Bank	20,000
			Oct. 1	By Depreciation	5, 897
				By P&L A/c (Loss)	52,728
			2010		
			Mar. 31	By Depreciation	34,688
			Mar. 31	By Balance c/d	1,96,562
		3,09,875			3,09,875

Illustration 11: On 1st January, 2000, Asha Ltd. purchased machinery for ₹ 12,00,000 and on 30 June, 2001, one more machine of worth ₹ 2,00,000. On 31 March, 2002, one of the original machinery which had cost ₹ 50,000 was found to have become obsolete and was sold as scrap for ₹ 7,000. It was replaced on that date by a new machine costing ₹ 80,000. Depreciation is to be provided @ 15% p.a. on W.D.V. method. Accounts are closed on 31 December every year. Show machinery A/c for 3 years.

Solution:

Machinery A/c

Date	Particulars	Amount (₹)	Date	Particulars	Amount (₹)
2000			2000		
Jan. 1	To Bank	12,00,000	Dec. 31	By Depreciation A/c	1,80,000
			Dec. 31	By Balance c/d	10,20,000
		12,00,000			12,00,000

Date	Particulars	Amount (₹)	Date	Particulars	Amount (₹)
2001			2001		
Jan. 1	To Balance b/d	10,20,000	Dec. 31	By Depreciation	1,68,000
June 30	To Bank	2,00,000	Dec. 31	By Bal. c/d	10,52,000
		12,20,000			12,20,000
2002			2002		
Jan. 1	To Balance b/d	10,52,000	Mar. 31	By Bank (sale)	7,000
March 31	To Bank	80,000	Mar. 31	By Depreciation A/c	13,50
			Dec. 31	By P&L A/c (Loss)	27,770
				By Depreciation (1,52,380 + 9000)	1,61,380
				By Bal. c/d	9,34,500
		11,32,000			11,32,000
2003 Jan. 1	To Balance b/d	9,34,500			

Illustration 12: Y Ltd. company purchased a second hand machinery on 1st January, 2009 for ₹ 3,70,000 and immediately spent ₹ 20,000 on its repairs and ₹ 10,000 for installation. On 1st July, 2010, it purchased another machine for ₹ 1,00,000.

On 1st July, 2011, it sold off the first machine for ₹ 2,50,000 and bought another for ₹ 3,00,000 Depreciation was provided on the machine @ 10% on original cost annually on 31st December. With effect from 1st January, 2012, the company changed the method of providing Depreciation and adopted the W.D.V. method and rate of Depreciation was 15% p.a.

Prepare machinery A/c for 4 years.

Solution: **Machinery A/c**

Date	Particulars	Amount (₹)	Date	Particulars	Amount (₹)
2009			2009		
Jan. 1	To Bank	3,70,000	Dec. 31	By Dep. A/c	40,000
	To Bank	30,000	Dec. 31	By Balance c/d	3,60,000
		4,00,000			4,00,000
2010			2010		
Jan. 1	To Balance b/d	3,60,000	Dec. 31	By Dep. (40000 + 5000)	45,000
July 1	To Bank	1,00,000	Dec. 31	By Balance c/d	4,15,000
		4,60,000			4,60,000
2011			2011		
Jan. 1	To Balance b/d	4,15,000	July 1	By Depreciation	20,000
July 1	To Bank	3,00,000	July 1	By Bank	2,50,000
			July 1	By P&L A/c (Loss)	50,000
			Dec. 31	By Depreciation (10,000 + 5000)	25,000
			Dec. 31	By Balance c/d (78,625 + 231,250)	3,70,000
		7,15,000			7,15,000
2012			2012		
Jan. 1	To Balance b/d	3,70,000	Dec. 31	By Depreciation	55,500
				By Balance c/d	3,14,500
		3,70,000			3,70,000

Illustration 13: M Ltd. which depreciates its machinery @ 10% p.a. according to D.B.M. (Diminishing Balance Method), had on 1st April, 2006 ₹ 4,86,000 balance in its machinery A/c. During 2004 the year ended 31st March, 2007, the machinery purchased on 1st April, 2004 for ₹ 60,000 was sold for ₹ 40,000. On 1st October, 2006 and a new machinery costing ₹ 70,000 was purchased and installed on the same date, installation charges ₹ 5000.

The Company wants to change its method of depreciation from W.D.V to Straight line method w.e.f. 1st April, 2004 and adjust the difference before 31st March, 2007, the rate of Depreciation remaining the same as before.

Show Machinery A/c for the year ended 31st March, 2007.

Solution: **In the books of M. Ltd.**

Machinery A/c

Date	Particulars	Amount (₹)	Date	Particulars	Amount (₹)
2006			2006		
April 1	To Balance b/d	4,80,000	Oct. 1	By Bank	40,000
			Oct. 1	By P&L A/c (Loss)	6,170
Oct. 1	To Bank	70,000			
Oct. 1	To Bank	5,000	2007	By Depreciation	60,180
			Mar. 31	By P&L A/c (Dep.)	5,400
				By balance c/d	4,49,250
		5,61,000			5,61,000

Working:

(*i*) Machinery sold on Oct. 1st, 2006

Cost on April, 2004	60,000
Less: Dep. for 2004–05	6,000
	54,000
Less: Dep. for 2005–06	5,400
	48,600
Less: Dep. for 06–07 for 6 months	2,430
	46,170
Less: Sale	(40,000)
Loss	6,170

(*ii*) Additional Depreciation

Cost of Machinery on April 1st, 2004	
$4,86,000 \times \frac{10}{9} \times \frac{10}{9}$	₹ 6,00,000
Less: Book Value of Machinery	
Sold on October 1 2006	₹ 60,000
Book value on April 1st, 2004	₹ 5,40,000
Dep. for 2004–05 & 2005–06 @ 10% p.a. (54,000 + 54,000)	1,08,000
Less: Dep. for 2004-05, 2005–06	
Already charged under W.D.V (54,000 + 48,600)	1,02,600
Difference	5,400

(*iii*) Dep. for 2006–07

On Machine sold	2,430
On New Machine	3,750
On old Machinery	54,000
	60,180

Illustration 14: Manoj Ltd. purchased a Computer Costing ₹ 80,000 on January 2000. The expected life is 5 years and scrap value ₹ 5000. Find the annual depreciation for 5 years by sum-of-years-digit methods.

Solution:

$C = 80,000$ $\quad S = 5000$ $\quad N = 5$

$$\text{Annual Depreciation} = \frac{N(C-S)}{\text{Sum}}$$

$$\text{Where Sum} = \frac{N(N+1)}{2}$$

$$\text{Sum} = \frac{5(5+1)}{2} = 15$$

Year	*Calculation*	*Depreciation*
1.	$\frac{5(75,000)}{15}$	₹ 25,000
2.	$\frac{4(75,000)}{15}$	₹ 20,000
3.	$\frac{3(75,000)}{15}$	₹ 15,000
4.	$\frac{2(75,000)}{15}$	₹ 10,000
5.	$\frac{1(75,000)}{15}$	₹ 5,000

Illustration 15: A bus was purchased by a Transport Company for ₹ 10,00,000 on 1st January, 2000. The scrap value is estimated at the end of 5 years ₹ 1,00,000. The rate of depreciation is 20% p.a. Calculate the annual Depreciation by Double Declining method.

Solution: The rate of Depreciation = 20 × 2 = 40% p.a.

End of Year	Asset Cost at Beginning of Year	Amount of Depreciation
1	1,00,000	4,00,000
2	6,00,000	2,40,000
3	3,60,000	1,44,000
4	2,16,000	86,400
5	1,29,600	51,840

4. Unit of Production Method: Under this method depreciation expense is allocated in proportion to the degree of asset used for production because estimation of useful life is done in terms of units of output or services hour and not a calender time period. A machine can produce a limited number of quantity or run for a limited hours. As a result of this limitation, the depreciation is related to usage and not to time. Under this method, the following is calculated:

Depreciation Per annum = Dep. expense Per unit × No. of units produced during the year

or

Dep. expense per hour × No. of hours used during the year

$$\text{Dep. per unit} = \frac{\text{Cost} - \text{Scrap value}}{\text{Total estimated unit of output or service hrs.}}$$

Illustration 16: X Ltd., bought a machine for ₹ 4,00,000 expected to run 72,000 hrs. Its salvage value is estimated at ₹ 40,000. Calculate depreciation for an accounting year in which it was used for 20,000 hrs.

Solution: $$\text{Dep. per hour} = \frac{4,00,000 - 40,000}{72,000}$$

$$= \frac{3,60,000}{72,000} = ₹\,5$$

Dep. Amount for Accounting period

= 2,0000 × 5 = ₹ 1,00,000

5. Annuity method: The main disadvantages of the different methods of depreciation discussed earlier are that they do not consider the interest on the capital invested on fixed assets. Annuity method deals with the effect of cost of capital in depreciation calculation. It makes treatment more explicit by showing the interest payment in the P&L A/c. Under this system the capital sum is assumed to earn a certain rate of interest. The assets is, therefore, charged with interest along with actual payment; interest is calculated on the debit balance of the assets on the commencement of the year. The following journal entry is made:

Assets A/c Dr.
To Interest A/c

At the same time, fixed amount is charged as a depreciation expense so that it eliminates the asset or brings down its salvage value, as the case may be. The important point to be noted is that the amount of depreciation to be charged every year must be calculated as to reduce the assets together with interest accumulated thereon to its salvage value at the end of the useful life of the assets.

Illustration 17: X Ltd. acquires a lease costing ₹ 2,00,000 on April 1st, 1997 for a term of 4 years. You find from annuity tables that in order to write off lease on the annuity method at 6% p.a. interest, the amount to be written off annually works out to be ₹ 2,88,591 for every rupee. Prepare lease A/c for 4 years. Books are closed on 31st March every year.

Solution: **Lease A/c**

Date	Particulars	Amount (₹)	Date	Particulars	Amount (₹)
1997			1998		
April 1	To Bank	2,00,000	March 31	By Dep.	57,718
	To Interest (6% of ₹ 20,000)	12,000		By Bal. c/d	1,54,282
		2,12,000			2,12,000
1998			1999		
April 1	To Bal. b/d	1,54,282	March 31	By Dep.	57,718
	To Interest (6% of ₹ 1,54,282)	9,527		By Bal. c/d	1,05,821
		1,63,539			1,63,539

Date	Particulars	Amount (₹)	Date	Particulars	Amount (₹)
1999			2000		
April 1	To Bal. b/d	1,05,821	Mar. 31	By Dep.	57,718
	To Interest	6,349		By Bal. c/d	54,452
	(6% of ₹ 1,05,821)	1,12,170			1,12,170
2000			2000		
April 1	To Balance b/d	54,452	Mar. 31	By depreciation	57,718
	To Interest (*Balancing fig.*)	3,266			
		57,718			57,718

Working: Depreciation = ₹ 2,00,000 × .288591
= ₹ 57,718.2

7. Sinking Fund Method: Under this method, the amount of depreciation goes on accumulating till the asset is completely worn out. This method provides necessary cash to replace the asset at end of its useful life. The amount of depreciation is fixed and remains same for every year and is charged to P&L A/c. The amount of depreciation is invested outside the business every year. The process of investing amount of depreciation and interest goes on till the time of replacement of asset. At the time of replacement all the investments are sold out and cash received, and the new asset purchased.

Journal Entries:

(*a*) At the end of first year.

(*i*) For setting aside amount of Depreciation

Depreciation A/c Dr.
To Sinking Fund A/c

(*ii*) For transfer of Depreciation A/c to P&L A/c

P &L A/c Dr.
To Depreciation A/c

(*iii*) For Investment of Amount

Sinking Fund Investment A/c Dr.
To Bank A/c

(*b*) Subsequent Year

(*i*) For receiving interest

Bank A/c Dr.
To sinking fund A/c

(*ii*) For setting aside amount of Depreciation

(*iii*) Depreciation A/c Dr.
To Sinking fund A/c

(*iv*) For transferring Depreciation A/c to P&L A/c

P&L A/c Dr.
To Depreciation A/c

(*v*) For investing amount of depreciation + interest received

Sinking fund investment A/c Dr.
To Bank A/c

(*c*) Last Year

(*i*), (*ii*) & (*iii*) entry remain same as in (*b*), but amount is not invested.

(*iv*) On sale of investment

Bank A/c Dr.
Sinking Fund A/c (if loss) Dr.
To Sinking Fund Investment A/c
To Sinking fund (in profit)

(*v*) On Sale of Asset

Bank A/c Dr.
To Asset A/c

(*vi*) Sinking Fund A/c balance is transferred to asset a/c and any balance left in the asset a/c is transferred to P&L A/c.

Illustration 18: X Ltd. Bought a, machinery for ₹ 2,00,000 on 1st January, 2000. The useful life was estimated at 3 years with a scrap value of ₹ 20,000. The Company uses Sinking Fund Investment Method, investment to carry 5% p.a. Interest. The sinking Fund Table shows that .31720 at 5% p.a. will in 3 years accumulate to Re. 1. Prepare Machinery A/c, Sinking Fund A/c & S.F. Investment.

Solution:

Machinery A/c

Date	Particulars	Amount (₹)	Date	Particulars	Amount (₹)
2002 Jan. 1	To Bal. b/d	2,00,000	2002 Dec. 31	By Sinking Fund A/c	1,80,000
				By cash	20,000
		2,00,000			2,00,000

Sinking Fund A/c

Date	Particulars	Amount (₹)	Date	Particulars	Amount (₹)
2000, Jan. 31	To Bal. c/d	57,097	2000, Dec. 31	By Dep. A/c	57,097
2001, Dec. 31	To Bal. c/d	1,17,053	2001, Jan. 31	By Bal. b/d	57,097
			Dec. 31	By Dep.	57,097
			Dec. 31	By Interest	2,859
		1,17,053			1,17,053
2002 Dec. 1	To Machinery A/c	1,80,000	2002 Jan., 31	By Bal. c/d	1,17,053
			Dec. 31	By Dep.	57,097
				By Interest	5,850
		1,80,000			1,80,000

Sinking Fund Investments A/c

Date	Particulars	Amount (₹)	Date	Particulars	Amount (₹)
2000, Jan. 1	To Bank	57097	2000, Dec. 31	By Bal. c/d	57,097
2002, Jan. 1	To Balance b/d	57097	2002, Dec. 31	By Bank	1,17,053
Jan. 1	To Bank	59,956			
		1,17,053			1,17,053

Illustration 19: (Insurance Policy Method) Y Ltd. purchased a Machinery for ₹ 4,00,000 on 1st January, 2007 to be replaced after 4 years. An Insurance Policy is taken to ensure availabilty of funds at the time of replacement, the annual premium being ₹ 90,000.

Prepare Machinery A/c, Dep. Fund A/c, Dep. Fund Policy A/c.

Solution:

Machinery A/c

Date	Particulars	Amount (₹)	Date	Particulars	Amount (₹)
2010 1 Jan.	To Bal. b/d	4,00,000	2010 Dec. 31	By Dep. Fund A/c	4,00,000

Depreciation A/c

Date	Particulars	Amount (₹)	Date	Particulars	Amount (₹)
2007 Dec. 31	To Bal. c/d	90,000	2007 Dec. 31	By Dep. A/c	90,000
2008 Dec. 31	To Bal. c/d	1,80,000	2008 Jan. 1	By Balance b/d	90,000
			Dec. 31	By Dep. A/c	90,000
		1,80,000			1,80,000
2009 Dec. 31	To Bal. c/d	2,70,000	2009 Jan. 1	By Bal. b/d	1,80,000
			Dec. 31	By Dep. A/c	90,000
		2,70,000			2,70,000
2010 Dec. 31	To Machinery A/c	4,00,000	2010 Dec. 31	By Bal. b/d	2,70,000
			Dec. 31	By Dep. A/c	90,000
			Dec. 1	By Dep. Fund Policy A/c	40,000
		4,00,000			4,00,000

Depreciation Fund Policy A/c

Date	Particulars	Amount (₹)	Date	Particulars	Amount (₹)
2007 Jan. 1	To Bank	90,000	2007 Dec. 31	By Bal. c/d	90,000
2008 Jan. 1	To Bal. b/d	90,000	2008 Dec. 31	By Bal. c/d	1,80,000
	To Bank	90,000			
		1,80,000			1,80,000
2009 Jan. 1	To Bal. b/d	1,80,000	2009 Dec. 31	By Bal. c/d	2,70,000
	To Bank A/c	90,000			
		2,70,000			2,70,000
2010 Jan. 1	To Bal. b/d	2,70,000	2010 Dec. 31	By Bank	4,00,000
	To Bank A/c	90,000			
		40,000			
	To depreciation Fund (Profit)	40,000			
		4,00,000			4,00,000

Illustration 20: General Manufacturers had a debit of balance of ₹ 8,00,000 in their machinery account on 1.1.2000. The concern was charging depreciation @ 15% p.a. on diminishing balance. On 31.3.2000, a part of the machinery purchased on 1.1.1997 at a cost of ₹ 70,000 was sold for ₹ 45,000. New machinery was purchased for ₹ 80,000 on 1.7.2000 and ₹ 6,700 was spent for installation. On 31.12.2000 the concern decided to change the depreciation method from

diminishing balance method to straight-line method. It was also decided to charge depreciation @ 10% p.a. under the new method. Prepare machinery account for the year 2000.

Solution:

Machinery A/c

Dr.		(₹)	Cr.		(₹)
1.1.2000	To Balance b/d	8,00,000	31.3.2000	By Bank	45,000
31.3.2000	To Profit & Loss A/c (Profit on sale) (1)	3,623	31.12.2000	By Depreciation (3)	1,29,214
1.7.2000	To Bank	86,700	31.12.2000	By balance	8,21,964
31.12.2000	To Profit and Loss A/c (Excess depreciation charged) (2)	1,05,855			
		9,96,178			9,96,178

1. Calculation of Profit/Loss on sale of machinery (₹)

	(₹)
Cost of machinery sold	70,000
Depreciation for 1997	10,500
	59,500
Depreciation for 1998	8,925
	50,575
Depreciation for 1999	7,586
	42,989
Depreciation for 2000 (*i.e.*, for 3 months)	1,612
	41,377
Realisation from sale	45,000
Book value at the time of sale	41,377
Profit on sale of machinery	3,623

2. Additional/Excess depreciation due to change in the method of depreciation (₹)

	(₹)
Book value of of machinery on 1.1.2000	8,00,000
Book value on 1.1.1997 (8,00,000) × (100/85) × (100/85) × (100/85)	13,02,666
Cost of machinery	70,000
	12,32,666
Depreciation for 1997 under WDV	1,84,900
	10,47,766
Depreciation for 1998 under WDV	1,57,165
	8,90,601
Depreciation for 1999 under WDV	1,33,590
	7,57,011
Depreciation under WDV @ 15% p.a. (1,84,900 + 1,57,165 + 1,33,590)	4,75,655
Depreciation under SLM @ 10% p.a. for 3 years	3,69,800
Excess depreciation charged	1,05,855

3. Depreciation for 2000 (₹)

	(₹)
Depreciation (on machinery sold) for 1997 for 3 months	1,612
Depreciation on remaining machinery purchased on 1.1.1996	1,23,267
Depreciation on newly purchased machinery for 6 months	4,335
	1,29,214

Illustration 21: A limited company purchased on 1st January, 1998 a second-hand plant for ₹ 12,000 and immediately spent ₹ 8,000 on its overhauling. On 1st July in the same year additional plant costing ₹ 10,000 is purchased. On 1st July, 2000 the plant purchased on 1st January, 1998 having become obsolete is sold for ₹ 4,000 and on the same date fresh plant is purchased at a cost of ₹ 24,000.

Depreciation is provided @ 10% per annum on original cost on 31st December every year. In 2001, however, the company changes the method of providing depreciation and adopts the method of writing off 15% per annum on the diminishing balance method.

Show the Plant Account from 1998 to 2001.

Solution:

Dr. **Plant Account** **Cr.**

Date	Particulars	Amount (₹)	Date	Particulars	Amount (₹)
1998 Jan. 1	To Bank A/c ₹ (12,000 + 8,000)	20,000	1998 Dec. 31	By Depreciation A/c ₹ (2,000 + 500)	2,500
1998 July 1	To Bank A/c	10,000		By Balance c/d	27,500
		30,000			30,000
1999 Jan. 1	To Balance b/d	27,500	1999 Dec. 31	By Depreciation A/c	3,000
				By Balance c/d	24,500
		27,500			27,500
2000 Jan. 1	To Balance b/d	24,500	2000 July 1	By Bank A/c	4,000
2000 July 1	To Bank A/c	24,000		By Depreciation A/c	1,000
				By Profit & Loss A/c Loss* 11,000 ₹ (20,000 – 5,000 – 4,000)	
			Dec. 31	By Depreciation A/c ₹ (1,000 + 1,200)	2,200
				By Balance c/d	30,300
		48,500			48,500
2001 Jan. 1	To Balance b/d	30,300	2001 Dec. 31	By Profit & Loss A/c* (Additional Depreciation)	1,416
				By Depreciation A/c (15% on ₹ 28,884)	4,332
				By Balance c/d	24,552
		30,300			30,300
2002 Jan. 1	To Balance b/d	24,552			

Working Notes:

*1 **Computation of Loss on Sale of machinery on 1.7.2000**

	₹
Cost of machinery sold (as on 1.1.98)	20,000
Less: Depreciation @ 10% p.a. for $2\frac{1}{2}$ years on original cost	5,000
Book value as on 1.7.2000	15,000
Less: Realised Value	4,000
Loss on Sale of Machinery	11,000

*2 **Computation of Depreciation on change of method on additional plant:**

	S.L.M. @ 10% (₹)	W.D.V. @ 15% (₹)
Cost of machinery in use on 1.7.1998	10,000	10,000
Less: Depreciation for 1998	500	750
Book Value on 1.1.1999	9,500	9,250
Less: Depreciation for 1999	1,000	1,387
Book Value on 1.1.2000	8,500	7,863
Add: Addition to Machinery on 1.7.2000	24,000	24,000
	32,500	31,863
Less: Depreciation	2,200	2,979
Book value on 1.1.2001	30,300	28,884

∴ Additional Depreciation ₹ (30,300 – 28,884) = ₹ 1,416

W.D.V. of machinery as per new method on 1.1.2001 = ₹ 28,884.

Illustration 22: On January 1, 2001 X Ltd. purchased a machine for ₹ 58,000 and spent ₹ 2,000 on its erection. On July 1, 2001, an additional machine costing ₹ 20,000 was purchased. On July 1, 2003 the machine purchased on 1.1.2001 was sold for ₹ 28,600 and on the same date a new machine was purchased at a cost of ₹ 40,000. Depreciation was provided for annually on December 31, at the rate of 10% p.a. on written down value of the machinery. In 2004 the company decided to change the method of depreciation from Written Down Value Method to Straight Line Method @ 5% p.a. with effect from 1st January, 2001. Prepare the Machinery Account from the first calender years.

Solution:

Dr. Machinery Account Cr.

Date	Particulars	₹	Date	Particulars	₹
01.01.01	To Bank A/c	58,000	31.12.01	By Depreciation A/c	7,000
01.01.01	To Bank A/c (erection charges)	2,000		By Balance c/d	73,000
01.07.01	To Bank A/c	20,000			
		80,000			80,000
01.01.02	To Balance b/d	73,000	31.12.02	By Depreciation A/c	73,000
				By Balance c/d	65,700
		73,000			73,000
01.01.03	To Balance b/d	65,700	01.07.03	By Bank A/c	28,600
01.07.03	To Bank A/c	40,000	01.07.03	By Depreciation A/c (on Machinery sold)	2,430
			01.07.03	By Profit & Loss A/c	17,570
			31.12.03	By Depreciation A/c	3,710
			31.12.03	By Balance c/d	53,390
		1,05,700			1,05,700
01.01.04	To Balance b/d	53,390	31.12.04	By Depreciation A/c	3,000
31.12.04	To P&L A/c* (Depreciation written back on account of change from WDV Method to Straight Line Method)	3,110		By Balance c/d	53,500
		56,500			56,500

Working Notes:

***1 Calculation of Short/Excess Depreciation on Existing Machines**

Year A	Machine B	Cost C	WDV as on 1.1.04 D	Dep. under WDV E = C – D	Dep. under SLM F
2001	II	20,000	(20,000 × 95/100 × 90/100 × 90/100) = 15,390	4,610	(20,000 × 5% × 2½ = 2,500
2003	III	40,000	(40,000 × 95/100) = 38,000	2,000	(40,000 × 5% × ½ = 1,000
		60,000	53,390	6,610	3,500

Excess Depreciation provided

= Depreciation under Old Method – Depreciation under New Method

= ₹ 6,610 – ₹ 3,500 = ₹ 3,110.

Illustration 23: The Plant and Machinery Account of a company had a debit balance of ₹ 1,47,390 on April 1st, 2006. The company was incorporated in April, 2003 and has been following the practice of charging full year's depreciation every year on Diminishing Balance System @ 15%. In 2006 it was, however, decided to change the method from Diminishing Balance to Straight Line with retrospective effect from April, 2003 and to give effect to the change while preparing the final accounts for the year ending 31st March, 2007, the rate of depreciation remaining same as before.

In 2006–07, new machinery was purchased at a cost of ₹ 50,000. All the other machines were acquired in 2003–04.

Show the Plant and Machinery Account from 2003–04 to 2006–07.

Solution:

Dr. **Plant and Machinery Account** **Cr.**

Date	Particulars	(₹)	Date	Particulars	(₹)
01.04.03	To Bank A/c*	2,40,000	31.03.04	By Depreciation A/c [15/100 × ₹ 2,40,000]	36,000
				By Balance c/d	2,04,000
		2,40,000			2,40,000
01.04.04	To Balance b/d	2,04,000	31.03.05	By Depreciation A/c [15/100 × ₹ 2,04,000]	30,600
				By Balance c/d	1,73,400
		2,04,000			2,04,000
01.04.05	To Balance b/d	1,73,400	31.03.06	By Depreciation A/c [15/100 × ₹ 1,73,400]	26,010
				By Balance c/d	1,47,390
		1,73,400			1,73,400
01.04.06	To Balance b/d	1,47,390	01.04.06	By Profit & Loss A/c* (Additional Depreciation)	15,390
	To Bank	50,000	31.03.07	By Depreciation A/c*	43,500
				By Balance c/d	1,38,500
		1,97,390			1,97,390

Working Notes:

*1 *Calculation of Cost Price of Plant on 1st April, 2003:*

	₹
Let Cost Price on 1st April, 2003	100.00
Less: Depreciation (2003–04) [15% of ₹ 100.00]	15.00

	85.00
Less: Depreciation (2004–05) [15% of ₹ 85.00]	12.750
	72.250
Less: Depreciation (2005–06) [15% of ₹ 72.250]	(approx.) 10.828
	61.412

$$\text{Cost Price on 1st April, 2003} = \frac{100}{61.412} \times (₹)\ 1,47,390 = (₹)\ 2,40,000 \text{ (approx)}$$

*2 *Calculation of Depreciation:*

	S.L.M. ₹	D.B.M. ₹
Cost (1.4.2003)	2,40,000	2,40,000
Less: Depreciation (2003–04)	36,000	36,000
	2,04,000	2,04,000
Less: Depreciation (2004–05)	36,000	30,600
	1,68,000	1,73,400
Less: Depreciation (2005–06)	36,000	26,010
	1,32,000	1,47,390

Difference on Account of change in method of Depreciation:

(₹ 1,47,390 – ₹ 1,32,000) = ₹ 15,390

∴ Additional Depreciation to be transferred to P&L A/c = ₹ 15,390

*3 *Calculation of Depreciation for 2006–07*

	₹
On Old Machinery	36,000
On New machinery [@ 15% of ₹ 50,000]	7,500
	43,500

Illustration 24: M/s Hot and Cold commenced business on 1st April, 2002 when they purchased a new machinery costing ₹ 8,00,000. On 1st October, 2003, they purchased another machinery for ₹ 6,00,000 and again on 1st July, 2006, machinery costing ₹ 15,00,000 was purchased. They adopted a policy of charging @ 20% p.a. on diminishing balance basis.

On April 1st, 2006, they, however, changed the method of providing depreciation and adopted the method of writing-off the machinery account at 15% p.a. under straight line method with retrospective effect from 1st April, 2002, the adjustment being made in the accounts for the year ended 31st March, 2007.

Show the Machinery Account for the year ending 31st March, 2007.

Solution: **Machinery Account**

Date	Particulars	₹	Date	Particulars	₹
2002 April 1	To Bank	8,00,000	2003 March 31	By Depreciation	1,60,000
				By Balance c/d	6,40,000
		8,00,000			8,00,000
2003			2004		
April 1	To Balance b/d	6,40,000	March 31	By Depreciation	1,88,000
October 1	6,00,000	6,00,000		By Balance c/d	10,52,000
		12,40,000			12,40,000

Date	Particulars	₹	Date	Particulars	₹
2004			2005		
April 1	To Balance b/d	10,52,000	March 31	By Depreciation	2,10,400
				By Balance c/d	8,41,600
		10,52,000			10,52,000
2005			2006		
April 1	To Balance b/d	8,41,600		By Depreciation	1,68,320
				By Balance c/d	6,73,280
		8,41,600			8,41,600
2006			2007		
April 1	To Balance b/d	6,73,280	March 31	By Depreciation	3,78,750
July 1	To Bank	15,00,000		By Balance c/d	18,16,250
2007	To Profit and Loss A/c				
March 31	(Depreciation written back)	21,720			
		21,95,000			21,95,000

Working Notes:

Machine No. 1

Depreciation for 4 years:	SLM	4,80,000
	WDV	4,72,320
Depreciation to be charged		7,680

Machine No. 2

Depreciation for 2½ years:	SLM	2,25,000
	WDV	2,54,400
Depreciation to be written back		29,400
Result: Depreciation to be written back in 2006–07		21,720

EVALUATION OF ACCELERATED METHODS

The use of accelerated methods of depreciation provide certain benefits and is useful to business enterprises in many respects. Some benefits which may occur to business entities are as follows:

1. Cash Flow: It terms of cash flow, initial depreciation serves the purpose of an interest free loan to the tax payer with respect to the year of erection of building or installation of machinery and plant. Since it results in postponement of the tax liability of the assesses, the amount of tax saved in the initial years results in a net addition to cash flow, which is repaid through a higher tax liability during the later year.

Depreciation is an expense that does not use funds currently. In the preparation of changes in financial position, depreciation is added back to net income in calculating funds provided by operations. Because it is added back to net income, the funds from operations is often defined as net income plus depreciation. However, depreciation is not a source of fund. Funds from other operations come from revenues from customers, not by making accounting entries.

In fact, depreciation expense result from an outflow of funds in an earlier period, that is only now being recognised as an operating expense. The following example explains the fact that depreciation does not produce funds.

Assume a company has net income in 2002 of ₹ 20,000 resulting from revenues of ₹ 1,25,000, expenses other than depreciation of ₹ 95,000 and ₹ 10,000 of depreciation. Now assume that depreciation increases to ₹ 25,000 while other expenses and revenues are unchanged: net income is ₹ 5,000 (ignore income tax in both instances). The following exhibit shows that changes in depreciation do not effect funds from operations; funds from operations would be the same ₹ 30,000 in both situations.

Impact of Depreciation on Funds from Operations

(i) Depreciation ₹ 10,000

Income Statement	(₹)	Funds from Operations	(₹)
Revenue	1,25,000	Net Income	20,000
Less: Expense except Depreciation	95,000	*Add*: Expenses not using capital: Depreciation	10,000
	30,000		
Depreciable expenses	10,000	Total funds from operations	30,000
Net income	20,000		

(ii) Depreciation ₹ 25,000

Income Statement	(₹)	Funds from Operations	(₹)
Revenue	1,25,000	Net Income	5,000
Less: Expense except Depreciation	95,000	*Add*: Expenses not using Capital Depreciation	25,000
	30,000		
	25,000	Total funds from operations	30,000
Net income	5,000		

Depreciation does help determine cash flow, however, by its effect on the measurement of taxable income and thus tax expenses. The more rapid the rate of depreciation charges for tax purposes, the slower the rate of tax payment. For this reason, accelerating depreciation for tax purposes stimulates acquisition of depreciable assets and is viewed as significant in increasing the rate of capital formation. In India, depreciation provision as a source of funds for joint stock companies accounted for more than 50 per cent of the funds utilised in gross fixed assets formation, and it thus plays an important role in the internal financing of industry. An increasing dependence on this source of finance would suggest lessening reliance of companies on the capital market.

2. Tax Advantage: Many companies may adopt accelerated depreciation methods for tax return purposes because of the tax advantage that they entail. Higher depreciation charges mean lower income and lower taxes. If accelerated methods are used for tax purposes they do not have to be used for financial reporting purposes. Every rupee that can be justified as a deduction saves the company about 50 per cent in tax money. Since the total tax deduction is limited to the total cost of the asset, the different depreciation methods merely shift the years in which the deduction is made. In so far as the deduction is made in earlier years rather than later, this saves interest but more than that it put the taxpayer into possession of funds at an earlier date and this increases his flexibility of financial management.

The actual tax-saving argument is sometimes short-sighted, but the saving of interest and the increased financial flexibility are actual and constitute the real pressure behind depreciation accounting. Thus, accelerated depreciation serves the purpose of an interest-free loan.

3. Benefit to Growing Company: The postponement of the liability under accelerated depreciation may be very useful for a growing firm investing more and more in fixed capital and more so for a new firm which may take some time to stabilise its business. When a company is expanding, the higher depreciation charges will help in expansion and investment which are essentially needed for the company.

4. Replacement of Assets: Accelerated depreciation may induce the tax payer to replace old machinery or equipment before the end of its useful life by new and improved models and also gain a tax advantage. But this would be just one of the considerations in deciding the proper time for replacement. Accelerated depreciation methods allow a business to recover more of the investments in a fixed asset in the first few years of the assets life. This is an important factor in any situation in which there is a high rate of technological change. It is also important when inflation is a factor and depreciation is limited to the original cost of a long-term asset.

Accelerated depreciation does provide an incentive to invest in fixed assets and it particularly helps a growing firm rather than a stationary or a declining one. As far as the form of accelerated depreciation is concerned, the diminishing balance or sum-of-the-years-digits method seems preferable to a straight-line method particularly with respect to plant and machinery. Selective use of initial depreciation and at varying rates for investment in priority sectors is likely to serve a better purpose than its general use. In case of underdeveloped economies, initial depreciation has a special role to play for encouraging investment in backward region and also in small and medium sized enterprises.

FACTORS INFLUENCING SELECTION OF DEPRECIATION METHOD

Depreciation has a significant effect in determining the financial position and result of operations of an enterprise via calculating net income as well as deduction from taxable income. The quantum of depreciation to be provided in an accounting period involves the exercise of judgement by management in the light of technical, commercial, accounting and legal requirements, and accordingly, may need periodical review.

If it is considered that the original estimate of useful life of an asset requires any revision, the unamortised depreciable amount of the asset is charged to revenue over the revised remaining useful life. Alternatively, the aggregate depreciation charged to date is recomputed on the basis of the revised useful life and the excess or short depreciation so determined is adjusted in the accounting period of revision.

There are several methods of allocating depreciation over the useful life of the asset. Those most commonly employed in industrial and commercial enterprises are the straight-line method and the reducing balance method. The management selects the most appropriate methods based on various important factors, *e.g.*, (*i*) type of asset, (*ii*) the nature of the use of such asset, and (*iii*) circumstances prevailing in the business. A combination of more than one method is sometimes used. In respect of depreciable assets which do not have material value, depreciation is often allocated full in the accounting period in which it is acquired.

The following factors influence the selection of a depreciation method:

1. Legal Provisions: The statute governing an enterprise may the basis for computation of depreciation. In India, in the case of company, the Companies Act, 1956, provides that the provision of depreciation, unless permission to the contrary is obtained from the central government, should either be based on reducing balance method at the rate specified in the Income-Tax Act/Rules or on the corresponding straight-line depreciation rates which would write off 95 per cent of the original cost over the specified period. Where the management's estimate of the useful life of an asset of the enterprise is shorter than that envisaged under the provision of the relevant statute, the depreciation provision is appropriately computed by applying a higher rate. If the management's estimate of the useful life of the asset is longer than that envisaged under the statute, depreciation rate lower than that envisaged by the statute can be applied only in accordance with the requirements of the statue.

For tax purposes, the asset should be written off as quickly as possible. Of course, a firm can deduct only the acquisition cost less salvage value, from the otherwise taxable income over the life of the asset. Earlier deductions are, however, worth more than later ones because a rupee of taxes saved today is worth more than a rupee of taxes saved tomorrow, *i.e.*, the goal of the firm in selecting a depreciation method for tax purpose should be to maximise the present value of the reductions in tax payments from claiming depreciation. When tax rates remain constant over time and there is a flat tax rate (*e.g.*, income is taxed at a 40 per cent rate), this goal can usually be achieved by maximising the present value of the depreciation deductions from otherwise taxable income.

2. Financial Reporting: The goal in financial reporting for long-life assets is to seek a statement of income that realistically measures the expiration of those assets. The only difficulty is that no one knows, in any satisfactory sense, just what portion of the service potential of a long-life asset expires in any one period. All that can be said is that financial statements should report depreciation charges based on reasonable estimates of assets' expiration so that the goal of fair presentation can more nearly be achieved.

3. Effect on Managerial Decision: The suitability of a depreciation method should not be argued only on the basis of correct portrayal of the objective facts but should also be decided in terms of their various managerial effects.

Depreciation and its financing effect take the less basic but still realistic approach that, regardless of any effect which depreciation may have upon the total revenue stream, the recognition of depreciation either through the cost of product or as an element in administration and marketing expenses, does cut down the showing of net income available for dividends, and thus, restricts the outflow of cash. The actual tax-saving argument is sometimes short sighted, but the saving of interest and the increased financial flexibility are actual and constitute the real pressure behind depreciation accounting.

Business managers consider these points, but they have the added responsibility of protecting management against the possible distortions of reported costs and misleading incomes which these pressures might engender.

A depreciation method which would lead to unwise dividends, distributing cash which was later needed to replace the asset, would be a poor method. A depreciation method which matches the asset costs distributed period by period against the revenues produced by the asset, thus helping management to make correct judgement regarding operating efficiency, would be a good method.

4. Inflation: Depreciation is a process to account for decline in the value of assets and for this many methods such as straight line, different accelerated methods are available. In recent years, inflation has been a major consideration in selecting a method of depreciation. To take an example, suppose one bought a car for ₹ 10,00,000 five years ago and wrote off ₹ 2,00,000 every year to account for depreciation using straight-line method, expecting that a new car can be purchased after five years. However, five years later, it is found that the same car costs ₹ 15,00,000 whereas only ₹ 10,00,000 has been saved through depreciation.

Why a new car or new asset cannot be purchased with the accumulated amount of depreciation? The difficulty has been created by the inflation. In fact, inflaction has eaten into the money saved through depreciation over the five years. This means that a business enterprise (or the owner of car) eats into the asset faster than the rate of depreciation as the cost of replacing the asset is increasing.

The accelerated methods of depreciation tend to write off ₹ 10,00,000 (the price of car in the above example) over the five years. But higher amounts are written off in the beginning as depreciation, and hence, larger amounts are accumulated through depreciation which increase the 'replacement capability' of a business enterprise.

The problem created by inflation in depreciation accounting has contributed in the emergence of the concept of inflation accounting. In inflation accounting, an attempt is made to increase the depreciation amount in line with inflation so that enough money to replace the asset at its current inflated cost can be accumulated.

5. Technology: Depreciation is vital because it decides the regenerating capacity of industry and enables enterprises to set aside an amount before submitting profits to taxation, for replacing machines. Realistically, the depreciation that enterprises are eligible for and capable of accumulating should cover the purchase price of assets, when the time comes for replacement.

But the critical question is, when exactly does the time for replacement come? Life of machine is no longer an engineering concept. Many electronic companies in the US had to write off their assets in three years because new technologies came in and old machines became scrap overnight. Commercial life of machine is decided by technological progress. The arrival of new machines is not governed by the depreciation policies of government. Therefore, the shorter the period over which the enterprise is able to recover depreciation, the better its chances to adapt to the new technology and survive. In an industry which are exposed to rapid technological progress, a fixed depreciation rate is the surest way to force it into bankruptcy.

Accumulating enough depreciation for buying new technology does not depend merely on a rate of depreciation. Business enterprises should have profit to provide for depreciation resulting into adequate money for replacement at the proper time. An industry in which profits are likely to be high in the initial years will have to provide more depreciation in those years than in the later years when the profit is likely to be low.

Technological progress as a dimension of depreciation has become more important than the engineering life of machines. A constant rate of depreciation may be followed when an enterprise is making profit at a constant rate. It is only when profits are fluctuating that the company in years of high profits will provide for higher depreciation. If it is not able to do that because of fixed rate of depreciation imposed by the government, it will be over-taxed. As a result, it will not be able to retain enough earnings after payment of tax and dividends to make up for its inability to provide normal depreciation in years of adversity. At the end of the useful life of machines the company will not have the resource to invest in new machines. It will succumb to technological progress.

6. Capital Maintenance: During inflation, depreciation, if based on historic cost of assets, helps a business firm to gather an amount equivalent to the historical cost of the asset less its salvage value. This treatment of depreciation facilities in maintaining only the 'money capital' or financial capital of business enterprises. However, this results into matching between historic amount of depreciation and sales in current Rupees. The result is that reported net income is overstated and dividends is distributed from the net income which is not real but fictitious. This way of income measurement and maintaining only financial capital during inflation results into erosion of real capital of business enterprises.

However, if depreciation is provided on replacement or current value of assets, it gives matching between current cost (depreciation) and current revenues. This does not involve any hoarding income as is found when depreciation is determined on historical cost. Depreciation on current value of assets provides real operating income in the profit and loss account. This means that capital of business enterprise would be maintained in real terms. Valuation of fixed cost in terms of current cost reflects the current value of operating capability of business enterprises.

CHANGE IN DEPRECIATION METHOD

The depreciation method selected should be applied consistently from the period to period. According to ICAI's AS 6, a change from one method of providing depreciation to another should be made only if the adoption of the new method is required by statute or for compliance with an accounting standard or if it is considered that the change would result in a more appropriate preparation or presentation of the financial statements of the enterprise. When such a change in the method of depreciation is made, the unamortised depreciable amount of the asset is charged to revenue over the remaining useful life by applying the new method.

When there is change from one method of depreciation to another, the unamortised cost of the asset should be written off over the remaining useful life on the new basis commencing with the period in which the change in made. The effect should be disclosed in the year of change, if material.

Depreciable amounts are allocated to each accounting period during the useful life of the asset by a variety of systematic methods. Whichever method of depreciation is selected, its consistent use is necessary irrespective of the level of profitability of the enterprise and of taxation consideration, in order to provide comparability of the result of operations of the enterprise from period to period.

DISCLOSURE ON DEPRECIATION

According to AS-6, the following information should be disclosed in the financial statements:

(*i*) the historical cost or other amount substituted for historical cost of each class of depreciable assets

(*ii*) total depreciation for the period for each class of assets, and

(*iii*) the related accumulated depreciation

The Accounting Standard 6 has proposed that the following information should also be disclosed in the financial statement alongwith the disclosure of other accounting policies:

(*i*) Depreciation methods used

(*ii*) Depreciation rates or the useful lives of the assets, if they are different from the principal rates specified in the statute governing the enterprise.

Also, in case the depreciable assets are revalued, the provision for depreciation is based on the revalued amount, on the estimate of the remaining useful life of such assets. In case the revaluation has a material effect on the amount of depreciation, the same is disclosed separately in the year in which revaluation is carried out.

Any adjustment for the excess or short depreciation made in any accounting period due to the revision in estimate of the useful lives of depreciable assets is treated as an extraordinary item and disclosed accordingly.

A change in the method of depreciation is treated as a change in an accounting policy and is disclosed accordingly.

THEORY QUESTIONS

1. List three major types of long-term (fixed) assets, present examples of each and indicates for each type the term that denotes the periodic write off to expense.

2. In what way is land different from other long-term assets?

3. In general, what amounts constitute the initial cost of fixed assets?

4. What is a basket purchase? What measurement problem does it pose?

5. Distinguish between depreciation, depletion and amortisation.

6. In computing depreciation, what factors or values must be known or estimated? Identify and explain the nature of each.

7. Which of the following qualities are characteristic of plant assets?

(*a*) Intangible

(*b*) Tangible

(*c*) Capable of repeated use in the operation of the business
(*d*) Held for sale in the normal course of business
(*e*) Used continuously in the operations of the business
(*f*) Long-lived.

8. Estimated useful life and residual value of a long-term asset relate to the current owner or user rather than to all potential users. Explain this statement.

9. Why is it useful to think of plant assets as a bundle of services?

10. Explain why the recognition of depreciation expenses is necessary to match revenues and expenses properly?

11. Explain the nature of depreciation.

12. "Depreciation is a process of allocation, not of valuation". Comment.

13. What kind of a depreciation expenses pattern is provided under the straight-line method? When would its use be appropriate?

14. What are accelerated methods of depreciation? What benefits are associated with these methods?

15. "The major purpose of depreciation accounting is to provide funds for the replacement of assets as they wear out." Do you agree? Explain.

16. "Accounting for depreciation assets would be greatly simplified if accounting periods were only long enough or the life of the assets short enough." What is the point behind the quotation?

17. Explain the benefit of accelerating depreciation when the total depreciation taken is no more than if straight-line depreciation is used.

18. What is the principal argument supporting accelerated depreciation methods?

19. How is disposal of fixed assets treated in accounting?

20. What factors should be considered while selecting a depreciation method?

21. Alpha Company borrowed ₹ 5 lakh to finance the purchase of a new office building which was ready for immediate use? May Alpha add a portion of the interest on ₹ 5 lakh to the building's cost? Explain.

22. Explain why the recognition of depreciation expenses is necessary to match revenue and expenses properly?

23. A company purchased a building five years ago. The market value of the building is now greater than it was when the building was purchased. Should the company stop depreciating the building?

24. Is the purpose of depreciation to determine the value of fixed asset?

25. What is the difference between depreciation for accounting purposes and for income tax purposes?

26. Are the amounts at which plant assets are reported in the balance sheet their approximate market values as of the balance sheet date? Discuss.

27. In what sections of the income statement are gains and losses from the disposal of plant assets presented?

28. Simon is in business as a demolition contractor. Most of the equipment which he started with (valued at ₹ 4 lakh) has a probable life of the eight to ten years. Until he received appropriate advice from his accountant, he had ignored depreciation. What have been the effect of continuing to do so?

29. List the factors which should be the basis for selecting a method of providing depreciation of any specific assets or group of assets.

30. Replacing the asset is not essential to the existence of depreciation. Depreciation is the expiration or disappearance of service potential from the time an asset is put into use until the time it is retired from service." Explain.
31. Discuss the disclosure guidelines given in AS 6 'Depreciation Accounting' about depreciation.
32. Why does an accountant provide for depreciation when he measures profit?
33. Contrast straight-line depreciation with accelerated depreciation in terms of the effect of each on reported net income.
34. Explain how charging depreciation affect:
    (*a*) the income statement, and
    (*b*) the balance sheet.
35. Why may depreciation for the financial statements be different from depreciation charged for income tax purposes?
36. Under what circumstances are accelerated methods of depreciation most appropriate?
37. If a company uses accelerated depreciation for a building rather than the straight-line method, what effect does that choice have on the financial statements in the year of acquisition?
38. "An accelerated depreciation method should be used because of the large decline in the value of an asset early in its life". Evaluate this statement.
39. The manager of an electricity company stated that since its transmission lines are kept in good condition by regular repairs and maintenance and their efficiency remains constant, the lines do not depreciate. Do you agree with this statement?
40. In a year in which the cost of replacing an asset rises, should depreciation be charged on that asset? Why?
41. Distinguish between Annuity Method and Sinking Fund Method of providing depreciation.
42. Explain the following Methods of Depreciation:
    (*i*) Service Hours Method
    (*ii*) Unit of Output Method
43. What are fixed assets? Examine the various methods of depreciation of fixed assets. **[MBA, JNTU, Hyderabad, Jan./Feb. 2007]**
44. What do you mean by straight line method of depreciation? Evaluate. **[MBA, JNTU, Hyderabad, 2006]**
45. Distinguish between straight line and diminishing balance methods of providing depreciation. **[BBA, GGSIP University, March 2000, Dec. 2010]**
46. Why do you consider it necessary to provide depreciation? Explain briefly. **[BBA, GGSIP University, Dec. 2000]**
47. Distinguish between depreciation, amortisation and depletion. **[BBA, GGSIP University, Dec. 2002]**
48. (*a*) Explain the need and significance of depreciation. What factors should be considered for determining the amount of depreciation?
    (*b*) Distinguish between "Straight Line Method" and "Diminishing Balance Method" of providing depreciation? Which one of the two you recommend to provide depreciation on plant and machinery. **[BBA, GGSIP University, Dec. 2004]**
49. What do you mean by depreciation? What are causes and objectives of providing depreciation? **[BBA, GGSIP University, Dec. 2006]**

50. "Depreciaton should be charged on replacement value of the asset." Comment.
[BBA, GGSIP University, Dec. 2007]

51. Explain the provisions of AS6 (Revised) Depreciation Accounting.
[BBA, GGSIP University, Dec. 2007]

52. "Depreciation is a process of allocation of cost, not of valuation of fixed assets." Comment.
[BBA, GGSIP University, Dec. 2008, Dec. 2010]

SELF-EVALUATION EXERCISES

I. Select the correct answer for the following multiple-choice questions:

1. Chain Hotel Corporation recently purchased Eligin Hotel and the land on which it is located with plans to tear down the Eligin and build a new luxury hotel on the site. The cost of the Eligin Hotel should be
   (*a*) Depreciated over the period from acquisition to the date due the hotel is scheduled to be torn down
   (*b*) Written off as an extraordinary loss in the year the hotel is torn down
   (*c*) Capitalised as part of the cost of the land
   (*d*) Capitalised as part of the cost of the new hotel
2. As generally applied to accounting, what is depreciation?
   (*a*) It is a process of asset valuation for balance sheet purposes
   (*b*) It applies only to long-lived intangible assets
   (*c*) It is used to indicate a decline in market value of long-lived asset
   (*d*) It is an accounting process which allocates long-lived asset cost to accounting periods
3. Which of the following principles best describes the conceptual rationale for the methods of matching depreciation expense with revenue?
   (*a*) allocating cause and effect
   (*b*) Systematic and rational allocation
   (*c*) Immediate recognition
   (*d*) Partial recognition
4. Which of the following statements is the assumption on which straight-line depreciation is based?
   (*a*) The operating efficiency of the asset decreases in later years
   (*b*) Service value declines as a function of time rather than use
   (*c*) Service value declines as a function of obsolescence rather than time
   (*d*) Physical wear and tear are more important than economic obsolescence
5. A principal objection to the straight-line method of depreciations is that it
   (*a*) Provides for the declining productivity of an ageing asset
   (*b*) Ignores variations in the rare of asset use
   (*c*) Tends to result in constant rate of return on a diminishing investments base
   (*d*) Gives smaller periodic write offs than decreasing charge methods
6. The straight-line method of depreciation is not appropriate for
   (*a*) A company that is neither expanding nor contracting its investments in equipment because it is replacing equipment as the equipment depreciates
   (*b*) Equipment on which maintenance and repairs increase substantially with age
   (*c*) Equipment with useful lives that are not affected by the amount of use
   (*d*) Equipment used consistently every period

7. Which of the following reasons provides the best theoretical support for accelerated depreciation?

(*a*) Assets are more efficient in early years and initially generate more revenue

(*b*) Expenses should be allocated in a manner that smooth earnings result

(*c*) Repairs and maintenance costs will probably increase in later period so depreciation should decline

(*d*) Accelerated depreciation provides easier replacement because of the time value of money

8. Accumulated depreciation is an example of

(*a*) An expense (*b*) An unrecorded revenue

(*c*) A liability (*d*) A contra account

9. Depreciation is to be calculated on

(*a*) Fixed assets (*b*) Outward charges

(*c*) Current assets (*d*) Intangible assets

10. The adjustment to be made for depreciation is

(*a*) Credit profit and loss account and deduct depreciation from fixed assets

(*b*) Credit profit and loss account and add depreciation to fixed assets

(*c*) Debit profit and loss account and add depreciation to fixed assets

(*d*) Debit profit and loss account and deduct depreciation from fixed assets

11. At cost a firm's assets were valued at ₹ 18,000. Three years later their book value is ₹ 10,000. The depreciation charge for the three years is

(*a*) ₹ 12,000 (*b*) ₹ 10,000 (*c*) ₹ 8,000 (*d*) ₹ 6,000

12. At cost a firm's assets are valued at ₹ 25,000. At the end of five years depreciation totals ₹ 15,000. The book value of the assets at the end of five years is

(*a*) ₹ 20,000 (*b*) ₹ 15,000 (*c*) ₹ 10,000 (*d*) ₹ 5,000

13. Which of the following is/are methods of depreciation?

1. Straight line 2. Reducing balance

3. Revaluation

(*a*) 1, 2 and 3 (*b*) 1 and 2 only (*c*) 1 only (*d*) 3 only

14. The initial cost of a plant asset is equal to the asset's implied cash price and

(*a*) Interest paid on any debt incurred to finance the asset's purchase

(*b*) Market value of any non-cash asset given up to acquire the plant asset

(*c*) Reasonable and necessary costs incurred to prepare the asset for use

(*d*) Asset's estimated salvage value

15. On January 1st, 2012, Alpha Co. purchased a delivery truck for ₹ 10,00,000. The company estimates the truck will be driven 80,000 miles over its eight-year useful life. The estimated salvage value is ₹ 2,00,000. The truck was driven 12,000 miles in 2012. Which method results in the latest depreciation expenses for 2002?

(*a*) Sum of the years digits (*b*) Written-down value

(*c*) Straight line (*d*) Double declining balance

16. Another name for the straight-line method is

(*a*) The equal instalment method (*b*) The reducing balance method

(*c*) The diminishing balance method (*d*) The revaluation method

17. What is the amount of depreciation, using the sum-of-the-years-digits method, for the first year of use for equipment costing ₹ 9,500, with an estimated residual value of ₹ 500 and an estimated life of 3 years?
(*a*) ₹ 4,500 (*b*) ₹ 3,166.67 (*c*) ₹ 3,000 (*d*) None of the above
18. A plant asset priced at ₹ 1,00,000 is acquired by trading in a similar asset that has a book value of ₹ 25,000. Assuming that the trade-in-allowance is ₹ 30,000 and that ₹ 70,000 cash is paid for the new asset. What is the cost basis for the new asset for financial reporting purposes?
(*a*) ₹ 1,00,000 (*b*) ₹ 70,000 (*c*) ₹ 30,000 (*d*) None of the above
19. The adjustment for depreciation is an example of
(*a*) Apportioning costs between two or more periods
(*b*) Apportioning revenues between two or more periods
(*c*) Recognising an accured expense
(*d*) Recognising an unaccured revenue
20. If the equipment account has a balance of ₹ 22,500 and the accumulated depreciation account has a balance of ₹ 14,000, the book value of the equipment is
(*a*) ₹ 36,500 (*b*) ₹ 22,500 (*c*) ₹ 14,000 (*d*) ₹ 8,500
21. An example of an accelerated depreciation method is
(*a*) Straight line (*b*) Sum-of-the-years-digits
(*c*) Units of production (*d*) None of the above
22. Plant assets are depreciated over their useful lives. Which basic principle of accounting does this procedure reflect?
(*a*) Historical cost (*b*) Matching expenses with revenue
(*c*) Consistency (*d*) Objectivity
23. Which of the following is/are advantages of the equal instalment method?
1. Easy to understand; calculation simple
2. Decreasing depreciation charges cancel out increasing repair charges
3. No re-calculation necessary when further assets are purchased
(*a*) 1, 2 and 3 (*b*) 1, and 2 only (*c*) 1 only (*d*) 3 only
24. Which of the following is/are disadvantages of the reducing balance method?
1. Percentage figure to be deducted annually is difficult to calculate
2. The charge against the profit and loss account increases over the years
3. If a further asset is purchased, the amount now required to be written off needs to be recalculated.
(*a*) 1, 2 and 3 (*b*) 1 and 2 only (*c*) 1 only (*d*) 3 only
25. Using the equal instalment method for depreciation the relevant formula is
(*a*) $\text{Annual charge against profits} = \dfrac{\text{Original cost} - \text{Residual value}}{\text{Number of years of active life}}$
(*b*) $\text{Annual charge against profits} = \dfrac{\text{Number of years of active life}}{\text{Original cost} - \text{Residual value}}$
(*c*) $\text{Annual charge against profits} = \dfrac{\text{Original cost} - \text{Residual value}}{\text{Estimated number of years remaining}}$
(*d*) $\text{Annual charge against profits} = \dfrac{\text{Estimated number of years remaining}}{\text{Original cost} - \text{Residual value}}$

26. Consider a piece of machinery costing ₹ 30,00,000 with an estimated life of 10 years. At the end of this time it can be sold for ₹ 3,00,000. Using the equal instalment method the annual charge against profits would be
    (*a*) ₹ 3,30,000 (*b*) ₹ 3,00,000 (*c*) ₹ 2,70,000 (*d*) ₹ 30,000
27. An asset was purchased for ₹ 12,50,000 and under the reducing balance method 20 per cent of the reducing value of the asset is written off each year. What is the value of the asset at the end of three years?
    (*a*) ₹ 8,00,000 (*b*) ₹ 7,50,000 (*c*) ₹ 6,40,000 (*d*) ₹ 5,00,000
28. A machine is purchased for ₹ 2,00,000. To achieve a residual value of ₹ 1,28,000 at the end of the second year (assuming that depreciation is calculated at the end of each year) the percentage depreciation using the reducing balance method must be
    (*a*) 72% (*b*) 36% (*c*) 20% (*d*) 12%
29. The book value of a machine is ₹ 20,00,000. Two years later the book value is ₹ 10,00,000. The straight-line percentage depreciation is
    (*a*) 50% (*b*) 33-1/3% (*c*) 25% (*d*) 20%
30. The provisions of Indian Companies Act require that
    (*a*) Assets are shown at cost
    (*b*) Assets are shown at cost less total depreciation to date
    (*c*) Assets are shown as at cost less last year's depreciation
    (*d*) Assets are shown at current net value

II. True or False:

1. Fixed assets is the broad general term for the long-term tangible economic resources used in the operation of a business.
2. The loss of value from the time of purchase to the time of disposal of a fixed asset is called depreciation.
3. In theory, no cost other than the actual purchase cost of a fixed asset should be capitalised.
4. Fixed asset costs that are capitalised benefit reported net income in the year the fixed asset is acquired, but hurt reported net income during the later years when the fixed asset is used.
5. Usually, the physical wear and tear on a fixed asset is the main factor used in estimating the useful economic life over which to depreciate the asset.
6. Salvage values can be ignored in depreciating fixed assets.
7. Land is the only fixed asset that is not depreciated.
8. If the value of land increases, such an appreciation of value should be recorded.
9. Assume that the estimated useful economic life of a fixed asset to the business is *N* years; therefore, the straight-line method would allocate 1/*n* of the total depreciate cost (purchase cost less salvage value) to each full year of using the asset.
10. The balance in the Accumulated Depreciation account at the end of the period after recording depreciation for the period normally is equal to the amount of depreciation expense recorded in the period.
11. The book value of a company's assets is equal to the original costs of the fixed assets less the total depreciation recorded on the assets up to the date of the balance sheet; this book value is the amount included in the total assets of the company at the balance sheet date.
12. The sum-of-the-years-digits (SYD) depreciation method puts more depreciation in the first half of the fixed asset's useful life and less in the second half.

13. According to the SYD depreciation method, the second year of a fixed asset's useful life would be charged with more depreciation than the first year.
14. The total depreciable cost of an eight-year fixed asset to compute depreciation for the third year of its useful life by the SYD method is 6/36.
15. Depreciation for 4 years has been recorded by the SYD method on a 10-years life fixed asset. So the accumulated depreciation at the end of the fourth year is 34/55 of the total depreciation to be recorded over its useful life.
16. According to the SYD method, the depreciation recorded in the last year of a four-year life fixed asset is 1/4 of its total depreciable cost.
17. Assume that a fixed asset that was being depreciated over a six-year useful economic life is sold after being used 3 years; there would be less gain (or more loss) recorded if the SYD method were used to record depreciation on the asset than if the straight-line method were used.
18. A fixed asset has an eight-year useful economic life; so 25 per cent would be multiplied by the book value of the fixed asset at the start of each year to determine the depreciation by the DDB method (until the accumulated depreciation of the asset equals its total depreciable cost).
19. A fixed asset has a 10-year useful economic life; using the DDB method its book value at the end of the second year is 80 per cent of its cost.
20. In contrast to the straight-line, SYD and DDB methods, it is not possible to know in advance exactly how much depreciation will be recorded in each future year while using a fixed asset if an activity-based depreciation method is used.
21. Fixed assets can be grouped together and depreciation recorded on a composite basis, or each individual fixed asset can be depreciated separately; either approach is acceptable.
22. A new fixed asset is bought on July 1, and the company's accounting year ends December 31, thus only 1/2 of the first full year's depreciation should be recorded.
23. On advantage of the SYD depreciation method is that the depreciation expense is comparable from year to year.
24. One argument for the SYD depreciation method is that the lower depreciation expense from year to year may be balanced by higher maintenance expenses on the fixed asset from year to year.
25. When an old fixed asset is traded-in on a new similar fixed asset, no gain or loss is ever recorded.
26. When an old fixed asset is sold for cash, a gain would result if the cash received is more than the book value of the fixed asset.
27. Assume that a fixed asset is sold for its book value; the proper entry is to debit (+) cash and to credit (–) the fixed assets account for the amount of money received.
28. The original estimated useful life of a fixed asset is never changed later.
29. The balance sheet of a company renting most of its fixed assets through operating leases would be comparable to that of another company that owns all its fixed assets.
30. There is a basic accounting similarity in depreciation, depletion, and amortisation, although different assets are involved in each.
31. Depreciation accounting is the systematic allocation of the cost of fixed assets (except land) over their useful lives, so that each year of use is charged with some expense.
32. Depreciation is not the result of particular transaction rather it is a summary charge for the whole period.

33. The amount of depreciation expenses for the period is usually reported separately in the income statement.
34. The amount of depreciation recorded for the period is credited (–) in the fixed assets account.
35. The balance in the accumulated depreciation account should never be larger than the balance in the fixed asset accounts.
36. Depreciation is a measure of the exact loss in the intrinsic value of an asset.
37. A well maintained asset need not to be depreciated.
38. All assets must be depreciated at the end of the year.
39. Goodwill is never depreciated.
40. Appreciation in the market value of assets must be taken into account if the correct profit of the year is to be determined.
41. The amount of depreciation remains constant over the years in the original cost method of depreciation.
42. The written-down value of an asset depreciated by the reducing balance method can never become zero.
43. The value of an asset falls faster in the reducing method than in the other.
44. If a motorcar is given out for repair for three months in a year, then depreciation should be charged for nine months only, and at the end of the year.
45. Depreciation is to be charged in the first year on the landed cost of the asset.
46. Profit on sale of a machine will appear on the credit side of the machinery account.
47. Reducing balance method of depreciation is best suited for assets with a long working life.

III. Fill in the Blanks:

1. Depreciation of assets is accounted to provide ________.
2. One of the reasons for charging depreciation is to provide funds for the ________ of the asset.
3. The total loss on account of wear and tear of most of the fixed assets is reflected in ________.
4. Depreciation is charged only on the ________ assets of a business.
5. Straight-line/fixed instalment method is the ________.
6. Depreciation is charged on the ________ and ________ values of the asset on the equal instalment and reducing balance methods, respectively.
7. Ten per cent depreciation on the reducing balance method on an asset costing ₹ 50,000 in the second year of its use will be ________.
8. The depreciated value after two years of an asset costing ₹ 10,000 depreciated at 10 per cent on fixed instalment method is ₹ ________ and on reducing balance method is ₹ ________.
9. Depreciation for the second year @ 10 per cent on ₹ 15,000 purchase price will be ________ on the fixed instalment whereas it will be ________ on the diminishing balance system.
10. Equipment valued in the books at ₹ 7,950 on April 1, 2001 will be valued at ₹ ________ when sold on July 15, 2001, if depreciation is charged @ 12-1/2 per cent on the diminishing balance method.
11. One of the few assets that is usually not depreciated is ________.
12. Depreciation of a ten-year lease is best done on the ________ method.
13. The depreciation account is closed at the end of the year by transfer to the ________.
14. Appreciation in the market value of a fixed asset will be recorded in the books of account only at the time of ________ of the asset.

15. The written-down value of an asset after three years of depreciation on the reducing balance method @ 10% p.a. is ₹ 36,450. Its original value must have been ________ and its brought down value after three years would have been ________ on the other method of depreciation.
16. The book value of an asset ________ if the depreciation method is changed from fixed instalment to diminishing balance, rate remaining the same.

IV. For each asset listed below, identify a code letter from the letter codes given here to indicate the allocation terminology for each asset.

Allocation Term

(A) Amortisation (D) Depreciation (P) Depletion (N) None of these

Assets

1. Patent 2. Land 3. Building 4. Cash 5. Oilwell
6. Trademark 7. Goodwill 8. Patents 9. Franchise 10. Plant
11. Copyright 12. Investment in common shares 13. Mineral deposit
14. Machinery 15. License right 16. Differed charge
17. Inventory of goods 18. Timber tract 19. Tools 20. Land and building

V. Match the definitions given below in List B with the terms given in List A.

Terms (List A)

1. Acquisition cost
2. Depreciation
3. Straight-line depreciation
4. Productive output depreciation
5. Tangible operational assets
6. Natural resource
7. Useful life
8. Depletion
9. Basket purchase
10. Book value
11. SYD depreciation
12. Residual value

Definition: (List B)

(A) Assets used in operations; have physical substance.
(B) Declining expense; numerator year of life in inverse order.
(C) Use cost is the same amount per year during useful life.
(D) Estimated recovery less costs of disposal.
(E) Cash equivalent amount.
(F) Periodic expense fluctuates with actual output.
(G) A timber tract.
(H) Estimated productive life to the current user.
(I) Systematic allocation of the cost of a natural resource.
(J) Must allocate a single purchase cost to two or more assets.
(K) Systematic allocation of the cost of a tangible operational asset.
(L) Acquisition cost minus accumulated allocation of original cost.

EXERCISES AND PROBLEMS

1. On 1st April, 2012, X Ltd. purchased a machinery for ₹ 3,00,000 and incurred ₹ 30,000 towards installation charges. It is estimated that the machinery will have a scrap value of ₹ 30,000 at the end of the useful life which is four years.

Prepare machinery A/c for first four years ending 31st March every year.
(*Depreciation* ₹ *75,000 p.a.*)

2. A Co. purchased a Machine for ₹ 40,000 on 1st April, 2012. It immediately spent ₹ 10,000 for installation. After using it for 5 years it was sold at ₹ 27,000. You are required to prepare Machine A/c. The rate of depreciation is 10% p.a. on straight line method. (*Profit* ₹ *2000*)

3. Gautam & Co. purchased Plant & Machinery for ₹ 1,00,000 on 1st July, 2012. The assets was to be depreciated at the end of each year at rate of 10% p.a. on written down value basis. The machinery was sold on 1 January, 2016 for ₹ 56,500.

Prepare Machinery A/C assuming accounting year to end on 30 June every year.
(*Loss* ₹ *12,755*)

4. A Co. had bought machinery for ₹ 1,10,000 on 1 January, 2012. This machinery was for the first four years credited for depreciation on written down value method at rate of 10% p.a. During the fifth year, the part of machine (original Cost ₹ 10,000) become useless and sold for ₹ 2,000 Prepare Machinery A/c.

(**Ans:** Loss ₹ 4,561 Balance ₹ 53,144).

5. On 1st January, 2012, a company purchased a, machinery costing ₹ 2,50,000, working life 20 years and scrap value ₹ 10,000. Addition are made on 1st January, 2013 to the value of ₹ 40,000, estimated life 20 years and scrap value ₹ 2000 and one more machine of ₹ 20,000, estimated life 20 yrs. and scrap value ₹ 1,000.

One Machine purchased on 1st January, 2006 sold on 31 December, 2016 at ₹ 1,35,000. Account are closed on 31st December. Prepare Machinery A/c for 5 years. (*Loss* ₹ 45,000)

6. A transport Co. purchases 5 Trucks at ₹ 2,00,000 each on 1st April, 2012, The company writes off depreciation @ 20% p.a. On original cost and accounts are closed on 31st December every year.

On 1st October, 2014, one of the trucks is involved in an accident and is completely destroyed. Insurance Company pays ₹ 90,000 in full settlement of the claim. On the same day the Co. purchased an old truck for ₹ 1,00,000 and spent ₹ 20,000 on its overhauling.

Prepare truck A/c for 3 years.

(**Ans:** Loss ₹ 10,000 Bal. ₹ 4,74,000).

7. Bajaj & Co. close their account on 31st March every year. They purchased the machines as follows:

(*i*) On 1.7.2000 Machines Costing 1,20,000
(*ii*) On 1.1.2001 Machines Costing 1,20,000
(*iii*) On 1.10.2001 Machines Costing ₹ 20,000
(*iv*) On 1.1.2002, Machines Costing ₹ 60,000

One Machine Costing ₹ 40,000 (Purchased on 1.7.2000) was sold for ₹ 12,000 on 1.4.2002. They charge depreciation @ 33-1/3%. On W.D.V. method. They have the practice to charge depreciation for the full year even if the machine used for a part of the year.

Prepare Machine A/c for 3 years

(**Ans:** Bal. ₹ 85,926 Loss ₹ 5,778).

8. The valuation of a group of assets (Plant & Machinery), on 1.1.2004 was ₹ 3,20,000 and its estimated life was 8 years. The following purchases and sales took place upto 31st December, 2006.

Purchases: 31st March, 2004, Cost ₹ 1,50,000 estimated life 10 yrs.
30th September, 2005, Cost ₹ 1,20,000 estimated life 6 yrs.
30th April 2006, Cost ₹ 2,00,000 estimated life 8 yrs.

Sales: Out of initial group of assets, a machine (whose valuation on 1st January, 2004 was ₹ 50,000 was sold for ₹ 47,000 on 30th June, 2006.

Assuming a break-up value of each asset to be 10% of initial cost, prepare the Assets A/c for 3 years.

(**Ans:** Profit ₹ 11,063 Bal. ₹ 5,74,250).

9. ABC Ltd. purchased on 1.1.2000 second-hand Machine for ₹ 4,00,000 overhauling and installation charges for the same were ₹ 1,00,000. Another machine was purchased for ₹ 2,00,000 on 17.2000.

On 1.7.2002, the machine installed on 1.1.2000 was sold ₹ 2,50,000. Dismantling charges for the machine sold on 1.7.2002 were ₹ 10,000. One the same date another machine was purchased for ₹ 8,000 and was commissioned on 30.9.2002. The company has adopted Calender year as its financial year. Under the existing practice, the company provides depreciation @ 10% p.a on original cost. In 2003, it has been decided that depreciation will be charged on D.B.M. @ 15% p.a. The charge is not to be made with retrospective effect.

Slow Plant A/c from 2000 to 2004

(**Ans:** Bal. on 31.12.2004 ₹ 6,71,925 & loss ₹ 1,35,000).

10. A Co. purchased 3 years Lease on January 1, 2000 for ₹ 25,000. It decided to provide for the replacement of the Lease at the end of 3 years by setting up a Sinking Fund. It's expected that investment will fetch interest @ 5%. Table shows that an annual payment of ₹ 1 @ 5% compound interest in 3 years accumulate ₹ 3.1525. Investment are made to the nearest rupee. On 31 December, 2002 Investment are sold for ₹ 15,250. Show Lease A/c, Sinking Fund A/c. Sinking Fund Investment A/c.

(**Ans:** ₹ 7,392.22 will be saved each year).

11. Mr. X takes a Lease, on 1.4.2001 for 5 years on a payment of ₹ 10,00,000. He proposes to provide for its replacement by means of an insurance policy for ₹ 10,00,000. The annual premium is ₹ 97,500. On 1st April, 2006, the Lease is renewed for a further period of 5 years for the same amount. Show necessary accounts.

(**Ans:** Profit ₹ 5,12,500).

12. A Co. purchased a Lease for 3 years for ₹ 30,00,000. On 1st January, 2000 it decided to provide for its replacement by taking an insurance policy for ₹ 3,00,000. The annual premium was ₹ 95,000.

On 1.1.2003, the Lease is renewed for a further period of 3 years for ₹ 3,00,000.

Show necessary accounts. (*Profit* ₹ 15,000)

ANSWERS TO SELF-EVALUATION EXERCISES

I.

1. (*c*)	**2.** (*d*)	**3.** (*b*)	**4.** (*b*)	**5.** (*b*)	**6.** (*b*)
7. (*a*)	**8.** (*d*)	**9.** (*a*)	**10.** (*d*)	**11.** (*c*)	**12.** (*c*)
13. (*b*)	**14.** (*c*)	**15.** (*d*)	**16.** (*a*)	**17.** (*a*)	**18.** (*d*)
19. (*a*)	**20.** (*d*)	**21.** (*b*)	**22.** (*b*)	**23.** (*c*)	**24.** (*c*)
25. (*a*)	**26.** (*c*)	**27.** (*c*)	**28.** (*c*)	**29.** (*c*)	**30.** (*b*)

II.

1. True	**2.** True	**3.** False	**4.** True	**5.** False	**6.** False
7. True	**8.** False	**9.** True	**10.** False	**11.** True	**12.** True
13. False	**14.** True	**15.** True	**16.** False	**17.** False	**18.** True

19. False	**20.** True	**21.** True	**22.** True	**23.** False	**24.** True
25. False	**26.** True	**27.** False	**28.** False	**29.** False	**30.** True
31. True	**32.** True	**33.** True	**34.** False	**35.** True	**36.** False
37. False	**38.** False	**39.** True	**40.** False	**41.** True	**42.** True.
43. False	**44.** False	**45.** True	**46.** False	**47.** True	

III.

1. For the loss is value of the asset due to wear and tear in use, passage of time, obsolescence, etc. to retain profits each year proportionate to the loss so as to provide funds to replace the assets at the end of its useful life time.

2. replacement **3.** depreciation **4.** Fixed

5. Method of estimating depreciation in which the amount of depreciation is calculated each year as a fixed percentage of original cost of asset.

6. original; written down **7.** ₹ 4,500 **8.** ₹ 8,000, ₹ 8,100

9. ₹ 1,500; ₹ 1,350 **10.** ₹ 7,660.15 **11.** goodwill/freehold land

12. straight line **13.** profit and loss account **14.** sale

15. ₹ 50,000; ₹ 35,000 **16.** increases

IV.

1. (A)	**2.** (N)	**3.** (D)	**4.** (N)	**5.** (P)	**6.** (N)
7. (N)	**8.** (N)	**9.** (N)	**10.** (D)	**11.** (N)	**12.** (N)
13. (P)	**14.** (D)	**15.** (N)	**16.** (N)	**17.** (N)	**18.** (P)
19. (D)	**20.** (D)				

V.

1. (E)	**2.** (K)	**3.** (C)	**4.** (F)	**5.** (A)	**6.** (G)
7. (H)	**8.** (I)	**9.** (J)	**10.** (L)	**11.** (B)	**12.** (D)

11

INVENTORY VALUATION

LEARNING OBJECTIVES

After reading this chapter, you should be able to:

- *Explain* the meaning and need of inventory.
- *List* the different types of inventory.
- *Discuss* the objectives of inventory measurement.
- *Explain* the different inventory costing methods such as first in-first out; last in-first out; average cost methods; specific identification method.
- *Discuss* the rule of 'lower of cost of market' in the valuation of inventory.
- *Present* ICAI's accounting standard on inventory valuation.
- *Discuss* the perpetual and periodic inventory system.

MEANING OF INVENTORY

Inventory includes tangible property that (*i*) is held for sale in the normal course of business, or (*ii*) will be used in producing goods or services for sale. Inventories are current assets and reported on the balance sheet. As current assets they can be used or converted into-cash within one year or within the next operating cycle of the business, whichever is longer.

According to Accounting Standard (AS)-2 (Revised), issued by the Institute of Chartered Accountants of India, inventories are assets.

(*i*) held for sale in the ordinary course of business;

(*ii*) in the process of production for such sale, or

(*iii*) in the form of materials or supplies to be consumed in the production process or in the rendering of services.

Inventories include goods purchased and held for resale, for example, goods purchased by a retailer and held for resale, computer software held for resale or land and other property held for resale.

Inventories are kept by manufacturing firms and merchandising (retailing) firms. For merchandising firms, inventories are often the largest or most invaluable current asset. The types of inventory usually held by these two kinds of enterprise are as follows:

(A) Manufacturing Enterprises

(*i*) Finished goods inventory—goods produced, completed and kept ready for sale.

(*ii*) Work-in-progress inventory—goods in the process of being produced but not yet completed as finished goods. When completed, work-in-progress inventory becomes finished goods inventory.

(*iii*) Raw material inventory—items purchased or acquired for using in making finished goods. Such items are known as raw material inventory until used. When raw materials are used, they become the part of the work-in-progress inventory (work-in-progress includes cost such as raw materials, direct labour and factory overhead).

(B) Merchandising Enterprises

In merchandising or retailing firms, inventory consists of goods (generally known as merchandise side) held for resale in the normal course of business. The goods are acquired in a finished condition and are ready for sale without further processing.

NEED FOR INVENTORIES

Inventory is one of the major problems that accountants face today. It is difficult to value it in terms of cash. It is almost impossible to assess its value in terms of future profits. The basic reason for holding inventories is that it is physically impossible and economically impractical for each inventory item to arrive exactly where it is needed and exactly when it is needed. Adam and Ebert[1] have listed the following reasons for carrying inventories:

Level	Reason
Fundamental (Primary)	Physical impossibility of getting the right amount of stock at the exact time of need. Economical impracticability of getting the right amount of stock at exact time need.
Secondary	Favourable return on investment. Buffer to reduce uncertainty. Decouple operations. Level or smooth production. Reduce material-handling costs. Allow production of family of parts. Price changes (can be disadvantageous). Bulk purchases. Display to customers.

Inventory is not purchased as investment or to hold or to realise a gain from possession but rather to sell and realise a gain from resale. In fact, each purchase of saleable goods is in anticipation of the very next sale. Inventory should be considered as an investment and should compete for funds with other investments contemplated by the business firm.

Inventory represents a type of business insurance which assures the company that it will not have to close down due to shortages of saleable goods. Inventory is a variable cost insurance. That is the cost of this insurance will vary in the same direction as the value of sales. As the sale increases the company will find it necessary to maintain a larger and larger inventory to meet the expanded sale volume.

It is often claimed that, for seasonal industries, it is advisable to have adequate opening inventories. If attractive quantity discounts are available, a business enterprises may prefer to buy in excess of its current sales requirements and can build up additional inventories. Many firms—especially those that sell in seasonal markets—buy in excess of their needs when supply prices are favourable. They store the goods and can then maintain sales during a period of unfavourable supply prices. Walgenbach *et al.*[2] observe:

1. Everett E. Adam, Jr. and Ronald J. Ebert, *Production and Operations Management*, Prentice Hall, 1992, p. 464.
2. Paul H. Walgenback, Ernst I. Hanson and Norman E. Dittrich, *Financial Accounting*, Harcourt Brace Jovana Vich, 1988, p. 329.

"Progressive firms take into account customer preferences, competitors, merchandising patterns, and favourable market situations in determining inventory size and balance, but they must also consider they cost of carrying large inventories. Often, savings obtained by purchasing in large quantities or under favourable market conditions may be more than off set by increased carrying costs. Storage and handling costs for large inventories can increase substantially. In addition, the firm may suffer losses from inventory deterioration and obsolescence. Finally, inventories tie up working capital that might be used more profitably elsewhere. These latter factors often cause merchandisers to contract inventory during recessionary periods."

OBJECTIVES OF INVENTORY MEASUREMENT

The measurement of inventory has a significant effect on income determination and financial position of a business enterprise. The American Institute of Certified Public Accountants (US) states:

"A major objective of accounting for inventories is the proper determination of income through the process of matching appropriate costs against revenues."[3]

It is significant to observe that a direct relationship exists between cost of goods sold and closing inventory. Cost of goods sold is measured by deducting closing inventory from cost of goods available for sale. Because of these relationships, it may be said that the higher the cost of closing inventory, the lower the cost of goods sold will be and the higher the resulting net income.

On the contrary, the lower the value of closing inventory, the higher the cost of goods sold and the lower the net income. Items which are not in the closing inventory are considered as sold and become the part of cost of goods sold. In this way, measurement of closing inventory influences the income statements (through influencing cost of goods, and net income) and balance sheet because inventory appears as current assets on the balance sheet.

Also, closing inventory influences net income of not only the current period but it also influences the net income of the next accounting period because closing inventory of the current period becomes the opening inventory for the next period and thus becomes cost of goods sold.

Since closing inventory determines cost of goods sold, the most common objective of inventory measurement is the attempt to match costs with related revenues in order to compute net income within the traditional accounting structure. The relationship of inventories to the process of income measurement is similar to the common characteristics of prepaid expenses and plant and equipment. The expression, matching costs against revenues, means determining what portion of the cost of goods available for sale should be as cost of the period and deducted from the revenue of the current period and what portion should be carried (as inventory) to be matched against the revenue of the following period.

Other things remaining the same, *i.e.*, if all other items appearing on an income statement are constant and also income-tax rates do not change, any change in the amount of closing inventory will bring similar change in the amount of reported net income. This is illustrated in the following data taken to explain this situation.

Effect of Inventory Value on Net Income

Data	Amounts (₹ in lakh)			
	Situations			
	A	B	C	D
Sale	50	50	50	50
Opening inventory	6	6	6	6

3. American Institute of Certified Public Accountants, *Accounting Research Bulletin No. 43*, AICPA, 1968.

Data	Amounts (₹ in lakh)			
	Situations			
	A	B	C	D
Purchases	40	40	40	40
Goods available for sale	46	46	46	46
Closing inventory	8	10	12	14
Cost of goods sold	36	36	34	32
Net Income	12	14	16	18

In the above example, it can be noticed that in all four situations (A, B, C, D) sale, opening inventory, purchases are identical. As the value of closing inventory changes among the four situations, net income also changes, to the extent the closing inventory increases or decreases. For instance, closing inventory increases by ₹ 2 lakh from situation A to B, from B to C, C to D, so net income also goes up by ₹ 2 lakh.

A second objective of inventory measurement is to state the fair value of inventory which appears as current assets on the balance sheet. This, alongwith other assets reflect the value of assets to the firm, and in turn, the financial position of a business enterprise.

Further, the value of inventory will help permit investors and other users to predict the future cash flows of the firm. This can be accomplished from two points of view. First, the amount of inventory resources available will support the inflow of cash through their sale in the ordinary course of business. Second, the amount of inventory resources available will, under normal circumstances, have an effect on the amount of cash required during the subsequent period to acquire the merchandise that will be sold during the period.

INVENTORY COSTING METHODS

The pricing or costing of inventory is one of the most interesting and most widely debated problems in accounting. Generally, inventories are priced at their cost in conformity with the cost concept. According to AICPA (US): "The primary basis of accounting for inventory is cost, which is the price paid or consideration given to acquire an asset. As applied to inventories, cost means in principle, the sum of the applicable expenditures and charges directly or indirectly incurred in bringing an article to its existing condition and location."

The cost of inventory, as per the above definition and in practice as well includes the following costs:

(*i*) Invoice price less cash discounts

(*ii*) Freight or transportation, insurance including insurance in transit

(*iii*) Applicable taxes and tariffs. Other costs such as these for purchasing, receiving and storage should theoretically be included in inventory cost. In practice, however, it is so difficult to allocate these costs to specific inventory items and also sometimes these costs are often not material in amount that they are in most cases considered an expenses of the accounting period instead of an inventory cost.

According to AS-2 (Revised) issued by The Institute of Chartered Accountants of India, the cost of inventories comprises all cost of purchases, cost of conversion and other cost incurred in bringing that inventories to their present location and condition (paragraph 6).

Inventory costing is quite simple when acquisition prices remain constant. When prices of identical lot of purchases vary in the accounting period, it is difficult to say which price should be used to measure the closing inventory. Also, when identical items are bought and sold, it is often impossible to tell which items have been sold and which are still in inventory. For this reason, it is necessary to make assumption about the order in which items have been sold.

Two terms-goods flow and cost flow–are useful in considering the problems of pricing inventories under fluctuating prices. Goods flow refers to the actual physical movement of goods in the firm's operations. Cost flow is the real or assumed association of costs with goods either sold or in inventory. The assumed cost flow may or may not be the same as the actual goods flow. Though this statement or practice may appear strange, there is nothing wrong or illegal about this practice. Generally Accepted Accounting Principles (GAAP) accept the use of an assumed cost flow that does not reflect the real physical movement of goods. In fact, the assumption about the cost flow is more important to goods flow as the former helps in determining net income which is the major objective of inventory valuation.

There are four generally accepted methods of inventory pricing, each based on a different assumption of cost flow:

1. First In First Out (FIFO)
2. Last In First Out (LIFO)
3. Average Cost Method
4. Specific Identification Method

The Accounting Standard No. 2 issued by The Institute of Chartered Accountants of India has recommended the use of FIFO (First in First out) or weighted average cost method for valuation of inventory. It also permits the use of specific identification method when specific costs are attributed to identified items of inventory.

The inventory costing methods are also known as cost flow assumptions. The specific identification method allocates costs according to the physical flow of goods. The other methods assume certain cost flow patterns that may or may not reflect the physical flow of goods.

1. First In First Out (FIFO)

The FIFO assumption of cost flow is recognised intuitively as being generally consistent with the physical flow of products and goods in most merchandising operations. This method follows the principle that goods received first are sold first. After the first lot or batch of goods purchased is exhausted, the next lot is taken up for sale. It does not suggest, however, that the same lot will be sold. Sometimes, all items are tagged with their arrival date and sold in date order specially with stocks that deteriorate. The inventory is priced at latest stock.

Arguments in Favour of FIFO: The FIFO method depends on the assumption that it is a good inventory management to sell or use the oldest goods first and maintain a current inventory representing the most recent purchases. It has the advantage that management has little or no control over the selection of units in order to influence recorded profits. It also has the advantage of not being influenced by the arbitrary choices of customers. As a result, it provides a more consistent and systematic determination of inventory and cost of goods sold. It also permits better comparison among different firms in the same industry and among several years.

Another benefit of FIFO is that it combines all elements of profit reported at the time of sale. Under FIFO, no separation can be made of gains and losses arising from price changes and income resulting from managerial decisions in the course of normal operations.

A third benefit of FIFO is the presentation of the ending inventory for balance sheet purposes in terms of the most recent costs which can be assumed to approximate replacement cost. The closeness of approximation to replacement cost depends on the stock turnover. When the stock turnover is rapid, the inventory valuation will reflect current prices unless prices change considerably after the recent purchases.

Arguments Against FIFO: With the FIFO method, the inventory is valued at costs that most closely represent the current cost. However, cost of goods sold is matched with costs that date back in time. If the prices of goods are rising rapidly, the cost of goods sold may be understated. If the sales price is fixed, then sale revenue may not produce enough income to cover the purchase of goods. The valuation of inventory in terms of current costs depend on the frequency of price changes and the stock turnover. In case stocks turn over rapidly, the inventory valuations will reflect current prices. But it is argued that the inventory valuations will hardly be identical with replacement costs under FIFO except accidently or under unusual conditions of stable prices from the date of acquisition of the ending inventory to the date of the balance sheet.

The objectives of matching current cost with current revenues is not achieved under the FIFO method. There are other limitations under the FIFO method. FIFO costing is improper if many lots of goods are purchased during the period at different prices. This method overstates profit especially with high inflation. It does not consider the cost of replacing used goods, a situation created by high inflation.

The FIFO method is suitable where (*i*) the size and cost of units are large, (*ii*) goods are easily identified as belonging to a particular purchased lot, and (*iii*) not more than two or three different receipts of the goods are on hand at one time.

Illustration 1: Explains the FIFO method of costing.

The following is a summary of the receipts and issue of materials in a factory during January:

January

1. Opening Balance 500 units @ ₹ 25 per unit
3. Issue 70 units
4. Issue 100 units
8. Issue 80 units
13. Received from supplier 200 units @ ₹ 24.50 per unit
14. Returned to store 15 units @ ₹ 24 per unit
16. Issue 180 units
20. Received from supplier 240 units @ ₹ 24.75 per unit
24. Issue 304 units
25. Received from supplier 320 units @ ₹ 24.50 per unit
26. Issue 112 units
27. Returned to store 12 units @ ₹ 24.50 per unit
28. Received from supplier 100 units @ ₹ 25 per unit.

Work out on the basis of First-in, First-out. This revealed that on the 15th there was a shortage of five units and another on the 27th of eight units.

Solution: (₹)

Date Jan.	Receipts Qty.	Receipts Rate	Receipts Amount	Issue Qty.	Issue Rate	Issue Amount	Stock Qty.	Stock Rate	Stock Amount
1	—	—	—	—	—	—	500	25.00	12,500
3	—	—	—	70	25	1,750	430	—	10,750
4	—	—	—	100	25	2,500	330	—	8,250
8	—	—	—	80	25	2,000	250	—	6,250
13	200 Refund	24.50	4,900	—	—	—	250 200	25.00 24.50	6,250 4,900

Date Jan.	Receipts			Issue			Stock		
	Qty.	Rate	Amount	Qty.	Rate	Amount	Qty.	Rate	Amount
14	15	24.00	360	—	—	—	250 200 15	25.00 24.50 24.00	6,250 4,900 360
15	—	—	Shortage	5	25	125	245 200 15	25.00 24.50 24.00	6,125 4,900 360
16	—	—	—	180	25	4,500	65 200 15	25.00 24.50 24.50	1,625 4,900 360
20	240	24.75	5,940	—	—	—	65 200 15 240	25.00 24.50 24.00 24.75	1,625 4,900 360 5,940
24	—	—	—	65 200 15 24	25.00 24.50 24.00 24.75	1,625 4,900 360 594	216	24.75	5,346
25	320	24.50	7:680	—	—	—	216 320	24.75 24.50	5,346 7,680
26	—	—	—	112	24.75	2,772	104 320	24.75 24.00	2,574 7,680
27	12	24.50	294	—	—		104 320 12	24.75 24.00 24.50	2,574 7,680 294
	—	—	—	—	—	—			
27	—	—	Shortage	8	24.75	198	96 320 12	24.75 24.00 24.50	12,376 7,680 294
28	100	2,500	2,500	—	—	—	96 320 12 100	24.75 24.00 24.50 25.00	2,376 7,680 294 2,500

Closing Stock 528 units = ₹ 12,750

2. Last in First Out

Under LIFO, latest stocks of goods flow into costs of goods sold and oldest stocks are included in stocks of inventories. This method is based on the assumption that cost of goods sold is charged at prices which almost correspond to the replacement cost of the goods. The main objective in LIFO is the matching of current cost against current revenues, resulting in an operating income which excludes gain and loss from the holding of inventories.

In LIFO, a distinction is often made between natural LIFO where cost flows demonstrably reflect physical flows, and artificial LIFO where cost flows demonstrably contradict physical flows. In fact, there is no necessary connection between physical flows and inventory valuation and the relation of one to the other is simply a convenient assumption. The actual flow of goods will more commonly follow the FIFO concept.

Advantages:

1. It is a cost method that prices goods sold in a systematic and realistic manner. It provides a better matching of current costs with current revenues.
2. It results in real income in time to rising prices by maintaining net income at a lower level than other costing methods.
3. In industries subject to sharp price fluctuations for goods, the method minimises unrealised inventory gains and losses and tends to stabilise reported operating profits. Income is reported only when it is available for distribution as dividends or for other purposes.
4. Probably the most important argument in favour of LIFO is its role in tax saving. It is generally considered a cheap form of tax avoidance by business firms. By valuing inventory at beginning-of-period price and calculating cost of sales at the prices of the period, the firm creates secret reserves which are not taxed. As long prices and inventory levels do not decline, this benefit remains, and in this case the tax saving will be eliminated by higher tax rates.
5. LIFO produces an income statement which shows correct profit or loses and financial position. It correlates current cost and sales and income statements show the result of operation, excluding profits or losses due to changing price levels.

Disadvantages:

1. The valuation of inventory for balance sheet purposes is out-of-date, as it reflect prices of some past period. Inventory valuations do not reflect the current prices, and therefore, are useless in the context of current conditions.
2. The argument that LIFO should be used for matching current costs with current revenue, is not sound. The recent purchase costs are matched against the revenue of the current period. However, unless both purchases and sales occur regularly in even quantities, the revenue will not be matched with the current costs at the time of sale. When purchases are irregular and unrelated to the timing of sales, the matching is illogical and unsystematic particularly if prices and costs are changing rapidly.
3. The profit of a firm can be manipulated with the LIFO method in operation. By timing purchases, a company can cause higher or lower costs to flow into the income statement, thus increasing or decreasing reported net income at will.
4. Another limitation which also results from LIFO's lowering of the earnings figure is the effect it will have on existing bonus and profit sharing plans. Employees and managers who are interested in the growth of these plans may have difficulty in understanding a drop in benefits created wholly, or partially, by an accounting change.

During a period of rising costs, LIFO produces the desirable effect of reducing taxable income and tax liability; thereby conserving cash. On the other hand, it also effects the profit reported in the financial statements. However, each business entity considering the adoption of LIFO should weigh the advantages and disadvantages as they affect the company's circumstances and environment and its future policies.

Timing the Adoption of LIFO: The decision as to when LIFO should be adopted depend on many factors which will be different in every case. Generally, the principal factors governing the question of 'when' include:

(*i*) Rice in price, because price increases paper profits in the inventory.
(*ii*) High taxes, because a tax saving (or deferment) is the most tangible benefit from choosing LIFO.

(*iii*) Normal inventory quantities, because if there is a substantial increase in inventory quantities during years of inflated prices, the equivalent of such increased quantities may remain indefinitely in the LIFO inventory at the high prices.

(*iv*) No foreseeable conditions that could cause the liquidation of the inventory during the high price and high tax period, because such liquidation would mean that the recognition of income was only temporarily deferred and the income may actually be taxed at a higher rate.

Sometimes, a question is asked as to whether, from a practical stand point, the LIFO principle can be incorporated in a financial accounting system and the commonly used form of statements of products or branch results and of departmental operations. It is argued that if the LIFO method results in a better reflection of income, it should be used for all management purposes. LIFO, however, can be used also alongwith other operating statements and cost systems.

Illustration 2: Prepare a stores ledger account from the following transactions under the LIFO method:

Jan.	1	Received 1,000 units @ ₹ 10 per unit
	10	Received 260 units @ ₹ 10.5 per unit
	20	Issued 700 units
Feb.	4	Received 400 units @ ₹ 11.5 per unit
	21	Received 300 units @ ₹ 12.5 per unit
March	16	Issued 620 units
April	12	Issued 240 units
May	10	Received 500 units @ ₹ 11.0 per unit
	25	Issued 380 units

Solution: **Stores Ledger Account (LIFO)**

	Receipts			Issue			Stock		
Date	**Qty.**	**Rate**	**Amount**	**Qty.**	**Rate**	**Amount**	**Qty.**	**Rate**	**Amount**
Jan. 1	1,000	10	10,000	—	—	—	1,000	10.0	10,000
10	260	10.5	2,730	—	—	—	1,260		12,730
20	—	—	—	260	10.5	2,730	560		5,600
				440	10.0	4,400			
Feb. 4	400	11.5	4,600	—	—	—	960		10,200
21	300	12.5	3,750	—	—	—	1,260		13,950
March 16	—	—	—	300	12.5	3,750	640		6,520
				320	11.5	3,680			
April 12	—	—	—	80	11.5	920	400		4,000
				160	10.0	1,600			
May 10	500	1.10	550	—	—		900		9,500
25	—	—	—	380	11.0	4,180	520		5,320

The Closing Stock consists of

120 units at ₹ 11.0 = 1,320

400 units at ₹ 11.0 = 4,000

₹ 5,320

3. Average Cost Methods

The use of average cost methods permits each purchase price to influence the inventory valuation and the cost of goods sold. The assumption is that the buying and selling operation results in the aggregation of costs and the assignment of these costs of goods sold and goods unsold on the basis of a single price. This single price is assumed to be a representative unit cost of all goods handled during a specific period. No specific flow of goods is assumed, unless it can be said that it represents a random selection of goods by customers so that any item handled during the period has an equal chance of appearing in the inventory at the end of the period. Usually, however, it is not thought to be in agreement with the physical flow of goods but in conflict with it.

Average costs do not reflect either the matching of current costs with current revenues or balance sheet valuations in terms of current costs. In this respect, they are somewhat neutral with regard to income determination and balance sheet valuation. But the extent to which they are neutral depends, in part, on how the average is computed.

Generally, simple average and weighted average price can be calculated for inventory costing under the average cost methods. Simple average price is an average of prices without having any regard to the quantities involved.

Under weighted average, total quantities and total costs are considered in computing the average price and not the total of rates divided by total number of rates as in simple average. The weighted average is calculated each time a purchase is made. The quantity bought is added to the stock in hand and the new revised balance is then divided by the new total value of the total stock.

Simple Average

This method is based on the principle that materials issued should be priced on an average price and not on exact cost price. The simple average is an average of prices without having regard to the quantities involved. It should be used when prices do not fluctuate very much and the stock value is small. The average under this method is calculated by dividing the total of rates of materials in the storeroom by the number of rates of prices. This method is easy to operate.

Illustration 3: Prepare a stores ledger account by following the simple average method on the basis of information given below:

Rate		Rate per unit (₹)
January 1st, 2012	Received 500 units	20
January 10th	Received 300 units	24
January 15th	Issued 700 units	—
January 20th	Received 400 units	28
January 25th	Issued 300 units	—
January 27th	Received 500 units	22
January 31st	Issued 200 units	—

Solution:

Stores Ledger Account
(Simple Average Price Method)

Date	Receipts			Issue			Stock		
Jan.	Qty.	Rate	Amount	Qty.	Rate	Amount	Qty.	Rate	Amount
2012									
Jan. 1		500	20	10,000	—	—	500	20	10,000
Jan. 10	300	24	7,200	—	—	—	500	20	10,000
							300	24	7,200
Jan. 15	—	—	—	700	22	15,400	100		1,800
Jan. 20	400	28	11,200	—	—	—	500		13,000
Jan. 25	—	—	—	300	26	7,800	200		5,200
Jan. 27	500	22	11,000	—	—	—	700		16,200
Jan. 31	—	—	—	200	25	5,000	500		11,200

Average price for different issues has been calculated as follows:

January 15th 700 units = 20 + 24/2 = ₹ 22 per unit

January 25th 300 units = 24 + 28/2 = ₹ 26 per unit

January 31st 200 units = 28 + 22/2 = ₹ 25 per unit

Weighted Average

Under this method, issue of materials is priced at the average cost price of the materials in hand, a new average being computed whenever materials are received. In this method, total quantities and total costs are considered while computing the average price and not the total of rates divided by total number of rates as in simple average. The weighted average is calculated each time a purchase is made. The quantity bought is added to the stock in hand, and the revised balance is then divided into the new cash value of the stock. The effect of early price is thus eliminated. This method avoids fluctuations in price and reduces the number of calculations to be made, as each issue is charged at the same price until a fresh, purchase necessitates the computation of a new average. It gives an acceptable figure for stock values.

Advantages: The following are the advantages of the weighted average method:

1. The method is logical and consistent as it absorbs cost while determining the average for pricing material issues.
2. The changes in the prices of materials do not affect much the materials issues and stock.
3. The method follows the concept of total stock and total valuation.
4. Both cost of materials issued and in stock tend to reflect actual costs.

Disadvantages: However, the weighted average method also has the following disadvantages:

1. Simplicity and convenience are lost when there is too much change in the prices of materials.
2. An average price is not based on actual price incurred, and therefore is not realistic. It follows only arithmetical convenience.

Illustration 4: Prepare a store ledger account on the basis of information given in Illustration 3 by following the weighted average method.

Solution:

Date	Receipts			Issue			Stock		
	Qty.	Rate	Amount	Qty.	Rate	Amount	Qty.	Rate	Amount
2012									
Jan. 1	500	20	10,000	—	—	—	500	20	10,000
Jan. 10	300	24	7,200	—	—	—	800	21.50	17,200
Jan. 15	—	—	—	700	21.50	15,050	100		2,150
Jan. 20	400	28	11,200	—	—	—	500	26.70	13,350
Jan. 25	—	—	—	300	26.70	8,010	200		5,340
Jan. 27	500	22	11,000	—	—	—	700	23.34	16,340
Jan. 31	—	—	—	200	23.34	4,668	500		11,672

4. Specific Identification Method

The specific identification method involves:

(*a*) Keeping track of the purchase price of each specific unit.

(*b*) Knowing which specific units are sold.

(*c*) Pricing the ending inventory at the actual prices of the specific units not sold.

The objective is to match the unit cost of the specific item sold with sales revenue. This method is based on the assumption that each unit purchased, sold or in inventory has its own identity, that it is separate and distinguishable from any other unit. Each unit sold or remaining in inventory is identified and its specific unit cost is used in calculating cost of goods sold or ending inventory cost. To take an example, assume that an art dealer purchased two seemingly identical pieces of pottery during a period.

The first piece is purchased for ₹ 3,000 and the second is purchased several months later for ₹ 3,500. Assume also that only one of these items is sold by the dealer during the period. The amounts assigned to cost of goods sold and ending inventory will depend on which specific piece of pottery is sold. If the item sold is the first piece of pottery, cost of goods sold is ₹ 3,000 and ending inventory is ₹ 3,500. On the other hand, if the second piece is sold, the numbers would be reversed; that is cost of goods sold will be ₹ 3,500 and ending inventory would be ₹ 3,000.

The specific identification method provides a highly objective procedure for matching costs with sales revenue because the costs flow pattern matches the physical flow of the goods. However, this method does not work for large volumes of identical low-cost items. This method is appropriate for companies that handle a relatively low volume of physical units, each having a high cost per unit, such as original oil paintings, antiques, diamonds, automobiles, jewellery, furs, etc. The specific identification method is not appropriate where each unit is the same in appearance but is differentiated from other units through serial numbers, such as the same model of washers, refrigerators or televisions.

To illustrate the specific identification method, an example is taken here. Assume the following data about the goods purchased and sold by a company.

Beginning inventory	60 units @	₹ 10	=	600
Purchase	100 units @	₹ 11	=	1,100
	100 units @	₹ 13	=	1,300
	40 units @	₹ 15	=	600
Total	300 units	₹		3,600
Unit sold	220	?		
Units in inventory	80	?		

In order to apply specific identification method, further assume that 80 unsold units which are in inventory, consist of 20 units from beginning inventory, 10 units from each of the first two purchase and all 40 of the last units purchased. Assuming this the costs of goods sold and cost of inventory under this method will be as follows:

Particulars	Units	Cost (₹)	Total (₹)
(A) Ending inventory	20	@ 10	200
	10	@ 11	110
	10	@ 13	130
	40	@ 15	600
	80		1,040
(B) Cost of goods sold	**Goods available**		
	Units	**Cost (₹)**	**Total (₹)**
Beginning inventory	60	@ 10	600
Purchases:	100	@ 11	1,100
	100	@ 13	1,300
	40	@ 15	600
	300		3,600
Cost of Goods available for sale			3,600
Less: Ending inventory			1,040
Cost of goods sold			2,560

Illustration 5: From the records of an oil distributing company, the following summarised information is available for the month of March 2012.

Sales of the month: ₹ 19,25,000

Opening Stock as on 1.3.2012: 1.25,000 litres @ ₹ 6.50 per litre

Purchases (including freight and insurance):

March 5th 150,000 litres @ ₹ 7.10 per litre

March 27th 100,000 litres @ ₹ 7.00 per litre

Closing stock as on 31.3.12: 1,30,000 litres.

General administrative expenses for the month: ₹ 45,000.

On the basis of the above information, work out the following using FIFO and LIFO methods of inventory valuation assuming that pricing of issues is being done at the end of the month after all receipts during the month:

(*a*) Value of closing stock as on 31.3.12

(*b*) Cost of goods sold during March 2012

(*c*) Profit or loss for March 2012.

Solution:

(A) FIFO METHOD OF PRICING ISSUES

Stores Ledger

Date	Particulars	Receipts			Issue			Stock		
		Qty. litre	Rate ₹ per litre	Value ₹	Qty. litres	Rate ₹ per litre	Value ₹	Qty. litres	Rate ₹ per litre	Value ₹
1.3.12	Balance b/d							1,25,000	6.50	8,12,500
5.3.12	Purchases	1,50,000	7.10	10,65,000				2,75,000		18,77,500
27.3.12	Purchases	1,00,000	7.00	7,00,000				3,75,000		25,77,500
	Issues				1,25,000	6.50	8,12,500	2,50,000		17,65,000
	(3,75,000 – 1,30,000 = 2,45,000 units)				1,20,000	7.10	8,52,000	1,30,000		9,13,000
		2,50,000		17,65,000	2,45,000		16,64,500			

(B) LIFO METHOD OF PRICING ISSUES

Stores Ledger

Date	Particulars	Receipts			Issue			Stock		
		Qty. litre	Rate ₹ per litre	Value ₹	Qty. litres	Rate ₹ per litre	Value ₹	Qty. litres	Rate ₹ per litre	Value ₹
1.3.12	Balance b/d							1,25,000	6.50	8,12,500
5.3.12	Purchases	1,50,000	7.10	10,65,000				2,75,000		18,77,500
27.3.12	Purchases	1,00,000	7.00	7,00,000				3,75,000		25,77,500
	Issues				1,00,000	7.00	7,00,000			
					1,45,000	7.10	10,29,500	1,30,000		8,48,000
		2,50,000		17,65,000	2,45,000		17,29,500			

Closing stock, cost of goods sold, profit under FIFO (₹)

(*a*) Value of closing stock 9,13,000

(*b*) Cost of goods sold (8,12,500 + 8,52,000) 16,64,500

(*c*) Profit

Sales		19,25,000
Less: Cost of goods sold		(16,64,500)
General Administration Expenses		(45,000)
Profit		2,15,000

Closing stock, cost of goods sold, profit under LIFO (₹)

(*a*) Value of closing stock		848,000
(*b*) Cost of goods sold (7,00,000 + 10,29,500)		17,29,500
(*c*) Profit:		
Sales		19,25,000
Less: Cost of goods sold	17,29,500	
General administration expenses	45,000	17,74,500
Profit		1,50,500

Illustration 6: From the following details of stores receipts and issues of material "EXA" in a manufacturing unit, prepare the Stock Ledger using "Weighted Average" method of valuing the issues:

Nov. 1 Opening stock 2,000 units @ ₹ 5 each.

Nov. 3 Issued 1,500 units to Production.

Nov. 4 Received 4,500 units @ ₹ 6.00 each.

Nov. 8 Issued 1,600 units to Production.

Nov. 9 Returned to stores 100 units by Production Department (from the issues of November, 3).

Nov. 16 Received 2,400 units @ ₹ 6.50 each.

Nov. 19 Returned to the supplier 200 units out of the quantity received on November, 4.

Nov. 20 Received 1,000 units @ ₹ 7.00 each.

Nov. 24 Issued to Production 2,100 units.

Nov. 27 Received 1,200 units @ ₹ 7.50 each.

Nov. 29 Issued to Production 2,800 units.

(use rates upto two decimal places).

Solution: Stores Ledger Material "EXE" (Weighted Average Method)

Date	References	Receipts			Issue			Stock		
		Qty. Units	Rate (₹)	Amount (₹)	Qty. Units	Rate (₹)	Amount (₹)	Qty. Units	Rate (₹)	Amount (₹)
Nov.										
1	Opening Balance							2,000	5.00	10,000
3	Issues to Production				1,500	5.00	7,500	500	5.00	2,500
4	Receipts	4,500	6.00	27,000				5,000	5.90	29,500
8	Issues to Production				1,600	5.90	9,440	3,400	5.90	20,060
9	Returns by production	100	5.00	500				3,500	5.87	20,560
16	Receipts	2,400	6.50	15,600				5,900	6.13	36,160
19	Returns to Supplier				200	6.00	1,200	5,700	6.13	34,960
20	Receipts	1,000	7.00	7,000				6,700	6.26	41,960
24	Issues to Production				2,900	6.26	13,446	4,600	6.26	28,814
27	Receipts	1,200	7.50	9,000				5,800	6.52	37,814
29	Issues to Production				2,800	6.52	18,256	3,000	6.52	19,558

Value of Closing Stock: ₹ 19,558

LOWER OF COST OR MARKET (LCM)

Different methods of inventory costing such as FIFO and LIFO, determine the value of inventory in terms of historical cost. However, according to conservatism concept, inventory should be reported on the balance sheet at the lower of its cost or its market value. Generally speaking, inventory is valued in terms of cost. But there should be a departure from the cost basis of valuing inventory and it should be reduced below cost when the utility of goods has declined and its sale proceeds or value of the items will be less than their cost. The decline in the value of inventory below cost can be due to different causes such as physical deterioration, obsolescence, drops in price level, etc. In these situations, inventory is reported at market value. The difference in value (cost–market value) is recognised as a loss of the current period.

It should be understood that the market value of inventory needs to be estimated as the inventory has not, in fact, been sold. As a rule, the market value concept is used in terms of current replacement cost of inventory, that is, what it will cost currently to purchase or manufacture the item. Thus, the LCM rule recognises a holding loss in the period in which the replacement cost of an item dropped, rather than in the period in which the item is actually sold. The holding loss as stated earlier is the difference between purchases cost and the subsequent lower replacement cost. If applicable the LCM rule simply measures inventory at the lower (replacement) market figure. As a result, net income decreases by the amount that the closing inventory has been written down. When the closing inventory becomes part of the cost of goods sold in a future period when selling prices are low, the lower carrying value of closing inventory helps in maintaining normal profit margins in the period of sale.

While applying the rule of 'lower of cost or market' the following upper and lower boundaries are used with regard to market value (current replacement cost) concept:

1. Market value should not be higher than the estimated net realisable value, *i.e.*, the estimated selling price of the item less the costs associated with selling it.
2. Market value should not be lower than the net realisable value less a normal profit margin.

The above rules on 'lower of cost or market' is summarised as follows:

"Use historical cost if the cost price is lowest; otherwise, use the next-to-lowest of the other three possibilities."

The following example presents the application of 'lower of cost of market' in different situation. In this example, four possible situations, A, B, C and D are assumed and historical cost, current replacement cost, net realisable value and net realisable value less profit margin figures of inventory are given.

The value at which inventory will be in these different situation is indicated by star*.

Situation	Historical cost (₹)	Current Replacement (₹)	Net Realisable value (Ceiling) (₹)	Net Realisable Value Less Profit Margin (Floor) (₹)
A	700*	800	1,000	900
B	900	800*	900	700
C	900	700	900	800*
D	1,000	900	800*	700

The above example proves that not all decreases in replacement prices are followed by proportionate reductions in selling prices (net realisable value). Therefore, the application of LCM rule is subject to the following additional guidelines:

(*i*) If selling price is not expected to drop, inventory may be priced at cost even though it exceeds replacement cost.

For example, assume that an item costing ₹ 80 is being sold for ₹ 100 during the year, yielding a gross profit of 20 per cent on sales. If the selling price remains at ₹ 100 and the replacement cost drops to ₹ 60 (a 25 per cent decline), inventory will not be written down.

However, if there is a proportionate decrease in the selling price, *i.e.*, selling price also declines by 25 per cent and becomes ₹ 75, then inventory will be shown at ₹ 60 replacement cost.

In this case, after showing the inventory at ₹ 60, the current period's income will be less by ₹ 20 (the difference between the historical cost and replacement cost). Further, when this item valued at ₹ 60 is sold in a subsequent period for ₹ 75, a normal gross profit of 20 per cent on sales will be reported (₹ 75 – ₹ 60 = ₹ 15 gross profit margin).

(*ii*) If selling price is expected to drop but less than proportionately to the decline in replacement cost, inventory is written down only to the extent necessary to maintain a normal gross profit in the period of sale. Taking the above example if the selling price drops from ₹ 100 to ₹ 90 and the replacement cost declines to ₹ 60, inventory will be shown at ₹ 72 (₹ 90 – 20 per cent of ₹ 90). This amount maintains a 20 per cent gross profit margin when the item is sold for ₹ 90.

Arguments in Support of LCM Rule

Supporters of the LCM Rule argue that an exception to the historical costs basis is desirable because it (LCM) serves the useful purpose of achieving better matching of costs and revenues and contributes to usefulness of periodic income measurement. The arguments in favour of LCM rule is that no assets should appear on a business enterprise's balance sheet in an amount greater than is likely to be recovered from the use or sale of that asset in the normal course of events. Unrecoverable amounts have no value and therefore are not assets. International Accounting Standards Committee (now IASB) observes:

> "The historical cost of inventories may not be realisable if their selling prices have declined, if they are damaged, or if they have become wholly or partially obsolete. The practice of writing inventories below historical cost to net realisable value accords with the view that current assets should not be carried in excess of amounts expected to be realised. Declines in value are computed separately for individual items, groups or similar items, an entire class of inventory (for example, finished goods), or items relating to a class of business, or they are computed on an over-all basis for all the inventories down based on a class of inventory, on a class of business, or on an over-all basis results in offsetting losses incurred against unrealised gains."

Depending on the character and composition of the inventory, the rule of cost or market, whichever is lower may properly be applied either directly to each item or to the total of the inventory (or in some case to the total of the components of each major category). The method should be that which most clearly reflects periodic income.

Criticism of LCM Rule

At the outset it may be noted that lower of cost or market is not a method of inventory costing but rather one of recognising measurable expected loss. The cost or market concept when applied to inventories is tied closely to the concept of realisation of revenue at the time of sale, but with the recognition of loss as soon as evidence of loss appears. The principal objections to the rule center around its violation of the historical cost principle. LCM rule is criticised on many grounds:

(*i*) It violates the concept of consistency because it permits a change in valuation base from one period to another and even within the inventory itself. It treats value increases and value decreases differently. If the market value of goods is greater than its cost, there is no recognition of the increased value on the balance sheet.

(*ii*) It is termed as a major cause of distortion of profit and loss.

(*iii*) Although it may be considered conservative with respect to the current period, it is unconservative with respect to the income of future period.

(*iv*) The current period may be charged with the result of inefficient purchasing and management, which should be included in the measurement of operating performance at the time of sale. However, it may also be argued that these should be recorded in the current period rather than in the period of sale.

(*v*) An increase in the market price in a subsequent period may result in an unrealised gain if the original cost is always used as the basis for comparison with the current market price (assuming of course that market in both periods is below the original cost).

(*vi*) The cost or market rule is said to permit excessive subjectivity in the accounts. This is a based on the assumption that market is always more subjective than cost.

ICAI's Guidelines on Inventory Valuation

The Institute of Chartered Accountants of India has revised Accounting standard (AS)-2: Valuation of Inventories in July 1999. The revised standard supersedes AS-2 issued in June 1981, and AS-2 (Revised) comes into effect in respect of accounting period commencing on or after 1 April, 1999 and it is mandatory in nature. The AS-2 (Revised) has listed the following guidelines.

1. Inventories should be valued at the lower of cost and net realisable value.

2. Net realisable value is defined as the estimated selling price in the ordinary course of business less the estimated cost of completion and estimated costs necessary to make the sale.

An assessment is made of net realisable value as at each balance sheet date.

3. The cost means historical cost comparising, (*i*) all costs of purchase (*ii*) cost of conversion and (*iii*) other costs incurred to bring the inventories to their present location and condition.

4. For the purpose of comparising historical cost with net realisable value each item in the inventory may be clear with separately, or similar items may be dealt with as a group.

5. The standards mentions the following formulas for determining the historical cost:

(*a*) Specific identification of cost,

(*b*) First in First out (FIFO) and

(*c*) Weighted average cost

6. The cost of inventories of items that are not ordinarily interchangeable and goods or services produced and segregated for specific projects should be assigned by specific identification of their individual costs (para 14).

7. The cost of inventories, other than those dealt with in paragraph 14, should be assigned by using First in First out, or weighted average cost formula.

8. Standard cost method or the retail method for the measurement of the cost of inventories, may be used for convenience if the results approximate the actual cost.

9. The historical cost of manufactured inventories may be arrived at on the basis of either direct costing or absorption costing where absorption costing has been used, the allocation of fixed assets of inventories should be based on the normal capacity of the production facilities.

10. When the costs of conversion of each product are not separately identifiable, they are allocated between the products on a rational and consistent basis.

11. Inventory of by-products should be valued at lower of cost and net realisable value where the by products, by their nature, are immaterial, they are measured at net realisable value and this value is deducted from the cost of main product.

12. The financial statements should disclose:

    (a) The accounting policies adopted in measuring inventories, including the cost formula used; and

    (b) The total carrying amount of inventories and its clarification appropriate to the enterprise.

Common classifications are raw materials, and components, work in progress, finished goods, stores and spares, and loose tools.

INVENTORY SYSTEMS

There are two principal ways of accounting for inventories.

Perpetual Inventory System

The perpetual inventory method requires a continuous records of addition to or reductions in materials, work-in-progress and cost of goods sold on a day-to-day basis. Such a record facilitates managerial control and preparation of interim financial statements. Physical inventory counts are usually taken at least once a year in order to check on the validity of the accounting records.

The perpetual inventory system may give such additional information as good ordered, expected delivery date and units costs. Usually, these records are maintained on a quantity basis but values can be included. It is an essential feature of the perpetual inventory method that items of stock are checked periodically, normally at least once or twice each year. This ensures that the stock records tally with the physical stocks, which is vital if the control procedure is to function properly.

The perpetual inventory method has the following advantages:

1. The stock-taking task which is long and costly is avoided under this method. On the other hand, the inventory of different items of materials in accordance with the stores ledger can be promptly prepared for the preparation of the income statement and balance sheet at interim periods, if required, without a physical inventory being taken.
2. Management may be informed daily of number of units and the value of each kind of material-on-hand-information which tends to eliminate delays and stoppage in production.
3. The investment in materials and supplies may be kept at the lowest point in conformity with operating requirements.
4. A system of internal check is always in operation and the activities of different departments, such as purchasing, stores and production are continuously checked against each other. This results into detailed and reliable checks on the stores also.
5. It is not necessary to stop production so as to carry out a complete physical stock-taking.
6. Perpetual inventory records provide details about material cost for individual products, jobs, processes, production orders or departments. This information is helpful to management in exercising control over costs.
7. Discrepancies and errors are promptly discovered and localised and remedial action can be taken to avoid their occurrence in the future.
8. This method has a moral effect on the staff; makes them disciplined and careful and acts as a check against dishonest actions.
9. The disadvantages of excessive stock are avoided, such as loss of interest on capital invested in stock, loss through deterioration, risk of obsolescence.

Periodic Inventory System

Under the periodic method, the entire book inventory is verified at a given date by an actual count of materials on hand. This physical inventory is usually taken near the end of the accounting period.

Some firms even suspend plant operations when this is done. This method provides for the recording of purchases, purchase returns and purchase allowances on a daily basis but does not provide for a continuous inventory or for a daily computation of the goods sold.

At the end of each accounting period, a physical count is made of the quantity of goods on hand and the value of the inventory is determined by using an inventory pricing method (FIFO, LIFO or average cost) and attaching costs to units counted. The cost of goods sold is computed by deducting closing inventory from the sum of opening inventory and purchases made during the current period. It is assumed that goods not on hand at the end of accounting period have been sold. There is no system and accounting for shrinkage, losses, theft and waste throughout the accounting period and they can be discovered only after the end of the period.

Taking a physical inventory at the year-end is an important task in the periodic inventory system. It must be ensured that all items have been counted accurately. Counting procedures usually involve teams of people assigned to specific sections of the factory, and to inventory storage areas. Large items are counted individually, while small items may be weight-counted. Counted items are tagged to prevent double counting and information from the tags concerning each item's description and quantity is recorded on the inventory sheet.

THEORY QUESTIONS

1. Define inventory and identify the costs that should be included as inventory costs.

2. What is meant by goods flow and cost flows?

3. Briefly describe each of the following inventory pricing methods under a periodic inventory system;

(*a*) First In First Out (FIFO) (*b*) Last In First Out (LIFO)

(*c*) Average cost method.

4. Why is inventory an important item to both internal management and external users of financial statements?

5. Explain the application of the cost principle to an item in the closing inventory.

6. When a perpetual inventory system is used, unit costs of the items sold are known at the date of each sale. In contrast, when a periodic inventory system is used, unit costs are known only at the end of the accounting period. Why are these statements correct?

7. Different inventory costing methods may be applied with either a periodic inventory system or a perpetual inventory system. Briefly explain how the methods are applied in each system.

8. Contrast the effects of LIFO versus FIFO on reported assets (*i.e.*, closing inventory) when (*a*) prices are rising, and (*b*) prices are falling.

9. Contrast the income statement effect of LIFO versus FIFO (*i.e.*, on reported net income) when (*a*) prices are rising, and (*b*) prices are falling.

10. The weighted average inventory costing method usually produces different results when a perpetual inventory system is used rather than a periodic inventory system. Explain why?

11. Explain the application of the LCM rule to the closing inventory and its effect on the income statement and balance sheet when market price is lower than cost.

12. When should net realisable value be used in costing an item in the closing inventory?

13. Why do relatively stable purchase prices reduce the significance of the choice of an inventory pricing method?

14. If prices have been rising, which inventory pricing method—FIFO, LIFO, weighted average, yields: (*a*) the lowest inventory amount (*b*) lowest net income (*c*) largest inventory amount (*d*) largest net income.

15. Discuss the effect on reported income of applying the lower of cost or market rule.

16. Contrast the accounting procedures for periodic and perpetual inventory system.

17. Which inventory pricing methods give the same results (closing inventory and total cost of goods sold) when applied under a perpetual inventory system and a periodic inventory system?

18. Under which method of cost flow are (*a*) the earliest costs assigned to inventory (*b*) latest cost assigned to inventory (*c*) average costs assigned to inventory.

19. What are the relative advantages and disadvantages of FIFO and LIFO from management point of view?

20. Which of the following companies would find a perpetual inventory system practical—a drug store, a grocery store, a restaurant, an automobile dealer, a wholesale auto parts? Why?

21. What methods can be used to determine lower of cost or market?

22. In the phrase 'lower of cost or market' what is meant by 'market'?

23. "Cost flow assumptions for inventory are required only because specific identification of item sold is costly. Specific identification is theoretically superior to any cost flow assumption and eliminates the possibility of income manipulation available with some cost flow assumption". Comment.

24. "LIFO provides a more meaningful income statement than FIFO, even though it provides a less meaningful balance sheet." Does it ever? Does it always?

25. Assume that the cost basis for inventory is changed from historical cost to current cost, the current costs exceed historical costs at the end of the year of change and that all year-end inventory is sold during the following year. What will be the impact of the change on net income for the year of change? On income for the following year. On total income over the two years.

26. Does the LIFO method mean that the items in the inventory are assumed to be the most recent (last) acquisitions? Explain.

27. "A departure from the cost basis of pricing the inventory is required when the utility of goods is no longer as great as it cost." In the light of this statement evaluate 'lower of cost or market' (LCM) rule.

28. Is the use of an appropriate valuation method for the inventory at the end of the year more important in producing a dependable income statement, or in producing a dependable balance sheet? Give arguments.

29. Why do some accountants consider the net income reported by business during a period of rising prices to be overstated?

30. Assume that a business uses the FIFO (First In First Out) method of inventory valuation during a prolonged period of inflation and that the business pays dividends equal to the amount of reported net income. Suggest a problem that may arise in continued successful operation of the business.

31. If costs are rising, which cost flow assumption will give the lowest net income in the current accounting period? The highest net income? The lowest ending inventory cost? The highest ending inventory costs? An ending inventory cost closest to the current replacement cost?

32. Why might the management of a company choose the LIFO cost flow assumption even though its use causes the company's net income to be lower?

33. If the ending inventory for 2003 is valued at market under the lower of cost or market rule, what is the effect on the financial statements for 2003? 2004? What is the meaning of the term market?

34. When a company changes from FIFO to LIFO, what effect does the change have on current net income and working capital?
35. Describe the calculation of cost of goods sold under the periodic inventory system.
36. The consistency principle means that the same accounting principles (or methods) used this period were also used last period. Does this mean that once a company decides to use FIFO, it can never switch to LIFO or weighted average?
37. Would there be any difference between using LIFO or FIFO if unit costs of inventory purchased remained constant over time? Explain.
38. Distinguish between LIFO and FIFO method. *(MBA, JNTU, Hyderabad, January 2006)*
39. "Inventory is valued at net realisable value or cost whichever is lower". Comment. *(BBA, GGSIP University, March 2000)*
40. Distinguish between periodic and perpetual systems of inventory valuation. *(BBA, GGSIP University, December 2002)*
41. (*a*) What are the objectives of inventory valuation?
    (*b*) What are the various methods of inventory valuation? Compare FIFO with LIFO. State the salient features of AS-2 regarding inventory valuation. *(BBA, GGSIP University, December 2004, December 2006)*
42. Differentiate between perpetual inventory system and periodic inventory system. *(BBA, GGSIP University, December 2007)*
43. Compare LIFO and FIFO methods of inventory valuation. Which one is better in periods of rising prices? *(BBA, GGSIP University, December 2010)*
44. State the limitations of LIFO method of inventory valuation. *(BBA, GGSIP University, March 2000)*
45. Explain provisions of AS2-Valuation of Inventories. *(BBA, GGSIP University, December 2007)*
46. Distinguish between perpetual and periodical systems of stock taking. *(BBA, GGSIP University, December 2006)*

SELF-EVALUATION EXERCISES

I. Select the correct answer for the following multiple-choice questions.

1. When valuing inventory at lower of cost or market, what is the meaning of the term market?
   (*a*) Net realisable value
   (*b*) Net realisable value less a normal profit margin
   (*c*) Current replacement cost
   (*d*) Discounted present value
2. If a unit of inventory has declined in value in original cost, but the market value exceeds net realisable value, the amount to be used for purpose of inventory valuation is
   (*a*) Net realisable value
   (*b*) Original cost
   (*c*) Market value
   (*d*) Net realisable value less a normal profit margin.
3. In no case can 'market' in the 'lower of cost or market rule' be more than
   (*a*) Estimated selling price in the ordinary course of business
   (*b*) Estimated selling price in the ordinary course of business less reasonably predictable costs of completion and disposal

(*c*) Estimated selling price in the ordinary course of business less reasonably predictable cost of completion and disposal and an allowance for an approximately normal profit margin

(*d*) Estimated selling price in the ordinary course of business less reasonably predictable costs of completion and disposal, an allowance for an approximately normal profit margin, and an adequate reserve for possible future losses.

4. When inventory declines in value below original (historical) cost, and this decline is considered other than temporary, what is the maximum amount that the inventory can be valued at?

(*a*) Sales price net of conversion costs

(*b*) Net realisable value

(*c*) Historical cost

(*d*) Net realisable value reduced by a normal profit margin.

5. An item of inventory purchased this period for ₹ 15 has been written down to its current replacement costs of ₹ 10. It sells for ₹ 30 with disposal cost of ₹ 3 and normal profit of ₹ 12. Which of the following statements is not true?

(*a*) The cost of sales of the following years will be understated

(*b*) The current year's income is understated

(*c*) The closing inventory of the current year is understated

(*d*) Income of the following year will be understated.

6. The cost of sale is equal to

(*a*) Opening stock minus purchases

(*b*) Opening stock plus purchases

(*c*) Opening stock minus purchases plus closing stock

(*d*) Opening stock plus purchases minus closing stock.

7. The item closing inventory is shown in balance sheet under

(*a*) Fixed assets (*b*) Current assets

(*c*) Current liabilities (*d*) Miscellaneous expenditure.

8. Which method of inventory pricing best approximates specific identification of the actual flow of cost and units in most situation?

(*a*) Average cost (*b*) LIFO

(*c*) FIFO (*d*) Specific identification.

9. An inventory pricing procedure in which the oldest costs incurred rarely have an effect on the ending inventory valuation is

(*a*) FIFO (*b*) LIFO

(*c*) Weighted average (*d*) Simple average.

10. Which inventory pricing method assumes that the goods most recently purchased are sold first?

(*a*) FIFO (*b*) Specific identifications

(*c*) Weighted average (*d*) LIFO.

11. Which inventory pricing method reflects the most recently incurred purchase costs in the ending inventory?

(*a*) FIFO (*b*) LIFO

(*c*) Simple average (*d*) Weighted average.

12. If the merchandise inventory at the end of the year is overstated by ₹ 7,500, the error will cause

(*a*) Overstatement of cost of merchandise sold for the year by ₹ 7,500
(*b*) Understatement of gross profit for the year by ₹ 7,500
(*c*) Overstatement of net income for the year by ₹ 7,500
(*d*) Understatement of net income for the year by ₹ 7,500.

13. The inventory system employing accounting records that continuously disclose the amount of inventory is called
(*a*) Periodic (*b*) Perpetual
(*c*) Physical (*d*) Retail.

14. The inventory costing method that is based on the assumption that costs should be charged against revenue in the order in which they were incurred is
(*a*) FIFO (*b*) LIFO
(*c*) Average cost (*d*) Perpetual inventory.

15. The following units of a particular commodity were available for sale during the period:
Beginning inventory 40 units at ₹ 20
First purchase 50 units at ₹ 21
Second purchase 50 units at ₹ 22
Third purchase 50 units at ₹ 23
What is the unit cost of 35 units on hand at the end of the period as determined under the periodic inventory system by the FIFO costing method?
(*a*) ₹ 20 (*b*) ₹ 21
(*c*) ₹ 22 (*d*) ₹ 23.

16. If inventory is being valued at cost and the price level is steadily rising, the method of costing that will yield the highest net income is
(*a*) LIFO (*b*) FIFO
(*c*) Average (*d*) Periodic

17. 'Lower of cost or market rule' is an example of which concept?
(*a*) Consistency (*b*) Conservatism
(*c*) Realisation (*d*) Matching.

18. Under which of the following inventory methods would a wholesaler most likely know the exact quantity in inventory of a particular item on hand in the middle of a month?
(*a*) Periodic inventory method
(*b*) Perpetual inventory method
(*c*) Either the periodic or perpetual inventory method
(*d*) Neither the periodic nor perpetual inventory method.

19. For an enterprise using the periodic inventory system, which of the following is added to merchandise inventory at the beginning of the period in computing the cost of merchandise sold?
(*a*) Purchase discounts
(*b*) Purchases returns and allowances
(*c*) Merchandise inventory at the end of the period
(*d*) None of the above.

20. The inventory system employing accounting records that continuously disclose the amount of inventory is called

(*a*) Periodic (*b*) Perpetual
(*c*) Physical (*d*) Retail.

21. The inventory costing method that is based on the assumption that costs should be charged against revenue in the order in which they were incurred is
(*a*) FIFO (*b*) LIFO
(*c*) Average cost (*d*) Perpetual inventory.

22. If merchandise inventory is being valued at cost and the price level is steadily rising, the method of costing that will yield the highest net income is
(*a*) LIFO (*b*) FIFO
(*c*) Average (*d*) Periodic.

II. Answer True or False

1. The work-in-progress inventories account of a manufactures is an 'in and out' account; manufacturing cost are first accumulated in this account and then when the products are completed, the cost are transferred out of the account to the finished-goods inventories account.
2. When the perpetual inventory method is used, the cost of goods sold is credited (–) in the inventories account at the time of sale, and the company would not have to make account of ending inventory to determine its cost of goods sold expenses for the period.
3. During a period for steadily rising costs, the average cost method will result in a cost of goods sold expenses for the period that is more than FIFO but less than LIFO.
4. During a period of steadily rising costs, FIFO will result in a lower ending inventory value than LIFO.
5. The name FIFO, meaning first-in first-out, refers to the sequence in which inventory acquisition costs are charged to cost of goods sold expense.
6. LIFO, meaning last-in first-out, refers to the manner of determining the cost of ending inventory; the last or most recent items purchased give the unit costs to be multiplied by the quantities of the items in ending inventory.
7. The actual physical flow (or movement) or the products out of inventory is not the main factor in deciding between FIFO and LIFO.
8. The selling price response of the company to increase in the unit cost of its products is not the main factor in deciding between FIFO and LIFO.
9. In a situation assume that cost increased steadily during the year and so did inventory (purchase were more than sales). In another situation, assume just the reverse-cost steadily decreasing during the year and inventory decreasing during the year; in this reverse situation, a comparison of FIFO and LIFO given just the reverse effects; that is, FIFO results in the highest cost of goods, sold expense and the lowest ending inventory.
10. When using the perpetual inventory, a physical inventory (counting and inspection) must be taken to determine inventory shortages and shrinkage; on the other hand, the periodic inventory method includes shortages and shrinkage as a part of the method.
11. A company using the periodic inventory method can estimate its inventory at any time during the period on the basis of the percentage of cost to sale price for its products.
12. One reason for using the periodic inventory method is to avoid the book-keeping cost of maintaining many detailed inventory records.
13. The periodic inventory method depends heavily on making a correct and accurate count of ending inventory.

14. If the total ending inventory cost is understated (too low) because certain items were overlooked and not counted in the stock of ending inventory, the cost of goods sold expense for the year would be overstated (too high).

15. If the total ending inventory cost is overstated (too high) because the unit cost used for certain items were higher than actual cost paid for the items, the cost of good sold expenses for the year would be overstated (too high).

16. Theoretically, freight-in (transportation-in) cost should be included in the cost of inventory.

17. Using the periodic inventory method requires that the company maintain up-to-date, detailed records for each item held in inventory.

18. Using the periodic inventory method requires that the company count and determine the cost value of its inventory at the end of the accounting period.

19. If the total cost value of ending inventory is higher than beginning inventory, then the total cost of purchases during the period must be more than the total cost of goods sold during the period.

20. If for some reason an error is made and its ending inventory is overstated, then the company's cost of goods sold expense for the period will be overstated, assuming that the entity uses the periodic inventory method.

21. The largest expenses of businesses that sell products is the cost of goods sold.

III. Match the terms given in List A with the definitions given in List B.

List A (Terms)

1. Specific identification
2. Work-in-progress inventory
3. Merchandise inventory
4. Periodic inventory system
5. Last In First Out
6. Weighted average
7. Finished good inventory
8. Comparability quality
9. Perpetual inventory system
10. Gross margin method
11. First In First Out
12. Net realisable value
13. Lower of cost or market
14. Raw materials inventory
15. Moving weighted average
16. Consignment

List B (Definitions)

(A) Prevents arbitrary changes from one accounting or measurement approach to another from one period to another.

(B) Goods held on this basis should be excluded from inventory because legal title still resides with the consignor.

(C) An account reported on the balance sheet as a current asset; represents goods completed in the manufacturing process.

(D) An inventory costing method that assumes that those items which have been in inventory the longest are sold first.

(E) Uses a ratio derived by dividing the gross margin amount by the net sales revenue to compute estimates.

(F) An inventory method that assumes that the units acquired most recently are sold first.

(G) Recognises a holding loss when replacement cost drops below costs.

(H) The inventory of a retailer or wholesaler.

(I) An inventory costing method in which a new average unit cost is computed at the time of each new purchase.

(J) Estimated selling price of a product in the ordinary course of business, less reasonably predictable costs of completion and disposal.

(K) Requires computation of the ending inventory by means of a physical count of the goods remaining on hand; CGS is computed as a residual amount.

(L) System that maintains a detailed daily inventory record throughout the period for each item stocked, and therefore, does not require a physical count at the end of each accounting period.

(M) Those items acquired by purchase, growth, or extraction of natural resources for further processing into finished goods.

(N) An inventory costing method that may be appropriate for 'big ticket' items but may be impractical when unit cost are low and unit cost changes frequently.

(O) An inventory costing method that weighs the number of units purchased and unit costs that prevailed during the period; used in conjunction with a periodic inventory system.

(P) As asset that includes the cost of raw material used, the direct labour incurred in the manufacturing process, and factory overhead cost.

EXERCISES AND PROBLEMS

1. You are presented with the following information by Sphix Engineering Co. relating to the first week of September, 2012:

Materials—The transactions in connection with the materials are as follows:

Days	Receipts Units	Rate per unit (₹)	Issues Units
1st	40	15.00	
2nd	20	16.50	
3rd			30
4th	50	14.30	
5th			20
6th			40

Calculate the cost of materials issued under FIFO method and Weighted Average Method of issue of materials.

Ans:

	Cost of materials issued		Stock	
	Units	Amount	Units	Amount
FIFO	90	1,359	20	286
Weighted Average	90	1,350	20	295

2. Show the stores ledger entries as they would appear when using:

(*a*) the weighted average method

(*b*) the LIFO method of pricing issues, in connection with the following transactions:

	April	Unit	Value (₹)
1.	Balance in hand	300	600
2.	Purchased	200	440
4.	Issued	150	
6.	Purchased	200	460
11.	Issued	150	
19.	Issued	200	
20.	Purchased	200	480
27.	Issued	250	

In a period of rising prices such as above what arc the effects of each method?

[**Ans:** (*a*) 150 units ₹ 342, (*b*) 150 units ₹ 300].

3. Explain the following two methods of pricing of materials issues and also the circumstances under which these methods are used—LIFO and FIFO. Draw a stores ledger card, recording the following transactions that took place in a month under the above two methods:

2012			
Jan.	1	Opening stock	200 pieces @ ₹ 20 each
Jan.	5	Purchases	100 pieces @ ₹ 22 each
Jan.	10	Purchases	150 pieces @ ₹ 24 each
Jan.	20	Purchases	180 pieces @ ₹ 25 each
Jan.	22	Issues	150 pieces
Jan.	25	Issues	100 pieces
Jan.	27	Issues	100 pieces
Jan.	28	Issues	200 pieces

[**Ans:** LIFO closing stock 80 units, ₹ 1,720
FIFO closing stock 80 units, ₹ 2,000].

4. The Fair Deal Granary was not maintaining a perpetual inventory system for its stocks unit recently. Only physical inventory was taken at the end of each month. The physical inventory at the end of December 2012 showed 200 bags of fine rice at ₹ 212.25 per bag. The following purchases were made in January, 2008:

3rd	400 bags at ₹ 218.00 per bag
10th	900 bags at ₹ 223.50 per bag
15th	400 bags at ₹ 220.00 per bag
28th	700 bags at ₹ 213.00 per bag
30th	300 bags at ₹ 224.00 per bag

On 31st January, 2013 the physical stock was 1,200 bags. You are required to calculate the value of the stock on 31st January, 2013 according to First-in, First-out, Last-in, First-out and Average Cost Method.

ANSWERS TO SELF-EVALUATION EXERCISES

I.

1. (*c*)	**2.** (*a*)	**3.** (*b*)	**4.** (*b*)	**5.** (*d*)	**6.** (*d*)
7. (*b*)	**8.** (*c*)	**9.** (*a*)	**10.** (*d*)	**11.** (*a*)	**12.** (*c*)
13. (*b*)	**14.** (*a*)	**15.** (*d*)	**16.** (*b*)	**17.** (*b*)	**18.** (*b*)
19. (*d*)	**20.** (*b*)	**21.** (*a*)	**22.** (*b*)		

II.

1. True	**2.** True	**3.** False	**4.** False	**5.** True	**6.** False
7. True	**8.** True	**9.** True	**10.** True	**11.** True	**12.** True
13. True	**14.** True	**15.** False	**16.** True	**17.** False	**18.** True
19. True	**20.** False	**21.** False			

III.

1. (N)	**2.** (P)	**3.** (H)	**4.** (K)	**5.** (F)	**6.** (O)
7. (C)	**8.** (A)	**9.** (L)	**10.** (E)	**11.** (D)	**12.** (J)
13. (G)	**14.** (M)	**15.** (I)	**16.** (B)		

PART – THREE

COMPANY ACCOUNTS

- **Chapter 12** Accounting for Shares
- **Chapter 13** Accounting for Debentures
- **Chapter 14** Company Final Accounts
- **Chapter 15** Accounting for Amalgamation
- **Chapter 16** Valuation of Goodwill

12

ACCOUNTING FOR SHARES

LEARNING OBJECTIVES

After reading this chapter, you should be able to:

- *Understand* the meaning of a share?
- *Describe* different types of shares.
- *Explain* Book Building and Dematerialisation.
- *Explain* accounting treatment with regard
  - — Issue of shares
  - — Forfeiture of shares
  - — Rights issue
  - — Issue of bonus shares
  - — Redemption of preference shares
  - — Underwriting commissions and brokerage on shares and debentures

WHAT IS A SHARE ?

The capital of a company is divided into a very large number of equal parts/units of small denomination. Each part or unit is called a share. For example a company has total capital ₹ 10,00,000 divided into 1,00,000 equal parts/units of the denomination of ₹ 10. Each unit part will be known as a share of ₹ 10 each.

According to Section 2 (46) of the Companies Act 1956 a share is defined as a share in the share capital of the company and includes stock except where a distinction between stock and shares is expressed or implied.

TYPES OF SHARES

In India, a limited company can issue shares which may be:

1. Preference shares
2. Equity/ordinary shares

A company may issue shares at its inception or at a later stage when it wants to raise further capital. A public limited company invites applications for its shares and debentures by issuing a prospectus. The allotment of shares takes place after the applications are received and the minimum subscription prescribed by the Companies Act is received.

Preference Shares

Preference shares are those shares which carry two preferential rights namely:

(*i*) right to receive dividend before any dividend is given on ordinary shares

(*ii*) right to receive back capital before any amount is to be paid to ordinary shareholders by way of refund of capital

The preference shares may be further subdivided as (*i*) cumulative and non-cumulative, (*ii*) participating and non-participating, (*iii*) redeemable and irredeemable shares, according to the provisions of the memorandum of association and/or the articles of association.

(*i*) Cumulative and Non-Cumulative Preference Shares: Cumulative preference shares are those shares in respect of which the amount of dividend accumulates if it is not paid in any one year or years. In the case of non-cumulative preference shares,dividend for the year lapses in case it is not paid in that year for any reason. If the articles of the company are silent, the assumption is that preference shares are cumulative.

(*ii*) Participating and Non-Participating Preference Shares: Participating preference shares are those preference shares which carry a right to participate alongwith equity shares in any (*i*) surplus of profits left after paying dividend to equity shareholders and/or (*ii*) the surplus of assets which may remain after the entire capital has been repaid on a winding up. Non-participating preference shares are those shares which do not carry any such right. If articles of the company are silent, preference shares are assumed to be non-participating preference shares.

(*iii*) Redeemable and Irredeemable Preference Shares: Irredeemable preference shares are those which can be redeemed only in the event of company's winding up. On the other hand, redeemable preference shares are redeemed within a stipulated period in accordance with the terms of the issue. After the amendment of the Companies Act in 1988, companies cannot issue irredeemable preference shares. The amendment of the Companies Act also provides for the redemption of such shares issued prior to the amendment of the Act in 1988.

Equity or Ordinary Shares

An equity shares is one which is not a preference shares. In other words, it has no priority as to the payment of dividend or refund of capital on winding up. These are normally risk bearing shares. They are entitled to all surplus of assets and profits after payment of creditors and preference shareholders.

BOOK BUILDING

Meaning of Book Building

Every business organisation needs funds for its business activities. It can raise funds either externally or through internal sources. When the companies want to go for the external sources, they use various means for the same. Two of the most popular means to raise money are Initial Public Offer (IPO) and Follow on Public Offer (FPO). During the IPO or FPO, the company offers its shares to the public either at fixed price or offers a price range, so that the investors can decide on the right price. The method of offering shares by providing a price range is called **book building method**. This method provides an opportunity to the market to discover price for the securities which are on offer.

Book Building may be defined as a process used by companies raising capital through Public Offerings-both Initial Public Offers (IPOs) and Follow-on Public Offers (FPOs) to aid price and demand discovery. It is a mechanism where, during the period for which the book for the offer is open, the bids are collected from investors at various prices, which are within the price band specified by the issuer. The process is directed towards both the institutional investors as well as the retail investors. The issue price is determined after the bid closure based on the demand generated in the process.

Book Building vs. Fixed Price Method

The main difference between the book building method and the fixed price method is that in the former, the issue price to not decided initially. The investors have to bid for the shares within the price range given. The issue price is fixed on the basis of demand and supply of the shares. On the other hand, in the fixed price method, the price is decided right at the start. Investors cannot choose the price. They have to buy the shares at the price decided by the company. In the book building method, the demand is known every day during the offer period, but in fixed price method, the demand is known only after the issue closes.

Book Building in India

The introduction of book-building in India was done in 1995 following the recommendations of an expert committee appointed by SEBI under Y.H. Malegam. The committee recommended and SEBI accepted in November 1995 that the book-building route should be open to issuer companies, subject to certain terms and conditions.

In January 2000, SEBI came out with a compendium of guidelines, circulars and instructions to merchant bankers relating to issue of capital, including those on the book-building mechanism.

Book Building Process

The principal intermediaries involved in a book building process are the companies, Book Running Lead Manager (BRLM) and syndicate members are the intermediaries registered with SEBI and eligible to act as underwriters. Syndicate members are appointed by the BRLM. The book building process is undertaken basically to determine investor appetite for a share at a particular price. It is undertaken before making a public offer and it helps determine the issue price and the number of shares to be issued. The following are the important points in book building process.

1. The Issuer who is planning an offer nominates lead merchant banker(s) as 'book runners'.
2. The Issuer specifies the number of securities to be issued and the price band for the bids.
3. The Issuer also appoints syndicate members with whom orders are to be placed by the investors.
4. The syndicate members put the orders into an 'electronic book'. This process is called 'bidding' and is similar to open auction.
5. The book normally remains open for a period of 5 days.
6. Bids have to be entered within the specified price band.
7. Bids can be revised by the bidders before the book closes.
8. On the close of the book building period, the book runners evaluate the bids on the basis of the demand at various price levels.
9. The book runners and the Issuer decide the final price at which the securities shall be issued.
10. Generally, the number of shares is fixed; the issue size gets frozen based on the final price per share.
11. Allocation of securities is made to the successful bidders. The rest bidders get refund orders.

How is the Price Fixed?

All the applications received till the last dates are analyzed and a final offer price, known as the cut-off price is arrived at. The final price is the equilibrium price or the highest price at which all the shares on offer can be sold smoothly. If the price quoted by an investor is less than the final price, he will not get allotment. If price quoted by an investor is higher than the final price, the amount in excess of the final price is refunded if he gets allotment. If the allotment is not made, full money is refunded within 15 days after the final allotment is made. If the investor does not get money or allotment in a month's time, he can demand interest at 15 per cent per annum on the money due.

Example: In this method, the company doesn't fix up a particular price for the shares, but instead gives a price range, *e.g.*, ₹ 80 to 100. When bidding for the shares, investors have to decide at which price they would like to bid for the shares, *e.g.*, ₹ 80, ₹ 90 or ₹ 100. They can bid for the shares at any price within this range. Based on the demand and supply of the shares, the final price is fixed. The lowest price (₹ 80) is known as the floor price and the highest price (₹ 100) is known as cap price. The price at which the shares are allotted is known as cut off price. The entire process begins with the selection of the lead manager, an investment banker whose job is to bring the issue to the public. Both the lead manager and the issuing company fix the price range and the issue size. Next, syndicate members are hired to obtain bids from the investors. Normally, the issue is kept open for 5 days. Once the offer period is over, the lead manager and issuing company fix the price at which the shares are sold to the investors. If the issue price is less than the cap price, the investors who bid at the cap price will get a refund and those who bid at the floor price will end up paying the additional money. For example, if the cut off in the above example is fixed at ₹ 90, those who bid at ₹ 80, will have to pay ₹ 10 per share and those who bid at ₹ 100, will end up getting the refund of ₹ 10 per share. Once each investor pays the actual issue price, the share are allotted.

Book Building vs. Reserve Book Building

While book building is used to raise capital for the company's business operations, reverse book building is used for buyback of shares from the market. Reverse book building is also a price discovery method, in which the bids are taken from the current investors and the final price is decided on the last day of the offer. Normally the price fixed in reverse book building exceeds the market price.

DEMATERIALISATION

Meaning

Dematerialisation ("Demat" in short form) signifies conversion of a share certificate from its physical form to electronic form. The term Demat, in India, refers to a dematerialised account for individual Indian citizens to trade in listed stocks or debentures, as required by The Securities Exchange Board of India (SEBI). In a Demat account, shares and securities are held electronically instead of the investor taking physical possession of certificates. An investor will have to first open an account with a Depository Participant and then request for the dematerialisation of his share certificates through the Depository Participant so that the dematerialised holdings can be credited into that account. This is very similar to opening a Bank Account. The Demat account number is quoted for all transactions to enable electronic settlements of trades to take place.

India has adopted this sytem of electronic book keeping thereby eliminating the need for paper and shares or securities are held in electronic form. Before the introduction of the depository system by the Depository Act, 1996, the process of sale, purchase and transfer of shares was difficult and there was a high risk of loss.

How Does the Depository System Operate?

The operations in the Depository System involve the participation of a Depository, Depository Participants (DP), Company/Registrars and Investors. The company is also called the *Issuer*. A *Depository* is an organisation that facilitates holding of securities in the electronic form and enables DPs to provide services to investors relating to transaction in securities. There are two depositories in India, namely NSDL and CDSL. As per SEBI guideline, the minimum net worth stipulated for a depository is ₹ 100 crores. NSDL (National Securities Depository Limited) was established in August 1996 and is the first depository in India. CDSL (Central Depository Securities Limited) is the other depository and was established in 1999.

A Depository Participant is the agent of the Depository and is the medium through which the shares are held in the electronic form. They are also the representatives of the investor, providing the link between the investor and the company through the Depository. A DP can be a financial organisation like—banks, brokers, financial institutions, custodians, etc., acting as an agent of the Depository to make its services available to the investors.

The Depository system functions very much like the banking system. A bank holds funds in accounts whereas a Depository holds securities in accounts for its clients. A bank transfers funds between accounts whereas a Depository transfers securities between accounts. In both the systems, the transfer of funds or securities happens without the actual handling of funds or securities. Both the banks and the Depository are accountable for safe keeping of funds and securities respectively.

Opening a Demat Account

In order to start dealing in securities in electronic form, one needs to open a demat account with a DP of his choice. An investor is allowed to open more than one account with existing DP or with different DPs. A maximum of three persons are allowed to open a joint demat account in their names. There is no stipulated minimum balance of securities to be kept in a demat account. Following is the procedure of opening a Demat account:

1. Choose a DP.
2. Fill up an account opening form provided by DP, and sign an agreement with DP in a standard format prescribed by the depository.
3. DP provides the investor with a copy of the agreement and schedule of charges for his future reference.

DP opens the account and provides the investor with a unique account number, also known as **Beneficiary Owner Identification Number (BOID)**.

Demat Conversion Process

Converting physical records of investments into electronic records is called *dematerialising securities*. An investor having securities in physical form must get them dematerialised, if he intends to sell them. In order to dematerialise physical securities investors must fill in a DRF (Demat Request Form) which is available with the DP and submit the same along with physical certificates. Every security has an ISIN (International Securities Identification Number). Separate DRFs must be filled for each ISIN Number. The complete process of dematerialisation is as follows:

1. Surrender of certificates by the investor for dematerialisation to the depository participant.
2. Depository participant intimates Depository of the request through the system.
3. Depository participant submits the certificates to the registrar of the Issuer Company.
4. Registrar confirms the dematerialisation request from depository.
5. After dematerialising the certificates, Registrar updates accounts and informs depository of the completion of dematerialisation.

6. Depository updates its accounts and informs the depository participant.
7. Depository participant updates the demat account of the investor.

Advantages of the Demat System: There are several benefits associated with the Demat system:

1. It is a safe and convenient way to hold securities.
2. It ensures immediate transfer of securities.
3. There is no stamp duty on transfer of securities.
4. Risks associated with physical certificates such as bad delivery, fake securities, delays, thefts, etc. are eliminated.
5. There is a major reduction in paperwork involved in transfer of securities, and reduction in transaction cost, etc.
6. No odd lot problem exists, even one share can be sold.
7. Change in address recorded with DP and gets registered with all companies in which investor holds securities eliminating the need to correspond with each of them separately.
8. Transmission of securities is done by DP eliminating correspondence with companies.
9. Automatic credit into demat account of shares, arising out of bonus/split/consolidation/merger etc. can take place.
10. Holding investments in equity and debt instruments in a single account is possible.

Besides the above benefits, there are some additional advantages listed as below:

Benefit to the Company: The depository system helps in reducing the cost of new issues due to lower printing and distribution costs. It increases the efficiency of the registrars and transfer agents and the Secretarial Department of the company. It provides better facilities for communication and timely services with shareholders, investors, etc.

Benefit to the Investors: The depository system reduces risks involved in holding physical certificates, *e.g.*, loss, theft, mutilation, forgery, etc. It ensures transfer settlements and reduces delay in registration of shares. It ensures faster communication to investors. It helps avoid bad delivery problems due to signature differences, etc. It ensures faster payment on sale of shares. No stamp duty is paid on transfer of shares. It provides more acceptability and liquidity of securities.

Benefits to Brokers: It reduces risks of delayed settlement. It ensures greater profit due to increase in volume of trading. It eliminates chances of forgery, bad delivery. It increases efficiency of trading, profitability and confidence in investors.

Disadvantages of the Demat System: The disadvantages of dematerialization of securities can be summarized as follows:

1. Trading in securities may become uncontrolled in case of dematerialized securities.
2. It is compulsory for the capital market regulator to keep a close watch on the trading in dematerialized securities and to check that trading does not act as a detriment to investors.
3. The role of key market players in case of dematerialized securities, such as stock-brokers, needs to be supervised as they have the capability of manipulating the market.
4. Multiple regulatory frameworks have to be followed, including the Depositories Act, Regulations and the various By-Laws of various depositories.
5. Additionally, agreements are entered at various levels in the process of dematerialization. Investors may find the process complicated.

ISSUE OF SHARES

A company may issue shares at their face value or at a price other than the face value. When shares are issued at a price equal to their face value it is termed as shares issued at par. When issue price of a share is more than its face value, it is known as shares issued at a premium. If issue price of a share is less than its face value, it is called as shares issued at a discount.

The issue price of a share is normally collected in stages—alongwith application, on allotment and later by making one or two calls. The shares become fully paid up only on receipt of all the money due on them.

The accounting entries pertaining to the issue of shares are as follows:

Issue of Shares at par

1. On receipt of applications money

Bank a/c Dr.
To share application a/c
(Being share application money received)

2. On allotment of shares

(*a*) Share application a/c Dr.
To share capital a/c
(Being appropriation of application money towards share capital)

(*b*) Share Allotment a/c Dr.
To share capital a/c
(Being allotment money due on shares @ ₹ per share)

3. When allotment money is received, the following entry is passed

Bank a/c Dr.
To share allotment a/c
(Being allotment money received)

4. (*a*) If any call is made on the shares, the following entries are passed

Share call a/c Dr.
To share capital a/c

(*b*) On receipt of call money

Bank a/c Dr.
To share call a/c

Issue of Share at Premium

Section 78 of the companies Act, as amended by the Companies Amendment Act 1999 provides that the amount of premium on the securities issued by the company shall be transferred to Securities Premium Account. Generally, premium money is received alongwith allotment money. In such a case, the following entries are passed.

(*a*) Bank a/c Dr.
To share application a/c
(Being application money received)

(*b*) Share application a/c Dr.
To share capital a/c
(Being application appropriated towards capital a/c)

(*c*) Share Allotment a/c Dr.
To share capital a/c
To *securities premium* a/c
(Being allotment money and premium money due on share)

Bank a/c Dr.
To share allotment a/c
(Being allotment money received)

The Companies Act does not impose any restriction on the issue of shares at a premium. However, it is only prosperous companies because of their financial strength and high earning capacity which are in a position to offer shares at a premium.

As per provisions of Companies Act, the premium money must be credited to a separate account called securities premium account. Under Section 78 of the Act, the amount of securities premium can be used wholly or in part for:

(*i*) paying up unissued shares of the company to be issued to members of the company as bonus shares

(*ii*) writing off the preliminary expenses of the company

(*iii*) writing off the expenses of or the commission paid or discount allowed on shares or debentures of the company

(*iv*) providing for the premium payable on the redemption of redeemable preference shares or debentures of the company.

Issue of Shares at a Discount

A company can issue shares at a discount only when the following conditions as laid down in Companies Act are satisfied:

(*a*) The shares must belong to a class already issued;

(*b*) The issue is authorised by an ordinary resolution in the general meeting and sanctioned by the company law board;

(*c*) The issue is made at a discount which is specified in the resolution but in no case the rate of discount should exceed 10 per cent or such higher percentage as the central government may permit;

(*d*) At least one year has elapsed since the company became entitled to commence the business; and

(*e*) Issues are made within two months after receiving the sanction of the Company Law Board.

Journal entry for the issue of shares at discount generally recorded at the time of allotment of share, is as follows:

Share Allotment a/c Dr.
Discount on issue of share a/c Dr.
To share capital a/c

Discount on issue of shares is a capital loss and is shown on the asset side of the balance sheet till it is written off.

Oversubscription of the Issue of Shares

When shares are over subscribed in certain cases, applications may be rejected and application money refunded, and in certain other cases allotment may be made for fewer shares than applied for. In the latter case, application money paid in excess is generally adjusted against money due on allotment. The relevant entries are:

(*a*) For refund of application money

Share application a/c Dr.
To bank a/c

(*b*) For adjustment of excess amount
Share Application a/c Dr.
To share allotment a/c
To calls-in-advance a/c

(*c*) On adjustment of calls-in-advance (if any)
Share call a/c Dr.
To calls-in-advance a/c

FORFEITURE OF SHARES

If a shareholder does not pay the allotment money or call money in time, the company, in accordance with the provisions of the articles of association, may proceed to forfeit the shares held by such a defaulting shareholder. Upon forfeiture of shares by the company, the person ceases to be the shareholder of the company and the money paid by him on the shares is forfeited to the company.

Accounting Entry for Forfeiture of Shares Issued at Par

When shares have been issued at par and are forfeited by the company, the following entry is passed:

Share capital a/c	Dr.	(with called up amount)
To forfeited shares a/c		(with the amount paid by the member)
To share call a/c		(with the amount due but not paid)

Example: X holds 100 shares of ₹ 10 each issued at par, on which he paid ₹ 2 on application but could not pay ₹ 3 on allotment and ₹ 2 on first call. His shares were forfeited by the company. Pass necessary entry to record the forfeiture of shares.

Solution:

Share capital a/c	Dr.	700	
To forfeited shares a/c			200
To share allotment a/c			300
To share first call a/c			200

(Being the forfeiture of 100 shares of ₹ 10 each, ₹ 7 per share called up, on account of non-payment of allotment money and first call @ ₹ 3 and ₹ 2 respectively)

Forfeiture of Shares which were Issued at Discount

When shares which were issued at discount are forfeited, the discount allowed on the issue of shares has to be cancelled, which is done by crediting the discount on issue of shares a/c.

Example: Y was holding 100 shares of ₹ 10 each issued at 10 per cent discount. He paid ₹ 2 on applications but could not pay allotment money @ ₹ 3 per share and first and final call @ ₹ 4 per shares. The director forfeited his shares. Pass the entry to record the forfeiture of shares.

Solution:

Share capital a/c	Dr.	₹ 1,000	
To forfeited share a/c			₹ 200
To share allotment a/c			₹ 300
To share first call a/c			₹ 400
To discount on issue of shares a/c			₹ 100

(Being the forfeiture of 100 shares of ₹ 10 each issued at 10 per cent discount for non payment of allotment money and first and final call @ ₹ 3 and ₹ 4 per share respectively)

Forfeiture of Shares which were Issued at Premium

Securities premium money is strictly regulated, by the provisions of Section 78 of Companies Act. Accordingly, premium money once collected cannot be cancelled even if that share is forfeited later on. But if a share, on which premium money has become due but has not been received is forfeited then any credit given to share premium account at the time of issue of shares must be cancelled on the forfeiture of shares by debiting share premium account.

Example: X Co. Ltd. issued 1,00,000 shares of ₹ 10 each at 10 per cent premium which is payable as follows:

on application	₹ 2
on allotment	₹ 3 (including premium)
on first call	₹ 2
on final call	₹ 4

Mr. R who was holding 100 shares did not pay his allotment money and first call and his shares were forfeited. Mr. S who was holding 200 shares did not pay his first call and his shares were also forfeited. Pass necessary entries to record the forfeiture of shares.

Solution:

1. Share capital account	Dr.	600	
Securities premium a/c	Dr.	100	
To forfeited shares a/c			200
To share allotment a/c			300
To share first call a/c			200

(Being the forfeiture of 100 shares of ₹ 10 each for non-payment of allotment money (including premium) and first call @ ₹ 3 and ₹ 2 respectively)

2. Share capital a/c	Dr.	1,200	
To forfeited shares a/c			800
To share first call a/c			400

(Being the forfeiture of 200 shares of ₹ 10 each for non-payment of first call @ ₹ 2)

Reissue of Forfeited Shares

The forfeited shares can be reissued by the company at any price. But in no case, the amount collected on the reissue of such shares plus the amount already forfeited be less than the amount credited as paid upon reissue of shares. For example, if a share of ₹ 10 on which ₹ 4 has already been paid, is forfeited and reissued as fully paid, then a minimum of ₹ 6 must be collected. The entry on the reissue of forfeited shares is

Bank a/c	Dr.	(with amount actually received)
Forfeited shares a/c	Dr.	(with discount)
To share capital a/c		(with the amount paid up)

At this stage, if some balance is left in the forfeited shares account, such balance is to be taken as capital profit on the reissue of forfeited shares and is to be transferred to capital reserve. The following entry is passed to transfer the amount to capital reserve:

Forfeited shares account Dr.
To capital reserve a/c

Where only a portion of forfeited shares are reissued, then only profit made on reissue of such shares transferred to capital reserve. Amount forfeited in respect of shares not yet reissued is to be kept intact in the forfeited shares a/c.

If shares originally issued at discount are reissued after forfeiture, the discount account is re-recorded. The entry is

Bank a/c Dr. (Amount actually received)
Discount on shares a/c Dr. (at old rate)
Forfeited shares a/c Dr. (excess over old rate)
To share capital account

Forfeited shares originally issued on premium where premium money was not received need not be reissued at premium. However, if reissue price is sufficient enough, then the share premium can be re-recorded and the balance can be transferred to capital reserve.

ISSUE OF RIGHT SHARES

Section 81 of the Companies Act requires that a public limited company, whenever it proposes to increase its subscribed capital after the expiry of two years from the date of its incorporation or after the expiry of one year from the date of allotment of shares in that company, made for the first time after its formation, whichever is earlier, shall be required to offer those shares to the existing equity shareholders in the proportion of paid-up capital as nearly as possible. Such shares are known as rights shares. The price at which these shares are offered to the existing shareholders is normally below the market price of the shares. The existing shareholders thus have a specific advantage in the sense that market price of the shares offered is more than its issue price. This specific advantage has a money value called as value of the right. The value of the right can be calculated as follows:

1. Ascertain the total market value of the shares which a shareholder is required to possess in order to get additional shares from of the fresh issue.
2. Add to the above market price, the amount to be paid to the company for additional shares of the fresh issue.
3. Find average price. This can be calculated by dividing the total prices calculated under step 2 by the total number of shares.
4. Deduct average price from market price. This difference is called value of the right.

Example: A company makes a rights issue of one shares of ₹ 100 at a premium of 10 per cent for every three shares held by the members of the company. Shares of the company are being sold in the market @ ₹ 150 per cent. Find the value of the right.

Solution: Market price for every 3 shares held by the shareholders

= 3 × 150 = ₹ 450

Add: Issue price of 1 right share = ₹ 110

Total price of 4 shares = ₹ 450 + 110 = 560

Average price = 560/4 = ₹ 140

Market price = ₹ 150 per share

Value of the right = 150 – 140 = ₹ 10

The accounting treatment of rights share is the same as that of issue of ordinary shares and is as follows:

Bank a/c Dr.
To Equity shares capital a/c

In case rights shares are being offered at a premium, the premium amount is credited to the securities premium account.

ISSUE OF BONUS SHARES

A company may issue bonus shares out of free reserves accumulated out of genuine profits or share premium collected. Reserves created by revaluation of fixed assets are not available for issue of bonus shares.

The bonus may be applied to convert partly paid shares into fully paid shares or may be issued as fully paid up bonus shares. The accounting entries in each of these cases would be as follows:

(A) For converting partly paid shares into fully paid shares

(*i*) Equity share final call a/c Dr.
To equity capital a/c
(Being call money due on ... shares)

(*ii*) P&L a/c Dr.
Securities Premium a/c
Reserve a/c Dr.
To bonus to shareholders a/c
(Being bonus declared)

(*iii*) Bonus to shareholders a/c Dr.
To equity share final call a/c
(Conversion of partly paid equity shares into fully paid equity shares)

(B) For fully paid bonus shares

(*i*) P&L a/c
Securities Premium a/c
Reserve a/c Dr.
To bonus to shareholders a/c

(*ii*) Bonus to shareholders a/c Dr.
To equity share capital a/c
(Being bonus utilised to issue fully paid up bonus shares)

REDEMPTION OF PREFERENCE SHARES

As per the Companies Act, 1956, as amended in 1988, only preference shares which are redeemable within 10 years can be issued. The preference shares may be redeemed at par or at premium. Redemption of preference shares may be carried out either out of undistributed profits otherwise available for distribution by way of dividend or from the proceeds of fresh issue of shares. It may be noted here that the term 'proceeds of fresh issue' does not include share premium money if fresh issue is being made at a premium. The premium on redemption of preference shares may be adjusted against the securities premium account or the profit and loss account. It is only fully paid preference shares which can be redeemed. Partly paid preference shares cannot be redeemed unless they are fully paid.

Accounting Entries on Redemption

1. Preference share capital a/c
   To preference shareholders a/c
   (Being the amount payable on redemption of preference shares transferred to shareholders)

2. Preference shareholders a/c
   To bank a/c
   (Being the amount due on redemption paid)

For premium on Redemption of preference shares

3. Premium on redemption of preference shares a/c To preference shareholders a/c (Being the amount of premium payable on redemption)			
4. P and L a/c Securities Premium a/c To premium on redemptions of preference shares a/c (Being the premium on redemption of preference shares adjusted against P and L a/c securities premium a/c)	Dr. Dr.		

Capital Redemption Reserve: When the preference shares are redeemed out of undistributed profits, it is necessary, as per provisions of Companies Act, that an amount equal to the face value of the preference share redeemed is transferred to capital redemption reserve. This is necessary in order to immobilise profit from being used for any other purpose such as declaration of dividend, redemption of debentures, etc. Capital redemption reserve can be utilised for the purpose of issuing fully paid-up bonus shares.

The accounting entry for the transfer of amount of profits to capital redemption reserve a/c is as follows:

P and L a/c/General reserve a/c Dr.
To capital redemption reserve a/c

Illustration 1: Moonshine Company Ltd. was newly formed with an authorised capital of ₹ 10,00,000 divided into 1,00,000 equity shares of ₹ 10 each. The company issued 50,000 shares at a premium of ₹ 2 per share payable ₹ 2 on applications ₹ 5 on allotment (including premium) and ₹ 5 on first and final call.

Application for 70,000 equity shares were received. Directors rejected applications for 10,000 shares and allotted shares to remaining applicants on prorate basis. All the shareholders paid allotment and call money except Mr. M who failed to pay allotment and call money on 800 shares. The directors forfeited these shares. The directors reissued the forfeited shares @ ₹ 9 per share fully paid up.

Pass necessary journal entries to record these transaction.

Solution: **(Amount in ₹)**

Bank a/c To share application a/c (Being the application money received on 70,000 shares of ₹ 10 each @ ₹ 2 per share)	Dr.	1,40,000	1,40,000
Share application a/c To equity share capital a/c To share allotment a/c To bank a/c (Being the transfer of application money on 50,000 shares to share capital a/c, excess application money being appropriated towards allotment and refund of application money on 10,000 shares)	Dr.	1,40,000	1,00,000 20,000 20,000
Share allotment a/c To share capital a/c To securities premium a/c (Being the allotment money due on 50,000 shares of ₹ 10 each @ ₹ 5 per share, premium being ₹ 2 per share as per board of director's resolution no ... dated ...	Dr.	2,50,000	1,50,000 1,00,000

Particulars		Dr. (₹)	Cr. (₹)
Bank a/c To share allotment a/c (Being the receipt of allotment money on 50,000 shares of ₹ 10, @ ₹ 5 per share each except 800 shares)	Dr.	2,26,320	2,26,320
Share first and final call a/c To equity share capital a/c (Being first and final call due on 50,000 shares @ ₹ 5)	Dr.	2,50,000	2,50,000
Bank a/c To share first and final call a/c (Being the receipt of call money on 50,000 shares less M's shares)	Dr.	2,46,000	2,46,000
Securities premium a/c Share capital a/c To forfeited share a/c To share allotment a/c To share first and Final call a/c (Being the forfeiture of 800 shares of ₹ 10 each on account of non-payment of allotment money @ ₹ 5 per share and call money @ ₹ 5 per share as per board of directors resolution no ... dated ...)	Dr. Dr.	1,600 8,000	 1,920 3,680 4,000
Bank a/c Forfeited shares a/c To equity share capital a/c (Being the reissue of 800 shares of ₹ 10 each @ 9 per share as fully paid up)	Dr. Dr.	7,200 800	 8,000
Forfeited shares a/c To capital reserve a/c (Being the transfer of profit on reissue of forfeited shares to capital reserve)	Dr.	1,120	1,120

Working Note 1. Calculation of allotment money received

Total allotment due	₹	2,50,000
Less: Already received	₹	20,000
		2,30,000
Less: Amount not paid by Mr. M		3,680
Amount received on allotment		2,26,320

2. Applicants for 60,000 shares received allotted 50,000 shares, Mr. M was allotted 800 shares. Since allotment was made on prorata basis, he must have applied for

$$\frac{800 \times 60,000}{50,000} = 960 \text{ shares}$$

Application money paid by him = ₹ 960 × 2 = ₹ 1,920

Excess money paid by him which was appropriated towards allotment

= ₹ 1,920 – 1,600 = ₹ 320

Total allotment money due on 800 shares

= ₹ 800 × 5 = ₹ 4,000

Net amount to be paid by Mr. M on allotment

= ₹ 4,000 – 320 = ₹ 3,680.

Illustration 2: Give journal entries for the forfeiture and reissue of forfeited shares.

(*a*) X Co. Ltd. forfeited 100 shares of ₹ 10 each fully called up, held by Mr. A for non-payment of allotment money of ₹ 3 per share and first and final call of ₹ 4 per share. He paid applications money @ ₹ 3 per share, these shares were reissued @ ₹ 9 per share as fully paid up.

(*b*) X Co. Ltd. forfeited 50 shares of ₹ 10 each, ₹ 7 called up on which the shareholder had paid applications and allotment money @ ₹ 5 per share. Out of these 50 shares, 30 shares were reissued as fully paid up @ ₹ 8 per share.

(*c*) X Co. Ltd. forfeited 100 shares of ₹ 10 each (₹ 6 called up) issued at a discount of 10 per cent on which the shareholder had paid ₹ 2 per share. All the shares were reissued as fully paid up @ ₹ 8 per shares.

Solution: **(Amount in ₹)**

Particulars		Dr.	Cr.
(*a*) Share capital a/c	Dr.	1,000	
To forfeited share a/c			300
To share allotment a/c			300
To share first and final call a/c			400
(Being the forfeiture of 100 shares of ₹ 10 of each fully called up for non payment of allotment money @ ₹ 3 and first and final call @ ₹ 4 per share)			
Bank a/c	Dr.	900	
Forfeited shares	Dr.	100	
To shares capital a/c			1,000
(Being the reissue of 100 forfeited shares as fully paid up @ ₹ 9)			
Forfeited shares a/c	Dr.	200	
To capital reserve a/c			200
(Being balance in forfeited shares a/c transferred to capital reserve a/c)			
(*b*) Share capital a/c	Dr.	350	
To forfeited shares a/c			250
To shares first call a/c			100
(Being the forfeiture of 50 shares of ₹ 100 each, ₹ 7 called for non-payment of first call @ ₹ 2)			
Bank a/c	Dr.	240	
Forfeited shares	Dr.	60	
To share capital a/c			300
(Being the reissue of 30 shares of ₹ 10 each @ ₹ 8 per share as fully paid up)			
Forfeited shares a/c	Dr.	90	
To capital reserve a/c			90
(Being the profit on reissue of forfeited shares transferred to capital reserve a/c)			
(c) Share capital a/c	Dr.	600	
To forfeited shares a/c			200
To share allotment a/c			300
To discount on shares a/c			100
(Being the forfeiture of 100 shares of ₹ 10 each (₹ 6 called up) for non-payment of allotment money @ ₹ 3 per share, discount being Re. 1 per share)			
Bank a/c	Dr.	800	
Forfeited shares	Dr.	100	
Discount on shares a/c	Dr.	100	
To share capital a/c			1,000
(Being the reissue of 100 shares of ₹ 10 each @ ₹ 8 per share as fully paid up)			
Forfeited shares a/c	Dr.	100	
To capital reserve a/c			100

Illustration 3: Bharat Limited invited applications for 1,00,000 shares of ₹ 100 each at a price of ₹ 110, payable ₹ 40 on application (including premium ₹ 10), ₹ 45 on allotment and balance on first and final call.

Applications were received for 1,20,000 shares. Allotment was made as:
To applicants of 80,000 shares: 100%
To applicants of 40,000 shares: pro-rata to all applicants

Excess application money was adjusted against further money payable. Mr. Rahul, to whom 1,000 shares were allotted on a pro-rata basis, failed to pay the allotment and call money. Mr. Sanjay, to whom 500 shares were allotted failed to pay the call money.

Prepare the following ledger accounts in the books of Bharat Ltd.:

(*i*) Equity share capital account
(*ii*) Share allotment account
(*iii*) Share call account
(*iv*) Securities premium account

Solution:

Dr. Equity Share Capital A/c Cr.

Particulars	(₹)	Particulars	(₹)
To balance c/d	1,00,00,000	By equity share application	30,00,000
		By equity share allotment	45,00,000
		By equity share call	25,00,000
	1,00,00,000		1,00,00,000

Dr. Share Allotment Account Cr.

Particulars	(₹)	Particulars	(₹)
To equity share capital	45,00,000	By equity share application	8,00,000
		By bank	36,95,000
		By balance c/d (allotment money in arrears)	5,000
	45,00,000		45,00,000

Dr. Share Call Account Cr.

Particulars	(₹)	Particulars	(₹)
To equity share capital	25,00,000	By Bank	24,62,500
		By balance c/d (calls in arrears on 1,500 shares)	37,500
	25,00,000		25,00,000

Dr. Securities Premium Account Cr.

Particulars	(₹)	Particulars	(₹)
To Balance c/d	10,00,000	By equity share application	10,00,000
	10,00,000		10,00,000

Illustration 4: A company made an issue of 30,000 shares of ₹ 10 each, payable ₹ 3 on application. ₹ 5 on allotment and ₹ 2 on call. A total of 93,200 shares were applied for and owing to this heavy oversubscription allotments were made as follows:

Applicants for 21,500 (in respect of applications for 2,000 or more) received 10,200 shares.

Applicants for 50,000 (in respect of application for 1,000 or more but less than 2,000) received 12,600 shares.

Applicants for 21,100 (in respect of applications for less than 1,000) received 7,200 shares. Cash then received after satisfying amount due on application was applied towards allotment and call money and any balance was returned. All moneys due on allotment and call were realised. Give journal entries including that of cash and write up the cash account and ledger accounts relating to this issue of shares in the books of the company.

Solution: **Journal Entries in the Books of Company**

			(₹)	(₹)
1.	Bank a/c To share application (Application money being received)	Dr.	2,79,600	 2,79,600
2.	Share application a/c To share capital (see workings) To bank (see workings) To share allotment (see workings) To calls-in-advance (see workings) (Being money received on application transferred)	Dr.	2,79,600	 90,000 25,800 1,32,900 30,900
3.	Share allotment a/c To share capital a/c (Money due on allotment)	Dr.	1,50,000	 1,50,000
4.	Bank a/c Share allotment a/c	Dr.	17,100	 17,100
5.	Final call a/c Share capital a/c	Dr..	60,000	 60,000
6.	Bank a/c To Final call a/c	Dr.	29,100	 29,100
7.	Calls-in-advance a/c To final call a/c	Dr.	30,00	 30,900

Dr. **Cash Book** **Cr.**

Particulars	(₹)	Particulars	(₹)
To share application	2,79,600	By share application (money returned)	25,800
To share allotment	17,100	By closing balance	3,00,000
To final call	29,100		
	3,25,800		3,25,800

Dr. **Share Application** **Cr.**

Particulars	(₹)	Particulars	(₹)
To share capital	90,000	By bank (93,200 × 3)	2,79,600
To bank	25,800		
To share allotment	1,32,900		
To calls-in-advance	30,900		
	2,79,600		2,79,600

Share Allotment

Particulars	(₹)	Particulars	(₹)
To share capital	1,50,000	By share application	1,32,900
		By bank	17,100
	1,50,000		1,50,000

Final Call

Particulars	(₹)	Particulars	(₹)
To share capital	60,000	By Bank By Call-in-advance	29,100 30,900
	60,000		60,000

Share Capital

Particulars	(₹)	Particulars	(₹)
To closing balance	3,00,000	By share application By share allotment By share final call	90,000 1,50,000 60,000
	3,00,000		3,00,000

Illustration 5: A limited company has an authorised capital of ₹ 2,50,000 in ₹ 10 shares. Of these, 4,000 shares were issued as fully paid in payment of building purchased, 8,000 shares were subscribed for by the public, and during the first year ₹ 5 per share was called up, payable ₹ 2 on application, Re. 1 on allotment, Re. 1 on first call and Re. 1 on second call. The amounts received in respect of these shares were as follows:

On 6,000 shares—full amount

On 1,250 shares—₹ 4 per share

On 500 shares—₹ 3 per share

On 250 shares—₹ 2 per share

The directors forfeited the 750 shares on which less than ₹ 4 per share had been paid.

Give journal entries recording the above transactions and set out the capital as it would appear in the company's balance sheet at the end of the first year.

Solution: **Journal Entries in the Books of the Company**

			(₹)	(₹)
1.	Buildings a/c To vendor a/c	Dr.	40,000	 40,000
2.	Vendor a/c To share capital a/c	Dr.	40,000	 40,000
3.	Bank a/c To share application a/c	Dr.	16,000	 16,000
4.	Share application a/c To share capital a/c	Dr.	16,000	 16,000
5.	Share allotment a/c To share capital	Dr.	8,000	 8,000
6.	Bank a/c To share allotment a/c (Allotment money on 250 shares not received)	Dr.	7,750	 7,750
7.	Share first call a/c To share capital a/c	Dr.	8,000	 8,000
8.	Bank a/c To share first call a/c	Dr.	7,250	 7,250
9.	Share second call a/c To share capital a/c	Dr.	8,000	 8,000

		(₹)	(₹)
10. Bank a/c	Dr.	6,000	
To share second call a/c			6,000
11. Share capital	Dr.	3,750	
To share forfeiture a/c			2,000
To share allotment a/c			250
To share first call a/c			750
To share second call a/c			750
(Forfeiture of 750 shares, ₹ 5 called up)			

Balance Sheet

Liabilities		(₹)	Assets	(₹)
Authorised capital:			Buildings	40,000
25,000 shares of ₹ 10 each		2,50,000	Bank	37,000
Issued capital:				
12,000 shares of ₹ 10 each		1,20,000		
Subscribed capital:				
4,000 shares of ₹ 10 each fully paid up		40,000		
7,250 shares of ₹ 10 each, ₹ 5 called up	36,250			
Less: Calls unpaid by other than directors	1,250			
	35,000			
Add: Share forfeited amount	2,000			
		37,000		
4,000 shares of ₹ 10 each fully paid up are issued to vendors for consideration other than cash				
		77,000		77,000

Illustration 6: The directors of a company with a subscribed capital of 20,000 equity shares of ₹ 25 each and 20,000 preference shares of ₹ 25 each, on both of which ₹ 20 per share were called up, forfeited 200 equity shares held by A on which he had failed to pay first and second calls of ₹ 5 per share each. They also forfeited 400 preference shares of B who failed to pay ₹ 5 per share on allotment, ₹ 5 per share on first call and ₹ 5 per share on second call. The directors further reissued the forfeited shares of A at ₹ 15 per share and those of B at ₹ 17.50 per share, all of which were taken up and paid for by C.

Pass the necessary journal entries to record the above transactions in the books of the company.

Solution: **Journal Entries**

		(₹)	(₹)
1. Bank a/c	Dr.	2,00,000	
To equity share application			1,00,000
To preference share application			1,00,000
2. Equity share application a/c	Dr.	1,00,000	
Preference share application a/c	Dr.	1,00,000	
To equity share capital a/c			1,00,000
To preference share capital a/c			1,00,000
3. Equity share allotment a/c	Dr.	1,00,000	
Preference share allotment a/c	Dr.	1,00,000	
To equity share capital a/c			1,00,000
To preference share capital			1,00,000

		(₹)	(₹)
4. Bank a/c	Dr.	1,98,000	
To equity share allotment a/c			1,00,000
To preference share allotment a/c			98,000
(All money due on allotment, except on 400 preference shares, received)			
5. Equity share first call a/c	Dr.	1,00,000	
Preference share first call a/c	Dr.	1,00,000	
To equity share capital a/c			1,00,000
To preference share capital a/c			1,00,000
6. Bank a/c	Dr.	1,97,000	
To equity share first call a/c			99,000
To preference share first call a/c			98,000
(All money due on first call, except on 200 equity shares and 100 preference shares, received)			
7. Equity share second call a/c	Dr.	1,00,000	
Preference share second call a/c	Dr.	1,00,000	
To equity share capital			1,00,000
To preference share capital			1,00,000
8. Bank a/c	Dr.	1,97,000	
To equity share second call a/c			99,000
To Preference share second call a/c			98,000
(All money due on second call, except on 200 equity shares and 400 preference shares, received)			
9. Equity share capital a/c	Dr.	4,000	
To equity share first call a/c			1,000
To equity share second call a/c			1,000
To equity share forfeiture a/c			2,000
(Forfeiture of 200 equity shares on which first and second calls were unpaid)			
10. Preference share capital a/c	Dr.	8,000	
To preference share allotment a/c			2,000
To preference share first call a/c			2,000
To preference share second call a/c			2,000
To preference share forfeiture a/c			2,000
(Forfeiture of 400 preference shares on which allotment, first and second calls were unpaid)			
11. Bank (200 × ₹ 15) a/c	Dr.	3,000	
Equity share forfeiture a/c	Dr.	1,000	
To equity share capital a/c			4,000
(Reissue of 200 equity shares at ₹ 15 per share as ₹ 20 called up)			
12. Bank (400 × ₹ 17.50) a/c	Dr.	7,000	
Preference share forfeiture a/c	Dr.	1,000	
To preference share capital a/c			8,000
(Reissue of 400 preference shares at ₹ 17.50 per share as ₹ 20 called up)			
13. Equity share forfeiture a/c	Dr.	1,000	
Preference share forfeiture a/c	Dr.	1,000	
To capital reserve a/c			2,000
(Transfer of balance in forfeiture account to capital reserve)			

Illustration 7: 'X' Co. Ltd. had an authorised capital of ₹ 20,00,000 divided into 20,000 shares of ₹ 100 each, out of which 15,000 shares were issued to the public for subscription. The

terms of issue were that ₹ 20 per share was payable on application. ₹ 20 per share on allotment, ₹ 30 per share on first call and the balance of ₹ 30 per share on second call. All the amounts were duly received except the following :

From A—holding 30 shares, on which the allotment money, and money due on first and second calls were in arrear.

From B—holding 20 shares, on which the first and second calls in arrear.

From C—holding 10 shares, on which the second call money was arrear.

The directors forfeited the shares and reissued the same to D on the following terms:

A's shares were issued at ₹ 90 per share
B's shares were issued at ₹ 70 per share
C's shares were issued at ₹ 50 per share

Give journal entries necessary to record the above transactions, assuming that D had paid the whole amount due from him.

Solution: **Journal Entries**

			(₹)	(₹)
1.	Bank a/c To share application a/c	Dr.	3,00,000	3,00,000
2.	Share application a/c To share capital a/c	Dr.	3,00,000	3,00,000
3.	Share allotment a/c To share capital a/c	Dr.	3,00,000	3,00,000
4.	Bank a/c To share allotment a/c (Allotment money on 14,970 shares received)	Dr.	2,99,400	2,99,400
5.	Share first call a/c To share capital a/c	Dr.	4,50,000	4,50,000
6.	Bank a/c To share first call a/c (First call money on 14,950 shares received)	Dr.	4,48,500	4,48,500
7.	Share second call a/c To share capital a/c	Dr.	4,50,000	4,50,000
8.	Bank a/c To share second call a/c (Second call money on 14,940 shares received)	Dr.	4,48,200	4,48,200
9.	Share capital (60 × ₹ 100) a/c To share allotment (30 × ₹ 20) a/c To share first call (50 × ₹ 30) a/c To share second call (60 × ₹ 30) a/c To share forfeiture (Forfeiture of 60 shares held by A, B and C)	Dr.	6,000	 600 1,500 1,800 2,100
10.	Bank a/c Share forfeiture (balancing figure) a/c To share capital	Dr. Dr.	4,600 1,400	 6,000
11.	Share forfeiture a/c To capital reserve a/c (Transfer of balance in share forfeiture account to capital reserve)	Dr.	700	700

Notes: (*i*) Calculation of share forfeiture amount:

Application money received from A on 30 shares	600
Application and allotment money received from B on 20 shares	800
Application allotment and first call money received from C on 10 shares	700
Total money forfeited	₹ 2,100
(*ii*) Calculation of amount received on reissue of shares:	
Money received on A's shares, 30 × ₹ 90	2,700
Money received on B's shares, 20 × ₹ 70	1,400
Money received on C's shares, 10 × ₹ 50	500
Total amount received on reissue of shares	₹ 4,600

Illustration 8: LLoyds Ltd. was registered with a nominal capital of 2,00,000 in equity shares of ₹ 100 each and 10,000 of these shares were issued to the public at a premium of 20 per cent. The amount payable was as follows:

₹ 20 on application

₹ 45 on allotment (including premium)

₹ 25 on first call

₹ 30 on final call

Applications were received for 13,000 shares and allotment was made as under:

To applicants of 12,000 shares: Pro-rata

To applicants of 1,000 shares: Nil

Amount overpaid on application was employed on account of sums due on allotment. X holding 200 shares paid the entire amount due on first call along with allotment, but failed to pay the final call.

Y holding 300 shares failed to pay the two calls and Z holding 400 shares failed to pay the final call only. All these shares were forfeited after the final call.

Of the shares forfeited 200 shares of Y and 300 shares of Z were sold to Mr P as fully paid for ₹ 90 per share. You are required to prepare the following ledger accounts:

(*i*) Share capital a/c

(*ii*) Share premium a/c

(*iii*) Share allotment a/c

(*iv*) Share first call a/c

(*v*) Share final call a/c

(*vi*) Share forfeiture a/c

Solution:

Dr. **LLoyds Limited: Equity Share Capital Account** **Cr.**

Particulars	(₹)	Particulars	(₹)
To equity share first call a/c	7,500	By equity share application a/c	2,00,000
To equity share final call a/c	27,000	By equity share allotment a/c	2,50,000
To forfeited shares a/c (900 × 100) – 7,500 –27,000)	55,500	By equity share first call a/c	2,50,000
		By equity share final call a/c	3,00,000
To balance c/d	9,60,000	By bank a/c (reissue of forfeited shares)	45,000
		By forfeited shares a/c (discount on reissue)	5,000
	10,50,000		10,50,000

Dr. Equity Share Premium A/c Cr.

Particulars	(₹)	Particulars	(₹)
To Balance c/d	2,00,000	By equity share allotment a/c	2,00,000
	2,00,000		2,00,000

Dr. Equity Share Allotment A/c Cr.

Particulars	(₹)	Particulars	(₹)
To equity share capital a/c	2,50,000	By equity share application a/c	40,000
To equity share premium a/c	2,00,000	By Bank A/c	4,10,000
	4,50,000		4,50,000

Dr. Equity Share First Call A/c Cr.

Particulars	(₹)	Particulars	(₹)
To equity share capital a/c	2,50,000	By bank a/c	2,37,500
		By calls in advance a/c (calls in advance of X)	5,000
		By equity share capital a/c (calls in arrears of Y)	7,500
	2,50,000		2,50,000

Equity Share Final Call A/c

Particulars	(₹)	Particulars	(₹)
To Equity share capital a/c	3,00,000	By bank a/c	2,73,000
		By equity share capital (calls in arrears of X, Y and Z)	27,000
	3,00,000		3,00,000

Forfeited Shares A/c

Particulars	(₹)	Particulars	(₹)
To equity share capital a/c (Discount on reissue)	5,000	By equity share capital a/c	55,550
To capital reserve a/c (see working)	25,000		
To balance c/d	25,500		
	55,500		55,500

Working

Balance in share forfeiture a/c		55,500
Less: Discount on reissue		5,000
Less: Balance to be retained for shares not reissued		50,500
200 shares of × @ 70 (100 – 30)	14,000	
100 shares of Y @ 45 (100 – 55)	4,500	
100 shares of Z @ 70 (100 – 30)	7,000	
		25,500
Transfer to capital reserve		25,000
Amount due on allotment		4,50,000
Less: Excess received on application		40,000
Money received on allotment		4,10,000

Illustration 9: Give Journal entries in each of the following cases:

(*i*) X Ltd. forfeited 100 equity shares of ₹ 10 each held by Vivek Ram on December 15, 2012, for non-payment of first call of ₹ 2 per share and the final call of ₹ 3 per share. These shares were reissued to Ghasita Ram on December 25, 2000 at a discount of ₹ 3.50 per share.

(*ii*) X Ltd. forfeited 200 equity shares of ₹ 10 each, issued at a premium of ₹ 5 per share, held by Motu Ram on December 15, 2012, for non-payment of the final call of ₹ 3 per share. These shares were reissued to Lok Nath on December 25, 2012, at the discount of ₹ 4 per share.

(*iii*) X Ltd. forfeited 150 equity share of ₹ 10 each, issued at a premium of ₹ 5 per share, held by Khotu Ram on December 15, 2012, for non-payment of allotment money of ₹ 8 per share (including share premium ₹ 5 per share), the first call of ₹ 2 per share and the final call of ₹ 3 per share. Out of these, 100 equity shares were reissued to Shree Bhagwan at ₹ 14 per share on December 5, 2012.

(*iv*) XY Ltd. forfeited 100 equity share of ₹ 10 each issued at a discount of 10% held by Raj Kumar on January 5, 2012 for non-payment of the first call of ₹ 2 per share and the final call of ₹ 3 per share. Of these, 50 equity shares were reissued to Shri Kishan at ₹ 8 per share on January 30, 2012, and the rest reissued on March 10, 2012, to Ram Nath at ₹ 7 per share.

(*v*) A company's share capital consists of 20,000 equity shares of ₹ 100 each, ₹ 50 paid up. The company has ₹ 15,00,000 in the reserve fund and ₹ 5,00,000 in the securities premium account. It was resolved that the reserve fund and the share premium account should be capitalized by (*i*) making the existing equity shares full paid without shareholders being required to pay anything, and (*ii*) issuing bonus shares to the shareholders (proportionate to their holdings) for the balance of the amount available, ₹ 100 shares being issued at ₹ 125 per share.

Solution: **Journal Entries**

Date	Particulars	L.F.	(₹)	(₹)
(*i*)				
2012	Share capital a/c	Dr.	1,000	
Dec. 15	To first call in arrears a/c			200
	To final call in arrears a/c			300
	To Share forfeiture a/c			500
	(100 shares of ₹ 10 each forfeited for non-payment of first call and final call of ₹ 2 and ₹ 3 each, respectively)			
2012				
Dec. 25	Bank a/c	Dr.	650	
	Share forfeiture a/c	Dr.	350	
	To share capital a/c			1,000
	(Forfeited shares reissued to Ghasita Ram at a discount of ₹ 3.50 per share)			
Dec. 25	Share forfeiture a/c	Dr.	150	
	To capital reserve a/c			150
	(Balance in share forfeiture a/c transferred To capital reserve a/c)			
(*ii*)				
Dec. 15	Share capital a/c	Dr.	2,000	
	To final call in arrears a/c			600
	To share forfeiture a/c			1,400
	(200 shares of ₹ 10 each held by Motu Ram forfeited for non-payment of final call of ₹ 3 per share)			

Date	Particulars	L.F.	(₹)	(₹)
Dec. 25	Bank a/c Dr. Share forfeiture a/c To share capital a/c (Forfeited share reissued to Lok Nath at a discount of ₹ 4 per share)		1,200 800	 2,000
Dec. 25	Share forfeiture a/c Dr. To capital reserve a/c (Balance in share forfeiture account transferred to capital reserve a/c)		600	 600
(iii) 2012 Dec. 15	 Share capital a/c Dr. Securities premium a/c Dr. To share allotment a/c To first call in arrears a/c To final call in arrears a/c To share forfeiture a/c (150 shares of ₹ 10 each issued at a premium of ₹ 5 per share forfeited for non-payment of allotment money of ₹ 8 including premium of ₹ 5, first call of ₹ 2 per share and final call of ₹ 3 per share)		 1,500 750	 1,200 300 450 300
Dec. 15	Bank a/c Dr. To share capital a/c To securities premium a/c (Of 150 shares forfeited, 100 shares reissued at ₹ 14 per share)		1,400	 1,000 400
Dec. 1	Share forfeited a/c Dr. To capital reserve a/c (Forfeited amount on 100 shares which have been reissued, is transferred to capital reserve a/c)		300	 300
(iv) 2012 Jan. 15	 Share capital a/c Dr. To discount on the issue of shares a/c To first call in arrears a/c To final call in arrears a/c To share forfeiture a/c (Being forfeiture of 100 equity shares of ₹ 10 each issued at a discount of 10% held by Raj Kumar for non-payment of first call of ₹ 2 per share and final call of ₹ 3 per share)		 1,000	 100 200 300 400
Jan. 30	Bank a/c Dr. Discount on the issue of shares a/c Share forfeiture a/c To share capital a/c (Reissue of 50 shares to Shri Kishan @ ₹ 8 per share)		400 50 50	 500
Jan. 30	Share forfeiture a/c Dr. To capital reserve a/c (Balance in share forfeiture a/c of reissued 50 shares transferred to capital reserve a/c)		150	 150
March 10	Bank a/c Dr. Discount on the issue of shares a/c Dr. Share forfeiture a/c Dr. To share capital a/c (Remaining 50 shares reissued @ ₹ 7 per share to Ram Nath)		350 50 100	 500

Date	Particulars	L.F.	(₹)	(₹)
March 10	Share forfeiture a/c To capital reserve a/c (Balance in share forfeiture account transferred To capital reserve account)	Dr.	100	100
(v)	Share call a/c To share capital a/c (Call on shares becomes due @ ₹ 50 per share)	Dr.	10,00,000	10,00,000
	Bonus to shareholders a/c To share call a/c (Bonus applied towards the call of shares)	Dr.	10,00,000	10,00,000
	Securities premium a/c Reserve fund a/c To Bonus to shareholders a/c (Bonus declared to shareholders to make equity shares fully paid without receiving cash)	Dr. Dr.	5,00,000 15,00,000	20,00,000
	Bonus to shareholders a/c To share capital a/c To securities premium a/c (Two Bonus shares issued to the existing shareholders for every 5 shares held)	Dr.	10,00,000	8,00,000 2,00,000

Illustration 10: Hindustan Manufacturing Co. Limited invited applications for 1,00,000 equity shares of ₹ 10 each at a premium of ₹ 2 per share. The shares are payable ₹ 2.50 on application, ₹ 4.50 on allotment (including premium), ₹ 2.50 on first call and ₹ 2.50 on final call.

There were over-subscriptions and applications were received for 1,50,000 equity shares. Pro-rata allotments were made to the applicant for 1,20,000 shares and the remaining applications were totally turned down. Excess money paid on application was adjusted against sums due on allotment.

A, who was allotted 200 equity shares, could not pay the sum due on allotment. B, holding 300 equity shares, could not pay the two calls. The company forfeited his share after the final call was made.

Show the entries in the company's journal.

Solution: **Journal Entries**

			(₹)	(₹)
1.	Bank a/c To share application a/c	Dr.	3,75,000	3,75,000
2.	Share application a/c To share capital a/c To share allotment a/c To bank a/c	Dr.	3,75,000	2,50,000 50,000 75,000
3.	Share allotment a/c To share capital a/c To securities premium a/c	Dr.	4,50,000	2,50,000 2,00,000
4.	Bank a/c To share allotment a/c	Dr.	3,99,200*	3,99,200
5.	Share first call a/c To share capital a/c	Dr.	2,50,000	2,50,000

			(₹)	(₹)
6.	Bank a/c To share first call a/c (First call received on 99,500 shares)	Dr.	2,48,750	 2,48,750
7.	Share capital a/c Securities premium a/c To share allotment a/c To share first call a/c To share forfeiture a/c (Forfeiture of 200 shares held by A)	Dr. Dr.	1,500 400	 800 500 600
8.	Share final call a/c To share capital a/c (Final call due on 99,800 shares)	Dr.	2,49,500	 2,49,500
9.	Bank a/c To final call a/c	Dr.	2,48,750	 2,48,750
10.	Share capital a/c To share first call a/c To share final call a/c To share forfeiture a/c (Forfeiture of 300 shares)	Dr.	3,000	 750 750 1,500

Notes:

(*i*) **Calculation of money received on allotment:**

Total money due on allotment	4,50,000
Less: Money received as advance on share application in respect of 20,000 shares whose money was not returned following pro-rata allotment	50,000
	4,00,000
Less: Calls in arrear in respect of 200 shares as per details given below:	800
	3,99,200

(*ii*) **Calculation of amount due on allotment in respect of 200 shares:**

A applied for $\frac{1,20,000}{1,00,000} \times 200$	240 shares
A remitted as a application money on 240 shares	600
A's application money adjusted towards capital following the allotment of 200 shares	500
A's application money treated as advance towards allotment money	100
Allotment money due from a (including premium)	900
Advance by A on application adjusted towards allotment	100
Net amount due on allotment (which was in arrear) ₹ 900 – ₹ 100	800

(*iii*) On the forfeiture of 300 shares, securities premium account will not be debited.

Illustration 11: Indo-Petro Company Ltd. with an authorised share capital of ₹ 90,00,000 divided into shares of ₹ 10 each issued a prospectus inviting applications for 6,00,000 equity shares of ₹ 10 each issued at a premium of ₹ 2 per share payable as to ₹ 3 with application ₹ 5 on allotment and the balance on first and final call to be made three months after the date of allotment.

Applications were received for 11,00,400 shares.

Applications for 400 shares were rejected, full allotment was made on applications for 1,00,000 shares while pro-rata allotment was made on the remaining applications.

All the allottees paid the allotment money due.

The call was made as scheduled. All the shareholders except one shareholder holding 500 shares paid the money on call. These five hundred shares were forfeited and later reissued as fully paid up shares @ ₹ 13 per share.

Prepare ledger accounts and Cash book.

Solution:

Ledger Accounts

Dr. Equity Share Applications A/c Cr.

Particulars	Amount (₹)	Particulars	Amount (₹)
To bank a/c (400 × 3)	1,200	By bank a/c (11,00,400 × 3)	33,01,200
To share capital a/c (6,00,000 × 3)	18,00,000		
To share allotment a/c (5,00,000 × 3)	15,00,000		
	33,01,200		33,01,200

Dr. Equity Share Allotment A/c Cr.

Particulars	Amount (₹)	Particulars	Amount (₹)
To share capital a/c (6,00,000 × 3)	18,00,000	By equity share applications a/c	15,00,000
To securities premium a/c	12,00,000	By bank a/c	15,00,000
	30,00,000		30,00,000

Dr. Equity Share First & Final Call A/c Cr.

Particulars	Amount (₹)	Particulars	Amount (₹)
To equity share capital a/c (6,00,000 × 4)	24,00,000	By bank a/c (5,99,500 × 4)	23,98,000
		By share capital a/c	2,000
	24,00,000		24,00,000

Securities Premium A/c

Particulars	Amount (₹)	Particulars	Amount (₹)
To balance c/f	12,01,500	By equity shares allotment a/c (6,00,000 × 2)	12,00,000
		By bank a/c (500 × 3)	1,500
	12,01,500		12,01,500

Dr. Equity Share Capital A/c Cr.

Particulars	Amount (₹)	Particulars	Amount (₹)
To equity shares first and final call a/c	2,000	By equity shares applications a/c (6,00,000 ×3)	18,00,000
To equity shares forfeited a/c	3,000		
To balance c/f (6,00,000 × 10)	60,00,000	By equity shares allotment a/c (6,00,000 × 3)	18,00,000
		By equity shares first & final call a/c (6,00,000 ×4)	24,00,000
		By bank a/c (500 × 10)	5,000
	60,05,000		60,05,000

Share Forfeited A/c

Particulars	Amount (₹)	Particulars	Amount (₹)
To capital reserve a/c	3,000	By equity shares capital a/c	3,000
	3,000		3,000

Dr. Capital Reserve A/c Cr.

Particulars	Amount (₹)	Particulars	Amount (₹)
To balance c/f	3,000	By Shares forfeited a/c	3,000
	3,000		3,000

Dr. Cash Book (Bank Column only) Cr.

Particulars	Amount (₹)	Particulars	Amount (₹)
To equity share applications a/c	33,01,200	By equity share applications a/c (400 × 3)	1,200
To equity share allotment a/c (30,00,000 – 15,00,000)	15,00,000	By balance c/d	72,04,500
To shares first & final call a/c (24,00,00 – 2,000)	23,98,000		
To share capital a/c (500 × 10)	5,000		
To securities premium a/c	1,500		
	72,05,700		72,05,700

Illustration 12: A company has decided to increase its existing share capital by making a rights issue to the existing shareholders in the proportion of one new share for every two old shares held. You are required to calculate the price of right if the market value of share at the time of announcement of right issue is ₹ 240. The company has decide to give one share of ₹ 100 each at a premium of ₹ 20 each.

Solution: (₹)

Money invested in purchasing the shares from the market for getting the right issue, 2 × ₹ 240	480
Add: Money paid to the company for getting one share	120
Total money invested for buying 3 shares	600
Average price per share, *i.e.*, 600/3	200
Value of right (*i.e.*, market price—average price)	400

Illustration 13: X Co. Ltd. had issued 2,00,000 6% redeemable preference shares of ₹ 100 each. Under the terms of the issue of shares, redemption was to take place on April 1, 2012. A general reserve of ₹ 1,25,00,000 had already been built up out of past profits. For the purpose of the redemption, 75,000 new 5% preference shares of ₹ 100 each were offered to the public at a premium of ₹ 50, payable in full on application. The new issue was fully subscribed and paid for. Thereupon 6% redeemable preference shares were redeemed. Make journal entries to record the above transactions.

Solution: **Journal Entries**

			(₹)	(₹)
1.	Bank a/c	Dr.	1,12,50,000	
	To 5% preference share capital a/c			75,00,000
	To securities premium a/c			37,50,000
	(Issue of 75,000 5% preference shares of ₹ 100 each at ₹ 50 per share premium)			

			(₹)	(₹)
2.	6% redeemable preference shares capital a/c To 6% redeemable preference share holder a/c	Dr.	2,00,00,000	2,00,00,000
3.	6% Redeemable preference shares holder a/c To Bank a/c (Redemption of preference shares)	Dr.	2,00,00,000	2,00,00,000
4.	General reserve a/c To capital redemption reserve account a/c (Transfer of general reserve to capital redemption reserve account)	Dr.	1,25,00,000	1,25,00,000

Note: The above redemption of preference shares is said to be (*i*) out of profit otherwise available for dividend to the extent of ₹ 1,25,00,000 and (*ii*) out of proceeds of fresh issue to the extent of ₹ 75,00,000.

Illustration 14: The balance sheet of Besto Ltd. as on March 31, 2012, disclosed the following information:

Authorised share capital:	(₹)
5% redeemable preference shares of ₹ 10 each	1,50,000
Ordinary shares of ₹ 10 each 5,00,000	
Paid up capital:	
5% Redeemable preference shares of ₹ 10 each fully paid	1,10,000
Ordinary shares of ₹ 10 each fully paid	3,00,000
Profit and loss account	2,00,000

On April 6, 2012 the preference shares were redeemed at a premium of ₹ 4 per share. The company could not yet trace holders of 1,200 preference shares. On April 8, 2012 a bonus issue of one fully paid ordinary share for every five shares was made.

Show the journal entries to record these transactions (including cash) and show these accounts as they would appear in the balance sheet on April 8, 2012.

Solution: **Journal Entries**

2012			(₹)	(₹)
April 6				
1.	5% Redeemable preference shares a/c Premium on redemption of shares a/c To preference shareholders a/c (Amount due on redemption of preference shares credited to shareholders account)	Dr. Dr.	1,10,000 44,000	1,54,000
2.	Preference shareholder a/c To bank a/c (Amount paid to preference shareholders)	Dr.	1,37,200	1,37,200
3.	Profit and loss a/c To premium on redemption of shares a/c (Premium on redemption of shares transferred to P and L a/c	Dr.	44,000	44,000
4.	Profit and loss a/c To capital redemption reserve account a/c (Transfer of profit to capital redemption reserve account)	Dr.	1,10,000	1,10,000
5.	Capital redemption reserve account a/c To bonus to shareholders a/c (Bonus of one share for five shares declared)	Dr.	1,00,000	1,00,000
6.	Bonus to shareholders a/c To ordinary share capital a/c (Issue of 10,000 ordinary shares)	Dr.	1,00,000	1,00,000

Illustration 15: The following is an extract from the balance sheet of Abhinav Ltd. as on December 31, 2011.

	(₹)	(₹)
Share Capital:		
20,000 12% preference shares of ₹ 50 each fully paid		10,00,000
1,00,000 equity shares of ₹ 10 each		
₹ 7.50 per share of called up	7,50,000	
Less: Calls unpaid	7,500	
		7,42,500
Securities premium account		50,000
General reserve		6,00,000
Calls in advance (Final call on equity shares)		2,500

On January 1, 2012, the board of directors decides the following:

(*i*) The fully paid preference shares are to be redeemed at a premium of 5% in February 2001 and, for that purpose, 50,000 equity shares of ₹ 10 each are to be issued at par to be paid for in full on application in January 2012.

(*ii*) The 1,000 equity shares owned by A, an existing shareholder, who has failed to pay the allotment money of ₹ 250 per share and the first call money of ₹ 2.50 per share, are to be forfeited in the month of March 2012.

(*iii*) The final call of ₹ 2.50 per share is to be made in April 2018.

All the above decisions were duly complied with according to the time schedule laid down.

The amount due on the issue of fresh equity shares and on final call were duly received except from B, who has failed to pay the first call money on his 1,000 shares, has failed to pay the final call money also. These shares of B were forfeited in the month of May 2012.

Of the total shares forfeited, 1,500 were issued to X in June 2012, credited as fully paid at ₹ 9 per share, the whole of A's shares being included.

Pass journal entries in the books of the company to record these transactions and show the relevant items on the liabilities side of the balance sheet (necessarily extract) according to the form prescribed by the Companies Act, 1956. Assume that the resources required for payment are available.

Solution:

Dr. **Journal Entries** **Cr.**

Date	Particulars		Amount (₹)	Amount (₹)
Jan. 2012	Bank A/c	Dr.	5,00,000	
	To equity shares application and allotment a/c			5,00,000
	(Being applications received for 50,000 equity shares, application money ₹ 10 per share)			
	Equity share application & allotment a/c	Dr.	5,00,000	
	To equity share capital a/c			5,00,000
	(Being shares allotted to all the applications)			
Feb. 2012	General Reserves A/c	Dr.	5,00,000	
	To capital redemption reserve a/c			5,00,000
	(Being ₹ 5,00,000 transferred to capital redemption reserve a/c)			

Date	Particulars		Amount (₹)	Amount (₹)
	12% preference share capital a/c Premium on redemption a/c To 12% preference shareholders a/c (Being 20,000 preference shares of ₹ 50 each fully paid due to be redeemed at a premium of 5%)	Dr. Dr.	10,00,000 50,000	 10,50,000
	12% preference shareholders a/c To Bank a/c (Being preference shares redeemed)	Dr.	10,50,000	 10,50,000
	Securities premium a/c To premium on redemption a/c (Being premium paid on redemption met out of the existing securities premium account balance)	Dr.	50,000	 50,000
Mar. 2012	Share Capital A/c To shares forfeited a/c To calls unpaid a/c (Being 1,000 shares held by A forfeited because of non-payment of allotment money and 1st call money of ₹ 2.50 per share each)	Dr.	7,500	 2,500 5,000
Apr. 2012	Share 2nd and final call A/c To share capital a/c (Being 2nd call made on 99,000 shares @ ₹ 2.50 per share)	Dr.	2,47,500	 2,47,500
	Bank a/c Call in advance a/c Call in arrears a/c To share 2nd & final call a/c (Being 2nd call money received except from B on 1,000 shares)	Dr. Dr. Dr.	2,42,500 2,500 2,500	 2,47,500
May 2012	Share capital A/c To shares forfeited a/c To calls in arrears or calls unpaid a/c (Being 1,000 shares of B forfeited because of non-payment of two calls)	Dr.	10,000	 5,000 5,000
June 2012	Bank A/c Share forfeited a/c To share capital a/c (Being 1,500 shares reissued to X @ ₹ 9 per share)	Dr. Dr.	13,500 1,500	 15,000
	Shares forfeited a/c To capital reserve a/c (Being unused balance of shares forfeited a/c in respect of A's 1,000 shares and B's 500 shares transferred to capital reserve a/c)	Dr.	3,500	 3,500

Balance Sheet of Abhinav Ltd.

Liabilities	Amount (₹)	Amount (₹)
Authorised Cop.:		
Preference shares		
Equity shares		
Issued and Subscribed Capital		
1,49,500 shares of ₹ 10 each fully paid	14,95,000	
[illegible]rfeited shares	2,500	14,97,500
[illegible]ital redemption reserve		5,00,000
[illegible]serve		3,500
[illegible] reserve		1,00,000

Illustration 16: The following is the balance sheet at Abhiprya Ltd. as on December 31, 2011.

Particulars	Amount (₹)	Particulars	Amount (₹)
Share capital:		Fixed assets	24,00,000
5,000, 12% redeemable preference shares of ₹ 100 each	5,00,000	Stock	5,00,000
		Debtors	50,000
10,000 equity shares of ₹ 100 each	10,00,000	Cash	50,000
Capital reserve	1,00,000		
Securities premium account	1,00,000		
General reserve	2,00,000		
Profit and loss account	1,00,000		
Current liabilities	10,00,000		
	30,00,000		30,00,000

The preference shares are to be redeemed on January 1, 2012 at 10 per cent premium.

On January 1, 2012, a fresh issue of equity shares was made to the extent it is required under the Companies Act for the purpose of the redemption of preference shares.

The shortfall in cash resources for the purpose of redemption after utilising the proceeds of fresh issue was met by raising a bank loan, the cash balance of ₹ 50,000 being the minimum the company requires for its trading operations.

Draft journal entries in the books of the company to record these share capital transactions and prepare the balance sheet, in the form prescribed by the Companies Act 1956, immediately after redemption.

Solution: Redemption of Preference Shares:

Dr. **Journal Entries** **Cr.**

Particulars		Amount (₹)	Amount (₹)
General reserve a/c	Dr.	2,00,000	
Profit and loss a/c	Dr.	1,00,000	
To capital redemption reserve a/c			3,00,000
(Being the balance of accumulated profits and reserve transferred to capital redemption reserve a/c)			
Bank a/c	Dr.	2,00,000	
To shares application & allotment a/c			2,00,000
(Being fresh issue of equity shares made)			
Shares application and allotment a/c	Dr.	2,00,000	
To shares capital a/c			2,00,000
(Being 2,000 equity shares allotted)			
Bank a/c	Dr.	3,50,000	
To bank loan a/c			3,50,000
(Being bank loan taken to redeem the 5,000 preference shares of ₹ 100 each at a premium of 10%)			
12% Redeemable preference share capital a/c	Dr.	5,00,000	
Premium on redemption a/c	Dr.	50,000	
To preference shareholders a/c			5,50,000
(Being 5,000 preference shares of ₹ 100 each due for redemption at a premium of 10%)			

Particulars		Amount (₹)	Amount (₹)
Preference shareholders a/c To bank a/c (Being preference shares redeemed)	Dr.	5,50,000	 5,50,000
Securities premium a/c To premium on redemption a/c (Being the premium paid on redemption met out of securities premium a/c)	Dr.	50,000	 50,000

Balance Sheet of Abhipraya Ltd.
(After Redemption)

Liabilities	Amount (₹)	Assets	Amount (₹)
Share capital:		Fixed assets	24,00,000
12,000 equity shares of ₹ 100 each	12,00,000	Stock	5,00,000
Capital reserve a/c	1,00,000	Debtors	50,000
Securities premium a/c	50,000	Cash	50,000
Capital redemption reserve a/c	3,00,000		
Current liabilities	10,00,000		
Bank loan a/c	3,50,000		
	30,00,000		30,00,000

Illustration 17: X Co. Ltd. issued 10,000 11% redeemable preference shares of ₹ 100 each at ₹ 105 on December 31, 2012. The terms of issue provide for (*a*), the conversion of ₹ 3,00,000 preference shares into equity shares of ₹ 100 each on December 31, 2014 and (*b*) the redemption of remaining preference shares at ₹ 103 on December 31, 2019. The company accordingly converts and redeems the preference shares.

Just before redemption, the company reserve and surplus comprises: Capital redemption reserve, ₹ 3,00,000, securities premium a/c 50,000, general reserve, ₹ 1,00,000 and P and L appropriation a/c ₹ 21,000.

Journalise since December 31, 2014. Assume that (*i*) the company raises minimum proceeds from fresh issue of shares for the purposes of redemptions and (*ii*) one per cent of the redeemed preference share remain unpaid.

Solution: **Journal Entries**

Date	Particulars		Amount (₹)	Amount (₹)
31.12.2012	Loss on issue of preference shares a/c Bank a/c To preference share capital a/c To securities premium a/c To premium on redemption of preference shares Shares capital a/c (Being the issue 10,000 11% redeemable preference share of ₹ 100 each at ₹ 105, 7,000 shares, being redeemable at a premium of ₹ 3 per share on December 31, 2019)	Dr.	21,000 10,50,000	 10,00,000 50,000 21,000
31.12.2014	11% preference share capital a/c To 11% preference shareholders a/c (Being ₹ 3,00,000 preference shares maturing for conversion into equity)	Dr.	3,00,000	 3,00,000

Date	Particulars		Amount (₹)	Amount (₹)
	11% preference shareholders a/c To equity share capital a/c (Being 11% preference shares of ₹ 3,00,000 converted into equity capital)		3,00,000	3,00,000
31.12.2019	General reserves a/c To capital redemption reserve a/c (Being the balance of general reserve transferred to capital redemption reserve a/c to carry out redemption of preference share capital of ₹ 7,00,000)	Dr.	1,00,000	1,00,000
	Bank a/c To equity share capital a/c (Being new capital issued to meet the requirements of redemption of preference capital of ₹ 7,00,000)	Dr.	6,00,000	6,00,000
	11% preference share capital a/c Premium on redemption of preference share capital a/c To 11% preference shareholders a/c (Being preference share capital of ₹ 7,00,000 maturing for redemption @ premium of 3%)	Dr. Dr.	7,00,000 21,000	7,21,000
	11% preference shareholders a/c To bank a/c (Being 11% preference shareholders paid back with the exception of 1%, *i.e.*, ₹ 7,210)	Dr.	7,13,790	7,13,790

Illustration 18: Determine the amount of fresh issue of shares from the following information relating to Shagoon Leather Works Ltd.

(*i*) Redeemable preference shares ₹ 2,00,000
(*ii*) Premium on redemption 10%
(*iii*) Divisible profits available ₹ 60,000
(*iv*) Balance on general reserve ₹ 40,000
(*v*) Securities premium a/c ₹ 15,000
(*vi*) Fresh issue to be made at a discount of 10%

Solution: Face value of preference shares to be redeemed = ₹ 2,00,000

Premium on redemption of preference shares (10%) = 20,000

Premium on redemption of preference shares amounting to ₹ 20,000 will be met out of securities premium money—₹ 15,000 and out of profits—₹ 5,000.

Profits available for redemption of preference shares

= ₹ 60,000 – ₹ 5,000 + 40,000 = ₹ 95,000.

Therefore, proceeds amounting to ₹ 1,05,000 have to be raised by making a fresh issue of shares. Nominal value of shares to be issued at a discount of 10%

$$= 1,05,000 \times \frac{100}{90}$$

= ₹ 1,16,670

Illustration 19: Swan Limited has a share capital of ₹ 20,00,000 in equity shares of ₹ 10 each. The company declared bonus out of its reserve fund of ₹ 12,00,000 and this bonus is to be paid by issue of fully paid equity shares at a premium of ₹ 5 per shares. Shares are quoted at ₹ 22 on the date of allotment of bonus shares.

Give Journal entries to record the above transaction.

Solution: **Journal Entries**

Particulars		Amount (₹)	Amount (₹)
1. Reserve fund a/c To bonus to shareholders a/c	Dr.	12,00,000	12,00,000
2. Bonus to shareholders a/c To share capital a/c To securities premium a/c (80,000 shares of ₹ 10 each issued as fully paid bonus shares at a premium of ₹ 5 per share as per directors resolution dated)	Dr.	12,00,000	 8,00,000 4,00,000

Note: The market value of ₹ 22 per share has not been considered because entries are to be recorded at the issue price in the books of the company.

Illustration 20: X Ltd. has resolved to utilise ₹ 3,00,000 out of the general reserve balance to declare bonus to the shareholders in the form of payment of final call @ ₹ 3 per share on 1,00,000 equity shares of ₹ 10 each. Alongwith this, the company further decided to utilise the balance of share premium account to issue fully paid-up bonus shares in the ratio of one equity share for every five equity shares held. Show journal entries in the books of X Ltd.

Solution: **Journal Book of X Ltd.**

Particulars		Amount (₹)	Amount (₹)
General reserve account Securities premium account To bonus to equity shareholders account (Utilisation of general reserve for declaring bonus on partly paid up shares and securities premium account for issuing fully paid up bonus shares)	Dr. Dr.	3,00,000 2,00,000	 5,00,000
Equity share final call account To equity share capital account (Final call of ₹ 3 per share on 1,00,000 shares)	Dr.	3,00,000	 3,00,000
Bonus to equity shareholders account To equity share final call account (Amount due from equity shareholders adjusted)	Dr.	3,00,000	 3,00,000
Bonus equity shareholders account To equity share capital account (Issue of fully paid bonus shares in the ratio of one equity share for every five shares held)	Dr.	2,00,000	 2,00,000

Illustration 21: The following is the balance sheet of Associated Enterprises Limited as December 31, 2012.

Liabilities	Amount (₹)	Assets	Amount (₹)
Share capital		Fixed assets	3,00,000
15,000 ordinary shares of ₹ 20 each ₹ 14 per share paid up	2,10,000	Current assets	3,00,000
General reserve	1,00,000		
Profit and loss account	1,00,000		
Securities premium account	20,000		
Capital redemption reserve	1,00,000		

Liabilities	Amount (₹)	Assets	Amount (₹)
Current liabilities	—		
Sundry creditors	60,000		
Bills payable	10,000		
	6,00,000		6,00,000

On January 1, 2014, the company decided:

1. That the partly paid shares are to be converted into fully paid by making a final call of ₹ 6 per share which was duly paid.
2. To issue three fully paid bonus shares for five shares held.
3. That for purpose of bonus issue, the minimum amount should be utilised from general reserve account.

Pass journal entries.

Solution: **Journal of Associated Enterprises Ltd.**

Date	Particulars		Amount (₹)	Amount (₹)
2014 Jan. 1	Equity share final call account To equity share capital account (Amount due on final call)	Dr.	90,000	90,000
	Bank account To equity share final call account (Amount received on account of final call)	Dr.	90,000	90,000
	Capital redemption reserve account Securities premium account Profit and loss account To bonus issue account (Declaration of bonus)	Dr. Dr. Dr.	1,00,000 20,000 60,000	1,80,000
	Bonus issues account To equity share capital account (Issue of equity shares in the ratio of 3 : 5)	Dr.	1,80,000	1,80,000

Illustration 22: The balance sheet of B Co. Ltd. as on March 31, 2012 disclosed the following information:

7% redeemable preference shares of ₹ 100 each, ₹ 70 paid up	2,10,000
Ordinary shares of ₹ 10 each, fully paid up	3,00,000
Profit and Loss a/c	2,10,000

It was decided to redeem preference share at a premium of ₹ 5 per share. The company made a first issue of 10,000 ordinary shares of ₹ 10 each at a premium of 10 per cent on April 7, 2012.

The issue was fully subscribed and paid for on April 15, 2012, the company redeemed all the preference shares. Pass necessary journal entries to record the transactions.

Solution:

Particulars		Amount (₹)	Amount (₹)
Preference share capital call a/c To 7 per cent redeemable preference share capital a/c (Being the final call due on 3,000 preference shares of ₹ 100 each @ ₹ 30 per share)	Dr.	90,000	90,000

Particulars		Amount (₹)	Amount (₹)
Bank a/c To preference share final call a/c (Being the receipt of final call on 3,000 preference shares of ₹ 100 each @ ₹ 30)	Dr.	90,000	 90,000
Bank a/c To share application and allotment a/c (Being the application and allotment money received on 10,000 ordinary shares of ₹ 10 each @ ₹ 11)	Dr.	1,10,000	 1,10,000
Share application and allotment a/c To equity share capital a/c To securities premium a/c (Being the transfer of application and allotment money to equity share capital a/c, premium credited to securities premium a/c)	Dr.	1,10,000	 1,00,000 10,000
Premium on redemption of preference shares a/c 7 per cent preference redeemable preference share capital a/c To preference shareholders a/c (Being the redemption of 3,000 preference shares of ₹ 100 each at a premium of ₹ 5 per share)	Dr. Dr.	15,000 3,00,000	 3,15,000
Preference shareholders a/c To bank a/c (Being the payment made to preference share-holders)	Dr.	3,15,000	 3,15,000
Securities premium a/c Profit and Loss a/c To Premium on redemption of preference Shares (Being the amount of premium on redemption of preference shares written off)	Dr. Dr.	10,000 5,000	 15,000
Profit and loss a/c To capital redemption reserve a/c (Being the transfer of profits to capital redemption reserve to the extent preference shares have been redeemed out of profits)	Dr.	2,00,000	 2,00,000

Illustration 23: X Co. Ltd. decided to redeem their preference shares as on March 31, 2012 on which date their position was as under:

Balance Sheet as on 31st March, 2012

Liabilities	Amount (₹)	Assets	Amount (₹)
Share Capital:		Cash and bank balances	2,00,000
5,000 equity shares of ₹ 100 each fully paid	5,00,000	Other assets	9,00,000
4,000 10% redeemable preference shares of ₹ 50 each, ₹ 25 per share paid	1,00,000		
2,000 9% redeemable preference shares of ₹ 100 each-fully paid up	2,00,000		
Reserves and Surplus:			
Securities premium a/c	10,000		
Capital redemption reserve a/c	1,00,000		
Dividend equalisation fund	1,10,000		
Sundry liabilities	80,000		
	11,00,000		11,00,000

The redemption of all preference shares is to be carried out at premium of 5 per cent. In order to carry out redemption of preference shares it was decided to issue sufficient number of equity shares of ₹ 100 each at a discount of 10 per cent. The new issue was fully subscribed and paid for. The redemption was duly carried out. Pass journal entries to record the above transaction and prepare the balance sheet after redemption.

Particulars		Amount (₹)	Amount (₹)
Preference share final call a/c	Dr.	1,00,000	
To 10% redeemable Preference share capital a/c			1,00,000
(Being the amount of final call due on 4,000 Preference shares of ₹ 50 each @ ₹ 25 per share)			
Bank a/c	Dr.	1,00,000	
To preference share final call a/c			1,00,000
(Being the receipt of final call money on 4,000 preference shares of ₹ 50 each @ 25)			
Bank a/c	Dr.	3,00,060	
To share application and allotment a/c			3,00,060
(Being the receipt of application and allotment money on 3334 equity shares of ₹ 100 each at discount of 10%)			
Share application and allotment a/c	Dr.	3,00,060	
Discount on shares a/c	Dr.	33,340	
To equity share capital a/c			3,33,400
(Being the transfer of application and allotment money on 3,334 shares of ₹ 100 each, discount being 10%)			
10% redeemable preference share capital a/c	Dr.	2,00,000	
9% redeemable preference share capital a/c	Dr.	2,00,000	
Premium on redeemable preference shares	Dr.	20,000	
To preference share holder a/c			4,20,000
(Being the transfer of 10% redeemable preference share capital and 9% redeemable pref. share capital alongwith 5% premium to preference share holders a/c)			
Preference shareholders a/c	Dr.	4,20,000	
To Bank			4,20,000
(Being the payment made to preference shareholders)			
Securities premium a/c	Dr.	10,000	
Dividend equalisation fund	Dr.	10,000	
To premium on redemption of preference			20,000
(Being the shares premium on redemption of preference shares written off)			
Dividends equalisation fund a/c	Dr.	1,00,000	
To capital redemption reserve			1,00,000
(Being the redemption of preference shares out of profit, equal amount transferred to capital redemption reserve a/c)			

Balance Sheet
(After Redemption)

Liabilities	Amount (₹)	Assets	Amount (₹)
8,334 equity shares of ₹ 100 each	8,33,400	Cash and Bank balances	1,80,060
Capital Redemption:		Other Assets	9,00,000
Reserve	2,00,000	Discount on shares	33,340
Sundry liabilities	80,000		
	11,13,400		11,13,400

Note 1: Total amount required to redeem:

Preference shares:

4,000 10% redeemable preference shares of ₹ 50 each	2,00,000
2,000 9% redeemable preference shares of ₹ 100 each	2,00,000
	4,00,000
Add: 5% premium	20, 000
	4,20,000

First securities premium on redemption of preference shares has to be provided out of share premium money and dividend equalisation fund. Thus, profits available for redemption of preference shares (in the form of balance in dividend equalisation fund) are ₹ 1,00,000. So, ₹ 3,00,000 has to be raised by making a fresh issue of equity shares.

Required number of equity share to be issued

$$= \frac{₹\ 3,00,000}{₹\ 90}$$

$$= 3,333 - 1/3 \text{ or } 3,334 \text{ shares}$$

Cash and bank account is prepared to find out cash and bank balance after redemption.

Note 2:

Cash and Bank A/c

Liabilities	Amount (₹)	Assets	Amount (₹)
To balance c/d	2,00,000	By preference shareholders a/c	4,20,000
To share final call a/c (pref. share)	1,00,000	By balance c/d	1,80,060
To share Application and allotment a/c (new issue)	3,00,060		
	6,00,060		6,00,060

UNDERWRITING COMMISSION AND BROKERAGE ON SHARES AND DEBENTURES

A company may enter into an underwriting or brokerage agreement for the sale of its shares and debentures. An underwriter guarantees that if the public do not take up all the shares, the underwriter will himself purchase the remaining shares and thus the company is able to obtain subscription for all the shares issued. The company undertakes to pay an underwriting commission for the services rendered by the underwriters. According to Companies Act, underwriting commission should not exceed 5 per cent of the nominal value of a share and 2½ per cent in the case of debentures.

A brokerage contract is different from an underwriting contract. A broker undertakes only to find buyers who are willing to buy shares and debentures and does not guarantee the sale of a specified number of securities (shares, debentures). Thus, if shares and debentures could not be sold by the company, the broker will not buy the securities which have not been subscribed for.

Illustration 24: Morrel Ltd. issues 10,000 equity shares of ₹ 100 each at par and 500 debentures of ₹ 1,000 each @ ₹ 950. The entire issue has been underwritten by Kapoor and Co., for a commission of 4 per cent on shares and 2 per cent on debentures (nominal value). The entire lot of shares was taken but only 400 debentures were applied for. All applications were accepted. Give journal entries and show the entries in the balance sheet, assuming all amounts have been received.

Solution:

Particulars		Amount (₹)	Amount (₹)
Bank account To equity shares capital account [The issue of ₹ 10,000 shares of ₹ 100 each (payment received) as per directors' resolution no ... dated ...]	Dr.	10,00,000	10,00,000
Bank account Discount on debentures account To debentures account (Issue of 400 debentures of ₹ 1,000 each, payment having been received @ ₹ 950, as per directors' resolution no ... dated ...)	Dr. Dr.	3,80,000 20,000	4,00,000
Kapoor & Co. Discount on debentures account To debentures account (The allotment of 100 debentures to the underwriters, being the debentures not taken up by the public, as per agreement dated ...)	Dr. Dr.	95,000 5,000	1,00,000
Commission on issue of debentures a/c Commission on issue of shares a/c To M/s Kapoor & Co. (The underwriting commission due to the underwriters @ 2% on ₹ 5,00,000 and 4% on ₹ 10,00,000 being respectively the nominal value of debentures and shares issued)	Dr. Dr.	10,000 40,000	50,000
Bank account To Kapoor & Co. (The amount due from the underwriters received)	Dr.	45,000	45,000

Balance Sheet

Liabilities	Amount (₹)	Assets	Amount (₹)
Share capital:		Bank	14,25,000
10,000 equity shares of ₹ 100 each, fully paid	10,00,000	Commission on issue of shares	40,000
		Commission on issue of debentures	10,000
500 debentures of ₹ 1,000 each	5,00,000	Discount on debentures	25,000
	15,00,000		15,00,000

When there is discount on debentures as well as commission or expenses on issue of debentures, it is usual to transfer both to one account named, cost of issue of debentures account. In the above illustration, the entry will be as follows:

Particulars		Amount (₹)	Amount (₹)
Cost of issue of debentures account To commission on issue of debentures a/c To discount on debentures a/c	Dr.	35,000	 10,000 25,000

Partial underwriting—Calculation of liability of underwriter: As explained earlier, if an underwriter underwrites the entire issue, the shares or debentures left unsubscribed by the public will have to be taken up by the underwriter. But if the underwriter undertakes responsibility for only part of the issue, the company will have to set off against the underwriter's undertaking applications received through him (marked applications). Suppose, out of an issue of 20,000 shares, only 12,000 shares are underwritten. Then, if the marked applications amount to 10,800 shares, the underwriter's liability will be 1,200 shares (12,000 – 10,800). But if all the shares are subscribed (even though the marked applications are less than the number underwritten) the underwriter has no liability.

Suppose, A and B, two underwriters, underwrite 4,000 and 6,000 shares. Total applications are for 8,000 shares out of which marked applications are for A 3,500 and for B 4,000. Then the liabilities of A and B for the 2,000 unsubscribed shares (10,000 – 8,000) will be determined as follows:

	A	B
Gross Liability	4,000	6,000
Less: Unmarked application* in the ratio of 4:6	200	300
	3,800	5,700
Less: Marked applications	3,500	4,000
	300	1,700

*Out of total applications for 8,000 shares marked applications are 3,500 for A and 4,000 for B (total 17,500 shares). Hence the remaining are unmarked. Unmarked applications should be 'credited' to the underwriters in the ratio of their gross liability.

If the marked applications for one underwriter exceed his liability, the surplus should be distributed among the other underwriters in the ratio of their gross liability or the ratio of the number of shares underwritten.

Another way of fixing the liabilities of the underwriters is to deduct the marked applications from the gross liability and to distribute the liability for unapplied shares in the ratio of the remaining liability. In the above example, the liabilities of A and B will be fixed as under:

	A	B
Gross liability	4,000	6,000
Less: Marked applications	3,500	4,000
Remaining liability	500	2,000
Liability for unapplied shares, (2,000) in the ratio of 5 : 20	400	1,600

If details of marked applications are not available, all the applications received should be 'credited' to various underwriters in the ratio of their gross liability; only the balance will have to be subscribed by them. It should be noted that if there is only one underwriter who underwriters only part of the issue, the company itself should be treated as an underwriter for the remaining part.

Illustration 25: Perfect Ltd. issues 1,000, 8% debentures of ₹ 1,000 each at a premium of 20 per cent. Sixty per cent of the issue was underwritten by Mehta & Co. 2½ per cent commission. Applications were received for 800 debentures which were accepted and payment for these was received in full. Give journal entries.

Solution: Since Mehta & Co. underwrite 60 per cent of the issue, the company must itself be treated as an underwriter of the remaining 40 per cent. In absence of any information, the application for 800 debentures must be deemed to have been marked 60 per cent in favour of the underwriters, viz. 480 debentures. The underwriters are, therefore, liable to take up 120 debentures (600 – 480).

The journal entries are as follows:

Journal

	Particulars		Amount (₹)	Amount (₹)
1.	Bank account	Dr.	9,60,000	
	To 8% debentures			8,00,000
	To premium on debentures account			1,60,000
	(Allotment of 800 debentures applied for payment being @ ₹ 1,200 per debenture, as per directors' resolution of ...)			

	Particulars		Amount (₹)	Amount (₹)
2.	M/s Mehta & Co. To 8% debentures To premium on debentures account (Allotment of 120 debentures to the underwriters in pursuance of their agreement, dated ...)	Dr.	1,44,000	1,20,000 24,000
3.	Commission on issue of debentures a/c To Mehta & Co. (The commission @ 2½ per cent (maximum allowed by law) on 600 debentures calculated at the issue price of ₹ 1,200 per debenture)	Dr.	18,000	18,000
4.	Bank account To Mehta & Co. (The amount received from the underwriters in settlement)	Dr.	1,26,000	1,26,000

THEORY QUESTIONS

1. What is a share? What are different types of shares?

2. Discuss the different types of preference shares.

3. Can a company issue shares at a discount? What conditions must a company satisfy for issuing shares at a discount?

4. What are the legal provisions as to the utilisation of securities premium money?

5. What do you understand by forfeiture of shares? Can forfeited shares be reissued?

6. What are legal provisions with regard to the redemption of preference shares?

7. What are provisions regarding reissue of forfeited shares?

8. What do you mean by underwriting of commission and brokerage contract.

9. How is the liability of an underwriter is determined?

10. Distinguish between equity shares and preference shares. *(BBA, GGSIP University, March, 2000)*

11. Write notes on Redemption of preference shares. *(BBA, GGSIP University, March, 2000)*

12. Explain the provisions under Companies Act related to rights issue. *(BBA, GGSIP University, December, 2008)*

13. Write notes on:

(*a*) Redemption of debentures

(*b*) Forfeiture of shares *(BBA, GGSIP University, December, 2008)*

14. Write short notes on:

Calls in advance and calls in arrears. *(BBA, GGSIP University, December, 2009)*

15. "Surrender of shares means the return of shares voluntarily by the shareholders". Comment. *(BBA, GGSIP University, December, 2010)*

16. (*a*) State legal provisions regarding issue of shares at discount.

(*b*) What are rights shares? When can these shares be issued?

(*c*) State the purposes for which money received on account of share premium can be used? *(BBA, GGSIP University, December 2010)*

17. What is Booking Building?

18. Explain the procedures under Book Building Process.

19. How is the price fixed under Book Building Process.

20. What is Reverse Book Building?
21. What is Dematerialisation?
22. How does the Depository System operate?
23. What is a Demat Conversion Process?
24. Discuss the advantages of Demat System.
25. How are company, investors and brokers benefited by Demat System?
26. Explain the disadvantages of Demat System.

SELF-EVALUATION EXERCISES

I. Select the correct answer for the following multiple-choice questions

1. A preference share is one which
   (*a*) Enjoys a preferential right regarding payment of dividend
   (*b*) Enjoys a preferential right regarding allotment of shares
   (*c*) Enjoys a preferential right regarding payment of dividend and return of capital
   (*d*) Enjoys a preferential right regarding return of capital.
2. Unless otherwise stated, a preference share is always presumed to be
   (*a*) Cumulative, participating and non-convertible
   (*b*) Non-cumulative, non-participating
   (*c*) Cumulative, non-participating and non-convertible
   (*d*) Non-cumulative, participating and non-convertible.
3. The amount of share premium can be used wholly or in part for
   (*a*) Writing off the preliminary expenses (*b*) Writing off Goodwill
   (*c*) Writing of advertising expenses (*d*) Purchasing fixed assets.
4. Upon forfeiture of shares, share capital account is debited by
   (*a*) Paid up amount (*b*) Calls-in-arrears
   (*c*) Nominal value of such shares (*d*) Called up amount.
5. The profit made on reissue of forfeited shares is transferred to
   (*a*) Capital reserve (*b*) Capital redemption reserve
   (*c*) General reserve (*d*) Profit and Loss a/c.
6. Upon forfeiture of shares originally issued at a discount, on the issue of such shares is
   (*a*) Debited to profit and loss a/c (*b*) Debited to discount on shares a/c
   (*c*) Credited to discount on shares a/c (*d*) Debited to forfeited shares a/c.
7. X Co. Ltd. forfeited 20 shares of ₹ 10 each on which ₹ 5 per share were paid. The company issued these shares @ ₹ 8 as fully paid up. Amount transferred to capital reserve will be
   (*a*) ₹ 40 (*b*) ₹ 60
   (*c*) ₹ 20 (*d*) ₹ 100.
8. X Co. Ltd. forfeited 100 shares of ₹ 10 each on which ₹ 4 per share paid. The company issued 40 shares @ ₹ 8 per share as fully paid. Amount transferred to capital reserve will be
   (*a*) ₹ 400 (*b*) ₹ 160
   (*c*) ₹ 240 (*d*) ₹ 80.
9. Preference shares can be redeemed
   (*a*) Out of profits only

(*b*) Out of proceeds of fresh issue only

(*c*) Out of capital profits only

(*d*) Out of proceeds of fresh issue and/or profits otherwise available for distribution by way and dividend.

10. To the extent preference shares have been redeemed out of profits, amount equal to the face value of preference shares redeemed should be transferred to

(*a*) Development Rebate Reserve (*b*) General Reserve

(*c*) Sinking Fund (*d*) Capital Redemption Reserve.

11. X Co. Ltd. has to redeem 1,000 preference shares of ₹ 100 each at 10 per cent premium. It issues 5,000 equity shares of ₹ 10 each at 10 per cent. Premium amount transferred to capital redemption reserve will be

(*a*) ₹ 1,00,000 (*b*) ₹ 50,000

(*c*) ₹ 55,000 (*d*) ₹ 1,10,000.

12. The liability of shareholders for a company is usually

(*a*) Unlimited

(*b*) Limited to the par or stated value of the share they hold

(*c*) Limited to the amount of their investment in the company

(*d*) Limited to the amount of the company's retained earnings.

13. Which type of share may have dividends in arrears?

(*a*) Cumulative preferred share (*b*) Common share

(*c*) Non-cumulative preferred share (*d*) Government securities.

II. Answer True or False

1. Because its shares have perpetual life and are negotiable, a company had continuous life.

2. Shareholders have limited liability; they may lose whatever they paid for their shares but no more.

3. The company's board of directors has fiduciary responsibilities to its shareholders which in basis terms means that the directors must watch over the shareholders's interests and rights.

4. Cash dividends are paid by companies on their taxable income.

5. Shares have the right to demand that the companies redeem the shares for cash.

6. Preferred share is usually issued only to managers and directors, not to the general public of investors.

7. Preferred share has preference in the claim on cash dividends over common share but the amount of dividends paid to preferred share is limited to a fixed amount per year.

8. Preferred share dividends, like interest on bonds payable, is legally guaranteed by the companies.

9. Common share usually is issued at a price equal to its par value.

10. When par value common share is issued, the amount of par value is put in one account and the excess over par is recorded in a second account, even though the total amount received for the shares may be the only amount reported in the company's balance sheet.

11. The preemptive right gives the shareholders the option of buying new shares to be issued by the company.

12. A company is legally required to pay cash dividends on its common shares every year when net income is earned.

EXERCISES AND PROBLEMS

1. ABC Co Ltd, issued 2,00,000 equity shares of ₹ 10 each at a premium of ₹ 2 per share and 20,000 10% preference shares of ₹ 100 each at a discount of 5% payable as follows:

	Equity shares (₹)	Preference shares (₹)
On Application	2	20
On Allotment	5 (Including Premium)	30
On 1st call	3	25
On Final Call	2	20

All the shares offered were subscribed for public and cash duly received.

Pass necessary journal entries to record the above issue of shares.

2. X Ltd., makes an issue of 10,000 ₹ 100 equity shares, payable as follows:

On Application and Allotment	₹ 50
On First Call	₹ 25
On Second Call	₹ 25

Members holding 400 shares do not pay the second call and the shares are duly forfeited, 200 of which are re-issued as fully paid up at ₹ 50 per share.

Pass journal entries in the books of the company.

[**Ans:** Capital Reserve ₹ 5,000].

3. Cream Ltd. issued 20,000 12% Preference shares of ₹ 100 each at a premium of ₹ 10 per share payable as follows:

On Application	₹ 20
On Allotment	₹ 40 (Including Premium)
On First Call	₹ 25
On Final Call	₹ 25

The application were received for 24,000 shares and the directors allotted 20,000 shares and rejected 4,000 shares with the moneys received there on refunded. The allotment money was duly received, while the first call money was received on 18,000 shares and the final call money on 16,000 shares.

Pass journal entries in the books of the company.

4. K Ltd. issued 1,50,000 shares of 10 each and 10,000 12% preference shares of ₹ 100 each payable as under:

	Equity shares (₹)	Preference shares (₹)
On application	2	20
On allotment	2	30
On first call	3	50
On second call	3	—

The company received application for 2,70,000 equity shares and 9,000 preference shares. Applications totalling 20,000 equity shares were rejected. Allotment on other applications for equity shares was made on pro-rata basis. All applications for preference shares were accepted in full. All moneys were duly received.

Show journal entries for the above mentioned transactions.

5. Wye Ltd. invited public to subscribe 10,000 equity shares of ₹ 100 each at premium of ₹ 10 per share, Payment was to be made as follows;

	(₹)
On application	20
On allotment	40 (including premium)
On first Call	30
On second Call	20

Application totalled for 13,000 shares, applications for 2,000 shares were rejected and allotment was made proportionately to the remaining applicants. The directors made both the calls and all the moneys were received except the final call on 300 shares which were forfeited after the required notice were served. Later 200 of the forfeited shares were issued as fully paid @ ₹ 85 per share.

Journalise these transactions including cash transactions.

6. A Company had forfeited 300 shares of ₹ 10 each of X for non-payment of second call of ₹ 3 per share and 200 shares of Y for non-payment of final call of ₹ 5 per share. It has reissued 400 shares (inclusive of all the forfeited shares of X) at ₹ 8 per share. Record the above in the books of the company.

(**Ans:** Capital reserve: ₹ 300).

7. Give Journal entries in the following:

(*i*) The Board of Directors forfeited 2,000 equity shares (issued at par) on account of non payment of final call of ₹ 2 per share. Later, these shares of ₹ 10 each are reissued as fully paid up at a premium of Re 1 per share.

(*ii*) The company allots 60,000 equity shares of ₹ 10 each as fully paid to the liquidator of V Co. in full satisfaction of purchase consideration of ₹ 6,60,000 for the business purchased from V Co.

(**Ans:** (*i*) Capital Reserve ₹ 16,000, (*ii*) Capital Reserve ₹ 60,000).

8. A company with an authorised capital of ₹ 50,00,000 divided into 50,000 shares of ₹ 100 each, issues the entire amount of shares payable as follows: ₹ 40 with application (including ₹ 20 as premium); ₹ 20 on allotment; ₹ 30 on first call and ₹ 30 on second call.

All the share money is received in full with the exception of the first call on 600 shares and the second call on 1,200 shares (including the 600 shares on which the first call has not been paid).

The above 1,200 shares are duly forfeited and are reissued at ₹ 80 per share payable by the purchase. Draw up the necessary journal entries and show the capital account after the above transactions have been given effect to.

9. Vishwas Ltd. with an authorised share capital of ₹ 90,00,000 divided into shares of ₹ 10 each issued a prospectus inviting applications for 6,00,000 equity shares of ₹ 10 each issued at a premium of ₹ 2 per share payable as to ₹ 3 with application, ₹ 5 on allotment and the balance of first and final call to be made three months after the date of allotment.

Applications were received for 11,00,400 shares. Applications for 400 shares were rejected, full allotment was made on application for 1,00,000 shares while pro-rata allotment was made on the remaining applications.

All the allottees paid the allotment money due.

The call was made as scheduled. All the shareholders except one shareholder holding 500 shares paid the money on call. These 500 shares were forfeited and later reissued as fully paid up shares @ ₹ 13 per share.

Prepare ledger accounts and cash book.

(**Ans:** Cash Book Balance: ₹ 72,04,500).

10. Inco. Ltd. had issued 50,000 redeemable preference shares of ₹ 10 each, ₹ 8 paid. In order to redeem these shares now being redeemable the Company issued for cash 30,000 equity shares of ₹ 10 each at a premium of ₹ 2 per share. Out of the Cash proceeds, the redeemable preference shares were paid and the balance was met out of the reserve fund which stood at ₹ 2,50,000.

Show the journal entries in the books of the company.

(**Ans:** Capital Redemption Reserve Account: ₹ 2,00,000).

11. Sonia Beauty Products Limited issued a prospectus inviting applications for 20,000 shares of ₹ 10 each at a premium of ₹ 2 per share payable as follows:

On Application	₹ 2
On Allotment	₹ 5 (including premium)
On first call	₹ 3
On second call	₹ 2

Applications were received for 30,000 shares and allotment made pro-rata to the applicants for 24,000 shares, the remaining applications being refused .

Money overpaid on applications was employed on account of sums due on allotment.

Reethika to whom 400 shares were allotted, failed to pay allotment money and her subsequent failure to pay the first call, her shares were forfeited. Bithika, the holder of 600 shares failed to pay the two calls, and her shares were forfeited, after the second call had been made. Of the shares forfeited, 800 shares were sold to Geethika credited as fully paid for ₹ 9 per share, the whole of Reethika's shares being included. Show journal and cash book entries and the balance sheet.

(**Ans:** Balance sheet total—₹ 2,40,360)

12. The ledger accounts of MN Ltd. show the following balances:

14% Preference share Capital	₹ 3,00,000
General Reserve	80,000
Securities Premium	20,000
Profit and Loss	38,600
Investment Allowance Reserve	50,000

The Company redeems preference shares at a premium of 10% by issue of equity shares of ₹ 10 each at a premium of 20%. Fresh issue of shares is made in lots of 100 shares for such amount as is necessary after utilising the available source to the maximum extent.

Calculate: (*i*) Number Fresh shares issued, (*ii*) Amount transferred to Capital Redemption Reserve and journal entry for transfer.

(**Ans:** (*i*) Number of Fresh shares issued—18,200, (*ii*) Amount transferred to Capital Redemption Reserve—₹ 1,18,000).

13. Determine the amount of fresh issue of shares from the following information relating to Shagoon Leather Works Ltd.: (*i*) Redeemable preference shares—₹ 2,00,000; (*ii*) Premium on redemption—10%; (*iii*) Divisible profits available—₹ 60,000; (*iv*) Balance in general reserve—₹ 40,000; (*v*) Securities Premium Accounts—₹ 15,000; (*vi*) Fresh issue to be made at a discount of 10%.

(**Ans:** Fresh issue of shares—₹ 1,16,667).

14. Footfault Ltd. had equity capital of ₹ 2,00,000 divided into shares of ₹ 100 each, 11% Cumulative redeemable preference shares of ₹ 100 each for ₹ 1,00,000 and ₹ 50,000 and ₹ 40,000 respectively to the credit of Profit and Loss Account and General Reserve as on 31st March 2009. It had also ₹ 8,000 to the credit of securities Premium Account.

As per the agreement with the preference shareholders, the Directors decided to redeem the shares on 1.4.2009 at a premium of 10%. It was also decided to sell certain investments whose book and market values on 31.3.09 were ₹ 40,000 and ₹ 50,000 respectively to enable redemption.

For purposes of redemption, the Board decided to utilise free reserve to the minimum extent possible. It was decided to issue right equity shares at a premium of 20% to finance the redemption.

After redemption, the Board decided to issue bonus shares to equity holders in the ratio 2 : 5. Holders of 100 preference shares were not traceable.

Show the necessary journal entries to record the above transactions in the books of company and also how the items will appear on the Balance Sheet of the Company.

(**Ans.:** Capital Redemption Reserve—₹ 50,000).

15. The following particulars are given from the books of Standard Products Ltd. relating to issue and forfeiture of equity shares during January to April 2008.

The amount per share was payable as ₹ 3 on application; ₹ 5 on allotment (including ₹ 2 as premium); ₹ 4 on First and Final Call.

	No. of shares allotted	**No. of shares applied for**
Category I	20,000	30,000
Category II	10,000	10,000
Category III	NIL	5,000
		(Application money refunded)

Allotments were made pro-rata in category I.

Mr. Giri who applied for 450 shares in Category I failed to pay Allotment and Call Money and his shares were forfeited by the Directors. Subsequently 200 forfeited shares were reissued to Mr. Puri as fully paid for ₹ 9/- per share.

Show the journal and Cash Book entries to record the above transactions.

(**Ans.:** Amount transferred to Capital Reserve—₹ 700).

ANSWERS TO SELF-EVALUATION EXERCISES

I.

1. (*c*)	**2.** (*c*)	**3.** (*a*)	**4.** (*d*)	**5.** (*a*)	**6.** (*c*)
7. (*b*)	**8.** (*d*)	**9.** (*d*)	**10.** (*d*)	**11.** (*b*)	**12.** (*c*)
13. (*a*)					

II.

1. True	**2.** True	**3.** True	**4.** False	**5.** False	**6.** False
7. True	**8.** False	**9.** False	**10.** True	**11.** True	**12.** False

13

ACCOUNTING FOR DEBENTURES

LEARNING OBJECTIVES

After reading this chapter, you should be able to:

- *Explain* the meaning of debentures
- *Discuss* the different types of debentures
- *Explain* the accounting treatment of issue of debentures, at premium, at discount
- *Understand* the treatment of discount on issue of debentures
- *Explain* the issue of debentures as a collateral security
- *Discuss* issue of debentures with conditions of redemption
- *Discuss* the redemption of debentures, sources of funds for redemption and methods of redemption
- *Discuss* non-convertible debentures with detachable warrants, secured premium notes

MEANING OF DEBENTURES

Debentures are popular means of raising funds by a company. A debenture is an instrument of acknowledgement of debt under the common seal of a company. Terms of the repayment of the principal sum and payment of interest are mentioned in the debenture certificates which are issued to debenture holders. It is usual to prefix a debenture with rate of interest that it carries. Suppose, debentures are issued carrying interest @ 13 per cent, then such debentures will be known as 13 per cent debenture.

CLASSIFICATION OF DEBENTURES

Debentures can be classified in different ways. Different types of debenture classified from various points of view are as follows:

1. Classification in Terms of Security

(*a*) **Secured Debentures/Mortgage Debentures:** These debentures carry some security with them. The security may be some particular asset. In this case, debentures are said to be secured by a fixed charge. Security offered for the debentures could be assets, in general. In that case, debentures are said to be secured by a floating charge.

(*b*) **Simple/Naked Debentures:** Simple or naked debentures are those which do not carry any security behind them.

2. Classification in Terms of Redemption

From redemption point of view, debentures can be classified as redeemable debentures and irredeemable debentures. Redeemable debentures are those debentures which will be repaid by the company at the end of a specified period or in instalments during the lifetime of the company. Repayment of principal sum is made in accordance with the terms already made known at the time of its issue. Irredeemable debentures are those which are repaid only when the company goes into liquidation.

3. Classification in Terms of Records Maintained

From records point of view, debentures can be classified as registered debentures or bearer debentures. Registered debentures are those in respect of which names, addresses and particulars of holding of the debenture holders are registered by the company. In this case, debentures can be transferred by executing a regular transfer deed.

Bearer debentures are those which are transferable by mere delivery. In this case, the company does not keep any record of the debenture holders.

4. Classification in Terms of Priority

From priority point of view, debentures are classified as first debentures and second debentures. First debentures are those which have to be repaid before other debentures are paid out. Debentures which will be repaid when first debentures have been redeemed are termed as second debentures.

5. Classification in Terms of Convertibility

From convertibility point of view, debentures are classified as convertible debentures or non-convertible debentures. Convertible debentures are those which can be converted into equity shares either wholly or in part at the option of the debenture holder. Nowadays convertible debentures are very popular. Non-convertible debentures are those which cannot be converted into equity shares.

ISSUE OF DEBENTURES

Procedure for issue of debentures is the same as that for issue of shares. The intending investors apply for debentures on the basis of prospectus issued by the company. The company may ask for the payment of entire amount of debenture on application or on both application and allotment.

Accounting entries for issue of debentures are as follows:

<table>
<tr><td>1.</td><td>Bank a/c
    To debenture application a/c
(Being the amount received as application money)</td><td>Dr.</td></tr>
<tr><td>2.</td><td>Debenture application a/c
    To debenture a/c
(Being application money transferred to debenture a/c)</td><td>Dr.</td></tr>
<tr><td colspan="3">When issue of debentures is over subscribed the above entry may be passed as under:</td></tr>
<tr><td></td><td>Debenture application a/c
    To debentures a/c
    To debentures allotment a/c
    To bank a/c
(Being the application money appropriated and excess application money refunded)</td><td>Dr.</td></tr>
</table>

3.	Debenture allotment a/c To debenture a/c (Being allotment money due on debentures)	Dr.
4.	Bank a/c To debenture allotment a/c (Being allotment money received)	Dr.

Debentures may be issued at par, at premium or at discount.

Issue of Debentures at Par: Debentures are said to be issued at par when amount collected on debentures is equal to the face value of debentures. In this case, accounting entries passed are the same as given earlier.

Issue of Debenture at Premium: When issue price of debentures is more than the face value of debentures they are said to be issued at premium. Generally, premium money is collected alongwith allotment money. In this case accounting entries are as under:

Bank a/c To debenture application a/c (Being application money received)	Dr.
Debenture application a/c To Debenture a/c (Being application money appropriated)	Dr.
Debenture allotment a/c To debentures a/c To debenture premium a/c (Being allotment money due on debentures and premium credited to debenture premium a/c)	Dr.
Bank a/c To debenture allotment a/c (Being allotment money received)	Dr.

Issue of Debentures at a Discount: When the issue price of the debenture is less than its face value the debenture is said to be issued at a discount. Amount of discount on issue of debentures is generally adjusted at the time of allotment. In this case, accounting entries are as follows:

Bank a/c To debenture application a/c (Being application money received)	Dr.
Debenture application a/c To debenture a/c (Being application money appropriated)	Dr.
Discount on debentures a/c Debenture allotment a/c To debenture a/c (Being allotment money due on debentures, and discount allowed on debentures)	Dr. Dr.
Bank a/c To debenture allotment a/c (Being allotment money received)	Dr.

TREATMENT OF DISCOUNT ON ISSUE OF DEBENTURES

Discount on issue of debentures is a loss of capital nature. It will appear on the asset side of balance sheet till it is written off. It is desirable that it is written off as quickly as possible.

Discount on issue of debentures, being a loss of capital nature, it can be written off in two ways.

First Method: In this case, the total amount of discount on debenture is spread over the life of debentures equally. Suppose the debentures are issued at discount, to be redeemed after five years. The amount of discount will be divided by five and the amount so arrived at will be charged to profit and loss account for five years. This method is followed where debentures are redeemed at the end of a specified period.

Second Method: In this method discount is written off every year in proportion to the amount of debentures used every year. This method is followed where debentures are redeemed every year by serving a notice and by draw of lots.

Accounting entry for writing off discount is as under:

Profit and loss a/c To discount on debenture a/c	Dr.

Example: X Co. Ltd. issues ₹ 1,00,000 debentures on Jan. 1, 2012, at 10 per cent discount. Calculate the amount of discount to be written off each year in each of the following cases:

1. Debentures are to be redeemed at the end of four years.
2. The company redeems ₹ 25,000 debentures each year by draw of lots beginning December 31, 2012.

Solution:

1. The company is to redeem debentures at the end of 4 years. Therefore, the amount of discount to be written off each year will be ₹ $\frac{10,000}{4}$ or ₹ 2,500.
2. The company redeems debentures worth ₹ 25,000 each year. Therefore, discount will be written off proportionately. It is calculated as under:

Year	Amount of debentures used (₹)	Ratio	Discount to be written
1	1,00,000	4	10,000 × 4/10 = 4,000
2	75,000	3	10,000 × 3/10 = 3,000
3	50,000	2	10,000 × 2/10 = 2,000
4	25,000	1	10,000 × 1/10 = 1,000
		10	10,000

ISSUE OF DEBENTURES FOR CONSIDERATION OTHER THAN CASH

Accounting entries which have been discussed above assume that debentures are issued for cash only. Sometimes debentures are issued for consideration other than cash. For example, debentures may be issued in payment of price for the purchase of fixed assets. In such a case accounting entries to be made are as under:

Assets a/c To vendor a/c (Being the purchase of assets)	Dr.

Vendor a/c To debenture a/c (Being the issue of debentures to vendor as payment of the price for assets purchased)	Dr.

ISSUE OF DEBENTURES FOR COLLATERAL SECURITY

Collateral security is secondary security or security in addition to principal security. The company may issue debentures as collateral security for a loan taken either from Bank or from some other institution. These debentures do not carry any rights so long as terms of loan agreement are not breached. In case the loan agreement is violated, the creditor may choose to activate these debentures and acquire the rights of a debenture holder.

Debentures issued as a collateral security may be dealt with in two ways in the books, as mentioned below.

(*i*) **First Method:** In this case, the fact of the issue of debentures as a collateral security may be shown in the balance sheet. For example, X Company has issued 9 per cent 10,000 debentures of ₹ 100 each for a loan of ₹ 10,00,000 taken from a bank. This fact may be shown in the balance sheet as under:

Balance Sheet

Liabilities	(₹)
Bank loan (Secured by the issue of 9 per cent 10,000 debentures of ₹ 10 each as collateral security)	10,00,000

(*ii*) **Second Method:** The issue of debentures as a collateral security may be recorded by means of journal entry:

Debenture suspense a/c To 9% debentures a/c (Being the issue of 10,000, 9% debentures of ₹ 100 each as collateral security for bank loan of ₹ 10,00,000)	Dr.	10,00,000	 10,00,000

Debenture suspense account will appear on the asset side of balance sheet. When the loan is repaid, the above entry will be cancelled by a reverse entry.

9% debenture a/c To debenture suspense a/c (Being the cancellation of 9% debentures a/c as collateral security on repayment of bank loan)	Dr.	10,00,000	 10,00,000

ISSUE OF DEBENTURES WITH CONDITIONS OF REDEMPTION

Debenture with specific conditions of redemption may be issued in any of the following six ways:

(*i*) Debentures issued at par, redeemable at par
(*ii*) Debentures issued at discount, redeemable at par
(*iii*) Debentures issued at premium, redeemable at par
(*iv*) Debenture issued at par, redeemable at premium
(*v*) Debentures issued at discount, redeemable at premium
(*vi*) Debentures issued at premium

Accounting entries for above six cases of issue of debentures are as follows:

(*i*) Debentures issued at par, redeemable at par

Bank a/c	Dr.	
To debentures a/c		

(*ii*) Debenture issued at discount but redeemable at par

Bank a/c	Dr.	(with amount actually received)
Discount on issue of debentures a/c	Dr.	(with discount on issue of debentures)
To debentures a/c		(with the face value of debentures)

(*iii*) Debentures issued at premium, redeemable at par

Bank a/c	Dr.	(with amount of debentures actually received)
To debentures a/c		(with face value of debentures)
To debenture premium a/c		(with premium money)

(*iv*) Debentures issued at par, redeemable at premium

Bank a/c	Dr.	(with amount of debentures actually received)
Loss on issue of debenture	Dr.	(with premium payable on redemption)
To debentures a/c		(With the face value of debentures)
To premium on redemption of debentures.		(with premium money payable on redemption)

(*v*) Debentures issued at discount redeemable at premium

Bank a/c	Dr.	(with amount of debentures actually received)
Loss on issue of debentures a/c	Dr.	(with amount of discount on issue plus premium payable in redemption)
To debentures a/c		(with face value of debentures)
To premium on redemption of debentures a/c		(with premium money payable on debentures)

(*vi*) Debentures issued at premium, redeemable at premium

Bank a/c	Dr.	(with amount of debentures actually received)
Loss on issue of debentures		(with premium payable on redemption)
To debentures a/c		(with face value of debentures)
To debenture premium a/c		(with premium money received)
To premium on redemption of debenture a/c		(with premium payable on redemption)

Interest on Debentures

Interest on debentures is generally paid every six months. Interest on debentures is paid even if company does not earn profit. It may be noted that a company paying interest on debentures is liable to deduct income tax at the prescribed rate from the gross amount of interest before any debenture interest is paid to debenture holders. Accounting entries for payment of interest are as follows:

1.	Debenture interest a/c To debenture holders a/c To income-tax payable a/c (Being the amount of interest due on debentures and income tax deducted at source)	Dr.
2.	Debenture holders To bank a/c (Being amount of interest paid to debenture holders)	Dr.

3. Income tax payable a/c To bank (Being the payment of income tax deducted from gross amount of debentures interest)	Dr.	

REDEMPTION OF DEBENTURES

Redemption of debentures means payment of the amount of debentures by the company. When debentures are redeemed, liability on account of debentures is discharged.

Amount of funds required for redemption of debentures is quite large and, therefore, prudent companies make sufficient provision out of profits and accumulate funds to redeem debentures.

In this connection, The Companies (Amendment) Act, 2000 has introduced section 117 C which provides that:

1. Where a company issues debentures after the commencement of this Act, it shall create a debenture redemption reserve for the redemption of such debentures, to which adequate amounts shall be credited, from out of its profits every year until such debentures are redeemed.
2. The amounts credited to the debenture redemption reserve shall not be utilised by the company except for the purpose aforesaid.

It should also be noted that before the introduction of this section, there was no provision in the Companies Act 1956 for the redemption of debentures. However Securities and Exchange Board of India has provided some guidelines. The relevant points of these guidelines are:

(*i*) Every company shall create DRR in case of issue of debentures redeemable after a period of more than 18 months from the date of issue.

(*ii*) The creation of DRR is obligatory only for non-convertible debentures and non-convertible portion of partly convertible debentures.

(*iii*) A company shall create DRR equivalent to 50% of the amount of debenture issue before starting the redemption of debenture.

(*iv*) Drawal from D.R.R. is permissible only after 10% of the debenture liability has already been redeemed by the company.

SEBI has no powers to administer the provisions of section 117 C. But Sec. 117 C does not specify the amount up to which D.R.R. should be created. In the absence of any such details, one may refer to guidelines issued by SEBI.

Sources of Funds for Redemption of Debentures

So, far as sources of funds for the redemption of debentures are concerned, the company may choose any one of following courses.

1. **Redemption of Debentures out of Capital:** Under this method the company may dispose off some fixed asset and may use the sale proceeds for redemption of debentures. However, it is a very unusual source of finance and is rarely followed.

   Again the company may utilise its working capital to redeem the debentures. This adversely effects the working capital of the company. In either case, the assets of the company are reduced. However, in view of the legal provisions with regard to creation of DRR, redemption of debentures purely out of capital is not possible. In this case, the basic entries for redemption of debentures are passed. They are as follows:

Debenture a/c To debenture holders a/c	Dr.	
Debenture holders a/c To bank a/c	Dr.	

2. **Redemption of Debentures out of Profits:** Redemption of debenture out of profits implies that an amount equal to the face value of the debentures redeemed is transferred to DRR. Thus, a part of the profits of company are withheld from distribution to shareholders.

Accounting entries in this case are as follows:

1. Debentures a/c To debenture holders a/c	Dr.
2. Debenture holders a/c To bank a/c	Dr.
3. Profit and loss appropriation a/c To debenture redemption reserve a/c	Dr.

Debenture redemption reserve account appears on the liabilities side of the balance sheet. The balance in Debenture Redemption Reserve a/c increases with each redemption. When all the debentures are redeemed, the DRR is closed by transferring its balance to general reserve.

Methods of Redemption of Debentures

Debentures may be redeemed in a number of ways. Procedure for redemption of debentures is laid down at the time of issue of debentures and it is in accordance with the provisions of articles of association. The following are the main methods of redemption of debentures:

I. Redemption of debentures in lumpsum at maturity
II. Redemption of debentures by draw of lots
III. Redemption of debentures by purchasing them in the open market
IV. Redemption of debentures by conversion

I. Redemption of Debentures in Lumpsum at Maturity: In this case, debentures are redeemed in one lumpsum at the end of stipulated period. The basic accounting entries for redemption of debentures are:

1. Debentures a/c To debenture holders a/c	Dr.
2. Debenture holders a/c To bank	Dr.

Debentures may be redeemed at par, at premium or at a discount.

When debentures are redeemed at par, the above two entries are passed. When debentures are redeemed at premium, the following accounting entries are passed.

Debenture a/c	Dr.	(with the face value of debentures to be redeemed)
Premium on redemption of debenture a/c	Dr.	(with premium payable on redemption)
To debenture holders a/c		

It may be noted here that 'premium on redemption of debentures a/c' may have opened and credited at the time of issue of debentures. If so, then premium payable on redemption of debentures has only to be transferred to debenture holders account as per first entry. If it has not been opened earlier, it will be debited now and later closed by transferring it to securities premium a/c or profit and loss account.

Debentures may be redeemed at discount though it is an unreal situation and not found in practice. However, in such a case the following entries are passed:

Debentures a/c	Dr.	(with the face value of debentures redeemed)
To debenture holders		(with the amount payable)
To profit on redemption of debentures		(with discount on redemption)

Profit on redemption of debentures is a capital profit. It is used to write-off discount on issue of debentures/shares, otherwise it will be transferred to capital reserve.

As explained earlier, debentures may be redeemed out of capital or out of profits. Prudent companies make arrangements for the redemption of debentures from the very beginning. They set aside a certain sum of money out of profits every year and invest an equivalent amount in first class securities so that necessary funds are available for redemption of debentures at the appropriate time. For investing funds outside the business, the company may follow any of the following two methods:

(*a*) Sinking fund method/debenture redemption fund method

(*b*) Insurance policy method

(*a*) *Sinking Fund Method/Debenture Redemption Fund Method*: Under this method every year the company sets aside a certain part of profits and credits the same to debenture redemption fund. To collect the required funds at the time of redemption, it invests the same in first-class securities. The interest earned in the investments is also invested when the debentures fall due for redemption; investments are sold and sale proceeds utilised for redeeming the debentures.

Under this method, the following accounting entries are passed:

1. Profit and loss appropriation a/c To debenture redemption fund a/c It may be noted that amount to be credited to DR Fund a/c is ascertained from sinking fund tables. 2. Debenture redemption fund investment a/c To bank a/c (Being the amount invested in securities)	Dr. Dr.

The above two entries are passed in the first year. At the end of second year and subsequent years, the following entries will be passed:

1. Bank a/c To Interest on DRF investment (Being interest received on DRF investment a/c)	Dr.
2. Interest on DRF investment a/c To DRF account (Being the interest credited to DRF a/c)	Dr.
3. Profit and loss appropriation a/c To DRF a/c (Being appropriation of profit to DRF a/c)	Dr.
4. DRF investment a/c To bank a/c (Being amount of annual appropriation of profit plus interest received invested in securities)	Dr.

Accounting for last year are as follows:

1. Bank a/c To interest on DRF investments a/c (Being the amount of interest received on investment)	Dr.
2. Interest on DRF investment a/c To DRF a/c (Being the interest credited to DRF a/c)	Dr.
3. Profit and loss appropriation a/c To DRF a/c (Being the amount of Profit transferred to DRF)	Dr.

4. Last year entry for purchase of investments will not be passed as investments are not purchased. Instead entry for sale of investment and redemption of debentures will be passed which are as follows:

Bank a/c	Dr.
To DRF investment a/c	
(Being the sale of investment)	
DRF investment a/c	Dr.
To DRF a/c	Dr.
(Being the profit on sale of investments transferred to DRF a/c)	

For loss on sale of investments reverse entry will be passed. On redemption of debentures, the following entries will be passed.

Debentures a/c	Dr.
To debenture holders a/c	
Debenture holders a/c	Dr.
To bank a/c	

The credit balance in DRF a/c will be transferred to general reserve account. It may be noted here that profit on sales of investment which was earlier transferred to DRF account will be transferred to capital reserve from DRF, these facts are recorded by means of following accounting entry.

Debenture Redemption Fund a/c	Dr.
To general reserve a/c	
To capital reserve a/c (Profit on sale of investment)	

(*b*) *Insurance policy method*: Under this method, the company instead of purchasing investments, takes an insurance policy for an amount which would be adequate for the redemption of debentures. Accounting entries, under this methods are as follows:

First year and subsequent years (including last year)

1.	Debenture redemption fund policy a/c	Dr.
	To bank a/c	
	(Being the payment of premium on DRF policy)	
2.	Profit and loss appropriation a/c	Dr.
	To debenture redemption fund a/c	
	(Being the appropriation of Profit to DR Fund a/c)	

In the last year, when policy amount is realised and debentures are redeemed, the following accounting entries are passed.

1.	Bank a/c	Dr.
	To DRF policy a/c	
	(Being the amount of policy realised)	
2.	Debentures a/c	Dr.
	To debenture holders a/c	
	(Being the amount of debentures transferred to debenture holders a/c	
3.	Debenture holders a/c	Dr.
	To bank	
	(Being payment made to debenture holders)	

4. DRF policy a/c To DRF a/c (Being the profit on insurance policy transferred to DRF a/c)	Dr.
5. DRF Fund a/c To general reserve (Being the balance in DRF transferred to general reserve a/c)	Dr.

II. Redemption of Debentures by Draw of Lots: Under this method, the company redeems debentures each year. The debentures to be redeemed are selected by draw of lots. Accounting entries for redemption of debentures are the same as passed in case debentures are redeemed out of profits. They are as follows:

1. Debenture a/c To debenture holders a/c	Dr.
2. Debenture holders a/c To bank a/c	Dr.
3. Profit and loss appropriation a/c To debenture redemption reserve a/c	Dr.

When all the debentures are redeemed, the balance in DRR account will be transferred to general reserve.

III. Redemption of Debentures by Purchasing them in the Open Market: Sometimes the company purchases the debentures in the open market at its convenience and redeems them. The company may purchase the debentures at par or at premium or at discount.

Accounting entries for the purchase of debentures at par will be as follows:

Debenture a/c To bank a/c	Dr.

If the company purchases the debentures at a premium, the amount paid in excess of the face value will be debited to 'loss on redemption of debentures' which will be transferred to profit and loss account and closed, the entry will be

Debentures a/c Loss on cancellation of debentures account To bank a/c	Dr. Dr.
P&L a/c To loss on cancellation of debentures (If capital reserve a/c or securities premium a/c is available)	Dr.

If the company pays a price which is less than the nominal value of the debentures, the company will make a profit. The entry will be

Debentures a/c To bank a/c To Profit on cancellation of debentures a/c	Dr.
Profit on cancellation of debentures a/c To capital reserve	Dr.

Own Debentures: Sometimes the company may purchase its debentures from the market and, instead of cancelling them, may keep them as investments. In such a case, the cost price of debentures purchased is debited to a new account known as 'own debentures account'. Own debentures may be utilised for reissue when needed afterwards.

Accounting entries for own debentures are:

Own debentures a/c	Dr.
To bank	
(Being the cost price of debentures purchased)	

On Cancellation of Own Debentures: When the actual price paid on purchase of own debentures is less than the face value of debentures, there will profit on cancellation of own debentures. Accounting entry will be:

Debentures a/c	Dr.
To own debentures	
To profit on cancellation of own debentures	
Profit on cancellation of own debentures a/c	Dr.
To capital reserve a/c	

However, if price paid on own debentures is more than the face value of debentures, company will make a loss on cancellations of own debentures. Accounting entry will be as under :

Debentures a/c	Dr.
Loss on cancellation of own debentures a/c	Dr.
To own debentures a/c	

Loss on cancellation of own debentures will be transferred to P&L account.

IV. Redemption of Debentures by Conversion: Sometimes a company redeems debentures by converting them into a new class of shares or debentures. If new debentures are issued in place of old debentures, the accounting entry will be

Debenture a/c	Dr.
To debentures a/c	(New)

In case debentures are redeemed by converting them into equity shares, the entry will be

Debentures a/c	Dr.	(nominal value of debentures
To equity share capital a/c		redeemed)

If the debentures are converted into equity shares at a premium the accounting entry will be

Debentures a/c	Dr.
To equity share capital a/c	
To securities premium a/c	

EX-INTEREST AND CUM-INTEREST QUOTATIONS

Sometimes debentures are purchased in the open market on a date other than the date of payment of interest on debentures. In such a case, distinction must be made between capital and revenue parts of the price paid for debentures. Of the price paid for the debenture, what is capital part and what is revenue part will depend upon the quotation made for the debentures. Quotation price of the debentures may be cum-interest or ex-interest. If the price quoted is cum-interest, it means price quoted for the debentures includes interest for the expired period. If the quotation is ex-interest, it means price of the debenture does not include interest for the expired period and, therefore, the buyer in addition to the quotation price, has to pay interest for the expired period.

At the time of passing entries for the purchase of own debentures, capital part of the price is debited to 'own debentures account' and revenue part of the price is debited to interest account.

Example: X Co. Ltd. buys its own 9 per cent debentures of the nominal value of ₹ 40,000 at ₹ 97 on March 31, 2002. Record the transaction in the books of the company if quotations price is (*i*) cum-interest (*ii*) ex-interest. Company pays interest on debentures on June 30, and December 31.

Solution:

(*i*) Cum-interest			
Own debentures a/c	Dr.	37,900	
Interest a/c	Dr.	900	
To bank a/c			38,800
(Being the purchase of own debentures of ₹ 97 cum-interest)			
(*ii*) Ex-interest			
Own debentures a/c	Dr.	38,800	
Interest a/c	Dr.	900	
To bank a/c			39,700
(Being the purchase of own debentures at ₹ 97 ex-interest)			

Note: Interest for the expired period $= ₹\ \frac{40,000 \times 9 \times 3}{100 \times 100 \times 12} = ₹\ 900$

NON-CONVERTIBLE DEBENTURES (NCD) WITH DETACHABLE WARRANTS

A recent innovation in the Indian stock market is the issue of non-convertible debentures with detachable warrants attached to them. These warrants can be exchanged by the investors for equity shares of the company. The number of equity shares that would be allotted to the investors against the warrants and the time period within which the option is to be exercised by the investors is specified by the company at the time of issue of the non-convertible debentures. When the time for exercising the option comes, the holders of these warrants who wish to exchange them for shares should pay the specified price and will be allotted the specified number of shares. The dividend warrants are intended to act as sweeteners to the NCD issue, and are considered beneficial to the investors because of the potential increase in the market prices of the company's shares.

For instance, Mangalore Refineries and Petrochemicals Ltd. came out with a large issue in May 1992 comprising the issue of equity shares, PCDs and NCDs with detachable warrants.

The terms of the issue of NCDs aggregating ₹ 500 crore were as follows:

NCDs—₹ 200 each

Rate of interest—17.5%

Redemption—5–9 years

Detachable equity warrants to carry the right to apply for one equity share of ₹ 10 at par between eighteen to twenty four months from the date of allotment.

The accounting entries would be as follows.

When the application money of ₹ 50 and the call money of ₹ 150 are received, the 17.5% non-convertible debentures account would show a credit balance of ₹ 500 crore. This would carry interest at 17.5 per cent and would be debited only on redemption between the fifth and the ninth year.

Between eighteen to twenty-four months, the NCD holders who are entitled to apply for equity shares will have to pay up ₹ 10 per share. Assuming that the holders of 2 crore NCDs of Mangalore

Refineries exercise such option, the company would pass the following entry:

		(₹ in crore)	
Bank a/c To equity share capital (Being the option on detachable equity warrants exercised by the NCD holders)	Dr.	20,000	20,000

Recognition of the Liability Under the Equity Warrant Exercisable by the Investor

The entries given above are under the assumption that the equity liability on the warrants are recognised in the company's books only when the option for the same is exercised by the debenture holders. However, an International Accounting Standard on 'Financial Instruments' has been formulated wherein a different treatment is suggested for the equity options. The IAS accounting standard requires a company to recognise the financial liability under the warrant option at the time of issuing the compound instrument (*i.e.*, the financial instrument consisting of the debentures, and the equity option) itself. The liability under the option may be determined by some options valuation model that are available. It is also required that the liability under the debentures and the equity option have to be segregated and shown separately—the debenture liability along with such similar bond instruments and that under the equity option under share capital.

However, since there is no such legal or accounting standard requirement in India and the equity warrants themselves are new instruments, it is yet to be seen how companies actually account for the same and whether they make any disclosure regarding the equity options in their balance sheets.

It is most desirable, however, that even if companies do not account for the equity options until such options are exercised, specific disclosures as to the number of such warrants issued, the price that is to be paid for converting them into shares and the time within which such options are to be exercised, etc. are given by way of a note to the Balance Sheet in order to facilitate analysis and future projections of the company's prospects and commitments.

Illustration 1: Show by means of journal entries how you will record the following issues. Also show how they will appear in their respective balance sheets:

(*a*) A Ltd. issues 5,000 10% debentures of ₹ 1,000 each at a discount of 5% redeemable at the end of 5 years at par.

(*b*) B Ltd. issues 5,000 11% debentures of ₹ 100 each at premium of 5% redeemable at the end of 5 years at par.

(*c*) C Ltd. issues 5,000 12% debentures of ₹ 100 each at a discount of 5% redeemable at the end of 5 years at a premium of 5%.

(*d*) D Ltd. issues 5,000 13% debentures of ₹ 100 each at a premium of 5% redeemable at the end of 5 years at a premium of 5%.

Solution:

(*a*) **In the Books of A Ltd.**

Journal Entries

		(₹)	(₹)
Bank a/c Discount on issue of debentures a/c To 10% debentures a/c (Issue of 5,000 10% debentures of ₹ 100 each at a discount of 5% redeemable at par as per board's resolution dated)	Dr. Dr.	4,75,000 25,000	5,00,000

Balance Sheet of A Ltd.
(as on ...)

Liabilities	(₹)	Assets	(₹)
Secured loan 10% debentures redeemable at par at the end of...	5,00,000	Balance at bank **Misc. Expenditures:** Discount on issue of debentures	4,75,000 25,000

(*b*) **In the Books of B Ltd.**
Journal Entries

		(₹)	(₹)
Bank a/c	Dr.	5,25,000	
To 11% debentures a/c			5,00,000
To premium on debentures a/c			25,000
(Issue of 5,000 11% debentures of ₹ 100 each at par redeemable at premium of 5% as per boards resolution dated ...)			

Balance Sheet of B Ltd.
(as on ...)

Liabilities	(₹)	Assets	(₹)
Reserves and Surplus: Premium issue of debentures	25,000	Balance at bank	5,25,000
Secured loans: 11% debentures	5,00,000		
	5,25,000		5,25,000

(*c*) **In the Books of C Ltd.**
Journal Entries

		(₹)	(₹)
Bank a/c	Dr.	4,75,000	
Discount on issue of debentures a/c	Dr.	25,000	
Loss on issue of debentures a/c	Dr.	25,000	
To 12% debentures a/c			5,00,000
To Premium on redemption of debentures a/c			
(Issue of 5,000 12% debentures of ₹ 100 each at a discount of 5% redeemable at a premium of 5% as per board's resolution dated ...)			25,000
Note: Alternatively, the entry may be			
Bank a/c	Dr.	4,75,000	
Loss on issue of debentures a/c	Dr.	50,000	
To 12% debentures a/c			5,00,000
To premium on redemption of debentures a/c			25,000

Balance Sheet of C Ltd.

Liabilities	(₹)	Assets	(₹)
Secured loans:		Balance at bank	4,75,000
12% debentures	5,00,000	**Misc. expenditure:**	
Current liabilities & provisions:		Discount on issue of debentures	25,000
Premium on redemption of debentures	25,000	Loss on issue of debentures	25,000
		Alternatively	
		Loss on issue of debentures	50,000

(*d*)

In the Book of D Ltd.
Journal Entries

		(₹)	(₹)
Bank a/c	Dr.	5,25,000	
Loss on issue of debentures a/c	Dr.	25,000	
To 13% debentures a/c			5,00,000
To premium on issue of debentures a/c			25,000
To premium on redemption of debentures a/c			25,000
(Issue of 5,000 13% debentures of ₹ 100 each at a premium of 5% redeemable at a premium of 5% as per board's resolution dated ....)			

Balance Sheet of D Ltd.
(as at.....)

Liabilities	(₹)	Assets	(₹)
Reserves & surplus:		**Misc. expenditure:**	
Premium on issue of debentures	25,000	Loss on issue of debentures	25,000
Secured loans:		Bank	5,25,000
13% debentures	5,00,000		
Current liabilities & provisions:			
Premium on redemption of debentures	25,000		

Illustration 2: X Ltd. issued for subscription 5,000 debentures of ₹ 100 each at a discount of 3%. The whole of the issue offered was underwritten by Paul and Co., commission being 2.5 per cent on nominal value. The public subscribed ₹ 4,00,000 worth of debentures, balance being allotted to Paul & Co. which on a subsequent date released their holdings in the market. The company took power to issue additional debentures worth ₹ 50,000 which were issued to its bank as collateral security against a loan of ₹ 10,000.

Show the entries in the cash book and ledger of the company and show how the entries would appear in the balance sheet.

Solution:

Debentures

	(₹)		(₹)
To closing balance	5,00,000	By Bank	3,88,000
		By Paul & Co.	97,000
		By Discount	15,000
	5,00,000		5,00,000

Paul & Co.

	(₹)		(₹)
To debentures	97,000	By commission	12,500
		By bank	84,500
	97,000		97,000

Cash Book

	(₹)		(₹)
To debentures	3,87,500	By Balance	5,12,500
To Paul & Co.	85,000		
To loan	40,000		
	5,12,500		5,12,500

Balance Sheet

	(₹)		(₹)
Debentures	5,00,000	Bank	5,12,500
Loan	40,000	Debentures discount	15,000
(Secured by the issue of ₹ 50,000 debentures as collateral security)		Underwriters commission on issue of debentures	12,500
	5,40,000		5,40,000

Note: Cash book and balance sheet should not ordinarily be totalled as the accounts shown there are only a part of the total picture.

Illustration 3: A limited company disbursed ₹ 1,00,000 worth of debentures, which were issued as follows:

(*a*) To sundry persons for cash at 90% 50,000 nominal
(*b*) To a creditor for ₹ 20,000 capital expenditure in satisfaction of his claim 25,000
(*c*) To bankers as collateral security 25,000

The issues 1 and 2 are redeemable at the end of 10 years at par. How should the debentures be dealt with in preparing the balance sheet of the company?

Solution:

(*a*) Debentures of ₹ 50,000 issued for cash to sundry persons at 90% will be shown on the liability side of the balance sheet. Discount on issue ₹ 5,000 will appear on the assets side under the main heading 'miscellaneous expenditure'. Cash received on them—₹ 15,000—will be merged with the cash of the company and final balance of cash will appear in the balance sheet.

(*b*) ₹ 25,000 debentures were issued for the capital expenditure of ₹ 20,000. It means debentures of ₹ 5,000 (₹ 25,000 – ₹ 20,000) were issued for goodwill. Assets of ₹ 20,000 and goodwill of ₹ 5,000 will be shown on the assets side. Debentures of ₹ 25,000 will be shown on the liability side.

(*c*) Loan of ₹ 25,000 will he shown on the liability side.

The equivalent amount will be added to the bank balance on the assets side. In addition to this on the liability side a narration will be given under the heading secured loan: "Loan is secured by the debentures of ₹ 25,000 issued as collateral security".

Illustration 4: A company issued debentures of the par value of ₹ 1,00,000 at a discount of 6%. The debentures were repayable by annual drawings of ₹ 20,000. How would you deal with the discount on debentures? Show discount account in the company's ledger for the period of duration of debentures.

Solution: Debenture discount can be written off in two ways:

(*a*) Equally over the life of the debentures. Since debentures are for five years, every year fifth of the discount can be taken to profit and loss account.

(*b*) In the ratio of amount used. Since in this case the plan of redemption is given it is possible to write off discount in the ratio of amount used. If it is done, then it will be written off as under:

Years	Debentures Outstanding	Ratio	Discount written off
1st year	1,00,000	5	5/15 × ₹ 6,000 = 2,000
2nd year	80,000	4	4/15 × ₹ 6,000 = 1,600
3rd year	60,000	3	3/15 × ₹ 6,000 = 1,200

Years	Debentures Outstanding	Ratio	Discount written off
4th year 5th year	40,000 20,000	2 1	2/15 × ₹ 6,000 = 800 1/15 × ₹ 6,000 = 400
		15	6,000

The debenture discount account in the second case will appear as under:

Debenture Discount

Date	Particulars	(₹)	Date	Particulars	(₹)
1st Year Jan. 1	To debenture	6,000	1st Dec. 31	By profit and loss By closing balance	2,000 4,000
		6,000			6,000
2nd year Jan. 1	To opening balance	4,000	2nd Dec. 3	By profit and loss By closing balance	1,600 2,400
		4,000			4,000
3rd year Jan. 1	To opening balance	2,400	3rd year Dec. 31	By profit and loss By closing balance	1,200 1,200
		2,400			2,400
4th year Jan. 1	To opening balance	1,200	4th year Dec. 31	By profit and loss By closing balance	800 400
		1,200			1,200
5th year Jan. 1	To opening balance	400	5th year Dec. 31	By Profit and loss	400
		400			400

Illustration 5: POR Ltd. issued 50,000 12% debentures of ₹ 100 each at par on April 2012. The issue was fully subscribed, interest is payable semi-annually on September 30 and March 31. On September 1, 2008, the company purchased 500 of its own debenture at ₹ 97 *ex-interest.* Again, on January 1, 1998 the company purchased 1,000 of its own debentures at ₹ 98 *cum-interest.* If all the 1,500 debentures were cancelled on March 31, 2013 the profit on redemption of debentures on cancellation will be:

(*a*) ₹ 3,500
(*b*) ₹ 9,000
(*c*) ₹ 6,500
(*d*) ₹ 6,000
(*e*) None of the above

Solution: Purchase value of debentures on 1.9.2012

500 × 97 = ₹ 48,500

Since it is quoted at ex-interest, ₹ 97 represents the price paid for the debentures, it does not include interest.

	(₹)
Purchase value of debentures on 1.1.2013	
100 × 98	= 98,000
Less: Interest @ 12% p. a. for the period 1.10.12–31.12.12	= 3,000
1,00,000 × 12/100 × 3/12 = 3,000	
Purchase value	95,000

Since the quote is cum-interest, the amount paid towards interest should be excluded.

Total purchase value of own debentures

= ₹ (48,500 + 95,000)

= ₹ 1,43,500

Face value of the debentures = ₹ 1,500 × 100 = ₹ 1,50,000

Profit and redemption = ₹ (1,50,000 – 1,43,500)

= ₹ 6,500

Choice (*c*) is correct

Illustration 6: X Co. Ltd. issued 10 per cent debentures for ₹ 6,00,000 on January 1, 2012. These debentures were to be redeemed after four years from the date of issues, *i.e.*, on Dec. 31, 2015. The company decided to create a debenture redemption fund for the purpose and purchased investment earning interest @ 5 per cent p.a. Sinking fund tables show that .232012 invested annually at 5 per cent amount to Re 1 in four years. On the due date, investment were sold for ₹ 4,40,000 and debentures were redeemed. Pass necessary journal entries to record the above transactions for 4 years. Also, prepare necessary accounts. Bank balance before redemption on the due date was ₹ 2,45,000.

Solution: The annual investment (excluding interest) required is

6,00,000 × .232012 = 1,39,207.20

Journal Entries **Amount in (₹)**

Date	Particulars		(₹)	(₹)
2012				
Jan.1	Bank a/c	Dr.	6,00,000	
	To 10% debentures a/c			6,00,000
	(Being the issue of 10% debentures a/c)			
Dec. 31	Profit and loss appropriation a/c	Dr.	1,39,207.20	
	To debenture redemption fund a/c			1,39,207.20
	(Being the amount of profit credited to DRF a/c)			
Dec. 31	Debenture redemption fund Investment a/c	Dr.	1,39,207.20	
	To bank a/c			1,39,207.20
	(Being the purchase of investments)			
2013				
Dec. 31	Bank a/c	Dr.	6,960.36	
	To interest on DRF investment a/c			6,960.36
	(Being interest received debentures)			
Dec. 31	Interest on DRF investment a/c	Dr.	6,960.36	
	To DRF a/c			6,960.36
	(Being interest received on DRF investment transferred to DRF a/c)			
Dec. 31	P&L appropriation a/c	Dr.	1,39,207.20	
	To DRF a/c			1,39,207.20
	(Being amount of profit transferred to DRF a/c)			
Dec. 31	DRF investment a/c	Dr.	1,46,167.56	
	To bank a/c			1,46,167.56
	(Being the purchase of investments)			

Date	Particulars		(₹)	(₹)
2014				
Dec. 31	Bank a/c	Dr.	14,268.74	
	To interest on DRF investment a/c			14,268.74
	(Being interest on investments received)			
Dec. 31	Interest on DRF investment a/c	Dr.	14,268.74	
	To DRF a/c			14,268.74
	(Being interest credited to DRF a/c)			
Dec. 31	Profit and loss approprition a/c	Dr.	1,39,207.20	
	To DRF a/c			1,39,207.20
	(Being amount of profit credited to DRF a/c)			
Dec. 31	DRF investment a/c	Dr.	1,53,475.94	
	To bank a/c			1,53,475.74
	(Being the purchase of investments)			
2015				
Dec. 31	Bank a/c	Dr.	21,942.53	
	To interest on DRF a/c			21,942.53
	(Being interests on investments)			
Dec. 31	Interest on DRF investments a/c	Dr.	21,942.53	
	To DRF a/c			21,942.53
	(Being interest on DRF investment a/c transferred on DRF a/c)			
Dec. 31	Profit and Loss appropriation a/c	Dr.	1,39,207.20	
	To DRF a/c			1,39,207.20
	(Being amount of profit credited DRF a/c)			
Dec. 31	Bank a/c	Dr.	4,40,000	
	To DRF investment a/c			4,40,000
	(Being the sale of investment)			
Dec. 31	DRF investment a/c	Dr.	1,149.30	
	To DRF investment a/c			1,149.30
	(Being the profit and sale of investment credited DRF a/c)			
Dec. 31	10% debentures a/c	Dr.	6,00,000	
	To debenture holders a/c			6,00,000
	(Being debentures transferred to debenture holders a/c)			
Dec. 31	Debenture holders a/c	Dr.	6,00,000	
	To bank a/c			6,00,000
	(Being payment made to debenture holders)			
Dec. 31	DRF a/c	Dr.	6,01,149.73	
	To general reserve a/c			6,00,000.43
	To capital reserve			1,149.30
	(Being transfer of balance in DRF a/c to general reserve a/c profit on sale of investments being transferred to capital reserve a/c)			

10% Debenture a/c

Date	Particulars	(₹)	Date	Particulars	(₹)
2012			**2012**		
Dec. 31	To balance c/d	6,00,000	Jan. 1	By bank a/c	6,00,000
2013			**2013**		
Dec. 31	To balance c/d	6,00,000	Jan. 1	By balance b/d	6,00,000

Date	Particulars	(₹)	Date	Particulars	(₹)
2014			**2014**		
Dec. 31	To balance c/d	600,000	Jan. 1	By balance b/d	6,00,000
2015			**2015**		
Dec. 31	To debenture holders	6,00,000	Jan. 1	By balance b/d	6,00,000

Debenture redemption fund a/c

Date	Particulars	(₹)	Date	Particulars	(₹)
2012			**2012**		
Dec. 31	To balance c/d	13,920.20	Dec. 31	By P&L appropriate a/c	13,920.20
2013			**2013**		
Dec. 31	To balance c/d	2,85,374.76	Jan. 1	By balance b/d	1,39,207.20
			Dec. 31	By interest on DRF	6,960.36
			Dec. 31	By profit and loss appropriation a/c	6,960.36
		2,85,374.76			2,85, 374.76
2014			**2014**		
Dec. 31	To balance c/d	4,38,850.70	Jan. 1	By balance b/d	2,85,374.76
			Dec. 31	By interest on DRF investment a/c	14,268.74
			Dec. 31	P&L appropriation a/c	13,920.20
		4,38,850.70			4,38,850.70
2015			**2015**		
Dec. 31	To G. reserve a/c	6,00,000.43	Jan. 1	By balance b/d	4,38,850.70
			Dec. 31	By Interest on DRF investment	21,942.53
	To capital reserve a/c	1,149.30	Dec. 31	By P&L appropriation a/c	1,39,207.20
			Dec. 31	By DRF investment a/c	1,149.30
		6,01,149.73			6,01,149.73

Debenture Redemption Fund Investment a/c

Date	Particulars	(₹)	Date	Particulars	(₹)
2012			**2012**		
Dec. 31	To bank a/c	1,39,207.20	Dec. 31	By balance c/d	1,39,207.20
2013			**2013**		
Jan. 1	To balance b/d	1,39,207.20	Dec. 31	By balance c/d	2,85,374.76
Dec. 31	To Bank a/c	1,46,167.56			
		2,85,374.76			2,85,374.76
2014			**2014**		
Jan. 1	To balance b/d	2,85,374.76	Dec. 31	By balance c/d	4,38, 850.70
Dec 31	To bank	1,53,475.94			
		4,38,850.70			4,38,850.70
2015			**2015**		
Jan. 1	To balance b/d	4,38,850.70	Dec. 31	By bank a/c	4,40,000
Dec. 31	To DRF a/c	1,149.30			
		4,40,000			4,40,000

Debenture Holders a/c

Date	Particulars	(₹)	Date	Particulars	(₹)
2015			**2015**		
Dec. 31	To bank a/c	6,00,000	Dec. 31	By 10% debenture a/c	6,00,000

Bank a/c

Date	Particulars	(₹)	Date	Particulars	(₹)
2015			**2015**		
Dec. 31	To balance b/d	2,45,000.00	Dec. 31	By 10% debenture a/c	6,00,000.00
Dec. 31	To interest DRF investment a/c	21,942.53		By balance c/d	1,06,942.53
Dec. 31	To DRF investment	4,40,000.00			
		7,06,942.53			7,06,942.53

Illustration 7: A company issued 20,000 9 per cent debentures of ₹ 100 each on Jan. 2012 redeemable after 3 years. The company took an insurance policy of ₹ 20,00,000 for redemption of debenture and paid ₹ 6,50,000 as annual premium. At the end of the third year, policy amount was received and debentures were redeemed. Prepare necessary ledger accounts.

Solution: **9% Debentures a/c**

Date	Particulars	(₹)	Date	Particulars	(₹)
2012			**2012**		
Dec. 31	To balance c/d	20,00,000	Jan. 1	By bank	20,00,000
2013			**2013**		
Dec. 31	To balance c/d	20,00,000	Jan. 1	By balance b/d	20,00,000
2014			**2014**		
Dec. 31	To debenture holders a/c	20,00,000	Jan. 1	By balance b/d	20,00,000

Debenture holders a/c

Date	Particulars	(₹)	Date	Particulars	(₹)
2012			**2012**		
Dec. 31	To bank a/c	20,00,000	Dec. 31	By 9% deb.	20,00,000

Debenture Redemption Fund a/c

Date	Particulars	(₹)	Date	Particulars	(₹)
2012			**2012**		
Dec. 31	To balance c/d	6,50,000.00	Dec. 31	By P&L appropriation	6,50,000.00
2013			**2013**		
Dec. 31	To balance	13,00,000.00	Jan. 1	By balance b/d	6,50,000.00
			Dec. 31	By P&L appropriation	6,50,000.00
		13,00,000,00			13,00,000.00
2014			**2014**		
Dec. 31	To general reserve	20,00,000	Jan. 1	By balance b/d	13,00,000
			Dec. 31	By P&L appropriation	6,50,000
			Dec. 31	By DRF Fund	50,000
		20,00,000			20,00,000

Debenture Redemption Fund Policy a/c

Date	Particulars	(₹)	Date	Particulars	(₹)
2012			**2012**		
Jan. 1	To bank (premium)	6,50,000	Dec. 31	By balance c/d	6,50,000
2013			**2013**		
Jan. 1	To balance b/d	6,50,000	Dec. 31	By balance c/d	13,00,000
Jan. 1	To bank	6,50,000			
		13,00,000			13,00,000
2014			**2014**		
Jan. 1	To balance b/d	13,00,000	Dec. 31	By bank a/c	20,00,000
Jan. 1	To Bank	6,50,000			
Dec. 31	To DRF Fund	50,000			
		20,00,000			20,00,000

Illustration 8: ABC Co. Ltd. had issued 9 per cent ₹ 5,00,000 debentures divided into 5,000 debentures of ₹ 100 each redeemable at any time by the company after giving three month's notice. Under the terms of the issue, the company had the power to purchase its own debentures and either resell them or cancel them. On Jan. 1, 2012 the following were the balances in the relevant accounts in the books of the company:

	(₹)		(₹)
Debentures issued	4,50,000	Debenture redemption fund a/c	3,00,000
Own debentures a/c (par value ₹ 5,000)	4,300	Debentures redemption fund investments a/c	2,80,000

During the year 2012, the following were the transactions relating to the above:

(*a*) Purchased 'own' debentures of par value ₹ 3,000 at ₹ 3,200

(*b*) Resold own debentures held at the beginning of the year for ₹ 5,000

(*c*) Interest received on DRF investments, ₹ 28,000

(*d*) Annual appropriation to debenture redemption fund a/c—₹ 50,000

(*e*) Purchased investments—₹ 75,000

(*f*) Own debentures held on 31.12.2004 were cancelled

Show ledger accounts relating to above.

Solution:

9% Debentures a/c

	(₹)		(₹)
To own debentures a/c	3,000	By balance b/d	4,50,000
To balance c/d	4,47,000		
	4,50,000		4,50,000
		By balance b/d	4,47,000

Own Debentures a/c

	(₹)		(₹)
To balance b/d (Fund value 5,000)	4,300	By Bank (Sale FV ₹ 5,000)	5,000
To Bank (Face value 3,000)	3,200	By 9% debenture a/c	3,000
To DRF a/c (Profit on sale of own debentures)	700	By DRF a/c (loss on cancellation)	200
	8,200		8,200

Debenture Redemption Fund

	(₹)		(₹)
To own debentures a/c	200	By balance b/d	3,00,000
To general reserve a/c	3,000	By own debentures a/c	700
To balance c/d	3,75,550	By bank (Int.)	28,000
		By P&L Approp. a/c	50,000
	3,78,700		3,78,700
		By balance b/d	3,75,500

Debenture Fund Investment a/c

	(₹)		(₹)
To balance b/d	2,80,000	By balance c/d	3,55,000
To bank	75,000		
	3,55,000		3,55,000
To balance b/d	3,55,000		

Note: Amount equal to the face value of own debentures cancelled is transferred to general reserve.

Illustration 9: On July 1, 2012, a company issued 2,000, 6% debentures of ₹ 100 each. The interest is payable on June 30 and December 31 every year. The company is allowed to purchase its own debentures which may be cancelled or kept or reissued at the company's option. The company made the following purchases by cheque in the open market.

On May 31, 2013 — 200 debentures @ ₹ 98 ex-interest

On September 30, 2014 — 100 debentures @ ₹ 97 cum-interest

The debentures, which were purchased on May 31, 2013, were cancelled on December 31, 2014. All payments were made on due dates.

Give journal entries to record the above transactions (including receipts and payments) and also the relevant items in the Balance Sheet as on December 31, 2014.

Solution: **Journal of ...Co. Ltd.**

Date	Particulars		Dr. (₹)	Cr. (₹)
2012				
July 1	Bank a/c	Dr.	2,00,000	
	To 6% debentures account			2,00,000
	(Issue of 2,000 6% debentures of ₹ 100 each at par)			
Dec. 31	Debenture interest account	Dr.	6,000	
	To bank account			6,000
	(Payment of the half-yearly interest on debentures)			
2013				
May 31	Own debentures account	Dr.	19,600	
	Debenture interest account	Dr.	500	
	To bank account			20,100
	(Purchase of 200 debentures ₹ 98 ex-interest; interest for 5 months paid in addition to purchase price)			
2014				
June 30	Debenture interest account	Dr.	5,500	
	To bank account			5,400

Date	Particulars		Dr. (₹)	Cr. (₹)
	To interest on own debentures a/c (Interest on 1,800 debentures paid and interest on own debentures for month credited to interest on own debenture)			100
2014 Sept 30	Own debentures a/c Interest a/c To bank (Being own debentures purchased at cum-interest)	Dr. Dr.	9,550 150	 9,700
2014 Dec. 31	6% debentures a/c To own debentures a/c To profit on redemption (Being the debentures purchased on May 31, 2013 cancelled ex-interest)	Dr.	20,000	 19,600 400

Balance Sheet as on December 31, 2014

Liabilities	(₹)	Assets	(₹)
6% debentures	2,00,000	Own debentures	95,500

Illustration 10: XYZ Ltd. had the following among their ledger opening balances as on January 2012.

11% debentures a/c (1993 issue)	₹ 50,00,000
Debenture redemption fund a/c	45,00,000
13.5% debenture in XX Ltd. a/c (Face value ₹ 20,00,000)	19,50,000
Own debentures a/c (Face value ₹ 20,00,000)	18,50,000

The face value of a debenture was ₹ 100.

As December 31, 2012, was the date for redemption of the 1993 debentures, the company started buying own debentures and made the following purchases in the open market.

1.2.2012 2,000 debentures at ₹ 98 cum-interest.

1.6.2012 2,000 debentures at ₹ 99 ex-interest. Half-yearly interest is due on the debentures on the June 30, and December 31, in the case of both the companies.

On December 31, 2012, the debentures in XYZ Ltd. were sold for ₹ 95 each *ex-interest.* On that date, the outstanding debentures of XYZ Ltd. were redeemed by payment or by cancellation.

Show the entries in the following ledger accounts of XYZ Ltd. during 2012.

(*a*) Debenture redemption fund a/c

(*b*) Own debenture a/c

(Round off calculations to the nearest rupee).

Solution: **In the Books of XYZ Ltd.**

Debenture Redemption Fund a/c

Date	Particulars	(₹)	Date	Particulars	(₹)
2012			**2012**		
Dec. 31	To debentures in XX Ltd. (Loss on sale of investment)	50,000	Jan. 1	By balance b/d	45,00,000
			Dec. 31	By interest on debenture in XY Ltd.	2,70,000
	To general	49,73,000		By interest on own debentures	2,53,000
		50,23,000			50,23,000

Own Debenture Account

Date	Particulars	(₹)	Date	Particulars	(₹)
2012			2012		
Jan. 1	To balance b/d	18,50,000	Dec. 31	By 11% debentures	24,00,000
Feb. 1	To bank a/c	1,94,167			
June 1	To bank a/c	1,98,000			
Dec. 31	To balance c/d	1,57,833			
	Transferred to debenture redemption fund				
		24,00,000			24,00,000

Working Note:

13.5% Debentures in XX Ltd.

Date	Particulars	(₹)	Date	Particulars	(₹)
2012			2012		
Jan. 1	To balance b/d (Face value 20,00,000)	19,50,000	June 30	By Bank (Half yearly interest)	1,35,000
Dec. 31	To debenture redemption fund	2,70,000	Dec. 31	By Bank (Half yearly interest)	1,35,000
			Dec. 31	By Bank (Sale @ 95 as ex-interest)	19,00,000
1992		(₹)		1992	(₹)
				By debenture redemption fund (Loss on sale)	50,000
		22,20,000			22,20,000

Illustration 11: On June 30, 2007, the following balances stood in the books of a company (₹)

6% first mortgage debentures 4,00,000

Debenture redemption reserve fund 4,26,160

The above fund was invested in the following securities:

₹ 2,40,000, 4.75% government loan, 2000 2,42,520

₹ 1,90,000, 4.5% government loan, 2008–2013 1,83,640

To redeem the debentures on June 30, 2007, the above investments were sold on the same day as under:

4.75% government loan, 2000 at par,

4.5% government loan 2008–2013 at ₹ 96

Draw up the necessary accounts; bring down their balance, if any, after the redemption of debentures and state how they will be disclosed in the balance sheet of the company.

Solution:

6% First Mortgage Debentures

2007	Particulars	(₹)	2007	Particulars	(₹)
June 30	To Bank	4,00,000	June 30	By opening balance	4,00,000

Debenture Redemption Reserve Fund

2007	Particulars	(₹)	2007	Particulars	(₹)
June 30	To debenture redemption reserve fund investments	3,760	June 30	By opening balance	4,26,160
	To general reserve	4,22,400			
		4,26,160			4,26,160

Debenture Redemption Reserve Fund Investments

2007	Particulars	(₹)	2007	Particulars	(₹)
June 30	To opening balance	4,26,160	June 30	By bank 4 3/2% government loan at par	2,40,000
				4.5% government loan at (96/100 × ₹ 1,90,000)	1,82,400
			June 30	By Debenture redemption reserve fund (transfer of loss on sale of investments)	3,760
		4,26,160			4,26,160

Note: General reserve account—₹ 4,22,400—will be shown in the balance sheet on the liability side under the main heading 'reserves and surplus'. All the above three accounts, *i.e.*, 6% first mortgage debenture account, debenture redemption reserve fund account and debenture redemption reserve fund investment account, will stand closed on the redemption of debentures.

Illustration 12: The following is the summarised balance sheet of Nalanda Steel Products Ltd. on December 31, 2012.

Liabilities	(₹)	Assets	(₹)
Share capital:		Freehold property	2,50,000
₹ 10 shares	2,50,000	Other fixed assets	2,00,000
General reserve	50,000	Current assets	2,50,000
Profit and loss a/c	2,50,000		
14% debentures	50,000		
Current liabilities	1,00,000		
	7,00,000		7,00,000

The company has had the freehold property professionally valued and decides to include it in the balance sheet at its valuation of ₹ 4,00,000.

At the same time, it is proposed to:

(*a*) Capitalise part of the undistributed profits by making a bonus issue to the shareholders of one ₹ 10 share for every five shares held;

(*b*) Create a reserve of ₹ 25,000 for the replacement of fixed asset (in addition to the aggregate depreciation of ₹ 50,000 already provided);

(*c*) Redeem one-half of outstanding debentures at a premium of 5 per cent.

Assuming that the appropriate resolutions have been adopted, pass journal entries in the books of the company to give effect to the above and set out the balance sheet as it would appear after the completion of all the transactions.

Solution: **Books of Nalanda Steel Products Ltd.**

Journal Entries

Particulars		Dr. Amount (₹)	Cr. Amount (₹)
Freehold property a/c	Dr.	1,50,000	
To capital reserve a/c			1,50,000
(Being revaluation of the property)			
Profit & loss a/c	Dr.	50,000	
To bonus to shareholders a/c			50,000
(Being bonus made out of undistributed profits)			

Particulars		Dr. Amount (₹)	Cr. Amount (₹)
Bonus to shareholders a/c	Dr.	50,000	
To equity share capital a/c			50,000
(Being bonus shares issued)			
Profit & loss a/c	Dr.	25,000	
To fixed asset replacement reserve a/c			25,000
(Being assets replacement reserve created)			
14% debentures a/c		25,000	
Premium on debentures redemption a/c		1,250	
To 14% debenture holders a/c			26,250
(Being redemption of 1/2 of the debentures at 5% Premium)			
14% debenture holders a/c	Dr.	26,250	
To bank a/c			26,250
(Being debenture holders paid)			
Profit & loss a/c	Dr.	25,000	
To general reserve a/c			25,000
(Being amount transferred to reserves a/c because of debentures having been redeemed)			
Profit & loss a/c	Dr.	1,250	
To Premium on debenture redemption a/c			1,250
(Being debenture redemption premium charged to the profit & loss a/c)			

Balance Sheet of Nalanda Steel Products Ltd.
(as on .....)

Liabilities	Amount (₹)	Assets		Amount (₹)
Share Capital 30,000 equity shares of ₹ 10 each	3,00,000	Freehold property	2,50,000	
		Appreciation	1,50,000	
Reserve & surplus: Assets replacement reserve	25,000			4,00,000
		Fixed assets		2,00,000
General reserve	75,000	Current assets	2,50,000	
Capital reserve	1,50,000	*Less*: Paid	26,250	
Profit & loss a/c	1,48,750			2,23,750
14% debentures a/c	25,000			
Current liabilities	1,00,000			
	8,23,750			8,23,750

Notes:

(*i*) The above balance sheet must be presented in the exact form prescribed.

(*ii*) The profit & loss a/c (utilisation) is as under:

Profit & Loss a/c

	(₹)		(₹)
To bonus shares	50,000	By balance b/f	2,50,000
To reserve a/c	25,000		
To asset replenishment reserve a/c	25,000		

	(₹)		(₹)
To premium on debentures redemption a/c	1,250		
To balance c/f	1,48,750		
	2,50,000		2,50,000

Illustration 13: On January 1, 2012 Shiwalik Breweries Ltd. had ₹ 8,00,000 5% debentures, outstanding in its books redeemable on December 31, 2012.

On January 1, 2012 the balance on sinking fund was ₹ 7,49,000 represented by:

(*i*) ₹ 1,00,000 own debentures purchased at an average price ₹ 99;

(*ii*) ₹ 6,60,000 nominal value of 3% war loan.

The amount annually credited to the sinking fund was ₹ 28,400.

The interest on debentures was paid by the company every year on December 31, and interest on war loan was received also on December 31 annually.

On December 31, 2012, the outside investments were realised at 98 per cent and all the outstanding debentures were redeemed on that date.

You are required to write up the necessary ledger accounts for the year 2012 in the books of the company.

Solution:

Books of Shiwalik Breweries Ltd.

Dr. **Sinking Fund a/c** **Cr.**

Date	Particulars	Amount (₹)	Date	Particulars	Amount (₹)
31.12.2012	To loss on sale of 3% war loan	3,200	01.01.2012	By balance b/f	7,49,000
			31.12.2012	By P&L a/c (Annual credit)	28,400
	To general reserves (Final transfer)	8,00,000		By interest on own debenture a/c	5,000
				By interest on 3% war loan a/c	19,800
				By profit on cancellation of own debentures a/c	1,000
		8,03,200			8,03,200

Dr. **5% Debentures a/c** **Cr.**

Date	Particulars	Amount (₹)	Date	Particulars	Amount (₹)
31.12.2012	To own debentures a/c	1,00,000	01.01.2012	By balance b/f	8,00,000
	To 5% debenture holders a/c	7,00,000			
		8,00,000			8,00,000

Dr. **Sinking Fund Investment a/c** **Cr.**

Particulars	Own debentures a/c	3% war loan	Particulars	Own debentures a/c	3% war loan
1.1.2012			31.12.2012		
To balance b/f	99,000	6,50,000	By 5% debentures a/c (Cancellation)	1,00,000	

Particulars	Own debentures a/c	3% war loan	Particulars	Own debentures a/c	3% war loan
31.12.2012					
To sinking fund a/c (profit)	1,000		By bank a/c (98%)		6,46,800
			By sinking fund a/c		3,200
	1,00,000	6,50,000		1,00,000	6,50,000

Working Notes:

1. Own debentures are shown as investments at cost, *i.e.*, at ₹ 93.3% war loan should have been purchased at ₹ 6,50,000 as total investments should equal to total balance of sinking fund a/c, *i.e.*, ₹ 7,49,000.
2. 3% war loan realises 98% of its face value, *i.e.*, ₹ 6,60,000 less 2% or ₹ 6,46,800 whereas it was acquired at ₹ 6,50,000.
3. Profit on cancellation of own of debentures is ₹ 1,000.

Illustration 14: The following was the balance sheet of Brite Ltd. as on March 31, 2012.

Liabilities	(₹)	Assets	(₹)
7,500 equity shares of ₹ 100 each	7,50,000	Fixed assets	7,80,000
2,000 15% preference shares of ₹ 100 each	2,00,000	Debenture redemption fund investments	88,500
General reserve	6,30,000	Stock	6,00,800
Profit and loss account	50,000	Debtors	2,60,700
Debenture redemption fund	88,480	Cash at bank	3,00,000
12% debentures	1,00,000		
Sundry creditors	2,11,520		
	20,30,000		20,30,000

On this date, the company redeemed at a premium of 5% all its preference shares and debentures. For the purpose, it sold all the investments for ₹ 90,000 and allotted to its existing equity shareholders 1,500 equity shares of ₹ 100 each at par the entire amount being received forthwith.

After the redemption of preference shares and debentures, the company issued one fully paid bonus share of ₹ 100 for every three shares held. Show journal entries for all the above mentioned transactions, including cash transactions, and prepare the balance sheet thereafter.

Solution:

Books of Brite Ltd.
Journal Entries

Particulars		Dr. Amount (₹)	Cr. Amount (₹)
Bank a/c	Dr.	90,000	
To debenture redemption fund investments a/c			88,500
To profit on DRF investments			1,500
(Being DRF investment sold for ₹ 90,000)			
Profit on DRF investments a/c	Dr.	1,500	
To debenture redemption fund a/c			1,500
(Being profit made on sale of DRF investments transferred to DRF a/c)			
Bank a/c	Dr.	1,50,000	
To equity shares applications and allotment a/c			1,50,000
(Being applications received for 1,500 equity shares of ₹ 100 each, the application money being ₹ 100 per share)			

Particulars		Dr. Amount (₹)	Cr. Amount (₹)
Equity share application and allotment a/c		1,50,000	
To equity share capital a/c			1,50,000
(Being 1,500 equity shares of ₹ 100 each allotted)			
General reserves a/c	Dr.	50,000	
To capital redemption reserve a/c			50,000
(Being transfer from general reserve)			
15% redeemable preference share capital a/c	Dr.	2,00,000	
Premium on redemption of Preference share capital a/c	Dr.	10,000	
To 15% Pref. share holders a/c			2,10,000
(Being 15% Pref. share holders paid back)			
15% Pref. share holders a/c	Dr.	2,10,000	
To bank a/c			2,10,000
12% debentures a/c	Dr.	1,00,000	
Premium on redemption of debentures a/c		5,000	
To 12% debentureholder a/c			1,05,000
(Being 12% debentures redeemed at a premium of 5%)			
12% debenture holders a/c	Dr.	1,05,000	
To bank a/c			1,05,000
(Being 12% debenture holders paid back)			
General reserve a/c	Dr.	10,000	
To Premium on redemption of RPS capital a/c			10,000
(Being premium paid on redemption of RPS capital met out of general reserves a/c)			
DR a/c	Dr.	5,000	
To premium on redemption of debentures a/c			5,000
(Being premium paid on redemption of debentures charged to DR fund a/c)			
DR a/c	Dr.	84,980	
To general reserve a/c			84,980
(Being the balance of DRF a/c transferred to general reserves as debentures are redeemed)			
General reserves a/c	Dr.	2,50,000	
To bonus to equity shareholders a/c			2,50,000
(Being bonus shares to be issued to equity shareholders in ratio of 1:3)			
Bonus equity shareholders a/c	Dr.	2,50,000	
To equity share capital a/c			2,50,000
(Being bonus shares allotted)			

Notes: It is presumed that bonus shares are issued only to the existing 7,500 equity shareholders. Otherwise, bonus shares to be issued will be of ₹ 3,00,000.

Balance Sheet of Brite Ltd.
(as on .....)

Liabilities	(₹)	Assets	(₹)
Equity share capital a/c 11,500 equity share of ₹ 100 each fully paid up	11,50,000	Fixed assets	7,80,000
		Stocks	6,00,800
Capital redemption reserves a/c	50,000	Debtors	2,60,700
General reserves a/c	4,04,980	Bank	2,25,000

Liabilities	(₹)	Assets	(₹)
Profit & Loss a/c	50,000		
Creditors	2,11,520		
	18,66,500		18,66,500

Illustration 15: The share capital of Mayur Industries Ltd. consisted of 50,000 equity shares of ₹ 10 each fully paid. The company has accumulated out of profits a reserve fund of ₹ 5,00,000. It issued further 10,000 equity shares during 2012 at a premium of ₹ 30 per share and the entire amount had been realised.

During 2012, an independent valuation of its assets increased the balance sheet values as follows:

Land and buildings by ₹ 6,00,000
Plant and machinery by ₹ 3,00,000
Stores and spares by ₹ 2,00,000

The valuation reduced the amounts of the following:

Goodwill by ₹ 1,50,000
Patents by ₹ 1,00,000

At the end of 2012, it was decided to redeem 3,000 debentures of ₹ 100 each at 5 per cent premium; to adopt the new valuation and to allot two equity shares of ₹ 10 each as fully paid bonus shares for every equity share held.

It was also decided that the balance of reserve fund, after carrying out all the above arrangements, was to be capitalised.

Pass journal entries to record these transactions in the books of Mayur Industries Ltd.

Solution: **Books of Mayur Industries Ltd.**

Journal Entries

Particulars		Dr. Amount (₹)	Cr. Amount (₹)
Bank a/c	Dr.	4,00,000	
To share applications and allotment a/c			4,00,000
(Being the money received on 10,000 shares)			
Share applications and allotment a/c	Dr.	4,00,000	
To share capital a/c			1,00,000
To securities premium a/c			3,00,000
(Being allotment made 10,000 shares of ₹ 10 each, premium being ₹ 30 per share)			
Land and buildings a/c	Dr.	6,00,000	
Plant and machinery a/c	Dr.	3,00,000	
Stores and spares a/c	Dr.	2,50,000	
To revaluation a/c			11,50,000
(Being upward revision in the values of above assets)			
Revaluation a/c	Dr.	2,50,000	
To goodwill a/c			1,50,000
To patents a/c			1,00,000
(Being downward revision of these assets)			
Revaluation a/c	Dr.	9,00,000	
To capital reserve a/c			9,00,000
(Being the profit made on the revaluations transferred to capital reserve a/c)			

Particulars		Dr. Amount (₹)	Cr. Amount (₹)
Debentures a/c Premium on redemption a/c To debenture holders a/c (Being 3,000 debentures of ₹ 100 each due for redemption at a premium of 5%)	Dr. Dr.	3,00,000 15,000	3,15,000
Reserve fund a/c To capital reserve a/c (Being an amount equal to that of debentures to be redeemed transferred to capital reserve a/c, redemption being out of profits)	Dr.	3,00,000	3,00,000
Securities premium a/c To Premium on redemption a/c (Being the premium payable on redemption of debentures met out of securities premium a/c)	Dr.	15,000	15,000
Debenture holders a/c To bank a/c (Being the payment to the debenture holders)	Dr.	3,15,000	3,15,000
Reserve fund a/c To capital reserve a/c (Being balance of the reserve fund ₹ 2,00,000 also transferred to capital reserve a/c)	Dr.	2,00,000	2,00,000
Capital reserve a/c To bonus to shareholders a/c (Being bonus shares to be allotted to the old 50,000 equity shares in the ratio of 2 equity shares of ₹ 10 each for every equity share held)	Dr.	10,00,000	10,00,000
Bonus to shareholders a/c To equity share capital a/c (Being bonus shares issued)	Dr.	10,00,000	10,00,000

Illustration 16: The balance sheet of a company as on December 31, 2012, contained the following items:

(*i*) Authorised capital—10,000 shares of ₹ 100 each.

(*ii*) Issued and subscribed capital of 5,000 shares fully paid.

(*iii*) 100 5% mortgage debentures of ₹ 1,000 each redeemable on October 1, 2013.

(*iv*) Profit and loss account (Cr.) ₹ 1, 17,350.

Given below are some of the company's transactions for the year 2013:

(*a*) On the recommendation of the directors the company at its annual general meeting held on June 15, 2013, decided to distribute ₹ 1,00,000 in the form of fully paid bonus shares which were to rank for dividend out of the profits of the company for the year 2013.

(*b*) With a view to raising funds for the redemption of debentures, the remaining shares were issued at a premium of ₹ 30 per share payable as to ₹ 80 on application and the balance on allotment which took place on September 1, 2013. The money due on allotment were all received by September 20, 2013. These right shares were to qualify for dividend from October 1, 2013.

(*c*) The debentures were redeemed on due date at a premium of 5 per cent but the payment on ten debentures remained unclaimed up to the end of the year. The premium on redemption on debentures was met out of the securities Premium Account.

(*d*) The net profits of the company for the year-ended December 31, 2013 after providing for taxation and depreciation amounted to ₹ 1,50,000 out of which the directors transferred ₹ 50,000 to general reserve and recommended a divided of 10 per cent for the year 2013.

You are required to:

(*i*) record the foregoing transactions in the company's journal and cash book, and

(*ii*) show the relevant balances in the sheet on December 31, 2013.

Solution: **Journal Entries**

	Particulars		**Dr. Amount (₹)**	**Cr. Amount (₹)**
1.	P&L appropriation a/c	Dr.	1,00,000	
	To bonus to shareholders a/c			1,00,000
	(Being bonus of ₹ 1,00,000 appropriated)			
2.	Bonus to shareholders a/c	Dr.	1,00,000	
	To share capital a/c			1,00,000
	(Being bonus declared)			
3.	Bank a/c	Dr.	3,20,000	
	To share appropriation allotment a/c			3,20,000
	(Being application money received on 4,000 shares @ ₹ 80 per share)			
4.	Shares allotment a/c	Dr.	5,20,000	
	To share capital a/c			4,00,000
	To security premium a/c			1,20,000
	(Being allotment made of 4,000 shares of ₹ 100 each at a premium of ₹ 30 each)			
5.	Bank a/c	Dr.	2,00,000	
	To share allotment a/c			2,00,000
	(Being money due on allotment received on 4,000 shares @ ₹ 50 each)			
6.	5% debentures a/c	Dr.	1,00,000	
	Premium on redemption of debenture a/c	Dr.	5,000	
	To 5% debenture holders a/c			1,05,000
	(Being 5% debentures redeemed at a premium of 5%)			
7.	5% debenture holders a/c	Dr.	94,500	
	To bank a/c			94,500
	(Being amount paid back to the debenture holders except on 10 debentures)			
8.	Securities premium a/c	Dr.	5,000	
	To premium on redemption of debenture a/c			5,000
	(Being premium on redemption of debenture met out of the securities premium a/c)			
9.	P&L appropriation a/c	Dr.	1,15,000	
	To general reserves a/c			50,000
	To dividends payable a/c			65,000
	(Being appropriations made out of profits for reserves and dividends @ 10% for 1992)			

Notes:

1. Dividends declared have been calculated as under:

For 1/2 year on Bonus Issue of ₹ 1,00,000	₹ 5,000
For full year on old capital of ₹ 5,00,000	₹ 50,000
For 3 months of Rights Equity Issue of ₹ 4,00,000	₹ 10,000
	₹ 65,000

2. Cash book has not been shown separately.
3. Balances in the balance sheet on December 31, 2013 will be as under:

Balance Sheet (liabilities side)

(i)	Authorised capital—10,000 shares of ₹ 100 each	₹ 10,00,000
(ii)	Issued and subscribed capital—10,000 shares of ₹ 100 each	₹ 10,00,000
(iii)	P&L a/c	₹ 52,350
(iv)	General reserves	₹ 50,000
(v)	5% debenture holders a/c (Amount not paid)	₹ 10,500
(vi)	Securities premium a/c	₹ 1,15,000
(vii)	Dividend payable a/c	₹ 65,000

Illustration 17: Following is the balance sheet of a company as on December 31, 2012.

Balance Sheet

Liabilities	Amount (₹)	Assets	Amount (₹)
5,000 equity shares of ₹ 100 each	5,00,000	Fixed assets	8,00,000
3,000 redeemable preference shares of ₹ 100 each	3,00,000	Investment	1,00,000
Securities premium	50,000	Cash	2,00,000
Capital reserve	1,00,000	Other current assets	5,00,000
Revenue reserve	2,00,000		
6% debentures	3,00,000		
Creditors	1,50,000		
	16,00,000		16,00,000

Both the redeemable preference shares and debentures are due for redemption. Company takes the following steps:

(i) 1,000 equity shares of ₹ 100 each at a premium of 10% are issued, subscribed and fully paid for.

(ii) investments are sold for ₹ 90,000

(iii) Bank overdraft is arranged to the extent necessary.

Now the redemption is carried out

Give the journal entries and the new Balance Sheet of the company.

Solution:

Journal Entries

Particulars		Amount (₹)	Amount (₹)
Bank a/c	Dr.	2,20,000	
To share capital a/c			2,00,000
To securities premium a/c			20,000
(Being 2000 equity shares of ₹ 100 each issued at a premium of 10%)			

Particulars		Amount (₹)	Amount (₹)
Bank a/c Revenue reserve a/c To investments a/c (Being investments sold for 90,000 the loss of ₹ 10,000 debited to revenue reserve a/c)	Dr. Dr.	90,000 10,000	 1,00,000
Revenue reserve a/c To capital redemption reserve a/c (Being amount transferred to capital redemption reserve a/c)	Dr.	100,000	 1,00,000
Bank a/c To bank overdraft a/c (Being bank overdraft arranged)	Dr.	90,000	 90,000
7% redeemable preference share capital a/c 6% debentures a/c To 7% RP share holders a/c To 6% debenture holders a/c (Being the amount payable to RPS and debenture holders)	Dr. Dr.	3,00,000 3,00,000	 3,00,000 3,00,000
7% RPS a/c 6% debenture holders a/c To bank a/c (Being payment made to RPS and debenture holders)	Dr. Dr.	3,00,000 3,00,000	 6,00,000

Balance Sheet of the Company after Redemption

Liabilities	Amount (₹)	Assets	Amount (₹)
7,000 equity shares of ₹ 100 each	7,00,000	Fixed assets	8,00,000
Capital reserve	1,00,000	Other current assets	5,00,000
Revenue reserve	90,000		
Capital redemption reserve	1,00,000		
Securities premium	70,000		
Creditors	1,50,000		
Bank overdraft	90,000		
	13,00,000		13,00,000

Illustration 18: The balance sheet of a limited company on December 31, 2012 was as follows:

	(₹)		(₹)
Share capital:		Freehold property	1,00,000
Authorised—		Stock	1,20,000
₹ 10 per share	3,00,000	Debtors	80,000
		Bank balance	2,20,000
Subscribed:			
20,000 shares of ₹ 10 each	2,00,000		
Profit and loss account	1,20,000		
10% debentures	1,20,000		
Creditors	60,000		
Proposed dividend	20,000		
	5,20,000		5,20,000

At the annual general meeting, it was decided:

(*i*) To pay a dividend in cash of 10 per cent

(*ii*) To issue one bonus share for every four shares held

(*iii*) To give existing share holders the option to purchase one ₹ 10 share at ₹ 15 for every four shares held prior to bonus distribution, this option being taken up by all share holders.

(*iv*) To repay debentures at a premium of 3 per cent

Enter these transactions in the books of the company by preparing the necessary ledger accounts.

Solution:

Dr. Ledger Accounts Proposed Dividend a/c Cr.

Particulars	Amount (₹)	Particulars	Amount (₹)
To dividends payable a/c	20,000	By balance b/f	20,000
	20,000		20,000

Dividends Payable a/c

Particulars	Amount (₹)	Particulars	Amount (₹)
To bank a/c	20,000	By proposed dividends a/c	20,000
	20,000		20,000

Bonus a/c

Particulars	Amount (₹)	Particulars	Amount (₹)
To equity share capital a/c	50,000	By P&L a/c	50,000
	50,000		50,000

10% Debentures a/c

Particulars	Amount (₹)	Particulars	Amount (₹)
To 10% debenture holders a/c	1,20,000	By balance b/f	1,20,000
	1,20,000		1,20,000

Dr. Equity Share Capital a/c Cr.

Particulars	Amount (₹)	Particulars	Amount (₹)
To balance c/f	3,00,000	By balance b/f	2,00,000
		By bonus a/c	50,000
		By bank a/c	50,000
	3,00,000		3,00,000

10% Debenture holders a/c

Particulars	Amount (₹)	Particulars	Amount (₹)
To bank a/c	1,23,600	By 10% debentures a/c	1,20,000
		By premium on redemption a/c	3,600
	1,23,600		1,23,600

Security Premium a/c

Particulars	Amount (₹)	Particulars	Amount (₹)
To premium		By bank	25,000
On redemption of debenture a/c	3,600		
To balance c/d	21,400		
	25,000		25,000

Premium on Redemption of Debentures a/c

Particulars	Amount (₹)	Particulars	Amount (₹)
To 10% debenture holders a/c	3,600	By Securities premium a/c	3,600
	3,600		3,600

Bank a/c

Particulars	Amount (₹)	Particulars	Amount (₹)
To balance b/d	2,20,000	By 10% debenture holders a/c	1,23,600
To share capital a/c	50,000	By dividends payable a/c	20,000
To securities premium a/c	25,000	By balance c/f	1,51,400
	2,95,000		2,95,000

Balance Sheet

Particulars	Amount (₹)	Particulars	Amount (₹)
Equity share capital:			
Authorised: ₹ 10 shares	3,00,000	Freehold property	1,00,000
		Stocks	1,20,000
		Debtors	80,000
Issued & subscribed:		Bank	1,51,400
30,000 shares of ₹ 10 each	3,00,000		
P&L a/c	70, 000		
Creditors	60,000		
Securities premium a/c	21,400		
	4,51,400		4,51,400

Illustration 19: Associated company Ltd. issues 10,000 equity shares of ₹ 100 each at par and 500 debentures of ₹ 1,000 each @ ₹ 950. The entire issue has been underwritten by Kapoor

and Co. for a commission of 4 per cent on shares and 2 per cent on debentures (nominal value). The whole of the shares were applied for but only 400 debentures were applied for, all applications were accepted. Give journal entries and show the entries in the balance sheet, assuming all amounts have been received.

Solution: **Journal Entries**

Particulars		Amount (₹)	Amount (₹)
Bank account To equity shares capital account (The issue of ₹ 10,000 shares of ₹ 100 each (payment received) as per directors resolution no dated...)	Dr.	10,00,000	10,00,000
Bank account Discount on debentures account To debentures account (Issue of 400 debentures of ₹ 1,000 each payment having been received @ ₹ 950 as per directors resolution no dated...)	Dr. Dr.	3,80,000 20,000	4,00,000
Kapoor & Co. Discount on debenture account To debentures account (The allotment of 100 debentures to the underwriters, being the debentures not taken up by the public, as per agreement dated....)	Dr. Dr.	95,000 5,000	1,00,000
Commission on issue of debentures a/c Commission on issue of shares a/c To M/s Kapoor & Co. (The underwriting commission due to the underwriters @ 2% on ₹ 5,00,000 and 4% on ₹ 10,00,000, being, respectively, the nominal value of debentures and shares issued)	Dr. Dr.	10,000 40,000	50,000
Bank account To Kapoor & Co. (The amount due from the underwriters received)	Dr.	45,000	45,000

Balance Sheet

Particulars	Amount (₹)	Particulars	Amount (₹)
Share capital		Bank	14,25,000
10,000 equity shares of ₹ 100 each fully paid	10,00,000	Commission on issue of shares	40,000
		Commission on issue of debentures	10,000
500 debentures of ₹ 1,000 each	5,00,000		

When there is discount on debentures as well as commission or expenses on issue of debentures, it is usual to transfer both to one account named, cost of issue of debentures account. In the above situation, the entry will be as follows:

Cost of issue of debentures account To commission on issue of debentures a/c To discount on debentures a/c	Dr.	35,000	 10,000 25,000

Illustration 20: As on July 1st, 2012 Progressive Ltd. has outstanding in its books of ₹ 1,000 debentures of ₹ 1,000 each carrying interest at 14% p.a. payable quarterly. The following transactions took place during the year ending June 30, 2010.

1. On 1.9.2015, the company acquired in the open market 100 debentures at ₹ 980 each (*cum interest*) and cancelled them immediately.

2. On 1.12.2015, the company acquired 200 debenture at ₹ 1,030 (*cum interest*) *as* an investment. Of this, 100 debentures were sold on 1.1.2010 at ₹ 1,015.

3. On 1.1.2016, persons holding 300 debentures exercised the option to convert them into 20,000 equity shares of ₹ 10 each face value.

Pass necessary journal entries.

Solution: **Journal Entries**

	Particulars		Amount (₹)	Amount (₹)
1.	14% debentures a/c	Dr.	1,00,000	
	Debentures interest a/c	Dr.	2,333	
	To bank a/c			98,000
	To profit on cancellation of debentures a/c			
	(Purchase and cancellation of 100 debentures at ₹ 980 inclusive of interest @ 14% p.a. for 2 months)			
2.	Own debentures a/c	Dr.	2,01,333	
	Interest on debentures a/c	Dr.	4,667	
	To bank a/c			2,06,000
	(Purchase of 200 own debentures as investment at ₹ 1.030 *cum-interest*)			
	Interest on debentures a/c	Dr.	2,333	
	To interest earned on own debentures a/c			2,333
	(Interest earned @ 14% on own debentures of face value of ₹ 2,00,000 for 1 month, *i.e.*, December 2015)			
	Bank a/c	Dr.	1,01,500	
	To own debentures a/c			1,00,666
	To profit on sale of investment a/c			834
	(Sale of 100 own debentures @ ₹ 1,015 per debenture)			
3.	14% debentures a/c	Dr.	3,00,000	
	To equity share capital a/c			2,00,000
	To securities premium a/c			1,00,000
	(Conversion of 300 debentures into 20,000 equity shares of ₹ 10 each face value)			

Illustration 21: The following details pertain to the rights offer made by a company. Pass necessary entries for the acquisition interest payment and redemption of the financial instruments arising under the Rights Offer:

(Assume that holders of 2,00,000 debentures exercised their equity warrant option and paid the requisite money).

The rights offer would be 16 per cent partly convertible debentures of ₹ 70 each, aggregating ₹ 177.21 crores in the ratio of one debenture for every two shares held.

Part A of the debenture would be compulsorily converted into one equity share of ₹ 10 each at a premium of ₹ 10 per share after six months from the date of allotment.

Part B—the non-convertible portion of the debenture worth ₹ 50 would be redeemed in three instalments on the expiry of the sixth, seventh and eight years from the date of allotment.

A detachable warrant would be attached to Part B which would entitle the holders to one equity share of ₹ 10 at a premium of ₹ 40 at any time between June 1, 2011, and June 30, 2012, as may be decided by the board of directors.

Solution: **Journal Entries** **(₹ in Crore)**

Particulars		Amount (₹)	Amount (₹)
For issue of debentures			
Bank a/c	Dr.	177.21	
To 16% partly convertible debentures			177.21
For conversion of Part A (see Note 1)			
16% PCD a/c	Dr.	50.63	
To equity share capital a/c			25.31
To securities premium a/c			25.32
On exercise of equity option by debenture holders:			
Bank a/c	Dr.	100.00	
To equity share capital a/c			20.00
To securities premium a/c			80.00
(Interest on the non-convertible portion (part B) in year 1 to 6)			
Interest on 16% PCDs a/c	Dr.	20.25	
To bank a/c			20.25
(Interest at 16% on ₹ 126.588 crores of Part B of the PCDs)			
Year 7			
Interest on 16% PCDs a/c	Dr.	13.50	
To bank			13.50
(Interest at 16% on ₹ 126.58 – 42.19 = 84.39 crores of PCDs) (see Note 2)			
Year 8			
Interest on PCDs a/c	Dr.	6.752	
To bank a/c			6.752
(Interest at 16% on ₹ 84.39 – 42.19 = 42 crores)			
Redemption			
End of year 6			
16% PCDs a/c	Dr.	42.19	
To bank a/c			42.19
End of year 7			
16% PCDs a/c	Dr.	42.19	
To bank a/c			42.19
End of year 8			
16% PCDs a/c	Dr.	42.20	
To bank a/c			42.20

Note:

1. ₹ $\frac{20 \times 177.21}{70}$ crore = ₹ 50.63 crores is converted into equity shares of ₹ 10 each at a premium of ₹ 10 per share

   The non-convertible portion = $\frac{50}{70} \times 177.21 =$ = ₹ 126.58 crore.

2. Redemption will be as follows:

   At the end of sixth year = ₹ 42.19 crore

   At the end of seventh year = ₹ 42.19 crore

   At the end of eight year = ₹ 42.20 crore

Illustration 22: Shareholders funds of M Ltd. as on January 1, 2012 comprise (*i*) 13.5 preference share capital—₹ 4,00,000; (*ii*) fully paid up equity share capital—₹ 5,00,000, and 60%

paid up equity share capital—₹ 3,00,000; and (*iii*) share premium—₹ 7,00,000. Profit before interest on 15% debentures of ₹ 10,00,000 and tax @ 60%) is ₹ 11,50,000 for the year ended December 31, 2012.

The company's board of directors recommendations include equity dividend @ 15% and capitalisation of profits for making partly paid equity shares as fully paid up.

Pass the necessary journal entries to incorporate the board's recommendations and duly show the aforesaid in the balance sheet.

Solution: **Journal Entries Books of M Ltd.**

Particulars		Amount (₹)	Amount (₹)
Interest on debentures a/c	Dr.	1,50,000	
To interest payable a/c			1,50,000
(Being interest payable on Debentures @ 15%)			
Profit & loss a/c	Dr.	7,50,000	
To interest on debentures a/c			1,50,000
To income-tax payable a/c or (provision for income-tax a/c)			6,00,000
(Being interest on debentures and income-tax payable charged to the P&L a/c)			
Profit & loss a/c	Dr.	4,00,000	
To P&L appropriation a/c			4,00,000
(Being the residual profits transferred to the P&L appropriation a/c)			
Profit & loss appropriation a/c	Dr.	20,000	
To general reserves a/c			20,000
(Being 5% minimum reserve created as dividend rate is 15%)			
P&L appropriation a/c	Dr.	1,74,000	
To preference dividend payable a/c			54,000
To equity dividend payable a/c			1,20,000
on fully paid shares 75,000			
on partly paid shares 45,000			
(Being 13.5% preference dividend and equity dividend)			
Equity shares final call a/c	Dr.	2,00,000	
To equity shares capital a/c			2,00,000
(Being final and remaining call on equity capital)			
P&L appropriation a/c	Dr.	2,00,000	
To bonus to shareholders a/c			200,000
(Being capitalisation of profits to make partly paid equity shares as fully paid)			
Bonus to shareholders a/c	Dr.	2,00,000	
To equity share final call a/c			20,000
(Being partly paid equity shares made as fully paid)			

Note:

(*i*) No tax deduction at source has been made either in case of debentures interest or in the case of dividends, both on preference share capital as well as on equity share capital.

(*ii*) Income-tax liability is 60% of the profits after providing for interest on debentures.

Balance Sheet (Position) of M Ltd.
(after incorporation of board's recommendations)

Liabilities	Amount (₹)	Assets	Amount (₹)
Share capital:		Sundry Assets (*Balancing figure*)	40,50,000
13.5% preference share capital	4,00,000		
Equity share capital (Fully paid-up)	10,00,000		
Securities premium a/c	7,00,000		
15% debentures a/c	10,00,000		
General reserves	20,000		
P&L appropriation a/c (Balance)	6,000		
Current liabilities:			
Interest on debentures payable a/c	1,50,000		
Income-tax payable a/c	6,00,000		
Preference dividend payable a/c	54,000		
Equity dividend payable a/c	1,20,000		
	40,50,000		40,50,000

Dr. **Profit & Loss a/c** **Cr.**

Particulars	Amount (₹)	Particulars	Amount (₹)
To interest on debenture a/c	1,50,000	By balance b/d (Given)	11,50,000
To income-tax payable a/c	6,00,000		
To P&L appropriation a/c (transfer)	4,00,000		
	11,50,000		11,50,000

Dr. **Profit & Loss Appropriation a/c** **Cr.**

Particulars	Amount (₹)	Particulars	Amount (₹)
To general reserve a/c (5% minimum as rate of equity dividend 15%)	20,000	P&L a/c	4,00,000
To preference dividend (13½%)	54,000		
To equity dividend:			
On fully paid shares	75,000		
On partly paid shares	45,000		
To bonus to shareholders a/c	2,00,000		
To balance c/f	6,000		
	4,00,000		4,00,000

Note: It is assumed that there are no other liabilities.

THEORY QUESTIONS

1. Define debentures. Briefly describe the different types of debentures.
2. Can debentures be issued as a collateral security? What is the accounting treatment in such a case?
3. Enumerate and describe the various ways of issuing debentures.
4. What do you understand by redemption of debentures? Describe the different ways in which debentures can be redeemed.

5. Explain the methods of writing discount on issue of debentures with reference to redemption plan.
6. Explain the following:
   (*i*) Redemption of debentures out of capital.
   (*ii*) Redemption of debentures out of profits.
7. Give the accounting treatment of redemption of debentures either through sinking fund method or insurance policy method.
8. Explain the terms, ex-interest and cum-interest in connection with purchase and sale of debentures. Give examples.
9. Write notes on:
   Issue of debentures and its redemption and how the issue of debenture loss is dealt in Books of Accounts. **[BBA, GGSIP University, December 2004]**
10. "Interest on debentures is payable only when profits are there". Comment. **[BBA, GGSIP University, December 2010]**
11. Give journal entries when the debentures are redeemed out of profits by using sinking fund method. **[BBA, GGSIP University, December 2002]**
12. What is a debenture? Describe various methods for redemption of debentures with illustrations. **[BBA, GGSIP University, December 2010]**

SELF-EVALUATION EXERCISES

I. Select the correct answer for the following multiple choice questions:

1. Debentures which are transferable by mere delivery are:
   (*a*) Registered debentures (*b*) First debentures
   (*c*) Bearer debentures
2. The following journal entry appears in the books of X Co. Ltd.:

Bank a/c	Dr.	4,75,000	
Loss on issue of debenture a/c	Dr.	75,000	
To 12% debentures a/c			5,00,000
To premium on Redemption of debentures a/c			50,000

   Debentures have been issued at a discount of:
   (*a*) 15% (*b*) 5% (*c*) 10%
3. X Co. Ltd. purchased assets with ₹ 28,80,000. It issued debentures of ₹ 100 each at a discount of 4 per cent in full satisfaction of the purchase consideration. The number of debentures issued to vendor of assets are
   (*a*) (*i*) 30,000 (*b*) (*ii*) 28,800 (*c*) (*iii*) 32,000
4. When all the debentures are redeemed, balance in the debentures redemption fund account transferred to
   (*a*) Capital reserve (*b*) General reserve
   (*c*) Profits and loss appropriation account
5. The nominal and book values of debenture redemption fund investments account are respectively ₹ 1,00,000 and ₹ 96,000. The company sold investments of the nominal value of ₹ 30,000 at a price which was just sufficient to redeem debentures of ₹ 30,000 at 10% premium, the profit on sale of investments is
   (*a*) ₹ 4,200 (*b*) ₹ 3,000 (*c*) ₹ Nil

6. Own debentures are those debentures of the company which

(*a*) The company allots to its own promotees

(*b*) The company allots to its director

(*c*) The company purchases from the market and keeps them as investments

7. Profit on cancellation of own debentures is transferred to

(*a*) Profit and loss appropriation a/c (*b*) General reserve

(*c*) Capital reserve

8. When debentures are redeemed out of profits, an equal amount is transferred to

(*a*) General reserve (*b*) Debenture redemption reserve

(*c*) Capital reserve

9. Profit on sale of debenture redemption fund investments in the first instance is credited to

(*a*) Debenture redemption fund account (*b*) Profit and loss appropriation account

(*c*) General reserve account

EXERCISES AND PROBLEMS

1. A company issues 20,000 equity shares of ₹ 100 each at par and 1000 debentures of ₹ 1,000 each @ ₹ 950. The whole of the issue has been underwritten by Bulls & Co. for a commission of 4 per cent on shares and 2 percent on debentures (nominal value). The whole of the shares were applied for but only 800 debentures were applied for. All applications were accepted. Give journal entries in the books of the company.

2. XYZ Ltd. issues 10,000 9% Debentures of ₹ 100 each. Give journal entries if the debentures are:

(*i*) issued at par;

(*ii*) issued at discount of 10%; and

(*iii*) issued at a premium of 10%; (redemption being in all these cases at par).

Also show the entries which will be made if the debentures are repayable at a premium of 5% but are issued

(*a*) at par; and

(*b*) at a discount of 10% .

In each case, show how the figures will appear in the Balance Sheet.

3. Give journal entries for the following:

(*i*) The company allots 1,000 12% debentures of ₹ 100 each at an issue price of ₹ 96 per debenture redeemable at a premium of ₹ 8 per debenture. (The liability of premium is also to be recorded at the time of issue of debentures).

(*ii*) 3,000 fully convertible debentures of ₹ 100 each are converted into 20,000 equity shares of ₹ 10 each at a premium of ₹ 5 per share.

4. Kite Ltd. raised a bank loan of ₹ 5,00,000 and issued by way of a collateral security 500 15%. Debentures of ₹ 1,000 each. The company further issued to public 16,000 12%. Debentures of ₹ 100 each at a discount of 2% payable as to ₹ 50 on application and the balance on allotment. The issue was underwritten by Bears & Co. for a commission of 2% of nominal value of debentures underwritten. The whole of the issue was subscribed to by the members of the public. The company paid the underwriting commission in the form of its 12% Debentures of ₹ 100 each issued at par. Pass journal entries for the above mentioned transactions.

5. SPY Limited purchases building worth ₹ 3,00,000 equipment worth ₹ 2,80, 000 and furniture for ₹ 20,000 from Lee & Co. and took over liabilities of ₹ 40,000 for a purchase consideration of ₹ 6,30,000. SPY Limited paid the purchase consideration by issuing 12% debentures of ₹ 100 each at a premium of 5%. Pass the necessary journal entries.
6. AB Co. Ltd. issued 500, 12% Debentures of ₹ 100 each at 98 on 1st January, 2012. Under the terms of issue: (*a*) debenture interest is annually payable on 31st December every year and (*b*) one-fifth of the debentures are annually redeemable by drawings, the first redemption occurring on 31st December, 2013. Show Debentures Account, Debenture Interest Account and Discount on Issue of Debentures Account (with working) up to 31st December, 2014 assuming that (*i*) company's accounting date is 31st December and (*ii*) all the terms of debenture issue are duly complied with.

   [**Ans:** Ratio of writing off the discount 5 : 5 : 4 : 3 : 2 : 1, Amount to be written off in 2000 – ₹ 250; 2001 – ₹ 250; 2002 – ₹ 200].
7. ABC Ltd. issued 1,000 12% debentures of ₹ 100 each. Assuming that the debentures were issued (*i*) at par, (*ii*) at a premium of 10% and (*iii*) at a discount of 10%. Calculate the net effective rate of interest on debentures.

   [**Ans:** (*i*) 12%; (*ii*) 10.90%; (*iii*) 13.33%].
8. A Ltd. had issued 2,000, 6% debentures of ₹ 100 each on 1st January, 2007. Interest was payable half yearly on 30 the June and 31st December each year. They are repayable at par on 31st Dec., 2010 with the option to redeem them at any time after 31st December, 2010 at ₹ 103. On January 1st, 2012, the balance in the Debenture Redemption Fund Account stood at ₹ 1,07,000 which was invested outside. On 30th June, 2012 a notice was given for redemption of the above debentures with the option to receive one new 9% debenture of ₹ 100 each at ₹ 98 and ₹ 5 in cash for each 6% debentures in place of ₹ 103 in cash.

   The holders of 1800 debentures exercised this option and the remaining were paid cash. The company sold the investments costing ₹ 72,000 for ₹ 87,400. The Company completed the redemption. Give necessary ledger accounts ignoring interest payments.

   [**Ans:** Amount transferred to General Reserve—₹ 1,12,800]
9. The following balances appeared in the books of a company on 1st April, 2012:

12% Debentures	₹ 4,00,000
12% Debentures Sinking Fund	₹ 3,00,000
12% Debentures Sinking Fund	₹ 3,00,000

   Investments represented by 10% ₹ 3,60,000 secured bonds of Government of India.

   Annual contribution to sinking fund was ₹ 64,000 made on 31st March each year. On 31st March 2013 balance at bank was ₹ 2,00,000 after receipts of interest. The company sold the investments at 80% as debentures were paid off. Journalise the transactions for 2012–13.
10. On 1st January, 2012, Neha Ltd. issued 2,500 10% debentures of ₹ 100 each at ₹ 95. Holders of these debentures have an option to convert their holding into 14% preference shares of ₹ 100 each at a premium of ₹ 25 per share at any time within three years.

    On 31st December, 2012, holders of 500 debentures notified their intention to exercise the option.

    Show the journal entries for the issue and conversion of debentures in the books of the company.
11. X Ltd. issued 2,000 12% Debentures of ₹ 100 each at par on April 1, 2011. These debentures are redeemable at the end of the fifth year at 10% premium. It was resolved that sinking Fund

should be formed and invested in 10%. Development Bonds of ₹ 100 each. Interest on Bonds is payable on 31st March every year.

Reference to Sinking Fund Table shows that ₹ .1638 invested at the end of every year at 10% compound interest will produce Re. 1 at the end of the fifth year.

10% Development Bonds of the required amount are purchased on different dates at the following prices:

On March 31, 2012	₹ 80
On March 31, 2013	₹ 90
On March 31, 2014	₹ 100

You are required to show Debenture Redemption Fund Account and Debenture Redemption Fund Investment Account for the first three years in the books of X Ltd. Accounting year of this company ends on 31st March.

12. In the books of Wood Ltd., the 6% Debentures Account showed a credit balance of ₹ 4,00,000 consisting of 4,000 debentures of ₹ 100 each as on 1st April, 2012. During the year debentures were purchased in the open market as follows:

1st August, 600 Debentures at ₹ 95 ex-interest.

1st November, 400 Debentures at ₹ 98 cum-interest.

The Debentures, thus, purchased were retained as investments of the company. Interest on debentures was payable half-yearly on 30th September and 31st March every year.

You are required to show the journal entries and the ledger accounts in the books of the Company.

13. On 31st March, 2012 Varun Ltd's Balance Sheet showed 10,000 12% debentures of ₹ 100 each outstanding. Interest on debentures is payable on 30th September and 31st March every year. On 1st August, 2012, the company purchased 500 of its own debentures as investment at ₹ 97 ex-interest.

Pass journal entries for purchase and disposal of own debentures in each one of the following cases:

(*i*) The company cancels all its own debentures on 1st March, 2013.

(*ii*) The company resells all its own debentures at ₹ 105 cum-interest on 1st March, 2013.

Also show journal entries relating to debenture-interest and interest on own debentures as on 31st March, 2013 in case (*i*) mentioned above.

14. On 1st January, 2012, Shiwalik Breweries Limited had ₹ 8,00,000 5% debentures outstanding in its books redeemable on 31st December, 2012. On 1st January, 2012, the balance on Sinking Fund was ₹ 7,49,000 represented by

(*i*) ₹ 1,00,000 Own Debentures purchased at an average price of ₹ 99; and

(*ii*) ₹ 6,60,000 nominal value of 3% War Loan.

The amount annually credited to the Sinking Fund was ₹ 28,400.

The interest an Debentures was paid by the company every year on 31st December and interest on war loan was received also on 31st December annually

On 31st December, 2012, the outside investments were realized at 98 per cent and all the outstanding Debentures were redeemed on that date.

You are required to write up the necessary ledger accounts for the year 2012 in the books of the company.

15. Modern Investors Ltd. issued on 1st April, 2012, 20,000 12% Debentures of ₹ 100 each redeemable at the option of the company after the second year at ₹ 104 upon giving two month's notice to the debenture holders. The company purchased the following debentures in the open market:

On 12th June, 2015, ₹ 4,000 nominal cum interest cost ₹ 4,025.

On 24th August, 2015, ₹ 7,000 nominal ex-interest cost ₹ 6,915.

These Debentures were retained as investment till 30th September, 2015 when these Debentures were cancelled. Show the respective ledger accounts as would appear in the books of the company for 2014–15 and for 2015–16. Interest is payable half yearly on 30th September and 31st March.

[**Ans:** Profit on redemption—₹ 156].

ANSWERS TO SELF-EVALUATION EXERCISES

I.

1. (*c*) **2.** (*b*) **3.** (*a*) **4.** (*b*) **5.** (*a*) **6.** (*c*)

7. (*c*) **8.** (*b*) **9.** (*a*)

14

COMPANY FINAL ACCOUNTS

LEARNING OBJECTIVES

After reading this chapter, you should be able to:

- *Identify* the final accounts of a company.
- *Explain* the requirements of the companies with regard to books of accounts maintained by a company.
- *Discuss* the legal provisions about the preparation of final accounts.
- *Discuss* the format and contents of balance sheet, as given in the Companies Act.
- *Discuss* the legal requirements with regard to preparation of profit and loss account of a company.
- *Explain* the accounting treatment of special items such as interest on debentures, preliminary expenses, calls-in-arrears, calls-in-advance, managerial remuneration, income tax, dividends, interest out of capital.

The Companies Act has made it compulsory for every Indian company to keep proper set of books for recording financial transactions and to prepare a set of financial statements in the prescribed form to periodically determine the profits earned and to know the financial position of the company as on a specified date. The Companies Act specifies the books of accounts to be maintained and also prescribes the format and content of the financial statements. The Companies (Amendment) Act 1988 has made it obligatory on all companies to maintain accounts on accrual basis and according to the double entry system of accounting.

The term final or annual accounts of companies is used to denote the preparation of two basic financial statements namely:

1. Balance Sheet
2. Profit and Loss Account

In addition, the Institute of Chartered Accountants of India has recommended that these two statements must be accompanied by a cash flow statement.

Since the owners or shareholders elect a board of directors to manage the company and rely on the ability and skills of these directors to conduct the business in the most profitable manner, the Companies Act tries to protect the shareholders interest by prescribing provisions and formats according to which the financial statements are to be prepared and presented to the shareholders.

The objective of the Companies Act in laying down various provisions with regard to accounts and audit is to ensure that adequate information is provided to the shareholders and other users in order to judge the performance of the company during an accounting period. The legal requirements laid down by the Companies Act, therefore, assume a great importance in the preparation of the financial statements of a joint stock company.

GENERAL REQUIREMENTS OF COMPANIES ACT

Books of Accounts

Section 209 of the Companies Act specifies the books of accounts to be maintained by a company. According to this section, every company should keep at its registered office proper books of accounts with respect to:

(*a*) all sums of money received and expended by the company and the matters in respect of which the receipt and expenditure take place

(*b*) all sales and purchases of goods by the company

(*c*) the assets and liabilities of the company

In the case of companies which are engaged in manufacturing, production, processing or mining activities, in addition to the financial accounts mentioned above, a set of cost accounts (if prescribed by the Central Government) must be maintained to show the utilization of material, labour and other items of cost.

This section also specifies that a company will not be deemed to be maintaining proper books of accounts unless,

(*i*) all the books necessary to give a true and fair view of the state of affairs of the company and to explain the transactions are maintained, and

(*ii*) the books of accounts are maintained on the accrual basis and according to the double entry system of accounting.

Preparation of Final Accounts

Sections 210–223 deal with the legal position having bearing on the preparation, presentation and publication of final accounts of a company. A brief description of the provisions contained in these sections is as follows:

1. **Section 210:** Deals with the preparation and presentation of the final accounts of a company at its annual general meeting.
2. **Section 211:** Prescribes 'form' and 'contents' of the balance sheet and Profit and Loss Account.
3. **Section 212:** Deals with the disclosure of certain details in the Balance Sheet of a holding company in respect of its subsidiaries.
4. **Section 213:** Provides for the financial year of the holding company and subsidiary company.
5. **Section 214:** Makes provisions regarding the rights of the representatives of the holding company to inspect books of account kept by any of its subsidiaries.
6. **Section 215:** Provides that the balance sheet and profit and loss account of a company shall be authenticated (signed) on behalf of the board of directors by its manager or secretary, if any, and by not less than two directors of the company, one of whom shall be a managing director, where there is one.
7. **Section 216:** Provides that the profit and loss account shall be treated as an annexure to the Balance Sheet and auditor's report as an enclosure there to.

8. **Section 217:** Provides that the report of the board of directors should be attached to every balance sheet laid before the shareholders at one general meeting.
9. **Section 218:** Provides for penalty for improper issue, circulation or publication of balance sheet or profit and loss account.
10. **Section 219:** Deals with the right of the members to copies of balance sheet and profit and loss account, auditor's report and every other document required by law to be annexed or attached to the Balanced Sheet which is to be presented in the general meeting.
11. **Section 220:** Provides that three copies of balance sheet, profit and loss account have to be sent to the registrar within 30 days after an annual general meeting.
12. **Section 221:** Requires the details of the particulars relating to the payments made to any director or other person by any other company, body corporate, firm or person.
13. **Section 222:** Provides that where any information which is required to be given in the accounts and is allowed to be given in the statement annexed to the accounts, it may be given in the board's report instead of in the account. Such a report of the directors shall be treated as an annexure to the accounts and the auditors shall report thereon only in so far as it gives the said information.
14. **Section 223:** Deals with certain companies like Banking Company, Insurance Company, etc. who are required as per this section, to publish a statement in the form in Table F in Schedule I of the Companies Act.

The Companies Act further specifies the following with regard to the annual accounts to be drawn up by a company.

(*i*) At every annual general meeting of the shareholders, the board of directors of the company should lay before the shareholders, a balance sheet as at the end of the accounting period which has just ended and also a profit and loss account for such accounting period.

(*ii*) The annual accounts of the company must be submitted in an annual general meeting within six months counted from the last day of the accounting period to which the accounts relate.

The period to which the accounts relate is known as the financial year and it may be less than, equal to or greater than 12 months but cannot exceed 15 months. Where special permission has been granted by the Registrar, the financial year may be extended to eighteen months.

REVISED SCHEDULE VI ON FINAL ACCOUNTS*

The forms and contents of Balance Sheet and Profit and Loss Account of companies are regulated as per Section 211 of the Companies Act 1956.

(*i*) Section 211 (i) states that every balance sheet of a company shall give a true and fair view of the affairs of the company as at the end of the financial year. The term true and fair view implies that there is no window dressing type of thing in respect of assets. In other words, it means that:

(*a*) the assets and liabilities are correctly stated,

(*b*) the provisions are adequate, that is, neither insufficient nor excessive,

(*c*) the stock has been valued on sound accounting principles, and

(*d*) all material contingent liabilities and assets are stated clearly in the form of Notes to Balance Sheet.

Every balance sheet must, subject to the provisions of this section, be in the form set out in Part I of Schedule VI.

* Materials taken from the website of Ministry of Corporate Affairs, Government of India. Notification No. S.0 447 (E) dated 28th February, 2011.

(*ii*) Sub-section (2) of above section 211 requires that every Profit and Loss account of a company must:

(*a*) give a true and fair view of the profit or loss of the company for the financial year, and

(*b*) comply, subject to the provisions of the section, with the requirements of Part II of Schedule VI so far as they are applicable thereto.

The revised schedule shall be effective from 01.04.2001 *i.e.*, FY 2011–2012 onwards.

Comparison Between Old Schedule VI and Revised Schedule VI

The following are the points of differences between old schedule VI and revised schedule VI.

(*i*) **Contents:** The contents of the Revised Schedule VI are as under:

(*a*) General instructions for preparation of Balance Sheet and Statement of Profit and Loss of a company.

(*b*) Form of Balance Sheet (only vertical format) with General Instructions for preparation of Balance Sheet (Part-I).

(*c*) Form of Statement of Profit and Loss with General Instructions for preparation of Statement of Profit and Loss (Part-II).

(*ii*) The contents of Old Schedule VI are as under:

(*a*) Form of Balance Sheet (including disclosure requirements) both in horizontal as well as vertical form with general instructions for its preparation (Part-I).

(*b*) Requirements as to Profit and Loss Account (Part-II).

(*c*) Interpretation (Part-III).

(*d*) Balance Sheet Abstract and Company's General Business Profile (Part-IV).

(*iii*) In revised Schedule, the following changes have been made:

(*a*) Balance Sheet Abstract and Company's General Business Profile as provided in Part-IV has been removed.

(*b*) Horizontal format of Balance Sheet known as conventional or customary form of Balance Sheet has been deleted. Accordingly, now onwards only vertical format is to be used.

(*c*) Form of Statement of Profit and Loss has been provided in Part II, which was not prescribed in old Schedule VI.

(*d*) Further Part III on Interpretation, which contained explanation of provision, reserve, etc. has been scrapped as these terms are already covered in the Accounting Standards. It has been stated in revised Schedule VI that for the purpose of this schedule, the terms used shall be as per the applicable Accounting Standards.

Disclosure Requirements in Revised Schedule

The disclosure requirements as specified in Part I and Part II of Revised Schedule VI are in addition to and not in substitution of the disclosure requirements specified in the Accounting Standards prescribed under the Companies Act, 1956.

Notes to accounts, which was earlier not specifically defined has been defined, as containing information in addition to that presented in the financial statements and shall provide where required (*a*) narrative descriptions or disaggregations of items recognised in those statements and (*b*) information about items that do not qualify for recognition in those statements.

As per revised Schedule VI each item on the face of the Balance Sheet and Statement of Profit and Loss shall be cross referenced to any related information in the notes to accounts. Accordingly, there is a column for stating the Note number in proforma for Balance Sheet as well as Statement of Profit and Loss. It is pertinent to mention here that in the old schedule VI there was a Column for indicating Schedule No. in the Balance Sheet. Accordingly the concept of schedules has been eliminated.

Form of Balance Sheet and General Instructions

As said earlier, Part I of the Revised Schedule VI prescribes the Form of Balance Sheet and general instructions for preparing the same. The important contents of the same are as under:

1. **Current/Non-current Classification:** The most important change in entire Revised Schedule VI is classification of all the assets and liabilities between current and non-current.

   The general instructions for preparation of Balance Sheet define current/non-current asset/ liability as under:

   An asset shall be classified as current when it satisfies any of the following criteria:

   (*a*) It is expected to be realised in, or is intended for sale or consumption in, the company's normal operating cycle;

   (*b*) It is held primarily for the purpose of being traded;

   (*c*) It is expected to be realised within 12 months after the reporting date; or

   (*d*) It is cash or cash equivalent unless it is restricted from being exchanged or used to settle a liability for atleast 12 months after the reporting date.

   All other assets shall be classified as non-current.

   A liability shall be classified as current when it satisfies any of the following criteria:

   (*a*) It is expected to be settled in the company's normal operating cycle;

   (*b*) It is held primarily for the purpose of being traded;

   (*c*) It is due to be settled within 12 months after the reporting date; or

   (*d*) The company does not have an unconditional right to defer settlement of the liability for atleast 12 months after the reporting date. Terms of a liability that could, at the option of the counter party, result in its settlement by the issue of equity instruments do not affect its classification.

   All other liabilities shall be classified as non-current.

   The above bifurcation of assets and liabilities between current and non-current would require major reclassifications in the Balance Sheets of all companies. Some examples are presented here about classification of assets and liabilities as current/non-current as per revised Schedule VI.

   (*a*) In old Schedule VI the current maturities to long term debt are shown as part of long term debt and only disclosure of amount due to be repaid within one year is made. However, as per revised Schedule VI current maturities to long term debt would be depicted as 'Other Current Liabilities'.

   (*b*) As per old Schedule VI interest accrued and due on long term loans were shown as part of the long term loans but in revised schedule VI the same is to be shown as current liabilities.

   (*c*) In old Schedule VI all loans and advances (except capital advances) are shown under Current Assets and Loans and Advances but now onwards the same needs to be bifurcated between current and non-current, accordingly the sub heading of long term loans and advances has been introduced in Revised Schedule VI.

   (*d*) The provisions also need to be bifurcated among long term and short term, the latter one being classified as current, and former being classified as non-current *e.g.*, employee related provisions; accordingly subheading of long term provisions has been introduced.

Under old Schedule VI all the provisions were being shown under Current Liabilities and Provisions.

(*e*) Under old Schedule VI the trade receivables (Debtors)/Trade payables (creditors) were always shown as Current, but in revised schedule VI, these can also be shown as Non-current. It appears that where the credit is offered on deferred credit basis or the payment is not/expected to be received from debtors within normal operating cycle/12 months from reporting period, the same needs to be disclosed as Non-current.

2. **Disclosure of current liabilities:** Under revised schedule VI the upper half is referred to as Equity and Liabilities and later half is shown as Assets whereas in old Schedule VI the same were referred as Sources of Funds and Application of Funds. Accordingly, the current liabilities (including short term provisions) are to be shown in upper half of balance-sheet under Equity and Liabilities whereas in old schedule VI (vertical form) it was shown as deduction from current assets, loans and advances and net current assets are disclosed on Assets side. Due to this the Balance Sheets totals would increase to the extent of the current liabilities.
3. **Disclosure of Accumulated Losses:** Debit balance of Profit and Loss shall be shown as a negative figure under the head 'Surplus'. Similarly, the balance of 'Reserve and Surplus' after adjusting negative balance of surplus, if any shall be shown under the head 'Reserve and Surplus' even if the figure is in the negative. As per old Schedule VI the accumulated losses were to be shown on Asset side after Miscellaneous Expenditure.
4. **Proposed Dividend:** Part I of Old Schedule VI requires 'proposed dividends' to be shown under "Provisions" and paragraph 3 (xiv) of Part II of the same requires the "proposed dividends" to be disclosed in the Profit and Loss Account.

   However, para 6(U) of the General Instructions for preparation of Balance Sheet of Part I of Revised Schedule VI does not require the provision for proposed dividend to be made and only desires disclosure of same in notes to accounts.
5. **Additional classification/disclosures/Changes:** The new schedule VI prescribes certain changes in disclosures, some of which are as under:

   (*i*) **Share capital:** Reconciliation of number of shares outstanding at beginning and at end of reporting period, shares in the company held by each shareholder holding more than 5 per cent shares specifying the number of shares held, etc.

   (*ii*) **Share Application Money** not exceeding the issued capital and to the extent not refundable shall be shown under head Equity and Share application money to the extent refundable *i.e.*, the amount in excess of subscription or in case of requirements of minimum subscription are not met, shall be separately shown under "Other current liabilities".

   (*iii*) **Reserves and Surplus:** Nature and purpose of each reserve to be stated only for those aggregated under "Other Reserves".

   (*iv*) **Long Term Borrowing:** Bonds/Debentures (along with rate of interest and particulars of redemption or conversion) shall be stated in descending order of maturity or conversion. Further period and amount of continuing default as on balance sheet date in repayment of loans and interest also needs to be disclosed, which was not required in old Schedule VI.

   (*v*) **Short Term Borrowing:** Period and amount of continuing default as on balance sheet date in repayment of loans and interest needs to be disclosed.

(*vi*) **Fixed Assets:** Details in respect of tangible and intangible assets needs to be given separately and their amount also depicted on the face of balance sheet separately, which was not earlier the case as a single schedule was prepared wherein the intangible assets were also included.

(*vii*) **Tangible Assets:** Assets under lease to be classified separately.

(*viii*) **Intangible Assets:** New head like mastheads and publishing rights, Mining Rights, Recipes, formulae, models, designs and prototypes introduced.

(*ix*) **Capital Advances** are required to be presented separately under the head "Long term loans and advances". In old Schedule VI they were being shown as part of fixed assets/ capital work in progress in absence of any heading available in existing Schedule VI for such advances.

(*x*) **Non-current Investment:** Against five heads available in old Schedule VI wherein there was no residual head the new one provides eight classifications, which includes the residual head of other non-current investments.

(*xi*) **Trade receivables:** The term sundry debtors has been replaced with trade receivables and instead of showing entire amount as current assets under old Schedule VI, bifurcation of same into non-current and current is now required. Further separate disclosure of trade receivables outstanding for a period exceeding six months from the date they become due for payment as against the billing/accounting date is required now.

(*xii*) **Cash and Cash Equivalents:** Bank deposits with more than 12 months maturity to be disclosed separately, which was not required till now. The bifurcation of bank deposits among scheduled and non-scheduled banks has been dispensed with.

(*xiii*) **Contingent liabilities and Commitments:** These were required to be disclosed as footnote to Balance Sheet under old Schedule VI and are now required to be disclosed in notes to accounts. Further disclosure of all financial commitments (not only capital commitment) are required under Revised Schedule VI.

Form of Statement of Profit and Loss and General Instructions

Form of Statement of Profit and Loss has been introduced in Revised schedule VI for the first time. The highlights of the form of Statement of Profit and Loss and general instructions for preparing the same are as under:

(*a*) The format of Statement of Profit and Loss does not depict any appropriation item on its face, as below the line adjustments *i.e.*, dividend, bonus shares and transfer to/from reserves, etc. are to be disclosed under "Reserve and Surplus" in the Balance Sheet. However, the amount set aside or proposed to be set aside to reserve/withdrawn from reserve needs to be disclosed as additional information in the notes.

(*b*) In respect of a company other than a finance company, revenue from operations shall disclose separately in notes revenue from (*i*) sale of products, (*ii*) sale of services, (*iii*) other operating revenues less, (*iv*) Excise Duty. In case of financial company, revenue from operations shall include revenue from: (*a*) Interest and (*b*) Other financial services. It has further been stated that revenue from each of the above heads shall be disclosed separately by way of notes to accounts to the extent applicable. The above disclosure is more detailed than old Schedule VI.

(*c*) Additional information regarding aggregate income or expenditure exceeding 1 per cent of the revenue from operatios or ₹ 1,00,000/-, whichever is higher, need to be disclosed by way of notes.

(*d*) The quantitative disclosure in respect of raw material, opening and closing stocks for each class of goods in case of manufacturing company and quantity details in respect of purchase made, opening and closing stock as required under the old Schedule VI has been removed.

Even the detailed quantitative information in respect of each class of goods manufactured in regard to the licensed capacity, installed capacity and actual production is not required.

(*e*) Prior Period items are to be separately disclosed.

(*f*) Payment to the auditor *inter alia* for reimbursement of expenses to be separately disclosed.

(*g*) Gain/Loss on foreign currency transactions and translations to be separated into Finance Costs and Other Expenses.

(*h*) Broad heads shall be decided taking into account the concept of materiality and presentation of true and fair view of financial statements.

Rounding Off of Figures

The limit of turnover and the extent of rounding off has been relaxed in the revised Schedule VI, which stipulates that financial statements of companies having turnover less than one hundred crore can be rounded off upto millions, whereas in old Schedule VI the rounding off could be made up to thousands only. Further for companies having turnover above hundred and less than five hundred crore, the rounding off can now be made up to crores, whereas in old Schedule VI the same was allowed upto millions.

PROFIT AND LOSS APPROPRIATION ACCOUNT

Sometimes, companies divide their income statement into three parts:

(*a*) Trading account—showing the gross profit earned

(*b*) Profit and loss account—showing the profit earned after tax and available for appropriation

(*c*) Profit and loss appropriation account.

The profit and loss appropriation account shows in detail the appropriations made from the profits in respect of dividends and transfer to reserves etc. The format of the Profit and Loss Appropriation Account is given below:

Dr. Profit and Loss Appropriation Account for the year ended Cr.

	(₹)		(₹)
To interim dividend To proposed final dividend To general reserve (or any transfers to reserves) To balance c/d (accumulated balance in profit & Loss Account carried forward)		By Balance b/d (Opening credit balance of profit and loss a/c in the trial balance) By profit and loss a/c (current year's profits)	

The balance in the profit and loss appropriation account, if it is a credit balance, will be shown on the liability side of the balance sheet under the heading 'Reserves and Surplus'. While in the case of sole proprietorships and partnerships, the balance in the Profit and Loss Account will be transferred to the proprietors' capital accounts, in the case of a company it will be carried forward as a part of reserves. If there is a closing debit balance in the profit and loss appropriation account (*i.e.*, a loss), then such balance will be shown on the Asset side under the heading 'Miscellaneous Expenditure'.

ACCOUNTING TREATMENT OF SPECIAL ITEMS

In addition to the provisions and general principles prescribed for the preparation of financial statements of a company, there are some items which require specific accounting treatment. Some important items are as follows:

1. Interest on Debentures: Debentures interest is a business expensed and therefore, it is a charge against profit and as such profit and loss account is debited with the total amount of interest payable during the accounting year whether the company has earned the profit or not.

Illustration

Dr. **Trial Balance of Sharp Ltd. as on 31.3.2012** **Cr.**

	(₹)	(₹)
14% Debentures		20,00,000
Interest on debentures	70,000	

Interest for the full year on ₹ 20,00,000 at 14 per cent p.a. is ₹ 2,80,000. Since an amount of ₹ 70,000 is shown in the trial balance against interest, we may assume that an amount of ₹ 2,10,000 is outstanding. Usually, debenture interest is payable every six months. In the given illustration we may assume the due dates of interest to be June 30 and December 31 of every year. While the interest due on June 30, 2011 has been paid, the amount due on December 31, 2011 has not been paid and in addition, interest has accrued for the three months period up to March 31, 2012. In the profit and loss account, the interest on debentures will be shown as follows:

Profit and Loss Account of Sharp Limited

	(₹)	(₹)
To debenture interest	70,000	
Add: Outstanding interest	2,10,000	2,80,000

The interest of ₹ 1,40,000 being the interest due for the six month period up to December 31, 2011, is termed as "interest accrued and due and though this outstanding amount is a short-term liability, as per Companies Act, it must be shown in the balance sheet along with the amount outstanding in respect of debentures. The interest of ₹ 70,000 being the interest due for the three month period up to March 31, 2012, is 'termed as interest accrued but not due' since the next due date for payment of interest is only June 30, 2012. Interest Accrued but not due should be shown in the Balance Sheet as a current liability.

Balance Sheet of Sharp Limited as on 31.3.2012

	(₹)	(₹)
Liabilities:		
Secured Loans 14% Debentures	20,00,000	
Add: Interest Accrued and Due	1,40,000	21,40,000
Current Liabilities and Provisions:		
Interest Accrued but not due on Debentures		70,000

2. Income Tax on Interest on Debentures: Payment of interest on debentures is subject to compulsory deduction of income tax at the current prescribed rates given in the Finance Act. The Accounting entry is

Interest on Debentures Account	Dr.	(with the gross amount)
To Debenture holders Account		(with the net amount payable)
To income-tax payable account		(with the amount of the tax on the gross amount)

3. Discount on the Issue of Debentures: Discount or costs, *e.g.*, commission, brokerage, etc. incurred on the issue of debentures should normally be written off as early as possible but in no case later than the date of redemption. The unwritten balance will be shown in the balance sheet under 'Miscellaneous Expenditure' on the Asset side.

4. Preliminary Expenses: Such expenses include the costs of formation of a company and since their amount is usually large, it is not desirable to write off them in one year. Instead preliminary expenses are spread over a number of years and profit and loss a/c is debited with certain fraction every year. The unwritten amount is shown under Miscellaneous Expenditures on the asset side of the Balance Sheet.

5. Call-in-Arrears: This item represents the amount not paid by the shareholders on the calls made on them by the company. If this item is given in the trial balance, it is shown in the balance sheet on the liabilities side as a deduction from the called up amount under the main head of share capital. But if this item is given outside the trial balance as an adjustment, it would mean that the trial balance shows only the paid up capital and not called up capital. The amount of call-in-arrears is then added to the paid up capital to make the later as called up capital and then deducted again.

6. Calls-in-Advance: It is a debt on the company until the calls are made and the amount received in advance is adjusted. A company may also pay interest on calls-in-advance and the rate of interest is usually stated in the articles. It should be treated as a current liability and shown under the heading current liabilities and provisions.

7. Auditors' Payments: Payments made to auditors for auditing the accounts and for doing any other work for the company should be mentioned separately.

8. Managerial Remuneration: The remuneration paid to managerial personal (*e.g.*, directors, managing directors or manager) of a company in any form or mode is a charge against profits and thus shown in the debit side of the profit and loss account. The mode of payment of the remuneration may include the fee for attending the meetings of the Board, monthly salary, a fixed percentage of profit and so on.

The Companies Act has imposed severe restrictions on the managerial remuneration payable by a public company or a private company which is a subsidiary of a public company.

Section 198 (i) provides that the total managerial remuneration in respect of any year is subject to an overall limit of 11 percent of the net profits of the company in that year.

9. Income-Tax: Dividends to both the equity and the preference shareholders can be paid only out of profits available after taking into account the income-tax. The profits on which income-tax is payable is termed as taxable profits and the calculation of taxable profits is based on the provisions as per the Income-Tax Act.

Though the actual amount of tax can be calculated only when the books of accounts are closed for the accounting period and profits are ascertained, the Income-Tax Act requires a business to pay advance tax by forecasting the likely profits that would accrue during the year. Another point to be noted in the case of Income-tax is that though a company may determine the tax liability, pay the tax and file its return,the income-tax officer will scrutinize the return and assess the tax payable by even recomputing the taxable profits. If the income-tax officer arrives at taxable profits which differ from that stated by the company in its return, then the tax assessed and to be settled will also differ. The process of assessment may take quite some time to be completed and until such completion the exact tax liability will not be known to the company. Thus, the accounting treatment of income-tax must take into account the following three stages:

(*i*) Payment of advance income-tax.

(*ii*) Determination of the tax liability by the company from its books of accounts, making a provision for such liability and payment of difference, if any, between advance tax and tax now computed.

(*iii*) Completion of the assessment by the income-tax officer.

The concepts of 'previous year' and 'assessment year' have also to be understood to follow the accounting treatment of income-tax. Assessment year means the period of twelve months starting from April 1 of every year and ending on March 31 of the next year.

The income of the previous year of a business is taxed during the following assessment year at the rates prescribed for such assessment year by the Finance Act. The previous year is defined as the financial year or the period of twelve months starting from April 1 of every year and ending on March 31 of the next year.

When advance tax is paid, the journal entry to record this would be

Advance Income-tax Accounts To Bank a/c	Dr.		

For example, if an advance tax of ₹ 3,50,000 is paid by a company for the previous year 2012 in 2012–13, the entry to record this would be

Advance Tax for Assessment Year 2012–13 Account	Dr.	3,50,000	
To Bank Account			3,50,000

Though the above transaction has been journalised to explain the dual aspects in reality, the payment of advance tax would be recorded in the cash book and the debit aspect posted into the ledger from the cash book. Thus, while preparing the trial balance as on March 31, 2012, the advance tax for assessment year, 2012–13, will be included in the trial balance at debit balance of ₹ 3,50,000.

Let us assume that in the example cited above, the company determines its tax liability as ₹ 3,42,500 after drawing up the Profit and Loss Account for the year ending March 31, 2012. This liability must be provided for by passing the entry as,

Profit and loss account	Dr.	3,42,500	
To provision for income-tax account (Assessment year 2012–13)			3,42,500

While the tax liability will appear as an expense in the profit and loss account, the provision for income-tax will be shown in the Balance Sheet as a current liability and the Advance Tax of ₹ 3,50,000 paid will be shown as an advance on the asset side of the balance sheet. Another acceptable method of presentation is to set off the advance and the provision relating to the same assessment year against each other and take only the net amount either to the liability or asset side of the balance sheet. In the example given above, since the advance exceeds the provision, the net amount would be presented as follows.

Balance Sheet as on March 31, 2012

Assets	(₹)	(₹)
Loans and Advances		
Advance tax for Assessment year 2012–13	3,50,000	
Less: Provision for tax for Assessment year 2012–13	3,42,500	7,500

Till such time the assessment is completed, the balances in the advance and provision accounts will be carried forward. To continue with the above example, if the assessment is completed in December 2012 and the tax liability is arrived at by the Income-tax Officer at ₹ 3,60,000, the accounting treatment will be as follows:

1. The provision for tax is short of the actual liability by ₹ 17,500. The company will have to provide for this extra liability. In the Profit and Loss Account for the year ended March 31, 2013 the increase in liability will be provided for by making the following entry.

Profit and Loss Account To provision for income-tax account (Assessment year 2012–13)	Dr.	17,500	17,500

The above entry will be in addition to the entry required to be passed in respect of tax payable for the financial year 2012–13.

2. Since the assessment has been completed, the advance tax account can be closed by transfer to the Provision account. The journal entry for the transfer will be:

Provision for Income-Tax a/c (Assessment year 2012–13) To advance tax for Assessment year 2012–13	Dr.	3,50,000	3,50,000

3. The balance of tax payable amounting to ₹ 10,000 (₹ 3,60,000 – 3,50,000) must be paid shortly after the completion of assessment. When the short-fall in tax is paid, the entry will be

Provision for Income-Tax a/c (Assessment year 2012–13) To bank a/c	Dr.	10,000	10,000

With the recording of the above entries, the balance sheet as on March 31, 2013, will not list any items pertaining to tax payable for Assessment Year 2012–13. The ledger accounts are given below:

Dr. Advance Tax for Assessment Year 2012–13 Cr.

2012	Particulars	(₹)	2013	Particulars	(₹)
April 1	To balance b/d	3,50,000	March 31	By provision for Income-tax Account	3,50,000
		3,50,000			3,50,000

Dr. Provision for Income-tax Account (Assessment Year 2012) Cr.

Date	Particulars	(₹)	Date	Particulars	(₹)
2012 Dec.	To bank a/c	10,000	2012 April 1	By balance b/d	3,42,500
2013 March 31	To Advance tax for Assessment year 2012–13	3,50,000	2013 Mar. 31	By Profit and Loss Account	17,500
		3,60,000			3,60,000

Note: Adjustments relating to income tax of the previous year is normally done by debiting or crediting the P/L appropriation a/c so that current operating profits are not distorted. Provision for current year's tax is, however, debited above the line.

10. Dividends: Dividends may be defined as the share of profits that is payable to each shareholder of the company. The Companies Act lays down that dividends can be paid out of profits only and prohibits the payment of any dividend out of capital. Also, dividends shall be paid in cash only. A company may pay dividends from any or all of the three following sources:

(*i*) profits of the current year

(*ii*) undistributed profits of previous years

(*iii*) moneys provided by the Central or any State Government for the payment of dividends in pursuance of a guarantee given by the government concerned.

The directors generally recommend the percentage of dividend payable on the equity shares. The shareholders in the annual general meeting may pass a resolution adopting the recommendation or may lower the percentage recommended. The shareholders do not have the power to enhance the dividend recommended by the Directors. The percentage adopted must be applied only on the paid-up capital.

For example, let us assume that the Directors of Sunshine Limited propose a dividend of 15 per cent for the equity shareholders which is adopted by the shareholders. The called up equity capital of the company is ₹ 50,00,000 and there are calls in arrears to the extent of ₹ 40,000. The dividend payable in the example would be calculated as (15/100) × (50,00,000 – 40,000) = ₹ 7,44,000. Of late, companies have started declaring dividends as a percentage of the Profit After Tax also.

The dividend recommended by the directors is termed as 'Proposed Dividend' till such time it is adopted by the shareholders in the annual general meeting. The entry to record proposed dividend is,

Profit and Loss A/c Cr.

To proposed dividend A/c

The proposed dividend will be classified as a provision and shown on the liability side of the balance sheet. The dividend finally decided by the shareholders in the annual general meeting as payable is termed as 'declared dividend'. Any dividend declared must be paid within forty-two days from the date of declaration. Hence, a declared dividend must be classified as a current liability in the balance sheet of the company.

Though dividends can be declared only by a resolution of the shareholders, if the articles of the company permit, the Directors can declare an interim dividend between two annual general meetings. When interim dividend is paid the entry to record the payment will be,

Interim Dividend A/c Dr.

To Bank A/c

The interim dividend paid during a year will appear in the Trial Balance of the Company as on the last date of the accounting period and will be transferred to the debit side of the profit and loss appropriation a/c as it is an item of appropriation of profits. Dividend is generally paid by posting the dividend warrants to the shareholders. The dividend warrants must then be presented to the company's bank which will make the payment. Sometimes, a portion of the dividend declared may remain as unpaid simply due to the fact that such dividend has not been claimed by certain shareholders. Any unpaid or unclaimed dividend is a current liability and is shown on the liabilities side of the balance sheet. The company should transfer any unpaid dividend within forty-nine days from the date of declaration of the dividend to a special bank account.

If the dividend is not claimed for a period of three years from the date of transfer to the special bank account, than the unclaimed amount must be transferred by the company to the general revenue account of the Central Government. After such a transfer, any shareholder entitled to claim such dividend may claim it from the Government.

11. Interest Out of Capital: Though the Companies Act provides that dividends to shareholders are payable only out of profits, in certain circumstances with the previous sanction of the Central Government, interest may be paid to shareholders out of capital. The circumstances as specified by Section 208 of the Companies Act are as below:

1. Where any shares in a company are issued for the purpose of raising money to defray the expenses of the construction of any work or building, or the provision of any plant, and
2. Such construction or provision of plant cannot be made profitable for a lengthy period.

In the above circumstances, if the company is authorised by the articles or by a special resolution, it may pay interest on so much of that share capital as is for the time being paid-up, for a specified period and charge such interest to capital as part of the cost of the construction of the work or building or the provision of the plant.

The payment of interest shall be made only for such period as may be determined by the central government. The period, in any case, cannot extend beyond the close of the half year next after the half year during which the work or building has been actually completed or the plant provided. The rate of interest cannot exceed four per cent per annum or such other rate as the Central Government may notify.

Illustration 1: A limited company has an authorised capital of ₹ 10,00,000 divided into 60,000 equity shares of ₹ 10 each and 4,000, 10% preference shares of ₹ 100 each out of which 50,000 equity share and 3,000 preference share were issued and fully paid up. The profit for the year 2012 being the first year of operation amounted to ₹ 1,80,000 after income tax. The directors decided to declare a dividend of 22% on the equity share capital after.

(*i*) statutory minimum requirement transfer to general reserve

(*ii*) provision of dividend on preference shares.

Prepare profit and loss appropriation account and show liabilities side of the balance sheet.

Solution:

Profit and Loss Appropriation Account for the Year Ended 31.12.2012

	(₹)		(₹)
To general reserve account	18,000	By balance b/d	1,80,000
To preference dividend	30,000		
To equity dividend	1,10,000		
To balance c/d	22,000		
	1,80,000		1,80,000

Since the dividend to be declared is more than 20% of the paid up capital, 10% of the net profit is to be transferred to reserve.

Balance Sheet as on 31.12.2012

Liabilities	(₹)
Share capital	
Authorised capital:	
60,000 equity shares of ₹ 10 each	6,00,000
4,000, 10 preference shares of ₹ 100 each	4,00,000
	10,00,000
Issued & paid-up capital:	
50,000 equity shares of ₹ 10 each	5,00,000
3,000, 10% preference shares of ₹ 100 each	3,00,000
Reserve & surplus:	
General reserve	18,000
Profit & loss appropriation account	22,000
Secured loans	—
Unsecured loans	—
Current liabilities & provision:	
(A) Current liabilities	—
(B) Provisions	—
Proposed dividend: Equity dividend	1,10,000
Preference dividend	30,000

Illustration 2: A company was registered with a nominal capital of ₹ 5,00,000 divided into shares of ₹ 10 each of which 20,000 shares had been issued and fully paid.

The following is the trial balance extracted on December 31, 2012.

Assets	(₹)	(₹)
Stock (January 1, 2007)	93,210	
Manufacturing wages	54,870	
Manufacturing expenses	9,620	
Purchases and sales	4,10,730	5,84,950
Machinery repairs	4,305	
Carriage inwards	2,455	
Carriage outwards	4,630	
Advance payment of income tax	7,145	
Bank loan (at 5%)		25,000
Interest on loan	625	
Debtors and creditors	82,200	46,110
Profit and loss account (January 1, 2012)		4,320
Bank current account	3,430	
Cash in hand	960	
Leasehold factory	32,105	
Plant and machinery	39,200	
Loose tools	6,250	
Share capital		2,00,000
Calls in arrear	500	
Rates and electricity (Factory–₹ 7,105; office–₹ 1,700)	8,805	
Director's fees and remuneration	6,000	
Office salaries and expenses	6,500	
Auditor's fees	625	
Office furniture	2,500	
Commission	4,320	
Returns	6,320	4,905
Preliminary expenses	3,000	
Transfer fees		20
Goodwill	75,000	
Total	8,65,305	8,65,305

You are required to prepare trading and profit and loss account for the year ended December 31, 2012, and a balance sheet as on that date after taking into consideration the following adjustments:

1. Write off one-third preliminary expenses
2. Depreciation: On plant and machinery at 20%; on office furniture at 10%
3. Manufacturing wages ₹ 945 and office salaries ₹ 600 had accrued due
4. Provide for interest on bank loan for 6 months
5. The stock was valued at ₹ 62,240 and loose tools at ₹ 5,000
6. Reserve ₹ 4,250 on debtors for doubtful debts
7. Reserve further ₹ 1,560 for discounts on debtors
8. The directors recommended dividend at 5% for the year ending December 31, 2012, after providing for taxes amounting to ₹ 11,500.

Solution:

Dr. **Trading and Profit and Loss Account for the year Ended December 31, 2012** **Cr.**

Particulars		Amount (₹)	Particulars		Amount (₹)
To opening stocks		93,210	By sales	5,84,950	
To purchases	4,10,730		*Less*: Return	6,320	5,78,630
Less: Returns	4,905	4,05,825	By closing stock		62,420
To Manufacturing wages	54,870				
Add: Accrued due	945	55,815			
To manufacturing expenses		9,620			
To machinery repairs		4,305			
To carriage inwards		2,455			
To rates & electricity:					
Factory		7,105			
To depreciation on:					
Plant and machinery (20% on ₹ 39,200)	7,840				
Loose Tools (₹ 6,250 – 5,000)	1,250	9,090			
To gross profit c/d		53,625			
		6,41,050			6,41,050
To carriage outwards		4,630	By gross profit b/d		53,625
To rates and electricity office		1,700	By transfer fees		20
To directors' fees and remuneration		6,000			
To office salaries and expenses	6,500				
Add: Accrued due	600	7,100			
To audit fees		625			
To commission		4,320			
To interest on bank loan @ 5% (on ₹ 25,000 for 6 months)		1,250			
To depreciation on office furniture @ 10% on ₹ 2,500		250			
To provision for doubtful debts		4,250			
To provision for discount on debtors		1,560			
To net profit c/d		21,960			
		53,645			53,645
To preliminary expenses written off (1/3rd of ₹ 3,000)		1,000	By balance b/f		4,320
			By net profit for the year		21,960
To provision for taxation		11,500			
To proposed dividend @ 5% on paid up capital on ₹ 1,99,500)		9,975			
By balance c/d		3,805			
		26,280			26,280

Balance Sheet as on December 31, 2012

Liabilities		Amount (₹)	Assets		Amount (₹)
Share capital:			**Fixed assets:**		
Authorised—50,000 shares of ₹ 10 each		5,00,000	Goodwill		75,000
			Leasehold factory		32,105
			Plant and machinery	39,200	
			Less: Depreciation	7,840	31,360
Issued—22,000 shares of ₹ 10 each		2,00,000	Office furniture	2,500	
Subscribed—20,000 shares of 10 each fully called up	2,00,000		*Less*: Depreciation	250	2,250
			Current assets, loans and advances:		
Less: Calls in arrear paid up	500	1,99,500	(A) Current assets:		
Reserve and Surplus:			Loose tools (as valued)		5,000
Profit and Loss a/c		3,805	Stock		62,420
Secured loans:			Sundry debtors	82,200	
Unsecured loans:			Outstanding for more than 6 months	—	
Bank loan at 5%	25,000				
Add: Interest accrued and due (₹ 1,250 – 645)	625	25,625	*Less*: Provisions for doubtful debts	4,250	77,950
Current Liabilities and Provisions:					
(A) **Current Liabilities:**			Bank current a/c (Scheduled bank)		3,430
Sundry creditors	46,110		Cash in hand		960
Outstanding expenses:			(B) **Loans and advances:**		
Manufacturing wages	945		Advance payment of income tax		7,145
Office salaries	600	47,655	Misc. expenditure (to the extent not written off or adjusted)		
(B) **Provisions:**					
Provisions for discount on debtors		1,560	Preliminary expenses (₹ 3,000 – 1,000)		
Provisions for taxation		11,500			2,000
Proposed dividends		9,975			
		2,99,620			2,99,620

Illustration 3: Following is the trial balance of Progressive Agencies Ltd., as on March 31, 2012. Prepare trading and profit and loss account as well as profit and loss appropriation account for the year ended on March 31, 2012, and a balance sheet on that date.

Trial Balance

Particulars	Debit (₹)	Credit (₹)
Authorised Capital		
50,000 equity shares of ₹ 10 each		
Subscribed and paid-up capital:		
25,000 equity shares of ₹ 10 each fully called up		2,50,000
Stock	50,000	
Sales		4,25,000
Purchase	3,00,000	
Wages (productive)	70,000	
Printing and stationery	2,400	
Advertising expenses	14,300	

Particulars	Debit (₹)	Credit (₹)
Debtors and creditors	48,700	35,200
Discount	4,200	3,150
Insurance premium	6,720	
Salaries (administrative staff)	18,500	
Rent	6,000	
Central expenses	8,950	
Profit and loss account	–	16,200
Plant and machinery	80,600	
Cash at bank	1,34,700	
Furniture	17,000	
General reserve		25,000
Loan from managing director (unsecured)		15,700
Bad debts	3,200	
Calls-in-arrears	5,000	
	7,70,270	7,70,270

Value of Stock on March 31, 2012, was ₹ 91,500, Depreciation is to be provided at 10% p.a. on plant and machinery, and at 20% p.a. on furniture. Outstanding liabilities are: Wages—₹ 5,200, salaries–₹ 1,200, rent–₹ 600. Insurance premium includes a sum of ₹ 800 being the charge for the quarter ended on June 30, 2012, No dividend payment is proposed and provisions for taxation are not considered necessary.

Solution:

Progressive Agencies Ltd
Trading and P&L a/c for the Year Ended 31.3.2012

Liabilities		(₹)	Assets	(₹)
To opening stock		50,000	By sales	4,25,000
To purchase		3,00,000	By closing stock	91,500
To wages	70,000			
Add: Outstanding	5,200	75,200		
To gross profit c/d		91,300		
		5,16,500		5,16,500
To printing & stationery		2,400	By G/P f/d	91,300
To advertising expenses		14,300	By discount received	3,150
To discount		4,200		
To insurance premium	6,720			
Less: prepaid	800	5,920		
To salaries	18,500			
Add: Outstanding	1,200	19,700		
To rent	6,000			
Add: Outstanding	600	6,600		
To general expenses		8,950		
To bad debts		3,200		
To depreciation:				
Plant & machinery	8,060			
Furniture	3,400	11,460		
To net profit c/d		17,720		
		94,450		94,450
To Balance c/d		33,940	By balance b/d	16,220
			By net profit	17,720
		33,940		33,940

Balance Sheet as at 31.3.2012

Liabilities		(₹)	Assets		(₹)
Share capital			**Fixed assets:**		
Authorised:			Plant & machinery	80,600	
50,000 equity shares of ₹ 10 each		5,00,000	*Less*: Depreciation	8,060	72,540
Paid up capital:			Furniture	17,000	
500 shares @ ₹ 10 each	2,50,000		*Less*: Depreciation	3,400	13,600
Less: Calls in arrears	5,000	2,45,000			
Reserve and surplus:			**Current asset:**		
General Reserve		25,000	Closing stock		91,500
Profit & Loss account		33,940	Debtors		48,700
Secured loans		Nil	Cash in bank		1,34,700
Unsecured loans:			Loans & advances		—
Loans from managing director		15,700	Prepaid insurance		800
			Misc. expenditure		Nil
Current liabilities:					
Creditor		35,200			
Outstanding expenses:					
Wages	5,200				
Salaries	1,200				
Rent	600	7,000			
		3,61,840			3,61,840

Illustration 4: From the following balances extracted from the books of Bharat Steel Ltd., you are required to prepare in the statutory forms, profit and loss account for the year ended March 31, 2012, and the balance sheet as on that date.

	(₹)
Share capital	
6,00,000 equity shares @ ₹ 10 fully paid	60,00,000
1,600 8% redeemable preference share @ ₹ 100	1,60,000
Securities premium account	1,00,000
General reserve	4,00,000
Preference share redemption	1,92,000
Block capital (at cost less depreciation)	38,20,000
Net profit for the year (before tax)	16,84,000
Debtors (unsecured, considered good)	1,20,000
Creditors	1,00,000
Profit and loss account (as on 31.3.2011) (Cr)	40,000
Interim dividend	3,00,000
Unpaid dividend	3,600
Other current assets	23,00,000
Investments	7,80,000
Outstanding expenses	24,400
Income tax paid under dispute for the year ending 30.3.2011	4,00,000
Provision for taxation for the above year	2,80,000
Advance payment of income-tax	8,80,000

You are given the following additional information:

1. Profit was calculated after charging ₹ 72,000 paid to the managing director as minimum remuneration. He is to be given a remuneration @ 5% of the net profit before tax, subject to the above minimum.

2. Preference shares were redeemed on October 1, 2011, at a premium of 20% but no entries were recorded in the books for giving effect thereto, except for the payment standing to the debit for preference share redemption account.
3. Income tax demanded for the year ended September 30, 2011, of ₹ 4,00,000 has not been provided in full, as an appeal is pending.
4. Market value of the investments is ₹ 7,10,000.
5. Income tax for the year is to be provided @ 55% on the year is book profits.

Solution: **Bharat Steel Ltd.**

P&L a/c for the Year Ending September 30, 2012

Liabilities	Amount (₹)	Assets	Amount (₹)
To managing directors Remuneration—5% of ₹ 17,56,000	87,800	By net profit*	17,56,000
To provision for taxation	9,17,510		
To profit for the year came down	7,50,690		
	17,56,000		17,56,000
To interim dividend	3,00,000	By balance b/d	40,000
To capital redemption reserve account	1,60,000	By net profit b/d	7,50,690
To balance c/d	3,30,690		
	7,90,690		7,90,690

* The net profit shown in the problem is ₹ 16,84,000; to this ₹ 72,000 paid as remuneration to the managing director has been added.

Balance Sheet of Bharat Steel Ltd. as on March 31, 2012

Liabilities		(₹)	Assets		(₹)
Share capital:			**Fixed Assets:**		
Authorised		—	Cost	—	
Issued & subscribed			*Less*: Depreciation	—	38,20,000
6,00,000 equity shares of ₹ 10 each fully paid		60,00,000	Investment at cost (Market value 7,10,000)		7,80,000
Preference shares of ₹ ... each redeemed during the year			Current asserts,loans & advances		
Reserve & surplus			(A) Current assets	23,00,000	
Share premium			Sundry debtors (Unsecured considered good)		
Balance as per balance sheet	1,00,000				
Less: Premium paid on redemption of preference shares	32,000	68,000	Outstanding for a period exceeding Others	1,20,000	24,20,000
Capital redemption reserve account	1,60,000		(B) Advance		
General reserve	4,00,000		Advance payment of income-tax (8,80,000 + 4,00,000)		12,80,000
Profit & loss a/c	3,30,690	8,90,690			
Current liabilities & provisions					
(A) Current liabilities					
Liabilities for goods and expenses	1,40,200				

Liabilities		(₹)	Assets	(₹)
Unclaimed concerns	3,600	1,43,800		
(B) Provisions				
Provision for taxation		11,97,510		
		83,00,000		83,00,000

Note: Income-tax demand for the previous year has been raised for ₹ 4,00,000 against which a provision of ₹ 2,80,000 had been created. An appeal against the demand is pending.

Illustration 5: Given below is a trial balance of Caps Ltd. as on December 31, 2012, which has an authorised capital of ₹ 6,00,000 in the equity shares of ₹ 10 each.

Particulars	Debit (₹)	Credit (₹)
Calls-in-arrears	7,500	
Premises	3,00,000	
Plant and machinery	3,30,000	
Interim dividend paid	37,500	
Stock	75,000	
Fixtures	7,200	
Sundry debtors	87,000	
Goodwill	25,000	
Cash in hand	750	
Cash with bank	39,900	
Purchases	1,85,000	
Preliminary expenses	5,000	
Wages	84,865	
General expenses	16,835	
Freight and carriage	13,115	
Salaries	15,000	
Director's fee	5,725	
Bad debts	2,110	
Debentures interest paid	9,000	
Subscribed and fully called up capital	—	4,00,000
6% debentures	—	3,00,000
Profit and loss account	—	15,000
Bills payable	—	38,000
Sundry creditors	—	50,000
Sales	—	4,45,000
General reserves	—	25,000
Advance income tax paid (Assessment year 2012–13)	30,000	
Provision for bad debts	—	3,500
	12,76,500	12,76,500

Prepare profit and loss account and balance sheet after making following adjustments:

1. Depreciate plant and machinery by 10%
2. Write off ₹ 500 from preliminary expenses
3. Make provision for bad debts at 5% on sundry debtors
4. Value of stock on 31.12.2012 ₹ 95,000
5. Provision for income tax to be made at 55% of the net profit

Solution:

Caps Ltd.–Trading and P&L a/c for the Year Ended 31.12.2012

Liabilities		(₹)	Assets	(₹)
To opening stock		75,000	By sales	4,45,000
To purchases		1,85,000	By closing stock	95,000
To wages		84,865		
To freight & carriage		13,115		
To gross profit c/d		1,82,020		
		5,40,000		5,40,000
To general expenses		16,835	By gross profit b/d	1,82,020
To salaries		15,000		
To debenture interest	9,000			
Add: Outstanding	9,000	18,000		
To Directors' fees		5,725		
To Preliminary Expenses		500		
To depreciation:				
Plant & machinery		33,000		
To provision for bad & doubt full debts on 1.1.2012	35,000			
Less: Bad debts	2,110			
	1,390			
Provision required on 31.12.2012, 5% of 87,000	4,350	2,960		
To provision for Income Tax (55% of 90,000)		49,500		
To net profit c/d		40,500		
		1,82,020		1,82,020
To interim dividend		37,500	Balance b/d	15,000
To balance c/d		18,000	Net profit b/d	40,500
		55,500		55,500

Balance Sheet as on 31.12.2012

Liabilities		(₹)	Assets		(₹)
Share capital:			**Fixed assets:**		
Authorised:			Goodwill		25,000
60,000 equity share of ₹ 10 each		6,00,000	Premises		3,00,000
Issued subscribed,			Plant & machinery	3,30,000	
Called up & Paid up:			*Less*: Depreciation	33,000	2,97,000
40,000 equity shares of ₹ 100 each fully called up	4,00,000		Fixtures		7,200
			Investments		Nil
Less: Calls in arrear	7,500	3,92,500	**Current assets:**		
Reserve and surplus:			Stock		95,000
General reserve		25,000	Debtors	87,000	
Profit & loss account		18,000	*Less*: Provision	4,350	82,650
Secured loans 6% debentures	3,00,000		Bank		39,900
Add: Interest	9,000	3,09,000	Cash		750

Liabilities		(₹)	Assets		(₹)
Unsecured loans		Nil	Loans & advances		Nil
(A) Current liabilities			**Misc. expenditure:**		
Bills payable		38,000	Preliminary		4,500
Creditors		50,000			
(B) Provision					
Taxation	49,500				
Less: Advance tax	30,000	19,500			
		8,52,000			8,52,000

Illustration 6: The balance sheet of Johnson Ltd. as on December 31, 2012 was as follows:

Liabilities	(₹)	Assets		(₹)
Share capital:		**Fixed assets:**		
1,000 6% redeemable preference shares of ₹ 10 each fully paid	10,000	Land and building		25,000
		Plant & machinery	15,000	40,000
5,000 equity shares of ₹ 10 each fully paid	50,000			
		Current assets:		
General reserve	11,000	Stock	30,000	
Profit and loss a/c	20,000	Debtors	16,000	
8% debenture	5,000	Cash and bank balance	24,000	70,000
Sundry creditors	14,000			
	1,10,000			1,10,000

The directors decided to:

1. Redeem preference shares at premium of 5%
2. Redeem debentures at a premium of 10%
3. Make a bonus issue to the equity shareholders of one ₹ 10 per equity share for every five ₹ 10 shares held in order to realise a part of the undistributed profit

The appropriate resolution having been passed, these transactions were completed. You are required to show:

1. The appropriate journal entries to record the transactions in the books of company
2. Balance sheet as it would appear after including the above transactions

Solution: **Journal Entries**

	Particulars		(₹)	(₹)
1.	General reserve a/c	Dr.	11,000	
	Profit and loss a/c	Dr.	5,000	
	To capital redemption reserve a/c			15,000
	To premium on redemption of debentures and shares			1,000
	(Being nominal value of preference shares redeemed out of undistributed reserves & surplus transferred to capital redemption reserve a/c and the premium payable on redemption transferred to premium on redemption of debentures and shares a/c)			
2.	6% redemption preference share capital a/c	Dr.	10,000	
	Premium on redemption of preference share capital a/c	Dr.	500	
	To preference shareholders a/c			10,500
	(Transfers of total liability on redemption to preference shareholders a/c)			

Particulars		(₹)	(₹)
3. 8% debenture a/c	Dr.	5,000	
Premium on redemption a/c	Dr.	500	
To 8% debenture holder's a/c			5,500
(Being transfer of total liability on redemption to 8% debenture holder's a/c)			
4. Preference shareholder's a/c	Dr.	10,500	
Debentureholder's a/c	Dr.	5,500	
To bank a/c			16,000
(Being payment in full to preference shareholders and debenture holders on redemption)			
5. Profit and loss a/c	Dr.	10,000	
To bonus to shareholder's a/c			10,000
(Amount transferred to bonus to shareholders a/c for issuing bonus shares in the ratio of 1:5) (Amount transferred to bonus to shareholders a/c for issuing shares in the ratio of 1:5)			
6. Bonus to shareholder's a/c Dr.		10,000	
To equity share capital a/c			10,000
(Issue of equity shares as bonus)			

Balance Sheet of Johnson Ltd. as on December 31, 2012

Liabilities		(₹)	Assets	(₹)
Share capital:			**Fixed assets:**	
Issued subscribed and paid up 6,000 equity shares of ₹ 10 each fully paid	60,000		Land and building	25,000
			Plant and machinery	15,000
(Out of the above 1,000 shares have been issued as bonus shares out of undistributed profit)			**Current assets:**	
			Stock in trade	30,000
			Sundry debtors	16,000
			Cash and bank balances	8,000
Capital redemption reserve		10,000		
General reserve	11,000			
Less: Transferred to capital redemption reserve	10,000			
	1,000			
Add: Transfer from profit and loss a/c	5,000	6,000		
Profit and Loss account:				
Balance b/fd	20,000			
Less: Issue of bonus shares	10,000			
Premium on redemption of debentures and shares	1,000			
Transfer to general reserve	5,000	4,000		
Secured loans		Nil		
Unsecured loans		Nil		
Current liabilities and provisions:		Nil		
Sundry creditors		14,000		
		94,000		94,000

Illustration 7: A company has an authorised capital of ₹ 5,00,000 divided into 5,000 equity shares of ₹ 100 each. On 31.3.2012, 2,500 shares were fully called up.

The following are the balances extracted from the ledger of the company as on 31.3.2012

Liabilities	(₹)	Assets	(₹)
Inventory	50,000	Advertisement	3,600
Sales	4,25,000	Bonus	10,500
Purchases	3,00,000	Accounts receivable	38,700
Wages (productive)	70,000	Accounts payable	35,200
Discount allowed	4,200	Plant and machinery	80,500
Discount received	3,150	Furniture	17,100
Insurance up to 30.6.2013	6,720	Cash and bank	1,34,700
Salaries	18,500	Reserve	25,000
Rent	6,000	Loan from managing director	15,700
General expenses	8,950	Bad debts	3,200
Profit & loss account	6,220	Calls-in-arrear	5,000
Printing and stationery	2,400		

You are required to prepare trading and profit and loss account for the year ended 31.3.2012 and the balance sheet as on that date. Also, the following information is given.

1. Closing inventory—₹ 91,500
2. Depreciation to be charged on plant and furniture at 15% and 10%, respectively
3. Outstanding liabilities—wages at ₹ 5,200, salary at ₹ 1,200 and rent at ₹ 600
4. Dividend on paid up share capital is to be provided.

Solution: **... Company Ltd.**

Trading and Profit and Loss Account for the Year Ended March 31, 2012

		(₹)		(₹)
To opening inventory		50,000	By sales	4,25,000
To purchase		3,00,000	By closing inventory	91,500
To wages		75,200		
To gross profit c/d		91,300		
		5,16,500		5,16,500
To salaries		19,700	By gross profit b/d	91,300
To discount allowed		4,200	By discount received	3,150
To insurance	6,720			
Less: Prepaid	1,680	5,040		
To rent + outstanding rent		6,600		
To general expenses		8,950		
To printing & stationery		2,400		
To advertisement		3,800		
To bonus		10,500		
To bad debts		3,200		
To depreciation:				
Plant and machinery	12,075			
Furniture	1,710	13,785		
To net profit c/d		16,275		
		94,450		94,450

	(₹)		(₹)
To proposed dividend 5% on ₹ 2,45,000 (*i.e.*, excluding calls in arrears)	12,250	By balance b/d	6,220
		By net profit for the year b/d	16,275
To balance c/d	10,245		
	22,495		22,495

Balance Sheet as on March 31, 2012

Liabilities		(₹)	Assets		(₹)
Share capital:			**Fixed assets:**		
Authorised: 5,000 shares of ₹ 100 each		5,00,000	Plant & machinery	80,500	
			Less: Depreciation	12,075	68,425
Issued and subscribed:					
2,500 shares of ₹ 100 each			Furniture	17,100	
fully called up	2,50,000		*Less*: Depreciation	1710	15,390
Less: Calls in arrear	5,000	2,45,000	Investments:		Nil
			Current assets loans and advances		
Reserves and surplus:					
Reserves		25,000	(A) Current assets:		
Profit & loss appropriation a/c		10,245	Stock (assumed at cost)		91,500
Secured loans:			Accounts receivable		38,700
Loans from managing director (assumed unsecured)		15,700	Cash and bank balance		1,34,700
			(B) Loans and advances:		
Current liabilities and provisions:			Prepaid insurance		1,680
Current liabilities;			Miscellaneous expenditure		Nil
Creditors		35,200			
Expenses outstanding		7,000			
Provisions:					
Proposed dividend		12,250			
		3,50,395			3,50,395

Illustration 8: From the following trial balance of a company as on 31.3.2012, prepare profit and loss a/c for the year ending 31.3.2012 and balance sheet as on that date.

	(₹)	(₹)
Paid-up share capital		3,00,000
(Issued share capital of 30,000 shares of ₹ 10 each)		
Gross profit		1,50,000
General reserve		30,000
Provision for taxation (1.4.2012)		44,100
Profit & loss account		57,385
Tax paid	36,540	
14% debentures		1,00,000
Bills receivable	44,800	
Interim dividend	17,250	
Debenture redemption reserve		20,000
Securities premium account		5,000
Director's fees	2,000	

	(₹)	(₹)
Prepaid expenses	3,000	
Debenture interest (Less tax @ 20%)	11,200	
Creditors		2,10,680
Cash in hand	500	
Cash at bank	25,800	
Tax deducted at source on income from investments	1,575	
Income from investment		5,000
Investments (market value, ₹ 47,375)	50,000	
Debtors (including ₹ 3,000 due for more than 9 months)	2,45,500	
Stock	1,66,000	
Buildings	1,06,000	
Plant and machinery	2,12,000	
	9,22,165	9,22,165

The following information is relevant:

1. Director's remuneration amounting to ₹ 11,500 was charged against trading account
2. Depreciation is to be provided on building @ 5% and plant & machinery @ 10%
3. Taxation provision required for the year is ₹ 50,000
4. ₹ 35,000 is to be transferred to general reserve
5. Directors recommended divided of 10% on paid-up capital subject to deduction of tax at appropriate rates
6. Authorised share capital of the company is ₹ 5,00,000 (50,000 shares of ₹ 10 each)
7. Assets are shown at their written-down values. The method of depreciation adopted by the management is written-down value method.

Solution:

Profit and Loss Account for the Year Ending March 31, 2012

Liabilities		(₹)	Assets	(₹)
To interest on debentures @ 14%		14,000	By gross profit b/d	1,50,000
To directors' fees		2,000	By income on investments (Gross of tax deducted at source)	5,000
To remuneration to director		11,500		
To depreciation:				
Building @ 5%	5,300			
Plant & machinery 10%	21,200	26,500		
To provision for taxation		50,000	By directors remuneration charged against trading account	11,500
To net profit c/d		62,500		
		1,66,500		1,66,500

Profit and Loss Appropriation Account

	(₹)		(₹)
To general reserve	35,000	By balance b/d	57,385
To interim dividend	17,250	By net profit	62,500
To proposed dividend	30,000	By excess provision for taxation written back (44,100 – 36,540)	7,560
To balance c/d	45,195		
	1,27,445		1,27,445

Balance Sheet as on March 31, 2012

Liabilities		(₹)	Assets		(₹)
Share capital:			**Fixed assets:**		
Authorised		5,00,000	Buildings	1,06,000	
50,000 shares of ₹ 10 each			*Less*: Depreciation (5%)	5,300	1,00,070
			Plant & machinery	2,12,000	
Issued, subscribed and paid up capital		3,00,000	*Less*: Depreciation (10%)	21,200	1,90,800
			Investment:		
Reserves and surplus:			Investment (Market value ₹ 47,375)		50,000
			Current assets		
Securities premium account		5,000	Loans and advances		
General reserve	30,000		(A) Current assets:		
Add: Transferred	35,000	65,000	Stock and work-in-progress		1,66,000
Debenture redemption reserve		20,000	**Debtors:**		
			Debtors outstanding for more than 9 months	3,000	
Profit & loss a/c		45,195	Other debts	2,42,500	2,45,500
Secured loans:					
14% debenture		1,00,000	Cash in hand		500
			Cash at bank		25,800
			(B) Loans and advance:		
			Bills receivable		44,800
Current liabilities and provisions:			Prepaid expenses		3,000
Current Liabilities:			Tax deducted at source and advance payment of tax		1,575
Sundry creditors		2,10,680			
Income-tax educated at sources on debenture		2,800	Miscellaneous expenditure		
Provisions: Provision for taxation		50,000			
Dividend		30,000			
		8,28,675			8,28,675

Illustration 9: The following balances are extracted from the books of the Polyester Trading Company Ltd. for the year ended Dec. 31, 2012.

	(₹)
Share capital: Authorised, issued and fully paid (50,000 equity shares)	5,00,000
General reserves (as at 1.1.2012)	1,50,000
Furniture (including addition of ₹ 5,000 during 2012)	35,000
Office equipment (as at 1.1.2012)	22,000
Motorcar purchased (on 31.12.2011)	30,000
Sundry debtors (unsecured)	8,50,000
Advances to staff (unsecured)	10,000
Balance with post office in saving account (on 28.12.2012)	20,000
Cash in hand	2,000
Balance with Bank of India (including fixed deposit ₹ 1,00,000)	1,20,000
Loans from directors (unsecured)	2,00,000
Liability for expenses and goods supplied	2,67,000

	(₹)
Depreciation written off up to 31.12.2011 (Furniture ₹ 5,000, office equipment ₹ 2,000)	7,000
Opening stock of cloth	1,50,000
Legal charges (including ₹ 3,000 paid to auditors for tax representation)	10,000
Salaries to staff	50,000
Miscellaneous expenses (including travelling expenses of ₹ 4,000 in India and ₹ 36,000 for visits abroad for exports by managing director)	2,00,000
Purchase of cloth	30,39,000
Audit fees	4,000
Interest on fixed deposits with bank	5,000
Sales	35,00,000
Provision for taxation (as on 1.1.2012)	1,00,000
Profit and loss account (on 1.1.2012)	3,000
Advance tax paid	1,90,000

The following further information is also given to you:

(*a*) Closing stock of cloth is ₹ 3,00,000.

(*b*) Rate of depreciation on written-down value for (*i*) furniture—10%, (*ii*) office equipment—15%, and (*iii*) Motorcar—20%.

(*c*) Managing director is entitled to a commission of 10% on net profits subject to a maximum of ₹ 45,000 per annum.

(*d*) Sundry debtors include ₹ 1,50,000 outstanding for more than 6 months, out of this, ₹ 20,000 is considered doubtful for which provision to be made in accounts for 2011–2012.

(*e*) Tax liability for 2012, is estimated at 55% for which provision is to be made.

(*f*) The directors have decided to transfer ₹ 50,000 out of the net profits to general reserve and have proposed to pay dividend at 6% on equity shares.

You are required to prepare balance sheet and profit and loss account for the year ended December 31, 2012, from the above information.

Solution: **Polyster Trading Company Ltd.**

Profit and Loss Account for the Year Ended December 31, 2012

Liabilities		(₹)	Assets	(₹)
To opening stock		1,50,000	By sales	35,00,000
To purchases		30,39,000	By closing stock	3,00,000
To gross profit c/d		6,11,000		
		38,00,000		38,00,000
To Salaries		50,000	By G/P b/d	6,11,000
To Misc. expenses		1,60,000	By Interest on fixed deposits	5,000
To legal charges		7,000		
To payment to auditors' Fees	4,000			
Tax representation	3,000	7,000		
To depreciation		12,000		
To travelling expenses		40,000		
To provision for doubtful debts		20,000		
To managing director's remuneration		34,000		
To provision for taxation (55% on 2,86,000)		1,57,300		

Liabilities	(₹)	Assets	(₹)
To net profit c/d	1,28,700		
	6,16,000		6,16,000
To general reserve	50,000	By balance b/d	3,000
To proposed dividend	30,000	By net profit b/d	1,28,700
To balance c/d	51,700		
	1,31,700		1,31,700

Balance Sheet of Polyster Trading Co. Ltd. as on December 31, 2012

Liabilities		(₹)	Assets		(₹)
Share capital:			**Fixed assets:**		
Authorised capital of 50,000 equity shares of ₹ 100 each		5,00,000	Office equipment at cost	22,000	
			Less: Depreciation	5,000	17,000
Subscribed & paid-up capital 50,000 equity shares of ₹ 10 each fully paid up		5,00,000	Furniture at cost	30,000	
			Additions	5,000	
				35,000	
			Less: Depreciation	8,000	27,000
			Motorcar at cost	30,000	
Reserve & surplus:					
General reserves as on 1.1.2012	1,50,000		*Less*: Depreciation	6,000	24,000
Add: Transfer	50,000	2,00,000			
			Investments		Nil
Profit & loss a/c		51,700	Current assets, loans & advances		
Secured loans:		Nil			
Unsecured loans:			(A) Current assets:		
Loans from director		2,00,000	Stock in trade		3,00,000
Current liabilities & provisions:			Sundry debtors		
Outstanding expenses		26,700	Less than 6 months	7,00,000	
Remunerations			More than 6 months	1,50,000	
Managing director		34,000			
Provision for taxation	1,57,300			8,50,000	
Less: Advance tax	90,000	67,300	*Less*: provision for doubtful debts	20,000	8,30,000
			Fixed deposits	1,00,000	
Proposed dividend		30,000	Cash at bank	20,000	
			Post office saving a/c	20,000	
			Cash	2,000	1,42,000
			(B) Loans and advances:		
			Advance to staff		Nil
		13,50,000			13,50,000

Notes: Net profit before Managing Director remuneration	3,20,000
Add: Provision for doubtful debts	20,000
	3,40,000
Managing Director remuneration @ 10% on ₹ 3,40,000	= ₹ 34,000

Illustration 10: From the following balances which appeared as on December 31, 2012, in the books of the True and Fair Ltd, prepare the profit and loss account for the year ended Dec. 31, 2012 its balance sheet as on that date in the prescribed form:

	Debit (₹)	Credit (₹)
Share capital:		
Authorised and issued shares of ₹ 10 each		30,00,000
General reserve		3,00,000
Provisions for taxation on Jan. 1, 2012		4,41,000
Profit and loss account		5,73,850
Taxation payment	3,65,400	
6% mortgage debentures, redeemable 2016–17 years		10,00,000
Balance from trading account		10,52,000
Interim dividend for the year	1,72,500	
Debenture redemption reserve		2,00,000
Securities premium account		50,000
Directors' fees	20,000	
Unexpired payments	30,000	
Debentures interest (Less tax @ 20%)	48,000	
Creditors and accured charges		20,34,800
Balance at bank	2,50,000	
Cash in hand	5,000	
Tax deducted at source on dividends on investments	15,750	
Dividends on investments		50,000
Investments at cost (Market value ₹ 4,73,750)	5,00,000	
Debtors (including ₹ 12,800 due for more than six months)	24,55,000	
Stock and work-in-progress	16,60,000	
Vehicles (cost ₹ 1,50,000)	1,00,000	
Furniture and equipment (cost ₹ 2,00,000)	1,60,000	
Plant and machinery (cost ₹ 30,00,000)	21,20,000	
Land and buildings (cost ₹ 10,00,000)	8,00,000	

1. Depreciation provision for the year charged against trading: leasehold land and building—₹ 50,000; plant and machinery—₹ 3,00,000; furniture and equipment—₹ 16,000 and vehicles—₹ 25,000.
2. Director's remuneration charged against trading: salaries—₹ 1,00,000 and pension to retired managing director—₹ 15,000.
3. Provision for taxation required ₹ 5,03,270.
4. Directors recommend:
   (*a*) Transfer of ₹ 2,00,000 to debentures redemption reserves
   (*b*) Transfer of ₹ 3,50,000 to general reserve
   (*c*) Payment of final dividend of 12% subject to deduction of tax at appropriate rates

Make such assumptions as you may think necessary.

Solution: **M/s True & Fair Ltd.**

P&L Account for the Year Ended December 31, 2012

	(₹)		(₹)
To Depreciation:		By gross profit b/d	15,58,000
Lease hold & building	50,000	By dividend on investment (gross-tax	
Plant & machinery	3,00,000	deducted at source–₹ 15,750)	50,000

		(₹)		(₹)
Furniture & equipment		16,000		
Vehicles		25,000		
To interest on debentures		60,000		
To director's fees		20,000		
To salaries to director		1,00,000		
To pension to retired managing director		15,000		
To provision for taxation provision required	5,03,270			
Less: Existing provision	4,41,000	62,270		
To net profit c/d		9,59,730		
		16,08,000		16,08,000

Profit & Loss Appropriation Account

	(₹)		(₹)
To interim dividend paid	1,72,500	By balance b/d	5,73,850
To transfer to debenture redemption reserve account	2,00,000	By net profit for the year	9,59,730
To transfers to general reserve	3,50,000		
To proposed dividend	3,60,000		
To balance c/d	4,51,080		
	15,33,580		15,33,580

M/s True & Fait Ltd. Balance Sheet as on December 31, 2012

		(₹)			(₹)
Share capital:			Fixed Assets (at cost less depreciation):		
Authorised–30,00,000 shares of ₹ 10 each		30,00,000			
Issued, subscribed and paid up–3,00,000 shares of ₹ 10 each fully paid up		30,00,000	Gross block (as per scheduled attached)	43,50,000	
Reserves and surplus:			*Less*: Depreciation (as per scheduled attached)	11,70,000	31,80,000
(*i*) Securities premium account		50,000	Investments (At cost quoted market value ₹ 4,73,750)		5,00,000
(*ii*) Debenture redemption reserve balance as per last balance sheet	2,00,000		**Current assets, loans and advances:**		
Add: Transferred during the year	2,00,000	4,00,000	(A) Current assets:		
(*iii*) General reserve Balance as per last balance sheet	3,00,000		(*i*) Stock and work-in-progress		16,60,000
Add: Transferred during the year	3,50,000	6,50,000	(*ii*) Sundry debtors		
(*iv*) Profit and loss a/c		4,51,080	(*a*) Debts outstanding for a period exceeding 6 months	12,800	
Secured loans:			(*b*) Other debts	24,42,200	24,55,000
6% mortgage debentures, 2004–05		10,00,000	(*iii*) Cash in hand		5,000
			(*iv*) Cash at Bank		2,50,000
			(B) Loans and advances:		
			(*i*) Unexpired payments		30,000
			(*ii*) Advance payment of tax and tax deducted at source		3,81,150

	(₹)		(₹)
Current liabilities and provisions:			
(A) Current liabilities:			
(*i*) Creditors and accrued charges	20,34,800		
(*ii*) Income-tax deducted at sources on debenture interest	12,000		
(B) Provisions:			
(*i*) Proposed dividend	3,60,000		
(*ii*) Provision for taxation	5,03,270		
	84,61,150		84,61,150

Notes:

1. Depreciation and directors' remuneration have been charged against trading, the gross profit figure has, therefore, been arrived at as follows:

Balance from the trading account	10,52,000.00
Add: Depreciation on Leasehold land and building	50,000.00
Plant and machinery	3,00,000.00
Furniture and equipment	16,000.000
Vehicles	25,000.00
Directors' remuneration: Salaries	1,00,000.00
Pension to retired managing director	15,000.00

2. It has been assumed that income tax deducted at source (of ₹ 12,000) from interest on debentures has not been paid so far.

3. It has been also assumed that taxation payments are advance payment of tax and no assessment has been completed requiring adjustment of advance payment of tax against provision for taxation.

4. Interim dividend of ₹ 1,72,500 is assumed to be gross.

5. Entry for tax deducted at source from dividends from investment is shown in the trial balance, dividend of ₹ 50,000 is therefore gross.

6. Additional provisions for taxation of ₹ 62,270 have been shown under profit and loss account and not under profit and loss appropriation account because it is customary these days to take it as a charge against profits and not as an appropriation of profits.

Schedule of Fixed Assets Attached and Forming Part of Account

	Gross block as on Jan. 1, 2012	Addition during the year	Gross block as on Dec. 31, 2012	Depreciation written off up to Jan. 1, 2012	Depreciation during the year	Total depreciation written off	Net block as on Dec. 31, 2012
1. Leasehold land and building	10,00,000	—	10,00,000	1,50,000	50,000	2,00,000	8,00,000
2. Plant and machinery	30,00,000	—	30,00,000	5,80,000	3,00,000	8,80,000	21,20,000
3. Furniture and equipment	2,00,000	—	2,00,000	24,000	16,000	40,000	1,60,000
4. Vehicle	1,50,000	—	1,50,000	25,000	25,000	50,000	1,00,000
Total	43,50,000	—	43,50,000	7,79,000	3,91,000	11,70,000	31,80,000

Illustration 11: The following is the trial balance of Ideal Manufacturers Ltd. as on September 30, 2013:

Debit Balances	(₹)	Credit Balances	(₹)
Opening stock	1,32,000	Sales	7,76,000
Purchases	1,84,000	Departmental orders and items used in works	90,400
Stores and spares consumed	10,000	Dividends	
Manufacturing & miscellaneous expenditure	1,65,000.	Profit on block sold	30,000
Salaries, wages, etc. to employees	1,90,000	Sundry receipts	3,000
Freight and insurance	57,000	Profit and loss a/c	20,000
Transfer to repairs reserves	52,000	Provision for depreciation on fixed assets	5,60,000
Interest on loans	22,500	Share capital	2,80,000
Depreciation	51,500	Securities premium	20,000
Interim dividend	28,000	General reserves	80,000
Fixed assets at cost:		Development rebate reserve	1,20,000
Opening balance	12,60,000	Repairs reserves	40,000
Addition	67,000	Secured loan	2,30,000
Investments	26,000	Unsecured loans	50,000
Debtors	1,02,400	Creditors	1,70,000
Interest on capital (during construction from last year)	15,000	Provision for taxation	75,000
Deposits	40,000	Outstanding expenses	5,000
Cash at bank	1,40,000		
Cash in hand	2,000		
Managing director's remuneration (minimum)	6,000		
	25,50,400		25,50,400

The following further information is available:

1. Closing stock was valued at ₹ 1,47,000.
2. Managing director is entitled to 5 per cent remuneration on the net profits of the company.
3. Profits on block sold u/s 349 of the Companies Act, 1956. ₹ 20,000
4. Depreciation allowed under Income-Tax laws, ₹ 65,000.
5. Repairs reserve balance of ₹ 40,000 has been arrived at as follows:

Opening balance	38,000
Add: Transfer during the year	52,000
	90,000
Less: Actual expenses	50,000
	40,000

6. Final dividend making a total of 20 per cent on the paid-up capital of the company less interim dividend already declared has been proposed by the board of directors.
7. Amount of share capital is composed of shares of ₹ 10 each, fully paid.

You are required to prepare the profit and loss account for the year ended September 30, 2013, and also draw up a balance sheet on that date. Show separately, the computation of managing director's remuneration. Also state which particulars could not be given in the absence of information.

Solution:

Trading and Profit and Loss Account of Ideal Manufacturers Ltd. for the Year Ended Sept. 30, 2013

	(₹)		(₹)
To opening stock	1,32,000	By sales	7,76,000
To purchase	1,84,000	By closing stock	1,47,000
To stores and spares	10,000	By departmental orders and items used in works	90,400
To manufacturing and misc. expenses	1,65,000		
To salaries and wages to employee	1,90,000	By dividends (Gross)	1,282
To freight and insurance	57,000	By profit on sale of block	20,000
To transfer to repairs reserves	52,000	By sundry receipts	3,000
To interest on loan	22,500		
To managing directors remuneration	8,109		
To depreciation	51,500		
To net profit c/d (Subject to taxation)	1,65,573		
	10,37,682		10,37,682

Profit and Loss Appropriation a/c

	(₹)			(₹)
To interim dividend	28,000	By balance from last year	1,10,000	
To proposed dividend	28,000	By Net profit (current year)	1,65,573	
To balance c/d	1,29,573		2,75,573	
		Less: Provision for taxation and development rebate	90,000	1,85,573
	1,85,573			1,85,573

Notes:

1. It has been presumed that provision for taxation of ₹ 75,000 and development rebate reserve of ₹ 20,000 relate to last year.
2. Computation of managing director's remuneration

Net profit before managing director remuneration (₹ 1,65,573 + ₹ 8,109)		1,73,682
Add: Expenditure not allowed: Depreciation	51,500	
Repairs reserve	52,000	1,03,500
		2,77,182
Less: Allowable expenditure: Depreciation	65,000	
Actual repair	50,000	1,15,000
Net profit for managing director's remuneration		1,62,182
Managing director's remuneration @ 5% = ₹ 8,109		

Balance Sheet of Ideal Manufacturers Ltd.

Liabilities	(₹)	Assets		(₹)
Share capital Authorised:		**Fixed assets:**		
		Cost as in the beginning of the year	12,60,000	

Liabilities		(₹)	Assets		(₹)
Shares of ₹ 10 issued, subscribed and paid up 28,000 shares of ₹ 10 each fully paid		2,80,000	Additions during the year	67,000	
				13,27,000	
			Less: Provision for depreciation	5,60,000	7,67,000
Reserve and surpluses:					
Securities premium		20,000	Investments (at cost) (Market value ...)		26,000
Capital reserve		10,000	**Current assets, loans and advances:**		
General reserve		80,000	(A) **Current assets:**		
Development rebate reserve as per last balance sheet	1,05,000		Stock	1,47,000	
			Sundry debtors	1,02,400	
Since added:	15,000		Cash at bank	1,40,000	
			Cash in hand	2,000	
	1,20,000			3,91,400	
Repairs reserve	40,000		(B) **Loans and advances:**		
Profit and loss account	1,29,573	3,89,573	Deposits	40,000	
Secured loans		2,30,000	Tax Deducted at source on dividends	282	4,31,682
Unsecured loans		50,000			
Current Liabilities and provisions:			Misc. expenses and losses:		
(A) Current liabilities			Interest on capital not yet adjusted		15,000
Creditors for goods and expenses		1,77,109			
(B) Provisions:					
Provision for taxation	75,000				
Proposed dividend:	28,000	1,03,000			
		12,39,682			12,39,682

Note: The particulars for the following items could not be given in the absence of information.

(*i*) Authorised capital
(*ii*) Nature of securities in case of secured loans
(*iii*) Market value of investments
(*iv*) Mode of valuation of closing stock
(*v*) Particulars about sundry debtors and loans and advances
(*vi*) Whether balance at bank is in a scheduled bank or otherwise
(*vii*) Previous year's corresponding figures for each item

Creditors for goods and expenses have been calculated as follows:

Creditors	₹ 1,70,000
Managing director remuneration (₹ 8,109–6,000)	2,109
Outstanding expenses	5,000
	₹ 1,77,109

Illustration 12: The following balances are extracted from the books of PQ Ltd. on March 31, 2013:

	(₹)
Share capital	30,00,000
Cash in hand	62,000
Repairs and maintenance	86,000
Raw materials at cost	26,70,000

Furniture	1,22,000
Sundry creditors	34,00,000
Directors' fees	4,000
Plant and machinery	43,00,000
Misc. expenses	6,10,000
General reserve	40,00,000
Land	3,00,000
Finished goods at cost	31,00,000
Sales	4,23,00,000
Development rebate reserve	10,00,000
Building	7,41,000
Cash at bank	80,000
Provision for taxation	21,00,000
Sundry debtors	14,00,000
Raw material consumption	2,86,00,000
Staff advances	53,000
Advance from customers	5,00,000
Salary & wages and bonus	1,16,00,000
Cash credit from bank	1,25,000
Power	88,000
Prepaid expenses	46,000
Rent	53,000
Travelling and conveyance	41,000
Auditors' fees	15,000
Misc. income	5,46,000
Income-tax advance	30,00,000

The following further information is also given:

1. The authorised share capital of the company is 80,000 equity shares of ₹ 100 each which has been issued and subscribed to the extent of 50 per cent during the year, each share which was called up to the extent of ₹ 75 was made fully paid up by capitalising the necessary amount from general reserves. No effect has been given in the account for this bonus issue.
2. During the year a pending income tax assessment for an earlier year was finalised and the tax payable, after given credit for advance tax paid for that year amounting to ₹ 7,00,000 was finalised at ₹ 8,50,000. the company did not dispute this tax assessment. A provision of ₹ 8,00,000 had been made for that year.
3. The tax provision is to be made on current year's profit at 60 per cent.
4. The directors recommend 5 per cent dividend on the share capital (after being fully paid up).
5. The closing stock of finished goods at cost is ₹ 56,00,000.
6. During the year there were no imports or exports or any transaction in foreign currency except a foreign tour by a Director on which net expenditure of ₹ 22,000 was incurred as follows:

	(₹)
Air Passage to and fro-tickets purchased in India	12,000
Cost of traveller cheques purchased in pound sterling	13,500
	25,500

Less: Foreign exchange surrendered by the Director on his return	3,500
	22,000

7. The development rebate reserve is no longer required.
8. Depreciation on assets amounting to ₹ 4,30,000 on plant and machinery, ₹ 13,000 on furniture and ₹ 38,000 on building has been debited to miscellaneous expenditure.
9. The surplus in profit and loss account is to be transferred to general reserve account.

Prepare profit and loss account and balance sheet indicating the extent to which information required to be disclosed under the Companies Act, 1956 has not been given.

Solution: Profit and Loss A/c for the Year Ended March 31, 2013

	(₹)		(₹)
To opening stock of finished goods	31,00,000	By sales	4,23,00,000
To raw materials consumed	2,86,00,000	By closing stock of finished goods	56,00,000
To salaries, wages and bonus	1,16,00,000	By miscellaneous income	5,46,000
To power	88,000		
To rent	53,000		
To repairs and maintenance	86,000		
To Directors' fees	4,000		
To Auditors' fees	15,000		
To travelling and conveyance	41,000		
To depreciation	4,81,000		
To miscellaneous expenditure	1,29,000		
To provision for taxation	25,49,400		
To net profit c/d	16,99,600		
	4,84,46,000		4,84,46,000
To provision for income-tax for earlier years	7,50,000	By net profit	16,99,600
To proposed dividend	2,00,000	By development rebate reserve written back	10,00,000
To general reserve transfer	17,49,600		
	26,99,600		26,99,600

PQ Limited
Balance Sheet as on March 31, 2013

Liabilities and Capital		(₹)	Assets		(₹)
Shares capital:			Fixed assets:		
Authorised:					
80,000 equity shares of ₹ 100 each		80,00,000	Land at cost		3,00,000
Issued subscribed and fully paid-up:			Buildings:		
40,000 equity shares of ₹ 100 each		40,00,000	Cost	7,79,000	
(out of the above 25 per share was paid-up by capitalising reserves without payment being realised in cash)			*Less*: Depreciation upto end of previous year	7,79,000	
			Less: Depreciation for the year	38,000	7,41,000
Reserves and surplus:			**Plant and machinery:**		
General reserve brought forward from previous year	40,00,000		*Less*: Depreciation written off up to end of previous year		

Liabilities and Capital		(₹)	Assets		(₹)
Less: Capitalised to make shares fully paid	10,00,000				
	30,00,000			47,30,000	
Add: Transferred from profit and loss account	17,49,600	47,49,600	*Less*: Depreciation written off this year	4,30,000	43,00,000
Development rebate reserve brought forward	10,00,000		Furniture Original cost	—	
			Less: Depreciation up to previous year	—	
				1,35,000	
Less: Transferred to P&L account	10,00,000	Nil	*Less*: Depreciation for the year	13,000	1,22,000
Secured loans:			**Investments:**		Nil
Cash credit from bank		1,25,000	Current assets, loans and advances:		
Unsecured loans:			Current assets		
			Raw materials at cost		26,70,000
Current liabilities:			Finished goods at cost		56,00,000
Sundry creditors		34,00,000	Sundry debtors		14,00,000
Income-tax payable		8,50,000	Cash at bank		80,000
Advances-from customers		5,00,000	Cash in hand		62,000
Provisions:			**Loans and advances:**		
Provision for taxation		38,49,400	Staff advances		53,000
Proposed dividend		2,00,000	Prepaid expenses		46,000
			Income-tax paid in* advance (30,00,000 – 7,00,000)		23,00,000
			Miscellaneous expenditure to the extent not year written off or adjusted		Nil
		1,76,74,000			1,76,74,000

* Alternatively, the amount may be deducted from the provision for taxation.

Statistical notes:

Foreign exchange earned	Nil
Foreign exchange used (on foreign tour of a director)	₹ 10,000

Provision for taxation is calculated as follows:

Profit before tax = ₹ 4,84,46,000 – ₹ 4,41,97,000 = 42,49,000

60% of ₹ 42,49,000 =	₹ 25,49,400
Add: (₹ 21,00,000 – 8,00,000) =	₹ 13,00,000
	₹ 38,49,400

Miscellaneous expenditure = ₹ 6,10,000 – (₹ 4,30,000 + ₹ 13,000 + ₹ 38,000) = ₹ 1,29,000

Note: Information regarding the following points as required under Schedule VI of the Companies Act, being not available,has not been given:

(*i*) Previous year's figures.

(*ii*) Details of security in respect of loan from bank.

(*iii*) Original cost, total depreciation and addition during the year, if any, to fixed assets.

(*iv*) The break-up of sundry debtors according to:

(*a*) security, and

(*b*) age.

(*v*) The break-up of repairs and maintenance into that for buildings and machinery.

(*vi*) Number of employees drawing salary above ₹ 2,00,000 per annum.

(*vii*) Licenced capacity, installed capacity, production, opening and closing stocks, turnover, raw material consumption and percentage of consumption of imported stock.

(*viii*) Break-up of payments made to the auditors.

Illustration 13: The Indian Implements Co. Ltd. has an authorised, issued, subscribed and paid up capital of ₹ 2,00,000 divided into 2,000 equity shares of ₹ 100 each. The following balances are taken out from its trial balance on 31.12.2012.

	(₹)	(₹)
Land & building	90,000	
Plant &machinery	1,65,600	
Loose tools	9,400	
Furniture & fittings	3,600	
Preliminary expenses	4,900	
Calls in arrears	1,500	
Cash in hand	500	
5% govt. bonds (Face value ₹ 10,000)	9,880	
Bills receivables	13,600	
Motor vehicles	3,000	
Goodwill	16,000	
Sundry debtors	20,800	
Sundry creditors		30,600
Reserve fund		15,000
P&L a/c balance		8,800
Bank overdraft		11,180
Purchases & purchase returns	2,40,000	5,000
Advertising	2,540	3,07,800
Sales & sale returns	7,000	
Legal charges	1,000	
Carriage inwards	3,700	
Wages	23,200	
Rent and rate and insurances	4,900	
Share capital		2,00,000
6% debenture of 100 each		1,00,000
Opening stock	47,600	
Income tax	2,800	
Trade expenses	1,500	
Repairs of plant & machinery	860	
Interim dividend for half year ending 30.6.2001	4,500	
	6,78,380	6,78,380

Prepare final accounts of the company creating a provision for bad debts of 5% on sundry debtors; charging 5% depreciation on plant and machinery, 7.5% on furniture and fittings, 10% on loose tools and 20% on motors. The stocks in trade as on 31.12.2012 was calculated at ₹ 44,200. On August 16, 2012, the directors had declared an interim dividend @ 5% for six months ending 30.6.2012.

Solution: **The Indian Implements Co. Ltd. Trading Account for the Year Ending Dec. 31, 2012**

Liabilities		(₹)	Assets		(₹)
To opening stock		47,600	By sales	3,07,800	
To purchase	2,40,000		Sales return	7,000	3,00,800
Purchase returns	5,000	2,35,000	By closing stock		44,200
To wages		23,200			
To carriage inwards		3,700			
To gross profits (Transfer to P&L a/c)		35,500			
		3,45,000			3,45,000

Profit and Loss a/c for the Year Ended December 31, 2012

Liabilities		(₹)	Assets	(₹)
To advertising		2,540	By gross profit from trading a/c	35,500
To legal charges		1,000	By interest accrued on govt. bonds @ 5%	500
To rent rates and insurances		4,900		
To trade expenses		1,500		
To repairs to plant machinery		860		
To interest on debentures outstanding		6,000		
To income tax		2,800		
To provision for bad debts at 5% on sundry debtors		1,040		
To depreciation: Plant and machinery @ 5%	8,280			
Furniture and fittings 7½%	270			
Loose tools @ 10%	940			
Motor vehicles @ 20%	600	10,090		
To net profit c/d		5,270		
		36,000		36,000

Profit and Loss Appropriation A/c

	(₹)		(₹)
To interim dividend	5,000	By balance b/d	8,800
To net profit carried to balance sheet	9,070	By net profit	5,270
	14,070		14,070

Balance Sheet as on December 31, 2012

Liabilities	Fig. for the current year (₹)	Assets		Fig. for the current year (₹)
Share capital:		**Fixed assets:**		
Authorised, issued & subscribed—2000 equity shares of ₹ 100 each	2,00,000	Goodwill		16,000
		Land & Building		90,000
		Plant and machinery	1,65,600	
		Less: Depreciation @ 5%	8,280	1,57,320

Liabilities		Fig. for the current year (₹)	Assets		Fig. for the current year (₹)
Called/paid-up capital	2,00,000				
Less: Calls in arrears	1,500	1,98,500	Furniture and fittings	3,600	
Reserve fund		15,000	*Less*: Depreciation 7½	270	3,330
Profit and loss a/c		9,070			
			Motor vehicles	3,000	
			Less: Depreciation @ 20%	600	2,400
Secured loans:					
6% debentures		1,00,000			
Bank overdraft		11,180			
Unsecured loans:			**Investments:**		
Current liabilities and provisions:			5% govt. bonds free of tax of the face		
Sundry creditors		30,600	value of ₹ 10,000		9,880
Unclaimed interim dividend		500			
Interest on debentures		6,000	**Current assets:**		
			Interest accrued on govt. bonds		500
			Loose tools	9,400	
			Depreciation @ 10%	940	8,460
			Stock		
			S/Debtors	20,800	
			Provision @ 5%	1,040	19,760
			Cash		500
			Bills receivables		13,600
			Closing stock		44,200
			Misc. expenditure		
			Preliminary expenses		4,900
		3,70,850			3,70,850

Illustration 14: A Co. was registered with an authorised capital of ₹ 10,00,000 divided into shares of ₹ 10 each of which 40,000 shares have been issued as fully paid. Following is the trial balance as on Dec. 31, 2012.

	(₹)		(₹)
Opening stock	1,86,420	Plant & machinery	78,400
Manufactures wages	1,09,740	Loose tools	12,500
Purchases	4,21,460	Share capital	4,00,000
Manufacture expenses	19,240	Calls in arrear	1,000
Machinery repairs	8,610	Rate & electricity–factory	14,210
Carriage inward	4,910	Office	3,400
Carriage outward	9,260	Directors' fees & remuneration	12,000
Advance payment for income tax	14,290	Office salaries & expenses	13,000
Bank loan 5%	50,000	Auditors' fees	1,250
Interest on bank loan	1,250	Office furniture	5,000
Debtors	1,64,400	Commission (Dr.)	8,640
Creditors	92,220	Returns inwards	12,640
P&L a/c opening Cr.	8,640	Returns outwards	9,810

	(₹)		(₹)
Bank current a/c	6,860	Preliminary expenses	6,000
Cash	1,920	Transfer fees	40
Leasehold factory	64,210	Goodwill	1,50,000
		Sales	7,69,900

Prepare final accounts of the period taking into account the following adjustments:

(i) Write off 1/3rd preliminary expenses.

(ii) Depreciation: on Plant & Machinery @ 10%, on office furniture @ 5%.

(iii) Manufactures wages ₹ 1,890 and office salaries, ₹ 1,200 had accrued due.

(iv) Provide for interest on bank loan for 6 months.

(v) Closing stock is valued at ₹ 1,24,840.

(vi) Loose tools at the end are valued at ₹ 10,000.

(vii) Provide ₹ 8,500 for doubtful debtors.

(viii) Provide further ₹ 3,120 for discount on debtors.

(ix) Directors recommended dividend @ 5% for the year ending December 31, 2012 after providing for taxes amounting to ₹ 23,000.

Solution: Trading Account for the Year Ending December 31, 2012

Particulars		Amount (₹)	Particulars		Amount (₹)
To opening stock		1,86,420	By sales	7,69,900	
To purchase	4,21,460		*Less*: Sales returns	12,640	7,57,260
Less: Purchase returns	9,810	4,11,650			
			By closing stock		1,24,840
To mfg. wages	1,09,740				
Outstanding	1,890	1,11,630			
To mfg. expenses		19,240			
To rates & electricity		14,210			
To carriage inward		4,910			
To gross profits (tr. to P&L a/c)		1,34,040			
		8,82,100			8,82,100

Profit & Loss a/c for the Year Ended Dec. 31, 2012

Particulars		Amount (₹)	Particulars	Amount (₹)
To office salaries & expenses	13,000		By gross profit	1,34,040
+Outstanding	1,200	14,200	By transfer fees	40
To machinery repairs		8,610		
To carriage outward		9,260		
To payment for income tax	14,290			
+ Payable	8,710	23,000		
To commission		8,640		
To interest on bank Loan	1,250			
+ Payable	1,250	2,500		
To Depreciation:				
Plant & machinery	7,840			

Particulars		Amount (₹)	Particulars	Amount (₹)
Loose tools	2,500			
Office furniture	250	10,590		
To rates & electricity		3,400		
To director's fees		12,000		
To auditors fees		1,250		
To preliminary expenses written off		2,000		
To provision for debts		8,500		
To provision for discount		3,120		
To net profits (after tax)		27,010		
		1,34,080		1,34,080

P&L Appropriation a/c

	(₹)		(₹)
To proposed dividend	19,500	By P&L a/c (opening balance)	8,640
To balance c/f	16,150	By P&L a/c (current)	27,010
	36,650		36,650

Balance Sheet as on December 31, 2012

Liabilities	Amount (₹)	Assets		Amount (₹)
Share capital:		Goodwill		1,50,000
Authorised		Fixed assets:		
10,00,000 shares of ₹ 10 each	10,00,000	Leasehold factory	78,400	64,210
Issued & subscribed:		Plant & machines	7,840	70,560
40,000 shares of ₹ 10 each	4,00,000	Office furniture	5,000	
		Depreciation	250	4,750
Calls in arrears	1,000			
Reserves & surplus	3,99,000			
		Current assets:		
P&L a/c (Balance)	16,150	Debtors	1,64,400	
		Provision for doubtful debts	8,500	
			1,55,900	
Provision & current Liabilities:		Provision for discount	3,120	1,52,780
Bank loans	50,000	Bank current a/c		6,860
Office salaries	1,200	Cash		1,920
Mfg. wages	1,890	Loose tools	12,500	
Interest on bank loan	1,250	Used	2,500	10,000
Creditors	92,220			
Dividends payable/proposed	19,500	Preliminary expenses	6,000	
Income-tax payable	8,710	Written off	2,000	4,000
		Stock		1,24,840
	5,89,920			5,89,920

Illustration 15: The following is the trial balance of Nakul Ltd. as on March 31, 2012.

	(₹)	(₹)
Stock April 1, 2011	75,000	
Purchase return		10,000
Purchases and sales	2,45,000	3,40,000
Wages	30,000	
Discount		3,000
Carriage inwards	950	
Furniture and fittings	17,000	
Salaries	7,500	
Rent	4,000	
Sundry expenses	7,050	
Profit and loss appreciation Account March 31, 2011		15,000
Dividend paid for 2011–12	9,000	
Share capital		1,00,000
Debtors and creditors	27,500	17,500
Plant and machinery	29,000	
Cash at bank	46,200	
General reserve		15,500
Patents and trademarks	4,800	
Bills receivable and bills payable	5,000	7,000
	5,08,000	5,08,000

Prepare trading account, profit and loss account and profit and loss appropriation account for the year ended March 31, 2012 and balance sheet as on that date. Take into consideration the following adjustments:

(*i*) Stock on March 31, was valued at ₹ 88,000.

(*ii*) Depreciate—Plant and machinery @ 15%; furniture and fittings @ 10% and patents and trademarks @ 5%.

(*iii*) Make a provisions for income tax @ 50%.

(*iv*) On March 31, 2012 outstanding rent amounted to ₹ 800 while outstanding salaries totalled ₹ 900.

(v) The directors proposed dividend @ 15% per annum for the year ended March 31, 2012, after the minimum transfer to general reserve as required by law.

(vi) Make a provision for doubtful debts amounting to ₹ 510.

(vii) Provide for managerial remuneration @ 10% of the net profit before tax.

Solution:

Trading and P&L a/c of M/s Nakul Ltd. for the Year Ended March 31, 2012

Particulars		Amount (₹)	Particulars	Amount (₹)
To stock on 1.4.2011		75,000	By sales	3,40,000
To purchase	2,45,000		By stock on 31.3.2012	88,000
Purchase returns	10,000	2,35,000		
To wages		30,000		
To carriage inward		950		

Particulars		Amount (₹)	Particulars	Amount (₹)
To gross profit		87,050		
		4,28,000		4,28,000
To Salaries	7,500		By gross profit b/d	87,050
+ outstanding	900	8,400	By discounts	3,000
To rent	4,000			
+ outstanding	800	4,800		
To sundry expenses		7,050		
To provision for doubtful debts		510		
To Depreciation:				
Plant	4,350			
Furnitures	1,700			
Patents & trademarks	240	6,290		
To managerial remuneration @ 10%		6,300		
To provision for tax		28,350		
To net profit (transfer to P&L app. a/c)		28,350		
		90,050		90,050

Profit & Loss Appropriation a/c

	(₹)		(₹)
To dividends for 2010–2011	9,000	By balance b/f	15,000
To general reserve 5% of ₹ 28,350	1,418	By P&L a/c	28,350
To proposed dividends for 2011–12	15,000		
To net profit (transfer to balance sheet)	17,932		
	43,350		43,350

Balance Sheet of M/s Nakul Ltd. as on March 31, 2012

Liabilities		Amount (₹)	Assets		Amount (₹)
Share capital:			**Fixed assets:**		
Authorised			Plant and machinery	29,000	
Issued & subscribed		1,00,000	Depreciation	4,350	24,650
Reserve & surplus:					
General reserve	15,500		Furniture & fittings	17,000	
+New reserve	1,418	16,918	Depreciation	1,700	15,300
P&L a/c (Balance)		17,932			
Current liabilities:			Patent & trademarks	4,800	
Creditors		17,500	Depreciation	240	4,560
Bills payable		7,000			
Outstanding:			**Current assets, loans & Advances:**		
Rent		800	Cash at bank		46,200
Salaries		900	Bills receivable		5,000
Provision for income-tax		28,350	Stocks		88,000
Proposed dividend for 2001–2002		15,000	Debtors	27,500	
			Less: Provision for doubtful debts	510	26,990
O/S managerial remuneration		6,300			
		2,10,700			2,10,700

Note: Managerial remuneration = 10/90 × 56,700 = ₹ 63,000

Illustration 16: The Auto Parts Manufacturing Co. Ltd. was registered with an authorised capital of ₹ 10,00,000 divided into shares of ₹ 10 each of which 40,000 shares had been issued and fully paid. The following is the trial balance extracted on March 31, 2012.

	Debit (₹)	Credit (₹)
Stock (April 1, 2011)	1,86,420	
Purchase and sales	7,18,210	11,69,900
Returns	12,680	9,850
Manufacturing wages	1,09,740	
Sundry manufacturing expenses	19,240	
Carriage inwards	4,910	
18% bank loans (Secured)		50,000
Interest on bank loan	4,500	
Office salaries and expenses	17,870	
Auditors fees	8,600	
Directors remuneration	26,250	
Preliminary expenses	6,000	
Freehold premises	1,64,210	
Plant and machinery	1,28,400	
Furniture	5,000	
Loose tools	12,500	
Debtors and creditors	1,05,400	62,200
Cash in hand	19,530	
Cash at bank	96,860	
Advance payments of tax	84,290	
P&L a/c on April 1, 2011		38,640
Share capital	—	4,00,000
	17,30,610	17,30,610

You are required to prepare trading and profit and loss account for the year ended March 31, 2012 and a balance sheet as on that date after taking into consideration the following adjustments:

(*i*) On March 31, 2012, outstanding manufacturing wages and outstanding office salaries stood at ₹ 1,890 and ₹ 1,200, respectively. On the same date, stock was valued at ₹ 1,24,840 and loose tools at ₹ 10,000.

(*ii*) Provide for interest on bank loan for 6 months.

(*iii*) Depreciation on plant and machinery is to be provided @ 15% while on office furniture it is to be @ 10%.

(*iv*) Write off one-third of balance of preliminary expenses.

(*v*) Make a provision for income tax @50%.

(*vi*) The directors recommended a maiden (first) dividend @ 15% for the year ending March 31, 2012, after a transfer of 5% of net profits to general reserve.

Solution: Trading and Profit & Loss a/c of Auto Parts Mfg Co. Ltd. for the Year Ending March 31, 2012

Particulars		Amount (₹)	Particulars		Amount (₹)
To stock 1.4.2011		1,86,420	By sales a/c	11,69,900	
To purchases	7,18,210		—Returns	12,680	11,57,220
—Returns	9,850	7,08,360	By stock (13.3.2012)		1,24,840

Particulars		Amount (₹)	Particulars	Amount (₹)
To wages	1,09,740			
+ outstanding	1,890	1,11,630		
To sundry mfg. expenses		19,240		
To carriage inwards		4,910		
To G/P c/d		2,51,500		
		12,82,060		12,82,060
To interest on bank loans	4,500		By Gross profit b/d	2,51,500
Add: Outstanding	4,500	9,000		
To office salaries & expenses	17,870			
+ outstanding	1,200	19,070		
To auditors fees		8,600		
To directors' remuneration		26,250		
To depreciation:				
Loose tools	2,500			
Plant and machinery	19,260			
Furniture	500	22,260		
To preliminary expenses		2,000		
To tax		82,160		
To net profit		82,160		
		2,51,500		2,51,500

Profit & Loss Appropriation a/c

Particulars	Amount (₹)	Particulars	Amount (₹)
To dividends (15%)	60,000	By P&L a/c (1.4.2001)	38,640
To general reserve (5% of net profit)	4,108	By P&L a/c	82,160
To balance c/d	56,692		
	1,20,800		1,20,800

Balance Sheet of Auto Parts Mfg. Co. Ltd. as on 31.3.2012

Liabilities	Amount (₹)	Assets		Amount (₹)
18% bank loan (secured)	50,000	Preliminary expenses	6,000	
Share capital	4,00,000	–Write/off	2,000	4,000
General reserves	4,108	Plant & machinery	1,28,400	
P&L a/c balance	56,692	–Depreciation	19,260	1,09,140
Proposed dividends	60,000	Freehold premises		1,64,210
Outstanding:		Furniture	5,000	
Interest on bank loan	4,500	–Depreciation	500	4,500
		Loose tools	12,500	
Mfg. wages	1,890	Depreciation	2,500	10,000
Office salaries	1,220	Debtors		1,05,400
Creditors	62,220	Cash in hand		19,530
		Cash at Bank		96,860
		Stock		1,24,840

Liabilities	Amount (₹)	Assets		Amount (₹)
		Advance tax	84,290	
			– 82,160	2,130
	6,40,610			6,40,610

Illustration 17: From the following trial balance of XYZ Ltd, as on March 31, 2012, you are required to prepare the final accounts of the company as on that date. The authorised capital of the Company is ₹ 10 lakh divided into 5,000 6% preference shares of ₹ 100 each and 50,000 equity shares of ₹ 10 each.

Trial Balance

	(₹)	(₹)
50,000 equity shares of ₹ 10 each fully paid up		5,00,000
5,000 6% preference shares of 100 each		5,00,000
Furniture & fixtures	4,00,000	
Buildings	2,00,000	
Goodwill	25,000	
Motor vehicles	4,00,000	
Plant & machinery	3,25,000	
General reserve		1,20,000
Stock-in-trade (April 1, 2011)	25,000	
Purchases and sales	2,40,000	7,00,000
Carriage inwards	10,000	
Returns inward and outward	2,400	1,450
Directors fee	450	
Salaries	10,000	
Wages	20,000	
Profit and loss account		80,000
Cash	40,000	
Accounts receivable & payable	1,00,000	80,000
Provision for depreciation:		
Building		2,000
Motor vehicles		20,000
Plant and machinery		16,250
Furniture & fixtures		8,000
Advances	1,00,000	
Closing inventory	29,850	
Audit fees	20,000	
Provision for taxation		70,000
Advances payment of income-tax	70,000	
Income-tax paid (under dispute)	80,000	
	20,97,700	20,97,700

The following additional information is relevant:

1. Provision @ 5% is to be made for bad debts reserve ₹ 2,000 to be written off as bad debts

2. Depreciation on written down value method should be provided as follows:

Plant and machinery	15%
Land & building	5%
Motor vehicles	25%
Furniture & fixture	10%

3. Interim dividend declared but not paid—₹ 10,000
4. Proposed final dividend 10% on equity shares.
5. Managing director is to be paid a commission of 5% on net profits subject to a maximum of ₹ 18,000.
6. Income tax to be provided @ 50%.

Solution: XYZ Company Ltd. Trading and Profit and Loss a/c for the Year Ending March 31, 2012

Particulars		Amount (₹)	Particulars		Amount (₹)
To opening inventory		25,000	By sales	7,00,000	
To purchase	2,40,000		*Less*: Returns	2,400	6,97,600
Less: Returns	1,450	2,38,550			
To carriage inwards		10,000			
To water		20,000			
To gross profit c/d		4,04,050			
		6,97,600			6,97,600
To director's fee		450	By gross profit b/d		4,04,050.00
To salaries		10,000			
To audit fees		20,000			
To bad debts		2,000			
To provision for bad debts		4,900			
To depreciation:					
Building	9,900				
Plant & machinery	46,313				
Motor vehicles	95,000				
To furniture & fixtures	39,200	1,90,413			
To managing directors commission (1)		9,060			
To provision for tax		83,613.50			
To net profit c/d		83,613.50			
		4,04,050.00			

Profit and Loss Appropriation Account

Particulars	Amount (₹)	Particulars	Amount (₹)
To interim dividend outstanding	10,000.00	By balance b/d	80,000.00
To proposed dividend on equity	50,000.00	By net profit b/d	83,613.50
To prefernce dividend	30,000.00		
To general reserve (3)	1,841.00		
To balance c/d	71,772.50		
	1,63,613.50		1,63,613.50

XYZ Company Ltd.
Balance Sheet as at March 31, 2012

Liabilities		Amount (₹)	Assets		Amount (₹)
Share capital:			**Fixed Assets:**		
Authorised capital			Goodwill		25,000
50,000 equity share of ₹ 10 each		5,00,000	Buildings	2,00,000	
5,000 6% preference share			*Less*: Accumulated depre-		
of ₹ 10 each		5,00,000	ciation (2,000 + 9,900)	11,900	1,88,100
Issued, subscribed and paid-up capital			Plant & Mach.	3,25,000	
50,000 equity shares of ₹ 10 each		5,00,000	*Less*: Accumulated dep.	62,563	2,62,437
5,000 6% preference shares of ₹ 100 each		5,00,000	Furniture & Fixture	4,00,000	
			(–) Accumulated dep.	47,200	3,52,800
Reserves and surplus:					
General reserve	1,20,000		Motor vehicle	4,00,000	
Add: transfer from profit &	1,841	1,21,841	*Less*: Accumulated dep.		
loss a/c			(20,000 + 95,000)	1,15,000	2,85,000
			Investments		Nil
			Current assets, loans and advances:		
Profit & loss a/c		71,772.50	**Current assets:**		
Secured loans		Nil	Stock		29,850.00
Unsecured loans		Nil	Debtors	1,00,000	
			Less: Bad debts	2,000	
				98,800	
Current liabilities and provisions:			*Less*: Provision	4,900	93,100.00
Current liabilities			Cash at bank		40,000.00
Sundry creditors		80,000.00	Loans and advances		1,00,000.00
Interim dividend		10,000.00	Income tax paid (under dispute)		80,000.00
MD's commission		9,060.00	Misc. expenditure		Nil
Provisions:					
Provisions for taxation		83,613.50			
Proposed dividend:					
Equity		50,000.00			
Preference		30,000.00			
		14,56,287.00			14,56,287.00

		₹
1. Calculations of managing director's commission gross profit as per trading a/c		4,04,050.00
Less:		
Director's fees	450	
Salaries	10,000	
Audit fee	20,000	
Bad debts	2,000	
Depreciation	1,90,413	2,22,863.00
		1,87,187.00

5% on ₹ 1,87,187 = ₹ 9,059.35 = ₹ 9,060 (approx)

Provision for tax is to be made after charging managing director commission.

2. The old provision for taxation is adjusted against the advance payment of income-tax and hence they do not appear in the balance sheet.

3. Transfer to reserves will be 2.5% of current profits as the divided declared and proposed, *i.e.*, 12%. Transfer to reserves = (2.5/100) × 73,613 = ₹ 1,841.

Illustration 18: The following are the balances of Johri & Co. Ltd. as on March 31, 2012:

Credit	Amount (₹)	Debit	Amount (₹)
Share capital	40,00,000	Premises	30,72,000
12% debenture	30,00,000	Plant	33,00,000
P&L account	2,62,500	Stock	7,50,000
Bills payable	3,70,000	Debtors	8,70,000
Creditors	4,00,000	Goodwill	2,50,000
Sales	41,50,000	Cash and bank	4,06,500
Generals reserve	2,50,000	Calls in arrear	75,000
Bad debt provision on 1.4.2011	35,000	Interim dividend paid	3,92,500
		Purchase	18,50,000
		Preliminary expenses	50,000
		Wages	9,79,800
		General expenses	68,350
		Salaries	2,02,250
		Bad debts	21,100
		Debenture interest paid	1,80,000
	1,24,67,500		1,24,67,500

Information:

(*a*) Depreciate plant by 15%

(*b*) Write off ₹ 5,000 from preliminary expenses

(*c*) Half year's debenture interest due

(*d*) Create 5% provisions on debtors for doubtful debts

(*e*) Provide for income tax @ 50%

(*f*) Stock on March 31, 2012, was ₹ 9,50,000

(*g*) A claim of ₹ 25,000 for workmen's compensation is being disputed by the company

Prepare final Accounts of the company.

Solution: **Trading and Profit & Loss Account of M/s Johri & Co. for the Year Ending March 31, 2012**

Particulars		Amount (₹)	Particulars	Amount (₹)
To opening stock		7,50,000	By sales	41,50,000
To purchase		18,50,000	By closing stocks	9,50,000
To wages		9,79,800		
To gross profit c/d		15,20,200		
		51,00,000		51,00,000
To salaries		2,02,250	By Gross profit b/d	15,20,200
To bad debts		21,100		
To debentures				
Interest Paid	1,80,000			

Particulars		Amount (₹)	Particulars	Amount (₹)
+Due	1,80,000	3,60,000		
To general expenses		68,350		
To prov. for doubtful debts	43,500			
–Existing provision	35,000	8,500		
To depreciation:				
Plant		4,95,000		
To preliminary expenses w/off		5,000		
To provision for tax		1,80,000		
To net profit		1,80,000		
		15,20,200		15,20,200

Profit & Loss Appropriation a/c of M/s Johri & Co. for the Year Ending March 31, 2012

Particulars	Amount (₹)	Particulars	Amount (₹)
To interim dividend paid	3,92,500	By balance b/d	2,62,500
To balance c/d	50,000	By P&L a/c	1,80,000
	4,42,500		4,42,500

Balance Sheet of M/s Johri & Co. as on 31.3.2012

Liabilities		Amount (₹)	Assets		Amount (₹)
Share capital:			**Fixed assets:**		
Authorised issued & subscribed 4,00,000 shares of ₹ 10% each	40,00,000		Goodwill		2,50,000
			Premises		30,72,000
			Plant	33,00,000	
Call-in-arrears	75,000		Depreciation	4,95,000	28,05,000
		39,25,000	**Current assets, loans & advances:**		
			Stocks		9,50,000
Reserves & surpluses:			Debtors	8,70,000	
General reserves		2,50,000	*Less*: Provision	43,500	8,26,500
P&L a/c		50,000	Cash at bank		4,06,500
Secured loans:			Loans & advances		—
12% debentures		30,00,000	**Misc. expenditure:**		
Add: Interest		1,80,000	Preliminary expenses	50,000	
Current liabilities & provisions:			W/off	5,000	45,000
Bills payable		3,70,000			
Creditors		4,00,000			
Tax provisions		1,80,000			
		83,55,000			83,55,000

Illustration 19: The following in the trial balance of ABC Company Ltd. as on June 30, 2012. Prepare trading and profit and loss account in the form prescribed under the Companies Act, 1956.

Dr.	Dr. (₹)	Cr. (₹)
Authorised Capital:		
50,000 shares at ₹ 10 per share		
Subscribed Capital:		1,00,000
10,000 shares at ₹ 10 share		
Calls-in-arrear	6,400	
Land	10,000	
Buildings	25,000	
Plant and machinery	15,000	
Furniture and fixture	3,200	
Carriage inwards	2,300	
Wages	21,400	
Salaries	4,600	
Bad Debts provision, July 1, 2011	—	1,400
Sales	—	80,000
Sales returns	1,700	
Bank charges	100	
Coal, gas & water	700	
Rates and taxes	800	
Purchases	50,000	
Purchase returns		3,400
Bills receivable	1,200	
General expenses	1,900	
Sundry debtors	42,800	
Sundry creditors		13,200
Stock, July 1, 2011	25,000	
Fire insurance	400	
Cash at bank	13,000	
Securities premium		6,000
Cash in hand	2,500	
General reserve	—	24,000
	2,22,800	2,22,800

Charge depreciation on Building @ 2½ per cent, on Plant and Machinery @ 10 per cent and Furniture and Fixture 10 per cent. Make a provision of 5 per cent on Sundry Debtors for Bad Debts. Carry forward the following unexpired amounts:

Fire Insurance 120

Provide the following outstanding liabilities:

Wages 3,200

Salaries 500

Rent and Rates and Taxes 200

The value of stock as on June 30, 2012 was ₹ 30,000

Solution:

ABC Company Ltd.
Trading and Profit and Loss Account for the Year ended 30.6.2012

Liabilities		Amount (₹)	Assets		Amount (₹)
To Opening Stock		25,000	By Sales	80,000	
To Purchases	50,000		*Less*: Returns	1,700	78,300
Less: Returns	3,400	46,600	By closing stock		30,000
To Carriage inwards		2,300			
To Wages	21,400				
Add: Outstanding	3,200	24,600			
To Coal, Gas & Water		700			
To Gross Profit c/d		9,100			
		1,08,300			1,08,300
To Salaries	4,600		By Gross profit b/d		9,100
Add: Outstanding	500	5,100	By Net loss		2,465
To Bank charges		100			
To Rent, Rates & Taxes	800				
Add: Outstanding	200	1,000			
To General Expenses		1,900			
To Bad Debts Provision					
Required	2,140				
Less: On 1.7.2001	1,400	740			
To fire Insurance	400				
Less: Prepaid	120	280			
To Depreciation:					
To Building		625			
To Plant & Machinery		1,500			
To Furniture & Fixture		320			
		11,565			11,565

Balance Sheet as on 30.6.2012

Particulars		Amount (₹)	Particulars		Amount (₹)
Share capital:			**Fixed Assets:**		
Authorised			Land		10,000
50,000 equity shares of ₹ 10 each		5,00,000	Building	25,000	
Issued, subscribed and called up:			*Less*: Depreciation	625	24,375
10,000 equity shares of ₹ 10	1,00,000		Plant & Machinery	15,000	
Less: Calls-in-Arrears	6,400	93,600	*Less*: Depreciation	1,500	13,500
Reserve & surplus:			Fixtures & Fitting	3,200	
Securities Premium Account		6,000	*Less*: Depreciation	320	2,880
General Reserve	24,000		Investments		
Less: Profit & Loss			**Current Assets:**		
Account (Dr.)	2,465	21,533	Closing Stock		30,000
Secured loans		—	Debtors	42,800	
Unsecured loans		—	*Less*: Provision	2,140	40,660

Particulars		Amount (₹)	Particulars	Amount (₹)
Current liabilities:			Bank	13,000
Creditors		13,200	Cash	2,500
Outstanding expenses			Loans & Advances	
Wages	3,200		Bills Receivable	1,200
Salaries	500		Prepaid Insurance	120
Rent	200	3,900	Miscellaneous Expenditure	
		1,38,235		1,38,235

Illustration 20: The trial balance of Pradeep Construction Ltd. as on March 31, 2012 as follows:

	Dr. (₹)	Cr. (₹)
Capital: Authorised and Issued (42,000 equity shares of ₹ 20 each)		8,40,000
Provision for depreciation (as on 1.4.2011)		
Leasehold property		42,000
Other properties		1,00,000
Motor van		20,000
Cash in hand	30,200	
Cash at bank	1,80,000	
Motor van	50,000	
Properties (at cost)	16,00,000	
Opening stock	2,40,000	
Administrative & selling expenses	3,53,000	
Purchases and sales	27,75,000	41,30,000
Managing director's remuneration	1,00,000	
Rent received		72,000
Investments at cost	1,35,000	
Investments income (net) (Tax deducted at source)		6,800
9% debentures		3,00,000
Debentures interest	21,000	
Bank interest	11,640	
Bank overdraft		14,600
Debtors and creditors	6,20,000	3,02,000
Interim dividend	33,600	
Profit & loss account as on 1.4.2001		1,15,040
Calls-in-arrears	2,000	
General reserve as on 1.4.2001		2,00,000
Share suspense		6,000
Unclaimed dividend		3,000
	61,51,440	61,51,440

The following further information is available:

(*a*) Closing stock at cost was ₹ 3,34,000.

(*b*) No effect has been given to the following resolutions of the Board:

(*i*) dated July 15, 2011 forfeiting 1,000 shares on which calls amounting to ₹ 2,000 remained unpaid;

(*ii*) dated September 18, 2011 reissuing the 1,000 forfeited shares for ₹ 6,000 as fully paid. The amount received was credited to Share Suspense Account.

(*c*) The directors have recommended a final dividend of ₹ 10 per share including the interim dividend already declared on December 25, 2011 and also to transfer ₹ 20,000 to general reserve.

(*d*) Depreciation is to provided as follows:

— Motor van 20 per cent on written down value.

— Properties other than leasehold 3 per cent on written down value.

— Leasehold property was purchased on April 1, 2005 for ₹ 2,80,000 for a period of 40 years.

(*e*) Managing directors are entitled to a remuneration of 10 per cent of the net profits subject to a minimum of ₹ 50,000.

(*f*) Provision for taxation is to be made at 60 per cent.

Ignoring figures for the previous year, prepare the profit and loss account for the year ended March 31, 2012 and the balance sheet on that date.

Solution: **Books of Pradeep Construction Ltd.**

Trading Profit and Loss Account for the Year Ended 31.3.2012

Particulars		Amount (₹)	Particulars	Amount (₹)
Opening Stock		2,40,000	Sales	41,30,000
Purchases		27,75,000	Closing stock	3,34,000
Administrative & selling expenses		3,53,000	Rent received	72,000
			Income from investments (6,800 × 100/90)	7,556
Bank interest		11,640		
Debenture interest	21,000			
Add: Outstanding	6,000	27,000		
Depreciation: Leasehold	7,000			
Other property	36,600			
Motor van	6,000	49,600		
Managing Directors remuneration		1,08,732		
Provision for taxation		5,87,150		
Balance c/d		3,91,434		
		45,43,556		45,43,556
General Reserve		20,000	Balance b/d	1,15,040
Interim Dividend		33,600	Net profit b/d (current year)	3,91,434
Proposed Dividend		3,86,400		
Balance c/d		66,474		
		5,06,474		5,06,474

Balance Sheet of Pradeep Construction Ltd. as on 31.3.2012

Particulars	Amount (₹)	Particulars		Amount (₹)
Share capital:		**Fixed Assets:**		
Authorised, Issued, Subscribed & paid up 40,000, Equity shares of ₹ 20 each	8,40,000	Property at cost	13,20,000	
		Less: Depreciation	1,36,600	11,83,400

Particulars		Amount (₹)	Particulars		Amount (₹)
Reserves & Surplus:			Leasehold Property at cost	2,80,000	
Capital Reserve (Surplus on forfeiture)		4,000	*Less*: Depreciation	49,000	2,31,000
General Reserve as on 1.4.2011	2,00,000		Motor Van at cost	50,000	
			Less: Depreciation	26,000	24,000
Add: Addition during the year	20,000	2,20,000	Investment at cost		1,35,000
Profit & Loss account		66,474	**Current Assets:**		
Secured Loans 9% deb.	3,00,000		Stock		3,34,000
Add: Interest outstanding	6,000	3,06,000	Debtors		6,20,000
Unsecured Loans		14,600	Bank		1,80,000
Current Liabilities & Provisions			Cash		30,200
A. **Current Liabilities:**			**Loan & Advances:**		
Creditors		3,02,000	Income Tax deducted at source		750
Unclaimed dividend		3,000	Miscellaneous Expenditure		
Managing Director's Remuneration		8,732			
B. **Provisions:**					
Provision for taxation		5,87,150			
Proposed dividend		3,86,400			
		27,38,356			27,38,356

Working Notes:

1. Depreciates (₹)

(*i*) Leasehold Property: Total cost	2,80,000
Depreciation upto 31.3.2011	42,000
Depreciation for 2012	7,000
(*ii*) Other Property: Total cost	16,00,000
Less: Leasehold	2,80,000
Cost	13,20,000
Less: Depreciation upto 31.3.2011	1,00,000
	12,20,000
Depreciation at 3% ₹ 36,600	
(*iii*) Motor van: Cost	50,000
Less: Depreciation upto 31.3.2011	20,000
W.D.V.	30,000
Depreciation @ 20%	6,000

2. Managing Director's remuneration

Net profit before remuneration and taxation ₹ 3,91,434 + ₹ 5,87,150 + 1,08,732 = ₹ 10,87,316
10% of ₹ 10,87,316 = ₹ 1,08,732.

3. Provision for taxation

Net Profits	10,87,316
Less: Remuneration of Managing Director	1,08,732
	9,78,574

60% ₹ 9,78,534 = ₹ 5,87,150

4. Interest on Debentures 9% of ₹ 3,00,000	27,000
Less: Already paid	21,000
Provision made for the balance	6,000

Illustration 21: Golden Traders Nagpur Ltd. has an authorised and subscribed capital of ₹ 8,00,000 divided into shares of ₹ 100 each. From the following balances which appear in the books of the company as on 31.12.2013, prepare:

(*a*) Profit and Loss Account

(*b*) Profit and Loss Appropriation Account for the year ended 31.12.2013, and

(*c*) Balance sheet as on that date in the form prescribed under the Companies Act 1956:

	Debit (₹)	**Credit (₹)**
Share capital		8,00,000
Land and building	3,40,000	
Plant and machinery	6,60,000	
Loose tools	40,000	
Preliminary expenses	20,000	
Furniture	29,000	
Calls-in-arrears	6,000	
Cash in hand	2,000	
5% government bonds (tax free), (Face value ₹ 40,000)	36,000	
Bills receivable	58,000	
Goodwill	36,000	
Motor vehicles	40,000	
Sundry debtors	83,000	
Interim dividend	18,000	
Repairs	3,000	
Sundry creditors		1,20,000
Reserve fund		60,000
Profit and loss account (1.1.2013)		35,400
Purchases and returns outwards	9,60,000	20,000
Sales and returns inwards	28,000	12,30,000
Advertisement	10,000	
Audit fees	4,000	
Carriage	15,000	
Wages	92,000	
Insurance	20,000	
Stock (1.1.2013)	1,90,000	
General expenses	17,000	
6% debentures of ₹ 100 each		4,00,000
Bank overdraft		50,000
Debenture interest (*Less*: tax at 30%)	8,400	
	27,15,400	27,15,400

You are required to consider the following adjustments:

1. Stock as on 31.12.2013, ₹ 1,80,000
2. Create Reserve for bad debts at 5% on sundry debtors

3. Provide depreciation: Plant and machinery at 5%
   Furniture at 10%
   Loose Tools at 15%
   Motor Vehicles at 20%
4. Prepaid Insurance ₹ 2,000
5. Reserve fund to be increased by ₹ 10,000
6. Directors declared on 30.9.2013 an interim dividend for six months ending June 30, 2013 at 3%
7. Wages outstanding ₹ 3,000
8. Interest on debentures for 6 months
9. Tax Rate is 55%

Solution: **Golden Traders Limited**

Trading and Profit and Loss Account for the Year Ended 31.12.2013

Particulars		Amount (₹)	Particulars		Amount (₹)
Opening stock		1,90,000	Sales	12,30,000	
Purchases	9,60,000		*Less*: Returns	28,000	12,02,000
Less: Returns	20,000	9,40,000	Closing stock		1,80,000
Wages	92,000				
Add: Outstanding	3,000	95,000			
Carriage		15,000			
Gross profit c/d		1,42,000			
		13,82,000			13,82,000
Repairs		3,000	Gross profit b/d		1,42,000
Advertising		10,000	Interest on Govt. bonds (5% of 40,000)		2,000
Audit fees		4,000			
Provision for doubtful debts		4,150			
Insurance	20,000				
Less: Prepaid	2,000	18,000			
General Expenses		17,000			
Debenture Interest (6% on ₹ 4,00,000)		24,000			
Depreciation plant		33,000			
Loose tools		6,000			
Furniture		2,900			
M. Vehicle		8,000			
		1,30,050			
Provision for tax 55% on (1,42,000 – 1,30,050) = 11,950		6,600			
Net profit c/d		7,350			
		1,44,000			1,44,000
To General Reserve		10,000	Balance b/d		35,400
To Interim Dividend (3% on 7,94,000)		23,820	Net profit b/d		7,350
To balance c/d		8,930			
		42,750			42,750

Balance Sheet as at 31.12.2013

Liabilities		Amount (₹)	Assets		Amount (₹)
Share capital:			**Fixed Assets:**		
Authorised, Issued, Subscribed, Called up and Paid up capital			Goodwill		36,000
			Land & Building		3,40,000
8,000 share of ₹ 100 each	8,00,000		Plant & Machinery	6,60,000	
Less: Call-in-Arrears	6,000	7,94,000	*Less*: Depreciation	33,000	6,27,000
			Furniture	29,000	
Reserves & Surplus:			*Less*: Depreciation	2,900	26,100
Reserve Fund		70,000			
Profit & Loss Appropriation Account		8,930	Motor Vehicle	40,000	
			Less: Depreciation Investments	8,000	32,000
Secured Loans: 6%					
Debentures	4,00,000		5% government bonds (face value		
Add: Interest outstanding	8,400	4,08,400	₹ 40,000)		36,000
(*Less*: 30% tax)			**Current Assets:**		
Bank overdraft		50,000	Interest outstanding on Govt. Bonds		2,000
Unsecured loans		nil			
Current liabilities:			Loose Tools (40,000 – 6,000)		34,000
Wages outstanding		3,000	Closing stock		1,80,000
Tax deducted at source		7,200	Debtors	83,000	
Unclaimed Interim Dividend (23,820, – 18,000)		5,820	*Less*: Provision	4,150	78,850
			Cash		2,000
Creditors		1,20,000	**Loans & advances:**		
Provision for taxation		6,600	Prepaid insurance		2,000
			Bills receivable		58,000
			Miscellaneous expenditure		
			Preliminary Expenses		20,000
		14,73,950			14,73,950

Working Notes:

Hints:

(*i*) Tax is not to be paid on interest income of ₹ 2,000 on Government bonds as these are tax free.

(*ii*) Though the tax at 55 per cent on ₹ 11,950 (13,950 – 2,000) is calculated at ₹ 6572.5, it is taken as ₹ 6,600).

(*iii*) Interim dividend is to be calculated on the paid up capital, *i.e.*, ₹ 8,00,000 – ₹ 6,000 calls in arrears, *i.e.*, 3 per cent of ₹ 7,94,000 for 6 months.

(*iv*) Interest on Government bonds is to be provided for.

THEORY QUESTIONS

1. What do you mean by final or annual accounts of a company?
2. Explain the legal requirements with regard to books of accounts maintained by a company.
3. Discuss briefly the legal provisions about the preparation of financial statements of a company.
4. Comment on the format of a balance sheet prepared by a company.

5. Explain the contents of balance sheet of a company as prescribed in the Companies Act.
6. What does the Companies Act say on the preparation of a profit and loss account?
7. Explain the accounting treatment of the following items:
   (*i*) Dividends
   (*ii*) Calls-in-arrears
   (*iii*) Call-in-advance
   (*iv*) Income tax
   (*v*) Interest on debentures
   (*vi*) Interest out of capital
8. Draw up a proforma balance sheet in horizontal form as per Schedule VI of the Companies Act.
9. State the requirements under Schedule VI (Parts I and II) of the Companies Act. 1956, in respect of:
   (*a*) Turnover
   (*b*) Managerial Remuneration
   (*b*) Foreign Exchange Transactions
   (*d*) Investments
   (*e*) Fixed Assets
10. Write short notes on any three of the following with reference to Schedule VI:
    (*a*) Secured and unsecured loans
    (*b*) Loans and advances
    (*c*) Miscellaneous expenses
    (*d*) Contingent liability
11. What information is required to be disclosed regarding the following items in the balance sheet of a company:
    (*a*) Unpaid dividends
    (*b*) Immovable property
    (*c*) Contingent liabilities
    (*d*) Debtors
    (*e*) Investments
12. State the statutory requirements relating to Profit and Loss Account with regard to the following items in case of a manufacturing company:
    (*a*) Raw material consumed
    (*b*) Foreign exchange earnings
    (*c*) Payments to auditors
    (*d*) Goods manufactured
    (*e*) Statement of net profit under Section 349.
13. Explain the provision relating to transfer of profits to reserves and declaration of dividends out of profits and reserves.
14. How are the contingent liabilities classified and shown in the balance sheet of a joint stock company?
15. What are the legal requirements, if any, regarding the preparation of Profit and Loss Appropriation Account?
16. Write a short note on the authentication of final accounts.
17. Explain the statutory requirements for the payment of interest out of capital.
18. "A company cannot make payment of dividend out of current profits without making good past losses."
19. Explain the nature of the following items and show how would you deal with them while preparing the final accounts of a company
    (*a*) Preliminary expenses
    (*b*) Arrears of dividend on cumulative preference shares.
    (*c*) Calls in arrear
    (*d*) Proposed dividend
    (*e*) Advance payment of tax. **(BBA, GGSIP University, December 2000)**

20. (*a*) Explain legal provisions of issue of shares at a discount by a company.

(*b*) Under what heads you will record the following items in the balance sheet of a company:

(*i*) Vehicles

(*ii*) Loose tools

(*iii*) Bills receivables

(*iv*) Securities premium account

(*v*) Interest due on secured loans

(*vi*) Provision for taxation

(*vii*) Discount on issue of Debentures **(BBA, GGSIP University, December, 2006)**

21. Comment on the following:

(*a*) "A public company must offer its share to general public for subscription". **(BBA, GGSIP University, December, 2007)**

(*b*) "A new company can not issue shares at a discount". **(BBA, GGSIP University, December, 2008)**

22. (*a*) Explain the difference between the balance sheet of a sole trader and that of adjoint stock company.

(*b*) For what purposes, the securities premium account be used as per Section 78 of the Companies Act. **(BBA, GGSIP University, December, 2009)**

SELF-EVALUATION EXERCISES

I. Select the correct answer for the following multiple choice questions:

1. On sale of old furniture, owners, equity would

(*a*) Increase (*b*) Decrease

(*c*) Remain unchanged (*d*) May or may not change

2. The liabilities of a firm are ₹ 16,000, the claim of the proprietors are ₹ 24,000. The total assets are

(*a*) ₹ 24,000 (*b*) ₹ 8,000 (*c*) ₹ 40,000 (*d*) ₹ 16,000

3. On a particular date the assets of a business are worth ₹ 2,00,000 and its capital is ₹ 70,000. Its liabilities on that date shall be

(*a*) ₹ 2,70,000 (*b*) ₹ 1,30,000 (*c*) ₹ 70,000 (*d*) ₹ 1,10,000

4. Withdrawals by the proprietor would

(*a*) Reduce both assets and owners equity

(*b*) Reduce assets and increase liabilities

(*c*) Reduce owners equity and increase liabilities

(*d*) Remains unaffected

5. Balance sheet discloses

(*a*) Cash position of the business (*b*) Financial position of the business

(*c*) Profit earning capacity of the business (*d*) Income position of the business

6. Final Accounts of complains means

(*a*) Balance sheet

(*b*) Profit and loss account

(*c*) Statement of changes in financial position

(*d*) Balance sheet and profit and less account

7. Indian companies are required to maintain their accounts on
   (*a*) Cash basis (*b*) Accrual basis
   (*c*) Accrual basis and double entry system (*d*) Double entry system
8. Which section of the companies Act requires the Indian Companies to maintain proper books of accounts
   (*a*) Section 209 (*b*) Section 211 (*c*) Section 214 (*d*) Section 217
9. The balance sheet of an Indian company should show, by way of notes, the following contingent liability(s)
   (*a*) Claim against the company not acknowledged as debts
   (*b*) Uncalled liability on shares partly paid
   (*c*) Arrears of fixed cumulative dividends
   (*d*) All of above
10. The Companies Act prescribes a format for preparing
    (*a*) Balance sheet (*b*) Profit and loss account
    (*c*) Statement of changes in financial position (*d*) All of the above
11. The credit balance of profit and loss appropriation account in the case of a company is transferred to
    (*a*) Capital account (*b*) Current account
    (*c*) Reserve and surplus (*d*) None of the above
12. Discount on the issue of debentures is written off
    (*a*) Before redemption of debentures
    (*b*) After redemption of debentures
    (*c*) In any period selected by the company
    (*d*) In no case later than the date of redemption
13. Calls-in-advance is a
    (*a*) Long term liability (*b*) Current liability
    (*c*) Contingent liability (*d*) None of the above
14. The total managerial remuneration in respect of any year should not exceed which per cent of the net profit
    (*a*) 7% (*b*) 9% (*c*) 13% (*d*) 11%
15. Dividend by a company can be paid from
    (*a*) Profit of the current year
    (*b*) Undistributed profits of previous years
    (*c*) Money provided by central government or any state government for the payment of dividend
    (*d*) All of the above

II. Answer True or False

1. Assets are concrete and real which may be touched and felt, whereas liabilities are not necessarily so.
2. In accounting as in common parlance, assets are desirable items for a business, whereas liabilities are not.
3. Half completed work need not always represent work-in-progress.
4. When a donation is received, it is not possible to reflect it in the balance sheet in accordance with the duality concept.

5. Losses and assets are alike just as profits and liabilities are alike.
6. Retained Earnings represent the amount of cash set aside in business.
7. Capitalising an expense implies showing an item in the balance sheet rather than in the profit and loss account.
8. Amortising an expense implies bringing a portion of an asset's cost from balance sheet to the profit and loss account.
9. Indian companies prepare their accounts on cash basis and accrual basis both.
10. Annual accounts of companies are required to be presented in annual general meeting of the shareholders.

EXERCISES AND PROBLEMS

1. Below is the Balance sheet of Exe Ltd. as at 31st March 2013:

Liabilities	Amount (₹)	Assets	Amount (₹)
Share Capital:		**Fixed Assets:**	
Authorised	15,00,000	Plant & Machinery	6,00,000
Issued and Subscribed 2,000 8% Redeemable Preference shares of ₹ 100 each, fully paid up	2,00,000	Furniture	75,000
50,000 equity shares of ₹ 10 each fully Paid up	5,00,000	Investments	1,00,000
		Current Assets,	
		Loans & Advances:	
		(*a*) **Current Assets:**	
Reserves and Surplus:		Stock	1,70,000
Capital Reserve	25,000	Debtors	65,000
Securities Premium	30,000	Cash at Bank	80,000
General Reserve	1,60,000	(*b*) **Loans and Advances:**	Nil
Profit & Loss Account	1,38,000		
Current Liabilities and Provisions:			
(*a*) **Current Liabilities:**			
Sundry Creditors	37,000		
(*b*) Provisions	Nil		
	10,90,000		10,90,000

On this date the Company decided to redeem its preference shares at a premium of 5%. For this purpose, Investments were sold for ₹ 1,10,000 and 10,000 equity shares of ₹ 10 each were issued at a premium of Re 1 each. After redemption of preference shares, the company issued one bonus share of ₹ 10 each for every five equity shares held.

Pass journal entries to record the above-mentioned transactions and prepare Balance-Sheet as it would appear thereafter.

[**Ans:** Number of Bonus shares Issued—12,000; Balance sheet total—₹ 10,00,000].

2. The following items appear on the liabilities side of the balance sheet of a limited company as on 1 April 2013:

	₹
(*a*) 13.5% Preference Share Capital	4,00,000
(*b*) Equity Share Capital—Fully paid up	5,00,000
(*c*) Equity Share Capital—60% paid up	3,00,000
(*d*) Securities premium account	7,00,000
(*e*) 15% Debentures	10,00,000

Profit (before interest on debentures and tax at 60%) is ₹ 11,50,000 for the accounting year ended 31, March 2014. The recommendation of the Company's board of directors include equity dividend of 15% and Capitalisation of profits for making partly paid equity shares as fully paid. Pass journal entries to incorporate board's recommendations and present the aforesaid items in the liabilities side of the balance sheet.

3. Calculate the managerial remuneration from the following particulars of Ankit & Co. Ltd, due to the managing directors of the company at the rate of 5% of the profits. Also determine the excess remuneration paid, if any;

Particulars	₹
Net Profit	2,00,000
Net Profit is calculated after considering the following:	
(*i*) Depreciation	40,000
(*ii*) Preliminary expenses	10,000
(*iii*) Tax Provision	3,10,000
(*iv*) Directors' Fees	8,000
(*v*) Bonus	15,000
(*vi*) Profit on sale of fixed assets (Original cost: ₹ 20,000; written down value: ₹ 11,000)	15,500
(*vii*) Provision for doubtful debts	9,000
(*viii*) Scientific research expenditure (for setting up new machinery)	20,000
(*ix*) Managing director's remuneration paid	30,000
Others information:	
(*i*) Depreciation allowable under Income Tax rules	35,000
(*ii*) Bonus liability as per payment of Bonus Act, 1965	18,000

[**Ans:** Managerial remuneration due to the managing director—₹ 28,725; Excess remuneration paid—₹ 1,275].

4. The following is the summarized Balance Sheet of Nalanda steel Products limited on 31st December, 2013:

Liabilities	Amount (₹)	Assets	Amount (₹)
Share Capital:		**Freehold:**	
₹ 10 Shares	2,50,000	Property	2,50,000
General Reserve	50,000	Other Fixed Assets	2,00,000
Profit & Loss Account	2,50,000	Current Assets	2,50,000
14% Debentures	50,000		
Current Liabilities	1,00,000		
	7,00,000		7,00,000

The Company has had the Freehold property professionally valued and decides to include it in the Balance sheet at its valuation of ₹ 4,00,000.

At the same time, it is proposed to—

(*a*) Capitalize part of undistributed profits by making a bonus issue to the shareholders of one ₹ 10 share for every five shares held;

(*b*) Create a reserve of ₹ 25,000 for the replacement of fixed assets (in addition to the aggregate depreciation of ₹ 50,000 already provided); and

(*c*) Redeem one-half of outstanding Debentures at a premium of 5 per cent.

Assuming that the appropriate resolutions have been adopted, pass journal entries in the books of the company to give effects to the above and set out the Balance sheet as it would appear after the completion of all the transactions.

[**Ans:** Balance Sheet total—₹ 8,23,750]

5. The paid up share capital of Exe Ltd. is ₹ 10,00,000 consisting of 60,000 Equity shares of ₹ 10 each fully paid up and 50,000 Equity shares of ₹ 10 each, ₹ 8 per share paid up.

It has ₹ 40,000 in securities Premium Account, ₹ 2,00,000 in Profit and Loss Account (Cr.), ₹ 3,00,000 in general Reserve and ₹ 60,000 in Capital Redemption Reserve Account.

By Way of Bonus Dividend the partly paid up shares are converted into fully paid-up shares and the holders of fully paid-up shares are also allotted fully paid-up Bonus shares in the same ratio.

Pass journal entries showing separately the two types of Bonus issues stated above. It is desired that there should be minimum reduction in free reserves.

6. The following is the Trial Balance of L. N. Manufacturing Co. Ltd. as at 31st March 2013:

	Debit (₹)	Credit (₹)
Stock 1st April 2012	7,50,000	
Sales		35,00,000
Purchases	24,50,000	
Wages	5,00,000	
Salaries	75,000	
Rent	49,500	
Discounts	70,000	50,000
General Expenses including Insurance	1,70,500	
Profit and Loss Account		1,50,300
Dividends paid	90,000	
Capital—1,00,000 shares of ₹ 10 each		10,00,000
Sundry Debtors and Creditors	3,75,000	1,75,000
Plant and Machinery	2,90,000	
Cash	1,62,000	
General Reserve		1,55,000
Bad Debts	48,300	
	50,30,300	50,30,300

You are required to prepare Trading Account, and Profit and Loss Account for the year ended 31st March, 2013 and the Balance sheet at that date. You are also to make provision in respect of the following:

(*a*) Stock on 31st March 2013: ₹ 8,20,000.

(*b*) Depreciate Plant and Machinery @ 15% p.a.

(*c*) Provide 5% discount on Debtors.

(*d*) Provide Managing Director's Commission @ 5% on the net profits before deducting his commission.

(*e*) Allow 2.5% discount on creditors.

(*f*) One month's rent @ ₹ 54,000 per annum was due on 31st March 2013.

(*g*) Six months Insurance was unexpired at ₹ 7500 per annum.

(*h*) Make a provision for Income Tax @ 50%.

[**Ans:** Gross Profit—₹ 6,20,000; Net Profit—₹ 93,750; Managing Director's remuneration—₹ 9,904; Balance sheet Total—₹ 15,88,500].

7. The promoters of proposed New Wave Ltd. purchased a running business on 1st January, 2012 from Mr. Altra Modern. New Wave Ltd. was incorporated on 1st May, 2012. The Combined Profit and Loss Account of the company prior to and after the date of incorporation is as under:

Profit and Loss Account for the year ended 31st Dec., 2012

Liabilities	Amount (₹)	Assets	Amount (₹)
To Rent, Rates, Insurance, Electricity & Salaries	12,000	By Gross Profit	1,50,000
To Director's Fees	3,600	By Discount Received from Creditors	6,000
To Preliminary Expenses	4,900		
To Carriage Outwards and Selling Expenses	5,500		
To Interest paid to vendors	10,000		
To Net Profit	1,20,000		
	1,56,000		1,56,000

Following further information is available :

(1) Sales upto 30th April, 2012 were ₹ 3,00,000 out of total sales of ₹ 15,00,000 of the year.

(2) Purchases upto 30th April, 2012 were ₹ 3,00,000 out of total purchases of ₹ 9,00,000 of the year.

(3) Interest paid to vendors on 1st Nov., 2012 @ 12% p.a. on ₹ 1,00,000 being purchase consideration.

From the above information, prepare Profit and Loss Account for the year ended 31st December, 2012, showing the profits earned prior to and after incorporation and also show the transfer of the same to the appropriate accounts.

[**Ans:** Pre-Incorporation Profit—₹ 22,900; Post-Incorporation profit—₹ 97,100].

8. From the following particulars furnished by Pioneer Ltd., prepare the balance sheet as at 31 March, 2013 as required by Part 1, schedule VI of the Companies Act. give notes at the foot of the balance sheet as may be found necessary:

		Debit (₹)	Credit (₹)
Equity Capital (face value of ₹ 100)			10,00,000
Calls-in-arrears		1,000	
Land		2,00,000	
Building		3,50,000	
Plant and machinery		5,25,000	
Furniture		50,000	
General reserve			2,10,000
Loan from State Financial Corporation			1,50,000
Stock:			
Finished goods	2,00,000		
Raw materials	50,000	2,50,000	
Provision for taxation			68,000
Sundry debtors		2,00,000	

	Debit (₹)	Credit (₹)
Advances	42,700	
Proposed dividend		60,000
Profit and loss account		1,00,000
Cash balance	30,000	
Cash at bank	2,47,000	
Preliminary expenses	13,300	
Loans (unsecured)		1,21,000
Sundry creditors (for goods and expenses)		2,00,000
	19,09,000	19,09,000

Following additional information is also provided

(*i*) Miscellaneous expenses included ₹ 5,000 audit fees and ₹ 700 for out of pocket expenses paid to the auditors.

(*ii*) 2,000 equity shares were issued for consideration other than cash.

(*iii*) Debtors of ₹ 52,000 are due for more than six months.

(*iv*) The cost of assets: Building—₹ 4,00,000; Plant and Machinery—₹ 7,00,000; Furniture—₹ 62,500.

(*v*) The balance of ₹ 1,50,000 in the loan account with State Financial Corporation is inclusive of ₹ 7,500 for interest accrued but not due. The loan is secured by hypothecation of the plant and machinery.

(*vi*) Balance at bank includes ₹ 2,000 with Perfect Bank Ltd., which is not a scheduled bank.

(*vii*) Bills receivable for ₹ 2,75,000 maturing on 30 June, 2013, have been discounted.

(*viii*) The company had contract for the erection of machinery at ₹ 1,50,000 which is still incomplete.

[**Ans:** Balance Sheet total—₹ 19,08,000].

9. Prepare a Balance sheet in vertical form as at 31st December, 2013 from the following information of ABC Limited as required under part 1B of Schedule VI of the Companies Act 1956:

	(₹)
Term Loan	10,00,000
Sundry Creditors	11,45,000
Advances	3,72,000
Cash and bank balances	2,75,000
Staff advances	55,000
Provision for taxation	1,70,000
Share Premium	4,75,000
Loose tools	50,000
Investments	2,25,200
Loss for the year	3,00,000
Sundry debtors	12,25,000
Miscellaneous expenses	58,000
Loans from debtors	2,00,000
Provision for doubtful debts	20,200
Stores	4,00,000

	(₹)
Fixed assets (WDV)	51,50,000
Finished goods	7,50,000
General reserve	20,50,000
Capital work in progress	2,00,000

Additional Information:

1. Share Capital consists of:
   (*a*) 3,000 equity shares of ₹ 100 each fully paid up.
   (*b*) 10,000 10% redeemable preference shares of ₹ 100 each fully paid up.
2. Term loans are secured.
3. Depreciation on assets ₹ 5,00,000.
4. Schedules need not be given. However, grouping should form part of the answer.

[**Ans:** Balance Sheet Total—₹ 77,25,00].

10. Sherry Engineering Ltd. have authorised capital of ₹ 50 lakhs divided into 5,00,000 equity shares of ₹ 10 each. Their books show the following balances as on 31st December, 2013:

Particulars	Amount (₹)	Particulars	Amount (₹)
Stock on 1.1.2013	6,65,000	Bank Current A/c	20,000
Discounts & Rebates	30,000	Cash in hand	8,000
Carriage Inwards	57,500	Debenture interest (for half year 31.6.2013)	10,000
Patterns	3,75,000		
Rates, Taxes and Insurance	55,000	Interest (Banks)	91,000
Furniture & Fixtures	1,50,000	Preliminary expenses	10,000
Material purchased	12,32,500	Calls in Arrears	10,000
Wages	13,05,000	Equity Share Capital (2,00,000 shares of ₹ 10 each)	20,00,000
Coal and Coke	63,000		
Freehold Land	12,50,000	4% Debentures (repayable after 10 years)	5,00,000
Plant & Machinery	7,50,000	Bank Overdraft	7,57,000
Engineering Tools	1,50,000	Sundry Creditors (for goods)	2,40,500
Goodwill	3,75,000	Sales	36,17,000
Sundry Debtors	2,66,000	Rent (Cr.)	30,000
Bills Receivables	1,34,500	Transfer Fees	6,500
Advertisement	15,000	Profit and Loss Account (Cr.)	67,000
Commission and Brokerage	67,500		
Business expenses	56,000		
Repairs	46,500		
Bad debts	25,500		

The stock (valued at Cost or market value, which is lower) as on 31st Dec. 2013 was ₹ 7,08,000. Outstanding liabilities for wages ₹ 25,000 and business expenses ₹ 25,000. Dividend declared @ 10% on paid-up capital. Charge depreciation: Plant and Machinery @ 5%; Engineering Tools @ 20%; Patterns @ 10%; and Furniture & Fixtures @ 10%. Provide 2% on debtors as doubtful debts after writing off ₹ 21,500 as bad debts. Write off preliminary expenses ₹ 5,000 and create debenture redemption reserve ₹ 50,000. Provide ₹ 2,40,000 for income tax. You are required to prepare:

(*a*) Profit & Loss account for the year ended 31st Dec. 2013; and (*b*) Balance sheet as on that date in vertical form.

[**Ans:** Net Profit after tax—₹ 1,90,610; Balance Sheet Total—₹ 33,15,610].

11. Fire Products Ltd. was registered with a nominal capital of ₹ 5,00,000 divided into shares of ₹ 100 each. The following Trial Balance is extracted from the books on 31st March, 2013:

Cr.

Particulars	Amount (₹)	Particulars		Amount (₹)
Buildings	2,90,000	Sales		5,20,000
Machinery	1,00,000	Salaries Outstanding		2,000
Closing Stock	90,000	Provision for Bad Debt (1.4.2012)		3,000
Purchases (adjusted)	2,10,000	Share Capital		2,00,000
Salaries	60,000	General Reserve		40,000
Directors Fees	10,000	Profit and Loss		25,000
Rent	26,000	Creditors		92,000
Depreciation	20,000	Provision for Deprecia-		
Bad Debts	6,000	tion on Building:	50,000	
Interest accrued on Investment	2,000	Machinery	55,000	1,05,000
12,000 shares of A Ltd. of ₹ 10 each ₹		14% Debentures		2,00,000
8 paid up	1,20,000	Interest on debentures accrued but not		
Debenture interest	28,000	due		14,000
Loose Tools	23,000	Interest on Investment		12,000
Advance Tax	60,000	Unclaimed Dividend		5,000
Sundry expenses	18,000			
Debtors	1,25,000			
Bank	30,000			
	12,18,000			12,18,000

You are required to prepare Trading and Profit and Loss Account for the year ending 31st March, 2013 and Balance Sheet as at that date after taking into consideration the following information:

(*i*) Closing stock is more than opening stock by ₹ 30,000.

(*ii*) Provide for bad and doubtful debts @ 4% on Debtors.

(*iii*) Make a provision for income tax @ 50%.

(*iv*) Depreciation expense includes depreciation of ₹ 8,000 on Buildings and that of ₹ 12,000 on Machinery.

(*v*) The directors recommend a dividend @ 25%.

[**Ans:** Gross Profit—₹ 3,10,000; Net Profit—₹ 76,000; Balance Sheet Total—₹ 7,30,000].

12. The balance sheet of a limited company on 31 March, 2013 was as under:

Liabilities	Amount (₹)	Assets	Amount (₹)
Share Capital:		Freehold Property	1,00,000
Authorised: ₹ 10 Shares	3,00,000	Stock	1,20,000
Subscribed: 20,000 shares of ₹ 10 each	2,00,000	Debtors	80,000
Profit and Loss Account	1,20,000	Bank Balance	2,20,000
10% Debentures	1,20,000		
Creditors	60,000		
Proposed Dividend	20,000		
	5,20,000		5,20,000

At the Annual Meeting, it was decided: (*i*) To pay a dividend in cash of 10 per cent (*ii*) To issue one Bonus Share for every four shares held. (*iii*) To give existing shareholders the option to purchase one ₹ 10 share at ₹ 15 for every four shares held prior to bonus distribution, this option being taken up by all shareholders. (*iv*) To repay Debentures at a premium of 3 percent. Enter these transactions in the books of the company by preparing the necessary ledger accounts.

ANSWERS TO SELF-EVALUATION EXERCISES

I.

1. (*d*)	**2.** (*c*)	**3.** (*b*)	**4.** (*a*)	**5.** (*b*)	**6.** (*d*)
7. (*c*)	**8.** (*a*)	**9.** (*d*)	**10.** (*a*)	**11.** (*c*)	**12.** (*d*)
13. (*b*)	**14.** (*d*)	**15.** (*d*)			

II.

1. False	**2.** True	**3.** True	**4.** True	**5.** True	**6.** False
7. True	**8.** True	**9.** False	**10.** True		

15

ACCOUNTING FOR AMALGAMATION

LEARNING OBJECTIVES

After reading this chapter, you should be able to:

- *Define* amalgamation and explain objectives and procedure of amalgamation.
- *Describe* types of amalgamation.
- *Discuss* the procedure of accounting for amalgamation.
- *Illustrate* the preparation of accounts.

In order to reap the benefits of large scale production or to eliminate competition, two or more firms may combine their undertakings and become one undertaking. It may be done in numerous ways viz. amalgamation, absorption and external reconstruction.

CONCEPT OF AMALGAMATION

Amalgamation is the blending of two or more existing companies into one company. For example, if two existing companies say, X Ltd. and Y Ltd. go into liquidation to form a new company XY Ltd., it is a case of amalgamation.

The Institute of Chartered Accountants of India has issued Accounting Standard (AS-14): "Accounting for Amalgamation" which has come into force in respect of accounting periods commencing on or after 1.4.1995 and is mandatory in nature. With the issue of this standard the terms used earlier viz. amalgamation, absorption and external reconstruction have lost their distinction. It should be noted that amalgamation includes absorption and reconstruction.

Objectives of Amalgamation

The main objective of amalgamation is to achieve synergetic benefits which arise, when two companies can achieve more in combination than when they are individual entities.

The other objectives of amalgamation are:

(*i*) To reap economies of scale

(*ii*) To eliminate competition

(*iii*) To build up goodwill

(*iv*) To reduce the degree of risk through diversification
(*v*) Managerial effectiveness.

PROCEDURE OF AMALGAMATION

The following procedure is followed in an amalgamation:

1. The terms of amalgamation are finalized by the board of directors of the constituent companies.
2. A scheme of amalgamation is prepared and submitted for approval to the respective High Court.
3. Approval of the shareholders of the constituent companies is obtained.
4. Approval of SEBI is obtained.
5. A new company is formed (where necessary) and issues shares to the shareholders of the transferor company.
6. The transferor company is liquidated and all assets and liabilities are taken over by the transferee company.

TYPES OF AMALGAMATION

For accounting purposes, AS-14 has categorized amalgamation into two:

1. Amalgamation in the nature of merger.
2. Amalgamation in the nature of purchase.

Amalgamation in the Nature of Merger

An amalgamation is considered as 'Amalgamation in the Nature of Merger' if all the following five conditions are satisfied:

1. All the assets and liabilities of the transferor company become the assets and liabilities of the transferee company after amalgamation.
2. Shareholders holding not less than 90% of the face value of the equity shares of the transferor company (other than the equity shares already held therein, immediately before amalgamation, by the transferee company or its subsidiaries or their nominees) become equity shareholders of the transferee company by virtue of amalgamation.
3. The consideration to the shareholders of the transferor company (who agree to become equity shareholders of the transferee company) is discharged by the transferee company wholly by issue of equity shares in the transferee company except that cash may be paid in respect of any fractional shares.
4. The business of the transferor company is intended to be carried on, after the amalgamation, by the transferee company.
5. No adjustment is intended to be made to the book values of the assets and liabilities of the transferor company when they are incorporated in the financial statements of the transferee company except to ensure uniformity of accounting policies.

AMALGAMATION IN THE NATURE OF PURCHASE

An amalgamation is in the 'Nature of Purchase' if any one or more of the five conditions specified for Merger is not satisfied. In such kind of amalgamation shareholders of the company which is acquired normally do not continue to have a proportionate share in the equity of the combined company. The transferee company may also not intend to continue the business of transferor company.

ACCOUNTING FOR AMALGAMATION

Accounting Standard AS-14 'Accounting for Amalgamation' issued by the Institute of Chartered Accountants of India states the procedure for accounting for amalgamation.

AS-14 uses and defines the various terms as under:

(*a*) **Amalgamation** means an amalgamation pursuant to the provisions of the Companies Act, 1956 or any other statute which may be applicable to companies.

(*b*) **Transferor Company** means the company which is amalgamated into another company.

(*c*) **Transferee Company** means the company into which a transferor company is amalgamated.

(*d*) **Reserve** means portion of earnings, receipts or other surplus of an enterprise (whether capital or revenue) appropriated by the management for a general or a specific purpose other than a provision for depreciation or diminution in the value of assets or for known liability.

(*e*) **Consideration** for the amalgamation means the aggregate of the shares and other securities issued and the payment made in the form of cash or other assets by the transferee company to the shareholders of the transferor company.

ACCOUNTING TREATMENT

Accounting for amalgamation of companies involves:

I. Computation of purchase consideration

II. Accounting Treatment in books of Transferor Company.

III. Accounting Treatment in books of Transferee Company according to the type of amalgamation.

I. Purchase Consideration

Purchase consideration means the price payable by Transferee Company to the Transferor Company for acquiring its business. According to AS-14, "Consideration for amalgamation means the aggregate of the shares and other securities issued and the payment made in the form of cash or other assets by transferee company to the shareholders of the transferor company."

This definition emphasises the following points which should be remembered while calculating 'Purchase Consideration':

1. Only payments to shareholders are to be taken into consideration.
2. Considerations for debenture holders and liquidation expenses or cost absorption are not included in the Purchase Consideration.

Method of Calculating Purchase Consideration: There are two methods of calculating the purchase consideration:

1. Net Payment Method
2. Net Assets Method

The choice of method depends on availability of information. If information is available on all modes of discharging the purchase consideration (*e.g.* preference shares, equity shares or cash payable to shareholders of transferor company) alongwith their amounts, then Net Payment Method should be used. In other cases 'Net Assets' Method should be used.

NET PAYMENT METHOD

'Purchase Consideration' under this method is taken as the aggregate of all payments made in the form of shares, debentures, other securities and cash to the shareholders of the transferor company.

Illustration 1: X Ltd. agrees to acquire the business of Y Ltd. on the following terms:

1. The shareholders of Y Ltd. are to be paid ₹ 25 in cash and are offered four shares of ₹ 10 each in X Ltd. for every share in Y Ltd. Y Ltd. has 50,000 equity shares outstanding as on the date of amalgamation.
2. The debenture holders holding 5,000 debentures of ₹ 100 each are to be redeemed at a premium of 10%.
3. Cost of liquidation amounting to ₹ 25,000 are to borne by X Ltd.

Calculate the value of purchase consideration.

Solution: Amount payable to Shareholders of Y Ltd.

	₹
1. Cash payment (₹ 25 × 50,000)	12,50,000
2. Shares Issued (50,000 × 4 × 10)	20,00,000
Total purchase consideration	32,50,000

Illustration 2: A Ltd. agrees to absorb B Ltd., the consideration being:

1. The assumption of trade liabilities of ₹ 50,000.
2. The payment of the costs of liquidation ₹ 2,000.
3. The redemption of 80% debentures of ₹ 6,00,000 at a premium of 10%.
4. The payment of ₹ 20 p.a. share in cash and the exchange of two fully paid ₹ 10 shares in A Ltd. for every share of ₹ 25 in B Ltd. The share capital of the vendor company consists of 20,000 shares of ₹ 25 each fully paid.

Calculate the purchase consideration as per AS-14.

Solution: **Amount payable to shareholders of B Ltd.**

	₹
1. Cash ₹ 10 × 20,000 shares	2,00,000
2. Equity Shares of A Ltd. (2 × 10 × 20,000)	4,00,000
Total	6,00,000

Note: According to AS-14, the amount paid by transferee company to discharge the debenture holders and the liquidation expenses of the vendor (transferor) company are not considered as part of purchase consideration.

Illustration 3: X Ltd. is acquired by Y Ltd., the consideration being the takeover of liabilities; the payment of cost of acquisition as a part of purchase consideration not exceeding ₹ 20,000 (actual cost ₹ 17,000); the payment of the debentures ₹ 1,00,000 at a premium of 10% in 9% debentures issued at par; and the payment of ₹ 16 per share in cash and allotment of one 145 preference share of ₹ 10 each and 6 equity shares of ₹ 10 each fully paid for every 4 shares in X Ltd. The number of shares of the vendor company (X Ltd.) is 2,00,000 of ₹ 10 each fully paid. Calculate purchase consideration as per AS-14.

Solution: **Payment to Equity Shareholders**

	₹
1. Cash ₹ 16 × 2,00,000	32,00,000
2. 14% Preference Shares—2,00,000/4 × ₹ 10	5,00,000
3. Equity Shares 2,00,000/4 × 6 × ₹ 10	30,00,000
Total	67,00,000

NET ASSETS METHOD

Net Assets Method is used when all the modes of discharging the purchase consideration (*e.g.* Pref. Shares, Equity shares or cash payable to shareholders of transferor company) are not given and hence where Net Payment Method cannot be adopted. Under this Method, purchase consideration is ascertained by aggregating the agreed values of only those assets which have been taken over by the transferee company and deducting it from the agreed value of liabilities taken over.

Illustration 4: The Balance Sheet of Digvijay Ltd. on 31st March, 2013 was as under:

Liabilities	(₹)	Assets	(₹)
Share Capital:		Land and Buildings	4,00,000
75,000 Equity Shares of ₹ 20 each fully paid	1,50,000	Plant and Machinery	2,56,000
		Sundry Debits	1,60,000
10% Debentures	4,00,000	Debenture fund investments	80,000
Outstanding interest on debentures	40,000	Cash	4,000
Sundry Creditors	1,20,000	Preliminary Expenses	20,000
General Reserve	80,000		
Debenture Redemption Fund (sinking fund)	80,000		
Profit & Loss Account	50,000		
	9,20,000		9,20,000

Sumant Ltd. absorbs Digvijay Ltd. on the following terms:

1. Sumant Ltd. to take over sundry creditors.
2. It will also take over land and buildings, Plant and Machinery and investments at 120% of book values, sundry debtors at 90% of book values and goodwill at ₹ 70,800.
3. Liability to debentures including interest to be met by issue of ₹ 5,00,000, 15% debentures by Sumant Ltd.

Calculate purchase consideration.

Solution: Agreed value of Assets taken over:

		₹
Land and Building		4,80,000
Plant and Machinery		3,07,200
Sundry Debtors		1,44,000
Debentures Fund Investments		96,000
Goodwill		70,800
		10,98,000
Less: Agreed Value of Liabilities taken over:		
Sundry Creditors	1,20,000	
10% Debentures	4,00,000	
Debenture Interest	40,000	–5,60,000
Purchase consideration		5,38,000

II. Accounting Treatment in the Books of Transferor/Vendor Company

So far as the books of the transferor company are concerned, the normal procedures are to be followed for closing the books of account through Realisation Account. It should be noted that the Accounting Standard (AS-14) deals with the accounting procedures only in the books of the transferee company. In case of amalgamation the transferor company has to wind up its business and hence it will dispose off its assets, pay its liabilities and distribute the surplus if any among its shareholders. It is done through opening a new account known as Realisation Account.

In order to close the books of account of the transferor company, the following steps (along with their journal entries) are required:

Step 1: Open a Realisation Account, transfer all assets and liabilities (excluding fictitious assets) to this account.

Journal Entry

For transferring different assets to Realisation Account.

1. Realisation A/c Dr. (with total)
   To Sundry assets (individually) (with their individual values)

Points to be noted:

(*a*) Fictitious assets, such as preliminary expenses, discount on issue of shares and debentures, debit balance of Profit and Loss Account etc. are not transferred to Realisation Account.

(*b*) In tangible assets such as goodwill, patents, trademarks etc. are also transferred to Realisation Account.

(*c*) The cash and bank balances should not be transferred to Realisation Account if these are not taken over by the purchasing company.

(*d*) An asset against which a provision or reserve has been created should be transferred at its gross figure and not at its net figure *e.g.* debtors.

Step 2: For transferring different liabilities to Realisation Account.

Sundry Liabilities Dr. [with their individual book values]
To Realisation A/c [with the total]

Points to be noted:

(*i*) Items in the nature 'Provisions' (*e.g.* Provision for taxation, Employees provident fund, Pension Fund, Provision for doubtful debts, Provision for Depreciation) should be transferred to Realisation Account.

(*ii*) Items in the nature of 'Reserve' are not to be transferred to Realisation Account. These are directly transferred to sundry shareholders account (*e.g.* workmen compensation fund, credit balance of profit and loss account).

(*iii*) A liability against which a provision or reserve has been created should be transferred at its gross figure *e.g.* creditors.

Step 3: For realising assets which have not been taken over by the purchasing company.

Cash or Bank Account Dr. (with the amount realised)
To Realisation account

Step 4: For discharging liabilities which have not been taken over by the purchasing company.

Realisation A/c Dr. (with the amount paid)
To Cash

Step 5: To record liquidation expenses

(*a*) If these expenses are borne by the transferor company	**Journal Entry** Realisation Account Dr. To Bank

(*b*)	If these expenses are paid by the purchasing companies directly	No Entry
(*c*)	If these expenses are first paid by the transferor company and later reimbursed by the transferee company 1. On Payment by the transferor company 2. On reimbursement	 Transferee company's account Dr. To Realisation Account Bank Account Dr. To Realisation Account

Step 6: For Receiving Purchase Consideration

Cash/Bank Account	Dr.	With cash received.
Preference Shares in Purchasing Company	Dr.	With issue price of preference shares
Equity Shares in Purchasing Company	Dr.	With issue price of equity shares
To Transferee Company		With the total

Step 7: Discharge the claims of preference shareholders and transfer the difference between the amount actually payable and the book figure to Realisation Account

Journal Entries for making the payment due:

If Preference shareholders are discharged at a premium		
Preference Share Capital Account	Dr.	With book value of preference share capital
Realisation Account	Dr.	With premium payable to preference shareholders
To Preference shareholders Account		With total
If Preference shareholders are discharged at a discount		
Preference Share Capital Account	Dr.	With book value of preference shares
To Realisation Account		With discount
To Preference Shareholders Account		
If Preference shareholders are discharged at par		
Preference Share Capital Account	Dr.	With book value of preference shares
To Preference shareholders Account		

For making payment to Preference Shareholders:

Preference Shareholders Account	Dr.	
To Cash/Bank Account		With cash paid
To Preference shares in Transferee Company		With issue price of preference shares given to preference shareholders

Step 8: Ascertain the profit/loss on realisation and transfer the same to equity shareholders account

In case of Profit	Realisation Account (with profit) To Equity Shareholders Account
In case of loss	Equity Shareholders Account To Realisation Account (with loss)

Step 9: Transfer Equity share capital, Accumulated profits and Reserves shown in the Balance Sheet (just before date of amalgamation) to Equity Shareholders Account

Equity Share Capital Account	Dr.	With paid up value of share capital
Profit and Loss Account	Dr.	With credit balance of profit and loss Account
General Reserve Account	Dr.	If any

Workmen Compensation Fund Account	Dr.	If any
Capital Reserve Account	Dr.	If any
Dividend Equalisation Fund Account	Dr.	If any
Securities Premium Account	Dr.	If any
Debenture Redemption Reserve Account	Dr.	If any
Capital Redemption Reserve Account	Dr.	If any
To Equity Shareholders Account		With total

Step 10: Transfer Accumulated losses (shown on debit side of Balance Sheet just before amalgamation)

Equity Shareholders Account	Dr.	
To Profit and Loss Account		Debit balance
To Preliminary Expenses Account		If any
To Discount on issue of shares/debentures		If any
To Deferred Revenue Expenditure Account		If any

Step 11: Make the final payment to equity shareholders

Equity Shareholders Account	Dr.	With total
To Equity Shares in transferee company's Account		No. of shares issued X issue price per share
To Cash/Bank Account		With cash paid

Notes:

1. After passing the above mentioned entries in books of transferor company, all the accounts will be closed and not a single account will show any balance.
2. The net amount payable to equity shareholders must be equal to the amount of shares in Transferee Company and cash and bank balance left after the discharge of all outsiders' liabilities and claims of preference shareholders.

III. Accounting Treatment in Books of Transferee Company or Purchasing Company

Accounting treatment in books of transferee company depends upon the type of amalgamation. As per AS-14, there are two methods of accounting for amalgamation:

1. **Pooling of Interest Method:** Applicable in case of Amalgamation in the nature of merger.
2. **Purchase Method:** Applicable in case of Amalgamation in the nature of Purchase.

Pooling of Interest Method (as per AS-14): The following are the salient features of pooling of interest method:

1. All assets, liabilities and reserves of the transferor company are recorded by the transferee company at their existing carrying amounts (book values) except in cases where these are to be adjusted to follow uniform set of accounting policies.
2. The identity of the reserves is preserved as they appear in financial statements of the transferee company. For example, the general reserve of the transferor company becomes the general reserve of the transferee company, the capital reserve of the transferor company becomes the capital reserve of the transferee company and the revaluation reserve of the transferor company becomes the capital reserve of the transferee company.
3. No goodwill account should be accounted for as a result of amalgamation in the books of the transferee company.

4. The difference between the amount of share capital issued (plus any additional consideration in the form of cash or other assets) and the amount of share capital of transferor company should be adjusted in reserves in the financial statements of the transferee company.
5. The balance of profit and loss account appearing in the financial statements of the transferor company is aggregated with the corresponding balance appearing in the financial statements of the transferee company.
6. Although AS-14 does not specifically state, the purchase consideration under this method is to be valued at par value of shares issued. The logic is that this method considers book values and not the fair values.

Accounting Entries in books of the Transferee Company (Pooling of Interest Method)

1. For amalgamation of the business	Business Purchase Account	Dr.	With the amount of purchase consideration
	To Liquidator of Transferor Company's A/c		
2. For acquisition of assets, liabilities and reserves	Sundry Assets Account	Dr.	With individual amounts at book value
	To Sundry Liabilities Account		Individually at book values
	To Reserves Account		See note below
	To Profit and Loss Account		
	To Business Purchase Account		With purchase consideration
Note: In this entry if the value of assets (debits) is more than the amount of liabilities and reserves (credits), the difference is added to reserves. Conversely, if the value of debits is less than the credits, the difference is debited to the reserves. It means any difference in the amount of debits and credits in this entry is suitably adjusted to reserves.			
3. For Payment of Purchase Consideration	Liquidator of the Transferor Company's A/c	Dr.	With total
	Discount on issue of shares Account	Dr.	If any
	To Equity share Capital Account		With paid up value of equity shares issued
	To Preference Share Capital Account		With paid value of preference shares issued
	To Securities Premium Account		With securities premium
	To Cash Account/Bank Account		For fractional shares and for dissenting shareholders
Note: The shares issued by way of purchase consideration must be recorded at their paid up values (and not at their issued price) after giving due credit to Securities Premium Account (in case the shares have been issued at premium) or after giving due debit to 'Discount on issue of shares Account' (in case the shares have been issued at discount).			
4. **For formation expenses of the new company (if formed) and reimbursement of the liquidation expenses of the vendor company (if paid by the transferee company)**	Preliminary Expenses Account	Dr.	For formation expenses
	Profit and Loss Account	Dr.	Reimbursed liquidation expenses
	To Cash Account/Bank Account		

Illustration 4: The following are the Balance Sheets as on 31st December, 2013 of X Ltd. and Y Ltd.:

Liabilities	X Ltd. (₹)	Y Ltd. (₹)	Assets	X Ltd. (₹)	Y Ltd. (₹)
Equity Share Capital (₹ 100 per share)	1,00,000	60,000	Land and Buildings	30,000	—
			Plant and Machinery	1,10,000	50,000
6% Debentures of ₹ 10 each	20,000	—	Stock	16,000	8,000
Reserve	34,000	—	Debtors	14,000	9,000
Dividend Equalisation Fund	4,000	—	Cash	3,000	1,000
Employees' P.F.	3,000	—			
Trade Creditors	10,000	8,000			
Profit and Loss A/c	2,000	—			
	1,73,000	68,000		1,73,000	68,000

In January, 2014, the two companies agree to amalgamate and form a new company called Z Ltd. which takes over the assets and liabilities of both the companies. The authorised Capital of Z Ltd. is ₹ 10,00,000, consisting of 1,00,000 Equity Shares of ₹ 10 each.

The purchase consideration is agreed at ₹ 1,20,000 and ₹ 60,000 for X Ltd. and Y Ltd. respectively. The entire purchase consideration is to be paid by Z Ltd. in its fully paid shares. In return for debentures in X Ltd. debentures of the same amount and denomination are to be issued by Z Ltd.

Give Journal Entries to close the books of X Ltd. and Y Ltd. and show the Opening entries in the books of Z Ltd. Also prepare the opening Balance Sheet of Z Ltd.

Solution:

In the Books of X Ltd.

Journal

Date	Particulars		LF	Dr. (₹)	Cr. (₹)
2014	Realisation A/c	Dr.		1,73,000	
Jan. 1	To Land and Buildings A/c				30,000
	To Plant and Machinery A/c				1,10,000
	To Stock A/c				16,000
	To Debtors A/c				14,000
	To Cash A/c				3,000
	(Being the transfer of different assets to Realisation Account as per the Sch. of amalgamation)				
	6% Debentures A/c	Dr.		20,000	
	Employees' P.F. A/c	Dr.		3,000	
	Trade Creditors A/c	Dr.		10,000	
	To Realisation A/c				33,000
	(Being the transfer of different liabilities to Realisation Account)				
	Equity Share Capital A/c	Dr.		1,00,000	
	Reserve A/c	Dr.		34,000	
	Dividend Equalisation Fund A/c	Dr.		4,000	
	Profit and Loss A/c	Dr.		2,000	
	To Sundry Equity Shareholders A/c				1,40,000
	(Being the transfer of Share Capital, Reserve and Surplus to Shareholders Account)				

Date	Particulars		LF	Dr. (₹)	Cr. (₹)
	Z Ltd. A/c	Dr.		1,20,000	
	To Realisation A/c				1,20,000
	(Being the purchase consideration due from Z Ltd.)				
	Sundry Equity Shareholders A/c	Dr.		20,000	
	To Realisation A/c (Note 1)				20,000
	(Being the loss on realisation transferred to Sundry Equity Shareholders Account)				
	Shares in Z Ltd. A/c	Dr.		1,20,000	
	To Z Ltd. A/c				1,20,000
	(Being purchase consideration received from Z Ltd.)				
	Sundry Equity Shareholders A/c	Dr.		1,20,000	
	To Shares in Z Ltd. A/c				1,20,000
	(Being the distribution of Shares in Z Ltd. among the existing Shareholders)				

In the Books of Y Ltd.
Journal

Date	Particulars		LF	Dr. (₹)	Cr. (₹)
2014	Realisation A/c	Dr.		68,000	
Jan. 1	To Plant and Machinery A/c				50,000
	To Stock A/c				8,000
	To Debtors A/c				9,000
	To Cash A/c				1,000
	(Being the transfer of different assets to Realisation Account as per the Sch. of amalgamation)				
	Trade Creditors A/c	Dr.		8,000	
	To Realisation A/c				8,000
	(Being the transfer of Trade Creditors to Realisation Account as per the Sch. of amalgamation)				
	Equity Share Capital A/c	Dr.		60,000	
	To Sundry Equity Shareholders A/c				60,000
	(Being the transfer of Share Capital to Shareholders Account)				
	Z Ltd. A/c	Dr.		60,000	
	To Realisation A/c				60,000
	(Being the purchase consideration due from Z Ltd.)				
	Shares in Z Ltd. A/c	Dr.		60,000	
	To Z Ltd. A/c				60,000
	(Being the purchase consideration received)				
	Sundry Equity Shareholders A/c	Dr.		60,000	
	To Shares in Z Ltd. A/c				60,000
	(Being the distribution of Shares in Z Ltd. among the existing Shareholders)				

In the Books of Z Ltd.
Journal

Date	Particulars		LF	Dr. (₹)	Cr. (₹)
2014	Business Purchase A/c	Dr.		1,80,000	
Jan. 1	To Liquidator of X Ltd. A/c				1,20,000
	To Liquidator of Y Ltd. A/c				60,000
	(Being the amount payable to the liquidators of X Ltd. and Y Ltd. as per agreement dated ...)				
	Land and Buildings A/c	Dr.		30,000	
	Plant and Machinery A/c	Dr.		1,10,000	
	Stock A/c	Dr.		16,000	
	Debtors A/c	Dr.		14,000	
	Cash A/c	Dr.		3,000	
	To 6% Debentures in X Ltd. A/c				20,000
	To Trade Creditors A/c				10,000
	To Employees P.F. A/c				3,000
	To Reserve A/c [See Note]				14,000
	To Profit and Loss A/c				2,000
	To Dividend Equalisation Fund A/c				4,000
	To Business Purchase A/c				1,20,000
	(Being the assets, liabilities, reserve, Profit and Loss Account taken over and the difference between the amount recorded as share capital issued and share capital of X Ltd. adjusted against reserve)				
	Plant and Machinery A/c	Dr.		50,000	
	Stock A/c	Dr.		8,000	
	Debtors A/c	Dr.		9,000	
	Cash A/c	Dr.		1,000	
	To Trade Creditors A/c				8,000
	To Business Purchase A/c				60,000
	(Being the assets and liabilities taken over)				
	Liquidator of X Ltd. A/c	Dr.		1,20,000	
	Liquidator of Y Ltd. A/c	Dr.		60,000	
	To Equity Share Capital A/c				1,80,000
	(Being the issue of 18,000 equity shares to transferor companies as fully paid-up for consideration other than cash)				
	6% Debentures in X Ltd. A/c	Dr.		20,000	
	To 6% Debentures A/c				20,000
	(Being the issue of necessary debentures to debenture-holders of X Ltd.)				

Note: It should be noted that reserve, dividend equalisation fund, Profit and Loss Account will be carried forward in the books of Z Ltd. However, the difference between the amount recorded as share capital and the share capital of X Ltd. will be adjusted against the Reserve. The amount to be adjusted has been calculated as follows.

Particulars	(₹)
Amount recorded as Share Capital	1,20,000
Less: Share Capital of X Ltd.	1,00,000
Amount to be adjusted in Reserve	20,000
Reserve of X Ltd.	34,000
Less: Amount to be adjusted (as calculated above)	20,000
Balance of Reserve to be shown in Balance Sheet of Z Ltd.	14,000

Balance Sheet of Z Ltd. as on 1st January, 2014

Liabilities	(₹)	Assets	(₹)
Share Capital:		**Fixed Assets:**	
Authorised Capital:		Land and Building	30,000
1,00,000 Equity Shares of ĵ 10 each	10,00,000	Plant and Machinery	1,60,000
Issued and Subscribed Capital		**Investments**	Nil
18,000 Equity Shares of ĵ 10 each	1,80,000	**Current Assets, Loans and Advances**	
(All the above shares have been allotted as fully paid up pursuant to a contract without payment being received in cash)		*(A) Current Assets:*	
		Stock	24,000
		Debtors	23,000
		Cash	4,000
Reserve and Surplus:		**Miscellaneous Expenditure:**	Nil
Reserve	14,000		
Profit and Loss Account	2,000		
Dividend Equalisation Fund	4,000		
Secured Loans			
6% Debentures	20,000		
Unsecured Loans	Nil		
Current Liabilities and Provisions			
A. Current Liabilities:			
Trade Creditors	18,000		
B. Provisions:			
Employees' P.F.	3,000		
	2,41,000		2,41,000

Working Notes:

Dr. **(1) Realisation Account** Cr.

Particulars	X Ltd. (₹)	Y Ltd. (₹)	Particulars	X Ltd. (₹)	Y Ltd. (₹)
To Land and Building A/c	30,000	—	By 6% Debentures A/c	20,000	—
To Plant and Machinery	1,10,000	50,000	By employee's PF A/c	3,000	—
To Stock A/c	16,000	8,000	By Trade Creditors A/c	10,000	8,000
To Debtors A/c	14,000	9,000	By Z Ltd. A/c	1,20,000	60,000
To Cash A/c	3,000	1,000	By Sundry Shareholders A/c	20,000	—
	1,73,000	68,000		1,73,000	68,000

Illustration 5: Zuari Ltd. agrees to absorb the business of Agro India Ltd. and to take over the Assets and Liabilities at their Balance Sheet value, in exchange for which it is to issue 12 shares of ₹ 10 each for every share of ₹ 100 in the Agro India Ltd. The expenses of absorption ₹ 10,000 will be paid by Zuari Ltd. On the date of absorption *i.e.*, 31st March, 2014, the Balance Sheets of the two companies were as under:

Zuari Ltd.

Liabilities	(₹)	Assets	(₹)
1,00,000 Equity Shares of ₹ 10 each	10,00,000	Land and Buildings	5,00,000
General Reserve	80,000	Machinery and Plant	3,00,000
Creditors	1,00,000	Goodwill	1,00,000

Liabilities	(₹)	Assets		(₹)
		Stock		60,000
		Debtors		1,20,000
		Bank		1,00,000
Total	11,80,000	Total		11,80,000

Agro India Ltd.

Liabilities	(₹)	Assets		(₹)
5,000 Equity Shares of ₹ 10 each	5,00,000	Land and Buildings		3,00,000
General Reserve	35,000	Machinery and Plant		2,00,000
Bills Payable	35,000	Sundry Debtors	55,000	
Creditors	40,000	*Less:* Provision	5,000	50,000
		Stock		25,000
		Bank		35,000
Total	6,10,000	Total		6,10,000

Show the Journal Entries in the books of the Zuari Ltd. and Agro India Ltd. Also prepare opening Balance Sheet of Zuari Ltd. immediately after absorption.

Solution:

1. Purchase Consideration:

5,000 × 12 = 60,000 shares × ₹ 10 = ₹ 6,00,000

2. Entries in books of Agro India Ltd. (Transferer Co.)

Particulars		Debit (₹)	Credit (₹)
1. Realisation A/c	Dr.	6,15,000	
To Land and Buildings			3,00,000
To Machinery and Plant			2,00,000
To Sundry Debtors			55,000
To Stock			25,000
To Bank			35,000
(Being transfer of assets to Realisation A/c)			
2. Provision on Debtors A/c	Dr.	5,000	
Bills payable A/c	Dr.	35,000	
Creditors A/c	Dr.	40,000	
To Realisation A/c			80,000
(Being transfer of liabilities to Realisation A/c)			
3. Zuari Ltd. A/c	Dr.	6,00,000	
To Realisation A/c			6,00,000
(Being purchase consideration due from transferee Co.)			
4. Equity Shares in Zuari Ltd. A/c	Dr.	6,00,000	
To Zuari Ltd. A/c			6,00,000
(Being receipt of purchase consideration) in form of 60,000 Equity Shares in Zuari Ltd. of ₹ 10 each)			
5. Realisation A/c	Dr.	65,000	
To Equity Shareholders A/c			65,000
(Being gain on realisation transferred to equity Shareholders A/c)			

Particulars		Debit (₹)	Credit (₹)
6. Equity Share Capital A/c	Dr.	5,00,000	
General Reserve A/c	Dr.	35,000	
To Equity Shareholders A/c			5,35,000
(Being transfer of Share Capital and General Reserve to Shareholders A/c			
7. Equity Shareholders A/c	Dr.	6,00,000	
To Equity Shares in Zuari Ltd.			6,00,000
(Being payment to Equity Shareholders)			

3. Entries in the books of Zuari Ltd. (Transferee Co.)

Particulars		Debit (₹)	Credit (₹)
1. Business Purchase A/c	Dr.	6,00,000	
To liquidators of Agro Ltd.			6,00,000
(Being the purchase consideration due to liquidator)			
2. Land and Buildings A/c	Dr.	3,00,000	
Machinery and Plant A/c	Dr.	2,00,000	
Sundry Debtors A/c	Dr.	55,000	
Stock A/c	Dr.	25,000	
Bank A/c	Dr.	35,000	
General Reserve A/c	Dr.	65,000	
To Bills payable A/c			35,000
To Creditors			40,000
To Provision for Doubtful Debts			5,000
To Business Purchase A/c			6,00,000
(Being entry for taking over assets and liabilities of Agro Ltd.)			
3. Liquidator of Agro Ltd.	Dr.	6,00,000	
To Equity Share A/c			6,00,000
(Being entry for allotment of 6,00,000 equity shares of ₹ 10 each as purchase consideration)			
4. Liquidation Expenses A/c	Dr.	10,000	
To Bank A/c			10,000
(Being payment of liquidation expenses of Agro Ltd.)			
5. General Reserve A/c	Dr.	10,000	
To Liquidation Expenses A/c			10,000
(Being transfer of liquidation expenses to reserve)			

Note: The contents of paragraph 35 of the standard (AS-14) are given effect to in the case of pooling of interest method applicable to an amalgamation in the nature of a merger as under:

1. Equity Share Capital of Agro Ltd.	5,00,000
—Equity Share Capital issued in Zuari Ltd.	6,00,000
Difference	1,00,000
Less: General Reserve in Agro Ltd.	35,000
Debit to General Reserve	65,000
2. General Reserve Balance in Zuari Ltd.	80,000
Less: Debit Balance as above	65,000
To be shown in Balance Sheet after amalgamation	15,000

Since liquidation expenses of ₹ 10,000 paid by the transferee company are to be charged to Profit and Loss Account, the same are set-off against the balance of reserve in the absence of Profit and Loss Account.

Balance Sheet of Zuari Ltd. as at 1st April, 2014

Liabilities	(₹)	Assets		(₹)
Share Capital:		**Fixed Assets:**		
Issued and Subscribed	16,00,000	Goodwill		1,00,000
1,60,000 equity shares of ₹ 10 each (of these 60,000 shares issued for consideration other than cash)		Land and Building		8,00,000
		Machinery and Plant		5,00,000
		Current Assets:		
Reserves and Surplus:		Stock		85,000
General Reserve	5,000	Debtors	1,75,000	1,70,000
Current Liabilities		*Less*: Provision	5,000	
Creditors	1,40,000	Bank		1,25,000
Bills payable	35,000			
Total	17,80,000			17,80,000

PURCHASE METHOD

The purchase method is applied in case of amalgamation in the nature of purchase. The salient features of this method are as follows:

1. **Recording of assets and liabilities:** The assets and liabilities of the transferor company should be incorporated at their existing carrying values or, alternatively, at their fair values (revised values) on date of amalgamation.
2. **Recording of reserves:**
   (*i*) **Statutory Reserves:** are those reserves which are required to be maintained as per the legal provisions, and there is restriction on its usage. If a statutory reserve is appearing in the Balance Sheet of a transferor company, the same should appear in the Financial Statements of the transferee company. For this purpose 'Amalgamation Adjustment Account' is debited and 'Statutory Reserve Account' is credited. Amalgamation Adjustment Account is shown on the assets side as a part of "Miscellaneous Expenditure" or other similar category in the Balance Sheet. When identity of the statutory reserves is no longer required to be maintained, both the reserves and the aforesaid account should be reversed. Examples of Statutory Reserves are: Investment allowance reserve; development rebate reserve, export profit reserve etc.).
   (*ii*) **Reserves other than statutory reserves:** The reserves (whether capital or revenue or arising on revaluation) of the transferor company, other than the statutory reserves, should not be included in the financial statements of the transferee company.
3. **Purchase Consideration:** Any excess of purchase consideration over net assets of the transferor company should be recognized as goodwill in the financial statements of transferee company. If the amount of consideration is lower than the value of net assets acquired, the difference should be treated as Capital Reserve.
4. **Goodwill** arising on amalgamation should be authorized systematically over its useful life. The authorization period should not exceed 5 years unless a somewhat longer period is justified.

Accounting Treatment in the Books of Transferee Company

1. For recording the acquisition of business from the Vendor Company:

Business Purchase A/c	Dr.	(with purchase consideration)
To liquidator of the Vendor Co.		

2. To record the Assets and Liabilities taken over at their respective agreed values and Debit Goodwill A/c if purchase consideration exceeds the net assets taken over or credit the Capital Reserve A/c if net assets taken over exceed the purchase consideration.

Individual Assets A/c	Dr.	(with respective agreed values of assets taken over)
Goodwill A/c	Dr.	(with excess of purchase consideration over the net assets) if any
To Individual Liabilities A/c		(with respective agreed values)
To Business Purchase A/c		(with purchase consideration)
To Capital Reserve		(with excess of Net Assets over the Purchase consideration)

3. For incorporation of Statutory Reserves:

Amalgamation Adjustment A/c	Dr.	[with total]
To Statutory Reserves A/c		[with the respective book values]

4. For discharge of Purchase consideration (same as in case of pooling of interest method).
5. For formation expenses of new company and to record the reimbursement of the liquidation expenses of the Vendor Company:

Preliminary expenses A/c	Dr.	(Formation expenses of Transferee Company)
Goodwill A/c		(Liquidation expenses of transferor company)
To Bank A/c		

Illustration 6: Following are the Balance Sheets of A Ltd. and B Ltd. as on 31.3.2013:

Liabilities	A (₹)	B (₹)	Assets	A (₹)	B (₹)
Equity Share:					
Capital (₹ 10)	50,00,000	20,00,000	Land and Building	29,00,000	12,00,000
14% Preference Share Capital (₹ 100 each)	20,00,000	10,00,000	Plant and Machinery	45,00,000	18,00,000
			Furniture	5,00,000	2,00,000
General Reserve	8,00,000	2,00,000	Stock	15,00,000	5,00,000
Investment Allowance	7,00,000	3,00,000	Debtors	10,00,000	7,00,000
Reserve:			Cash at Bank	5,00,000	3,00,000
Profit and Loss A/c	10,00,000	5,00,000			
12% Debenture (₹ 100)	5,00,000	3,00,000			
Creditors	5,00,000	3,00,000			
Other Current Liabilities	4,00,000	2,00,000			
	1,09,00,000	47,00,000		1,09,00,000	47,00,000

A Ltd. takes over B Ltd. as on 31.3.2013 on the following terms:

1. To issue 2,00,000 Equity Shares of ₹ 10 each at ₹ 12.50 to the Equity Shareholders of B Ltd.
2. To issue 15% preference shares of ₹ 100 each to discharge preference shares of B Ltd. at par.
3. To convert debentures of B Ltd. into equivalent number of debentures of A Ltd. of ₹ 100 each.
4. To maintain investment allowance reserve for two years.
5. The fair value of Plant and Machinery is ₹ 15,00,000.

Pass Journal Entries in the books of the transferee company (if the intention is not to carry on the business of transferor company).

Solution: Purchase consideration:

Equity Shares in A Ltd. = 2,00,000 × 12.50	= 25,00,000
Preference Shares in A Ltd.	10,00,000
	₹ 35,00,000

Books of A Ltd.

Particulars		Debit (₹)	Credit (₹)
1. Business Purchase A/c		35,00,000	
To liquidators of B Ltd. A/c			35,00,000
(For purchase consideration payable to B Ltd.)			
2. Land and Building A/c		12,00,000	
Plant and Machinery A/c		15,00,000	
Furniture A/c		2,00,000	
Stock A/c		5,00,000	
Debtors A/c		7,00,000	
Bank A/c		3,00,000	
To Creditors A/c			3,00,000
To other Current Liabilities A/c			2,00,000
To 12% Debentures A/c (B Ltd.)			2,00,000
To Business Purchase A/c			35,00,000
To Capital Reserve (*Balancing figure*)			2,00,000
(For recording fair values of Assets and Liabilities and taking the excess of net asset value over purchase consideration as capital reserve)			
3. Amalgamation Adjustment Account A/c	Dr.	3,00,00	
To Investment Allowance Reserve A/c			3,00,000
4. Liquidator of B Ltd. A/c		35,00,000	
To Equity Share Capital A/c			20,00,000
To Securities Premium A/c			5,00,000
To Preference Share Capital A/c			10,00,000
(For discharge of Purchase consideration)			
5. 12% Debenture (in B Ltd.) A/c		2,00,000	
To 12% Debenture A/c			2,00,000
(For conversion of debentures in new debentures)			

Balance Sheet of A Ltd. (after Purchase)

Liabilities	(₹)	Assets	(₹)
Equity Share Capital	70,00,000		
14% Preference Share Capital	20,00,000	Land and Building	41,00,000
15% Preference Share Capital	10,00,000	Plant and Machinery	60,00,000
General Reserve	8,00,000	Furniture	7,00,000
Investment Allowance Reserve	10,00,000	Stock	20,00,000
Securities Premium	5,00,000	Debtors	17,00,000
Capital Reserve	2,00,000	Bank	8,00,000

Liabilities	(₹)	Assets	(₹)
Profit and Loss A/c	10,00,000	Amalgamation Adjustment Account	3,00,000
12% Debentures	7,00,000		
Creditors	8,00,000		
Other Current Liabilities	6,00,000		
Total	1,56,00,000		1,56,00,000

Illustration 7: The Balance Sheet of A Co. Ltd. after amalgamation as at 31st March, 2013 was as under:

Liabilities	(₹)	Assets	(₹)
Equity Share of ₹ 10 each	6,00,000	Goodwill	1,00,000
Retained Earnings	2,80,000	Land and Building	6,40,000
15% Debentures	1,00,000	Stock	1,68,000
Creditors	20,000	Debtors	36,000
		Cash	56,000
Total	10,00,000		10,00,000

Note: Contingent Liability in respect of a pending suit ₹ 10,000.

On 1st April, 2013 B Co. Ltd. absorbed the business of A Co. Ltd. The Purchase Consideration was agreed as:

1. A cash payment of ₹ 2.50 for every ₹ 10 share in A Co. Ltd.
2. The issue of 1,35,000 equity shares of ₹ 10 each fully paid in B Co. Ltd.
3. The issue of such an amount of fully paid 14% debentures in B Co. Ltd. at 96% as is sufficient to discharge 15% debentures in A Co. Ltd. at a premium of 20%.

B Co. Ltd. valued land and building at ₹ 12,00,000; stock at ₹ 1,42,000; and debtors at book value subject to 5% provision for doubtful debts. B Co. Ltd. also agreed to take over the contingent liability, which ultimately materialized for ₹ 7,000. Prepare Ledger Accounts in the books of A Co. Ltd. and pass journal entries in the books of B Co. Ltd.

Solution: It is an amalgamation in the nature of purchase because the assets of A Co. Ltd. are not taken over at book value and purchase consideration will be satisfied by issue of shares and cash payment.

1. **Calculation of Purchase Consideration:**

For Equity Shareholders	₹
Cash (₹ 2.50 × 60,000)	1,50,000
Equity Shares (₹ 10 × 1,35,000)	13,50,000
Purchase Consideration	15,00,000

Note: Issue of 14% debentures to pay-off 15% debentures in A Co. Ltd. is not to be included while calculating purchase consideration. Such debentures will be taken over by B Co. Ltd. and then discharged.

2. **Calculation of Goodwill/Capital Reserve**

Assets taken over:	₹
Land and Building	12,00,000
Stock	1,42,000
Debtors (₹ 36,000 – 1,800)	34,200
Total	13,76,200

Less: **Liabilities taken over**		
15% debentures at a premium of 20%		1,20,000
Creditors		20,000
Total		1,40,000
Net Assets taken over	= 13,76,000 – 1,40,000	= ₹ 12,36,000
Less: Purchase Consideration		– 15,00,000
Goodwill =		(–) 2,63,000

In the Books of A Co. Ltd.
Realisation Account

Date	Particulars	Dr. (₹)	Particulars	Cr. (₹)
2007	To Goodwill A/c	1,00,000	By 15% debentures	1,00,000
April 1	To Land and Building	6,40,000	By Creditors	20,000
	To Stock A/c	1,68,000	By B Co. Ltd A/c (Purchase consideration)	15,00,000
	To Debtors A/c	36,000		
	To Cash A/c	56,000		
	To Equity Shareholder's A/c	6,20,000		
	Total	16,20,000	Total	16,20,000

Equity Shareholder's A/c

Date	Particulars	Dr. (₹)	Particulars	Cr. (₹)
2013	To Equity Shares in B Co. Ltd.	13,50,000	By Equity Share Capital A/c	6,00,000
April 1	To Cash	1,50,000	By Retained Earnings A/c	2,80,000
			By Realisation A/c	6,20,000
	Total	15,00,000		15,00,000

In the Books of B Co. Ltd.

Date	Particulars		Dr. (₹)	Cr. (₹)
1. 2013	Business Purchase A/c	Dr.	15,00,000	
April 1	To liquidators of A Co. Ltd.			15,00,000
	(Being the purchase consideration payable to liquidator of A Co. Ltd.)			
2.	Goodwill A/c (*Balancing figure*)	Dr.	2,63,800	
	Land and Building A/c	Dr.	12,00,000	
	Stock A/c	Dr.	1,42,000	
	Debtors A/c	Dr.	36,000	
	To Provision for Doubtful Debts A/c			1,800
	To 15% Debentures in A Co. Ltd. A/c			1,20,000
	To Creditors A/c			20,000
	To Business Purchase A/c			15,00,000
	(Being the different assets and liabilities taken over and the difference between the net assets and purchase consideration transferred to goodwill)			
3.	Liquidator of A Co. Ltd.		15,00,000	
	To Equity Share Capital A/c			13,50,000
	To Cash A/c			1,50,000
	(Being purchase consideration discharged by issue of 1,35,000 equity shares of ₹ 10 each, balance payment in cash)			

Date	Particulars		Dr. (₹)	Cr. (₹)
4.	15% Debentures in A Co. Ltd. A/c	Dr.	1,20,000	
	Discount on Issue of Debenture	Dr.	5,000	
	To 14% Debentures			1,25,000
	(Being 15% Debentures in A Co. Ltd. discharged by issue of 14% Debentures at a discount of 4%)			
5.	Goodwill A/c	Dr.	7,000	
	To Cash A/c			7,000
	(Being the contingent liability paid-off)			

Illustration 8: To companies Weak Ltd. and Feeble Ltd. amalgamate and form a new company Recovery Ltd. The Balance Sheets of two companies are as under:

Liabilities	Weak Ltd. (₹)	Feeble Ltd. (₹)	Assets	Weak Ltd. (₹)	Feeble Ltd. (₹)
Equity Shares of ₹ 10 each	8,00,000	5,00,000	Goodwill	1,40,000	
Profit and Loss Account	1,00,000	2,00,000	Stock	3,10,000	3,00,000
10% Debentures	1,20,000	—	Debtors	7,50,000	5,00,000
Creditors	1,80,000	1,00,000			
	12,00,000	8,00,000		12,00,000	8,00,000

The past average profits of Weak Ltd. and Feeble Ltd. were ₹ 60,000 and ₹ 40,000 respectively.

Recovery Ltd. agreed to take over the two companies for the sum of ₹ 15,00,000 and to discharge all liabilities. ₹ 3,00,000 of the purchase consideration be paid in cash and balance in equity shares. It is agreed that before being amalgamated, the debtors of the two companies will be written-down to the extent of 10%. The profit on conversion is to be divided between the two companies in the same proportion as to the profit previously earned by them.

Show Business Purchase Account in the books of Recovery Ltd. Also show how the Equity Shareholders Account of Weak Ltd. and Feeble Ltd. be closed.

Solution: It is an amalgamation in the **Nature of Purchase** because the purchase consideration has not been satisfied fully in equity shares. ₹ 3,00,000 was paid in cash out of total purchase consideration of ₹ 15,00,000.

Working Notes:

(1) Calculation of Goodwill/Capital Reserve

Particulars	Weak Ltd. (₹)	Weak Ltd. (₹)	Feeble Ltd. (₹)	Feeble Ltd. (₹)
Assets taken over:				
Stock	3,10,000		3,00,000	
Debtors (*less:* 10%)	6,75,000	9,85,000	4,50,000	7,50,000
Less: Liabilities taken over:				
10% Debentures	1,20,000		—	
Creditors	1,80,000	3,00,000	1,00,000	1,00,000
Net Assets taken over		6,85,000		6,50,000

Total net assets taken over = ₹ (6,85,000 + 6,50,000) = ₹ 13,35,000.

Purchase consideration = ₹ 15,00,000.

Profit on conversion = ₹ (15,00,000 – 13,35,000) = ₹ 1,65,000. This is also the goodwill paid by Recovery Ltd.

Again, profit sharing ratio between Weak Ltd. and Feeble Ltd. is : ₹ 60,000 : ₹ 40,000 = 3 : 2. Therefore, profit on conversion of ₹ 1,65,000 will be shared by the two companies as under: Weak Ltd.—₹ 1,65,000 × 3/5 = ₹ 99,000; Feeble Ltd. – ₹ 1,65,000 × 2/5 = ₹ 66,000.

(2) Calculation of Purchase Consideration of each Company

Particulars	Weak Ltd. (₹)	Feeble Ltd. (₹)
Net Assets taken over (as above)	6,85,000	6,50,000
Add: Profit on conversion	99,000	66,000
Purchase consideration	7,84,000	7,16,000

(3) Statement Showing Mode of Payment

The above purchase consideration will be satisfied as under assuming that the equity shares of Recovery Ltd. is divided equally and the balance by cash:

Particulars	Weak Ltd. (₹)	Feeble Ltd. (₹)
Equity Shares in Recovery Ltd. (equally)	6,00,000	6,00,000
Cash (*Balancing figure*)	1,84,000	1,16,000
	7,84,000	7,16,000

In the Books of Recovery Ltd.
Business Purchase Account

Dr. Cr.

Date	Particulars	(₹)	Date	Particulars	(₹)
	To 10% Debentures in Weak Ltd. A/c	1,20,000		By Goodwill A/c	99,000
	To Creditors A/c (Liabilities taken over from Weak Ltd.)	1,80,000		By Stock A/c	3,10,000
	To Creditors A/c (Liabilities taken over from Feeble Ltd.)	1,00,000		By Debtors A/c (Net assets taken over from Weak Ltd.)	6,75,000
	To Equity Share Capital A/c	12,00,000		By Goodwill A/c	66,000
	To Bank A/c	3,00,000		By Stock A/c	3,00,000
				By Debtors A/c (Net assets taken over from Feeble Ltd.)	4,50,000
		19,00,000			19,00,000

In the Books of Weak Ltd.
Equity Shareholders Account

Dr. Cr.

Date	Particulars	(₹)	Date	Particulars	(₹)
	To Goodwill A/c (written-off)	1,40,000		By Equity Share Capital A/c	8,00,000
	To Debtors A/c (written-off)	75,000		By Profit and Loss A/c	1,00,000
	To Equity Shares in Recovery Ltd. A/c	6,00,000		By Realisation A/c (profit on conversion)	99,000
	To Bank A/c	1,84,000			
		9,99,000			9,99,000

In the Books of Feeble Ltd.

Dr. **Equity Shareholders Account** **Cr.**

Date	Particulars	(₹)	Date	Particulars	(₹)
	To Debtors A/c (written-off)	50,000		By Equity Share Capital A/c	5,00,000
	To Equity Shares in Recovery Ltd. A/c	6,00,000		By Profit and Loss A/c	2,00,000
	To Bank A/c	1,16,000		By Realisation A/c (profit on conversion)	66,000
		7,66,000			7,66,000

Illustration 9: The abridged Balance Sheet of P Ltd. as at 31st December, 2014 is as follows.

Liabilities	(₹)	Assets	(₹)
5,000 Equity Shares of ј 100 each fully paid	5,00,000	Patents	70,000
2,000, 10% Preference Shares of ј 100 each	2,00,000	Freehold Premises	2,50,000
15% Debentures	2,00,000	Machinery	1,35,000
Unsecured Loan	1,00,000	Stock	2,00,000
Creditors	1,50,000	Debtors	1,80,000
Accrued Interest on Debentures	30,000	Bank	50,000
		Profit and Loss Account	2,95,000
	11,80,000		11,80,000

The following scheme of reconstruction was passed and approved by the court:

(*i*) A new company PK Ltd. to be formed to take over the entire business of P Ltd.

(*ii*) PK Ltd. to issue one equity share of ₹ 100, ₹ 60 paid-up in exchange of every two shares in P Ltd. to the shareholders who agree with the scheme. Shareholders, who do not agree with the scheme, to be paid @ ₹ 20 per share in cash. Such shareholders hold 400 equity shares.

(*iii*) Preference shareholders to get 15, 11% preference shares of ₹ 10 each in exchange of 2 preference shares of P Ltd.

(*iv*) Liability in respect of 15% debentures and interest accrued thereon to be taken over and discharged directly by PK Ltd. by issue of equity shares of ₹ 100 each fully paid-up.

(*v*) The creditors of P Ltd. will get from PK Ltd. 50% of their dues in cash and 25% in equity shares of ₹ 100 each and the balance to be foregone by them.

(*vi*) The freehold premises to be revalued at 20% more. The value of machinery to be reduced by 331/3% and that of debtors by 10%. The value of stock to be reduced to ₹ 1,60,000 and patents to have no value.

(*vii*) The preliminary expenses amounted to ₹ 5,000.

You are required to prepare necessary Ledger Account in the books of P Ltd. and pass opening journal entries in the books of PK Ltd.

Solution: Working Note:

(1) Calculation of Purchase Consideration

Particulars	(₹)	(₹)
For Equity Shareholders:		
Equity Shares (5,000 – 4,000)/2 × ₹ 60	1,38,000	
Cash (400 × ₹ 20)	8,000	1,46,000
For Preference Shareholders:		
11% Preference Shares (2,000/2 × 15 × ₹ 10)		1,50,000
Purchase Consideration		2,96,000

In the Books of P Ltd.

Realisation Account

Dr. Cr.

Date	Particulars	(₹)	Date	Particulars	(₹)
2015 Jan. 1	To Patents A/c	70,000	2015 Jan. 1	By 15% Debentures A/c	2,00,000
	To Freehold Premises A/c	2,50,000		By Unsecured Loan A/c	1,00,000
	To Machinery A/c	1,35,000		By Creditors A/c	1,50,000
	To Stock A/c	2,00,000		By Accrued Interest on Debentures A/c	30,000
	To Debtors A/c	1,80,000		By PK Ltd. A/c (Purchase consideration)	2,96,000
	To Bank A/c	50,000		By Preference Shareholders A/c	50,000
				By Equity Shareholders A/c (loss on realisation)	59,000
		8,85,000			8,85,000

PK Ltd. Account

Dr. Cr.

Date	Particulars	(₹)	Date	Particulars	(₹)
2015 Jan. 1	To Realisation A/c	2,96,000	2015 Jan. 1	By Equity Shares in PK Ltd. A/c	1,38,000
				By Bank A/c	8,000
				By 11% Preference Shares in PK Ltd. A/c	1,50,000
		2,96,000			2,96,000

Preference Shareholders Account

Dr. Cr.

Date	Particulars	(₹)	Date	Particulars	(₹)
2015 Jan. 1	To 11% Preference Shares in PK Ltd. A/c	1,50,000	2015 Jan. 1	By 10% Preference Share Capital A/c	2,00,000
	To Realisation A/c	50,000			
		2,00,000			2,00,000

Equity Shareholders Account

Dr. Cr.

Date	Particulars	(₹)	Date	Particulars	(₹)
2015 Jan. 1	To Profit and Loss A/c	2,95,000	2015 Jan. 1	By Equity Share Capital A/c	5,00,000
	To Realisation A/c (Loss)	59,000			
	To Equity Shares in PK Ltd. A/c	1,38,000			
	To Bank A/c	8,000			
		5,00,000			5,00,000

In the Books of PK Ltd.

Journal

Date	Particulars		LF	Dr. (₹)	Cr. (₹)
2015 Jan. 1	Business Purchase A/c	Dr.		2,96,000	
	To Liquidator of P Ltd. A/c				2,96,000
	(Being the amount payable to the liquidator of P Ltd. as per agreement dated...)				

Date	Particulars		LF	Dr. (₹)	Cr. (₹)
	Freehold Premises A/c (₹ 2,50,000 + ₹ 50,000)	Dr.		3,00,000	
	Machinery A/c (₹ 1,35,000 – ₹ 45,000)	Dr.		90,000	
	Debtors A/c (₹ 1,80,000 – ₹ 18,000)	Dr.		1,62,000	
	Stock A/c	Dr.		1,60,000	
	Bank A/c	Dr.		50,000	
	To 15% Debentures in P Ltd. A/c				2,30,000
	To Unsecured Loan A/c				1,00,000
	To Creditors A/c (₹ 1,50,000 – ₹ 37,500)				1,12,500
	To Business Purchase A/c				2,96,000
	To Capital Reserve A/c				23,500
	(Being the different assets and liabilities taken over)				
	Liquidator of P Ltd. A/c	Dr.		2,96,000	
	To Equity Share Capital A/c				1,38,000
	To Bank A/c				8,000
	To 11% Preference Share Capital A/c				1,50,000
	(Being the discharge of purchase consideration)				
	15% Debentures in P Ltd. A/c	Dr.		2,30,000	
	To Equity Share Capital A/c				2,30,000
	(Being 15% Debentures in P Ltd. discharged by the issue of 2,300 equity shares of ₹ 100 each fully paid-up)				
	Creditors A/c	Dr.		1,12,500	
	To Bank A/c				75,000
	To Equity Share Capital A/c				37,500
	(Being the creditors of P Ltd. paid-off)				
	Capital Reserve A/c	Dr.		5,000	
	To Bank A/c				5,000
	(Being the preliminary expenses paid-off)				

Note: It is an amalgamation in the **Nature of Purchase** because the value of different assets and liabilities are to be adjusted.

Illustration 10: The Balance Sheet of Moon Limited as on 31st December, 2013 was as follows:

Liabilities	(₹)	Assets	(₹)
Share Capital:		Building	2,00,000
5,000 Equity Shares of ₹ 100 each	5,00,000	Plant	1,60,000
Reserve	10,000	Stock	30,000
9% Debentures	1,00,000	Debtors	1,20,000
Creditors	90,000	Bank	25,000
		Preliminary Expenses	35,000
		Profit and Loss Account	1,30,000
	7,00,000		7,00,000

On 1st January, 2014 Sun Limited was formed to take over the business of Moon Limited on the following terms:

(*i*) Debentures will be discharged by the issue of sufficient number of 12% Debentures of Sun Limited as would bring the same amount of interest.

(*ii*) Shareholders will be issued 2,400 Equity Shares of ₹ 100 each of Sun Limited.

(*iii*) Liquidation expenses of ₹ 2,000 will be paid by Sun Limited.

Prepare the necessary Ledger Accounts to close the books of Moon Limited.

Pass the opening journal entries in the books of Sun Limited and prepare the Balance Sheet of Sun Limited assuming that the assets of Moon Limited are taken over at 25% discount.

Solution:

Calculation of Purchase consideration	(₹)	Calculation of Goodwill/ Capital Reserve	(₹)	(₹)
Equity Shares: 2,400 × ₹ 100 Issue of 12% debentures to pay-off 9% debentures is not to be included while calculating purchase consideration. Such debentures will be taken over by Sun Ltd. and then discharged. Likewise, liquidation expenses will also not to be included	2,40,000	Assets taken over:		
		Building	1,50,000	
		Plant	1,20,000	
		Stock	22,500	
		Debtors	90,000	
		Bank (Note 2)	25,000	4,07,500
		Less: Liabilities taken over 9% Debentures (Note 1)	75,000	
		Creditors	90,000	1,65,000
				2,42,500
		Less: Purchase consideration		2,40,000
		Capital Reserve		2,500

In the Books of Moon Ltd.

Dr. Realisation Account Cr.

Date	Particulars	(₹)	Date	Particulars	(₹)
2014 Jan. 1	To Building A/c	2,00,000	2014 Jan. 1	By 9% Debentures A/c	1,00,000
	To Plant A/c	1,60,000		By Creditors A/c	90,000
	To Stock A/c	30,000		By Sun Ltd. A/c (Purchase Consideration)	2,40,000
	To Debtors A/c	1,20,000			
	To Bank A/c	25,000		By Sundry Equity Shareholders A/c (Loss on realisation)	1,05,000
		5,35,000			5,35,000

Dr. Sun Ltd. Account Cr.

Date	Particulars	(₹)	Date	Particulars	(₹)
2014 Jan. 1	To Realisation A/c	2,40,000	2014 Jan. 1	By Equity Shares in Sun Ltd. A/c	2,40,000

Dr. Equity Shares in Sun Ltd. Account Cr.

Date	Particulars	(₹)	Date	Particulars	(₹)
2014 Jan. 1	To Sun Ltd. A/c	2,40,000	2014 Jan. 1	By Sundry Equity Shareholders A/c	2,40,000

Dr. Sundry Equity Shareholders Account Cr.

Date	Particulars	(₹)	Date	Particulars	(₹)
2014 Jan. 1	To Preliminary Expenses A/c	35,000	2014 Jan. 1	By Equity Share Capital A/c	5,00,000
	To Profit and Loss A/c	1,30,000		By Reserve A/c	10,000

Date	Particulars	(₹)	Date	Particulars	(₹)
	To Equity Shares in Sun Ltd. A/c	2,40,000			
	To Realisation A/c (Loss)	1,05,000			
		5,10,000			5,10,000

In the Books of Sun Ltd.
Journal

Date	Particulars	LF	Dr. (₹)	Cr. (₹)
2014 Jan. 1	Business Purchase A/c Dr.		2,40,000	
	To Liquidator of Moon Ltd. A/c			2,40,000
	(Being the amount payable to Moon Ltd. as per agreement dated...)			
	Building A/c Dr.		1,50,000	
	Plant A/c Dr.		1,20,000	
	Stock A/c Dr.		22,500	
	Debtors A/c Dr.		90,000	
	Bank A/c Dr.		25,000	
	To 9% Debentures in Moon Ltd. A/c (Note 1)			75,000
	To Creditors A/c			90,000
	To Business Purchase A/c			2,40,000
	To Capital Reserve A/c			2,500
	(Being the different assets and liabilities taken over as per agreement dated... the difference between the net assets taken over and purchase consideration transferred to capital reserve)			
	Liquidator of Moon Ltd. A/c Dr.		2,40,000	
	To Equity Share Capital A/c			2,40,000
	(Being the purchase consideration discharged by the issue of 2,400 equity shares of ₹ 100 each)			
	9% Debentures in Moon Ltd. A/c Dr.		75,000	
	To 12% Debentures A/c			75,000
	(Being 9% debentures in Moon Ltd. discharged by the issue of 12% debentures)			
	Capital Reserve A/c Dr.		2,000	
	To Cash A/c			2,000
	(Being the liquidation expenses paid-off)			

Balance Sheet of P Ltd. as at Ist January, 2014

Liabilities	(₹) ('000)	Assets	(₹) ('000)
Share Capital		**Fixed Assets**	
Authorised Capital:		Building	1,50,000
... Equity Shares of ₹ 100 each	***	Plant	1,20,000
Issued, Subscribed and Paid-up Capital:		**Investments**	Nil
2,400 Equity Shares of ₹ 100 each	2,40,000	**Current Assets, Loans and Advances**	
(All these shares are allotted as fully paid-up pursuant to a contract without payments being received in cash)		(*A*) *Current Assets:*	
		Stock	22,500
		Debtors	90,000

Liabilities	(₹) ('000)	Assets	(₹) ('000)
Reserve and Surplus		Bank (₹ 25,000 – 2,000)	23,000
Capital Reserve (₹ 2,500 – 2,000)	500	Miscellaneous Expenditure	Nil
Secured Loans			
12% Debentures	75,000		
Unsecured Loans	Nil		
Current Liabilities and Provisions			
(*A*) *Current Liabilities:*			
Creditors	90,000		
	4,05,500		4,05,500

Working Notes:

1. Face value of Debentures of Moon Ltd was ₹ 1,00,000. Interest payable @ 9%. Therefore, the debentureholders were getting interest of ₹ 9,000 (9% of ₹ 1,00,000).

   Sun Ltd. will issue 12% Debentures of such value which will result in same amount of interest. Therefore, the face value of 12% Debentures of Sun Ltd. will be: ₹ 9,000/12 × 100 = **₹ 75,000.**

   In the books of Sun Ltd., debentures will be recorded at ₹ 75,000 only.
2. Bank will be taken at book value since it is a monetary asset.

Illustration 11: Following is the Balance Sheet of Star Ltd. as on 31st March, 2013:

Liabilities	(₹)	Assets	(₹)
Share Capital:		Plant and Machinery	9,00,000
1,20,000 Equity Shares of ₹ 10 each	12,00,000	Furniture and Fittings	1,50,000
Capital Reserve	20,000	Stock	4,00,000
Long-term Loan	3,60,000	Debtors	2,20,000
Creditors	3,00,000	Bank	1,00,000
		Profit and Loss Account	1,10,000
	18,80,000		18,80,000

On 1st April, 2013 a new company Suraj Ltd was incorporated which took over fixed assets and stock of Star Ltd for ₹ 12,60,000 payable as ₹ 9,00,000 in the form of 1,80,000 equity shares of ₹ 5 each and ₹ 3,60,000 in the form of 3,600, 12% Mortgage Debentures of ₹ 100 each. Lender accepted the debentures in Suraj Ltd in discharge of the loan. Debtors realised ₹ 2,05,000. Expenses of liquidation amounted to ₹ 8,000 and were met by Star Ltd. The available cash was distributed among creditors in full satisfaction of their claim.

Show necessary Ledger Account to close the books of Moon Ltd. and draw the opening Balance Sheet of Suraj Ltd.

Solution:

***(i)* Calculation of Goodwill/Capital Reserve** | ***(ii)* Calculation of Purchase Consideration**

Liabilities	(₹)	(₹)	Assets	(₹)
Assets taken over:			Equity Shares: 1,80,000 × ₹ 5	9,00,000
Plant and Machinery	9,00,000		Issue of 12% mortgage debentures to pay-off loan is not to be included while calculating purchase consideration. Such loan will be taken over by Suraj Ltd. and then discharged.	
Furniture and Fixture	1,50,000			
Stock	4,0,000	14,50,000		
Less: Liabilities taken over:				
Long-term Loan		3,60,000		
Net Assets taken over		10,90,000		
Less: Purchase Consideration		9,00,000		
Capital Reserve		1,90,000		

In the Books of Star Ltd.

Dr. **Realisation Account** Cr.

Date	Particulars	(₹)	Date	Particulars	(₹)
2013	To Plant and Machinery A/c	9,00,000	2013	By Loan A/c	3,60,000
April 1	To Furniture and Fixture A/c	1,50,000	April 1	By Suraj Ltd. A/c	9,00,000
	To Stock A/c	4,00,000		By Creditors A/c (Profit on payment)	3,000
	To Debtors A/c (Loss on realisation)	15,000		By Sundry Equity Shareholders A/c (Profit on realisation)	2,10,000
	To Bank A/c (Realisation expenses)	8,000			
		14,73,000			14,73,000

Dr. **Suraj Ltd. Account** Cr.

Date	Particulars	(₹)	Date	Particulars	(₹)
2013 April 1	To Realisation A/c	9,00,000	2013 April 1	By Equity shares in Suraj Ltd. A/c	9,00,000

Dr. **Equity Shares in Suraj Ltd. Account** Cr.

Date	Particulars	(₹)	Date	Particulars	(₹)
2013 April 1	To Suraj Ltd. A/c	9,00,000	2013 April 1	By Equity Shareholders A/c	9,00,000

Dr. **Debtors Account** Cr.

Date	Particulars	(₹)	Date	Particulars	(₹)
2013	To Balance b/d	2,20,000	2013	By Bank A/c	2,05,000
April 1			April 1	By Realisation A/c	15,000
		2,20,000			2,20,000

Dr. **Bank Account** Cr.

Date	Particulars	(₹)	Date	Particulars	(₹)
2013	To Balance b/d	1,00,000	2013	By Realisation A/c (expenses)	8,000
April 1	To Debtors A/c	2,05,000	April 1	By Creditors A/c	2,97,000
		3,05,000			3,05,000

Dr. **Creditors Account** Cr.

Date	Particulars	(₹)	Date	Particulars	(₹)
2013	To Bank A/c	2,97,000	2013	By Balance c/d	3,00,000
April 1	To Realisation A/c	3,000	April 1		
		3,00,000			3,00,000

Dr. **Sundry Equity Shareholders Account** Cr.

Date	Particulars	(₹)	Date	Particulars	(₹)
2013	To Profit and Loss A/c	1,10,000	2013	By Equity Share Capital A/c	12,00,000
April 1	To Equity Shares in Suraj Ltd. A/c	9,00,000	April 1	By Capital Reserve A/c	20,000
	To Realisation A/c	2,10,000			
		12,20,000			12,20,000

Note: It is an amalgamation in ***Nature of Purchase*** because all the assets and liabilities are not taken over by the transferee company.

Balance Sheet of Suraj Ltd. as at 1st April, 2013

Liabilities	(₹) ('000)	Assets	(₹) ('000)
Share Capital:		**Fixed Assets:**	
Authorised Capital:		Plant and Machinery	9,00,000
... Equity Shares of ₹ 5 each		Furniture and Fixture	1,50,000
Issued, Subscribed and Paid-up Capital:		**Investments**	Nil
1,80,000 Equity Shares of ₹ 5 each (All these shares are allotted as fully paid-up pursuant to a contract without payments being received in cash)	9,00,000	**Current Assets, Loans and Advances**	
		(A) Current Assets:	
		Stock	4,00,000
		Miscellaneous Expenditure	Nil
Reserve and Surplus			
Capital Reserve [Note (*ii*)]	1,90,000		
Secured Loans			
12% Mortgage Debentures	3,60,000		
Unsecured Loans	Nil		
Current Liabilities and Provisions	Nil		
	14,50,000		14,50,000

Illustration 12: (Apportionment of purchase consideration – Merger and Purchase)

On 1st April, 2013 the Balance Sheets of R Ltd. and S Ltd. were as under:

Liabilities	R Ltd. (₹)	S Ltd. (₹)	Assets	R Ltd. (₹)	S Ltd. (₹)
12% Preference Share Capital (Shares of ₹ 100 each)	2,50,000	—	Fixed Assets	11,50,000	6,50,000
			Current Assets	8,30,000	6,70,000
Equity Share Capital (Shares of ₹ 10 each)	12,50,000	9,00,000	Preliminary Expenses	—	20,000
General Reserve	40,000	90,000			
Export Profit Reserve	60,000	40,000			
Investment Allowance Reserve	—	20,000			
Profit and Loss A/c	1,50,000	1,20,000			
13% Debentures	1,00,000	70,000			
Sundry Creditors	1,30,000	1,00,000			
	19,80,000	13,40,000		19,80,000	13,40,000

A new company RS Ltd., was formed to takeover the business of R Ltd. and S Ltd. on the following terms:

(*i*) RS Ltd. to takeover both the companies at a total price of ₹ 24,00,000 to be discharged by issue of equity shares of ₹ 10 each at a premium of 20%.

(*ii*) The shareholders of R Ltd. and S Ltd. to get shares in RS Ltd. in the ratio of net assets value of their respective shares.

(*iii*) The debentures of both companies are to be converted into equivalent number of 12% Debentures in RS Ltd.

(*iv*) Statutory Reserves are to be maintained for 3 more years.

(*v*) The Fixed assets of R Ltd. and S Ltd., are valued at ₹ 12,00,000 and ₹ 7,00,000 respectively.

Record journal entries in the books of RS Ltd. and prepare a Balance Sheet if:

(*a*) It is a case of amalgamation in nature of merger.

(*b*) It is an amalgamation in nature of purchase.

Solution:

(*a*) Amalgamation in the nature of merger.

Calculation of Purchase/Consideration

	R Ltd.		S Ltd.
Fixed Assets (Revised Value)	12,00,000		7,00,000
Current Assets	8,30,000		6,70,000
	20,30,000		13,70,000
Less: Liabilities	2,30,000		1,70,000
Net Assets	18,00,000		12,00,000
Ratio	18	:	12

Hence total purchase consideration of ₹ 24,00,000 to be divided in the ratio of 3 : 2

Purchase consideration for R Ltd. $\left(₹\ 24{,}00{,}000 \times \frac{3}{5}\right)$ = ₹ 14,40,000

No. of shares to be issued (₹ 14,40,000 ÷ 12) = 1,20,000 Shares

Purchase consideration for S Ltd. $\left(₹\ 24{,}00{,}000 \times \frac{2}{5}\right)$ = ₹ 9,60,000

No. of Shares to be issued (₹ 9,60,000 ÷ 12) = 80,000 Shares

Books of RS Ltd.
Journal Entries

Particulars		LF	Dr. (₹)	Cr. (₹)
Business Purchase A/c	Dr.		24,00,000	
To Liquidator of R Ltd.				14,40,000
To Liquidator of S Ltd.				9,60,000
(Being purchase consideration payable on taken over)				
Fixed Assets A/c	Dr.		18,00,000	
Current Assets A/c	Dr.		15,00,000	
Preliminary Expenses A/c	Dr.		20,000	
To 13% Debentures				1,70,000
To Sundry Creditors				2,30,000
To Export Profit Reserve				1,00,000
To Investment Allowance Reserve				20,000
To Profit and Loss A/c				2,70,000
To General Reserve (B.F.)				1,30,000
To Business Purchase A/c				24,00,000
(Being assets and liabilities taken over at book values)				
Liquidator of R Ltd. A/c	Dr.		14,40,000	
Liquidator of S Ltd. A/c	Dr.		9,60,000	
To Equity Share capital A/c				20,00,000
To Securities Premium A/c				4,00,000
(Being shares allotted to liquidators)				

Particulars		LF	Dr. (₹)	Cr. (₹)
13% Debentures A/c	Dr.		1,70,000	
To 12% Debentures				1,70,000
(Being 13% Debentures converted into 12% Debentures)				

Balance Sheet of RS Ltd. as on 1st April, 2013

Liabilities	(₹)	Assets	(₹)
Authorised Capital ...		Fixed Assets	18,00,000
Issued and Subscribed Capital		Current Assets	15,00,000
2,00,000 Shares of j 10 each	20,00,000	Miscellaneous Expenditures:	
Reserve and Surplus:		Preliminary Expenses	20,000
Securities Premium	4,00,000		
Export Profit Reserve	1,00,000		
Investment Allowance Reserve	20,000		
General Reserve*	1,30,000		
Profit and Loss A/c	2,70,000		
Secured Loans:			
12% Debentures	1,70,000		
Current Liabilities:			
Trade Creditors	2,30,000		
	33,20,000		33,20,000

* Verification

	₹
Total Purchase consideration	24,00,000
Total Share Capital (₹ 2,50,000 + 12,50,000 + 9,00,000)	24,00,000
Difference	Nil

Hence, accumulated profits are not be affected and will be maintained in the same form as before.

(*b*) Amalgamation in the nature of purchase.

Journal Entries

Particulars		LF	Dr. (₹)	Cr. (₹)
Business Purchase A/c	Dr.		24,00,000	
To Liquidator of R Ltd.				14,40,000
To Liquidator of S Ltd.				9,60,000
(Being purchase consideration payable to liquidators)				
Fixed Assets A/c	Dr.		19,00,000	
Current Assets A/c	Dr.		15,00,000	
To 13% Debentures				1,70,000
To Sundry Creditors				2,30,000
To Business Purchase				24,00,000
To Capital Reserve (B.F.)				6,00,000
(Being assets and liabilities takenover at revised values)				
Liquidator of R Ltd. A/c	Dr.		14,40,000	
Liquidator of S Ltd. A/c	Dr.		9,60,000	
To Equity Share Capital A/c				20,00,000

Particulars		LF	Dr. (₹)	Cr. (₹)
To Securities Premium A/c (Being shares allotted to liquidators at premium)				4,00,000
Amalgamation Adjustment A/c To Export Profit Reserve A/c To Investment Allowance Reserve A/c (Being statutory reserves maintained)	Dr.		1,20,000	 1,00,000 20,000
13% Debentures A/c To 12% Debentures (Being 13% Debentures converted into 12% Debentures)	Dr.		1,70,000	 1,70,000

Balance Sheet of RS Ltd. as on 1st April, 2013

Liabilities	(₹)	Assets	(₹)
Authorised Capital ...		Fixed Assets	19,00,000
Issued and Subscribed Capital		Current Assets	15,00,000
2,00,000 Shares of ₹ 10 each	20,00,000	Miscellaneous Expenditures:	
Reserves and Surplus:		Amalgamation Adjustment A/c	1,20,000
Securities Premium	4,00,000		
Capital Reserve	6,00,000		
Export Profit Reserve	1,00,000		
Investment Allowance Reserve	20,000		
Secured Loans:			
12% Debentures	1,70,000		
Current Liabilities:			
Sundry Creditors	2,30,000		
	35,20,000		35,20,000

Inter-company Transactions

Often there maybe certain transactions between transferor and the transferee companies at time of amalgamation whereby the transferor company maybe a debtor or creditor of the transferee company or vice-versa. This may be due to following reasons:

(*i*) Loan given by one company to the other company.

(*ii*) Bills accepted by one company, drawn by other company and vice-versa.

(*iii*) Goods purchased from the other company.

(*iv*) Goods sold to one company by other company.

The above mentioned transactions require adjustment which can be explained under two heads:

1. Cancellation of common debts
2. Cancellation of unrealized profits.

It may be noted that no adjustment is required in the books of transferor company in any of the situations mentioned above.

Treatment in Books of Transferee Company

1. **Cancellation of common debts:** Inter company debts represented by common debtors and/ or bills of exchange or loan are cancelled by passing an additional entry in the books of the transferee company. The Journal entries are as follows.

In case of loan:

Loan (from one company) A/c Dr.
  To Loan (to other company) A/c

In case of bills

Bills payable (of one company) Dr. [with common part of B/R and B/P]
  To Bills Receivable (of other company)

In case of debtors and creditors

Creditors (of one company) Dr.
  To Debtors (of other company)

2. **Cancellation of Unrealised Profit:** If certain goods were purchased by the transferor company from the transferee company and remain unsold at the time of acquisition of business then the unsold stock of Transferor Company becomes the part of stock of the transferee company. Since transferee company had sold the goods at "cost plus profit" the same cannot be taken back or included in the stock at this price. Hence the profit element which is included in the unsold stock of the transferor company is treated as unrealized profit and has to be eliminated there from. The journal entry required for this is:

(*i*) Profit and Loss A/c Dr. [in case of merger]
  To Stock A/c

(*ii*) Goodwill A/c [in case of amalgamation in the nature of purchase]
  To Stock A/c

OR

Capital Reserve A/c
  To Stock A/c

Illustration 13: X Ltd. is absorbed by Y Ltd., on the following terms and conditions:

1. Y Ltd. to take over all assets and liabilities of X Ltd.
2. To pay cost of liquidation not exceeding ₹ 8,000.
3. To issue 15% Debenture of ₹ 14,90,000 for debenture holder of X Ltd.
4. To pay ₹ 15 per share in X Ltd.
5. To allot one 12% preference share of ₹ 100 each and five equity shares of ₹ 100 each for every four equity shares in X Ltd.
6. Actual cost of liquidation amounted to ₹ 10,000.

Stock of X Ltd. included ₹ 56,000 for goods purchased from Y Ltd. which Y Ltd. supplied at cost + 1/3 of cost. Creditors of X Ltd. included ₹ 10,000 due by X Ltd. to Y Ltd.

The balance sheet of X Ltd. on the date of absorption was as follows:

Liabilities	Amount	Assets	Amount
Equity Share Capital (₹ 100)	20,00,000	Fixed Assets (including goodwill ₹ 4,00,000)	37,50,000
General Reserve	5,00,000		
Debenture Sinking Fund	1,00,000	Sinking Fund Investments	1,00,000
Workmen Compensation Fund	50,000	Stock	2,00,000
Employees Profit Sharing Fund	1,00,000	Debtors	3,60,000
Staff Provident Fund	1,50,000	Cash	30,000
Sundry Creditors	1,40,000		
12% Debentures	14,00,000		
	44,40,000		44,40,000

A claim of ₹ 9,000 by a worker was admitted by X Ltd. but not recorded in the books.

You are required to closed the books of X Ltd. and pass journal entries in the books of Y Ltd.

Solution: *Calculation of Purchase Consideration*

Cash (20,000 × 15)	3,00,000
Preference Shares in Y Ltd. (20,000/4 × 1 × 100)	5,00,000
Equity Shares in Y Ltd. (20,000/4 × 5 × 100)	25,00,000
	33,00,000

Dr. **Realisation Account** **Cr.**

Particulars	(₹)	Particulars	(₹)
To Fixed Assets A/c	37,50,000	By Creditors A/c	1,40,000
To Sinking Fund Investment A/c	1,00,000	By 12%, Debentures A/c	14,00,000
To Stock A/c	2,00,000	By Provident Fund A/c	1,50,000
To Debtors A/c	3,60,000	By Profit Sharing Fund A/c	1,00,000
To Cash A/c	30,000	By Worker's Claim A/c	9,000
To Cash (expenses) (10,000 – 8,000) A/c	2,000	By Y Ltd. A/c	33,00,000
To Equity Shareholders A/c (Profit)	6,57,000		
	50,99,000		50,99,000

Dr. **Equity Shareholders Account** **Cr.**

Particulars	(₹)	Particulars	(₹)
To Preference Shares in Y Ltd. A/c	5,00,000	By Equity Share Capital A/c	20,00,000
To Equity Shares in Y Ltd. A/c	25,00,000	By General Reserve A/c	5,00,000
To Cash (3,00,000 – 2,000 Exp.) A/c	2,98,000	By Debenture Fund A/c	1,00,000
		By Workmen Accident Fund A/c (50,000 – 9,000)	41,000
		By Realisation (Profit) A/c	6,57,000
	32,98,000		32,98,000

Notes:

1. Accident liability ₹ 9,000 is provided out of accident fund and then it is transferred to realisation account as all liabilities are taken over. The balance of fund account is transferred to equity shareholders account.
2. Only book value of debentures is transferred to realisation account as it is assumed to have been taken over in first place and then discharged directly by Y Ltd.

Journal of Y Ltd.

Particulars		LF	Dr. (₹)	Cr. (₹)
Business Purchase A/c	Dr.		33,00,000	
To Liquidator of X Ltd.				33,00,000
(For purchase consideration payable to X Ltd.)				
Goodwill (*Balancing figure*)	Dr.		11,49,000	
Fixed Assets A/c (excluding goodwill)	Dr.		33,50,000	
Investments A/c	Dr.		1,00,000	
Stock A/c	Dr.		2,00,000	
Debtors A/c	Dr.		3,60,000	

Particulars		LF	Dr. (₹)	Cr. (₹)
Cash A/c	Dr.		30,000	
To Creditors A/c				1,40,000
To 12% Debentures A/c in X Ltd.				14,90,000
To Accident Liability A/c				9,000
To Provident Fund A/c				1,50,000
To Profit Sharing Fund A/c				1,00,000
To Business Purchase A/c				33,00,000
(For acquisition of business and taking goodwill as balancing figure)				
Goodwill A/c	Dr.		16,000	
To Stock Reserve A/c				8,000
To Cash A/c (1/7 × 56,000)				8,000
(For creation of stock reserve and reimbursement of realisation expenses)				
12% Debentures A/c in X Ltd.	Dr.		14,90,000	
To 15% Debentures A/c				14,90,000
(For payment to debentureholders of X Ltd. by issue of 5% debentures)				
Liquidator of X Ltd.	Dr.		33,00,000	
To Equity Share Capital A/c				25,00,000
To Preference Share Capital A/c				5,00,000
To Cash A/c				3,00,000
(For discharge of purchase consideration)				
Creditors A/c	Dr.		10,000	
To Debtors A/c				10,000
(For cancellation of common debt)				

THEORY QUESTIONS

1. Define amalgamation, absorption and reconstruction.
2. Distinguish between, "amalgamation in the nature of merger" and "amalgamation in the nature of purchase."
3. Explain the conditions to be satisfied in amalgamation in the nature of merger as per AS-14.
4. Define purchase consideration as per AS-14.
5. Write a note on treatment of realisation expenses.
6. When amalgamation adjustment account is opened and why?
7. Write a note on "pooling of interest method" and "purchase method".
8. Write short notes :

   Statutory Reserves Vs. Capital Reserve; Transferor Vs. Transferee Company; External Reconstruction Vs. Amalgamation; Book Value Vs. Intrinsic Value.

EXERCISES AND PROBLEMS

1. A Ltd. is absorbed by B Ltd. on that date the Balance Sheet of A Ltd. was as follows:

Liabilities	(₹)	Assets	(₹)
12% Preference Shares of ₹ 100 each	5,00,000	Sundry Assets	20,00,000
7,500 Equity Shares of ₹ 100 each	7,50,000		
General Reserve	3,00,000		

Liabilities	(₹)	Assets	(₹)
Profit and Loss A/c	1,50,000		
6% Debentures	2,00,000		
Sundry Creditors	1,00,000		
	20,00,000		20,00,000

B Ltd. agrees to:

(*i*) Issue 9% Preference Shares of ₹ 100 each in the ratio of 3 : 4 to preference shareholders.

(*ii*) Issue to the debentureholders of AS Ltd. 9% Debentures at ₹ 96 in lieu of 6% Debentures in the old company.

(*iii*) Pay ₹ 10 per share in Cash and to issue six equity shares of ₹ 100 each at the market price of ₹ 125 in exchange for every 5 shares held in A Ltd., and

(*iv*) Assume liability to creditors.

Calculate Purchase Consideration.

Ans: ₹ 15,75,000.

2. X Ltd. absorbs Y Ltd. as on 31st March, 2013 when its Balance Sheet was as follows:

Liabilities	(₹)	Assets	(₹)
70,000 Equity Shares of j 10 each	7,00,000	Net Assets	6,80,000
9% Preference Shares of j 100 each	1,00,000	Profit and Loss A/c	1,20,000
	8,00,000		8,00,000

X Ltd. agrees to takeover assets of X Ltd. An equity share in Y Ltd. is valued at ₹ 7 for the purpose of absorption. X Ltd. agrees to pay ₹ 1,00,000 cash to preference shareholders and the balance in the form of equity shares valued at ₹ 12.50 each.

Calculate Purchase consideration.

Ans: ₹ 5,90,000.

Hint: ₹ 1,00,000 Cash to Preference Shareholders and Equity shares worth ₹ 4,90,000 to Equity Shareholders.

3. The two Companies Abad Ltd. and Nabad Ltd. amalgamate and form a new company called Kamyab Ltd. The position of two Companies was as under:

Liabilities	Abad Ltd. (₹)	Nabad Ltd. (₹)	Assets	(₹)	(₹)
Paid-up Capital:			Goodwill	70,000	—
Shares of ₹ 10 each fully paid	3,00,000	2,00,000	Stock	1,80,000	80,000
Profit and Loss A/c	50,000	42,000	Debtors	2,00,000	2,20,000
5% Debentures	70,000	—			
Sundry Creditors	30,000	58,000			
	4,50,000	3,00,000		4,50,000	3,00,000

The average profits of Abad Ltd. and Nabad Ltd. have been ₹ 30,000 and ₹ 20,000 respectively. Kamyab Ltd. agrees with the two companies to takeover both the companies for the sum of ₹ 6,00,000 and in addition to discharge all liabilities; ₹ 1,00,000 to be paid in cash and the balance in shares at face value.

It is further agreed that the Debtors of both the companies before being taken over by Kamyab Ltd. will be written off to the extent of 10% of their respective book figures. The profit on conversion is to be divided between the shareholders of Abad Ltd. and Nabad Ltd. in the same proportion as to profits previously earned by them.

Calculate purchase consideration and prepare Realisation A/c and Shareholders' A/c in the books of Abad Ltd. and Nabad Ltd. and prepare Business Purchase A/c in the books of Kamyab Ltd.

	Abad Ltd.	Nabad Ltd.
	₹	₹
Ans: Purchase Consideration (₹)	3,60,000	2,40,000
Profit (Loss) on Realisation A/c	10,000	(2,000)
Profit on Conversion	30,000	20,000

Goodwill arising from Business Purchase A/c ₹ 1,20,000

4. Following is the Balance Sheet of Resham Ltd. as on 1st April, 2013:

Liabilities	(₹)	Assets	(₹)
12% Preference Share Capital (Shares of ₹ 100 each)	3,00,000	Fixed Assets	15,00,000
		Investments	2,50,000
Equity Share Capital (Shares of ₹ 10 each)	12,00,000	Current Assets (Other than Cash and Bank)	7,50,000
Foreign Project Reserve (Statutory Reserve)	1,50,000	Cash and Bank Balance	2,00,000
General Reserve	3,50,000		
11% Debentures	5,00,000		
Current Liabilities	2,00,000		
	27,00,000		27,00,000

Rashmi Ltd. takes over Resham Ltd. on the following terms:

1. Preference Shareholders of Resham Ltd. are to be discharged at a premium of 25% by issuing the necessary number of 13% preference shares of ₹ 100 each.
2. Equity Shareholders of Resham Ltd. are to be issued on the basis of intrinsic values of shares of both the Companies. The intrinsic value of Resham Ltd. was ₹ 20 per share and of Rashmi Ltd. was ₹ 30 each. However, it was agreed to record the entry on the basis of par value only. The nominal value of Rashmi Ltd. was ₹ 10 per share.
3. The debentures of Resham Ltd. are to be redeemed by Rashmi Ltd. by issuing 13% own debenture of ₹ 100 each at ₹ 120 per debenture.

Record entries in the books of Rashmi Ltd.

Ans: Purchase consideration = ₹ 11,60,000.

5. A Ltd. was absorbed by B Ltd. as on 31st March, 2013. The purchase consideration was agreed at ₹ 3,36,000 to be discharged in fully paid equity shares of ₹ 10 each. Balance Sheets of both the companies were as under:

Liabilities	A Ltd. (₹)	B Ltd. (₹)	Assets	A Ltd. (₹)	B Ltd. (₹)
Share Capital (Issued & Subscribed) Shares of ₹ 10 each	2,00,000	7,50,000	Goodwill	60,000	2,00,000
			Plant and Machinery	1,00,000	3,12,000
General Reserve	50,000	1,50,000	Stock	80,000	2,65,000
Profit and Loss A/c	12,900	20,500	Debtors	56,000	2,21,200
Workmen Compensation Fund	9,000	12,000	Prepaid Insurance	700	—
Sundry Creditors	30,460	58,570	Income Tax Refund Claim	6,000	—

Liabilities	A Ltd. (₹)	B Ltd. (₹)	Assets	A Ltd. (₹)	B Ltd. (₹)
Staff Provident Fund	4,000	10,000	Cash at Bank	8,300	14,000
Provision for Taxation	5,000	12,000	Cash in Hand	360	870
	3,11,360	10,13,070		3,11,360	10,13,070

Prepare necessary ledger accounts in the books of A Ltd. and pass journal entries in the books of B Ltd. Also prepare a Balance Sheet after amalgamation.

Ans: Realisation A/c Profit = ₹ 64,700

General Reserve (Dr.) ₹ 73,700 after adjustment 76,300

6. The following is the summarised Balance Sheet of A Ltd. as at 31st March, 2013:

Liabilities	(₹)	Assets	(₹)
20,000 Equity Shares of ₹ 10 each	2,00,000	Land and Building	1,00,000
10% Debentures	1,00,000	Plant and Machinery	50,000
Reserve	90,000	Furniture	40,000
Profit and Loss A/c	30,000	Stock	20,000
Creditors	10,000	Debtors	30,000
		Bank	1,50,000
		Cash	40,000
	4,30,000		4,30,000

On 1st April, 2013, B Ltd. took over the business of A Ltd. The terms and conditions are as under:

(*a*) Debentures are to be discharged at a premium of 5% by B Ltd.

(*b*) Creditors are to be paid-off by B Ltd.

(*c*) B Ltd. will issue 5 equity shares of ₹ 10 each (market value ₹ 11) for every 4 equity shares of A Ltd.

(*d*) Cost of liquidation of ₹ 5,000 is to be paid by B Ltd.

You are required to:

(*i*) Close the books of A Ltd.

(*ii*) Pass opening journal entries in the books of B Ltd., assuming that the amalgamation is in the nature of (*a*) merger; and (*b*) purchase.

Ans: Purchase Consideration = ₹ 2,75,000

7. With a view of effecting economy in working the United Mills Limited agrees to takeover the business of the Bharat Hosiery Limited as on 31st March, 2013.

Liabilities	(₹)	Assets	(₹)
Share Capital:		Land and Building	1,80,000
12,000 Shares of ₹ 50 each	6,00,000	Plant and Machinery	1,25,000
Reserve Fund	1,20,000	Stock	2,50,000
Reserve for doubtful debts	10,000	Debtors	2,90,000
Profit and Loss A/c	65,000	Cash and Bank	25,000
S. Creditors	75,000		
	8,70,000		8,70,000

The purchasers took over all assets and liabilities of the vendor company excepting a sum of ₹ 10,000 to provide for cost of liquidation and payment to any dissentient shareholders.

The purchase price was to be discharged by the allotment to the shareholders of the Vendor Company of the share of ₹ 100 (₹ 90 paid up) of the United Mills Ltd. for every two shares in the Bharat Hosiery Ltd. The expenses of liquidation amount to ₹ 30,000. Dissentient shareholders of 100 shares are paid out at ₹ 70 per share.

Pass journal entries in the books of respective companies to give effect to the above transactions. Also prepare Balance Sheet after absorption.

Ans: Purchase Consideration — ₹ 5,35,500

Loss on Realisation — ₹ 2,44,500

Capital Reserve — ₹ 2,39,500

Balance Sheet Total — ₹ 8,60,000

EXTERNAL RECONSTRUCTION

8. Ess Ltd. is taken-over by, Zed Ltd., newly formed Company. The Balance Sheet of Ess Ltd. as on 31st March, 2013 was as follows:

Liabilities	(₹)	Assets	(₹)
9% Preference Share Capital	9,00,000	Freehold Property	6,00,000
Shares of ₹ 100 each		Plant and Machinery	3,00,000
Equity Share Capital	12,00,000	Stock	1,50,000
Shares of ₹ 10 each		S. Debtors	2,25,000
Current Liabilities	3,00,000	Profit and Loss A/c	11,25,000
	24,00,000		24,00,000

There was a contingent liability of ₹ 45,000 on account of legal dispute. Zed Ltd. agrees to take over the assets as follows:

Freehold property — 90% of book value

Plant and Machinery — 60% of book value

Stock — 30% of book value

S. Debtors are considered — 40% bad.

The purchase consideration was satisfied by issuing equal number of equity shares and preference shares in Zed Ltd., both having a face value of ₹ 10 each. The contingent liability materialised only to the extent of ₹ 30,000. It was taken over by Zed Ltd., and settled by issue of equity shares.

Record journal entries in the books of Ess Ltd. and Zed Ltd.

Ans: Realisation Profit — ₹ 2,10,000

Purchase Consideration — ₹ 5,70,000

9. The following is the Balance Sheet of Frank Ltd. on 31st March, 2013. The Company went into voluntary liquidation on 1.4.2013 and a new Company was formed to takeover the assets and liabilities of the old Company.

Liabilities	(₹)	Assets	(₹)
9% Preference Shares Capital Shares of ₹ 100 each	9,00,000	Goodwill	1,50,000
		Building	4,50,000
Equity Share Capital Shares of ₹ 100 each	15,00,000	Plant and Machinery	6,00,000
10% Debentures (₹ 100)	6,00,000	Furniture	75,000
Unsecured Loans	3,00,000	Patents	1,50,000

Liabilities	(₹)	Assets	(₹)
S. Creditors	1,50,000	Investments	3,00,000
		Stock	3,00,000
		S. Debtors	2,25,000
		Cash and Bank	75,000
		Profit and Loss A/c	9,75,000
		Preliminary Expenses	1,50,000
	34,50,000		34,50,000

Preference dividend is in arrear for three years. Debenture interest has not been paid for last two years.

A company named Franklin Corporation was formed with an authorised capital of ₹ 18,00,000 divided into equity shares of ₹ 100 each. The New Company and stakeholders of old company agreed on the following terms:

1. Preference shareholders waived the dividend and accepted one equity share in the new company for two shares held by them in old company.
2. Equity shareholders accepted one equity share of ₹ 100 each ₹ 50 paid for every four shares held by them in the old company and agreed to bring ₹ 50 per share to be used for paying creditors.
3. Debentureholders accepted one equity share of ₹ 100 for one debenture of ₹ 100 and also for interest due to them by way of equity shares.
4. Loan creditors agreed to waive interest for next two years.
5. S. Creditors accepted to receive half in cash in full settlement of their claims.
6. Building is taken at 1/3rd more in value, Plant and machinery 25% less, Furniture 50% less, Stock at ₹ 1,50,000 Investment at book value and Cash and Bank.

Prepare opening Balance Sheet.

Ans: Purchase Consideration — ₹ 6,37,500

Capital Reserve — ₹ 30,000

Balance Sheet (Total) — ₹ 19,50,000

10. Unable to meet liabilities the court sanctioned a scheme of reconstruction as on 31st March 2013 when the assets and liabilities of C Ltd. were as under:

Liabilities	(₹)	Assets	(₹)
Equity Share Capital Shares of ₹ 10 each	19,20,000	Land and Building	6,91,200
12% Debentures	17,60,000	Plant and Machinery	6,56,000
Sundry Creditors	3,48,800	Stock	9,72,800
O/s Liabilities	6,40,000	S. Debtors	14,40,000
		Bank	14,700
		Profit and Loss A/c	8,94,100
	46,68,800		46,68,800

Note: Debenture interest for one year had not been paid and is included in the figures of outstanding liabilities shown in the Balance Sheet.

The broad features of the sanctioned scheme are as under:

(*i*) CEE Ltd. will have a share capital of ₹ 25,00,000 divided into equity shares of ₹ 10 each.

(*ii*) Arrears of debenture interest will be satisfied by issue of fully paid up equity shares.

(*iii*) For every ₹ 100 due to creditors an immediate cash payment of ₹ 50 be made. In addition they would be allotted 3 equity shares in the company as fully paid up. Creditors will not have any other claims against the company.

(*iv*) Outstanding liabilities other than interest on debentures, would receive 75 paise in the rupee in full settlement.

(*v*) For every two equity shares in the company the holders will receive one share fully paid up.

(*vi*) 12% debentures will be replaced by 8% debentures.

(*vii*) Balance of equity shares will be fully paid up in cash by the holders.

(*viii*) Sundry debtors would be written off to the extent of ₹ 12,00,000. Any balance on adjustment under the scheme of reconstruction, will be utilised to adjust the value of Land and Building.

Close the books of C Ltd. and pass opening entries and give effect to the above in the Balance Sheet of CEE Ltd.

[**Ans:** Purchase Consideration — ₹ 9,60,000
Realisation A/c (Loss) — ₹ 65,900
Balance Sheet — ₹ 42,60,000].

16

VALUATION OF GOODWILL

LEARNING OBJECTIVES

After reading this chapter, you should be able to:

- *Understand* meaning of goodwill, its distinguishing features
- *Describe* types of goodwill; factors affecting goodwill.
- *Describe* the procedure of accounting for goodwill.
- *Explain* methods of valuation of goodwill.

MEANING OF GOODWILL

Goodwill may be described as the aggregate of those intangible attributes of a business which contributes to its superior earning capacity over a normal return on investment. It may arise from such attributes as favourable locations, the ability and skill of its employees and management, quality of its products and services, customer satisfaction etc.

Some definitions of goodwill are:

1. According to SSAP-22, UK Accounting Standard on Accounting for Goodwill, "Goodwill is the difference between the value of a business as a whole and the aggregate of the fair values of its separable net assets."
2. If time value of money is taken into account, goodwill may be defined as the present value of the firm's anticipated excess earnings.
3. "Goodwill is nothing more than the profitability that the old customers will resort to the old place."
   —Lord Eldon
4. According to Lord Macraughton "Goodwill is a thing very easy to describe, very difficult to define. It is the benefit and advantage of good name, reputation and connection of a business. It is the attractive force which brings in customers. It is one thing which distinguishes an old established business from a new business at its start."

Distinguishing Features of Goodwill

The following are the features of goodwill:

1. Goodwill is an intangible asset. It is non-visible but it is not a fictitious asset.

2. It cannot be separated from the business and therefore cannot be sold like other identifiable and separable assets, without disposing off the business as a whole.
3. The value of goodwill has no relation to the amount invested or cost incurred in order to build it.
4. Valuation of goodwill is subjective and is highly dependent on the judgement of the valuer.
5. Goodwill is subject to fluctuations. The value of goodwill may fluctuate widely according to internal and external factors of business.

Types of Goodwill

Goodwill is generally of two types:

(*a*) Purchased goodwill; and

(*b*) Non-Purchased or Inherent goodwill.

(*a*) Purchased goodwill: Purchased goodwill arises when a business concern is purchased and the purchase consideration paid exceeds the fair value of the separable net assets acquired. The purchased goodwill is shown on the assets side of the Balance sheet. Para 36 of AS-10 'Accounting for fixed assets' states that only purchased goodwill should be recognised in the books of accounts.

(*b*) Non-Purchased goodwill/Inherent goodwill: Inherent goodwill is the value of business in excess of the fair value of its separable net assets. It is referred to as internally generated goodwill and it arises over a period of time due to good reputation of a business. The value of goodwill may be positive or negative. Positive goodwill arises when the value of business as a whole is more than the fair value of its net assets. It is negative when the value of the business is less than the value of its net assets.

FACTORS AFFECTING GOODWILL

The important factors that give rise to goodwill are as follows:

1. Outstanding quality of products/services.
2. Locational factors—If a business is located at a favourable place; it enhances the value of goodwill.
3. The period for which the business has been in business.
4. Special advantages—A company that enjoys special advantages such as favourable contracts, assured supply of raw material at low rates, possession of trademarks, patents, copyrights, technical know how and research and development, well known collaborators etc. contribute to higher value of goodwill.
5. Nature of Business—A business having stable continuous demand for its products such as consumer goods is able to earn more profits and hence has more goodwill. If the business is risky, profits will be uncertain. The monopoly condition or limited competition enables the enterprise to earn higher profits which leads to higher value of goodwill.
6. Good relations with customers, suppliers, labour and government.
7. Efficiency of Management—A firm having efficient management enjoys advantages of high productivity and cost of efficiency. This leads to higher profits which in turn increases the value of goodwill.
8. Capital Required—If two businesses have same rate of profit, the business which requires lesser amount of capital tends to enjoy more goodwill.

ACCOUNTING FOR GOODWILL

The various ways in which goodwill can be accounted for are as follows.

(*a*) Carry it as an asset and write it off over a period of years through the profit and loss account.

(*b*) Write it off against profits or accumulated reserves immediately.

(*c*) Retain it as an asset with no write-off unless a permanent diminution in value becomes evident.

(*d*) Show it as a deduction from shareholders funds which may be authorized carried forward indefinitely.

In this connection, it is important to state that goodwill should be recognised and recorded in business only when some consideration in money or money's worth has been paid for it.

METHODS OF VALUATION OF GOODWILL

The valuation of goodwill depends upon assumptions made by the valuer. Methods to be adopted in valuation of goodwill would depend on circumstances of each case and is often based on the customs of the trade. The various methods that can be adopted for valuation of goodwill are follows:

1. Average Profit Method
2. Super Profit Method
3. Capitalisation Method
4. Annuity Method.

1. **Average Profit Method:** Under this method the value of Goodwill is calculated by multiplying the Average Future profit by a certain number of year's purchase.

Goodwill = Future maintainable profit after tax × No. of years purchase

The first step under this method is the calculation of average profit based on past few years' profit. Past profit are adjusted in respect of any abnormal items of profit or loss which may affect future profit. Average profit may be based on simple average or weighted average. If profits are constant, equal weightage may be given in calculating the average profits i.e., simple average may be calculated. However, if the trend shows increasing or decreasing profit, it is necessary to give more weightage to the profits of recent years.

Number of year's purchase: After calculating future maintainable average profits, the next step is to determine the number of years' purchase. The number of years of purchase is determined with reference to the probability of new business to catch up with an existing business. It will differ from industry to industry and from firm to firm. Normally the number of years ranges between 3 to 5.

Steps involved under Average Profits Method

(*i*) Calculate past profits before tax.

(*ii*) Calculate future-maintainable profit before tax after making past adjustments.

(*iii*) Calculate Average Past adjusted Profits (taking simple average or weighted average as applicable).

(*iv*) Multiply Future Maintainable Profits by number of years' purchase.

Value of Goodwill = Future Maintainable Profits × No. of years' purchase.

Illustration 1: X Ltd. agreed to purchase business of a sole trader. For that purpose, goodwill is to be valued at 3 years' purchase of average profits of last 5 years.

Profits for these years are:

Years	Profits (₹)
I	24,000
II	20,000
III	22,000
IV	26,000
V	24,000

Solution:

$$\text{Average profit} = \frac{₹\ 24,000 + 20,000 + 22,000 + 26,000 + 24,000}{5}$$

= 1,16,000/5

= ₹ 23,200

Goodwill = 3 year's purchase of average profit of last 5 years

= ₹ 23,200 × 3 = ₹ 69,600

Illustration 2: Y Ltd. proposed to purchase business carried on by Mr. A. Goodwill for this purpose is agreed to be valued at 3 year's purchase of the weighted average profits of the past four years. The profit for these years and respective weights to be assigned are as follows:

Years	Profits (₹)	Weight
2010	20,200	1
2011	24,800	2
2012	20,000	3
2013	30,000	4

On a scrutiny of the accounts, the following matters are revealed:

(*a*) On 1st September, 2012 a major repair was made in respect of plant incurring ₹ 6,000 which was charged to revenue, the said sum is agreed to be capitalised for goodwill calculation subject to adjustment of depreciation of 10% p.a. on reducing balance method.

(*b*) The closing stock for the year 2011 was over valued by ₹ 2,400; and

(*c*) To cover management cost an annual charge of ₹ 4,000 should be made for the purpose of goodwill valuation.

Required: Compute the value of goodwill of the firm.

Solution: Before calculating goodwill, it is necessary to compute adjusted profit on the basis of information given.

Calculation of Adjusted Profit (₹)

Particulars	2010	2011	2012	2013
Profit (as given)	20,200	24,800	20,000	30,000
Less: Management cost	4,800	4,800	4,800	4,800
	15,400	20,000	15,200	25,200
Less: Over valuation of closing stock		2,400		
Add: Over valuation of opening stock (Note 1)			2,400	
	15,400	17,600	17,600	25,200

Particulars	2010	2011	2012	2013
Add: Capitalisation of repairs			6,000	
	15,400	17,600	23,600	25,200
Less: Depreciation (Note 2)			200	580
	15,400	17,600	23,400	24,620

Calculation of Average Profit

Year	Profit	Weights	Profit × Weight
2010	15,400	1	15,400
2011	17,600	2	35,200
2012	23,400	3	70,200
2013	24,620	4	98,480
Sum total	—	10	2,19,280

Weighted Average Profit = ₹ 2,19,280/10
= ₹ 21,928

Goodwill = 3 years' purchase of weighted average profit
= ₹ 21,928 × 3
= ₹ 65,784

Notes:

(*i*) Closing Stock of 2011 becomes Opening Stock of 2012.

(*ii*) Depreciation of 2012 = 10% of ₹ 6,000 for 4 months ending on 31st December, 2012.
= 200

Depreciation of 2013 = 10% of (₹ 6,000 – ₹ 200)
= ₹ 5,800

2. Super Profit Method: Super profit is the excess of estimated future maintainable profits over normal profits. An enterprise may possess some advantages which enable it to earn extra profits over and above the normal profit that would be earned if the capital of the business was invested in some other business with similar risks. The goodwill under this method is ascertained by multiplying the super profits by certain number of year's purchase.

Steps involved in calculating goodwill under Super Profit Method

Step 1: Calculate capital employed (it is the aggregate of Shareholders' equity and long term debt or fixed assets and net current assets).

Step 2: Calculate Normal Profits by multiplying capital employed with normal rate of return.

Step 3: Calculate average maintainable profit.

Step 4: Calculate Super Profit as follows:

Super Profit = Average maintainable profits – Normal Profits.

Step 5: Calculate goodwill by multiplying super profit by number of year's purchase.

Illustration 3: From the following information calculate the value of goodwill on the basis of 3 years purchase of super profits of the business calculated on the average profit of the last four years (simple average and weighted average):

(*i*) Capital employed – ₹ 50,000

(*ii*) Trading profit (after tax):

2010 ₹ 12,200;

2011 ₹ 15,000;
2012 ₹ 2,000 (loss); and
2013 ₹ 21,000

(*iii*) Rate of interest expected from capital having regard to the risk involved is 10%.

(*iv*) Remuneration from alternative employment of the proprietor (if not engaged in business) ₹ 3,600 p.a.

Solution: (Simple Average)

(*i*) **Calculation of Average Profits**

Year	Profits (₹)
2010	12,200
2011	15,000
2012	(2,000)
2013	21,000
Total	46,200

Average Profit = ₹ 46,000/4 = ₹ 11,550

(*ii*) **Calculation of Super Profits**

Particulars	₹
Average profits	11,550
Less: Remuneration	3,600
Average Trading Profit	7,950
Less: Normal Return @ 10% on capital employed *i.e.*, ₹ 50,000	₹ 5,000
Super Profits	2,950

Goodwill = 3 years' purchase of Super Profit
= ₹ 2,950 × 3
= ₹ 8,850

Weighted Average

Year	Profit (₹)	Adjusted Profit		Weight	Product
2010	12,200	12,200 – 3,600	8,600	1	8,600
2011	15,000	15,000 – 3,600	11,400	2	11,400
2012	(2,000)	[(2,000) – 3,600)]	(5,600)	3	(16,800)
2013	21,000	21,000 – 3,600	17,400	4	69,600
				Total	84,200

Average Profit = 84,200/10
= 8,420

Normal Profit = 5,000 (As Calculated Earlier)

Super Profit = ₹ 8,420 – 5,000 = 3,420

Goodwill = Super profit × 3
= ₹ 3,420 × 3
= ₹ 10,260.

3. Capitalisation Method: Goodwill under this method can be calculated by capitalizing average normal profit or capitalizing super profits.

(*i*) **Capitalisation of Average Profit Method:** Under this method goodwill is ascertained by deducting Actual Capital Employed (*i.e.*, Net Assets as on the valuation date) from the capitalised value of the average profits on the basis of normal rate of Return (also known as value of the firm or capitalised value of business)

Goodwill = Capitalised Value – Net Assets of Business

Steps involved in calculating goodwill as per capitalisation of Average Profits Method:

Step 1: Calculate Average future maintainable profits

Step 2: Calculate Capitalised value of business on the basis of Average Profits

$$\text{Capitalised Value} = \frac{\text{Average Future maintainable profits} \times 100}{\text{Normal Rate of Return}}$$

Step 3: Calculate the value of Net Assets on the valuation date

Net Assets = All Assets (other than goodwill, fictitious assets and non-trade investments) at their current values – Outsider's Liabilities

Step 4: Calculate Goodwill

Goodwill = Capitalised Value – Net assets of business.

Illustration 5: From the following calculate the value of goodwill according to capitalisation of Average Profits Method:

(*i*) Average Capital employed in the business ₹ 7,00,000.

(*ii*) Net trading profit of the firm for the past three years

Years	Profits (₹)
2011	1,47,600
2012	1,48,100
2013	1,52,500

(*iii*) Rate of interest expected from Capital having regard to the risk involved –18%

(*iv*) Sundry Assets (excluding goodwill) – ₹ 7,54,762

Sundry liabilities – ₹ 31,329

(*v*) Fair remuneration to the partners for the services – ₹ 12,000 p.a.

Solution: **Calculation of Average Future Profit**

Years	Profit (₹)
2011	1,47,600
2012	1,48,100
2013	1,52,500
Total	4,48,200

Average Profit = 4,48,200/3	= ₹ 1,49,400
Less: Fair Remuneration to Partners	–12,000
Average Future Maintainable Profit	= ₹ 1,37,400

Capitalised Value

$$\text{(Normal Capital Employed)} = \frac{\text{Average Future Profits} \times 100}{\text{Normal Rate of Return}}$$

= 1,37,400/18 × 100

= ₹ 7,63,333

Actual Capital Employed = Sundry Assets – Sundry Liabilities
= ₹ 7,54,762 – 31,329
= ₹ 7,23,433

Goodwill = Capitalised Value (Normal Capital Employed) – Net Assets
= 7,63,333 – 7,23,433 = ₹ 39,900

(*ii*) **Capitalisation of Super Profit Method:** The goodwill under this method is ascertained by capitalizing the super profits on the basis of normal rate of return. This method assesses the capital needed for earning the super profit. The value of goodwill is computed as follows:

$$\text{Goodwill} = \frac{\text{Average Annual Super Profits} \times 100}{\text{Normal Rate of Return}}$$

Illustration 6: Balance Sheet of X Ltd. on 31st March, 2013 was as under:

Liabilities	(₹)	Assets	(₹)
Capital	2,50,000	Land and Building	1,80,000
Creditors	80,000	Machinery	1,10,000
Bills payable	20,000	Furniture	2,000
		Stock	8,000
		Cash at Bank	50,000
Total	3,50,000	Total	3,50,000

The profit of the business for the last five years ending 31st March, 2013 is:

Year	Profit (₹)
2009	40,000
2010	42,000
2011	45,000
2012	50,000
2013	53,000

The assets are revalued as follows. Land and Building ₹ 19,400, Machinery ₹ 1,18,000 and Furniture ₹ 1,000. Find out goodwill by capitalisation of Super Profit Method.

Solution: **Calculation of Average Profit**

Year	Profit (₹)
2009	40,000
2010	42,000
2011	45,000
2012	50,000
2013	53,000
Total	2,30,000

Average Profit = 2,30,000/5
= ₹ 46,000

Capital Employed

Current Value of Assets	(₹)
Land and Building	1,94,000
Machinery	1,18,000

Furniture		1,000
Stock		8,000
Cash at Bank		50,000
Total Assets		3,71,000
Less: Outside Liabilities		
Creditors	80,000	
Bills payable	20,000	–1,00,000
		2,71,000

Normal Profit = Capital Employed × Normal Rate of Return
= 2,71,000 × 10/100
= ₹ 27,100

Super Profit = Future Average Profits – Normal Profit
= ₹ 46,000 – ₹ 27,100 = ₹ 18,900

Value of Goodwill by Capitalisation of Super Profit Method
= ₹ 18,900 × 100/10
= ₹ 1,89,000

4. **Annuity Method:** Under this method, goodwill is calculated by taking average super profit as the value of an annuity over a certain number of years. The present value of this annuity is computed by discounting at the given rate of interest (normal rate of return). This discounted present value of the annuity is the value of goodwill.

The value of annuity for Rupee 1 can be known by reference to the annuity tables. If the value of annuity is not given, it can be calculated with the help of following formula:

$$A = \frac{1 - (1 + r/100)^{-n}}{r/100}$$

where, A = Present Value of Annuity of Rupee 1
r = Normal Rate of Return
n = Number of Years

Value of Goodwill = Average Super Profit × A (Present Value of annuity for Rupee at given rate of interest)

Illustration 7: The net profit of a company after providing for taxation for the past five years is:

Year	Profit (₹)
2009	40,000
2010	50,000
2011	30,000
2012	70,000
2013	80,000

The net tangible assets in the business are ₹ 4,00,000 on which the normal rate of return is expected to be 10%. It is also expected that the company will be able to maintain its super profits for next five years. Calculate the value of goodwill of the business on the basis of an annuity of super profits, taking present value of an annuity of ₹ 1 for five years at 10% interest is ₹ 3.78.

Solution: **Calculation of Average Profits**

Year		**Profit (₹)**
2009		40,000
2010		50,000
2011		30,000
2012		70,000
2013		80,000
Total		2,70,000
Average Profit	= 2,70,000/5	
	= ₹ 54,000	

Calculation of Super Profit

Particulars		**Profit (₹)**
Average Profit		54,000
Less: Normal Profit (10% of 4,00,000)		40,000
Super Profit		14,000
Value of Goodwill	= Super Profit × Value of an Annuity	
	= ₹ 14,000 × 3.78 = ₹ 52,920.	

THEORY QUESTIONS

1. Define goodwill and discuss the factors that affect the value of goodwill of a company.
2. What are super profits? In what ways super profits can be used for the purpose of valuation of goodwill?
3. What points will you keep in mind while estimating the future maintainable profit of a joint stock company?
4. What is goodwill? State the various methods of valuation of goodwill.

EXERCISES AND PROBLEMS

1. The following information is available in respect of business carried on by a trader:

(*i*) Profits earned for the years:

	(₹)
2010–11	50,000
2011–12	60,000
2012–13	55,000

(*ii*) Normal rate of return 10%.

(*iii*) Capital employed ₹ 3,00,000.

(*iv*) Present Value of an annuity of one rupee for five year's at 10% = ₹ 3.78.

(*v*) Profits included non-recurring profits on an average basis of ₹ 3,000.

You are required to calculate the value of goodwill:

(*a*) As per five years' purchase of super profits.

(*b*) As per capitalisation of super profits method.

(*c*) As per Annuity Method.

Ans: (*a*) ₹ 1,10,000 (*b*) ₹ 2,20,000 (*c*) ₹ 83,160.

Hint: Treat Capital employed as average capital employed.

2. The Balance Sheet of A Ltd. as on 31st March, 2013:

Liabilities	(₹)	Assets	(₹)
Equity Share Capital	6,00,000	Fixed Assets	3,60,000
General Reserve	2,16,000	Current Assets	4,88,000
Current Liabilities	1,52,000	Investments	1,20,000
	9,68,000		9,68,000

The Normal Rate of Return (NRR) is 10%. The profits earned during the last four years including interest of ₹ 8,000 on investment were as under :

Year ending 31st March	(₹)
2009–10	1,28,000
2010–11	1,44,000
2011–12	1,72,000
2012–13	1,80,000

Compute the amount of goodwill at two year's purchase of average super profits of four years presuming that each year's profit was fully distributed as dividend to shareholders.

Ans: Weighted Average Profits ₹ 1,57,200

Average Capital Employed 7,80,000

Goodwill at 2 year's purchase 2,37,600

Hint: Since all the profits are distributed as dividend, add half of the current year's operating profits to the capital employed to find out the average capital employed.

3. On 31st March, 2013 A Ltd. proposes to purchase the business carried on by M/s X Ltd. Goodwill for this purpose is agreed to be valued at three year's purchase of the weighted average profits for last four years. The appropriate weights to be used were decided as follows.

2009–2010	1
2010–2011	2
2011–2012	3
2012–2013	4

The profits for these years are:

2009–2010	₹ 10,10,000	2011–2012	10,00,000
2010–2011	₹ 12,40,000	2012–2013	14,00,000

On a scrutiny of the accounts, the following facts are revealed:

(*i*) On 1st December, 2011 major repairs were carried out is respect of the Plant, spending ₹ 3,00,000; the amount was charged to revenue. The said sum is agreed to be capitalised for the purpose of calculation of goodwill subject to the adjustment for depreciation @ 10% p.a. on reducing balance method.

(*ii*) The Closing Stock for the year 2010–2011 was over valued by ₹ 1,20,000.

(*iii*) To Cover management cost an annual charge of ₹ 2,40,000 is to be made while calculating goodwill.

Compute the value of goodwill of X Ltd.

Ans: Goodwill = ₹ 31,69,200.

4. The following particulars are available in respect of the business of Lucky Ltd.:

(*i*) Profits earned for the years: (₹)

	(₹)
2010–2011	5,00,000
2011–2012	6,00,000
2012–2013	5,50,000

(*ii*) Normal rate of return = 10%.

(*iii*) Capital employed = ₹ 30,00,000.

(*iv*) Present value of an annuity of one rupee for 5 years at 10% = ₹ 3.78.

(*v*) The profits included non-recurring profits on an average basis of ₹ 30,000 a year.

You are required to calculate the value of goodwill of the company:

(*i*) as per five year's purchase of super-profits;

(*ii*) as per capitalisation of super-profits method; and

(*iii*) as per annuity method.

5. A Ltd. agreed to purchase business of a sole trader. For that goodwill is to be valued at three year's purchase of the average of previous four years adjusted profits. The profits for the years ending 31.12.2010 to 31.12.2013 were as follows: ₹ 20,200; ₹ 24,800; ₹ 25,000; ₹ 30,000. Following additional information is available as under:

(*i*) On 01.9.2012 a major repair expenditure to plant and machinery for ₹ 6,000 was charged to revenue. This was agreed to be capitalised for goodwill subject to 10% p.a. depreciation on diminishing balance method.

(*ii*) The closing stock for the year ending 31.12.2011 was over valued by ₹ 2,400.

(*iii*) In order to cover cost of management, an annual charge of ₹ 4,800 should be made for valuation of goodwill.

Compute value of goodwill.

Ans: Goodwill ₹ 64,515.

PART–FOUR

FINANCIAL ANALYSIS

- **Chapter 17** Statement of Changes in Financial Position
- **Chapter 18** Cash Flow Statement
- **Chapter 19** Financial Statement Analysis

17

STATEMENT OF CHANGES IN FINANCIAL POSITION

LEARNING OBJECTIVES

After reading this chapter, you should be able to:

- *Understand* concept of statement of changes in financial position (SCFP), concept of funds, funds defined as working capital.
- *Explain* sources and uses of working capital.
- *Describe* effects of transactions on funds flow statement.
- *Explain* the procedural steps in preparing funds flow statement.
- *Illustrate* the preparation of funds flow statement.

Financial statement of a business enterprise, *i.e.*, income statement and balance sheet are important statements to judge the results of business operation and financial position at the beginning and end of year. The income statement sets forth the enterprise's revenues, expenses, gains and losses. The balance sheet portrays the overall financial position of a business enterprise at a specific date during the recurring cycles of investment, recovery of investment and reinvestment. The income statement, however, does not show the effects of all the events which affected an enterprise's liquidity—its ability to meet its cash obligations on time—nor does it reflect all the flows of resources into or out of the enterprise during the period. Also, the correct appraisal of performance requires knowledge about movement of funds during a year and their impact on the financial position; this is not achieved in balance sheet as it depicts only summarised financial position on a particular date. To overcome these deficiencies, a second performance related statement needs to be prepared which is popularly known as Statement of Changes in Financial Position, or Funds Statement.

CONCEPT OF STATEMENT OF CHANGES IN FINANCIAL POSITION (SCFP)

A statement of changes in financial position (funds statement) helps us to understand how and why a business enterprise has acquired its resources and what those resources were used for. The objectives of funds statement are (1) to summarise the financing and investing activities of the entity, including the extent to which the enterprise has generated funds from operations during the period, and (2) to complete the disclosure of changes of financial position during the period.

CONCEPT OF FUNDS

A statement of changes in financial position can be prepared using different concepts of funds as a basis. For instance, statement of changes in financial position may focus on changes in working capital, cash, or total financial resources of a business enterprise. Accordingly, this chapter discusses the preparation of the following types of statement of changes in financial position:

1. Statement of changes in working capital, popularly known as Funds Flow Statement or Statement of Sources and Applications of Funds.
2. Statement of Changes in Cash, popularly known as Cash Flow Statement.
3. Statement of Changes in Total Financial Resources.

FUNDS DEFINED AS WORKING CAPITAL

In common usage, the term funds means cash. However, accountants and financial executives think of 'funds' in a broader sense. They view the funds available to a business enterprise as its working capital. Working capital is defined as current assets minus current liabilities and thus, is a broader definition of funds than is cash.

Since funds have been defined as the difference between current assets and current liabilities, it is necessary to know which accounts are covered and which are not covered by this definition.

1. **Current Assets:** The term current assets is used to mean cash and other assets or resources generally identified as those which are reasonably expected to be realised in cash or sold or consumed during the normal operating cycle of the business. These include: (1) cash and bank balances; (2) temporary investments, bills receivables, debtors, and stock in trade; (3) prepayments like salary paid in advance, unexpired insurance, prepaid rent, prepaid interest which can be consumed during the normal operating cycle of business.
2. **Current Liabilities:** The term 'current liabilities' is used to denote obligations such as: (*i*) ones which are payable within one year, and (*ii*) which are paid out of current assets or by clearing current liabilities. These include amounts payable to (*a*) creditors, (*b*) bills payable, (*c*) bank overdraft, and (*d*) outstanding bills on account of wages, salary, commission, rent, royalties etc.
3. **Non-Current Accounts:** For the purpose of preparing funds flow statement all accounts which are not current accounts are treated as non-current accounts. Examples of such accounts are as follows :

Non-current accounts on the liabilities side of the Balance Sheet	Non-current accounts on the assets side of the Balance Sheet
1. Equity share capital	1. Goodwill
2. Preference share capital	2. Land
3. Redeemable preference share capital	3. Building
4. Long-term loans	4. Machinery
5. Debentures	5. Furniture
6. Security premium account	6. Long-term investments
7. Share forfeited account	7. Patent right
8. Profit and Loss Account (credit balance)	8. Trade mark

Non-current accounts on the liabilities side of the Balance Sheet	Non-current accounts on the assets side of the Balance Sheet
9. Appropriation to profit, *e.g.*, transfer to general reserve, dividend equalisation fund, insurance fund, compensation fund, debentures sinking fund, capital redemption reserve account.	9. Profit and Loss Account (debit balance)
10. Provision like provision for tax, provision for depreciation on fixed assets, proposed dividend.	10. Discount on issue of shares and debentures
11. Capital reserve.	11. Preliminary expenses 12. Other deferred expenditure like advertisement cost.

The basic objective of the statement of changes in financial position, working capital basis, is to explain the changes in the working capital for a specified period of time. In the process of achieving this objective, the statement should enable the user to identify the changes as they relate to three basic causes.

(*a*) Amount of changes in working capital associated with the operating activities of the firm.

(*b*) Long term financing or other sources that cause an increase in the working capital.

(*c*) Long term investment activities or other uses that cause a reduction in the working capital.

If the amount of working capital increases during a given fiscal period, this means that more working capital was generated than was used for various business purposes; if a decrease in working capital occurred, the reverse is true. One of the key purposes of statement of changes in financial position is to explain fully the increase or decrease in working capital during an accounting period.

SOURCES AND USES OF WORKING CAPITAL

Any transaction that increases the amount of working capital is a source of working capital. For example, the sale of merchandise at a price greater than its cost is a source of working capital, because the increase in cash or receivable from the sale is greater than the decrease in inventory. Any transaction that decreases working capital is a use of working capital. For example, either incurring current liability to acquire a non-current asset or using cash to pay expenses represents a decrease in working capital.

The principal sources and uses of working capital are listed below:

SOURCES OF WORKING CAPITAL

The following are the sources of working capital:

1. **Funds from Business Operations:** If the inflow of funds from sales exceeds the outflow of funds to cover the cost of merchandise purchases and expenses of doing business, current operations will provide a net source of funds. If the inflow of funds from sales is less than these outflows, operation will result in a net use of funds. Working capital provided by operations is the net increase or decrease in working capital resulting from the normal business activities of earning revenue and paying expenses. However, not all the expenses require the use of funds in the current period; therefore the amount of funds provided by operations is not the same as the amount of net income earned during the period.

The following points explain this situation:

(*i*) Some expenses do not reduce working capital. Some expenses, such as depreciation and amortisation of intangible assets reduce net income but have no immediate effect on the amount of working capital provided by operations, *i.e.*, these items do not reduce working capital. The net income figure therefore understates the amount of working capital provided by operations by amount of depreciation expenses recorded during the period. Thus funds provided by operations would be computed in the following manner:

Funds from Operations:

Net income

Add: Depreciation expense

Funds provided by operations

The addition of depreciation expense to the net income figure has led some people to believe that depreciation expenses is a source of funds. However, it is important for the users of financial statement to understand that depreciation is neither a source nor a use of working capital (funds). No funds flow into business as a result of recording depreciation expense. It is shown in the statement of changes in financial position merely to explain one of the differences between the concept of net income and the concept of working capital provided by operations.

(*ii*) Some items increase income but do not increase working capital—some items in the income statement increase net income without increasing working capital; such items must be deducted from net income in arriving at working capital provided by operations.

(*iii*) Non-operating gains and losses—non-operating gains and losses, if material in amount, should be eliminated from net income in order to show the working capital provided by 'normal' operations. For example, assume that plant costing ₹ 1,00,000 is sold at ₹ 1,20,000, at a net gain of ₹ 20,000. In the statement of changes in financial position, the entire ₹ 1,20,000 as proceeds from sale will be reported as funds provided by the sale of plant. The ₹ 20,000 non-operating gain, however, is included in the net income for the period. In determining the amount of working capital provided by operations, this ₹ 20,000 non-operating gain must be deducted from the net income figure because the entire proceeds from sale of the plant are reported elsewhere in the statement of changes in financial position.

As a separate example, assume that the same plant is sold for ₹ 90,000; then the non-operating loss of ₹ 10,000 should be added back to net income to arrive at working capital provided by operations and the working capital provided through sale of plant should be reported at ₹ 90,000.

Briefly, the procedure of computing funds provided by operations can be summarised as follows:

Funds from Operations

Net profit (or loss) as per the Profit and Loss Account		
Add:	(*i*)	Depreciation expense.
	(*ii*)	Amortisation of goodwill, patents and other intangible assets.
	(*iii*)	Amortisation of extraordinary losses occurred in previous periods.
	(*iv*)	Amortisation of discount on debentures.
	(*v*)	Loss on sale of non-current assets such as plant, equipment etc.
Less:	(*i*)	Gain on sale of non-current assets such as plant, equipment etc.
	(*ii*)	Profit or revaluation surplus of non-current assets.
	(*iii*)	Dividends and interest on investments (earned but not received)
	(*iv*)	Amortisation of premium received on debentures
		= Fund from Business Operations

2. Sales of Non-current Assets: A business may obtain working capital by selling non-current assets, such as plant and equipment or long term investments, in exchange for current asset. As long as current assets are received, the sale is a source of funds regardless of whether the non-current assets are sold at a gain or loss. For example, assume that a business firm sells for

₹ 2,50,000 a plant which cost ₹ 3,00,000. Although the plant was sold at a loss, the firm has increased its current assets by ₹ 2,50,000 by selling the plant. Thus, the transaction is a source of working capital.

3. **Long-term borrowing:** Long-term borrowing, such as issue of debentures and bonds result in an increase in current assets, thereby increasing working capital. Short-term borrowing, however, does not increase working capital. When a company borrows cash on short term credit or by signing a short-term note payable, working capital is unchanged because the increase in current assets is offset by an increase in current liabilities of the same amount.
4. **Issue of additional equity capital:** The issue of additional equity shares results in an inflow of current assets, thereby increasing working capital. In a similar manner, additional investments of current assets by owners represent source of funds in single proprietorship and partnership.

USES OF WORKING CAPITAL

The following are the uses of working capital:

(*i*) **Declaration of Cash Dividend:** The declaration of a cash dividend results in a current liability (dividend payable) and is therefore a use of funds. It should be understood that it is the declaration of dividend, rather than the payment of the dividend which is the use of funds. Actual payment of the dividend reduces current assets and current liabilities by the same amount and thus has no effect upon the amount of working capital. Issue of shares in lieu of dividend does not involve any distribution of assets and, therefore, are not a use of funds.

(*ii*) **Purchase of non-current assets:** Purchases of non-current assets, such as plant and equipment, reduce current assets or increase current liabilities. In either case, working capital is reduced.

(*iii*) **Repayment of long-term debt:** Working capital is decreased when current assets are used to repay long-term debt. However, repayment of short-term debt is not a use of funds, since current assets and current liabilities decrease by the same amount.

EFFECT OF TRANSACTIONS ON FUNDS FLOW STATEMENT

In preparing a statement of changes in financial position, on working capital basis or funds flow statement, it is convenient to classify business transactions into three categories:

(*a*) Both debit and credit aspects of the transaction affecting current accounts only.

(*b*) Both debit and credit aspects of the transaction affecting non-current accounts only.

(*c*) One aspect of the transaction affecting current account and another aspect affecting a non-current account (non-current asset or non-current liability).

The effect of above mentioned categories of transactions on the funds flow statement can be analysed with the help of following examples:

1. **Transactions affecting current accounts only—do not result in flow of fund:** These transactions produce changes in working capital accounts but do not change the amount of working capital. Few examples of such transactions are given below:

S. No.	Transaction	Journal entry		Effect on current asset/current liability	Net effect on working capital
1.	Bills receivable collected	Bank A/c To Bills receivable	Dr.	Increase in C.A. Decrease in C.A.	Nil
2.	Goods purchased for cash	Purchases A/c To Cash	Dr.	Increase in C.A. Decrease in C.A.	Nil

S. No.	Transaction	Journal entry		Effect on current asset/current liability	Net effect on working capital
3.	Goods purchased on credit	Purchases A/c To Creditors	Dr.	Increase in C.A. Increase in C.L.	Nil
4.	Bills payable paid	Bills payable A/c To Cash	Dr.	Decrease in C.L. Decrease in C.A.	Nil

Hence, such transactions would not be reflected as a source or use in a working capital basis statement of changes in financial position.

2. **Transactions affecting non-current accounts only—do not result in flow of fund:** These transactions have no direct effect on the amount of working capital. The entry to record depreciation is an example of such a transaction. Such transactions may not be considered in preparing a statement of changes in financial position on working capital basis. Few examples of such transactions are:

S. No.	Transaction	Journal entry		Effect on current asset/ current liability	Net effect on working capital
1.	Building purchased and shares issued in satisfaction of purchase price	Building A/c To Share Capital	Dr.	Nil	Nil
2.	Preliminary expenses written off	Profit and Loss A/c To Preliminary expenses	Dr.	Nil	Nil
3.	General reserve created	Profit and Loss Appropriation A/c To General Reserve	Dr.	Nil	Nil

3. **Transactions affecting non-current account and current account result in flow of fund resulting either in a source of fund or application of fund:** These transactions bring about either an increase or a decrease in the amount of working capital.

If changes in non-working capital accounts are analysed, these events are brought to light, and their effect on working capital will be reported in the statement of changes in financial position. Few examples of such transactions and their effects on working capital are shown below:

S. No.	Transaction	Journal entry		Effect on current asset/current liability	Net effect on working capital
1.	Building sold for cash	Bank A/c To building	Dr.	Increase in C.A. Non-C.A.	Increase in working capital
2.	Redeemable preference shares redeemed	Redeemable preference shares A/c To bank	Dr.	Non-current liability Decrease in C.A.	Decrease in working capital
3.	Loan repaid	Loan A/c To Bank	Dr.	Non-current liability Decrease in C.A.	Decrease in working capital
4.	Issue of share capital (for cash)	Bank A/c To Share Capital	Dr.	Increase in C.A. Non-Current A/c	Increase in working capital
5.	Debentures redeemed	Debentures A/c To Bank	Dr.	Non-current liability Decrease in C.A.	Decrease in working capital

MAIN STEPS IN PREPARING THE STATEMENT

In order to prepare a statement of changes in financial position on a working capital basis, it is necessary to have balance sheets at two points in time and an income statement covering that span of time. The steps involved in preparing the statement are as follows:

1. Determine the change (increase or decrease) in working capital.
2. Determine the adjustments account to be made to net income.
3. For each non-current account on the balance sheet, establish the increase or decrease in that account. Analyse the change to decide whether it is a source (increase) or use (decrease) of working capital.
4. Be sure the total of all sources including those from operations minus the total of all uses equals the change found in working capital in Step 1.

General Rules for Preparing Funds Flow Statement: The following general rules should be observed while preparing funds flow statement:

1. Increase in a current asset means increase (plus) in working capital.
2. Decrease in a current asset means decrease (minus) in working capital.
3. Increase in a current liability means decrease (minus) in working capital.
4. Decrease in a current liability means increase (plus) in working capital.
5. Increase in current asset and increase in current liability does not affect working capital.
6. Decrease in current asset and decrease in current liability does not affect working capital.
7. Changes in fixed (non-current) assets and fixed (non-current) liabilities affects working capital.

SCHEDULE OF CHANGES IN WORKING CAPITAL

Many business enterprises prefer to prepare another statement, known as schedule of changes in working capital, while preparing a funds flow statement, on a working capital basis. This schedule of changes in working capital provides information concerning the changes in each individual current assets and current liabilities accounts (items). This schedule is a part of the funds flow statement and increase (decrease) in working capital indicated by the schedule of changes in working capital will be equal to the amount of changes in working capital as found by funds flow statement. The schedule of changes in working capital can be prepared by comparing the current assets and current liabilities at two periods. The format of schedule of changes in working capital is as follows:

Schedule of Changes in Working Capital

Items	As on	As on	Changes	
			Increase	Decrease
A. Current Assets:				
Cash Balance				
Bank Balance				
Accounts Receivable (Debtors)				
Marketable Securities				
Stock				
Prepaid Expenses				
B. Current Liabilities:				
Bank Overdraft				
Accounts payable (Creditors) outstanding expenses				
Total				
Net increase/decrease in working capital				

FORMAT OF FUNDS FLOW STATEMENT

A funds flow statement can be prepared in statement form or 'T' form. Both the formats are given below:

Funds Flow Statement (Statement Form)

A. Sources of Funds:

(*i*) Funds from Business Operations
(*ii*) Sale of Fixed Asset
(*iii*) Issue of Shares
(*iv*) Issue of Debentures
(*v*) Long-term borrowings

Total Sources

B. Application of Funds:

(*i*) Loss from Business Operation
(*ii*) Payment of Dividend
(*iii*) Payment of Tax
(*iv*) Purchase of Fixed Asset
(*v*) Payment of Long-term Loans
(*vi*) Redemption of Debentures
(*vii*) Redemption of Preference Shares

Total uses

Not increase/decrease in Working Capital
(Total sources minus Total uses)

Funds Flow Statement ('T' Form)

Source of Funds	₹	Application of Funds	₹
(*i*) Funds from Business Operations		(*i*) Loss from Business Operations	
(*ii*) Sale of Fixed Assets		(*ii*) Payment of Dividend	
(*iii*) Issue of Shares		(*iii*) Payment of Tax	
(*iv*) Issue of Debentures		(*iv*) Purchase of Fixed Assets	
(*v*) Long-term Borrowings		(*v*) Payment of Long-term Loans	
(*vi*) Decrease in Working Capital (If application amount is more than the sources amount)		(*vi*) Redemption of Debentures	
		(*vii*) Redemption of Preference Shares	
		(*viii*) Increase in Working Capital (if sources are more than the application amount)	
Total		Total	

TREATMENT OF PROVISION FOR TAXATION AND PROPOSED DIVIDENDS

Provision for Taxation

There are two possible treatment about the provision for taxation:

1. Provision for taxation can be treated as a current liability and it will decrease the working capital in the schedule of changes in working capital. However, payment of tax does not affect working capital because it involves both current asset and current liability account, *i.e.*,

payment decreases cash or bank balance on the one hand and decreases the current liability (tax provision) by the equivalent amount on the other hand.

2. Provision for taxation may be considered as non-current item. Such a treatment does not change working capital position. Provisions made for taxation during the current year is transferred to adjusted profit and loss account. The amount paid as tax is shown as an application of fund.

Proposed Dividends

There are also two treatments about the proposed dividend:

1. Proposed dividends can be considered as current liability and hence will decrease working capital in the schedule of changes in working capital. However, when dividends are paid, it is not treated as uses of funds.
2. Proposed dividend can be treated as non-current item. In this case, proposed dividend for current year is added back to retained profit in order to find out funds from operations. Then, payment of dividend, will be shown as application of funds. Generally, it is treated as non-current item.

Illustration 1: Compute funds from Operations from the following income statement:

Income Statement

Particulars	(₹)	Particulars	(₹)
To Salaries	10,000	By G/P b/d	2,000
To Rent	4,000	By Rent	10,000
To Depreciation	2,000	By Interest Amount	8,000
To Preliminary Expenses	4,000	By Net Loss	10,000
To Loss on Sale of Furniture	10,000		
	30,000		30,000

Solution: **Funds from Operations**

	(₹)	(₹)
Net loss as per Income Statement		(10,000)
Add: Items which do not decrease funds:		
Depreciation	2,000	
Preliminary Expenses	4,000	
Loss on Sale of Furniture	10,000	16,000
Funds from Operations		6,000

Note: Rent and interest on investment, alternatively can be considered as non-operating income and in such case, they will have to be excluded (deducted) while calculating funds from operations. Also, then, these items will be shown under 'non-operating income' in the funds flow statement.

Illustration 2: From the following balance sheets for the years 2012 and 2013 find out funds from operations:

	2012 (₹)	2013 (₹)
General Reserve	10,000	12,500
Goodwill	5,000	2,500
Provision for Depreciation on Plant	5,000	6,000
Preliminary Expenses	3,000	2,000
Profit and Loss Appropriation A/c	15,000	20,000

Solution: **Funds from Operations**

		(₹)
	Profit and Loss Appropriation Account as on December 31st, 2013	20,000
Add:	Items not decreasing funds:	
	Transfer to General Reserve	2,500
	Goodwill written off	2,500
	Provision for Depreciation on Plant	1,000
	Preliminary Expenses written-off	1,000
		27,000
Less:	Profit and Loss Appropriation Account Balance as on December 31st, 2012	15,000
	Funds from Operations	12,000

The funds from operations can also be found by preparing adjusted profit and loss account as given below:

Adjusted Profit and Loss Account

Particulars	(₹)	Particulars	(₹)
To Transfer to General Reserve	2,500	By Balance b/d	15,000
To Goodwill written-off	2,500	By Funds from Operations	12,000
To Preliminary Expenses written-off	1,000	*(Balancing figure)*	
To Provision for Depreciation	1,000		
To Balance c/d	20,000		
	27,000		27,000

Illustration 3: The following are the balance sheet of a company for the years 2012 and 2013 and income statement for the year 2013:

Balance Sheets as on December 31st, 2012 and December 31st, 2013

Assets	Dec. 31st 2013 (₹)	Dec. 31st 2012 (₹)	Increase (decrease) (₹)	Liabilities and Equity	Dec. 31st 2013 (₹)	Dec. 31st 2012 (₹)	Increase (decrease) (₹)
Current Assets:				**Current Liabilities:**			
Cash	19,000	17,400	1,600	Creditors	33,600	32,400	1,200
Debtors	24,600	24,000	600	Salaries Payable	600	1,000	(400)
Inventory	33,000	34,000	(1,000)	Income-taxes Payable	4,400	3,400	1,000
Prepaid Insurance	4,000	3,600	400	Long-term Loan	46,000	40,000	6,000
Long-term Assets			10,000	Equity Capital	1,00,000	1,00,000	—
Machinery	3,60,000	3,50,000		Retained Earnings	87,200	86,200	1,000
Less: Accumulated Depreciation	(1,68,800)	(1,66,000)	(2,800)				
Total Assets	2,71,800	2,63,000	8,800	**Total Liabilities**	2,71,800	2,63,000	8,800

Income Statements for the Year Ending 2013

	(₹)
Sales	63,800
Expenses:	
Cost of Goods Sold	45,600

	(₹)
Salaries	8,400
Rent	1,200
Depreciation	2,800
Insurance	600
Interest	400
Income-tax	1,000
Total Expenses	60,000
Net Income	3,800
Statement of Retained Earnings	(₹)
Retained earnings for the year 2012	86,200
Add: Net income for the year 2013	3,800
	90,000
Less: Dividends	2,800
	87,200

You are required to prepare a Funds Flow Statement, on a working capital basis.

Solution:

Funds Flow Statement (Working Capita Basis)

	(₹)	(₹)	(₹)
(A) Sources of Funds:			
(*i*) Funds from operations:			
Net income	3,800		
Add: Non-cash charges:			
Depreciation	2,800		
Funds provided by Operations		6,600	
(*ii*) Other sources:			
Long-term borrowings		6,000	12,600
(*B*) Uses of Funds:			
(*i*) Purchase of Machinery		10,000	
(*ii*) Dividends		2,800	
Total uses			12,800
Changes in Working Capital			(200)

The above statement presentation is a two parts statement; the sources are first detailed and then totalled, followed by the detail information and total for uses. The difference between the sources and uses must equal the change in working capital.

It can be noticed that sources of funds (working capital) is sub-divided into two parts; the first part is concerned with sources from operations, and the second part deals with other sources.

Uses of working capital in the above statement do not include any uses for operations, such as salaries and rent, because these have been included automatically by starting the funds flow statement with the net income rather than with revenue. Generally, the most common uses of funds shown are for the firm's investment activities such as the purchase of the new equipment, declaration of dividends, or payment of long-term liabilities.

Using the figures given in the Illustration 3, the Schedule of Changes in Working capital can be prepared as follows.

Schedule of Changes in Working Capital
(changes in current assets and current liabilities)

	Dec. 31st 2013 (₹)	Dec. 31st 2012 (₹)	Increase (Decrease) (₹)		Dec. 31st 2013 (₹)	Dec. 31st 2012 (₹)	Increase (Decrease) (₹)
Current Assets:				**Current Liabilities:**			
Cash	19,000	17,400	1,600	Accounts payable	33,600	32,400	1,200
Accounts Receivable	24,600	24,000	600	Salaries Payable	600	1,000	(400)
Inventory	33,000	34,000	(1,000)	Income-taxes Payable	4,400	3,400	1,000
Prepaid Insurance	4,000	3,600	400				
Total Current Assets	80,600	79,000	1,600	**Total Current Liabilities**	38,600	36,800	1,800
				Working Capital	42,000	42,200	(200)

Illustration 4: Following are the summarised Balance Sheet of A. Co. Ltd. as on 31st December, 2012 and 2013:

Liabilities	2012 (₹)	2013 (₹)	Assets	2012 (₹)	2013 (₹)
Share Capital	2,00,000	2,50,000	Land and Buildings	2,00,000	1,90,000
General Reserve	50,000	60,000	Machinery and Plant	1,50,000	1,69,000
Profit and Loss A/c	30,500	30,600	Stock	1,00,000	74,000
Bank Loan	70,000	—	Sundry Debtors	80,000	64,200
Sundry Creditors	1,50,000	1,35,200	Cash	500	600
Provision for Taxation	30,000	35,000	Bank	—	8,000
			Goodwill	—	5,000
	5,30,500	5,10,800		5,30,500	5,10,800

Additional information supplied:

During the year ended 31st December, 2013:

(*a*) Dividend of ₹ 23,000 was paid.

(*b*) Assets of another company were purchased for a consideration of ₹ 50,000 payable in shares. The following assets were purchased: Stock ₹ 20,000: Machinery ₹ 25,000.

(*c*) Machinery was purchased for ₹ 8,000.

(*d*) Depreciation written off: Building ₹ 10,000, Machinery ₹ 14,000.

(*e*) Income-tax paid during the year ₹ 28,000. Provision of ₹ 33,000 was charged to Profit and Loss A/c.

Prepare a Statement of Sources and Applications of funds for the year ended 31st December, 2013.

Solution: **Statement of Sources and Applications of Funds**

Sources	(₹)	Applications	(₹)
Issue of Shares	20,000	Dividend paid	23,000
Funds from operation	90,100	Purchase of Machinery	8,000
	1,10,100	Income-tax paid	28,000
Decrease in working capital (as per statement)	18,900	Bank Loan paid	70,000
	1,29,000		1,29,000

Statement of Changes in Working Capital

	2012 (₹)	2013 (₹)	Increase (₹)	Decrease (₹)
Current Assets:				
Stock	1,00,000	74,000		26,000
Sundry Debtors	80,000	64,200		15,800
Cash	500	600	100	
Bank	—	8,000	8,000	
Total (A)	1,80,500	1,46,800		
Current Liabilities:				
Sundry Creditors	1,50,000	1,35,200	14,800	
Total (B)	1,50,000	1,35,200		
Working Capital (A – B)	—	18,900	18,900	
	30,500	30,500	41,800	41,800

Adjusted Profit and Loss A/c

Particulars	(₹)	Particulars	(₹)
To Depreciation:		By Balance b/d	30,500
Land and Building	10,000	By Funds from operation	90,100
Machinery	14,000	*(Balancing figure)*	
To General Reserve	10,000		
To Dividend	23,000		
To Provisions for Tax	33,000		
To Balance c/d	30,600		
	1,20,600		1,20,600

Share Capital A/c

Particulars	(₹)	Particulars	(₹)
To Balance c/d	2,50,000	By Balance b/d	2,00,000
		By Machinery Purchase	25,000
		By Stock	20,000
		By Goodwill *(Balancing figure)*	5,000
	2,50,000		2,50,000

Machinery A/c

Particulars	(₹)	Particulars	(₹)
To Balance b/d	1,50,000	By Depreciation	14,000
To Share Capital (Purchase)	25,000	By Balance c/d	1,69,000
To Cash (Purchase)	8,000		
	1,83,000		1,83,000

Provision for Income-tax

Particulars	(₹)	Particulars	(₹)
To Cash (Tax paid)	28,000	By Balance b/d	30,000
To Balance c/d	35,000	By Profit and Loss A/c	33,000
	63,000		63,000

Illustration 5: From the following Balance Sheets of A Ltd. make out the statement of sources and uses of funds:

Liabilities	2012 (₹)	2013 (₹)	Assets	2012 (₹)	2013 (₹)
Equity Share Capital	3,00,000	4,00,000	Goodwill	1,15,000	90,000
8% Redeemable			Land and Building	2,00,000	1,70,000
Preference Shares	1,50,000	1,00,000	Plant	80,000	20,000
General Reserve	40,000	70,000	Debtors	1,60,000	2,00,000
Profit and Loss A/c	30,000	48,000	Stock	77,000	1,09,000
Proposed Dividend	42,000	50,000	Bills Receivable	20,000	30,000
Creditors	55,000	83,000	Cash in Hand	15,000	10,000
Bill Payable	20,000	16,000	Cash at Bank	10,000	8,000
Provision for Taxation	40,000	50,000			
	6,77,000	8,17,000		6,77,000	8,17,000

Additional information:

(*i*) Depreciation of ₹ 10,000 and ₹ 20,000 have been charged on plant account and land and buildings account respectively in 2013.

(*ii*) An interim dividend of ₹ 20,000 has been paid in 2013.

(*iii*) Income-tax ₹ 35,000 was paid during the year 2013.

Solution: **Statement of Sources and Applications of Funds for the year ended 31st December, 2013**

Sources	(₹)	Applications	(₹)
Issue of Equity Share Capital	1,00,000	Redemption of Preference Share Capital	50,000
Sale of Land	10,000	Purchase of Plant	1,30,000
Funds from Operation	2,18,000	Dividend paid (42,000 + 20,000)	62,000
		Income-tax	35,000
		Increase in Working Capital	51,000
	3,28,000		3,28,000

Schedule of Changes in Working Capital

	2012 (₹)	2013 (₹)	Increase (₹)	Decrease (₹)
Current Assets:				
Cash in Hand	15,000	10,000	—	5,000
Cash in Bank	10,000	8,000		2,000
Bills Receivable	20,000	30,000	10,000	—
Stock	77,000	1,09,000	32,000	—
Debtors	1,60,000	2,00,000	40,000	—
Total (A)	2,82,000	3,57,000	82,000	7,000
Current Liabilities:				
Creditors	55,000	83,000	—	28,000
Bills Payable	20,000	16,000	4,000	—
Total (B)	75,000	99,000		
Working Capital (A – B)	2,07,000	2,58,000		
Increase in Working Capital	51,000	—	—	51,000
	2,58,000	2,58,000	86,000	86,000

Adjusted Profit and Loss Account

Particulars	(₹)	Particulars	(₹)
To Goodwill	25,000	By Balance b/d	30,000
To Depreciation: Land and Building	20,000	By Funds from Operation	2,18,000
Plant	10,000		
To General Reserve	30,000		
To Proposed Dividend	50,000		
To Interim Dividend	20,000		
To Provision for Taxation	45,000		
To Balance c/d	48,000		
	2,48,000		2,48,000

Goodwill

Particulars	(₹)	Particulars	(₹)
To Balance b/d	1,15,000	By Adjusted Profit and Loss A/c	25,000
		By Balance c/d	90,000
	1,15,000		1,15,000

Land and Buildings

Particulars	(₹)	Particulars	(₹)
To Balance b/d	2,00,000	By Adjusted Profit and Loss A/c (Depreciation)	20,000
		By Bank	10,000
		By Balance c/d	1,70,000
	2,00,000		2,00,000

Plant A/c

Particulars	(₹)	Particulars	(₹)
To Balance b/d	80,000	By Adjusted Profit and Loss A/c	10,000
To Bank (*Balancing figure*)	1,30,000	By Balance c/d	2,00,000
	2,10,000		2,10,000

General Reserve

Particulars	(₹)	Particulars	(₹)
To Balance c/d	70,000	By Balance c/d	40,000
		By Adjusted Profit and Loss A/c	30,000
	70,000		70,000

Proposed Dividend

Particulars	(₹)	Particulars	(₹)
To Dividend paid	42,000	By Balance b/d	42,000
To Balance c/d	50,000	By Adjusted Profit and Loss A/c	50,000
	92,000		92,000

Provision for Taxation

Particulars	(₹)	Particulars	(₹)
To Income-tax	35,000	By Balance b/d	40,000
To Balance c/d	50,000	By Adjusted Profit and Loss A/c	45,000
	85,000		85,000

SIGNIFICANCE OF STATEMENT OF CHANGES IN FINANCIAL POSITION—WORKING CAPITAL BASIS

A better understanding and analysis of the affairs of a business enterprise requires the knowledge about the movements in assets, liabilities and capital which have taken place during the year and their consequent effect on its financial position. This information is not specifically disclosed by a profit and loss account and balance sheet but can be made available in working capital based funds flow statement.

The funds flow statement is in no way a replacement for the profit and loss account and balance sheet although the information which it contains is a selection, reclassification and summarisation of information contained in these two statements. The balance sheet gives a "snapshot" view at a point in time of the sources from which a firm has acquired its funds and the uses which the firm has made of these funds. The equities side of the balance sheet delineates these sources, and the asset side shows the uses. The income statement is a flow statement; it explains changes that occurred in the retained earnings account by summarizing the increases (revenues) and decreases (expenses) in retained earnings during the accounting period. A funds flow statement explains the changes that took place in a balance sheet accounts or group of accounts during the period between dates of two balance sheets "snapshots." It shows the manner in which the operations of an enterprise have been financed and in which its financial resources have been used. It also distinguishes the use of funds for the long-term from the short-term. For example, it distinguishes the use of funds for the purchase of new fixed assets from funds used in increasing the working capital of the company. Thus, it provides a meaningful link between the balance sheets at the beginning and at the end of a period and profit and loss account for that period. It should be understood, however, that a funds statement does not purport to indicate the requirements of a business for capital.

The concept of working capital is in conformity with normal accrual accounting procedures. Hence, a funds flow statement based on the concept of net working capital fits well with other statements. Above all, working capital is also a measure of the short-term liquidity of the firm. Therefore, an analysis of factors bringing about a change in the amount of net working capital is useful for decision-making by shareholders, creditors, lenders and management.

LIMITATIONS OF STATEMENT OF CHANGES IN FINANCIAL POSITION—WORKING CAPITAL BASIS

The working capital concept of funds enlarges the problem of valuation because it includes inventory and prepaid items. Thus, the measurement of working capital flows is less precise than for cash. A fund statement based on the working capital concept is usually a brief presentation, and many significant inter-firm transactions are not disclosed. For example, significant addition to inventories financed by short-term credits would not be shown because the two items are offset in the computation of the net change in working capital. Furthermore, transactions not affecting working capital, such as the acquisition of plant and equipment by the issuance of equity capital, would not be included in the statement. Therefore, the funds statement in this presentation would not disclose structural changes in the financial relationships in the firm or major changes in policy regarding investments in current assets and short term financing.

RELATIONSHIP BETWEEN WORKING CAPITAL BASIS STATEMENT OF CHANGES IN FINANCIAL POSITION AND INCOME STATEMENT

The income statement is based on the accrual principle: Cash significant events are reported, whether or not they coincide with actual cash flows. The accrual principle necessarily involves the use of estimates and artificial allocations in seeking to predict future cash effects of current events, and attempting to measure the current consequences of the past cash flows.

Working Capital provided by operations is derived from the income statement by omitting certain items that do not affect working capital. For this reason, working capital provided by operations depends on many of the same estimates and conventions that enter into the measurement of net income. Over time, cumulative amounts of income, working capital, and cash should coincide—the only difference should be the timing of the reported flows. Because most financial decisions must be based on annual data, and timing differences between the reported annual flows can be substantial, these differences have a significant impact on the actions taken by decision-makers.

THEORY QUESTIONS

1. Explain why an adequate amount of working capital is essential to the successful operation of a business enterprise?
2. What are the primary ways in which an enterprise generates working capital and the primary ways in which a firm uses working capital?
3. Explain the different concepts of funds used in the preparation of statement of changes in financial position.
4. How does a funds flow differ from a balance sheet and income statement?
5. What information/statements are required to prepare a statement of sources and application of funds?
6. Define the following, giving suitable examples:
   (*i*) Current Assets
   (*ii*) Current Liabilities
   (*iii*) Non-Current Accounts.
7. Discuss the different sources and uses of working capital.
8. Explain effect of different transactions on working capital.
9. List the different steps in preparing funds flow statement.
10. How are taxes and proposed dividends treated in preparing working capital basis funds flow statement.
11. Explain the importance of statement of changes in financial position/working capital basis.
12. What do you mean by statement of changes in working capital? Also explain the process of preparation of funds flow and cash flow statement.

EXERCISES AND PROBLEMS

1. From the following particulars of M/s Tushar Ltd. prepare Funds Flow Statements and Schedule of Changes in Working Capital.

Liabilities	2012 (₹)	2013 (₹)	Assets	2012 (₹)	2013 (₹)
Equity Share Capital	2,10,000	1,50,000	Fixed Assets	3,72,000	3,06,000
Profit and Loss A/c	1,62,000	66,000	Investments	48,000	18,000
14% Debentures	1,80,000	2,10,000	Debtors (all good)	45,000	24,000
Creditors	60,000	30,000	Other Current Assets	1,80,000	1,20,000
Proposed Dividend	15,000	6,000	Discount on Issue of		
Provision for Tax	12,000	6,000	Debentures	3,000	6,000
Provision for Doubtful Debt	9,000	6,000			
	6,48,000	4,74,000		6,48,000	4,74,000

Additional Information :

(*a*) The provision for depreciation stood at ₹ 90,000 on 31.12.2011 and at ₹ 1,14,000 on 31.12.2012. A fixed asset costing ₹ 42,000 (Book value ₹ 24,000) was disposed off for ₹ 15,000.

(*b*) An Interim dividend @ 15% was paid on equity shares. New equity shares were issued on 31.12.2012.

(*c*) Tax provided during the year ₹ 9,000.

(*d*) Some Investments were sold for ₹ 30,000 at a profit of 25% on cost.

[**Ans:** Net increase in working capital ₹ 51,000; Funds from operations ₹ 1,93,500; Purchase of fixed assets for cash ₹ 1,32,000; Tax paid during the year ₹ 3,000; Profit on sale of investments ₹ 6,000. Loss on sale of fixed assets ₹ 9,000].

2. From the following particulars, prepare Funds Flow Statement:

Assets	Mar. 2012 (₹)	Mar. 2013 (₹)	Liabilities	Mar. 2012 (₹)	Mar. 2013 (₹)
Current Assets	64,000	64,000	Current Liabilities	36,000	41,000
Fixed Assets:			Bank Loan	30,000	45,000
Land	20,000	30,000	Capital	1,48,000	1,49,000
Buildings	50,000	55,000			
Machinery	80,000	86,000			
	2,14,000	2,35,000		2,14,000	2,35,000

During the year, drawings by the proprietor for personal use amounted to ₹ 25,000. ₹ 9,000 was charged as depreciation on Machinery during the year ending March 31st, 2013.

[**Ans:** Net decrease in working capital ₹ 5,000; Funds from operations ₹ 26,000 + 9,000 = ₹ 35,000; Machinery purchased for cash ₹ 15,000].

3. From the following Summarised Balance Sheets of M/s G. Ltd., prepare the Funds Flow Statement for the year ended on 31st March, 2013:

Liabilities	Year Ending: 31st March		Assets	Year Ending: 31st March	
	2012 (₹)	2013 (₹)		2012 (₹)	2013 (₹)
Share Capital	10,00,000	10,50,000	**Fixed Assets:**		
Capital Reserve	50,000	50,000	Cost Less Depreciation	12,30,000	13,75,000
Loans	5,00,000	6,50,000	Stock in Trade	4,10,000	5,60,000
Sundry Creditors	6,00,000	7,85,000	Sundry Debtors	3,40,000	2,10,000

Liabilities	Year Ending: 31st March		Assets	Year Ending: 31st March	
	2012 (₹)	2013 (₹)		2012 (₹)	2013 (₹)
			Cash at Bank	20,000	5,000
			Discount on Issue of Shares	—	5,000
			Profit and Loss A/c	1,50,000	3,80,000
	21,50,000	25,35,000		21,50,000	25,35,000

The company issued share capital to a firm against the following assets purchased: Fixed Assets: ₹ 25,000, Stock in Trade: ₹ 20,000, During 2012–13; Depreciation was provided on Fixed Assets as ₹ 1,15,000.

[**Ans:** Decrease in working capital ₹ 1,80,000; Total sources ₹ 1,70,000; Total uses ₹ 3,50,000. Loss from business operations ₹ 1,15,000].

4. Following are the Balance Sheet of M/s X Co. Ltd. for the two years:

Liabilities	Mar. 2012 (₹)	Mar. 2013 (₹)	Assets	Mar. 2012 (₹)	Mar. 2013 (₹)
Share Capital	5,00,000	7,00,000	Plant and Machinery	5,00,000	8,00,000
Profit and Loss A/c	1,00,000	1,60,000	Land and Buildings	80,000	1,20,000
General Reserve	50,000	70,000	Stock	1,00,000	75,000
S. Creditors	1,03,000	1,20,000	S. Debtors	1,50,000	1,60,000
Bills Payable	20,000	25,000	Cash in Hand	20,000	20,000
Outstanding Exp.	7,000	5,000			
Provision for Taxation	20,000	25,000			
Proposed Dividend	50,000	70,000			
	8,50,000	11,75,000		8,50,000	11,75,000

Additional information:

(*i*) An interim dividend of ₹ 20,000 was paid during the year.

(*ii*) Income-tax ₹ 15,000 was paid in 2012–13.

(*iii*) During the year ₹ 50,000 was charged as depreciation on Plant and Machinery.

(*iv*) One machine costing ₹ 12,000 (on which ₹ 7,000 has been written off as depreciation) was sold for ₹ 8,000 during the year.

Prepare the Schedule of Changes in Working Capital and the Funds Flow Statement. Also show the detailed workings clearly.

[**Ans:** Net decrease in working capital ₹ 35,000; Funds from operation ₹ 2,37,000].

5. From the following information, prepare a statement of Sources and Applications of Funds for the year ended December 31st, 2013.

(*i*) Increase in working capital ₹ 4,000.

(*ii*) Net profit ₹ 10,750 before writing off goodwill.

(*iii*) Depreciation provided on fixed assets ₹ 1,750.

(*iv*) Dividend paid ₹ 3,500.

(*v*) Goodwill ₹ 5,000 written off out of profits.

(*vi*) ₹ 5,000 share capital was issued for cash.

(*vii*) Machinery was purchased for ₹ 10,000.

[**Ans:** Funds from operations ₹ 12,500; Total sources ₹ 17,500; Total applications ₹ 13,500].

6. Following are the Balance Sheets of X Co. Ltd. as on 31st March, 2012 and 2013:

Liabilities	2012 (₹)	2013 (₹)	Assets	2012 (₹)	2013 (₹)
Pref. Share Capital	—	2,00,000	Goodwill	20,000	30,000
Equity Share Capital	4,20,000	5,20,000	Buildings	6,00,000	5,80,000
General Reserve	1,00,000	1,10,000	Machinery	3,00,000	3,38,000
Creditors	4,40,000	2,68,000	Stock	2,00,000	1,48,000
Profit and Loss A/c	61,000	71,200	Debtors	1,40,400	1,08,000
14% Debentures	2,00,000	—	Cash/Bank	20,600	37,200
Unclaimed Dividend	—	2,000			
Provision for Tax	60,000	70,000			
	12,81,000	12,41,200		12,81,000	12,41,200

Additional Information:

(*i*) Dividend paid in cash ₹ 50,000 during the year.

(*ii*) Assets acquired for ₹ 1,00,000 payable in equity shares: stock ₹ 50,000, Machine ₹ 40,000 and goodwill.

(*iii*) Machine purchased for cash ₹ 12,000.

(*iv*) Provision for tax during the year ₹ 66,000.

(*v*) Debenture-Holders accept preference shares in settlement of their claims.

(*vi*) Depreciation on building ₹ 20,000.

Prepare Funds Flow Statement and Schedule of Changes in Working Capital.

[**Ans:** Net increase in working capital ₹ 92,200; Funds from operations ₹ 1,06,200; Depreciation on machinery ₹ 14,000].

[**Hint:** Dividend proposed during the year ₹ 52,000 (paid ₹ 50,000 + Unclaimed ₹ 2,000)].

7. From the following particulars of M/s Evergreen Ltd., prepare Funds Flow Statement and a Statement of Changes in Working Capital:

Liabilities	2012 (₹)	2013 (₹)	Assets	2012 (₹)	2013 (₹)
Share Capital	1,50,000	2,10,000	Fixed Assets	3,06,000	3,72,000
Profit and Loss A/c	66,000	1,62,000	Investments (long-term)	18,000	48,000
14% Debentures	2,10,000	1,80,000	Debtors (all good)	24,000	45,000
Creditors	30,000	60,000	Other Current Assets	1,20,000	1,80,000
Proposed Dividend	6,000	15,000	Discount on the Issue of Debentures	6,000	3,000
Provision for Tax	6,000	12,000			
Provision for Doubtful Debts	6,000	9,000			
	4,74,000	6,48,000		4,74,000	6,48,000

Additional Information:

(*i*) The provision for depreciation stood at ₹ 90,000 on 31.12.2012 and at ₹ 1,14,000 on 31.12.2013. A fixed asset costing ₹ 42,000 (Book Value ₹ 24,000) was sold at ₹ 15,000.

(*ii*) An interim dividend @ 15% was paid on equity shares. New equity shares were issued on 31.12.2013.

[**Ans:** Increase in Working Capital ₹ 51,000; Funds from operations ₹ 1,93,500; Total Sources ₹ 2,98,500; Total uses ₹ 2,47,500].

8. From the Balance Sheets given below as on March 31st, 2012 and 2013 of M/s Tulsi & Co., prepare a statement of change in working capital and a statement showing sources and uses of Funds.

Liabilities	Year Ending: 31st March 2012 (₹)	Year Ending: 31st March 2013 (₹)	Assets	Year Ending: 31st March 2012 (₹)	Year Ending: 31st March 2013 (₹)
Share Capital	5,00,000	7,00,000	Land and Building	80,000	1,20,000
General Reserves	50,000	70,000	Plant and Machinery	5,00,000	8,00,000
Profit and Loss A/c	1,00,000	1,60,000	Stock	1,00,000	75,000
Sundry Creditors	1,53,000	1,90,000	Sundry Debtors	1,50,000	1,60,000
Bills Payable	40,000	50,000	Cash at Bank	20,000	20,000
Outstanding Exp.	7,000	5,000			
	8,50,000	11,75,000		8,50,000	11,75,000

Additional information:

(*i*) During the year ending March 31st, 2013, the company purchased machinery against which the payment to the extent of ₹ 1,00,000 was made through the issue of share capital and the balance in cash.

(*ii*) Depreciation on Plant and Machinery was charged ₹ 50,000 during the current year. A piece of machinery was sold for ₹ 8,000 during the year ending on March 31st, 2013 which costed ₹ 12,000 to the company. The accumulated depreciation on this machinery was ₹ 7,000.

[**Ans:** Decrease in working capital ₹ 60,000; Total Sources ₹ 2,35,000; Total uses ₹ 2,95,000].

9. From the particulars of X Co. Ltd. as on March 31st, prepare funds flow statement and schedule of changes in working capital:

Liabilities	2013 (₹)	2012 (₹)	Assets	2013 (₹)	2012 (₹)
Equity Share Capital	7,00,000	5,00,000	Fixed Assets	12,40,000	10,20,000
14% Debentures	6,00,000	7,00,000	Investments	1,60,000	60,000
Profit and Loss A/c	5,40,000	2,20,000	Debtors (All good)	1,50,000	80,000
Creditors	2,00,000	1,00,000	Other Current Assets	6,00,000	4,00,000
Proposed Dividend	50,000	20,000	Discount on issue of Debentures	10,000	20,000
Provision for Tax	40,000	20,000			
Provision for Doubtful Debts	30,000	20,000			
	21,60,000	15,80,000		21,60,000	15,80,000

Additional Information:

(*i*) Tax provided during the year, ₹ 30,000.

(*ii*) Some investments were sold for ₹ 1,00,000 at a profit of 25% on cost.

(*iii*) An interim dividend @ 15% was paid on equity shares. New equity shares were issued on 31st March, 2013.

(*iv*) Provision for depreciation stood at ₹ 3,00,000 on 1st April, 2012 and at ₹ 3,80,000 on 31st March, 2013. A fixed asset costing ₹ 1,40,000 (Book Value ₹ 80,000) was sold for ₹ 50,000.

[**Ans:** Increase in Working Capital ₹ 1,70,000; Total Sources ₹ 9,95,000. Total uses ₹ 8,25,000].

10. Following are the summarised balance sheets of a Limited Co. as at March 31st, 2012 and March 31st, 2013.

Liabilities	On March 31st 2012 (₹)	On March 31st 2013 (₹)	Assets	On March 31st 2012 (₹)	On March 31st 2013 (₹)
Sundry Creditors	39,010	41,135	Cash at Bank	3,000	2,700
Bills Payable	33,780	11,525	Sundry Debtors	85,175	72,625
Bank Overdraft	60,000	Nil	Sundry Advances	2,315	735
Provision for Income Tax	40,000	49,000	Stock	1,09,040	97,370
Reserves	48,000	50,000	Land and Buildings	1,48,000	1,54,250
Profit and Loss A/c	39,690	41,220	Plant and Machinery	1,12,950	1,16,200
Share Capital	2,00,000	2,60,000	Goodwill	Nil	9,000
	4,60,480	4,52,880		4,60,480	4,52,880

Additional Information:

(*i*) An interim dividend of ₹ 26,000 and a final dividend of ₹ 54,000 were paid during 2012–13.

(*ii*) The assets of another company were purchased for ₹ 60,000 payable in fully paid shares of the company. The assets purchased comprised of Stock: ₹ 22,000 and Machinery: ₹ 29,000.

(*iii*) Additional plant purchased worth ₹ 6,000.

(*iv*) Depreciation provided during the current year:
Land and Buildings—₹ 3,750; Plant and Machinery—₹ 12,000.

(*v*) Income Tax paid during the year ₹ 30,000.

You are required to prepare the Funds Flow Statement and a statement of Change in Working Capital for the year ending on March 31st, 2013.

[**Ans:** Funds from operations ₹ 1,38,280; increase in working capital 54,030].

11. Following are summarised Balance Sheets of X Ltd. as on 31st December, 2012 and 2013:

Liabilities	2012 (₹)	2013 (₹)	Assets	2012 (₹)	2013 (₹)
Equity Share Capital	2,00,000	2,50,000	Bank	35,000	16,000
12% Debentures	1,00,000	80,000	Stock	40,000	75,000
10% Pref. Share Cap.	50,000	80,000	B/R	20,000	50,000
Public Deposits	20,000	30,000	Debtors	70,000	1,00,000
Loans	50,000	80,000	Machinery	75,000	60,000
Reserves	20,000	25,000	Furniture	10,000	8,000
Profit and Loss A/c	50,000	60,000	Land	1,70,000	2,80,000
Provision for Dep. on Machinery	10,000	15,000	Buildings	1,40,000	99,000
			Goodwill	30,000	25,000
Dividend Proposed	20,000	25,000			
Creditors	40,000	50,000			
B/P	30,000	18,000			
	5,90,000	7,13,000		5,90,000	7,13,000

Additional Information:

(*i*) Depreciation charged during 2013 was ₹ 4,000 on Furniture, ₹ 12,000 on Machinery and ₹ 20,000 on Buildings.

(*ii*) Redemption of debentures was made at 10% premium.

(*iii*) Part of machinery was sold for ₹ 15,000 at a loss of ₹ 4,000.

(*iv*) During 2013, interim dividend was paid ₹ 10,000 and income tax was paid ₹ 5,000.

You are required to prepare Fund Flow Statement and Schedule of Changes in Working Capital from the above particulars. Working notes are also required.

[**Ans:** Increase in working capital ₹ 78,000. Funds from operations 1,02,000. Total Source 2,58,000, Total uses ₹ 1,80,000].

12. From the following Balance Sheets of A Ltd. as on March 31st, prepare Funds Flow Statement and a schedule of changes in working capital:

Liabilities	As on 2012 (₹)	As on 2013 (₹)	Assets	As on 2012 (₹)	As on 2013 (₹)
Equity Share Capital	2,00,000	2,80,000	Fixed Assets	4,08,000	4,96,000
Profit and Loss A/c	88,000	2,16,000	Investments	24,000	64,000
14% Debentures	2,80,000	2,40,000	Debtors (all good)	32,000	60,000
Creditors	40,000	80,000	Other Current Assets	1,60,000	2,40,000
Proposed Dividend	8,000	20,000	Discount on issue of		
Provision for Tax	8,000	16,000	Debentures	8,000	4,000
Provision for Doubtful Debts	8,000	12,000			
	6,32,000	8,64,000		6,32,000	8,64,000

Additional Information:

(*a*) The provision for depreciation stood at ₹ 1,20,000 on 31.12.2012 and at ₹ 1,52,000 on 31.12.2013. A fixed asset costing ₹ 56,000 (book value ₹ 32,000) was sold for ₹ 20,000.

(*b*) An interim dividend @ 15% was paid on equity shares. New equity shares were issued on 31.12.2013.

(*c*) Tax provided during the year ₹ 12,000.

(*d*) Some of the investments were sold for ₹ 20,000 at a profit of 25% on cost.

[**Ans:** Funds from operations ₹ 2,62,000; Increase in working capital ₹ 68,000].

18

CASH FLOW STATEMENT

LEARNING OBJECTIVES

After reading this chapter, you should be able to:

- *Understand* concept of cash flow statement.
- *Describe* different types of cash inflows and cash outflows.
- *Distinguish* between cash flow statement and cash receipts and disbursements, and income statement.
- *Discuss* methods of presentation of cash flow statement.
- *Explain* significance and limitations of cash flow statement.

CONCEPT

A cash flow statement discloses net increase (or decrease) in cash during an accounting period. As per AS-3 (Revised) the objective of cash flow statement is to provide information about cash flows of an enterprise which is useful in providing the users of financial statements with a basis to assess the ability of an enterprise to generate cash and cash equivalents to utilise those cash flows. The statement deals with the provisions of information about the changes in cash and cash equivalents during the accounting year. It classifies cash flows into operating, investing and financing activities.

DEFINITIONS IN AS-3

The following terms are used in this Statement with the meanings specified:

Cash comprises cash on hand and demand deposits with banks

Cash equivalents are short-term, highly liquid investments that are readily convertible into known amounts of cash and which are subject to an insignificant risk of changes in value.

Cash flows are inflows and outflows of cash and cash equivalents.

Operating activities are the principal revenue-producing activities of the enterprise and other activities that are not investing or financing activities.

Investing activities are the acquisition and disposal of long-term assets and other investments not included in cash equivalents.

Financing activities are activities that result in changes in the size and composition of the owner's capital (including preference share capital in the case of a company) and borrowings of the enterprise.

Cash and Cash Equivalents

1. Cash equivalents are held for the purpose of meeting short-term cash commitments rather than for investment or other purposes. For an investment to qualify as a cash equivalent, it must be readily convertible to a known amount of cash and be subject to an insignificant risk of changes in value. Therefore, an investment normally qualifies as a cash equivalent only when it has a short maturity of, say, three months or less from the date of acquisition. Investments in shares are excluded from cash equivalents unless they are, in substance, cash equivalents; for example, preference shares of a company acquired shortly before their specified redemption date (provided there is only an insignificant risk of failure of the company to repay the amount at maturity).
2. Cash flows exclude movements between items that constitute cash or cash equivalents because these components are part of the cash management of an enterprise rather than part of its operating, investing and financing activities. Cash management includes the investment of excess cash in cash equivalents.

CLASSIFICATION OF CASH INFLOWS AND OUTFLOWS

A cash flow statement focuses on various activities and items which bring about changes in the cash balance between two balance sheet dates. This statement covers all items which increase or decrease the cash of a business enterprise. For example, this statement includes items like receipts from debtors and payments to creditors. On the contrary, this statement will not cover items which have no immediate effect on cash increase or decrease. For instance, goods purchased on credit and goods sold on credit will not be included in this statement as these transactions have no effect on inflow and outflow of cash.

A cash flow statement aims to determine the effects on cash of different types of cash inflows and outflows. In this process, all cash flows, *i.e.,* activities resulting into cash flows are classified into different categories. The ICAI's AS 3 'Cash Flow Statement' has classified cash flows into three categories:

1. Operating Activities (or Flows)
2. Investing Activities (or Flows)
3. Financing Activities (or Flows).

Figure 18.1 displays the classification of cash inflows and cash outflows relating to operating activities, investing activities and financing activities.

1. **Operating Activities**—Operating activities are those transactions which are considered in the determination of net income. Examples of cash inflows in this category are cash received from debtors for goods and services, interest and dividend received on loans and investment. Examples of cash outflows in this category are cash payments for goods and services; merchandise; wages; interest; taxes; supplies and others.

   AS 3 Cash Flow Statement states:

   (*i*) The amount of cash flows arising from operating activities is a key indicator of the extent to which the operations of the enterprise have generated sufficient cash flows to maintain the operating capability of the enterprise, pay dividends, repay loans and make new investments without recourse to external sources of financing. Information about the specific components of historical operating cash flows is useful, in conjunction with other information, in forecasting future operating cash flows.

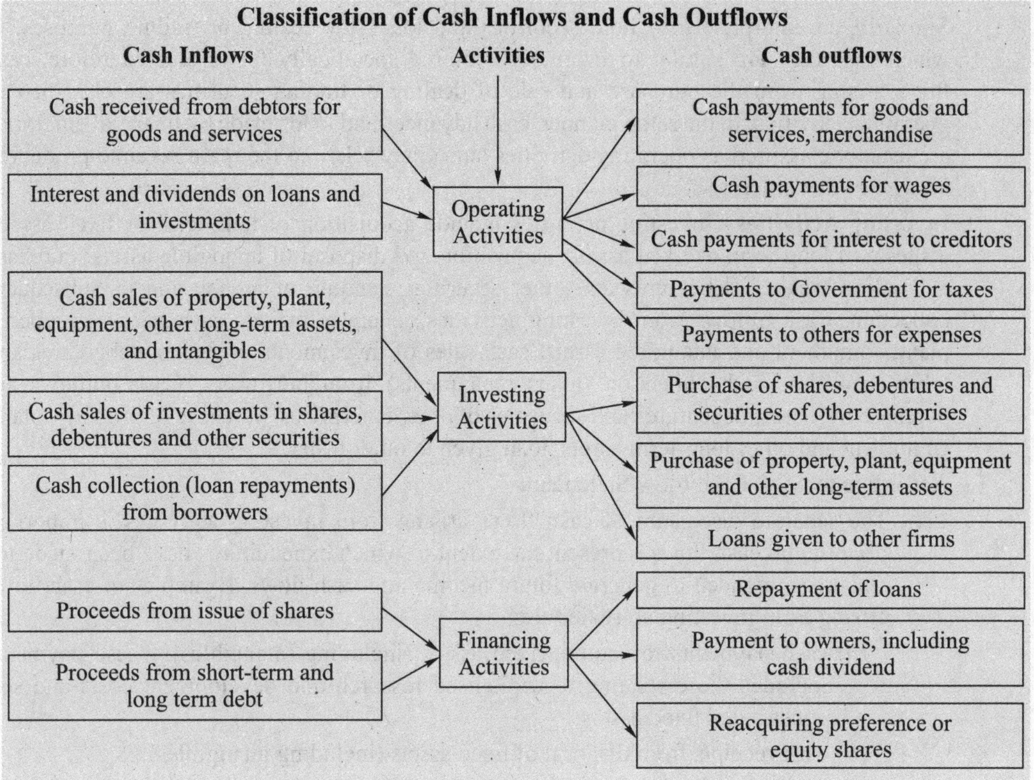

Fig. 18.1 Classification of cash inflows and out flows relating to operating activities, investing activities and financing activities

(*ii*) Cash flows from operating activities are primarily derived from the principal revenue-producing activities of the enterprise. Therefore, they generally result from the transactions and other events that enter into the determination of net profit or loss. Examples of cash flows from operating activities are:

(*a*) cash receipts from the sale of goods and the rendering of services;

(*b*) cash receipts from royalties, fees, commissions and other revenue;

(*c*) cash payments to suppliers for goods and services;

(*d*) cash payments to and on behalf of employees;

(*e*) cash receipts and cash payments of an insurance enterprise for premiums and claims, annuities and other policy benefits;

(*f*) cash payments or refunds of income-taxes unless they can be specifically identified with financing and investing activities; and

(*g*) cash receipts and payments relating to future contracts, forward contracts, option contracts and swap contracts when the contracts are held for dealing or trading purposes.

(*iii*) Some transactions, such as the sale of an item of plant, may give rise to a gain or loss which is included in the determination of net profit or loss. However, the cash flows relating to such transactions are cash flows from investing activities.

(*iv*) Cash flows from operating activities are determined according to the activities relating to the business in which the enterprise deals in e.g. interest and dividend received by financial institutions will be treated as operating cash flow.

Similarly, an enterprise may hold securities and loans for dealing or trading purposes, in which case they are similar to inventory acquired specifically for resale. Therefore, cash flows arising from the purchase and sale of dealing or trading securities are classified as operating activities. In the same manner, cash advances and loans made by financial enterprise are usually classified as operating activities since they relate to the main revenue-producing activity of that enterprise.

2. **Investing Activities**—Investing activities include acquisition of long-term or fixed assets; disposal of long-term or fixed assets; acquisition and disposal of intangible assets; purchase and sale of shares, debentures and other securities; lending of money and its subsequent collection. Cash inflows from investing activities generally include cash sales of property, plant, equipment and intangible assets, cash sales of investments in shares, debentures and other securities, cash collection (loans repayments) from borrowers. Cash outflows are purchase of shares, debentures and securities of other enterprises, purchase of property, plant, equipment and other long-term assets, loan given to other firms.

According to AS-3 Cash Flow Statement:

(*i*) The separate disclosure of cash flows arising from investing activities is important because the cash flows represent the extent to which expenditures have been made for resources intended to generate future income and cash flows. Examples of cash flows arising from investing activities are:

(*a*) cash payments to acquire fixed assets (including intangibles). These payments includes those relating to capitalised research and development costs and self constructed fixed assets;

(*b*) cash receipts from disposal of fixed assets (including intangibles);

(*c*) cash payments to acquire shares, warrants or debt instruments of other enterprises and interests in joint ventures (other than payments for those instruments considered to be cash equivalents and those held for dealing or trading purposes);

(*d*) cash receipts from disposal of shares warrants or debt instruments of other enterprises and interests in joint ventures (other than receipts from those instruments considered to be cash equivalents and those held for dealing or trading purposes);

(*e*) cash advances and loans made to third parties (other than advances and loans made by a financial enterprise);

(*f*) cash receipts from the repayment of advances and loans made to third parties (other than advances and loans of a financial enterprise);

(*g*) cash receipts from future contracts, forward contracts, option contracts and swap contracts excepts when the contracts are held for dealing or trading purposes, or the payments are classified as financing activities; and

(*h*) cash receipts from future contracts, forward contracts, option contracts and swap contracts except when the contracts are held for dealing or trading purposes, or the receipts are classified as financing activities.

(*ii*) When a contract is accounted for as a hedge of an identifiable position, the cash flows of the contract are classified in the same manner as the cash flow of the position being hedged.

3. **Financing Activities**—Financing activities relate to long-term liability and equity capital. A firm engages in financing activities when it obtains resources from owners, returns resources

to owners, borrows resources from creditors and repays amounts borrowed. Cash inflows include proceeds from issue of shares and short term and long term borrowings. Cash outflows include repayment of loans and payments to owners, including cash dividends. Repayment of accounts payable or accrued liabilities are not considered repayment of loans under financing activities but are classified as cash outflows under operating activities. AS-3 Cash Flow Statement observes:

The separate disclosure of cash flows arising from financing activities is important because it is useful in predicting claims on future cash flows by providers of funds (both capital and borrowings) to the enterprise. Examples of cash flows arising from financing activities are:

(*a*) cash proceeds from issuing shares or other similar instruments;

(*b*) cash proceeds from issuing debentures, loans, notes, bonds and other short or long-term borrowings; and

(*c*) cash repayments of amounts borrowed.

CASH FLOW STATEMENT AND CASH RECEIPTS AND DISBURSEMENTS

A cash flow statement differs from the summary of cash receipts and disbursements. A cash flow statement is prepared by a rearrangement of items on the income statement and balance sheet, rather than from entries made to the cash account. Cash flow statement may also highlight the amount of cash generated by the firm's operations. This is not reported in statement of cash receipts and disbursements.

CASH FLOW AND INCOME STATEMENT

Cash flow statement apparently differs from income statement. An income statement includes adjustments in respect of expenses accrued in the calculation of periodic income, whereas cash flow statement excludes such adjustments. The largest item of difference between them is the allocation of fixed assets costs as depreciation. Also, the procedures adopted in the two statements are reflected in changes in balance sheet items. These would include changes in balances of trade debtors and trade creditors.

CASH PROFIT (CASH NET INCOME)

Accrual-based profit and loss account reveals accrual net income. By adjusting the items on the profit and loss account, one can arrive at cash profit or cash net income. It should be noted that cash profit relates to operating activities in the same way as profit and loss account focuses on net income determination from operating activities. But profit and loss account does not show cash inflow and outflow relating to operating activities because profit and loss account is prepared on accrual basis.

Cash profit and cash flow is not the same thing. Cash profit is confined to indicating cash flow relating to operating activities. But cash flow is a total concept indicating total inflows and outflows. Fox example, issue of equity shares is a source of cash inflow but will not be used for determining cash profit. Similarly, plant purchased will be cash outflow for its full value, but will not be used for determining cash profit.

PRESENTATION OF CASH FLOW STATEMENT

A cash flow statement can be presented in either the direct or indirect format. The investing and financing sections will be the same under either format. However, the operating section will be different.

DIRECT METHOD

Direct method is that method whereby major classes of gross cash receipts and gross cash payments are disclosed. Enterprises that utilise the direct method should report separately the following classes of operating cash receipts and payments:

1. Cash collected from customers, including lessees, licensee, and other similar items.
2. Interest and dividends received.
3. Other operating cash receipts, if any.
4. Cash paid to employees and other suppliers of goods or services, including supplies of insurance, advertising, and other similar expenses.
5. Interest paid.
6. Income-taxes paid.
7. Other operating cash payments, if any.

Companies that use the direct method must provide a reconciliation of net income to net cash flow from operating activities in a separate schedule in the financial statements.

According to AS 3 cash flow Statement:

The direct method provides information which may be useful in estimating future cash flows and which is not available under the indirect method and is, therefore, considered more appropriate than the indirect method. Under the direct method, information about major classes of gross cash receipts and gross cash payments may be obtained either:

(*a*) from the accounting records of the enterprise; or

(*b*) by adjusting sales, cost of sales (interest and similar income and interest expense and similar charges for a financial enterprise) and other items in the statement of profit and loss for:

(*i*) changes during the period in inventories and operating receivables and payables;

(*ii*) other non-cash items; and

(*iii*) other items for which the cash effects are investing or financing cash flows.

Illustration 1: From the following Profit and Loss Account of ABC Ltd. for the year ended 31st March, 2013. Calculate cash generated from "Operating Activities" by Direct Method:

Profit and Loss Account for the year ended 31st March, 2013

		(₹)		(₹)
To Opening Stock		1,60,000	By Sale (Cash)	42,50,000
To Purchases (Cash)		31,00,000	By Commission accrued	40,000
To Wages	4,40,000		By Dividend received	60,000
Add: Outstanding	60,000	5,00,000	By Profit on Sale of Plant (Sale proceeds 22,40,000 – Book Value 2,00,000)	2,40,000
To Salaries	2,20,000			
Add: Outstanding	20,000		By Closing Stock	2,20,000
	2,40,000			
Less: Prepaid	10,000	2,30,000		
To Office Expenses		80,000		
To Selling Expenses		1,20,000		
To Depreciation		1,10,000		
To Income Tax paid		20,000		
To Goodwill Written		44,000		
To Preliminary of expenses written off		20,000		
To Net Profit		4,26,000		
		48,10,000		48,10,000

Solution: **Cash Flow from Operations**

Particulars	(₹)	(₹)
A: Cash Receipts from Operating Activities:		
Cash Sales		42,50,000
Less:		
B: Cash payments due to Operating Activities:		
Purchases	31,00,000	
Wages	4,40,000	
Salaries	2,20,000	
Office Expenses	80,000	
Selling Expenses	1,20,000	39,60,000
Cash Flow from Operations before Tax		2,90,000
Less: Income Tax paid		20,000
Net Cash inflow from Operations		2,70,000

Notes:

1. Non-cash charges such as depreciation, Goodwill written off, Preliminary expenses written off have been ignored as these do not involve any outflow of cash.
2. Dividend received and profit on sale of Plant are to be treated under cash flow from 'Investing activities'.
3. Commission Accrued does not involve any cash inflow, hence ignored.
4. Changes in current assets and current liabilities are ignored.

Illustration 2: From the following Profit and Loss A/c and additional information of M/s Anurag Enterprise, compute cash flow from operations:

Profit and Loss Account for the year ended 31st March, 2013

		(₹)			(₹)
To Opening Stock		1,60,000	**By Sales:**		
To Purchases			Cash		6,00,000
Cash	2,00,000		Credit		10,00,000
Credit	6,00,000	8,00,000	By Closing Stock		2,08,000
To wages		48,000	By Commission		1,12,000
To Office Expenses		1,76,000	By Royalties		80,000
To Selling Expenses		96,000	By Discount Received		40,000
To Bad Debts		16,000			
To Discount Allowed		32,000			
To Depreciation		1,20,000			
To Provision for Tax		2,40,000			
To Net Profit		3,52,000			
		20,40,000			20,40,000

Additional Information:

Particulars	March 31st 2012 (₹)	March 31st 2013 (₹)
Debtors	1,20,000	1,44,000
Creditors	1,12,000	80,000
O/S Selling Expenses	24,000	32,000

Particulars	March 31st 2012 (₹)	March 31st 2013 (₹)
Prepaid Office Expenses	16,000	24,000
Accrued Royalties	96,000	88,000
Advance Commission	72,000	64,000
Provision for Tax	3,20,000	4,80,000

Solution: **Cash Flow from Operations**

Particulars	(₹)	(₹)
(A) Receipts from Operations:		
Cash Sales		6,00,000
Cash Received from Debtors*[1]		9,76,000
Cash from Royalties*[2]		88,000
Cash from Commission*[3]		1,04,000
		17,68,000
Less: **(B) Operating Cash Payments:**		
Cash Purchases	2,00,000	
Cash paid to Creditors*[4]	6,32,000	
Cash Selling Expenses	88,000	
Cash Office Expenses	1,92,000	11,12,000
Cash Inflow from Operations before tax		6,56,000
Less: Income Tax paid (on Operating Incomes)		80,000
Net Cash flow from Operations		5,76,000

*[1]Cash Received from debtors → prepare debtors A/c.

Debtors A/c

Particulars	(₹)	Particulars	(₹)
To Balance b/d	1,20,000	By Cash Received (*Bal. figure*)	9,76,000
To Sales (Credit)	10,00,000	By Bal. c/d	1,44,000
	11,20,000		11,20,000

***[2]Cash from Royalties**

Opening Balance + Royalties as per Profit and Loss A/c – Closing Balance

= Cash from Royalties

96,000 + 80,000 – 88,000 = ₹ 88,000.

***[3]Cash from Commission**

Closing Bal. of Advance + Commission as per Profit and Loss A/c – Opening Bal. of Advance

= Cash from Commission

64,000 + 1,12,000 – 72,000 = 1,04,000.

***[4]Cash paid to Creditors**

Opening Balance + Purchases – Closing Balance

= Cash paid to Creditors

80,000 + 6,00,000 – 1,12,000 = ₹ 6,32,000

INDIRECT METHOD

Under the indirect method, the net cash flow from operating activities is determined by adjusting net profit or loss for the effects of:

(*a*) changes during the period in inventories and operating receivables and payables;

(*b*) non-cash items such as depreciation, provisions, deferred taxes, and unrealised foreign exchange gains and losses; and

(*c*) all other items for which the cash effects are investing or financing cash flows.

Alternatively, the net cash flow from operating activities may be presented under the indirect method by showing the operating revenues and expenses excluding non-cash items disclosed in the statement of profit and loss and the changes during the period in inventories and operating receivables and payables.

The indirect method starts with net income and reconciles it to net cash flow from operating activities. The cash flow from operating activities is found by adjusting net income for (*i*) changes in current assets and current liabilities, and (*ii*) depreciation expense. Depreciation expense is not a cash flow. Because it decreases net income, it is added back to net income in order to arrive at the operating cash flow. The following summarizes the process:

Change	Adjustment to Net Income
Decrease in a current asset	Add
Increase in a current asset	Subtract
Decrease in a current liability	Subtract
Increase in a current liability	Add

The indirect method is more widely used, since it shows the relationship between the income statement and the Balance Sheet and therefore aids in the analysis of these statements.

REPORTING CASH FLOWS FROM INVESTING AND FINANCING ACTIVITIES

An enterprise should report separately major classes of gross cash receipts and gross cash payments arising from investing and financing activities.

Both the approaches, direct and indirect result in the same amount for cash flow from operations after making necessary adjustments. However, both the approaches have the arguments, pros and cons.

The arguments in favour of direct approach are that it identifies the major categories of cash receipts and cash payments arising from operating activities; it provides a more useful basis for estimating future cash flows; and it provides information that is not otherwise available in the balance sheet and profit and loss account. The direct method is a better indicator of company solvency, has a sounder conceptual framework and reflects accepted business practice. It permits an evaluation of cash flow relating to specific line items of income statement such as sales and cost of goods sold. The empirical evidence indicates that the direct method is superior over the indirect method in predicting future operating cash flows and future net operating cash flows.

On the other hand, followers of the indirect approach argue that indirect method is less costly and more convenient to use by firms. It is argued that the direct approach would require information that is hard to collect and sensitive. One difficulty with the direct approach is that some of the cash flows may have characteristics of more than one category of cash flow.

However, the indirect method has also been criticised on two grounds. First, it contains unnecessary detail and may confuse the users. Another limitation of the indirect method is that the adding of expenses such as depreciation suggests that expenses are a source of cash. The conceptual and practical problems which underline the indirect method are as follows:

(*i*) Ambiguity in the definition of "operations."

(*ii*) Diversity in reporting practices.

(*iii*) Impact of changes in the reporting entity on the non-cash current accounts.

(*iv*) Use of absorption costing in accounting for manufactured inventory.

(*v*) Measurement of current portion of long-term leases.

(*vi*) Reclassifications between current and non-current accounts.

Figures 18.2 and 18.3 shows respectively direct and indirect method of preparing cash flow statement.

ABC Company for the year Ended December 31st, 2013

Particulars	(₹)	(₹)
(A) Cash Flow from Operating Activities:		
Cash Receipts from:		
Sales		
Interest Received		
Cash Payments for:		
Purchases		
Operating Expenses		
Interest Payments		
Income Taxes		
Net Cash Flow from Operating Activities		
(B) Cash Flows from Investing Activities:		
Sale of Plant Assets		
Sale of Investments		
Purchase of Plant Assets		
Purchase of Investments		
Net Cash Flows used by investing Activities		
(C) Cash Flows from Financing Activities:		
Repayment of Bonds and Debentures		
Issue of Common shares		
Dividends Paid		
Net Cash Flows from Financing Activities		
Net Increase (Decrease) in Cash		

Fig. 18.2 Cash Flow Statement (Direct Method)

ABC Company for the Year Ended December 31st, 2013

Particulars	(₹)	(₹)
(A) Cash Flows from Operating Activities:		
Net Income		
Adjustments to Reconcile Net Income to Net		
Cash provided by Operating Activities		
Depreciation		
Gain on Sale of Investments		

Particulars	(₹)	(₹)
Loss on Sale of Plant Asset		
Decrease in Accounts Receivable		
Increase in Inventory		
Decrease in Prepaid Expenses		
Increase in Accounts Payable		
Increase in Accrued Liabilities		
Decrease in Income Taxes Payable		
Net Cash Flows from Operating Activities		
(B) Cash Flows from Investing Activities		
Sales of Plant Assets		
Sale of Investments		
Purchase of Plant Assets		
Purchase of Investments		
Net Cash Flows Used by Investing Activities		
(C) Cash Flows from Financing Activities		
Repayment of Bonds and debentures		
Issue of common shares		
Dividends Paid		
Net Cash flows from Financing Activities		
Net Increase (Decrease) in cash		

Fig. 18.3 Cash flow Statement (Indirect Method)

PREPARING CASH FLOW STATEMENT

Before preparing cash flow statement, first of all, the following three steps have to be completed:

1. Determining cash flows from operations or operating activities.
2. Determining cash flows from investing activities.
3. Determining cash flows from financing activities.

After obtaining information regarding the above, a cash flow statement can be prepared. The three steps have been discussed below:

Cash Flow from Operations

The profit and loss account focuses on net income determination from operating activities. However, it does not show cash inflow and outflow relating to operating activities because the profit and loss account is prepared on accrual basis. In preparing profit and loss account, revenues are recorded even though cash for them has not been received. Similarly, expenses are recorded even though they may not have been paid. Therefore, to find cash flows from operations, one need to convert accrual basis income statement figures to cash basis by making adjustments. By way of adjustments, earned revenues will be converted into cash received from sales or customers and incurred expenses will be converted into cash expended, *i.e.,* expenses actually paid in cash.

The conversion of accrual basis income statement to cash basis income statement along with required adjustment has been shown in Fig. 18.4. The conversion process displayed in Figure 18.4 can be described as follows, using a short-cut calculation.

Accrual-Basis Net Income

↓

Deduct Increase in Accounts Receivable (or Add Decrease in Accounts Receivable)

Deduct Increase in Merchandise Inventory (or Add Decrease in Merchandise Inventory)

Deduct Increase in Prepaid Expenses (or Add Decrease in Prepaid Expenses)

Add: Increase in Accounts Payable (or Deduct Decrease in Accounts Payable)

Add: Increase in Accrued Expenses (or Deduct Decrease in Accrued Expenses)

Add: Depreciation and Amortization Expenses for the year

↓

Cash-Basis Net Income

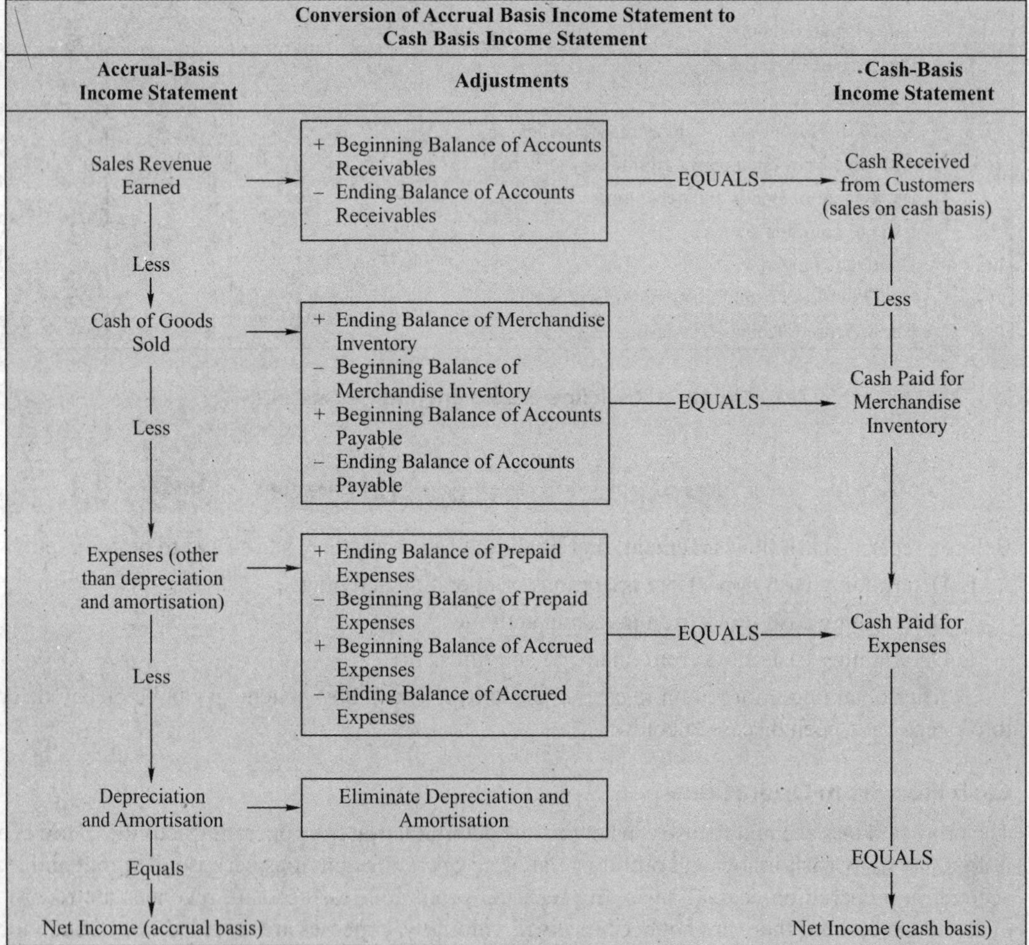

Fig. 18.4 Relationship of Accrual Basis and Cash Basis of Accounting

While making conversion, one should know the relationship between income statement accounts and balance sheet changes. Each individual item on the income statement should be viewed as it relates to a balance sheet account. On the accrual basis of accounting, the explanation for the difference between the amount of sales revenue and the receipts from those sales is found in the changes in accounts receivable and debtors account. Similarly, the difference between the amount of an expense and the amount of payments for that expense is found in the changes of its associated asset or liability, such as prepaid rent or rent payable. If there is no associated balance sheet account for an item on the income statement, it is presumed that the amount shown on the income statement resulted in a cash flow exactly equal to that revenue or expense. Figure 18.5 shows relationship between some income statement accounts and balance sheet accounts.

Financial Statement Relationship

Income Statement Accounts	Related to Balance Sheet Accounts
1. Sales	Debtors
2. Cost of goods sold	(Inventory) (Creditors)
3. Salaries expenses	Salaries payable
4. Rent expense	Rent payable
5. Depreciation expense	Accumulated depreciation
6. Insurance expense	Prepaid insurance
7. Interest expense	Interest payable
8. Income-tax expense	Income-taxes payable

Fig. 18.5 Relationship between Income Statement and Balance Sheet

PROVISIONS OF AS-3 ON TREATMENT OF CERTAIN ITEMS

1. **Interest and Dividend:** Cash flows from interest and dividends received and paid should be disclosed separately and classified on the basis of nature of the enterprise as shown below:

   For Financial enterprises
   - interest paid and received, dividend received as operating activities.
   - dividend paid as financing activities.

   For Other enterprises
   - interest and dividend received as investing activities.
   - interest and dividend paid as financing activities.

2. **Extra Ordinary items:** The cash flows associated with extra ordinary items should be classified as arising from operating, investing or financing activities as appropriate. It should be disclosed separately. Few examples of such items are:
   (*i*) Claim for loss of stock—Operating activity
   (*ii*) Claims for loss of assets—Investing activity
   (*iii*) Recovery of bad debts—Operating activity
   (*iv*) Damages paid/received for breach of contract—Operating activity
   (*v*) Winnings from lotteries—Investing activity
   (*vi*) Cost of legal action to protect property title—Investing activity.

3. **Taxes on Income:** Cash flows arising from taxes on income should be separately disclosed and should be classified as cash flows from operating activities unless they can be specifically identified with financing and investing activities.

   For instance:
   (*i*) Provision for Taxation for the current year—Non-cash charge under operating activity
   (*ii*) Tax paid—Operating cash outflow
   (*iii*) Income tax refund—Cash inflow from operating activity

(*iv*) Capital gains tax—Cash outflow from investing activity

(*v*) Corporate dividend tax—Cash outflow from financing activity.

4. **Foreign Currency cash flows:** Foreign currency cash flows should be converted at the exchange rate of the date of cash flow. Exchange gain/loss on cash and cash equivalents held in foreign currency will be reported as part of reconciliation of change in cash and cash equivalents for the period and hence, not reported in cash statement.

5. **Non-cash transactions:** Investing and financing transactions that do not require the use of cash or cash equivalents are not shown in the cash flow statement. Examples of such non-cash transactions are:

   (*i*) Issue of shares or debentures for a consideration other than cash *i.e.*, against building, machinery etc.

   (*ii*) Conversion of debentures into equity shares.

   (*iii*) Purchase of business by issue of shares.

   AS-3 (Revised) recommends that such transactions may be disclosed under footnote to cash flow statement.

6. **Investments in Subsidiaries, Associates and Joint Venture:** Acquisition of interest in any Subsidiary, associates or in any joint venture is treated as "Investing Activity". Similarly, sale or disposal of such interest and receipt of interest or dividends on such investments is treated as "Investing Activity".

Illustration 3: (Classification of Cash Flows)

Giving reason, classify the following into cash flows from:

1. Operating Activities;
2. Investing Activities; and
3. Financing Activities;

   (*i*) Cash sales of goods-in-trade;

   (*ii*) Cash paid to suppliers of raw materials;

   (*iii*) Cash payments of salaries and wages to employees;

   (*iv*) Cash payments to acquire a fixed asset, say, machinery;

   (*v*) Cash proceeds from issuing shares at a premium;

   (*vi*) Payment of dividends;

   (*vii*) Interest received on investment;

   (*viii*) Interest paid on debentures;

   (*ix*) Payment of income tax; and

   (*x*) Cash repayment of a long-term loan.

Solution:

1. **Cash Flows from Operating Activities:**

   (*i*) Cash sales of goods-in-trade: Normal business activity of selling inventories or goods-in-trade (cash inflow).

   (*ii*) Cash paid to suppliers of raw materials: Routine payments for purchasing the goods (cash outflow).

   (*iii*) Cash payments of salaries and wages: Cash payments to staff for their services in the office (cash outflow).

   (*iv*) Payment of income tax: Payment of tax on business income (cash outflow).

2. Cash Flows from Investing Activities:

(*i*) **Cash payment to acquire a fixed asset, say, machinery:** Purchase of long term asset (cash outflow).

(*ii*) **Interest received on investment:** It is an income on investments (cash inflow).

3. Financing Activities:

(*i*) **Cash proceeds from issuing shares at premium:** Issue of share capital along with the premium (cash inflow).

(*ii*) **Payment of dividends:** It is related to issue of share capital, a financing activity (cash outflow).

(*iii*) **Interest paid on debentures:** Payment associated with loan (or borrowed) capital (cash outflow).

(*iv*) **Cash repayment of a long term loan:** Redemption of loan or borrowed capital (cash outflow).

Illustration 4: The net income reported on the income statement for the year was ₹ 1,10,000 and depreciation of fixed assets for the year was ₹ 44,000. The balances of the current asset and current liability accounts at the beginning and end of the year are as follows.

Particulars	End of the year (₹)	Beginning of year (₹)
Cash	1,30,000	1,40,000
Debtors	2,00,000	1,80,000
Inventories	2,90,000	3,00,000
Prepaid Expenses	15,000	16,000
Accounts Payable	1,02,000	1,16,000
Calculate total cash from operating activities		

Solution: **Cash from Operating Activities**

Particulars	(₹)	(₹)
Net Income		1,10,000
Add: Depreciation		44,000
Operating profit before working capital changes		1,54,000
Add: Decrease in Inventories	10,000	
Decrease in prepaid expenses	1,000	11,000
		1,65,000
Deduct: Increase in Debtors	20,000	
Decrease is Accounts Payable	14,000	34,000
Net Cash Flow from Operating Activities		1,31,000

Illustration 5: **(Cash flow from operation-Indirect Method)**

From the following, calculate cash from operation by Indirect Method:

Profit and Loss Account for the year ended 31st March, 2013

		(₹)		(₹)
To Opening Stock		2,00,000	By Sales	45,00,000
To Purchases		36,40,000	By Closing Stock	2,40,000
To Wages	2,25,000			

		(₹)		(₹)
+ Outstanding	25,000	2,50,000		
To Manufacturing Expenses		75,000		
To Gross Profit c/d		5,75,000		
		47,40,000		47,40,000
To Salaries	1,37,500		By Gross Profit b/c	5,75,000
Add: Outstanding	62,500	2,00,000	By Rent Received	37,500
To Insurance	30,000		By Commission Accrued	17,500
Less: Prepaid	7,500	22,500	By Net Loss	55,000
To Office Expenses		1,17,500		
To Selling Expenses		1,45,000		
To Depreciation		1,25,000		
To Share Issue Expenses w/o		75,000		
		6,85,000		6,85,000

Solution: Calculation of Cash from Operating Activities
Indirect Method

Particulars	(₹)	(₹)
Net Loss as per Profit and Loss A/c (before tax and Extraordinary item)		(55,000)
Adjustments for Non-cash charges and Non-operating items		
Add: Depreciation	1,25,000	
Add: Share Issue Expenses w/o	75,000	2,00,000
		1,45,000
Less: Rent Received (Non-operating)		(37,500)
Operating Profit before Working Capital Changes		1,07,500
Adjustment for Current Assets/Liabilities:		
Add: Increase in Current Liabilities:		
Wages O/s	25,000	
Salaries	62,500	87,500
		1,95,000
Less: Increase in Current Assets		
Stock	40,000	
Prepaid Insurance	7,500	
Accrued Commission	17,500	(65,000)
Net Cash from Operating Activities		1,30,000

Illustration 6: (Cash Flows from Operating Activities)

X Ltd. has the following balance on 01.01.2013:

Particulars	(₹)	(₹)
Fixed Assets	15,00,000	
Less: Depreciation	(5,00,000)	10,00,000
Bank		87,500
Other Current Assets		6,25,500
Current Liabilities		2,50,000

Next year's estimate are:

(*i*) The company will acquire fixed assets costing ₹ 2,50,000 after selling one machine for ₹ 70,000, costing ₹ 1,50,000 on which depreciation provided will amount to ₹ 90,000.

(*ii*) The net profits will be ₹ 1,75,000 after providing for a depreciation of ₹ 1,50,000.

(*iii*) Current assets and current liabilities (other than bank balance) at 31.12.2013 are estimated to be ₹ 7,50,000 and ₹ 4,00,000 respectively.

At the end of the accounting year, the company deposits all the cash into the bank. Calculate the cash flows from operations and investing activities for the year 2013.

Solution: **Cash Flows from Operating Activities**

Particulars	(₹)	(₹)
Net Profit after Depreciation	1,75,000	
Add: Depreciation provided	1,50,000	
Less: Profit on Sale of Machinery	(10,000)	
Operating profit before working capital changes	3,15,000	
Less: Increase in Assets	(1,25,000)	
Add: Increase in Current Liabilities	1,50,000	
Net cash from operating activities		3,40,000

Cash Flows from Investing Activities

Particulars	(₹)	(₹)
Sale of Machine	70,000	
Purchase of Machine	(2,50,000)	
Net cash used in Investing Activities		(1,80,000)

Working Notes:

Calculation of Profit on Sale of Machinery: 70,000 – (1,50,000 – 90,000) = ₹ 10,000.

Illustration 7: (Cash from operating and Extra Ordinary Activities)

From the following information calculate cash from operations.

Profit and Loss A/c for the year ended 31st March, 2013

	(₹)		(₹)
To Opening Stock	1,50,000	By Sales	32,75,000
To Purchases	14,50,000	By Closing stock	3,25,000
To Wages	70,000		
To Gross Profit c/d	19,30,000		
	36,00,000		36,00,000
To Operating Expenses	11,10,000	By Gross Profit b/d	19,30,000
To Interest on Debentures	18,000	By Interest on Investments	15,000
To Depreciation	1,20,000	By Dividend Received	18,000
To Loss on Sale of Plant	40,000	By Profit on Sale of Land	20,000
To Discount on Issue of Shares	10,000	By Rent Received	12,000
To Goodwill w/o	15,000	By Refunds of Tax	8,000
To Provision for tax	30,000	By Insurance claims for Loss of Stock	1,25,000
To General Reserve	25,000		

	(₹)		(₹)
To Proposed Dividend	1,80,000		
To Interim Dividend	70,000		
To Net Profit	5,10,000		
	21,28,000		21,28,000

Additional Informations:

Particulars	31.03.12 (₹)	31.03.13 (₹)
Stock	1,40,000	1,00,000
Debtors	25,000	1,00,000
Creditors	15,000	50,000
Provision for Tax	50,000	60,000
Prepaid Expenses	18,000	20,000
Outstanding Salaries	20,000	25,000
Accrued Commission	15,000	30,000

Solution: **Cash Flow from Operating Activities**

Particulars	(₹)	(₹)
Net Profit before Tax and Extraordinary Items (1)		6,82,000
Adjustment for: Non-cash Charges and Non-operating Items		
Add: Depreciation	1,20,000	
Goodwill	15,000	
Discount on Issue of Shares	10,000	
Loss on Sale of Plant	40,000	
Interest on Debentures (2)	18,000	2,03,000
Less: Profit on Sale of Land (3)	20,000	8,85,000
Interest Received (3)	15,000	
Dividend Received (3)	18,000	(53,000)
Operating Profit before Working Capital Changes		8,32,000
Adjustment for Working Capital:		
Add: Decrease in Current Assets and Increase in Current Liabilities:		
Stock	40,000	
Debtors	35,000	
O/s Salaries	5,000	80,000
		9,12,000
Less: Increase in Current Assets and Decrease in Current Liabilities:		
Debtors	75,000	
Accrued Commission	15,000	
Prepaid Expenses	2,000	(92,000)
		8,20,000
Less: Tax Paid		(12,000)
Cash flow before Extraordinary Items		8,08,000
Add: Cash from Extraordinary Items [Insurance claims for loss of Stock (4)]		1,25,000
Net Cash Flow from Operations		9,33,000

Working Notes:

	Particulars	(₹)	(₹)
1.	Net Profit as per Profit and Loss A/c		5,10,000
Add:	Tax and Appropriations:		
	Provision for Tax	30,000	
	Proposed Dividend	1,80,000	
	Interim Dividend	70,000	
	General Reserve	25,000	3,05,000
			8,15,000
Less:	Tax Refund and Extra Ordinary Receipts (8,000 + 1,25,000)		1,33,000
			6,82,000

2. Interest on Debentures to be adjusted against Financing Activities.
3. Interest Received, Dividend Received, Profit on sale of Fixed Assets are covered by Investing Activities.
4. Insurance claims for loss of Stock is treated under Operating Activities while loss of assets under "Investing Activities".

Illustration 8: (Indirect Method)

The following data are provided for ABC Ltd:

Income Statement Data for 2013

Particulars	(₹)
Revenues	84,000
Cost of Goods sold	(48,000)
Depreciation Expense	(4,000)
Interest Expense	(6,000)
Other Expenses	(22,000)
Net Income	4,000

Comparative Balance Sheet Data

Liabilities	2013 (₹)	2012 (₹)	Assets	2013 (₹)	2012 (₹)
Liabilities			*Current Assets*		
Creditors	12,000	14,000	Cash	20,000	16,000
Non-current Note Payable	20,000	20,000	Debtors (net)	12,000	7,000
Less: Discount on Note	(1,600)	(2,000)	Stock in Hand	16,000	14,000
	30,400	32,000	*Non-current Assets*		
Owner's Equity			Plant and Machinery	24,000	20,000
Equity Share Capital	24,000	14,000	*Less:* Accumulated	(8,000)	(4,000)
Retained Earnings	9,600	7,000	Depreciation		
	33,600	21,000	Total Assets	64,000	53,000

Required: Prepare statement of cash flows using the Indirect Method as per AS-3 (Revised).

Solution:

ABC Ltd.
Cash Flow Statement for the Year ended 31st December, 2013
[AS-3 (Revised)] (Indirect Method)

	Particulars	(₹)	(₹)
(A)	**Cash Flows from Operating Activities**		
	Net Income before Tax	4,000	
	Adjustments for:		
	Depreciation	4,000	
	Amortisation of Discount on Note Payable	400	
	Interest Expense	6,000	
	Operating Profit before Working Capital Changes	**14,400**	
	Increase in Debtors	(5,000)	
	Increase in Inventories	(2,000)	
	Decrease in Creditors	(2,000)	
	Net cash provided by Operating Activities		**5,400**
(B)	**Cash Flows from Investing Activities**		
	Purchase of Plant and Machinery	(4,000)	
	Net Cash used in Investing Activities		**(4,000)**
(C)	**Cash Flows from Financing Activities**		
	Issue of Share Capital	10,000	
	Interest Paid	(6,000)	
	Dividends Paid	(1,400)	
	Net cash from Financing Activities		2,600
	Net increase in cash and cash equivalents (A + B + C)		4,000
	Cash and cash equivalents at the beginning of the period		16,000
	Cash and cash equivalents at the end of the period		20,000

Note: Dividends paid have been calculated as under:

Particulars	(₹)
Retained earnings at the beginning	7,000
Add: Net Income	4,000
	11,000
Less: Retained earnings at the End	9,600
Dividend paid	1,400

Illustration 9: (Direct and Indirect Methods)

From the following particulars, prepare Cash Flow Statement for the year ended 31st March, 2013 using:

(*a*) Direct Method

(*b*) Indirect Method

(a) Income Statement of Reliance Ltd. for the year ended 31st March, 2013

Particulars	(₹)	(₹)
Turnover		12,80,000
Less: Cost of Goods Sold		8,00,000
Add: Other Receipts		4,80,000
Insurance Claims for loss of Stock due to Fire		20,000
		5,00,000

Particulars	(₹)	(₹)
Less: Operating Expenses	3,16,000	
Interest on Debentures	6,000	
Depreciation	84,000	
Discount on Debentures w/o	400	4,06,400
Profit before Tax		93,600
Less: Provision for Tax		36,800
Profit after Tax		56,800

(*b*) The Asset and Liabilities as on 31.3.2012 and 31st March, 2013 were as under:

Particulars	30.03.2012 (₹)	31.03.2013 (₹)
Stock	72,000	88,000
Debtors	16,000	15,200
Bills Receivable	12,000	22,000
Cash and Bank Balance	44,800	99,200
Creditors	31,200	38,000
Bills Payable	8,000	6,000
O/s Expenses	12,400	17,600

(*c*) **Additional Information:**

(*i*) Fully paid Equity shares of the face value of ₹ 80,000 were allotted at a premium of @ 20%

(*ii*) Fixed assets were acquired for ₹ 60,000 and the payment was made in 6% convertible debentures at par.

(*iii*) Income Tax paid during the year amounted to ₹ 38,000.

(*iv*) Company paid a dividend and corporate dividend tax there on for the year ended 31st March 2012 amounting to ₹ 44,000.

(*v*) 9% Debentures for ₹ 1,20,000 were redeemed at a premium of 2%

Solution: (*a*) Cash Flow Statement (Direct Method)

Particulars	(₹)	(₹)
Cash Flow from Operating Activities:		
(*a*) Operating Cash Receipts:		
Cash from Customers (1)	12,70,800	
(*b*) Operating cash Payments (2)	11,22,000	
Cash Flow from Operations (a – b)	1,48,800	
Income Tax Paid	(38,000)	
	1,10,800	
Cash Flow from Extra Ordinary Items:		
Add: Claims Received	20,000	
Net Cash Flow from Operating Activities:		1,30,800
Cash Flow from Financing Activities:		
Issue of Shares at Premium (3)	96,000	
• Redemption of Debentures	(1,22,400)	
• Interest on Debentures	(6,000)	
• Dividend and Corporate Dividend Tax	(44,000)	

Particulars	(₹)	(₹)
Net Cash used in Financing Activities		(76,400)
Net Increase in Cash and Cash Equivalents		54,400
Cash and Cash equivalents in the beginning		44,800
Cash and Cash equivalents at the end		99,200
Financing and Investing Activities not affecting Cash flow—Issue of Deben-tures against Acquisition of Land		60,000

Working Notes:

(1) Receivables A/c (Debtors + Bills Receivables)

	(₹)		(₹)
To Balance b/d	28,000	By Cash Received (B.F.)	12,70,800
To Sales (Credit)	12,80,000	By Balance c/d	37,200
	13,08,000		13,08,000

(2) Payables A/c (Creditors + Bills Payable)

	(₹)		(₹)
To Cash paid	8,11,200	By Balance b/d	39,200
To Balance c/d	44,000	By Purchases*	8,16,000
	8,55,200		8,55,200

Operating Expenses A/c

	(₹)		(₹)
To Cash Paid (*Balancing figure*)	3,10,800	By Balance b/d	12,400
To Balance c/d	17,600	By Profit and Loss Account (Income Statement)	3,16,000
	3,28,400		3,28,400

*Purchases = Closing Stock + Cost of Goods sold – Opening Stock

Purchases = 88,000 + 8,00,000 – 72,000 = 8,16,000

Thus operating cash payment = 8,11,200 (To creditors)

and operating Expenses paid 3,10,800

11,22,000

	(₹)
(3) Face Value of Shares issued	80,000
Add: Premium @ 20%	16,000
	96,000

(3) Cash Flow Statement as per AS-3 (Revised) (Indirect Method)

Particulars	(₹)	(₹)
I. **Cash Flow from Operating Activities:**		
Net Profit before Tax and Extraordinary Item	73,600	
Adjustment for Non-cash and Non-operating Items Depreciation	84,000	

Particulars	(₹)	(₹)
Discount on Issue of Debentures	400	
Interest on Debentures	6,000	
Operating Profit before Working Capital Changes	1,64,000	
Adjustment for Current Items		
– Increase in Stock	(16,000)	
– Increase in Bills Receivable	(10,000)	
– Decrease in Bills Payable	(2,000)	
+ Decrease in Debtors	800	
+ Increase in Creditors	6,800	
+ Increase in o/s Expenses	5,200	
Cash generated from Operation	1,48,800	
Less: Income Tax Paid	38,000	
Cash Flow from Operation before Extraordinary Item	1,10,800	
Add: Insurance Claim for Loss of Stock	20,000	
Net Cash generated from Operation		1,30,800
II Cash Flow from Investing Activities	—	—
III Cash Flow from Financing Activities		
Issue of Shares at Premium	96,000	
Redemption of Debentures	(1,22,400)	
Interest on Debentures	(6,000)	

Particulars	(₹)	(₹)
Dividend and Corporate Dividend Tax	(44,000)	
Net Cash used in Financing Activities		(76,400)
Net Increase in Cash and Cash Equivalents		54,400
Cash and Cash Equivalents in the Beginning		44,800
Cash and Cash Equivalents at the end		99,200

Illustration 10: From the following details relating to the Accounts of Grow More Ltd. prepare Cash Flow Statement:

Liabilities	31.03.2013 (₹)	31.03.2012 (₹)	Assets	31.03.2013 (₹)	31.03.2012 (₹)
Share Capital	10,00,000	8,00,000	Plant and Machinery	7,00,000	5,00,000
Reserve	2,00,000	1,50,000	Land and Building	6,00,000	4,00,000
Profit and Loss Account	1,00,000	60,000	Investments	1,00,000	—
Debentures	2,00,000	—	Sundry Debtors	5,00,000	7,00,000
Provision for Taxation	1,00,000	70,000	Stock	4,00,000	2,00,000
Proposed Dividend	2,00,000	1,00,000	Cash on Hand/Bank	2,00,000	2,00,000
Sundry Creditors	7,00,000	8,20,000			
	25,00,000	20,00,000		25,00,000	20,00,000

(*i*) Depreciation @ 25% was charged on the opening value of Plant and Machinery.

(*ii*) During the year one old machine costing 50,000 (WDV 20,000) was sold for ₹ 35,000.

(*iii*) ₹ 50,000 was paid towards income tax during the year.

(*iv*) Building under construction was not subject to any depreciation.

Prepare Cash flow Statement.

Solution: **Grow More Ltd.**

Cash Flow Statement for the year Ended 31st March, 2013

Particulars	(₹)	(₹)
(A) Cash Flows from Operating Activities		
Net Profit before Tax and Extra-ordinary items*	3,20,000	
Adjustment for:		
Transfer to General Reserve	50,000	
Depreciation	1,25,000	
Profit on Sale of Plant and Machinery	(15,000)	
Operating Profit before Working Capital Changes	**4,80,000**	
Increase in Stock	(2,00,000)	
Decrease in Debtors	2,00,000	
Decrease in Creditors	(1,20,000)	
Cash generated from Operations	**3,60,000**	
Income Tax Paid	(50,000)	
Net cash provided by Operating Activities		**3,10,000**
(B) Cash Flows from Investing Activities		
Purchase of Fixed Assets	(3,45,000)	
Expenses on Building	(2,00,000)	
Increase in Investments	(1,00,000)	
Sale of Old Machine	35,000	
Net Cash used in Investing Activities		**(6,10,000)**
(C) Cash Flows from Financing Activities		
Proceeds from Issue of Shares .	2,00,000	
Proceeds from Issue of Debentures	2,00,000	
Dividend Paid	(1,00,000)	
Net Cash provided by Financing Activities		**3,00,000**
Net increase in Cash and Cash Equivalents (A + B + C)		Nil
Cash and Cash equivalents at the beginning of the year		2,00,000
Cash and Cash equivalents at the end of the year		2,00,000

Working Notes:

Provision for Taxation Account

	(₹)		(₹)
Bank (Paid)	50,000	Balance b/d	70,000
Balance c/d	1,00,000	Profit and Loss Account (B.F.)	80,000
	1,50,000		1,50,000

*₹ 40,000 + ₹ 2,00,000 (Provision for dividend) + ₹ 80,000 (Provision for Tax).

Plant and Machinery Account

	(₹)		(₹)
Balance b/d	5,00,000	Depreciation	1,25,000
Bank (*Balancing figure*)	3,45,000	Bank (Sale)	20,000
		Balance c/d	7,00,000
Total	8,45,000	Total	8,45,000

Illustration 11: (Loss on Machinery discarded)

Following are the Balance Sheets of Suhani Ltd. as on 31st March, 2012 and 2013:

Liabilities	2013 (₹)	2012 (₹)	Assets	2013 (₹)	2012 (₹)
Share Capital	4,00,000	3,00,000	Goodwill	90,000	1,00,000
General Reserve	1,00,000	80,000	Plant and Machinery	4,29,250	2,98,000
Profit and Loss A/c	50,000	30,000	Investments	60,000	1,00,000
Debentures	1,00,000	1,50,000	S. Debtors	1,10,000	1,60,000
Provision for Taxation	40,000	50,000	Stock	80,000	50,000
Proposed Dividend	40,000	30,000	Prepaid Expenses	5,750	4,000
Trade Creditors	70,000	90,000	Cash and Bank Balance	20,000	10,000
			Discount on Debentures	5,000	8,000
	8,00,000	7,30,000		8,00,000	7,30,000

Additional Information:

(*i*) Depreciation on Plant and Machinery has been charged @ 15%.

(*ii*) A machine costing ₹ 10,000 (W.D.V. ₹ 3,000) has been discarded. An old machine costing ₹ 50,000 (W.D.V. ₹ 20,000) has been sold for ₹ 35,000.

(*iii*) A profit of ₹ 10,000 has been earned by sale of investments.

(*iv*) Debentures have been redeemed at 5% premium.

(*v*) ₹ 45,000 income tax has been paid and adjusted against provision for taxation. Prepare Statement of changes in Financial Position-cash basis.

Solution: Statement of changes in Financial Position (Cash basis) for the year ended 31st March, 2013

Particulars	(₹)	(₹)
I. Cash Flow from Operating Activities		
Net Profit before tax and extraordinary items	1,75,000	
Adjustment for Non-cash and Non-operating Items:		
Depreciation	75,750	
Goodwill w/o	10,000	
Loss on Machine discarded	3,000	
Profit on Sale of Investment	(10,000)	
Profit on Sale of Machine	(15,000)	
Loss (Premium) on Redemption of Debentures	2,500	
Discount on Issue of Debentures	3,000	
Cash generated from Operation before Tax	1,84,250	
Less: Tax paid	45,000	
Cash generated from Operating Activities before Working Capital	1,39,250	
Adjustments for Working Capital		
Decrease in Debtors	50,000	
Increase in Stock	(30,000)	
Increase in Prepaid Expenses	(1,750)	
Decrease in Trade Creditors	(20,000)	
Net Cash Flow from Operating Activities		1,37,500
II. Cash Flow from Investing Activities:		
Sale of Investments	50,000	

Particulars	(₹)	(₹)
Sale of Machinery	35,000	
Purchase of Machinery	(2,30,000)	
Net Cash used in Investing Activities		(1,45,000)
III. Cash Flow from Financing Activities:		
Issue of Shares	1,00,000	
Redemption of Debentures	(52,500)	
Payment of Dividend	(30,000)	
Net Cash generated from Financing Activities		17,500
Net Increase in Cash and Cash Equivalents		10,000
Cash and Cash Equivalents at the Beginning		10,000
Cash and Cash Equivalents at the end		20,000

Working Notes:

(1) Profit and Loss A/c (Adjusted)

	(₹)		(₹)
To Provision for Tax	35,000	By Balance b/d	30,000
To General Reserve	20,000	By Net Profit before Tax and Extraordinary items	1,15,000
To Proposed Dividend	40,000		
To Balance c/d	50,000		
	1,45,000		1,45,000

(2) Plant and Machinery A/c

	(₹)		(₹)
To Balance b/d	2,98,000	By Depreciation*	75,750
To Profit on Sale (Tr. to P&L A/c)	15,000	By Bank (Sale)	35,000
To Bank (Purchased) (*Balancing figure*)	2,30,000	By Loss on Sale (Tr. to P&L A/c)	3,000
		By Balance c/d	4,29,250
	5,43,000		5,43,000

	(₹)
*W.D.V. as on 1.4.2012	2,98,000
Less: W.D.V. of Machine sold (20,000 + 3,000)	23,000
	2,75,000
*Depreciation @ 15%	41,250
W.D.V. after Depreciation	2,33,750
Cost of Machinery acquired	2,30,000**
*Depreciation on Machinery Purchased	34,500
W.D.V.	1,95,500
*Thus total Depreciation charged ₹ (41,250 + 34,500) =	75,750

**₹ (4,29,250 – 2,33,750) = $\left(1,95,500 \times \frac{100}{85}\right)$ = ₹ 2,30,000

Provision for Taxation Account

	(₹)		(₹)
To Bank	45,000	By Balance b/d	50,000
To Balance c/d	40,000	By Profit and Loss A/c (*Bal. figure*)	35,000
	85,000		85,000

Illustration 12: (Cash Flow Statement Indirect Method)

Presented below is the comparative Balance Sheets for Jyoti Ltd. at 31st March:

Particulars	2013 (₹)	2012 (₹)
Cash	40,000	57,000
Accounts Receivable	77,000	64,000
Inventory	1,32,000	1,40,000
Prepaid Expenses	12,140	16,540
Land	1,25,000	1,50,000
Equipment	2,00,000	1,75,000
Accumulated Depreciation-Equipment	(60,000)	(42,000)
Building	2,50,000	2,50,000
Accumulated Depreciation-Building	(75,000)	(50,000)
	7,01,140	7,60,540
Accounts Payable	33,000	45,000
Bonds Payable	2,35,000	2,65,000
Equity Share Capital (₹ 10 shares)	2,80,000	2,50,000
Retained Earnings	1,53,140	2,00,540
	7,01,140	7,60,540

Additional information:

(*i*) Operating expenses include depreciation expense of ₹ 70,000 and amortisation of prepaid expenses of ₹ 4,400.

(*ii*) Land was sold for cash at book value.

(*iii*) Cash dividends of ₹ 74,290 were paid.

(*iv*) Net income for 2006 was ₹ 26,890.

(*v*) Equipment was purchased for ₹ 65,000 cash. In addition equipment costing ₹ 40,000 with a book value of ₹ 13,000 was sold for ₹ 15,000 cash.

(*vi*) Bonds were redeemed at face value by issuing 3,000 Equity Shares of ₹ 10 at par.

Instructions: Prepare a Statement of Cash Flows for 2013 using the indirect method [AS-3 (Revised)].

Solution:

Jyoti Ltd.
Cash Flows Statement for the Year Ended 31st December, 2013
[As-3 (Revised)] (Indirect Method)

Particulars	(₹)	(₹)
(A) Cash Flows from Operating Activities		
Net Income	26,890	
Adjustments for:		
Depreciation	70,000	

Particulars	(₹)	(₹)
Amortisation of Prepaid Expenses	4,400	
Gain on Sale of Equipment	(2,000)	
Operating Profit before Working Capital Changes	**99,290**	
Increase in Accounts Receivable	(13,000)	
Decrease in Inventories	8,000	
Decrease in Accounts Payable	(12,000)	
Net Cash from Operating Activities		**82,290**
(B) Cash Flows from Investing Activities		
Sale of Land	25,000	
Sale of Equipment	15,000	
Purchase of Equipment	(65,000)	
Net Cash used in Investing Activities		**(25,000)**
(C) Cash Flows from Financing Activities		
Dividends Paid	(74,290)	
Net Cash used in Financing Activities		**(74,290)**
Net Decrease in Cash and Cash Equivalents (A + B + C)		(17,000)
Cash and Cash Equivalents at the beginning of the period		57,000
Cash and Cash Equivalents at the end of the period		40,000

Significant Non-cash Transaction

Redemption of Bonds in exchange for Equity Share Capital ₹ 30,000

Working Note:

Equity Share Capital Account

	(₹)		(₹)
Balance c/d	2,80,000	Balance b/d	2,50,000
		Bonds Payable Account	30,000
	2,80,000		2,80,000

Bonds Payable Accounts

	(₹)		(₹)
Equity Share Capital Account	2,35,000	Balance b/d	2,65,000
Balance c/d	30,000		
	2,65,000		2,65,000

SIGNIFICANCE OF CASH FLOW STATEMENT

Cash flow statement is important for a number of reasons.

1. First, by focusing on cash flows, it explains the nature of the financial events which have affected the cash position. This statement explains the reason for the difference between opening and closing cash balance.
2. The statement is important for financial planning purposes. For example, budgeted cash statements are a crucial element in the process of budget plans. These surpluses and shortfalls

are expressed sequentially over the planning period and require management to deal with the forecasted cash surplus or deficit, the former involving a short-term investment of surplus cash, the latter a short-term borrowing arrangement.

3. This statement bring into sharp focus the enterprise's earning capacity with its spending and operating activity. Accounting principles restrict the income statement to matching periodic revenues with the cost of earning those revenues. Statement of changes in cash is not restricted in this way; hence, it provides an extended view of the financial inflows and outflows by including both capital and revenue flows.
4. Cash flow statement provides an insight into the critical areas of financial management by identifying two important classes of cash flows, namely, operating cash flows and financing cash flows. This distinction draws attention to the net cash flows from operations and the net financing cash flows. The net operating cash flows classify the capability of the firm to support dividend payments to shareholders. It is these net cash flows which are of critical importance to investors and shareholders in predicting the amount of cash likely to be distributed in the future in the form of liquidation distributions or repayment of principal and in the evaluation of risk.
5. The significance of cash flow statement lies in the increased complexity of business activity. This complexity results in a greater disparity between the time when income and expense items are reported and the time when the related cash flows occur. It may also result in a greater variability of cash flows.

ICAI's AS-3 Cash Flow Statement contains the following explanations on the utility of cash flow statement:

1. Information about the cash flows of an enterprise is useful in providing users of financial statements with a basis to assess the ability of the enterprise to generate cash and cash equivalents and the needs of the enterprise to utilise those cash flows. The economic decisions that are taken by users require an evaluation of the ability of an enterprise to generate cash and cash equivalents and the timing and certainty of their generation.
2. Users of an enterprise's financial statements are interested in how the enterprise generates and uses cash and cash equivalents. This is the case regardless of the nature of the enterprise's activities and irrespective of whether cash can be viewed as the product of the enterprise, as may be the case with a financial enterprise. Enterprises need cash for essentially the same reasons, however different their principal revenue-producing activities might be. They need cash to conduct their operations, to pay their obligations, and to provide returns to their investors.
3. A cash flow statement, when used in conjunction with the other financial statements, provides information that enables users to evaluate the changes in net assets of an enterprise, its financial structure (including its liquidity and solvency) and its ability to affect the amounts and timing of cash flows in order to adapt to changing circumstances and opportunities. Cash flow information is useful in assessing the ability of the enterprise to generate cash and cash equivalents and enables users to develop models to assess and compare the present value of the future cash flows of different enterprise. It also enhances the comparability of the reporting of operating performance by different enterprises because it eliminates the effects of using different accounting treatments for the same transactions and events.
4. Historical cash flow information is often used as an indicator of the amount, timing and certainty of future cash flows. It is also useful in checking the accuracy of past assessments of future cash flows and in examining the relationship between profitability and net cash flow and the impact of changing prices.

LIMITATIONS OF CASH FLOW STATEMENT

Cash flow can be more precisely measured than can other concepts of funds because the valuation problem of cash are not as great as for other financial resources. However, movement of cash may be easily influenced. For example, payment of liabilities, may be temporarily delayed or marketable securities may be sold, increasing cash flow for a given period. This statement, since it does not cover non-cash items, is not useful in analysing changes in financial position of an enterprise. Cash and changes in cash are not adequate to measure change in financial position. For instance, an enterprise may possess very satisfactory financial (cash) position during a particular month. But if the firm has to pay creditors next month, or make payments for the plant purchased in the near future the cash position of the firm will be adversely affected. In this way statement of changes in financial position measured through cash only has drawbacks and does not indicate accurately the changes in financial position. The statement has utility for making short-term financial planning but for long-term planning this statement would not be useful. Because of the limited usefulness of statement of changes in cash, the preparation of statement of changes in working capital (popularly known as funds flow statement) has been suggested.

THEORY QUESTIONS

1. Why is cash flow statement a useful statement?
2. Identify the three major types of activities classified on a cash flow statement and gives examples of cash inflows and cash outflows in each classification.
3. What limitations of funds flow statement are overcome by a cash flow statement?
4. What are the purposes of cash flow statement?
5. Discuss the procedures in preparing a cash flow statement.
6. What are the two methods of determining cash flows from operations? Generally, which of these methods is preferable?
7. "A cash flow statement is required to explain changes in cash account balances between balance sheet dates." Explain this statement.
8. List the common sources and uses of cash in each activity area: operating, investing and financing.
9. Discuss the guidelines as contained in AS-3 on Cash Flow Statement.
10. Discuss the main features of AS-3. What changes have been made in this standard?
11. Distinguish between cash and cash equivalent.
12. Distinguish between cash flow from operating, investing and financing activities. Provide examples of each type of activity as per AS-3, show a preform a statement of cash flows.
13. Discuss the Direct Method and Indirect Method of preparing Cash Flow Statement.

EXERCISES AND PROBLEMS

1. **(Cash Flow from Operating Activities)**

   The following is the financial position of Aruna Limited:

Liabilities	2012 (₹)	2013 (₹)	Assets	2012 (₹)	2013 (₹)
Equity Share Capital	4,50,000	5,00,000	Goodwill	1,15,000	90,000
General Reserve	40,000	70,000	Land and Building	2,00,000	1,70,000
Profit and Loss Account	30,000	48,000	Plant	80,000	2,00,000

Liabilities	2012 (₹)	2013 (₹)	Assets	2012 (₹)	2013 (₹)
Proposed Dividend	42,000	50,000	Debtors	1,60,000	2,00,000
Creditors	55,000	83,000	Stock	77,000	1,09,000
Bills Payable	20,000	16,000	Bills Receivable	20,000	30,000
Provision for Taxation	40,000	50,000	Cash	25,000	18,000
	6,77,000	8,17,000		6,77,000	8,17,000

Additional Information:

(*i*) Depreciation of ₹ 15,000 and ₹ 25,000 have been charged on Plant, and Land and Building respectively.

(*ii*) An interim dividend of ₹ 20,000 has been paid in 2013.

(*iii*) An income-tax of ₹ 35,000 was paid during 2013.

Calculate cash from operating activities as per AS-3 (Revised).

[**Ans:** ₹ 1,35,000].

2. From the following particulars Calculate Cash from operating activities by applying:

(*a*) Direct Method

(*b*) Indirect Method.

Profit and Loss A/c for the Year Ended 31st March, 2013

	(₹)		(₹)
To Opening Stock	60,000	By Sales	6,00,000
To Purchases	3,00,000	By Stock (Closing)	85,000
To Wages	75,000		
To Gross Profit c/d	2,50,000		
	6,85,000		6,85,000
To Salaries	50,000	By Gross Profit b/d	2,50,000
To General Expenses	15,000		
To Insurance	10,000		
To Depreciation	75,000		
To Provision for Tax	30,000		
To Net Profit	70,000		
	2,50,000		2,50,000

Additional Information as on March 31st:

Particulars	2012 (₹)	2013 (₹)
Salaries o/s	5,000	7,500
Prepaid Insurance	5,000	5,000
Debtors	50,000	70,000
Bills Receivable	25,000	15,000
Creditors	35,000	25,000

Income Tax paid during the year amounted to ₹ 25,000.

[**Ans:** ₹ 97,500].

3. (Investing and Financing activities not affecting Cash)

The Following are the Balance Sheets of Huda Ltd. as on 31st March, 2012 and 31st March, 2013:

Liabilities	2012 (₹)	2013 (₹)	Assets	2012 (₹)	2013 (₹)
Share Capital	4,00,000	5,20,000	Goodwill	—	40,000
General Reserve	1,00,000	1,00,000	Land and Building	2,97,000	2,88,500
Profit and Loss Account	79,380	82,440	Plant and Machinery	2,25,900	2,32,400
S. Creditors	79,000	82,270	Stock	2,22,080	1,94,740
Bills Payable	67,560	23,050	Advances	4,630	1,470
Bank Overdraft	1,19,020	—	Debtors	1,70,350	1,45,250
Provision for Tax	80,000	1,00,000	Cash at Bank	5,000	5,400
	9,24,960	9,07,760		9,24,960	9,07,760

Additional Information:

(*i*) During the year ended 31st March, 2013, an additional dividend of ₹ 52,000 was paid.

(*ii*) The assets of another company were purchased for ₹ 1,20,000 payable in fully paid shares of the company. The assets consisted of Stock ₹ 43,280, Machinery ₹ 36,720 and Goodwill ₹ 40,000. In addition plant was purchased amounting to ₹ 11,300.

(*iii*) Income tax paid during the year was ₹ 50,000.

(*iv*) The net-profit for the year before tax amounted to ₹ 1,25,060.

Prepare Cash Flow Statement as per AS-3 (Revised).

Ans: Cash from operating activities: ₹ 1,82,720 Cash from investing activities: ₹ (11,300) Net-increase in cash and cash equivalents ₹ 400.

4. (Cash Flow Statement – General)

From the following particulars prepare a Cash Flow Statement as per AS-3 (Revised):

Liabilities	2012 (₹)	2013 (₹)	Assets	2012 (₹)	2013 (₹)
Share Capital – Shares of ₹ 10 each	4,00,000	4,00,000	Fixed Assets (Depreciating)	4,28,000	4,88,000
			Less: Provision for Dep.	(1,08,000)	(1,44,000)
Profit and Loss A/c	1,92,000	1,96,000		3,20,000	3,44,000
Loan from Bank	1,20,000	1,00,000	Fixed Assets (non-Dep.)	2,80,000	3,40,000
S. Creditors	1,44,000	2,44,000	Stock in Trade	1,00,000	88,000
			Debtors	1,40,000	1,53,600
			Cash and Bank	16,000	14,400
	8,56,000	9,40,000		8,56,000	9,40,000

*During the year the company paid a dividend of ₹ 1,04,000.

[**Ans:** Cash flow from operations: ₹ 1,62,400, Net decrease in cash and cash equivalents: ₹ (1,600)].

5. From the following Profit and Loss A/c Calculate Cash from operating activities:

	(₹)		(₹)
To Salaries	1,80,000	By Gross Profit b/d	5,40,000
To Rent	90,000	By Profit on Sale of Land	28,000
To Office Expenses	30,000	By Dividend Received	20,000
To Depreciation	24,000	By Income Tax Refund	8,000
To Loss.on Sale of Plant	12,000	By Rent Received	40,000
To Goodwill w/o	30,000		
To Discount on Issue of Debentures w/o	10,000		
To Preliminary Expenses w/o	8,000		
To Proposed Dividend	60,000		
To Provision for Tax	60,000		
To Net Profit c/d	1,32,000		
	6,36,000		6,36,000

Income Tax paid during the year amounted to ₹ 50,000.

[**Ans:** Cash generated from operating activities ₹ 1,98,000].

6. From the following information compute:

1. Cash flow from Operating activities
2. Cash flow from Investing activities
3. Cash flow from Financing activities.

(*i*) Sales made during the year (₹)

Cash—	2,00,000
Credit—	3,50,000
Purchases Cash—	Nil
Credit—	3,00,000

(*ii*) Salaries incurred during the year 62,500

(*iii*) Depreciation 1,50,000

(*iv*) Goodwill w/o 12,500

(*v*) Issue of 1,00,000 equity shares of ₹ 10 each at premium of 20%.

(*vi*) Issue of equity shares of ₹ 25,00,000 as purchase consideration of Building of ₹ 30,00,000

(*vii*) Purchase of Machinery for cash—4,20,000

(*viii*) Dividend of last year amounting to ₹ 1,00,000 was paid. Dividend of ₹ 2,50,000 was declared but not yet paid.

(*ix*) An equipment (Book value ₹ 50,000) sold for ₹ 60,000

(*x*) Closing Balances Debtors ₹ 85,000

Creditors—₹ 1,00,000, Salaries o/s ₹ 12,500

[**Ans:** Cash from Operating activities — ₹ 2,15,000

Cash used in Investing activities — ₹ (3,60,000)

Cash Flow from Financing Activities — ₹ 11,00,000

7. Following are the Balance Sheets of Rungta Ltd. as on 31st March, 2012 and 2013:

Liabilities	2012 (₹)	2013 (₹)	Assets	2012 (₹)	2013 (₹)
Equity Share Capital	12,00,000	12,75,000	Fixed Assets	11,10,000	12,60,000
Profit and Loss			Stock	1,35,000	1,05,000
Appropriation A/c	2,17,500	3,67,500	Debtors	2,47,500	2,92,500
Mortgaged Loans	—	75,000	Cash and Bank Balance	60,000	1,35,000
S. Creditors	1,35,000	75,000			
	15,52,500	17,95,500		15,52,500	17,92,500

Prepare Cash Flow Statement as per AS-(Rev.)

[**Ans:** Cash from Operating Activities — ₹ 75,000

Cash used in Investing Activities — ₹ (1,50,000)

Cash flow from Financing Activities — ₹ 1,50,000

Increase in Cash and Cash Equivalents — ₹ 75,000

8. (From Trial Balance: Indirect Method)

Usha Ltd. had the following condensed Trial Balance at the end of 31 March, 2013:

	(₹)		(₹)
Cash	7,500	Current Liabilities	15,000
Accounts Receivable	30,000	Long-term Notes Payable	25,500
Investments	20,000	Bonds Payable	25,000
Plant Assets	67,500	Capital Stock	75,000
Land	40,000	Retained Earnings	24,500
	1,65,000		1,65,000

During 2012–13 the following occurred:

(*i*) A tract of land was purchased for ₹ 7,750 cash.

(*ii*) Bonds payable in the amount of ₹ 6,000 were retired for cash at face and book value.

(*iii*) An additional ₹ 20,000 equity shares were issued at par for cash.

(*iv*) Dividends totalling ₹ 9,375 were paid.

(*v*) Net income for 2012–13 was ₹ 28,450 after allowing for depreciation of ₹ 9,500.

(*vi*) Land was purchased through the issuance of ₹ 22,500 in bonds.

(*vii*) Usha Ltd. sold part of its investments portfolio for ₹ 12,875 cash. This transaction resulted in a gain of ₹ 1,375 for the firm.

(*viii*) Current liabilities increased to ₹ 18,000 at 31.03.2013.

(*ix*) Accounts receivable at 31 March 2013 total ₹ 38,000.

(*x*) The cash balance at 31 March 2013 is ₹ 48,825.

Instructions: Prepare a statement of cash flows for 2012–13 with the indirect method [AS-3 (Revised)]. **[B. Com. (Hons.) Delhi 2003 (Adapted)]**

[**Ans:** Net cash from operating activities ₹ 31,575.

Net cash from investing activities ₹ 5,125

Net increase in cash and cash equivalent ₹ 41,325].

9. From the following Balance Sheets of Twenty First Century Ltd. and additional information prepare a Cash Flow Statement as per AS-3 (Revised):

Liabilities	2012 (₹)	2013 (₹)	Assets	2012 (₹)	2013 (₹)
Equity Share Capital	12,00,000	15,00,000	Building	8,00,000	7,60,000
General Reserve	3,00,000	3,50,000	Machinery	5,00,000	7,20,000
Profit and Loss A/c	1,00,000	1,50,000	Short-term Investments	3,00,000	4,50,000
9% Debentures	6,00,000	4,00,000	Inventories	4,00,000	4,70,000
Creditors	4,90,000	5,60,000	Debtors	6,70,000	5,30,000
Proposed dividends	1,20,000	1,80,000	Cash at Bank	2,20,000	3,30,000
Provision for Taxation	1,00,000	1,30,000	Prepaid Expenses	20,000	10,000
	29,10,000	32,70,000		29,10,000	32,70,000

Additional Information:

(*i*) Debenture were redeemed at a premium of 10% on 1st April, 2012.

(*ii*) Income tax paid during the year amounted to ₹ 1,40,000.

(*iii*) A machine which appeared at a W.D.V. of ₹ 80,000 was sold for ₹ 1,30,000 and a new machine costing ₹ 3,60,000 was acquired during the year.

[**Ans:** Net cash flow from operating activities: ₹ 5,66,000
Net cash used in investing activities ₹ (3,80,000).
Net increase in cash and cash equivalents ₹ 1,10,000].

10. From the summary cash account of X Ltd. prepare Cash Flow Statement for the year ended 31st March, 2013 in accordance with AS-3 (Revised) using the direct method and indirect method. The company does not have any equivalents.

Summary Cash Account for the Year Ended 31st March, 2013

(₹ '000)

	(₹)		(₹)
Balance on 01.04.2012	50	Payment to Suppliers	2,000
Issue of Equity Shares	300	Purchase of Fixed Assets	200
Receipt from Customers	2,800	Overhead Expenses	200
Sale of Fixed Assets	100	Wages and Salaries	100
		Taxation	250
		Dividend	50
		Repayment of Bank Loan	300
		Balance on 31.03.2013	150
	3,250		3,250

[**Ans:** Net cash from operating activities in ₹ (000): ₹ 250
Net cash used in investing activities ₹ (100)
Net increase in cash: ₹ 100].

11. From the following Balance Sheet of Kishore Ltd. prepare a Cash Flow Statement:

Liabilities	2012 (₹)	2013 (₹)	Assets	2012 (₹)	2013 (₹)
12% Preference Share Capital	—	90,000	Fixed Assets	7,38,000	7,20,000
			Less: Provision for Dep.	(1,98,000)	(2,70,000)
Equity Share Capital	7,20,000	8,10,000		5,40,000	4,50,000
General Reserve	36,000	45,000	Stock	5,40,000	6,30,000

Liabilities	2012 (₹)	2013 (₹)	Assets	2012 (₹)	2013 (₹)
Profit and Loss Account	18,000	21,600	Debtors	3,60,000	4,32,000
15% Debentures	1,08,000	1,17,000	Prepaid Expenses	5,400	9,000
S. Creditors	2,16,000	1,98,000	Cash and Bank	21,600	63,000
Bank Overdraft	2,25,000	1,22,400			
Provision for Taxation	54,000	75,600			
Proposed Dividend	90,000	1,04,400			
	14,67,000	15,84,000		14,67,000	15,84,000

Interest paid on debentures—₹ 16,200

Prepare Cash Flow Statement.

[**Ans:** Cash from Operating Activities — ₹ 43,200

Cash from Investing Activities — ₹ 18,000

Cash used in Financing Activities — ₹ 82,800

Net Increase in Cash and Cash equivalent — ₹ 1,44,000].

12. From the following condensed comparative Balance Sheets of Bangalore Mills Ltd. and additional information, prepare a Cash Flow Statement for the year 2013:

Liabilities	2012 (₹)	2013 (₹)	Assets	2012 (₹)	2013 (₹)
Share Capital	70,000	80,000	Plant and Machinery	62,000	66,000
Security Premium	9,000	11,000	Accumulated Dep. on Plant and Machinery	(37,000)	(26,200)
Retained earnings	23,820	30,820			
7% Mortgage loan	—	20,000	Building	95,000	1,16,000
Creditors	6,900	6,000	Accumulated dep. on building	(43,000)	(45,000)
Outstanding Salaries	2,000	1,400			
Provision for taxation	1,000	1,400	Land	10,000	12,000
			Stock	10,220	9,620
			Debtors	8,600	7,600
			Prepaid Expenses	720	800
			Cash	6,180	9,800
	1,12,720	1,50,620		1,12,720	1,50,620

Additional information:

1. Plant costing ₹ 16,000 (accumulated depreciation ₹ 14,800) was sold during the year for ₹ 1,200.
2. Building was acquired during the year at a cost of ₹ 21,000. In addition to cash payment of ₹ 1,000, a 7% mortgage loan was raised for the balance.
3. Dividend of ₹ 8,000 was paid during the year.
4. A sum of ₹ 13,900 was transferred to provision for taxation account in 2013.

[**Ans:** Net cash generated from operations: ₹ 21,420

Net cash used in investing activities ₹ (21,800)

Net cash from financing activities: ₹ 4,000

Net increase in cash ₹ 3,600].

13. Balance sheets of M/s Ram and Shyam as on January 1st, 2013 and 31st December, 2013, were as follows:

Liabilities	2013 (₹)	2013 (₹)	Assets	2013 (₹)	2013 (₹)
Creditors	40,000	44,000	Cash	10,000	7,000
Mrs. Ram's Loan	25,000	—	Debtors	30,000	50,000
Loan from Bank	40,000	50,000	Stock	35,000	25,000
Capital	1,25,000	1,53,000	Machinery	80,000	55,000
			Land	40,000	50,000
			Building	35,000	60,000
	2,30,000	2,47,000		2,30,000	2,47,000

During the year a machine costing ₹ 10,000 (accumulated depreciation ₹ 3,000) was sold for ₹ 5,000. The balance of provision for depreciation against machinery as on 1st January, 2013 was ₹ 25,000 and on 31st December, 2013 ₹ 40,000. Net profit for the year amounted to ₹ 45,000.

Required: Prepare a Cash Flow Statement [AS-3 (Revised)].

[**Ans:** Net cash generated from operations: ₹ 59,000

Net cash used in investing activities ₹ (30,000)

Net cash used in financing activities: ₹ (32,000)

Net decrease in cash: ₹ (3,000)].

19

FINANCIAL STATEMENT ANALYSIS

LEARNING OBJECTIVES

After reading this chapter, you should be able to:

- Understand meaning and objectives of financial statement analysis.
- Explain various techniques of financial statement analysis: horizontal analysis, vertical analysis, trends analysis, ratio analysis.
- Discuss meaning, significance and computation of different ratios of liquidity, movement of current assets, profitability, capital structure, market strength, growth and stability.
- Explain limitations of financial ratios.

MEANING OF FINANCIAL STATEMENT ANALYSIS

Financial Statement Analysis is an analysis which highlights important relationships in the financial statements. Financial Statement analysis embraces the methods used in assessing and interpreting the results of past performance and current financial position as they relate to particular factors of interest in investment decisions. It is an important means of assessing past performance and in forecasting and planning future performance. According to Lev[1]:

"Financial Statement Analysis is an information processing system designed to provide data for decision making models, such as the portfolio selection model, bank lending decision models, and corporate financial management models."

OBJECTIVES OF FINANCIAL STATEMENT ANALYSIS

The major objectives of financial statement analysis is to provide decision makers information about a business enterprise for use in decision-making. Users of financial statement information are the decision makers concerned with evaluating the economic situation of the firm and predicting its future course. Financial statement analysis can be used by the different users and decision makers to achieve the following objectives:

1. **Assessment of Past Performance and Current Position:** Past informance is often a good indicator of future performance. Therefore, an investor or creditor is interested in the trend

1. Baruch Lev, *Financial Statement Analysis, A New Approach*, Prentice Hall, 1974, p. 5.

of past sales, expenses, net income, cash flow and return on investment. These trends offer a means for judging management's past performance and are possible indicators of future performance. Similarly, the analysis of current position indicates where the business stands today. For instance, the current position analysis will show the types of assets owned by a business enterprise and the different liabilities due against the enterprise. It will tell what the cash position is, how much debt the company has in relation to equity and how reasonable the inventories and receivables are.

2. **Prediction of Net Income and Growth Prospects:** The financial statement analysis helps in predicting the earning prospects and growth rates in the earnings which are used by investors while comparing investment alternatives and other users interested in judging the earning potential of business enterprises. Investors also consider the risk or uncertainty associated with the expected return. The decision makers are futuristic and are always concerned with the future. Financial statements which contain information on past performances are analysed and interpreted as a basis for forecasting future rates of return and for assessing risk.

3. **Prediction of Bankruptcy and Failure:** Financial statement analysis is a significant tool in predicting the bankruptcy and failure probability of business enterprises. After being aware about probable failure, both managers and investors can take preventive measures to avoid/minimise losses. Corporate managements can effect changes in operating policy, reorganise financial structure or even go for voluntary liquidation to shorten the length of time losses.

   In accounting and finance area, empirical studies conducted have suggested a set of financial ratios which can give early signal of corporate failure. Such a prediction model based on financial statement analysis is useful to managers, investors and creditors. Managers may use the ratios prediction model to assess the solvency position of their firms and thus can take appropriate corrective actions. Investors and shareholders can use the model to make the optimum portfolio selection and to bring changes in the investment strategy in accordance with their investment goals. Similarly, creditors can apply the prediction model while evaluating the creditworthiness of business enterprises.

4. **Loan Decision by Financial Institutions and Banks:** Financial statement analysis is used by financial institutions, loaning agencies, banks and others to make sound loan or credit decision. In this way, they can make proper allocation of credit among the different borrowers. Financial statement analysis helps in determining credit risk, deciding terms and conditions of loan if sanctioned, interest rate, maturity date etc.

TECHNIQUES OF FINANCIAL STATEMENT ANALYSIS

Various techniques are used in the analysis of financial data to emphasise the comparative and relative importance of data presented and to evaluate the position of the firm. Among the more widely used of these techniques are the following:

1. Horizontal Analysis
2. Vertical Analysis
3. Trend Analysis
4. Ratio Analysis.

1. Horizontal Analysis: The percentage analysis of increases and decreases in corresponding items in comparative financial statements is called horizontal analysis. Horizontal analysis involves the computation of amount changes and percentage changes from the previous to the current year. The amount of each item on the most recent statement is compared with the corresponding item on one more earlier statements. The increase or decrease in the amount of the item is then listed, together with the per cent of increase or decrease. When the comparison is made between two statements, the earlier statement is used as the base. If the horizontal analysis includes three or more statements, there are two alternatives in the selection of the base. First, the earliest date or period may be used as the basis for comparing all later dates or periods; or second, each statement may be compared with the immediately preceding statement.

Figures 19.1 and 19.2 present the comparative balance sheet and profit and loss account respectively of a company with the amount of increase or decrease and percentage changes shown. The per cent change is computed as follows:

$$\text{Percentage change} = \frac{\text{Amount of change}}{\text{Previous year amount}} \times 100$$

Comparative Balance Sheet with Horizontal Analysis
ABC Company Ltd., Balance Sheet
December 31, 2013 and December 31, 2012

	(₹ in '000)		Increase Amount (₹)	Decrease percentage
	2013 (₹)	2012 (₹)		
Assets:				
Current Assets:				
Cash	161	192	(31)	(16.1)
Marketable securities	652	819	(167)	(20.4)
Receivables	2,346	2,050	296	14.4
Inventories	1,940	1,758	182	10.4
Prepaid Expense and deferred charges	578	312	266	85.3
Total Current Assets	5,677	5,131	546	10.6
Properties:				
Land, Buildings, Machinery and equipment less accumulated depreciation of ₹ 5,386 and ₹ 4,801	5,977	5,389	588	10.9
Long-term receivables and other non-current assets	488	258	230	89.1
	12,142	10,778	1,364	12.7
Liabilities:				
Current Liabilities:				
Payables	2,989	1,828	1,161	63.5
Taxes payable	156	268	(112)	(41.8)
Dividends payable	180	210	(30)	(14.3)
Total current Liabilities	3,325	2,306	1,019	44.2
Long-term Liabilities:				
Long-term Debentures	988	409	579	141.6
Other long-term Liabilities	219	203	16	7.9
Deferred Income-tax Liabilities	1,048	723	325	45.0
Total Liabilities	5,580	3,641	1,939	53.3
Ownership:				
Equity Capital	621	414	207	50.0
Preference Capital	312	520	(208)	(40.0)
Govt. Securities at Cost	(1,081)	(728)	(353)	48.5
Total Ownership	6,562	7,137	(575)	8.1
Total Liabilities and Ownership	12,142	10,778	1,364	12.7

Fig. 19.1 Comparative Balance Sheet with Horizontal Analysis

2. **Vertical Analysis:** Vertical Analysis uses percentages to show the relationship of the different parts to the total in a single statement. Vertical analysis sets a total figure in the statement equal to 100 per cent and computes the percentage of each component of that figure. The figure to be used as 100 per cent will be total assets or total liabilities and equity capital in the case of balance sheet and revenue or sales in the case of the profit and loss account.

Comparative Profit and Loss Account with Horizontal Analysis
ABC Company Ltd.
Income Statement for the year ended December 31, 2012 and December 31, 2013

	(₹ in '000)		Increase Amount	Decrease percentage
	2013	2012		
Sales	10,631	10,600	31	0.3
Costs and Expenses:				
Cost of Goods Sold	7,129	6,887	242	3.5
Selling and Administration Expenses	2,378	2,166	212	9.8
Total Costs and Expenses	9,507	9,053	454	5.0
Earnings from Operations	1,124	1,547	(423)	(27.3)
Unusual Charges	(563)	—	(563)	NA
Other Income and Expenses including Interest Expenses of ₹ 183 and ₹ 114	(31)	77	(108)	(140.3)
Earnings before Income Taxes	530	1,624	(1,094)	(67.4)
Provision for Income Taxes	198	701	(503)	(71.8)
Net Earnings	332	923	(591)	(64.0)

Fig. 19.2 Comparative Income Statements with Horizontal Analysis

3. **Trend Analysis:** Using the previous year's data of a business enterprise, trend analysis can be done to observe percentage changes over time in selected data. In trend analysis, percentage changes are calculated for several successive years instead of between two years. Trend analysis is important because, with its long-run view, it may point to basic changes in the nature of the business. By looking at a trend in a particular ratio, one may find whether that ratio is falling, rising or remaining relatively constant. From this observation, a problem is detected or the sign of a good management is found.

   Trend analysis uses an index number over a period of time. For index numbers, one year, the base year is equal to 100 per cent. Other years are measured in relation to that amount For example, an analyst may be interested in sales and earnings trends for the past five years. For this purpose, sales and earnings data of a company are given to prepare further the trend analysis or percentages.

ABC Company

Annual Performance					(₹ in '000)
	Year 1	Year 2	Year 3	Year 4	Year 5
Sales	202.0	215.0	243.0	320.0	415.0
Net Earnings	10.9	11.7	13.5	15.4	18.8

The above data show a fairly healthy growth pattern but the pattern of change from year to year can be determined more precisely by calculating trend percentages. To do this, a base year is selected and then the data are divided for each of the other years by the base year data. The resultant figures are actually indexes of the changes occurring throughout the period. If year 1 is chosen as the base year, all data for year 2 through 5 will be related to year 1, which is represented as 100%.

To create the following table, each year sales is divided—from year 2 through years 5—by ₹ 202, the year 1 sales. Similarly, the net earnings for years 2 through 5 were divided by ₹ 10.9, the year 1 net earnings.

Annual Performance (Percentage of base year)

	Year 1	Year 2	Year 3	Year 4	Year 5
Sales	100	106	120	158	205
Net Earnings	100	107	124	141	172

The trend percentages reveal that the growth in earnings outstripped the growth in sales for years 2 and 3, then fell below the sales growth in the last two years. It is clear in this analysis of comparative statements that a disproportionate increase in operating expenses emerged in year 5. One may analyse the year 4 data to determine if net income was affected for the same reason or if the reduced growth was caused by other factors.

4. **Ratio Analysis:** Ratio analysis is an important means of expressing the relationship between two numbers. A ratio can be computed from any pair of numbers. To be useful, a ratio must represent a meaningful relationship, but use of ratios cannot take the place of studying the underlying data.

   Ratios are guides or shortcuts that are useful in evaluating the financial position and operations of a company and in comparing them to previous years or to other companies. The primary purpose of ratios is to point out areas for further investigation. They should be used in connection with a general understanding of the company and its environment.

   Comparison of income statement and balance sheet numbers, in the form of ratios, can create difficulties due to the timing of the financial statements. Specifically, the profit and loss account covers the entire fiscal period, whereas the balance sheet is for a single point in time, the end of the period. Ideally then, to compare an income statement figure such as sales to a balance sheet figure such as receivable, we usually need a reasonable measure of average receivables for the year that the sales figure cover. However, these data are not available to the external analyst. In some cases, the analyst should take the next best approach, by using an average of beginning and ending balance sheet figures. This approach smooths out changes from beginning to end, but it does not eliminate problem due to seasonal and cyclical changes. It also does not reflect changes that occur unevenly throughout the year.

COMMON SIZE STATEMENTS

Common size statements involve expressing comparisons in percentages. Common size statements may be prepared in order to compare percentages of a current period with past periods, to compare individual business, or to compare one business with industry percentages published by trade associations and financial information services.

Common size financial statements contain the percentages of a key figure alone, without the corresponding amount figures. The use of percentages is usually preferable to the use of absolute figures. An illustration will make this clear. If company A earns ₹ 10,000 and Company B earns ₹ 1,000, which is more profitable? The answer is likely to be company A. However, the total shareholders equity of company A is ₹ 10,00,000 and company B is ₹ 10,000 the return on equity will be as follows:

$$\text{Return on Equity} = \frac{\text{Earnings}}{\text{Equity}}$$

$$\text{Company A} = \frac{₹\ 10,000}{₹\ 10,00,000} = 1\%$$

$$\text{Company B} = \frac{₹\ 1,000}{₹\ 10,000} = 10\%$$

Comparing the return on equity, it can be clearly said that company B is more profitable than company A.

The use of common size statements can make comparisons of business enterprises of different sizes much more meaningful since the numbers are brought to common base, *i.e.,* per cent. Such statement allows an analyst to compare the operating and financing characteristics of two companies of different sizes in the same industry.

Care must be exercised in the use of common size statements when the absolute figures are small, because a small absolute change can result in a very substantial percentage change. For example, if net profits last year amounted to ₹ 1,000 and increased this year to ₹ 5,000, this would be an increase of only ₹ 4,000 in net profits, but it represents a substantial increase in percentage terms.

Common size statements can be prepared in vertical analysis and horizontal analysis formats. In vertical analysis format, a figure from a year is compared with a base selected from the same year. For example, if advertising expenses were ₹ 10,000 in 2008 and sales were ₹ 10,00,000, the advertising expenses will be 1% of sales. In horizontal analysis format, the amount of an item (an account) is expressed in terms of that same account figure for a selected base year. For example, if sales were ₹ 8,00,000 in 2008 and ₹ 12,00,000 in 2009 then sales increased to 150% of the 2008 level in 2009, an increase of 50%.

FOCUS OF FINANCIAL STATEMENT ANALYSIS

Financial Statement Analysis involves evaluating different aspects of a business enterprise which are of great importance to different users such as management, investors, creditors, bankers, analysts, investment advisers etc. Generally, the following analyses are made while making financial statement analysis:

I. Liquidity or Short-Term Solvency Analysis
II. Analysis for Measuring the Movement of Current Assets
III. Profitability Analysis
IV. Capital Structure or Gearing Analysis
V. Market Strength or Investor Analysis
VI. Growth and Stability Analysis.

I. Liquidity or Short-term Solvency Analysis (or Ratios)

Liquidity or short-term solvency analysis aims to determine the ability of a business to meet its financial obligations during the short-term and to maintain its short-term debt-paying ability. The aim of liquidity analysis is for a company to have adequate funds on hand to pay bills when they are due and to meet unexpected needs for cash. If a business enterprise cannot maintain its short-term debt paying ability, obviously it cannot maintain a long-term debt-paying ability or long-term solvency. Shareholders also will not be satisfied with such a state of affairs of the company. Even a business enterprise on a very profitable course will find itself bankrupt if it fails to meet its obligations to short-term creditors.

Liquidity analysis mainly focuses on balance sheet relationships that indicate the ability of a business to liquidate current and non-current liabilities. The ratios that evaluate liquidity relate to working capital or some part of it, because it is out of working capital that debts are paid as they mature. The comparisons and ratios related to evaluating liquidity or short term solvency are as follows:

1. **Working Capital Position:** The working capital of a business is the excess of current assets over current liabilities; this is computed by subtracting current liabilities from the current assets. The resulting working capital figure is taken as one of the primary indications of the short-term solvency of the business. The working capital formula is as follows:

$$\text{Working Capital} = \text{Current assets} - \text{Current liabilities}$$

The current working capital amount should be compared with past amounts to determine if working capital is reasonable. Caution must be exercised, because the relative size of the firm may be expanding or contracting. Further, the absolute amounts of working capital are difficult to use in comparing companies of different sizes or in comparing such amounts with industry figures.

2. **Current Ratio:** Current ratio is sometimes referred to as working capital ratio or banker's ratio. Current ratio expresses the relationship of current assets to current liabilities. It is widely used as a broad indicator of a company's liquidity and short-term debt-paying ability. The current ratio formula is as follows:

$$\text{Current ratio} = \frac{\text{Current Assets}}{\text{Current Liabilities}}$$

Current ratio is a more dependable indication of solvency than is working capital. For many years, the guideline for the minimum current ratio has been 2:1. The assumption is even if the value of current assets declines by 50%, the firm can still pay its current liabilities. But now-a-days there has been a decline in the liquidity of many firms. It can be said that in some industries, a current ratio substantially below 2 is adequate, while some other industries may require a ratio much larger than 2. In general, the shorter the operating cycle, the lower the normal current ratio. The longer the operating cycle, the higher the normal current ratio. A higher current ratio enables a firm to pay off current obligations and thus provides adequate margin of safety to the creditors.

A company's current ratio can be compared with the company's past current ratios and with industry averages as well. Such comparisons can help in determining if the current ratio is high or low at this period in time. However, these comparisons do not indicate why the current ratio is high or low. Possible reasons for unsatisfactory current ratio can be found from an analysis of the individual accounts and items which make up the current assets and current liability.

Example: The following are the current assets and current liabilities in respect of two companies, Company A and Company B.

	Company A (₹)	Company B (₹)
Current Assets	4,50,000	1,60,000
Current Liabilities	1,50,000	80,000

The current ratio will be as follows:

$$\text{Current ratio} = \frac{\text{Current Assets}}{\text{Current Liabilities}}$$

$$\text{Company A} = \frac{₹\ 4{,}50{,}000}{₹\ 1{,}50{,}000} = 3{:}1$$

$$\text{Company B} = \frac{₹\ 1{,}60{,}000}{₹\ 80{,}000} = 2{:}1$$

3. **Acid Test Ratio or Quick Ratio:** The current ratio is generally used to evaluate an enterprise's overall short-term solvency or liquidity position. The current ratio does not take into account the make-up or composition of current assets. For example, a rupee of cash or debtor is considered more readily available to meet obligations than a rupee of inventory. The quick ratio is designed to overcome this problem by relating the most liquid assets to current liabilities. Cash, marketable securities or short-term investments, receivables and prepaid are included within the meaning of most liquid assets; inventory is excluded. The acid test ratio is as follows.

$$\text{Acid Test} = \frac{\text{Current Assets} - \text{Inventory}}{\text{Current Liabilities}}$$

It may be preferable to have a better view of liquidity by excluding some other items in current assets that may not represent relatively current cash flow. Examples of items to be excluded are prepaid and miscellaneous items such as assets held for sale. This is considered a more conservative manner of computing the acid test ratio and the formula of acid test ratio in this situation will be as follows:

$$\text{Acid Test} = \frac{\text{Cash + Marketable Securities + Net Receivable and Debtors}}{\text{Current Liabilities}}$$

Inventory should be removed from current assets when computing the acid test ratio. Some of the reasons for this are that inventory may be slow moving or possibly obsolete and parts of the inventory may have been pledged to specific creditors. For example, a winery has inventory that requires considerable time for aging and therefore a considerable time before sale. To include the wine inventory in the test computation would overstate the liquidity. There is also a valuation problem with inventory, because it is stated at a cost figure that is likely to be materially different from a fair current valuation. In summary, inventory should be left out of the computation because of possible misleading liquidity indications[2].

The usual guideline for the acid test ratio is 1.00. However, some industries may find that a ratio less than 1.00 is adequate, while others need a ratio greater than 1.00. For example, a typical grocery store sells only for cash and therefore does not have receivables. This type of business can have an acid test substantially below the 1.00 guideline and still have adequate liquidity.

Example: A firm has the following current assets and current liabilities:

	(₹)
Debtors	5,000
Inventory	20,000
Cash	5,000
Total current assets	40,000
Total current liabilities ₹ 20,000	

2. Charles H. Gibson, *Financial Statement Analysis*. South-Western Publishing Co. 1992, p. 236.

The acid test or quick ratio is as follows:

$$\text{Quick ratio} = \frac{\text{Quick Assets}}{\text{Current Liabilities}}$$

$$= \frac{₹\ 10{,}000}{₹\ 20{,}000}$$

$$= 0.5 : 1.$$

4. Cash Ratio: Liquidity of a firm can be viewed from an extremely conservative point of view and the short-term liquidity of a company may be measured through cash ratio. The cash ratio relates cash and marketable securities to current liabilities. The cash ratio is computed as follows:

$$\text{Cash Ratio} = \frac{\text{Cash + Marketable Securities}}{\text{Current Liabilities}}$$

Cash ratio is not given much importance unless a firm is in deep financial trouble. It is not considered pragmatic to expect a business enterprise to have enough cash and marketable securities to cover current liabilities. However, in the case of very slow-moving inventories and receivables and highly speculative companies, cash ratio is of great importance. A high cash ratio indicates that a business enterprise is not using its resource cash to best advantage. A low cash ratio reflects an immediate problem with paying bills.

II. Analysis for Measuring the Movement of Assets—Activity Ratios

Activity ratios also known as turn over ratios indicate the efficiency with which an enterprises's resources are to utilised. Liquidity or short-term analysis (current ratio and acid test ratio) will show misleading results if debtors are too high because of slow collections. Similarly, the current ratio will be misleading if inventory is not sold and thus remains at high levels. Since liquidity ratios (*i.e.,* Current ratio and acid test ratio) ignore the movement of current assets, it is necessary for short-term creditors to make an analysis of how fast the debtors and stock are turned into cash so that their claims can be met timely. Moreover, the over all profitability of the business depends upon: (1) the rate of returns of capital employed; and (2) the turnover, *i.e.,* the speed at which the capital employed in the business rotates. Hence, in order to find out which part of capital (*i.e.,* assets) is efficiently employed and which part not, different activity or turnover ratios are calculated. Mainly activity ratios include:

1. Capital turnover ratio
2. Assets turnover ratio
3. Net working capital turnover ratio
4. Inventory turnover ratio
5. Debtor's turnover ratio or Receivables turn over.

1. Capital Turnover Ratio: This ratio measures the effectiveness with which a firm uses its financial resources. It indicates the number of times the capital has been rotated in the process of doing business. This ratio is computed as follows:

$$\frac{\text{Net Sales (or cost of goods sold)}}{\text{Capital employed or Owners' Equity}}$$

Net Sales = Total Sales less returns (if any)

Cost of goods sold = Opening Stock + Purchases + Direct Expenses – Closing Stock

OR

Sales – Gross Profit

Illustration 1: A firm has opening and closing stock of ₹ 30,000 and ₹ 20,000 respectively. Its administrative and selling expenses are ₹ 10,000; Purchases ₹ 3,10,000; Sales ₹ 5,00,000; Debentures ₹ 50,000 (representing one-third of owner's equity). The capital turnover ratio is as follows:

$$\text{Capital turnover ratio} = \frac{\text{Cost of goods sold}}{\text{Owner's Equity}}$$

Cost of goods sold = Opening Stock + Purchases – Closing Stock

= 30,000 + 3,10,000 – 20,000

= ₹ 3,20,000

Capital or owner's equity = 3 times Debentures

= 3 × 50,000 = ₹ 1,50,000

$$\text{Capital turnover ratio} = \frac{3,20,000}{1,50,000} = 2.133 \text{ times.}$$

2. Asset Turnover Ratio: This ratio reveals the number of times the net tangible assets (*i.e.*, total assets less current liabilities less intangibles) are turned over during the year. Strictly speaking, average net tangible assets should be used in calculating this ratio. But, invariably net tangible assets at the end of the year is used.

$$\text{Asset Turnover} = \frac{\text{Turnover}}{\text{Net Tangible Assets}}$$

An improvement in asset turnover ratio as compared to the previous year indicates that the turnover of the company has improved. In cases where assets are not revalued or replaced, its magnitude will be decreasing over the years due to depreciation. Then, obviously, the ratio will be higher as turnover figures for the future will reflect an increasing trend.

Another form of assets turnover ratio can be computed as **fixed assets turnover ratio.** This ratio indicates the extent to which the investment in fixed assets have contributed to sales. If compared with a previous period, it indicates whether investment in fixed assets has been judicious or not.

The higher this ratio, better it is because it indicates higher efficiency indicating that investment in fixed assets has resulted in higher sales. A lower ratio may point to the under utilisation or non-utilisation of certain assets. The ratio is calculated as follows:

$$\frac{\text{Net Sales}}{\text{Fixed Assets less Depreciation}}$$

Illustration 2: The following details have been given for Messers ABC Ltd. for two years. You are required to find out Fixed Assets Turnover Ratio and comment on it.

	2012 (₹)	**2013 (₹)**
Fixed assets at written down value	15,00,000	30,00,000
Sales less returns	60,00,000	80,00,000

Solution: $\text{Fixed Assets Turnover Ratio} = \frac{\text{Sales}}{\text{Fixed Assets}}$

For 2012

= 60,00,000 ÷ 15,00,000

= 4 times

For 2013

= 80,00,000 ÷ 30,00,000

= 2.67 times

Comment: There has been decline in the Fixed Assets Turnover Ratio though absolute figures of sales have gone up. It indicates that increase in the investment in Fixed Asset has not brought about proportionate gain. However, before concluding, results for next two to three years must also be seen.

3. Net-Working Capital Turnover Ratio: This ratio indicates whether or not working capital has been effectively utilised in making sales. This ratio is computed by dividing the net sales or cost of goods sold by net working capital. Net working capital signifies the excess of current assets over current liabilities. The ratio is calculated as follows:

$$\frac{\text{Net Sales}}{\text{Networking Capital}}$$

A high net working capital ratio (if it is expressed in percentage) indicates efficient use of working capital and quick turnover of current assets like stock and debtors. A low ratio indicates low turnover of these assets.

4. Inventory Turnover Ratio: Inventory turnover measures the relative size of inventory and influences the amount of cash available to pay liabilities. A smaller, faster-moving inventory means that the company has less cash tied up in inventory. On the contrary, a build up in inventory means that a recession or some other factor is preventing sales from keeping pace with purchasing and production. Ideally, inventory should be maintained at an optimum level to support production and sales. Inventory turnover ratio is calculated by using the following formula:

$$\text{Inventory turnover} = \frac{\text{Cost of goods sold}}{\text{Average inventory}}$$

Average inventory is obtained using a simple average process by dividing the opening and closing inventory by the two. Cost of goods sold is obtained by deducting gross profit from sales.

Illustration 3: A firm has opening and closing inventory of ₹ 56,000 and ₹ 44,000 respectively. The firm has sold goods for ₹ 5,00,000 at gross profit margin of 20%. The inventory turnover ratio is as follows:

$$\text{Inventory Turnover} = \frac{\text{Cost of goods sold}}{\text{Average inventory}}$$

$$= \frac{₹\ 5{,}00{,}000 - ₹\ 1{,}00{,}000}{1/2\ (₹\ 56{,}000 + 44{,}000)}$$

$$= \frac{₹\ 4{,}00{,}000}{₹\ 50{,}000}$$

$$= 8 \text{ times per year}$$

5. Receivables Turnover Ratio: The ability of a company to collect for credit sales in a timely way affects the company's liquidity. The relationship between credit sales and accounts receivables may be stated as the receivable turnover. Receivables or debtors turnover determines the liquidity of one item of current assets and finds out how faster debts are being collected. The formula for computing receivables turnover is as follows:

$$\text{Receivable Turnover} = \frac{\text{Net Credit Sales}}{\text{Average Accounts Receivables or Debtors}}$$

Receivables turnover shows how many times, on average, the receivables were turned into cash during the period. A high debtors turnover ratio indicates shorter time span between credit sales and cash collection. This ratio requires one balance sheet account and one profit and loss account item. In case, credit sales figure is not given, total sales figure can be used to compute receivables turnover.

Illustration 4: A firm has opening and closing debtors of ₹ 40,000 and ₹ 75,000 respectively and credit sales of ₹ 3,45,000. The debtors turnover ratio is as follows.

$$\text{Debtors turnover ratio} = \frac{\text{Credit Sales}}{\text{Average Debtors}}$$

$$= \frac{₹\ 3,45,000}{₹\ 57,500}$$

$$= 6 \text{ times per year}$$

$$\text{Debt Collection period} = \frac{12 \text{ months}}{\text{Debtors turnover}}$$

$$= \frac{12 \text{ months}}{6 \text{ times}}$$

$$= 2 \text{ months.}$$

III. Profitability Analysis (Or Ratios)

The long-term survival of a business enterprise depends on satisfactory income earned by it. An evaluation of a company's past profits may give the investors, creditors and others a better understanding for decision-making. The profitability position also affects the liquidity position which is vital to creditors as well. These ratios are:

1. **Earnings margin:** It is the ratio of net income to turnover, expressed as a percentage.

$$\text{Earnings Margin} = \frac{\text{Net income}}{\text{Turnover}} \times 100\%$$

Earnings margin is not the same as margin of profits. Margin of profits refers to the direct operating results only and is the amount before income-tax and before non-operating income and charges. In earnings margin, only the final net profit is used.

Illustration 5: The Profit and Loss Account of ABC Pvt. Ltd. is given as follows:

ABC Pvt. Ltd.
Profit and Loss Account

Particulars	(₹)	Particulars	(₹)
Cost of Goods sold	30,00,000	Sales	50,00,000
Interest on Debentures	1,00,000	Income from Investments	1,00,000
Provision for Taxation	10,00,000		
Net Profit after Tax	10,00,000		
	51,00,000		51,00,000

Calculate Earnings margin.

$$\text{Earnings Margin} = \frac{\text{Net Profit after tax}}{\text{Sales (Turnover)}} \times 100\%$$

$$= \frac{₹\ 10,00,000}{50,00,000} \times 100 = 20\%$$

2. **Return on Capital Employed or Return on Investment (ROI):** This ratio measures profitability in relation to the total capital employed in a business enterprise. The terms invested capital, capital funds and total capital may be used interchangeably. It is a useful ratio when comparing the overall performances of companies, particularly where they have

different proportions of debt in their capital structure. This ratio would also show whether the company's borrowing policy is wise economically and whether the capital had been employed fruitfully. For example, funds have been borrowed at 8% and return on capital is 7½%, it would be better not to borrow (unless it is essential). It would also show that the firm had not been employing the funds efficiently. The business can survive only when the return on capital is more than the cost of capital employed in the business.

$$\text{Return on Capital} = \frac{\text{Profit before Interest and Tax}}{\text{Total Capital Employed}} \times 100$$

According to some analysts, short-term borrowings, such as bank loans, commercial paper, and deferred tax liability, should be included under capital. Current accrued payables which are not interest bearing should be excluded because their interest component is not observable.

Illustration 6: Given below is the Balance Sheet of ABC Co. Ltd. as on 31st March, 2013:

Liabilities	(₹)	Assets	(₹)
Equity Share Capital	20,00,000	Fixed Assets	30,00,000
Reserves	5,00,000	Current Assets	25,00,000
Surplus-Profit for the year	5,00,000	Discount on issue of Debentures	1,00,000
10% Debentures	10,00,000		
Current Liabilities	16,00,000		
	56,00,000		56,00,000

Find out Return on Capital Employed/ROI.

Solution: Return on Investment

$$= \frac{\text{Profit before Interest etc.}}{\text{Capital Employed}} \times 100$$

Profit before interest = Profit (given in b/s) + Interest on debentures
= 5,00,000 + 1,00,000 (10% of 10,00,000)
= ₹ 6,00,000

Capital Employed = Fixed Assets + Working Capital
= 30,00,000 + (25,00,000 – 16,00,000) = ₹ 39,00,000

OR

Capital Employed = Equity Share Capital + Reserves + Surplus
+ Long Term Debts – Discount on issue of Debentures
= 20,000 + 5,00,000 + 5,00,000 + 10,00,000 – 1,00,000
= 39,00,000

$$\text{Return on Capital/ROI} = \frac{6,00,000}{39,00,000} \times 100 = 15.4\%$$

3. **Return on Equity:** Return on equity is derived by taking net income and dividing it by the shareholders' equity. This indicates the return which the management is realising from the shareholders' equity and shows how effectively ordinary shareholder funds are being utilised by the management. As long as it is above the current interest rates, a company is doing fairly well.

$$\text{Return on Equity} = \frac{\text{Profit after taxation – Preference Dividends}}{\text{Ordinary Shareholders' funds}} \times 100\%$$

It is obvious that both the ratios—return on capital and return on equity—will be influenced when a company has raised new capital during the course of the year. That is, in other words, the ratios will be artificially low. Also, the ratios do not take into account the effect of financial leverage which undesirably tends to increase the variability of earnings for the ordinary shares. In fact, ordinary shareholders of a company having higher dose of borrowings expect large returns to compensate for the high levels of risk. Financial analysts, sometimes in such cases, find out the trade-off between higher earnings and increased variability of earnings to determine whether the management has chosen the optimum amount of financial leverage.

Illustration 7: Calculate Return on Equity (ROE) from the following information:

	(₹)
10% Preference Share Capital (fully paid-up)	10,00,000
1,60,000 Equity Shares of ₹ 10 each fully paid	16,00,000
Reserves and Surplus	64,00,000
Net Profit after tax	23,75,000

Solution: Returns on Equity $= \dfrac{\text{Net Profit} - \text{Preference dividend}}{\text{Equity Shareholders' Fund}}$

Preference dividend = 10% on 10,00,000 = ₹ 1,00,000

Equity Shareholders' funds:

	(₹)
Paid-up Equity Share Capital	16,00,000
Reserves and Surplus	64,00,000
	80,00,000

$$\text{Return on Equity} = \frac{23,75,000 - 1,00,000}{80,00,000} \times 100$$

$$\frac{22,75,000}{80,00,000} \times 100 = 28.44\%$$

IV. Capital Structure or Gearing Analysis (Ratios)

Gearing ratio, *i.e.*, the relationship of long-term debt to total capital is considered the most important by many investors and financial analysts. Popularly known as debt-equity ratio, this ratio has utility to many including shareholders creditors, business managers, suppliers and other user groups. Gearing ratios are used to indicate:

(*i*) The cushion of assets/profits available to holders of fixed income capital should assets/profits decline.

(*ii*) The gearing advantage of potentially higher assets/profits attributable to ordinary shareholders and the correspondingly higher risk which is incurred.

(*iii*) The scope for raising additional fixed-income capital at reasonable costs, from the point of view of the company.

The debt-equity ratio is computed as follows:

$$\text{Debt-equity ratio} = \frac{\text{Loan Capital} + \text{Preference Share Capital}}{\text{Net Tangible Assets}} \times 100$$

Net tangible assets (or total capital) is obtained by subtracting the intangible assets and the current assets from total assets. Loan capital plus preference capital constitute the amount of long-term debt. Alternatively, long-term debt can be derived by subtracting current liabilities from total liabilities. Other variants of Debt-Equity Ratio are as follows:

1. $\dfrac{\text{Long term Liabilities}}{\text{Equity (or net worth)}} \times 100$

2. $\dfrac{\text{External Equities}}{\text{Internal Equities}}$

3. $\dfrac{\text{Long-term Debts}}{\text{Owner's Equities}}$

4. $\dfrac{\text{Long-term Debts}}{\text{Shareholder's funds + Long term Debt}}$

Sometimes capital gearing is calculated in terms of debt to equity ratio and not total capital. Capital gearing ratios, calculated in these two manners, provide essentially the same information. It is desirable that the investors select a standard method and follow it consistently throughout. It is said that as a rule of thumb, one should not opt for a company whose long-term debt exceeds two-thirds of its total capitalisation. Debt equity ratio is very helpful in assessing a company—whether the company is marching steadily into or out of debt. In younger and aggressive companies, comparatively speaking the long-term debts may at times exceed the shareholders equity which means that a company will not be able to get out of the difficult situation easily. A company depending on large amounts of debt should manage and perform well to avoid any worse contingencies. Debt equity ratios should be analysed not for one but for many years to determine a trend. If it is found that equity component is continuously increasing than the long-term debt, there may not be any cause for concern.

Illustration 8: From the following, calculate debt-equity ratio:

	(₹)
Equity Share Capital:	
10,000 Equity Shares of ₹ 100 each	10,00,000
General Reserve	4,50,000
Accumulated Profits	3,00,000
Debentures	7,50,000
Sundry Trade creditors	4,00,000
Outstanding Expenses	1,00,000

Solution: 1. Debt-Equity Ratio

$$= \frac{\text{External equities}}{\text{Internal equities}}$$

$$= \frac{\text{Debentures + Trade Creditors + Outstanding Expenses}}{\text{Equity Share Capital + General Reserve + Accumulated Profit}}$$

$$= \frac{7,50,000 + 4,00,000 + 1,00,000}{10,00,000 + 4,50,000 + 3,00,000} = \frac{12,50,000}{17,50,000} = 0.71:1$$

2. Debt-Equity Ratio $= \dfrac{\text{Long term debts}}{\text{Owner's equity}}$

$$= \frac{\text{Debentures}}{\text{Equity Share Capital + General Reserve + Accumulated Profit}}$$

$$= \frac{7,50,000}{17,50,000} = 0.43:1$$

3. Debt-Equity Ratio $= \dfrac{\text{Long term debts}}{\text{Shareholder's funds + long term loans}}$

$$= \frac{7,50,000}{17,50,000 + 7,50,000} = \frac{7,50,000}{25,00,000} = 0.3:1$$

Interest Coverage Ratio: Interest coverage ratio determines the debt servicing capacity of a business enterprise keeping in view fixed interest on long-term debt. The formula for this ratio is:

$$\text{Interest Coverage ratio} = \frac{\text{Earnings before Interest and Taxes (EBIT)}}{\text{Interest}}$$

If a business enterprise is able to earn a return on the assets higher than the rate of interest on long-term debt, the enterprise makes an overall profit. However, if the enterprise runs the risk of not earning a return on assets equal to the interest cost of the long-term loan, the enterprise makes an overall loss. The interest coverage ratio measures the degree of protection creditors have from default on the payment of interest by the company.

Illustration 9: ABC Ltd. has earned net profit of ₹ 3,50,000 during the year 2012–2013. It has paid income tax ₹ 1,50,000 and interest on debentures as ₹ 1,25,000. The interest coverage ratio may be calculated as follows:

$$\frac{\text{Earnings before Interest and Taxes (EBIT)}}{\text{Interest}}$$

$$\frac{3,50,000 + 1,50,000 + 1,25,000}{1,25,000}$$

$$= \frac{6,25,000}{1,25,000} = 5 \text{ times}$$

V. Market Strength Analysis or Investor Analysis

The market strength analysis or investor analysis are especially important for investors while analysing information about a company. This analysis helps the investors to decide about a company as an investment opportunity at a point of time. These ratios are also known as stock market ratios, investment ratios or market test ratios. The ratios under this category are as follows:

1. **Earnings per share:** Earnings per share is derived by dividing the profit of a company by the total number of shares outstanding. Earnings here means the net profit, net income or the net earnings. This is the amount by which the total revenues exceed the total expenses for the year.

$$\text{Earnings after Tax} = \frac{\text{Earnings after tax} - \text{Preference dividends}}{\text{Number of ordinary shares}}$$

The net earnings figure is the amount which is completely free from any obligations and the company can plough it back into the company, pay to the ordinary shareholders as dividends or a combination of both. This amount is also known as the earnings available for ordinary shareholders.

Illustration 10: Net profit before tax ₹ 1,00,000

Tax rate –40% of Net Profit

10% Preference Share Capital (₹ 10 each)	₹ 1,00,000
Equity Share Capital (₹ 10 per share)	₹ 1,00,000

$$\text{Earnings per Share} = \frac{\text{Net Profit after Tax and Pre. Dividend}}{\text{Number of Equity Shares}}$$

$$= \frac{₹\ 1,00,000 - 40,000\ (\text{Tax}) - 10,000\ (\text{Pref. Div.})}{10,000}$$

$$= \frac{50,000}{10,000} = ₹\ 5 \text{ per share}$$

Earnings per share can either be primary or diluted. Primary earnings per share is the earnings per share for the number of ordinary shares outstanding as on the beginning of the report period. Diluted earnings per share, on the other hand, is calculated after taking into account convertible debentures, bonds etc. (which have been converted into ordinary shares) during the year. It is computed in the same manner as primary earnings per share except that it assumes that all investments with the convertibility clause were converted at the beginning of the year. In case a company has bonds and debentures which are convertible into ordinary shares, it is always useful to compute fully diluted earnings per share (assuming full conversion) as well as earnings per share on a normal basis. This implies adding back the interest paid on the convertibles, recalculating the numerator and then dividing by the total number of ordinary shares on the assumption that conversion has taken place.

2. **Dividend per share:** The dividend per share can be net or gross, Net dividend per share is the dividend declared on a single ordinary share for the year, the net of basic rate tax.

$$\text{Net Dividend Per share} = \frac{\text{Ordinary dividends paid to ordinary shareholders}}{\text{Number of ordinary shares}}$$

Gross Dividend Per share is net dividend per share together with the associated tax credit.

$$\text{Gross Dividend Per share} = \frac{\text{Net dividend per share}}{\text{1-Basic rate of tax}}$$

Alternatively Gross Dividend Per Share = Net Dividend Per Share + Associated Tax Credit

3. **Gross Dividend yield:** The gross dividend yield is the gross dividend per share divided by the ordinary share price, expressed as percentage.

$$\text{Gross Dividend yield} = \frac{\text{Gross dividend per share}}{\text{Ordinary share price}} \times 100\%$$

For example, it a company declares dividend at 20% on its shares, each having a paid-up value of ₹ 8 and market price of ₹ 25, the dividend yield ratio will be calculated as follows:

$$\text{Dividend per share} = \frac{20}{100} \times 8 = ₹\ 1.60$$

$$\text{Dividend yield ratio} = \frac{\text{Dividend per share}}{\text{Market price per share}} \times 100 = \frac{1.6}{25} \times 100 = 6.4\%$$

The gross dividend yield indicates the current level of income from a share. Dividend yields are normally calculated using gross dividends rather than net dividends because it helps in better analysis and comparison with other types of investments. Also, investors pay income-tax at rates other than the basic rate. If the dividend yield is calculated on a net basis, the level of tax rate which has been deducted should be made clear.

Besides indicating the general level of the market, dividend yield reflects the market estimates of future dividend growth and risk. The higher the dividend growth expectations for a given share, the lower the current yield; the higher the market's estimate of risk, the greater the current yield.

4. **Dividend Cover:** Dividend cover denotes the number of times the dividend per share is covered by earnings per share

$$\text{Dividend cover} = \frac{\text{Earnings per share}}{\text{Dividend per share}}$$

Dividend cover helps in assessing the prospects for dividend increases. Or, alternatively, the possibility of a dividend cut, should profits decline. For the purpose of dividend cover, full distribution earnings per share is normally taken into account. In other words, it is assumed that all profits are distributed as dividends. The gross dividends per share should be taken to ensure consistency in the resulting figure of dividend cover.

5. **Payout ratio:** Payout ratio measures the proportion of earnings per share which are paid out as dividends.

$$\text{Payout ratio} = \frac{\text{Net dividend per share}}{\text{Net earnings per share}} \times 100\%$$

The percentage of available earnings paid out as ordinary dividends has a vital influence on the market's behaviour towards those issues which are not in the growth category. For those companies which have paid dividends in the form of stock dividends and cash, only the cash dividend should be included in calculating the payout ratio, In the case of dividends paid out as stock dividends, the investor receives nothing that was not already owned and the company gives up nothing of value.

Illustration 11: Compute the Pay-out-Ratio and Retained Earning Ratio from the following data:

	(₹)		(₹)
Net Profit	20,000	No. of Equity Shares	3,000
Provision for tax	10,000	Dividend per Equity Share	Re 0.80
Preference Dividend	4,000		

Solution: Payout ratio

$$= \frac{\text{Dividend per equity share}}{\text{Earnings per equity share}} \times 100$$

$$\text{Earnings per share} = \frac{\text{Profit available to equity Shareholders}}{\text{No. of equity share}}$$

$$= \frac{20,000 - 10,000 - 4,000}{3,000} = \frac{6,000}{3,000}$$

$$= 2$$

$$\text{Dividend Payout Ratio} = \frac{₹\ 0.80}{2} \times 100 = 40\%$$

$$\text{Retained Earnings Ratio} = \frac{\text{Retained Earnings}}{\text{Total Earnings (after tax and pref. div.)}} \times 100$$

Retained Earnings = Profit available for Equity shareholders – Dividends paid

= 6,000 – 2,400 = ₹ 3,600

$$\text{Retained Earnings Ratio} = \frac{3,600}{6,000} \times 100 = 60\%$$

6. **Dividends to Cashflow:** Dividends to cash flow is a more useful ratio than the payout ratio. It helps in understanding the past trend in this regard and is greatly helpful in estimating future dividends, than the conventional payout ratio.

$$\text{Dividend to Cash flow} = \frac{\text{Dividend paid on ordinary shares}}{\text{Net earnings available for ordinary share}}$$

7. **Price/Earnings (P/E) Ratio:** It is the market price of shares expressed as a multiple of earnings per share.

$$\text{Price Earnings (P/E) Ratio} = \frac{\text{Price per ordinary share}}{\text{Earnings per share}}$$

Many investors consider P/E ratio as the best indicator of the ongoing performance of a company. This ratio along with the payout ratio indicates the market estimates of future dividend growth and risk. High growth shares have high P/E ratios as investors are willing to pay a greater multiple of current earnings to achieve a higher future growth. If high risk is found in a share, it reduces its market price and hence automatically reduces its P/E ratio. Payout ratios can have a positive influence on P/E ratio. High P/Es are not always bad. If investors are willing to pay a high price for a share in relation to its earnings, then they are doing so in the belief that the company has a bright future. That it will continue to strengthen and grow in future. Buying a share with a high P/E is described as buying a security with a high multiple. It should be understood that the common share dividends come out of the earnings per share. A drop in earnings could mean that a dividend is in trouble.

The elements which govern the P/E ratio are:

(*i*) Those factors that are fully reflected in the financial data (tangible factors)—Growth of earnings and sales in the past; profitability or rate of returns on invested capital; stability of past earnings; Dividend rate and record, and; financial strength or credit standing.

(*ii*) Those factors that are reflected to an indefinite extent in the data (intangible factors)—Quality of management; Nature and prospects of the industry, and competitive position and individual prospects of the company.

8. Net asset value per share: This ratio is also known as the book value per share. Net asset value per share is the value of net tangible assets attributable to one ordinary share. Net asset value is, simply put, the shareholders' equity. Net asset value or book value has nothing to do with the market value as share usually sell in the stock market at several times its net asset or book value.

Net Asset Value per share

$$= \frac{\text{Ordinary share capital + Reserves − Intangibles}}{\text{Number of ordinary shares outstanding at Balance Sheet date}}$$

Net asset value applies to ordinary shares only. However, it does not mean that investors can get that amount if the company is liquidated. The amounts attributed to the assets are only attempts at fair and systematic evaluation, not at guessing what these assets would bring if sold in the market place. Net asset or book value can be considered only as the theoretical value of ordinary shares if the assets of the company were liquidated at the amounts attributed to them on the balance sheet. It is not unusual for a share price to be very different from the net asset value per share, even where assets in the balance sheet have recently been revalued. In general, the market price of a share will be influenced by earnings and the dividend-paying potential. Share price will not be significantly influenced by the net asset value per share except where:

(*a*) The company is an investment vehicle for specific types of assets (*e.g.*, investment trusts, property companies).

(*b*) It seems probable that the company will be liquidated.

(*c*) A takeover bid of the company seems likely.

The net asset value per share figure is useful while comparing shares of one company with shares of other companies operating in the same industry. If it is found that a company is selling shares at a much lower ratio of market price to book value than other companies in the same industry, it indicates a good investment opportunity. When a share can be bought for less than its net asset value, it is an indication that share will have good value in the future. In case of mutual funds, net asset value ratio is important as it is determined at or near the price at which the mutual fund will buy and sell its shares. In the stock market, it is often found that a share is selling five times, seven times (and more) its book value. The lower the multiple, the greater will be probable value of the share.

9. **Cash flow per share:** Cash flow per share is a useful indicator of a company's general ability to leverage itself, to pay dividends, to convert accounting earnings into cash and to enjoy financial flexibility.

$$\text{Cash flow per share} = \frac{\text{Cash flow from operations after taxes}}{\text{Ordinary shares outstanding at Balance Sheet date}}$$

The amount of cash flow does not totally belong to ordinary shareholders, as the earnings belong; it is also meant to pay the expenses and claims prior to the payment of dividend.

VI. Growth and Stability Analysis or Ratios

Growth and stability ratios measure the performance and financial strength of a company apart from market valuation. Stability ratios are useful in evaluating the quality of bonds, debentures, preference shares, etc. These ratios are calculated over time and relate to sales, total returns, and earnings per share. Such ratios are:

(1) Growth in sales $= \dfrac{\text{Sales in final period}}{\text{Sales in base period}}$

(2) Growth in Total Returns $= \dfrac{\text{Net earned for total capital in final period}}{\text{Net earned for total capital in base period}}$

(3) Growth in earnings $= \dfrac{\text{Earnings per share in final period}}{\text{Earnings per share in base period}}$

(4) Maximum decline in coverage of interest charges

$$= \frac{\text{Worst year (or lowest year)}}{\text{Average of previous three years}}$$

Normally interest charges may include any of the following combinations:

— Interest on short and long-term debts, including capital leases.

— Interest on expenses plus an interest component for Operating leases.

— Interest on expenses on short and long-term debts plus rentals on both capital and operating bases.

— Total fixed charges, rentals and preferred dividends.

(5) Per cent decline in return on total capital

$$= \frac{\text{Worst year (or lowest year)}}{\text{Average of previous three years}}$$

(6) Per cent decline in return on ordinary capital

$$= \frac{\text{Worst year (or lowest year)}}{\text{Average of previous three years}}$$

(7) Percentage decline in earning per share

$$= \frac{\text{Worst year (or lowest year)}}{\text{Average of previous three years}}$$

LIMITATIONS OF FINANCIAL RATIOS

Financial statement analysis through ratios is useful because they highlight relationships between items in the financial statements. However, they have a number of limitations which should be kept in mind while preparing or using them.

1. Ratios are based on accounting figures given in the financial statements. However, accounting figures are themselves subject to deficiencies, approximations, diversity in practice or even manipulation to some extent. Therefore ratios are not very helpful in drawing reliable conclusions.
2. Ratios have inherent problem of comparability. Companies otherwise similar may employ different accounting methods, which can cause problems in comparing certain key relationships. For example, inventory turnover can be different for a company using FIFO than for the other company using LIFO method of inventory valuation. Similarly the differences in accounting methods relating to depreciation, estimates of the life of asset, amortisation of intangibles and preliminary expenses, treatment of extraordinary items etc. can create the problem of comparability among the companies even in the same industry.
3. Inflation may limit the utility of accounting ratios. Due to inflation, historical cost-based financial statements and accounting figures do not reflect current value figures, especially in the case of assets purchased at different dates by the different enterprises. Since financial statements are not adjusted in terms of inflation effect, accounting ratios calculated (using varying cost or prices) have distortions and become deceptive. Sometimes, gains (reflected through ratios) over time in sales, net income and other key figures disappear when the accounting data are adjusted for changes in price levels.
4. Accounting ratios are not totally dependable and they must be used after giving due weightage to general economic conditions, industry situation, position of firms within the industry, mode of operations, size of firm, diversity of product which can make the business enterprises completely dissimilar and thus affect the computation of accounting ratios.
5. The different methods of computation also influence the utility of accounting ratios. The different concepts used for determining numerator and denominator in a particular accounting ratio will not help in drawing reliable conclusions even in identical situations.

Illustration 12: The working capital of ABC Ltd. has deteriorated in recent years and now stands as under:

Currents Assets	(₹)	Current Liabilities	(₹)
Inventory	5,60,000	Creditors	4,90,000
Debtors	3,50,000	Bank loan	2,10,000
Cash	70,000		
	9,80,000		9,80,000

(*a*) Compute the current and quick ratios.

(*b*) A further bank loan of ₹ 50,000 against debtors is under negotiation. Assuming the loan is received, calculate the revised current and quick ratios.

(*c*) There is also a negotiation going on for discounting the debtors of ₹ 3,50,000 for ₹ 3,15,000 to a collection agency for immediate cash. Also obsolete stocks worth ₹ 1,25,000 are being sold for ₹ 80,000. Of the cash to be realised by the two transactions, the bank loan is proposed to be reduced to ₹ 1,00,000. Calculate the current ratio after the transactions are put through.

Solution:

(*a*) Current ratio $= \dfrac{\text{Current Assets}}{\text{Current Liabilities}} = \dfrac{9,80,000}{7,00,000} = 1.4$

Quick ratio $= \dfrac{\text{Liquid Assets}}{\text{Current Liabilities}} = \dfrac{4,20,000}{7,00,000} = 0.6$

(*b*) Revised current ratio $= \dfrac{10,30,000}{7,50,000} = 1.37$

Revised quick ratio $= \dfrac{4,70,000}{7,50,000} = 0.63$

(*c*) Financial position after the transactions:

Current Assets	(₹)	Current Liabilities	(₹)
Inventory	4,35,000	Creditors	4,90,000
Debtors		Bank Loan	1,00,000
Cash	3,55,000		
	7,90,000		7,90,000

New current ratio $= \dfrac{7,90,000}{5,90,000} = 1.34$

New quick ratio $= \dfrac{3,55,000}{5,90,000} = 0.6$

Cash balance = ₹ 70,000 + ₹ 3,15,000 + ₹ 80,000 – ₹ 1,10,000
= ₹ 3,55,000

Illustration 13: From the following annual account of New Horizon Limited you are required to calculate the following ratios and comment on the results, indicating what other information you require:

(*i*) Gross profit percentage
(*ii*) Net profit percentage
(*iii*) Return on total assets
(*iv*) Quick assets ratio
(*v*) Debtors collection period
(*vi*) Stock turnover
(*vii*) Fixed assets turnover
(*viii*) Return on shareholders' funds
(*ix*) Current ratio
(*x*) Debt ratio.

Balance Sheet at 31st December, 2013

	(₹ '000)
Share capital	450
Retained profits	240
	690
12% Debentures	700

	(₹ '000)
Trade Creditors	620
Proposed Dividend	45
	2,055
Fixed assets net of depreciation	875
Stocks	310
Debtors	770
Bank Balance	100
	2,055

Extracts from year's Profit and Loss Account

	(₹)
Sales for the year	31,00,000
Gross profit	17,25,000
Expenses	8,05,000
Depreciation	2,50,000

Solution:

(*i*) Gross profit percentage $= \dfrac{1725}{3100} \times 100\% = 55.6\%$

(*ii*) Net profit percentage $= \dfrac{670}{3100} \times 100\% = 21.6\%$

(*iii*) Return on total assets $= \dfrac{670}{2055} \times 100\% = 32.6\%$

(*iv*) Quick ratio $= \dfrac{870}{665} = 1.3 : 1$

(*v*) Debtors collection period $= \dfrac{770}{3100} \times 365 = 91$ days

(*vi*) Stock: turnover $= \dfrac{3100}{310} = 10$ times

(*vii*) Fixed assets: turnover $= \dfrac{3100}{875} = 3.5$ times

(*viii*) Return on shareholders' funds $= \dfrac{586}{690} \times 100\% = 84.9\%$

(*ix*) Current ratio $= \dfrac{1180}{665} = 1.8 : 1$

(*x*) Debt ratio $= \dfrac{1365}{2065} \times 100\% = 66.4\%$

Very few ratios have an absolute value but they are used in a relative way in intra and inter-firm comparisons. Both gross and net margins are calculated using the profit before tax and interest to identify the trading profit, irrespective of the capital structure in force. Both these figures seem satisfactory but knowledge of the industry is necessary. Also the returns on shareholders' funds and on total assets both appear quite satisfactory.

The quick ratio exceeds the 1 : 1 norm and the current ratio is near the 2 : 1 norm, but this requirement varies widely. On the other hand the debt ratio seems high, as two-thirds of all assets are financed by debt.

Asset turnover rates also need comparisons to make any judgment but the debtors collection period of 91 days would seem too long for most industries, especially if credit is granted on a net monthly basis.

Illustration 14: XYZ Company's financial statements contain the following information:

	2012 (₹)	2013 (₹)
Cash	2,00,000	1,60,000
Sundry Debtors	3,20,000	4,00,000
Temporary investments	2,00,000	3,20,000
Stock	18,40,000	21,60,000
Prepaid expenses	28,000	12,000
Total current assets	25,88,000	30,52,000
Total assets	56,00,000	64,00,000
Current Liabilities	6,40,000	8,00,000
Loans	16,00,000	16,00,000
Capital	20,00,000	20,00,000
Retained earnings	4,68,000	8,12,000

Statement of Profit for the current year

	(₹)
Sales	40,00,000
Less: Cost of goods sold	28,00,000
Less: Interest	1,60,000
Net Profit	10,40,000
Less: Taxes @ 50%	5,20,000
Profit after taxes	5,20,000
Profit distributed	2,20,000

From the above, appraise the financial position of the company from the point of view of: (*i*) Liquidity, (*ii*) Profitability, and (*iii*) Activity.

Solution:

1. Liquidity Ratios:

(*a*) Current Ratio (2013) $= \dfrac{\text{Current Assets}}{\text{Current Liabilities}} = \dfrac{₹\ 30,52,000}{₹\ 8,00,000} = 3.81$

(*b*) Acid test Ratio (2013) $= \dfrac{\text{Liquid Assets}}{\text{Current Liabilities}} = \dfrac{₹\ 30,52,000 - 21,72,000}{₹\ 8,00,000} = 1.1$

2. Leverage Ratios:

(*a*) Debt Equity Ratio (2013) $= \dfrac{\text{Long term debts}}{\text{Equity Funds}} = \dfrac{₹\ 16,00,000}{₹\ 28,12,000} = 0.57$

(*b*) Interest Coverage Ratio (2013) $= \dfrac{\text{EBIT}}{\text{Interest Charge}} = \dfrac{₹\ 12,00,00}{₹\ 1,60,000} = 7.5$ times

3. Profitability Ratios:

(*a*) Gross Profit Ratio (2013) $= \frac{\text{Gross Profit}}{\text{Sales}} \times 100 = \frac{₹\ 12,00,000}{₹\ 40,00,000} \times 100 = 30\%$

(*b*) Net Profit Ratio (2013) $= \frac{\text{Net Profit}}{\text{Sales}} \times 100 = \frac{₹\ 5,20,000}{₹\ 40,00,000} \times 100 = 13\%$

(*c*) Return on Total Assets (2013)

$$= \frac{\text{Profit after Tax}}{\text{Total Assets}} \times 100 = \frac{₹\ 5,20,000}{₹\ 64,00,000} \times 100$$

$$= 8.12\%$$

(*d*) Return on Cap. Emp. (2013)

$$= \frac{\text{PAT + Int. } (1 - T)}{\text{Total Cap. Emp.}} \times 100$$

$$= \frac{₹\ 5,20,000 + 80,000}{₹\ 44,12,000} \times 100 = 13.6\%$$

(*e*) Return on Equity Funds (2013)

$$= \frac{\text{Profit after Tax}}{\text{Equity Funds}} \times 100 = \frac{₹\ 5,20,000}{₹\ 28,12,000} \times 100$$

$$= 18.5\%$$

3. Activity Ratios:

(*a*) Debtors Turnover (2013) $= \frac{\text{Sales}}{\text{Average Debtors}} = \frac{₹\ 40,00,000}{₹\ 3,60,000} = 11.1$ times

(*b*) Stock Turnover (2013) $= \frac{\text{Cost of goods sold}}{\text{Average Stock}} = \frac{₹\ 28,00,000}{₹\ 20,00,000} = 1.4$ times

(*c*) Total Assets Turnover (2013) $= \frac{\text{Sales}}{\text{Average Assets}} = \frac{₹\ 40,00,000}{₹\ 60,00,000} = .67$ times

On the basis of the above ratios, it can be said that the firms positions is sound from the point of view of liquidity, solvency and profitability. However, its activity ratios do not represent a satisfactory position. Better position will be reflected only if the ratios are compared with the performance of other firms in the same industry.

Illustration 15: The Balance Sheet of XYZ company is given below:

Liabilities	Amount (₹ in lacs)	Assets	Amount (₹ in lacs)
Equity Share Capital	250	Fixed Assets	400
General Reserve	280	Investment	50
P&L A/c (current year)	30	Stock	460
Secured Loans—Long term	300	Debtors	460
Secured Loans—Short term	360	Cash in Hand	10
Creditors	150	Misc. Expenditure (not written-off)	20
Other Liabilities	30		
	1,400		1,400

Additional Information:

(*a*) From the Profit and Loss Account ₹ 90 lacs was transferred to General Reserve during the year.

(*b*) Interest cost amounted to ₹ 120 lacs.

(*c*) Taxation @ 40%.

You are required to calculate: (*i*) Debt equity ratio (*ii*) Current ratio (*iii*) Interest coverage ratio.

Solution:

$$\text{Current ratio} = \frac{\text{Current Assets}}{\text{Current Liabilities}} = \frac{₹\ 930 \text{ lacs}}{₹\ 540 \text{ lacs}} = 1.73$$

$$\text{Debt Equity Ratio} = \frac{\text{Debt}}{\text{Equity}} = \frac{₹\ 300 \text{ lacs}}{₹\ 560 \text{ lacs}} = 0.54$$

$$\text{Interest Coverage Ratio} = \frac{\text{EBIT}}{\text{Interest}} = \frac{₹\ 320 \text{ lacs}}{₹\ 120 \text{ lacs}} = 2.66$$

Working Notes:

Current Assets	(₹ in lacs)	Debt	Equity	(₹ in lacs)
Stock	460	Term loan ₹ 300 lacs	Capital	250
Debtors	460		Reserve	280
Cash	10		P&L A/c	30
	930			560

Current Liabilities	(₹ in lacs)	EBIT	(₹ in lacs)
Short term loan	360	Profit for the year (30 + 90)	120
Trade Credit	150	Interest	120
Other Liabilities	30	Tax @ 40% $\frac{120 \times 40}{60}$	80
	540		320

Illustration 16: Calculate the P/E ratio from the following: (₹)

	(₹)
Equity Share Capital (₹ 20 each)	50,00,000
Reserves and Surplus	5,00,000
Secured Loans at 15%	25,00,000
Unsecured Loans at 12.5%	10,00,000
Fixed Assets	30,00,000
Investments	5,00,000
Operating Profit	25,00,000
Income-tax Rate	50%
Market price/share	50

Solution:

	(₹)	(₹)
Operating Profit		25,00,000
Less: Interest on:		
Secured Loans @ 15%	3,75,000	

	(₹)	(₹)
Unsecured Loans @ 12.5%	1,25,000	5,00,000
Profit before Tax (PBT)		20,00,000
Less: Income Tax @ 50%		10,00,000
Profit after tax (PAT)		10,00,000
No. of Equity Shares		2,50,000

$$\text{EPS} = \frac{\text{Profit after tax}}{\text{No. of Equity Shares}} = \frac{₹\ 10,00,000}{2,50,000} = ₹\ 4$$

P/E ratio = Market price per share/EPS = ₹ 50/₹ 4 = 12.50.

Illustration 17: ABC Distributors has the following Balance Sheet and Income Statement:

Balance Sheet

Liabilities	(₹)	Assets	(₹)
Shareholders Equity (50,000 shares)	3,00,000	Long Term Assets	3,50,000
Long term Debt	1,00,000	Cash	25,000
Account Payable	80,000	Accounts Receivables	60,000
Other Current Liabilities	20,000	Inventory	65,000
	5,00,000		5,00,000

Income Statement

Particulars	Amount (₹)
Sales	9,00,000
Cost of Goods Sold	4,00,000
General, Administrative and Selling Expenses	1,00,000
Other Expenses	2,50,000
Net Income (PAT)	1,50,000

You are required to:

(*a*) Determine ABC Distributor's liquidity position by calculating the Current ratio, Working Capital, the ratio of Current Assets to Total Assets, the ratio of Current Liabilities to Total Assets and the Cash Conversion cycle.

(*b*) Calculate the current market price per share of ABC's Stock if its P/E ratio is eight.

Solution: Various Ratios of ABC Distributors may be found as follows:

Current Assets = Cash + Accounts receivable + Inventory
= 25,000 + 60,000 + 65,000 = 1,50,000

Current Liabilities = Accounts payable + Other current liabilities
= 80,000 + 20,000 = 1,00,000

Current Ratio = Current assets/Current liabilities
= 1,50,000/1,00,000 = 1.5

Net working capital = 1,50,000 – 1,00,000 = 50,000

Current assets/Total assets = 1,50,000/5,00,000 = 0.30

Current liabilities/Total assets = 1,00,000/5,00,000 = 0.20

Receivables Turnover = Sales/Accounts receivables = 15.00

Inventory Turnover = Cost of goods sold/Inventory = 6.15

Payable Turnover $= \dfrac{\text{Cost of goods sold}}{\text{Accounts payable}} = 5.00$

Average collection period = 365/Receivables turnover = 24.33 days

Inventory conversion period = 365/Inventory turnover = 59.35 days

Payable Deferral period = 365/Payables turnover = 73 days

Cash conversion cycle = 10.68 days (24.33 + 59.35 – 73)

Calculation of Market price of Share of ABC Distributors

EPS = PAT/No. of Shares = 1,50,000/50,000 = 3.00

Price = (EPS) × (P/E) = (3.00 × 8) = ₹ 24.00

Illustration 18: Following is the Balance Sheet of M/s Bintex Co. Ltd., Bangalore, as on 31st December, 2013:

Liabilities	(₹)	Assets	(₹)
Share Capital:		Land	4,00,00
Authorised, issued and fully paid-up:		Building	21,00,000
50,000 9% preference shares of ₹ 100 each	50,00,000	Plant and Machinery	1,19,00,000
5,00,000 Equity Shares of ₹ 10 each	50,00,000	Furniture and Fittings	1,50,000
	1,00,00,000	Office cars, trucks	1,50,000
Capital Reserves	5,00,000	Stock	1,50,00,000
General Reserves	10,00,000	Accounts receivable	6,00,000
Sinking Fund Reserves	15,00,000	Cash and Bank	2,00,000
7% Debentures	50,00,000		
Bank Overdraft	85,00,000		
Notes Payable	15,00,000		
Account Payable	25,00,000		
	3,05,00,000		3,05,00,000

Compute the following from the above balance sheet:

1. Net worth
2. Total value of equity
3. Shareholders reserves
4. Total fixed assets
5. Total current assets
6. Working capital
7. Long-term liabilities

(Show the workings, where necessary).

Solution:

1. **Net Worth:** This represents the net assets of the company. It is also equivalent to proprietors' fund, *viz.*, paid up capital plus reserves. This can be obtained by calculating both ways Assets Approach and Liabilities Approach as given below:

	(₹)	(₹)
(*a*) Gross Assets as per Balance Sheet		3,05,00,000
Less: Liabilities		
7% Debentures	50,00,000	

	(₹)	(₹)
Bank Overdraft	85,00,000	
Notes Payable	15,00,000	
Accounts Payable	25,00,000	
		1,75,00,000
Net Worth		1,30,00,000
Alternatively		
(*b*) Paid-up Capital		
Preference Share Capital	50,00,000	
Equity Share Capital	50,00,000	
		1,00,00,000
Reserves:		
Capital Reserve	5,00,000	
General Reserve	10,00,000	
Sinking Fund Reserve	15,00,000	30,00,000
Net worth		1,30,00,000

2. **Total value of equity:** This can be obtained by adding up Equity Paid up Capital with reserves and surpluses belonging to equity shareholders. Alternatively the same can be obtained by subtracting from net worth of the company what is due to preferences shareholders:

	(₹)	(₹)
Net worth as calculated under (1)		1,30,00,000
Less: Preference Share Capital		50,00,000
Total value of equity		80,00,000
(3) Shareholder's Reserves		
Capital Reserve		5,00,000
General Reserve		10,00,000
Sinking Fund Reserve		15,00,000
Total		30,00,000
(4) Total Fixed Assets		
Land		4,00,000
Building		21,00,000
Plant and Machinery		1,19,00,000
Furniture and Fittings		1,50,000
Office Cars and Trucks		1,50,000
Total		1,47,00,000
(5) Total Current Assets		
Stock		1,50,00,000
Account Receivable		6,00,000
Cash at Bank		2,00,000
Total		1,58,00,000
(6) Working Capital		
This represents excess of Current Assets over Current Liabilities:		
Current Assets as calculated under (5)		1,58,00,000
Less: Current Liabilities	(₹)	
Bank Overdraft	85,00,000	
Notes Payable	15,00,000	

		(₹)
Accounts Payable	25,00,000	1,25,00,000
Working Capital		33,00,000
(7) Long-term Liabilities		
7% Debentures		50,00,000
		50,00,000

Illustration 19: Calculate and comment on the rate of return on total assets from the following data of two companies:

	Go Slow Co.	Go Fast Co.
Sales		2,52,75,000
Total Assets	42,50,000	
Net Profit in Sales	6%	4%
Turnover of Assets	6 times	6 times
Gross Margin	20,68,000	12%

Solution:

	(₹)	(₹)
Sales	42,50,000 × 6 = 2,55,00,000	2,52,75,000
Total Assets	42,50,000	2,52,75,000 ÷ 6 = 42,12,500
Net Profit in Sales	6% of 2,55,00,000 = ₹ 15,30,000	4% of 2,52,75,000 = ₹ 10,11,000
Rate of return on total assets	₹ 15,30,000 / ₹ 42,50,000 = 36%	₹ 10,11,000 / ₹ 42,12,500 = 24%

The rate of return on total assets in respect of Go Fast Co. is less than that of Go Slow Co. as the total assets are same (approx.) in both the Cos. Net profit in sales in Go Fast Co. is 2/3rd of net profit of Go Slow Co. and similar is the case of rate of return on total assets.

Illustration 20: The capital of E Co. Ltd., is as follows:

	(₹)
9% Preference shares of ₹ 10 each	3,00,000
Equity Shares of ₹ 10 each	8,00,000
	11,00,000

The accountant has ascertained the following information:

Profit (after tax at 60%) ₹ 2,70,000: Depreciation ₹ 60,000; Equity dividend paid 20%: market price of equity shares ₹ 40. You are required to state the following, showing the necessary workings:

(*a*) Dividend yield on the equity shares.

(*b*) Cover for the preference and equity dividends.

(*c*) Earnings for equity shares.

(*d*) Price-earnings ratio.

Solution:

(*a*) Dividend yield on the equity shares:

$$= \frac{\text{Dividend per Share}}{\text{Market Price per Share}} \times 100$$

$$= \frac{₹\ 2\ (20\%\ \text{of}\ ₹\ 10) \times 100}{₹\ 40} \times 100 = 5\%.$$

(*b*) Dividend coverage ratio:

(*i*) Preference

$$= \frac{\text{Profits after taxes}}{\text{Dividend payable to preference shareholders}}$$

$$= \frac{₹\ 2{,}70{,}000}{₹\ 27{,}000\ (9\%\ \text{of}\ ₹\ 3{,}00{,}000)}$$

$$= 10 \text{ times}$$

(*ii*) Equity

$$= \frac{\text{Profits after taxes} - \text{Preference share dividends}}{\text{Dividend payable to equity shareholders at current rate of ₹ 2 per share}}$$

$$= \frac{₹\ 2{,}70{,}000 - ₹\ 27{,}000}{₹\ 1{,}60{,}000\ (80{,}000 \text{ shares} \times ₹\ 2)}$$

$$= \frac{₹\ 2{,}43{,}000}{₹\ 1{,}60{,}000} = 1.52 \text{ times}$$

(*c*) Earnings for equity shares:

$$= \frac{\text{Earnings available to Equity Shareholders}}{\text{Number of the Equity Share Outstanding}}$$

$$= \frac{₹\ 2{,}43{,}000}{80{,}000} = ₹\ 3.04 \text{ per share}$$

(*d*) Price-earning (P/E) ratio:

P/E ratio

$$= \frac{\text{Market Price per Share}}{\text{Earning per Share}}$$

$$= \frac{₹\ 40.00}{₹\ 3.04} = 13.2 \text{ times.}$$

Illustration 21: With the help of the following ratios regarding Indu Films, draw the Balance Sheet of the Company for the year 2013.

Current Ratio	2.5
Liquidity Ratio	1.5
Net Working Capital	₹ 3,00,000
Stock Turnover Ratio (Cost of Sales/Closing Stock)	6 times
Gross Profit Ratio	20 per cent

Fixed Assets Turnover Ratio (on cost of sales)	2 times
Debt Collection Period	2 months
Fixed Assets to Shareholders Net worth	0.80
Reserve and Surplus to Capital	0.50

Solution: **Balance Sheet as on ...**

Liabilities	(₹)	Assets	(₹)
Share Capital	5,00,000	Fixed Assets	6,00,000
Reserve and Surplus	2,50,000	Stock	2,00,000
Long-term borrowings (*Balancing figure*)	1,50,000	Debtors	2,50,000
Current Liabilities	2,00,000	Bank	50,000
	11,00,000		11,00,000

Working Notes:

If Current Liabilities	= 1
Current Assets	= 2.5
It means the difference of Working Capital	= 1.5
Working Capital is 1.5	= ₹ 3,00,000
Therefore, Current Assets	= ₹ 5,00,000
Current Liabilities	= ₹ 2,00,000
Liquidity ratio	1.5
Therefore, the liquid assets (Bank and Debtors (2,00,000 × 1.5)	= 3,00,000
Stock (5,00,000 – 3,00,000, *i.e.*, Current Assets – Liquid Assets)	= 2,00,000
Cost of Sales (as stock turnover ratio is 6)	= 12,00,000
Sales as G/P Ratio is 20 per cent, 12,00,000 + 20/80 × 12,000)	= 15,00,000
Fixed Assets are ₹ 12,00,000/2 since fixed assets turnover is ratio 2	= 6,00,000
Debtors are ₹ 15,00,000/6 since debt collection period is 2 months	= 2,50,000
Shareholders Net worth $\left(\dfrac{6,00,000 \times 1}{0.80}\right)$	= 7,50,000
Out of Shareholders net worth, reserves and surplus	= 2,50,000
Therefore, Share Capital	= 5,00,000

Illustration 22: With the following ratios and further information given below prepare a Trading Account, Profit and Loss account and Balance Sheet of Shri Narain:

(*i*) Gross Profit Ratio	25 per cent
(*ii*) Net Profit/Sales	20 per cent
(*iii*) Stock-turnover Ratio	10
(*iv*) Net Profit to Capital	1/5
(*v*) Capital to Total Liabilities	1/2
(*vi*) Fixed Assets/Capital	5/4
(*vii*) Fixed Assets/Total Current Assets	5/7
(*viii*) Fixed Assets	₹ 10,00,000
(*ix*) Closing Stock	₹ 1,00,000

Solution: **Trading and Profit and Loss Account for the year ended...**

	(₹)		(₹)
To Opening Stock	20,000	By Sales	8,00,000
To Purchases (*Balancing figure*)	6,80,000	By Closing Stock	1,00,000
To Gross Profit c/d	2,00,000		
	9,00,000		9,00,000
To Expenses	40,000	By Gross Profit b/d	2,00,000
To Net Profit	1,60,000		
	2,00,000		2,00,000

Balance Sheet as on ...

	(₹)		(₹)
Capital:			
Opening Balance	6,40,000	Fixed Assets	10,00,000
Add: Net Profit	1,60,000	Closing Stock	1,00,000
	8,00,000	Other Current Assets (*Balancing figure*)	13,00,000
Liabilities	16,00,000		
	24,00,000		24,00,000

Working Notes:

1. Fixed Assets are ₹ 10,00,000

$$\frac{\text{Fixed Assets}}{\text{Capital}} = \frac{5}{4}$$

$$\text{Capital} = \frac{1,00,000}{5} \times 4 = ₹\ 8,00,000$$

2. Capital is 1/2 of total liabilities

   Liabilities = 8,00,000 × 2 = 16,00,000

3. Net profit is 1/5 of Capital

   Net profit = 8,00,000 × 1/5 = ₹ 1,60,000

4. Net Profit is 20 per cent of sales

   Sales = 1,60,000 × 100/20 = ₹ 8,00,000

5. Gross Profit Ratio is 25 per cent of Sales

   Gross Profit = ₹ 2,00,000

6. Stock Turnover Ratio (*i.e.*, Cost of Sales/Average Inventory) is 10

   Cost of Sales = Sales – Gross Profit
   = ₹ 8,00,000 – 2,00,000
   = ₹ 6,00,000

   Average Inventory is ₹ 60,000

7. Closing Stock is ₹ 1,00,000

   Average Inventory is ₹ 60,000

   Opening Stock is ₹ 20,000

8. Fixed Assets are ₹ 10,00,000

   Fixed Assets/Total Current Assets = 5/7

   Total Current Assets are 10,00,000 × 7/5 = ₹ 14,00,000

   Stock is ₹ 1,00,000

   Other Current Assets are ₹ 13,00,000.

THEORY QUESTIONS

1. What do you mean by financial statement analysis? What are its purposes?
2. Discuss the importance of financial ratios.
3. Explain the financial ratios:
   (*a*) Liquidity ratios
   (*b*) Profitability ratio
   (*c*) Capital structure ratio.
4. In what way market strength ratios are useful to investors?
5. Discuss the computation and significance of the following financial ratios:
   (*a*) Current ratio
   (*b*) Quick ratio
   (*c*) Inventory turnover ratio
   (*d*) Debt-equity ratio
   (*e*) Accounts receivables ratio
   (*f*) Earnings margin
   (*g*) Earning per share.
6. What are the limitations of accounting ratios?
7. What is meant by horizontal and vertical analysis of financial statement? Explain giving suitable examples.
8. What is asset turnover? What influence does a higher asset turnover tend to have on the rate of return on assets?
9. What is the key question in assessing liquidity? What ratios are used in this regard?
10. What are trend percentages and how are they calculated?
11. Distinguish between horizontal analysis and vertical analysis of financial statements.
12. What are common size percentages and how are they used?
13. Discuss the significance of equity ratio and explain how it is computed.
14. What similarities and differences exist in the objectives of investors and creditors in using financial statement analysis?
15. "Net income based on historical financial statements is a useless measurement because it is influenced by so many arbitrary decisions." Examine the rationale of this statement.
16. What are the objectives associated with horizontal and trend analysis of a company's financial statements?
17. Company A and Company B both have net income of ₹ 10,00,000. Is it possible to say that these companies are equally successful? Why or why not?
18. Explain the utility of ratio analysis and its significance. [*MBA, JNTU, Hyderabad, 2007*]
19. Write note on Leverage Ratios. [*MBA, JNTU, Hyderabad, 2006*]
20. Explain the utility of Ratio Analysis. Differentiate between horizontal analysis and vertical analysis. [*MBA, JNTU, Hyderabad, Feb. 2007*]
21. Explain the significance of Ratio Analysis in the financial decision making. [*MBA, JNTU, Hyderabad, Jan. 2006*]

EXERCISES AND PROBLEMS

1. From the following annual statement of Pioneer Ltd. calculate the following ratios:
   (*a*) Gross Profit Ratio;

(*b*) Current Ratio;
(*c*) Liquid Ratio;
(*d*) Debt-Equity Ratio; and
(*e*) Return on Equity Ratio.

Trading and Profit and Loss Account for the year ended 31st December, 2013

	(₹)		(₹)
Materials Consumed:		Sales	85,000
Opening Stock	9,050	Profit on Sale of Investments	600
Purchases	54,525	Interest on Investments	300
	63,575		
Closing Stock	14,000		
	49,575		
Carriage Inwards	1,425		
Office Expenses	15,000		
Sales Expenses	3,000		
Financial Expenses	1,500		
Loss on Sale of Assets	400		
Net Profit	15,000		
	85,900		85,900

Balance Sheet as on 31st December, 2013

		(₹)			(₹)
Share Capital:			**Fixed Assets:**		
2,000 Equity Shares of ₹ 10 each		20,000	Buildings	15,000	
Reserves		9,000	Plant	8,000	23,000
Profit and Loss Account		6,000	**Current Assets:**		
Bank overdraft		3,000	Stock in Trade	14,000	
Sundry Creditors:			Debtors	7,000	
for expenses	2,000		Bills Receivable	1,000	
for others	8,000	10,000	Bank	3,000	25,000
		48,000			48,000

[**Ans:** (*a*) Gross Profit Ratio 40%; (*b*) Current Ratio 1.92 : 1; (*c*) Liquid Ratio 1.1 : 1 Bank overdraft has not been taken as a current liability; (*d*) Debt-Equity Ratio:

(*i*) $\frac{\text{All Debts}}{\text{Equity}} = 0.371 : 1$

(*ii*) $\frac{\text{All Debts}}{\text{All Debts + Equity}} = 0.271 : 1$

(*iii*) Return on Investment Ratio $= \frac{\text{Net Profi}}{\text{Capital Employed}} = \frac{15,000}{35,000} = 42.85$

2. Following is the Profit and Loss Account and balance sheet of A Limited for the year ended 31st December, 2002 and balance sheet as on that date. Calculate the different ratios and comment on the financial position of the company.

Profit and Loss Accounts for the year ended 31 December, 2013

	(₹)	(₹)
Net Sales		3,00,000
Less: Cost of Goods sold		2,58,000
Gross Profit		42,000
Operating Expenses:		
Selling	2,200	
General and Administration	4,000	
Rent of Office	2,800	
		9,000
Gross Operating Profit		33,000
Depreciation		10,000
		23,000
Other Income:		
Interest on Government Securities		1,500
Gross Income		24,500
Other Expenses:		
Interest on Bank Overdraft	300	
Interest on Debentures	4,200	
		4,500
Net Income before Tax		20,000
Tax @ 50 per cent on Net Income		10,000
Net Income after Tax		10,000

Balance Sheet as on 31 December 2013

Liabilities	(₹)	Assets		(₹)
Sundry Creditors	6,000	Cash		5,000
Bills Payable	10,000	Investments (Govt. Securities)		15,000
Outstanding Expenses	1,000	Sundry Debtors		20,000
Provision for Taxation	13,000	Stock		30,000
Total Current Liabilities	30,000	Total Current Assets		70,000
6 per cent Mortgage Debentures	70,000	Fixed Assets	1,80,000	
7 per cent Preference Shares	10,000	*Less:* Provision for dep.	50,000	
Equity Shares	50,000			1,30,000
Reserve and Surplus	40,000			
Total Claim on Assets	2,00,000			2,00,000

[**Ans:** Gross Profit Ratio 14 per cent. Net Profit Ratio (after considering interest on bank overdraft): 7.56 per cent ROI 13.53 per cent, stock turnover Ratio 8.6. Debt Collection Period 24 days. Fixed Assets Turnover 2.3, Fixed Assets Ratio 7.6, Debt-equity ratio 70/100 = .7, Current ratio 2.3].

3. Following is the balance sheet of C Ltd. as on 31st December, 2013:

Liabilities	(₹)	Assets	(₹)
Equity Share Capital	20,000	Goodwill	12,000
Capital Reserve	4,000	Fixed Assets	28,000
8% Loan on Mortgage	16,000	Stocks	6,000

Liabilities		(₹)	Assets	(₹)
Trade Creditors		8,000	Debtors	6,000
Bank Overdraft		2,000	Investments	2,000
Taxation: Current		2,000	Bank	6,000
Future		2,000		
Profit and Loss A/c				
Profit for 2013 after taxation and interest on Fixed Deposits	12,000			
Less: Transfer to Reserve	4,000			
Dividend	2,000	6,000		
		60,000		60,000

Sales amounted to ₹ 1,20,000

Calculate ratio for:

(*i*) Testing liquidity

(*ii*) Testing solvency

(*iii*) Testing profitability

(*iv*) Testing capital gearing and

(*v*) Comment on the significant thereof.

4. From the following particulars extracted from the financial statements of Sun and Co. Ltd. Compute: (*a*) Current Ratio, (*b*) Acid Test Ratio, (*c*) Stock Turnover Ratio, (*d*) Debtors Turnover Ratio and (*e*) Creditors Turnover Ratio for the two years 2012 and 2013 independently and comment on the liquidity position of the company:

	2012 (₹)	2013 (₹)
Opening Stock	47,000	53,000
Closing Stock	53,000	67,000
Sales less returns	2,52,000	3,65,000
Provision for Bad Debts	2,000	3,000
Sundry Creditors	32,000	35,000
Purchases	1,80,000	1,90,000
Sundry Debtors	42,000	63,000
Cash	10,000	15,000
Bank	8,000	10,000
Bills Receivable	15,000	20,000
Bills Payable	29,000	30,000
Marketable Securities	8,000	8,000

5. A Ltd. and B Ltd. produce and sell the same product but under different brand names. Their profit and loss statements and Balance Sheets are given below for the year ending 2013.

Profit and Loss Statement (Figures in ₹ lakhs)

	A Ltd.	B Ltd.
Sales	25.00	30.00
Less: Costs: Materials	4.00	2.00
Labour	2.00	7.00

	A Ltd.	B Ltd.
Overheads: Fixed	9.00	2.00
Variable	2.00	9.00
Total cost	17.00	20.00
Gross margin	8.00	10.00
Interest	2.00	4.00
Profit before Taxes	6.00	6.00
Taxes	3.00	3.00
Profit after Taxes	3.00	3.00
Dividends declared	2.00	2.00
Retained earnings	1.00	1.00

Balance Sheet **(Fig. in ₹ lakhs)**

		A Ltd.	B Ltd.
A.	**Capital and Liabilities:**		
	1. Equity Capital	10.00	20.00
	2. Debenture Capital	8.00	20.00
	3. Creditors	5.00	15.00
	4. Reserves	17.00	5.00
		40.00	60.00
B.	**Assets:**		
	1. Plant and Machinery	8.00	34.00
	2. Buildings	6.00	16.00
	3. Inventories	18.00	2.00
	4. Debtors	7.00	1.00
	5. Cash	1.00	7.00
		40.00	60.00

Required: Evaluate the performance of two organisations for the current year and assess the expected problem by using the relevant ratios.

6. A condensed balance sheet and other financial data for Alpha Company appear below:

Alpha Company
Balance Sheet December 31st, 2012

Liabilities and Equity	(₹)	Assets	(₹)
Current Liabilities	1,00,000	Current Assets	1,00,000
Long-term Liabilities	75,000	Plant Assets	1,40,000
Total Liabilities	1,75,000		
Common Equity	75,000		
Total Liabilities and Equity	2,50,000	Total Assets	2,50,000

Income Statement Data

Net Sales	3,75,000
Interest Expense	4,000
Net Income	22,500

The following account balances existed at December 31st, 2011. Total Assets, ₹ 2,00,000; Equity, ₹ 65,000. The tax rate is 35 per cent.

Industry norms as of December 31st, 2012 were:

Debt-equity ratio	1.75
Profit margin	0.12
Return on total assets	0.15
Return on stockholders' equity	0.30
Total asset turnover	1.71

Calculate and evaluate the following ratios for Alpha Company as of December 31st, 2012:

(*a*) Debt-equity ratio

(*b*) Profit margin

(*c*) Return on total assets

(*d*) Return on stockholders' equity

(*e*) Total asset turnover.

7. Here are the income statements and balance sheets of A Company and B Company, taken from their annual reports for the year ended December 31st, 2013.

Income Statement for the year 2013

	A Company (₹)	B Company (₹)
Sales	80,00,000	70,00,000
Cost of goods sold	60,00,000	47,00,000
Selling, General, and Administrative Expenses	12,00,000	19,00,000
Interest on debt:	—	70,000
Income before Taxes	8,00,000	3,30,000
Income Taxes	3,90,000	1,60,000
Net Income	4,10,000	1,70,000
Dividends declared	1,00,000	70,000

Condenses Balance Sheets as on December 31st, 2013

Liabilities and Equity	A Company (₹)	B Company (₹)	Assets	A Company (₹)	B Company (₹)
Accounts Payable	7,10,000	4,00,000	Cash	3,00,000	3,00,000
Taxes Payable	3,90,000	1,60,000	Accounts receivable	8,00,000	6,50,000
Long-term debt	—	14,00,000	Inventory	13,00,000	8,50,000
Common Equity	22,00,000	8,00,000	Net Plant and Equipment	21,00,000	15,00,000
Retained earnings	12,00,000	5,40,000			
Total Liabilities and Equity	45,00,000	33,00,000	Total Assets	45,00,000	33,00,000

On the basis of the available information, which do you consider to be:

(*i*) more liquid,

(*ii*) more solvent,

(*iii*) more profitable?

Explain your conclusions.

PART–FIVE

SPECIALISED TOPICS

- **Chapter 20** Corporate Financial Reporting
- **Chapter 21** Computerised Accounting (How to use Tally)

20

CORPORATE FINANCIAL REPORTING

LEARNING OBJECTIVES

After reading this chapter, you should be able to:

- *Understand* concept of financial reporting, users in financial reporting.
- *Define* specific purpose report.
- *Discuss* qualitative characteristics of accounting information.
- *Explain* some specific issues in financial reporting: Segment Reporting, Social Reporting, Value added reporting, Interim Reporting.

CONCEPT OF FINANCIAL REPORTING

Financial reporting may be defined as communication of published financial statements and related information from a business enterprise to third parties (external users) including shareholders, creditors, customers, governmental authorities and the public. It is the reporting of accounting information of an entity (individual, firm, company, government enterprise) to a user or group of users. Company financial reporting is a total communication system involving the company as issuer (preparer); the investors and creditors as primary users, other external users; the accounting profession as measurers and auditors; and the company law regulatory or administrative authorities.

OBJECTIVES OF FINANCIAL REPORTING

An evaluation of company financial reporting requires some agreement on its objectives. Financial reporting is not an end in itself but is a means to certain objectives. The objectives of financial reporting and financial statements have been discussed for a long time. While there is no final statement on objectives, to which all parties (of financial reporting) have agreed, some consensus has been developing on the objectives of financial reporting. At present, the following may be described as the primary objectives of financial reporting:

(*a*) Investment Decision-Making

(*b*) Management Accountability.

(*a*) Investment Decision-Making: The basic objective of financial reporting is to provide information useful to investors, creditors and other users in making sound investment decisions.

These decisions concern the efficient allocation of investment funds and the selection among investment opportunities. The Trueblood Committee of USA stated that "...the basic objective of financial statements is to provide information useful for making economic decisions." Recently, the FASB (USA) in its Concept No. 1 also concluded that "financial reporting should provide information that is useful to present and potential investors and creditors and other users in making rational investment, credit and similar decisions".

Investment decision and investment values, both, are comparative, not absolute. In all investment decisions, comparison is made in order to determine the most attractive (greatest) returns in relation to risk. Comparison requires uniform standards of measurement. Where different accounting measurements are used in similar situations, investors and financial analysts make their own accounting adjustments to achieve comparability, provided adequate information is available to do so. But the attribute of comparability can be achieved at a lower cost (associated with financial reporting system), and with equal benefit for all investors, by eliminating the alternatives.

(*b*) Management Accountability: A second basic objective of financial reporting is to provide information on management accountability to judge management's effectiveness in utilising the resources and running the enterprise. Management of an enterprise is periodically accountable to the owners not only for the custody and safe-keeping of enterprise resources, but also for their efficient and profitable use and for protecting them to the extent possible from unfavourable economic impacts of factors in the economy such as technological changes, inflation or deflations.

Management accountability is of very great interest not only to existing shareholders and other users but also to potential shareholders, creditors and users. A company generally offers shares, debentures etc., to the prospective investing public and therefore it should accept accountability responsibilities to prospective investors also. Certainly annual and other financial statements is intended to play a major role in this regard.

To conclude, the above two basic objectives associated with company financial reporting contribute in making wise economic decisions and determining the economic performance. Both these objectives lead to broader social goals of efficient allocation of investment funds and proper selection among alternative investment opportunities. Thus, accomplishment of these financial reporting objectives influence capital formation and flow of funds and perform a vital role in the successful functioning of an economy.

GENERAL PURPOSE FINANCIAL REPORTING

Generally speaking, the term 'financial reporting' is used to mean general purpose external financial reporting. Often it is said that the purpose of financial reporting is the preparation of general purpose reports for external users. Despite the fact that financial reports are mainly intended (legally) for share holders, they can be, and are, used by a number of other external users.

The users of financial statements include present and potential investors, employees, lenders, suppliers and other trade creditors, customers, governments and their agencies and the public. They use financial statements in order to satisfy some of their different needs for information. These needs include the following:

(*a*) **Investors:** The providers of risk capital and their advisors are concerned with the risk inherent in, and return, provided by their investments. They need information to help them determine whether they should buy, hold or sell. Shareholders are also interested in information which enables them to assess the ability of the enterprise to pay dividends.

(*b*) **Employees:** Employees and their representative groups are interested in information about the stability and profitability of their employers. They are also interested in information which enables them to assess the ability of the enterprise to provide remuneration, retirement benefits and employment opportunities.

(*c*) **Lenders:** Lenders are interested in information that enables them determine whether their loans, and the interest attaching to them, will be paid when due.

(*d*) **Suppliers and other trade creditors:** Suppliers and other creditors are interested in information that enables them to determine whether amounts owing to them will be paid when due. Trade creditors are likely to be interested in an enterprise over a shorter period than lenders unless they are dependent upon the continuation of the enterprise as a major customer.

(*e*) **Customers:** Customers have an interest in information about the continuance of an enterprise, especially when they have a long-term involvement with, or are dependent on, the enterprise.

(*f*) **Governments and their agencies:** Governments and their agencies are interested in the allocation of resources and, therefore, the activities of enterprises. They also require information in order to regulate the activities of enterprises, determine taxation policies and as the basis for national income and similar statistics.

(*g*) **Public:** Enterprises affect members of the public in a variety of ways. For example, enterprises may make a substantial contribution to the local economy in many ways including the number of people they employ and their patronage of local suppliers. Financial statements may assist the public by providing information about the trends and recent developments in the prosperity of the enterprise and the range of its activities.

SPECIFIC PURPOSE REPORT

Financial reporting objectives in accounting literature so far has focused on general purpose financial reporting which aims to satisfy the information needs of all potential users. Company law provisions in almost all countries of the world have consistently accepted the utility of general purpose financial reporting. Due to this the separate (specific) needs of specific users have been largely ignored on the assumption that general purpose reports can satisfy the information needs of all external users. However, a reasoning has also been made suggesting that the needs of specific users may be better served by presenting specific purpose reports to help them in their separately identifiable decision functions. For instance, financial reports submitted to obtain credit or loans, or government, or financial reports given to trade and industry, may not satisfy other users' needs and expectations.

However, the proposal of specific purpose reports in company financial reporting is criticised on some counts.

Firstly, the cost of the developing specialised reports to satisfy special requirements of specific users may exceed the benefits when the company financial reporting policy is determined in its totality.

Secondly, specialised needs of specific users cannot be ascertained with any degree of certainty.

Thirdly, issuing multiple reports about the financial results of an enterprise can create confusion among various users. Multiple reports increase the perceived complexity of the environment. Such changes in perceived environment complexity induce changes in decision-makers' cognitive processing capabilities and, in turn, can decrease the effectiveness of decision-making by users.

Fourthly, multiple reports may not be desirable and practicable from the standpoint of information economics.

To conclude, company financial reporting, in future, will continue to adhere to general purpose reporting system to aid investors, creditors, and other external users in their economic decisions. Meanwhile, in order to achieve the objectives of financial reporting (through general purpose reports) there is a continuous need to investigate many vital aspects relating to general purpose financial reports such as identifying potential users and user groups, identifying information needs of such users, determining the feasibility of providing general purpose information to meet these needs, determining the manner of reporting such information, and having a feedback from the users regarding the use and relevance of general purpose information.

QUALITATIVE CHARACTERISTICS OF FINANCIAL REPORTING INFORMATION

Qualitative characteristics or qualities necessary for information serve a major supporting role in the decision usefulness, decision model approach to accounting theory. Qualitative characteristics are the tributes that make the information provided in financial statements useful to users. Accounting information that is reported to facilitate economic decisions should possess certain characteristics or normative standards. The informational qualities which has been accepted by FASB (USA) in its Concept No. 2 "Qualitative Characteristics of Accounting Information" is displayed in Table 1.

Table 1 : A Hierarchy of Accounting Qualities

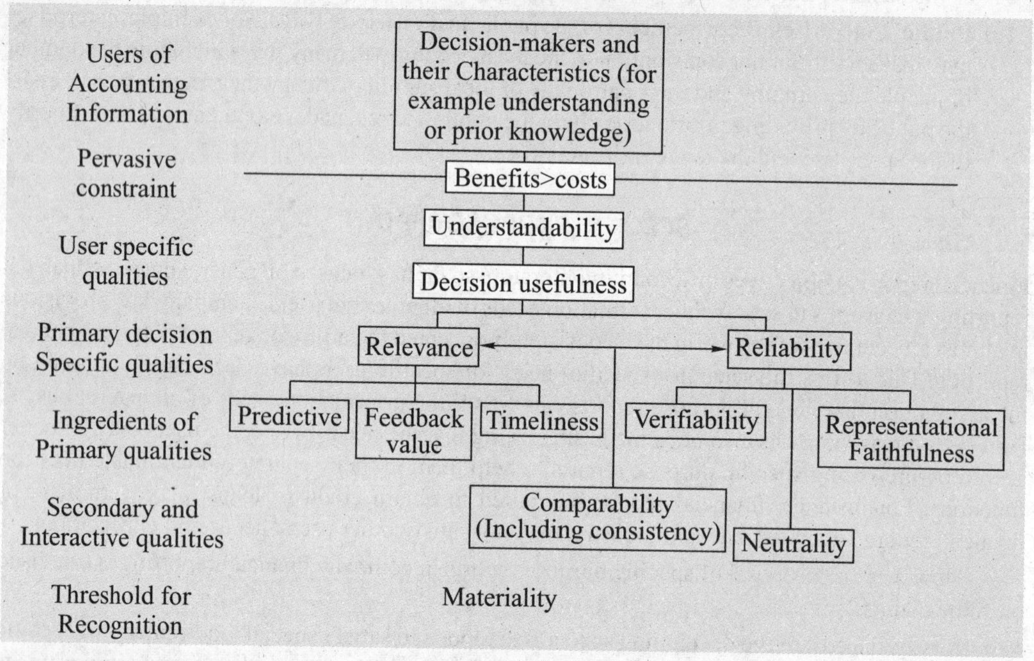

Users of Accounting Information	Decision-makers and their Characteristics (for example understanding or prior knowledge)
Pervasive constraint	Benefits>costs
User specific qualities	Understandability; Decision usefulness
Primary decision Specific qualities	Relevance ↔ Reliability
Ingredients of Primary qualities	Relevance: Predictive, Feedback value, Timeliness; Reliability: Verifiability, Representational Faithfulness
Secondary and Interactive qualities	Comparability (Including consistency); Neutrality
Threshold for Recognition	Materiality

Source: Financial Accounting Standards Board, Statement of Financial Accounting Concept No. 2, Qualitative Characteristics of Accounting Information, Stamford : FASB, p. 15.

International Accounting Standards Board (IASB) has recognised the four principal qualitative characteristics of accounting information.

1. Understandability
2. Relevance
3. Reliability
4. Comparability.

The other qualities suggested by IASB are materiality, faithful representation, substance over form, neutrality, prudence, completeness, timeliness.

The qualitative characteristics that have been found possessing wider acceptance and recognition in accounting literature are as follows:

1. Relevance: Relevance is closely and directly related to the concept of useful information Relevance implies that all those items of information should be reported that may aid the users in making decisions and/or predictions. In general, information that is given greater weight in decision-making is more relevant. Specially, it is information's capacity to make a difference that identifies it as relevant to a decision. American Accounting Association's Committee to Prepare A Statement of Basic Accounting Theory defines relevance as "the primary standard and requires that information must bear upon or be usefully associated with actions it is designed to facilitate or results desired to be produced".

Financial Accounting Standards Board in its Concept No. 1 (para 47, 1978) comments:

"Relevant Accounting information must be capable of making a difference in a decision by helping users to form predictions about the outcomes of past, present and future events or to confirm or correct expectations."

2. **Reliability:** Reliability is described as one of the two primary qualities (relevance and reliability) that make accounting information useful for decision-making. Reliable information is required to form judgments about the earning potential and financial position of a business firm. Reliability differs from item to item. Some items of information presented in an annual report may be more reliable than others. For example, information regarding plant and machinery may be less reliable than certain information about current assets because of differences in uncertainty of realisation. Reliability is that quality which permits users of data to depend upon it with confidence as representative of what it purports to represent. FASB Concept No. 2 concludes:

   "The reliability of a measure rests on the faithfulness with which it represents what it purports to represent, coupled with an assurance for the user that it has that representational quality. To be useful information must be reliable as well as relevant. Degrees of reliability must be recognised. It is hardly ever a question of black or white, but rather of more reliability or less. Reliability rests upon the extent to which the accounting description or measurement is verifiable and representationally faithful. Neutrality of information also interacts with those two components of reliability to affect the usefulness of the information."

3. **Understandability:** Understandability is the quality of information that enables users to perceive its significance. The benefits of information may be increased by making it more understandable and hence useful to a wider circle of users. Presenting information which can be understood only by sophisticated users and not by others, creates a bias which is inconsistent with the standard of adequate disclosure. Presentation of information should not only facilitate understanding but also avoid wrong interpretation of financial statements. Thus, understandable financial accounting information presents data that can be understood by users of the information and is expressed in a form and with terminology adopted to the user's range of understanding.

4. **Comparability:** Economic decision requires making choice among possible courses of actions. In making decisions, the decision-maker will make comparisons among alternatives, which is facilitated by financial information. Comparability implies to have like things reported in a similar fashion and unlike things reported differently. FASB (USA) Concept No. 2 (para 115, 1980) defines comparability, "... as the quality or state of having certain characteristics in common, and comparison is normally a quantitative assessment of the common characteristics. Clearly, valid comparison is possible only if the measurements used– the quantities or ratios–reliably represent the characteristic that is the subject of comparison".

   Comparable financial accounting information presents similarities and differences that arise from basic similarities and differences in the enterprise or enterprises and their transactions, and not merely from difference in financial accounting treatment. Information, if comparable, will assist the decision-maker to determine relative financial strengths and weaknesses and prospects for the future, between two or more firms or between periods in a single firm.

5. **Consistency:** Consistency of method over a period of time is a valuable quality that makes accounting numbers more useful. Consistent use of accounting principles from one accounting period to another enhances the utility of financial statements to users by facilitating analysis and understanding of comparative accounting data. It is relatively unimportant to the investor what precise rules or conventions are adopted by a company in reporting its earnings, if he knows what method is being followed and is assured that it is followed consistently from year to year. Lack of consistency produces lack of comparability. The value of inter-company comparisons is substantially reduced when material differences in income are caused by variations in accounting practices.
6. **Neutrality:** Neutrality is also known as the quality of 'freedom from bias' or objectivity. Neutrality means that, in formulating or implementing standards, the primary concern should be the relevance and reliability of the information that results, not the effect that the new rule may have on a particular interest or user(s). A neutral choice between accounting alternatives is free from bias towards a predetermined result. The objectives of (general purpose) financial reporting serve many different information users who have diverse interests, and no one predetermined result is likely to suit all users' interests and purposes. Therefore, accounting facts and accounting practices should be impartially determined and reported with no objective of purposeful bias toward any user or user group. If there is no bias in selection of accounting information reported, it cannot be said to favour one set of interests over another. It may, in fact, favour certain interests, but only because the information points that way.
7. **Materiality:** The concept of materiality permeates the entire field of accounting and auditing. The materiality concept implies that not all financial information need or should be communicated in accounting reports–only material information should be reported. Immaterial information may and probably should be omitted. Information should be disclosed in the annual report which is likely to influence economic decisions of the users. Information that meets this requirement is material.
8. **Timeliness:** Timeliness means having information available to decision-makers before it loses its capacity to influence decisions, Timeliness is an ancillary aspect of relevance, If information is either not available when it is needed or becomes available long after the reported events that it has no value for future action, it lacks relevance and is of little or no use, Timeliness alone cannot make information relevant, but a lack of timeliness can rob information of relevance it might otherwise have had.

   Clearly, there are degrees of timeliness, Some reports need to be prepared quickly, say in case of takeover bid or strike. In some other contexts, such as routine reports by a business firm of its annual results, a longer delay in reporting information may materially affect the relevance and, therefore, the usefulness of information. But in order to have gain in relevance that comes with increased timeliness, it may involve sacrifices of other desirable characteristics of information, and as a result there may be an overall gain or loss in usefulness. For example, it may sometimes be desirable to sacrifice precision for timeliness, for an approximation produced quickly is often more useful than precise information that is reported after a longer delay.
9. **Verifiability:** The quality of verifiability contributes to the usefulness of accounting information because the purpose of verification is to provide a significant degree of assurance that accounting measures represent, what they purport to represent. Verification does not guarantee the suitability of method used, much less the correctness of the resulting measure. It does convey some assurance that the measurement rule used, whatever it was, was applied carefully and without personal bias on the part of the measurer.

According to FASB, "Verifiability means no more than that several measurers are likely to obtain the same measure. It is primarily a means to attempting to cope with measurement problems stemming from the uncertainty that surrounds accounting measures and is more successful in coping with some measurement problems than others. Verification of accounting information does not guarantee that the information has a high degree of representational faithfulness and a measure with a high degree of verifiability is not necessarily relevant to the decision for which it is intended to be useful."

10. **Conservatism:** There is a place for a convention, such as conservatism - meaning prudence in financial accounting and reporting, because business and economic activities are surrounded by uncertainty, but it needs to be applied with care. Conservatism in financial reporting should no longer connote deliberate consistent, understatement of net assets and profits. Conservatism is a prudent reaction to uncertainty to try to ensure that uncertainties and risks inherent in business situations are adequately considered. Thus, if two estimates of amounts to be received or paid in the future are about equally likely, conservatism dictates using the less optimistic estimates. However, if two amounts are not equally likely, conservatism does not necessarily dictate using the more pessimistic amount rather than the more likely one. Conservatism no longer requires deferring recognition of income beyond the time that adequate evidence of its existence becomes available, or justifies recognising losses before there is adequate evidence that they have been incurred.

Specific Issues in Financial Reporting

There are many specific issues which have gained vital importance and wider recognition in company financial reporting in the recent years. In this chapter, some such specific issues have been discussed.

SEGMENT REPORTING

Concept of Segment Reporting

The concept of segment reporting is applicable to a diversified enterprise. A diversified company may be defined as a company which has diversified operations, *i.e.,* activity or operations in different industries and/or foreign operations and sales where those activities (or operations) are significant in terms of sales revenue, profit or losses generated or assets employed. It is also true that segmentation along industry and geographical lines subject to different profitability, different risks and different growth prospects are likely to be found in most diversified companies.

The diversified companies and their operations indifferent industries, activities and geographical areas raise questions as to whether modifications are necessary to the existing framework of corporate accountability and financial reporting practices. Are consolidated financial statements meaningful where company's operations comprise a number of activities in different geographical areas with different profitability, risk and growth characteristics? Although a business enterprise's total or aggregated financial information is useful, the financial 'statements users find segment information more valuable in assessing an enterprise's standing—its past results and future prospects.

Need for Segment Reporting

Diversified companies present a peculiar and special problem for investment decision-making. The progress and success of a diversified company are composites of the progress and success of its several segments. Proponents of segment reporting contend that information about separate segments contributes to investor evaluations of diversified companies.

1. **Segment Disclosure and Investment Decision-Making:** A major argument in support of segmental reporting is that if investors are provided with information about the profitability, risk and growth of the different segments of a company's operations, they will be better able to assess the earnings potential and the risk of the company as a whole. They will be able to predict more accurately a firm's future earnings and cash flows than can be done by using consolidated data alone. Investor uncertainty about company prospects will thus be reduced, share prices will be set more accurately, and a more efficient allocation of resources will be promoted.
2. **Segments Disclosure and Other Users (Other than Investors):** Besides the investors, it has been suggested that segmental reports are likely to be useful to employees and trade unions, consumers, the general public, government and also for the purpose of promoting managerial efficiency. Employees and trade unions are interested in the performance and prospects of the firm from the standpoint of wage negotiations and job security and hence, segmental reports may be just as relevant to them as to investors. There is also a need for information on segmental performance so that policy decisions by management to develop or curtail particular activities can be verified and understood. Lack of information, on the other hand, may lead to distrust and labour relations problems.

   The interests of consumers and the public may also be promoted by segmental disclosure in the sense that social responsibility in terms of the removal of price discrimination could be encouraged by disclosure of profits by segment. Consumers may also benefit from the increased competition that may result.

   Governments, at national and also international level in the case of multinational companies, are becoming increasingly concerned by the activities of large companies and the balance of payments. Segmental disclosures by geographical location seem likely to promote a better understanding of corporate strategy and its impact, and will thus provide a more reliable base for governmental policy-making. Furthermore, legislation relating to mergers and acquisition and competition policy seems likely to be more effective if based on more comprehensive information.

Difficulties in Segment Reporting

The difficulties involved in segment reporting relate to implementation of segment reporting rather than to its concept and theory. Some difficulties are listed as follows:

1. **Base (or Bases) of Segmentation:** How a diversified company would be fractionalised for reporting purposes, is a problem in segment reporting. A diversified company may be divided for segment reporting purposes in terms of organisation division, industry, market, customer product, etc. Each base of segmentation may create segments that differ significantly in profitability, growth and risk and each implies a different basis for identifying segments. Moreover, more than one form of diversification may be present in the same. Unless the base (or bases) selected actually represent the company and the way it operates, unless they reflect the difference within the company regarding rate of profit, degree of risk, and potential for growth, reports-of operating data by segments are unlikely to be of any real use.
2. **Allocation of Common Costs:** In a business enterprise producing more than one product or engaged in different activities, there are likely to be costs which are common to two or more of the products. Examples of common costs are general administrative and selling expenses, legal expenses, general advertising etc. Because these costs are common to more than one segment, they cannot be associated in entirety with a single segment.

   The problem of allocating common costs is greater for some items than for others. It is particularly great for assets, liabilities, and equity so that reporting for business segments is suggested less often for information from the balance sheet, statement of shareholders equity, and funds statements than for information from the income statement. Because of the diversity of methods employed, cross-company comparison of similar segments are likely to be misleading and the reliability of segment operating results varies depending on how closely the basis of allocation approximates results that would have been produced by market transactions.

3. **Pricing Inter-segment Transactions:** A diversified company composed of disparate parts, each of which goes its own way, might have very few inter-company transactions. On the other hand, there might be some diversified business enterprises which may have very substantial transactions among and between the segments. There are different methods for inter-segment transfers such as cost, cost plus, market price, and negotiated price. The basic purpose (in selecting a method of transfer pricing) is to motivate employees, and to actually measure the success of the several segments as accurately as possible. Different methods results in different operating results for the segments. For a meaningful segment reporting, there is a need for selecting a reasoned method for inter-segment transfers.
4. **Costs of Segment Disclosure:** Further arguments against segmental reporting are concerned with the costs of disclosure. The provision of additional information will, undoubtedly, increase a firm's operating costs in terms of the costs of collection, processing, audit and dissemination.

   Another important cost argument relates to the increased competition that may result from segmental disclosures. It is argued that the disclosure of profitable segments will attract competitors, whilst loss-making segments may become the subject of take-over bids or put pressure on management to sell them off, with the purpose of improving profits in the short-term and to take on less risky projects. A competitive disadvantage may also occur where foreign companies are not required to provide segmental reports.
5. **Management Conservatism:** Another argument is that, where there is no regulatory provision to disclose segmental reports, voluntary disclosures are likely to be perceived by managements to be beneficial only in certain instances; for example, where management believes that the company's attractiveness to investors will be enhanced and the costs of finance reduced. Few companies are likely to take voluntary action that may benefit their competitors or reveal weaknesses.

Segment Reporting in India

The Institute of Chartered Accountants of India has issued AS 17 titled 'Segment Reporting' in October 2000. AS 17 is mandatary in respect of companies who are listed on the stock exchange or who are in the process of issuing equity or debt securities and will be accordingly listed on the stock exchange in India. Therefore, Indian companies are giving segmental information in compliance with AS 17 Segment Reporting issued by Accounting Standards Board of ICAI. AS 17 Segment Reporting has the following guidelines on identifying reportable segments:

(*i*) Primary and Secondary Segment Reporting

(*ii*) Business and Geographical Segment

AS 17 suggests the disclosure of following information in segment reports:

(*i*) Segment revenue

(*ii*) Segment expense

(*iii*) Segment profitability

(*iv*) Assets

(*v*) Liabilities

(*vi*) Accounting policies.

To illustrate segment disclosure practices in India, an example is given here of Indian Oil Corporation Ltd. and Gujarat State Petronet Ltd. for segmental disclosures made by them (Tables 2 and 3 respectively).

Table 2
Indian Oil Corporation Ltd.
Unaudited Financial Results for the Quarter Ended 30th June, 2011

(₹ in crore)

	Quarter ended 30.06.2011 (Unaudited)	Quarter ended 30.06.2010 (Unaudited)	Previous year ended 31.03.2011 (Audited)
I. Financial:			
1. **Gross Turnover**	**99757.39**	**77972.20**	**328744.27**
Less: Excise Duty	7657.22	6690.37	25789.90
Net Sales	92100.17	71281.83	302954.37
2. Subsidy from Government of India (as per scheme)	422.83	397.59	1676.66
3. **Net Sales/Income from Operations**	**92523.00**	**71679.42**	**304631.03**
4. Grant from Government of India	8200.85	0.00	22604.84
5. Other Operating Income	560.66	230.20	1617.32
6. Total Expenditure			
(*a*) (Increase)/Decrease in Stocks	(2370.10)	(166.00)	(4972.93)
(*b*) Purchase of Products and Crude for resale	49064.26	36118.88	155648.10
(*c*) Consumption of Raw Materials	51290.45	34691.89	143000.32
(*d*) Employee Cost	1165.03	983.15	6435.55
(*e*) Depreciation	1223.49	1034.60	4546.67
(*f*) Other Expenditure	3996.71	2967.66	15470.38
	104369.84	75630.18	320128.09
7. **Profit from Operations before Other Income and Interest (3 + 4 + 5 – 6)**	**(3085.33)**	**(3720.56)**	**8725.10**
8. Other Income	404.22	903.34	3040.59
9. **Profit before Interest (7 + 8)**	**(2681.11)**	**(2817.22)**	**11765.69**
10. Interest	1037.59	571.17	2669.83
11. **Profit before Tax (9 – 10)**	**(3718.70)**	**(3388.39)**	**9095.86**
12. Provision for Taxation	0.00	0.00	1650.38
13. **Net Profit (11 – 12)**	**(3718.70)**	**(3388.39)**	**7445.48**
14. Paid-up Equity Share Capital (Face value-₹ 10 each)	2427.95	2427.95	2427.95
15. Reserves excluding revaluation reserves			52904.37
16. Earnings per Share (₹) (Basic and Diluted) (Face value-₹ 10 each)	(15.32)	(13.96)	30.67
17. Aggregate of Public Shareholding			
(*a*) Number of Shares	511796772	511796772	511796772
(*b*) Percentage of Shareholding (%)	21.08	21.08	21.08
18. Promoters and Promoter Group Shareholding			
(*a*) Pledged/Encumbered			
— Number of Shares	—	—	—
— Percentage of Total Promoters and Promoter Group Shareholding (%)	—	—	—
— Percentage of Total Share Capital of Company (%)	—	—	—
(*b*) Non-Encumbered			
— Number of Shares	1916155710	1916155710	1916155710

	Quarter ended 30.06.2011 (Unaudited)	Quarter ended 30.06.2010 (Unaudited)	Previous year ended 31.03.2011 (Audited)
— Percentage of Total Promotoers and Promoter Group Shareholding (%)	100.00	100.00	100.00
— Percentage of Total Share Capital of Company (%)	78.92	78.92	78.92
II. Physical (In MMT)			
1. Product Sales:			
— Domestic	18.226	17.254	67.932
— Export	1.033	1.058	4.988
2. Refineries Throughput	14.306	13.278	52.962
3. Pipelines Throughput	19.281	16.489	67.841

Note:

1. The above results have been reviewed and recommended by the Audit Committee and approved by the Board of Directors at its meeting held on 10th August, 2011.
2. The Financial Results have been reviewed by the Statutory Auditors as required under clause 41 of the listing agreement.
3. Average Gross Refining Margins for the quarter April-June, 2011 was $ 4.71 per bbl (April-June 2010: $ 3.00 per bbl).
4. (*a*) MOP&NG has approved discount of ₹ 7932.32 crore on crude oil/petroleum products purchased ONGC/GAIL/OIL/CPCL, towards part of the under recovery suffered by IOC on sale of HSD, SKO (PDS) and LPG April-June 2010, ₹ 3671.26 crore on sale of MS, HSD, SKO (PDS) and LPG (Domestic).

   (*b*) The company has accounted for Budgetary Support of ₹ 8200.85 crore (April-June 2010: ₹ NIL) towards under-recovery on sale of HSD, SKO (PDS) and LPG (Domestic) in the Profit and Loss Account as Revenue Grants. This amount has been accounted for based on the advice from Government of India, pending receipt of compensation.

   (*c*) Consequent to non-revision of retail selling prices in line with international prices, the Company has suffered net under-realization of ₹ 7672.59 crore on sale of HSD, SKO (PDS) & LPG (Domestic) [April-June 2010: ₹ 7342.59 crore on sale of MS, HSD, SKO (PDS) and LPG (Domestic)].
5. Impact, if any, on account of impairment of assets will be reviewed at the year end.
6. In view of loss for the quarter and due to uncertainty in estimation of profit for the year pending clarity on the extent of compensation for the under recoveries suffered on sale of HSD, SKO (PDS) & LPG (Domestic), no provision has been made for Current Tax and Deferred Tax for the current quarter.
7. Company has received 359 complaints from investors during the quarter which were all resolved. No complaint was pending at the beginning or end of the quarter.
8. Figures for the previous periods have been regrouped wherever necessary.

Segment-wise Results (₹ in crore)

	Quarter ended 30.06.2011 (Unaudited)	Quarter ended 30.06.2010 (Unaudited)	Previous year ended 31.03.2011 (Audited)
1. Segment Revenue			
(*a*) Sale of Petroleum Products	91167.42	67124.58	299830.58
(*b*) Sale of Petrochemicals	1748.41	844.46	5747.04

	Quarter ended 30.06.2011 (Unaudited)	Quarter ended 30.06.2010 (Unaudited)	Previous year ended 31.03.2011 (Audited)
(*c*) Other Business Activities	10624.47	5425.22	29160.81
Sub-total	**103540.30**	**73394.26**	**334738.43**
Less: Inter-segment Revenue	2255.79	1484.64	5885.24
Total Revenue	**101284.51**	**71909.62**	**328853.19**
2. **Segment Results:**			
(*a*) Profit Before Tax, Interest income, Interest expense and Dividend from each segment			
(*i*) Sale of Petroleum Products	(2395.42)	(2979.59)	11324.82
(*ii*) Sale of Petrochemicals	(408.90)	(483.99)	(1706.22)
(*iii*) Other Business Activities	5.55	7.46	(384.58)
Sub-total of (*a*)	**(2798.77)**	**(3456.12)**	**9234.02**
(*b*) Interest Expenditure	1037.59	571.17	2669.83
(*c*) Other un-allocable expenditure (Net of un-allocable income)	(117.66)	(638.90)	(2531.67)
Profit before Tax (a-b-c)	**(3718.70)**	**(3388.39)**	**9095.86**
3. **Capital Employed (Segment Assets-Segment Liabilities)**			
(*a*) Sale of Petroleum products	90400.92	60794.58	79023.93
(*b*) Sale of Petrochemicals	16949.52	17004.91	16937.97
(*c*) Other Business Activities	24.42	359.01	157.28
(*d*) Unallocable-Corporate	(55761.50)	(30994.10)	(40786.86)
Total	**51613.36**	**47164.40**	**55332.32**

Notes:

(*a*) Segment Revenue comprises Turnover (Net of Excise Duties), Subsidy and Grants received from Government of India and other Operating Income.

(*b*) Other Business segment of the Corporation comprises; Sale of Imported Crude Oil, Sale of Gas, Oil and Gas Exploration Activities, Explosives and Cryogenic Business and Wind Mill Power Generation.

(*c*) Figures for the previous periods have been rearranged wherever necessary.

Source: The Times of India, New Delhi, August 11, 2011.

Table 3

Gujarat State Petronet Ltd.

Unaudited Financial results for the Quarter Ended 30th June, 2011

(₹ in Lakhs)

Sr. No.	Particulars	For the Quarter ended 30.06.2011 (Unaudited)	For the Quarter ended 30.06.2010 (Unaudited)	For the Year ended 31.03.2011 (Audited)
1.	(*a*) Net Sales/Income from Operations	28429.14	25179.26	103910.02
	(*b*) Other Operating Income	331.33	271.48	741.81
	(*c*) **Total**	**28760.47**	**25450.74**	**104651.83**
2.	Expenditure			
	(*a*) Staff Cost	561.70	257.23	1528.71
	(*b*) Operation and Maintenance expenses	1085.19	816.71	3573.89
	(*c*) Administrative and other expenses	588.95	292.49	2613.59

Sr. No.	Particulars	For the Quarter ended 30.06.2011 (Unaudited)	For the Quarter ended 30.06.2010 (Unaudited)	For the Year ended 31.03.2011 (Audited)
	(*d*) Depreciation	4526.74	6871.64	12992.40
	(*e*) **Total**	**6762.58**	**8238.07**	**20708.59**
3.	**Profit from operations before other Income, Interest and Exceptional Items (1-2)**	**21997.89**	**17212.67**	**83943.24**
4.	Other Income	785.13	298.32	2163.43
5.	**Profit before Interest and Exceptional Items (3+4)**	**22783.02**	**17510.99**	**86106.67**
6.	Interest and Financial Charges	3238.45	2243.44	9606.25
7.	**Profit after Interest but before Exceptional Items (5–6)**	**19544.57**	**15267.55**	**76500.42**
8.	Exceptional Items	0.00	0.00	0.00
9.	**Profit (+)/Loss (–) from Ordinary Activities after Tax (7+8)**	**19544.57**	**15267.55**	**76500.42**
10.	Tax Expense	**5808.01**	**4757.92**	**25862.20**
	— Income Tax	4849.71	4757.79	13509.32
	— Deferred Tax	958.30	0.13	12352.88
11.	**Net Profit (+)/Loss (–0) from Ordinary Activities after Tax (9–10)**	**13736.56**	**10509.63**	**50638.22**
12.	Extraordinary Items (net of tax expenses)	0.00	0.00	0.00
13.	**Net Profit (+)/Loss (–) for the period (11–12)**	**13736.56**	**10509.63**	**50638.22**
14.	Paid-up Equity Share Capital (face value of ₹ 10/- each)	56261.42	56248.42	56258.25
15.	Reserves excluding revaluation reserves			144241.72
16.	(*a*) Basic and diluted EPS before Extraordinary Items for the period, for the year to date and previous year			
	Basic EPS (₹)	2.44	1.87	9.00
	Diluted EPS (₹)	2.44	1.87	8.97
	(face value of ₹ 10/- each)	(not annualised)	(not annualised)	
	(*b*) Basic and diluted EPS after Extraordinary Items for the period, for the year to date and previous year			
	Basic EPS (₹)	2.44	1.87	9.00
	Diluted EPS (₹)	2.44	1.87	8.97
	(face value of ₹ 10/- each)	(not annualised)	(not annualised)	
17.	Public Shareholding			
	— No. of Shares	350,308,905	350,178,891	350,277,198
	— Percentage of Shareholding	62.26%	62.26%	62.26%
18.	Promoters and Promoter Group Shareholding			
	(*a*) Pledged/Encumbered			
	— Number of shares	Nil	Nil	Nil
	— Percentage of shares (as a % of the total shareholding of promoter and promoter group)	Nil	Nil	Nil
	— Percentage of shares (as a % of the total share capital of the Company)	Nil	Nil	Nil
	(*b*) Non-encumbered			
	— Number of shares	212,305,270	212,305,270	212,305,270
	— Percentage of shares (as a % of the total shareholding of the promoter and promoter group)	100.00%	100.00%	100.00%
	— Percentage of shares (as a % of the total share capital of the Company)	37.74%	37.74%	37.74%

Segment-wise Revenue, Results and Capital Employed for the Quarter Ended 30th June, 2011

(₹ in Lakhs)

Sr. No.	Particulars	For the Quarter ended 30.06.2011 (Unaudited)	For the Quarter ended 30.06.2010 (Unaudited)	For the Year ended 31.03.2011 (Audited)
1.	Segment Revenue (Net Sales/Income)			
	(*a*) Gas Transportation	27,196.29	25,217.47	103,305.92
	(*b*) Sale of Electricity	1,588.28	238.63	1,389.19
	Total	28,784.57	25,456.10	104,695.11
	Less: Inter-Segment Revenue	—	—	—
	Sales/Income from Operations	**28,784.57**	**25,456.10**	**104,695.11**
2.	**Segment Results:**			
	Profit(+)/Loss(–)			
	(*a*) Gas Transportation	22,335.77	17,493.68	88,672.22
	(*b*) Sale of Electricity	449.24	74.00	(1,531.74)
	Total	**22,785.01**	**17,567.68**	**87,140.48**
	Less: (*i*) Interest and Financial Charges	3,238.86	2,243.44	9,606.25
	(*ii*) Other Un-allocable Expenditure	762.61	349.65	3,153.96
	Add: (*iii*) Other Un-allocable Income	761.03	292.96	2,120.14
	Total Profit before Tax	**19,544.57**	**15,267.55**	**76,500.42**
3.	**Capital Employed:**			
	(Segment Assets Less Segment Liabilities)			
	(*a*) Gas Transportation	315,652.36	285,813.90	315,559.75
	(*b*) Sale of Electricity	27,407.70	20,219.72	25,706.32
	(*c*) Un-allocable	52,476.40	18,070.16	33,592.06
	Total	**395,536.46**	**324,103.78**	**374,858.13**

Notes:

1. The above results were recommended by the Audit Committee and approved by the Board of Directors of the Company in their meeting held on 9th August, 2011.
2. The statutory auditors have carried out a limited review of the above results.
3. Segment Revenue includes Other Income which is directly attributable to each segment.
4. During the quarter, the Company has allotted 31707 equity shares of ₹ 10 each to eligible employees pursuant to ESOP Plan 2005.
5. Because of change in depreciation rate on Gas Transmission Pipeline(s) from 8.33% SLM to 3.17% SLM the depreciation amount for corresponding quarter is not comparable.
6. The status of the investor complaints for the quarter ended on 30th June 2011 was as follows:

	Opening	Received	Disposed Off	Closing
No. of Complaints:	0	93	93	0

7. The Gas volumes transported is as follows: (in MMSCM)

Year/period	Qtr. 1
Financial Year 2011-12	3344.80
Financial Year 2010-11	3303.54

8. Figures of the previous years have been regrouped/rearranged wherever considered necessary.

Source: The Economic Times, New Delhi 11th August, 2011.

SOCIAL REPORTING

What is Social Reporting?

Social reporting is defined as reporting of some meaningful, definable domain of a business enterprise's activities that have social impact. Put another way, social reporting implies the measurement and reporting, internal or external, of information concerning the impact of a business enterprise and its activities on society. The Trueblood Committee Report (AICPA, USA, 1973) observes that "an objective of financial statements is to report on those activities of the enterprise affecting society which can be determined and described or measured and which are important to the role of the enterprise in its social environment." Social reporting aims at measuring (either in monetary or non-monetary units) adverse and beneficial effects of an enterprise's activities both on the firm and/or those affected by the firm; it measures social costs and benefits.

Uses of Social Responsibility Information

Social responsibility information about business enterprises is mainly useful to internal users (management), external users (shareholders and other investors), and in influencing the share prices of a company.

1. **Internal Users:** Within a company, the greatest need and the greatest demand for social responsibility information comes from top management, or board of directors. Top management, especially the chief executive officer, needs social performance information to respond to a critical press, to answer shareholders questions, and to ensure that company policies are followed. Corporate directors, especially because of their growing legal liability, need to know in some detail what sort of social programmes the company is having, and what result it is getting. Directors also need complete information about the effects of the company on society, it is probably more important that they be fully informed as to negative effects, since this is where the criticism will be directed and this is where the directors may have to defend themselves. Labour unions can also be expected to seek social performance information about their companies.
2. **External Users:** The external users demand for social accounting information is even more diverse. Social accounting and reporting are needed by present and potential investors, by large institutions and individuals. Some studies conducted in this area show the impact of social disclosure on investment decisions. There are ethical investors who are concerned with not only economic performance but also with social responsibility performance of business enterprises while making investment decisions.
3. **Impact on Share Prices:** The disclosure of social information helps investors in studying the negative effects of social awareness expenditures on earnings per share alongwith any compensating positive effects that reduce risk or create interest for a particular investment. Between firms competing in the capital markets those perceived to have the highest expected future earnings in combination with the lowest expected risk from environmental and other factors will be most successful at attracting long term funds. Others believe that ethical investors form a clientele that would like to avoid particular investments entirely for ethical reasons and would prefer to favour socially responsible companies in their investment decisions.

Scope of Social Responsibility Reporting

The areas for the purpose of social reporting have been identified in the financial accounting literature. Generally, such areas are as follows:

1. Net income contribution
2. Human resource contribution

3. Public contribution
4. Environmental contribution
5. Product or service contribution.

The term contribution includes both benefits and costs associated with an organisation's activities. Implicit in this definition of the scope of corporate social responsibility are a variety of users having different purposes in using accounting information.

1. **Net Income Contribution:** The growing attention which other social objectives are receiving does not reduce the importance of the income objective. A business organisation cannot survive without an adequate financial surplus; long-range planning includes calculating the minimum return to shareholders. There is a clear correlation between income and other objectives. The failure to recognise a social responsibility may well affect the organisation's income performance either in the short term or the long term. Thus, excessive hours of work under bad working conditions may damage the ability of workers to maintain the level of output. Failure to pay adequate attention to the quality of the product and customer's reactions to poor product quality may ultimately affect sales and income.
2. **Human Resource Contribution:** This contribution reflects the impact of organisational activities on the people who constitute the human resources of the organisation. These activities include: recruiting practices; training programmes; experience building—job rotation; job enrichment; wage and salary levels; fringe benefit plans; management-union relations; employee skills; employee knowledge; employee attitudes; employee self actualisation; congruence of employee and organisational goals; mutual trust and confidence; job security, stability of work force, layoff and recall practices; transfer and promotion policies; occupational health; freedom from undue stress; on-the-job physical environment, and on-the-job safety.
3. **Public Contribution:** This area considers the impact of organisational activities on individuals generally outside the organisation. For example, general philanthropy—contributions to educational, cultural, or charitable organisations; financial or manpower support for public transportation; health services, urban housing, day-care centres, minority business, community problem solving, minority group programmes and general volunteer community activities; equal opportunity employment practices; training and employment of handicapped persons; and taxes paid.
4. **Environmental Contribution:** This area involves the environmental aspects of production, covering the use of resources, the production process and the product itself, including recycling and other positive environmental activities. Attention has been drawn in recent years to the negative aspects of organisational activities such as the pollution of air and water, noise and spoiling of the environment. Moreover, industrial activities lead to a net use of irreplaceable resources and a net production of solid wastes.
5. **Product or Service Contribution:** This area concerns the qualitative aspects of the organisation's product or service, for example, product utility, product life-durability, product safety, serviceability as well as the welfare role of the product or service. Moreover, it includes customer satisfaction, truthfulness in advertising, completeness and clarity of labelling and packaging. Many of these considerations are important already from a marketing point of view.

VALUE-ADDED REPORTING

Value-added statement (VAS) or reporting is a modified version of the profit and loss account. Like profit and loss account, the VAS reveals the operating performance of a company at a given point in time, using both accrual and matching procedures. However, the VAS does not aim to provide a profit (or loss) figure as in the case of profit and loss account but a figure or return to a larger group of capital and labour providers (*i.e.*, owners, employees), other claimants or interested parties.

The term 'value added' means the market price of the output of an enterprise less cost of bought-in goods and services. The resulting balance money is known as the value added by an enterprise and this money can he divided among the various parties who have contributed in the production of goods and services of the enterprise in the form of factor inputs. Thus, the owners (or shareholders), creditors and governments (through taxation) are recipients of the enterprise income. Thus, the value-added income would include wages, rent, interest, taxes, dividends paid to shareholders and retained income of the company.

As stated earlier, the value added statements can be derived from the profit and loss account. Generally, the profit and loss account is expressed as follows:

$$RE = S - B - DP - W - I - DD - T \quad ...(1)$$

where

RE = Retained Earnings
S = Sales Revenue
B = Bought in materials and services
DP = Depreciation
W = Wages
I = Interest
DD = Dividends
T = Taxes

Equation (1) expresses the profit as a return to shareholders. The value-added statement can be obtained by rearranging Equation (1), as follows:

$$S - B = W + I + DD + T + DP + RE \quad ...(2)$$

or

$$S - B - DP = W + I + DD + T + RE \quad ...(3)$$

Equation (2) indicates the gross value added and Equation (3) indicates the net value added. In both the cases (equation) the left part of the equation indicates the value-added (net or gross) and the right part of the equation divides the value added among the groups involved.

Tables 4 shows the preparation of a value-added statement and also indicates as to how a VAS can be derived from the profit and loss account.

The value-added statement reflects a broader view of an enterprise's role and objectives than profit does. Profit is considered by some to convey narrow, sectional interpretation. Value-added reflects the performance of a team, *i.e.*, employees, managers, shareholders, creditors. VAS helps the employees to perceive them as responsible participators in a team effort with management and thus may motivate them to work harder. Based on the value added and maximised productivity incentives can be given to employees. VAS provides a better measure of the size and importance of companies. Value added-based ratios are interpreted as more indicative and predictive of the strength of the company than conventional ratios. The value-added concept is useful in the context of large companies that influence a large sections of society and have a general economic and social importance besides the limited interests of shareholders.

Profit and Loss Account

	(₹)	(₹)
Sales		20,00,000
Less: Materials	2,00,000	
Wages	4,00,000	
Services purchased	6,00,000	
Interest paid	1,20,000	
Depreciation	80,000	
		14,00,000

	(₹)	(₹)
Profit before tax		6,00,000
Income (assuming 50% tax rate)		3,00,000
Profit after tax		3,00,000
Less: Dividends payable		1,00,000
Retained Earnings		2,00,000

Table 4 Value-added Statement

	(₹)	(₹)
Sales		20,00,000
Less: Bought-in materials and services and depreciation		8,80,000
Value Added (available for Distribution or Retention)		11,20,000
Distributed as follows:		
To Employees		4,00,000
To Providers of Capital:		
Interest	1,20,000	
Dividends	1,00,000	2,20,000
To Government		3,00,000
Retained earnings		2,00,000
Value Added		11,20,000

INTERIM REPORTING

Concept and Need

Interim reporting is the financial reporting made by a company on a less than annual basis, such as half yearly or quarterly financial reports.

Annual data are insufficient to evaluate developments in general economic, industry, and company activities and making or revising projections of earnings and financial position as a basis for investment decisions. Investment decisions are made on the basis of information disclosed in company annual reports. These economic decisions are made throughout the year rather than at year-end reporting dates. Although annual reporting has been accepted by accountants and/or law, investment decisions based on financial data are made daily and require current financial information. No doubt the annual report will continue as a report on management's stewardship for the full year and a benchmark or measurement of financial progress over several years. But, neither the dynamics of the internal organisation, nor outside economic forces stop and start over at each new accounting year. Therefore, it is suggested that company financial reporting should continuously measure and report on the firm's progress and provide information on a less than annual basis for the benefit of shareholders and other external users.

The FASB's (USA) has found the following five possible objectives and uses for interim reporting:

1. To estimate annual earnings.
2. To make projections.
3. To identify turning points.
4. To evaluate management performance.
5. To supplement the annual report.

Problems in Interim Reporting

Basically two problems—Accounting Problems and Conceptual Problems are involved in interim financial reporting.

Accounting Problems

Accounting Problems are of the following types:

1. **Inventory Problems:** In a business enterprise, inventory is a major element in the generation of income. Inventory problem in interim reporting has three types of problems; determination of inventory quantities, valuation of inventories, and adjustments of valuation. The development of inventory data for interim reporting depends largely on the making of accurate physical counts and its costing procedure. However, the valuation problem is more important than the quantity problem. It is almost invariably considered impractical to count and price the inventory every quarter or every month, so estimates of gross profit must be used to determine cost of goods sold. Alternatively, the company may have perpetual inventory records integrated with the accounting records, allowing direct determination of cost of goods sold, but the perpetual records may not be verified by cycle counts, and some interim allowance will be needed for annual physical inventory adjustments.
2. **Matching Problem:** Business operations are not similar and uniform throughout the year. Resources are acquired and output is done in advance of sales. Some costs related to current sales do not mature into liabilities or readily measurable expenses until a subsequent time. Because of various lead and lag relationships between cost and sales, difficulties are created in matching costs and revenues. The relationship between costs and revenues becomes unclear. Interim accruals for various selling expenses, general and administrative expenses, allowances for doubtful accounts, and deferrals and contingencies are illustrations of items that normally require companies to rely heavily on estimates.

   Many techniques and procedures are available in accounting for allocating costs between different periods. But the allocation procedures appear to be highly arbitrary which raise serious questions as to the reliability and usefulness of the results. For example, depreciation and property taxes may be allocated to months on a time basis, but deducting a constant amount each period when sales fluctuate, tend to increase the amplitude of fluctuations in reported profits. Some expenses to be incurred during a period may be uncertain at the time when revenues are reported, e.g., maintenance and repairs, employee vacations, various taxes, etc. Income tax is also a complex area in interim reporting requiring considerable attention. In order to calculate interim income taxes, a company must estimate such items as the annual pretax income, and other permanent differences for the full year.
3. **Extent of Disclosure Problem:** There is a problem of deciding the quantity of disclosures in interim financial reports. Generally speaking, disclosure requirements applicable for annual reporting are not applicable to interim reporting. In the absence of mandatory interim disclosures, the interim disclosure practices are likely to vary. There is a problem of determining materiality criteria for deciding the information to be disclosed in interim reports. The treatment to be given in respect of prior period adjustments, extraordinary items and earning per share can create difficulties in interim reporting.

Conceptual Issues

The primary conceptual issue is whether the interim period is part of a longer period or is a period in itself. The former position is known as the integral view, the latter as the discrete view. Under the integral view, revenue and expenses for interim periods are based on estimates of total annual revenues and expenses. The discrete view holds that earnings for each period are not affected by projections of the annual results; the methods used to measure earnings are the same for any period, whether a quarter or a year. As a practical matter some elements of both positions are recognised in current reporting practices.

Those who favour the second, the integral approach, view each interim period primarily as being an integral part of the annual period. Under this view deferrals, accruals, and estimates at the end of each interim period are affected by judgements made at the interim date as to the results of operations for the balance of the annual period.

Proponents of the discrete approach, on the other hand, argue that users are interested in a report of the actual realisations of the interim period itself in order to monitor management's (and the firm's) performance during this period. Consequently, they argue against any allocation of costs based upon annual results that would lead to a smoothing effect in which turning points and short-term fluctuations are obscured from investors.

For the purpose of interim reporting, discrete approach is preferred for some items (issues) whereas integral view is suggested for the other items. This combination approach has been recognised by FASB (USA) when it states:

"Users may be interested both in making predictions for various future periods and in detecting changes in profit trend and liquidity. It may not be necessary ... to place emphasis on one of these or on other possible uses. The integral and discrete views may seem to have both advantages and disadvantages. Therefore a more reasoned approach is to attempt to obtain the advantages and minimise the disadvantages of each of these views."

Audit of Interim Reporting

Interim period reporting is inevitably an attempt to ensure that report users have reliable information on which to base their decisions. Interim reporting present particular problems in the context of audit. The urgency of timely reporting both precludes a full external audit, and increases the chance of the inaccuracies arising through estimations and allocations. Furthermore, narrative comments are less easily validated or assessed for accuracy and completeness than well-defined numerical disclosures.

Interim Reporting in India

In India, earlier, the companies were required to provide financial information by way of annual reports to their shareholders. Recently it was felt that there is a wide time gap between the two annual reports and during this time gap investors do not get information to make sound investment and other decisions. On the other hand, rational investment decisions cannot be made on the basis of rumours, hearsay, liking or disliking. The publication of the interim results of the companies may prove a reliable source to evaluate the strengths and weaknesses of the company.

AS 25 Interim Financial Reporting issued by Accounting Standards Board of ICAI in February 2002 observes:

"Timely and reliable interim financial reporting improves the ability of investors, creditors and others to understand an enterprise's capacity to generate earnings and cash flows, its financial condition and liquidity."

AS 25 comes into effect in respect of accounting periods commencing on or after April 1, 2002. The objective of AS 25 is to prescribe the minimum content of an interim financial report and to prescribe the principles for recognition and measurement in a complete or condensed financial statements for an interim period.

The Securities and Exchange Board of India (SEBI) has issued the guidelines on February 4, 2000 requiring the stock exchanges to amend the listing agreements to incorporate quarterly financial reporting.

As per SEBI's guidelines, a company should furnish unaudited financial result on a quarterly basis in the prescribed proforma within one month of the expiry of the period to the Stock Exchanges and will make an announcement forthwith to the Stock Exchanges where the company is listed and also with in 48 hours of the conclusion of the Board Meeting at least in one English daily newspaper circulating in the whole or substantially the whole of India and in a newspaper published in the language of the region, where the registered office of the company is situated.

In addition, a company has to prepare half yearly results in the same proforma. The half yearly results are subject to limited audit review by the auditors of the company.

AS 25 Interim Financial Reporting (issued in February 2002) has made the following recommendations with regard to interim financial information:

1. A complete set of financial statements normally includes:
   (*a*) balance sheet
   (*b*) statement of profit and loss
   (*c*) cash flow statement
   (*d*) notes including those relating to accounting policies and other statements and explanatory material that are an integral part of the financial statements.
2. In the interest of timeliness and cost considerations and to avoid repetition of information previously reported, an enterprise may be required to or may, elect to present less information at interim dates as compared with its annual financial statements.
3. An interim financial report should include, at a minimum, the following components:
   (*a*) Condensed balance sheet
   (*b*) Condensed statement of profit and loss
   (*c*) Condensed cash flow statement
   (*d*) Selected explanatory notes.
4. Selected explanatory notes should include the following information, as a minimum, in the notes to its interim financial statements, if material and if not disclosed elsewhere in the interim financial report:
   (*a*) a statement that the same accounting policies are followed in the interim financial statements
   (*b*) explanatory comments about the seasonability of interim operations
   (*c*) nature and amount of item affecting assets, liabilities, equity, net income or cash flows that are unusual because of their nature, size or incidence
   (*d*) nature and amount of changes in estimates of amounts reported in prior interim periods of the current financial year or changes in estimates of amount reported in prior financial years, if those changes have a material effect in the current interim period
   (*e*) issuances, buybacks, repayments and restructuring of debt equity and potential equity shares
   (*f*) segment revenue, segment capital employed and segment result for business segments or geographical segments, whichever is the enterprise's primary basis of segment reporting
   (*g*) dividends, aggregate or per share separately for equity shares and other shares
   (*h*) effect of changes in the composition of the enterprises during the interim period such as amalgamations, acquisitions or disposal of subsidiaries and long-term investments, restructuring, and discontinuing operations
   (*i*) material changes in contingent liabilities since the last annual balance sheet date.

The above informations should normally be reported on a financial year-to-date basis. However, the enterprise should also disclose any events or transactions that are material to an understanding of the current interim period.

Table 5 display, quarterly unaudited financial result of Escorts Ltd. as published in national newspaper.

Table 5
Escorts Ltd.
Unaudited Financial Results for the Quarter Ended 30th June, 2011

(₹ in Lakhs)

Sl. No.	Particulars	For the Quarter ended		For the Nine Months ended		Previous Year ended
		30.06.2011 Unaudited	30.06.2010 Unaudited	30.06.2011 Unaudited	30.06.2010 Unaudited	30.06.2010 Audited
1.	(*a*) Net Sales/Income from Operations	72,896.53	80,621.27	2,44,656.74	2,07,811.45	2,74,573.25
	(*b*) Other Operating Income	1,059.89	463.95	3,254.56	1,216.40	1,894.08
	Total Net Operating Income	**73,956.42**	**81,085.22**	**2,47,911.30**	**2,09,027.85**	**2,76,467.33**
2.	**Expenditure**					
	(*a*) (Increase)/decrease in stock in trade and work in progress	2,003.78	(3,300.57)	446.19	(5,631.60)	(5,503.43)
	(*b*) Consumption of Raw Materials	46,034.96	54,147.90	1,56,549.92	1,36,916.12	1,78,719.86
	(*c*) Purchase of Traded Goods	4,679.72	4,249.44	19,944.35	9,484.05	13,052.82
	(*d*) Employees Cost	8,438.54	8,606.78	25,080.62	22,638.75	28,923.80
	(*e*) Depreciation and Amortisation	905.16	955.87	2,917.40	3,384.68	4,348.38
	(*f*) Other Expenditure	9,373.37	9,549.74	32,309.46	25,991.31	38,153.74
	Total Expenditure	**71,435.53**	**74,209.16**	**2,37,247.94**	**1,92,783.31**	**2,57,695.17**
3.	**Profit from Operations before other Income, Interest, Exceptional Items and Tax (1-2)**	**2,520.89**	**6,876.06**	**10,663.36**	**16,244.54**	**18,772.16**
4.	Other Income	—	—	—	—	10.00
5.	**Profit before Interest, Exceptional Items and Tax (3-4)**	**2,520.89**	**6,876.06**	**10,663.36**	**16,244.54**	**18,782.16**
6.	Interest, Bank and Finance charges (Net)	759.13	(27.61)	1,752.96	335.89	1,173.50
7.	**Profit after Interest but before Exceptional Items & Tax (5-6)**	**1,761.76**	**6,903.67**	**8,910.40**	**15,908.65**	**17,608.66**
8.	Exceptional Items (Net)	(105.03)	64.25	(40.73)	355.35	(1,193.11)
9.	**Profit (+) from Ordinary Activities before tax (7-8)**	**1,866.79**	**6,839.42**	**8,951.13**	**15,553.30**	**18,801.77**
10.	Tax Expense	544.99	2,255.69	(2,241.81)	4,482.69	5,047.22
11.	**Net Profit(+)/Loss(–) from ordinary activities after tax (9-10)**	**1,321.80**	**4,583.73**	**11,192.94**	**11,070.61**	**13,754.55**
12.	Extraordinary Item (net of tax expense)	—	—	—	—	—
13.	**Net Profit (+)/Loss (–) for the period (11-12)**	**1,321.80**	**4,583.73**	**11,192.94**	**11,070.61**	**13,754.55**
14.	Paid-up equity share capital (Face Value ₹ 10/- each)	10,561.80	10,142,22	10,561.80	10,142.22	10,561.80
	Less: Amount recoverable from Escorts Employees Benefit and Welfare Trust	331.36	361.16	331.36	361.16	334.36
	Paid-up equity share capital (Face Value ₹ 10/- each)	**10,230.44**	9,781.06	**10,230.44**	9,781.06	10,227.44

Sl. No.	Particulars	For the Quarter ended		For the Nine Months ended		Previous Year ended
		30.06.2011 Unaudited	30.06.2010 Unaudited	30.06.2011 Unaudited	30.06.2010 Unaudited	30.06.2010 Audited
15.	Reserves excluding Revaluation Reserves	—	—	—	—	1,57,108.01
16.	Earnings Per Share (EPS)					
	(*a*) Basic EPS (not annualized)	**1.29**	4.86	**10.94**	11.70	14.67
	(*b*) Diluted EPS (not annualized)	**1.29**	4.70	**10.85**	11.33	14.42
17.	Public shareholding					
	— Number of shares	7,73,45,538	7,31,50,160	7,73,45,538	7,31,50,160	7,73,46,038
	— Percentage of shareholding	73.23	72.13	73.23	72.13	73.23
18.	Promoters and Promoter Group Shareholding					
	(*a*) Pledged/Encumbered					
	Number of shares	56,00,000	63,60,892	56,00,000	63,60,892	57,84,892
	— Percentage of shares (as a % of the total shareholding of promoter and promoter group)	19.81	22.50	19.81	22.50	20.46
	— Percentage of shares (as a % of the total share capital of the company)	5.30	6.27	5.30	6.27	5.48
	(*b*) Non-encumbered					
	Number of shares	2,26,72,498	2,19,11,106	2,26,72,498	2,19,11,106	2,24,87,106
	— Percentage of shares (as a % of the total shareholding of promoter and promoter group)	80.19	77.50	80.19	77.50	79.54
	— Percentage of shares (as a % of the total share capital of the company)	21.47	21.60	21.47	21.60	21.29

Notes:

1. The above results have been subjected to limited review by the statutory auditors. After review by the Audit committee, these results have been approved and taken on record by the Financial Results Committee of the Board of Directors at its meeting held on 5th August, 2011.
2. At the beginning and end of the quarter here were no investor complaint pending for disposal. During the quarter, the Company received 5 complaints from investors, which were disposed off within the quarter itself.
3. Previous year figures have been regrouped/rearranged wherever necessary.

Segment-wise Revenue, Results and Capital Employed, for the Quarter Ended 30th June, 2011

(₹ in Lakhs)

Sl. No.	Particulars	For the Quarter ended		For the Nine Months ended		Previous Year ended
		30.06.2011 Unaudited	30.06.2010 Unaudited	30.06.2011 Unaudited	30.06.2010 Unaudited	30.06.2010 Audited
1.	**Segment Revenue:**					
	(*a*) Agri Machinery Products	66,861.91	74,754.70	2,25,926.23	1,87,748.93	2,47,378.77
	(*b*) Auto Ancillary Products	3,055.90	2,813.94	9,329.15	8,326.56	11,088.66
	(*c*) Railway Equipments	4,368.06	4,148.46	13,702.92	14,265.12	19,775.91
	(*d*) Unallocable	155.15	156.20	398.96	427.55	455.70
	Total	**74,441.02**	**81,873.30**	**2,49,357.26**	**2,10,768.16**	**2,78,699.04**

Sl. No.	Particulars	For the Quarter ended		For the Nine Months ended		Previous Year ended
		30.06.2011 Unaudited	30.06.2010 Unaudited	30.06.2011 Unaudited	30.06.2010 Unaudited	30.06.2010 Audited
	Less: Inter Segment Revenue	484.60	788.08	1,445.96	1,740.31	2,231.71
	Net sales/Income from Operations	**73,956.42**	**81,085.22**	**2,47,911.30**	**2,09,027.85**	**2,76,467.33**
2.	**Segment Results:**					
	(*a*) Agri Machinery Products	3,574.20	8,323.98	13,883.73	18,040.41	22,336.16
	(*b*) Auto Ancillary Products	(449.29)	(713.99)	(1,164.47)	(1,286.67)	(1,733.28)
	(*c*) Railway Equipments	364.58	10.82	1,334.83	1,649.75	2,283.95
	Total	**3,489.49**	**7,620.81**	**14,054.09**	**18,403.49**	**22,886.83**
	Less:					
	— Interest, Bank and Finance charges (Net)	759.13	(27.61)	1,752.96	335.89	1,173.50
	— Exceptional Items	(105.03)	64.25	(40.73)	355.35	(1,193.11)
	— Other unallocated expenditure (*Net of unallocated income*)	968.60	744.75	3,390.73	2,158.95	4,104.67
	Profit before Tax	**1,866.79**	**6,839.42**	**8,951.13**	**15,553.30**	**18,801.77**
3.	**Capital Employed** (*Segmented assets – Segment Liabilities*)					
	(*a*) Agri Machinery Products	1,05,035.49	96,562.20	1,05,035.49	96,562.20	99,246.39
	(*b*) Auto Ancillary Products	4,836.01	4,663.47	4,836.01	4,663.47	4,584.26
	(*c*) Railway Equipments	9,224.86	9,943.89	9,224.86	9,943.89	10,042.22
	(*d*) Unallocable	1,00,563.40	94,018.16	1,00,563.40	94,018.16	89,769.82
	Total	**2,19,659.76**	**2,05,187.72**	**2,19,659.76**	**2,05,187.72**	**2,03,642.69**

***Source*:** The Economic Times, New Delhi, 10th August, 2011.

THEORY QUESTIONS

1. Define financial reporting.
2. Explain the objectives of financial reporting.
3. List users in general purpose financial reporting.
4. What is specific purpose report? What are its limitations?
5. Discuss qualities of accounting information.
6. Write explanatory notes on:
   (*a*) Relevance
   (*b*) Reliability
   (*c*) Understandability
   (*d*) Comparability
   (*e*) Consistency
   (*f*) Materiality.
7. What is segment reporting? Discuss the usefulness of segmental disclosures to investors and other users.
8. What are the difficulties in providing segmental information in company annual reports?
9. What is social reporting?
10. What are the uses of social responsibility information?

11. Identify the areas for the purpose of social reporting.
12. What is a value added statement? What are its format?
13. Distinguish between profit and loss account and value added statement.
14. How is value-added statement derived from the profit and loss account?
15. Using imaginary figures, prepare a value-added statement.
16. What are the advantages and disadvantages of value-added statement?
17. What is interim reporting? What are its objectives?
18. Discuss the position of interim reporting in India.
19. Explain the problems in interim reporting.

21

COMPUTERISED ACCOUNTING (HOW TO USE TALLY)

LEARNING OBJECTIVES

After reading this chapter, you should be able to:

- *Distinguish* between computerised and manual accounting.
- *Describe* steps in Tally for the preparation of financial statements.
- *Explain* the essentials in company creation.
- *Know* how to open ledger accounts in Tally.
- *Discuss* entering Vouchers in Tally.

Keeping accurate accounting records is an important part of managing an organization. Smaller firms can usually manage with simple book-keeping procedures but bigger firms juggling with larger sum of money and more complex financial transactions may find their workload eased by using a computerised accounting system. The computerised accounting system provides better record keeping and improved reporting.

Computerized vs Manual Accounting

In manual accounting one first has to record accounting transactions in journal (subsidiary books) and cash book. The transactions from journal and cash book are then transferred to the respective ledgers. Ledgers balances (difference of debit and credit total) are transferred to Trial balance. For preparation of final accounts, from trial balance, nominal accounts are posted to Profit and Loss Account and real and personal accounts are posted to balance Sheet.

Since all posting, totaling and balancing—all are done manually, there are chances of error.

When computerized accounting is used all work of recording and preparation of final accounts can be done in the following three simple steps:

1. Create Company.
2. Open ledger accounts under (Predefined) groups with opening balance (in case of an existing company).
3. Make Voucher entry (entering the transaction in different vouchers depending upon the nature of transaction).

Posting of transactions to ledgers, preparation of trial balance, final accounts etc. is done automatically by software. All above three steps are discussed in detail later in this chapter.

Starting Tally

Tally is a financial package developed by Tally Solutions Pvt. Ltd. Tally 3.0, 4.5 are DOS based where as Tally 5.4, 6.3, 7.2, 8.1 and 9 are window based version.

Either by clicking at Tally from its icon on computer desktop or running it from window Explorer, you can run Tally to get the initial screen of Tally as shown in Figure 1.

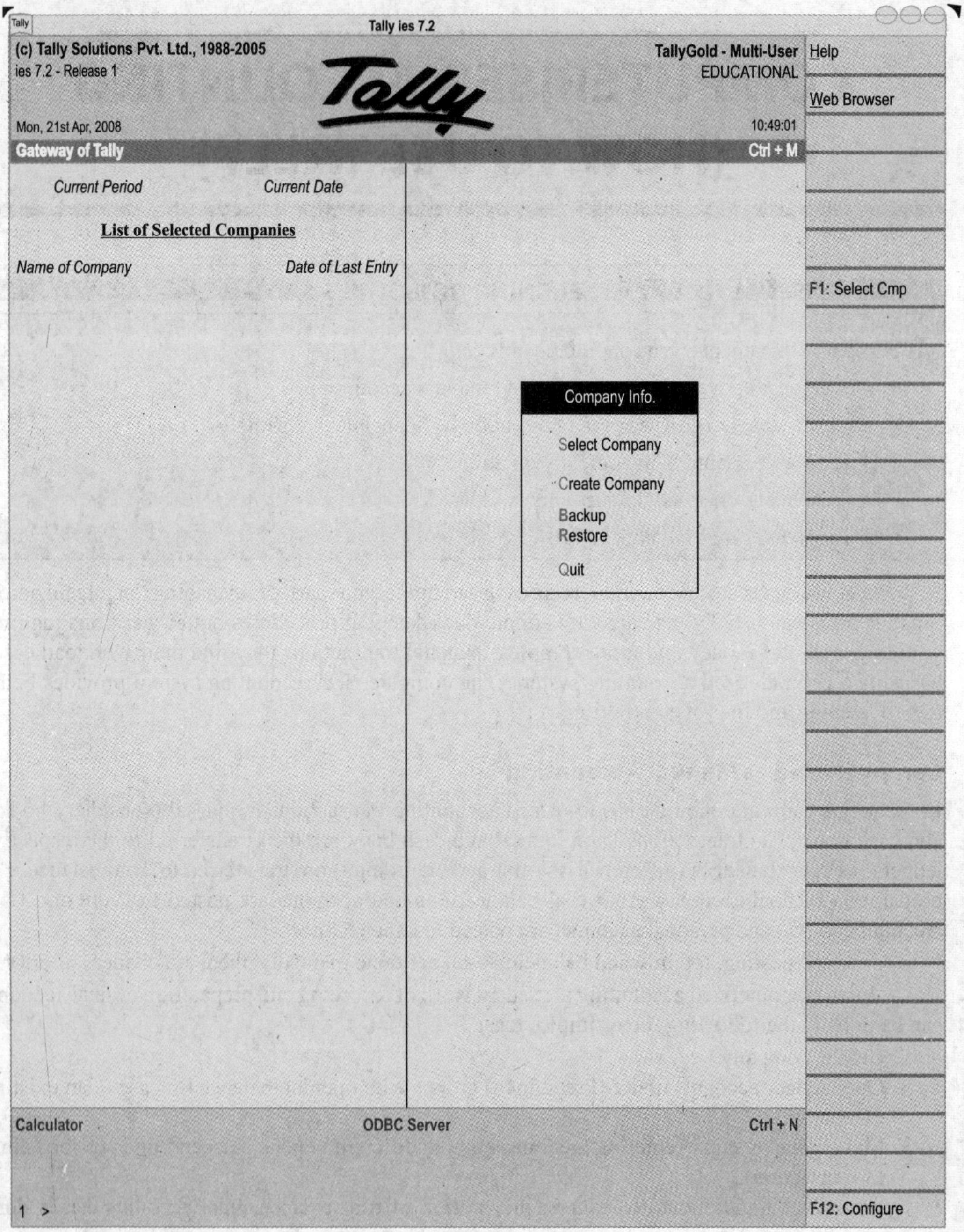

Fig. 1

Items on Tally Screen

Tally ies 7.2

(c) Tally Solutions Pvt. Ltd., 1988-2005
ies 7.2 - Release 1

Tally

TallyGold - Multi-User
EDUCATIONAL

Mon, 21st Apr, 2008 11.59:11

Gateway of Tally Ctrl + M

Current Period	*Current Date*
1-4-2012 to 31-3-2013	**Fri, 1st Apr, 2013**

List of Selected Companies

Name of Company	*Date of Last Entry*
M/s Aman & Co	***1-Apr-2013***

Gateway of Tally .....

Company Info.

Select Company
Shut Company
Create Company
Security control
Alter
Change Rally Vault
Split Company Data
Backup
Restore
Quit

Help
Web Browser
F1: Select Cmp
F1: Shut Cmp
F11: Features
F12: Configure

Calculator ODBC Server Ctrl + N

1 >

Fig. 2

1. **Title Bar** is self-explanatory, showing developer of software, version of software and date.
2. **Gateway of Tally** is the area in which you will actually work. It is divided into two parts:

   The left part contains the current period (financial period one is working with), the current date (user last worked in the current period) and the list of loaded companies. The active company is shown in bold letters.

   The right part contains the menu options. The options are:
   - Select Company
   - Shut Company
   - Create Company
   - Create Group Company
   - Alter
   - Change Tally Vault
   - Split Company Data
   - Back up
   - Restore
   - Quit.

   Since you have not created a Company, you would not be able to select any company and also you do not want to quit. So the only logical selection here would be to create a Company.
3. **Button Bar** contains buttons which perform various useful functions. For example, the button in this area has a caption: "F_1: Select Comp.", this means that in order to select one of the companies whose accounts you are maintaining can be selected by using this button. Similarly, you have "$\underline{F}_1$: Shut Comp.". [$\underline{F}_1$: F_1 + Alt].
4. **Calculator**, by default the calculator remains inactive. It can be made active by clt + N.

STEPS FOR PREPARATION OF FINAL ACCOUNTS IN TALLY

The following are the steps in the preparation of financial statements through Tally:

1. Company Creation
2. Opening of Ledger Accounts
3. Voucher Entry.

The above steps are being discussed through solving the illustration given below:

Illustration: From the following transaction of M/s VEE KAY ENTERPRISES, write up the journal in proper form, post a ledger, take out a trail balance and prepare final accounts using Tally:

2013

April 1 **Assets:** Cash in Hand ₹ 10,000, Cash at Bank ₹ 34,000, Stock of Goods ₹ 20,000, Machinery ₹ 50,000, Furniture ₹ 20,000, M/s Surya Bros. owe ₹ 30,000, M/s Balu Bros. owe ₹ 40,000.

Liabilities: Loan ₹ 1,00,000, sum owing to Jain Ltd. ₹ 20,000 and S Bros ₹ 10,000

		₹
April 1	Bought goods from R & Co.	30,000
April 1	Sold goods for cash	40,000
April 1	Sold goods to Surya Bros. on Credit	20,000
April 2	Cash deposited in the Bank	2,000
April 2	Received from Surya Bros. in full Settlement of amount due on April 1st	28,000
April 2	Payment made to Jain Bros. Ltd. by cheque	19,750
	They allowed discount	250

April 4	Purchase Furniture for cash	10,000
April 5	Bought goods	10,000
April 9	Balu Bros. pay by cheque. Cheque deposited in Bank	40,000
April 15	Bought goods of Jain Bros. Ltd.	10,000
	Paid carriage on these goods	500
April 16	Received cheque from Surya Bros. cheque deposited in Bank	19,500
	Discount allowed to them	500
April 17	Paid cheque to Jain Bros. Ltd.	10,000
April 19	Sold goods to Surya Bros.	60,000
April 24	Paid Municipal Taxes in cash	500
April 25	Borrowed from Navya Investment Co. Ltd. for constructing own premises Money deposited with bank for the time being.	50,000
April 30	Paid rent in cash	2,500
	Paid Salaries for the month	5,000
	Drew for Private use	2,500
	An old amount, written-off as Bad debt in 2011 is recovered	1,500

Step I–Company Creation

Company in Tally does not only mean company registered under Companies Act, but any entity which maintains set of books *i.e.*, an individual firm, partnership firm, a Hindu undivided family or non-profit organization.

To create the company, click creates company on company information option under Gateway of Tally. This opens the company creation screen as shown in Fig. 3.

Various items on the screen are described below:

Directory: Shows where in the hard disk, your data is being stored.

Name: Type here the name of the company you want to create. This name is displayed at company selection lists and internal reports.

Mailing Name: Type here the mailing name of the company. By default this name is the same as the name of the Company but if you wish you can specify a different may be a short name.

Address: Type here the address of your company. You can enter any number of lines for the address. This field is optional. If you don't want to give address move to next field by pressing <Enter>.

State: Type here the state in which you are going to work. It is very important in case, you are considering VAT because different rates apply in different states.

Pin code: It is portal code given by portal authorities to various areas in the country.

E-mail Address: Give e-mail address of the company.

Use Indian VAT: If VAT applies say yes, but in our case it is no.

Local Sales Tax Number: Enter the Registration Certification No., if company is registered under sales tax office. This field is optional.

Inter State Sales Tax Number: Enter the registration no., if you transact with the parties of the other states and have been granted Central Sales Tax Registration.

Income-Tax Number: Enter the Company's Income Tax PAN (Permanent Account Number) or GIR No. (General Index Register Number) whichever is available.

Currency Symbol: Enter the currency symbol. For our purpose is ₹

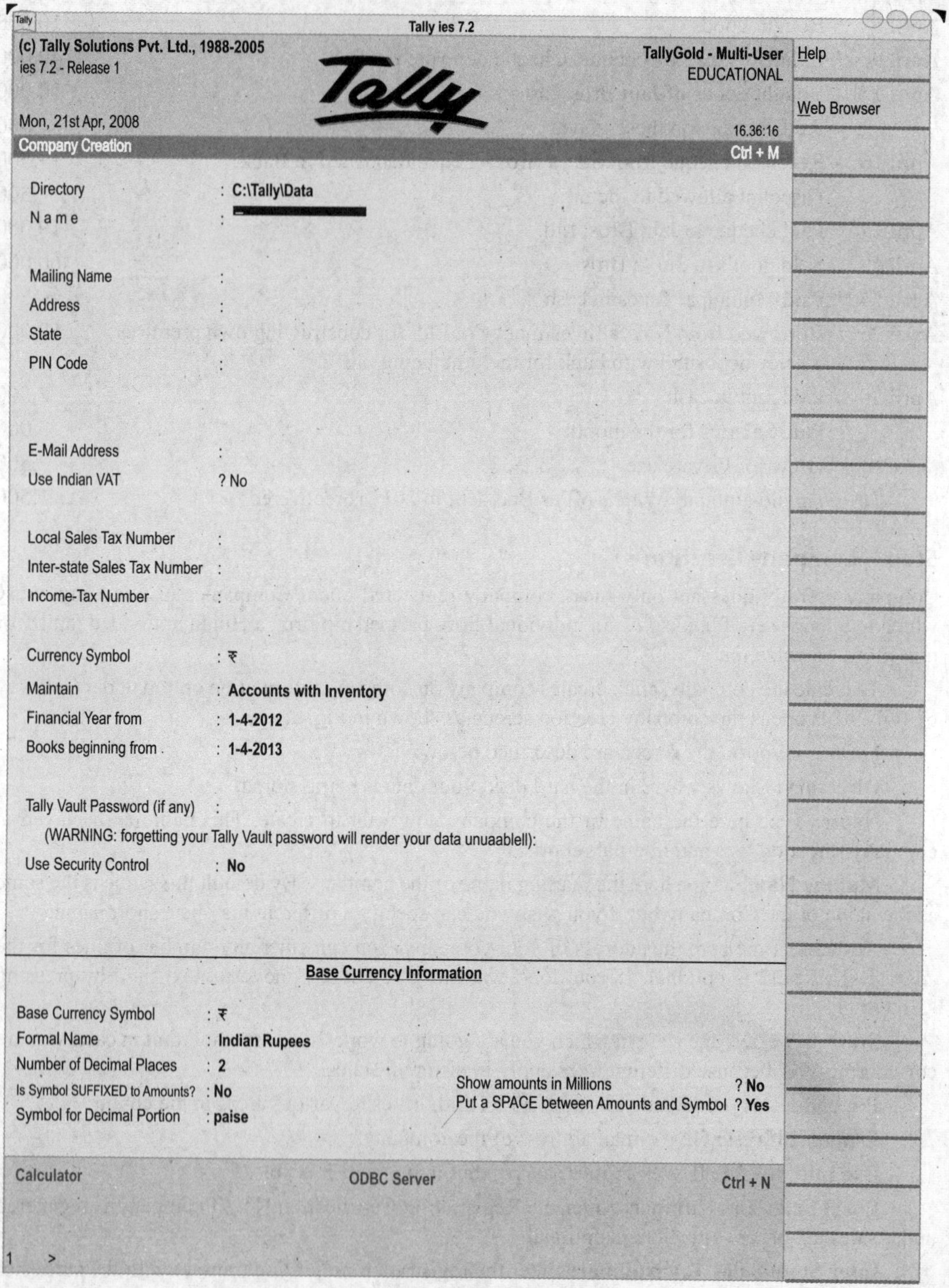

Tally ies 7.2

(c) Tally Solutions Pvt. Ltd., 1988-2005
ies 7.2 - Release 1

Tally

TallyGold - Multi-User
EDUCATIONAL

Help

Web Browser

Mon, 21st Apr, 2008

16.36:16

Company Creation Ctrl + M

Directory : **C:\Tally\Data**
Name :

Mailing Name :
Address :
State :
PIN Code :

E-Mail Address :
Use Indian VAT ? No

Local Sales Tax Number :
Inter-state Sales Tax Number :
Income-Tax Number :

Currency Symbol : ₹
Maintain : **Accounts with Inventory**
Financial Year from : **1-4-2012**
Books beginning from : **1-4-2013**

Tally Vault Password (if any) :
(WARNING: forgetting your Tally Vault password will render your data unuaablell):
Use Security Control : **No**

Base Currency Information

Base Currency Symbol : ₹
Formal Name : **Indian Rupees**
Number of Decimal Places : **2**
Is Symbol SUFFIXED to Amounts? : **No**
Symbol for Decimal Portion : **paise**

Show amounts in Millions ? **No**
Put a SPACE between Amounts and Symbol ? **Yes**

Calculator ODBC Server Ctrl + N

1 >

Fig. 3

Maintain: There are two different ways you can use Tally:

— Accounts only

— Accounts with inventory.

By default, accounts with inventory are selected but you can always differ to use your own option. Using this option you would be able to use both financial as well as inventory management. For our purpose, we use accounts only.

Financial Year from: Type here the financial year.

Books Beginning from: Type here the date by which you actually want Tally to maintain your accounts.

	Financial Year from	Book Beginning from
1. New Company starting business on 01.04.2012 and starting computerised A/c's on 01.04.2012	01.04.2012	01.04.2012
2. New Company starting business on 01.02.2013 and starting computerised A/c's on 01.02.2013	01.04.2012	01.02.2013
3. Existing Company starting computerised A/c's on 01.04.2013	01.04.2013	01.04.2013
4. Existing Company starting computerised A/c's on 01.06.2013	01.04.2013	01.06.2013

Tally/Vault Password (if any): Tally Vault is an enhanced security system, which allows for, encryption of the company data. Encryption means converting normally accessible Tally information into unrecognisable information which can only be reconverted by authorized person. Give a password here and repeat the same. By doing this, name of the company will be shown as *****. Once vault password is entered while selecting the company, name of company appears.

Use Security Control: By default it is no, but if you want to provide security control, enter yes. This will allow only authorised users to access the data. For availing this option enter name of the administrator & password and repeat the password.

Base Currency Information: In Tally you can work in foreign currency too. This section provides information related to this.

Base Currency Symbol: Specify symbol for base currency.

Formal Name: Formal name of currency.

Number of decimal places: Means fractional part of currency. In our case are 2 (because of paisa).

Is symbol Suffixed to Amounts: By default it is no but if you want currency symbol to be suffixed before the amount say yes.

Show Accounts in Millions: By default it is no.

Put Space between Amounts and Symbol: By default it is yes.

Keep pressing enter in order to move from one field to another. After filling all the entries Tally asks to save the company profile by showing message at right bottom corner, accept "Yes or No" Press "Y" for yes and "N" for No. When you save the company's profile, Tally automatically creates two accounts namely **Cash and Profit & Loss Account.**

In our illustration name of the company is Vee Kay Enterprises. So Company is created as shown in Fig. 4.

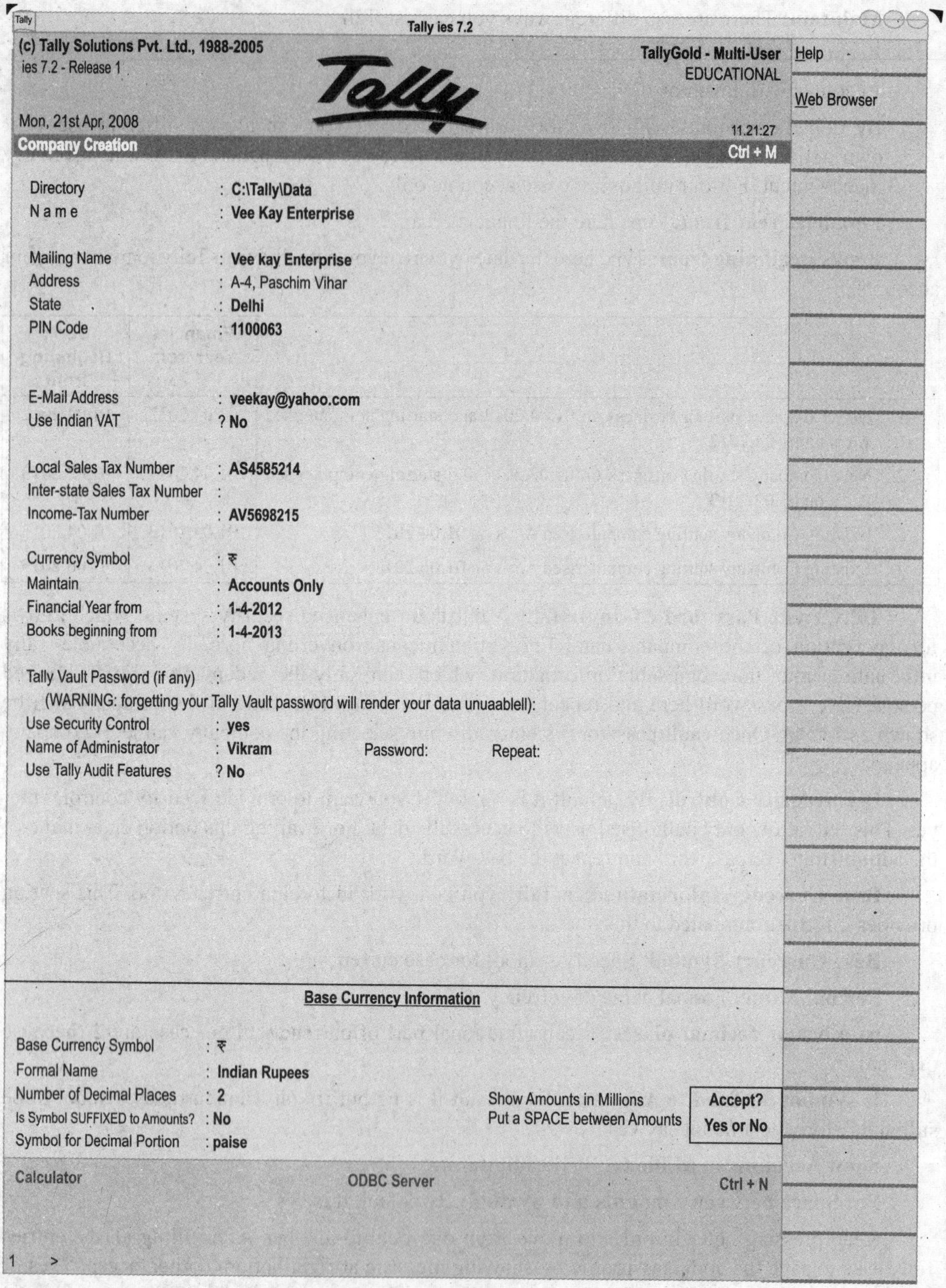

Tally ies 7.2

(c) Tally Solutions Pvt. Ltd., 1988-2005
ies 7.2 - Release 1

Tally

TallyGold - Multi-User
EDUCATIONAL

Help
Web Browser

Mon, 21st Apr, 2008 11.21:27

Company Creation Ctrl + M

Directory : C:\Tally\Data
Name : Vee Kay Enterprise

Mailing Name : Vee kay Enterprise
Address : A-4, Paschim Vihar
State : Delhi
PIN Code : 1100063

E-Mail Address : veekay@yahoo.com
Use Indian VAT ? No

Local Sales Tax Number : AS4585214
Inter-state Sales Tax Number :
Income-Tax Number : AV5698215

Currency Symbol : ₹
Maintain : Accounts Only
Financial Year from : 1-4-2012
Books beginning from : 1-4-2013

Tally Vault Password (if any) :
(WARNING: forgetting your Tally Vault password will render your data unuaablell):
Use Security Control : yes
Name of Administrator : Vikram Password: Repeat:
Use Tally Audit Features ? No

Base Currency Information

Base Currency Symbol : ₹
Formal Name : Indian Rupees
Number of Decimal Places : 2
Is Symbol SUFFIXED to Amounts? : No
Symbol for Decimal Portion : paise

Show Amounts in Millions
Put a SPACE between Amounts

Accept?
Yes or No

Calculator ODBC Server Ctrl + N

1 >

Fig. 4

Let us discuss other options on screen.

Select Company: This option permits you to load another company which you may have created earlier from the list of companies listed.

Shut Company: This allows you to shut an existing company.

Create Company: This allows you to create a new company as done earlier.

Security Control: You can provide security control with more users and their respective password.

Alter: This allows you to alter information about the existing company.

Change Tally Vault: This allows you to change Tally Vault password, if provided earlier.

Split Company Data: Tally allows user to specify the date from which the company has to be split and Tally will split the company to form two companies as per period specified.

Backup/Restore: Tally has Backup and Restore option. The user can take a backup in the local hard disk or in any external media.

Quit: This allows you to quit the screen.

The Buttons:

F1: Select Comp. Already discussed.

F1: Shut Comp. Already discussed.

F11: Features: F 11 will open Company Operations Alteration Screen as shown in Fig. 5.

On the Top Part

Allow Multi Currency: Tally allows you to use more than one currency at a time, if your company has accounts in more than one country.

Maintain Budgets & Controls: If you want to make budgets, set this option yes.

Allow 0 valued Entries in Voucher: If you want to enter any voucher with 0 values, set it yes.

Accounting Features

Maintain Bill wise Details: This option allows you to keep track of an account, on bill to bill basis. If you don't need bill wise detail, let this option be set to its default value which is no. In this case you will only get net closing balances of ledger without any bill wise details.

(For non-trading A/c's also): You can use the bill wise details not only for trading accounts such as creditors or debtors, but also for non-trading accounts like Loan and Advances. If required, enter yes.

Maintain Cost Centres: If you want to do center wise allocation say yes otherwise set it to remain at its default value *i.e.*, no.

More than one cost category: If you have set yes to previous option, you can allocate the transaction to more than one cost center by entering yes.

Use Reverse Journals & Optional Vouchers: For use of reversing journals set this option to yes, else let it no. (its default value.)

Use Debit/credit Notes: Response yes if you want to use debit/credit notes instead of journal vouchers.

Activate Interest Calculation: By this feature you can have your interest calculation on or off.

Income & Expenses Statement instead of P&L: Opt for this option if you wish to maintain accounts of non-profit organization.

Tally ies 7.2

(c) Tally Solutions Pvt. Ltd., 2012-13
ies 7.2 - Release 1

Tally

TallyGold - Multi-User
EDUCATIONAL

Help
Web Browser

Tue, 22nd Apr, 2013
16.38:24

Company Operations Alteration
Ctrl + M

Company: Vee Kay Enterprise

Allow Multi-Currency	? No	Maintain Budgets and Controls	? No
		Allow 0 valued entries in Vouchers	? No
		Enable TDS	? No

Accounting Features		Inventory Features	
Maintain Billwise Details	? Yes	Maintain Stock Categanes	? No
(for Non-Trading A/cs also)	? No	Maintain Batch Wise Details	? No
Maintain Cost Centres	? No	(set Expiry Dates for Batches)	? No
(more than ONE Cost Category)	? No	Maintain Multiple Godowns	? No
Use Rev. Journals and Optional Vouchers	? No	Use Tracking Numbers	?No
Use Debit/Credit Notes	?No	Use Rejection Notes	? No
Activate Interest Calculation	? No	Use different Actual & Billed Qty	? No
(use advanced parameters)	? No	Track additional costs of Purchase	? No
Income/Expense Stmt instead of P & L	? No		

Set/Modify other Company Feature? **No**

Calculator   ODBC Server   Ctrl + N

1 >

Fig. 5

F 12-Configure: F 12 opens the configuration menu as shown in Fig. 6.

Licensing: Gives information about Tally license server.

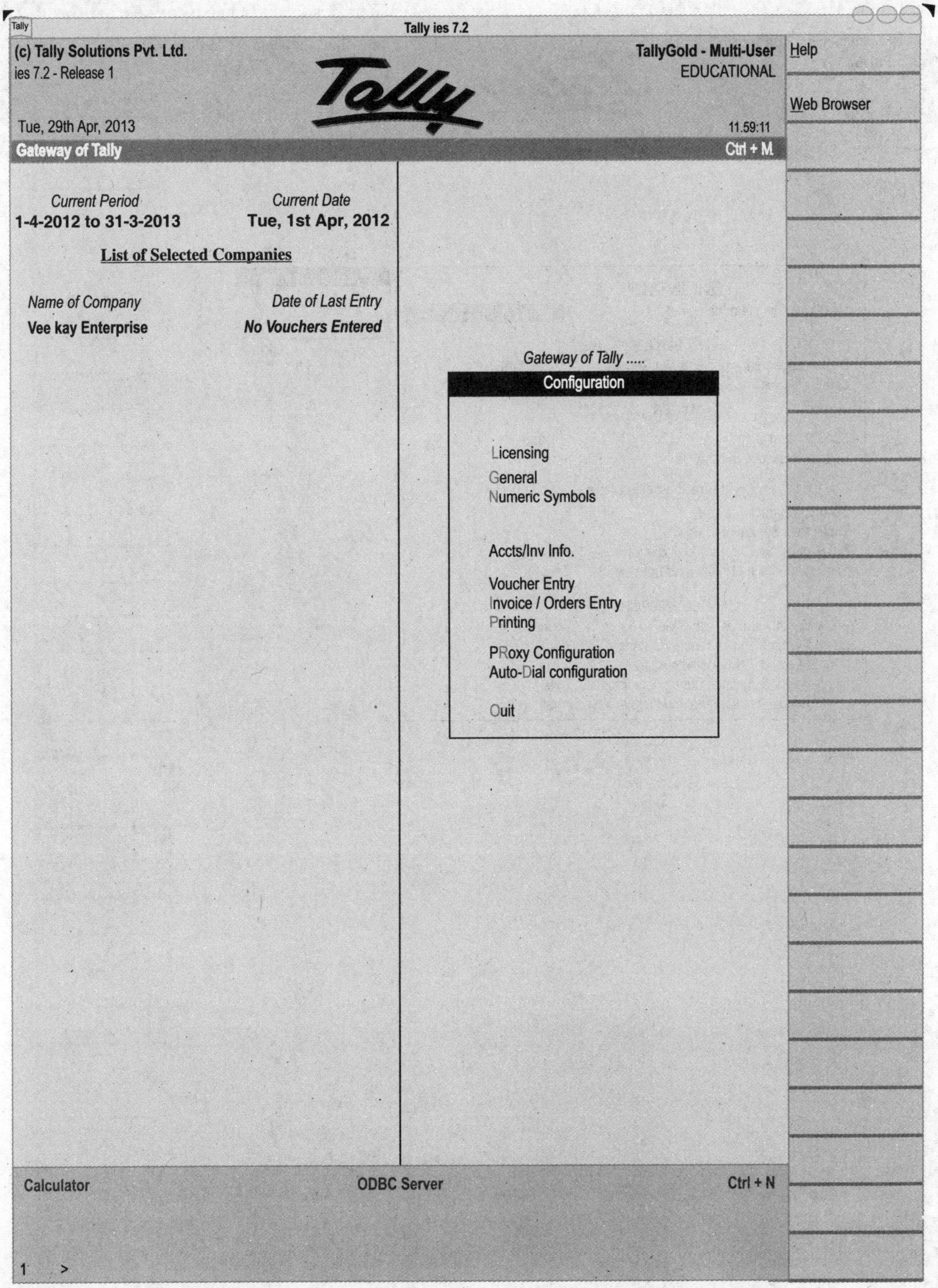

Tally ies 7.2

(c) Tally Solutions Pvt. Ltd.
ies 7.2 - Release 1

TallyGold - Multi-User
EDUCATIONAL

Help

Web Browser

Tally

Tue, 29th Apr, 2013 11.59:11

Gateway of Tally Ctrl + M

Current Period
1-4-2012 to 31-3-2013

Current Date
Tue, 1st Apr, 2012

List of Selected Companies

Name of Company Date of Last Entry
Vee kay Enterprise No Vouchers Entered

Gateway of Tally .....

Configuration

Licensing
General
Numeric Symbols

Accts/Inv Info.

Voucher Entry
Invoice / Orders Entry
Printing

PRoxy Configuration
Auto-Dial configuration

Quit

Calculator ODBC Server Ctrl + N

1 >

Fig. 6

General: Discuss country details, style of names, style of dates, configuration of numbers and other options as shown in Fig. 7.

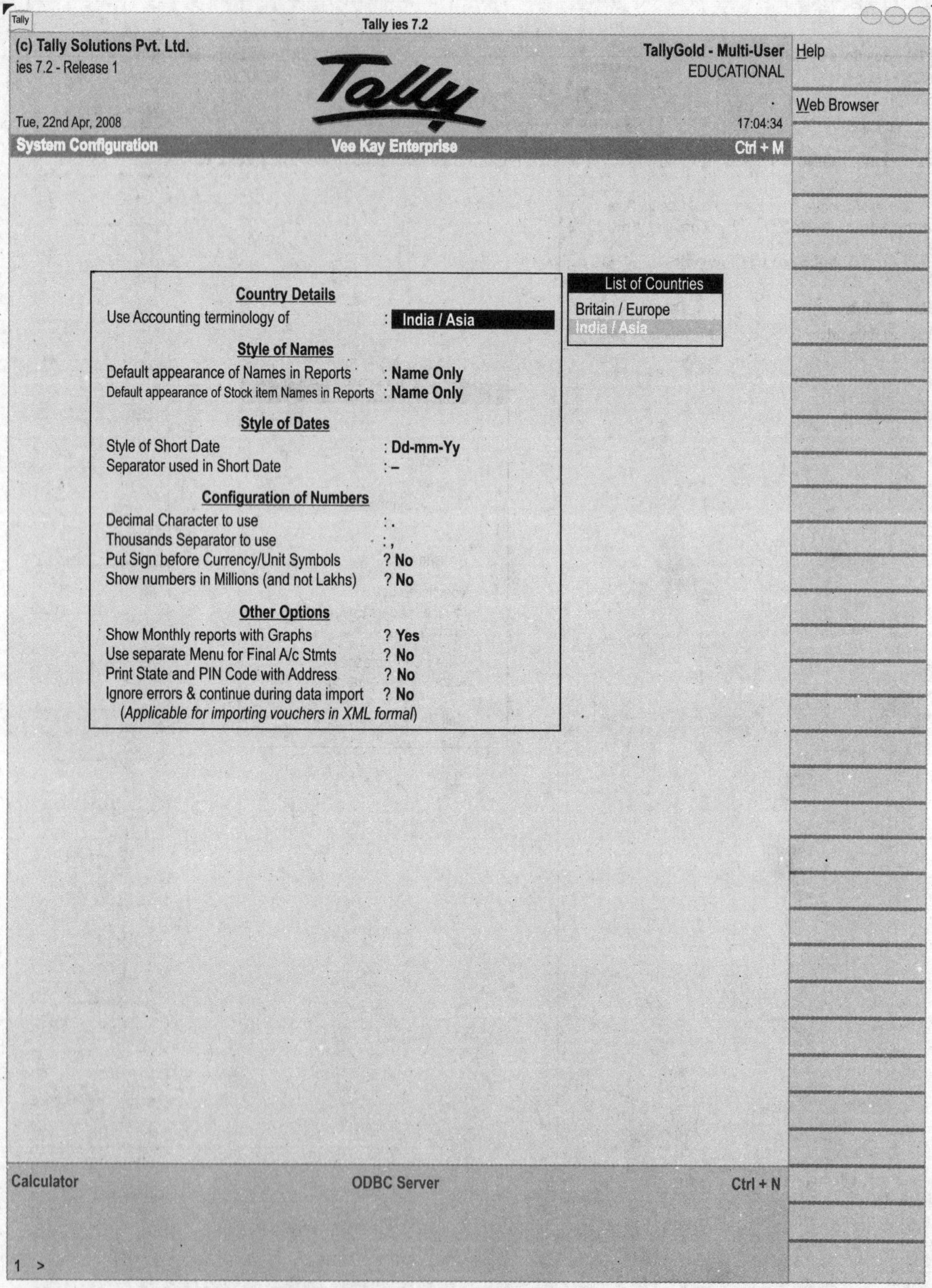

Tally ies 7.2

(c) Tally Solutions Pvt. Ltd.
ies 7.2 - Release 1

TallyGold - Multi-User
EDUCATIONAL

Help

Web Browser

Tue, 22nd Apr, 2008 17:04:34

System Configuration Vee Kay Enterprise Ctrl + M

Country Details

Use Accounting terminology of : India / Asia

Style of Names

Default appearance of Names in Reports : Name Only
Default appearance of Stock item Names in Reports : Name Only

Style of Dates

Style of Short Date : Dd-mm-Yy
Separator used in Short Date : –

Configuration of Numbers

Decimal Character to use : .
Thousands Separator to use : ,
Put Sign before Currency/Unit Symbols ? No
Show numbers in Millions (and not Lakhs) ? No

Other Options

Show Monthly reports with Graphs ? Yes
Use separate Menu for Final A/c Stmts ? No
Print State and PIN Code with Address ? No
Ignore errors & continue during data import ? No
(Applicable for importing vouchers in XML formal)

List of Countries
Britain / Europe
India / Asia

Calculator ODBC Server Ctrl + N

1 >

Fig. 7

Numeric Symbols: This configures number styles. The defaults setting are for normal user; do not alter items as shown in Fig. 8.

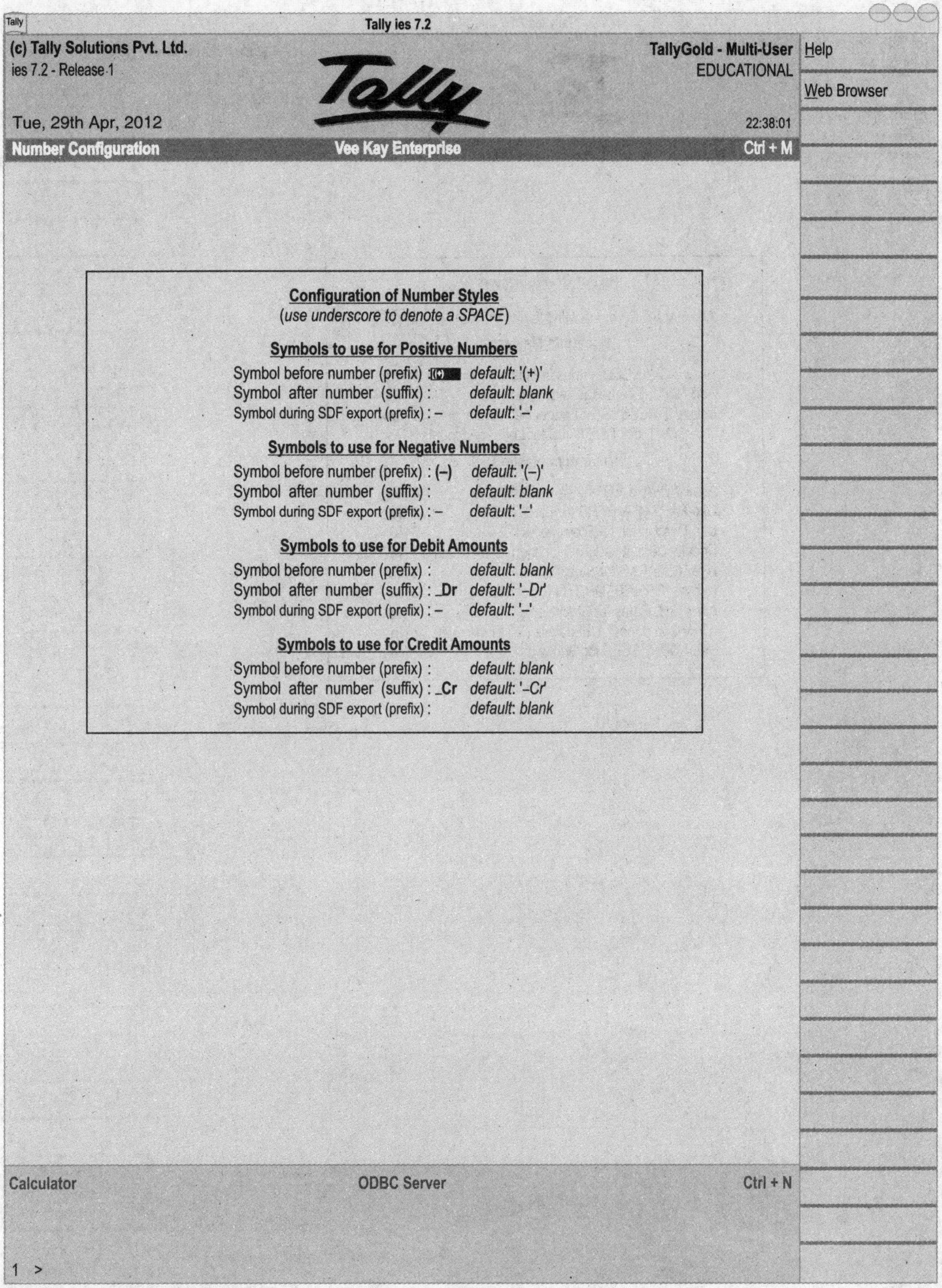

Tally ies 7.2

(c) Tally Solutions Pvt. Ltd.
ies 7.2 - Release 1

TallyGold - Multi-User
EDUCATIONAL

Tue, 29th Apr, 2012 22:38:01

Number Configuration | Vee Kay Enterprise | Ctrl + M

Help
Web Browser

Configuration of Number Styles
(*use underscore to denote a SPACE*)

Symbols to use for Positive Numbers

Symbol before number (prefix) : (+) *default*: '(+)'
Symbol after number (suffix) : *default*: *blank*
Symbol during SDF export (prefix) : – *default*: '–'

Symbols to use for Negative Numbers

Symbol before number (prefix) : (–) *default*: '(–)'
Symbol after number (suffix) : *default*: *blank*
Symbol during SDF export (prefix) : – *default*: '–'

Symbols to use for Debit Amounts

Symbol before number (prefix) : *default*: *blank*
Symbol after number (suffix) : _Dr *default*: '–Dr'
Symbol during SDF export (prefix) : – *default*: '–'

Symbols to use for Credit Amounts

Symbol before number (prefix) : *default*: *blank*
Symbol after number (suffix) : _Cr *default*: '–Cr'
Symbol during SDF export (prefix) : *default*: *blank*

Calculator | ODBC Server | Ctrl + N

1 >

Fig. 8

Account/Inventory Information: This menu allows to configure accounts and inventory masters, since inventory is not part of our syllabus. So we need to discuss master configuration and accounts masters which are self explanatory (Fig. 9).

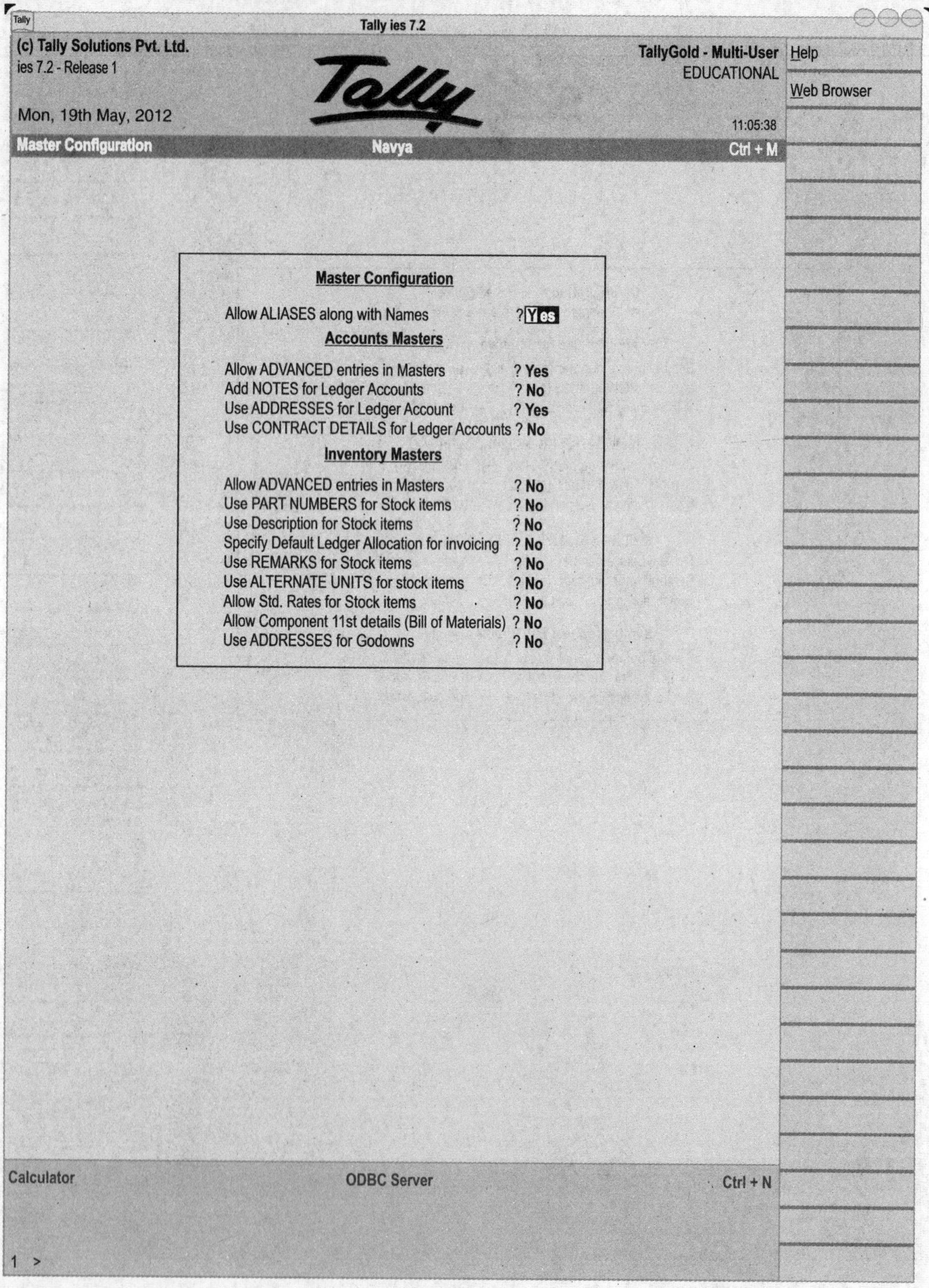

Tally ies 7.2

(c) Tally Solutions Pvt. Ltd.
ies 7.2 - Release 1

Tally

TallyGold - Multi-User
EDUCATIONAL

Mon, 19th May, 2012

11:05:38

Help
Web Browser

Master Configuration | Navya | Ctrl + M

Master Configuration

Allow ALIASES along with Names ? Yes

Accounts Masters

Allow ADVANCED entries in Masters ? Yes
Add NOTES for Ledger Accounts ? No
Use ADDRESSES for Ledger Account ? Yes
Use CONTRACT DETAILS for Ledger Accounts ? No

Inventory Masters

Allow ADVANCED entries in Masters ? No
Use PART NUMBERS for Stock items ? No
Use Description for Stock items ? No
Specify Default Ledger Allocation for invoicing ? No
Use REMARKS for Stock items ? No
Use ALTERNATE UNITS for stock items ? No
Allow Std. Rates for Stock items ? No
Allow Component 11st details (Bill of Materials) ? No
Use ADDRESSES for Godowns ? No

Calculator | ODBC Server | Ctrl + N

1 >

Fig. 9

Voucher Entry: This allows you to configure voucher entry in Tally as shown in Fig. 10.

Tally ies 7.2

(c) Tally Solutions Pvt. Ltd.
ies 7.2 - Release 1

TallyGold - Multi-User
EDUCATIONAL

Help

Web Browser

Tue, 22nd Apr, 2012

17:15:53

Voucher Configuration | Vee Key Enterprise | Ctrl + M

Accounting Vouchers

Skip Date field in Create Mode (faster entry)	? Yes
Use Single Entry mode for Pymt/Rcpt/Contra	? No
Show Cost Centre Details	? Yes
Show Inventory Details	? Yes
Show Table of Bill Details for Selection	? Yes
Show Bill-wise Details	? Yes
Expand into multiple lines	? Yes
Show Ledger Current Balances	? Yes
Show Balance as on Voucher Date	? No
Use Payment/Receipt as Contra	? No
Allow Cash Accounts in Journals	? No
Use Cr/Dr instead of To/By during entry	? Yes
Warn on Negative Cash Balance	? Yes
Pre-Allocate Bills for Payment/Receipt	? No
Allow Expenses/Fixed Assets in Purch. Vouchers	? No
Allow income Accounts in Sales Vouchers	? No

Inventory Vouchers

Show Batch-wise Details	? Yes
Show Godown-wise Details	? Yes
Use Ref. Number in Stock-Journal	? No
Warn on Negative Stock Balance	? Yes
Honor Expiry Dates usage for Batches	? Yes
Show Balances as on Voucher Dates	? No

Calculator | ODBC Server | Ctrl + N

1 >

Fig. 10

All the options under vouchers entry configure set at default are for normal user except the following:

1. **Use Single Entry mode for payment/Rect./Contra.:** Set it no as we are using double entry system.
2. **Use Cr./Dr. instead of to/by during entry:** By default, to and by appears during vouchers, however if you find Dr./Cr more convenient set this option yes.

Invoice/Order Entry: Configure invoices/delivery notes/orders. Options set at default are for normal user, so need not to change.

Printing: Configure the dimension and details of payment vouchers. Default options are ok, so need not to modify.

Step II–Opening of Ledger Accounts

After creating a company and setting features and configuration, next step is opening of ledger accounts.

Tally sets 28 predefined groups. These groups determine whether ledger effects P&L A/c item or capital item or asset or liability item. These predefined groups are:

- Fixed Assets
- Investments
- Current Assets
- Bank Account
- Cash in hand
- Deposits (Asset)
- Loan and Advances (Asset)
- Stock in hand
- Sundry Debtors
- Capital Account
- Reserve and Surplus
- Loan (Liability)
- Bank OD Accounts
- Bank OCC Accounts
- Secured Loans
- Unsecured Loans
- Current Liabilities
- Duties and Taxes
- Provisions
- Sundry Creditors
- Branch/Division
- Miscellaneous Expenses (Asset)

- Suspense Account
- Sales Account
- Direct Income
- Indirect Income
- Purchase Account
- Direct Expenses
- Indirect Expenses.

CREATING A LEDGER

Select Account Info (under Gateway of Tally), then Press Enter Key, dialog box will display. Select ledger by arrow key then press Enter Key.

Accounts info
Group Ledger Voucher Types Quit

Select create in single ledger by arrow key and press <enter>. This will open the ledger creation screen as shown in Fig. 11.

Following are the options of the screen:

Name: Enter the name of the ledger you wish to create.

Alias: This option will present, if you had configured master configuration menu for aliases. Give here an alternate name for the ledger account.

Under: Select the parent group from specified groups under Tally.

Opening Balance: Specify here the opening balance in ledger as on date of beginning of books. This is obviously the opening balance of the account taken from the previous year's balance sheet. You have to specify whether it is a debit or credit balance by saying D or C. By default Tally assumes that assets have debit balances and liabilities have credit balances. In case of a new company you can leave it as blank.

Mailing and Related Details: This option is relevant only in the case of groups like Sundry Debtors, Creditors and Loan & Advances. Here you can give the complete name and address of the party along with its Income Tax and Sales Tax Number.

After filling the entire field and pressing <Enter> a dialogue box will appear, 'Accept' Yes or No. After pressing 'Y' ledger account is saved and again a blank field screen appears to create next ledger.

It is advisable first to create all ledger of the question. In our illustration the ledger accounts needed are: Cash at bank. Stock in Hand, Machinery, Furniture M/s Surya Bros. (Debtors), M/s Balu Bros. (Debtor), loan, Jain Ltd. (Creditor), S Bros (creditor), Capital, Bad Debt, Discount Received, Purchase, Sales, Carriage, Discount Allowed, Municipal Taxes, Navya Investment Co. Ltd., Rent, Salaries, Drawings, Bad Debt Recovered. Some of ledger accounts created for illustrations as shown below.

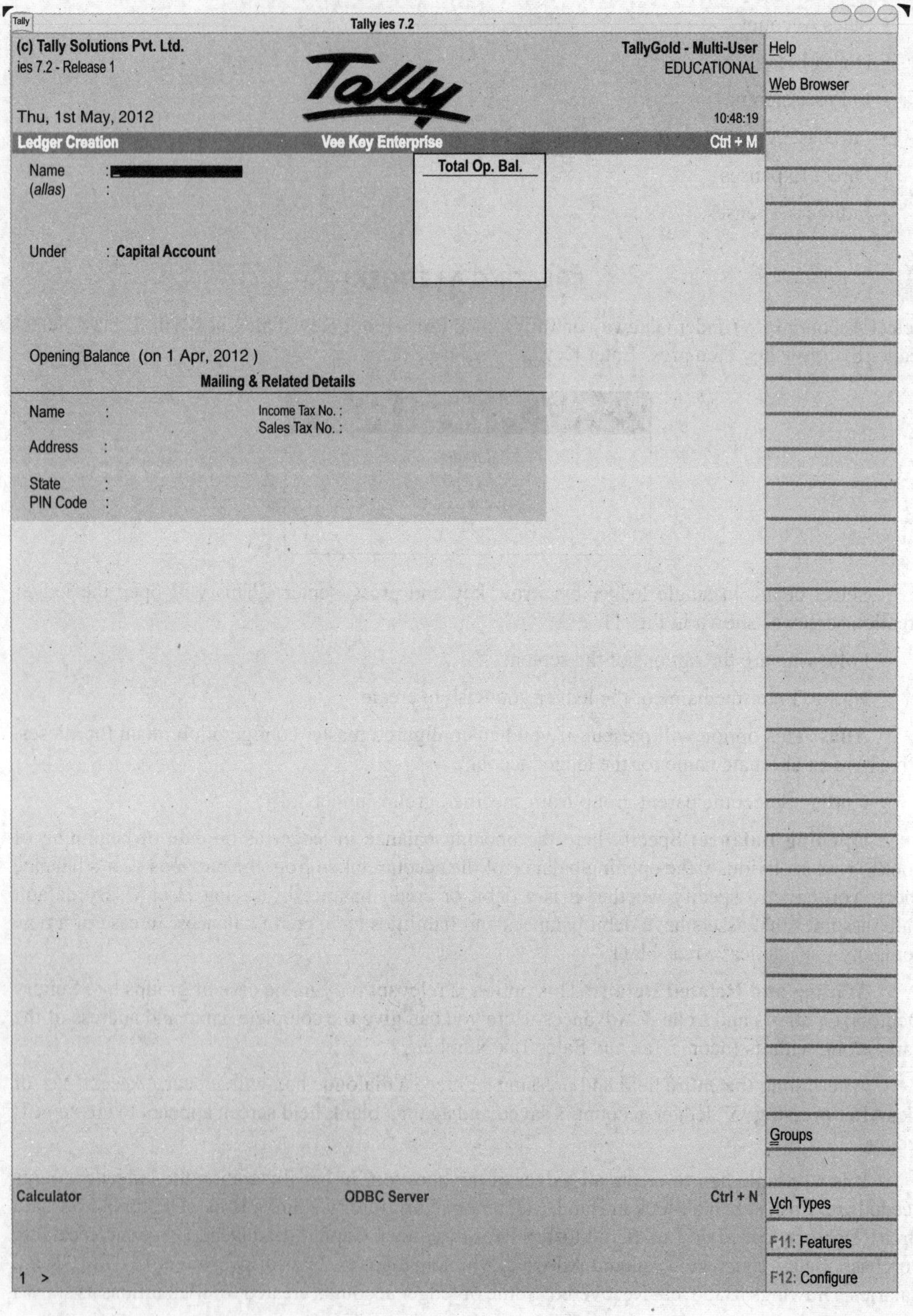

Tally ies 7.2

(c) Tally Solutions Pvt. Ltd.
ies 7.2 - Release 1

TallyGold - Multi-User
EDUCATIONAL

Tally

Thu, 1st May, 2012

10:48:19

Help
Web Browser

Ledger Creation | Vee Key Enterprise | Ctrl + M

Name :
(alias) :

Total Op. Bal.

Under : Capital Account

Opening Balance (on 1 Apr, 2012)

Mailing & Related Details

Name :
Address :
State :
PIN Code :

Income Tax No. :
Sales Tax No. :

Groups

Calculator | ODBC Server | Ctrl + N

Vch Types

F11: Features

1 >

F12: Configure

Fig. 11

Cash-at-Bank

See Fig. 12.

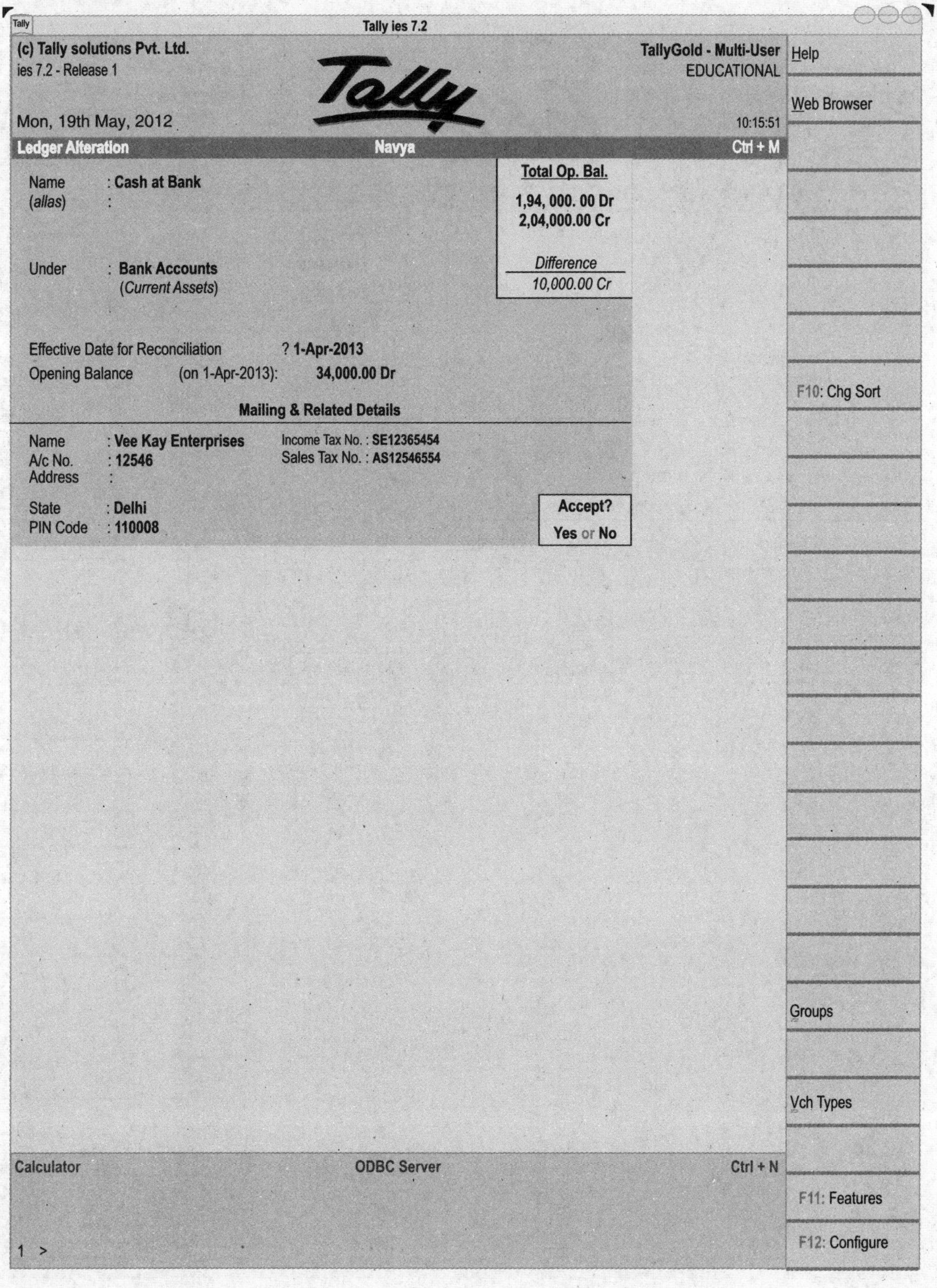

Tally ies 7.2

(c) Tally solutions Pvt. Ltd.
ies 7.2 - Release 1

TallyGold - Multi-User
EDUCATIONAL

Mon, 19th May, 2012 10:15:51

Ledger Alteration | Navya | Ctrl + M

Name : Cash at Bank
(alias) :

Under : Bank Accounts
(Current Assets)

Total Op. Bal.
1,94, 000. 00 Dr
2,04,000.00 Cr
Difference
10,000.00 Cr

Effective Date for Reconciliation ? 1-Apr-2013
Opening Balance (on 1-Apr-2013): 34,000.00 Dr

Mailing & Related Details

Name : Vee Kay Enterprises
A/c No. : 12546
Address :
Income Tax No. : SE12365454
Sales Tax No. : AS12546554

State : Delhi
PIN Code : 110008

Accept?
Yes or No

Help
Web Browser
F10: Chg Sort
Groups
Vch Types
F11: Features
F12: Configure

Calculator | ODBC Server | Ctrl + N

1 >

Fig. 12

Surya Bros.

See Fig. 13.

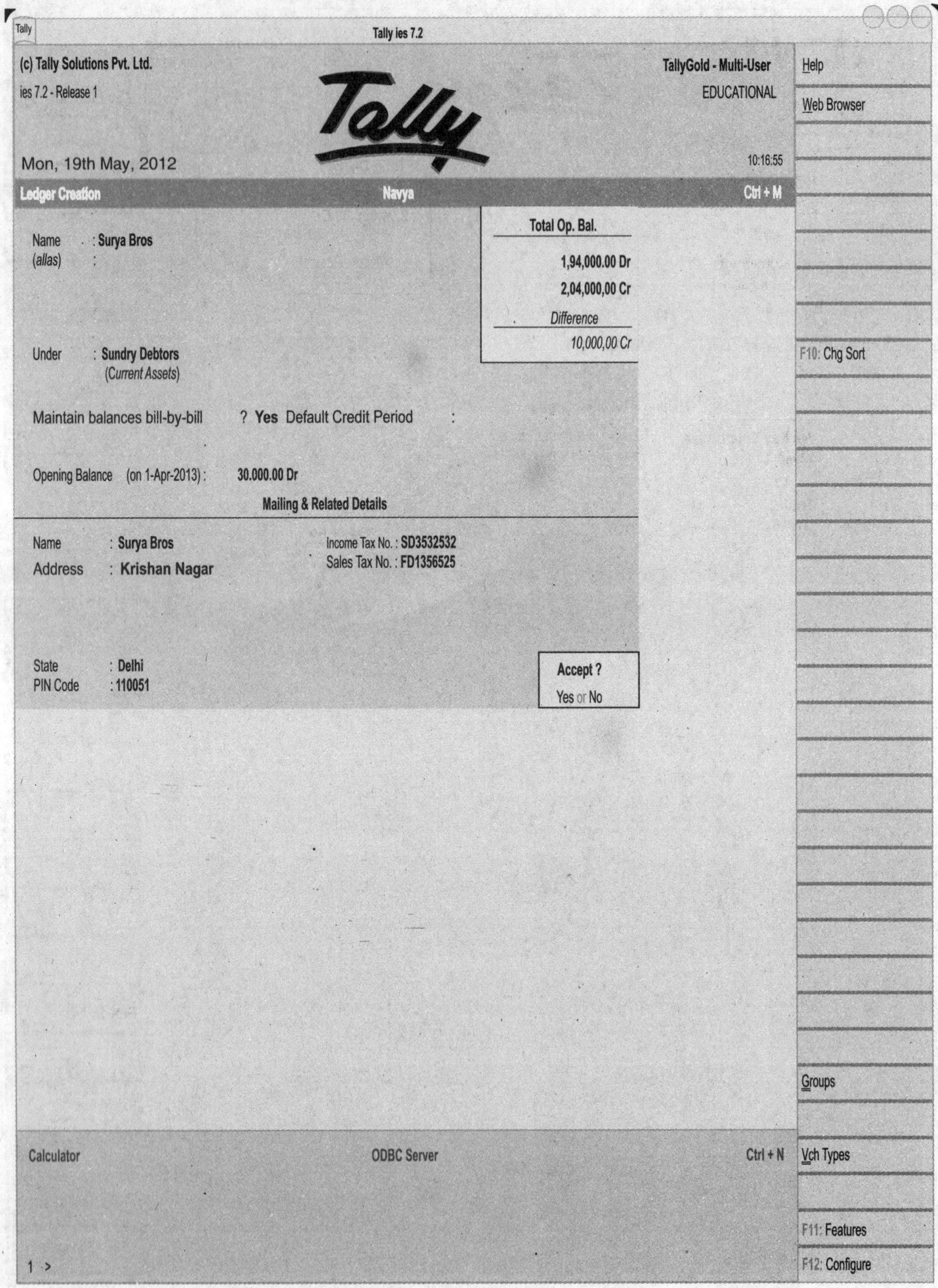

Tally ies 7.2

(c) Tally Solutions Pvt. Ltd.
ies 7.2 - Release 1

TallyGold - Multi-User
EDUCATIONAL

Tally

Mon, 19th May, 2012 10:16:55

Ledger Creation Navya Ctrl + M

Name : Surya Bros
(alias) :

Under : Sundry Debtors
(Current Assets)

Total Op. Bal.
1,94,000.00 Dr
2,04,000,00 Cr
Difference
10,000,00 Cr

Maintain balances bill-by-bill ? **Yes** Default Credit Period :

Opening Balance (on 1-Apr-2013) : 30.000.00 Dr

Mailing & Related Details

Name : Surya Bros
Address : Krishan Nagar

Income Tax No. : SD3532532
Sales Tax No. : FD1356525

State : Delhi
PIN Code : 110051

Accept ?
Yes or No

Help
Web Browser
F10: Chg Sort
Groups
Vch Types
F11: Features
F12: Configure

Calculator ODBC Server Ctrl + N

1 >

Fig. 13

Jain Ltd.

See Fig. 14.

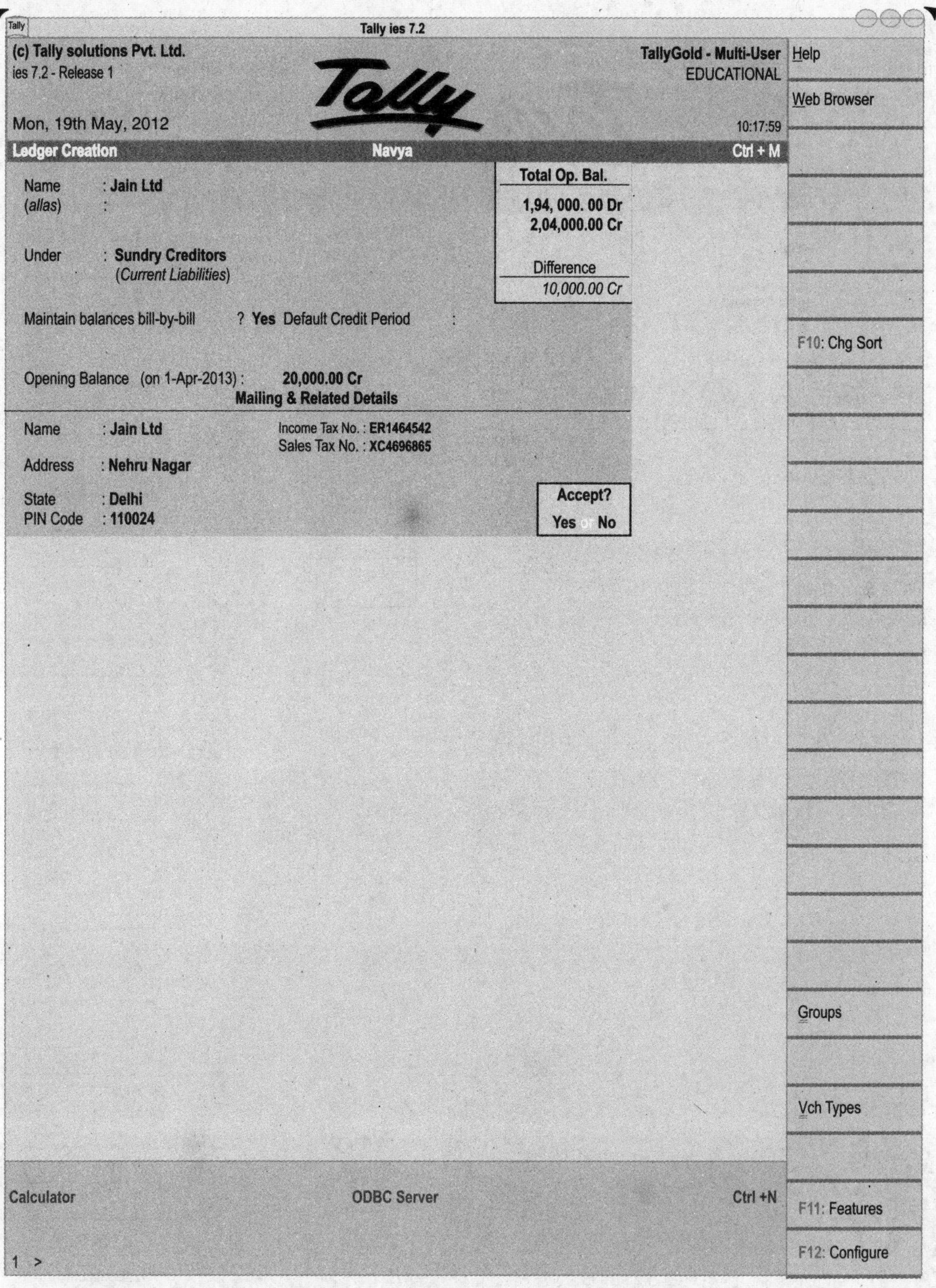

Fig. 14

Capital Account

See Fig. 15.

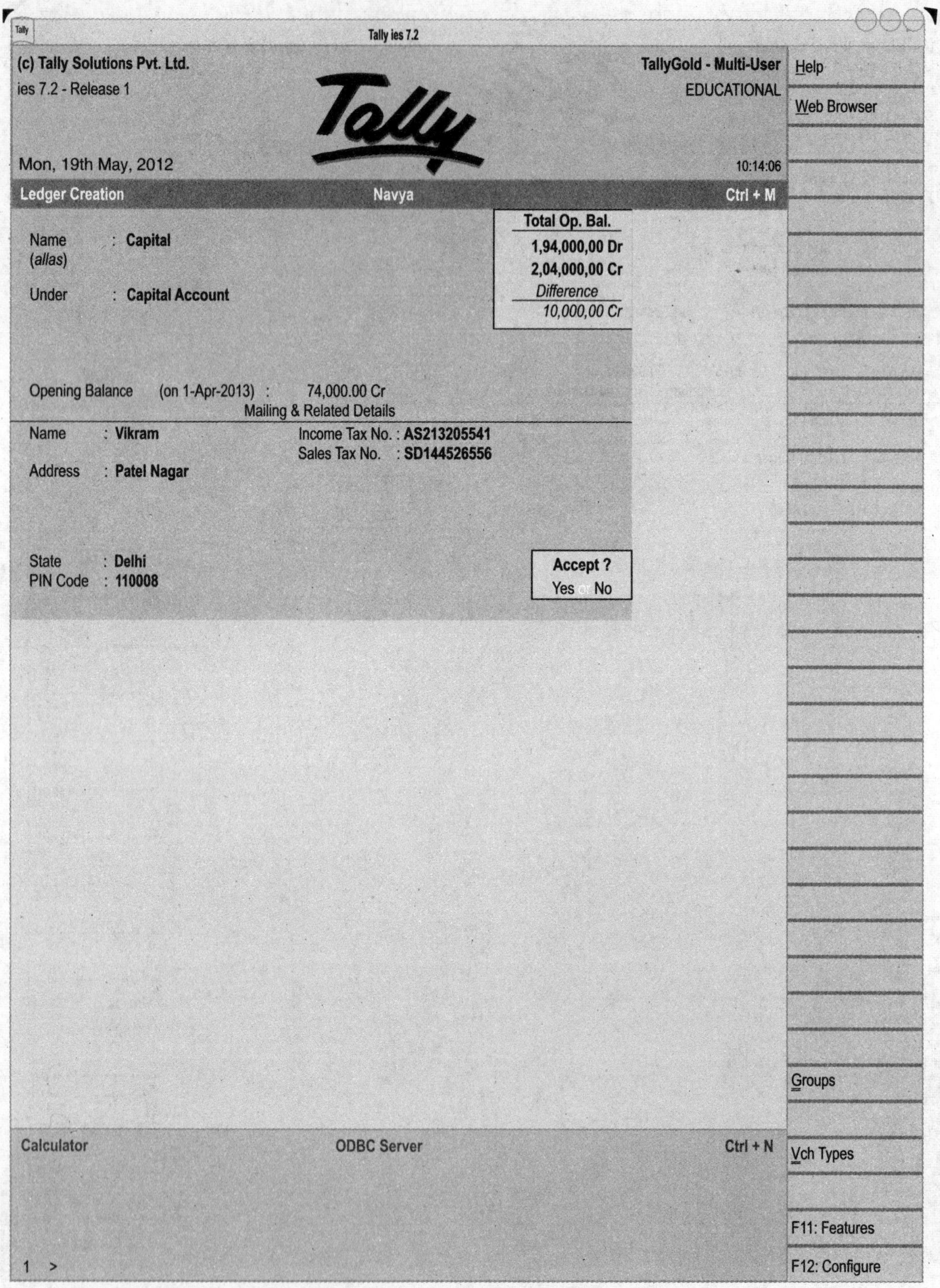

Tally ies 7.2

(c) Tally Solutions Pvt. Ltd.
ies 7.2 - Release 1

TallyGold - Multi-User
EDUCATIONAL

Tally

Mon, 19th May, 2012 10:14:06

Ledger Creation Navya Ctrl + M

Name : Capital
(alias)

Under : Capital Account

Total Op. Bal.
1,94,000,00 Dr
2,04,000,00 Cr
Difference
10,000,00 Cr

Opening Balance (on 1-Apr-2013) : 74,000.00 Cr

Mailing & Related Details

Name : Vikram
Income Tax No. : AS213205541
Sales Tax No. : SD144526556
Address : Patel Nagar

State : Delhi
PIN Code : 110008

Accept ?
Yes or No

Help
Web Browser
Groups
Vch Types
F11: Features
F12: Configure

Calculator ODBC Server Ctrl + N

1 >

Fig. 15

Salaries

See Fig. 16.

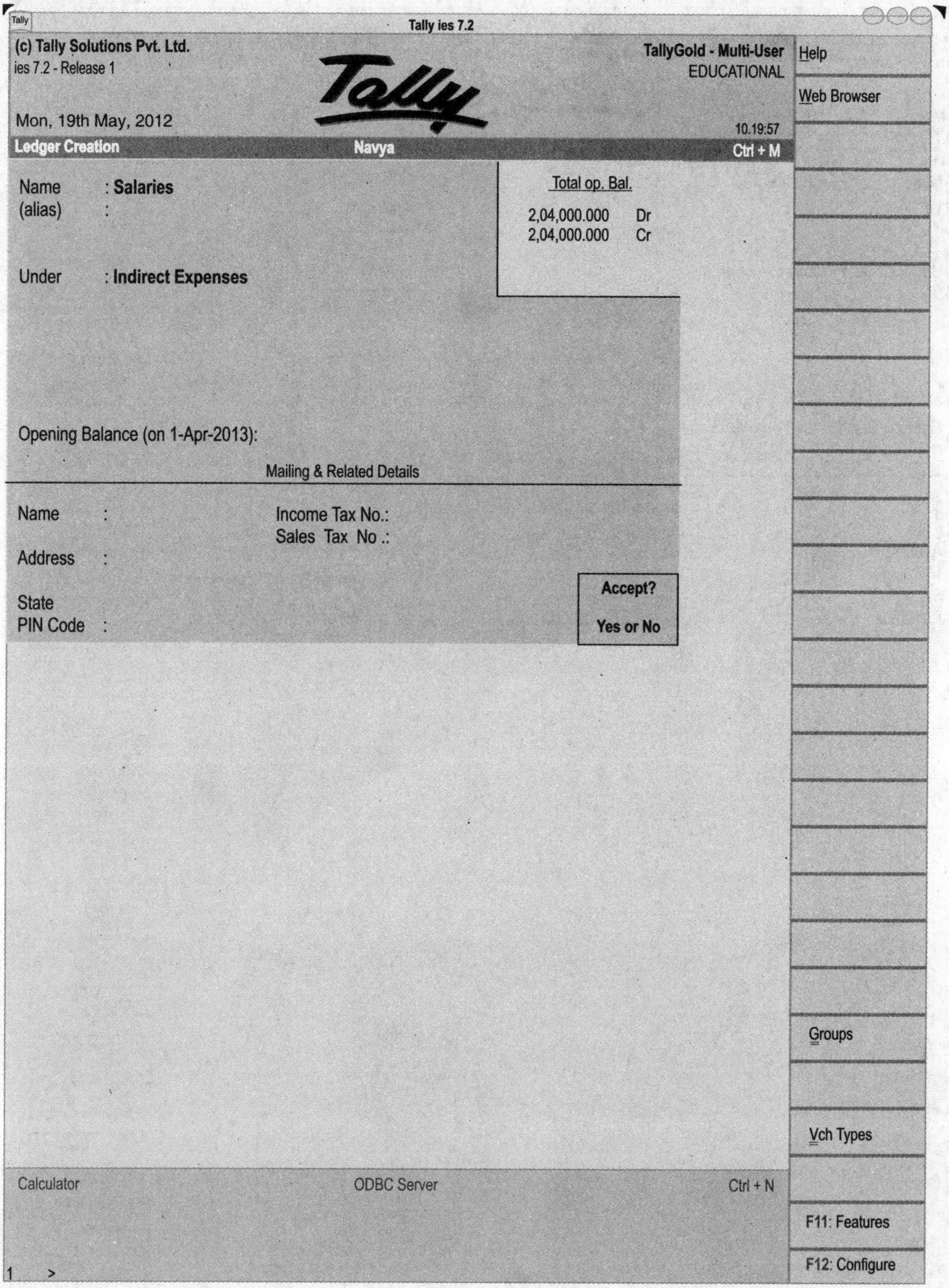

Tally ies 7.2

(c) Tally Solutions Pvt. Ltd.
ies 7.2 - Release 1

TallyGold - Multi-User
EDUCATIONAL

Tally

Mon, 19th May, 2012

10.19:57

Ledger Creation | Navya | Ctrl + M

Help
Web Browser

Name : **Salaries**
(alias) :

Under : **Indirect Expenses**

Total op. Bal.
2,04,000.000 Dr
2,04,000.000 Cr

Opening Balance (on 1-Apr-2013):

Mailing & Related Details

Name :
Address :
State
PIN Code :

Income Tax No.:
Sales Tax No .:

Accept?
Yes or No

Groups
Vch Types
F11: Features
F12: Configure

Calculator | ODBC Server | Ctrl + N

1 >

Fig. 16

Purchase

See Fig. 17.

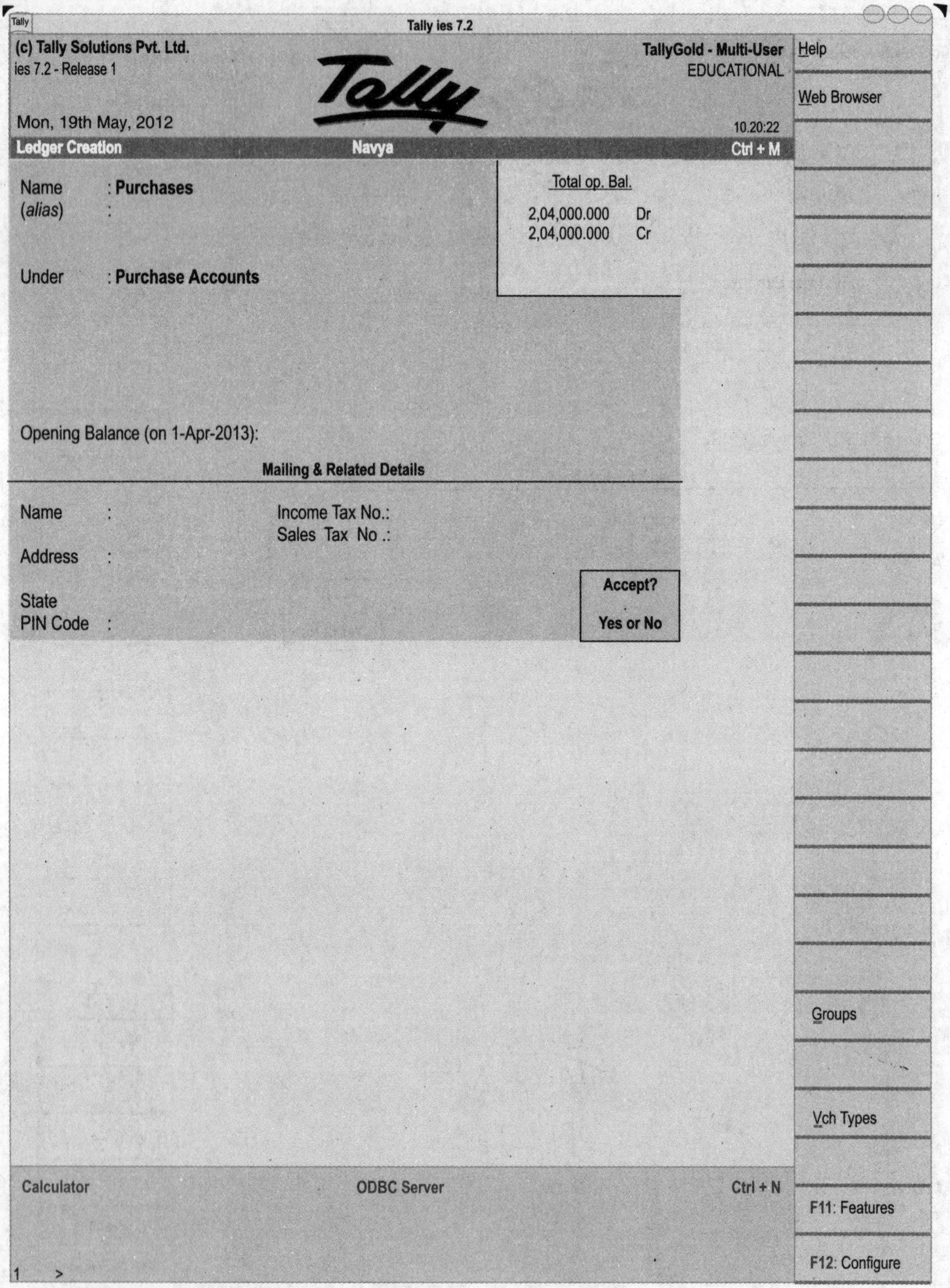

Tally ies 7.2

(c) Tally Solutions Pvt. Ltd.
ies 7.2 - Release 1

TallyGold - Multi-User
EDUCATIONAL

Tally

Mon, 19th May, 2012 10.20:22

Ledger Creation Navya Ctrl + M

Help
Web Browser

Name : **Purchases**
(*alias*) :

Under : **Purchase Accounts**

Total op. Bal.
2,04,000.000 Dr
2,04,000.000 Cr

Opening Balance (on 1-Apr-2013):

Mailing & Related Details

Name :
Income Tax No.:
Sales Tax No .:
Address :
State
PIN Code :

Accept?
Yes or No

Groups
Vch Types

Calculator ODBC Server Ctrl + N

1 >

F11: Features
F12: Configure

Fig. 17

Display of individual ledger: You can display any ledger account on the screen by selecting Display from the menu. You would be next given a choice to display any of the ledger account, list of which comes on the screen. Remember the account is just displayed and cannot be altered.

Alteration of Account: For alteration of an account select alter from menu. You would be next given a choice to select any of the ledger account, list of which comes on the screen and then you can do alteration.

Deletion of Ledger: You can delete a ledger by pressing Alt + D in the ledger alteration screen. Your confirmation would be sought from you before deleting any record in the form of Yes of No. Click yes, if you are very sure of deleting. However, if the ledger is transacted in any voucher, ledger cannot be deleted.

STEP III–VOUCHER ENTRY

Accounting is based on the vouchers that make. They form the main input for the accounting, both for manual as well as for computerized accounting.

Types of Vouchers

To display all types of vouchers in Tally, select Voucher Types from Accounting Info menu. The display of voucher type shows the following as given in Fig. 18.

We will discuss only those types of vouchers which are needed.

1. **Contra Voucher (F_4):** This voucher is used when out of cash/Bank balance, one increases & other decreases.
2. **Payment Voucher (F_5):** All the payment transactions (*i.e.*, cash/bank balance decreases) are entered through payment voucher, for e.g. Salaries paid, Rent paid etc.
3. **Receipt Voucher (F_6):** Receipt voucher is created for recording all receipts (where cash/bank balance increases). For examples. Cash received from debtors, rent received etc.
4. **Journal Voucher (F_7):** Journal voucher is used for recording that transaction in which cash/bank balance and stock do not change. For example. Depreciation charged, rent outstanding etc.
5. **Sales Voucher (F_8):** All the sales of the company, including cash sales are entered using this voucher.
6. **Purchase Voucher (F_9):** All purchase transactions are entered in purchase voucher, including cash purchases.
7. **Credit Notes:** If you set yes to option use Debit/Credit Notes in F_{11}: Features, you can select this voucher upon clicking either F 7 : journal or F 8 : sales button. It is actually entered when buyer returns some goods that was sold to him or when you grant him credit due to rate difference of discount/rebate.
8. **Debit Note:** If you activate the option use Debit/Credit notes for the company under features, you can select this voucher upon clicking either F 7 : journal and F 9 : Purchase buttons. It is entered when you make purchase return or suppliers have granted credit to you on account of rate difference, discounts etc.

Voucher Entry: To create voucher, click at Accounting Vouchers in Gateway of Tally. This will open the screen as shown in Fig. 19.

Voucher Type: Shows the type of voucher selected. By default it chooses payment voucher. You can select other types of vouchers by buttons given on right.

Voucher Number: A unique number is provided to each voucher.

Reference (not available for receipt and payment vouchers): You can enter a reference such as purchase order numbers or invoice number.

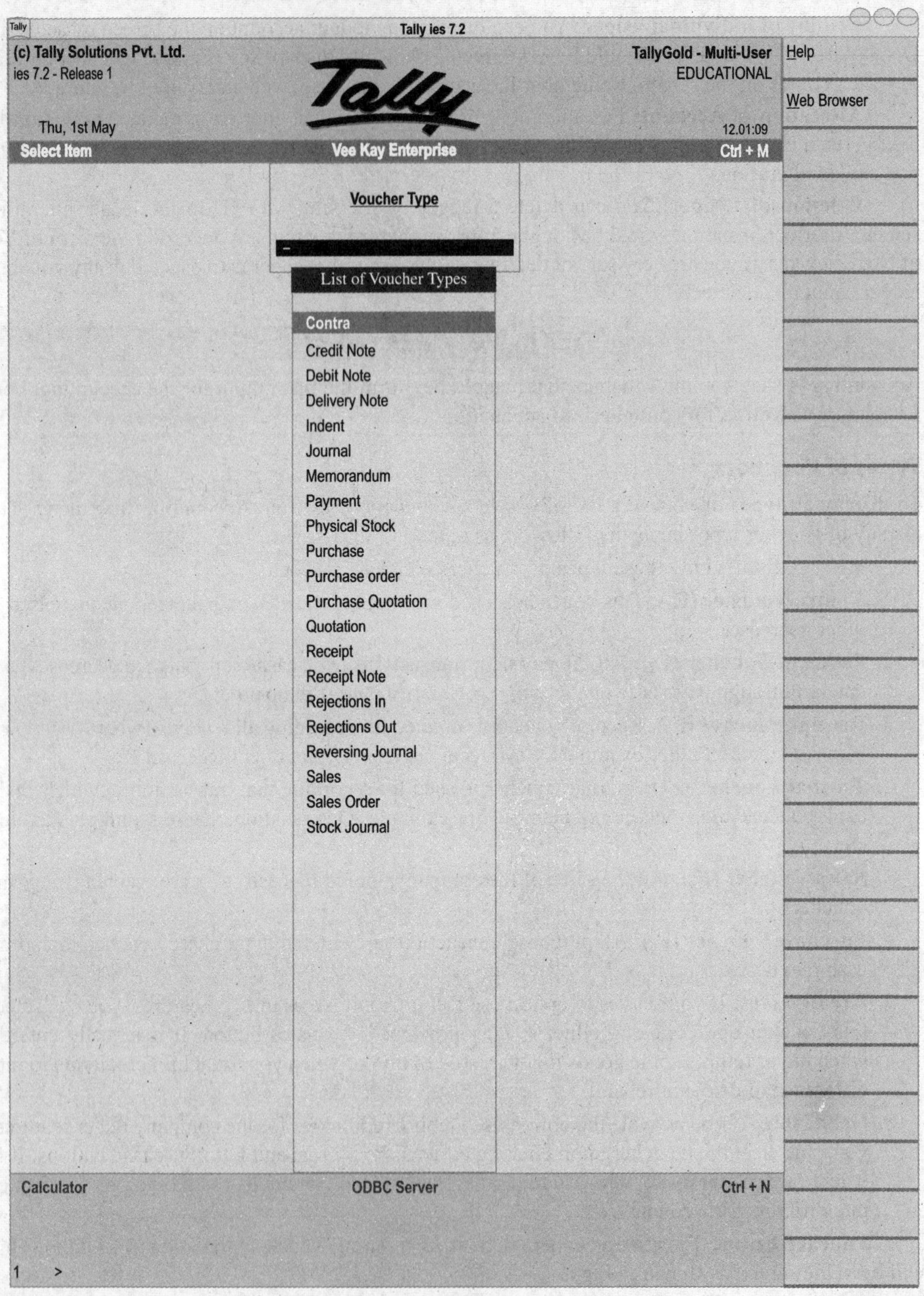

Fig. 18

Date of Voucher: The date of the voucher is entered at the top right of the voucher creation screen. The date is taken initially current date, you can change the date using the F2: Date button on the button bar.

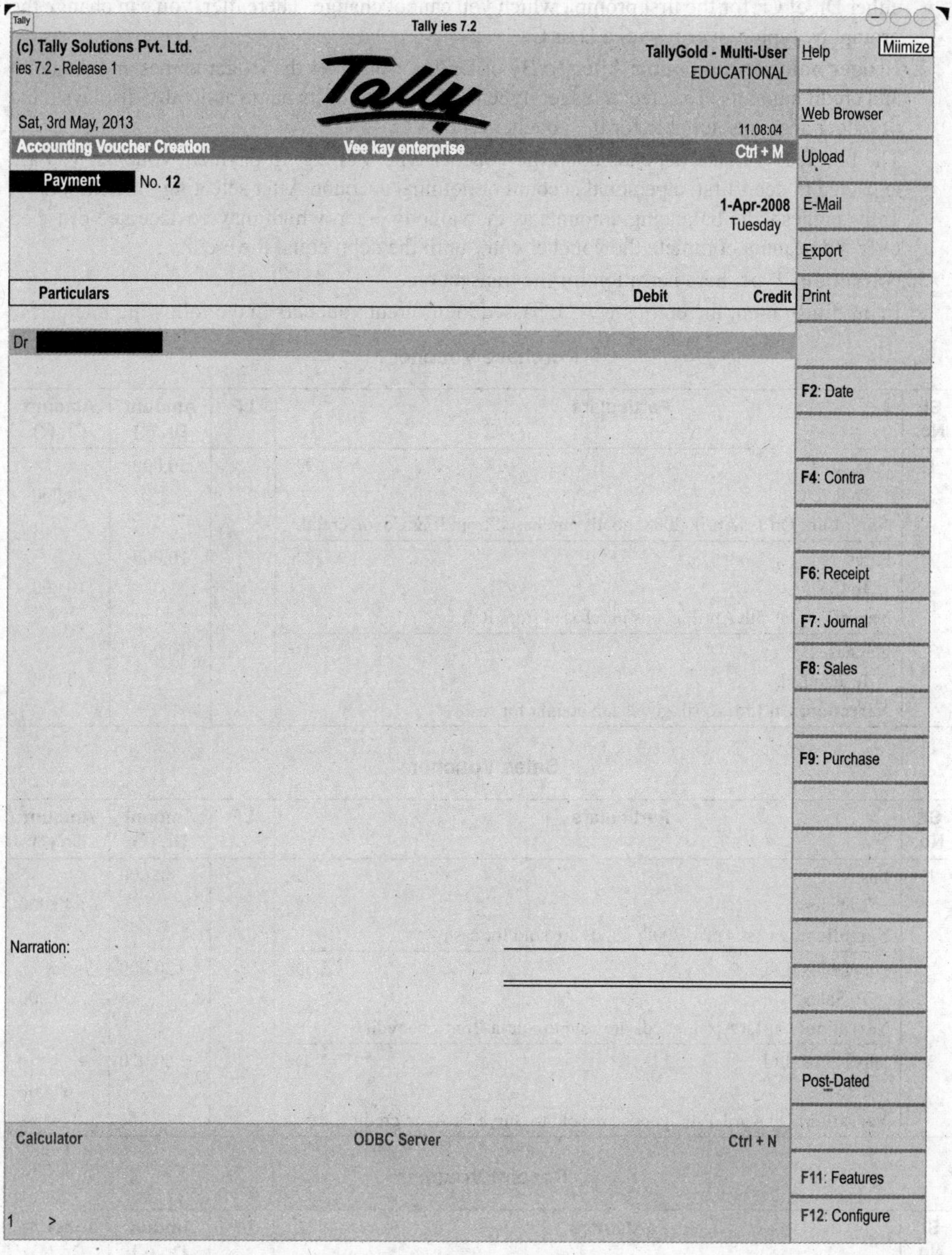

Tally ies 7.2

(c) Tally Solutions Pvt. Ltd.
ies 7.2 - Release 1

Tally

TallyGold - Multi-User
EDUCATIONAL

Sat, 3rd May, 2013 11.08:04

Accounting Voucher Creation Vee kay enterprise Ctrl + M

Payment No. 12

1-Apr-2008
Tuesday

Particulars Debit Credit

Dr

Narration:

Calculator ODBC Server Ctrl + N

1 >

Help
Miimize
Web Browser
Upload
E-Mail
Export
Print
F2: Date
F4: Contra
F6: Receipt
F7: Journal
F8: Sales
F9: Purchase
Post-Dated
F11: Features
F12: Configure

Fig. 19

Day of Voucher: Self explanatory.

Body of voucher:

1. **To/By or Dr./Cr.:** Tally defaults To/By, but this can be changed to Dr. and Cr. by selecting F12: Configure in the voucher creation screen. Depending on the voucher type, Tally selects

either Dr. of Cr. for the first prompt, which you cannot change. Thereafter, you can change the prompt by typing over it with a D or C.

2. **Ledger name and amount:** After To/By or Dr./Cr., you enter the ledger names and the debit and credit amounts. To select a ledger, type the first letter of its name and Tally displays a list of ledger accounts suitable for the voucher type.

   The first ledger name depends upon the voucher type. For e.g. in payment voucher, you are expected to debit first, a personal account or nominal account. After selecting the next ledger, Tally suggests the balancing amounts as the value to enter, which may be accepted or typed over. You cannot complete the voucher entry until the debit equal the credits.

3. **Narration:** Type, here narration for the transaction.

   In our illustration, the entries will be passed in different vouchers in the following manner:

Purchase Voucher

Sl. No.	Particulars		LF	Amount Dr. (₹)	Amount Cr. (₹)
1.	Purchases	Dr.		30,000	
	To R & Co.				30,000
	Narration: On 1st April, 2008, goods purchased from R & Co. on credit.				
2.	Purchases	Dr.		10,000	
	To Cash				10,000
	Narration: On 5th April, goods purchased from R & Co.				
3.	Purchases	Dr.		10,000	
	To Jain Ltd.				10,000
	Narration: On 15th April, goods are bought for cash.				

Sales Voucher

Sl. No.	Particulars		LF	Amount Dr. (₹)	Amount Cr. (₹)
1.	Cash	Dr.		40,000	
	To Sales				40,000
	Narration: On 1st April, 2008, goods are sold for cash				
2.	Surya Bros. Ltd.	Dr.		20,000	
	To Sales				20,000
	Narration: On 1st April, goods are sold to Surya Bros. on credit				
3.	Surya Bros. Ltd.	Dr.		60,000	
	To Sales				60,000
	Narration: On April 19th, goods are sold to Surya Bros. on credit				

Receipt Voucher

Sl. No.	Particulars		LF	Amount Dr. (₹)	Amount Cr. (₹)
1.	Cash	Dr.		28,000	
	Discount allowed	Dr.		2000	
	To Surya Bros.				30,000
	Narration: On 2nd April, received from Surya Bros. and allowed him discount				

Sl. No.	Particulars		LF	Amount Dr. (₹)	Amount Cr. (₹)
2.	Bank	Dr.		40,000	
	To Balu Bros.				40,000
	Narration: On 9th April, cheque received from Balu Bros.				
3.	Bank	Dr.		19,500	
	Discount allowed	Dr.		500	
	To Surya Bros.				20,000
	Narration: On 16th April, cheque received from Surya Bros. and we allowed them discount				
4.	Bank	Dr.		1,00,000	
	To Navya Investment Co. Ltd.				1,00,000
	Narration: On 25 April, loan is taken from Navya Investment Co.				
5.	Cash	Dr.		1,500	
	To Bad Debt recovered				1,500
	Narration: Bad Debt written-off last year received				

Payment Voucher

Sl. No.	Particulars		LF	Amount Dr. (₹)	Amount Cr. (₹)
1.	Jain Bros.	Dr.		20,000	
	To Bank				19,750
	To Discount Received				250
	Narration: On 2nd April, payment made to Jain Bros., they allowed us discount				
2.	Furniture	Dr.		10,000	
	To Cash				10,000
	Narration: On 4th April, Furniture is Purchased for Cash				
3.	Carriage	Dr.		500	
	To Cash				500
	Narration: On 15th April, carriage is paid for goods purchase from Jain Bros.				
4.	Jain Bros.	Dr.		10,000	
	To Bank				10,000
	Narration: On 17th April, payment to Jain Bros. is made by cheque				
5.	Municipal Taxes	Dr.		1,000	
	To Cash				1,000
	Narration: On 24th April, Municipal taxes are paid				
6.	Rent	Dr.		2,500	
	To Cash				2,500
	Narration: On 31st April, rent paid				
7.	Salaries	Dr.		5,000	
	To Cash				5,000
	Narration: Salaries for month is paid				
8.	Drawing	Dr.		2,500	
	To Cash				2,500
	Narration: On 31st April, drew for private use				

Contra Voucher

Sl. No.	Particulars		LF	Amount Dr. (₹)	Amount Cr. (₹)
1.	Cash at Bank To Cash **Narration:** On 2nd April, Cash deposited to Bank	Dr.		2,000	2,000

Some of Voucher Entries are shown below :

1. Purchaes from R & Co.

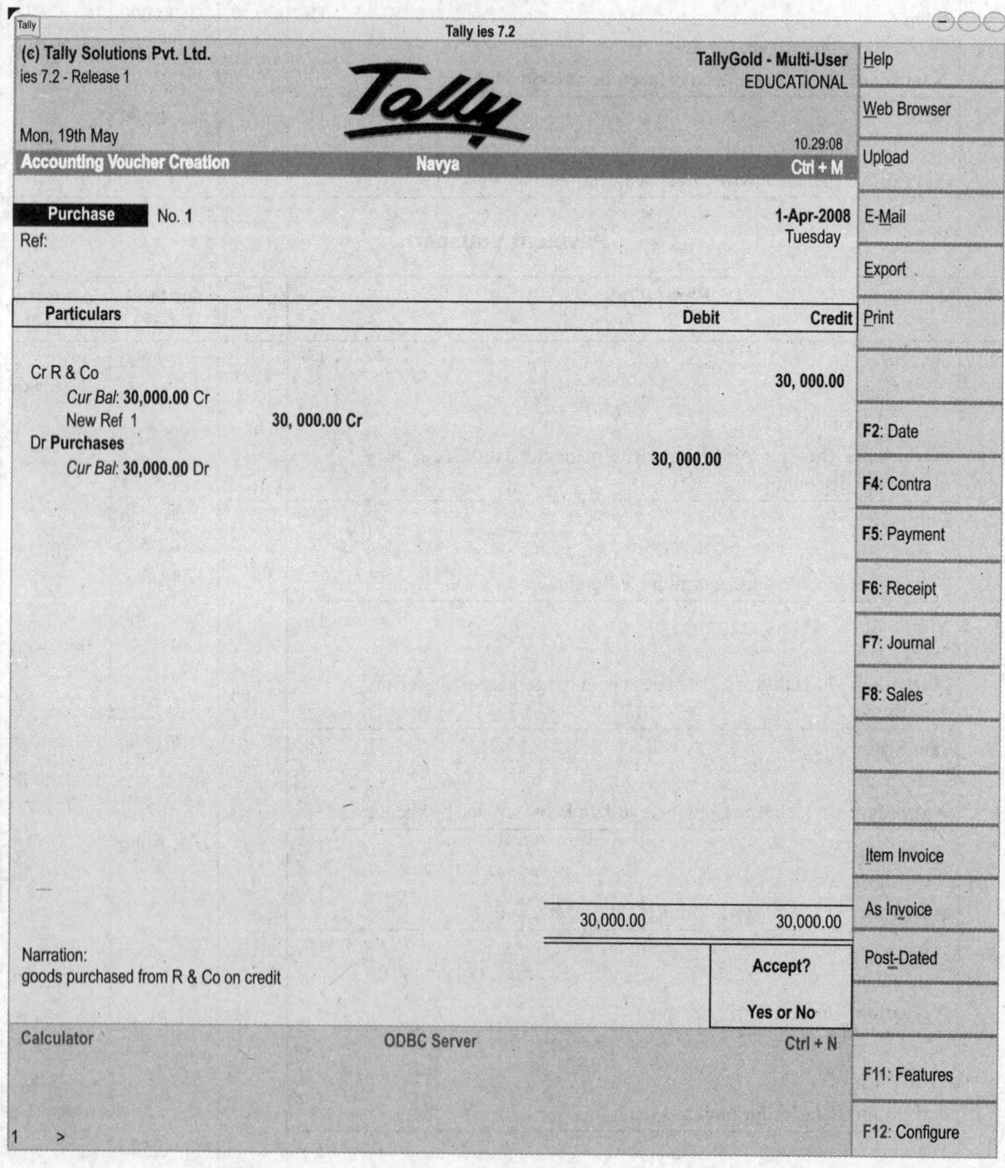

Fig. 20

2. Cash Sales

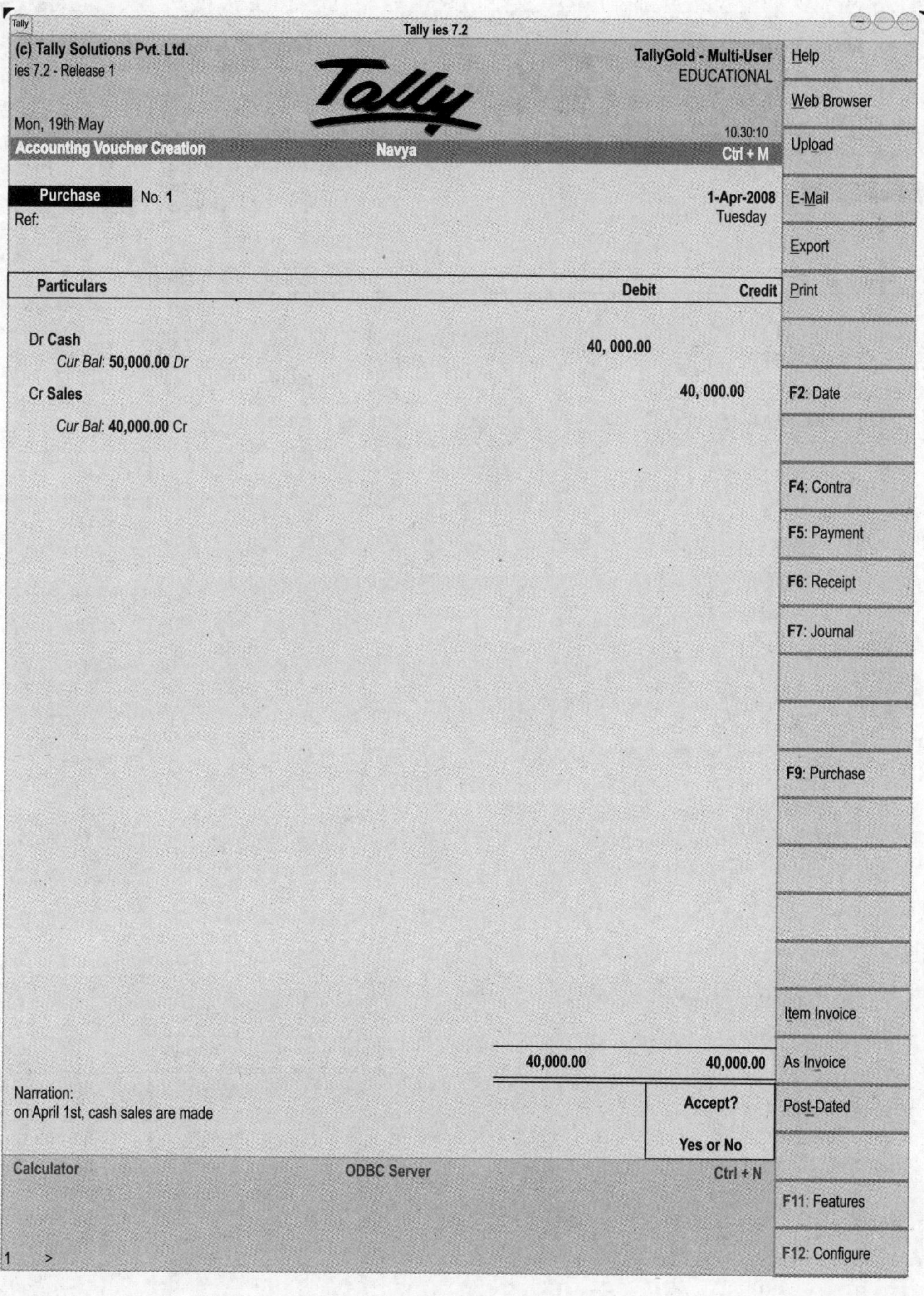

Fig. 21

3. Cash Deposited in the Bank

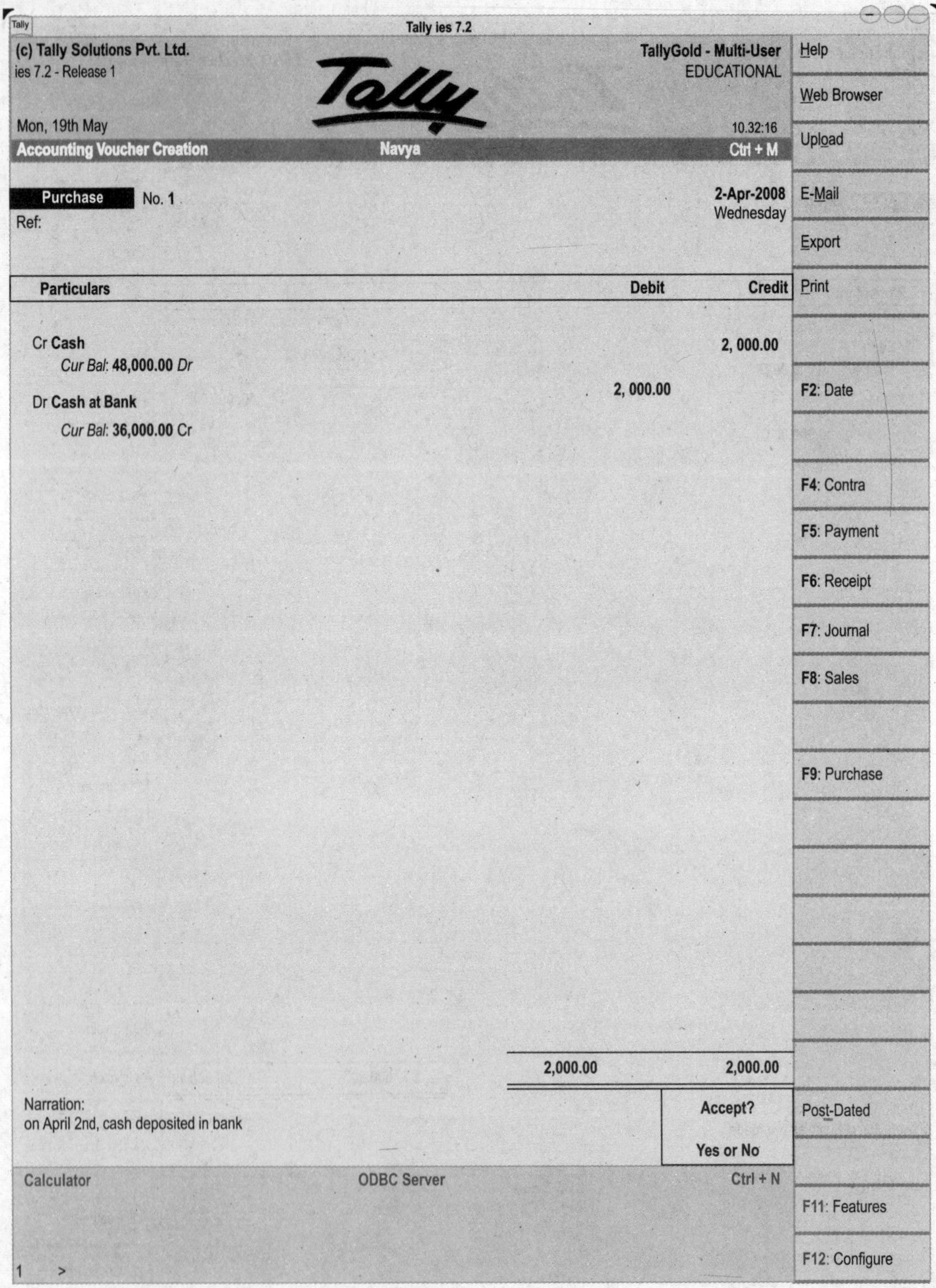

Tally ies 7.2

(c) Tally Solutions Pvt. Ltd.
ies 7.2 - Release 1

TallyGold - Multi-User
EDUCATIONAL

Mon, 19th May 10.32:16

Accounting Voucher Creation Navya Ctrl + M

Purchase No. 1 2-Apr-2008
Ref: Wednesday

Particulars	Debit	Credit
Cr **Cash**		**2, 000.00**
Cur Bal: **48,000.00** *Dr*		
Dr **Cash at Bank**	**2, 000.00**	
Cur Bal: **36,000.00** Cr		
	2,000.00	**2,000.00**

Narration:
on April 2nd, cash deposited in bank

Accept?
Yes or No

Calculator ODBC Server Ctrl + N

1 >

Help | Web Browser | Upload | E-Mail | Export | Print | F2: Date | F4: Contra | F5: Payment | F6: Receipt | F7: Journal | F8: Sales | F9: Purchase | Post-Dated | F11: Features | F12: Configure

Fig. 22

4. Receipt from Surya Bros.

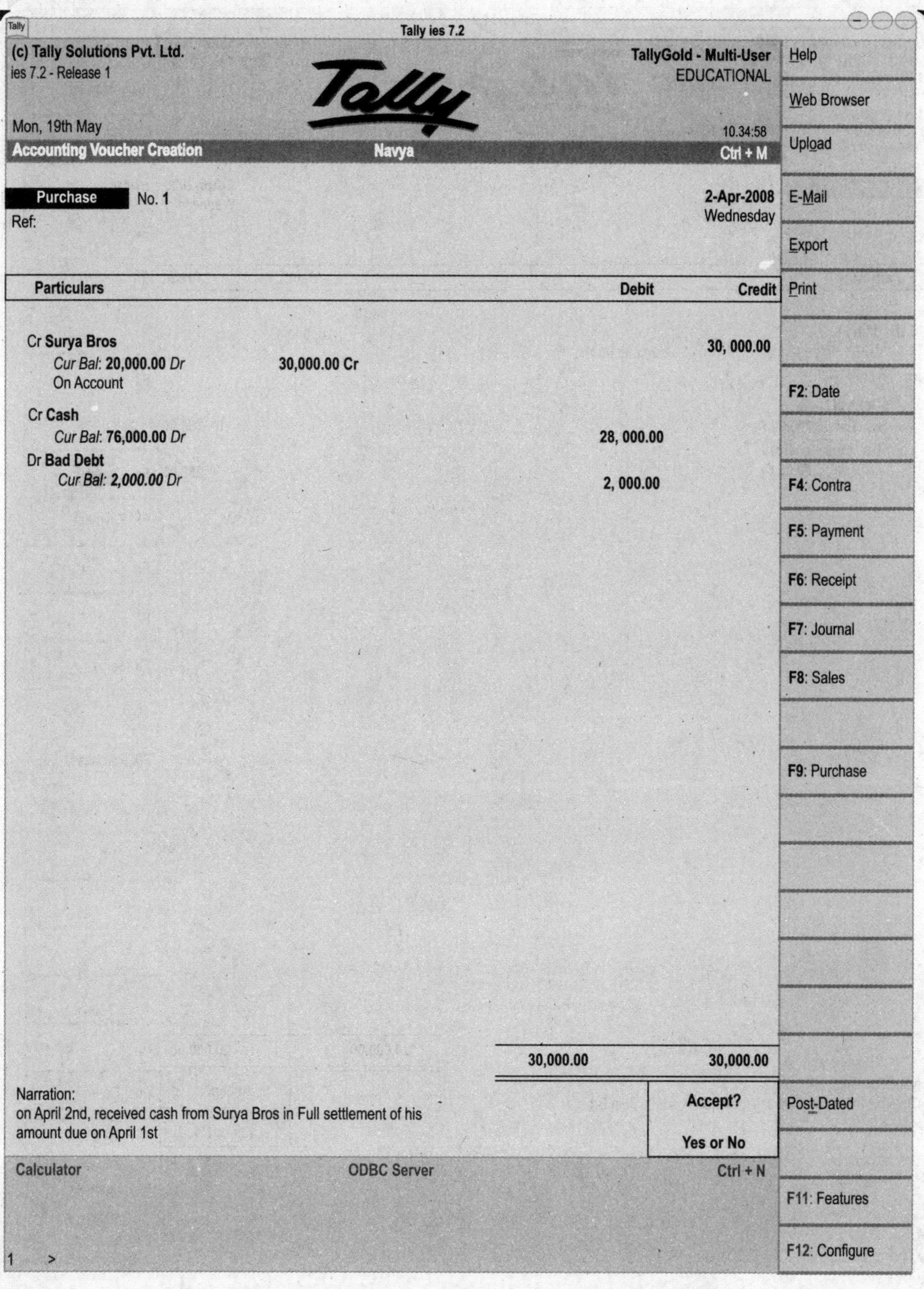

Fig. 23

5. Payment made to Jain Bros.

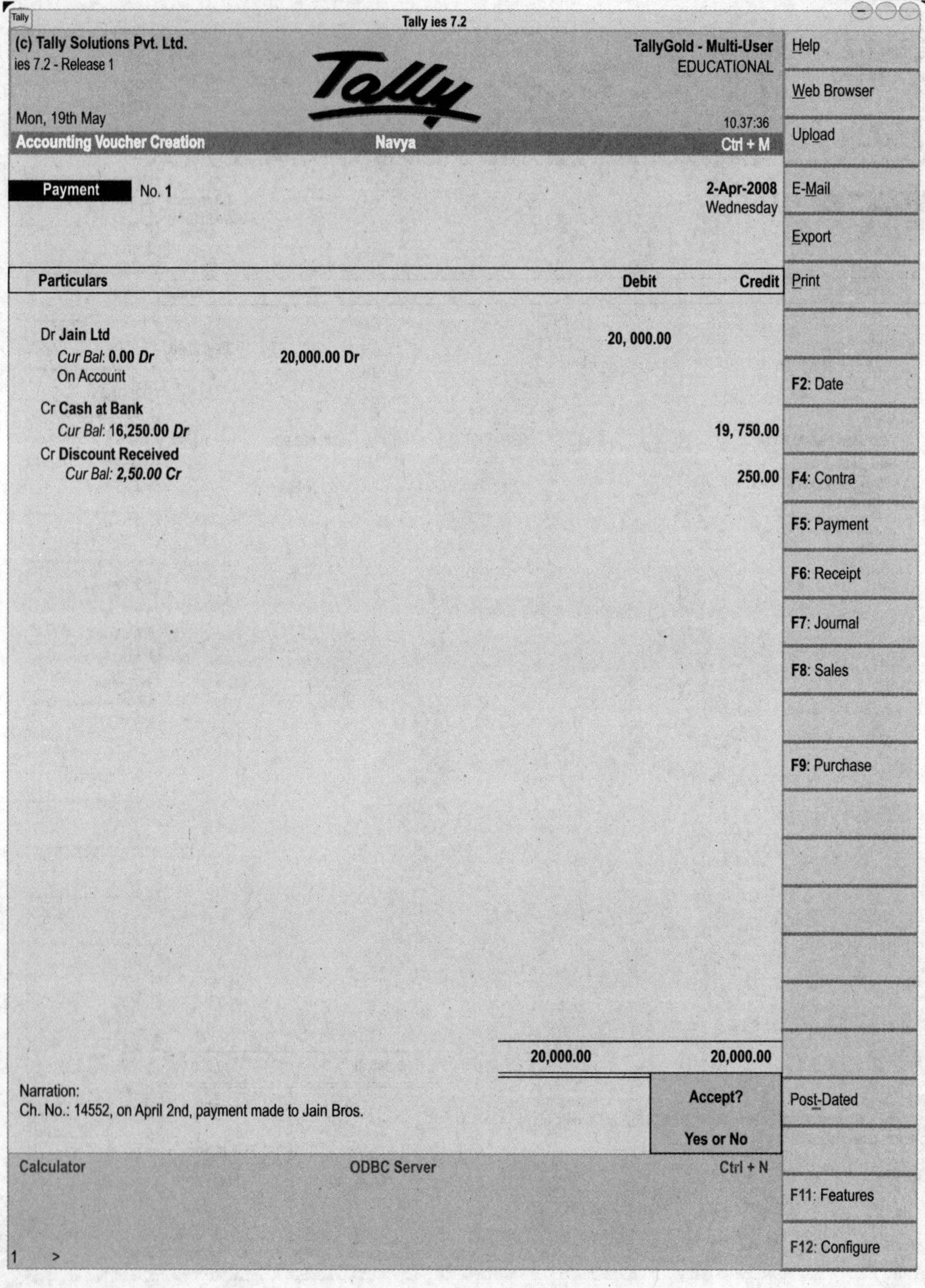

Fig. 24

After entering all vouchers, Trial **Balance, Profit and Loss Account and Balance Sheet** for the respective company is automatically created in condensed and detailed form.

Trial Balance of VEE KAY Enterprises is shown in Fig. 25.

Tally ies 7.2

(c) Tally Solutions Pvt. Ltd.
ies 7.2 - Release 1

Tally

TallyGold - Multi-User
EDUCATIONAL

Mon, 19th May, 2012

10.50:02

Trial Balance — Navya — Ctrl + M

Particulars	Navya 1-Apr-2013 to 30 Apr-2013 Closing Balance Debit	Credit
Capital Account	**2,500,00**	**74,000,00**
Capital		*74,000,00*
Drawings	*2,500,00*	
Loans (Liability)		**1.50.000.00**
Loan		*1.00.000.00*
Navya Investment Co Ltd		*50.000.00*
Current Liabilities		**40,000.00**
Sundry Creditors		40,000.00
Fixed Assets	**80,000.00**	
Furniture	*30,000.00*	
Machinery	*50,000.00*	
Current Assets	**2,42,250.00**	
Opening Stock	20,000.00	
Sundry Debtors	60,000.00	
Cash-in-hand	45,500.00	
Bank Accounts	1,15,750.00	
Sales Accounts		**1,20,000.00**
Sales		*1,20,000.00*
Purchase Accounts	**50,000,00**	
Purchases	*50,000,00*	
Direct Expenses	**500.00**	
Carriage	*500.00*	
Indirect Incomes		**1,750.00**
Bad Debt Recovered		*1,500.00*
	7 more ...	
Grand Total	**3,85,750.00**	**3,85,750.00**

Help | Web Browser | Upload | E-Mail | Export | Print | F1: Condensed | F2: Period | F4: Group | F5: Led-wise | F7: Vouchers | New Column | Alter Column | Auto Column | F8: Other Rep | F9: Inv Rep | F10: Acc Rep | F11: Features | F12: Configure | F12: Range | F12: Value

Calculator — ODBC Server — Ctrl + N

1 >

Fig. 25

PROFIT AND LOSS ACCOUNT

Tally ies 7.2

(c) Tally Solutions Pvt. Ltd. TallyGold - Multi-User
ies 7.2 - Release 1 EDUCATIONAL

Tally

Mon, 19th May, 2012 10.50:22

Profit & Less A/c Navya Ctrl + M

Particulars		Navya 1-Apr-2012 to 30 Apr-2013	Particulars		Navya 1-Apr-2012 to 30 Apr-2013
Opening Stock		20,000.00	**Sales Accounts**		1,20,000.00
Stock of Goods	20,000.00		*Sales*	1,20,000.00	
Purchase Accounts		50,000.00	**Closing Stock**		20,000.00
Purchases	50,000.00			20,000.00	
Direct Expenses		500.00			
Carriage	500.00				
		69, 500.00			
		1,40, 000.00			1,40,000.00
		10, 500.00	***Gross profit b/f***		***69,500.00***
Indirect Expenses			**Indirect Incomes**		1,750.00
Bad Debt	2,000.00		*Bad Debt Recovered*	1,500.00	
Discount Allowed	500.00		*Discount Received*	250.00	
Municipal Taxes	500.00				
Rent	2,500.00				
Salaries	5,000.00				
Nett Profit		60,750,.00			
Total		71,250.00	**Total**		71,250.00

Calculator ODBC Server Ctrl + N

1 >

Help | Web Browser | Upload | E-Mail | Export | Print | F1: Condensed | F2: Period | New Column | Alter Column | Auto Column | F8: Other Rep | F9: Inv Rep | F10: Acc Rep | F11: Features | F12: Configure | F12: Range | F12: Value

Fig. 26

Balance Sheet (Condensed form)

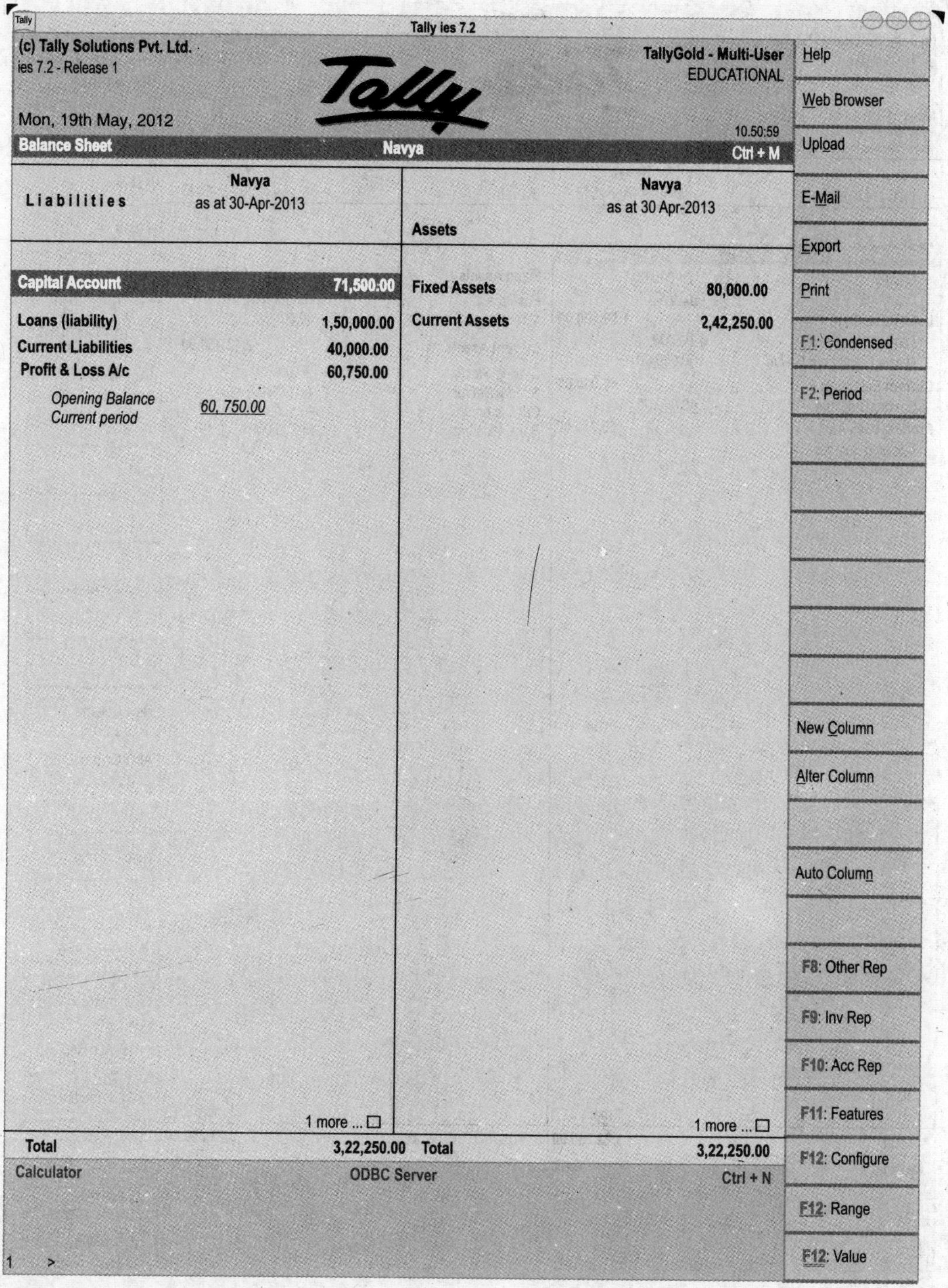

Tally ies 7.2

(c) Tally Solutions Pvt. Ltd.
ies 7.2 - Release 1

TallyGold - Multi-User
EDUCATIONAL

Tally

Mon, 19th May, 2012

10.50:59

Balance Sheet | Navya | Ctrl + M

Liabilities	Navya as at 30-Apr-2013	Assets	Navya as at 30 Apr-2013
Capital Account	71,500.00	Fixed Assets	80,000.00
Loans (liability)	1,50,000.00	Current Assets	2,42,250.00
Current Liabilities	40,000.00		
Profit & Loss A/c	60,750.00		
Opening Balance			
Current period *60, 750.00*			
1 more ...		1 more ...	
Total	3,22,250.00	Total	3,22,250.00

Calculator ODBC Server Ctrl + N

1 >

Help
Web Browser
Upload
E-Mail
Export
Print
F1: Condensed
F2: Period
New Column
Alter Column
Auto Column
F8: Other Rep
F9: Inv Rep
F10: Acc Rep
F11: Features
F12: Configure
F12: Range
F12: Value

Fig. 27

Balance Sheet (Detailed form)

Tally ies 7.2

(c) Tally Solutions Pvt. Ltd. — TallyGold - Multi-User
ies 7.2 - Release 1 — EDUCATIONAL

Tally

Mon, 19th May, 2012 — 10.50:40

Balance Sheet — Navya — Ctrl + M

Liabilities		Navya as at 30-Apr-2013	Assets		Navya as at 30 Apr-2013
Capital Account		**71,500.00**	**Fixed Assets**		**80,000.00**
Capital	*74,000.00*		*Furniture*	*30,000.00*	
Drawings	*(–)2,500.00*		*Machinery*	*50,000.00*	
Loan (Liability)		**1,50,000.00**	**Current Assets**		**2,42,250.00**
Loan	*1,00,000.00*		*Closing Stock*	*20,000.00*	
Navya investment Co Ltd	*50,000.00*		*Sundry Debtor*	*60,000.00*	
Current Liabilities		**40,000.00**	*Cash in hand*	*46,500.00*	
Sundry Creditors	40,000.00		*Bank Accounts*	*1,15,750.00*	
Profit & Loss A/c		**60,750.00**			
Opening Balance					
Current Period	*60,750.00*				
		1 more ...			1 more ...
Total		**3,22,250.00**	**Total**		**3,22,250.00**

Help | Web Browser | Upload | E-Mail | Export | Print | F1: Condensed | F2: Period | New Column | Alter Column | Auto Column | F8: Other Rep | F9: Inv Rep | F10: Acc Rep | F11: Features | F12: Configure | F12: Range | F12: Value

Calculator — ODBC Server — Ctrl + N

1 >

Fig. 28

Illustration 2: Pass necessary entries and prepare final accounts of M/s Naman & Co.

Date	Particulars	(₹)
April, 1st	Naman started business with cash	5,00,000
May, 1st	Purchased Furniture	72,000
May, 1st	Opened new Bank Account in SBI	2,00,000
May, 31st	Purchased Goods	1,40,000
May, 31st	Sold Goods	1,80,000
July, 10th	Purchased Stationary	14,000
July, 25th	Withdrawn from SBI	50,000
July, 31st	Rent paid for April to September by Cheque	30,000
August, 31st	Purchased Goods on Credit from Ram	1,60,000
September, 24th	Received Commission	10,000
October, 12th	Purchased Gods from Mohan	80,000
November, 24th	Paid cash to Ram	56,000
December, 10th	Sold Goods to Kapil	1,88,000
December, 21st	Paid to Ram in Full Settlement	1,00,000
January, 25th	Received from Kapil in full settlement: Cash	46,000
	Cheque	1,34,000
February, 1st	Sold Goods to Ravi	1,60,000
February, 10th	Purchase Goods from Mohan	1,04,000
March, 1st	Rent paid for October to February by Cheque	25,000
March, 15th	Stationary Bill paid by Cheque	12,600

Adjustments:

1. Closing Stock was valued at 1,60,000
2. Depreciate Furniture @ 10% p.a.
3. Rent o/s for March.

Solution: The following entries will be passed in the different vouchers:

Receipt Voucher

Sl. No.	Particulars		LF	Amount Dr. (₹)	Amount Cr. (₹)
1.	Cash	Dr.		5,00,000	
	To Naman				5,00,000
	Narration: On 1st April, Naman started business with cash				
2.	Cash	Dr.		10,000	
	To Commission				10,000
	Narration: On September 24th, received commission				
3.	Cash	Dr.		46,000	
	Bank	Dr.		1,34,000	
	Bad Debt	Dr.		8,000	
	To Kapil				1,88,000
	Narration: On January 25th, Received from Kapil in full settlement of his account				

Payment Voucher

Sl. No.	Particulars		LF	Amount Dr. (₹)	Amount Cr. (₹)
1.	Furniture	Dr.		72,000	
	To Cash				72,000
	Narration: On May 1st, Purchased Furniture for cash				
2.	Stationary	Dr.		14,000	
	To cash				14,000
	Narration: On July 10th, Purchased Stationary for cash				
3.	Rent	Dr.		30,000	
	To Bank				30,000
	Narration: On July 31st, Paid rent for the month of April to September				
4.	Ram	Dr.		56,000	
	To Cash				56,000
	Narration: On November 24th, paid Cash to Ram				
5.	Ram	Dr.		1,04,000	
	To cash				1,00,000
	To Discount Received				4,000
	Narration: On December 21st, paid to Ram in Full Settlement				
6.	Rent	Dr.		25,000	
	To Bank				25,000
	Narration: On March 1st, paid rent by Cheque for October to March				
7.	Stationary	Dr.		12,600	
	To Bank				12,600
	Narration: On March 15th, Stationary Bill is paid				

Journal Voucher

Sl. No.	Particulars		LF	Amount Dr. (₹)	Amount Cr. (₹)
1.	Depreciation	Dr.		7,200	
	To Furniture				7,200
	Narration: On March 31st, Depreciation Charged on Furniture @ 10%				
2.	Rent	Dr.		5,000	
	To Rent o/s				5,000
	Narration: Rent outstanding for the month of March				

Contra Voucher

Sl. No.	Particulars		LF	Amount Dr. (₹)	Amount Cr. (₹)
1.	Bank	Dr.		2,00,000	
	To Cash				2,00,000
	Narration: On 1st May, opened a new Account with SBI Bank				

Sl. No.	Particulars		LF	Amount Dr. (₹)	Amount Cr. (₹)
2.	Cash	Dr.		50,000	
	To Bank				50,000
	Narration: On July 25th, withdraw Cash from Bank				

Purchase Voucher

Sl. No.	Particulars		LF	Amount Dr. (₹)	Amount Cr. (₹)
1.	Purchases	Dr.		1,40,000	
	To Cash				1,40,000
	Narration: On 31st May, Purchased Goods for cash				
2.	Purchases	Dr.		1,60,000	
	To Ram				1,60,000
	Narration: On August 31st, Purchased Goods on Credit from Ram				
3.	Purchases	Dr.		80,000	
	To Mohan				80,000
	Narration: On October 2nd, Purchased Goods on Credit from Mohan				
4.	Purchases	Dr.		1,04,000	
	To Mohan				1,04,000
	Narration: On February 10th, Purchased Goods on Credit from Mohan				

Sales Voucher

Sl. No.	Particulars		LF	Amount Dr. (₹)	Amount Cr. (₹)
1.	Cash	Dr.		1,80,000	
	To Sales				1,80,000
	Narration: On 31st May, sold Goods for Cash				
2.	Kapil	Dr.		1,88,000	
	To Sales				1,88,000
	Narration: On January 25th, sold Goods on Credit to Kapil				
3.	Ravi	Dr.		1,60,000	
	To Sales				1,60,000
	Narration: On February 1st, sold Goods to Ravi on Credit				

Journal Voucher entries in Tally are shown below:

1. Depreciation on Furniture (Fig. 29).

Tally 9

(c) Tally Solutions FZ-LLC

TallyGold - Multi-User

Tally

http:www.tallysolutions.com

EDUCATIONAL

P: Print | E: Export | M: E-mail | O: Upload | K: Keyboard | H: Help

Accounting Voucher Creation — Naman & Co — Ctrl + M

Journal No. 1 — 31-Mar-2012 Monday

Particulars	Dedit	Credit
Dr **Depreciation**	7,200,00	
*Cur Bal : **7,200.00 Dr***		
Cr **Furniture**		
*Cur Bal : **64,800.00 Dr***		**7,200.00**
Narration:	7,200.00	7,200.00

depreciation charged on furniture @10%

Accept ?
Yes or No

F2: Date
F4: Contra
F5: Payment
F6: Receipt
F8: Sales
F9: Purchase
T: Post-Dated
F11: Features
F12: Configure

Calculator — ODBC Server — Ctrl + N

1 >

Gateway of Tally--> Accounting Voucher Creation — 9 - Release 1.11 (English) — Sat, 17 May, 2013 — 10:29:17

Fig. 29

2. Rent outstanding (Fig. 30).

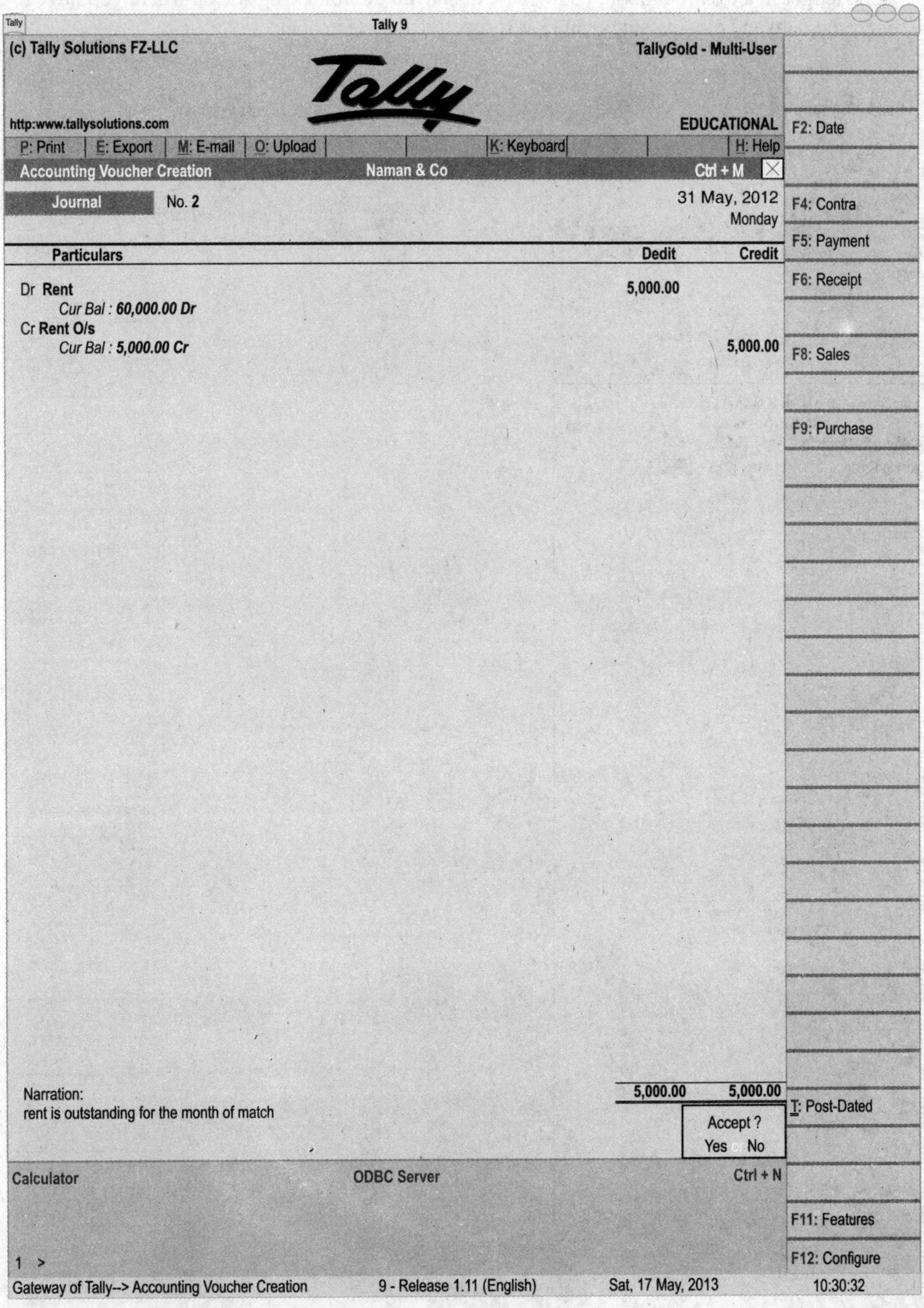

Tally 9

(c) Tally Solutions FZ-LLC TallyGold - Multi-User

Tally

http:www.tallysolutions.com EDUCATIONAL

P: Print | E: Export | M: E-mail | O: Upload | K: Keyboard | H: Help

Accounting Voucher Creation Naman & Co Ctrl + M

Journal No. 2 31 May, 2012 Monday

Particulars	Dedit	Credit
Dr Rent	5,000.00	
Cur Bal : ***60,000.00 Dr***		
Cr **Rent O/s**		
Cur Bal : ***5,000.00 Cr***		5,000.00
	5,000.00	5,000.00

Narration:
rent is outstanding for the month of match

Accept ?
Yes or No

Calculator ODBC Server Ctrl + N

1 >

Gateway of Tally--> Accounting Voucher Creation 9 - Release 1.11 (English) Sat, 17 May, 2013 10:30:32

F2: Date
F4: Contra
F5: Payment
F6: Receipt
F8: Sales
F9: Purchase
T: Post-Dated
F11: Features
F12: Configure

Fig. 30

3. **Closing stock:** You need not to pass Journal Voucher for Closing Stock. Instead select closing stock ledger in alteration mode, you will be displayed the following screen where you have to enter the date and closing stock value at respective date (Fig. 31).

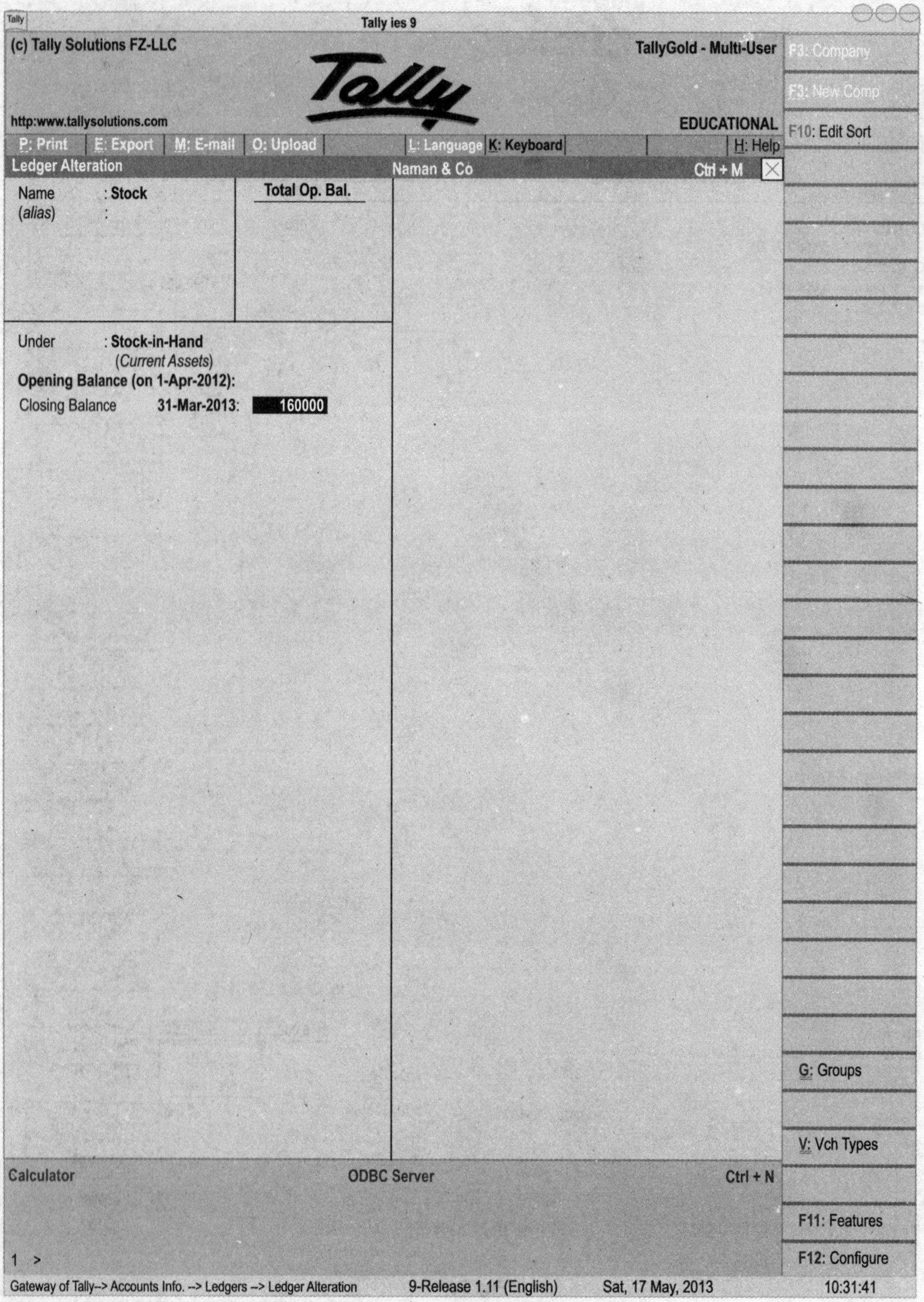

Tally ies 9

(c) Tally Solutions FZ-LLC

TallyGold - Multi-User

Tally

http:www.tallysolutions.com

EDUCATIONAL

P: Print | E: Export | M: E-mail | O: Upload | L: Language | K: Keyboard | H: Help

Ledger Alteration | Naman & Co | Ctrl + M

Name : Stock

(alias) :

Total Op. Bal.

Under : Stock-in-Hand

(Current Assets)

Opening Balance (on 1-Apr-2012):

Closing Balance 31-Mar-2013: 160000

F3: Company

F3: New Comp

F10: Edit Sort

G: Groups

V: Vch Types

F11: Features

F12: Configure

Calculator | ODBC Server | Ctrl + N

1 >

Gateway of Tally--> Accounts Info. --> Ledgers --> Ledger Alteration | 9-Release 1.11 (English) | Sat, 17 May, 2013 | 10:31:41

Fig. 31

Having entered the value, it will be shown in Profit and Loss Account and also in Balance Sheet as shown in Figs. 32 and 33.

Profit and Loss Account

Tally ies 9

(c) Tally Solutions FZ-LLC TallyGold - Multi-User

Tally

http:www.tallysolutions.com EDUCATIONAL

P: Print | E: Export | M: E-mail | O: Upload | L: Language | K: Keyboard | H: Help

Profit & Loss A/c | Naman & Co | Ctrl + M

Particulars		Naman & Co. 1-Apr-2012 to 31-Mar-2013	Particulars		Naman & Co. 1-Apr-2012 to 31-Mar-2013
Opening Stock			**Sales Accounts**		5,28,000.00
Stock			*Sales*	*5,28,000.00*	
Purchase Accounts		4,84,000.000	**Closing Stock**		1,60,000.00
Purchases	*4,84,000.000*		*Stock*	*1,60,000.00*	
Gross Profit c/o		2,04,000.00			6,88,000.00
		6,88,000.00	***Gross Profit b/f***		2,04,000.00
Indirect Expenses		1,01,800.00	**Indirect Incomes**		14,000.00
Bad Debts			*Commission*	*10,000.00*	
Depreciation	*8,000.00*		*Discount Received*	*4,000.00*	
Rent	*7,200.00*				
Stationary	*60,000.00*				
	26, 600.00				
Nett profit		1,16,200.00			
Total		2,18,000.00	**Total**		2,18,000.00

F1: Condensed
F2: Period
F3: Company
F7: Valuation
C: New Column
A: Alter Column
D: Del Column
N: Auto Column
F9: Inv Rep
F10: Acc Rep
F11: Features
F12: Configure
F12: Range
F12: Value

Calculator | ODBC Server | Ctrl + N

1 >

Gateway of Tally--> Profit & Loss A/c | 9-Release 1.11 (English) | Sat, 17 May, 2013 | 10:32:38

Fig. 32

Balance Sheet

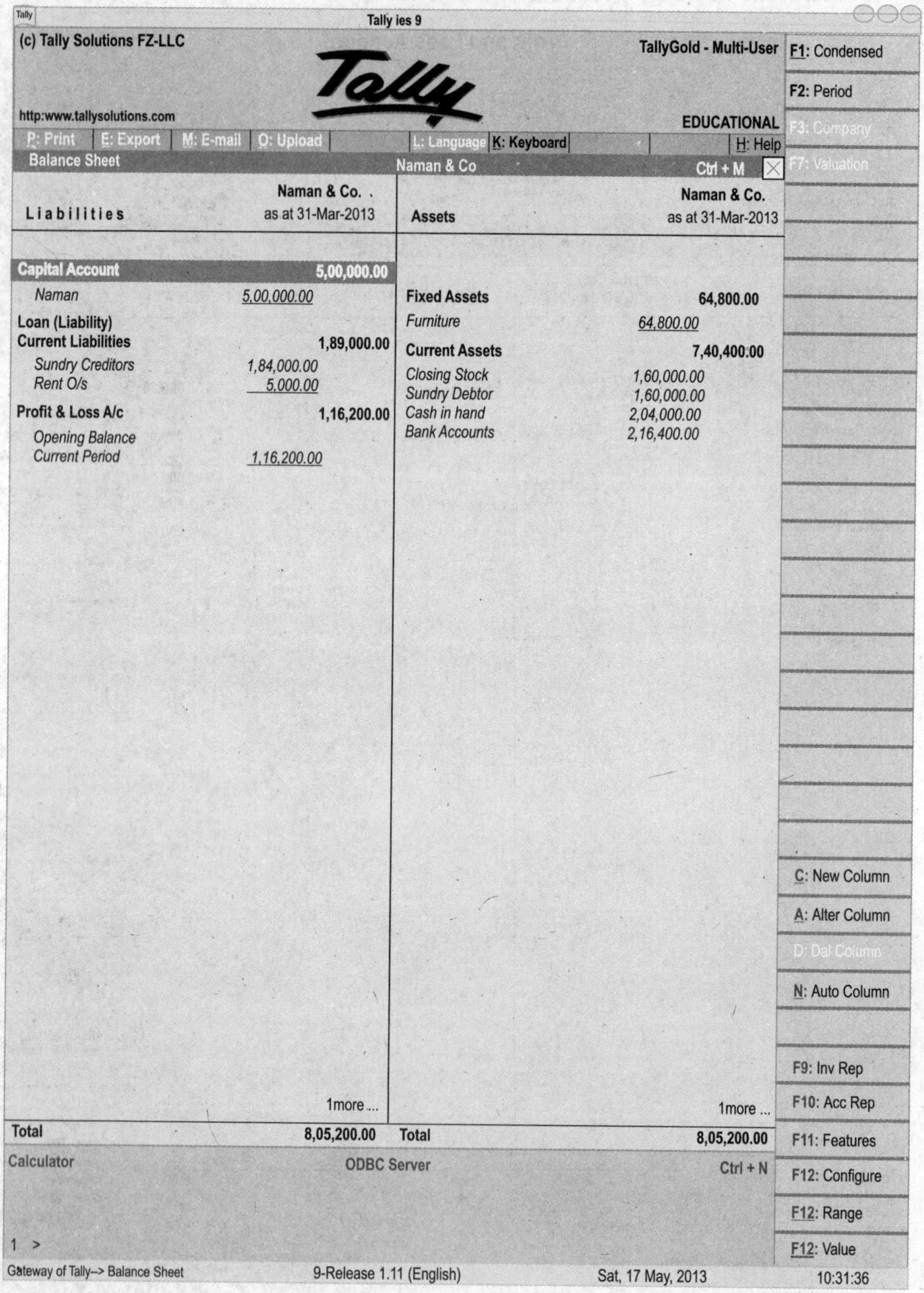

Tally ies 9

(c) Tally Solutions FZ-LLC

TallyGold - Multi-User

http:www.tallysolutions.com

EDUCATIONAL

P: Print | E: Export | M: E-mail | O: Upload | L: Language | K: Keyboard | H: Help

Balance Sheet — Naman & Co — Ctrl + M

Liabilities		Naman & Co. as at 31-Mar-2013	Assets		Naman & Co. as at 31-Mar-2013
Capital Account		**5,00,000.00**	**Fixed Assets**		**64,800.00**
Naman	*5,00,000.00*		*Furniture*	*64,800.00*	
Loan (Liability)					
Current Liabilities		**1,89,000.00**	**Current Assets**		**7,40,400.00**
Sundry Creditors	*1,84,000.00*		*Closing Stock*	*1,60,000.00*	
Rent O/s	*5,000.00*		*Sundry Debtor*	*1,60,000.00*	
Profit & Loss A/c		**1,16,200.00**	*Cash in hand*	*2,04,000.00*	
Opening Balance			*Bank Accounts*	*2,16,400.00*	
Current Period	*1,16,200.00*				
		1more ...			1more ...
Total		**8,05,200.00**	**Total**		**8,05,200.00**

F1: Condensed
F2: Period
F3: Company
F7: Valuation
C: New Column
A: Alter Column
D: Del Column
N: Auto Column
F9: Inv Rep
F10: Acc Rep
F11: Features
F12: Configure
F12: Range
F12: Value

Calculator — ODBC Server — Ctrl + N

1 >

Gateway of Tally--> Balance Sheet — 9-Release 1.11 (English) — Sat, 17 May, 2013 — 10:31:36

Fig. 33

Trial Balance

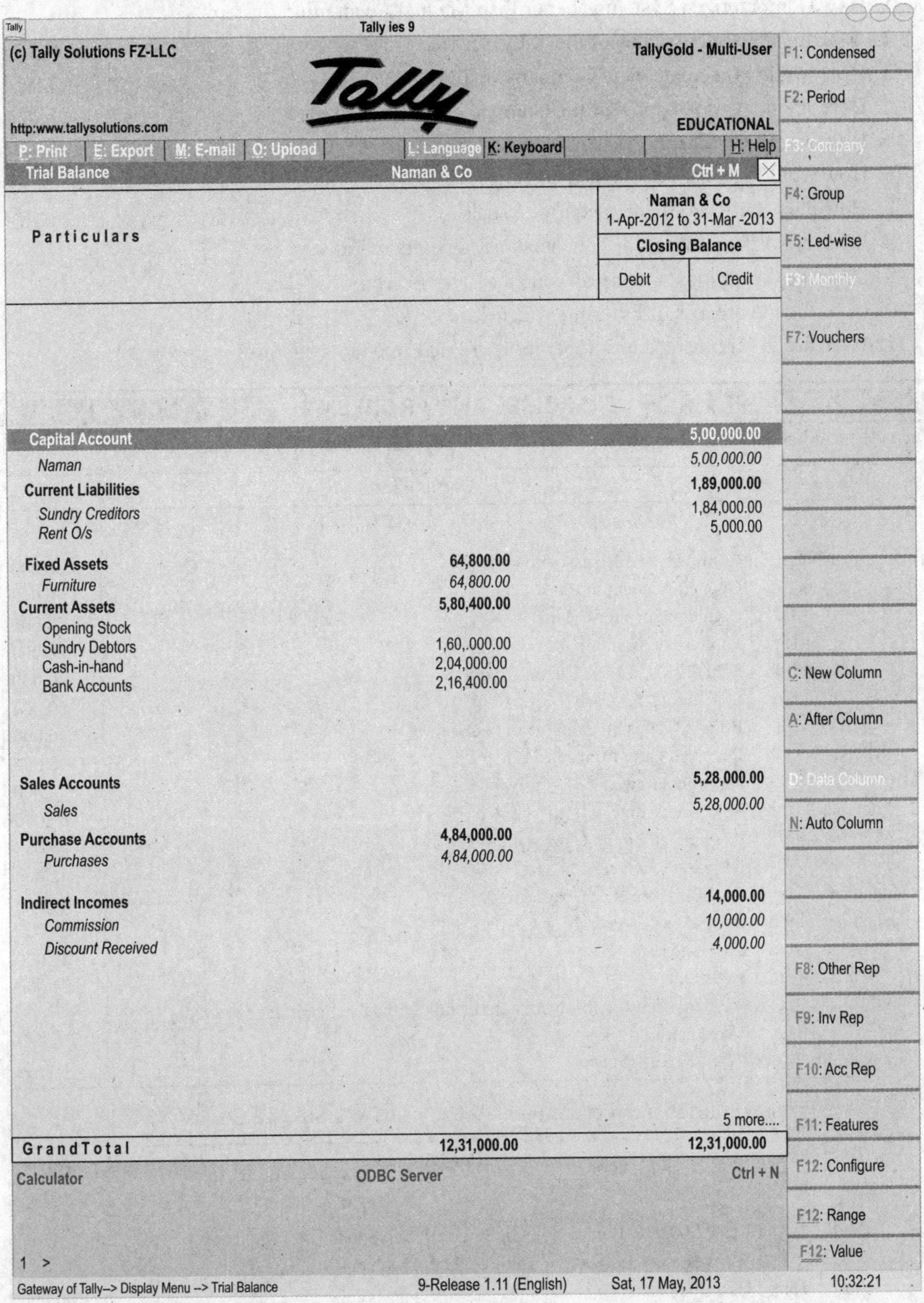

Tally ies 9

(c) Tally Solutions FZ-LLC — TallyGold - Multi-User

Tally

http:www.tallysolutions.com — EDUCATIONAL

P: Print | E: Export | M: E-mail | O: Upload | L: Language | K: Keyboard | H: Help

Trial Balance — Naman & Co — Ctrl + M

Particulars	Naman & Co 1-Apr-2012 to 31-Mar -2013 Closing Balance Debit	 Credit
Capital Account		**5,00,000.00**
Naman		*5,00,000.00*
Current Liabilities		**1,89,000.00**
Sundry Creditors		1,84,000.00
Rent O/s		5,000.00
Fixed Assets	**64,800.00**	
Furniture	*64,800.00*	
Current Assets	**5,80,400.00**	
Opening Stock		
Sundry Debtors	1,60,.000.00	
Cash-in-hand	2,04,000.00	
Bank Accounts	2,16,400.00	
Sales Accounts		**5,28,000.00**
Sales		*5,28,000.00*
Purchase Accounts	**4,84,000.00**	
Purchases	*4,84,000.00*	
Indirect Incomes		**14,000.00**
Commission		*10,000.00*
Discount Received		*4,000.00*
5 more....		
Grand Total	**12,31,000.00**	**12,31,000.00**

Calculator — ODBC Server — Ctrl + N

1 >

Gateway of Tally--> Display Menu --> Trial Balance — 9-Release 1.11 (English) — Sat, 17 May, 2013 — 10:32:21

F1: Condensed | F2: Period | F3: Company | F4: Group | F5: Led-wise | F6: Monthly | F7: Vouchers | C: New Column | A: After Column | D: Data Column | N: Auto Column | F8: Other Rep | F9: Inv Rep | F10: Acc Rep | F11: Features | F12: Configure | F12: Range | F12: Value

Fig. 34

THEORY QUESTIONS

1. How Computerized System is better than Manual Accounting System?
2. Describe the various items of the Tally Screen.
3. How would you create New Company in Tally?
4. Describe the various items of the Company Creation Screen.
5. How would you Display, Alter, Delete a Ledger from Tally?
6. How would you create a Ledger in Tally?
7. How does Tally handle the Security Issue?
8. What are different kinds of vouchers available under Tally?
9. Describe the various options of Voucher Entry Screen.
10. Describe the process of Entering Vouchers.
11. What are different steps for preparation of Final Accounts in Tally?

EXERCISES AND PROBLEMS

1. Journalise the following transactions of JK Co. and create the Final Accounts:

Date		Particulars	(₹)
2012			
April	1st	Commenced business with cash	5,00,000
	2nd	Opened Account in Bank	1,00,000
	3rd	Bought Goods for Cash	50,000
	15th	Purchased Furniture	20,000
May	3rd	Sold Goods to M & Co. on Credit	40,000
June	1st	Sold Goods for Cash	50,000
July	10th	Bought Goods on Credit from S & Co.	1,00,000
August	16th	Received Cash from M & Co.	38,000
		Discount allowed	2,000
September	10th	Sold Goods on Credit to M & Co.	80,000
October	15th	Paid to S & Co. by Cheque	95,000
		Discount received	5,000
November	10th	Sold Goods to R & Co. on Credit	30,000
December	30th	Bought Goods from N & Co. on Credit	50,000
January	30th	Cash Sales	20,000
March	16th	Paid Rent	24,000
	25th	R & Co. becomes insolvent a dividend of 50 paisa in a rupee received	
	31st	Taxes paid	2,000
(Gross Profit: 20,000, Net Loss: 18,000)			

2. Pass necessary Entries and prepare Final Accounts of M/s Silky & Co.

Date		Particulars	(₹)
2012			
April	1st	Cash 2,00,000, Bank 1,50,000, Stock 50,000, Sohan (Dr.) 10,00,000, Investment 1,00,000, Furniture 50,000, Mohan (Cr.) 70,000	
April	15th	Cash Purchases	1,00,000
May	20th	Sold goods, Cheque received	2,00,000
June	15th	Sold Goods to Ram	50,000

Date		Particulars	(₹)
July	10th	Purchase Stationary	1,000
August	12th	Purchased Goods on Credit from Shyam	1,00,000
September	15th	Rent paid by Cheque	18,000
October	20th	Sold for Cash	20,000
November	30th	Received from Sohan in full settlement	90,000
January	20th	Issued cheque to Mohan in full settlement	65,000
February	10th	Sold to Sohan	50,000
March	30th	Rent paid	18,000
		Salary paid	10,000

Adjustments:

1. Depreciate furniture @ 10% p.a.
2. Provide for outstanding salaries ₹ 5,000.
3. Closing Stock valued at ₹ 30,000.

(Gross Profit: 1,00,000, Net Profit: 38,000).

GLOSSARY

A

Abridged Accounts: Any balance sheet or profit and loss account relating to a financial year of a Company other than as part of full accounts.

Abstract: A summary of information.

Accelerated Depreciation: Any depreciation method under which the amounts of depreciation expenses taken in the early years of an asset is life are larger than those amounts taken later.

Account: A recording device used for sorting accounting information into similar groups.

Accountability: The state or condition of being accountable.

Accounting: The set of rules and methods by which financial and economic data are collected and transformed into useful reports for decision making.

Accounting Concepts: Necessary assumptions or conditions upon which accounting is based.

Accounting Equation: The statement in relation to an accounting entity: Assets = Liability + Equity.

Accounting Income: Net profit or loss of an accounting entity for a period, including extraordinary items as reported in the profit and loss account, before deducting relating payments of tax or adding amounts of tax recoverable.

Accounting Standard: A rule when it is widely accepted should be followed in accounting, propounded by an accounting or professional body.

Accounts Payable: Amounts payable by the firm to persons from whom goods have been purchased. Syronymous with sundry creditors.

Accounts Receivable: Amounts due to the firm from people to whom goods have been sold. Synonymous with sundry debtors.

Accrual Basis of Accountings: The basis that assumes that revenue is realised at the time of the sale of goods or services regardless of when the cash is received.

Expenses are recognised at the time the services are received and utilised or an asset is consumed in the production of revenue, regardless of when payment of these services or assets is made.

Accrual Principle: The basis that assumes that revenue is realised at the time of the sale of goods or services, regardless of when the cash is received.

Expenses are recognised at time the services are received and utilised or an asset is consumed in the production of revenue, regardless of when payment for these services or assets is made.

Administrative Expenses: Classification of expenses incurred in the general direction of an enterprise as a whole such as salaries, postage, stationery and insurance.

Allotment: Assignment of previously unissued shares to particular holders, giving them an unconditional right to be entered in the register of members in respect of those shares.

Amalgamation: An arrangement under which the entire business and undertaking of two or more companies are transferred to another company newly formed for the purpose and old companies are dissolved.

Amortisation: This term is used in two senses; (*i*) repayment of loan over a period of time; (*ii*) write-off of an expenditure (like issue cost of shares) over a period of time.

Annual Report: The report issued annually by a company to this shareholders. It contains primarily the financial statements. In addition, it presents the management's view of the operations of the previous year and the prospects for future.

Annuity: A series of periodic cash flows.

Assets: A thing of value owned by an economic enterprises.

Auditing: Independent review of an entity's accounting reports usually made by a certified public accountant/Chartered Accountant.

Auditor: One who audits books of account and records kept by others.

Authorised Share Capital: The maximum share capital the company is authorised to issue as per its articles of association.

B

Bad Debts: Uncollectable receivable.

Balance Sheet: The statement that summarise the assets, liabilities and owner's equity of a business unit as of a specific date.

Bank Reconciliation Statement: Statement showing items of difference between the balance of an account reported by bank and balance appearing on the books of customer.

Bankruptcy: A state in which a firm (or individual) is unable to meet its obligations and, hence, its assets are surrendered to a court for administration.

Bill of Exchange: A general term for a note demanding payment.

Bill of Lading: A document which represents ownership of goods in transit.

Bills Payable: A bill showing that a firm owes money to those whose names are mentioned in the bill.

Bills Receivable: A bill showing that money is due to the firm from those whose names are mentioned in the bill.

Bonus Shares: Share issued to existing shareholders a result of capitalisation of reserves.

Book-keeping: The process of analysing, classifying and recording transactions in a systematic manner in various set of books.

Book of Original Entry: The record used by accountants to initially enter transactions. It is called a journal.

Book Value: The accounting value. The book value of an asset is its historical cost less accumulated depreciation. The book value per share is the net worth of the company divided by the number of outstanding shares.

Brought Down (b/d): Term used to present the opening balance of an account (may be used as a synonym for the term 'Brought Forward').

Brought Forward (b/f): Terms used to open an account for the current year by posting the closing balance of previous year.

Capital Expenditure: Cost incurred to acquire fixed assets, the benefit from which is spread over several accounting periods.

Capital Work-in-Progress: Investment made in fixed assets which are not yet ready for use.

Carried Down (c/d): Term used to balance an account (may be used as a synonym for the term carried forward).

Carried Forward (c/f): Transferring the balance of an account from one period to another period.

Carriage Inwards: Expenses incurred for transporting the goods/direct material purchased by a firm.

Carriage Outwards: Expenses incurred for transporting the goods in the course of a sale.

Cash: Currency, coins, cheque and any other items that a bank will accept for deposit.

Cash Accounting Basis: A basis of keeping accounts, whereby revenue and expenses are recorded in the books of account when received and paid without regard to which they apply.

Cash at Bank: Balance of deposit with a bank.

Cash book: A book of entries for cash receipts and payments.

Cash flow statement: A statement showing a firm's cash inflows and outflows, classified into operating, investing and financing categories.

Cash on Hand: Balance of cash available and undeposited.

Closing stock/closing inventory: Balance of goods at the end of an accounting period.

Convertism Principle: This principle says, 'anticipate no profits but provide for all possible losses'.

Contingent liability: Potential liability that has arisen as the result of a past event, not an effective liability until some future event occurs.

Conversion Price: The Price, in terms of rupees of par of the convertible security paid per share of equity stock obtained through conversion.

Conversion Ratio: The number of equity share exchangeable per bond or preferred stock at the time of conversion.

Convertible Security: Bond or preferred stock which is convertible into equity shares at the option of the holder.

Commission: Remuneration for services related to sales, purchases etc.

Cost: The amount paid or payable in either cash or its equivalent for goods, services or other assets purchased.

Credit: The right hand side of the T form of an account or the process of placing an amount on the right hand side of an account.

Credit Note: A note sent by the seller to the purchaser informing the latter of the reduction in the amount due from him. Eg: When goods are returned by the purchaser as not conforming to specifications the seller will issue a credit note on receipt of the goods.

Creditors: Persons to whom the business owes certain amounts.

Cum Dividend: With dividend.

Cum Rights: With rights.

Cumulative Dividends: A feature of preferred stock that requires all past dividends on preferred stock to be paid before any equity dividends are paid.

Cumulative Preference Shares: A preference share is a cumulative preference share when the arrears of dividends are accumulated and such arrears are paid first of all whenever dividend is declared.

Current Assets: Assets which normally get converted into cash during the operating cycle of the firm.

Current Liabilities: Liabilities that are normally payable within a year.

Current Ratio: A liquidity measure defined as current assets dividend by current liabilities.

Debenture: An instrument for long-term debt. Debentures in India are typically secured.

Debit: The left hand side of the form of an account or the process of placing an amount on the left side of an account.

Debit Note: A note sent by the purchaser to the seller informing the latter of the reduction in the amount due to him. Eg. When the purchaser returns goods he issues a debit note at the time of such despatch of goods.

Debtors: Persons who owe the business certain amounts.

Depreciation: The accounting process adopted for the gradual conversion of asset cost into expenses.

Discount: A reduction in price offered by the seller.

Discount on Debtors (cash discount): Rebate offered to customers to induce them to pay the dues within a stipulated time period.

Dividend: A share of earnings distributed to the owners of a business.

Dividend Yield: The ratio of the current dividend to the current market price of a share.

Double Entry: Recording of transaction which takes into account the debit and credit aspects of each transaction.

Doubtful Debts: A debt, the collectibility of which is doubtful.

Drawings: Withdrawal of cash or goods by the owners from the business for personal use.

Dual Aspect Principle: A fundamental principle of accounting according to which the total of assets and the total of equities are always equal.

Due Point System: A system of financial analysis, pioneered by the Du Pont Company, which helps in understanding profitability in terms of profit margin and assets turnover.

Ebit: Abbreviation for earnings before interest and taxes.

Efficient Market Hypothesis: The concept that the prices in the securities market reflect all available information.

Entity Principle: For purpose of accounting, the business firm is regarded as a separate entity.

Equity: The net worth of a firm consisting of paid up equity capital plus reserves and surplus.

Equity Shares: These shares receive the residue of the distributed profit after commitments on preference shares and any other shares carrying priority have been met. Equity shareholders have voting rights.

Exchange Rate: The rate at which one currency may be exchanged for another.

Expenses: Expired cost: the materials used and services utilised in the production of revenue during a specific period.

External Financial Report: Reports the income statement, balance sheet and other related information-prepared for to meet the information needs of those who do not have direct access for the business entity's records.

Face Value: The amount the firm promises to pay the bondholder or preference stockholder at the time of maturity. It is also referred to as the par value or principle value.

Financial Assets: A price of paper representing claim on real assets.

Financial Ratio: A ratio based on figures obtained from the firm's financial statements and supposedly reflects some aspects of the firm's financial condition and performance.

Financial Statement: A balance sheet, income statement. Funds statement or other presentation of financial data derived from accounting records.

Fixed Assets: Assets purchased for use in the operation of the business and not intended for resale to consumers. Eg. Premises, Plant and Machinery, Furniture, Land and Building etc.

Fixed Charge: A payment by a firm which is required under a contract. Example: Interest on debt.

Freehold Premises: Premises not subject to any charge.

Funds Flow Statement: A statement showing the flow of funds through a business over a period of time. Funds may be defined as total resources, or net working capital or cash.

Furniture and Fittings: Assets like Chairs, Tables, Lights and attachment thereto.

General/Miscellaneous Expenses: Expenses not classifiable as manufacturing, selling, administrative etc.

Generally Accepted Accounting Principles: The ground rules used by economic entities in presenting financial information.

General Reserve: Segregated portion of the retained earnings of a business. It may be utilised for future needs.

Going Concern Principle: Accounting is based on the premises that the business firm will remain a going concern for an indefinitely long period.

Goodwill: Intangible assets represented by the excess of purchase price over book value.

Gross Cost: The acquisition value of a fixed asset (with no reduction for accumulated depreciation) used in calculating return on capital.

Gross Profit: The difference between net sale and cost of goods sold.

Gross profit Margin: Gross profit/net sales. A ratio denoting the gross profit of the firm as a percentage of net sales.

Holding Company: A company which holds a controlling interest in one or more other companies which are referred to as subsidiaries.

Imprest: Cash maintained for paying sundry expenses.

Income: Money or money equivalent earned or accrued during an accounting period.

Income Due but not Received: Income receivable but not yet received (*i.e.*, outstanding).

Income Received but not Due: Income received during an accounting period, through due to be received only at a future date.

Income Statement: A basic accounting statement that measures the results of a firm's operations over a specified period commonly one year. Also known as the profit and loss statement. The bottom line of the income statement shows the firm's profit or loss for the period.

Insolvency: The inability of a firm to meet its debt obligations.

Insurance: For payment of a premium the insurer agrees to compensate the insured in the event of the latter 'suffering a specified loss.

Intangible Assets: Non-physical but valuable resources like goodwill, patents, and copyrights owned by the firm.

Interest-Rate Risk: The uncertainty that envelops the expected returns from a security caused by changes in interest rates. Price changes induced by interest-rate changes are greater for long-term than for short-term financial instruments.

Internal Financing: Funds generated internally. Internal financing consists of retained earnings plus depreciation and other non-cash charges.

Inventory: Stock of goods.

Investment Allowance Reserve: Reserve created at the time of making investment in plant and machinery to avail tax benefits.

Investment: Purchase of shares, debentures or other securities.

Issued share: Total shares that have been issued by a company.

Journal: A record of transactions, showing for each transaction the debits and credits to be entered in specific ledger accounts.

Lease: An agreement to rent assets for a period of time, often several years.

Leasehold premised: Holding of premises under an agreement (lease) for specific purpose, rent and period.

Ledger: Record containing all the individual accounts of business.

Lessee: The individual receiving the right to use the leased assets.

Lessor: The owner of the asset being leased.

Liability: Obligation of a business on a creditor's claim against the assets of a business.

Lien: A lender's claim on assets offered as security for a loan.

Lighting and Heating: Expenses incurred for lighting and heating.

Liquidation Value: The rupee amount that could be realised if an asset were sold independently of the going concern.

Liquidity: A firm's liquidity refers to its ability to meet its obligations in the short run (defined usually as a period of one year). An asset's liquidity refers to how quickly it can be sold at a reasonable price.

Lower of cost or market: A companion of the cost of inventory with the replacement cost of the same inventory to determine if there has been a loss in the value of inventory that should be recorded.

Marketable securities: Security investment that the firm can quickly convert into cash balances.

Market value: The value observed in the market place, where buyers and sellers negotiate a mutually acceptable price for the assets.

Matching Principle: According to this principle, expenses are matched with revenue.

Miscellaneous Expenditure: Expenditure such as preliminary expenses and development expenditure which are expected to bring in benefits during several accounting periods.

Monetary Items: Claims (assets) or obligations (liabilities) that are fixed in terms of a specified amount.

Money Measurement Principle: Financial accounting is concerned with only those facts which are expressible in monetary terms.

Mortgage: A pledge of specific property offered as security for a loan.

Multinational Company: A company which had direct investment in two or more countries.

Multiple Discriminant Analysis: A statistical technique for determining a discriminant function which provides a reasonable basis for classifying an items into various categories (for example debtors may be classified into good debtors and bad debtors) based on certain obserable, quantifiable characteristics.

N

Net Assets: Total assets less total liabilities. Net assets are equal to owner's equity.

Net Block: Capitalised cost of assets less accumulated depreciation.

Net Current Assets: Excess of current assets over current liabilities.

Net Income: A figure representing the firm's profit or loss for the period. It also represents the earnings available to the firm's common and preferred shareholders.

Net profit margin: Net income/sales. A ratio that measures the net income of the firm as a percent of sales.

Net Reliable Value: An asset measure computed by substracting the expected completion and disposal costs from the asset's estimated selling price.

Net Worth: It consists of paid up capital plus reserve and surplus.

Nominal Accounts: Accounts of various expenses and income.

Non-Monetary Items: Assets or liabilities whose prices are not fixed in terms of a specified amount.

Owner's Equity: The interest or claim of an entity's owners in the entity assets; equal to the excess of assets over liabilities.

Opening Stock/Opening Inventory: Balance of stock at the beginning of accounting period.

Operating Profit Margin: Net operating income/sales. A firm's earnings before interest and taxes. This ratio serves as an overall measure of operating effectiveness.

Outstanding Expenses: Expenses remaining unpaid.

Overdraft: Amount by which a cheque or other demand for payment exceeds the amount of credit against which it is drawn.

Paid up Capital: Share capital which has been paid up by the shareholders.

Partnership: A business owned by two or more owners (partners) who agree on how the profits (losses) and obligations of the business will be shared.

Par Value: See face value.

Patent: Exclusive right to manufacture and sell, or use a product.

Personal Accounts: Accounts opened to enter all transactions with persons.

Petty Cash Book: Record of entries for payment of small amount.

Petty Expenses: Expenses of small amount.

Plant and Machinery: Tangible assets held for use in the production of goods and services.

Postage: Amount paid for postal services.

Posting: The formal transcribing of amounts from the journals to the ledger(s) used in an accounting system.

Power and Fuel: Coal, Electricity etc.

Preference Dividend: A fixed amount payable each year to the holders of preference shares.

Preference Shares: Class of shares usually having preference as to dividends and in the distribution of assets in the event of liquidation.

Prepaid Expenses: Expenses paid in respect of which benefits are yet to be received.

Present Values: The estimated current worth of amounts to be received (or paid) in the future from which appropriate amounts of discount have been deducted.

Printing and Stationery: Expenses incurred for printing and stationery items.

Profit: The excess of a firms operating revenue over the expenses of producing that revenue in a given fiscal period.

Profit and Loss Account: A statement showing all revenue and expenses items for a given period, arranged so that total expenses are substracted from total revenues to reveal the net income earned during that period.

Pro-forma Financial Statements: Literally, 'according to form' financial statements. They are the basic financial statements projected to the end of the next fiscal period in accordance with the provisions of the planning budget.

Profit Margin: The ratio of profit to sales. Several profit margin ratios are used. The two most commonly used are: gross profit margin (gross profit divided by sales) and net profit margin (net profit divided by sales).

Proposed Dividends: Dividend proposed as return on investment made by equity shareholders.

Prospectus: A document issued to describe a new security issue.

Provision for Doubtful debts: Providing for those debts whose collection is doubtful.

Provision for Tax: Providing for tax payment which is calculated on profits earned.

Public Company: A corporate body other than a private company. In a public company there is no upper limit on the number of shareholders and there is no restriction of transfer of shares.

Purchase Book: A record of entries made for purchase on credit.

Purchases Returns Book: A record of entries made for return of purchased goods.

R

Rate: Municipal Tax.

Real Accounts: Accounts relating to assets and liabilities.

Realisation Principle: According to this principle, revenue is deemed to be earned/realised when the goods or services are exchanged for cash or claims to cash.

Redeemable Preference Shares: Preference shares which are repayable at par at a certain date or at some time between two stated dates.

Refunding: The issuance of new securities to retire outstanding securities.

Rent: Expenses for using the land or building.

Reserves and Surplus: Accumulated profits of a business.

Retained Earnings: The portion of net income which is ploughed back in the business.

Return on Equity: The ratio of equity earnings to net worth.

Revenue Expenditure: An expenditure charged against income.

Revenue Recognition: To recognise revenue in the form of an inflow of assets resulting from the profit oriented activities of business.

Rights Issue: Issue of securities offered to existing shareholders on a pre-emptive basis.

Risk: Risk refers to variability. It is measured in financial analysis generally by standard deviation or by beta coefficient.

S

Salary: Compensation paid periodically for services like managerial, administrative and professional services.

Sales Book: A record of entries of sales made on credit.

Segment Reporting: Showing separately in financial statements the financial position and results of a business enterprise attributable to different segments of the business.

Sales Returns Book: A record of entries for goods returned by customers.

Secured Loans: Loans against which specific assets have been pledged or guarantees given.

Segment: Activities of a business enterprise concerned with separate major lines of business.

Selling Expenses: Class of expenses incurred in selling or marketing.

Share Application Money: Money received by the company along with application for share debentures.

Share Capital: Capital of a company represented by shares.

Shareholders' Funds: Funds owned by the shareholders *i.e.*, share capital, retained earning and reserves.

Single Entry: System of keeping only records of cash and personal accounts.

Sinking Fund: A required annual payment that allows for the periodic retirement of debt.

Software: A term that describes the programmes, written procedures and other documentation associated with use of computers.

Stable Monetary Unit Principle: Financial accounting is based on the assumption that the monetary unit remains stable.

Staff welfare Expenses: Expenses incurred for the welfare of employees.

Statement of changes in Financial Position: A basic accounting statement, also known as a sources and use of funds statement, identifying how the firm acquired its funds for the period and what it did with those funds.

Stock Accretion/Decretion: Difference between opening and closing stock.

Straight-Line Depreciation Method: Allocates uniform amounts of depreciation expenses to each full period of an asset's useful life.

Subsidiary Books: Books such as Journal, Sales Book, Purchase Book, Returns Book, Bills Book, Cash Book etc.

Sundry Expenses: General Miscellaneous Expenses.

Taxable Income: Gross from all sources, except for allowable exclusions, less any tax deductible expenses.

Tax: A levy backed by the force of laws which unilaterally determine the payers and terms of payment to a government unit.

Telephones: Telephone charges.

T Form: Preparing the account in the form of letter 'T'.

Times Interest Earned Ratio: Earnings before interest and taxes (EBIT)/interest expenses. A ratio that measures the firm's ability to meet its interest payments from its annual operating earnings.

Total Assets Turnover Ratio: The ratio of net sales to total assets.

Trade Discount: The differences between suggested retail prices and the prices at which wholesale purchasers are able to buy merchandise.

Transaction: An event the recognition of which give rise to an entry in accounting records; or a business activity or event which has taken place.

Trend Analysis: An analysis of a firm's financial ratios over time.

Trial Balance: Trial balance is a statement in which debit and credit balances of all the accounts of the ledger are listed to test the arithmetical accuracy of books of accounts.

Turnover Ratio: Turnover ratio, also referred to as activity ratio or asset management ratios, measure how efficiently the assets are employed by the firm.

Underwriting: The purchase and subsequent resale of a new security issue. The risk of selling the new issue at a satisfactory (profitable) price is assumed by investment banker or underwriter.

Unsecured Loans: Loans for which the creditors hold no security.

Vertical Form: Preparing the account in the form of statement.

Wages: Compensation paid to workmen.

Working Capital: Current assets minus current liabilities.

Written Down Value Method: A depreciation method according to which the depreciation charge is a certain percentage of the written down value of the assets.

Zero-Base budgeting: A method of drawing up budgets in which each budgeted expenditure must be justified for each budget period without reference to the fact that there was a similar expenditure in the previous period.

NOTES

NOTES

NOTES

NOTES

NOTES

NOTES